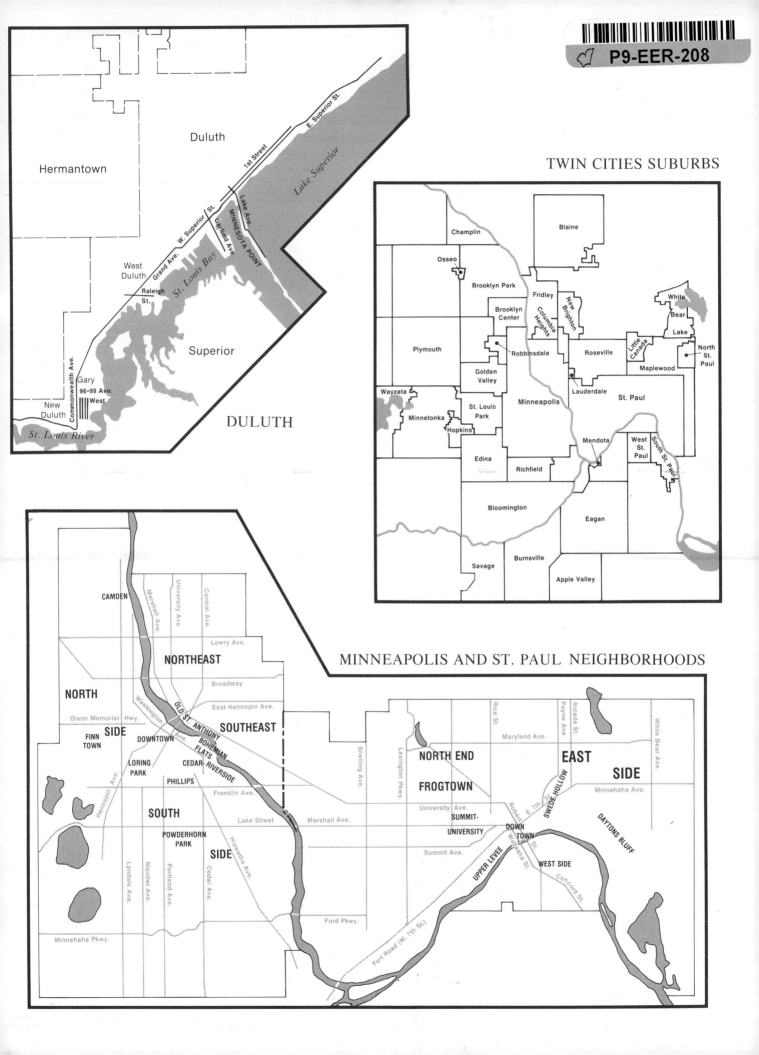

Duluth

Hermantown

Duluth

Lake Superior

E. Superior St.

1st Street

W. Superior St.

Lake Ave.

Grand Ave.

Garfield Ave.

MINNESOTA POINT

West Duluth

St. Louis Bay

Raleigh St.

Superior

Commonwealth Ave.

Gary

96-99 Ave. West

New Duluth

St. Louis River

DULUTH

TWIN CITIES SUBURBS

Champlin

Blaine

Osseo

Brooklyn Park

Fridley

New Brighton

White Bear Lake

Brooklyn Center

Columbia Heights

Plymouth

Robbinsdale

Roseville

Little Canada

Maplewood

North St. Paul

Wayzata

Golden Valley

Lauderdale

St. Paul

Minnetonka

St. Louis Park

Minneapolis

Hopkins

Mendota

West St. Paul

South St. Paul

Edina

Richfield

Bloomington

Eagan

Savage

Burnsville

Apple Valley

MINNEAPOLIS AND ST. PAUL NEIGHBORHOODS

CAMDEN

Marshall Ave.

University Ave.

Central Ave.

Lowry Ave.

NORTHEAST

Broadway

NORTH

Washington

East Hennepin Ave.

Rice St.

Arcade St.

Payne Ave.

White Bear Ave.

Olson Memorial Hwy.

OLD ST. ANTHONY

SOUTHEAST

Maryland Ave.

SIDE

BOHEMIAN FLATS

FINN TOWN

DOWNTOWN

CEDAR RIVERSIDE

Snelling Ave.

Lexington Pkwy.

NORTH END

EAST

LORING PARK

FROGTOWN

SIDE

PHILLIPS

Franklin Ave.

University Ave.

SUMMIT-UNIVERSITY

Robert St.

E. 7th St.

SWEDE HOLLOW

Minnehaha Ave.

Hennepin Ave.

SOUTH

Lake Street

Marshall Ave.

DOWN TOWN

DAYTONS BLUFF

POWDERHORN PARK

Hiawatha Ave.

SIDE

Summit Ave.

Wabasha St.

WEST SIDE

Lyndale Ave.

Nicollet Ave.

Portland Ave.

Cedar Ave.

UPPER LEVEE

Concord St.

Ford Pkwy.

Minnehaha Pkwy.

Fort Road (W. 7th St.)

Publications
of the

MINNESOTA
HISTORICAL SOCIETY

RUSSELL W. FRIDLEY, *Director*

JUNE DRENNING HOLMQUIST, *Assistant Director*
for Publications and Research

THEY CHOSE MINNESOTA

A Survey of
The State's Ethnic Groups

June Drenning Holmquist, *Editor*

MINNESOTA HISTORICAL SOCIETY PRESS · ST. PAUL · 1981

Copyright © 1981 by the Minnesota Historical Society

Library of Congress Cataloging in Publication Data:

Main entry under title:
They Chose Minnesota.
   (Publications of the Minnesota Historical
Society)
   Includes index.
   1. Minorities—Minnesota.   2. Minnesota—
History.   3. Minnesota—Ethnic relations.
I. Holmquist, June Drenning.   II. Series.
F615.A1T45   977.6′004   81-14124
                        AACR2

International Standard Book Number 0-87351-155-7

Manufactured in the United States of America

The Authors

MICHAEL ALBERT, assistant professor of geography at the University of Wisconsin, River Falls, wrote his Ph.D. dissertation on Japanese Americans in Chicago and the Twin Cities. He is a cultural geographer interested in east Asia, ethnic communities, and the American landscape.

HYMAN BERMAN is professor of history at the University of Minnesota, Minneapolis, and a senior fellow at the Minnesota Historical Society. His specialties include labor and Jewish history in America and Minnesota. He is co-author of *The American Worker in the Twentieth Century: A History through Autobiographies* (1963).

C. WINSTON CHRISLOCK is associate professor of history at the College of St. Thomas, St. Paul. Along with Czech culture and Slavic immigrant history, his special areas are American foreign policy and central and eastern Europe.

LOUIS M. deGRYSE is a historian whose research areas include the social and cultural history of the medieval and renaissance Low Countries. He has taught at the University of Minnesota, Minneapolis, and the College of St. Thomas, St. Paul. His Ph.D. dissertation and several articles have explored Flemish judicial and diplomatic history.

SUSAN M. DIEBOLD, who earned a master's degree in history at the University of Minnesota, Minneapolis, was a research assistant on the Minnesota Ethnic History Project in 1976–77. She is a registered nurse and member of the Human Rights Commission of Robbinsdale.

KEITH P. DYRUD, who teaches history at Concordia College, is co-editor and the author of a chapter on the Greek Catholic church in America in a book on *The Other Catholics* (1978) and of a study of the Rusins at the turn of the 20th century. He is active in the American Association for the Advancement of Slavic Studies and the Upper Midwest Ethnic Studies Association.

JON A. GJERDE is a doctoral candidate in history at the University of Minnesota, Minneapolis, where he is analyzing the cultural adaptation of Norwegian immigrants in Minnesota and Wisconsin. He was a research assistant and statistician on the Minnesota Ethnic History Project.

JUNE DRENNING HOLMQUIST, head of the Minnesota Historical Society's publishing program from 1956 to 1981 and the first woman to be named an assistant director of the society, served as editor of the Minnesota Ethnic History Project. She is the author or editor of half a dozen books and numerous articles on subjects related to Minnesota and midwestern history.

HILDEGARD BINDER JOHNSON, a specialist in historical geography, taught from 1947 to 1975 at Macalester College, St. Paul, where she chaired the geography department. She is an authority on German settlement in Minnesota and the Midwest and on the genesis and pictorial representation of the American landscape.

ANNE R. KAPLAN is an assistant editor at the Minnesota Historical Society and a doctoral candidate in folklore at the University of Pennsylvania. Her research interests include ethnicity, social and cultural history, and foodways.

PAUL KIRCHNER, a native of Hungary and a naturalized United States citizen, is tutor in the Paracollege and a member of the German department at St. Olaf College, Northfield. He is the author of literary articles and reviews and co-author of several rhetoric textbooks.

SARAH R. MASON is director of the Hmong Oral History Project at the Minnesota Historical Society, where she was a research assistant for the Minnesota Ethnic History Project. Her doctoral dissertation and subsequent work with oral and recorded archival materials focused on Asian and Asian-American history.

DEBORAH L. MILLER (formerly Stultz), an assistant editor at the Minnesota Historical Society, served as research co-ordinator for the Minnesota Ethnic History Project. Graduate work in Scandinavian studies sparked her interest in ethnic history.

KENNETH B. MOSS, who was a research assistant on the Minnesota Ethnic History Project, has taught American and diplomatic history at the Universities of Alabama at Huntsville, Nebraska at Lincoln, and Minnesota at Minneapolis. He is the author of articles and reviews on international relations, especially during the World War II era.

CARLTON C. QUALEY, emeritus professor of history at Carleton College, Northfield, and editor of *Immigration History Newsletter*, initiated the Minnesota Ethnic History Project. His early book, *Norwegian Settlement in the United States* (1938), was a landmark in the field of immigration studies. He has written extensively and lectured internationally on immigration and ethnic history.

ANN REGAN is an assistant editor at the Minnesota Historical Society. She earned a bachelor of arts degree in history and the Russian language at the University of Montana, Missoula.

FRANK RENKIEWICZ is editor of *Polish American Studies*, the journal of the Polish American Historical Association. He has been a professor of history at the College of Saint Teresa, Winona, has written broadly on Poles in the United States, and is active in local, state, and national ethnic associations.

JOHN G. RICE is a professor of geography at the University of Minnesota, Minneapolis. His numerous published works reflect his major research interests in the areas of historical demography, Scandinavia and Finland, and immigration to the Upper Midwest. He is the author of *Patterns of Ethnicity in a Minnesota County, 1880–1905* (1973).

TIMO RIIPPA is a graduate student in Scandinavian studies and library sciences at the University of Minnesota, Minneapolis, and associate editor of *Finnish Americana: A Journal of Finnish American History and Culture*. In addition to teaching the Finnish language, he has written, translated, or edited a number of published works on Finns in the United States.

MITCHELL E. RUBINSTEIN is a researcher and analyst for the Minnesota Higher Education Coordinating Board, St. Paul. He holds a doctoral degree in European history and international relations and was a research assistant on the Minnesota Ethnic History Project.

SARAH P. RUBINSTEIN was a research assistant for the Minnesota Ethnic History Project before she joined the staff of the Minnesota Historical Society as an assistant editor. She is a doctoral candidate in British and European history.

THEODORE SALOUTOS (1910–80) was professor emeritus at the University of California, Los Angeles, specializing in the history of immigration and agriculture, and a founder of the Immigration History Society. Before his untimely death, he had approved the edited manuscript of his contribution to this book.

JOSEPH STIPANOVICH, who holds a Ph.D. degree in history from the University of Minnesota, Minneapolis, has specialized in American social and economic history and immigration studies of South Slavs in America. He directed the Historical-Cultural Survey of the Minnesota Iron Mining Regions (1978–79), contributed a chapter to *The South Slavs in Utah: A Social History* (1974), and is the author of a forthcoming history of the Twin Cities.

M. MARK STOLARIK is executive director of The Balch Institute for Ethnic Studies, Philadelphia. He is the author of three books and many articles on Slovaks in America, immigration, acculturation, and interethnic relations.

DAVID VASSAR TAYLOR is director of the Minority/Special Services Program at Macalester College, St. Paul. He was a research assistant for the Minnesota Ethnic History Project and in 1974 and 1975 directed the Minnesota Historical Society's Minnesota Black History Project. He has taught in Black and minority studies programs at the State University of New York, New Paltz, and St. Olaf College, Northfield.

RUDOLPH J. VECOLI is professor of history at the University of Minnesota, Minneapolis, and director of its Immigration History Research Center in St. Paul. He has lectured and written extensively on Italian-American life, immigration history, and ethnicity. Among his books is *The People of New Jersey* (1965).

ALAN R. WOOLWORTH is former chief archaeologist and research fellow at the Minnesota Historical Society and the editor of the *Minnesota Archaeologist*. He has directed archaeological and historical field surveys of Indian and fur trade sites and written several ethnohistorical studies of Indian land use and ownership.

Preface

THIS BOOK is the result of an eight-year Minnesota Ethnic History Project begun by the Minnesota Historical Society in 1973 at the suggestion of Carlton C. Qualey, MHS research fellow, after his retirement as professor of history at Carleton College, Northfield. The project's objective was to bring together in a single volume information on the major ethnic population elements that have resided in Minnesota during the 130 years from 1850 to 1980. More than 60 ethnic groups are discussed in the 32 chapters that follow and at least a half dozen others are touched on more briefly.

The text is divided into four sections based on the geographic origins of Minnesota's population groups: (1) North Americans, (2) Northern and Western Europeans, (3) Central and Southern Europeans, (4) Middle Easterners and Asians. Because of the interest present-day members of each population stock have in their group's role in the story of Minnesota, the chapters were organized within these broad geographical units by national and racial origins. While this arrangement has limitations, especially for readers interested in topics that cut across group lines, we believe the comprehensive index will lead searchers to the material they seek. Information on patterns of settlement nationally and within the state, organizations, politics, language retention, acculturation, mobility, and other economic, social, religious, and political aspects are among the topics incorporated in the chapter essays. Full documentation is provided at the end of each essay, and a comprehensive bibliography was therefore omitted for reasons of economy.

We regard this book as a beginning. It is not, and was never intended to be, an exhaustive treatment of Minnesota's ethnic history. While the project sometimes exhausted all those involved, we are well aware that we have neither exhausted all the ethnic elements represented in the state, nor treated definitively those which were included. The immigration history of even a single state was, we found, an often uncharted labyrinth, cutting across many subject areas and a vast array of sources, as the extensive references cited make abundantly clear.

Although we know that we have not said the last word, we are pleased that so many chapters have been able to say a first word. We hope other researchers will be stimulated to help fill in the many gaps and to explore some of the fascinating byways suggested in the comprehensive source notes. If the project's efforts trigger additional research and writing, improved documentation, and further probing of the myriad approaches to the study of the people who chose Minnesota,

it will have fulfilled the principal hopes of its sponsor, the Minnesota Historical Society.

That organization's interest in immigration history was not new. When Qualey proposed that the society produce such a book for Minnesota, he did so in a receptive milieu. With varying degrees of intensity, the Minnesota Historical Society has pursued themes relating to the state's peoples both before and after the fertile years of the 1930s when Qualey and Theodore C. Blegen wrote their books on Norwegian immigration and, serving as the society's directors (Blegen 1931–39 and Qualey 1947–48), encouraged the collection of ethnic source materials. The pages of *Minnesota History*, the institution's quarterly, have for over 60 years carried articles on ethnic topics. Staff members over the decades also projected their interests to such organizations as the Folk Arts Foundation, the International Institute of Minnesota, and the Norwegian-American Historical Association.

Accentuated emphasis within the society came again in the 1970s with the execution of projects for collecting materials relating to Mexican Americans and Blacks in the state, and for the production of curriculum resource units on the Ojibway Indians and the immigrant experience. For a time an active Folklife Center was part of the MHS program, and since 1973 the institution has housed the office of the Immigration History Society's *Newsletter* edited by Qualey.

Thus the MHS, drawing upon its own collections, those of Minnesota's regional research and local historical networks, and such other depositories as the Immigration History Research Center (IHRC) of the University of Minnesota, launched the Minnesota Ethnic History Project in two phases. Phase 1, directed by Qualey in 1973–78, involved the creation of a statistical base and the gathering of additional pertinent research on all groups for the period from the beginnings of settlement to 1930. Phase 2, carried out from January, 1978, to 1981 under the direction of the editor with the able assistance of Deborah L. Miller, research co-ordinator, assembled data on all groups from 1930 to the 1980s.

Phase 1, completed by the end of 1977, was supported by a grant from the Minnesota legislature ($30,000), matching funds from the Bush Foundation of St. Paul, and an additional grant ($30,000) from the National Endowment for the Humanities in 1975–77. A second legislative grant ($25,000) plus generous support from the Minnesota Historical Society's private endowment funds completed the project and provided compensation for the 27 authors selected at the beginning of Phase 2.

In making the chapter assignments, a deliberate effort was made to obtain a mix of experienced historians and young scholars, representatives of other appropriate disciplines, and talented researchers on the society's own staff, several of whom had participated in Phase 1. The results of such multiple authorship are inevitably uneven, but we hope that fault is compensated for by the variety in points of view presented.

The book's framework is basically demographical and geographical. The statistical base was derived from state and federal censuses from 1850 to 1970, supplemented by the scant preliminary data for 1980 available at press time. These essential, but frequently unsatisfactory and contradictory, figures were bolstered by extensive research in government records, manuscripts collections, newspaper files, local histories, church archives, biographical literature, theses, monographs, and plat maps, and by personal interviews.

The body of research assembled by both phases of the Minnesota Ethnic History Project (abbreviated throughout this volume as MEHP) is preserved in the MEHP Papers in the society's Division of Archives and Manuscripts. It is hoped that these files will prove useful to future researchers, for they contain numerous leads awaiting exploration as well as considerable information which did not find its way into the final chapters prepared by the various authors.

Although the project made very little use of computerized information, the demographic data it gathered has been prepared in such a way that it can be readily computerized. Initially, it was hoped the project could rely extensively on computers, but it quickly became apparent that this would not only be expensive but also unnecessary. Instead a team of researchers, composed of graduate students at the University of Minnesota, was employed to extract and record the relevant statistics from various census schedules, an essential first step in any case. The page-by-page transcribing from the 1880 federal manuscript census schedules, which revealed many differences from the published figures, for example, was accomplished by six research assistants in four months. These were supplemented by additional statistics derived from printed censuses and from a computer analysis of the 1970 census. In this way a comprehensive body of statistical information was established, which was used to create the distribution maps and tables throughout the book. Taken together the tables and maps, although based on statistics possessing severe limitations which are discussed in the Appendix below, offer for the first time detailed, collected outlines of population distribution by ethnic origin in Minnesota.

To list the many people who aided this work would require many pages. We have tried to call attention to their contributions in the bylines and footnotes throughout the volume. Especially important were the hundreds of people who generously agreed to share their experiences in oral history interviews. Without their insights and photographs, this book would have been far less interesting.

We also wish to thank our cheerful colleagues on the MHS staff, particularly librarians Alice Grygo and Alissa Wiener, who patiently ferreted out or obtained countless books for authors and editors. And we especially want to acknowledge the work of our research crews. The Phase 1 crew consisted of part-time workers Maurycey Czerwonka, Susan M. Diebold, Lynn Laitala, Byron J. Nordstrom, Kathleen A. O'Brien, Robert C. Ostergren, James A. Quirin, Mitchell E. Rubinstein, Sarah P. Rubinstein, Steven D. Strandmark, Deborah L. Miller (Stultz), and David V. Taylor. The Phase 2 crew included Jon A. Gjerde, Marjorie Hoover, Sarah R. Mason, Kenneth B. Moss, and Dennis Tachiki.

The dedicated editorial staff, which was often called upon to supply additional research, deserves a special vote of thanks. It was composed of Jean A. Brookins, Mary Cannon, Kenneth Carley, Anne R. Kaplan, Lucile M. Kane, Helen T. Katz, Deborah Miller, Ann Regan, and Sarah Rubinstein. Design and production were carried out under the supervision of Alan Ominsky, who with the help of Ann Regan also prepared the country-of-origin maps. Statistical maps for 1880 and 1905 were the work of Robert Ostergren, now of the University of Wisconsin. Advice was provided throughout the project by Dr. Qualey and during Phase 2 by James S. Griffin of St. Paul and Professors John G. Rice of the University of Minnesota and La Vern Rippley of St. Olaf College. To all who helped us in any way, we say a sincere "Thank you."

The following four abbreviations were used throughout the references in this book:

IHRC — Immigration History Research Center, University of Minnesota

IRRC — Iron Range Research Center, Chisholm

MEHP — Minnesota Ethnic History Project

MHS — Minnesota Historical Society.

St. Paul

JUNE DRENNING HOLMQUIST, *Editor*

Contents

Maps and Tables

MAPS

xi

TABLES

Introduction

THIS SURVEY of Minnesota ethnic groups has been organized in four broad categories — those whose antecedents had roots in North America, northern and western Europeans whose migrations affected countries from Iceland to Switzerland, central and southern Europeans who left homelands stretching from the Baltic Sea to the Mediterranean, and representatives of the diverse lands and religions of the Middle East and Asia. Whether they were among the Indian people who had arrived first, Blacks from the American South whose roots reached back to Africa, restless New England Yankees who were among those we have called Old-Stock Americans, or the thousands that arrived by sailing ship or jet plane, all those who chose Minnesota were at some time immigrants, emigrants, or migrants.

An immigrant (or in-migrant) is one who voluntarily *comes into* another country, intending to make it his or her home, although involuntary immigration was also a common occurrence in the early history of the nation. An emigrant (or out-migrant) is one who *goes from* his or her country of origin, while a migrant is a person who moves from place to place within a region or travels in either direction between countries. The last is the broadest of the three terms, and it can be applied to the movement of peoples from, to, or within areas. The key element among all three words is mobility.

The earliest migrants discussed in this book are Minnesota's two principal Indian tribes, the Dakota and the Ojibway. Both had well-established societies based upon hunting and gathering when white traders arrived to plant fur posts among them. Changes in the ways of life of Indian people further accelerated after Fort Snelling rose on the heights above the junction of the Mississippi and Minnesota rivers in the 1820s, bringing an Indian agent to represent the United States government as well as missionaries to preach a new religion. But the Dakota and Ojibway withstood the 19th-century invasion by European peoples and in 1980 were present in numbers nearly twice as large as when white men first visited the Upper Mississippi River Valley. In the Twin Cities they formed the third largest urban Indian concentration in the United States, and in northern Minnesota the Ojibway still occupied one of the few unallotted and unceded reservations in the nation.

Spaniards were the earliest European explorers of the New World, but their descendants were relative latecomers to Minnesota. Just as the lure of gold drew the conquistadors to America in earlier times, economic opportunities drew thousands of Mexicans north to work, chiefly in agriculture, in the early 20th century. By their own estimate, people of Spanish heritage constituted the largest minority in the state in the 1970s.

In the early 1800s the area's economy was based upon the fur trade, which had been established by French Canadians. French priests were also the first to introduce Christianity to what is now Minnesota. Later in the 19th century French Canadians followed the old fur trade routes to become settlers, and in the 1980s Minnesota had more French Canadians than any state outside of New England.

As the first sizable wave of settlement reached Minnesota in the 1850s and 1860s, the townsite developers, timber speculators, small businessmen, grassroots politicians, and organizers of churches and schools were often New England Yankees. They flocked to Minnesota Territory, which was established in 1849, hoping to create a New England of the West. Yankee enterprise determined the shape of Minnesota's institutions, but its early citizens were a varied lot who made their way west from the older areas to the south and east. Among them were free Blacks who reached the new state after the Civil War. They chose to live primarily in the Twin Cities of Minneapolis and St. Paul, where they have since the 1860s consistently accounted for about 1% of Minnesota's population.

In the 156 years from 1820 through 1975 at least 47,000,000 immigrants reached the United States from the Americas, Europe, Asia, and other parts of the world; millions more scattered to Canada, Australia, New Zealand, South Africa, and South America. These movements constituted perhaps the greatest folk migration in the known history of humanity. Over 9,500,000 persons moved from the British Isles (including 4,700,000 from Ireland) to the United States. Almost 7,000,000 Germans, at least 5,000,000 Italians, and between 3,000,000 and 4,500,000 people from the Austro-Hungarian Empire, the Netherlands, Russia, and Canada departed for the United States. Almost 2,500,000 people left from the small northern nations of Norway, Sweden, and Denmark, while hundreds of thousands departed from Belgium, France, Greece, Portugal, Romania, Spain, and Switzerland, as well as from China, Japan, and the Middle East. More than 1,000,000 Mexicans entered the country legally, while fewer than 3,000 immigrants arrived from each of the small countries of Albania, Latvia, Lithuania, and Luxembourg. An estimated 399,000 Blacks were carried to English North America and the United States by 1861, perhaps 51,000 of them involuntarily and illegally after the slave trade was prohibited in 1808. Deducting an estimated 13,000,000 or so migrants who returned to their homelands or emigrated elsewhere between 1820 and 1950, the net immigration to the

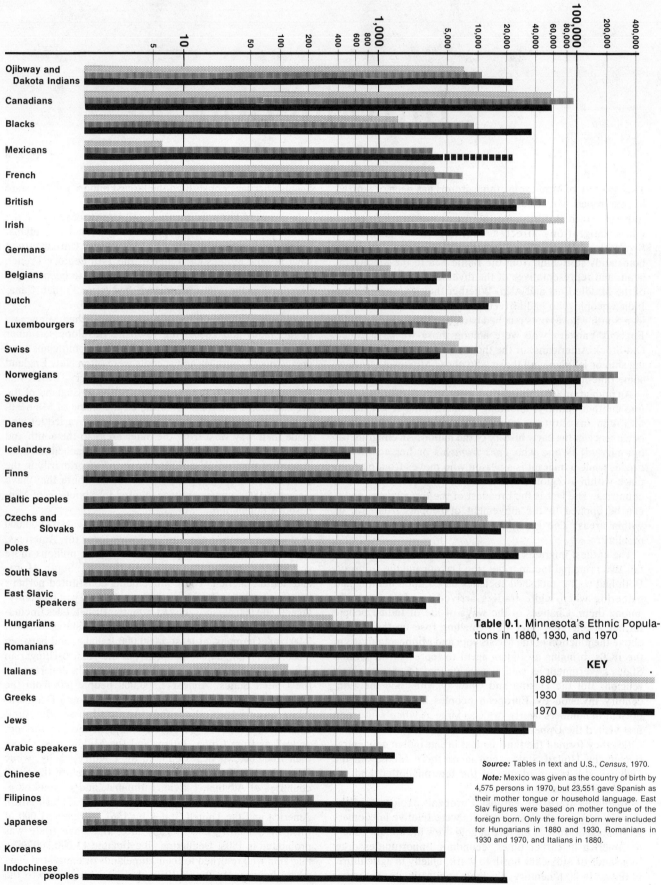

Table 0.1. Minnesota's Ethnic Populations in 1880, 1930, and 1970

KEY
1880
1930
1970

Source: Tables in text and U.S., *Census*, 1970.

Note: Mexico was given as the country of birth by 4,575 persons in 1970, but 23,551 gave Spanish as their mother tongue or household language. East Slav figures were based on mother tongue of the foreign born. Only the foreign born were included for Hungarians in 1880 and 1930, Romanians in 1930 and 1970, and Italians in 1880.

United States was somewhat over 32,000,000. At a guess perhaps 1,000,000 or so of the gross total made their way to or through Minnesota (see Table 0.1). In the 1980s the three largest ethnic groups represented in the state's population were Germans, Swedes, and Norwegians.[1]

From the 1820s, when the first permanent white settlers arrived to live among well-established Indian communities, until about 1890, the people who chose Minnesota emigrated principally from the British Isles, Germany, and Scandinavia (see Table 0.2). Small groups of Czech and Polish farmers took up land, which in 1980 some of their descendants still owned, and less numerous Swiss, Dutch, Belgians, and Luxembourgers added to the rural mix before 1890. In his inaugural address of 1876 Governor John S. Pillsbury said: "In a young frontier State, recognizing labor as its prime necessity, there can be few more legitimate objects of legislation than those which contemplate the early peopling of its unoccupied territory and the culture of its idle soil." Many of these northern Europeans responded to the lure of free or cheap land, staking claims in the southern half of the state and founding numerous small trading centers along the principal rivers and rail lines.[2]

From 1890 to 1920 the immigrants who arrived were predominantly from southern, central, and eastern Europe (see Table 0.2). Landing in the United States largely without capital, these people gravitated to American urban and industrial centers, including the iron ranges of Minnesota. They reached the United States just as the amount of free or cheap agricultural land was running low, and the huge new industrial and transportation systems were experiencing an acute need for workers. Minnesota's share of these immigrants included many people from the Russian and Austro-Hungarian empires, while Italy and Greece sent smaller numbers. From Russia Minnesota received Russian Germans, Poles, Jews, Ukrainians, Finns, and a few Rusins. Czechs, Poles, Jews, Slovaks, Rusins, and Magyars left

Austria-Hungary, as did South Slavs — Slovenes, Croats, Serbs, and Bulgars — and Romanians (see Table 0.1).[3]

During this period, Germans and Scandinavians also continued to pour in. In fact, more Norwegians arrived in Minnesota between 1900 and 1909 than in any previous decade. By 1900 the combined flood of Scandinavians outnumbered the previously dominant Germans. Irish, British, Anglo-Canadians, Swiss, Dutch, Belgians, Luxembourgers, and Blacks also continued to settle in the state as they had since before the Civil War.

Few Europeans arrived during the period between World Wars I and II, but larger numbers of Mexicans and Mexican Americans, who traveled to the state as migrant workers, put down roots in St. Paul in the 1930s. Immediately after World War II large numbers of other migrants — political refugees displaced by war — were admitted after they refused to return to eastern European homelands by then under Soviet control. Among them were Baltic peoples — Estonians, Latvians, Lithuanians — as well as Hungarians, Ukrainians, Jews, Czechs, Slovaks, Poles, and South Slavs. About 7,000 of these Displaced Persons were destined for Minnesota between 1948 and 1952, when the program ended. Slightly less than half were Poles. In the 1950s and 1960s small additional numbers of refugees fled Soviet repression in Hungary and Czechoslovakia to settle in the state.

The post-World War II era also saw the immigration of professionals and intellectuals, who were drawn by better employment opportunities in the United States in such numbers that the phenomenon came to be called the "brain drain." In that period greater numbers of university students also arrived from the Middle East, Asia, and Africa, some of whom chose to remain in Minnesota.

The first community of Asian people was composed of Chinese, who began to migrate from the West to Minnesota in 1876. Filipinos appeared in the 1920s, and their numbers were augmented after World War II. The nucleus of the

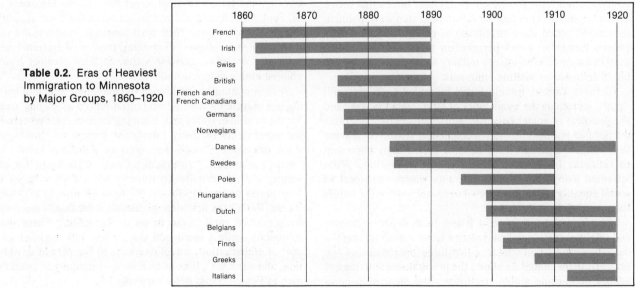

Table 0.2. Eras of Heaviest Immigration to Minnesota by Major Groups, 1860–1920

Source: U.S., *Census,* 1860–1920; based on country-of-origin data.
Note: Each bar begins at the approximate year in which the number of foreign born in the nationality group equalled half of the largest figure reported by the U.S. *Census* in the year marked by the end of the bar.

Japanese community was formed by a small group that attended military language school in the state during World War II. Koreans began to live in St. Paul and Minneapolis after 1965, and in the second half of the 1970s Indochinese refugees from Southeast Asia streamed in by the thousands. In 1980 the Twin Cities had the largest single Hmong settlement in the United States.

Why Did They Emigrate?

What causes people to leave familiar ancestral homelands for a relatively unknown land? In the age of sail it was an act of considerable courage, for the dangerous and uncomfortable sea voyage might take as long as three months. Later, steamships shortened the trip and made it safer, but emigration nevertheless meant great individual risks and changes. There were, of course, many personal reasons for departure — among them discontent, the desire to accompany one's family, or the lure of a vision of a Land of Canaan across the sea, to name only a few. But underlying much of the movement from Europe after 1820 were three principal "push" factors: the pressure of increased population, the Industrial Revolution, and changes in farming systems which produced large numbers of landless workers and caused agrarian crises in many countries. Although the population imbalance was partially eased by migration to the rising European industrial centers, such as the English Midlands or the Rhine provinces, industrialization in most countries was not sufficiently advanced to absorb the greatly expanded labor supply. Despite the emigration and fairly high death rates, Europe's population almost tripled in the century after 1815.[4]

Poverty in various degrees characterized much of rural Europe, and it was from there that most of the emigrants went to the United States. Conditions in industrial centers were also grim. Ties to the homeland and its culture were compelling reasons to stay, but when disaster in one form or another — famine in Ireland and Finland, for example, or large-scale unemployment in the Rhineland — was added to poverty, emigration meant survival. Other forces that drove smaller numbers of people to this radical step were political inequality, social class stratification, rebellion against state church dictation, direct persecution (such as the Jews in eastern Europe), compulsory military service, and the example of returned or visiting emigrants.

To these various forces should be added such powerful "pull" factors as the availability of land, higher wages, and the prospect of social equality. Most 19th-century migrants did not find political freedom a compelling reason for leaving their homes, although it did become increasingly important to refugees in the last half of the 20th century. What attracted many 19th-century migrants was the prospect of social equality, a fact mentioned over and over in the letters they sent back to Europe.

The enormous influence of letters from departed friends and relatives (the so-called America letters) were among the most powerful "pull" factors that lured people across the seas. To them should be added the promotional activities of agents of various states, railroads, and steamship companies; a growing number of emigrant guidebooks in various languages; and the "herd instinct" that affected some people who would not otherwise have had the courage to tear themselves away from accustomed environments. Increasingly information reached Europe about the opportunities in America. As public education spread, more and more Europeans were able to read about the millions of acres of land and the jobs waiting in the United States. To a farmer tilling less than 20 acres, frequently less than five, the prospect of owning 80 or 160 acres or more was enticing. To the landless worker from Europe, Asia, or Mexico, the possibility of earning as much as $.50 to $1.00 a day seemed like a fortune; a skilled laborer could make as much in an hour as he or she made at home in a day.[5]

Without question, however, the most potent factor in bringing migrants across the oceans was remittances. Usually sent by earlier immigrants to family members at home, such remittances, in the form of bank drafts or postal money orders after the 1890s, provided funds for tickets, support for parents, help for relatives, or the means to pay off a mortgage. Increasingly they took the form of prepaid tickets. While no calculation has yet been made of the total amount of money sent back to Europe, Asia, the Middle East, or Mexico, estimates for some countries add up to millions of dollars per year and several hundred million dollars for the periods studied. To these remittances must be added money supplied by philanthropists and appropriations by governments to send out indigents and hopeless debtors.[6]

The communities established by the firstcomers became another important pull factor. They offered points of certain destination in which a prospective emigrant could hope to find a refuge while becoming familiar with the language and customs of the New World. These transitional settlements frequently became permanent ethnic communities — Brown and Stearns counties for the Germans, the St. Croix Valley for the Swedes, Houston and Fillmore counties and the Red River Valley for the Norwegians, Ramsey and Dakota counties for the Irish, the iron ranges for the Finns and Yugoslavs, McLeod, Scott, and Le Sueur counties for the Czechs, and the Mississippi River flats for the Mexicans of St. Paul. Most immigrant groups clustered together, supporting clerics who spoke their own language, meeting in their own halls and saloons, organizing their own fraternal and insurance societies, and for a time at least creating transplanted ethnic neighborhoods.

Such communities cushioned the inevitable shock of leaving one culture for another and often served as staging areas for the next leap westward. Forming an important pattern in the movements of many immigrant groups to Minnesota, these intermittent stops were part of a process known as "staged migration." In practice Croatian peasants, for example, did not usually go directly from their villages in Yugoslavia to mining jobs on northern Minnesota's Mesabi Range. Rather the first step might take some family members from the old rural home to an urban center, where they frequently made a prolonged stop. Then they might go to a port of embarkation, travel overseas to the port of destination, and work for a time at an inland community of countrymen in Pennsylvania before moving on.

In pursuit of land and jobs, people were far more likely to move to places where they had old acquaintances or relatives (especially if the latter had sent money to pay the new-comer's fare) than they were to venture to an area with jobs but no known countrymen. Thus New World settlement — whether in rural areas or city neighborhoods — often reflected Old World ties. Rather than a sudden "uprooting," it was more often a transplantation from one community to another, with retention of much of the old in the new.

Some studies show that ethnic homogeneity decreased with the westward spread of American settlement. Much of New England and the South in the early days had large areas of cohesive ethnic composition, and "Even in heterogeneous Pennsylvania, specific groups would tend to dominate specific counties." By the time the Middle West became the target of European settlement, however, "rural immigrant blocs seldom prevailed beyond the township scale, giving rise to intricately meshed mosaics." Much of Minnesota would seem to fit the mosaic pattern, but one scholar declared in 1973 that "large parts of Minnesota and the Dakotas" were among the few large areas in the United States where foreign (in this case, Scandinavian) immigration "brought about major modification" in "the American culture." [7]

As the families of immigrants in the United States reached the second and third generations, correspondence with friends and relatives became sporadic or broke off completely. Fewer and fewer America letters crossed the seas. Deaths on both sides of the ocean or of the Rio Grande or the St. Lawrence rivers might bring brief renewals of contact, especially if an inheritance was involved. Studies of America letters revealed that it frequently took less than a single generation for ties to break or dissolve. Distance, the time required for the exchange of letters, the prevalence of illiteracy in some groups, and the fact that entire families had emigrated, all lessened the influence of emigrants on countries of origin. While an awareness of America persisted in the homelands, it was distant, and the image was to some extent unreal. Immigrant America increasingly became a New World of its own.

The Migrants' Travel Routes

Having once decided to emigrate, the routes prospective settlers followed to Minnesota depended almost entirely upon when they chose to make the trip. Relatively few immigrants trickled into the Midwest before the mid-1820s. The United States was as yet little known abroad, much of it had not been explored, and transportation methods were primitive, inadequate to carry more than a few hundred persons per year. By the mid-1820s, however, a combination of circumstances started the regular flow of emigrants to the New World, and eventually to what later became Minnesota Territory. In the 1820s a Swiss group reached Fort Snelling by traveling south over the Red River Trails connecting present Winnipeg with what became St. Paul. And in 1823 the first Mississippi River steamboat to push so far upstream docked at the fort.[8]

Of the various ports, Boston and New York were important for Irish immigrants, while English and continentals also landed at the latter, especially if they sailed from Liverpool. Germans and others departing from Hamburg and Bremen reached Baltimore, while those whose ships left from Le Havre docked at New Orleans. Chinese, many of whom sailed from Hong Kong, entered through West Coast ports, as did most other Asians. Many immigrants remained in the cities where they landed simply because they had no money to go elsewhere; others, slightly more prosperous, got farther inland before their money gave out.

Four main routes led from the East and South to the Midwest (see Map 0.1). Regular steamboats leaving New Orleans offered the most direct one up the Mississippi, and some Germans used this method of reaching the Midwest. The finishing of the Erie Canal in 1825 enabled New Englanders and New Yorkers to journey by water through the Great Lakes to Detroit, Chicago, and Milwaukee, and, after the canal at Sault Ste. Marie began operating in 1855, to continue to Duluth at the extreme western end of Lake Superior. Travel from Montreal up Lake Ontario and through the Welland Canal to Lake Erie also put migrants on the Great Lakes route, an entrance to the American Midwest used by numerous Norwegians. The fourth major early path led overland from Philadelphia across the Allegheny Mountains to Pittsburgh, then along the Ohio River to the Mississippi, or over the National Road to Illinois.

Creeping westward at what seemed a snail's pace to people of that day, railroads at last reached Chicago in 1852 and the Mississippi River at Galena, Illinois, in 1853. Those who wished to investigate prospects in Minnesota quickly abandoned toll roads and slow canals in their pell-mell pursuit of farmland in the trans-Mississippi West. From the early 1850s onward most of the migrants would travel by train.

In that decade railroads from Chicago and Milwaukee terminated on the banks of the Mississippi, the former at Galena and Dunleith (East Dubuque), Illinois, and the latter after 1858 at La Crosse, Wisconsin. From there travelers could continue their journeys on regularly scheduled steamboats to such Minnesota ports as Winona, Wabasha, Red Wing, or

EUROPEANS from many nations passed through the Emigrant Halls at the port of Hamburg, Germany, bound for the United States. The words painted on the wall read, "My realm is the world."

AT ELLIS ISLAND, in New York Harbor, immigrants arriving about 1907 underwent a series of tests — including the dreaded trachoma examination — before they could enter the United States.

St. Paul. The boat trip from the end of the rail line at Galena up the river to St. Paul took about three days, depending on weather, fuel supplies, snags, and the number of tows. From La Crosse the trip was shorter, but there were fewer boats. During the summer navigation season, two boats a day usually left Galena for Minnesota, sometimes with as many as 800 persons crowded on board. Smaller Minnesota

Map 0.1. Routes to Minnesota in the 19th Century

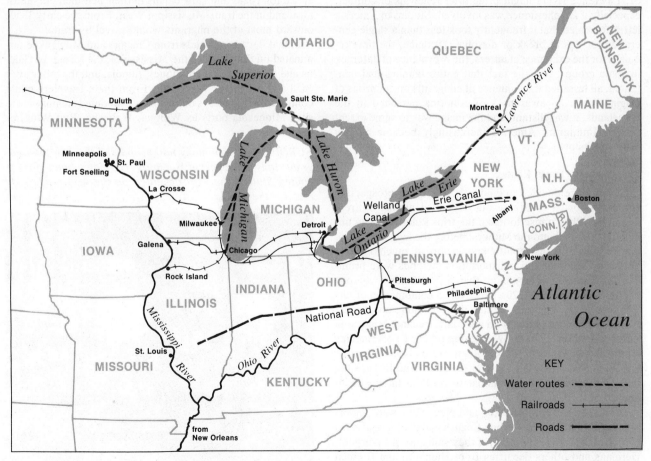

streams, such as the Root, Blue Earth, Minnesota, and St. Croix rivers, served as highways of pioneer settlement within the state.

By the 1870s the heyday of the steamboat was over, and patterns of migration to and in Minnesota had shifted to overland transport usually via railroad. The first all-rail line connecting Minneapolis and Chicago opened in 1867. In the boom years which culminated in the panic of 1873, track was laid through Wisconsin to St. Paul and from the Twin Cities to five locations on Minnesota's western border. Three years before the panic, the railroad reached Duluth, and immigrants, having arrived by Great Lakes steamer, funneled through that city on their way to the fertile Red River Valley. The chief advantage of a Great Lakes passage over a total rail journey, according to one settler, was that the steamer rates were cheaper.

In the last third of the 19th century, railroad companies constructing tracks across Minnesota promoted and sold lands along their lines that at first supplemented and then supplanted the earlier settlement patterns along rivers. From concentrations in the southeastern corner, land seekers moved southwest onto the prairies and westward to the Red River Valley and the Dakotas. After the Civil War a railroad construction boom threaded the state with 6,795 miles of track by 1900. In the late 19th and early 20th centuries the exploitation of iron ore, the northward movement of sawmilling, and the promotion of cutover lands for agricultural use drew people into the northeast region neglected by the early railroad builders. Most southern, central, and eastern Europeans entered the state by rail; some helped lay the tracks and then decided to stay.[9]

Rails dominated the transportation picture for many decades. Eventually Minnesota was the headquarters of no fewer than four transcontinentals, which spanned the nation

THE IMMIGRANT HOUSE in Duluth, built in 1872 and operated by the Northern Pacific Railroad, provided quarters for newly arrived immigrants in the port city while they waited for transportation to other areas of the state.

EARLY 20th-century immigrants carrying food baskets, beverage jugs, and bedrolls disembarked from a Minneapolis, St. Paul, and Sault Ste. Marie train in the Milwaukee Railroad sheds, probably in Minneapolis.

to the Pacific and connected through other lines with port cities elsewhere. In the 1920s rails began to give way to the auto and the airplane. By 1930 Minnesota had some 2,800 miles of paved and bituminous roads, a network that continued to grow in succeeding decades. From Wold-Chamberlain Airport, opened near the Twin Cities in 1923, the oldest and the second oldest air carriers in the United States (Western and Northwest Airlines) began operations in 1926. With others added in the 1940s, air routes stretched from Minnesota around the world. More and more immigrants arrived by plane in the second half of the 20th century at the same time that railroad passenger service virtually disappeared.[10]

The Minnesota They Chose

Yielding to white pressures, the Indians successively ceded a small area where Fort Snelling was built, the triangle between the Mississippi and St. Croix rivers, most of southern Minnesota, and then tract after tract to the north until only a few reservations remained to them (see Map 1.1). In the mid-19th century Minnesota lay in the pathway of a westward migration that would carry new settlers into regions as yet sparsely populated but rich in natural resources. Within the 84,068 square miles that became the North Star State, migrants found waterways that provided not only an initial transportation system but also power to turn mills, forests of white pine and hardwoods, fertile land in part covered by tough prairie sod, and hidden beneath the surface of its rocky northern reaches the ores of the Vermilion, Mesabi, and Cuyuna iron ranges.

When Minnesota became a territory in 1849, it had a recorded population of 4,852. Lumbering had begun in the St. Croix Valley in 1839, and the hamlets that became the cities of St. Paul and Minneapolis had been founded in the 1840s. In the 1850s the number of settlers pushing into the ceded Indian lands created a population explosion of 2,831% — by far the highest rate in the nation. When Minnesota joined the Union as the 32nd state in 1858, it counted 150,037 people. A host of Irish carpenters and tavernkeepers, Swiss and Welsh laborers, German butchers and cigarmakers, English masons, and Scots bakers joined farmers from Germany, Canada, and older areas of the United States, wagonmakers from New York, hotelkeepers from Virginia, lawyers and merchants from Pennsylvania, millwrights from Ohio, ministers, teachers, and tailors from New England, and French-Canadian voyageurs and blacksmiths to spread over its southeastern quarter and cluster in more than 400 cities, towns, and villages.[11] Although the growth rate never again reached the pinnacle of the 1850s and has continuously declined since that decade, it remained strong in the 19th century, ranging from 155.6% in the 1860s (despite the interruptions of the Civil and Dakota wars) to 33.7% in the 1890s. During the half century that closed in 1900, the state's population grew to 1,751,394. Eighty years later it was recorded as 4,077,148.

Until the mid-20th century over 50% of Minnesota's people were rural; 22% of them were engaged in farming as late as 1950. From 1860 to 1880 this figure exceeded 50%. Hospitable land laws, among them the Homestead Act of 1862, had

encouraged them to farm. Its provision for granting 160 acres free to a bona fide settler was important in a state embracing millions of acres of federally owned land.

At first the area's pioneer farmers concentrated upon the cultivation of wheat, but by the 1880s poor prices and soil exhaustion had convinced them of the wisdom of diversified farming. They grew corn, barley, oats, hay, sugar beets, flax, soybeans, potatoes, and vegetables, as well as raising livestock and poultry (especially turkeys in the mid-20th century) and developing dairying. A surprising number of farms has remained in the hands of the same families for over 100 years. But the efforts by many Finns and South Slavs to cultivate the cutovers of northern Minnesota after the trees had been removed were not equally successful.

A strong urban movement, begun in the industrial age following the Civil War, accelerated sharply in the 1880s when the urban population grew from 19.1% to 33.8% of the total. Many pre-World War I immigrants arrived intending only to amass a fortune and quickly depart. They had no desire to invest in land or anything else that implied permanence. Still others, like the Greeks, embittered by agricultural disasters in their homelands, scrupulously avoided rural life. In the last quarter of the 19th century, these factors, combined with the ready availability of urban jobs, attracted a polyglot population to Minnesota's industrial centers. When the 1930 and 1940 censuses were taken, the state's urban-rural population struck an almost even balance. It swung to 54.5% urban in 1950 and climbed to 66.4% in 1970.[12]

Although many Minnesota communities served as trading centers, the most prominent by far were the Twin Cities of St. Paul and Minneapolis. By 1890 they boasted a total population of 297,894 encompassing about 23% of the state's inhabitants. In that year Minneapolis ranked as the 18th largest city in the nation, and St. Paul was in 23rd place. The Twins' influence as an economic and cultural center intensified with the expansion of transportation and communication facilities. Their position was recognized and strengthened in 1914 when Minneapolis became the headquarters of the 9th Federal Reserve District, embracing not only Minnesota but also the Dakotas, Montana, and portions of Wisconsin and Michigan. By 1970 the two cities, with a combined population of 744,380, were the core of a seven-county metropolitan area inhabited by 1,704,423 people. It had numerous colleges and a diversified manufacturing base that included the headquarters or plants of four of the world's leading computer firms. With about 100 additional electronics companies plus internationally renowned medical centers in the state, they proved an irresistible magnet that drew many professionals in the brain drain era of the 1950s and 1960s.[13]

On both the national and state levels, attitudes toward immigrants have fluctuated widely. For many years, for example, Minnesota was not satisfied to capture what population increments might come its way in the course of westward movement. Official encouragement to immigrants got under way in 1855 when the territory appointed a commissioner of immigration, and continued, with varying degrees of intensity, into the 1920s. Laboring in New York City, the first commissioner combated the allegations of rival agents that immigrants who went to Minnesota Territory would risk their lives among the "mountains of ice" there.[14]

The official attitude of the United States toward the admission of immigrants has varied over four major periods in the country's history thus far. What might be called the Unrestricted Era, covering the years from the nation's founding until about 1875, saw policy and law favoring the free admission of needed workers. So eager was the United States to receive the newcomers, who in that period were largely from northern and western Europe, that it repeatedly passed laws encouraging ship owners to improve steerage conditions on the vessels carrying them across the seas.[15]

By 1886, when Emma Lazarus' famous sonnet was engraved upon the pedestal of the Statue of Liberty, attitudes were already changing. No longer entirely applicable were its famous lines:

> Give me your tired, your poor,
> Your huddled masses yearning to breathe free,
> The wretched refuse of your teeming shore.
> Send these, the homeless, tempest-tost to me.

The Qualitative Era, 1875 to 1920, beginning with passage of the first federal law restricting immigration, placed ever more selective restraints upon who could be admitted. By 1917, when a literacy test was added, the list was extensive. Excluded, for example, were paupers, convicts, mentally and physically diseased persons, polygamists, anarchists, contract laborers, and virtually all Asians.

These restrictions were codified and extended in the Quantitative or Quota Era from 1920 to 1965. An influx of southern and eastern Europeans just before and after World War I led to the addition of numerical restrictions to the already lengthy list of proscriptions. First imposed in 1921, numerical quotas were tightened by the Immigration Act of 1924, often referred to as the National Origins Act or the Quota Law, which set limits based upon the total number from a given country counted in the United States census of 1920. This system, which favored immigrants from northwestern Europe and the British Isles, took effect in 1929; it remained, with minor revisions, the basis of United States immigration law for over 35 years. A recodification in 1952 abolished race as a barrier to entrance and permitted small quotas for various previously barred Asians. Not until 1965, however, was the national origins system scrapped in favor of broad hemisphere allotments on a first-come, first-served basis. Although revised from time to time since, the 1965 law was still essentially in force in 1980.

The fourth period, which overlapped the third, might be called the Refugee Era, for the existing laws proved inadequate to cope with the humanitarian concerns that surfaced in connection with Displaced Persons in the 1940s, refugees from the Hungarian Revolution in the 1950s, Cubans in the 1960s, and Southeast Asians and Middle Easterners in the 1970s. The Displaced Persons Act of 1948, later extended, permitted the admission of over 400,000 people from Germany, Austria, Italy, and Eastern Europe. The Refugee Act of 1980, the latest attempt to cobble together a coherent policy, removed the anti-Communist bias of earlier laws,

established uniform rules for admissions, and provided for a domestic resettlement program to be financed largely by the federal government rather than the states.

Certain groups other than refugees have also received special treatment within the framework of various laws. Among them have been people from Western Hemisphere countries, who have been rather generously treated, and those from Asian countries, who were for many decades excluded. The opening years of the 1980s, however, witnessed increased anxiety over the rising numbers of illegal aliens (largely Mexicans) who filtered across the border in search of work. No one knew how many had arrived. Estimates ranged as high as 12,000,000 or more nationally and perhaps as many as 5,000 in Minnesota. During the severe labor shortages of World War II, Mexican field workers were welcomed by the hundreds of thousands under the Bracero Program, which functioned from 1942 to 1964. Since then policies and programs concerning such contract workers, who are important to the agriculture of many states including Minnesota, have varied almost from year to year. Since few could be admitted legally, many skilled as well as unskilled Mexicans made their way across the unguarded border as best they could.

A Select Commission, which examined the Immigration and Naturalization Act and various related laws and submitted its recommendations to the president in March, 1981, commented that it "was well aware of the widespread dissatisfaction among U.S. citizens with an immigration policy that seems to be out of control." Among the numerous changes recommended were establishment of increased ceilings, a "fixed-percentage limit to the independent immigration from any one country," expansion of those eligible for preference as relatives of United States citizens, streamlining of refugee resettlement agencies, stricter enforcement of existing laws, and adoption of a program to legalize "a substantial portion" of the "undocumented illegal aliens now in the United States."[16]

As for Asians, a large body of federal legislation has concerned them for more than a century. Beginning with the first restriction passed in 1875, Chinese and Japanese were specifically barred and companies were prohibited from importing them as contract laborers. The Chinese Exclusion Act of 1882 suspended the immigration of Chinese laborers for 10 years and prevented all Chinese from obtaining citizenship. The time period specified was extended again and again, and the restrictions were supplemented by additional discriminatory provisions denying Chinese visiting the homeland the right to re-enter the United States, requiring certificates of residence, etc.

In 1917 and 1924 Congress not only reinforced the exclusion of Chinese but broadened it to refuse virtually all Asians. The Immigration Act of 1917, passed over two vetoes by President Woodrow Wilson, established "barred zones" which included China and most other Asian countries. The 1924 Quota Law expanded the restrictions, making it especially difficult for women to qualify as immigrants. Not until 1943, when China was an American ally during World War II, did Congress enact repeal, provide a small quota (105 annually), and grant Chinese the right to naturalization. The repeal stimulated a call to end exclusion of people from other Asian countries, but extensive revision was not attempted until 1965.

An even more unusual situation prevailed regarding Japanese immigrants. From 1907, when President Theodore Roosevelt negotiated a Gentleman's Agreement with Japan, until 1924, when Congress passed the Quota Law, Japan decided who among its citizens was to receive a passport allowing him or her to go to the United States. Under the terms of the Gentleman's Agreement of 1907, Japan agreed to limit voluntarily the number allowed to emigrate, and it continued to regard those who did so as Japanese citizens. In 1922 the United States Supreme Court ruled that Japanese were not eligible for naturalization, and this prohibition was incorporated into the 1924 law, effectively barring all Japanese immigration. The prohibition was not lifted until 1952.

Just as the law's attitudes toward immigrants varied over time, so did those of American society. One of the most extreme national reactions concerned the Japanese, who by President Franklin D. Roosevelt's executive order were evacuated from West Coast states in 1942 and placed in camps in desolate areas of the United States, where they remained until 1945. Of the approximately 110,000 Japanese thus driven from their homes during World War II, 64% were American citizens.[17]

A blatant Minnesota example of legalized discrimination was the massive attack on immigrant groups launched during World War I by a special state agency known as the Minnesota Commission of Public Safety. With an appropriation of $1,000,000, the seven-man body was created by the legislature in April, 1917, only a few days after the United States entered World War I. It functioned until December, 1920, chaired by Governor Joseph A. A. Burnquist. Possessing sweeping powers, the commission set up local units throughout the state, saturated it with speakers, bulletins, news reports, and spies and informers, required all aliens to register, and banned strikes and union activity. Although German-speaking persons and institutions were its chief prey, other ethnic groups, Socialists, and members of labor unions were also spied upon and otherwise intimidated. Co-operating with the commission were women's clubs and local units of the American Protective League, a zealous volunteer organization which sought to ferret out "slackers" and people deemed subversives — a network almost impossible to escape.[18]

Non-English-speaking groups were especially caught up in the effort that came to be called Americanization — a campaign to save the immigrants from such philosophies as Socialism, teach them to speak English, acquaint them with America's history and ideals, and urge them to become naturalized American citizens. In Minnesota the wartime effort was waged by dozens of organizations, among them city-wide Americanization committees in Minneapolis, St. Paul, and Duluth, the University of Minnesota's Americanization training course, the local women's committee of the Council of National Defense, and the Minnesota State Americanization Committee, which was created by the Public Safety Commission to co-ordinate the multifarious activities of the others.[19]

Although the antiforeign hysteria of the World War I period accentuated the Americanization movement, it had begun earlier. Spurring activity was the federal naturalization law of 1906, which laid down a standard procedure, restricted the granting of naturalization to certain courts, created a Division of Naturalization in the United States Department of Labor, and required applicants to speak English. Important, too, was the establishment in 1914 of an Immigrant Education Division in the United States Bureau of Education, which included in its program the distribution of printed materials.[20]

Ten years earlier, however, large-scale Americanization efforts were begun by the public school systems of Minnesota's range towns, which pioneered adult night classes in the early 1900s — at that time a trail-blazing innovation. Virginia was operating a night school in 1904–05; in 1909 Hibbing and half a dozen other range cities inaugurated experimental programs to teach English to the adult foreign born, including the 6% who were illiterate. In succeeding years many

IMMIGRANT children participated in Americanization activities provided by the Pillsbury Settlement House, Minneapolis, about 1925.

THE POWERFUL *Minnesota Commission of Public Safety, about 1918.*

FOREIGN *men and women prepared for American citizenship at a night school in Eveleth, about 1915.*

other subjects were added, including home classes for women and "classes in citizenship for applicants for Second Papers," in which the United States Bureau of Immigration in Duluth and St. Louis County federal judges took a keen interest. Eventually a passing grade in these courses was a requirement for naturalization in St. Louis County.[21]

Although these endeavors were backed by the mining companies, they were funded by the local school boards. Not until 1917, after Congress passed the literacy test law, were state and federal appropriations for vocational education made to support this work. That employers exerted pressure upon foreign-born miners to become citizens was apparent in the attitude of the Oliver Iron Mining Company. In 1916 a company spokesman favored "making it clear to our men that when we make promotions . . . the man with full citizenship has a better chance . . . and will be favored over the one without citizenship." It seems abundantly evident that during the period of World War I at least, the immigrant in Minnesota could not enjoy the assumed and then unquestioned benefits of the American system without accepting, theoretically at least, its values.[22]

Writing during the final months of the war, Carol Aronovici, an immigrant who was chairman of the Minnesota State Committee on Americanization, observed, "It is almost the fashion now to talk, write or organize in the interest of Americanization work. Every existing organization has an Americanization committee . . . and folks who used to be just human beings are being classified into American and unAmerican, according to their willingness to agree or disagree with the Americanizers as to what their social, economic and political ideals should be." The fashion did not fade after the war, when a nationwide movement, taking various forms in various states, got under way. A multitude of federal, state, municipal, and private agencies joined the schools' efforts, which became even more extensive. Indicative of Minnesota's participation in the movement was the broad representation of organizations in Americanization conferences held in the state and the formation in 1920 of the Americanization Council of Minnesota as a co-ordinating agency.[23]

Among the private agencies in the forefront of the effort were settlement houses, such as Neighborhood House, founded in 1897 on St. Paul's West Side to serve the Jewish people there but later reorganized to include the Mexican community, and North East Neighborhood House, established among the Slavs of Minneapolis in 1915. The social settlement movement and the newly spawned philosophy of social work, both products of the Progressive reform era, were responses to an "industrialism which created a large working class and brought about an influx of immigrants with numerous problems of assimilation." The movement focused especially upon recently arrived immigrants, striving to achieve what one author called "100 per cent Americanism and 100 per cent conformity." Another wrote of its objectives: "somehow the immigrant must be shown the peculiar genius of the American way; then somehow America must be taught the cultural enrichment it stood to gain from new immigrant contributions." The settlement house attempted to bridge the gap.[24]

Like the night schools on the iron ranges, settlement houses came to appreciate some of the varied cultural elements in the immigrant communities. Ironically, however, Minnesota's earliest general ethnic cultural preservation effort did not originate with the immigrants themselves. Rather it came out of the vision of social worker Alice Sickels. The International Institute, founded in St. Paul and in Duluth in 1919, sponsored its first Festival of Nations in St. Paul as a showcase for the various ethnic groups in 1932.

In view of organized efforts to "melt" the immigrants into the American mold, it is not surprising that the ways they viewed themselves changed and how others regarded them also wavered. Some changes would, of course, have occurred in any case. Culture is far from static, and people adapt to radical changes in their environment by means of cultural shifts. Some immigrants had completed major identity shifts before they reached Minnesota. Descendants of French who had immigrated to Quebec some generations earlier, for example, already thought of themselves as French Canadians rather than French. Blacks too had remained in North America, coming to view themselves as African Americans by the time they moved to Minnesota rather than Africans. On the other hand, most immigrants, including such diverse groups as Norwegians and Lebanese, who had arrived directly from Europe, Asia, or the Middle East, often underwent the transformation from an immigrant group to an ethnic one only after reaching Minnesota. This could be a gradual process that affected second and third generations as well.

Definitions of ethnicity, or of what constitutes an ethnic group, vary greatly. Few of the authors whose work is included in this book would agree upon all the elements possible in such a definition. Some approach it from the viewpoint of a group with common origins; others prefer to emphasize ethnicity as one of many roles in the lives of individual Americans somewhat akin to age, religious affiliation, or political persuasion. Still another segment of late 20th-century scholarship uses the word ethnic to refer to any minority group.

Perhaps we can do no better than to follow the *Harvard Encyclopedia of American Ethnic Groups* in this thorny matter. "All the groups treated here are characterized," it said, "by some of the following features, although in combinations that vary considerably:

(1) common geographic origin;
(2) migratory status;
(3) race;
(4) language or dialect;
(5) religious faith or faiths;
(6) ties that transcend kinship, neighborhood, and community boundaries;
(7) shared traditions, values, and symbols;
(8) literature, folklore, and music;
(9) food preferences;
(10) settlement and employment patterns;
(11) special interests in regard to politics in the homeland and in the United States;
(12) institutions that specifically serve and maintain the group;
(13) an internal sense of distinctiveness;
(14) an external perception of distinctiveness."[25]

Still another attitude found among some Americans, who do not care where their ancestors came from, is hostility to the whole idea of ethnicity in the United States. Perhaps they reason that such an idea seems to exclude them, or they see it as a threat to their view of the United States as a nation and Americans as one people. Others searching for their roots are eagerly tracing genealogies and researching their countries of origin. Whatever one may think of ethnicity, ethnic groups, and the tendency of some people to identify in ethnic terms, however, it is not possible to dismiss the subject completely. Scholars in recent years have supplanted filiopietists in studying the phenomenon. Many chapters in the following pages clearly indicate that ethnicity in various forms and degrees continues to exist in Minnesota in the 1980s.

"The characteristics and symbols that set off one category of people from another are not relics from the past but a result of the creative process involved when people take on different, or reaffirm the same, ethnic attributes," wrote George L. Hicks.[26] Ethnicity, it seems, is an open-ended, ongoing process, not always without conflict — one which will invite serious study tomorrow, the day after tomorrow, and onward into the future. Change, often but not always gradual, is a key element in it, opening a wide field for continuing research. Indeed many aspects of the state's ethnic history touched on in this book offer rich avenues for further exploration. The sponsors and authors associated with the Minnesota Ethnic History Project hope that their work will stimulate scholars to pursue further the complex and fascinating stories of the people who chose Minnesota.

Reference notes

[1] Stephan Thernstrom, ed., *Harvard Encyclopedia of American Ethnic Groups*, 1049 (Cambridge, Mass., 1980); Philip D. Curtin, *The Atlantic Slave Trade: A Census*, 75, 231, 234 (Madison, Wis., 1969). For background information and charts, see Philip A. M. Taylor, *Distant Magnet: European Emigration to the U.S.A.*, chapters 1–6 (London, 1971); Maldwyn A. Jones, *American Immigration*, chapters 4, 7 (Chicago, 1960).

Statistics of emigration and immigration are generally inaccurate because of unreported migrants, recording errors, lack of information from many ports, the flow through Canada, classification of passengers, and repeaters who returned to the homeland and re-emigrated several times. The percentage of returnees varied with each group, from relatively high figures for Greeks and Italians, to low ones for Norwegians. The number of returnees also varied by period, with higher return rates for urban migrants. Calculations of the number departing from the U.S. were based on Walter F. Willcox, ed., *International Migrations*, 2:88, 89, 103 (Reprint ed., New York, 1969), and Thernstrom, ed., *Harvard Encyclopedia*, 1036. See also Appendix, below.

[2] Minnesota, *Executive Documents*, 1875, 1:13.

[3] The terms "old emigrants" referring to northern and western Europeans and "new emigrants" referring to those from southern and eastern Europe were applied by the U.S. Immigration Commission in 1911. During the period of controversy before. numerical quotas were enacted in the 1920s, the terms took on discriminatory overtones, and "new" often became synonymous with inferior. The terms were avoided throughout this book. See John Higham, *Strangers in the Land: Patterns of American Nativism, 1860–1925*, chapter 7 (New Brunswick, N.J., 1955). For time lines, elementary and secondary booklets, and other curriculum materials useful to teachers, see Minnesota Historical Society, Education Division, *The Immigrant Experience: A Minnesota History Resource Unit* (St. Paul, 1979).

[4] On transatlantic voyages and the push-pull factors discussed below, see Marcus L. Hansen, *The Immigrant in American History*, chapter 2 (Cambridge, Mass., 1940); Taylor, *Distant Magnet*, chapters 7, 8; Alfred J. Lotka, "Modern Trends in the Birth Rate," in American Academy of Political and Social Science, *Annals*, 188:2 (November, 1936); Brinley Thomas, *Migration and Economic Growth: A Study of Great Britain and the Atlantic Economy* (Cambridge, Eng., 1954); Sten Carlsson, "Chronology and Composition

of Swedish Emigration to America," 114–148, and Hans Norman, "The Causes of Emigration: An Attempt at a Multivariate Analysis," 149–164, both in Harald Runblom and Hans Norman, eds., *From Sweden to America: A History of the Migration* (Minneapolis, 1976).

[5] Information on why the writers emigrated may be found in collections of America letters, such as Charlotte Erickson, ed., *Invisible Immigrants: The Adaptation of English and Scottish Immigrants in Nineteenth-Century America*, 81–226, 266–389, 411–482 (Coral Gables, Fla., 1972); Theodore C. Blegen, ed., *Land of Their Choice: The Immigrants Write Home*, 19–31, 35–88 (Minneapolis, 1955); H. Arnold Barton, ed., *Letters from the Promised Land: Swedes in America, 1840–1914*, 22–103 (Minneapolis, 1975); Alan Conway, ed., *The Welsh in America: Letters from the Immigrants*, 17–50 (Minneapolis, 1961). For descriptions of the many Minnesota guidebooks available in both Europe and America, see Carlton C. Qualey, "A New Eldorado: Guides to Minnesota, 1850s–1880s," in *Minnesota History*, 42:215–224 (Summer, 1971). For a summary of promotion by railroads, see Harold F. Peterson, "Early Minnesota Railroads and the Quest for Settlers," in *Minnesota History*, 13:25–44 (March, 1932).

[6] For Sweden alone, it was estimated that $100,000,000 was returned in postal money orders from 1885 to 1937 and that $8,000,000 went back annually from 1906 to 1930. Another scholar estimated that $260,000,000 was sent to the United Kingdom from 1848 to 1900. See Franklin D. Scott, "The Study of the Effects of Emigration," in *Scandinavian Economic History Review*, 8:164 (April, 1960); Arnold Schrier, *Ireland and the American Emigration, 1850–1900*, 105, appendix tables 18, 19 (Minneapolis, 1958).

[7] Wilbur Zelinsky, *The Cultural Geography of the United States*, 26, 28 (Englewood Cliffs, N.J., 1972).

[8] On travel routes here and five paragraphs below, see John F. Stover, *Iron Road to the West: American Railroads in the 1850s*, 143, 149, 153, 160–176 (New York, 1978); Louis C. Hunter, *Steamboats on the Western Rivers: An Economic and Technological History*, 45, 181–189 (Cambridge, Mass., 1949); William J. Petersen, *Steamboating On the Upper Mississippi: The Water Way to Iowa*, 224–226, 316–380 (Iowa City, Ia., 1937); Richard S. Prosser, *Rails to the North Star*, 12, 17–24 (Minneapolis, 1966). For one of many descriptions of a Great Lakes trip, see John Stewart, *Building Up the Country on the Northwest Frontier*, 7–18 (n.p., [1967?]), photocopy in MHS.

[9] John R. Borchert and Donald P. Yaeger, *Atlas of Minnesota Resources and Settlement*, chapter 9 (St. Paul, 1968); R[obert] W. Murchie and M[errill] E. Jarchow, *Population Trends in Minnesota*, 7–18 (University of Minnesota Agricultural Experiment Station, *Bulletin No. 327* — [St. Paul], 1936); Mildred L. Hartsough, *The Development of the Twin Cities (Minneapolis and St. Paul) as a Metropolitan Market*, 206 (Minneapolis, 1925); Theodore C. Blegen, *Minnesota: A History of the State*, 326, 328 (Minneapolis, 1963).

Particularly important among the railroads promoting immigration was the Northern Pacific, which in the 1870s conducted a well-organized campaign to bring settlers to its lands. Area after area from Duluth westward across Minnesota owed its development to this company.

[10] Blegen, *Minnesota*, 484, 485; Mildred L. Hartsough, "Transportation as a Factor in the Development of the Twin Cities," in *Minnesota History*, 7:225–229 (September, 1926); James W. Lydon, "History of the Soo Line Railroad," 109, undated manuscript in MHS; *Commercial West*, April 17, 1909, p. 32; Harold R. Harris, "Minnesota in the World of Aviation," in *Minnesota History*, 33:240–242 (Summer, 1953).

[11] For population data here and three paragraphs below, see William W. Folwell, *A History of Minnesota*, 1:352, 359 (Reprint ed., St. Paul, 1961); Patricia C. Harpole and Mary D. Nagle, eds., *Minnesota Territorial Census, 1850* (St. Paul, 1972); U.S., *Census, 1860, Population*, IV, 599; 1970, vol. 1, part 25, p. 7; Blegen, *Minnesota*, 177, 253, 339, 390–394; Lowry Nelson, Charles E. Ramsey, and Jacob Toews, *A Century of Population Growth in Minnesota*, 5 (University of Minnesota Agricultural Experiment Station, *Bulletin No. 423* — [St. Paul], 1954). The 1980 figure was reported as final in *St. Paul Pioneer Press*, March 29, 1981, Metro sec., 2; slightly smaller figures appear in U.S., *Census, 1980, Preliminary Reports, Population and Housing*, part 25, pp. 1, 2.

[12] U.S., *Census, 1970, Population*, vol. 1, part 25, p. 7. Because of a change in urban definition, percentages for 1950 and 1970 are not precisely comparable to those of earlier years.

[13] U.S., *Census, 1890, Population*, lxvi, lxvii; 1970, vol. 1, part 25, p. 42; Hartsough, *Development of the Twin Cities*, 177; Ronald Abler, John S. Adams, and John R. Borchert, *The Twin Cities of St. Paul and Minneapolis*, 19 (Cambridge, Mass., 1976); Don W. Larson, *Land of the Giants: A History of Minnesota Business*, 161 (Minneapolis, 1979).

[14] The quotation is from Theodore C. Blegen, "Minnesota's Campaign for Immigrants," in Swedish Historical Society of America, *Yearbook*, 11:6 (St. Paul, 1926).

[15] Information not otherwise documented in the following summary of immigration law was based on Marion T. Bennett, *Immigration Policies: A History* (Washington, D.C., 1963); Thernstrom, ed., *Harvard Encyclopedia*, 486–495; *Indochinese Refugee Reports*, March 11, 1980, p. 1; U.S. Displaced Persons Commission, *The DP Story: The Final Report* (Washington, 1952).

[16] For a summary of the Select Commission's recommendations and the comments of its chairman, Father Theodore M. Hesburgh, see *Congressional Record*, 97 Congress, 1 session, 1683–1690. On post-1964 immigration, see Roy S. Bryce-Laporte, ed., *Sourcebook on the New Immigration*, 2 vols. (New Brunswick, N.J., and Washington, D.C., 1979).

[17] Thernstrom, ed., *Harvard Encyclopedia*, 566.

[18] Carol Jenson, "Loyalty As a Political Weapon," in *Minnesota History*, 43:44–57 (Summer, 1972); Franklin F. Holbrook and Livia Appel, *Minnesota in the War with Germany*, 2:27–37 (St. Paul, 1932); Minnesota Commission of Public Safety, *Preliminary Report to J. A. A. Burnquist, Governor of Minnesota*, 19 ([St. Paul, 1919]); Minnesota State Americanization Committee, Minutes, December 18, 1918, in File 236, Minnesota Commission of Public Safety (PSC) Records, Minnesota State Archives, MHS. See also Robert K. Murray, *Red Scare: A Study in National Hysteria, 1919–1920* (Minneapolis, 1955).

[19] Timothy L. Smith, "Educational Beginnings, 1844–1910," 11, typed paper, 1963, copy in MHS; Holbrook and Appel, *Minnesota in the War*, 2:7, 13, 79, 83, 86; Albert E. Jenks, "The Americanization Training Course at the University of Minnesota," in *Minnesota State Americanization Conference, Papers and Resolutions*, 122, 127 ([Duluth], 1921); three pamphlets by Jenks, *The Goal of Americanization Training, The Spirit of Americanization* (both 1919), and *Americanization — A Brief Summary* (1920), in University of Minnesota Archives, Minneapolis. Jenks, an anthropologist, directed the course. Frank V. Thompson, *Schooling the Immigrant*, 1, 40 (New York, 1920) and Albert A. Owens, *Adult Immigrant Education: Its Scope Content and Methods* (New York, 1925) were contemporary texts, offering insight into the era's thinking and multiple definitions of Americanization.

[20] Holbrook and Appel, *Minnesota in the War*, 2:83; U.S. Division of Immigrant Education, miscellaneous literature, in File 236, PSC Records. On naturalization procedures, see U.S. Department of Labor, *Historical Sketch of Naturalization in the United States*, 8–12 (Washington, D.C., 1926).

[21] On the ranges, see R. K. Doe, "Where the Melting Pot Doth Melt," 8, 9, in Dept. of Labor, Immigration and Naturalization

Services, General Education Correspondence files, National Archives Record Group 85 (NARG 85), copy in MEHP Papers; P. P. Colgrove, "Night Schools of the Iron Range in Minnesota," and J. Vaughan, "The Evening Schools of Chisholm," in *Immigrants in America Review*, January, 1916, pp. 68, 83; Timothy L. Smith, "School and Community: The Quest of Equal Opportunity, 1910–1921," 27–35, typed paper, 1963, copy in MHS. See also C. C. Alexander, "Survey of Hibbing Night Schools from 1909 to 1922," 1, 2, 4; anonymous, "Americanizing the Immigrant Woman," 8; Herbert Blair to J. W. Richardson, April 8, 1924; and a pamphlet entitled *Evening School Review* (Chisholm) containing short autobiographical reminiscences of those attending English and citizenship classes in the 1920s — all in Grace Lee Nute Papers, University of Minnesota-Duluth Library, used with permission. Similar pamphlets were printed by various other range school systems, and the *Hibbing Tribune* devoted a monthly page to "Schools of Our New Americans" in 1923–24.

[22] Minnesota, *Statutes, Supplement*, 1917, 283; R. K. Doe, ["History of the Americanization Movement in Northern Minnesota, 1906–1924"], 1, 9, in NARG 85; John F. McClymer, "The Federal Government and the Americanization Movement, 1915–24," in *Prologue, The Journal of the National Archives*, 10:23–41 (Spring, 1978); Edward G. Hartmann, *The Movement to Americanize the Immigrant*, 216–266 (New York, 1948). The quotation is from L. R. Salsich to George W. Morgan, May 22, 1916, in Oliver Iron Mining Company Records, MHS.

[23] Carol Aronovici, *Americanization*, 46 (St. Paul, 1919); *Proceedings at the Third Minnesota State Americanization Conference*, 11–16, 128–131 (Duluth, 1921).

[24] Winifred W. Bolin, "Heating Up the Melting Pot," in *Minnesota History*, 45:58 (Summer, 1976); Clarke A. Chambers, *Seedtime of Reform: American Social Service and Social Action, 1918–1933*, 14 (Minneapolis, 1963). See also the papers of these and other Twin Cities' settlement houses, in MHS. On the YMCA and YWCA on the ranges, see Clarke A. Chambers, "Social Welfare Policies and Programs on the Minnesota Iron Range — 1880–1930," 54–60, 64, typescript, 1963, in MHS. The papers of the International Institute of Minnesota in St. Paul are in the IHRC; those of the International Institute of Duluth are in the Northeast Minnesota Historical Center, Duluth. See also Alice L. Sickels, *Around the World in St. Paul* (Minneapolis, 1945).

[25] Thernstrom, ed., *Harvard Encyclopedia*, vi.

[26] George L. Hicks and Philip E. Leis, *Ethnic Encounters: Identities and Contexts*, 18 (North Scituate, Mass., 1977).

NORTH AMERICANS

CHAPTER 1

The Dakota and Ojibway

Mitchell E. Rubinstein and Alan R. Woolworth

WHILE AMERICAN INDIAN people from many tribal cultures now make their homes in Minnesota, the Dakota and Ojibway are the "old-stock" native people in the state. In retrospect what is called Minnesota history before the middle of the 19th century is really their history, even though explorers and fur traders have received favored treatment in print. In the years since then, both tribal groups have witnessed the breath-taking speed with which white settlement gobbled up the land and developed present-day Minnesota, and both were profoundly affected by these historical events. This chapter sketches the broad outlines of Dakota (or Sioux) and Ojibway (or Chippewa) experience from the period of early Minnesota statehood to the present time.[1]

Prelude: Ancient People

From the perspective of western culture, history began in Minnesota with the arrival of the first European who left or generated a written record of the visit. Everything preceding this event is called prehistory, and in varying degrees tends to be ignored by historians as irrelevant to the main thrust of the story of Minnesota. The effect, if not the intent, of this approach has been to deny the longevity of Indian experience and provide modern readers with a distorted notion that meaningful human experience began in the region with the arrival of Europeans.

How long the Dakota have been living in what is now Minnesota is not really known, but most scholars interested in their earliest beginnings believe the Dakota culture was flourishing long before the arrival of Daniel Greysolon, sieur du Luth, and Father Louis Hennepin in 1678–80. The Ojibway, on the other hand, by their own tribal traditions as well as historical accounts, are known to be latecomers from an eastern Great Lakes location who probably reached northern Minnesota in the late 1600s and early 1700s. In addition, the Assiniboin, who are distant relatives of the Dakota, lived and hunted in the state, and at a more remote time the Cheyenne and several other tribes later associated with the Great Plains very likely lived in the area.[2]

Antedating these historic tribes, native people about whom very little is known made Minnesota their home. The earliest of them may have settled in the region as long ago as 6000 B.C. A thousand or so years later people of the "Old Copper Culture" established themselves in the Great Lakes region, where they persisted from about 5000 B.C. to about 1500 B.C. Their handsome copper artifacts, which are found primarily in Minnesota, Wisconsin, Michigan, and Ontario, represented the first known use of fabricated metal in either North or South America.[3]

More is known about the Woodland and Mississippian peoples, who span the period from 1000 B.C. to 1700 A.D. in historic times. For some seven centuries before the arrival of French explorers in the 1600s, the occupants of much of Minnesota are thought to have been representatives of these two cultures. They customarily buried their dead in mounds, and they seem not to have been numerous until about 800 A.D. when wild rice became a food staple, fostering more permanent settlements in the Mississippi Valley. To the north along the Rainy River of present Koochiching County a Woodland people, whose life-style archaeologists have called the Laurel culture, were Minnesota's earliest known potterymakers. Although most researchers are convinced that such prehistoric peoples were the ancestors of later Indian tribes, tracing tribal connections has proven difficult.

By the time of white settlement the Assiniboin and some other tribes encountered by French explorers and fur traders had departed westward, leaving two major groups of Indian people in control of the area — the Dakota on the prairie and hardwood lands of the southern portion and the Ojibway in the pine forests of northern Minnesota. Both societies were seminomadic, moving as the seasons changed and various foods were ready to harvest.

Dakota and Ojibway Before 1850

The term "Indian" should not be used to obscure the differences among the peoples it describes. Although a subsistence life-style led the Dakota and Ojibway to develop fairly similar economic and political systems, each tribe maintained a distinctive culture and language. Before white contact, they lived in different parts of the continent, the Ojibway apparently on the East Coast near the mouth of the St. Lawrence River, the Dakota in an unknown location in the Midwest from which they migrated west and south of Lake Superior. As the Ojibway also gradually moved west, the first direct encounters of the two tribes, perhaps occasioned by the fur trade, seem to have occurred in the Minnesota country.[4]

From oral tradition, the accounts of early observers, and 20th-century ethnohistories a picture of Indian cultures before white contact may be reconstructed. The social, political, economic, and religious systems that composed Ojibway and Dakota life derived from their intimate association with the natural environment. Sociocultural activities appeared to have followed the dictates of each tribe's mixed economy of hunting, gathering, and agriculture.[5]

By 1680 the Dakota (or Allies, as they called themselves) consisted of seven tribal groups, later classified into three divisions: the Santee (Eastern), the Wiciyela (Middle), and the Teton (Western). It was the Santee, composed of four related tribes — the Mdewakanton (meaning Spirit Lake Village), Wahpekute (Shooters Among the Leaves), Wahpeton (Village of the Leaf), and Sisseton (Lake or Fishscale Village) — who lived in present Minnesota. The Yanktonai and Yankton (Middle tribes) inhabited what is now North and South Dakota.

As late as the 17th century the Dakota were established at and around Mille Lacs Lake. Most lived in a belt of hardwood forest, where the wealth of vegetation supported a large population of animals and birds and a wide variety of plants. In this environment they followed a seasonal cycle of food gathering, fishing, hunting, and limited agriculture, based on a profound understanding of the habits, habitats, and growth cycles of all parts of the ecological system. They sought muskrat and maple sugar in spring, waterfowl and berries in summer, deer and other game from early summer through January, and wild rice in the fall. Agriculture was, of course, confined to the warm months. Corn, the staple, was planted in May.

According to Ojibway tradition, the westward-moving tribe stopped for many years at Sault Ste. Marie at the eastern end of Lake Superior. About 1680, however, it divided into what were later called the northern, southwestern, southeastern, and Plains Ojibway. Between 1680 and 1736 the northern and southwestern tribes traveled west along the south shore of Lake Superior, arriving in what is now Minnesota in the area of the later Grand Portage Reservation near the Pigeon River boundary with Ontario. By that time their participation in the fur trade provided the Ojibway with certain technological advantages, such as the gun, which made them formidable enemies and enhanced their ability to exploit game resources.[6]

Like the Dakota, the Ojibway practiced a mixed subsistence economy of hunting, fishing, and harvesting wild food in season. They too gathered maple sugar in the spring and wild rice in the fall. In addition the cultivation of corn, potatoes, beans, pumpkins, and squash was a prominent part of their food system.[7]

Observers have subdivided the Dakota and the Ojibway into tribes, bands, clans, and villages. To the surprise of white people who tried to negotiate with them, political organization and lines of power were very egalitarian and presented many difficulties to outsiders who were accustomed to more rigid and authoritarian political systems. The family was the vital unit of activity. In the normal course of events, families assembled and dispersed depending on the season. During the winter months they hunted singly or in small groups, for resources were not sufficient to support large numbers. Village life commenced with the spring sugaring

season and carried through ricing in the fall. Consequently most social activity was confined to that period. Harvests were occasions for celebration, and village life was also the setting for organized games, informal visiting, and religious ceremonies.[8]

Subsistence depended upon co-operation, and group decision-making was done by arriving at a consensus. Families were generally headed by the eldest male; villages, which were usually made up of extended families, and bands were led by what whites called chiefs. These men gained their status by demonstrating unusual wisdom and particular skills, as well as by having large personal followings. As leaders they might propose courses of action, but they had neither absolute authority nor formal mechanisms of enforcement. Their suggestions were followed if village or band members had confidence in the leader's ability. While chieftainships often passed from father to son or to another male relative, they were not absolutely hereditary. Civil chiefs shared responsibility for the well-being of their bands with religious leaders and war chiefs of demonstrated fighting skills.

As the fur trade era dawned, Dakota-Ojibway relations were at first peaceful. In 1679 Sieur Du Luth engineered a treaty between the Ojibway, who were his allies, and the Dakota, Cree, and Assiniboin of the Lake Superior region. As a result, a system developed wherein the Ojibway became middlemen for the French, thus assuring the Dakota a steady supply of trade goods and the Ojibway access to Dakota hunting and fishing grounds. These resources drew the Ojibway from Sault Ste. Marie to La Pointe (Madeline Island) near the eastern end of Lake Superior. At the same time, the Dakota were attracted to the rich bison-hunting grounds farther west, and many began to dwell in those regions. In 1736 trade relations deteriorated when the French established a post in southeastern Minnesota, thereby undercutting the Ojibway middlemen and their claim to use of Dakota lands.

There ensued a long intertribal fight for control of northern Minnesota which lasted until about 1825. By the 1780s, however, Ojibway were in possession of the area from present-day Red Lake to Little Falls, including Big Sandy and Leech lakes. By 1800 many Dakota had resettled along the lower Minnesota and the Mississippi below the Falls of St. Anthony. Others journeyed west of the Red River or north into Canada.[9]

At this time only a few years remained for the Dakota and Ojibway as free and independent people. Already the fur-bearing animals on which they had become so heavily dependent were becoming scarce. Soon American frontier settlements would creep into their midst, marking the close of one chapter and the beginning of another in tribal experiences with the white man. Only this time, settlers and developers were interested in the land itself, and their impact on the Dakota and Ojibway would be devastating.

Except for two small parcels of land sold to the United States in 1805, all of what is now Minnesota belonged to the Dakota and the Ojibway when white settlement reached the area in 1837. One of the pieces, bought by Zebulon M. Pike on behalf of the United States government, was the future site of Fort Snelling, the area's first military post, built in the 1820s. In 1825 under the auspices of government agents, the Dakota and Ojibway agreed to the establishment of a diagonal demarcation between their tribal areas. It ran northwest across Minnesota from the St. Croix River on the east to the Red River a bit north of present Moorhead (see Map 1.1).[10]

This division endured until 1837, when the United States negotiated substantial cessions with the Ojibway and Dakota that opened to white settlement the first portion of the present state, a triangle of land between the Mississippi and St. Croix rivers which included the sites of the future cities of Minneapolis and St. Paul. Ten years later another treaty ceded lands west of the Mississippi in central Minnesota as a temporary residence for the Winnebago and Menominee,

Map 1.1. Indian Land Cessions in Minnesota, with 1980 Reservations and Communities

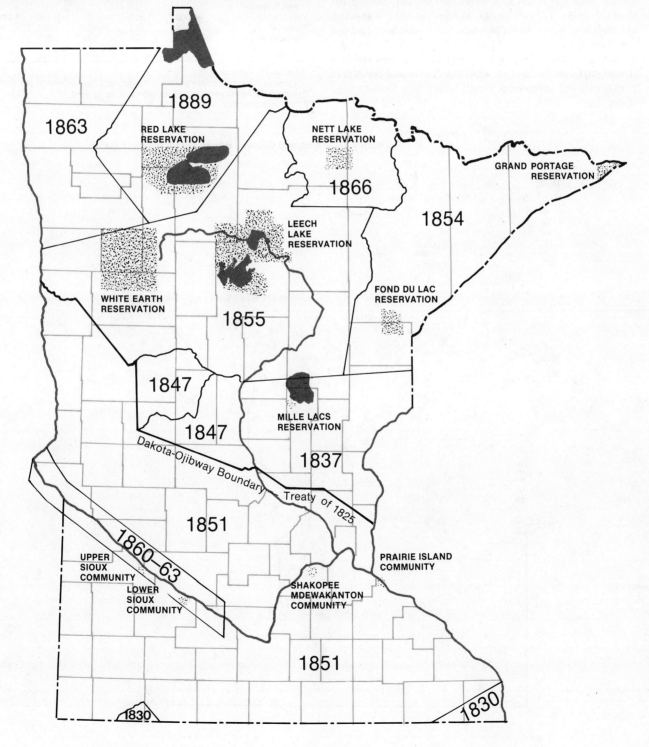

who never occupied it. In 1850 the Ojibway still controlled most of the forested northern third of the state, and the Dakota remained in possession of the prairie southern section.

Five well-defined subtribes, numbering from 5,400 to 8,000 people, inhabited different parts of the Dakota domain in the 1830s and 1840s (see Table 1.1). In the Minnesota country the Mdewakanton, the most sedentary group, lived in the southeast along the Mississippi northward to its confluence with the Minnesota River and up that stream for about 25 miles. Farther up the Minnesota were Wahpeton and Sisseton, some bands of whom also lived near Lac qui Parle, Big Stone Lake, and Lake Traverse. The Wahpekute hunted in the area of southern Minnesota between the Des Moines and Cannon rivers, while the Yanktonai (or North Yankton) lived in eastern North and South Dakota (see Map 1.2).

The Ojibway, who numbered about 4,800 people in 1843 (see Table 1.2), were divided into two major bodies — the Lake Superior and the Mississippi tribal groups. Among the

Table 1.1. Dakota Indian Bands, 1805–46

Tribe	1805	1834	1836	1839	1846
Mdewakanton	2,105	1,999	1,488	1,658	2,141
Wahpeton	1,060				
Wahpeton, North Yankton, and Sisseton*		490	627		627
Yankton	4,300**	1,820	1,781	2,150	1,781
Sisseton	2,160	3,211	1,188	1,256	1,188
Wahpekute	540	560	555	325	555
Total	10,165	8,080	5,639	5,389	6,292

Source: See notes on p. 35.
*Listed as Wahpeton in 1834 and North Yankton and Sisseton in 1836 and 1846. Perhaps these Dakota were included in 1839 figure for Yankton.
**Includes Yanktonai

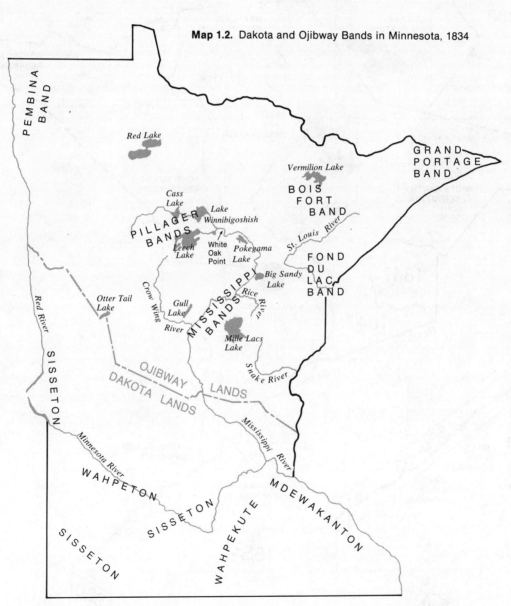

Map 1.2. Dakota and Ojibway Bands in Minnesota, 1834

Table 1.2. Ojibway Indian Bands, 1843–1920

		1843	1866	1885	1900	1911	1920
Mississippi Bands	Crow Wing	429					
	Gull Lake	59					
	Pokegama Lake	173					
	Sandy Lake	278	2,166	2,664	3,835	4,538	5,643
	Snake River	172					
	Mille Lacs Lake	151					
	Rice River	132					
Pillager Bands	Otter Tail			596	741	742	876
	Leech Lake	1,000		1,169	1,201	1,087	1,063
	Winnibigoshish Lake	200	1,899	387	499	508	537
	Cass Lake	300					
Bois Fort Bands	Red Lake	315	1,183	1,069	1,350	1,413	1,522
	Pembina		931	218	318	386	472
	Vermilion Lake	200					
	Hunters Island	500	869	698	808	622	587
	Rainy Lake	325					
	Grand Portage	145		298	337	326	346
	Fond du Lac	433	518	400	904	1,065	1,227
	Total	4,812	7,566	7,499	9,993	10,687	12,273

Source: See notes on p. 35.

former were the Fond du Lac band at the eastern end of Lake Superior and the Grand Portage band part way up the north shore. Sometimes also listed in this group was the Bois Fort band, so named because of the almost impenetrable, fortresslike forest in the Rainy River watershed of northern Minnesota where they lived. The Mississippi Ojibway occupied the Upper Mississippi Valley north of the present Twin Cities. They included bands at Crow Wing River, Gull, Pokegama, and Sandy lakes, Snake River, Mille Lacs Lake, and Rice River. Other smaller Ojibway bands included those who lived farther north and west near Red Lake and Lake Winnibigoshish, the Pillager near Leech, Cass, and Otter Tail lakes and the Pembina Ojibway on the plains of the Red River Valley and in northern Dakota Territory and southern Manitoba. By 1856 there were over 6,000 Ojibway living in Minnesota Territory.[12]

During the 1850s when the tide of white settlement rolled westward from the Mississippi, the Dakota were forced to give up most of what is now southern Minnesota in treaties signed at Traverse des Sioux and Mendota in 1851, leaving these Indian people with only narrow reservations along the upper Minnesota River. In 1854 the Mississippi, Lake Superior, and Bois Fort bands of Ojibway ceded their territory surrounding the western tip of Lake Superior and north to the Canadian border. In 1855 the Mississippi, Pillager, and Winnibigoshish bands gave up their claims to the area from Mille Lacs Lake north to the Canadian border and west to the Red River. Not until 1863 did the Red Lake and Pembina bands cede lands on both sides of the Red River north to the Canadian border. Three years later the Bois Fort relinquished additional territory south of the Rainy River.

Thus by the mid-1860s much of the once vast domain of these two tribes had been transferred to the United States government for sale to white settlers. Under the terms of the various treaties, the Indians had usually been paid much less than the land was worth, had been allotted reservations, and had been promised various benefits. The results for both tribes were catastrophic, although in different ways.[13]

The Dakota Experience after 1850

The story of the Dakota after 1851 is particularly sad. Neither they nor the government kept their word. Congress refused to establish the reservation stipulated in the treaties, although the president by executive order provided the Dakota people with provisional reserves on the upper Minnesota. Attempts to remove the various bands to these reservations in 1853 and 1854 met with little success. The late arrival of annuity payments promised by the government, failure to provide agricultural aid, and dissatisfaction with the restrictions of reservation life prompted many Dakota to return to their old homes near Wabasha (Wabasha County), Red Wing (Goodhue County), and Faribault (Rice County). These areas were now occupied by white settlers, and distrust between the earlier and later masters of the land deepened as the decade wore on.[14]

The killing of whites at Spirit Lake, Iowa, and in Jackson County, Minnesota, by Inkpaduta and his followers in 1857 heightened tensions between the two peoples. Friction and local outbreaks of violence, spurred by the whites' growing intolerance of the Indians and the Dakotas' increasing disrespect for the United States government, created an inflammable situation. Indian Agent Joseph R. Brown and missionary Stephen R. Riggs failed in their attempts to establish Dakota self-government in the form of the Hazelwood Republic and to arrange for the allotment of lands to heads of families under a treaty negotiated in 1858.

In August, 1862, driven by hunger and disgusted by unfulfilled promises, the Dakota attacked settlements in the Minnesota River Valley in what rapidly became a desperate attempt to drive the whites out of southern Minnesota. The Dakota War of 1862 lasted only a few weeks, but it had far-reaching repercussions for Indian-white relations in the three decades that followed. The deaths of about 500 whites and the widespread destruction of property evoked cries for the removal, if not the extermination, of all Dakota from the state. Thirty-eight were hanged at Mankato for their part in the conflict. Those who had not already fled to Dakota Territory or to Canada were exiled to an unsatisfactory reservation at Crow Creek (now South Dakota). Many died before they were able to move again to the Santee Reservation in northeastern Nebraska in 1866.

From a population of upward of 7,000 the number of Dakota in Minnesota dropped to 374 in 1866; most of them were part-time residents allowed to return under permits. By 1870 even these had largely departed, leaving 176 Dakota who had remained friendly to the whites during the 1862 conflict. These Indian people lived chiefly in Nicollet and Rice counties at Traverse des Sioux and Faribault under the wings of Episcopal Bishop Henry B. Whipple, who devoted much of his life to aiding Minnesota's Indians, and fur trader Alexander Faribault, who went into debt to help them. Smaller groups were located in the Shakopee-Prior Lake area (Scott County) along the lower Minnesota River, on Grey Cloud Island in the Mississippi River (Washington County), and at Bloomington (Hennepin County), the residence of Gideon H. Pond, one of the first missionaries to the Dakota. There was also a remnant of a Dakota scout camp in Chippewa County.[15]

From this low point in the early 1870s, the population slowly increased (see Table 1.3). Because they refused to move to the designated reservation outside the state, those who remained in Minnesota at first received no government benefits. Despite the fact that they had to scrape out a meager existence, their numbers grew to about 300 by 1889. By then their principal settlements were Birch Coulee (now Morton in Redwood County) near the old Lower Agency in the Minnesota Valley with a population of 86, Prior Lake-Shakopee with 62, and Prairie Island in the Mississippi River just north of Red Wing with 46. Even smaller numbers lived at Wabasha, Bloomington, Grey Cloud Island, and Hastings and Mendota (Dakota County), while those at Faribault were about to relocate at Birch Coulee.

With the help of Bishop Whipple, government agents in the late 1880s prevailed upon Congress to allocate funds to purchase lands for the Mdewakanton in order to establish a colony at Birch Coulee. There, near the site of a skirmish during the 1862 war, a Dakota named Good Thunder bought land in 1884. Others joined him, and with the help of government appropriations for land and farm implements, the colony eventually became the Lower Sioux Community under the Indian Reorganization Act of 1934.

Whipple, who had hoped to create a home at Birch Coulee for all the Minnesota Dakota, unintentionally paved the way for other Dakota reservations in the state. In 1886 the government appropriated money to buy land for them at Prairie Island, Prior Lake, and Wabasha. Those who settled at Prairie Island were largely exiles who, after living for more than a decade on the Santee Reservation, had begun making excursions to visit their former homes. The length of these visits gradually increased so that within 10 years many of the former Mdewakanton inhabitants of the Red Wing area had taken up virtually permanent residence on Prairie Island, the only nearby tract which had not been occupied by whites. Government appropriations for this group in the late 1880s and 1890s provided *de facto* recognition of Prairie Island as a permanent Dakota community. Official affirmation followed in the 1934 act.

DAKOTA INDIANS at work at Pipestone Quarry about 1893. Near the quarry, now part of Pipestone National Monument, Ojibway pipe maker George Bryan (right) demonstrates his craft at the visitor's center.

Table 1.3. Dakota Indians in Selected Minnesota Counties, 1866–1980

County	1866	1870	1880	1885	1890	1899	1900	1910	1920	1930	1940	1950	1960	1970	1980
Brown			5			10							3	6	
Chippewa		34	1										16	15	
Dakota		2	44	24	52	112	75	90	1	53	9	19	61	277	
Freeborn			3		1						1	73	116	42	
Goodhue (Prairie Island)			11		60	49	65	56	43	83	111	121	160	132	212
Hennepin		32	71	20	40	70	48	27	45	199	172	505	2,391	6,722	
Le Sueur		12	4			5							28	36	
Nicollet		31	2		1								8	12	
Pipestone							110	220	23	56	103	254	46	44	
Ramsey		1	26	33	12	204	5	10	32	174	60	200	585	2,146	
Redwood (Lower Sioux)		2	28		101	69	139	167	137	156	230	170	130	116	268
Rice	65	39	53		6	36			2	16	32	53	27	17	
Scott (Shakopee)		10	47	47	35	48	12	4	7	10	21	16	18	81	150
Wabasha	12		34	40	15	83							1	2	
Washington		13	18		74	66	28	30	2	50	28	36	115	198	
Yellow Medicine (Upper Sioux)	158		2		18	5	59	57	68	79	104	111	104	84	212
Miscellaneous	139			73	82	222							124	397	
Total*	374	176	349	237	497	979	541	661	360	876	871	817	842	1,261	842

Source: See notes on p. 35.
*Excluding Hennepin, Ramsey, and Washington counties, 1950–70.

About the same time, the Upper Sioux colony was beginning to form at Granite Falls in Yellow Medicine County. In 1887 a few Dakota people ventured into that area from Redwood County to gather ginseng roots. The next year Lazarus Skyman obtained title to land near Granite Falls. He was followed by Big Eagle, a Dakota leader who had served four years in federal prison for his participation in the 1862 war.

Over the next 50 years they were joined by small numbers of Santee from Nebraska and Sisseton and Yankton, who had been forced into exile after 1862 and had returned from South Dakota. The community received no official sanction or aid, however, until the federal government bought land for its members in 1938. Similar migrations and land purchases led to the creation of the Shakopee-Mdewakanton Community near Prior Lake and its formal recognition in 1969.[16]

Population data for these small Dakota centers during the 20th century are confusing and often unreliable. The pattern, however, seems to have been a slow rise to a total of about 500 people among them and then a decline by the 1950s as members moved. All four communities were agricultural, and employment of any other kind had to be found in nearby towns or in the Twin Cities. Although the Dakota in Minnesota in 1973 numbered only one-sixth of their pre-1862 total, they had increased sevenfold since 1870. In 1973 about 300 were said to live outside the Twin Cities — 105 at Lower Sioux, 60 at Shakopee-Mdewakanton, 90 at Prairie Island, and 56 at Upper Sioux. Estimates by Indian leaders in the same year, however, indicated a reservation population of about 525 — 225 at Lower Sioux and 100 each at the other locations.[17]

The Ojibway Experience after 1850

The Ojibway tragedy in Minnesota was acted out over a longer period of time. Unlike the Dakota, they were able to avoid major warfare with Minnesotans and its consequences. Nevertheless they lost most of their land, were relegated to reservations, experienced severe disruptions in their traditional life, and were subjected to vacillating government policies that failed to protect their rights and promote their general welfare. Recovery for the Ojibway was impossible until the ideas and principles underlying 19th-century Indian-white relations faded into history.

As white settlement in Minnesota spread northward in the 1850s and 1860s, the Ojibway ceded considerable portions of their land in smaller parcels than did the Dakota in 1851. The Grand Portage band reserved an area for themselves at the tip of northeastern Minnesota, and the Fond du Lac band retained a reservation on the St. Louis River west of Duluth. The Mississippi bands had reservations set aside at Pokegama, Sandy, Rabbit, Gull, and Mille Lacs lakes. The Winnibigoshish group obtained lands on the north shore of the lake bearing their name. The Pillager held small reserves on the north shore of Cass Lake and on the south and east shores of Leech Lake. Only the Bois Fort and Red Lake bands for a time preserved substantial tracts south of the Rainy River and in the Red River Valley.[18]

During the 1860s, in response to growing demands for Ojibway land and timber resources, government officials tried to consolidate the disparate bands within fewer and larger reserves. An attempt in 1863 failed to persuade the various Mississippi bands to join the Pillager at Cass and Leech lakes. In 1867, however, leaders of Mississippi bands agreed to occupy jointly a large block of land located in Becker, Mahnomen, and Clearwater counties and known as the White Earth Reservation.

Ojibway people were reluctant to go to White Earth because they preferred their old, familiar homes. Less than half had moved west by the mid-1870s. Of those who did, many located at White Oak Point on Leech Lake rather than at White Earth. Most of the Pembina, Otter Tail Pillager, and Mille Lacs bands resisted relocation. Because they would not go to White Earth, these people received few government benefits and their condition was dismal.[19]

Those who did move in the 1860s and 1870s fared little better, and the government's hope of gathering all the Ojib-

THE MOCCASIN GAME, played to the accompaniment of a traditional drum, captured the attention of festively attired men at White Earth about 1910. A teacher and his young students engaged in another traditional pastime, the hand game, at St. Paul's Red School House in 1980.

way at White Earth was not to be. In 1873 the Leech Lake Reservation was assigned its own agent, and its boundaries were extended to include Leech and Cass lakes, Lake Winnibigoshish, and later White Oak Point. The Red Lake band successfully retained its reservation, as did the Bois Fort and Superior Ojibway. By 1875 the territorial outlines of Ojibway reserves in Minnesota had been set, and with few exceptions (most notably Red Lake) they have remained so to this day.[20]

Between 1871 and 1890 the geographic distribution of Minnesota's Ojibway was affected by additional changes in federal Indian policy. After 1871 the United States abandoned its earlier system of making treaties with Indian tribes and largely dealt with their affairs by simply enacting legislation in Congress. Having followed a policy of consolidating tribes on large reservation tracts during the 1860s and 1870s, the government reversed course in the mid-1880s in the face of pressure to release reservation lands for white settlement. In 1887 Congress passed the Dawes Allotment Act, which authorized the Indian Office to allot from 80 to 160 acres of land to enrolled members of any reservation for the ostensible purpose of engaging in farming and ranching. The unallotted lands were then sold to the general public.[21]

To implement the main features of the Dawes Act in Minnesota, Congressman Knute Nelson successfully sponsored in 1888 a bill that provided for the concentration of all Ojibway (except those at Red Lake) on the White Earth Reservation and for the allotment of the reserve's land, including timberland, to them. An amendment to the bill diluted the consolidation policy, however, by permitting the Red Lake Reservation to remain "closed" (that is, unallotted to individual tribal members) and by allowing other Ojibway to take up allotments on their old reservations

rather than at White Earth. The government made no serious attempt to relocate the Bois Fort and Lake Superior bands. By 1900 White Earth had become the home of 3,800 of the state's 10,000 Ojibway. Only 91 persons from Fond du Lac, 88 of the 743 members of the White Oak Point community, 51 of 499 from Cass Lake and Lake Winnibigoshish, and 309 of the 1,201 enrolled members of the Leech Lake group had moved (see Table 1.4).[22]

The Mille Lacs band again resisted. Under the provisions of the Nelson Act, its members had the right to take up allotments on their old reservation at Mille Lacs Lake. Nevertheless tensions ran so high among white settlers near the lake, many of whom were Scandinavian immigrants, that an Indian uprising was rumored in 1903. The rumor prompted an Ojibway newspaper editor at White Earth to complain: "If Indians are so obnoxious to these foreigners the latter should have remained in Europe where there are no Indians, instead of coming to this country and dispossessing the original owners of it of their homes.

"Scandinavians are, in some respects, all right, but they have no regard for the rights of the Indians, and their influence with Minnesota Congressmen, who want their votes, is too strong for the Indians to look for much justice."[23]

By 1900 only 323 of the 1,212 members of the Mille Lacs band were living at White Earth. After the turn of the century, however, others moved in small groups, so that by 1911 the figures were reversed and only 374 enrolled members of the band still resided at Mille Lacs Lake and, in accordance with the Nelson Act, selected allotments on their old lands. The government then purchased additional land near the lake. A new reservation was officially established there under the 1934 Indian Reorganization Act, but it "has no defined original boundaries."[24]

On the White Earth Reservation there was a tendency for the migrant groups to settle together. Many of the original inhabitants were from Mississippi bands. The United States government then brought to the reservation the Otter Tail Pillager and the Pembina — two groups who had not been parties to the treaty establishing White Earth. The Pembina, who first entered the reservation in 1873, settled in what is now Pembina Township of Mahnomen County. The 500 Otter Tail Pillager, who also arrived in 1873, made their homes at Pine Point. Later some of them moved nearer White Earth village and the Pembina group.[25]

Members of the Mille Lacs band who went to the reservation in 1892 settled northeast of White Earth village around Twin Lakes. About half of the 30 or so Christian Ojibway living at Cass Lake moved, and 37 families, mostly Christians from Leech Lake, resettled at Pine Point, which in the mid-1970s was still predominantly Pillager. The tendency of incoming Ojibway to settle in their own communities in outlying areas of the reservation left such population centers as White Earth village to the older reservation residents, who were often mixed-bloods and more accustomed to the ways of whites.[26]

Passage of the Dawes Act in 1887 and other statutory measures seemed to indicate that the federal government expected Indian people to become assimilated into American society, thus eliminating any further need for an Office of Indian Affairs. These hopes were shared by a newspaper called The Progress, the first to be published in English on a Minnesota reservation. Issued at White Earth from 1886 to 1889 by Gus H. and Theodore H. Beaulieu, The Progress was highly critical of the Office of Indian Affairs, which it regarded as arbitrary and authoritarian, and almost equally critical of the existing tribal leadership, which it labeled "nonprogressive." The paper supported assimilation into white society and favored an end to the tribal system, advocating its replacement by a self-governing body. Its motto was "A Higher Civilization: The Maintenance of Law and Order."[27]

In his next journalistic enterprise, Gus Beaulieu in 1903 launched The Tomahawk, a weekly paper again attacking the Office of Indian Affairs, defending allotment, and promoting assimilation and the distribution of all tribal funds and lands. He reasoned that if these steps were taken, Indian people would be freed of the restraints of reservation life and assimilation would gradually result. The Tomahawk, edited by Gus Beaulieu until his death in 1917 and then by C. H. Beaulieu until the paper's demise in 1926, spoke for the mixed-bloods among the Ojibway. It opposed what it called "warehouse Indians" because of their insistence upon federal compliance with the annuity system and other support provided for in previous treaties and agreements. In this group it placed the Red Lake "full-bloods," particularly those living north of the lake. The core issue of the quarrel throughout World War I and on into the interwar period involved tribal or band rights versus those of individual members in the distribution of reservation lands. A policy favoring distribution to individuals was advocated by mixed-bloods in general.[28]

Much of the land on Ojibway reservations initially allotted to individuals under the Dawes and Nelson acts passed into the hands of white settlers. Some Indians sold as soon as possible to obtain cash; others tried farming, found it unsatisfactory, and sold out. Unallotted land remained for a time in tribal hands, but eventually much of it too wound up in white ownership, often fraudulently. Only relatively small areas of arable land existed on Ojibway reservations; much of the rest was swamp, lakes, or forests, some with desirable standing timber. Government promises of implements and training for farming were only partially fulfilled. In addition, a series of dams erected by the federal government in the 1880s on the upper reaches of the Mississippi River flooded Ojibway rice beds, garden plots, and homes upstream.[29]

Table 1.4. Ojibway Reservation Population — Removals and Nonremovals, 1885–1920

	1885	1900	1911	1920
Mississippi Bands	2,664	3,835	4,538	5,643
White Oak Point	582	743	727	819
At White Oak Point Leech Lake Res.		655	465	504
Removals on White Earth Res.		88	262	315
Mille Lacs	942	1,212	1,439	1,591
At Mille Lacs		889	374	283
Removals on White Earth Res.		323	1,065	1,308
Gull Lake, on White Earth Res.		336	408	469
White Earth	922	1,544	2,064	2,764
Pembina Band, on White Earth Res.	218	318	386	472
Pillager Bands	2,152	2,441	2,337	2,476
Cass and Winnibigoshish	387	499	508	537
At Cass and Winnibigoshish Lakes, Leech Lake Res.		448	447	476
Removals on White Earth Res.		51	61	61
Leech Lake	1,169	1,201	1,087	1,063
At Leech Lake, Leech Lake Res.		892	809	782
Removals on White Earth Res.		309	278	281
Otter Tail, on White Earth Res.	596	741	742	876
Fond du Lac Band	400	904	1,065	1,227
At Fond du Lac		813	954	1,114
Removals on White Earth Res.		91	111	113

Source: U.S. Office of Indian Affairs, Annual Report, 1885, 344, 353, 362, 368; 1900, 642, 654; 1911, 60, 69; 1920, 67.

MILLE LACS OJIBWAY constructed round wigwams in 1932. Nearly 50 years later a worker outside the American Indian Center in Minneapolis looped poles together for Dakota tepees.

When the disastrous results of the allotment policy became evident on other reservations, the allotments scheduled at Red Lake met with stiff opposition from band leaders and were postponed indefinitely. That reservation has remained in common tribal ownership, closed to settlement by outsiders, and exempt from county and state jurisdiction. Nevertheless its boundaries were reduced. In 1889 and 1904 the band ceded lands between Upper Red Lake and the Canadian border as well as others east of the Thief River. But it still retained ownership in 1981 of over 721,000 acres of land, an area about the size of Rhode Island, and 370,532 acres of water. Much of the Red Lake band lived in the villages of Red Lake and Redby on the southern shore and at Ponemah on the northern shore of Lower Red Lake.[30]

20th-Century Dakota and Ojibway Challenges

The independent course followed by Red Lake Ojibway has given rise to a different experience for members of that reservation in the 20th century. In 1918 the band adopted a written constitution, which combined American and traditional Ojibway political features. Under this system, which was not changed until 1958, the Red Lake people were able to avoid many of the problems visited upon their brethren elsewhere. They have, however, experienced their own share of struggles to preserve their reservation from outside interests and adverse governmental policies.

The failures of the federal government as trustee of the interests of the Ojibway as well as all other Indian tribes had become notorious by the 1920s. The scandals associated with White Earth's allotment and subsequent orgy of fraudulent land and timber sales were part of a larger story which D'Arcy McNickle, dean of American Indian scholars, eloquently summarized.

"The preceding one hundred years had wrought incalculable damage to Indians, their property, and their societies," McNickle wrote in 1976. "Tribes had been moved about like livestock until, in some cases, the original homeland [was] no more than a legend in the minds of the old men and women. Children had been removed from the family, by force at times, and kept in close custody until they lost their mother tongue and all knowledge of who they were, while parents often did not know where the children had been taken or whether they even lived. Tribal religious practices when they were not proscribed outright were treated as obscenities. Land losses . . . were catastrophic, while the failure of government to provide economic tools and training for proper land use left the remaining holdings untenable or leased to White farmers at starvation rates. The bureaucratic structure had penetrated the entire fabric of Indian life, usurping the tribal decision-making function, demeaning local leadership, obtruding into the family — and yet was totally oblivious of its inadequacies and its inhumanity."[31]

The larger story suggested by this quotation compelled public action and led to demands for reform. In 1928 a report prepared under the direction of Lewis Meriam urged greater emphasis upon Indian education. Under the leadership of Indian Commissioner John C. Collier, much of this advice found its way into the Johnson-O'Malley Act passed by Congress in 1934. Collier also pressed for the restoration of lands to Indian tribes and advocated a revival of pride in their heritage. In 1934, at his urging, Congress passed the Indian Reorganization Act. Among other things this legislation sought to stop the further breakup of reservations, acquire new lands to be held in trust for the tribe or the reservation as a whole, give more authority to tribal councils, and allow tribes to incorporate in order to facilitate business ventures. Under its provisions the Ojibway on all Minnesota reservations (see Table 1.5) except Red Lake voted to organize and later, in 1964, incorporated as the Minnesota Chippewa Tribe. Each of the six reservations chose to be governed by

Table 1.5. Ojibway Population by Reservation, 1930–73

	1930		1942		1950	1960		1970	1973 (estimate 1)		1973 (estimate 2)	
	Total enrolled	Residing where enrolled	Total enrolled	Residing where enrolled	Total enrolled	Total enrolled	Residing where enrolled	Residing where enrolled	Residing on or near reservation	Residing where enrolled	Total enrolled	Residing where enrolled
White Earth	8,584	4,627	9,021	6,245	9,390	2,550	2,150	1,474	2,571	1,983		3,600
Leech Lake			2,212	1,935	2,403	2,750	2,350	1,985	2,874	2,059		4,000
1) White Oak Point	564	451										
2) Cass Lake	500	424										
3) Leech Lake	897	773										
Mille Lacs	321	187	408	354	452	800	500	303	757	501		350
Red Lake	1,799	1,605	2,329	2,112	2,923	3,200	2,900	2,741	3,163	3,093	5,500	5,200
Fond du Lac	1,480	523	1,365	749	1,450	850	650	391	687	458		750
Nett Lake	648	322	724	576	809	600	400	289	669	483		350
Grand Portage	414	137	394	267	399	325	175	83	191	154		225
Total	15,207	9,049	16,453	12,238	17,826	11,075	9,125	7,266	10,912	8,731	30,000	14,475
Per cent Residing Where Enrolled		60%		74%			82%			80%		48%

Source: See notes on p. 35.

an elected Reservation Business Committee; Red Lake opted for a tribal council. The Dakota communities had also organized tribal councils duly elected by enrolled members; in 1977 they were loosely joined in the Minnesota Sioux Tribe, Inc.[32]

The federal policies initiated in the 1930s continued in force into the 1980s, paving the way for a new era of self-determination. They did not, however, reduce dissatisfaction among either Indians or whites with the operations of the reorganized and renamed (in 1948) Bureau of Indian Affairs. Frequently attacked and constantly criticized, its liquidation was suggested from time to time by congressional committees. In the 1950s termination of the special legal status of Indian tribes and federal support services — a move which opponents hoped would eventually make the bureau unnecessary — was seriously considered, but tribal and public opposition prevented the large-scale application of the termination policy's main features. Although its intent was to lift federal restrictions which impeded Indian participation in national life, its effects were just the opposite. Where the policy was applied, as in the case of the Menominee Indians in neighboring Wisconsin, the results were so disastrous that it was reversed. In 1975 the government restored the Menominee to their original status as a federally recognized tribe.

Underlying the debate over termination was the issue of assimilation versus cultural adaptation to the larger society within reservation enclaves, a matter unresolved in 1981 in Minnesota and elsewhere. A special aspect of termination-era thinking brought Minnesota's Dakota communities and all Ojibway reservations except Red Lake under state criminal and civil jurisdiction in 1953, a change which in the long run created as many problems for the state and the affected areas as it solved. In a concomitant move, the Bureau of Indian Affairs in 1955 turned over to the Department of Health, Education, and Welfare the responsibility for health services on reservations. Generally speaking, the transfer resulted in improved health care through hospitals, field clinics, and educational programs dealing with medical problems. Seeking to handle effectively issues resulting

from changes in policy, Minnesota in 1963 inaugurated what became the Indian Affairs Intertribal Board. By so doing it became the first state to create an agency to serve as a liaison between its legislature and its various Indian communities. The board's members included the chairman of each of the 11 territorial units, five urban residents, and two representatives of non-Minnesota tribes living in the state.[33]

Among the many problems facing the board and the Indian people, economic ones loomed large. Minnesota's reserved lands have never provided sound economic bases for the Dakota and Ojibway. The very idea of reservations contradicted traditional Indian existence, which depended upon freedom of movement. The constraints of the reservation and the loss of customary hunting and gathering areas to encroaching white settlement damaged the basis of the Indian way of life. Some of the reservation areas were inaccessible and their lands were unsuited to cultivation. The Nett Lake Reservation, for example, was described by one Indian agent as "out of reach and good for nothing." Like other northern reservations, however, it offered lakes for wild rice, maple trees for sugar, and abundant fish.[34]

The Minnesota Ojibway have shown little enthusiasm for farming. Many preferred hunting, trapping, and fishing to the daily labor of tending fields or cattle. Accustomed to their traditional ways, they found it difficult to make a wholesale shift to agriculture. Nor was the northern Minnesota climate encouraging. In 1900 at Red Lake 275 acres were under cultivation, at Leech Lake 400 acres, and at White Earth 6,000 out of 1,091,523 acres. By 1920 Indian people had under cultivation 2,150 acres at Red Lake, 4,320 at Leech Lake, and 9,440 at White Earth. The number of cultivated acres per person, however, remained small.[35]

Some Indian lands with marketable timber were cut over beginning in the 1840s, and the government either ignored the destruction or advised the Indians to make the best deals they could get. They were often cheated, most notoriously in the early 1900s when the federal government permitted the sale of allotted timberlands on the White Earth Reservation. The Red Lake Ojibway were more successful than most other bands in developing their resources. The Red Lake

HARVESTING wild rice on the Leech Lake Reservation the traditional way in 1939 and, in 1980, when more modern, commercial methods were used.

Indian Mill at Redby was started with over $80,000 in government funds in 1924 and, with brief interruptions, has continued to operate. In 1924 the state of Minnesota constructed a fish hatchery and encouraged commercial fishing on Red Lake. When the state withdrew from this activity in 1929, the Red Lake Fisheries Association was organized and carried on by the Ojibway residents. Wild-rice harvesting and maple-sugar gathering have also been developed to commercial proportions on various reserves.[36]

From the mid-19th century to the present, the Indians of Minnesota have been economically depressed. Although their lands were capable of supporting such renewable resources as trees and fish, they have usually been both physically and economically isolated, offering few means of obtaining cash incomes. Some residents earned money from the sale of craftwork like basketweaving, beadwork, and wood carving. Some had jobs with the Indian service; a smaller number managed to find work in private industry. The more assimilated mixed-bloods often lived in urban communities near the reservations or in the major cities. The remainder lived in inferior housing on the reservations. Without steady and remunerative means of support, many relied on government aid simply to survive.[37]

The situation did not improve after World War I. The Mille Lacs band was a case in point. During the war its members profited from high prices for the hay and other produce they raised. While they did not live far above subsistence levels, neither did many whites in the vicinity. The agricultural depression of the 1920s ruined this economic base.[38]

The Depression of the 1930s worsened conditions, curtailing the availability of off-reservation employment. Decreasing tourism hurt areas like Mille Lacs Lake, where craft sales evaporated and the boat factory closed. In the southern part of the state, Dakota farming settlements near Morton and at Prairie Island suffered severely from drought.[39]

Beginning in 1933, as part of the New Deal program, the Civilian Conservation Corps (CCC) Indian Division established at least 14 camps and projects at various locations in the state. Between 1933 and 1939 they employed a total of 2,536 Indians. Depending upon the camp, wages ranged from $30 to $45 a month for unskilled and $130 for skilled workers. CCC forestry programs increased fire prevention and improved the condition and amount of timber on Red Lake and other reservations. At Rice Lake on the White Earth Reservation facilities were constructed to make the harvesting of wild rice easier and less injurious to the health of the harvesters. CCC workers also laid out new roads, trails, and telephone lines on the Nett Lake and White Earth reserves.

But neither the New Deal programs nor World War II brought real prosperity to Minnesota's Indians. Individuals returning to reservations from the war and war-related work found it hard to get jobs. Lack of land and modern equipment made farming difficult. Even the reservation-owned wood-products and commercial-fishing enterprises at Red Lake failed to provide continuous employment. In 1950 and 1951 there were periods when both were closed, leaving people to seek such other jobs as harvesting potatoes in the Red River Valley or working at a cannery at Fairmont. On the Grand Portage, Mille Lacs, and Leech Lake reservations postwar tourism provided limited employment. But off-reservation opportunities were not numerous, and discrimination was widespread. Businesses in rural areas and small towns hired few Indians. More openings existed in urban areas, where Indians obtained sales, clerical, skilled, and unskilled work.[40]

The Urban Migration

The post-World War II period was marked by a major shift of Indian population to the state's urban centers, especially Minneapolis and St. Paul. A federal voluntary relocation program for Indians begun in 1953 greatly influenced the movement. In some respects the situation of these migrants was not unlike that of earlier immigrants. They were generally poor, clustered together in areas of substandard housing, had difficulty finding suitable employment, and carried with them certain cultural and ethnic attributes that differed from the larger society. Of a total Minnesota Indian population of 15,496 in 1960, about a fifth lived in the Twin Cities and Duluth. By 1980 over one-third did so. Probable undercounts in the census of 1940 listed only 145 Indian residents in Minneapolis; in 1950 the figure given was 426. By 1960 it was recorded as 2,077, and the total reached 8,932 by 1980 (see Table 1.6).[41]

In 1980 most Minneapolis Indians were of Ojibway ancestry, and their numbers were growing both by migration from reservations and by natural increase. Housing surveys and school attendance indicated that most lived either on the south or north sides of the downtown area. It was estimated that about half were Roman Catholic.[42]

Table 1.6. Urban Indian Population, 1950–80

	1950	1960	1970	1973 (estimate)	1980
Minneapolis	426	2,077	5,828	6,500	8,932
St. Paul	163	524	1,906	4,300	2,538
Duluth	186	402	615	2,200	1,344

Source: See notes on p. 35.

The St. Paul Indian community differed from that of Minneapolis in several respects. It was smaller, numbering 2,538 in 1980, and its composition was not the same. About one-fourth were Dakota, one-fourth Winnebago, and the rest Ojibway. Some had migrated from other states — the Dakota from Nebraska and South Dakota and the Winnebago from Wisconsin. Each tribal group had its own organization and council. All lived primarily in inner city low rent areas, but as one Indian leader said, "Unlike Minneapolis, St. Paul has no identifiable Indian community."[43]

Retaining Indian culture in an urban environment and educating a white society to its values have been problems for reservation migrants. In a series of efforts beginning in the 1960s and 1970s, Minneapolis and St. Paul Indian people have used political action to enhance individual and family life. For much of this heightened awareness, the Upper Midwest Indian Center, the Division of Indian Work of the Minnesota Council of Churches, and the American Indian Movement (AIM), all headquartered in Minneapolis, provided the impetus. In the early 1970s American Indian centers under various sponsorships were established in both cities to serve the social, cultural, educational, and advisory needs of urban Indians. *The Circle*, a monthly newspaper published in Minneapolis beginning in 1980, contained news items, art work, notices of jobs and services, interviews, and poetry. The centers have also sponsored annual celebrations of Indian Week and educational programs in the public schools. Indian-sponsored and staffed alternative schools — Heart of the Earth Survival School in Minneapolis and Red School House in St. Paul — taught Indian languages and culture and English reading and math skills in Indian contexts. Similar themes were on the agenda of the second annual Minnesota Indian Education Conference held at Bemidji State University in 1980.[44]

In order to provide job training, business development, and housing and meet health needs, Minneapolis Indians created new agencies. The American Indian Opportunities Industrialization Center, the "first program of its kind in the country," and the Comprehensive Employment Training Act (CETA), a federal program which developed a special segment for Indians, tried to deal with preparing the hardcore unemployed for available jobs in the 1970s. At the same time, the American Indian Business Development Corporation, formed in 1975, began a six-year battle to build a shopping center in Minneapolis on Franklin Avenue in the midst of the Indian neighborhood, thus providing both employment and a needed service. Local leaders hailed the mall as the "only urban Indian economic development of its kind" in the United States. Similar efforts supported the Urban Indian Housing Program, another pioneering local undertaking which provided for Indian-owned houses, and a townhouse development of the Little Earth Housing project managed by the Little Earth of United Tribes, Inc. The Indian Health Board, established in 1971, provided comprehensive health and dental care for Twin Cities Indians. It also has been singled out for praise as one of the model Indian health care programs in the nation.[45]

A series of surveys made since 1945 indicated that Minnesota Indians living in urban areas were somewhat better off than those on or near reservations. But in 1969, 29.2% of Minnesota's Indian families in the cities and 41.7% of those in rural areas were still below the poverty level. For Indian males 16 years of age and older in 1969 the state-wide median income was $3,486. With a mean family size of 4.53 in urban centers and 5.45 in rural areas, the respective mean family incomes were $7,226 and $5,592.[46]

For the entire population of Minnesota in 1971 average per capita income was $4,020; for northern counties containing reservations it ranged from $2,200 to $2,900. As late as 1973 the highest per capita income on reservations was $1,123 at Red Lake; industry there consisted of a fishery, a wood-products factory, and other timber-related businesses. For a time Mille Lacs operated a tribal electronics plant started in 1968, and the Grand Portage band maintained a hotel and marina tourist complex which opened in 1975. The lowest per capita income on Minnesota reservations in 1973 was $581 at Nett Lake. The highest unemployment rate, however, was 63% at Fond du Lac; on other reserves it varied from 36% to 48% in that year. Among the Dakota communities unemployment rates ranged from 30% at Morton to 49% at Prairie Island.[47]

A major reason often assigned to explain such figures has been inadequate education and lack of training for Minnesota Indians. The merits of education have been advocated and debated by private and public agencies and elements of the Indian community virtually since the advent of white settlement. The debate has largely centered on what type of education was most desirable and what its objectives should be. Initially Indian education was in the hands of missionaries who established schools and missions in the 1830s and fanned out across the state in the decades that followed. By the 1890s the federal government had entered the picture, operating day schools and boarding schools on various reservations for both the Ojibway and Dakota. Since the 1920s Indian children have attended public schools near their reservations, but they have encountered problems in coping with white values and racial discrimination.[48]

Of 1,118 children of school age on the White Earth, Red Lake, and Leech Lake reservations in 1880, only 250 attended school. In 1911 only 1,545 of the 2,641 Ojibway children on the state's reservations were in classes, but even so the capacity of available classrooms barely accommodated the number attending. By 1930 most children were enrolled in local public schools; 4,499 of the 4,738 eligible were attending. Enrollment figures were, however, misleading, for few Indian students were present regularly. Moreover, since very limited opportunities existed for those who did manage to finish school, the incentive to do so was greatly reduced.[49]

Twentieth-century efforts to provide education for Minnesota Indian children have met with modest success. In 1945 there were only 8 high school graduates, but by 1946 the figure had risen to 64 and to 509 in 1979. In 1950 only half of the state's Indian population (exclusive of the Dakota and the Red Lake Ojibway) had at least 7.6 years of education. By 1970 the median number of school years completed by Indian people 25 years of age and older was 10.1 state wide, 11.1 in urban centers, and 9.0 in rural areas. The percentage of high school graduates was 32.5% state wide, 41.7% in urban areas, and 22.6% in rural ones. Nevertheless dropout rates remained high into the 1980s. At Cloquet near the Fond du Lac Reservation the estimated rate for 1972–73, for example, was 70%.[50]

On the other hand, more and more Indian students were persisting not only through high school but also through college and on to professional training. In 1955 the state of Minnesota established a scholarship fund to aid Indians enrolled at accredited institutions of higher learning. In that year a total of 43 students attended college or received vocational training; 15 of them were on state scholarships. Between 1956 and 1973 over 300 completed four years of college, and at least 35 received master's degrees. In 1971–72 state aid for higher education was being received by 1,025 Indian students. In 1973 a total of 42 scholarship recipients received four-year degrees, 29 earned two-year degrees, and 20 completed vocational training. There was a 10% failure rate among scholarship recipients from 1969 to 1973.[51]

In 1973 the Bureau of Indian Affairs assisted 384 Minnesota Indians under the federal Vocational Training Program. In addition some 3,000 adults took courses under the auspices of a state program called Opportunities Unlimited for Minnesota Indians. From 1970 to 1973 nearly 530 earned general education certificates. Of these, 80 went on to college, 33 went to vocational schools, and 240 obtained new jobs, promotions, or pay increases.[52]

In post-secondary education, programs aimed specifically at the Indian student led to a 15% increase in enrollment between 1974 and 1979. The biggest jump came in numbers attending the Area Vocational-Technical Institutes, particularly at Detroit Lakes. Rainy River Community College and Bemidji State University also drafted courses of study for Indian students. In 1969 the University of Minnesota inaugurated an American Indian Studies Department which offered a bachelor's degree. In that year there were 44 Indian students in attendance, about 350 in 1976, and an estimated 283 in 1979. The program was still in existence in the 1980s at reduced levels.[53]

Unresolved Problems and Future Directions

Since the 1960s, a considerable change has taken place in the relationship between Minnesota's Indian tribes and the state and federal governments. Generally the tribes have experienced increases in authority and responsibility as a

PREPARATIONS *for a pony race were under way at the 42nd annual Ojibway-Dakota celebration on the White Earth Reservation in 1910. The Dakota encampment of tents and tepees is in the background. Dancers participated in a summer powwow at Little Earth of United Tribes, Inc., Minneapolis Indian housing project, in the 1970s.*

result of legal rights guaranteed to them in the past and newer policies adopted in the Indian Self-Determination and Education Reform Act of 1975. These changes have enabled Red Lake and the six other member reservations of the incorporated Minnesota Chippewa Tribe to develop and run many of their own programs. Transfers of state authority and responsibility, as in the case of Johnson-O'Malley Funds, have been made to the tribes. On the federal level, the Bureau of Indian Affairs' responsibility for higher-education funds and other programs has been shifted to reservation authorities. Under tribal direction, these and many other federal programs have been modified to meet the special needs of reservation people in health, education, economic development, and social services.

Like other governments, Red Lake and the Minnesota Chippewa Tribe attempted to meet a wide variety of needs. In education, for example, projects devised under tribal auspices have resulted in several alternative schools such as the Bug-o-nay-ge-shig School on the Leech Lake Reservation. Recreation programs have been developed in most areas, and beginning in 1974 the Minnesota Chippewa Tribe supported the publication of *Ni-Mi-Mah-Kwa-Zoo-Min (Speaking of Ourselves)*, a newspaper which served not only reservation residents but also Indian people throughout the region. In 1981 Red Lake Reservation held a grand opening of a new hospital complex. By that time the corporations of Red Lake and the Minnesota Chippewa Tribe were handling multimillion-dollar budgets, which played important roles in the economy of northern Minnesota.[54]

This is a far cry from the 19th century when the state's Indians were not considered citizens. In 1870 Minnesota Winnebago could become citizens if they had been self-sufficient for five years and had adopted a "civilized" way of life. Given the small number of Winnebago in Minnesota, this obviously did not help many. There were three other ways for Indians to attain citizenship: marry a citizen (applied to women only), serve in the armed forces, or obtain a land patent in fee simple. These methods still prevented most members of the Red Lake Reservation from becoming citizens. In 1924, however, citizenship was granted to all American Indians and in 1940 to Canadian-born Indians dwelling in the United States.[55]

The question, "Who is an Indian?" has troubled tribal life, Indian-white relationships, and all who undertake to describe Indian demographic patterns. Three approaches have been attempted over the years: the biological, the legal, and the cultural. The first viewed anyone of Indian descent as Indian; the second sought to define "Indian" by the degrees of Indian ancestry or blood quantum; the third employed life-style and cultural expression as primary criteria. The federal government has been continuously involved in this problem, chiefly because of treaty obligations regarding lands, money, goods, and services to those eligible to receive them. Officials therefore compiled lists of individuals and families belonging to signatory tribes for the purpose of fulfilling treaty provisions.

By 1860 most of Minnesota's Indian bands were enrolled with the United States Office of Indian Affairs. Problems arose because some bands were not party to any treaty, some persons failed to be registered on annuity rolls, and some individuals remained on those rolls even though they had moved away from a reservation. More serious was the growing number of mixed-bloods, descendants of earlier enrollees. Because Congress usually appropriated funds for tribes in lump sums to be divided on a per capita basis, many enrollees of full to one-quarter blood resented the inclusion of those with little Indian ancestry and only minimal associations with the tribal group. By 1900 blood quantum had become the primary criterion in determining Indian identity, and to some degree it still obtains.[56]

Concern with blood lines led to complicated and even ridiculous situations. The policy of allotting reservation lands to individual Indian families and selling nonallotted lands to outsiders led to a major scandal on the White Earth Reservation in 1905 when many Ojibway were defrauded of valuable timberlands. As a result of its investigation of this episode, the Office of Indian Affairs published a list showing the proportion of Indian blood of White Earth landholders. More than 90% of the 2,500 enumerated surnames of mixed-bloods were English, Scottish, French Canadian, or those of other European groups. Of the 1,000 full-bloods, only about 10% did not have Indian names. The Office of Indian Affairs carried the blood-quantum principle to absurd extremes with fractions like 1/16, 15/32, 23/64, and even 63/128.[57]

In numerous lawsuits arising from the allotment of White Earth timberlands the question of blood quantum became a central issue. The federal government established a commission that attempted to trace ancestry and to sort out blood lines. Recorded genealogical data were often unavailable or subject to dispute, so the courts relied upon physical anthropology. Professor Albert E. Jenks, an anthropologist at the University of Minnesota, was consulted. From 1914 to 1916 Jenks measured skin, hair, faces, eyes, teeth, heads, noses, hands, and feet of whites, mixed-bloods, and full-bloods. Based on these measurements, he concluded that a blending of racial characteristics occurred in mixed-bloods, making them identifiably different from full-bloods. The "evidence" he compiled seems to have helped settle eight of nine allotment cases. With Jenks the definition and classification of Indians on a purely physical and biological basis reached an extreme.[58]

In the 1980s there was no single answer to the question of Indian identity. A commonly held definition maintained that "An Indian is a person of sufficient Indian blood to be recognized as an Indian in the community." The legal definition, widely used in the United States, has been that an Indian is a person having no less than one-fourth Indian blood. A 1967 Minnesota state commission recommended that this be changed to "Indians duly enrolled with any Indian group." An alternate criterion holds that one is an Indian if he or she accepts the customs, traditions, beliefs, and way of life of the tribe, regardless of how much Indian blood he or she may have. Under this definition, of course, persons with little or no Indian ancestry qualify.[59]

Enough has been said to suggest some reasons why Indian population statistics are both misleading and unreliable. The problem of definition is part, but only part, of the reason for the incomplete and inconsistent data collected over the decades, especially in the 20th century. Although United States census figures are available, they appear to have substantially undercounted Minnesota's Indian people (see Table 1.7). Nor do they seem to reflect accurately the proportions of the migration to the cities. For Minneapolis, St. Paul, and Duluth, census figures indicated an Indian population of 171 in 1920 and 918 in 1930, but as early as 1925 the secretary of the Twin Cities Indian Association estimated that there were 1,000 Indian people in the Twin Cities alone. As America rearmed for entry into World War II, many Ojibway left their reservations to work in defense industries throughout the country. The statistics take no cognizance of this development, and it is probable that reservation populations in the 1940s were considerably less than the official counts show.

Table 1.7. Indian Population of Minnesota, 1890–1980

1890	—	10,096	1940	— 12,528
1900	—	9,182	1950	— 12,533
1910	—	9,053	1960	— 15,496
1920	—	8,761	1970	— 23,128
1930	—	11,077	1980	— 35,026

Source: U.S., *Census*, 1960; Minnesota Indian Affairs Commission, *Report*, 17 (1974); Minnesota Analysis and Planning System, "Final Report on the 1980 Census," telephone information, April 10, 1981.

The statistics of the Bureau of Indian Affairs, while difficult to use, may be more accurate, at least for the Ojibway. Its agents on the scene were perhaps more aware of the true situations on their reservations. In any case, lists and estimates were necessary for the administration of federal and state laws affecting Indian people, and the researcher must use them — albeit cautiously — to arrive at any conception of the numbers and fortunes of Indian people over the years.[60]

Whatever one's approach to the story of the Ojibway and Dakota of Minnesota, be it demographic, historical, social, economic, or anthropological, the basic facts underline a complex and unresolved relationship with American society and culture. The stories of the Dakota and Ojibway since World War II have been neglected by scholars, offering fertile areas for investigation. Until that is done, the period can be only superficially reconstructed from the scattered and incomplete sources available. What can be pieced together, however, suggests a portrait of gradual recovery from the past and an accommodation to the larger society which indicates that the Dakota and Ojibway are no more willing than their ancestors were to reject fully their tribal heritages as the price of full participation in American society and culture.

Under the Indian self-determination policies of recent years and the questioning in American society of past and present attitudes, beliefs, and practices inimical to racial and cultural groups, cultural themes, long submerged among the Dakota and Ojibway people, have experienced a renaissance. Understanding and knowledge of the tribal languages, history, and cultures have been woven into health, education, and social service programs, both to enhance pride and to provide a meaningful alternative to the poverty, discrimination, and personal and social disorganization often surrounding urban and reservation life. The basic premise of these programs is that one need not choose between being Indian and assimilating into the larger society, but that one can be both a successful Dakota or Ojibway and a successful American at the same time. Among members of both tribes in the 1980s there are varying degrees of tradition and acculturation, pride in ancestry, and interest in tribal languages.

In the political realm, the policy of Indian self-determination has meant greater control and decision-making authority for tribal political bodies in matters affecting reservation or group life; for other Indian organizations, it has enhanced their voice in decisions affecting how Indian people live. Both the Red Lake Reservation and the Minnesota Chippewa Tribe have used their tribal sovereignty and Indian self-determination policies to assume responsibility for federal services previously administered by the Bureau of Indian Affairs, to work out intergovernmental agreements with the state of Minnesota over such matters of mutual jurisdiction and authority as hunting and fishing, and to promote effectively and protect forcefully the rights and interests of members living both on and off the reservations. For the Dakota communities, the Minnesota Sioux Tribe similarly advocates their interests and safeguards their political rights.

In the fields of art, music, literature, and poetry, both traditional and newer methods and techniques are serving as mediums for the transmission of tribal heritages and as ways of exploring new meanings of the concept of being "Indian" in the modern world. Indeed in a political and social climate more understanding of cultural differences and supportive of Indian self-determination, the Dakota and Ojibway of the 1980s were creating new approaches to life. Tested by tragedy and born out of the will of people to survive oppression, these dynamic new efforts promise to enrich not only tribal life but American society and culture as well.

Reference notes

[1] This chapter was condensed from much longer drafts in the MEHP Papers, MHS, prepared by Rubinstein on the reservations, Woolworth on the Dakota, and Deborah L. Miller on urban Indians, which contain additional details and statistics. The authors wish to acknowledge the help and advice of W. Roger Buffalohead.

[2] On the Assiniboin and other early tribal groups, see Walter M. Hlady, "Indian Migrations in Manitoba and the West," in Historical and Scientific Society of Manitoba, *Papers*, 24–53 (Winnipeg, 1964); William W. Folwell, *A History of Minnesota*, 1:80–88, 308–320 (Reprint ed., St. Paul, 1956); Joseph R. Estabrook, "The Winnebago Indians, 1634–1863," master's thesis, University of Minnesota, 1936. For a good overview for elementary and secondary students, see Minnesota Historical Society Curriculum Committee, *The Land of the Ojibwe*, 4–11 (St. Paul, 1973).

For bibliographies, see Helen H. Tanner, *The Ojibwas: A Critical Bibliography* (Bloomington, Ind., 1976); Minnesota Historical Society, *Chippewa and Dakota Indians: A Subject Catalog of Books, Pamphlets, Periodical Articles, and Manuscripts in the Minnesota Historical Society* (St. Paul, 1969); MHS Educational Services Division, comp., *Bibliography of Ojibwe Resource Materials* (Minnesota Archaeological Society, *Occasional Publications*, no. 8 — St. Paul, 1981).

[3] Here and below, see Elden Johnson, *The Prehistoric Peoples of*

Minnesota, 1, 5–24 (St. Paul, 1969); Elden Johnson, ed., *Aspects of Upper Great Lakes Anthropology: Papers in Honor of Lloyd A. Wilford*, 8–39 (St. Paul, 1974); James B. Stoltman, *The Laurel Culture in Minnesota* (St. Paul, 1973); Elden Johnson, *The Arvilla Complex* (St. Paul, 1973); Richard S. MacNeish, "Early Man in the New World," in *American Scientist*, 64:316–327 (May–June, 1976).

[4] Timothy G. Roufs, *The Anishinabe of the Minnesota Chippewa Tribe*, 39–45 (Phoenix, Ariz., 1975).

[5] For concise accounts, here and below, see Roufs, *Anishinabe*, 1–39; Alan Woolworth, "The Eastern or Santee Dakota Indians of the Minnesota Region," 1–6, undated typescript in MEHP Papers.

[6] Roufs, *Anishinabe*, 44; Edmund J. Danziger, Jr., *The Chippewas of Lake Superior*, 8 (Norman, Okla., 1978). The northern tribes initially remained in the vicinity of Lake Superior, while the southwestern Ojibway occupied the interior of the region.

[7] Roufs, *Anishinabe*, 16–36.

[8] On the Ojibway, here and below, see Dean A. Crawford, David L. Peterson, and Virgil Wurr, *Minnesota Chippewa Indians: A Handbook for Teachers*, 71 (St. Paul, 1967); W. Vernon Kinietz, *Chippewa Village: The Story of Katikitegon*, 69–110 (Bloomfield Hills, Mich., 1947); Danziger, *Chippewas of Lake Superior*, 11, 23; on the Dakota, see Woolworth, "Eastern or Santee Dakota," 2. Although a family might return to the same hunting, fishing, or gathering places year after year, neither the Dakota nor Ojibway believed in private land ownership.

[9] Roufs, *Anishinabe*, 26, 45–57.

[10] Here and below, see Folwell, *Minnesota*, 1:91–94, 133–136, 140, 143–147; Estabrook, "The Winnebago."

[11] Edmund C. and Martha C. Bray, *Joseph N. Nicollet on the Plains and Prairies: The Expeditions of 1838–39 with Journals, Letters, and Notes on the Dakota Indians*, 252–262 (St. Paul, 1976); Woolworth, "Eastern or Santee Dakota."

Some indication of the proportion of mixed-bloods about this time was suggested by Thomas S. Williamson, a missionary at Lac qui Parle, who estimated that of the 386 Dakota near his mission just under 5% were part white, while less than 2% were half white. See Williamson to Amos J. Bruce, August 5, 1840, in Letters Received, St. Peter's Agency, U.S. Office of Indian Affairs, National Archives Record Group (NARG) 254, roll 759, microfilm in MHS.

[12] Erminie Wheeler-Voegelin and Harold Hickerson, "The Red Lake and Pembina Chippewa," Hickerson, "Ethnohistory of Mississippi Bands and Pillager and Winnibigoshish Bands of Chippewa," and Hickerson, "Ethnohistory of Chippewa of Lake Superior," all in David A. Horr, comp. and ed., *Chippewa Indians*, 1:25–175, 2:4–308, 3:25–180 (New York, 1974). These volumes give the population estimates by various traders and explorers.

Mixed-bloods made up approximately 10% of the Ojibway population of Minnesota in the early 1840s; some bands had a large proportion of mixed-bloods while others had none or virtually none. W. T. Boutwell *et al.* to David Greene, March 6, 1843, in Correspondence, American Board of Commissioners for Foreign Missions Papers, typed copies in MHS; U.S. Office of Indian Affairs, *Annual Report, 1856*, 41; "Census of the Chippewas of the Mississippi and Lake Superior, within the La Pointe Sub-Agency, 1843," in Letters Received, U.S. Office of Indian Affairs, NARG 75, roll 388.

[13] Roy W. Meyer, *History of the Santee Sioux: The United States Indian Policy on Trial*, 72–87 (Lincoln, Neb., 1967); Folwell, *Minnesota*, 1:266–308, 4:191 (Reprint ed., St. Paul, 1969).

[14] Here and two paragraphs below, see Meyer, *Santee Sioux*, 88–154; Kenneth A. Carley, *The Sioux Uprising of 1862*, 1–5 (Revised ed., St. Paul, 1976).

[15] Here and three paragraphs below, see Meyer, *Santee Sioux*, 258–284; Roy W. Meyer, "The Prairie Island Community: A Remnant of Minnesota Sioux," in *Minnesota History*, 37:271–282 (September, 1961).

[16] Carl and Amy Narvestad, *A History of Yellow Medicine County, Minnesota, 1872–1972*, 25–40 (Granite Falls, 1972); Meyer, *Santee Sioux*, 350–353.

[17] Governor's Interracial Commission, *The Indian in Minnesota*, 37 (St. Paul, 1947); Ethel Nurge, ed., *The Modern Sioux Social Systems and Reservation Culture*, 304 (Lincoln, Neb., 1970); League of Women Voters of Minnesota, *Indians in Minnesota*, 29 (St. Paul, 1974); Meyer, *Santee Sioux*, 343, 352n; Minnesota Indian Affairs Commission, *Report*, 1973.

[18] Folwell, *Minnesota*, 4:192.

[19] Folwell, *Minnesota*, 4:193–196; Joel B. Bassett to N. G. Taylor, October 29, 1867, and John Johnson (Enmegahbow) to Alexander Ramsey, January 27, 1870, in Letters Received, Chippewa Agency, U.S. Office of Indian Affairs, NARG 75, rolls 156, 157; U.S. Office of Indian Affairs, *Annual Report, 1869*, 423–425; *1872*, 208–211; *1873*, 12, 179.

[20] U.S. Office of Indian Affairs, *Annual Report, 1866*, 293; *1867*, 341–343; *1868*, 300–302, 379; *1869*, 423–425, 430–432; *1870*, 304–308, 311; *1871*, 588–594, 597–600; *1872*, 18, 22–25, 86, 208–211; *1873*, 178–182; *1874*, 195–198; *1875*, 295–298.

[21] U.S., *Statutes at Large*, 16:566, 570, 24:388–391. On federal allotment policy, see Henry E. Fritz, *The Movement For Indian Assimilation, 1860–1890* (Philadelphia, 1963). On the Northwest Indian Commission, an attempt in 1886 to consolidate Minnesota's Ojibway, see Folwell, *Minnesota*, 4:198–219.

[22] U.S., *Statutes at Large*, 25:642; U.S. Office of Indian Affairs, *Annual Report, 1900*, 642; Folwell, *Minnesota*, 4:219–226. For the process of allotment in Minnesota, see Folwell, 4:226–235; "Chippewa Indians in Minnesota," 51 Congress, 1 session, *House Executive Documents*, no. 247 (serial 2747), known as the Rice Report.

[23] *Tomahawk*, July 9, 1903, p. 1; S. M. Brosius, *The Urgent Case of the Mille Lacs Indians* (Philadelphia, 1901).

[24] U.S. Office of Indian Affairs, *Annual Report, 1900*, 642; *1911*, 60; League of Women Voters, *Indians in Minnesota*, 33.

[25] U.S. Office of Indian Affairs, *Annual Report, 1873*, 179; *1880*, 104; *1883*, 95; U.S. Office of Economic Opportunity, *A Comprehensive Evaluation of OEO Community Action Programs on Six Selected American Indian Reservations*, 297 (1966).

[26] *Detroit Record*, October 25, 1895; *Chippeway Herald* (White Earth), December, 1902, p. [3]; U.S. Office of Economic Opportunity, *Comprehensive Evaluation*, 297.

[27] *The Progress*, November 26, 1887, March 9, June 8, 1889. For a study of the newspaper, see Gerald R. Vizenor, "A Brief Historical Study and General Content Description of a Newspaper Published on the White Earth Reservation in Becker County, Minnesota," master's starred paper, University of Minnesota, 1965, copy in MHS.

For the various directions American Indian policy has taken, see S. Lyman Tyler, *A History of Indian Policy* (Washington, D.C., 1973).

[28] *Tomahawk*, April 13, 1916, p. 1; August 16, 1917, p. 1; May 30, p. 1, June 6, p. 1, September 19, p. 1, October 31, p. 1, November 7, p. 1 — all 1918; February 21, 1924, p. 1.

[29] Folwell, *Minnesota*, 4:261–264; 51 Congress, 1 session, *House Executive Documents*, no. 247 (serial 2747).

[30] Here and below, see League of Women Voters, *Indians in Minnesota*, 34; Folwell, *Minnesota*, 4:297–306; Minnesota Indian Affairs Commission, *Report*, 1974, pp. 10, 11; Indian Affairs Intertribal Board, *Report*, 1978, p. 6.

[31] American Indian Policy Review Commission, "Tentative Final Report," 1:32 (1976), mimeographed copy in MEHP Papers.

[32] U.S., *Statutes at Large*, 48:984; League of Women Voters, *Indians in Minnesota*, 36–38; Institute for Government Research, *The Problem of Indian Administration*, 346–429 (Baltimore, 1928), known as the Meriam Report; Meyer, *Santee Sioux*, 295; Indian

Affairs Intertribal Board, *Report*, 1978, p. 6. The Lower Sioux Community at Morton had withdrawn from the joint organization by 1981.

[33] Tyler, *Indian Policy*, 151–216; League of Women Voters, *Indians in Minnesota*, 47–53, 156; Indian Affairs Intertribal Board, *Report*, 1978, p. 5.

[34] U.S. Office of Indian Affairs, *Annual Report, 1880*, 173. A survey of Minnesota's reservations published in 1974 indicated that Fond du Lac was covered by secondary and tertiary growth and had significant sand and gravel deposits. Grand Portage's land was too poor for farming, but there were seasonal trapping, fishing, and timbering occupations. Nett Lake was in an isolated area with too many lakes and swamps for farming but with some timberlands. Leech Lake was swampy with rocky ledges and many lakes; it was not good for farming and the timber had been cut over. Mille Lacs was on timberland, but the timber was of inferior grade. Red Lake was largely timberland and lakes with a fishing industry. White Earth had lakes and forests in the east and good farmlands in the west. Prairie Island had submarginal farmland. The Lower Sioux Community at Morton had good farmland. The Upper Sioux Community had farmland but subleased much of it. League of Women Voters, *Indians in Minnesota*, 30–36; Governor's Interracial Commission, *The Indian in Minnesota*, 27–34.

[35] U.S. Office of Indian Affairs, *Annual Report, 1880*, 266; *1900*, 662; *1920*, 119.

[36] Mary M. Kirkland and Clarence W. Ringey, "Indians at Red Lake, Minnesota, Meet Problems of a Changing World," in *Indians at Work*, May, 1939, pp. 30–34; U.S. Office of Indian Affairs, *Annual Report, 1911*, 42; Folwell, *Minnesota*, 4:235–295; Governor's Interracial Commission, *The Indian in Minnesota*, 20–23.

[37] U.S. Office of Indian Affairs, *Annual Report, 1911*, 118, 132, 138, 144, 149; *1915*, 115, 135, 138, 146. Notable lacework was produced by Dakota women at Morton in the late 19th and early 20th centuries; samples were given to England's Queen Victoria and Queen Alexandra. E. Whipple, "The Church and the Dakotas of Birch Coolie," in *Spirit of Missions*, 74:203–207 (March, 1909).

[38] Harvey Klevar, "The Mille Lacs Band of Chippewa: Children of Government Policy and White Prejudice," 3–7, 13–17, seminar paper, University of Minnesota, 1968, copy in MHS.

[39] Here and below, see Meyer, *Santee Sioux*, 345–350; Calvin G. Gower, "The CCC Indian Division: Aid for Depressed Americans, 1933–1942," in *Minnesota History*, 43:3–13 (Spring, 1972); Klevar, "The Mille Lacs Band of Chippewa," 7; Consolidated Chippewa Agency, *Minnesota Chippewa Bulletin* (Duluth), November 21, 1938–August 21, 1942; Sister M. Inez Hilger, *A Social Study of One Hundred Fifty Chippewa Indian Families of the White Earth Reservation of Minnesota*, 27–29 (Washington, D.C., 1939).

[40] Governor's Interracial Commission, *The Indian in Minnesota*, 30, 64–69; Frell M. Owl to Harold C. Hagen, September 11, 1950; Information Bulletin, Red Lake Agency, September 5, 1950; Otto Thunder to Hagen, May 17, 1951; D. S. Myer to Hagen, June 22, 1951; Louis F. Stately to Hagen, July 11, 1951 — all in Correspondence, Harold C. Hagen Papers, in MHS.

[41] League of Women Voters, *Indians in Minnesota*, 38–43, 88, 178; League of Women Voters of Minneapolis, *Indians in Minneapolis*, 2 (Minneapolis, 1968); Minnesota Analysis and Planning System (MAPS), "Final Report of the 1980 Census," telephone information, April 10, 1981.

[42] League of Women Voters of Minneapolis, *Indians in Minneapolis*, 7; *Minneapolis Tribune*, December 5, 1980, p. 1A.

[43] Arthur M. Harkins and Richard G. Woods, *Indian Americans in St. Paul: An Interim Report* (Minneapolis, 1970); *The Circle* (Minneapolis), June, 1980, p. 11; MAPS, "Final Report."

[44] *The Circle*, April, 4; May, 1; June, 11; December, 10 — all 1980; January, 1981, p. 6.

[45] *The Circle*, March, 3; April, 5, 18; July, 3; September, 5; December, 5, 13 — all 1980.

[46] U.S. Bureau of the Census, *Subject Reports: American Indians, 1970*, 31, 124, tables 4, 9.

[47] League of Women Voters, *Indians in Minnesota*, 30–38, 83.

[48] For a summary of the debates on Indian education, see U.S. Office of Indian Affairs, *Annual Report, 1885*, cxi–cxiii; League of Women Voters, *Indians in Minnesota*, 58–82. Minnesota Indians first began receiving government-administered funds for education under the treaties of 1842, 1854, and 1867; by 1885 there were schools operating on the Ojibway reservations; U.S. Office of Indian Affairs, *Annual Report, 1885*, lxxx.

[49] U.S. Office of Indian Affairs, *Annual Report, 1880*, 246, 254; *1897*, 159–161; *1911*, 161, 167; *1930*, 52; Governor's Interracial Commission, *The Indian in Minnesota*, 64–68; Institute for Government Research, *Problem of Indian Administration*, 356–358.

[50] U.S. Dept. of Health, Education and Welfare, *Indians on Federal Reservations in the United States, a Digest; Aberdeen Area*, part 3, p. 41 (Washington, D.C., 1958); Minnesota Indian Affairs Commission, *Report*, 1967, p. 32; League of Women Voters, *Indians in Minnesota*, 59, 72; U.S. Bureau of the Census, *Subject Reports: American Indians, 1970*, 22, table 3; Minnesota Higher Education Coordinating Board, *A Report on the Status of Hispanic/Latino Students . . . and other Minority Students in Post-Secondary Education*, 16 (St. Paul, 1981), copy in MEHP Papers.

[51] Interim Commission on Indian Affairs, *Report*, 1959, p. 49C; League of Women Voters, *Indians in Minnesota*, 76; Minnesota Dept. of Education, "Supplemental Report on State-Wide Conference on Indian Affairs, June 1, 1956, to the Governor's Human Rights Commission," 3, copy in MHS.

[52] League of Women Voters, *Indians in Minnesota*, 80.

[53] Higher Education Coordinating Board, *Report on the Status of Hispanic/Latino Students*, 1981, pp. 22, 53, 67; *The Circle*, December, 1980, p. 6.

[54] Wilfred D. Antell, "A Model for the Distribution of Johnson-O'Malley Funds Based on Educational Needs," Ph.D. thesis, University of Minnesota, 1973; *Ni-Mi-Mah-Kwa-Zoo-Min*, February, 1981 (called *Ourselves* beginning March, 1981); League of Women Voters, *Indians in Minnesota*, 112–120, 157–159; Indian Affairs Intertribal Board, *Report*, 1978; *The Pioneer* (Bemidji), March 8, 1981, pp. 1, 17; Tyler, *Indian Policy*, 200, 218, 221; *Congressional Record*, 93 Congress, 2 session, 41,396–41,405. The Red Lake tribe handled the complete $9,700,000 hospital project, the first of its kind in the U.S.

[55] Governor's Interracial Commission, *The Indian in Minnesota*, 44–46; U.S., *Statutes at Large*, 16:361, 25:392, 41:350, 43:253, 54:715.

[56] Governor's Interracial Commission, *The Indian in Minnesota*, 8; League of Women Voters, *Indians in Minnesota*, 17–20, 22, 194–196; Minnesota Indian Affairs Commission, *Report*, 1967, p. 17.

[57] U.S. Office of Indian Affairs, *Lists Showing the Degree of Indian Blood of Certain Persons Holding Land upon the White Earth Reservation in Minnesota and a List Showing the Date of Death of Certain Persons Who Held Land Upon Such Reservation* (Washington, D.C., 1911).

[58] The enrollment commission established in 1913 recorded information on residence, proportion of Indian blood, ancestry and ancestors' proportion of Indian blood, and identity of siblings. See Correspondence and Miscellaneous Papers, Ransom Judd Powell Papers, in MHS. See also Albert E. Jenks, *Indian-White Amalgamation: An Anthropometric Study* (University of Minnesota, *Studies in the Social Sciences*, no. 6 — Minneapolis, 1916); *Tomahawk*, March 2, 1916, p. 1; "Report in the Matter of the Investigation of the White Earth Reservation," in 63 Congress, 3 session, *House Report*, no. 1336, pp. iii–xxii (serial 6337).

[59] Governor's Interracial Commission, *The Indian in Minnesota*, 8; League of Women Voters, *Indians in Minnesota*, 17–20, 22, 194–196; Minnesota Indian Affairs Commission, *Report*, 1967, p. 17.

[60] Minnesota Governor's Human Rights Commission, *Minnesota's Indian Citizens (Yesterday and Today)*, 41 (St. Paul, 1965); Minnesota Dept. of Social Security, Division of Social Welfare, *Indian Study*, 5 (St. Paul, 1948); *Tomahawk*, January 8, 1925, p. 1.

Table Sources

Table 1.1: Elliott Coues, ed., *The Expeditions of Zebulon Montgomery Pike, 1805–07*, 1:346 (Reprint ed., Minneapolis, 1965); "Census of Sioux Indians, St. Peters Agency, September 1, 1834," "Statistical Return of the Various Tribes or Bands of Sioux, within the Agency of St. Peters, September 30, 1836," Lawrence Taliaferro to T. Hartly Crawford, September 30, 1839, "Statistical Returns Showing the Number of the Bands or Tribes of the Dakota . . . within the Agency of St. Peters," September 1, 1846 — all in U.S. Office of Indian Affairs, Letters Received, rolls 757, 758, 760, National Archives Record Group (NARG) 75, microfilm in MHS. The reliability of figures for all but the Mdewakanton is questionable; Roy W. Meyer, *History of the Santee Sioux*, 68 (Lincoln, Neb., 1967).

Table 1.2: "Census of the Chippewa of the Mississippi & Lake Superior, within the La Pointe Sub-Agency, September, 1843," in U.S. Office of Indian Affairs, Letters Received, roll 388, NARG 75;

U.S. Office of Indian Affairs, *Annual Report, 1866*, 350; *1885*, 344, 352, 362, 368; *1900*, 642, 654; *1911*, 60, 69; *1920*, 67.

Table 1.3: Meyer, *Santee Sioux*, 264, 273; U.S., manuscript census schedules, 1870, 1880, microfilm in MHS; "Census of Mdewakanton Sioux of Minnesota," March 15, 17, 1899, in Sioux Annuity and Census Rolls, 1849–1935, U.S. Office of Indian Affairs, NARG 75, microfilm in MHS; Bureau of Indian Affairs, telephone information, January 19, 1981. Published sources were U.S., *Census, 1890, Population*, 533; *1910*, 2:995; *1920*, 3:507; *1940*, 2:75; *1950*, 1:122; *1960*, vol. 1, part 25, pp. 162–168; *1970*, vol. 1, part 25, pp. 160–162.

Table 1.5: U.S. Office of Indian Affairs, *Annual Report, 1930*, 41, and *Statistical Supplement to the Annual Report*, 7 (1942; U.S. Dept. of Health, Education and Welfare, *Indians on Federal Reservations in the United States, a Digest: Aberdeen Area*, part 3, p. 41 (Washington, D.C., 1958); League of Women Voters of Minnesota, *Indians in Minnesota*, 29 (St. Paul, 1974); U.S. Bureau of the Census, *Subject Reports: American Indians, 1970*, 190, table 17; Minnesota Indian Affairs Commission, *Report* (1973).

Table 1.6: Governor's Human Rights Commission, *Minnesota's Indian Citizen (Yesterday and Today)*, 41 (St. Paul, 1965); League of Women Voters of Minnesota, *Indians in Minnesota*, 27 (St. Paul, 1974); Minnesota Indian Affairs Commission, *Report* (1973); Minnesota Analysis and Planning System, "Final Report on the 1980 Federal Census," telephone information, April 10, 1981.

CHAPTER 2

The French Canadians and French

Sarah P. Rubinstein

TWO DIVERSE STRAINS of French immigrants appeared early in North America. One went directly from France to the American colonies and to the later United States; the other went to Canada in the last half of the 17th century. From there a secondary migration moved from a base in Quebec southeast to New England, south to Michigan and Illinois, and southwest to Minnesota. Over the years French Canadians have constituted a small but significant segment of Minnesota's population, a segment more than five times larger than that from France.

Exactly how many French Canadians traveled to the United States is impossible to determine because existing statistics before 1890 made no attempt to differentiate them from Anglo-Canadian immigrants. One estimate placed the number who emigrated before 1890 at 450,000. The United States census of that year counted 302,496 French-Canadian foreign born and 513,428 of mixed parentage. About 75% of them lived in New England and New York, the chief concentrations. In the northern Midwest, Minnesota ranked second to Michigan with 10,910 foreign born and 21,895 of mixed parentage. These percentages and rankings remained unchanged in 1930 when Minnesota had 6,484 foreign-born and 23,300 foreign-stock French Canadians. No figures were recorded after 1950.[1]

As for the French, 729,516 (or an average of only 4,707 yearly) left France for the United States between 1821 and 1976. The peak decade, when 77,262 arrived, occurred in the 1840s, much earlier than that of other European groups. The year of heaviest immigration was 1851 with 20,126, distantly followed by 1872 with 13,782. By 1920 there were 152,890 foreign-born French; in 1930 the figure for foreign stock was 336,373 — the high points in these categories. Minnesota attracted few of these people; their principal areas of concentration in the 1860s were New York and Louisiana. By the 1950s New York and California were the leaders. In 1890 foreign-born French in the state numbered 1,869, the highest point their population reached. In 1920 the foreign born totaled 1,463; 10 years later the census counted 7,248 of foreign stock.[2]

The earliest French and French Canadians to reach what is now Minnesota were explorers and fur traders. Beginning in the late 1600s, men from New France penetrated the heart of the continent by using the rivers and lakes as their highways. French priests like Fathers Jacques Marquette and Louis Jolliet were the first white men to travel the Mississippi River. Explorer-fur traders like Daniel Greysolon, sieur du Luth, pushed westward in canoes paddled by French-Canadian voyageurs, trading with the Indian peoples along their routes and setting up posts among them. A Minnesota city is named for Du Luth and major Minneapolis streets recall such French explorers as Marquette and Joseph N. Nicollet. A county, a town, and an island in the Mississippi are also named for Nicollet, the French scientist who was the first to map accurately the upper Mississippi and Missouri rivers in the 1830s. And other French names on the Minnesota landscape bear testimony to the presence of these people — Frontenac, the St. Croix River, Lac qui Parle, Mille Lacs Lake, and many more.[3]

From the 1820s to the 1870s the métis, who were the offspring of French Canadians and Indians, helped develop Minnesota's first overland roads. Driving two-wheeled, wooden oxcarts, they carried furs south to St. Paul and returned with goods and supplies for the Selkirk Colony near present Winnipeg and the trading posts located in between. This lucrative exchange was a mainstay of the Minnesota economy in the late 1840s and 1850s. When the heyday of the fur trade passed, many of those who had participated in it turned to farming.[4]

THE FRENCH CANADIANS

Most French Canadians, including voyageurs, were descendants of peasants who migrated to New France on the St. Lawrence River in the 17th century during the reign of Louis XIV. Relatively few arrived after 1700. They left largely from the provinces of Normandy, Aunis, Saintonge, and Poitou in western France (see Map 2.1), where agriculture was still primitive and produce was heavily taxed. Many more men than women emigrated, chiefly by enlisting in the army or becoming *engagés* to serve under contract to such commercial enterprises as fur companies for a specified number of years. Although these people were not drawn from the lowest levels of society, they left heavily populated but poor regions "nearly destitute and virtually landless." The French-Canadian community of Quebec grew from this population base, augmented by Parisian women shipped over by the French government after 1660, demobilized soldiers who elected to stay, fur traders, and scattered others attracted by kinfolk. At the end of the 17th century it numbered perhaps 15,000. By 1754 it had grown, largely through natural increase, to about 55,000. By the late 19th century French Canadians in Quebec had become an isolated minority in a predominantly British country, where they preserved a 17th-century religion, language, culture, and legal system.[5]

The pre-eminent initial formulating factors in the development of the community along the St. Lawrence were the abundance of cheap land and access to the river. Given the absence of roads in New France, the only means of travel was by water, and even marginal land was valuable if it had river frontage. There the French Canadian cleared only enough land to sustain his family and no more. Lacking markets, he had no incentive to produce a cash crop. On the banks of the St. Lawrence and many other streams along which French Canadians later settled, their farmhouses were characteristically set on long, narrow pieces of land fronting rivers, interspersed by an occasional church or mill. The farmer built his house near the shore, and in succession behind it came his garden, his fields, his pasture, and his woods.[6]

The French Canadians followed the practice of dividing inheritances among their children. They also married young and had large families. These customs inevitably led to the breakup of family lands and the overpopulation of rural

French Canada. By the early 19th century young people were leaving family farms in search of jobs in Montreal, Three Rivers, and Quebec, as well as in New England lumber camps and mill towns. These trends intensified after the rebellions of 1837 and 1838 when the government followed an unduly repressive policy toward French Canadians who rose against English dominance. Moreover, Canada did not recover so quickly as the United States from the economic panic of 1837. Thus when the Upper Mississippi Valley opened for settlement about that time, it drew an increasing number of land- and income-hungry French Canadians, many of whom found employment in its infant lumbering industry. Industrial jobs in New England, the Homestead Act of 1862, and two decades of depression in Canada following the panic of 1873 induced others to migrate to the United States. Frequently, the younger men or women went first, to be followed after a season or two by other family members.[7]

By the time permanent white settlement got under way in Minnesota in the 1850s, French Canadians who had earlier worked in the fur trade or in the lumbering industry knew the river valleys intimately, and it was there they chose to settle. With few exceptions the pioneers among them homesteaded in the valleys of the Minnesota, Mississippi, Crow Wing, Red Lake, and Red rivers, where their fathers had traded with the Indians or traveled over the Red River Trails. Later immigrants from Canada followed the same pattern. By 1900 the principal concentrations of French Canadians were to be found in the river and lake cities of St. Paul, Minneapolis, and Duluth, and in Polk and Red Lake counties of western Minnesota (see Table 2.1).

The Fort Snelling-Mendota Hub

The hub of French-Canadian settlement in Minnesota, and indeed of settlement in the state generally, was the military post of Fort Snelling and the fur-trading center of Mendota. Located on opposite shores of the Mississippi River at its

Map 2.1. Historic Provinces of France

Table 2.1. French Canadians in Minnesota by County, 1900–30

County	1900 foreign born	1910 fb	1910 foreign mixed	1930 fb	1930 fm
Aitkin	142	107	140	72	179
Anoka	212	127	238	106	332
Becker	28	55	58	14	91
Beltrami	112	214	204	86	285
Benton	32	38	53	23	88
Big Stone	24	15	21	11	54
Blue Earth	34	12	17	7	59
Brown	5	4	5	4	13
Carlton	385	432	457	203	461
Carver	4	2	5	7	15
Cass	84	71	75	26	87
Chippewa	10	5	7	3	16
Chisago	42	26	30	15	41
Clay	101	30	53	35	130
Clearwater		7	7	10	34
Cook	41	31	20	9	31
Cottonwood	12	6	12	1	20
Crow Wing	212	146	259	99	407
Dakota	124	89	96	41	243
Dodge	6	15	6	1	13

Table 2.1. French Canadians in Minnesota (continued)

County	1900 foreign born	1910 fb	1910 foreign mixed	1930 fb	1930 fm
Douglas	7	10	10	4	16
Faribault	44	36	69	11	103
Fillmore	29	9	7	6	37
Freeborn	18	14	15	5	41
Goodhue	13	4	6	6	33
Grant	3				6
Hennepin	2,060	1,866	2,324	1,517	5,505
Houston	9	12	11	3	14
Hubbard	62	56	65	11	58
Isanti	6	6	4	1	9
Itasca	125	294	298	143	443
Jackson	7	4	1	2	6
Kanabec	7	3	5	3	19
Kandiyohi	24	15	35	15	36
Kittson	50	22	25	25	90
Koochiching		101	50	148	349
Lac qui Parle	5	4	7	1	4
Lake	99	170	100	20	70
Lake of the Woods				12	39
Le Sueur	33	22	28		27
Lincoln	4	1	4	2	12
Lyon	100	76	214	39	210
McLeod	61	49	58	8	72
Mahnomen		20	18	15	27
Marshall	383	177	317	94	336
Martin	18	9	21	4	447
Meeker	44	12		5	18
Mille Lacs	51	27	38	20	69
Morrison	342	317	433	140	440
Mower	17	29	22	11	44
Murray	36	26	56	13	89
Nicollet	30	23	30	10	70
Nobles	5	7	6	4	22
Norman	10	1		2	15
Olmsted	20	11	20	34	121
Otter Tail	50	56	23	16	70
Pennington		62	87	27	97
Pine	108	43	48	31	86
Pipestone	1	6	10	5	23
Polk	749	663	891	337	1,186
Pope	30	12	42	4	34
Ramsey	1,098	1,216	1,484	795	3,416
Red Lake	1,259	735	1,269	345	1,137
Redwood	14	7	20	6	34
Renville	26	6	4	7	28
Rice	291	226	353	108	516
Rock	7	2	3	1	11
Roseau	59	70	47	23	58
St. Louis	1,703	2,295	1,971	1,224	3,388
Scott	23	23	20	5	32
Sherburne	42	20	41	11	62
Sibley	57	27	35	9	41
Stearns	56	39	20	33	131
Steele	14	17	11	4	32
Stevens	8	9	12	5	22
Swift	69	44	55	19	71
Todd	81	34	45	18	96
Traverse	5	6	11	4	24
Wabasha	44	19	23	15	46
Wadena	18	9	10	10	50
Waseca	10	11	12	6	27
Washington	467	331	402	163	516
Watonwan	14	2	1	4	27
Wilkin	50	34	42	22	69
Winona	37	10	16	20	75
Wright	326	161	359	98	385
Yellow Medicine	7	2	3	2	14
White Earth (Ind. res.)	8				
Total	12,063	11,062	13,430	6,484	23,300
Published census figures	(12,063)	(11,062)	(13,442)	(6,484)	(22,900)

Source: See Appendix

junction with the Minnesota, Fort Snelling and Mendota early became the linchpins of white movement into the Minnesota country. At Mendota the American Fur Company in the 1830s established a headquarters post for trade with the Dakota Indians, and there numerous voyageurs, *engagés*, clerks, and others found employment. As they retired or decided to take up land after the trade declined, some of them chose to remain at Mendota or at other posts where they had been active. They were not numerous, however, and they were quickly outnumbered by later arrivals.[8]

Several traders of French-Canadian ancestry became naturalized citizens and well-known pioneers. Alexis Bailly, who left Mendota to establish a fur post at Wabasha on the Mississippi River in 1836, lived there until his death in 1861 in a district that became known as French Hill. Louis Provençalle, after a long career as a Minnesota Valley trader, died at Mendota in 1850. Joseph Rolette, a territorial legislator from Pembina who saved the capital for St. Paul, lived the rest of his life near his old post at what is now Pembina, North Dakota, after Minnesota became a state in 1858. Joseph Renville, for whom Renville County was named, lived out his years on Lac qui Parle Lake. Louis Robert, a trader credited with having built the first frame house in St. Paul, became a well-known businessman there before his death in 1874. A street is named for him.[9]

Another trading family who chose to remain in Minnesota was responsible for the development of the only French-Canadian colony in the southeastern part of the state. Born near Quebec, Jean Baptiste Faribault was trading in the Minnesota country before 1805. He and his family were undoubtedly among its earliest permanent residents, and the stone house he built in 1839–40 at Mendota has been preserved as a historic site. From this impressive base, Faribault's operations ranged up the Minnesota River Valley. In 1844 Alexander, his eldest son, launched the earliest known effort to establish a French-Canadian colony in the state.[10]

Like Jean Baptiste, Alexander built a substantial house (also preserved) in what is now the city of Faribault, which was named for him. He bought land and encouraged others, including his father, to move to Rice County. Alexander was also responsible for the presence in Minnesota of Nicholas and Edmund N. La Croix, for he invited these pioneers in the development of the middlings purifier to move from Montreal to oversee his flour mill on the Cannon River in 1861. There they installed a European milling process and experimented with the purifier, which made it possible to produce white flour from hard, spring wheat. Their discoveries later established Minneapolis for a time as the milling capital of the nation. By 1857 the efforts of Faribault and others had attracted 364 Canadians to Rice County, many of whom "were undoubtedly of French ancestry." They had also resulted in the organization of a Catholic parish, which was served by French-speaking clergy at least until 1938.[11]

Elsewhere in Rice County French Canadians were to be found along with Irish settlers in Erin, Cannon City, Shieldsville, Walcott, Wells, and Wheatland townships. In wooded, lake-studded Wheatland Township northwest of Faribault, a group of French Canadians arrived in 1855. Three years later they founded the second Catholic church in the county. At one time it was attended by 40 families, but by 1906, when the church was abandoned, the number had dwindled to only 15. Many of the French Canadians who moved out sold to incoming Bohemian (Czech) farmers, especially in Wheatland Township. Some remained, however, and in the 1970s French names were still present in Faribault and in Wells and Walcott townships.[12]

The Fort Snelling-Mendota hub also spawned the future cities of St. Paul and St. Anthony (now part of Minneapolis). Settlement at what became St. Paul began when the fort's commandant in 1840 ordered the immediate eviction from the Fort Snelling Military Reserve of numerous civilian squatters. Among them were French Canadians, some of whom had taken up residence there in the 1820s and 1830s as refugees from the ill-fated Selkirk Colony in the lower Red River Valley. Summarily evicted by the soldiers, they moved downriver to join such whisky-selling countrymen as Pierre Parrant at a spot then known as Pig's Eye, the ignominious beginning of the future city of St. Paul.[13]

When Bishop Mathias Loras of Dubuque traveled up the Mississippi in 1839, he counted 185 Catholics at Pig's Eye and Mendota. Ten years later a traveler noted in his journal that the settlements at Mendota, "St. Pauls," and St. Anthony were mostly inhabited by French, French Canadians, and mixed-bloods served by Catholic priests. By 1850 Mendota had a population of 154, over 100 of whom were of French-Canadian stock, while St. Paul and Ramsey County had a total of 344 Canadians, many of whom possessed French surnames.[14]

Father Lucien Galtier and his successor Father Augustin Ravoux, the missionary priests who ministered to these people, had both been born in France. Galtier recommended that the new settlement's name be changed from Pig's Eye to St. Paul. Ravoux organized the construction of what is now the oldest church in continuous use in Minnesota, St. Peter's Catholic Church at Mendota. Another French cleric, Joseph Cretin, was named as the first bishop of the newly created diocese of St. Paul in 1851, and two French teaching orders — the Sisters of St. Joseph of Carondelet and the Brothers of the Holy Family — opened schools in the community in the 1850s. The sisters also started the first hospital in the city. In 1853 Cretin observed that no one objected to sermons being delivered in both French and English. But by 1860, with the arrival of the first waves of Irish and German immigrants, French dominance began to fade, and the Catholic church assumed the strong Irish aspect it was to retain.[15]

Both old and new arrivals from French Canada began to move beyond the St. Paul-Mendota hub as early as 1844 to take up land in northern Ramsey County. Among them was former Red River Valley resident Benjamin Gervais, who operated one of the first two privately owned gristmills in Minnesota. Five men who emigrated together from Sorel, Quebec (see Map 2.2), found new homes in what is now the suburb of Little Canada on Lake Gervais in 1847. Others followed, and in 1850 the census recorded 116 Canadian-born persons in a population of 194; their names indicated that most of them were French. As late as 1924 services in Little Canada's St. John's Catholic Church (established in 1852) were still conducted entirely in French; thereafter both French and English were used. In the schools, however, English became the language of instruction as early as 1853.

Settlers from Quebec continued to be drawn to Little Canada at least until 1900. They were primarily farmers and truck gardeners, but a sprinkling of hotelkeepers, real estate salesmen, and blacksmiths also appeared. By the 1970s many families had lived there for four and five generations, comfortably intermingled with several German and a few Austrian, Swedish, and, since 1900, Italian families.[16]

From Little Canada, French Canadians spread northward in Ramsey County to Vadnais Heights and to Centerville across the border in Anoka County. In 1854, two years after the first settlers arrived at Centerville, they formed a Catholic congregation, which numbered 190 members in 1857. Though both settlements continued to receive newcomers throughout the next three decades, much of their growth occurred by natural increase. From 1866 to 1891 the parish priest at Centerville recorded 1,366 baptisms, 210 marriages, and 114 funerals. In 1887 the population remained two-thirds French Canadian. Plat maps of Anoka County showed a continuing French concentration at Centerville as late as 1975, as did the records of St. Genevieve's Cemetery, which go back 100 years. Gravestone inscriptions ceased to appear in French, however, after about 1900.[17]

Map 2.2. Provinces and Towns of Canada from which Emigrants Reached Minnesota

That the French-Canadian population continued to grow in the 1880s and 1890s is suggested by Catholic parish development not only in northern Ramsey County but also in adjoining Washington County. In 1880 some members of the Little Canada congregation established a church at White Bear Lake. Most of them were French and Irish railroad workers, but since only two-fifths of them knew English, the parish of St. Mary's of the Lake, as it was called, used French during its first five years. To serve the influx of French-Canadian workers attracted by the lumbering industry in nearby Washington County (some had been there since before 1850), a French-language church was established at Stillwater in 1882. By 1898 it boasted a membership of 110 families and 600 persons. Its services were conducted in French until 1920, by which time many French Canadians were moving away and the congregation was becoming Italian. Farther north in Washington County, French Canadians who had moved from the Centerville area became sufficiently numerous to found a parish at Hugo in 1902. A comparison of the names of French landowners there in 1901 with those in 1976 showed that many family names had persisted.[18]

From the St. Paul-Mendota hub other fur trader-settlers of French-Canadian stock moved to St. Anthony, the nucleus of Minneapolis. A stopping place for Red River oxcart caravans plying between St. Paul and points north, St. Anthony began to assume a more stable air after Pierre Bottineau and others settled there in 1845. The son of a French trader and an Ojibway mother, Bottineau was born in the Red River Settlement in 1817. He moved to the Fort Snelling area in 1837, where he worked for the American Fur Company as an interpreter, guide, and scout. He was among those evicted from the military reservation in 1840, living for a time in St. Paul before going to St. Anthony.[19]

Bottineau embodied much of the French-Canadian experience in Minnesota. His mixed Indian and French heritage, his childhood spent in the Red River Valley, his involvement in the fur trade, and his employment as a scout and interpreter were experiences shared by most of the French Canadians of the prestatehood period. Like all French Canadians he supported the Catholic church, at one time donating 14 lots to St. Anthony of Padua Church in St. Anthony. His role as a leader of the French-Canadian community is amply demonstrated in his colonization efforts. The three settlements he founded — St. Anthony, Osseo, and Red Lake Falls — are still centers of French-Canadian life. Bottineau and Antoine Le Count, who had shared many fur-trading and exploring experiences, led the way to a new settlement in northern Hennepin County. In 1852 Bottineau laid claim to land at Osseo, which was quickly dubbed Bottineau's Prairie, while Le Count settled not far away at Medicine Lake in Plymouth Township. Over the next 20 years other French Canadians followed them to take land at Maple Grove, Corcoran, and Hamel. Many of their descendants still live in these areas.[20]

Again the religious activity of these French-Canadian Catholics provided a clue to their numbers and their language retention. In 1855 they organized the Church of St. Louis at Osseo and three years later that of St. Francis at Medicine Lake. Forty years later Osseo's membership was still three-fourths French Canadian, and two sermons a month were given in French. This practice continued until 1914, by which time the parishioners were part French and part German.

An equally strong French-Canadian tradition developed nearby at the junction of the Rum and Mississippi rivers, where the counties of Hennepin, Wright, Sherburne, and Anoka adjoin. To this area French Canadians also made their way in the 1850s, founding a Catholic parish at Dayton in 1856. At the turn of the century the Dayton church was composed of some 150 families, almost all of whom were French Canadian. As late as the mid-1930s the sacrament was still administered in French. To the east across the Mississippi, where the city of Anoka evolved from a ferry crossing on the Red River Trail, French Canadians from southern Canada helped found a church in 1856. Testimony to their continuing presence may be found in Anoka's Calvary Cemetery, where tombstones bearing French names range in date from the 1890s to the 1970s.[21]

Up the Mississippi in adjoining Wright County, homesteading began as early as 1854 when a family group located in Otsego Township at the mouth of the Crow River to operate a trading post and open small farms. By the end of the decade French Lake and Marysville townships held a few French Canadians. The ever-active Pierre Bottineau made an apparently unsuccessful attempt to start a French colony in Wright County in 1879 when he tried to persuade 200 to 300 families from Ontario to dwell at Maple Lake. A few miles farther west, the village, township, and body of water known as French Lake were named by those who had arrived in the late 1850s and early 1860s.[22]

In keeping with their convictions, these French Canadians organized congregations soon after arriving. Catholic church services occurred at East Maple Lake in 1862, Marysville in 1866, French Lake in 1874, and Buffalo in the early 1870s. All used French occasionally during the beginning years. The first two listed, however, soon merged with neighboring congregations — the Maple Lake church with the Irish to form St. Timothy's and Marysville with the Germans of St. Mary's in Waverly. A French priest remained at St. Timothy's until 1905 when an Irish one replaced him. At St. Mary's the French priest departed in 1899, after which 75 French-Canadian families reportedly withdrew their memberships and began attending church in Buffalo. In the 20th century French names continued to appear in lists of Waverly war veterans, members of the Knights of Columbus and the volunteer fire department, and parishioners of St. Mary's. Elsewhere in Wright County, French Canadians sold out to incoming Germans.[23]

The French Canadians Spread Out

Moving with the tides of settlement, French Canadians in the 1850s and 1860s took lands farther northward and westward along the Mississippi and Minnesota rivers and their tributaries and in the Park Region of central Minnesota. By the 1870s they were becoming established in a major concentration in the Red River Valley, and by the 1880s they were also to be found on the prairies of the southwest and in the forests of the northeast. Their migrations seem to have resulted from a combination of factors. Some followed the routes of the Red River Trails which wound up the river valleys and through the Park Region. For others who occupied a strip of counties from Morrison on the north to Nicollet on the south, the move was a natural extension from the Hennepin-Wright-Anoka triangle. Those who ventured into southwestern and northeastern Minnesota initiated a new pattern by becoming part of communities founded by other Catholic groups, while the northwestern concentrations continued the earlier practice of forming exclusively French-Canadian enclaves.

The heritage of the fur trade was also an important influence at certain times and places. For example, south of modern Brainerd in present Crow Wing County stood the fur post of Crow Wing. Located at the junction of the Crow Wing and Mississippi rivers, the spot had been a major trading center since 1837, and it had also become a prosperous village and stopping place on one of the major Red River Trails by the 1850s. Using Crow Wing as a kind of anchor, homesteading French Canadians spread down along the east bank of the Mississippi to Little Falls and Belle Prairie in Morrison County, which had between 30 and 40 families by the end of the 1850s. More continued to arrive during the next three decades. Besides having the access to the river preferred by French Canadians, the land, they found, was relatively easy to break though not of top quality. It was also possible for many of the men to obtain employment as lumberjacks and river drivers for logging companies in this forested region. By 1881 French Canadians constituted a majority in the population of Belle Prairie, and in 1895 they totaled a third of that of Little Falls.[24]

Both became stable communities. Belle Prairie's Catholic chapel was also attended by French Canadians from Little Falls until 1871. Belle Prairie's Convent and Academy of St. Anthony, founded in 1872, was operated by the Franciscan Sisters who taught all the classes in French. The language continued to be used for some services in Belle Prairie's Holy Family Catholic Church until World War II. By 1963 the congregation numbered 160 families, some of whom were members of the sixth generation in the community. Land records show that Belle Prairie, Little Falls, and Ripley townships in Morrison County had numerous landowners with French surnames in 1892, and that many of the same names persisted into the late 1970s.[25]

Along the Minnesota River Valley, French Canadians joined other settlers at Henderson and Jessenland in Sibley County in the 1850s. By the following decade they could be found in the next tier of counties to the west at Glencoe, Helen Township, Hutchinson, and Rocky Run (just west of Winsted) in McLeod County and Roseville Township in Kandiyohi County. A few families from Canada joined the Roseville group by the end of the century. In addition to operating small farms, they fished, trapped, did painting and carpenter work, and occasionally owned a store or hotel. But in none of these places were they numerous, and they were soon dominated by Germans, Bohemians, and Poles who formed a clear majority in the Catholic churches. Many of their children left the area for the Twin Cities, North

Dakota, or Canada. After 1860 Catholic communities at Luxemburg (Stearns County) and Forest City (Meeker County) included only a few French Canadians. Perhaps it was members of these families who moved to St. Cloud, where they formed part of a growing body of railroad and granite workers.[26]

Farther to the northwest, among the hills and lakes of the Park Region in Otter Tail, Becker, and Mahnomen counties, representatives of the older French-Canadian fur trading community were to be found. Some had worked for both British and American fur companies over several generations, choosing their wives among the Ojibway and Dakota Indians. An analysis of 56 members of French-surnamed families living in Otter Tail County in 1860 revealed that the group was predominantly male (61%), young (80% aged 30 or less), Minnesota born (79%), and of mixed blood (68%). A total of 12 persons or 21% had been born in Canada. Twelve gave their occupations as laborers, six as farmers, and one was a trader. Eleven women were married and 11 were single, while there were 11 married and 23 single men. Their ages were:[27]

Ages	Female	Male
0–18	11	14
18–30	8	12
31–40	2	3
41–50	1	3
51–		2

In 1867 a large group of Canadian natives migrated to this area from Edmonton, Alberta. Some members of the party took claims near Breckenridge on the Red River in Wilkin County to the west, while others went east to Fergus Falls or north to the White Earth Indian Reservation, where they claimed a mixed-blood's right to reservation land.[28]

After the creation of the White Earth Reservation (in Becker, Clearwater, and Mahnomen counties) in 1867, the Ojibway reluctantly began the long trek from their old homes near Crow Wing and Leech Lake. One estimate placed the number who moved at 700 Ojibway, of whom 150 were mixed-bloods from Crow Wing. Beaulieu Township within the Mahnomen County portion of the reservation was named for families of French-Canadian and Indian descent who owned farms there following the Civil War. After 1906 when mixed-bloods were allowed to sell their reservation land allotments, white settlers, many of them from Stearns County, moved in. A 1933 population study of the Beaulieu parish listed "64 new families and 34 Indian families"; by 1960 it was said to be 95% German and French. Many French names were still current in 1976.[29]

The major French-Canadian influx into the northwestern corner of the state, however, began in the 1870s when the restless Pierre Bottineau made yet another move. This time he built the red brick home in which he lived out the remaining years of his life on the banks of the Red Lake River in what is now Red Lake Falls. There near the Old Crossing of the Red River Trail, he and one of his sons in 1877–78 purchased nearly 9,000 acres using half-breed scrip. And there on the rolling prairies along the wooded courses of the Clear-

PIERRE BOTTINEAU, the founder of numerous French-Canadian settlements in Minnesota, is pictured here in his distinguished old age along with the brick house in Red Lake Falls where he died in 1895.

water and Red Lake rivers in Polk and Red Lake counties the highest concentration of rural French-Canadian settlement in Minnesota developed (see Map 2.3).[30]

In their efforts to establish the new colony, Bottineau and his son were soon joined by Louis Fontaine, who had operated a mercantile business in St. Paul and traveled the Red River Valley. While living in Crookston, Fontaine served as chief propagandist for the colony. He also started a store there, which was for a time the largest in the area. The French-Canadian families who followed these men migrated largely from southeastern Minnesota and from Quebec, in part because of Fontaine's efforts and the promotional advertising he placed in such French-language newspapers as *Echo de l'Ouest*, published in Minneapolis.[31]

From Oklee on the Lost River near the route of the Min-

neapolis, St. Paul and Sault Ste. Marie Railway (now the Soo Line), their farms followed both banks of the Clearwater River as it meandered first southward then westward to join the Red Lake River at the village of Red Lake Falls. They then fanned out along the Red Lake River and the line of the Great Northern Railroad westward and southwestward to East Grand Forks on the Red River. French Canadians settled in the townships of Red Lake Falls, Gervais, Emardville, Terrebonne, Poplar River, Lambert, and Louisville in Red Lake County, as well as in Huntsville, Gentilly, Crookston, and Kertsonville townships in adjacent Polk County. At Crookston the characteristic landholding pattern appeared along the Red River, where French Canadians acquired long strips with narrow frontages and built their homes close to the bank. (Elsewhere in Crookston the land was divided in the more usual block pattern.)[32]

The arrival of both the Great Northern and Northern Pacific railroads in the Grand Forks area by 1880 gave a tremendous boost to colonization. After that emigrants from Quebec could travel by water to Duluth and take the train to Polk County. In 1889 a parish census at Gentilly revealed that 55 of 142 French-Canadian families had moved directly from Quebec. Moreover, at least 125 of them were living near relatives or neighbors from their former villages.[33]

Again the success of French-Canadian colonization can be traced in the proliferation of Catholic churches. Congregations were organized at Gentilly, Crookston, and Red Lake Falls by 1879. Two years later that at Gentilly had 118 French-Canadian and only two Irish families. From that day to this all its priests have been of French descent. Seven years after being established, the parishes of Crookston and Red Lake Falls split, with the English-speaking members forming new churches. From 1880 to 1920 four more French parishes appeared at Oklee (1881), Terrebonne (1882), Brooks (1916), and Louisville Township (1918). Like Crookston and Red Lake Falls these remained French speaking through the 1930s with gradual additions of English thereafter. At Gentilly, however, no services were conducted in English until 1958.[34]

Initially the colony's farmers raised wheat, but its exclu-

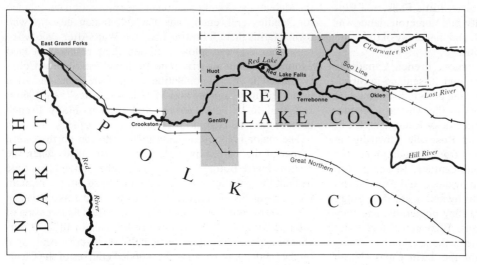

Map 2.3. French-Canadian Settlement in Polk and Red Lake Counties

THE GOTHIC-STYLE Church of St. Peter in Gentilly was built in 1915 with funds raised by the French-Canadian parishioners. This view of the Red Lake River Valley town is from the church steeple.

sive production quickly depleted even the fertile Red River Valley soil. Then in 1892, after a hailstorm wiped out the crop, Father Elie Theillon, the pastor of St. Peter's in Gentilly, began a campaign to introduce diversified farming. He gathered information from a variety of sources including the University of Minnesota State Farmers Institutes and helped to found a cheese factory, which was so successful that it won a national reputation for quality. Other neighboring communities followed Gentilly's example and prospered by diversifying.[35]

Various population estimates, all open to question, suggest the continuing residence of French Canadians in Polk and Red Lake counties. One historian estimated that 5,000 French Canadians were living between Crookston and Red Lake Falls about 1885. French-language newspapers in 1895 claimed that Crookston had 950 French Canadians, and the Catholic church at East Grand Forks in 1915 listed 70 families in its membership. Parishes in Red Lake County in the 1930s reported 633 French-Canadian members at Terrebonne, 578 in Poplar River Township (Brooks), 920 at Red Lake Falls, and 90 families in Louisville Township. In the late 1970s strong survival of the French-Canadian identity existed, especially in Gentilly.[36]

Many persons of French-Canadian descent could also still be found in the Argyle area of adjoining Marshall County, where their forebears had begun to settle in 1878. Within five years they had become so numerous that a section of Argyle, which was oriented toward the Middle River, was known as "Frenchtown," a Societé Union Canadienne Française had been organized, and St. Rose of Lima Catholic Church had been built. By the turn of the century, the parishioners opened a school staffed by Benedictines, but it failed within a year for lack of community support. The diocese tried again with the Sisters of St. Joseph of Bourg who had recently left France to escape religious persecution. This effort was well received. One Benedictine nun, in writing a history of

Catholic missions in northern Minnesota, commented that "As French Sisters in a French community in America, they met with considerable [*sic*] more success."[37]

In 1915 the Argyle church split, and the English-speaking members formed St. Mary's. Over the next three decades, as the people became Americanized, more and more English was used. "The French identity was gradually subdued," wrote the church historian, "and the parish forsook this ethnic trait." By 1946 the need for two churches no longer existed, and St. Mary's rejoined St. Rose. All of the priests of St. Rose, however, had been of French descent up to the late 1970s, an indication of the stability of the French-Canadian community over five generations.[38]

Another example of its continuity may be found in a couple who left Quebec and settled at Argyle in 1879. The land they claimed was still in the family 100 years later. Seven of their ten children stayed in the vicinity, as did nine grandsons, five great-grandsons, and four great-great-grandsons.[39]

Migration to Argyle continued as late as 1919. Not all were young people; many arrived with grown families. Some had lived in the Twin Cities or southern Minnesota. Others moved west from Wisconsin, Michigan, New England, and Quebec. Most were farmers, but a few operated such businesses as stores, hotels, boardinghouses, livery stables, smithies, restaurants, barbershops, dray lines, saloons, pool halls, and carpenter shops. Some worked seasonally on the railroads or in the lumber camps to earn the cash necessary to sustain them while they were establishing farms.

By the third generation some changes were noticeable. Young people were marrying outside the French-Canadian ethnic group but still within the geographic area and within the Catholic church. They were also ceasing to use French given names for their children, who were moving with more frequency to other locations in northwest Minnesota, the Twin Cities, Canada (Manitoba, Alberta, or Saskatchewan), or to the Pacific Northwest.[40]

A dramatically different settlement pattern developed in the 1870s and 1880s when skilled French-Canadian farmers from Canada and Illinois joined three Catholic colonies on the fertile but initially forbidding prairies of southwestern Minnesota. Their descendants were still to be found in that region 100 years later. The promotional efforts of Catholic Bishop John Ireland of St. Paul and John Sweetman, the visionary organizer of the Irish-American Colonization Society, induced French Canadians to join a Belgian community at Ghent in Lyon County and two Irish ones at Currie in Murray County and Clontarf in Swift County. By 1880 the latter had at least 20 French-speaking families who emigrated directly from Canada with sufficient capital to buy farms larger than the ones they had left.[41]

A secondary migration of larger numbers of second- and third-generation French Canadians from Kankakee and Iroquois counties, Illinois, settled near Ghent and Currie. After touring the prairie states looking at land in Iowa, Dakota Territory, and Minnesota, two Kankakee men chose Lyon County because Ghent had an established Catholic parish with a French-speaking priest. As a result, 50 prosperous farmers bought land there in 1882 and paid cash for it. Not only did these families require an entire train to deliver their possessions to Ghent, they also displayed a one-to-one ratio of people to horses, a level of affluence almost unheard of among immigrant groups at that time. In 1885–86 an additional 40 French-Canadian "men of substance" moved from Kankakee to the Sweetman colony at Currie. Other blue-collar workers were drawn to Swift County by employment opportunities on the St. Paul and Pacific Railroad (now the Burlington Northern Railroad), which was built through the area in 1870.[42]

The mixed groups seem to have adjusted fairly well. Serious difficulties occurred, however, at Ghent, where so acrimonious a feud developed within the parish that some of the French sold out and moved. Five miles away at Green Valley, a mixed group of French and Belgians founded St. Clotilde Catholic Church in 1912. By 1949 it had 100 French and Belgian families in its membership; many of the same names continued into the 1950s and 1960s.[43]

Nearby Marshall, the seat of Lyon County, had received an infusion of French Canadians after 1895, some from the old French town of Bourbonnais, Illinois. In the mid-1890s "of the 100 families," a historian of the Catholic parish stated, "40 were French and Belgian, and it was thought at that time that Marshall would become a predominantly French parish." In order to attract new Catholic members, these parishioners placed advertisements in Illinois newspapers. As a further inducement to French settlers, the priest started a school and recruited the Sisters of St. Joseph of Carondelet to staff it, thus satisfying the "great demand for instruction in the French language." By 1910 of the 250 families in the parish, about one-third were French, a fourth Belgian, and another fourth mixed. In that year, however, the departure of the French priest "marked the beginning of four years of unsettledness, dissatisfaction and disappointments." Three years later, when the noted French architect Emmanuel L. Masqueray drafted plans for a new Holy Re-

deemer Church in Marshall, the parish had only 200 families.[44]

Northeastern Minnesota, the last major area of French-Canadian settlement in the state, was one of the first to have been visited by French explorers and fur traders. At Grand Portage, famous in the late 18th century as the headquarters of the British North West Company, Frenchmen crossed the portage as early as 1731. Later a French-Canadian family lived for many years on the island in Grand Portage Bay near the old fur post and Ojibway village. They farmed, fished, and trapped there until the 1920s. But northeastern Minnesota was ill suited by soil and climate for farming, and most of the people were employed as laborers on the railroad and in the lumbering and mining industries that began to develop north of Duluth in the 1880s and 1890s.[45]

French Canadians were among the first to arrive, trickling in singly and in families, but there is little reliable information on them. Range town parish records bear out the fact that they were present early but were not numerous. At Tower in 1888 there were 12 French families and 300 Slovenian ones. At Two Harbors, the Lake Superior port city for the mine at Tower, the early priests were French, but the settlement became predominantly Scandinavian. At Eveleth the French Canadians worshiped with the Irish, Germans, and native-born Americans, while the more numerous Slavs had their own church. A 1909 study of 13 towns on the Mesabi Range showed 875 (1.7%) French Canadians in a total population of 50,191. On both the Mesabi and Vermilion ranges the French Canadians reportedly "worked out of the unskilled occupations" and were "found holding such positions as foremen, master mechanics, machinists, and steam engineers." In lumbering, too, they were said to have "moved up into the higher positions" or followed the pine to the Pacific Northwest by 1909.[46]

Concentrations of French-Canadian loggers lived at Cloquet and Cromwell in Carlton County just west of Duluth, where by the 1880s they were using a skill learned in the pineries of Quebec, New Brunswick (Canada), Maine, or Michigan. In Cloquet they lived on the western edge of town in "Little Canada" and painted their houses blue. One observer commented that a payroll of the logging companies sounded remarkably like a roster of the old North West Company, including such names as Bouche, Beaupre, Roy, Paul-Joseph, Loisel, Chartier, Bernier, La Vasseur, La Tulip, Brouseau, de la Rushe, Cyrette, Le Fleur, and Chapados. Frequently they also farmed a few acres among the stumps and raised field peas, potatoes, and other garden crops.[47]

These families also supported the Catholic church where they expected to have a French priest. By 1906 the Cloquet priest was trying to please a mixed congregation by using the English and French languages on alternate Sundays. He was a little miffed when his English-speaking parishioners complained to the bishop. It happened, wrote a man who grew up in Cloquet, that "shortly afterward lightning struck the tall steeple of the church . . . and it burned to the ground. Good Father Giraux never really implied that Somebody Up There was less than pleased with his fickle flock, but he never discouraged the idea either."[48]

French Canadians were among the earliest settlers at Duluth-Superior, the port cities which later served as gateways to the camps and mines. From about 1860 to the turn of the century they attended Duluth's Sacred Heart Cathedral. In 1884, when they were outnumbered by other groups in that congregation, they were allowed to organize their own French national parish of St. Jean Baptiste. By 1888 Duluth was said to have 200 French-Canadian families, and in 1902 the estimate was 500. The national parish claimed 900 members in 1885 and 1,400 members or 250 families in 1893. West Duluth, which is now part of the city, reported a French-Canadian population of 524 or 121 families in 1894. Later figures for Duluth listed a 1920 population of 3,680 of French-Canadian stock, 1,093 of whom were born in Canada. Ten years later there were 3,219 of French-Canadian stock, of whom 872 were Canadian born.[49]

A Catholic directory published in 1892 provided information on the occupations of members of St. Jean Baptiste who were employed outside the home. Of the 317 men, 101 (32%) were laborers and another 92 (30%) were in various building trades. There were 46 (15%) in white-collar jobs and three (1%) in professions. Of the 23 women listed, 19 were dressmakers or milliners.[50]

By 1905 the parish established a school, which in 1936 had an enrollment of 385 pupils. Two organizations were particularly active. The Union of St. Jean Baptiste, founded in 1882 as a mutual benefit society, helped start the French church; in 1936 it had 200 members. Even more active with 500 members in 1936 was the French Naturalization Club, which "assisted many men and women to secure citizenship papers and . . . instructed them to take an active and intelligent part in matters pertaining to the welfare of our city, county, state, and country."[51]

French Canadians in the Twin Cities

As the French-Canadian population of Duluth grew, that of Minneapolis and St. Paul increased even more. During the last four decades of the 19th century some of the newcomers immigrated directly from Quebec; others lived briefly or for several years in New England, Michigan, or Wisconsin before going west to Minnesota. Members of the younger generations moved from smaller communities throughout the state to the Twin Cities.[52]

St. Paul in 1866 reported 476 French Canadians and Pembina French and 115 French in the city. The heaviest concentration was in Ward 2, the downtown area, with 229 Canadian and Pembina French and 53 French. Spotty figures for the next 30 years, gleaned from parish records and French-language newspapers, ranged from 4,000 in 1887 to 10,000 in 1898. One report listed 6,000 French-speaking St. Paul residents in 1888, of whom 4,500 were French Canadian. For Minneapolis estimates ran the gamut from 80 families in 1879 to 5,000 people in 1887 and 12,000 in 1893.[53]

More reliable figures on French Canadians in the Twin Cities broken down by decades may be found in the following table for the period from 1900 to 1930:

	Minneapolis		St. Paul	
	foreign born	foreign and mixed parentage	foreign born	foreign and mixed parentage
1900	1,702	4,845	1,015	2,842
1910	1,637	5,341	1,096	3,582
1920	1,016	4,104	587	2,770
1930	1,373	6,182	720	3,727

The decline in 1920 reflected the effects of World War I.[54]

French-Canadian Roman Catholic churches were maintained in the Twin Cities well into the 20th century, although ultimately the French language lost out due to the increasing numbers of Irish and German Catholics. With other nationalities already crowding the cathedral parish in St. Paul, French Canadians in 1868 established the Church of St. Louis at 10th Street and Cedar Avenue. When rebuilding in 1909, they selected architect Masqueray, the French immigrant who also designed the St. Paul Cathedral. Most of the parishioners were from Quebec; only a small minority had immigrated directly from France. The peak of the parish's membership was reached in 1910 with 900 families; in 1936 it

THE MANSARD-ROOFED French Catholic Ecole St. Louis stood on 10th Street in St. Paul next to St. Louis Church from 1886 until about 1965.

had 600 members. As late as 1959 about 25% of the church's list of patrons had French surnames. In 1873 the church founded the famous Ecole St. Louis, which continued the tradition of instruction in French until the 1960s. The school's catalog for 1907–09, for example, listed the names and addresses of 325 students, most of whom had French surnames and a few French first names.[55]

In Minneapolis three French national parishes have existed, but only one — Our Lady of Lourdes Church, which faces the Mississippi River on Main Street Southeast — has retained its French traditions for a century. (The other two churches were St. Anthony of Padua, built in 1849 on land donated by the ubiquitous Bottineau, and St. Clotilde, founded in 1884.) In 1877 the French Canadians bought the 20-year-old First Universalist Church and renamed it Our Lady of Lourdes. In 1900, its peak year, the congregation had 2,200 members. By World War I a decline was evident as families moved to other parts of the city and were not replaced by new arrivals from Canada. Nevertheless in 1948 the congregation included immigrants from France, Belgium, and the French colonies, and it remained a French national parish. English was added to the service in 1917; by 1952 the French language had totally disappeared.[56]

In 1959 the parish school, operated since 1888, closed. Ten years later the church itself was in imminent danger of being disbanded, but revived interest in the Minneapolis river front brought renewal. The building was placed on the National Register of Historic Places, and in 1979 Our Lady of Lourdes drew 400 people for Sunday Masses.

THE FRENCH

France was an anomaly among the European nations which sent people to the United States in the 19th and 20th centuries, because it did not suffer from the pressures of overpopulation. From 1800 to 1850 its population was relatively stable, increasing only about one-third. In the next 60 years, it grew by 14% from 36,500,000 to 41,500,000, while Great Britain's, for example, doubled. During the French Revolution, the lands of the Catholic church had been auctioned off and feudal dues abolished. In the post-Napoleonic era, the French peasant had no desire to see his hard-won privileges jeopardized by dividing his lands among many sons. Thus peasant families were small. In 1860 France had the lowest birth rate in Europe. Any surplus population was easily absorbed by growing industry or the French colonies.[57]

Consequently, compared to other Europeans, few French emigrated either directly or permanently. Those who arrived in North America during the colonial period were primarily refugees, either religious or political. French Protestants, called Huguenots, had been forced to convert to Catholicism or leave France in 1685; some of those who fled went directly to the American colonies while others arrived after stays in the Rhineland, the Netherlands, or England. Political dissidents of all persuasions left France during the Revolution, the Napoleonic era, and the Bourbon restoration. As individuals these immigrants to the United States assimilated readily, and even in groups they lost most of their French characteristics in the second generation. Unlike the French Canadians, few of them settled in New England.[58]

Minnesota's small numbers of French migrants are difficult to identify, for they, too, seem to have assimilated quickly. Census data show that they were concentrated largely in the Twin Cities with a few scattered elsewhere in the state, where they seem to have mixed with Germans or Belgians as well as with French Canadians (see Table 2.2). Another problem in discussing them occurs in determining just who were "the French." As the preface to the United States census said of them in 1860, "It should be remarked that a large number are natives of the provinces of Alsace and Lorraine, who are really Germans by descent, and speak the German language, although they have been enumerated indiscriminately with the other natives of France." The proclivity of the census thus to classify immigrants solely by country of origin in certain years, rather than by language, makes it impossible to sort out with exactness either the ethnic French or the ethnic Germans.[59]

According to the 1850 Minnesota census there were only 29 natives of France in the territory. Ten years later the number had risen to 829. For 50 years after 1880 the number of foreign-born French in the state remained fairly constant; the peak year was 1890 when the population reached 1,869. The largest concentrations were in Minneapolis (353 in 1920) and St. Paul (355 in 1890). Skimpy figures for the 20th century indicate that they remained in the Twin Cities area, but that their numbers were never large.

Existing statistics also suggest that the French in the United States were not a cohesive group and that those in Minnesota were even less so. Using the 1890 census, one finds that of 4,606 persons of French stock in the state, 2,151 or 46.7% were born of mixed marriages compared to only 29.4% for the United States as a whole. Of these persons 1,133 or 52.7% had one German parent, while 347 had one French Canadian. Corresponding figures for the nation were 56.8% (43,262) and 6% (4,598), respectively.[60]

This hypothesis can be tested by examining manuscript censuses of Minnesota counties with French populations in 1870 and 1880. A sample of 46 couples in Stearns County in 1870, for example, revealed that in one-third of the marriages both partners were French, while in two-thirds they were mixed. Half of the latter were French-German combinations. A survey of 52 couples in Stearns, Carver, Winona, and Wright counties in 1880 produced 29% pure French, 44% French-German combinations, and the rest intermarried with Luxembourgers, Swiss, French Canadians, and Belgians. The names of many of those in the samples listed as born in France suggest German ancestry, and their farms were thoroughly interspersed with German ones. Perhaps they were among the immigrants from Alsace-Lorraine who were counted with the French and who are thus impossible to trace.[61]

A study of the 1880 census for St. Paul yielded similar results. In a sample of 60 marriages, 15% of the couples were French, 41.6% were French and German, and 40% of the remaining French marriages were split evenly among native-born Americans, French Canadians, English, Swiss, and Irish. The other two in the sample involved a Luxem-

Table 2.2. French in Minnesota by County, 1860–1970

County	1860 foreign born	1860 foreign mixed	1880 fb	1880 fm	1895 fb	1905 fb	1905 fm	1930 fb	1930 fm	1970 fb	1970 fm
Aitkin			2		2	5	5	5	39	8	
Anoka	7	6	10	10	17	5	24	9	43	38	128
Becker	1		2	11	9		30	4	27		7
Beltrami						8		11	40	7	25
Benton	7	1	27	27	29	16	25	11	30		9
Big Stone			4	6	5	2	18	5	28		
Blue Earth	53	41	41	108	37	22	114	15	120		50
Brown	18	7	22	30	13	13	31	6	59		12
Carlton	1		2	1	9	6	34	5	19		36
Carver	93	24	58	93	18	16	45	5	40	14	
Cass					3		41	4	29		13
Chippewa			1	4			3		14		6
Chisago	6	4	6	9	4	7	22	1	9		
Clay			10	23	20	15		7	36		12
Clearwater						1	4	1	6		8
Cook						1	2	1	5		
Cottonwood				1	1	1	8	3	14		
Crow Wing	5		12	13	21	22	76	10	60	21	18
Dakota	44	55	46	83	22	24	104	21	93	11	61
Dodge	8	12	14	38	12	11	43	8	32	7	
Douglas			3	22	2	3	20	3	27		25
Faribault	2		50	80	20	20	74	16	70	5	12
Fillmore	10		23	58	9	8	50	4	36		11
Freeborn	7	2	4		5	2	17	4	24		7
Goodhue	10	5	16	24	9	3	8	3	39	12	25
Grant				1			5	1	11		
Hennepin	63	45	144	318	264	258	917	308	1,415	266	947
Minneapolis			94		235	239	841	279	1,257	115	384
Houston	17	12	29	33	17	7	15	4	28		7
Hubbard					1	6	17	9	21	11	19
Isanti							5		2	9	
Itasca					6	8	48	16	71		7
Jackson			6	2	5	4	17	3	17		11
Kanabec					3	1	3	2	10		
Kandiyohi			3	9	1	1	15	1	18		21
Kittson	2	3	4	14	2	2	9		2		
Koochiching								8	35		6
Lac qui Parle			2	8	1	1	2	1	20		8
Lake			1	1	6	6	10	4	8		
Lake of the Woods								1	12		
Le Sueur	18	6	22	64	26	7	28	10	58		22
Lincoln			6	7	2			1	5		13
Lyon			18	14	6	21	50	8	36		14
McLeod	12	5	40	127	17	10	49	5	41		6
Mahnomen	1	5							4		10
Marshall			1		14	26	43	13	38		33
Martin			7	15	6	15	55	12	57		7
Meeker			10	26	4		14	4	23		26
Mille Lacs						1	2	5	26		17
Morrison	2	5	4	15	6	5	32	7	35		29
Mower	2	3	11	41	11	4	65	3	56	7	54
Murray			2	2	4	4	18	3	24		13
Nicollet	17	11	28	71	26	13	47	18	76		
Nobles			8	6	7	3	20	12	40		10
Norman					7	7	25		8		
Olmsted	5	6	14	22	5	7	19	14	66	18	34
Otter Tail			16	36	16	9	68	14	61		
Pennington								4	21	10	7
Pine	2		1	8	3	4	16	7	52		16
Pipestone			1	9	2	3	13	7	23		
Polk	2		24	16	45	22	41	26	50		11
Pope			10	13	1	1	4	3	12		7
Ramsey	121	73	119	208	281	272	810	270	1,160	104	583
St. Paul			109		268	272	783	256	1,098	91	439
Red Lake						10	59	3	17		13
Redwood			7	35	7	1	3	6	27	15	44
Renville	6	8	2	12	15		56	7	58		6
Rice	12	8	54	147	55	32	124	14	80		27
Rock			1	6	2	2	12	2	12		5
Roseau						7	33	5	22		10
St. Louis	7	2	13	30	84	86	358	104	397	42	228
Duluth					57	86	221	45	218	38	108
Scott	60	33	53	84	20	23	76	5	40	7	39
Sherburne			7	15	5	3	19	1	28	9	5
Sibley	41	21	13	21	9	5	2	8	22		

Table 2.2. French in Minnesota by County, 1860–1970 (*continued*)

County	1860 foreign born	1860 foreign mixed	1880 fb	1880 fm	1895 fb	1905 fb	1905 fm	1930 fb	1930 fm	1970 fb	1970 fm
Stearns	71	36	58	100	58	41	99	22	177	10	81
Steele	1	2	13	18	8	5	20	7	17		
Stevens			5	6	5	5	12	8	28	9	20
Swift			9	33	5	2	17		5		
Todd			14	30	11	19	29	7	59		23
Traverse			1	1	1	1	6	5	31		11
Wabasha	27	14	29	75	11	10	23	6	51		24
Wadena			6	3	6		11	4	21		
Waseca	7	5	10	49	11	3	20	1	16		8
Washington	9	2	24	42	13	33	44	13	51	12	56
Watonwan			18	25	18	9	26	4	19		27
Wilkin			3	1	2	3	13	5	29	15	
Winona	32	22	49	93	34		62	25	109	15	24
Wright	20	17	51	101	40	34	108	13	86		25
Yellow Medicine			1	3		4	20	5	19	5	
Total	829	501	1,325	2,657	1,482	1,277	4,532	1,246	6,002	687	3,079
Published census figures	(867)		(1,351)		(1,492)	(1,277)	(4,532)	(1,246)	(6,002)	(687)	(3,079)

Source: See Appendix

bourger and an Austrian. Again some supposedly French names sounded quite German.[62]

The survey also revealed that the French, unlike other groups in St. Paul, did not cluster in any single location. Rather they seemed to have spread throughout the city, living primarily among native-born Americans, Irish, and Germans. A few resided in the French-Canadian neighborhoods. Almost none could be found in the flats along the Mississippi River or among the Polish squatters on railroad land.

The occupations for 57 of the 60 persons in the group proved to be principally in the white-collar and small-business categories. A slightly smaller number could be found in the professions and the building trades. Three men were grocers; two each were saloonkeepers, machinists, shoemakers, carpenters, and basketmakers. Other occupations listed included lawyer, dentist, stone mason, butcher, baker, and trunkmaker. Only two men listed themselves as laborers. Women in the sample, other than housewives, were dressmakers (5), nuns (5), teachers (3), or servants (2). Similar findings were reflected in French alien registrations in Hennepin and Ramsey counties in 1918 and in a national study based on United States census figures for the years from 1890 to 1920. The latter confirmed the unusually high proportion of French in the professions and in personal service employment. Frenchmen were rarely to be found farming, although they appeared as gardeners. Women were employed chiefly as dressmakers and domestic help.[63]

One of the few rural settings in which French and French Canadians lived side by side was Todd County. A look at this central Minnesota area west of the Mississippi River shows little interaction between the two groups in the period between the Civil War and World War II. Most of the French Canadians arrived in 1868 from Faribault and Wheatland in Rice County; they settled in a heavily wooded section of Eagle Valley Township. The French took up claims at the same time, but they chose land farther south in Little Sauk and Long Prairie townships. Most of the adult men were farmers at one time or another. Many of the French Cana-

dians, however, were also active in some phase of the lumbering industry, various building trades, or similar crafts, while the French favored the professions or businesses in the town. The two groups tended not to intermarry. Rather their children seemed generally to have married outsiders, often either native-born Americans or people of German stock. By World War II most of the French had left the area, but descendants of the French Canadians were still living in Eagle Valley and Staples townships.[64]

French and French-Canadian Organizations

Like many national groups in Minnesota, the French and French Canadians created a proliferation of social, insurance, literary, dramatic, and political organizations from the 1850s to the 1920s. A search of the available files of locally published French-language newspapers revealed a vigorous group life. As early as 1857 French Canadians in St. Paul had organized the Société de Bienfaisance Franco-Canadienne de Saint Paul, and, ten years later, the Union Française. Both were mutual benefit societies which financed burials and aided widows and orphans and members who fell ill. On the occasion of the union's 25th anniversary in 1892, it reported cumulative payments over the years of $445 for funerals, $6,491 for members who were sick, and $9,266 for widows and orphans. The reasonably healthy balance on hand was $4,322. Minneapolis had its own mutual benefit societies — the Union Nationale and the Union St. Joseph.[65]

Some organizations were strictly Catholic in their orientation. Union St. Jean Baptiste lodges, which celebrated their saint's day annually on June 24, existed in St. Paul, Minneapolis, Duluth, Crookston, Little Canada, and other strongly French-Canadian parishes. The Union Catholique de l'Abstence Totale, a temperance group, was formed in 1871, and the Catholic Foresters, a mutual aid insurance society, were also active in the Twin Cities. Although it was not formally Catholic, the Woodmen of the World, a secret fraternal group, had a French-Canadian chapter in each of the Twin Cities. An advertisement in *Le Canadien* (St. Paul) for January 20, 1898, boasted: "It is one of the rare secret societies that the Catholic Church does not condemn." A list of officers and members indicated that many St. Paul French-Canadian tradesmen and workers had joined.[66]

French-language newspapers also reported the activities of a plethora of reading, music, and drama clubs, most of which were short-lived. Among those which came and went were the French American Literary Club of the Sister Cities, a French-Canadian Dramatic Club in Minneapolis, a Union Dramatique in St. Paul, and in Minneapolis the Club des Bons-Vivants, which was said to be open to persons of good nature with smiling faces and happy characters.[67]

The period from the 1880s to the early years of the 20th century marked the high point of organizational activity. In mid-1888 Minnesota had 21 French societies out of 287 in the United States with a total national membership of 43,051. (The Minnesota membership figures were not reported.) From the mid-1890s until after the turn of the century was the heyday of political clubs. Groups of Democrats existed in both St. Paul and Minneapolis as early as 1888, and in March, 1894, a combined Club Democratie Franco-Americaine was organized. Two Republican clubs that originated in 1892 combined in May, 1898, as the Lafayette-Papineau Republican League of Minneapolis. A rash of naturalization clubs made their appearance in 1897, and at least one group of Franco-Canadienne Populists was known to exist in this period.[68]

After 1900 the obituary columns of newspapers in Minnesota were crowded with notices of the deaths of pioneers, and organizational life seemingly died with them. It was perhaps symptomatic that a new assemblage, formed in Duluth in July, 1911, was called in translation the Association of French-Canadian Pioneers at the Head of the Lakes. Its purpose was to bring together old-timers and perpetuate the French-Canadian heritage there.[69]

French-language newspapers survived in the state only a decade or so longer. Over the years 60 were published in the Upper Midwest — 33 in Michigan, 15 in Illinois, and 12 in the Minnesota cities of Minneapolis (6), St. Paul (4), and Duluth (2). Of the latter *Le Canadien* in St. Paul and *Echo de l'Ouest* in Minneapolis were the longest lasting. *Le Canadien*, established in 1877, went through several changes of ownership before it ceased publication in 1904. *Echo de l'Ouest*, founded in 1883 by Zéphirin Demeules, was carried on by members of the Demeules family until January 4, 1929.[70]

Le Canadien followed a dual editorial policy of strongly endorsing any movement enhancing the French-Canadian heritage as well as urging greater participation in Minnesota politics. It supported naturalization as a means of increasing the political impact of French Canadians, and at the same time it attempted to hold fast to French language and customs. In the issue of October 25, 1888, for example, the editor urged his readers to shake off their apathy and run for political office. A year later he deplored the lack of a state-wide celebration of St. Jean Baptiste Day and followed up this complaint in the issue of August 7, 1890, by criticizing *Echo de l'Ouest* for suggesting that July 4, rather than June 24, should be the national holiday of French Canadians. Pursuing his quest for the maintenance of French, the editor on

LOCAL DANCERS in costume performed a French bourrée in St. Paul in 1937.

May 4, 1893, went so far as to reproach his readers for not insisting upon being served by French-speaking store clerks. The paper regularly campaigned for state conventions of French Canadians, predicting that "without union, without national spirit, we are fatally condemned to disappear as a nationality." In a similar vein, it disapproved of "the same apathy for French-Canadian parochial schools" in the Twin Cities that it had observed in politics.

Beginning on September 5, 1895, *Le Canadien* for a short time published an English edition in addition to the French one, an experiment that was not a success. As its circulation dwindled, the paper's editorials became more stridently critical of French Canadians for failing to retain their language. *Le Canadien* merged with a Chicago French-Canadian paper in 1903.[71]

From first to last *Echo de l'Ouest* was concerned with French-Canadian matters throughout the United States as well as in Minnesota. On August 14, 1896, it reported that it had 5,000 subscribers. Its contents were more or less consistent: a serialized novel, a directory of French Canadians engaged in Minneapolis public affairs, a large number of advertisements, several columns of news items, commercial reports, and an editorial page listing meetings of French-Canadian organizations. In general *Echo* was Republican in politics, Catholic in religion, puritanical in manners and morals, and a strong supporter of French-Canadian interests.

In an address to the Societé Jean Baptiste in Duluth on September 1, 1887, the *Echo*'s editor urged his listeners to preserve an identifiable community by supporting French-

Canadian schools, actively participating in French-Canadian organizations, and using the French language in everyday life. The paper consistently advocated parochial education, especially if French were taught. It appealed to parents in the issue of August 4, 1887, to send their children to Our Lady of Lourdes school in Minneapolis, where French was required for admission. Too many French Canadians, the paper charged, did not encourage their children to acquire educations. As an example it noted that only one French Canadian, a medical student, was listed among the 1903 graduates of the University of Minnesota.[72]

Strong advocacy of the retention of the French language to stave off assimilation appeared repeatedly in its pages. In editorial commentary on the national convention of French Canadians, held in Nashua, New Hampshire, in the summer of 1888, the paper maintained that they must strive to preserve their identity. As an aspect of this campaign, an article later that year decried the practice of changing family names and supplied a list of French names that had been Anglicized: Allard to Lord, Larue to Street, Dubois to Wood, Leblanc to White, Lenoir to Black, Lefebvre to Bean, Roy to King, Lamoureaux to Love. In its opposition to linguistic assimilation it lashed out in the issue of February 23, 1893, at Irish Catholics who insisted on the use of English, asserting aggressively that speaking English did not make the Irish any better Americans. A decade later an editorial sadly offered three reasons for the declining use of French: workers seeking employment must speak English, English was the language of American politics, and learned French people stayed in Quebec and did not migrate.[73]

Both *Le Canadien* and *Echo de l'Ouest* published a wide range of news reports from French-Canadian communities throughout the state and advertisements, mostly in French, for all manner of goods and services. Both favored businesses owned by fellow countrymen, complained of the lack of French Canadians in the professions, and printed literary classics acceptable to middle-class readers.

Since World War II most French organizational activities in the state have continued to focus on language use. In these efforts French and French Canadians have mingled freely. The French section of the International Institute's Festival of Nations, a St. Paul program begun in 1932, has borrowed liberally from both traditions. Such organizations as the French Club of St. Paul were open to natives of France as well as students of the language. Both the Alliance Française and Les Amis du Theatre were active in the Twin Cities in 1980, promoting French culture and language. Further evidence that the French language did not totally disappear existed in the 1970 census, which listed 28,413 French, French Canadians, and others in the state for whom French was a mother tongue. Nearly half (13,187) of them lived in Hennepin and Ramsey counties. Other large groups were listed in the counties of Anoka (1,414), Dakota (899), Polk (1,076), Red Lake (856), and St. Louis (2,242). Slightly under 10% (2,385) of the total were foreign born.[74]

By the 1970s the state's French Canadians were becoming conscious of their history. A multivolume biographical dictionary was in progress, and a few reminiscences had appeared recalling such family customs as New Year's Day visiting, when the entire family would gather in the parental home for music, dancing, and eating. Thick pea soup was always on the menu along with such pork dishes as *tortiere* and ragout (meat pie and pig's feet in gravy.) The calendar year ended soberly with midnight Mass on Christmas Eve and a quiet family day on Christmas.[75]

Some old customs seem to have survived in Minnesota, especially in the Gentilly area. For the most part, however, it can be said that the French and French-Canadian people have been so thoroughly assimilated that they are difficult to trace. Nevertheless they are still very much a part of Minnesota's population. When the city of St. Paul celebrated its 125th anniversary in 1979, for example, direct descendants of Jean Baptiste Faribault and others took part in the festival parade. Perhaps in the years to come these long-time Minnesotans will reach back to reclaim additional segments of their past. As this is written a locally organized Union Métis is hard at work researching the history and culture of its members' colorful forebears. It is to be hoped that others will follow their example.[76]

Reference notes

[1] Yolande Lavoie, *L'émigration des Québécois aux États-Unis de 1840 à 1930*, 45 (Quebec, 1979); United States, *Census*, 1890, *Population*, clxvi, clxxiii; 1930, 2:236, 274.

[2] Virginia B. Kunz, *The French in America*, 83 (Minneapolis, 1966); U.S., *Census*, 1880, *Population*, 461–463; 1860, p. 620; 1890, part 1, p. 608; 1920, 3:18, 47; 1930, 2:234, 268, 281; U.S. French statistics, in MEHP Papers, MHS, compiled by Jon A. Gjerde from U.S. Justice Dept., Immigration and Nautralization Service, *Annual Reports*, 1940–75.

[3] Warren Upham, *Minnesota Geographic Names*, 143–147, 219, 371, 373, 480, 601, 602, 605 (Reprint ed., St. Paul, 1969); Mary W. Berthel, "French Names That Stuck," in *Gopher Historian*, April, 1951, p. 14.

[4] On the Red River Trails, see Rhoda R. Gilman, Carolyn Gilman, and Deborah M. Stultz, *The Red River Trails: Oxcart Routes Between St. Paul and the Selkirk Settlement, 1820–1870* (St. Paul, 1979).

[5] R. Cole Harris, "The Extension of France into Rural Canada," in James R. Gibson, ed., *European Settlement and Development in North America: Essays on Geographical Change in Honor and Memory of Andrew Hill Clark*, 27–45 (Toronto, 1978); G. E. Marquis, "The French Canadians in the Province of Quebec," in American Academy of Political and Social Science, *Annals*, 107:7–12 (May, 1923). For a brief account, see Alfred L. Burt, *A Short History of Canada for Americans*, chapters 2–4 (Minneapolis, 1942). The classic narrative is Francis Parkman, *France and England in North America*, 9 vols., several editions (Boston, 1867–92). For the French period, see also Gustave Lanctot, *A History of Canada*, 3 vols. (Cambridge, Mass., 1963–65). A summary statement is Mason Wade, *The French Canadians, 1760–1967*, vol. 1, chapter 1 (Rev. ed., Toronto, 1968). In comparison, there were about 1,500,000 people in the British North American colonies on the eve of the French and Indian War.

[6] Here and below, see Harris, in Gibson, ed., *Essays*, 27–45; Richard C. Harris, *The Seigneurial System in Early Canada: A Geographical Study*, 127 (Madison, 1966). See also Hildegard B. Johnson, *Order Upon the Land: The U.S. Rectangular Land Survey and the Upper Mississippi Country*, 22–24, 104 (New York, 1976).

[7] Marcus L. Hansen, *The Mingling of the Canadian and Amer-*

ican Peoples, 115–117, 124–135, 164 (New Haven, Conn., 1940); Georges J. Joyaux, "French Language Press in the Upper Mississippi and Great Lakes Areas," in *Mid-America*, 43:243 (1961).

[8] For French fur traders, see A. G. Morice, *Dictionnaire Historique des Canadiens et des Métis français de l'Ouest* (2nd ed., Quebec, 1912); Joseph Tassé, *Les Canadiens de l'Ouest*, 2 vols. (2nd ed., Montreal, 1878).

[9] *History of Winona and Wabasha Counties*, 591–599, 646 (Chicago, 1884); Franklyn Curtiss-Wedge, ed., *History of Wabasha County, Minnesota*, 49 (Winona, 1920); Catholic Archdiocese of St. Paul and Minneapolis, Parish Questionnaires, 1948, Wabasha County, originals in the Catholic Historical Society, St. Paul Seminary, St. Paul, microfilm in MHS, hereafter cited as Parish Questionnaires; Warren Upham and Rose B. Dunlap, eds., *Minnesota Biographies, 1655–1912*, 28, 617, 634, 646, 654 (St. Paul, 1912). Bailly's descendants are vintners at Hastings, Minnesota.

[10] Louise P. Kellogg, "Jean Baptiste Faribault," in *Dictionary of American Biography*, 6:272 (New York, 1931); June D. Holmquist and Jean A. Brookins, *Minnesota's Major Historic Sites: A Guide*, 13–15 (Revised ed., St. Paul, 1972).

[11] Here and below, see Kenneth Bjork, "The Alexander Faribault House," in *Minnesota History*, 35:320–324 (September, 1957); Sister Mary G. Kelly, *Catholic Immigrant Colonization Projects in the United States, 1815–1860*, 201 (New York, 1939); Johanna M. O'Leary, *Historical Sketch of the Parish of the Immaculate Conception, Faribault, Minnesota*, 5–10, 93 (Faribault, 1938); I. Domestici, *A Brief History of the Church of the Sacred Heart of Faribault, Minnesota* (Faribault, 1922); *Echo de l'Ouest* (Minneapolis), June 24, 1904; Works Projects Administration, Minnesota, Historical Records Survey: Churches, 1936–41, Rice County, in MHS, hereafter cited as WPA, Church Records; Lester E. Swanberg, ed., *Then and Now: A History of Rice County, Faribault and Communities*, 3, 68 ([Faribault?], 1976); Margaret Snyder, *The Chosen Valley: The Story of a Pioneer Town*, 318 (New York, 1948); Richard J. Steinman, "The Wapacootas and the White Man: The Story of the Early Development of Faribault," typed paper, St. John's University, 1971, copy in MHS; Arthur J. Larsen, "Various Nations Contributed to Early Settlement of Rice County," in *Faribault Daily News*, May 19, 1933, pp. 3, 4; Arthur H. Durand, *Autobiography of Msgr. Arthur H. Durand*, 3–5 (St. Paul, 1978). Many French churches took the names of French patron saints — St. Louis, St. Anne, St. Jean Baptiste, St. Clotilde; thus the church name can be a key to the ethnic identity of the parish. The Faribault church was initially named for St. Anne.

[12] Swanberg, *Then and Now*, 29, 109, 247, 282, 283, 284, 330, 340; Larsen, "Various Nations," 4; *Plat Book of Rice County, Minnesota*, 7, 11, 13, 14, 17, 19 ([St. Paul?], 1900); *Atlas and Plat Book, Rice County, Minnesota*, 13, 18 (Rockford, Ill., 1976); Franklyn Curtiss-Wedge, ed., *History of Rice and Steele Counties, Minnesota*, 1:557–562 (Chicago, 1910); WPA, Church Records, Rice County; *Echo de l'Ouest*, March 24, 1911; Parish Questionnaires, Rice County.

[13] "Isaac Labissonniere," in *Acta et Dicta*, 3:185–188 (July, 1911); Benjamin Backnumber, "St. Paul Before This: Vital Guerin, Early Settler and Liberal Giver," in *St. Paul Daily News*, March 14, 1920, Sunday Magazine and Story sec., 5; J. Fletcher Williams, *A History of the City of St. Paul and of the County of Ramsey, Minnesota*, 69, 100 (*Minnesota Historical Collections*, vol. 4 — St. Paul, 1876). Parrant, a French-Canadian trading post operator, carried the nickname "Pig's Eye" because of the appearance of his blind eye; Williams, 64.

[14] M. M. Hoffmann, "New Light on Old St. Peter's and Early St. Paul," in *Minnesota History*, 8:27–51 (March, 1927); "Major William Williams' Journal of a Trip to Iowa in 1849," in *Annals of Iowa*, 12:260–268 (April, 1920); Williams, *City of St. Paul*, 140–144, 291;

Patricia C. Harpole and Mary D. Nagle, eds., *Minnesota Territorial Census 1850* (St. Paul, 1972).

[15] M. M. Hoffmann, *The Church Founders of the Northwest*, 163, 174, 192, 333, 337 (Milwaukee, 1937); Upham and Dunlap, eds., *Minnesota Biographies*, 149, 246, 449, 628; Helen Angela Hurley, *On Good Ground: The Story of the Sisters of St. Joseph in St. Paul*, 24–32, 74–79 (Minneapolis, 1951).

[16] Alice Coloizy, "Notes on the Gervais Family, 1786–1949," undated typed manuscript, in MHS; Margaret W. Wall, "Village In the Wilderness: Little Canada — Heritage from the French," in *Ramsey County History*, Fall, 1964, pp. 8–11; *Pioneer Chronicles*, 14–17 (Minneapolis, 1976); Harpole and Nagle, eds., *Census, 1850*; Parish Questionnaires, Ramsey County; WPA, Church Records, Ramsey County; Edward D. Neill, *History of Ramsey County and the City of St. Paul*, 288–295 (Minneapolis, 1881); *Minnesota Weekly Democrat* (St. Paul), August 12, 1851; *Echo de l'Ouest*, July 19, 1918; *Minneapolis Tribune*, June 23, 1979, p. 6B; *Vadnais Heights, A History, 1845–1976* ([Vadnais Heights?, 1976?]).

[17] *Vadnais Heights, A History*, 9–14; *Centerville School, 1976* (n.p., 1976?); Parish Questionnaires, Anoka County; *Le Canadien* (St. Paul), August 4, 1887; Joseph E. Krause, "The History of Catholicity in Anoka County, Minnesota, 1670 to 1891," master's thesis, St. Paul Seminary, 1954; *Atlas and Farmers' Directory of Anoka County and the Eleven Northern Townships of Hennepin County, Minnesota* (St. Paul, 1914); *Atlas & Plat Book, Anoka County, Minnesota* (Rockford, Ill., 1975); Anoka County Historical Society, *Silent Cities: A Survey of Anoka County Minnesota Cemeteries*, 183–191 (Anoka, 1977).

[18] Parish Questionnaires, Ramsey and Washington counties; WPA, Church Records, Ramsey and Washington counties; *Stillwater Trades Review*, January, 1898, p. 19; *Plat Book of Washington County, Minnesota*, 14, 16 (Minneapolis, 1901); *Atlas and Plat Book, Washington County, Minnesota*, 20, 23 (Rockford, Ill., 1976); Augustus B. Eaton, *History of the St. Croix Valley*, 18, 30, 847, 915 (Chicago, 1909). Unfortunately, little information about French Canadians in logging and lumbering seemed to exist in 1980.

[19] Here and below, see Upham and Dunlap, eds., *Minnesota Biographies*, 66; Margareth Jorgensen, "Life of Pierre Bottineau," term paper, University of Minnesota, 1925, copy in MHS; Robert Hazel, *Notre Dame de Minneapolis*, 9 (Minneapolis, 1977).

[20] Here and below, see George E. Warner, *History of Hennepin County*, 271, 276, 294–297, 302–305, 317–326, 329, 332 (Minneapolis, 1881); WPA, Church Records, Hennepin County; Parish Questionnaires, Hennepin County; *Echo de l'Ouest*, January 27, September 1, 22, 1887, February 8, 1894. See also *Map of Hennepin County, Minnesota* (St. Paul, 1873) for the heavy concentration of French names in the northeastern part of Hennepin County.

[21] Albert M. Goodrich, *History of Anoka County and the Towns of Champlin and Dayton in Hennepin County, Minnesota*, 23–28 (Minneapolis, 1905); Parish Questionnaires, Anoka County; Anoka County Historical Society, *Silent Cities*, 21–40; Krause, "Catholicity in Anoka County," 12.

[22] Franklyn Curtiss-Wedge, ed., *History of Wright County, Minnesota*, 2:750, 758, 977 (Chicago, 1915); *Pioneer Chronicles*, 106–116; *Le Canadien*, April 6, 1899. Only one French name appears on the 1894 plat map of Maple Lake Township; *The Standard Township Map and Gazeteer of Wright County, Minnesota*, 14 (Minneapolis, 1894).

[23] Here and below, see *1869–1969 Waverly Centennial*, 2, 23, 27, 30, 31, 33 ([Waverly?, 1969?]); Wright County Historical Society, *D[aniel] R. Farnham's History of Wright County*, 139, 266, 267, 271, 289, 295, 351–353 (Buffalo, 1976); John A. St. Hilaire, "Maple Lake, Wright County, Minnesota," typed paper, 1975, copy in MHS; Parish Questionnaires, Wright County; WPA, Church Records, Wright County. The identity of the priest is usually a clue to the

ethnic composition of early Catholic churches. Fr. Joseph Guillot, a French priest, went from Waverly, 1884–98, to Marshall, 1898–1910, Minneapolis (Our Lady of Lourdes), 1910–18, Faribault (Sacred Heart), 1918; all were French churches.

[24] Clara K. Fuller, *History of Morrison and Todd Counties, Minnesota, Their People, Industries, and Institutions*, 1:68–71 (Indianapolis, 1915); *History of the Upper Mississippi Valley*, 591 (Minneapolis, 1881); Harold L. Fisher, *The Land Called Morrison*, 85, 112–115, 135 (St. Cloud, 1972); *Echo de l'Ouest*, November 14, 1895, July 23, 1897.

[25] Parish Questionnaires, Morrison County; WPA, Church Records, Morrison County; *Pioneer Chronicles*, 275–277; Holy Family parish files, in *St. Cloud Visitor* office, St. Cloud; C. M. Foote and J. W. Henion, *Plat Book of Morrison County, Minnesota* (Minneapolis, 1892); *Morrison County, Minnesota: Land Atlas & Plat Book, 1978* (Rockford, Ill., 1978). On the convent school, see *Minneapolis Tribune*, August 20, 1950, Women's sec., 1, 9; and Sister Mary Assumpta Ahles, *In the Shadow of His Wings: A History Of The Franciscan Sisters*, 67–72 (St. Paul, 1977). Little Falls received its own French church in 1871; it held services in French, causing dissension as the number of Germans and Poles in the parish increased. By 1886 the latter groups had split off to form their own churches.

[26] *Illustrated Album of Meeker and McLeod Counties, Minnesota*, 510, 551, 630 (Chicago, 1888); WPA, Church Records, McLeod County; Parish Questionnaires, McLeod, Sibley, Meeker, and Stearns counties; Harold Albrecht, *This Is Our Town*, 266 (n.p., n.d.); Victor E. Lawson, *Illustrated History and Descriptive and Biographical Review of Kandiyohi County, Minnesota*, 358, 361 (St. Paul, 1905); Joseph D. Varley, *A Brief History of The Church of St. Louis of Paynesville, Minnesota* ([Paynesville?], 1949).

[27] John W. Mason, ed., *History of Otter Tail County, Minnesota*, 86–89 (Indianapolis, 1916). For recent efforts to trace mixed-blood families, see Virginia Rogers, "MHS Collections: The Indians and the Métis: Genealogical Sources on Minnesota's Earliest Settlers," in *Minnesota History*, 46:286–295 (Fall, 1979).

[28] "Narrative secured from Mrs. Rose Barbeau of Fergus Falls by Charles R. Wright," typed manuscript, March 16, 1933, in MHS; Parish Questionnaires, Wilkin and Becker counties.

[29] Alvin H. Wilcox, *A Pioneer History of Becker County, Minnesota*, 241, 248, 253, 257–261, 262, 700, 732, 741–743 (St. Paul, 1907); Parish Questionnaires, Becker County; *Our Northland Diocese* (Crookston), September, 1960, p. 13; *Land Atlas and Plat Book, 1976, Mahnomen County, Minnesota* (Rockford, Ill., 1976).

A list of persons showing the proportion of Indian blood on the White Earth Reservation in 1911 includes such names as Beaulieu, Bellecourt, Brunette, St. Clair, Dufault, La Duke, and Trotochaud, as well as non-French-Canadian names such as McDougall, Fairbanks, Aitkin, Anderson, McArthur, Morrison, Murphy, Peavy, Sloan, Sullivan, Starkey, and Thompson. See U.S. Office of Indian Affairs, *Lists Showing the Degree of Indian Blood of Certain Persons Holding Land upon the White Earth Reservation in Minnesota* (Washington, D.C., 1911).

[30] Here and below, see Virgil Benoit, "Gentilly: A French-Canadian Community in the Minnesota Red River Valley," in *Minnesota History*, 44:279–281 (Winter, 1975); *History of the Red River Valley, Past and Present*, 2:871 (Chicago, 1909); Jorgensen, "Bottineau," 15.

[31] *Echo de l'Ouest*, March 16, 1893, September 30, 1910.

[32] *Plat Book of Polk County, Minnesota* (Minneapolis, 1902). A pamphlet produced by a French-Canadian committee in 1883 described Polk County and its colony, its railroad connections, principal crops and yields, the possibilities for acquisition of land, church and market facilities, climate, topography, and schools. Several letters from settlers praising opportunities available in the

region appeared in an appendix. The pamphlet's purpose was to attract settlers from eastern Canada. See *Description de la Colonie Canadienne du Comté de Polk* (Crookston, 1883).

[33] Benoit, in *Minnesota History*, 44:280; *St. Paul Daily Globe*, March 14, 1880.

[34] Parish Questionnaires, Polk and Red Lake counties; WPA, Church Records, Polk and Red Lake counties; *The Oklee Community Story*, 51, 66–68, 90 (Oklee, 1960); *History of the Red River Valley*, 2:896.

[35] Benoit, in *Minnesota History*, 44:282, 284–286; *Echo de l'Ouest*, May 4, 1893.

[36] Gerald Foley, *The History of the Diocese of Crookston*, 41 ([Crookston?], n.d.); *Le Canadien*, December 5, 1895; *Echo de l'Ouest*, April 30, 1915; WPA, Church Records, Red Lake County.

[37] *First 100 Years: St. Rose of Lima, Argyle, Minnesota, 1879–1979*, 10, 11, 30 ([Argyle?, 1979?]); *Standard Atlas of Marshall County, Minnesota*, 16 (Chicago, 1909); Sister Bernard Coleman and Sister Verona LaBud, *Masinaigans: The Little Book*, 216 (St. Paul, 1972); *Our Northland Diocese*, September, 1960, p. 14; WPA, Church Records, Marshall County; Parish Questionnaires, Marshall County; Foley, *Diocese of Crookston*, 53; *Echo de l'Ouest*, March 20, 1896, August 13, 1897.

[38] *First 100 Years*, 14, 16; *Our Northland Diocese*, September, 1960, p. 14. Red Lake Falls, which was like Argyle in ethnic composition, had a similar experience. After the creation of an English church in 1883, the bishop prohibited the English from attending St. Joseph's French Church, nor could the French go to St. Mary's English Church. A mixed family had to choose one parish and stick with it; *St. Joseph's Parish, Red Lake Falls, Minn., U.S.A.* ([Red Lake Falls?, 1889?]). St. Mary's closed in 1952 and all Catholics once again attended St. Joseph's; Red Lake County Historical Society, *A History of Red Lake County*, 120 (Dallas, 1976).

[39] Here and below, see *First 100 Years: Atlas of Marshall County, Minnesota* (Moorhead, 1956); Cecile S. Belland, "The Schillers of Argyle, MN," typed paper, 1970, copy in MHS.

[40] French Canadians were among early settlers of Stephen and Oslo, also in Marshall County. Nancy Solum, ed., *Self Portrait of Marshall County*, 212 (Dallas, 1976); Gladys Halfmann, ed., *Our Town, Stephen, Minnesota, 1878–1978*, 147, 205 (Stephen, 1978). Kittson, Roseau, and Lake of the Woods counties on the border with Canada had long felt the influence of the French Canadians. Early arrivals were traders and trappers; later ones worked in the lumber industry. Badger organized a Catholic church in 1898 which was served by priests from Red Lake Falls, but the mixed congregation used English. In Warroad, French services existed in the early days. *History of the Red River Valley*, 2:265; Parish Questionnaires, Kittson and Roseau counties; WPA, Church Records, Kittson and Roseau counties; *Echo de l'Ouest*, October 21, 1910.

[41] Here and below, see James P. Shannon, *Catholic Colonization on the Western Frontier*, 136, 139, 140, 147 (New Haven, 1957); Irish-American Community Study, interviews of Alex and Leona Benoit, July 27, 1977, Mrs. Ernest Goulet, July 21, 1977, tapes and transcripts in West Central Minnesota Historical Center, Morris; Edward D. Neill, *History of the Minnesota Valley*, 969 (Minneapolis, 1882); Arthur P. Rose, ed., *An Illustrated History of Lyon County, Minnesota*, 97, 100, 214 (Marshall, 1912); *Echo de l'Ouest*, January 15, 1904; *Le Canadien*, November 14, 1899; *Standard Atlas of Swift County, Minnesota*, 15, 17 (Chicago, 1907); *Atlas and Plat Book, Swift County, Minnesota*, 28, 29 (Rockford, Ill., 1972); *Standard Atlas of Murray County, Minnesota*, 35 (Chicago, 1908); *Atlas of Murray County, Minnesota*, 17 (Fergus Falls, 1961); Nettie Wunderlich to Jarle Leirfallom, December 30, 1947, in responses from County Welfare Boards to Inquiry Regarding Displaced Persons, Minnesota Displaced Persons Commission files, Minnesota Dept. of Public Welfare Records, State Archives, MHS.

[42] Parish Questionnaires, Lyon, Murray, and Swift counties; Richard S. Prosser, *Rails to the North Star*, 11 (Minneapolis, 1966).

[43] Parish Questionnaires, Lyon County; *Dedication: Church of St. Clotilde, Green Valley, Minnesota, June 4, 1956*, 14, 42, 43, 46 (Marshall, 1956); *Plat Book of Lyon County, Minnesota*, 17 (Minneapolis, 1902); *Atlas of Lyon County, Minnesota* (Milbank, S. Dak., [1967?]). Archbishop Ireland named the parish after a sixth-century French Christian queen because "the original members of the new parish were predominantly French"; *Dedication*, 14.

[44] Donald Rubertus, "History of Holy Redeemer Catholic Church, 1869–1916, Marshall," 35, 46, 49, 61, 62, 65, typescript, 1956, in Southwest Minnesota Historical Center, Marshall, copy in MEHP Papers. Second-generation French Canadians from Marshall were prominent in the founding of the church of St. Genevieve in 1897 at Lake Benton in Lincoln County; Parish Questionnaires, Lincoln County. Masqueray, a native of Dieppe, came to New York in 1886; he designed the Cathedral of St. Paul and many other churches and residences and achieved a national reputation before his death in St. Paul in 1917; Upham and Dunlap, eds., *Minnesota Biographies*, 493; *Echo de l'Ouest*, June 1, 1917. An examination of Marshall telephone directories for the 1950s and a city directory for 1972 revealed few French names but many Belgian.

[45] Holmquist and Brookins, *Minnesota's Major Historic Sites*, 152.

[46] U.S. Immigration Commission, *Immigrants in Industries*, 78:300, 301, 314, 339, 343, 377 (61 Congress, 2 session, *Senate Documents*, no. 633 — serial 5677); J. Zarilli, ed., *Holy Ghost Church, 40th Anniversary Historical and Souvenir Record, 1890–1930*, 15 (Two Harbors, 1930); Coleman and LaBud, *Masinaigans*, 167, 168, 170, 177. Parish records indicated the presence of scattered French Canadians at Floodwood in St. Louis County where railway workers were served by priests from Cloquet, at Remer in Cass County where former White Bear Lakers established a church which used the French language for the first five years, at Sandstone in Pine County, and at Mora in Kanabec County. *History of St. Louis Church, Floodwood, Minnesota, 1903–1953* (Floodwood, 1953); Parish Questionnaires, St. Louis, Cass, Pine, and Kanabec counties; WPA, Church Records, Cass County.

[47] Walter O'Meara, *We Made It Through The Winter: A Memoir of Northern Minnesota Boyhood*, 3, 11, 12 (St. Paul, 1974); Bennett A. Beck, *Brief History of the Pioneers of the Cromwell, Minnesota, Area*, 12, 20, 26–28, 42, 169 ([Cromwell?, 1962?]). Descendants of some of these early residents are still present among the owners of small farms. See *Triennial Atlas & Plat Book, Carlton County, Minnesota, 1967* (Rockford, Ill., 1967).

[48] O'Meara, *We Made It Through The Winter*, 12.

[49] Leon Truesdell, *The Canadian Born in the United States*, 35, 87 (New Haven, Conn., 1943); Parish Questionnaires, St. Louis County; *Echo de l'Ouest*, April 26, 1888, January 19, 1893, February 8, 1894; *Le Canadien*, December 1, 1887, February 28, 1902; Raymond J. Cossette, "The Catholic Church in the City of Duluth, 1869–1890," 9, 33–35, 72, master's thesis, St. Paul Seminary, 1965; Patrick J. Lydon, "Notes on the History of the Duluth Diocese," in *Acta et Dicta*, 5:258–260 (July, 1918). A national parish is one organized for a single immigrant group. It has a priest conversant in the native language to deliver the homily and hear confessions. Duluth boasted two French-language newspapers in the early 1890s, *Le Courrier de Duluth* and *La Voix du Lac*; Maximilienne Tétrault, *Le Role de la Presse dans l'Évolution du Peuple Franco-Américain de la Nouvelle Angleterre*, 35, 37 (Marseilles, Fr., 1935).

[50] *Catholic Directory of Duluth*, 87–105 (Duluth, 1892). A similar sample from the German parish showed 37% laborers but 14% in building trades and 25% as shopowners or in personal services. For women, 64% were domestics. In the Polish parish, 84% of the men were laborers; women's occupations did not appear. Irish men in the cathedral parish were 28.9% laborers and 25% in trade; women were dressmakers and domestics.

[51] "St. Jean-Baptiste Parish Book," and "Annual Messenger, 1936, St. Jean-Baptiste Parish, Duluth, Minnesota," both in Vertical File: Churches, and Gertrude Anderson, "French-Canadian Folk Customs," 1936, in Vertical File: French Activities — all in Northeast Minnesota Historical Center, Duluth.

[52] *Echo de l'Ouest*, April 21, 1892, July 24, 1903, March 11, 1904, June 10, 1910, January 27, March 3, November 24, 1911, May 25, 1917, November 26, 1920; *Le Canadien*, December 19, 1895; *Minneapolis Tribune*, December 18, 1877; *Pioneer Chronicles*, 121.

[53] *St. Paul Directory, 1866*, 263, 265, 268, 270, 273; *Echo de l'Ouest*, July 6, 1893, November 3, 1887; *Le Canadien*, April 12, 1888, January 13, 1898. Pembina French would be those who came from the Minnesota-North Dakota-Canada border area.

[54] Truesdell, *Canadian Born*, 87, 88.

[55] Parish Questionnaires, Ramsey County; WPA, Church Records, Ramsey County; Paroisse St. Louis, St. Paul, Minn., *École Saint Louis* (Minneapolis, 1908); *Echo de l'Ouest*, June 1, 1917; "Golden Jubilee, St. Louis Church, St. Paul, Minnesota, 1909–1959," copy in parish files of Catholic Historical Society Library, St. Paul.

[56] Here and below, see Parish Questionnaires, Hennepin County; WPA, Church Records, Hennepin County; Nicholas A. Weber, *A Short History of the French Catholic Congregation of East Minneapolis in Minnesota (1849–1949)* (Minneapolis, 1949); Hazel, *Notre Dame; Riverfront News* (Minneapolis), October, 1979, p. 1; Theodore Guminga, "Some Aspects of the Catholic Immigration of the Nineteenth Century with Reference to Minnesota," master's thesis, St. Paul Seminary, 1958.

[57] Philip Taylor, *The Distant Magnet: European Emigration to the U.S.A.*, 43, 47 (London, 1971); U.S., *Census*, 1860, *Population*, xxxix; Walter F. Willcox, ed., *International Migrations*, 2:201–236 (Reprint ed., New York, 1969).

[58] Lucian J. Fosdick, *The French Blood in America*, 125–127, 211, 311–315 (New York, 1906); Frances S. Childs, *French Refugee Life in the United States, 1790–1800: An American Chapter of the French Revolution*, 45–47, 63 (Baltimore, 1940); Arthur H. Hirsch, *The Huguenots of Colonial South Carolina* (Durham, N.C., 1928). Descendants of at least one refugee family were prominent in early St. Paul; see August L. Larpenteur, "Recollections of the City and People of St. Paul, 1843–1898," in *Minnesota Historical Collections*, 9:363–394 (St. Paul, 1901).

[59] U.S., *Census*, 1860, *Population*, xxix.

[60] U.S., *Census*, 1890, *Population*, part 1, p. 698.

[61] U.S., manuscript census schedules, 1870, Stearns County, T132, roll 11; 1880, Carver County, Dahlgren and Laketown townships, rolls 616, 617; Stearns County, Brockway and St. Augusta townships, roll 634; Winona County, Mt. Vernon and Wilson townships, rolls 637, 638; Wright County, French Lake and Marysville townships, roll 638, microfilm in MHS.

[62] Here and below, see U.S., manuscript census schedules, 1880, Ramsey County, St. Paul, rolls 630, 631.

[63] E. P. Hutchinson, *Immigrants and Their Children, 1850–1950*, 136, 177, 246 (New York, 1956); Alien Registration forms, 1918, Hennepin, Ramsey, and St. Louis counties, in Minnesota Commission of Public Safety Records, State Archives, MHS.

[64] Here and below, see Todd County Bicentennial Committee, *Todd County Histories*, 30, 73, 93, 104, 106, 118, 119, 123, 133, 142, 148, 158, 183, 202, 208, 214, 215, 216, 228, 231, 239, 241, 242, 243, 268, 397, 402, 410, 424, 426, 430 (Long Prairie, 1976).

[65] *Minnesota Pioneer and Democrat*, March 14, 1857; *Le Canadien*, August 4, 1887; *Echo de l'Ouest*, June 30, 1892.

[66] *Le Canadien*, June 23, 1887, May 28, 1896; *Echo de l'Ouest*, August 12, 1885, August 11, 25, September 29, 1887, May 3, 1894,

May 5, 1899. The Union St. Jean Baptiste had chapters in French-Canadian communities throughout the United States. How many chapters existed through the years in Minnesota and the exact dates are unknown. In Minneapolis and St. Paul they organized in the mid-1870s and by the mid-1890s had been replaced by the Woodmen of the World and the Catholic Order of Foresters. See Minneapolis and St. Paul, *City Directories, 1870–1900.*

An early resident of Crookston claimed that there was no sense celebrating the 4th of July because nothing could surpass the parade, floats, music, and songs of the French Canadians who had just 10 days earlier observed St. Jean Baptiste Day; *History of the Red River Valley,* 2:897.

[67] *Echo de l'Ouest,* October 19, 1893, February 1, 1895; *Le Canadien,* March 17, 1887, September 13, 1888.

[68] *Echo de l'Ouest,* October 6, 1892, January 5, 1893, April 5, 1894, June 19, 1896, November 19, 1897, May 6, 13, 1898; *Le Canadien,* January 12, May 31, June 7, August 30, September 13, 1888, March 8, 1894, May 12, 1898.

[69] *Echo de l'Ouest,* July 28, 1911.

[70] Tétrault, *Role de la Presse,* 21–40. The Minnesota papers were: *L'Etoile du Nord* (St. Paul, 1874–76), *Le Franco-Canadien* (St. Paul, 1876), *Le National* (St. Paul, 1876–77), *Le Canadien* (St. Paul, 1877–1904), *Le Citoyen Américain* (Minneapolis, 1884), *Le Progrés* (Minneapolis, 1877, 1884–87), *Echo de l'Ouest* (Minneapolis, 1883–1929), *Le Courrier de Duluth* (Duluth, 1890), *La Voix du Lac* (Duluth, 1892), *L'Oeil* (Minneapolis, 1892–?), *La Voix du Peuple* (Minneapolis, 1900–03), and *Les Veillées Canadiennes* (Minneapolis, 1890). Of these the MHS has files of *Le Canadien* and *Echo de l'Ouest.*

[71] *Le Canadien,* June 25, July 16, 1891; Tétrault, *Role de la Presse,* 25.

[72] *Echo de l'Ouest,* August 4, 1887, May 29, 1903.

[73] *Echo de l'Ouest,* May 31, December 6, 1888, May 22, 1903.

[74] International Institute, *Festival of Nations,* programs for 1939, 1942, 1949, 1952, 1955, 1964, 1967 (St. Paul); International Institute of Minnesota Collection, French Club, 1953–55, Nationality Groups folder, IHRC; *Southeast: A Journal of a Minneapolis Community,* February, 1979, p. 8; *The [St. Anthony] Park Bugle* (St. Paul), December, 1979, p. 1; Minnesota Analysis and Planning System, *Minnesota Socio-Economic Characteristics From the 4th Count Summary Tape of the 1970 Census,* vol. 3, n.p. (St. Paul, 1972).

[75] Irish-American Community Study, Benoit and Goulet interviews; Stella H. LeBlanc interview, November 23, 1973, typescript, in Northwest Minnesota Historical Center, Moorhead; O'Meara, *We Made It Through The Winter,* 12.

[76] *Saint Paul Area Downtowner,* September 6, 1979, p. 1; *Notre/Our Héritage* (St. Paul, 1979), copy in MEHP Papers; *Minneapolis Tribune,* September 3, 1978, p. 1B.

CHAPTER 3

The Old-Stock Americans

John G. Rice

THE OLD-STOCK AMERICANS were members of white European families whose ancestors had resided in North America for a number of generations before they made the trek to Minnesota. Most were little more than 200 years removed from their homelands across the Atlantic. They differed from the newer immigrants who were part of the Great Atlantic Migration of the 19th century in at least two respects. First, their culture was founded primarily, though not exclusively, on the cultures of the British Isles. Second, after the Revolutionary War, the regional subcultures of Colonial America began to come together west of the Appalachian Mountains to form a distinctive national culture. Clearly British in origin, this emerging synthesis nevertheless contained new values developed in the American environment.[1]

According to some interpretations, Old-Stock Americans in the 19th century did not comprise an ethnic group. They were not a minority consciously preserving a distinctive culture in the midst of an alien society. They *were* the host society, the bearers of a new national culture. For them there was no foreign language to preserve, no national church to form, no debate within the group about cultural issues. They took it for granted that their ways would become the ways of all Americans. Their literary skills enabled them not only to record their own story but also to impress their own interpretation upon the stories of other groups. Since they had nothing to be defensive about, the Old-Stock Americans produced no self-conscious "ethnic" literature.[2] Nevertheless they represented a distinctive culture group. No work on Minnesota's people would be complete without them.

Central to the significance of the Old-Stock Americans was their singular ideology, to which United States citizens eventually subscribed. This political philosophy involved sovereignty for the individual, delegation of powers to the central government, protection of civil liberties, sanctity of private property, freedom of enterprise, and separation of church and state. Their convictions and optimism regarding the perfectability of man were embodied in the American constitutional system.[3]

The term "Old-Stock Americans" hides, as do virtually all other such rubrics used in this volume, a great deal of cultural diversity. Although a national culture was developing in the 19th century, strong regional differences were still in evidence. Three, or possibly four, primary culture hearths

and at least two secondary ones can be identified along the eastern seaboard in colonial times. A culture hearth or cultural core may be defined as a place where a community of people developed a set of cultural characteristics which made the group distinctive. One was located in southern New England, including Rhode Island and eastern Massachusetts and Connecticut; a second lay in the rich farming country of southeastern Pennsylvania, and a third embraced the tidewater estuaries of the western shore of Chesapeake Bay in Maryland and Virginia. A fourth primary core has been postulated in the coastal lowlands of South Carolina, but its connections with subsequent westward movements are little understood (see Map 3.1).[4]

Of the three identifiable hearths, southern New England spawned the most homogeneous culture — highly literate, strongly middle class, and rooted in the nonconformist, Calvinist teachings which gained strength in England in the 17th century. In America its religious institution became the Congregational church, where the ritual of the Church of England was replaced by a simple service and supervision by bishops yielded to government by the congregation.

New England was the home of Puritan ethics, and its culture had a mission. These settlers had turned their back on England, sailing west determined to set their "city upon a hill" somewhere in the wilderness. Their zeal for democracy in church government was mirrored in their concern for representative civil government. From the start individual settlements conducted their affairs in democratic town meetings. To the New Englander, a democratic society meant an educated society, and his passion was the school. A large number of the colonists were very well educated for the day. Many, especially the leaders, had attended a university, while others were drawn from the minor landholders and bourgeoisie. In some ways New England "Yankees" comprised a true ethnic group in Colonial America. Not only was their culture distinctive but they themselves were acutely conscious of it. When they began to move westward in the 19th century, they were intent on making their values the values of the entire nation.

In strong contrast to Yankee culture stood that of Tidewater Virginia and Maryland, where life was deeply rural and the economy was narrowly based on the production of tobacco. Heavy dependence on the English market meant that Tidewater society, far from turning its back on the mother country, maintained close ties with it. Virginia was a refuge for hundreds of Cavaliers fleeing Puritan England after 1649, and many founded what were to become the colony's leading families.[5] The Church of England remained the established religious body until the Revolutionary War. Nonconformist ideas, espoused especially by the descendants of white indentured servants and Black slaves, were expressed through the Baptist and Methodist movements. Religious diversity was furthered by the arrival in the 18th century of numbers of Scots and Scotch-Irish whose Calvinist convictions led them to maintain Presbyterianism in the face of the Episcopal state church.

The Maryland Tidewater differed from that of Virginia principally in the degree of religious freedom for Christians which existed there after the passage of the Toleration Act in 1649. In spite of momentary lapses, this principle remained a foundation stone of the Maryland colony, which long served as a refuge for dissidents from other regions. Though not as homogeneous or as mission-conscious as the Yankees, the people of the Tidewater nonetheless developed a distinctive southern subculture that subsequently made its contribution

to the emerging national culture in the Trans-Appalachian West.

Between the Tidewater and New England lay the lands beyond the Delaware River granted to William Penn in 1681. Penn had conceived his colony as a haven for English Quakers, who, in spite of earlier Swedish and Dutch settlements, dominated Pennsylvania in its early years. By the middle of the 18th century, however, his policies of religious toleration had drawn large numbers of Rhineland Germans, who settled the rich farmlands west of Philadelphia. Most of these "Pennsylvania Dutch" were Lutheran and Reformed, but some, like the Amish, Mennonites, and Moravians, were the spiritual descendants of the Anabaptist movement. On the mountainous western fringes of the Pennsylvania culture hearth settled a third group, the Scots and Scotch-Irish, bringing with them their Presbyterian church. Out of these diverse peoples, working together to build a commercial economy with a strong urban as well as rural component, developed what came to be called Midland culture, which was clearly more heterogeneous than the other two.

From the Tidewater and Pennsylvania hearths settlement

Map 3.1. Movements of Culture Core Groups in the United States

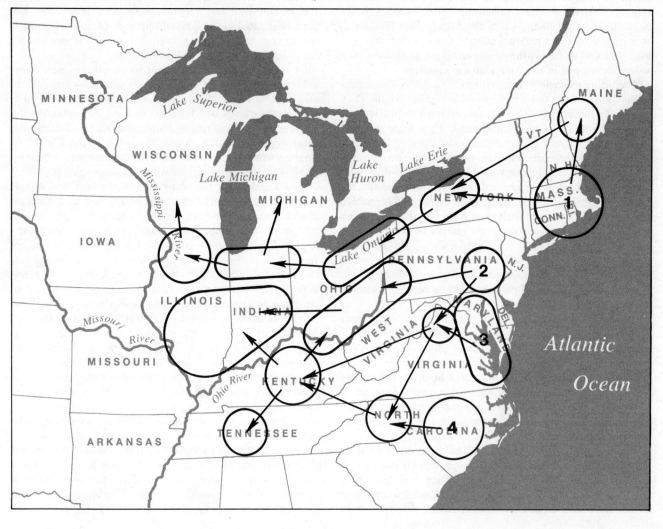

spread inland, where two secondary culture cores were established. In the Shenandoah Valley of western Virginia, Scots, Scotch-Irish, and Germans following the longitudinal valleys out of Pennsylvania met a largely English population moving upcountry from the shores of Chesapeake Bay. Some of these people continued southward into the Piedmont country of western North Carolina, which was simultaneously receiving settlers from the coastal regions. There in the valley and on the Piedmont an early mixing of Southern and Midland traits took place, producing a culture subsequently carried into Kentucky and Tennessee.

By the end of the colonial period, then, five culture hearths may be identified, each with its own distinctive blend of people. During the years following the Revolution, these areas would act as springboards for the early settlement of the Trans-Appalachian Midwest, including Minnesota. There additional cultural mixing would occur, laying the groundwork for a national culture with strong persisting regionalisms.

West of the mountains in the early years of the republic six additional tertiary culture cores may be identified. New Englanders flocked to (1) the Genesee country in western New York and (2) Connecticut's Western Reserve in what would become northeastern Ohio, taking with them Congregationalism and town meetings and planting relatively faithful reproductions of Yankee culture.[6] Midlanders crossed the Appalachians via the National Road and moved into the Ohio Valley, establishing their culture in (3) southwestern Pennsylvania and (4) Ohio, where it mingled with southern influences. People moving from the Shenandoah Valley through the Cumberland Gap settled the fertile bluegrass region of (5) central Kentucky. From there some trekked north across the Ohio River, while others went south into (6) the Nashville basin of Tennessee, which also received influences from the North Carolina Piedmont to the east (see Map 3.1).

MINNESOTA descendants of New England families dressed as Puritans for the 1934 Festival of Nations of the International Institute in St. Paul.

The Old-Stock Americans in the Middle West

In the years following 1830 the lands of the Northwest Territory, lying north of the Ohio and east of the Mississippi, received people from the three primary culture groups. By far the strongest contrast was that between the New Englander on the one hand and the Midlander and Southerner on the other. (Indeed it is often difficult to distinguish between the latter two.) As the Midlanders followed the National Road out of western Maryland and Pennsylvania, they joined the "Upland" Southerners making their way from Kentucky into southern Ohio, Indiana, and Illinois. There a mixed Southern-Midland culture, described by its bearers as "Western," was well established by 1830. Then the Yankee deluge hit. Although New Englanders had been settling in the Western Reserve since the turn of the century, few had ventured far from the shores of Lake Erie. Now they came by the thousands, and by 1860 nearly half of the Yankees then living had left New England.[7]

Among these migrants were what Stewart H. Holbrook called "Come-Outers," who left because of religious controversies, and "Go-Awayers," who went off to seek better economic opportunities. The Yankees regarded the Westerners as uneducated, irreligious, lazy, and a threat to the most fundamental values their forefathers had brought to America. It was the duty of God-fearing Yankees, they believed, to migrate to the West, establish churches and colleges, and spread their culture through Sunday schools, missions, and temperance organizations. For, as Harriet Beecher Stowe put it, the New England Puritan was "especially called and chosen by God for some great work on earth." The distaste many Westerners felt for the Yankee was rooted in his inability not to meddle, for "the typical New Englander was entirely unable, when there were wrongs to be corrected, to mind his own business."[8]

In his turn, the New Englander was unfavorably impressed by the religious fragmentation, poverty, and lack of literacy among the Southerners he encountered in the Midwest. Compared to the Yankee, the man from south of the Ohio did indeed display a lack of learning and an absence of "fixings." For one thing, the tradition of education, so fundamental to New England life, was weak in the South. For another, the Southerner's long and arduous journey over mountain roads did not permit him to take along the quantity of personal possessions the New Englander could readily carry on canal and lake steamers to the Old Northwest. Then, too, the more expensive travel on the Yankee's water route tended to select somewhat more affluent migrants.

Before the development of railroads, which did not amount to much in Ohio, Indiana, and Illinois before 1850 and in Minnesota until the 1860s, the chief avenues of travel were rivers, canals, lakes, and roads. The Ohio-Mississippi River route offered a ready water approach to Minnesota for Midlanders and Southerners. Working steadily to make the country's great river arteries more navigable, army engineers in 1830 built a canal to bypass the rapids in the Ohio River at Louisville, Kentucky. Because of the rapids at Keokuk, Iowa, however, the Upper Mississippi remained inaccessible to the very largest steamboats.[9]

By 1854, when the frontier of settlement began to press into Minnesota Territory, two distinct waves could be observed. Moving along the Ohio Valley were the Midlanders and Southerners, the bearers of what we have called Western culture. Fragmented in religion and Democratic in politics, these people were oriented to river trade and southern markets. Their city was St. Louis. Following the chain of Great Lakes were the New Englanders, Puritan in religion, Republican in politics, and tied by rail and ship to eastern markets. Their city was Chicago.[10]

Table 3.1 shows the eastern and southern origins of the population of seven midwestern states according to the census of 1860. Old-Stock Americans of the Lower Midwest (Ohio, Indiana, Illinois, and Iowa) showed a preponderance of Midlanders and Southerners, while those of the Upper Midwest (Michigan, Wisconsin, and Minnesota) exhibited a strong New England element. Within the Upper Midwest, however, Minnesota recorded a higher percentage of Midlanders and Southerners than was registered by its two neighbors to the east. A partial explanation may be found in the established routes of travel. Although the state lay directly in the path of the advancing Yankees, the Mississippi River channeled to it a significant leaven of Midlanders and Southerners. Thus Minnesota's Old-Stock Americans were not quite so thoroughly dominated by New Englanders as were those of Michigan and Wisconsin.

Nevertheless the large proportion of Mainites among the Yankees is especially striking. This can be explained by the presence of the lumbering frontier in Minnesota at the time of these migrations. Having begun in northern New England in the 17th century, loggers swept across the Great Lakes states with the advance of population. From earliest times Maine lumbermen dominated the industry. When they reached Minnesota, however, the great forest ended. Beyond lay a sea of grass. By the time the industry made the jump to the Pacific Northwest, many Mainites had taken up farming or entered other occupations in Minnesota. In no other midwestern state was the heritage of Maine so strong.

Minnesota shared with Wisconsin a large proportion of Vermonters and New Hampshiremen among its Old-Stock Americans. With Maine, these states represented the New England farming frontier, a stony land supporting what Timothy Dwight, president of Yale College, regarded as an overly large population "too talkative, too passionate, too prodigal, and too shiftless to acquire either property or character." Commented Holbrook, "few men have been so mistaken in their judgment."[11] When more fertile lands became available, these New Englanders flocked to Wisconsin and Minnesota in droves. They were enthusiastically joined by Yorkers, until in 1860 just over half of the total northeastern-born population of Minnesota was made up of these Yankees "one step removed."

Old-Stock Americans led the settlement of Minnesota. Table 3.2 shows that for all the groups (except Southerners) the decade of the 1850s saw a larger total increment than any subsequent 10-year period. By 1860 almost 37% of the population born outside the state had originated in the East and South. In succeeding years, in-migration gradually dropped until between 1890 and 1900 deaths exceeded new arrivals, and the absolute number of first-generation Old-Stock Americans began to decline. At their population peak in 1890 (at 111,343), their distribution among the major subgroups had changed only slightly from that in 1860. While the Yankee surge of the 1850s slackened rapidly, a strong in-migration of Yorkers continued in the 1860s. By 1890 the latter had somewhat increased their representation at the expense of Yankees. Unlike the others, the small Southern-born group continued to grow slowly right up to 1920.[12]

It was the settlers from the East, especially Yankees and Yorkers, who laid the groundwork for the future state of

Table 3.1. Eastern and Southern Origins of the Midwest Population, 1860 (in percentages)

	Ohio	Indiana	Illinois	Iowa	Michigan	Wisconsin	Minnesota
Maine	0.7	0.5	1.7	1.8	0.8	4.2	12.6
Upper New England (Vermont, New Hampshire)	3.4	1.7	5.8	6.2	6.6	12.3	12.9
Lower New England (Connecticut, Rhode Island, Massachusetts)	7.7	2.4	7.3	6.4	7.2	10.1	11.3
New York	16.8	11.8	27.3	26.4	73.8	58.8	42.2
Total Northeast	28.6	16.4	42.1	40.8	88.4	85.4	79.0
Pennsylvania and New Jersey	42.7	24.8	22.3	32.2	9.6	11.9	16.3
Upper South	28.7	58.8	35.6	27.0	2.0	2.7	4.7
Total East and Upper South	100.0	100.0	100.0	100.0	100.0	100.0	100.0

Source: U.S., *Census*, 1860.

Table 3.2. Population Change Among Old-Stock Americans in Minnesota, 1860–1920 (in thousands)

	1850–60	1860–70	1870–80	1880–90	1890–1900	1900–10	1910–20
Yankees	+ 18.8	+ 9.9	+ 6.0	+ 1.3	− 5.9	− 6.8	− 6.1
Yorkers	+ 21.6	+ 17.9	+ 7.5	+ 1.3	− 4.0	− 8.9	− 8.5
Midlanders	+ 8.4	+ 4.9	+ 3.6	+ 2.0	− 0.2	− 0.4	− 1.7
Southerners	+ 2.4	+ 2.8	+ 1.3	+ 1.7	+ 0.7	+ 0.3	+ 0.8
Total	+ 51.2	+ 35.5	+ 18.4	+ 6.3	− 9.4	− 15.8	− 15.5

Source: U.S., *Census*, 1850, 1870, 1890–1920; Manuscript Census, 1860, 1880.

Minnesota. They built and managed towns, founded industries, and established important institutions. They were acutely aware of their role as builders of a civilization in the wilderness and confident that Minnesota would become the New England of the West.[13]

In 1857, at the first anniversary banquet of the New England Society of the Northwest, held in the Cataract Hotel in Minneapolis, one speaker hoped that Minnesota might "imitate the heroic virtues of her foster mother, till New England industry, New England enterprise, and New England thrift shall build here a glorious super-structure of education and Gospel truth, till Sabbath bells shall echo from hill-top to hill-top, and forests now untrodden shall be filled with the murmur of the common school, ensuring the intelligence and integrity of our people, and making the land we live in like the land we left."[14]

These hopes, however, were dampened by the panic of 1857, the Civil War, and the arrival of thousands of emigrants from Europe. If anything, Minnesota became a New Scandinavia. By 1890 when the Old-Stock American population peaked, less than 15% of the Minnesota population born outside the state was from the East and South, and by 1920 the figure had dropped to 7%. Their influence, however, far outweighed their numbers. In the years before World War I, 14 of Minnesota's 18 governors were of eastern birth or descent. Similar percentages obtained for the other top elected officials, supreme court justices, and prominent lawyers.[15]

Yankees and Yorkers

By 1880 many Old-Stock Americans in Minnesota had retired from their farms and moved to town. Table 3.3 shows their distribution in 1880, along with that of the foreign born, among farming areas, outstate towns, and the Twin Cities (see Map 3.2). Of the three subcultures, the Yankees had become by then the most town-oriented. Mainites and the people from Lower New England were also especially heavily represented in the Twin Cities. The strong showing of Mainites in Minneapolis is related to their preoccupation with sawmilling, much of which was concentrated near the Falls of St. Anthony. These patterns are explainable in terms of the business opportunities they sought in addition to their farming enterprises. They had the advantage of speaking the national language, so it was they who opened the shops, operated the banks, published the newspapers, and ran the government. Among the Old-Stock Americans, mixing farm-

ing with commerce was a tradition which explains their willingness to move to town and open a business. Those with a persistent rural tradition were the Southerners.

Map 3.2 shows those townships whose rural populations were predominantly Old-Stock American in 1880. Yorkers have been grouped with other Yankees because the two groups represent essentially a single culture and they frequently settled together. Indeed they were often members of the same families, the result of stepwise migration out of New England and into the fertile river valleys of upstate New York.[16] Mainites have been treated separately because their occupational interests drew them to the timberlands and mill sites; thus, they seldom settled with Yankee farmers. Southerners, too, tended to form relatively compact, homogeneous settlements.

The Yankees and Yorkers appeared to be fairly evenly distributed across the then-settled parts of the state. Numerically, however, they were quite heavily concentrated in the southeastern counties (see Tables 3.4 and 3.5), where they were among the earliest settlers on the scene and where the density of rural population was then much greater than elsewhere in the state. The agricultural frontier approached Minnesota from the southeast, and it was there in the maple-basswood forests and oak openings west of the Mississippi that the first major farming settlements were made. Place names alone suggest what an enormous contribution the people of the Northeast made to the settlement of this region: Burlington and Danville (Vermont), Concord and Dover (New Hampshire), Haverhill, Lexington, and Lynn (Massachusetts), Meriden and New Haven (Connecticut), Elmira, Rochester, Saratoga, and Utica (New York), and Greenbush, Maine Prairie, and Stillwater (Maine). Even the unlikely name of Yucatan in Houston County bespeaks a Yankee heritage. Originally called Utica, it was changed — to avoid confusion with Utica Township in nearby Winona County — to a word with a "somewhat similar sound" but found nowhere else in the United States at the time.[17]

The advent of such a large number of Yankees and Yorkers in the southeast during the 1850s created some major problems for the territorial government as it pursued its quest for statehood. Before the farming frontier swept up the Mississippi more than half of the territory's slightly over 6,000 people in 1850 lived in the St. Paul-St. Anthony triangle between the Mississippi and St. Croix rivers. At first the government was controlled by settlers and fur traders who had lived for some time in the Minnesota country under the

Table 3.3. Location of Old-Stock Americans and Foreign Born in Minnesota, 1880 (in percentages)

	Farm	Town	Twin Cities	Total
Maine	42.1	29.7	28.2	100.0
Upper New England (Vermont, New Hampshire)	50.0	34.4	15.6	100.0
Lower New England (Connecticut, Rhode Island, Massachusetts)	43.6	31.3	25.1	100.0
New York	54.5	32.2	13.3	100.0
Total Northeast	50.6	31.9	17.5	100.0
Pennsylvania and New Jersey	54.1	29.3	16.6	100.0
Upper South and Indiana	58.2	25.3	16.5	100.0
Foreign Born	71.0	17.7	11.3	100.0

Source: U.S., Manuscript Census, 1880.

Map 3.2. Minnesota Rural Settlement by Old-Stock Americans and Others, 1880

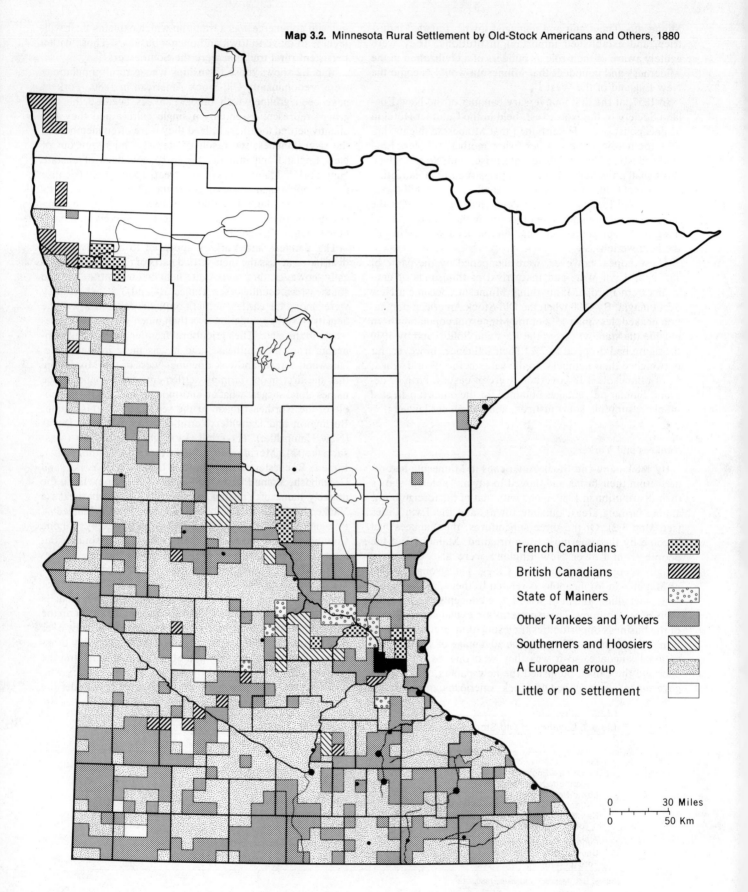

French Canadians

British Canadians

State of Mainers

Other Yankees and Yorkers

Southerners and Hoosiers

A European group

Little or no settlement

0   30 Miles

0   50 Km

Table 3.4. Minnesotans Born in New England, 1850–80*

County	1850	1860	1880	Concentrations
Aitkin		1	41	
Anoka		670	1,033	Anoka
Becker		1	348	
Beltrami			3	
Benton	43	157	158	Sauk Rapids
Big Stone			240	Ortonville
Blue Earth	19	462	854	Mankato
Brown		33	167	
Carlton		2	62	
Carver		232	114	
Cass		3	49	Montevideo
Chippewa			166	
Chisago		170	141	Taylors Falls
Clay			300	Moorhead
Cook			2	
Cottonwood			191	
Crow Wing	15		178	Brainerd
Dakota	19	964	809	
Dodge		487	568	Dodge Center
Douglas			175	
Faribault		156	563	
Fillmore		967	674	Chatfield, Preston, Spring Valley
Freeborn		265	395	Albert Lea
Goodhue		955	801	Red Wing, Zumbrota
Grant			91	
Hennepin	247	3,093	7,242	St. Anthony, Minneapolis, Richfield
Houston		480	348	Houston, Caledonia
Isanti		52	179	
Itasca	5		11	
Jackson		4	127	Jackson
Kanabec		17	43	
Kandiyohi		20	183	
Kittson	4	10	22	
Lac qui Parle			96	
Lake		3		
Le Sueur		301	377	
Lincoln			104	
Lyon			359	Marshall
McLeod		152	323	Hutchinson, Glencoe
Mahnomen		21		
Marshall			41	
Martin		17	270	
Meeker		201	497	
Mille Lacs		15	232	
Morrison		112	300	
Mower		357	589	Austin
Murray		2	151	
Nicollet		198	223	
Nobles			241	
Olmsted		915	1,139	Rochester
Otter Tail		28	469	Fergus Falls
Pine		14	96	
Pipestone		31	156	
Polk			273	Crookston
Pope			118	
Ramsey	125	781	1,978	St. Paul
Redwood			235	Redwood Falls
Renville		16	220	
Rice		914	1,060	Northfield, Faribault
Rock			130	
St. Louis		15	157	Duluth
Scott		319	208	Shakopee
Sherburne		250	522	Elk River
Sibley		126	145	
Stearns		542	724	St. Cloud
Steele		515	617	Owatonna
Stevens			257	Morris
Swift			313	Appleton
Todd		48	207	
Traverse		19	89	
Wabasha	7	816	839	Lake City, Wabasha
Wadena			151	
Waseca		199	342	Waseca
Washington	154	954	1,298	Stillwater
Watonwan			180	
Wilkin			117	
Winona		1,150	1,110	Winona
Wright		784	801	Monticello
Yellow Medicine			125	
Total	623	19,031	34,157	
Published census figures		(18,882)	(34,363)	

Source: U.S., *Census*, 1850; Manuscript Census, 1860, 1880.
* The states covered are Maine, New Hampshire, Vermont, Massachusetts, Rhode Island, and Connecticut.

Table 3.5. Minnesotans Born in Middle Atlantic States, 1850–80*

County	1850	1860	1880	Concentrations
Aitkin		1	31	
Anoka		244	478	Anoka
Becker		1	390	
Beltrami			1	
Benton	24	118	247	Sauk Rapids
Big Stone			446	Ortonville
Blue Earth	39	962	2,314	
Brown		98	428	
Carlton		4	106	
Carver		334	370	
Cass		8	44	
Chippewa			350	Montevideo
Chisago		209	332	Taylors Falls
Clay			400	Moorhead
Cook			2	
Cottonwood			435	Windom
Crow Wing		18	284	Brainerd
Dakota	34	1,434	1,329	Hastings
Dodge		1,043	1,580	Dodge Center
Douglas			594	Alexandria
Faribault		355	1,966	Blue Earth City
Fillmore		3,285	2,890	Rushford, Lanesboro, Preston, Chatfield
Freeborn		805	1,275	Albert Lea
Goodhue		1,725	1,721	Cannon Falls, Zumbrota, Red Wing
Grant			141	
Hennepin	35	1,620	6,654	Minneapolis
Houston		929	833	Houston, Caledonia
Isanti		33	133	
Itasca	1		6	
Jackson		38	384	Jackson
Kanabec		2	27	
Kandiyohi		43	332	Willmar
Kittson		27	30	
Lac qui Parle			259	
Lake		6		
Le Sueur		747	957	Le Sueur
Lincoln			287	Lake Benton
Lyon			868	Tracy, Marshall
McLeod		198	714	Hutchinson, Glencoe
Mahnomen		40		
Marshall			79	
Martin		37	817	Fairmont
Meeker		131	712	Litchfield,
Mille Lacs		14	156	Princeton

Table 3.5. Minnesotans Born in Middle Atlantic States, 1850–80*
(continued)

County	1850			Concentrations
Morrison		55	443	Little Falls
Mower		893	2,102	Austin
Murray		11	398	
Nicollet		360	480	St. Peter
Nobles			676	Worthington
Olmsted		2,955 *	3,211	Rochester
Otter Tail		21	1,350	Fergus Falls
Pine		6	152	
Pipestone		1	352	
Polk		43	605	Crookston
Pope			230	
Ramsey	134	1,759	3,838	
Red Lake	3			
Redwood			588	
Renville		41	576	
Rice		1,393	2,002	Northfield, Faribault
Rock			469	Luverne
St. Louis		57	354	Duluth
Scott		572	590	Shakopee
Sherburne		90	410	
Sibley		466	430	
Stearns		416	1,195	St. Cloud
Steele		679	1,355	Owatonna
Stevens			429	Morris
Swift			540	Appleton
Todd		54	662	
Traverse		18	160	
Wabasha	27	1,836	2,158	Lake City, Wabasha
Wadena			305	
Waseca		520	999	Waseca
Washington	141	780	1,581	Stillwater
Watonwan			315	Madelia
Wilkin			197	Breckenridge
Winona		2,166	2,575	Winona
Wright		598	1,234	Monticello
Yellow Medicine			430	Granite Falls
Total	438	30,299	64,793	
Published census figures		(30,075)	(64,089)	

Source: U.S., Census, 1850; Manuscript Census, 1860, 1880.
*The states covered are New York, New Jersey, Pennsylvania, and Delaware.

protection of Fort Snelling. Like most frontiersmen, these people were Democrats. As fiercely abolitionist Republicans, the Yankees and Yorkers resented the political power wielded by Democrats in St. Paul. They further resented the representational imbalance which grew daily as more and more settlers poured into the southeastern corner.[18] When the number of people in the territory had increased sufficiently to petition Congress to admit Minnesota as a state, Republican forces championed the creation of a long east-west state tied to markets in Chicago, while Democrats, led by fur trader Henry Mower Rice, successfully advocated a state longer from north to south, which would enhance the position of St. Paul and St. Anthony.[19]

Individual families were largely responsible for transplanting New England culture to Minnesota. An analysis of their birthplace information in the 1880 census for the 50 townships where the rural Old-Stock American population was largest showed that most of these families had left New York or New England only a few years before. Of those born outside Minnesota who had at least one Yankee or Yorker parent, 63.6% were themselves born in New York or New

England, while the rest were born in one of the five states of the Old Northwest, a majority in Wisconsin. By contrast only 43.9% of the Midlanders were born in Pennsylvania or New Jersey and 49.7% of the Southerners in the South. This birthfield pattern suggests that the migration from the Northeast to the Upper Midwest was, for the most part, accomplished in only one or two stages. The bulk of the settlers went directly to Wisconsin and Minnesota, where they were joined by compatriots who had settled earlier in parts of the Lower Midwest.

The migration to Minnesota was stimulated in part by letters sent home to friends and relatives by new settlers, but some active recruitment was apparently carried on by state authorities working with the railroad companies. The writer of an article entitled "The Star of the North — Minnesota," which appeared in a Vermont newspaper about 1870, reported on the visit of the "Traveling Immigrant Agent" for the state of Minnesota. From him, he wrote, "we learn of a lively emmigration [sic] west to the above named State, which, is not at all surprising, as we know that our Vermont people generally get on the right track, and in going for Minnesota, they go to a land of promise, to where there is openings for all, and where all will succeed who go there with a will to do their utmost . . . in that health giving State, with such a clime, and such openings, there is no such word as fail." Such promotional articles were aimed chiefly at Civil War veterans who, in Minnesota, settled along the Northern Pacific line.[20]

The healthful climate was much emphasized in the early propaganda. The damp, raw air of New England was thought to be very unhealthy, and indeed the rate of consumption (tuberculosis) there was high. It was even said that placing a guest in a northeast bedroom (where he or she was exposed to cold sea air) was tantamount to murder. Minnesota, in direct contrast to Florida, was praised for the dryness of its air as well as for the absence of the "foul emanations of the earth" then thought to cause malaria.[21]

A letter to the Northampton (Massachusetts) Courier of March 7, 1854, commented that "Respecting the health of the country, it exceeds all my expectations. To live in a town containing over 2000 people for 6 months in succession and hear of no sickness and of hardly a death, surprises me." A writer in the Boston Congregationalist of October 3, 1856, reported, "The air is pure and bracing, and there is almost an entire absence of those unfavorable causes that so often produce sickness." Some years later a new settler in Mower County informed the Boston-based New England Farmer of June 24, 1865, of the rapid progress being made by New Englanders in his township. He was also careful to add that the water was very good and that a dozen people had been cured of consumption since taking up residence there. The search for better health led many Easterners of education and means to Minnesota, and one observer has suggested that "If through the years Minnesota's most important natural resource has been the unusual caliber of its citizenry, the period when Minnesota was Florida's rival [as a resort for Yankee convalescents] made a substantial contribution to that asset."[22]

While the virtues of its climate attracted some, far more

MEMBERS of Zumbrota's Old Settlers Association in 1905.

migrants sought economic opportunities, intent on using their Yankee skills and ingenuity to build another New England in the West. In the *Congregationalist* of September 12, 1856, a writer observed that the New Englanders in Minnesota had taken "with them to their new homes, all their associations and attainments, . . . all that has made New England what she is today."

These settlers felt strongly that the church and the school were the two institutions which had made New England. One newcomer wrote home that "The men who have come this year are those who love the church and the schoolhouse, and they will not do without these. The Majority are New-Englanders, and they come with the good old Pilgrim spirit." They arrived, however, without sufficient teachers or women who could become teachers. To rectify the lack, Easterners formed the Ladies' Society for the Promotion of Education at the West to send "to the Western States Competent female teachers of unquestionable piety, belonging to Congregational churches in New England." Under the auspices of a similar organization, the National Board of Popular Education, St. Paul in 1847 obtained its first public school teacher, Vermont native Harriet Bishop.[23]

Sometimes bits of New England culture were even visible in the landscape. In 1850 a visitor to Cottage Grove described one farm of "about forty acres in cultivation, with an old-fashioned New England fence around it, all neat and trim."[24] Most, but not all, of the rural settlers had farming backgrounds. A report to the *New York Daily Tribune* of May 23, 1853, on a colony of Easterners at Minnesota City in Winona County observed that "It has a select population, having twice been sifted. . . . Most of those who left were

mechanics and artisans, principally from New York City, who knew nothing about farming, or the wants of a new settlement." An 1857 visitor to Garden City, a Yankee settlement in Blue Earth County, noted that "most of these people had come from Boston, Massachusetts, and knew very little of wild western life or how to handle an ax."[25]

The Rollingstone colony at Minnesota City was an organized effort of the Western Farm and Village Association of New York City. Although such colonies were not as prevalent in Minnesota as they were in Michigan and Wisconsin, other prominent examples included Hutchinson, an idealistic effort founded by a Yankee family of singing entertainers; Excelsior, started by the Excelsior Pioneer Association of New York; Zumbrota, sponsored by the Strafford Western Emigration Company; a colony sent from Northampton, Massachusetts, and known by that name; and Detroit Lakes, begun by a Civil War veterans' group known as the Western Land Improvement Association.[26]

Neither these nor the numerous smaller ventures which resembled them fulfilled the dreams of their initiators. Indeed the Northampton experiment never resulted in the establishment of a true colony. According to the *Northampton Courier* of June 14, 1853, "when the Colony reached St. Paul, they were furiously beset by those pests to the Territory, the land speculators," who deflected many from the previously chosen site on the Cannon River. Thus "Even . . . *before seeing* the country selected for them by their agent, they broke up and scattered."[27]

The unreasonable expectations of the colonists and the cold and rainy weather that greeted them were blamed for the failure. "The members were impatient, and undoubtedly many of them had wrong impressions of the country, supposing that they should find it possessing all the excellencies and luxuries of New England, with ten-fold its productiveness and beauty," explained the *Courier*. They expected to find it all "suitably divided into mowing, pasturage, tillage and wood land." Some of the colonists did settle at the Cannon River site, but most apparently melted into the mass of Yankee settlers.

Usually after a suitable location was agreed upon, the colonists went about the task of laying out the kind of village they had known in New England. A report in the *Congregationalist* of October 3, 1856, submitted by a traveler recently returned from Zumbrota, noted that "One quarter of a section has been laid out in blocks and each block divided in village lots."[28] Thirteen years later a local historian speculated about the thoughts of the colony's leaders when they first saw the Zumbro Valley. "What visions of future greatness arose in their excited imaginations as they gazed at the prospect before them! . . . A city had already arisen in the center of the valley. A half score of church spires glisten in the rays of the morning sun. Mills and manufacturing establishments lined the banks of the river in the distance. A college stands on yonder hill, and the busy hum of a populous town falls upon their ears."[29] This would truly have been a New England landscape transplanted to the Middle West, but no such grand design came to fruition because of the financial panic of 1857 and the heterogeneous flood of settlers that subsequently inundated the Yankees. Zumbrota today looks little different from any other Minnesota small town.

Like all migrants, the New Englanders took with them a fondness for the foods or "fixings" and customs of home. A Connecticut native "filled a really gnawing need" in Minnesota by starting a cracker factory in 1856 because his compatriots "were not quite whole without a supply of crackers." A woman sent back to Maine to obtain seed for her cherished dandelion greens. And a new arrival commented that St. Anthony was truly a New England town; you could tell by the pies that appeared on the breakfast tables.[30]

News of the old home state was important to the settlers and several eastern papers, such as the *New England Farmer*, had subscribers in Minnesota. New England customs also appeared. One of the earliest to be transplanted was the Thanksgiving celebration, held in the mid-1850s in December rather than November. New Englanders writing home, however, said they made Thanksgiving "as much *Eastern* as our circumstances would permit."[31]

Another native institution the New Englander established in Minnesota was the township as a unit of local government. The New England town had its origins in the small land grants made by the English crown to groups of settlers. Within them the democratic town meeting provided government. Thus, while the county was the unit of regional government in most parts of the country, the belt of northern states stretching from New York to Nebraska where Yankees settled provided another, more local, level of administration.

The strength of the township vis-à-vis the county varied from state to state. In Minnesota the governing body, as in New England, was the town meeting. Held annually, it elected a board to carry on the everyday business of the township — the maintenance of roads, the administration of public assistance, and some taxation and licensing. Most of these "civil" townships were coextensive with the boundaries of the six-mile-square "congressional" townships, which as a result of the Ordinance of 1785 were primary units in the survey system. In the much greater mobility of the 20th century, the townships have lost many of their functions to the counties, but their names remain with us, and over much of rural Minnesota the town meeting halls are still in use as reminders of Yankee democracy.[32]

We have noted that the separation of Mainite communities from other New England settlements in Minnesota occurred largely as a result of the special affinity these people had for lumbering. After the Minnesota Indian land cession in 1837, by which the United States government acquired the triangle between the Mississippi and St. Croix rivers, lumbermen began to pour into the region in search of the highly valued

HOMES on 3rd Street, Marine on St. Croix, in 1972 retained the New England style brought to the village by Yankee settlers beginning in the 1840s.

white pine. The first sawmill was built at Marine on St. Croix in 1839. By 1844 the Stillwater Lumber Company had been formed, and Stillwater, the "Queen of the St. Croix," became the premier milling center. In the 1850s the quest for pine spread into the valleys of the Mississippi and the Rum, and a sawmilling industry sprang up at the splendid power source created by the Falls of St. Anthony in what is now Minneapolis.

. A chronicler of the lumbering industry in Minnesota wrote: "The lumbermen who established themselves at St. Anthony came largely from Maine. . . . as though drawn by a magnet. Maine and Minnesota had much in common. The climate, much of the topography, and the natural resources of Minnesota were like those of Maine. The men who had learned lumbering firsthand on the banks of the Penobscot, on the Androscoggin, the turbulent St. Croix, easily transplanted themselves to the business of rolling logs on the Mississippi, the Rum, or the St. Croix in Minnesota. 'I'm from Maine' was all the reference necessary to secure a job in and around St. Anthony in the lumber days."[33]

Fresh recruits to serve as sawyers, teamsters, and choppers were constantly sought by placing advertisements in Maine newspapers. That state's "stalwart sons" responded, observed a Maine congressman in 1852, "marching away by scores and hundreds to the piny woods of the Northwest."[34] By 1880 they were well concentrated in the four lumbering centers of Stillwater, Minneapolis, Anoka, and St. Cloud, where their representation was significantly higher than the average for all urban places, as shown in Table 3.6. By that time these cities contained 59.3% of all the urban Mainites in Minnesota but only 29.3% of the other urban New Englanders.

Table 3.6. First-Generation Yankees and Yorkers in Principal Minnesota Towns, 1880 (in percentages of town population)

	Mainites	Other Yankees	Yorkers	Total
Minneapolis	6.3	6.0	7.8	20.1
St. Paul	1.0	3.7	5.8	10.5
Winona	1.1	3.2	7.8	12.1
Stillwater	6.5	2.7	5.4	14.6
Red Wing	1.1	3.6	6.3	11.0
Mankato	1.0	4.1	8.5	13.6
Faribault	0.8	6.9	7.9	15.6
Rochester	0.7	5.7	13.9	20.3
Hastings	2.2	4.2	9.5	15.9
Duluth	1.2	2.5	5.8	9.5
Owatonna	1.3	6.1	14.9	22.3
St. Peter	0.6	2.2	5.7	8.5
Anoka	16.9	5.3	6.1	28.3
Lake City	1.0	6.9	13.2	21.1
New Ulm	0.1	0.8	1.1	2.0
St. Cloud	4.9	3.3	7.1	15.3
Austin	1.1	6.3	13.1	20.6
Northfield	1.7	10.8	10.6	23.1
Moorhead	1.7	3.6	4.7	10.0
Wabasha	0.3	3.8	7.6	11.7
Shakopee	0.9	3.3	3.4	7.6
Albert Lea	0.7	2.9	9.7	13.3
Brainerd	2.8	3.4	8.4	14.6
Waseca	0.4	5.3	10.9	16.6
Fergus Falls	3.2	3.7	9.7	16.6
Sauk Centre	3.4	4.6	14.1	22.1
Total Urban	2.8	4.5	8.2	15.5

Source: U.S., Manuscript Census, 1880.

That Yankee influence had made itself felt as early as the territorial period was suggested by the legislature's passage in 1852 of a temperance or "Maine law," outlawing the manufacture or sale of intoxicating liquors except for "medicinal purposes." The measure, upon being sent to the people in a referendum, passed by a vote of 853 to 662, with Stillwater giving it the largest majority of any town in Minnesota.[35]

At one point during its consideration in the legislature a facetious amendment was proposed, calling for the death penalty as punishment for violation. It was voted down, and the Maine law itself was subsequently ruled unconstitutional. Nevertheless the temperance issue remained a real one in Minnesota for many years. In early Anoka, where the influence of Mainites was substantial, it was recorded that "a vigilante group attacked the Empire Saloon operated by Daniel D. Dudley — likely a Yankee too — broke door and windows, then poured his stocks of liquor into the street. Dudley promptly reopened, and this time his place was destroyed by fire 'of undetermined origin.' It was possibly a coincidence, but the First Methodist Church of Anoka was presently destroyed by fire, the origin of which was as mysterious as that of the disaster to Dudley's dramshop."[36]

Few towns possessed the distinctly Maine flavor of Anoka. By 1880 most "Yorker towns" like Owatonna, Rochester, Lake City, and Austin were located in southeastern Minnesota amid the farmlands so heavily settled by that group (see Table 3.5). Sauk Centre, made famous by Sinclair Lewis' *Main Street*, was an island of Yorkers in the German and Norwegian sea of Stearns County. In general Yorkers and New Englanders often tended to settle together. Only in Northfield did the Yankees (excluding Mainites) outnumber the New York born. There in Rice County Yankee settlement was especially strong (note the large New England component in Faribault's population), and Northfield became the site of Carleton College, a Congregational school founded in 1866, which was one of a chain of institutions established as Yankee "beacons in the wilderness."[37]

The Yankee-Yorker population was also strong in Minneapolis. Among those drawn to the sawmilling industry were members of the Washburn family, who were also subsequently successful in diverse business ventures including, most notably, flour milling. Other New Englanders, however, were also quick to grasp the opportunities afforded by the power of the falls. The Pillsburys, who migrated from Sutton, New Hampshire, accumulated considerable wealth in a variety of enterprises before making their name in the flour-milling world.

Few families became as successful and famous as these, but the rapidly growing industry and commerce of Minneapolis attracted a host of Yankee entrepreneurs whose business acumen helped build the city. The guiding hand of the Yankee may be seen in the extensive system of Twin Cities parks conceived by Horace W. S. Cleveland, who was born in Massachusetts and first visited Minnesota in 1872. The Minneapolis aspect of his plans was implemented by Charles M. Loring, another Yankee, who became president of the newly formed board of park commissioners in 1883.[38]

Midlanders and Southerners

Compared with the flood of settlers into Minnesota from the northeastern states, the flow of Midlanders and Southerners appeared small. As we have seen, however, their migration had been proceeding more slowly than that of the Yankees, and many settlers born in the states of the Lower Midwest (Ohio, Indiana, Illinois, Iowa) probably should be included in their numbers. Except in the case of Indiana, where the Southern element was pronounced, this is difficult to do. Census data alone do not allow us to separate the Ohio born whose roots are in New England from those whose forefathers trekked along the National Road. The long residence of many of these families in the Lower Midwest also makes it difficult to distinguish Midlanders from Southerners. The 1880 census reveals only seven townships in the state which contained 50 or more persons born in Pennsylvania.[39] Nor is there any assurance that these people bore a Midland culture, for the extreme northern counties of Pennsylvania were outposts of New England. In view of these problems any discussion of Old-Stock Americans in Minnesota other than Yankees and Yorkers must center on the more easily identified Southerners with their Hoosier cousins.

Southerners, as has been pointed out, were drawn more to rural areas than to towns (see Table 3.3). They were also concentrated to a remarkable degree in only a few areas in the state. The largest of these extended from western Wright into eastern Meeker and northern McLeod counties.[40] The 1880 census showed 1,866 first- and second-generation Southerners living in this area. Of these almost two-fifths were from Virginia, a third from Kentucky, a sixth from West Virginia, and just under a tenth from North Carolina. An analysis of the birthplaces of parents and children enumerated suggested three fairly distinct populations. One had its 18th-century roots in North Carolina. Early in the 19th century these people were moving through Kentucky and crossing the Ohio River into Indiana. Of those in the 1880 census born outside Minnesota of North Carolina-born parents, only 34.9% had themselves been born in North Carolina, while 12.3% had been born in Kentucky, and 37.7% in the Lower Midwest (24% in Indiana).

Although the evidence is scanty, it seems likely that the bulk of this group was Quaker. A historian of the Society of Friends in Minnesota recorded that the first Quaker to arrive at St. Anthony in 1851 "brought his wife and family from Indiana," although he "was a native of North Carolina."[41] During the next two decades, the membership of the Minneapolis Quaker meeting increased substantially. The St. Paul *Weekly Minnesotian* of October 22, 1853, reported "Quite a procession of emigrant wagons passing through . . . from Indiana," and added that the group intended to settle in Hennepin County.

By 1870 "most of the newcomers had taken up farms in the counties west of the city. Wright County in particular experienced a Quaker immigration so large as to warrant the establishment of several meetings for worship." The migration, which continued through the 1870s, was traceable in the clusters of North Carolinians in Independence Township in western Hennepin County, then in Middleville and Albion in west-central Wright County, and finally in Collinwood Township in southeastern Meeker County. By 1905 few remained. "The Quaker farmers sold their Minnesota lands and went elsewhere. It was with them as it had been with their ancestors for a century and more." Having pushed west into Iowa, Kansas, and Minnesota, where "they were rooted . . . neither by time nor tradition, the depression of the nineties set them moving again."[42]

The second group migrated from Kentucky and Virginia. It is difficult to determine to what extent those born in the two states differed from each other, since there was reciprocal movement between these states through the Cumberland Gap. Of those whose parents were Virginia born, 14.2% were born in Kentucky, while of those whose parents were Kentucky born, 14.1% were born in Virginia. In contrast to the Carolinians, only 12.8% of those with Virginia and Kentucky parents were born in the Lower Midwest, most of them (7.8%) in Ohio.

These people appear to have moved much more directly to Minnesota than the Carolina Quakers, but few arrived before the 1860s. An editorial in the *Daily Minnesotian* (St. Paul) of November 15, 1854, reported rumors that a colony of Virginians was planning to move into Minnesota Territory with their slaves and expressed disgust at the prospect of the introduction of this institution. More charitable was the May 4, 1861, observation in the *Blue Earth City News* that "Some emigrants from Virginia passed through this place last Wednesday. Let them come — we have room enough for them all, just as long as they behave themselves."[43]

Unfortunately the inability or lack of enthusiasm for writing about themselves, which had earlier characterized this group in the Old Northwest, was carried into Minnesota, leaving us with little insight into this post-Civil War migration. A hint may be offered by the Todd County historian who described the arrival in Reynolds Township in 1866 of one Benjamin Maynard, a native of Kentucky. A soldier in the Union Army mustered out of service in Louisville, he concluded that he would not be welcome among his former neighbors, most of whom sympathized with the Southern cause. Therefore he traveled directly to Minnesota without ever going home. Several other Kentuckians joined him.[44] Mixed allegiances within communities and even families were, of course, common in the lands on both sides of the Ohio River during the Civil War. The 118% increase between 1860 and 1870 in the Southern-born population of Minnesota, compared to an increase of 65% for Yankees and Yorkers, may in part at least be attributable to war-nurtured antagonisms.

A third group of Southerners-Midlanders, who appear to have been settled in West Virginia in the early 19th century, began moving to Minnesota in the 1860s with little stopping along the way. Of those born outside Minnesota of West Virginia parents, 86.9% were born in West Virginia and only 2.6% in the Lower Midwest. The birthplace information on the remaining 10.5% reveals more interaction with Pennsylvania, Maryland, and Ohio than with the Southern states. Because of proximity to the National Road, this group may be more Midland than Southern; their location on the border between the Union and the Confederacy, coupled with the timing of their migration, once again suggests that the Civil War may have acted as a stimulus.

The concentration of at least three distinctive Southern and Midland groups in a relatively compact area raises questions which are not easy to answer. Historians of the westward migration have taught us to view the Yankee as literate, goal oriented, and well organized. He was contrasted with the Western man who could neither read nor write, had no cultural horn to blow, and lived from day to day. Yet we are faced here with a well-functioning mechanism, which by 1880 had brought almost 2,000 of these Westerners together in 16 adjacent townships in the Meeker-McLeod-Wright county triangle and located between 600 and 800 miles from home. That communication systems were operating within the individual groups is shown by the clustering of Kentuckians in Kingston and Dassel townships, for example, of West Virginians in Victor and Marysville, and of Virginians in Collinwood and Albion. Given the speed with which settlement spread through central Minnesota following the Civil War, and the competition for land among so many groups, this concentration is remarkable and demands some explanation. Unfortunately little research has been done. The Yankee has monopolized the spotlight. The story of the Western man in the settlement of Minnesota remains to be told.[45]

The Religious Contribution

One of the most lasting imprints which the Old-Stock Americans made on the cultural fabric of Minnesota was the religious diversity they supported. The variety of denominations, all of them Protestant, ranged from rigidly hierarchical to evangelical and included Episcopalians, Methodists, Presbyterians, Congregationalists, and Baptists. Each group relied heavily on eastern support during the Minnesota missionary years.[46]

The Presbyterians began to cultivate the Minnesota mission field as early as 1834, sending Connecticut natives Samuel W. and Gideon H. Pond to preach to the Dakota Indians. The Methodists and Episcopalians quickly followed suit. In 1849, when Minnesota Territory was created, these three groups plus the Congregationalists broadened their efforts to include the newly arrived Easterners.[47]

Because of doctrinal similarities between Congregationalism and Presbyterianism, these two bodies worked together under the auspices of the American Home Missionary Society. An 1860 article in the *Congregationalist* observed that "there is many a neighborhood and village in which there is no church, but where the population is waiting for the missionary, the sanctuary, the church and the ordinances after the manner of the Fathers of New England." The church in Minnesota was young and in need of "the fostering care of its New England mother, of whom it is a legitimate and hopeful child."[48]

In the territorial period, churches sprang up throughout southern Minnesota. Co-operation between Presbyterians and Congregationalists meant that the two denominations respected each other's "priority rights . . . so that neither body would enter where the other had already established a work." Nevertheless, judging by the reports sent from ministers in the field to their eastern supporters, the competition for members among the five major denominations must have been intense. Ministers such as the Reverend Edward D. Neill, a Presbyterian from Pennsylvania, noted with pride the first services held or first church built. On the other hand, the settlers themselves seem not to have been too particular about who preached to them. Often the first churches formed were union churches or Sunday schools, and the communicants accepted the ministrations of the first qualified man who rode through. New Hampshire Congregationalist Richard Hall, superintendent of missions for the American Home Missionary Society, commented in 1856, "Many have I found whose desire for a preached gospel is far stronger than their desire for any particular form of church polity."[49]

This mission to take the established religion to the pioneers and, thereby, create a New England in the West underwent subtle modifications as the numbers of non-English-speaking immigrants increased in Minnesota. Clusters of Easterners still clamored for ministers and church support from their various missionary agencies, but the rationale for assistance often hinged on being the only English-language church in the town.[50]

Organizing churches was not enough to occupy the zealous Yankees. They took notice of the number of saloons in each growing town and embarked on a crusade for temperance. Enforcement of Sabbath observance was another popular cause with them.[51]

The New Englanders' sense of mission carried them into a new field — that of ministering to Minnesota's immigrant community. All five of the major Protestant denominations were active in this enterprise. By the mid-1850s the Episcopalians had a mission for the Swedes and Norwegians in St. Paul. In 1903 they were supporting nine Swedish churches. The Presbyterians in their home missions to the foreign-language groups organized Sunday schools to teach English and preach the gospel to Scandinavians, Germans, Czechs, and Chinese. Finding missionaries was difficult, for few Presbyterians spoke any of these languages and most immigrants lacked Presbyterian training. The efforts, therefore, met with limited success.[52]

Congregational attempts at founding Scandinavian, Czech, and German churches fared little better, but this denomination enjoyed a curious success among Finns. Attracted by the free church atmosphere of the Congregationalists, Finns were attending 14 mission stations by 1926.[53]

Neither the Congregationalists nor the Presbyterians increased their numbers in Minnesota as greatly as the Methodists. It has been suggested that the latter became the largest non-Lutheran Protestant denomination in the state because they were not opposed to the "use of emotionalism, lay preaching, camp meetings, and circuit-riding ministers as a means to an end." Rather they were "unhampered by tradition and class consciousness and utilized these techniques to its best advantage." Far from stressing elegance in their services, the Methodists sought to involve themselves in the everyday lives of the common people, holding prayer meetings, sponsoring excursions, ice cream socials, and picnics.[54]

In this way, they competed quite successfully with the

Congregationalists and Presbyterians and managed to draw into their fold many Old-Stock Americans whose roots lay in other denominations. One historian observed that during the 19th century the Methodists were more adept than any other denomination in "transcending barriers of class, language, point of origin, and former religious affiliation to win adherents throughout the Middle West." The base, then, was Old Stock, but more varied than in the case of its more traditional competitors. Methodism did take hold among some non-English-speaking groups in Minnesota, notably the Swedes and Germans.

In sharp contrast to Methodism, the Episcopal church in Minnesota has been cited as a "prime example of a major religious denomination . . . which failed to succeed as a significant missionary force." As the daughter of the Church of England and the established religion in some of the southern colonies, it suffered after the Revolutionary War from its English connections, retaining the image of an "upper class church to be avoided by the anti-bureaucratic, anti-mercantilistic population of the frontier." As Bishop Henry B. Whipple of Minnesota observed in 1863, "The work has had peculiar difficulties [in part] growing out of . . . the prejudices which immigrants bring with them from their Eastern homes." To an even greater degree than the three more successful Protestant denominations, the Episcopal church failed to attract non-English-speaking immigrants. Most of the clergy, hampered by weak financial support in the mission field, expended their energy on people who had been Episcopalians before arriving in Minnesota, "leaving to others the evangelization of the unchurched."[55]

The Baptist church was the only one among the major "English" denominations whose main support in Minnesota was not in the Old-Stock American population. The Baptists showed strength only in areas such as Isanti County, where a large community of Swedish Baptists developed, or north of Albert Lea, where a Danish group settled. Early Baptist work in Minnesota, however, was certainly accomplished by Easterners, especially by people from New England. The Freewill movement, in particular, was associated with Yankee settlers, but the church as a whole never had the following among Northeasterners that the other Protestant denominations did. Nor did the Southern settlers in the state appear to bring with them this religion, which came to be dominant in the South.[56]

According to the religious census of 1906, Congregationalists were heavily concentrated in Rice County, the heart of New England settlement and the location of Carleton College. They were also well represented in the southeastern counties of Mower, Dodge, Olmsted, Winona, and Wabasha. When Congregationalism was able to make converts, they tended to be among those with some wealth and education. Because of this, and because of the large Yankee population in and around Minneapolis, Hennepin County formed another area of Congregational strength. The Twin Cities also were the location of most of the small groups of Christian Scientists, Unitarians, and Universalists. The latter's liberal views on theology had caused them to part ways with the Congregationalists. The 1906 combined membership of these three groups was 4,767 while the Congregationalists numbered 22,264.[57]

The distribution of the 27,569 Presbyterians who lived in Minnesota in 1906 reflected the phenomenon of co-operation with Congregationalists and the fact that the two groups tended to stay out of each other's way. While the Presbyterians showed some strength in the heavily Yankee-Yorker southeast, it was relatively not as great as that of the Congregationalists. The largest concentrations were instead in the southwestern counties of Watonwan, Nobles, Lyon, and Pipestone, areas of considerable Midland and Yorker as well as Scottish and Welsh settlement. Presbyterian strength in Blue Earth County also rested to some degree upon the presence of a large Welsh community, while in Redwood County a few settlements of Scottish Canadians explained their importance. Like the Congregationalists, the Presbyterians were well represented among the better-educated middle and upper classes of the Twin Cities. A minister commented that the First Presbyterian Church in St. Paul was "highly favored. . . . the very cream of the community: the piety, the zeal, the intelligence, the wealth and the controling [sic] social element."[58]

The distribution of the 47,637 Methodists in the state in 1906 reflected the group's wide appeal. They were most numerous among the Yorkers of Olmsted and Dodge counties, well represented in the southwest, in Wright County with its Southern (and German) population, and across northern Minnesota. Their strength in outstate areas gave them a substantial edge over the Congregationalists and Presbyterians in almost all the major towns. Even in the Twin Cities they outnumbered these two rivals, though their *relative* strength there was nowhere near as great (24% as opposed to 38.5% to 44.4% for the others).

The Episcopal church in Minnesota in 1906 had 18,763 members distributed very unevenly over the state. As with the Congregationalists their stronghold lay in Rice County, largely because a seminary and cathedral, seat of the Episcopal bishop, were located at Faribault. They extended into Goodhue County. But in no other part of outstate Minnesota was the denomination particularly well represented among Old-Stock Americans.

The social and economic biases in its membership also gave the Episcopal church considerable strength in the Twin Cities. Its ranks were swelled by British and Canadian immigrants and by Episcopalians who originally settled in other parts of the state and then were among the first to move to the metropolitan area. Indeed this depletion of population probably was a serious problem for many outstate parishes whose records often showed a gradually declining membership necessitating first the sharing of a priest with other parishes and then perhaps the complete extinction of the congregation.[59]

An examination of the 1906 religious census also shows that in none of the four counties of large Southern settlement were Baptists well represented. Lacking a solid base of "natural" members, the denomination was in a poor position to recruit new people, and divisiveness within it may also have hindered missionary activity. By 1906 there were

A GROUP of Hennepin County Territorial Pioneers awaited transportation to Fort Snelling for a 1905 excursion.

24,309 Baptists in Minnesota, many of foreign birth or parentage. As was the case with all Protestant groups except the Methodists, they were disproportionately well represented in the Twin Cities.

Toward the end of the 19th century, the Old-Stock Americans made their contribution to the rapidly increasing number of special interest organizations. Minneapolitans who had migrated from eastern states gathered to reminisce in such groups as the New England Society, the Sons of Maine, or the Vermont or Massachusetts or New York society. St. Paulites formed the Ohio Society and the Keystone League "composed exclusively of persons born in Pennsylvania." Many of these same people found the centenary of the signing of the Declaration of Independence a profoundly moving occasion, a sentiment, they felt, shared by too few of their fellow citizens. As great numbers of Old-Stock Americans were direct descendants of Revolutionary War soldiers, these sons and daughters believed it their duty to teach all Americans about their mutual heritage. In 1892 chapters of the Sons of the American Revolution and the Daughters of the American Revolution were organized in the Twin Cities. Other groups such as the Patriotic Order of the Sons of America, the Society of Colonial Wars, the Native Sons and Daughters of America, and the Society of Colonial Dames followed.[60]

In 1895 the Minnesota Society of the Sons of the American Revolution issued a yearbook which contained 378 biographical sketches of the members. Analysis of this material provides an interesting profile of a patriotic organization's supporters. Of the total, three-fourths (74.9%) lived in the Twin Cities, three-fifths (61.4%) in St. Paul, almost one-fifth (17.4%) in other Minnesota towns, and the balance elsewhere in the United States. The members' occupations, with two exceptions, fell into the white-collar category. The greatest number were in the legal profession — 77 lawyers and 9 judges. The next three largest groups were merchants (25), realtors (25), and physicians (21). Also included were 13 journalists, 6 librarians, 2 United States senators, one congressman, and the speaker of the Minnesota House of Representatives.[61]

Birthplace information echoed the census data. About one-fourth (98) were natives of New England (ranging from 13 from Connecticut to 28 from New Hampshire); 113 migrated from the Middle Atlantic states (76 from New York, 30 from Pennsylvania); 67 moved from the Old Northwest (30 from Ohio); 18 were Southerners, and 62 were Minnesota born.

The New England origins of this sample were even more obvious when the places of residence of their ancestors were tallied. A whopping 257 (68%) were from New England; Massachusetts led with 94, followed closely by Connecticut with 82, New Hampshire with 42, Rhode Island with 17, Vermont with 13, and Maine with 9. The Middle Atlantic states had one-fourth; Pennsylvania led with 41, followed by New York with 30. Virginia accounted for all but one of the Southerners.

The family histories of these people illustrated the east-to-west migration pattern. Many Revolutionary War veterans died at locations inland from their birthplaces. Their sons and grandsons lived farther west — many of them in upstate New York. The Minnesota sons, although their families may have been in North America for several generations, had family traditions of moving on to find a better place to live.

The Old-Stock Americans have made important contributions, both religious and secular, to the settlement and culture history of Minnesota. It is easy to take them for granted because they are the contributions of Americans to another part of America. In this age of ethnic awakening there is little celebration of the Yankee or Yorker. Few Minnesotans descended from the original Old-Stock settlers would today think of themselves as New Englanders or Southerners in the way that increasing numbers are remembering their Swedish, German, or Norwegian roots. If ethnicity is the awareness of a cultural identity different from that of the nation as a whole, the Old-Stock Americans clearly form no ethnic group. This is not, however, to deny the distinctiveness of their cultures among the many which have been carried to Minnesota since the early days of settlement.

Reference notes

[1] To some extent this was true also of the Canadians in Minnesota, but there were important differences between them and the Old-Stock Americans. For this reason French and British Canadians are dealt with elsewhere in this volume. See Chapters 2, 6.

[2] A case could be made for a Yankee ethnic literature, produced by people whose roots lay in the New England colonies. However, although they were keenly aware of their distinctive culture, the New Englanders never thought of themselves as a minority group. Their expression of attitudes and values is better thought of as a plan for the new nation than as an attempt to preserve one culture among many. See below.

[3] For a discussion of Old-Stock Americans' ideas, see Perry Miller, *The New England Mind: The Seventeenth Century* (New York, 1939).

[4] The following discussion of early culture cores is based largely upon the argument in Robert D. Mitchell, "The formation of early American cultural regions: an interpretation," in James R. Gibson, ed., *European Settlement and Development in North America: Essays on geographical change in honour and memory of Andrew Hill Clark*, 66–90 (Toronto, 1978).

[5] Charles I, king of England, was executed in 1649; the Puritans then established their own governments, the Commonwealth and Protectorate.

[6] The Genesee country was the core of the Yorker culture. People from downstate New York were not known as Yorkers.

[7] Here and below, see Stewart H. Holbrook, *The Yankee Exodus: An Account of Migration from New England*, 4, 10 (New York, 1950); Richard Lyle Power, "Planting Corn Belt Culture: The Impress of the Upland Southerner and Yankee in the Old Northwest," in Indiana Historical Society, *Publications*, 17:1–56, 92–126 (Indianapolis, 1953). The Northwest Territory, created by the Congressional Ordinance of 1787, comprised the present states of Ohio, Indiana, Michigan, Illinois, and Wisconsin, as well as that part of Minnesota east of the Mississippi River.

[8] Constance M. Rourke, *Trumpets of Jubilee*, 122 (New York, 1927).

[9] John F. Stover, *Iron Road to the West: American Railroads in the 1850s*, 164–167 (New York, 1978); Louis C. Hunter, *Steamboats on the Western Rivers: An Economic and Technological History*, 45, 181–189 (Cambridge, Mass., 1949).

[10] George H. Miller, *Railroads and the Granger Laws*, 4, 7 (Madison, 1971).

[11] Holbrook, *Yankee Exodus*, 108.

[12] The continuation of Southern immigration into the 20th century to some degree reflects the later northward movement of Blacks. See Chapter 4.

[13] This view was advanced avidly by James M. Goodhue, a New England-born journalist who published the *Minnesota Pioneer* in St. Paul between 1849 and his death in 1852. Theodore C. Blegen, *Minnesota: A History of the State*, 184, 203 (Minneapolis, 1963); Mary

W. Berthel, *Horns of Thunder: The Life and Times of James M. Goodhue* (St. Paul, 1948).

[14] Carlton C. Qualey, "Some National Groups in Minnesota," in *Minnesota History*, 31:20 (March, 1950).

[15] Holbrook, *Yankee Exodus*, 185. Of the Eastern stock, three were New York natives (Davis, Hubbard, Merriam), three Pennsylvanians (Ramsey, Miller, McGill), two New Hampshiremen (Pillsbury, Clough), and one each for Michigan (Sibley), Ohio (Swift), Illinois (Van Sant), Connecticut (Austin), Massachusetts (Hammond), and Missouri (Marshall); *Gopher Historian*, Fall, 1964, p. 13.

[16] Holbrook, *Yankee Exodus*, Chapters 2 and 3.

[17] William W. Folwell, *A History of Minnesota*, 1:353–356 (Reprint ed., St. Paul, 1956); Warren Upham, *Minnesota Geographic Names*, 28, 59, 172, 240, 302, 318, 344, 386, 387, 525, 533, 571, 583 (Reprint ed., St. Paul, 1969).

[18] The story of this political-cultural confrontation is told in William Anderson and Albert J. Lobb, *A History of the Constitution of Minnesota, with the First Verified Text*, 44–68 (Minneapolis, 1921); Folwell, *Minnesota*, 1:352, 388–421.

[19] Although born in Vermont, Rice had gone to the Minnesota country as a fur trader 10 years before the creation of the territory and was a thoroughly "Western" man.

[20] MHS has several collections containing such letters; see, for example, a young Connecticut man writing to a woman in his home town, "All the settlers there [*Cannon Falls*] are New Englanders. The country about there is splendid, the soil almost fabulously rich, and the whole beauties must be seen to be appreciated." David Humphrey to Mrs. Seth King, July, 1855, in David W. Humphrey Papers, MHS. Undated newspaper clipping, Immigration file, Governors — Main Series, Austin, 1870, Governors files, Minnesota State Archives, MHS; Soldiers Colonies, in Letters Received, Land Dept., Northern Pacific Railway Papers, MHS. One colony established was at Detroit Lakes.

[21] The early perceptions of Minnesota's climate are discussed in Ralph H. Brown, "Fact and Fancy in Early Accounts of Minnesota's Climate," and Helen B. Clapesattle, "When Minnesota Was Florida's Rival," both in *Minnesota History*, 17:243–261 (September, 1936), 35:214–221 (March, 1957).

[22] Clapesattle, in *Minnesota History*, 35:221.

[23] *Independent* (New York City), November 20, 1856, and *New England Puritan* (Boston), September 12, 1856, typed copies in MHS; Winifred D. W. Bolin, "Harriet E. Bishop: Moralist and Reformer," in Barbara Stuhler and Gretchen Kreuter, eds., *Women of Minnesota: Selected Biographical Essays*, 7, 8 (St. Paul, 1977). The board also sent teachers who established the first schools in Stillwater (1848) and St. Anthony (1849); Willard E. Rosenfelt, *Washington: A History of the Minnesota County*, 196 (Stillwater, 1977).

[24] Robert Watson, *Notes on the Early Settlement of Cottage Grove and Vicinity, Washington Co., Minn.*, [3] (Northfield, 1924). The farm belonged to Maine native Joseph Haskell.

[25] Theodore E. Potter, "Captain Potter's Recollections of Minnesota Experiences," in *Minnesota History*, 1:432 (November, 1916).

[26] Alvin H. Wilcox, *A Pioneer History of Becker County, Minnesota*, 315–371 (St. Paul, 1907); Franklyn Curtiss-Wedge, *The History of Winona County, Minnesota*, 149–176 (Chicago, 1913); and the following articles in *Minnesota History*: Philip D. Jordan, "The Hutchinson Family in the Story of American Music," 22:113 (June, 1941); Donald B. Marti, "The Puritan Tradition in a 'New England of the West'," 40:10 (Spring, 1966); and Charles W. Nichols, "Henry Martyn Nichols and the Northampton Colony," 19:132–147 (June, 1938); "The Northampton Colony and Chanhassen," 20:140 (June, 1939); "New Light on the Northampton Colony," 22:169–173 (June, 1941).

[27] Charles W. Nichols, historian of the colony and grandson of one of the founders, found no corroboration for this story; *Minnesota History*, 22:171.

[28] For town plat maps, see A. T. Andreas, *An Illustrated Historical Atlas of the State of Minnesota* (Reprint ed., Evansville, Ind., 1976).

[29] W. H. Mitchell, *Geographical and Statistical Sketch of the Past and Present of Goodhue County*, 147 (Minneapolis, 1869). A student of the Zumbrota colony has examined the original plat of the town and tried to ascertain whether it bore close resemblance to the plat of Lowell, Massachusetts, a planned industrial community from which several leading members of the company emigrated. Her conclusion was that a certain similarity was apparent, but its degree was dependent on the suggestibility of the observer. Joan Seidl, "Paper," n.p., March 12, 1978, copy in MEHP Papers.

[30] Holbrook, *Yankee Exodus*, 180; Lucy L. W. Morris, ed., *Old Rail Fence Corners*, 37, 186 (Reprint ed., St. Paul, 1976).

[31] Letters to the editor, *New England Farmer*, March, 1858, typed copy in MHS; Charles W. Nichols, "Henry M. Nichols and Frontier Minnesota," in *Minnesota History*, 19:248 (September, 1938); *Puritan Recorder* (Boston), January 15, 1857, typed copy in MHS. The *Puritan Recorder*, March 12, 1857, carried a notice of a Minnesota celebration of the Pilgrims' Plymouth landing. The toast drunk after dinner was to "Our Puritan Ancestors: They planted the religious institutions of New England; may we transplant them to the New England of the West."

[32] For the Ordinance of 1785, see Hildegard B. Johnson, *Order Upon The Land: The U.S. Rectangular Land Survey and the Upper Mississippi Country*, 40–49 (New York, 1976). This ordinance provided for surveying public lands and dividing them into townships of six square miles.

[33] Agnes M. Larson, *History of the White Pine Industry in Minnesota*, 15, 18, 32–37 (Minneapolis, 1949).

[34] Larson, *White Pine Industry*, 74; Theodore C. Blegen, "Sources for St. Croix Valley History," in *Minnesota History*, 17:393 (December, 1936). See also Richard Hall and Family Papers, in MHS.

[35] Theodore C. Blegen, "The Day of the Pioneer," in *Minnesota History*, 14:138 (June, 1933); Larson, *White Pine Industry*, 19.

[36] Holbrook, *Yankee Exodus*, 173. See also Nichols, in *Minnesota History*, 19:265–267.

[37] Holbrook, *Yankee Exodus*, 43; Leal A. Headley and Merrill E. Jarchow, *Carleton: The First Century*, 1–8 (Northfield, 1966). The other colleges in the Yankee chain were Berea (Ky.), Hillsdale (Mich.), Ripon (Wis.), and Grinnell and Tabor (Ia.). Hamline University, founded by Methodists in 1854 at Red Wing, was Minnesota's first college. Merrill E. Jarchow, *Private Liberal Arts Colleges in Minnesota: Their History and Contributions*, 7–12 (St. Paul, 1973).

[38] Blegen, *Minnesota*, 498. Loring also was an early president of Lakewood Cemetery Assn. The organization had several Yankees on its executive committee, was in the mainstream of the rural cemetery movement, and hired C. W. Folsom, superintendent of Mt. Auburn Cemetery, Boston, to draw up the plans. *Rules and Regulations of the Lakewood Cemetery Association* (Minneapolis, 1875) and *Lakewood Cemetery Association, Minneapolis, Minnesota* (Minneapolis, 1911). On the rural cemetery movement, see Naomi R. Remes, "The Rural Cemetery," in *Nineteenth Century*, 52–55 (Winter, 1979).

[39] The seven townships were New Haven (Olmsted County), Mt. Pleasant and Gillford (Wabasha), Shell Rock (Freeborn), Blakeley (Scott), and Woodland and Corinna (Wright).

[40] Southerners also formed small concentrations in the townships of Ward, Hartford, and Eagle Valley (Todd County), Sharon and Waterville (Le Sueur), and Le Ray (Blue Earth).

[41] Thomas E. Drake, "Quakers in Minnesota," in *Minnesota History*, 18:249 (September, 1937). The first Quaker's name was William W. Wales.

[42] Drake, in *Minnesota History*, 18:254, 258; Minnesota Manuscript Census Schedules, 1905, rolls 119–128, 135, 164, microfilm in MHS.

[43] *Blue Earth City News* quoted in *St. Paul Daily Press*, May 15, 1861.

[44] Clara K. Fuller, *History of Morrison and Todd Counties, Minnesota: Their Peoples, Industries and Institutions*, 1:225 (Indianapolis, 1915); Todd County Bicentennial Committee, *Todd County Histories*, 95 ([Long Prairie], 1976).

[45] Another aspect of the story awaiting attention is the matter of remigration from Minnesota to the eastern states. A historian of the Detroit Lakes colony commented that "a majority of them returned at an early date to their old homes in New England"; Wilcox, *Becker County*, 327. The Kinkeads, founders of Alexandria (Douglas County), had gone back to their former home in Delaware by the mid-1860s; Jeanette Eckman, ed., *The Kinkeads of Delaware as Pioneers in Minnesota, 1856–1868* (Wilmington, 1949).

[46] Some of the Old-Stock Americans were probably Catholic, but their numbers are unknown.

[47] Marti, in *Minnesota History*, 40:1–11; Theodore C. Blegen, "The Pond Brothers," in *Minnesota History*, 15:273–281 (September, 1934); Merrill E. Jarchow, "The Social and Cultural Aspects of the Methodist Church in Pioneer Minnesota," master's thesis, University of Minnesota, 1933; George C. Tanner, "Early Episcopal Churches and Missions in Minnesota," in *Minnesota Historical Collections*, 10:203–231 (St. Paul, 1905).

[48] Isaac P. Langworthy, "Congregationalism in the Northwest," in *Congregationalist* (Boston), October 5, 1860, p. 157. See also Hall Papers. Many Congregational churches testify to their New England heritage by having "Plymouth," "Mayflower," or "Pilgrim" as part of the church name or of a group within the church.

[49] Maurice D. Edwards, *History of the Synod of Minnesota Presbyterian Church U.S.A.*, 103 (St. Paul, 1927); Marti, in *Minnesota History*, 40:4–11; Richard Hall to American Home Missionary Society, July 8, 1856, in Hall Papers.

[50] One church historian stated that rural Congregational churches managed to remain open because they offered the only English-language services in the town; he cited the examples of Ellsworth (Nobles County), Lyle (Mower), and Glenwood (Pope). Edgar L. Heermance, "List of Churches founded from 1881 to 1890," in Warren Upham Papers, MHS.

[51] Bolin, in Stuhler and Kreuter, eds., *Women of Minnesota*, 12; Letter to the Editor, *Boston Recorder*, November 15, 1860; Edwards, *Minnesota Presbyterian Church*, 286.

[52] Tanner, in *Minnesota Historical Collections*, 10:227; George Tanner, *Fifty Years of Church Work in the Diocese of Minnesota, 1857–1907*, 379, 503 (St. Paul, 1909); Edwards, *Minnesota Presbyterian Church*, 106, 168, 179, 226, 232, 248. For Chinese in Presbyterian churches, see Chapter 28.

[53] George J. Eisenach, *A History of the German Congregational Churches in the United States*, 18, 21, 57, 253 (Yankton, S. Dak., 1938); Archibald Hadden, *Congregationalism in Minnesota, 1851–1891*, 14 (Minneapolis, 1891); Arvel M. Steece, "A Century of Minnesota Congregationalism," 336–338, Ph.D. thesis, Harvard University, 1957.

[54] Here and below, see Neil A. Markus, "Areal Patterns of Religious Denominationalism in Minnesota, 1950," 142–144, master's thesis, University of Minnesota, 1961.

[55] Markus, "Areal Patterns," 122; Tanner, *Fifty Years of Church Work*, 207; Edward R. Hardy, Jr., "Kemper's Missionary Episcopate: 1835–1859," in Protestant Episcopal Church, *Historical Magazine*, 4:217 (September, 1935). The unusually large number of

Episcopalians in Meeker County is related to the success the church had there in bringing Swedes into the fold. See Chapter 12.

[56] Markus, "Areal Patterns," 149, 152–154.

[57] Here and four paragraphs below, see U.S. Census Bureau, *Special Reports, Religious Bodies: 1906*, 1:327–329.

[58] "Early presbyterianism In the Twin Cities, St. Paul & Minneapolis," 2, undated sermon, in John G. Riheldaffer and Family Papers, MHS.

[59] Protestant Episcopal Church, Diocese of Minnesota, Papers, MHS.

[60] For dates and officers of these societies, see *Minneapolis City Directory, 1867–1912*; *St. Paul City Directory, 1856–1932*.

[61] Here and three paragraphs below, see William H. Grant, comp., *Minnesota Society, Sons of the American Revolution, Year Book, 1889–1895*, 182–499 (St. Paul, 1895).

CHAPTER 4

The Blacks

David Vassar Taylor

AFRICAN AMERICANS, often referred to as Black Americans, make up the largest racial minority in the United States. According to the 1970 census they numbered more than 22,500,000 or 11.1% of the national population.[1] In the past, African Americans, for largely political reasons, were defined as persons with any visible African physical traits regardless of the degree of racial mixture. Although the definition is essentially the same today, Black Americans are here understood to be persons having ancestors from any of the ethnic or racial groups of Black Africa or descendants of those groups found in the western hemisphere.

Black Americans are not only a racial but also an ethnically distinct group within American society, having well-defined cultural characteristics that reflect a synthesis of African and European heritages. Although history has exhibited ambivalence toward their integration into the main stream, as a people they have contributed immeasurably to the physical expansion, economic development, and cultural attainments of the United States. Their urban communities have achieved a high degree of cohesion through well-developed institutions such as Black churches, newspapers, fraternal, social, and political organizations.

In 1970 a total of 34,868 Black Americans were residents of Minnesota, or just under 1% of the state's population. This proportion has remained more or less constant for 100 years. Black Americans constitute relatively small numbers in 82 of the state's 87 counties; however, 97.3% of them reside in urban areas — 19,005 (54.5%) in Minneapolis, 10,930 (31.3%) in St. Paul, and 857 (2.5%) in Duluth (see Table 4.1).

Black Americans are the only racial or national group almost wholly brought involuntarily to North America as slave labor for the emerging agrarian economy. During the entire period of the Atlantic slave trade from 1510 to the 1880s, approximately 8,000,000 to 10,500,000 Africans were imported into South America, the islands of the Caribbean, and the North American continent. It has been estimated that at least 348,000 slaves were brought from the west coast of Africa to British North America from 1619 to 1808. Their importation into the United States was legally prohibited in 1808, but another 51,000 are thought to have been smuggled into the southern states between 1808 and the outbreak of the Civil War. In 1861 the country had about 4,000,000 Black Americans. In the years following the Civil War many of them migrated from the South in search of greater economic opportunities and political freedom. In the succeeding century such migrations ebbed and flowed to industrial cities of the Northeast, Midwest, and West.[2]

Pioneers and Beginnings

Although Minnesota was less affected by these migrations than Michigan and Illinois, for example, Black people have long been present there. The earliest records of them in what is now Minnesota date from the closing years of the 18th century when the British still effectively controlled the fur trade of the region. The best known of the free Black traders of that era are Pierre Bonga (or Bungo) and his son George, who was born near the site of Duluth about 1802. Bungo Township and Bungo Brook in Cass County were named for this family. More than 100 of their descendants lived in the Leech Lake region as late as 1900.[3]

The next small group of Black people to reach Minnesota were slaves owned by officers stationed at Fort Snelling after 1820 and by southern families who vacationed in Minnesota during the summer months in the 1850s and 1860s. History has accorded varying degrees of attention to five of them — Rachael, a slave who spent the years 1831–34 at various army posts in Minnesota and Wisconsin and sued for her freedom before the Missouri Supreme Court in 1835; Dred Scott and his wife Harriet, whose two-year residence at Fort Snelling from 1836 to 1838 led to a celebrated United States Supreme Court decision in 1857; Eliza Winston, who accompanied her vacationing master to the state in 1860 and obtained her freedom there with the help of local abolitionists; and James Thompson, who arrived at Fort Snelling as a slave in 1827 and remained to become the only Black member of the St. Paul Old Settlers Association.[4]

After Minnesota was officially organized as a territory in 1849, its first census recorded 40 free persons of African descent, 30 of whom lived in St. Paul. The community there consisted of seven families, having six male heads of households employed as barbers and cooks; 15 other persons lived outside of family groups. Four of the other 10 Blacks resided in Washington County, two each at Fort Snelling and Sauk Rapids, and one in what was then called Wabashaw County. A woman, Maria Haynes, was the only Black resident recorded in St. Anthony (now Minneapolis). Eleven states

Table 4.1. Blacks in Minnesota by County and Major Urban Areas, 1860–1970, and Selectively for 1980

County	1860	1870	1880	1910	1930	1970	1980
Aitkin			3	46	11	9	
Anoka		15	21	41	25	178	
Becker			1	4	1	3	
Beltrami				11	14	25	
Benton		1		2		2	
Big Stone				3	1	2	
Blue Earth	1	20	25	8	6	84	
Brown			4	2	3	5	
Carlton						8	
Carver		1	2	4	1	7	
Cass	13	12		36	16	17	
Chippewa			2	5	1		
Chisago	12	1	1	4	1	18	
Clay			8	15	20	73	
Clearwater					1	1	
Cook					15	14	
Cottonwood				2	5	5	
Crow Wing			2	2	4	33	
Dakota	39	46	38	40	23	182	
Dodge		5	11	27	3	7	
Douglas				5	10	4	
Faribault		2	3	9	5	1	
Fillmore		17	12	11		8	
Freeborn		7	9	7	15	67	
Goodhue	6	22	54	45	31	48	
Grant					1	2	
Hennepin	13	190	476	2,646	4,257	20,044	
Minneapolis			144	2,592	4,176	19,005	28,433
Houston		10	12	1	1	7	
Hubbard				15	1	1	
Isanti				4	2	49	
Itasca	1			12	4	7	
Jackson		2		2	2		
Kanabec						8	
Kandiyohi			1	5	6	15	
Kittson			1	2	10	2	
Koochiching				10	15	6	
Lac qui Parle				5		1	
Lake					3	26	
Lake of the Woods						19	
Le Sueur	20	5	32	23	6	4	
Lincoln				1			
Lyon			2	5		46	
McLeod			1	12	3	2	
Mahnomen	1					4	
Marshall			1	3		1	
Martin				4	4	8	
Meeker		2	11	3	1	8	
Mille Lacs	2	2		6	4	9	
Morrison	1			6	1	5	
Mower	1		12	21	11	19	
Murray				1	1	12	
Nicollet	1	4	1	11	42	83	
Nobles					5	62	
Norman				2		1	
Olmsted		27	13	33	38	222	
Otter Tail			6	52	82	25	
Pennington				7	3	2	
Pine	16	2	2	11	16	145	
Pipestone			1	1		2	
Polk			59	27	6	15	
Pope		1		3	2	2	
Ramsey	70	198	491	3,154	4,026	11,525	
St. Paul				3,144	3,981	10,930	13,305
Red Lake					4		
Redwood		1		11	15	3	
Renville				1	3	6	
Rice	11	19	41	21	15	107	
Rock				3	7		
Roseau				2	1	3	
St. Louis		22	13	439	453	1,000	
Duluth				410	416	857	768
Scott		8	8	1	4	15	
Sherburne				9	31	114	
Sibley		1		6		3	
Stearns	3	5	2	14	23	125	
Steele		13	32	20	19	9	
Stevens		3	2			5	
Swift			1		5	6	
Todd		1		2	2	2	
Traverse			1	2		1	
Wabasha	14	23	23	11	7	6	
Wadena		1		1		24	
Waseca	1	2	5	5	9	1	
Washington	7	21	43	71	64	139	
Watonwan			3	1	5	1	
Wilkin			1	3	3	5	
Winona	19	50	68	22	7	32	
Wright	7		3	18	2	19	
Yellow Medicine				1	1	2	
Total	259	759	1,564	7,084	9,445	34,868	53,342

Source: U.S. Census, 1860–80, 1910, 1930, 1970; Minnesota Analysis and Planning System (MAPS), "Final Report on the 1980 Federal Census," telephone information, April 10, 1981.

were given as places of birth, with Virginia and Kentucky listed most frequently. According to the census, 95.4% of the Black adults were literate.[5]

During the 1850s free Blacks and fugitive slaves continued to migrate to Minnesota, where they engaged the attention of the territorial legislature. A St. Paul newspaper characterized the early arrivals as industrious and "attentive to their business," but some legislators feared that the Mississippi River was becoming a conduit for those expelled or fleeing from the South, that Black people would compete for jobs customarily held by unskilled whites, or that they would become paupers and wards of the territory. As early as 1849 they were barred from voting in congressional, territorial, county, and precinct elections, and this prohibition was extended to village elections in 1851 and to town meetings in 1853. The following year a bill, modeled on similar legislation in Ohio, would have required the posting of a personal bond of $300 to $500 as a guarantee of good behavior for every Black person intent upon becoming a permanent resident. The bill was defeated.[6]

By the time Minnesota accumulated enough people to apply for statehood in 1857, the national issue of slavery and the sociopolitical divisiveness it engendered found a refrain in the debates of the Minnesota constitutional convention. Convened in the summer of 1857, the body soon deadlocked over the issue of nonwhite suffrage which was strongly advocated by a vocal group of Republicans. Unable to muster sufficient support, the Republicans compromised by restricting suffrage to white males in exchange for Democratic support of a simpler method by which the constitution could be amended in the future.[7]

In 1860 bills were proposed in the Minnesota legislature to grant Black suffrage, protect persons claimed as fugitive slaves, and prohibit the confinement of fugitives in the jails of the state. These measures failed to pass, and the House of Representatives defeated one which would have prevented the migration of free Blacks and mulattoes to Minnesota and required the registration of those already in residence. Further attempts to allow nonwhites to vote were made in 1865 and 1867. Two state-wide referendums seeking to amend the constitution on this matter failed — that in 1865 by 2,513 votes and that in 1867 by 1,298 votes. By 1868,

ROBERT T. HICKMAN, cofounder and first minister of St. Paul's Pilgrim Baptist Church.

MEMBERS of the Minnesota Federation of Afro-American Women's Clubs posed on the steps of Pilgrim Baptist Church, St. Paul, about 1907.

however, attitudes and political loyalties had shifted sufficiently to carry the issue by 9,372 votes. Thus on March 6, 1868, the legislature amended the state constitution by granting the franchise to male Blacks, "civilized" Indians, and mixed-bloods over the age of 21. By so doing, Minnesota became one of the few states to enfranchise its Black citizens voluntarily — two years before adoption of the 15th Amendment to the United States Constitution permitted them to vote nationally. In 1869 the legislature also abolished segregation in the Minnesota public schools, a practice that had existed in St. Paul for over 10 years.[8]

The early legislators' fears concerning Black migration to the river towns of Minnesota were not unfounded. The state's Black population nearly tripled from 259 in 1860 to 759 in 1870. Doubtlessly included in the latter figure were numbers of former slaves who accompanied Minnesota soldiers returning home from the conflict. It should be noted, too, that although the legislature passed a law in 1858 establishing a state militia from which Black citizens were excluded, 104 Black men from Minnesota served in the Union forces during the Civil War.[9]

Other Black migrants reached the state as the result of a severe labor shortage engendered by repeated calls for volunteers during the war. In 1962 the St. Paul and Galena Packet Company sent agents to St. Louis to hire Blacks as deck hands. The St. Paul Daily Press of May 16, 1863, suggested that as many as 5,000 were needed to supply the region with dependable labor. During the same year, Henry H. Sibley, commanding the state's effort to put down the rebellious Dakota Indians, asked for and received from St. Louis teamsters, mules, and "contraband" laborers to be employed by the military at Fort Snelling. When the steamboat "Northerner" approached St. Paul on May 5, 1863, laden with the laborers Sibley had requested, it had in tow a crudely constructed raft containing an additional 76 Black

men, women, and children. The raft and its occupants had been found adrift on the Mississippi near Jefferson, Missouri, where the "Northerner" collected it and towed it upstream. The people on board the raft were led by Robert Thomas Hickman, a slave preacher.[10]

Another large contingent of "contrabands" reached St. Paul on May 15, 1863, aboard the steamboat "Davenport." Numbering 218 in all, this group included about 100 women and children. They had been sent north under the protective custody of Chaplain J. D. White, and they were escorted by Company C of the 37th Iowa Regiment. Both groups were harassed by Irish dock workers, until the boats departed for Fort Snelling. A portion of these people settled near the fort, where they found employment as teamsters and laborers. Some returned to St. Paul under the leadership of Robert Hickman.

The Twin Cities

In general, Black migrants probably moved to Minnesota for much the same economic reasons European immigrants did: jobs and opportunities in urban areas and an abundance of land to homestead. They also followed many of the same migratory routes as the Europeans, with a significant number of Blacks immigrating from Canada. St. Paul quickly developed an indigenous community that was to be the center of Black social and cultural activity in the state well into the 20th century. Not until after 1910 was St. Paul's hegemony slowly eclipsed by the growth of a Minneapolis enclave. Later St. Paul, Minneapolis, and Duluth exerted a strong magnetic pull on Black youths in rural areas. As the children of homesteaders began to come of age, they sought the excitement of the cities. As a result the state's rural Black population has remained marginal (while over 90% lived in the urban areas).[11]

It was the settlers of St. Anthony who formed the first

formal Black religious organization in Minnesota. The village of St. Anthony, settled in 1849, was the earliest municipal unit in what later became the city of Minneapolis, with which it was consolidated in 1872. There sometime in 1857 eight families of free Blacks from Missouri, Arkansas, and Illinois are said to have settled near the Falls of St. Anthony. Because houses were in short supply, they stayed in the basement of a hotel known as the Winslow House and at Fort Snelling until shelters could be erected. It seems probable that the founding members of St. James African Methodist Episcopal Church of St. Anthony were among this group.[12]

In any case, it is known that a few Black people, wanting to worship as Methodists, met in the home of Paul Brown on 4th Avenue Southeast in 1860. They continued to meet in various St. Anthony homes until 1863, by which time their numbers had doubtless been augmented by new arrivals. Two years later the combined Black population of St. Anthony and Minneapolis totaled 78 persons, 50 of whom lived in St. Anthony. In 1863 some of them formally organized the St. James African Methodist Episcopal Church, but not until 1869 was the congregation sufficiently affluent to take possession of a house of worship formerly occupied by a white congregation at 6th Avenue Southeast and 2nd Street.[13]

Meanwhile in St. Paul at least two Black churches — Pilgrim Baptist and St. Mark's Episcopal — had been founded, and one of them, led by Robert Hickman, had erected a building in which to worship. Calling themselves "pilgrims," Hickman's little band met as a religious prayer group, first in the home of Mrs. Caroline Nelson on 5th Street and then in other residences until November, 1863, when they succeeded in renting the lodge room of the Good Templars, a temperance society that met in Concert Hall on 3rd Street. Unable to incorporate as a formal congregation without an ordained minister, and wanting closer bonds with the existing white Baptist community, Hickman and Thomas Scott sought and received mission status from the First Baptist Church of St. Paul in January, 1864.

Between 1864 and 1866 the Black parishioners continued to worship separately under Hickman's direction. Lacking resources, they successfully petitioned the trustees of the First Baptist Church in 1866 to intercede and purchase in trust for them a lot located at 13th and Cedar streets upon which they wanted to construct a house of worship. On November 15, 1866, the Pilgrim Baptist Church was formally organized. Its first structure was built in 1870, probably of used lumber salvaged from the demolition of the old First Baptist Church in St. Anthony. In 1877 Hickman was ordained, and three years later he at last became the congregation's official pastor.[14]

Four other St. Paul religious groups came into existence before 1895; two were Episcopal, a third was Methodist, and the fourth was Catholic. A short-lived Episcopal congregation of St. Mark's was organized in 1867 and disbanded about 1870 or 1871; not until 1894 was the more stable St. Philip's Episcopal Church formed. St. James African Methodist Church of St. Paul, which may have existed as a prayer group as early as 1870, disbanded about 1876, reorganized in 1878, and was able to purchase a permanent home in 1881. The last of the group — St. Peter Claver Catholic Church — began in an unstructured way in 1889. With the help of Archbishop John Ireland, a new building was erected for the segregated congregation at Aurora and Farrington avenues in 1892.[15]

From the 1860s until nearly the end of the century these churches served a Black population distributed throughout St. Paul's five wards, but most heavily concentrated in the city's commercial district in Ward 2 along lower Jackson Street and in Ward 3 along West 3rd, 4th, and 5th streets between Jackson and Franklin (see Map 4.1). As late as May, 1866, a local newspaper complained of a health hazard existing in the "old rookery" on Wabasha Street. The sanitary inspector found the building "inhabited solely by negroes . . . of all ages, sexes and shades. In one room thirteen persons were sleeping every night." A month later a group of whites attacked the "negro rookery," destroying the meager personal possessions of the Black people living there. In October white neighbors forced the removal of a Black family living on 7th Street because of an alleged outbreak of smallpox among them.[16]

Initial settlement in St. Paul had developed on a bend in the Mississippi River, where the lower levee was located. Into this basin during the early years poured immigrants of ethnically diverse backgrounds — Irish, Germans, Norwegians, Swedes, Jews, and Blacks — creating a potpourri of merging ethnic boundaries and residential life. Although there was no discernible pattern of residential segregation, enclaves existed. Locked into a rigid socioeconomic class structure, Black people were generally unable to procure employment above low wage levels. Although many male and female heads of households owned substantial amounts of real and personal property by 1870, they were forced to reside in the commercial district where employment existed nearby and rents were generally cheaper. A majority of St. Paul Black families lived in single dwellings; a few occupied multiple-family units with white and Black neighbors.[17]

In 1870 St. Paul had a total population of 20,030; by 1905 it had become a major urban center with 197,023 people, 28.8% of whom were foreign born. As members of various ethnic groups began to ascend the socioeconomic ladder, they abandoned the commercial district of initial settlement near the river for residential areas on the bluffs, where they re-established enclaves. This movement was accelerated by the extension of horsecar trolley lines in the 1880s and electric streetcars in the 1890s. Among the last groups to leave the commercial district were the city's Blacks, who remained there until after the turn of the century.[18]

The physical growth of the Black neighborhood was limited by other ethnic residential areas that grew up around the city's commercial core. To the west, where Blacks were not welcome, Germans expanded along 7th Street. To the east and below Dayton's Bluff, upper-class white Protestants and French and Irish Catholics developed a fashionable lower-town neighborhood by the 1870s. To the northeast lived Germans, Swedes, and a few Norwegians. Discrimination and racial antagonism being what they were, the only direction for Black expansion lay along the immediate north

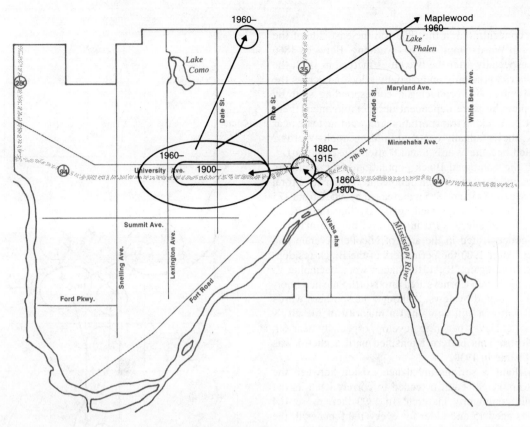

Map 4.1. St. Paul Black Neighborhoods, 1860–1980

and northwest corridors leading to residential areas on the western plateau. There the path of least resistance lay through the Jewish community.

During the early 1880s German Jews, who had arrived in St. Paul in the 1850s, began to leave the neighborhood from 8th to 14th streets for more fashionable homes on Dayton and Summit avenues. They were replaced by more recent Russian-Jewish immigrants and Blacks. By 1900 the pressures of population, coupled with the greater commercialization of the core city, forced Blacks farther north and west onto the plateau along Rondo and adjacent streets from Rice to Lexington. Rondo, St. Anthony, Central, Carroll, and University avenues east of Dale Street became principal centers of Black residential life. The movement out of downtown was almost completed by World War I; by 1930 the Rondo area was 47.8% Black.

Between 1870 and 1890 the Black community had grown over sixfold. The greatest increase occurred among young males from the upper South, attracted in part by expanding employment opportunities. This in-migration added to the imbalance between the sexes; by 1910, 60.5% (1,904 out of 3,144) were Black males, a demographic characteristic similar to that of other northern urban centers, which was reflected in such indexes of stability as employment characteristics, marital status, homeownership, and institutional development.[19]

Although Black males could be found in a range of occupations by 1910, the majority were unskilled workers employed as porters and waiters. Their largest St. Paul employer in

1880 was the Metropolitan Hotel. It was eclipsed in 1886 by the newly opened Hotel Ryan, most of whose waiters, porters, and cooks were Black. Beginning in 1880 the railroad lines headquartered in St. Paul became major employers.[20]

Most of the single men roomed in private homes, boardinghouses, or hotels close to their places of work. Their presence created a highly transient population along lower Cedar, Minnesota, and Robert streets. Those who worked for the railroads usually lived in the commercial district or later on the plateau to the west. Only 41.9% of the eligible Black males in Minnesota were married in 1890. By 1910 the figure had risen to 45% for men and 58% for eligible women living in St. Paul. The low incidence of marriage among males might have been the result of a low wage scale that retarded the establishment of independent households. An 1890 survey revealed more Blacks rooming or boarding than residing in their own homes. Nevertheless the *Appeal*, a Black newspaper, reported on August 24, 1901, that St. Paul had a larger percentage of Black homeowners in 1900 than any other city in the United States. Only 14.1% were unencumbered by a mortgage. Ten years later out of 748 dwelling units occupied by Black families, 71.3% were rented.[21]

Early Minneapolis

A similar pattern of neighborhood development near the commercial center is suggested by an examination of the city directories for St. Anthony and Minneapolis. Very little is known of the early Black community there, but it seems to have been concentrated in the 1860s on the east side of the Mississippi in Wards 3 and 4 of St. Anthony. Between 1866 and 1875, especially after the two cities merged in 1872, the business district gradually and partially relocated across the river in Minneapolis, producing a corresponding shift by Black people who were dependent upon employment there (see Map 4.2). Lacking transportation and wanting to be near their work, they gradually centered in Minneapolis Wards 2 and 3 (which became Wards 6 and 8 after consolidation).[22]

By 1870 the combined Black population of St. Anthony and Minneapolis had more than doubled in 10 years to a total of 162. Between 1875 and 1885 it increased by 385% from 175 to 673, and by 1895 it doubled again. By that time Black people resided in every ward in the city, but the majority were still concentrated in the area of Nicollet Avenue and 10th Street. After 1900 the perimeters of the Black residential area shifted again. By 1910 Blacks were beginning to move from the Seven Corners area into North Side neighborhoods being vacated by Jews. Although the southern wards close to downtown still contained a majority of the city's Blacks, new enclaves began to develop, especially near 6th Avenue North. This pattern intensified until a ghetto was clearly definable in 1930.

Like St. Paul, a serious imbalance existed between the sexes, but unlike St. Paul, it tended to correct itself as the Minneapolis community matured. In 1890 there were 164 Black males aged 15 and older for every 100 females in the same age group. By 1910 the ratio had fallen to 146 to 100 in Minneapolis, but St. Paul still had 166 men to 100 women. Only 44% of eligible Black Minneapolis males over the age of 15 were married in 1910. Similar employment and homeownership patterns also existed. Men worked as porters, waiters, cooks, and janitors in hotels, restaurants, jobbing houses, and on railroad lines, while Black women worked as personal or domestic servants to augment the family's income. By 1910, 75.3% of the dwelling units occupied by Black people in Minneapolis were rented. Only 24.7% were owned.[23]

As the population increased and the neighborhoods changed, Black churches relocated to meet the spiritual needs of their congregations. Initially located in Ward 4, St. James African Methodist Episcopal Church moved several times and by 1874 was located at 5th Avenue Southeast and 2nd Street in the consolidated city. An African Baptist church was located at various addresses on Harrison Street, and a Free Will Baptist church stood on 1st Avenue South at the corner of 7th Street.[24]

In 1881 a schism developed in the St. James Church because a portion of its congregation wanted to relocate closer to the downtown area, while others preferred to remain in Southeast Minneapolis. As a result, those in favor of a downtown location withdrew to establish St. Peter's African Methodist Church, which was officially organized in 1886. By 1890 it was able to erect a new building at a cost of $7,000 capable of seating 450 persons. Three additional congregations were established before 1910. They included Bethesda Baptist, organized in 1889; Zion Baptist Mission, organized in the 1880s, reorganized in 1906, and formed into a full-fledged church in 1910; and St. Thomas Episcopal Mission,

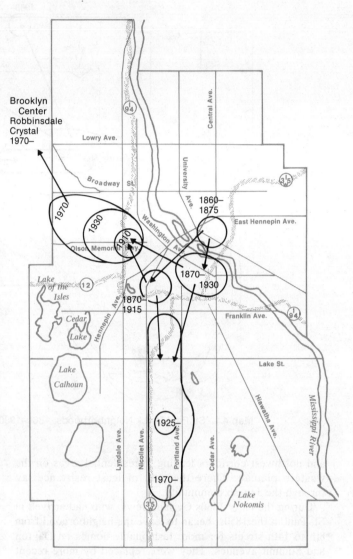

Map 4.2. Minneapolis Black Neighborhoods, 1860–1980

organized in 1898. In a larger sense, the churches in Minneapolis and St. Paul functioned as community centers offering a wide range of social and recreational activities. Their buildings were used as public meeting halls where issues of the day were discussed. In neither city, however, did Black church leaders assume the commanding positions they occupied in other northern urban centers before the turn of the century.[25]

Leadership and Organizations

In 1870 Black community leadership was provided by a small but cohesive group of St. Paul men and women. Later they were augmented by a Black professional class recruited to serve the needs of the Twin Cities' community. Much of the early leadership elite was composed of mulattoes, who, although small in number compared with the over-all Black population, exercised considerable influence as a class within the Black community. The first generation of leaders responsible for the remarkable institutional growth and diversification of the St. Paul community were for the most part men and women without extended formal schooling. Some had arrived in Minnesota during the territorial period. Others were among the migrants of 1863 or later. Some derived income from various businesses or from land speculation. Many more were hard-working, unskilled laborers.[26]

An article published in the *St. Paul and Minneapolis Pioneer Press* of December 11, 1887, described 13 Black leaders with assets of between $5,000 and $100,000. Among them were Thomas H. Lyles and James K. Hilyard. Lyles arrived in St. Paul in 1874 and went into business as a barber. In 1887 he opened a real-estate agency, and by 1906 he became a mortician and established a funeral parlor, which his wife Amanda continued to operate after his death in 1920. Hilyard settled in the city in 1866. He operated a used-clothing store, sold real estate and insurance, and served as bandmaster for a popular group of musicians who played in the city and on the riverboats.

Both Hilyard and Lyles were organizers. Lyles was active in numerous Republican political clubs, especially in the 1880s. He is credited with convincing the mayor that St. Paul should hire a Black policeman in 1881 and that it should have an all-Black fire company in 1885. Hilyard was the prime mover in founding Black Masonic lodges in St. Paul and Minneapolis in the 1860s, as well as the short-lived St. Mark's Episcopal congregation. Lyles was a charter member and first president of the Robert Banks Literary Society in 1875, and the first grand master of the African Grand Lodge of Minnesota when it was formed by six existing lodges in 1894. The Banks Society, which was perhaps the first flowering of intellectual life in the St. Paul Black community, was composed of men and women who met to discuss issues of philosophical and practical importance to the race. A local newspaper placed its membership at approximately 40 persons in 1875.[27]

Lyles and Hilyard may also have played roles in abortive efforts in 1876 and 1880 to publish a Black newspaper in St. Paul. It is certain that they quickly became involved in a third, more successful attempt launched in June, 1885, which produced the *Western Appeal*. Frederick Douglass Parker, recently arrived from Washington, D.C., was hired as editor, and the paper appeared until 1886, when a financial crisis forced dissolution of the original partnership. Lyles and Hilyard then stepped in to form the Appeal Publishing Company.[28]

The two men were also instrumental in luring professional people to the city. In the 1880s both St. Paul and Minneapolis lacked trained Black doctors, lawyers, dentists, and teachers. In the hope of attracting such people, an article was placed in the *New York Globe* of November 24, 1883, emphasizing the potential business opportunities and desirability of living in St. Paul. More directly fruitful, however, were Hilyard's successful efforts to lure John Quincy Adams, former editor of the *Louisville Bulletin*, to the city in 1886. A year later Adams replaced Parker as editor of the *Western Appeal*. Hilyard was also responsible for the arrival in 1889 of Frederick L. McGhee, the state's first Black criminal lawyer, and Dr. Valdo Turner, one of its earliest Black physicians.[29]

The combined efforts of these men as well as those of concerned citizens of both cities attracted other professionals. In 1889 William R. Morris, a young lawyer from Tennessee, and Dr. Robert S. Brown, a recent graduate of Bennett Medical College in Chicago, settled in Minneapolis. The latter became the first Black physician licensed to practice in that city. J. Frank Wheaton, a lawyer who joined the Minneapolis group, became the first Black elected to the Minnesota legislature, where he represented the 42nd district in the House of Representatives in 1899. Two other arrivals were Charles W. Scrutchin and William T. Francis. Scrutchin took up residence in 1899 in the northern Minnesota town of Bemidji, where he established a reputation as a criminal lawyer. Francis, who became a well-known attorney in St. Paul before World War I, served as a presidential elector in 1920 and was appointed United States minister to Liberia in 1927.[30]

The presence of a growing professional class and the founding of the *Western Appeal* marked a major watershed in the history of the Twin Cities' Black community. John Q. Adams' rise to a position of prominence between 1887 and 1920 signaled the advent of a new generation of leadership, and the *Appeal*, which disseminated news of and protested injustices to Blacks, quickly became the people's paper. It defended the race against malicious propaganda, accorded recognition for individual achievement, and spoke out

HOME of John Q. Adams, journalist and civil rights advocate, on St. Anthony Avenue, St. Paul, about 1910.

against proscriptive legislation on the national and state levels, while waging a militant local battle for civil rights. Moreover the *Appeal* was an important advertising medium for Black businessmen, for it encouraged its subscribers to patronize them. Under Adams' capable editorship, the *Appeal*, which became a newspaper with a national readership by 1900, engendered pride and served as a strong unifying force in the Black communities of the Twin Cities. Through the doors of Adams' spacious home on St. Anthony Avenue in St. Paul passed Booker T. Washington, William E. B. DuBois, William Monroe Trotter, and other prominent Black national leaders.[31]

When the *Western Appeal* made its appearance, the Black population of Minneapolis and St. Paul had grown to approximately 1,400 persons, almost equally divided between the two cities. St. Paul, the older twin, remained the more progressive. As early as 1869 five Black men had served on a jury in the Ramsey County Court of Common Pleas, and 10 years later St. Paul had a Black dramatic club which helped Black citizens of Stillwater stage a benefit for the relief of Kansas refugees. The influence of Lyles had opened the St. Paul police and fire departments to Black men in the 1880s and 1890s. After a city militia was authorized in 1880, a Black company known as the Rice Guards was formed. The Minnesota Women's Christian Temperance Union established a mission among Blacks in 1884, an effort in which Mrs. Lyles was active and which continued on and off until its demise in 1937.[32]

In the 1880s St. Paul Blacks also formed organizations designed to combat local *de facto* segregation and lend support to court tests of proscriptive legislation in the South. The first of these grew out of a suggestion made by Adams in 1887. Upset over a recent court decision that awarded a visiting Black architect only $25 in damages because the Clarendon Hotel refused to provide lodgings for him, Adams proposed in the pages of the *Appeal* of October 22, 1887, that a state convention of Black people be assembled to formulate a plan to protect their civil rights. Representatives from 15 counties gathered in St. Paul in December, 1887, and out of their deliberations the Minnesota Protective and Industrial League was formed.[33]

Two years later, rallying to a call for the formation of a national group to act on behalf of the race, a similar community-wide organization known as the Afro-American League came into being. Additional leagues were established in Anoka, Duluth, Faribault, Minneapolis, and Stillwater. Adams and McGhee were sent as delegates to a conference in Chicago that led to the formation of the National Afro-American League in 1890, the first national attempt to secure affirmation of Black political and civil rights through judicial process. Still a third group — the Minnesota Citizens Civil Rights Committee — grew out of league efforts to raise funds to test the legality of Tennessee's Jim Crow law in 1891. Undaunted by its lack of success in Tennessee, the committee went on to raise funds for a second attempt in Oklahoma.

Adams and McGhee, who served on the national executive committee, were also undoubtedly responsible for the fact that the renamed National Afro-American Council's

convention was held in St. Paul in 1902. But McGhee, disillusioned by Booker T. Washington's attempt to dominate the council's affairs, bolted the organization in 1903 and closed ranks with W. E. B. DuBois to form the Niagara Movement two years later. McGhee and Adams again teamed up, however, to found the Twin City Protective League, an organization interested in improving living conditions for Blacks in the Twin Cities. In 1912 McGhee and Dr. Turner were chosen to represent this organization at the annual conference of the National Association for the Advancement of Colored People (NAACP) in Chicago. Their trip helped lay the groundwork for the birth of a St. Paul chapter of the NAACP in September, 1913, a year after McGhee's death.[34]

In addition to participating in civil rights organizations that sprang up during the closing decades of the 19th century, Black men formed Republican political clubs in the 1880s. As the Black electorate grew, its leaders and political clubs were taken seriously by white Republicans. Although Blacks never wielded major political strength at the polls, their votes were assiduously cultivated and in close city elections became the margin of victory. Incumbent officials as well as aspiring candidates accepted invitations to address Black audiences at political rallies. Republicans courted these voters, but they rarely delivered lucrative local patronage appointments. Some Black leaders were, however, elected as delegates and alternates to national Republican and Democratic conventions. As early as 1888 the *Appeal* sometimes questioned the unswerving allegiance of Blacks to the Republican party, and in the early 1900s independent political clubs were formed that refused to endorse a candidate until his position on race issues was clarified. Such clubs began to wane by 1912, but Blacks continued to support the Republican party until the ascendancy of Franklin D. Roosevelt.[35]

In spite of the fact that Black leaders in St. Paul made impressive strides toward organizational and institutional development between 1870 and 1915, the community lagged far behind other northern urban areas. It is the opinion of the present writer that Blacks did not possess the resources to support their existing organizations and institutions, nor could they bring into being new agencies adequate to serve the community's needs. Discrimination in employment, the failure or inability of Blacks to support Black businesses, and the indifference of the white community to them prevented the accumulation of surplus capital. For Blacks, St. Paul was a working-class community. Social class distinctions as they were known in the East were slow in arriving; the city had no wealthy Blacks and no social Brahmins who could claim three generations of free birth. Class differentiation in St. Paul was based upon type of employment rather than upon wealth or breeding.

The Twin Cities from 1910 to 1980

As the years went by, an extended Black community was created that included both St. Paul and Minneapolis. Judging by newspapers published in each city, there were few differences between the two by 1910. Although separate social groupings existed, they were closely bound by marriage and family relationships. The number of Blacks in both cities was

SIXTH Avenue North in Minneapolis before wrecking began for construction of the Sumner Field Project, 1936.

small enough for almost all of the members to be known. Newspapers based in each city circulated freely in the other, and many activities were held jointly.[36]

The genesis of this commonality went back to 1868, when the 30th anniversary of Great Britain's emancipation of West Indian slaves was celebrated in St. Paul on August 1. Attended by Black people from St. Anthony and Minneapolis, the event became an annual one, featuring a picnic, commemorative services, and a grand ball. These celebrations continued at least until 1932, frequently attracting visitors from as far away as Duluth. The emancipation of American slaves was also celebrated annually in January, beginning in 1869 after the passage of the Minnesota nonwhite suffrage law, and a state-wide organization known as the Sons of Freedom came into being the same year. Supposedly composed of all the Black men in the state, its purpose was to monitor the general welfare of Black residents and provide information on employment, housing, farms for lease, and trade apprenticeships available to them.[37]

After about 1915 the initiative and leadership seems to have shifted from St. Paul to Minneapolis. As World War I broke over an unprepared America, Minneapolis began to replace its older sister as the center of Black intellectual, social, and cultural life in the state. The advent of war stemmed the flow of European immigrants and created an acute labor shortage in the United States. To meet the demands of a wartime economy between 1915 and 1920, recruiters scoured the South for Blacks willing to move to northern industrial centers in return for promises of free transportation, higher wages, and a better standard of living. It is estimated that from 300,000 to 1,000,000 Black people left the South in these years, forerunners of an exodus repeated during World War II and the succeeding decades of the 1950s and 1960s.[38]

The Twin Cities were only mildly affected by this massive migration, for the area at that time lacked employment opportunities. The Black population of St. Paul grew by only 7.3% from 3,144 to 3,376 between 1910 and 1920; Minneapolis registered a hefty 51.5% increase from 2,592 to 3,927, while Detroit jumped an astounding 611.3% and Cleveland gained 307.8%. The over-all growth of the state's Black population also remained relatively small — 7,084 in 1910 to 8,809 in 1920. Nevertheless by the latter year 49.1% of the Blacks in Minnesota had been born in various southern states.[39]

Many of these migrants found work on the railroads and in the meat-packing plants. Others took traditional nonunion jobs as redcaps, porters, janitors, waiters, cooks, and barbers. Among those who reached St. Paul in 1912 was Gordon Parks, later famous as a photographer and film producer. The influx of southern migrants generated feelings of hostility among established members of the Black community in both cities. Unfamiliar with urban living and with the subtle nuances of northern racial détente, they were castigated for their shortcomings by both Blacks and whites. Often the Black community placed them at the bottom of its social hierarchy.[40]

By 1920 restrictive housing covenants were being used extensively to contain and isolate Blacks of both cities. As a result, ghettos were created. The years between 1920 and 1930 saw a decided shift away from the city centers and a clustering of Black people in adjacent wards (see Maps 4.1 and 4.2). In Minneapolis the near North Side and Seven Corners became the principal ghetto areas. By 1930 they contained 2,100 (50.2%) of the city's 4,176 Black people and had the highest incidence of blighted and deteriorating housing, poverty, vice, and crime. A third concentration along South 4th and 5th avenues between East 35th and 41st streets was a fairly stable neighborhood of lower-middle-class Blacks living in standard housing. The general areas of concentration in Minneapolis did not change greatly during the 1960s and 1970s. Blacks on the near North Side moved west from Fremont Avenue to tract 33, along Penn Avenue and north to tracts 27 and 28, while those residing in South Minneapolis moved farther south, nearly to the city limits.[42]

In St. Paul the movement out of the downtown district accelerated after World War I. The concentration along Rondo Avenue and the adjacent streets constituted a lower-middle-class residential neighborhood of predominantly single-family dwellings. More affluent residents continued to move westward toward Lexington Avenue. The section west of Dale Street (upper Rondo) became known as "Oatmeal Hill," a term indicative of high social standing, while that east of Dale Street (lower Rondo) was called "Cornmeal Valley," a reference to the growing poverty and greater social dislocation that became apparent in the 1930s. One newspaper in 1926 compared Rondo Avenue to State Street in Chicago and to Lennox Avenue in New York's Harlem because of the variety of cultural expression it exhibited. In the 1920s it was still relatively free of blighted housing, and it still had a low population density.[42]

Two additional Black neighborhoods existed in St. Paul: the river flats and a tenement district in the shadow of the state Capitol, where Jews, Italians, and Blacks lived in a deteriorating slum. A shanty district along the levee on the west bank of the Mississippi, the flats were inhabited by representatives of 19 ethnic and racial groups, the most notable being Russian Jews, Italians, Irish, Blacks, and later Mexicans. All shared a culture of extreme poverty.

While detractors are quick to point out that urban moral ills are directly related to the poverty and illiteracy of delinquent youths under the corrupting influence of criminally minded adults, that does not seem to be the case in Minneapolis. A study of the Minneapolis ghetto conducted in 1923–25 showed that its Black residents did not commit major crimes out of proportion to their numbers, as had been alleged. The most frequent arrests were for misdemeanors usually associated with vagrancy, drunkenness, gambling, disorderly conduct, and prostitution.[43]

Nor were the Black residents of Twin Cities ghettos illiterate. By 1930 their illiteracy rate was one of the lowest for Blacks in the nation, and it was significantly lower than that for foreign-born white, Mexican, and Chinese residents. In Minneapolis only 1.7% of Blacks over 10 years of age were illiterate; in St. Paul the figure was 1.2%. (For the country as a whole, the rate was about 16.3%.) By 1970 census figures for urban areas showed 51.3% of Blacks over 25 years old had four or more years of high school and 66.5% between the ages of 18 and 24 had that much schooling.[44]

The Twin Cities were unusual among northern urban areas in another respect. The wave of racial unrest that swept the nation in the aftermath of World War I did not affect Minneapolis and St. Paul. Although all of the elements of strife were present, Black and white leaders, fearing riots like those in Chicago, Detroit, and Omaha, worked to keep the peace. In this period Blacks arriving in the Twin Cities did not have the benefit of community-based agencies to help them secure housing and employment. Usually such assistance was handled by Black churches, social clubs, civic organizations, or referrals made by Black barbers who obtained information from their patrons. In St. Paul, the St. James Church in 1915 began publication of the *Helper*, an organ of church news which soon contained job and housing references. The Hall Brothers Barbershop also served as an employment center by posting jobs available, and the Negro Business leagues of both cities aided in opening new areas of employment.[45]

These combined efforts, however, were not sufficient to process all the new arrivals. As a result, in 1923 the Twin Cities Urban League, a community-wide agency, was founded over the objections of the Chamber of Commerce, whose members felt that such an organization would only encourage further Black migration. The joint league functioned until 1938 when separate units were formed for each city.[46]

A second city-wide agency came into being in Minneapolis in 1924 when Phyllis Wheatley House opened its doors on October 17 at 808 Bassett Place North in a building that had formerly housed a frame manufacturing plant and Talmud Torah School. W. Gertrude Brown was hired as the first director. In addition to providing recreational activity, the settlement house sponsored baby and dental clinics and classes in Black history and culture.[47]

St. Paul had no less than three centers, only one of which was not church sponsored. Neighborhood House, located at Indiana and Robertson streets, had been established in 1897 to serve the West Side flats across the river from downtown St. Paul. Originally formed as an outgrowth of Mount Zion Temple's efforts to provide assistance for Russian-Jewish immigrants, it was reorganized on a nonsectarian basis in 1903. For years Black youths participated in its programs. In 1916 Zion Presbyterian Church, a Black mission congregation sponsored by several white Presbyterian congregations, opened Welcome Hall Community Center adjacent to the church at the corner of St. Anthony and Farrington avenues. Under the leadership of the Reverend George W. Camp and his wife Anna, the center offered recreational activities, Bible classes, a girls' club, and the first day-care facility in the Black community. Christian Center, founded on February 7, 1926, was the dream of the Reverend Joseph Walter Harris, who wished to provide a nondenominational center for religious education and wholesome recreation. The

SEAMSTRESSES worked on a WPA project in 1936 at Minneapolis' Phyllis Wheatley Settlement House.

$40,000 structure, completed in 1927 at 603 West Central Avenue, featured classrooms, a library, a music room, social and reading rooms, cafeteria and dining hall, guest rooms, and an apartment for the resident director. Until it burned 10 years later, the center sponsored many social, intellectual, cultural, and religious programs for its patrons.[48]

Two additional facilities were developed in the 1920s as a result of studies conducted by the newly formed Urban League. Convinced of the legitimate need for another community center in St. Paul, the Young Women's Christian Association (YWCA) reorganized its limited "colored" program in 1923 and established a branch at 598 West Central Avenue which continued to function until 1928. When it closed, the Community Chest empowered the Urban League to organize a new center along racial lines. The result was the Hallie Q. Brown Community Center, which opened under the direction of I. Myrtle Cardin in Union Hall at the corner of Aurora and Kent streets. The structure had originally been built in 1914 by Black Masons to house lodge functions and had served as a community meeting hall in earlier years.[49]

Hallie Q. Brown opened only a few months before the 1929 stock-market crash precipitated the Great Depression of the 1930s. By 1931 more than 6,000,000 unemployed workers milled about the streets of the nation's cities looking for work. The Twin Cities were no exception. Black people of Minneapolis and St. Paul had never fully participated in the prosperity of the 1920s. (As early as 1919 it was estimated that the median wage of a Black male head of household in the Twin Cities was only $22.55 per week at a time when the United States Bureau of Labor Statistics regarded $43.51 per week as the amount necessary for a family of five.) As the Depression lengthened, Pullman porters, redcaps, and others were laid off by the 11 railroad lines operating out of the Twin Cities. Undercapitalized Black businesses were forced to close their doors, and lawyers and doctors kept creditors at bay only because of their white clients. The sole Black group possessing economic security was composed of postal workers employed by the federal government. At a meeting sponsored by the St. Paul Urban League in May, 1938, a speaker pointed out that approximately 69% of the city's Blacks were either on direct relief or participating in such federal help programs as the Civilian Conservation Corps or the Works Progress Administration. Discrimination seems to have been pervasive in the administration of relief, in the placement of persons on government-sponsored projects, and in working conditions.[50]

The dramatic drop in real income had an adverse effect upon community institutions. As church revenues declined, programs were curtailed, ministers were forced upon the relief rolls, and church buildings suffered from lack of maintenance. In spite of economic conditions, however, two Black newspapers and one literary magazine were started in Minneapolis. The *Minneapolis Spokesman*, edited by Cecil E. Newman, began publication in 1934 following the failure of his effort to establish a literary magazine called the *Timely Digest* in 1932. The *Spokesman* survived to become the longest-lived Black newspaper in Minnesota. Only the *Appeal* had a comparable longevity. The second newspaper,

the *Northwest Monitor*, was edited by William Helm. Like Newman's magazine, it failed after only one year.[51]

Not everyone took the events of the Depression passively. Ostensibly angered over the political and economic status of Black people in the United States, many of those in the Twin Cities flirted with the Communist party. In June, 1932, 15 Black delegates from Minneapolis, Duluth, and St. Paul participated in the Minnesota State Ratification Convention of the Communist party that nominated Robert Turner, a Black worker from St. Paul, as its candidate for the position of Minnesota secretary of state. James W. Ford, the Communist vice-presidential candidate, spoke to an audience at the Hallie Q. Brown Center in September, 1932. The party was also active in Minneapolis; in April, 1933, Asa Mitchell, a Black, was a candidate for fourth-ward alderman on the Communist ticket. But the party's attempt to mobilize Black workers met with limited success. They seemed preoccupied by such practical concerns as food, clothing, and jobs rather than by revolt against a political system. Some were more upset by charges of alleged fraternization of Black men and white female workers in the party than they were by the diminution of their political rights.[52]

Even if they could afford them, recreational and entertainment facilities for Black people were limited in the 1930s. None of the major hotels in the Twin Cities allowed them to rent halls for dances or private parties, and none of the better restaurants served them. Much of the entertaining that took place thus necessarily occurred at home or in the Hallie Q. Brown or Phyllis Wheatley centers. Out of this experience social clubs evolved which were based on specific recreational interests. By 1935 more than a dozen fraternal and secret orders and two dozen clubs of various kinds existed in the Twin Cities.[53]

Among them was the Credjafawn Social Club, an acronym fashioned from the first letters of the names of the members, which was founded in 1928. Two years later a junior club for

WORKERS and shoppers at St. Paul's Credjafawn Co-op Store, Rondo Street, about 1950.

those under the age of 20 was started. As these youths came of age, they were inducted into the senior organization. The club, which still existed in 1980, provided the Twin Cities Black community with lectures, recitals, and other social, cultural, and recreational affairs. It also started its own credit union and pioneered the first Black Neighborhood Co-operative Store in St. Paul. Because banks usually refused to loan cash or extend credit to Black people, the club in 1936 or 1937 also offered a savings and loan facility. The store was an outgrowth of a public meeting sponsored by the club to discuss the practical application of co-operative principles. To purchase a grocery on the corner of Rondo and St. Albans streets, $7,000 was raised, and in September, 1945, Neighborhood Co-operative Store No. 3 opened. It offered low-cost but nutritious foods at discount prices to club members and others who invested in the co-op. It also provided a few badly needed jobs for Black people.[54]

In 1939 unemployment remained a critical problem in the Twin Cities. Fully 60% of Blacks were unemployed, compared to 25% of whites. Although the quickening pace of events in Europe would involve that continent in a global conflict before the year ended, no immediate effects were felt by the American economy. Not until 1941, with United States entry into World War II, did wartime mobilization at last end the dreary course of unemployment and Depression. Companies with sizable government contracts began to hire or rehire workers.[55]

Initially the large industries refused to hire Black people for war-related work above the level of matrons and janitors. Such a blatantly discriminatory policy, supported by tax dollars and ostensibly sanctioned by the federal government, led A. Phillip Randolph to threaten a march on Washington by 100,000 Blacks to protest discrimination in war-contract industries. On June 25, 1941, President Franklin D. Roosevelt issued Executive Order No. 8802 forbidding discrimination in defense industries and setting up a federal regulatory body called the Fair Employment Practice Committee (FEPC) to ensure that the directive was obeyed.

In the Twin Cities some industries and businesses, which had refused to hire Black workers before the war and were not recipients of federal contracts, still refused to hire them. Four of the major breweries — Hamm, Schmidt, Grain Belt, and Gluek — were the targets of a one-year consumer boycott initiated by Cecil Newman and the *Minneapolis Spokesman* in 1935–36. But the companies continued generally to refuse to employ Black people throughout and after World War II. Nor were they hired by major department stores in the Twin Cities, except as porters, matrons, elevator operators, or stock clerks, until 1948, when eight large stores hired a total of 14 Black salespeople.[56]

Significant break-throughs took place, however, in plants that had never before considered hiring Black workers. More than 1,000 were employed by the Twin City Ordnance Plant of the Federal Cartridge Corporation at New Brighton. Disavowing the prevailing discriminatory policies of others, the firm assigned Blacks at all levels according to their skills, education, and training. At one time this plant employed 20% of the state's adult Black population. More than a dozen other firms had favorable records, including the meat-packing industry.[57]

The employment gains made during the war years were sustained in the postwar period. Additional break-throughs were achieved in retail sales, public utilities, printing, and manufacturing. Efforts were also made to introduce FEP legislation on the state level, although none was passed until 1955. In the area of housing, however, racial discrimination continued unabated. Although restrictive covenants in real-estate transactions were limited by a state law passed in 1937, unwritten agreements often prevented Blacks from obtaining houses or inflated their cost far above actual market value. Home loans and insurance were difficult to obtain from commercial firms, and the Federal Housing Administration (FHA) and Veterans Administration often discriminated against Black applicants. With the upswing in employment, there came a corresponding increase in Black homeownership.[58]

By 1960 most St. Paul Blacks lived in an area that extended west from the central downtown business district, with University Avenue serving as a northern boundary and Selby Avenue being roughly the southern limit. Between 1960 and 1970 there was a slight change in their dispersion in the city because of the dislocations caused by freeway construction and urban renewal. Two additional areas emerged, one along Wheelock Parkway and the other in suburban Maplewood.[59]

The war period did more than open up jobs for Blacks. It also enabled them to gain skills and training that allowed them to retain those jobs after peace came. They sent their children to college and supported community institutions that would be important in mobilizing resources for the civil rights struggles of the late 1950s and early 1960s.

In spite of the economic progress made by Black Minnesotans during World War II, other problems — notably a shortage of housing — were exacerbated with the return of veterans. The Governor's Interracial Commission found in the mid-1940s that "the overwhelming number" of Blacks could not hope to buy or rent outside of definite neighborhoods to which white persons "expect Negroes to be restricted." Urban renewal, Model Cities planning, and freeway construction displaced many residents of these Twin Cities' restricted areas in the late 1950s and early 1960s. In their attempts to revitalize the inner cities, urban planners altered socioeconomic and political bases, undermining the stability of neighborhoods, irrevocably damaging certain institutions, and compounding the housing problem.[60]

Between 1950 and 1970 the Black population in Minnesota increased from 13,775 to 34,868, a gain of 153%. Minneapolis experienced a record 436% increase in its Black population, while St. Paul registered an impressive 388%. The largest jump occurred between 1960 and 1970, the decade in which the struggle for civil rights reached its greatest intensity in the United States. The majority of these migrants to Minnesota were from the South and from the north-central states.[61]

The reason for this heavy migration to Minnesota is not completely understood. Belief in Minnesota's liberal racial climate, expanded employment opportunities, more generous public assistance, and progressive legislation such as the Fair Employment Practice Act have been credited with influencing some to move to the state. Moreover the Twin Cities had been identified as a training ground for Black professional, technical, and managerial people employed by national and international corporations headquartered there. Existing data suggest, however, that the racial climate in the Twin Cities was not qualitatively better than in other northern cities. Moreover employment opportunities for unskilled and undereducated Blacks had not improved dramatically. During the prosperity of the 1960s a large number of Blacks were absorbed in the service and menial sector of the economy. By 1970 only 18% were classified as professional, technical, managerial, or administrative. The median income for Black families in Minneapolis and St. Paul in 1950 was $2,160 and $2,294, respectively. Although this figure increased to $7,353 and $7,250 in 1970, almost 67% of Black families in both cities earned less than $10,000 per year in 1970. Approximately 21% were receiving public assistance.

Against this backdrop of discrimination and limited opportunities, it is not difficult to understand why the Twin Cities experienced serious civil disorder during the volatile 1960s. The Black population of the two cities was becoming progressively younger with a median age of 25 in 1960. The average employed Black male earned $1,000 less in 1970 than his white counterpart. Unemployment in St. Paul's Summit-University area in 1965 was estimated at 9.2% for Blacks and 6% for whites. In what has been described as a decade of rising expectations, the Black urban population of Minnesota was becoming increasingly resentful of its exclusion from the general prosperity.[62]

The outbreak of civil disorder in the Twin Cities on Labor Day weekend in 1968 was influenced by national events. Although the extent of local rioting never reached the levels experienced in Detroit, Newark, the Watts area of Los Angeles, Cleveland, or New York, it produced thousands of dollars in property damage and scores of personal injuries. The civil unrest of the 1960s helped to underscore the disparity in opportunity accorded Black Minnesotans. It was responsible in part for legislation and special programs designed to counteract racism. The bulk of the gains in the decade of the 1970s were registered, unfortunately, by a small but cohesive Black middle class, leaving the undereducated and unskilled not much more advanced than they were in the 1960s. Although Blacks have been elected to the state legislature — the first since 1899 — and have been appointed to the University of Minnesota Board of Regents, discrimination against Black people continues effectively to prevent their full participation in the social, economic, and political life of the state in the 1980s.

Blacks in Duluth

The city of Duluth, a railroad and shipping center possessing one of the finest deep-water harbors on Lake Superior, developed as the largest city of northern Minnesota in the closing decades of the 19th century after iron ore was found on the nearby Vermilion and Mesabi ranges. The opening of the Vermilion mines in the 1880s and larger ones on the

Mesabi in the 1890s attracted a polyglot group of native-born Americans and immigrants from many nations. Evidence suggests that small numbers of Blacks were also drawn to the new range communities, but the scope of their involvement in the mining and lumbering industries of the region remains a fertile field for future study. It is known that John Nichols, an enterprising Black man, migrated from Chester, Pennsylvania, to the newly founded mining village of Tower in 1884. For a number of years he worked as a cook in the Vermilion Hotel there. After it was destroyed by fire, he opened the City Hotel, which he operated until his death in 1907. Nichols derived a handsome income from his business. He married an Irish immigrant woman and raised a family of seven children.[63]

More is known about Duluth's slowly evolving Black community. At the time of the city's incorporation in 1857, at least two Black men were working as barbers. St. Louis County, in which Duluth is situated, listed 11 Black people, seven of whom belonged to the Bonga family. By 1870 there were only 22 Blacks in a county population of more than 4,000, and all lived within Duluth's city limits. Thirteen Blacks were listed there in 1880, 220 in 1890, and 385 in 1895. Sizable numbers lived in Wards 1 and 3, but the majority in 1886–87 clustered in Ward 4 — an area comprising all of the city west of 12th Avenue West and south of 4th Street, and including Rices Point, later known as Central Hillside. Unlike St. Paul-Minneapolis, a relatively stable ratio of males (211) to females (205) existed as late as 1930.[64]

It is not known to what extent racial discrimination molded the condition of the community's Black residents during this period. The city's population was characterized by extreme ethnic diversity, and new immigrants continued to arrive in the 20th century. In this structured environment, Black men were relegated to such jobs as porters, waiters, messengers, janitors, and valets in the city's hotels, at the Kitchi Gammi Club, or on the railroads. A few established themselves as independent barbers, and some opened restaurants during the first decade of the 20th century. At least one person is known to have secured employment in the police department and another in the post office before 1910. In short, the patterns discernible in Duluth are virtual duplicates of those already described for the Twin Cities.[65]

Like the Twin Cities, too, as the Duluth Black community continued to grow, institutions arose to meet its needs. In August, 1890, the Reverend Richmond Taylor established St. Mark's African Methodist Episcopal Church on the corner of 4th Street and 4th Avenue West. A year later its congregation totaled 13 adults and 30 children. Writing in the *Western Appeal* of August 29, 1891, Pastor Taylor reported with pride the organizing of a Black Masonic chapter as one of the congregation's accomplishments.[66]

Other Black groups in Duluth included Florence L. Williams Chapter No. 22 of the Eastern Star, the Household of Ruth Lodge No. 3586 of the Grand United Order of Odd Fellows — both formed in 1896 — and a Knights of Pythias group which apparently held regular meetings. By 1910 Doric Lodge No. 3 had been added. Most of these organizations were offshoots of established lodges in the Twin Cities and often fell under their jurisdiction. Black citizens of Duluth maintained close ties with those in St. Paul and Minneapolis, regularly taking part in the annual West Indies emancipation celebrations and later the yearly Union Picnic held there. Among the political clubs organized in Duluth to deliver votes for Republican candidates were the Federation of Colored Men of St. Louis County, the Colored Political Club of Duluth, and the Colored Men's Morris and McKinley Club.[67]

As early as 1895 Duluth could also boast a Black newspaper, the *World*. Originally published by P. O. Gray, it had subscribers across the bay in Superior, Wisconsin, as well as in Minneapolis and St. Paul. In May, 1896, the main office of the *World* was moved to Minneapolis, leaving a branch in Duluth. Nominally independent in its political posture, the paper competed with the *Appeal* and editorially criticized Adams' leadership in community affairs. A second newspaper, the *Progressive News Review*, was initiated and published monthly by Henry Williams after his arrival in Duluth in 1904. Williams also taught violin and was the only Black to direct the Duluth municipal band and a children's orchestra.[68]

Despite the flurry of organizational activity, the city's Black population did not grow after 1895, remaining stabilized at about 400 persons from 1910 to 1930. During the early 1920s the United States Steel Corporation recruited unskilled Black laborers from Texas, Louisiana, Mississippi, and Georgia for its plant in the company-built suburb of Morgan Park, but few of these workers stayed. Inferior wages, substandard and segregated housing, discrimination, and harsh weather were cited among the reasons for leaving. While white workers were housed in cinderblock homes constructed by the company in Morgan Park, Blacks lived either in company barracks or in substandard houses located in Gary, then a predominantly Black enclave. A lifelong resident pointed out that the steel plant was a major employer of Blacks into the 1950s.[69]

Long-time Black residents of the port city, interviewed in 1974–75, emphasized the steel industry's role in bringing them to the community. One described recruitment procedures used by the steelmakers to secure Black workers from Texas for the Morgan Park mill. He regarded their importation as an antiunion effort on the company's part.[70]

After World War I race relations in Duluth became progressively worse. Restaurants, hotels, and theaters, which had reluctantly served Blacks before the war, refused to do so or attempted to establish segregated seating. Growing racial antipathy culminated in violence on June 15, 1920, when three Black laborers associated with a traveling circus were lynched for the alleged rape of a white girl on a complaint filed by the girl's escort. A crowd variously estimated at between 1,000 and 10,000 stormed the city jail, seized three of the six accused Blacks, and hanged them from a street lamp. State troops were dispatched to quell the disturbance, and a grand jury was immediately impaneled to investigate the outrage. Eighteen members of the mob responsible for the lynching were indicted, but only two received jail sentences. Ten Black men were arrested, two were indicted, and one was sentenced to Stillwater State

Prison for a crime few believed ever took place. The St. Paul and Minneapolis NAACP chapters hired lawyers to defend the accused, and the circumstances surrounding the lynching and the ensuing trial received national publicity. This lynching was the only incident of its kind against Blacks in the state's history, and it resulted in the passage of an antilynching law by the Minnesota legislature in 1921. It also resulted in a decrease in the Black population of the port city, as some moved to neighboring Superior or to the Twin Cities. Those who chose to remain helped to establish a local branch of the NAACP, a step they had opposed before the lynching took place.[71]

The decline of Duluth's Black population continued after 1930, hitting its lowest point in 50 years in 1940 with only 314 persons. Following World War II, however, more Blacks migrated to the northern port, so that by 1960 they numbered 565 with nearly 300 more by 1970, a 53% increase. (The white population of Duluth decreased 6% from 106,884 to 100,578 in the same decade.) Their mobility within the city is difficult to assess, because census listings by wards have not been available since 1910. Moves to suburban areas were probably minimal because, as one authority noted, "Duluth has a great deal of open space . . . [so that] the suburbanizing trend has been substantially accommodated without the creation of extra-city settlements." Examination of census tract schedules for 1960 and 1970 indicated no substantial shift of the Black population; increases in various tracts chiefly reflected the growth in the number of Blacks.[72]

It has been suggested that the growth in Duluth's Black population since 1950 was spurred when the local airport was placed under the jurisdiction of the Central Air Defense Force of the Aerospace Defense Command in May, 1951. Along with adding Black military and civilian personnel, the air base required construction work, supplies and equipment, and other services which boosted the local economy; federal guidelines concerning discrimination probably helped to increase the employment of Blacks.

Many Black Duluthians in the 1970s felt that theirs was an aging group and that the younger members of the community were leaving to seek opportunities elsewhere. The 1970 census, however, showed that out of 857 persons, 307 (35.8%) were between the ages of 19 and 44; only 117 (13.6%) were in the over-45 age bracket. Ostensibly at least 50.5% of the population was age 19 or under, but these youthful figures might in part be explained by the presence of military personnel and their dependents, a transient population. Continued patterns of discrimination in employment, housing, and racial hostility in the public school system were cited by Black residents as contributing factors to the exodus of young people, who often moved to the Twin Cities.[73]

Although the 1970 census suggested a low incidence of unemployment among Black adults in Duluth, they were still relegated to service and marginally skilled jobs. Fully 34% were employed as service workers, 20% as clerical, 9% as laborers, and 14% as machinery operators. Only 16% were classified as professional and managerial, with nearly half being elementary and secondary schoolteachers. In 1969 the average Black male over 16 years of age earned $6,357, the average Black female only $3,500 yearly.

In the past the strength and vitality of urban Black communities was measured by the growth and development of community institutions. Although the Black churches in Duluth have remained stable and the fledgling NAACP chapter survived, most of the fraternal societies in the late 1970s were affiliates of Twin Cities organizations, a Black press did not exist, and social, cultural, or civic clubs had virtually disappeared — all suggesting a community in decline.

The Rural Folk

Of the 39 Black or mulatto citizens of Minnesota Territory in 1850, only nine did not live in Ramsey County. Twenty years later Blue Earth, Dakota, Goodhue, Le Sueur, Rice, and Winona counties each had more than 15 Blacks (see Table 4.1), with concentrations in Hastings (24), Northfield (19), and Winona (37). By the turn of the century only 10 of the state's 82 established counties listed no Black persons. The largest enclaves, as we have seen, were in Minneapolis, St. Paul, and Duluth, but significant numbers were also clustered in 14 nonurban counties — Aitkin, Anoka, Blue Earth, Dakota, Dodge, Goodhue, Le Sueur, Olmsted, Otter Tail, Polk, Rice, Steele, Washington, and Winona.[74]

Ten years later 8.7% of Minnesota's Black people lived in rural areas, but only 29 farms out of 156,137 were operated by Black families. Of these, 16 were owned by the operator, 12 were farmed by tenants, and one was managed. The combined acreage owned by Black farmers in 1910 was only 2,362, a decrease of nearly 2,000 acres from 1900. The total value of land, buildings, and farm equipment amounted to $128,910. Between 1910 and 1920 both national and state farm operations increased slightly. In the latter year 33 farms, having a total value of $134,670, were operated by Black families.[75]

The types of agricultural operations varied. Some were truck farms located near large urban centers, others produced various cash crops, and a few were homesteads with subsistence agriculture. Among the rare recorded instances of homesteading by Blacks in Minnesota was that of the Hosey Posey Lyght family. Dissatisfied with life in a Pennsylvania mining community, Lyght and his wife Stella decided to try their hand at farming in South Dakota. A change of plan took them to Duluth in 1913. From there they traveled by steamer up the north shore of Lake Superior to a site near Lutsen in Cook County, where with their three children they spent the first winter in a one-room cabin. They supported themselves by hunting, fishing, and subsistence farming, supplemented by the wages Lyght was able to earn as a laborer to make ends meet. In addition to the three children brought from Pennsylvania, 12 more were born on the homestead. Later the family owned Northern Lights Resort on Caribou Lake. Most of its patrons were white tourists, but Blacks from the Twin Cities, Duluth, Chicago, and Iowa made annual visits to hunt and fish there. Late in the 1960s John R. Lyght was named deputy sheriff of Cook County, and in 1972 he was elected Minnesota's first Black sheriff and one of only about a dozen in the United States.[76]

Large numbers of Black families attempted to homestead near Fergus Falls in Otter Tail County. Approximately 18 family groups from Kentucky made their way to that north-central Minnesota region as the result of an unusual series of events. In the summer of 1896 the Grand Army of the Republic held a national encampment on the state fairgrounds in St. Paul. Two real-estate agents distributed promotional materials among Black veterans from Kentucky extolling the virtues of Fergus Falls. Representatives of a Greenwood, Kentucky, group visited the city later that year, and about 50 persons arrived in April, 1897, intending to settle there. Unable to find suitable homesteads or steady employment, some left at the end of the summer, moving to Aitkin County, Akeley and Nevis in Hubbard County, or to Sioux Falls, South Dakota. According to the census, the Black community of Fergus Falls numbered 56 in 1900, declining to 34 in 1910 and only 15 by 1970. Most of the members were employed as laborers, while a few farmed. Two businesses are known to have existed, a hairdressing salon and a shoeshine parlor operated by Frank and Minnie Penick.[77]

The Kentuckians were not, however, the first Blacks in Fergus Falls. That distinction belongs to Prince Honeycutt, who had lived there since the close of the Civil War. Having served as camp boy for Captain James Compton during the conflict, Honeycutt returned home with Compton at the war's end. He became a barber, married a white woman who died in a few years, and much later in life took a Black woman as his second wife. His children were known for their musical ability, and some of them became schoolteachers in Otter Tail County.

Initially the 1897 migrants to Fergus Falls attended the Swedish Baptist Church, but that proved unrewarding because the services were conducted in Swedish. Some joined the Seventh-Day Adventist congregation and others the Methodist Episcopal Church. Not until February 22, 1919, did the Blacks organize their own Central Baptist Church. After it was officially incorporated on April 2, 1919, with a membership of 22, it bought Bethania Hall, a building formerly occupied by the Bethania Lutheran congregation at 226 Washington Avenue East. The Black Baptists remained active until the mid-1940s; after that services were held infrequently.[78]

The Kentuckians who moved from Fergus Falls to Aitkin County seem to have been joined by 25 additional Greenwood families who were persuaded to homestead in Wealthwood, an undeveloped township laid out by a Mille Lacs County real-estate man in 1899. The effort failed, and many of these people settled in Aitkin the following spring. Although predominantly Baptist, some joined the First Methodist Episcopal Church there. In 1914, however, the Black parishioners withdrew under the leadership of C. S. Kathan, a white minister, and in October, 1915, they organized a nondenominational Mission Church with 55 charter members. At first, services were held in the homes of members, but the following year a building was erected and formally dedicated. The congregation continued to meet until 1921 when Calvary Baptist Church was organized. The Mission Church then disbanded, and its remaining membership merged with that of Calvary.[79]

The Dakota County city of Hastings had a growing Black population at the end of the Civil War. About the turn of the century some members of the community erected an African

Methodist Church at East 5th and Sibley streets. In October, 1907, the church was burned to the ground, the work of "incendaries," said the local papers. Whether a hostile act was responsible is impossible to say, but the Black population of Hastings dropped sharply between 1905 and 1910. By 1970 there were only eight Blacks listed in the federal census for the city.[80]

In the 20th century other outstate communities showed decreases in the number of Black citizens. Stillwater in Washington County had a population of 56 in 1910 but only one in 1970. Redwood Falls (Redwood County), which had 39 Blacks in 1905, had a Black population of one in 1970.[81]

In other areas, however, there have been equally dramatic increases in numbers of Blacks. Rochester in Olmsted County grew from 27 in 1910 to 186 in 1970; both St. Cloud in Stearns County (12 Blacks in 1910) and Red Wing in Goodhue County (20 in 1910) increased to nearly 50 by 1970; and Moorhead on the western edge of Clay County grew from eight to 73 Blacks in the same period. Although Blacks lived in all but five Minnesota counties by 1970 (see Table 4.1), no other concentrations as significant as those in the Twin Cities have developed, and none is known to have evolved such numerous cultural institutions around which organized community life, religious and secular, distinct from the white social milieu, could be built.

Reference Notes

[1] Here and two paragraphs below, see United States, *Census, 1870, Population*, 40; 1890, part 1, p. 416; 1900, 1:544; 1970, vol. 1, part 25, pp. 130–162.

[2] Estimates of slaves imported as well as information on their areas of origin on the west coast of Africa between the Senegal and Niger rivers appear in Philip D. Curtin, *The Atlantic Slave Trade: A Census*, 150–158, 231 (Madison, Wis., 1969). Here and below, see also Florette Henri, *Black Migration: Movement North, 1900–1920* (Garden City, N.Y., 1976); John Hope Franklin, *From Slavery to Freedom* (New York, 1947).

[3] George Bonga, "Letters of George Bonga," and Kenneth W. Porter, "Relations Between Negroes and Indians Within the Present Limits of the United States," in *Journal of Negro History*, 12:53, 17:361 (January, 1927, July, 1932); Porter, "Negroes and the Fur Trade," in *Minnesota History*, 15:423, 425 (December, 1934); Earl Spangler, "The Negro in Minnesota, 1800–1865," in Historical and Scientific Society of Manitoba, *Papers*, 3rd series, 20:15 (1963–64); Warren Upham, *Minnesota Geographic Names*, 88 (Reprint ed., St. Paul, 1969).

[4] L[ivia] A[ppel], "Slavery in Minnesota," in *Minnesota History*, 5:40–43 (February, 1923); Jeffrey A. Hess, *Dred Scott: From Fort Snelling to Freedom*, 2–6 (*Historic Fort Snelling Chronicles*, no. 2 — St. Paul, 1975); Helen T. Catterall, "Some Antecedents of the Dred Scott Case," in *American Historical Review*, 30:67 (October, 1924); Earl Spangler, *The Negro in Minnesota*, 19–21, 29–31 (Minneapolis, 1961).

[5] The total number is approximate at best, for the methods used to determine race were imprecise, especially for people of mixed parentage. The category "mulatto," for example, which was listed for 25 persons, was really a catch-all and served merely as an indication of color. See Patricia C. Harpole and Mary D. Nagle, eds., *Minnesota Territorial Census, 1850*, 2, 5, 13, 14, 43–45, 47, 49, 50, 53, 66, 72, 80, 88, 90 (St. Paul, 1972); Joseph Alexander, "Blacks in Minnesota, 1850–1870," 13–16, term paper, University of Minneso-

ta, 1970, a quantitative study based upon U.S. census data; a partial copy is in the MEHP Papers, MHS.

[6] Gary Libman, "Minnesota and the Struggle for Black Suffrage, 1849–70," pp. 13–15, Ph.D. thesis, University of Minnesota, 1972; *Minnesota Pioneer* (St. Paul), September 30, 1852; *St. Paul Daily Minnesotian*, October 2, 1856, July 18, 1857; Minnesota Territory, *House Journal*, 1854, p. 255.

[7] William Anderson, *A History of the Constitution of Minnesota*, 99–101 (Minneapolis, 1921); Libman, "Black Suffrage," 16–37.

[8] Libman, "Black Suffrage," 37–41, 96, 101, 137, 169; Minnesota, *Laws*, 1868, p. 149; William Gillette, *The Right to Vote: Politics and the Passage of the Fifteenth Amendment*, 26, 145 (Baltimore, 1965). A segregated facility was established in February, 1859, with Moses Dixon as teacher. *St. Paul Weekly Pioneer and Democrat*, November 5, 1857; *St. Paul Daily Minnesotian*, March 9, 1859; Minnesota, *Laws*, 1869, p. 7; interview of Edward Nichols by author, July 17, 1974, in MHS. Nichols married into the Joseph Farr family who had migrated to St. Paul in the 1850s. See [A. Hermina Poatgieter], "The Story of Afro-Americans in the Story of Minnesota," in *Gopher Historian*, vol. 23, Winter, 1968–69, p. 10.

The interviews cited in this chapter here and below were taped as part of the Minnesota Black History Project, 1974–76, and are in MHS.

[9] Spangler, *Negro in Minnesota*, 25, 46–50; Minnesota, *Laws*, 1858, p. 232. For example, Charles Jackson, a 14-year-old former slave from Georgia, was among those who arrived in the state with the returning 2nd Minnesota Regiment. He became a barber in Stillwater, where he lived until his death in 1903. On Jackson and the small Washington County Black community, see *Stillwater Daily Gazette*, May 5, 1903, p. 3; interview of Jackson's daughter, Mattie J. Rhodes, by author, June 26, 1974.

[10] Here and below, see Spangler, *Negro in Minnesota*, 50–53, for a discussion of various versions of the arrival of the Hickman group. See also Alfred M. Potekin, "Rev. Robert Thomas Hickman: Preacher, (col'd) rail splitter and Slave liberator," 2, in Works Progress Administration (WPA), Annals of Minnesota, Negroes in Minnesota, in MHS.

[11] [U.S. Bureau of the Census], *Negro Population in the United States, 1790–1915*, 87–89 (New York, 1968); U.S., *Census, 1920, Population*, 3:518, 523, 524.

[12] Marion D. Shutter, ed., *History of Minneapolis, Gateway to the Northwest*, 1:85, 101, 113 (Chicago and Minneapolis, 1923); *Minneapolis Spokesman*, September 29, 1939, p. 3.

[13] State of Minnesota, *Census, 1865*, 94; Thomas L. Dynneson, "The Negro Church in Minnesota, 1860–1967," 26, master's thesis, Macalester College, 1968; Spangler, *Negro in Minnesota*, 56. The *Minneapolis Chronicle*, August 4, 1866, noted "quite an addition to our colored population recently, by arrivals from the sunny south." An account of the church's founding by Robert Hickman's grandson, John Hickman, appears in *Minneapolis Spokesman*, April 25, 1958, pp. 1, 4.

[14] Minnesota Baptist State Convention, *Minutes of the Forty-First Anniversary*, 13 (Minneapolis, 1900); Spangler, *Negro in Minnesota*, 52–55; *St. Paul Daily Press*, November 7, 1863; *St. Paul and Minneapolis Pioneer Press*, December 11, 1887; Thomas Scott and R. Hickman to First Baptist Church, January 17, 1864; "Report," January 6, 1865, to members of the First Baptist Church, St. Paul; Records of the Board of Trustees, vol. 13, p. 72, all in First Baptist Church Records, MHS; Norma Sommerdorf, *A Church in Lowertown: The First Baptist Church of Saint Paul*, 40 (St. Paul, 1975); Jon H. Butler, "Communities and Congregations: The Black Church in St. Paul, 1860–1900," in *Journal of Negro History*, 56:119–121 (April, 1871).

[15] *St. Paul and Minneapolis Pioneer Press*, December 11, 1887; *St. Paul City Directory, 1869*, 242, *1870*, 269, *1871*, 248; *St. Paul*

Echo, January 16, 1926, p. 3; Butler, in *Journal of Negro History*, 121–123; Dynneson, "Negro Church in Minnesota," 29, 39, 42, 45, 49.

[16] *St. Paul City Directory, 1866*, 263–275, gives a breakdown by wards of ethnic and racial groups based upon the 1865 state census; these figures, which differ from those in Minnesota, *Census, 1865*, 101, have been used here. See also Spangler, *Negro in Minnesota*, 56, 73; *St. Paul Pioneer*, May 31, June 9, October 7, 1866.

[17] Alexander, "Blacks in Minnesota," 22–24. On the development of neighborhoods here and below, see a useful summary in Virginia B. Kunz, *St. Paul: Saga of an American City*, 54–65 (Woodland Hills, Calif., 1977).

[18] Here and two paragraphs below, see U.S., *Census, 1870, Population*, 1:16; Minnesota, *Census, 1905*, 38, 171; Kunz, *St. Paul*, 69, discusses the extension of streetcars. Maps compiled from data in the *St. Paul City Directory* on ethnic neighborhoods about 1870 and for Blacks in 1896 may be found in David V. Taylor, "Pilgrim's Progress: Black St. Paul and the Making of an Urban Ghetto," 44, 45, 47, Ph.D. thesis, University of Minnesota, 1977. See also *St. Paul Pioneer Press*, September 26, 1875; W. Gunther Plaut, *The Jews in Minnesota: The First Seventy-Five Years*, 157, 158 (New York, 1959); Calvin F. Schmid, *Social Saga of Two Cities: An Ecological and Statistical Study of Social Trends in Minneapolis and St. Paul*, 148, 155, 157, 162, 163, 177–182, 184 (Minneapolis, 1937). The *St. Paul Echo*, September 18, 1926, p. 2, described Rondo Street as "a riot of warmth, and color, and feeling, and sound." On the distribution of other ethnic groups in St. Paul, see James M. Reardon, "The Church of St. Mary of St. Paul," in *Acta et Dicta*, 5:234, 235 (October, 1934).

[19] Here and below, see U.S., *Census, 1870, Population*, 1:16; [U.S. Bureau of the Census], *Negro Population*, 156. Abram L. Harris, *The Negro Population in Minneapolis: A Study of Race Relations*, 11 (Minneapolis, [1926?]), contains useful data on states of origin of Minnesota's Black population from 1880 to 1920.

[20] On occupations, see [U.S. Bureau of the Census], *Negro Population*, 518; *Western Appeal*, June 27, 1885. The author obtained the information here and below by compiling Black addresses and occupations given in the *St. Paul City Directory, 1880, 1890*, and in the 1895 manuscript state census schedules and transcribing that data onto city maps. According to the 1880 directory, 59–61, railroads based there were the Chicago, Minneapolis and Omaha, the Northern Pacific, the St. Paul and Duluth, and the St. Paul, Minneapolis and Manitoba.

[21] Alexander, "Blacks in Minnesota," 22–24; [U. S. Bureau of the Census], *Negro Population*, 252, 273, 471; *Appeal* (St. Paul-Minneapolis), August 24, 1901, p. 3. From 1885 to 1888, this was the *Western Appeal*. See note 28, below.

[22] Here and below, see Thomas E. Reinhart, "The Minneapolis Black Community, 1863–1926," p. 16, unpublished paper, St. John's University, 1970, copy in MHS; U.S., *Census, 1870, Population*, 1:10; Minnesota, *Census, 1885*, 25, *1895*, 95; Schmid, *Social Saga of Two Cities*, 78, 179, 183.

[23] [U.S. Bureau of the Census], *Negro Population*, 156, 273, 471, 518.

[24] *Minneapolis City Directory, 1873–74*, 25, 28; *1875*, 24, 27; *1878–79*, 28, 30.

[25] Dynneson, "Negro Church," 40, 48–51; Butler, in *Journal of Negro History*, 56:124, 133; Reinhart, "Minneapolis Black Community," 12; Taylor, "Pilgrim's Progress," 32–37.

[26] Addison R. Fenwick, ed., *Sturdy Sons of Saint Paul*, 93 ([St. Paul?], 1899); *St. Paul City Directory, 1877–78*, 198; *1880–81*, 388; *1906*, 1155; *Western Appeal*, July 18, 1885, September 8, 22, October 6, 1888; *Appeal*, September 1, 1894, July 31, September 25, October 9, 25, 1897, March 26, 1898, May 24, 1902, p. 3, September 11, 1920, p. 3.

[27] [Poatgieter], in *Gopher Historian*, Winter, 1968–69, pp. 17, 18; Spangler, *Negro in Minnesota*, 71; James S. Griffin, *Blacks in the St. Paul Police and Fire Departments, 1885–1976*, 31 ([St. Paul], 1978). Griffin is deputy chief of police in St. Paul and the only Black to hold that position in Minnesota. See also *Western Appeal*, September 8, 22, 1888; *Appeal*, September 1, 1894; *St. Paul Daily Dispatch*, February 25, 1875; *Minneapolis Tribune*, March 20, 24, 1875.

[28] On September 23, 1876, the *St. Paul Daily Dispatch* announced the commencement of a colored newspaper called the *Western Appeal*, which was Republican in its politics. Another paper, possibly called the *St. Paul Review*, or *Northwest Review*, edited by E. P. Wade was announced in 1880. See *Minneapolis Tribune*, February 11, 1880.

On the beginnings of the second, successful *Appeal* in 1888, see David V. Taylor, "John Adams and the Western Appeal: Advocates of the Protest Tradition," 10, 14, master's thesis, University of Nebraska at Omaha, 1971. Portions of this thesis appeared under the title "John Quincy Adams, St. Paul Editor and Black Leader," in *Minnesota History*, 43:283–296 (Winter, 1973). See also *Appeal*, September 24, 1910, p. 4.

[29] *Appeal*, September 24, 1910, p. 4, September 11, 1920, p. 2; Taylor, in *Minnesota History*, 43:285–287. On McGhee and Turner, see Fenwick, ed., *Sturdy Sons of Saint Paul*, 95; [Poatgieter], in *Gopher Historian*, Winter, 1968–69, pp. 18, 20. *St. Paul City Directory, 1897*, 423, lists Dr. T. S. Cook who apparently preceded Turner by a year. See also *St. Paul City Directory, 1898*, 406, 1342.

[30] [Poatgieter], in *Gopher Historian*, Winter, 1968–69, pp. 19–21; *Minneapolis Spokesman*, May 27, 1949, p. 13.

[31] Taylor, in *Minnesota History*, 43:288–290. For a list of leaders in the Twin Cities Black community, see Taylor, "Pilgrim's Progress," 89.

[32] U.S., *Census, 1880, Population*, 687, 696; [Poatgieter], in *Gopher Historian*, Winter, 1968–69, p. 18; Minnesota Adjutant General, *Annual Report, 1880*, 4 (St. Peter, 1881); Griffin, *Blacks in the St. Paul Police and Fire Departments*, 31; *Minneapolis Daily Tribune*, March 25, 1869, December 4, 1881; *Stillwater Gazette*, May 7, 1879; Bessie L. Scovell, *A Brief History of the Minnesota Woman's Christian Temperance Union . . . 1877 to 1939*, 211 (Minneapolis, 1939).

[33] Here and below, see *Western Appeal*, December 24, 1887; Taylor, in *Minnesota History*, 43:291–295; Spangler, *Negro in Minnesota*, 78. The name of the National Afro-American League was changed in 1898.

[34] *Appeal*, October 19, 1901, p. 3, September 13, 1913, p. 3; Taylor, in *Minnesota History*, 43:294–296. On the NAACP, see its *Fourth Annual Report*, 1913, p. 57, *Sixth Annual Report*, 1916, p. 20 (New York, 1913, 1916); *St. Paul Dispatch*, November 27, 1969, p. 1. By 1916 the St. Paul chapter had 135 members.

[35] *Minneapolis Tribune*, June 15, 1880; *Western Appeal*, September 8, 22, 1888. In the city elections of 1876, Major John Becht was elected Ramsey County sheriff with a plurality of 186 votes, exactly the number of registered Black voters turned out by T. H. Lyles in that election. Fenwick, ed., *Sturdy Sons of Saint Paul*, 93. In 1892 F. L. McGhee was nominated as a presidential elector of the Republican party. Later he was an alternate delegate to the Democratic national convention at Kansas City. He is believed to have been the first Black in the state to be so elected by Democrats. *Svenska Amerikanska Posten*, September 20, 1892; *Appeal*, June 23, 1900, p. 3. See also Spangler, *Negro in Minnesota*, 81; Taylor, "Pilgrim's Progress," 145, 206–211.

[36] Community events in both cities received equal attention in the press. See, for example, *Appeal*, August 14, 1909, p. 3, January 22, 1910, pp. 1, 3, July 16, 1910, p. 3. Between 1888 and 1919, 13 newspapers competed with the *Appeal*; each lasted only a short

time. They were *Afro-American Advance*, 1899; *Afro-Independent*, 1888; *Colored Citizen*, 18??; *Minneapolis Observer*, 1890; *National Advocate*, 1917; *Negro World*, 1892; *Northwestern Vine*, 1902; *Protest*, 1892; *Twin City American*, 1899; *Twin City Star*, 1910; *Twin City Guardian*, 1895; *Voice of the People*, 1888; and *World*, 1895. Daniel P. Mikel, "A History of Negro Newspapers in Minnesota, 1876–1963," 12–14, 52–54, master's thesis, Macalester College, 1962.

[37] *St. Paul Daily Press*, August 4, November 13, December 31, 1868; *Minneapolis Daily Tribune*, December 20, 1868, January 4, 1870; Convention of Colored Citizens of the State of Minnesota, *Proceedings . . . in Celebration of the Anniversary of Emancipation*, 8, 29–31 (St. Paul, 1869); *Twin City Herald*, July 30, 1932, p. 2.

[38] Schmid, *Social Saga*, 123; Henri, *Black Migration*, 68–70.

[39] [U.S. Bureau of the Census], *Negro Population*, 99; U.S., *Census, 1920, Population*, 3:60; Harris, *Negro Population of Minneapolis*, 11; Henri, *Black Migration*, 69.

[40] Spangler, *Negro in Minnesota*, 67. Parks's autobiography, *A Choice of Weapons*, was published in 1965. Other autobiographical accounts of this period are Dr. Anna A. Hedgeman's *The Trumpet Sounds* (New York, 1964) which described her family's migration from the South to Anoka, and Taylor Gordon's *Born To Be* (New York, 1929) which depicted St. Paul. On the struggle to admit Blacks to labor unions, see *St. Paul Echo*, February 13, 1926, p. 1; *Northwestern Bulletin* (St. Paul-Minneapolis), April 22, 1922, p. 2; *Minneapolis Spokesman*, January 12, p. 2, January 19, p. 1, 1940.

[41] Schmid, *Social Saga*, 180, 185; Brian Storton, "Analysis of Minority Dispersion in Minneapolis and St. Paul," 2, term paper, University of Minnesota, 1973.

[42] Here and below, see Schmid, *Social Saga*, 180; *St. Paul Echo*, September 18, 1926, p. 2; "Twin Cities Map," in *Fortune*, April, 1936, pp. 112–119.

[43] Maurine Boie, "A Study of Conflict and Accommodation in Negro-White Relations in the Twin Cities," 81, 82, 83, 86, master's thesis, University of Minnesota, 1932; Spangler, *Negro in Minnesota*, 93.

[44] Schmid, *Social Saga*, 176; U.S., *Census, 1970, Population*, vol. 1, part 25, p. 235.

[45] For a general account of postwar unrest, see Louis E. Lomax, *The Negro Revolt* (New York, 1971). See also *Appeal*, April 7, 1923, [p. 1]; Whitney M. Young, Jr., "History of the St. Paul Urban League," 19, 20, Plan B paper, University of Minnesota, 1947, copy in MHS. Copies of the *Helper*, which later became the *Bulletin*, are in the Eva Neal and Family Papers, MHS.

[46] Young, "St. Paul Urban League," 22–25, 31; Spangler, *Negro in Minnesota*, 105.

[47] Phyllis Wheatley House, "History," notes and typed manuscripts, in Phyllis Wheatley Settlement House Records, MHS.

[48] Plaut, *Jews in Minnesota*, 154; *Neighborhood House, 1897–1947; Welcome Hall; A Community House for Colored People; Testimonial as to Welcome Hall and Welcome Hall Playground*; and *Glimpses of the Christian Center, Inc.* — all four pamphlets in MHS library. See also Chapter 26, below.

[49] Alice S. Onqué, "History of the Hallie Q. Brown Community House," 12–34, Plan B paper, University of Minnesota, 1959, copy in MHS.

[50] *Twin City Herald*, February 25, 1933, p. 1; Boie, "A Study of Conflict," 111; Harris, *Negro Population of Minneapolis*, 28, 29; *Minneapolis Spokesman*, May 6, 1938, pp. 1, 6.

[51] L. E. Leipold, *Cecil E. Newman: Newspaper Publisher*, 67, 69, 73 (Minneapolis, 1969); Mikel, "History of Negro Newspapers," 17, 63, 121.

[52] *Twin City Herald*, May 21, p. 1, June 25, p. 3, August 27, p. 1, September 10, p. 1 — all 1932, and April 15, 1933, p. 1.

[53] *Minneapolis City Directory, 1935*, 2060–2065; *St. Paul City Directory, 1935*, 1895–1898.

[54] Credjafawn Club, "Report of the President," [1937?], in Credjafawn Social Club Papers, roll 2, microfilm in MHS; "Successful Co-op in St. Paul," in *Eyes: The Negroes' Own Picture Magazine*, June, 1946, p. 13. The first two co-operatives were at 384 North Prior Ave. and 989 Payne Ave.; *St. Paul City Directory, 1942*, 251, *1946*, 233. The parent organization of these stores was Co-ops, Inc. of St. Paul, established about 1940; it was through this group that the Credjafawn Club established Neighborhood Store No. 3. Information from Arthur W. Sternberg, secretary of the corporation from 1945 to 1969, April 30, 1978.

[55] Here and below, see Governor's Interracial Commission, *The Negro Worker in Minnesota*, 6, 16 ([St. Paul], 1945); Governor's Interracial Commission, *The Negro and His Home in Minnesota: A Report*, 49 ([St. Paul], 1947); Franklin, *From Slavery to Freedom*, 561; *Code of Federal Regulations Title 3 — The President, 1933–43, Compilation*, 957 (Washington, D.C., 1968).

[56] Leipold, *Cecil E. Newman*, 92–95; Minnesota Governor's Interracial Commission, *The Negro Worker's Progress in Minnesota: A Report*, 21, 26 ([St. Paul], 1949); *Minneapolis Spokesman*, May 10, p. 1, July 12, p. 1, 1935, and February 14, p. 1, July 24, p. 2, 1936. One brewery reportedly employed a token Black as a result of the boycott.

[57] Governor's Interracial Commission, *Negro Worker*, 12–14 (1945); Leipold, *Cecil E. Newman*, 94–100; Spangler, *Negro in Minnesota*, 109. Other plants were Brown and Bigelow, Inc., Griggs, Cooper and Co., International Harvester, Minneapolis Honeywell Regulator Co., Munsingwear, Inc., Northwest Airlines, Northwestern Aeronautical Corp., D. W. Onan and Sons, Raymond Laboratories Inc., Seeger Refrigerator Co., A. O. Smith Corp., Strutwear Knitting Co., and Superior Metal Products Co.

[58] Spangler, *Negro in Minnesota*, 151–153; Minnesota, *Laws*, 1955, pp. 802–812. For earlier attempts to obtain FEP legislation, see, for example, Minnesota, *Senate Journal*, 1947, p. 363; 1949, p. 94; 1953, p. 231. On housing, see Governor's Interracial Commission, *Negro and His Home*, 41–49; Minnesota, *Laws*, 1937, p. 852.

[59] Here and below, see Storton, "Analysis of Minority Dispersion," 2; Governor's Interracial Commission, *Negro Worker's Progress*, 9, 15–19; U.S., *Census, 1970, Population*, vol. 1, part 25, pp. 596–599.

[60] Governor's Interracial Commission, *Negro and His Home*, [3], 18; St. Paul Urban Coalition, *The 1968 Labor Day Weekend in St. Paul: The Events and Their Causes*, 35–46 (St. Paul, 1969).

[61] Here and below, see U.S., *Census, 1950, Population*, vol. 2, part 23, pp. 64, 143–145, 248; 1970, vol. 1, part 25, pp. 68, 81–92, 241, 325–328.

[62] Here and below, see U.S., *Census, 1960, Population*, vol. 1, part 25, pp. 333–335; 1970, vol. 1, part 25, pp. 93–96, 321–324, 329–332; St. Paul Urban Coalition, *1968 Labor Day Weekend*, 28–32, 68; *St. Paul Pioneer Press*, September 3, p. 13, September 4, p. 4, 1968; *St. Paul Recorder*, September 5, 1968, p. 8. See also Minnesota, *Legislative Manual 1977–78*, 143, 146; Scott Publishing Co., *Minnesota's Black Community*, 63 (Minneapolis, 1976); Ethel V. Mitchell, ed., *Contributions of Black Women to Minnesota History*, 83 (St. Paul, 1977).

[63] Interview of Nichols' son, Edward, by author, July 17, 1974.

[64] U.S., *Census, 1870, Population*, 1:17; 1890, 1:235, 1930, vol. 3, part 1, p. 1217; *Duluth City Directory, 1886–87*, 36; Minnesota Manuscript Census Schedules, 1857, pp. 95, 99, 102, 107, 114, roll 5, microfilm in MHS; Minnesota, *Census, 1885*, 65, *1895*, 126.

[65] Interview of Ethel Ray Nance by author, May 25, 1974; Nichols interview, July 17, 1974.

[66] *Appeal*, February 22, 1890. A second Black congregation was

organized about 1890 by Rev. Frederick Lomack, who moved from Minneapolis to Duluth and established a short-lived Mount Olivet Baptist Church. It failed to survive, and more than 20 years elapsed before Calvary Baptist Church was formed about 1913. *Minneapolis City Directory, 1890*, 786; *Duluth City Directory, 1914*, 72.

[67] Duluth visitors to Twin Cities events appeared in social columns of the *Appeal*. See, for example, July 28, 1900, p. 3, August 4, 1906, p. 5, August 3, 1907, p. 3. See also *World* (Minneapolis and St. Paul — Duluth and West Superior), April 25, May 30, June 6, 13, July 4, September 12, 1896; *Duluth City Directory, 1910*, 118–120. Union picnics were so called because they were sponsored by all the Twin Cities Black congregations with the support of other agencies.

[68] *World*, April 25, May 9, June 6, 1896, May 29, August 28, 1897. On Williams, see *Duluth Sunday News-Tribune*, May 16, 1976, Accent North sec., p. 11; interview of William F. Maupins, Jr., by W. J. Musa Foster, Malik Simba, and Seitu Jones, July 31, 1975; *Duluth City Directory, 1906*, 875, *1925*, 729. The duration of his publication is not known.

[69] U.S., *Census, 1910, Population*, 2:1010; 1930, vol. 3, part 1, p. 1209; author's interviews of Fred D. and Lillian V. Bell, July 9, 1975, and Charles M. and Geraldine H. Stalling, July 30, 1975; Maupins interview, July 31, 1975. See also Gus Turbeville, "The Negro Population in Duluth, Minnesota, 1950," in *Sociology and Social Research*, 36:231–238 (March-April, 1952).

[70] Bell interview, July 9, 1975; Maupins interview, July 31, 1975; Stalling interview, July 30, 1975.

[71] Spangler, *Negro in Minnesota*, 100–103; Minnesota, *Laws*, 1921, p. 612. See also Michael W. Fedo, *'They Was Just Niggers'* (Ontario, Calif., 1979), a recent account of the Duluth incident. Earlier concern about lynching had led to the establishment in 1898 of the American Law Enforcement League of Minnesota; Taylor, in *Minnesota History*, 43:294. Duluth's Black population decreased by 42 between 1920 and 1930 while the total population of the city increased by more than 2,000. U.S., *Census, 1920, Population*, 3:518; 1930, vol. 3, part 1, p. 1253.

[72] Here and below, see U.S., *Census, 1940, Population*, vol. 2, part 4, p. 166; 1950, vol. 2, part 23, p. 11; 1960, vol. 1, part 25, p. 103; 1970, vol. 1, part 25, p. 80. The *Duluth City Directory, 1915–16*, 89, listed "election districts" rather than wards. See also Daniel J. Elazar, "Constitutional Change in a Long-Depressed Economy: A Case of the Duluth Civil Community," 10, 15, mimeographed article, [1964?], copy in MHS; Bureau of the Census, *Census Tracts: Duluth-Superior*, 1961, 14–17; 1972, 1–4; "History of Duluth International Airport," mimeographed summary, copy

in MHS. In April, 1978, Major John W. Volpel, director of information at the base, gave the Black military population as 103 and said there was no minority group data for the 1950 to 1970 period.

[73] Here and below, see Bureau of the Census, *Census Tracts: Duluth-Superior*, 1970, 5; U.S., *Census*, 1970, *Population*, vol. 1, part 25, pp. 81–92, 321–324.

[74] Harpole and Nagle, eds., *Territorial Census, 1850*, 2, 5, 13, 14, 80, 88, 90; U.S., *Census*, 1900, *Population*, 1:544. The 10 counties were Benton, Houston, Kittson, Lincoln, Marshall, Mille Lacs, Murray, Todd, Wadena, and Yellow Medicine.

[75] [U.S. Bureau of the Census], *Negro Population in the United States*, 588, 607, 656; U.S., *Census*, 1920, *Agriculture*, vol. 6, part 1, pp. 19, 487.

[76] Interview of Norman P. Lyght by author, June 25, 1974. Another Black family, that of George Moses, arrived in Cook County from Chicago before 1920. They homesteaded near Good Harbor Bay and were known locally as fine musicians; information from Lyght, April 6, 1978.

[77] Here and below, see Elmer E. Adams, "The Coming of Colored People," in *Fergus Falls Daily Journal*, September 16, 1933, p. 2; Grand Army of the Republic, *Journal of the Thirtieth Encampment . . . St. Paul, Minnesota*, 3 (Indianapolis, 1896); *Fergus Falls City and Rural Directory, 1919*, 104; U.S., *Census*, 1970, *Population*, vol. 1, part 25, p. 148.

[78] WPA, Minnesota, Historical Records Survey: Church Records, Otter Tail County, in MHS. Rev. M. W. Withers, a "missionary Evangelist of the Baptist Church, from Minneapolis," served the church during 1918–25, 1928–29, and 1931–36, but it is not certain whether the congregation ever had a resident pastor.

[79] Spangler, *Negro in Minnesota*, 67n; WPA, Church Records.

[80] Minnesota, *Census, 1865*, 12; U.S., *Census*, 1870, *Population*, 1:18; 1970, vol. 1, part 25, pp. 130–159; Lucille H. Doffing, *Hastings-on-the-Mississippi*, 113 (Hastings and Kilkenny, 1976); *Hastings Gazette*, November 2, 1907, p. 3; *Hastings Democrat*, October 31, 1907, p. 2.

[81] Here and below, see Minnesota, *Census, 1905*, 71; U.S., *Census*, 1910, *Population*, 3:997–1012; 1970, vol. 1, part 25, pp. 130–159, 160–162. On Blacks in the Moorhead area, see Earl Lewis, "Pioneers of a Different Kind," in *Red River Valley Historian*, Winter, 1978–79, pp. 14–16. While Stillwater's population decreased, nearby Bayport had 131 Blacks in 1970. It is possible to speculate that industrial diversification and the growth of outstate educational institutions have been responsible in part for increases in some rural Black communities.

CHAPTER 5

The Mexicans

Susan M. Diebold

MEXICAN AMERICANS immigrated to Minnesota in sizable numbers largely in the 20th century. But they were not recent foreigners nor strangers to the United States; rather, they were early colonists. For over 200 years, the Southwest belonged to Mexico. At the end of the Mexican War, the United States acquired not only Mexican territory, but about 100,000 Mexican citizens. No Mexicans were counted in Minnesota Territory in 1850, but two were listed in the state 10 years later and the figure grew to six by 1880. In that decade Luis Garzón, who may have been the first Mexican resident of Minneapolis, arrived with the Mexican National Band to perform at the city's Industrial Exposition in 1886; he remained for more than 50 years. At the turn of the century Mexican residents of the United States numbered 103,410, comprising 1% of the total national census, while in Minnesota they totaled 24 — less than 1/1000 of 1%.[1]

Like other immigrants from certain European countries, Mexicans were drawn to the United States by the promise of work — in this case, chiefly agricultural field work. Unsettled political conditions created by the Mexican Revolution (1911–17) and the increased demand for labor in the United States during World War I caused many to move north. They migrated to Minnesota's Red River and Minnesota River valleys from the agricultural central states of Mexico — Guanajuato, Michoacán, Jalisco, San Luis Potosí, Zacatecas, and to the north and northwest, Coahuila and Nuevo León — and from the southwestern United States — Texas, New Mexico, and Oklahoma (see Map 5.1).[2]

Initially most of the Mexicans and Mexican Americans in Minnesota were migrant or seasonal workers who arrived early in the spring and spent only a few weeks or months employed in the fields before moving on. Over the years, however, some "settled out" of the migrant stream and became permanent residents of the state. The story of the Minnesota Mexican community is complicated by the differing patterns of the two groups — the transient migrant workers who have continued to visit each season and the year-round residents of the state. Most of the latter group, it may be noted, are descendants of settled-out migrants.

Rapid expansion of the sugar beet industry in the United States was responsible for the first extensive importation of Mexican workers into Minnesota. First grown in the state in

the 1880s, beets were not used for the production of sugar until a factory was built at St. Louis Park in 1897. Although it burned down a few years later, it was "so successful that other cities in Minnesota clamored for the privilege of being the site of future plants." Initially the industry relied on German and Russian immigrants to work the beet fields, but World War I and the quota laws enacted by the United States in the 1920s effectively cut off that labor supply (see Introduction). The Mexicans provided a satisfactory alternative.[3]

In the first decade of the 20th century the Chaska plant of the Minnesota Sugar Company (later the American Crystal Sugar Company) was the largest employer of Mexican labor. As soon as the plant was built in 1907, recruiters for the firm set up offices in Texas and other southwestern states to hire Mexicans as well as Americans of Mexican descent and assist them in traveling north. Those who were hired during this period, "the first Mexican and Mexican-American migrant farmers to come to Minnesota, went to work on beet farms around Albert Lea, Chaska and Savage." In 1912 only about 200 field workers were employed; few remained over the winter. Census figures for 1900, 1910, and 1920 indicate that 24, 52, and 237 Mexican-born persons, respectively, resided in Minnesota during those years.[4]

A sharp increase occurred in the 1920s. Between 1921 and 1930 some 459,000 Mexicans (11.1% of the United States total) immigrated legally; thousands more arrived illegally, either "wet" by wading the Rio Grande River to Texas or "dry" by crossing into Arizona and New Mexico. Mexican labor had "proved so satisfactory" that the demand for it remained high after World War I ended. Recruitment of seasonal workers, numbering in thousands rather than hundreds, continued throughout the decade. A sugar-beet company representative estimated the total Minnesota Mexican population in 1927 at 5,000 and in 1928 at 7,000, adding that beet acreage had doubled in the year and that the firm was "having a hard time securing enough Mexican workers." A Texas agent wrote that he had sent them to "over 200 different places in Minnesota" during the 1928 season. Another reported that "1,933 Mexicans were shipped by 2 labor agencies during 2 months only" and that there were "10 agencies in San Antonio alone."[5]

St. Paul Beginnings

At first these Mexicans were largely Mestizos (Spanish and Indian) workers who stayed only the 16 to 24 weeks they were needed in the beet fields. Gradually, however, more and more of them remained over the winter. They settled principally in St. Paul. A possible explanation for the nucleus of St. Paul's Mexican colony may be the fact that a number of its earliest residents were employed by railroad companies — many of which were headquartered in that city.[6]

The first elements of the colony, formed between 1912 and 1916, found winter housing in the Riverview district, locally referred to as the "West Side." The heart of the "primary settlement," which was to attract so many, was at Fairfield, State, and Indiana streets. Other workers sought shelter on the low land between the 3rd and 6th Street bridges, in Swede Hollow along Phalen Creek below the 7th Street Bridge, on the east bank of the Mississippi behind the public market, and in boxcars along the Burlington Railroad tracks.

The Mexicans were merely the most recent of the many immigrant groups to settle on "the flats" of St. Paul's lower West Side. When they arrived about 1915, the predominant ethnic enclave there was composed of eastern European Jews with whom they coexisted in harmony. By the early 1920s the Jewish people began leaving the flats. This migration accelerated in the 1930s; the Jewish population decreased from 72% in 1917 to 36% in 1931, and gradually the area became predominantly Mexican American.

Of 237 Mexicans in Minnesota in 1920, 70 were living in St. Paul. By 1925 the city's winter population was estimated at 350. By 1930 there were 3,636 (2,069 males and 1,557 females) in the state, or 0.1% of the total population. Seventeen per cent, or 630, were living in St. Paul and adjacent Ramsey County, 151 or 4% in Minneapolis. Many of them continued to go out to work the fields in such rural areas as Le Sueur, Chaska, Cokato, Albert Lea, Glencoe, East Grand Forks, and Hollandale. The official policy of the Minnesota Sugar Company encouraged the winter layover by erecting housing in Albert Lea, Le Sueur, and East Grand Forks. By 1930 eight counties in addition to Ramsey had sizable numbers of Mexicans: Blue Earth 345, Faribault 292, Freeborn 159, Hennepin 164, Martin 245, Nobles 276, Polk 237, and Waseca 135. This pattern seems to have continued with some interruption during the Depression of the 1930s (see Table 5.1).[7]

The Minnesota Sugar Company's treatment of migrants

Map 5.1. Areas in Mexico from which Immigrants Arrived in Minnesota

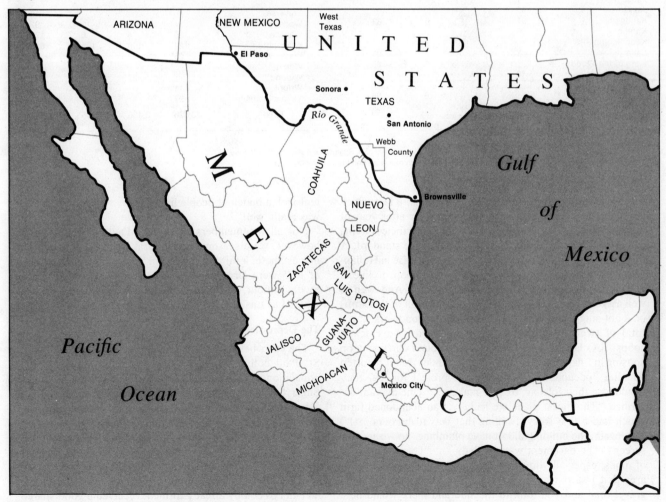

Table 5.1. Mexicans in Minnesota by County and Major Urban Areas, 1930–70

County	1930 foreign stock	1960 foreign stock	1970 foreign stock	1970 Spanish language*	County	1930 foreign stock	1960 foreign stock	1970 foreign stock	1970 Spanish language*
Aitkin				44	Martin	245			5
Anoka		40	89	644	Meeker	49			65
Becker	1				Mille Lacs		4		
Beltrami		19		22	Morrison				36
Benton	5	15	7	44	Mower		20	9	116
Blue Earth	345	64	22	250	Murray			7	94
Brown	8	3		47	Nicollet	92	5		44
Carlton				161	Nobles	276		7	105
Carver	51				Norman	11			
Cass	1		6	20	Olmsted	1	19	89	588
Chippewa	11			36	Otter Tail				12
Chisago		8		64	Pennington	12	12		5
Clay	80	16	188	330	Polk	237	36	69	248
Cottonwood		5		16	Pope				18
Crow Wing	3		53	189	Ramsey	630	1,593	1,912	7,433
Dakota	84	109	401	1,162	St. Paul	628	1,440	365	6,512
Dodge	7				Redwood	11			7
Douglas				13	Renville	88			14
Faribault	292	49	46	332	Rice		30	42	200
Freeborn	159	269	275	740	Roseau				9
Goodhue	2	11		34	St. Louis	14	36	55	696
Grant				12	Duluth	14	19	33	353
Hennepin	164	821	937	6,595	Scott	3	19		199
Minneapolis	151	690	167	3,940	Sherburne	4	16		28
Houston				10	Sibley	82			34
Hubbard				42	Stearns		21	26	218
Isanti		16	5	52	Steele	60	8	22	130
Itasca	1	8	27	52	Todd		6		6
Jackson	90			7	Traverse				18
Kandiyohi	91		6	83	Wadena		12	11	92
Kittson	19				Waseca	135	4	5	173
Koochiching			7		Washington	24	109	191	850
Lake	1		7	101	Watonwan	20			20
Lake of the Woods			8	33	Wilkin			21	70
Le Sueur	3	17		40	Winona		27	8	227
Lincoln				8	Wright	11			61
Lyon			6	95	Yellow Medicine	97			5
McLeod	17			94	Total	3,626	3,436	4,575	23,198
Marshall	89								

Source: See Appendix

*Persons of Spanish mother tongue and all others whose head of family gave Spanish as his/her mother tongue, 1970.

Note: Foreign stock here includes foreign born and native born of foreign and mixed parentage.

was apparently better than that of many firms, a fact which helps to account for the frequent return year after year of Mexican migrant families to Minnesota. Nevertheless living conditions were still appalling by any objective standard. A former migrant worker recalled "one specific case in Hollandale where this farmer gave us two chicken coops to live in and we had to clean all the excrement out of it. And even as well as you can wash a chicken coop that is full of this stuff, on a hot muggy day it still seeps out of the woodwork. . . . a total of twelve people . . . had to live in two chicken coops." As late as 1957 a state agency found chicken coop housing in "flagrant violation" of state codes, but it reported that the "occupants refused to . . . protest for fear they would lose their jobs as 'trouble-makers.'" One migrant described "The nicest place we had . . . an abandoned farm which had a two story dwelling that was to be ours. . . . But, again, the building didn't have plumbing, no wiring, nor screens. The basement was flooded. . . . There were a lot of times, especially down in Hollandale, this was the worst area that I saw, when you would be driving down the dirt gravel road and you look to the side and there would be a

tent with a bunch of people living in . . . just a little tent. It was really sad!"[8]

Not all the members of the St. Paul Mexican colony, however, were seasonal agricultural workers. According to one estimate, a third of the 350 in St. Paul during the winter of 1925 were farm laborers; others were employed by the Swift, Armour, and Cudahy meat-packing houses, and some worked as unskilled laborers for the railroads.[9]

The Depression Years of the 1930s

The years between 1930 and 1938 were a watershed for the St. Paul colony. Nearly a third of the state's Mexican population lived in Ramsey County by 1936. The Minnesota Sugar Company, which had been the largest employer of Mexican labor, had stopped recruiting in Texas in 1929 when that state began to collect license fees for workers hired to leave its borders. As the Depression continued, the company further curtailed its activities; by 1933 it stopped guaranteeing wages, transportation, and credit. This resulted in a build-up of workers remaining in the state, and St. Paul, with an embryo colony already formed, received a good share.[10]

In January, 1931, a West Side social worker noted "A new development: There are 600 or 700 Mexicans in the neighborhood." Her figures may be exaggerated, but it is known that between 1930 and 1933 about 220 Mexicans settled in the capital city, 165 of them on the Lower West Side. One man who moved there during those years emphasized that "In 1930, there weren't any jobs in St. Paul, not until 1933," and he credited "that good man" Franklin D. Roosevelt with providing "jobs for poor people." In the next five years some 700 more Mexicans arrived, about 200 of whom settled on the Lower West Side, but at least six families found homes on the East Side.

There is some indication that certain differences existed between Mexican Americans in these two neighborhoods. One East Side resident recalled that while the "kids [on the West Side] spoke Spanish . . . most of us didn't, on the East Side." He also reported that as a child he was keenly aware of being "different." "I was darker," he said, "and I felt that in order to be American, you had to be white, you had to speak English well, and you had to eat American food. . . . I was ashamed to bring people to my house," he remembered; "they would smell the 'tortillas' and 'frijoles' in my house. Even though I couldn't speak Spanish well, I still had an accent and I could tell it. . . . So, I was embarrassed that I was a Mexican American. . . . I think I was very successful by the time I got to high school in . . . behaving like the American kids around me at that time." [11]

With the deepening of the Depression, the problems of the Mexican American increased. Growing competition for jobs and the subsequent displacement of the Mexican migrant worker by white labor resulted in a movement to deport Mexicans who were not naturalized citizens of the United States. Railroads, which had provided some employment, now took a new position; one Great Northern official wrote that as far as he was concerned, "we are not going to have any Mexicans on the line in the future." The United States Department of Labor began to ask railroad companies to co-operate "in permitting us to have Mexican laborers questioned with a view to determining whether or not they are in the United States legally." In 1934 some 328 persons were deported to Mexico from Ramsey County "at the request of relief authorities." Included were many children who had been born in the United States and were thus citizens. [12]

Such episodes made Mexicans reluctant to seek relief during the Depression of the 1930s for fear of "being returned to the place of their legal settlement, or if they were aliens to Mexico." Despite their hesitancy, however, most of those in St. Paul were finally forced to do so. And their numbers were increased by the arrival of families from outstate areas and from neighboring states, especially Wisconsin. One report revealed that in February, 1936, "it was found that 233 cases, including 1,152 persons, were on relief" — 76.8% of the total St. Paul Mexican community. [13]

A glance at the earnings of employed Mexicans is sufficient to show why this was so. The average yearly wages "per family for beet-field work in Minnesota in 1936 were $315.68"; in 1937 they were $329.19. The average family numbered 5.62 persons. State relief agencies assumed that the beet-field workers could supplement their wages with

other farm work, but such additional earnings provided only $48.41 per family in increased income in 1936 and $47.42 in 1937. These wages were earned by working in the onion fields and picking peas, corn, and potatoes in southern Minnesota. One interviewee summed up the situation during this period when he said: "We worked in sugar-beet fields in 1933 in Lake Lillian. In the winter we would come to St. Paul and go on welfare. Of course, that was pretty common in those days." [14]

By 1935 the employment situation was desperate, both because of the increased size of the colony and the scarcity of jobs. Most of St. Paul's 136 families were still agricultural workers; only 38 heads of households were recorded as having urban employment. The three meat-packing plants of South St. Paul, paying an average of 25 cents per hour, were a source of jobs from fall until February for from 80 to 100 persons, but during the summer months the number so employed dwindled to about 25. From 23 to 30 Mexicans worked on the Burlington Railroad the year around, and the Twin City "Street Railway Company employed a maximum of thirty Mexicans." But in 1935 the "major source of employment for the Mexican was still the beet field." [15]

A number of state and local agencies expressed concern for the future of the city's Mexican residents. One writer noted that "In addition to the disruptions caused by the Depression," they also "faced the problems of adjusting to a settled way of life in an urban community . . . not an easy task." The International Institute, founded in St. Paul in 1919 as an information center and service bureau for foreign people of all nationalities, considered "race prejudice a threat to the employment future of the Mexican young people." It expressed the opinion that prejudice and lack of education appeared to be "the two outstanding problems" faced by the Mexicans in this period. [16]

Despite the fact that most migrants had been born in the southwestern United States, many did not speak English, a decided drawback in the local job market. Because of the frequent dislocations caused by the mobility of migrant life, school attendance was sporadic. One man recalled that he had attended 68 schools between 1930 and 1941, and his was by no means an unusual case. [17]

Although information about Mexicans residing in communities other than St. Paul during the 1930s is limited, there is some evidence that life was even more difficult for them. One woman who lived with her family in the Minnesota Sugar Company's hotel at Chaska for three years during this period remembered that "the children had to walk into town to go to school in the cold and snow" and that "some . . . had nothing to eat." Urged by friends, this family and others moved from Chaska to St. Paul and "we never went back." Another woman, recalling field work near Mankato, Jordan, and Sleepy Eye, said "It is terrible. Now that I remember, I get the chills!" [18]

While it seems probable that a similar pattern was followed by other Mexican Americans throughout the state during the Depression years, it is impossible, on the basis of available data, to list all the communities or to give exact numbers. The Minneapolis Mexican population had grown, but not as much as that of St. Paul; Duluth had only 14

Mexicans in 1930. Apparently, life in St. Paul, difficult as it was in the 1930s, at least offered some compensations to the Mexicans who flocked there in ever-increasing numbers. Foremost, perhaps, was the opportunity to live among friends and relatives who, if short on material assistance, could generally be relied upon for emotional support. Another reason may have been the tangible and intangible assistance offered by two organizations on the West Side — Our Lady of Guadalupe Church and Neighborhood House.

Long to be a focal point for the Mexican-American community, Our Lady of Guadalupe began in 1931 as a small Catholic mission serving about a dozen families of sugar-beet workers. Part of a building was rented at 186 East Fairfield, a chapel was set up in the basement, and the mission, with the support of the Guild of Catholic Women, established a food and clothing distribution center to relieve the acute distress of its parishioners. It also recorded and assembled birth and baptismal records, attempting to obtain information from churches in Mexico to help its members establish claims for Social Security. For many years it sponsored celebrations of Mexican national holidays, and "During the 1940's, large and colorful parades were held on the West Side during [Mexican] Independence Day." A church-sponsored credit union, formed in 1948, was helpful to the community in encouraging saving habits and granting small loans unobtainable elsewhere.[19]

Perhaps most importantly, however, the church, which was formally incorporated as a parish and purchased its building in 1939, served as a center of community life for Mexican Americans living not only on the West Side (where 41% of the population was Catholic) but also throughout the Twin Cities. Even those who resided in different parishes looked to Guadalupe for such significant services as marriages, baptisms, and funerals. The priest, a non-Mexican, took the trouble to learn the Spanish language, and the church encouraged its members to observe such traditional Mexican festivals as *Posadas* (a Christmas Nativity re-enactment) and *El Dia de la Raza* (Race Day). As one member of the community noted: "I think one thing that I'm very, very proud of, and I think that anyone who is a Mexican who's been here would say, 'We have a lovely church.'"[20]

Neighborhood House, founded in 1897 to assist recent Jewish immigrants and reorganized on a nonsectarian basis in 1903, recognized the special needs of Mexicans as early as World War I by developing a program which included Americanization and citizenship classes. Instruction was also offered in sewing, cooking, health education, handicrafts, and athletics. A new gymnasium, added to existing facilities in 1928, was open 16 hours a day during the Depression; it doubled as a place to celebrate festivals, weddings, and baptisms. In the field of employment service, the house was instrumental in helping Mexican Americans find work in the beet fields as well as with such firms as Minnesota Mining and Manufacturing Company, Seeger Refrigerator Company, and Twin City Street Railway Company. In 1933 only about half of the Mexicans in St. Paul were reached by Neighborhood House, but by 1938 seven-eighths were participating in its programs.[21]

"Neighborhood House has been so good to me and my

A PROCESSION of young Mexican Americans at Our Lady of Guadalupe Roman Catholic Church on St. Paul's West Side in 1950.

family," said one woman. "We come from Texas. My husband he work for packing company. Neighborhood House help get him job. Neighborhood House teach he and I to speak American. Neighborhood House make us citizens of United States, help us get start here. At Neighborhood House I learn to sew and cook American way. . . . Neighborhood House our first real friend here."

The most comprehensive information on St. Paul Mexicans during the Depression years comes from a report compiled in 1936 by Neighborhood House and the International Institute. Of the 1,459 individuals in the community on whom data was assembled, 5 were Europeans married to Mexicans; 496 were born in Mexico, including 239 men, 166 women, and 91 children under 21 years of age; and 834 (36 men, 59 women, and 739 children) or 61.7% of those responding, were born in the United States. For every 100 adult women, there were 122 men. Virtually all of them had been in the United States more than five years and the vast majority had spent at least 10 years in the country. Most of the families had arrived in Minnesota before the 1930s, but they had settled in St. Paul only between 1931 and 1935, a fact which lends support to the suggestion made earlier that Mexican Americans residing outstate moved to that city during the Depression years. (In Minneapolis, on the other hand, a survey made by the city planning engineer in 1934 listed only 41 families of Mexican heritage.) The capital city community, 92.8% of whom replied to the survey, was largely composed of young people; 856, or 63%, were under 21 years of age. Of these, 755, or 55%, were children less than 16 years old. There were 116 more males than females in the community as a whole, and among those over 50 years of age there were twice as many men as women.[22]

The War Years of the 1940s

With the advent of World War II and its concomitant labor shortage, the demographic outlines of the Minnesota community changed when the recruiting of workers resumed in Mexico and Texas in 1941. Although information on the number of Mexican and Mexican-American migrants is scanty, it is possible to piece together a fragmentary outline of the situation in the 1940s. In the Crookston area the Catholic church started diocese-wide "mission activities for Spanish-speaking migrants from Texas" and made a "complete census" of such families. During the summer of 1942 a church-based migrant committee opened work centers at Fisher, Moorhead, and Mapleton and reported some 3,000 Spanish-speaking persons — most of whom were Mexican Americans. By 1943 about 350 Mexican nationals were harvesting Minnesota beet fields, while perhaps 1,000 more were employed by the Minnesota Valley (Green Giant) and Fairmont Canning companies.[23]

Figures on the Mexican nationals are contradictory, however. An official of the Great Northern Railway reported that the American Crystal Sugar Company was importing 1,000 to work in the Red River Valley. (The railroad was interested in acquiring Mexicans for track-laying and repair during times they could be spared from agricultural work.) From 1944 through 1946 approximately 4,000 were imported, and in 1947, 13 canneries requested 2,255, while 225 went to the beet fields. During 1948 in Clay County alone nearly 2,000 migrants arrived — double the figure for 1947. A study made in 1950 indicated still higher figures for the six "main employers of 'foreign' and Latin-American labor": American Crystal Sugar, 5,000 to 6,000; Green Giant, 500 to 1,200; Fairmont Canning, 300 to 1,200; Faribault Canning, 110 to 180; Owatonna Canning, 100 to 150; and Hollandale Farm Labor Association, 750 to 2,000. Both the Northern Pacific and the Great Northern railroads recruited track laborers from Mexico during the war.

Because of transportation problems created by the war, fewer workers were able to bring their families with them, and single workers — mainly young men from 18 to 25 years of age — largely replaced the family groups. An employment agent of the Minnesota Valley Canning Company stated that approximately 240 Mexican nationals arrived at Le Sueur about June 15 each year to work with the peas and sweet corn, remaining until mid- or late September. "These men do not bring their families as a rule," the agent said in 1947. During the pea pack, they "live in quarters provided for them on the Canning Company property, or at the various vining stations in the area which supplies the factory with peas." Between the pea and corn packs, the Mexicans were employed by the producers of hybrid seed corn to detassel corn in Iowa. According to the agent, their educational backgrounds ranged from "highly educated" to "practically no schooling." Those from Texas "speak, read and write English very well," he said, and "bring their families, who receive accommodations in the ample family quarters provided by the Canning Company."[24]

Another report, however, maintained that "the housing and sanitary facilities provided by employers are very often totally inadequate for normal, healthful living. In one area the average amount of space provided in 1944 was about one room to a family of six or seven. To be sure, some families had more space, but in other instances several families lived in one or two rooms!" In 1950 investigators found some deplorable conditions but felt that, on the whole, Minnesota had "better housing than any [they had] visited" elsewhere in the country.[25]

Given the crowded living conditions and an average work week of at least 60 hours, it is small wonder that the migrants were eager to spend their spare time at a Mexican dance or socializing with friends. Places like Maple Island near Hollandale, Albert Lea, Brownton, and Litchfield often had Mexican bands, offered some recreational activities, and sold Mexican foods at local grocery stores, although many outstate Mexican Americans went to St. Paul about once a month to "stock up." There is also some evidence that local merchants took advantage of the migrant workers. One recalled that a store in Hollandale had "a time of the week that prices were for the local people and a time of week when prices were much, much higher when the migrants would go in. . . . Growers would arbitrarily just take this [money] out of their checks and make sure that the local people got paid."[26]

There were three full-time missionaries among the Mexican and Mexican-American migrant workers in Minnesota in 1944. In Crookston and Fisher in Polk County Protestant missionaries associated with the Home Missions Council of North America served approximately 600 Spanish-speaking Americans, while Moorhead in Clay County had about 500 Spanish-speaking Mexican Americans in 90 families. The Minnesota Migrant Committee, an agency of the Minnesota Council of Religious Education (later the Minnesota Council of Churches) associated with the Home Missions Council, counted 10 additional counties where it believed missionary work to be needed among Mexican Americans and Mexicans, many of whom were young men "away from home in an unfamiliar environment for the first time." The committee hoped to add new missionaries, and in 1944 missionary work was begun at Ortonville in Big Stone County, where Spanish-speaking migrants had been going "for several years to serve as field laborers for the Big Stone Canning factory." By 1946 the agency had workers at eight locations.[27]

Missionary efforts had initiated summer school programs in 1951 for migrant children in East Grand Forks, at Fairmont, and in Faribault County where three schools were established. The following year Fairmont was the location of "a vacation school for Texas Mexicans." As the migrant population increased, efforts in the missionary field extended to Glencoe and Hector in 1956, Buffalo Lake in 1957, and Owatonna in 1959. Three years later a Minnesota Council of Churches committee reported that 95% of the migrants worked in six major areas: Blue Earth, Faribault, Hector, Hollandale, Owatonna, and the Red River Valley. In 1970 the Coalition of Churches for Migrant Concerns, which included both Protestants and Catholics, was established to better serve the state's migrant workers.

Some information has been found on wages during the 1940s. One migrant who returned to Texas at the end of each season reported that during the early 1940s beet work paid

$18.50 to $21.50 per acre depending on the type of labor. Another, who lived in St. Paul during the winter and worked near Hollandale in the late 1940s weeding and picking onions during the summer months, described average earnings of $.70 per hour for adult members of the family and $.40 per hour for youngsters. According to the 1953 revised report of the Governor's Interracial Commission, the rate of pay for beet harvesting was $23.00 per acre; workers who remained in the field for the entire season usually received a bonus of $3.00 per acre. A survey of vegetable-crop earnings, made by the Minnesota Industrial Commission in 1950, revealed that onion weeding paid $.60 per hour for adults and $.40 for children; onion picking was worth $.10 a bushel and potato picking $.08. Average earnings per day for an adult and a family ranged from $20.00 to $25.00. In 1952 string-bean harvesting paid workers $.03 per pound, and in most areas corn "snapping" was worth $2.25 per ton. In the canning industry hourly pay ranged from $.90 to $1.20. More than 20 years later, one newspaper reported the rate for asparagus pickers as $.08 to $.15 per pound.[28]

The war years also brought changes for Mexican Americans who were permanent residents of the state. One estimate placed the number living in St. Paul in 1946 at 3,100. As far as the Governor's Interracial Commission of 1948 could ascertain, there were about 300 living in Minneapolis — double its 1930 population. Others were to be found in Blue Earth, Clay, Dakota, Faribault, Freeborn, Martin, Nicollet, Polk, Renville, Sibley, Waseca, and Washington counties, although little is known about them. One source noted that many of the Mexicans and Mexican Americans who had remained in rural areas throughout the Depression moved in the 1940s to the Twin Cities, where they could find work in defense plants. Some of these settled on St. Paul's Lower West Side. Many older residents of that area also found employment. A sample of 295 Mexican workers in St. Paul in 1946 showed 110 men and 14 women employed in meat-packing plants, 66 men in beet fields, 30 on the railroads, 20 men and 5 women in textile mills, and 44 men and 6 women in other miscellaneous jobs. Those who did not find jobs in the Twin Cities worked in the outstate beet fields in the spring and summer months and returned to the Lower West Side for the winter, but the trend was away from the fields and toward industrial employment. Employment opportunities increased at the beginning of the 1950s; the sugar beet industry, to augment the local and Texas-Mexican labor supply, imported 1,400 Mexican nationals, "by far the best workers they ever had."[29]

The changing pattern from seasonal to year-round work, and the fact that young Mexican women were also finding jobs in meat-packing and textile plants while their husbands were in service were factors in the improved condition of the community. In 1946 only 82 Mexican-American families (265 individuals) in St. Paul requested relief. Ten years earlier the total had been 1,152 persons. A 1947 survey covering 33 counties in which Mexicans lived or worked confirmed that few applied for assistance when employment was available.[30]

In 1946 Neighborhood House and the International Insti-

tute again made a detailed study of the St. Paul colony. Of the 1,612 persons studied, 378 were born in Mexico; 1,234 (189 men, 173 women, and 872 children under 18 years of age) or 76.5% were born in the United States. Once again, the age distribution showed that the community was composed of numerous young people. About 50%, or 887 persons, were under 18 years of age. Only 725 adults were counted, of whom 329 were "men of the working years between 21 and 55, and 362 women of the reproductive years between 16 and 50." There was an average of 4.1 children per family. While the children were inclined to marry somewhat later than their parents had, they still tended to marry young — 16 to 20 years of age for women, 18 to 23 for men. Generally Mexicans tended to marry other Mexicans, but 33 mixed marriages were listed. Almost all the mixed marriages involved Mexican men and non-Mexican women. Few Mexican women married outside the group.[31]

The 1946 study made some mention of the health problems of the Mexican-American community. The migrant missionaries had earlier noted that tuberculosis was the leading cause of death. Of 261 Mexicans in five counties who were given the Mantoux test in 1946, 37.9% reacted positively; 11.9% were eventually found to show definite evidence of the disease. The study also noted that "While known cases of feebleminded represent about 1% of the estimated total population of 3,000, no cases of mental breakdown were reported by the public welfare agencies."[32]

Health problems like tuberculosis were undoubtedly exacerbated by the poor housing conditions of Mexican Americans in the cities as well as in rural areas. On St. Paul's West Side they often lived in dwellings "entirely unfit for habitation . . . usually old houses of frame structure that have been converted . . . to accommodate three or four families." Inside plumbing and central heating were usually lacking, and most cooking was done by coal or kerosene. One member of the community remembered that when she arrived in St. Paul in 1945 "most of the landlords in the West Side were Jewish people. The place where we lived was called 'Little Mexico' because it had three floors. What they called a 'Cold water flat.' No hot water. . . . a table, stove, two chairs, and a bed and one closet. And this is how most of the houses were. There were very few houses in good condition."[33]

Of the 300 homes covered in a 1946 study, only 40 were owned by their Mexican-American occupants. Many were overcrowded, in part because Mexican Americans retained a strong sense of family bonds and responsibility. It was not uncommon for them "to take in children, sometimes related, sometimes not, who [were] left . . . homeless." One man recalled his close family ties. "Even as a child we'd always visit our relatives," he said. "My mother talked to the parents in Spanish. The kids hung together even when we worked sugar beets during the depression."[34]

When he was interviewed in 1975, the man quoted above noted that this sense of family was still a part of his heritage. He said that during holidays "we all get together. . . . we all make 'Tamales'. . . . It is a family project." Another interviewee expressed the belief that "Mexicans have always been the extended family type. . . . By extended family, I mean a kid just doesn't have a mother or father. He has a

MEXICAN-AMERICAN migrant workers from Texas (left) thinning sugar beets in the Red River Valley in 1979, and (right) packing asparagus near Owatonna in the 1950s.

grandfather, grandmother, his aunts, uncles and cousins. Everybody is interested in his present and his future. They are all going to take part in enhancing it. . . . the language, the food, different customs."[35]

During the 1940s the social life of the predominantly Roman Catholic Mexican Americans on the Lower West Side continued to center on Our Lady of Guadalupe Church and Neighborhood House. Those across the river worshiped at St. Mary's and in the French Church of St. Louis. Non-Catholics continued to attend the First Baptist Church at Wacouta and 9th streets. The 1946 study counted 574 heads of families; 511 were Roman Catholic, 24 were non-Catholic, and 39 expressed no preference in religious beliefs.[36]

Despite their poverty, Mexican Americans had a low incidence of crime. St. Paul Police Department records and statistics on the population of Minnesota penal institutions showed that Mexican offenses "seldom involve[d] any persons but themselves and other Mexicans. The two most common offenses [were] drunkenness and fights with one another." There were very few robberies or sex crimes. As recently as 1980 a St. Paul police sergeant called the West Side "one of the lowest crime areas in the city," but other estimates suggest the rate is only a little below the average. Reports from the smaller Minneapolis population and from rural areas showed an equally impressive record. An employment agent for the Minnesota Valley Canning Company commented that Mexican nationals working during the summer months in the Le Sueur area were "law-abiding people" who as a rule "cause no disturbance." At Fergus Falls, where large numbers were employed in the beet fields, federal district court records showed only three cases concerning Mexicans in six years, all of which involved illegal entry into the United States.[37]

In 1946 Neighborhood House reported that there were 283 noncitizens out of the total of 378 born in Mexico. This "startling figure" was probably a consequence of the fact that so many were unable to prove legal entry and continued residence in the United States and thus were afraid to apply for citizenship. One resident, who spent summers working in

Hollandale, indicated that these fears were not unfounded. "One thing that really bothered me in those days," he said, "was that on payday or a day before payday, the Immigration officers would come by and pick up a whole bunch of people. I always wondered how they knew." The man obviously suspected the growers of turning in the names of Mexican aliens to avoid paying their wages.[38]

When alien registration began in 1940, Mexicans who could prove they had arrived in the United States before July 1, 1924, and had continued in residence could legalize their status. No matter what their arrival date, Mexican spouses of American citizens or parents of minor children born in the United States could petition Congress on hardship grounds and then apply for citizenship through the usual channels. International Institute, Neighborhood House, and Our Lady of Guadalupe Church were instrumental in informing Mexicans of these facts and in helping them secure the records necessary to prove continued residence. Illiteracy remained a drawback (see Introduction). The St. Paul report listed 725 heads of families, 293 of whom were literate in Spanish, 227 in English, and 205 were illiterate.

Nevertheless, in the area of education the 1940s were a distinct improvement over the Depression years when few Mexican Americans reached the ninth grade. In 1946, 468 Mexican children were attending St. Paul public and parochial schools; 75 were in high school, and two were in colleges. The same general pattern held true for Minneapolis. In nonlanguage tests, Mexican-American children there showed "virtual equality" in scores when compared to white Americans. While few of the returning Mexican-American World War II veterans took advantage of the GI Bill to attend college in 1946, "a considerable number [were] using it for vocational training, especially in radio engineering and the mechanical trades generally." Indeed, "ambition for his children" was given as the "impelling motive" for the Mexican American's "shift from purely agricultural activities to steady employment in urban centers."[39]

In the rural areas of Clay, Polk, Sibley, Faribault, Dakota, Marshall, and Waseca counties, the information collected was sketchy, but some data were gathered on an educational project begun in 1944 by the Sisters of St. Benedict at St. Joseph's Parochial School in Moorhead. The sisters there conducted a six-week summer school for the children of migrant workers which laid great stress "upon Americanism and the learning of English." Centers at Fisher and Mallory also offered educational programs for children, and some attempted adult education — English classes, health information, and recreational courses. At Moorhead, for example, a summer center was opened for Spanish-speaking families, who "on their trips to town . . . had no place to gather except in alleys or at the back of stores. On the first Saturday that the Center was opened, 32 Spanish-speaking people came. Just two Saturdays later, 110 were there!"[40]

The Continuing Urban Shift

The 1940s saw an accelerating shift from agricultural to urban employment among resident Mexican Americans, a trend that continued in succeeding decades. Of the 950 Mexican-born Minnesotans listed in the 1950 census, 751 or 79% were city dwellers. The Bureau of Employment and Security estimated that there were about 4,800 permanent Mexican-American residents of the state in 1953, and less than 20% were of Mexican birth; 3,800 lived in St. Paul, 300 in Minneapolis, 400 in the metropolitan area of Anoka, Dakota, Hennepin, and Ramsey counties, and about 300 were scattered in the 16 counties of Benton, Blue Earth, Clay, Faribault, Freeborn, Kandiyohi, Le Sueur, Martin, Morrison, Nicollet, Pennington, Pipestone, Polk, St. Louis, Sibley, and Waseca. According to the 1960 census, 3,436 Mexicans were permanent residents of Minnesota in that year (see Table 5.1). Of these 846 were foreign born, and 2,590 were native born of foreign or mixed parentage. Only 367 were listed as living in rural areas; 3,069 were living in urban areas — 2,672 of them in the Minneapolis-St. Paul metropolitan area.[41]

These figures may be deceptive. Sparse information for the 1950s and 1960s hints that migrant workers continued to settle out during the period either in St. Paul or by finding year-round work in other parts of the state. In the 1960s, for example, a Jenny-O turkey-processing plant at Litchfield "wanted to hire Mexicans," and apparently a number of migrant workers seized the opportunity to stay there. Others settled in the East Grand Forks area, Blooming Prairie, and Winona.[42]

Urban living affected Mexican-American cultural patterns, producing changes in attitudes toward family life, work, and education. Generally speaking, in the 1930s the husband and father was the dominant figure in the home and the wife and mother was definitely subordinate. It was the Mexican-American man's primary duty to provide for his parents and listen to their advice. As children, boys had few domestic responsibilities and far more personal freedom than girls, who were destined for "a very restricted life at home." The Depression, World War II, and the shift to urban centers began the "development of a more 'democratized' family structure with the wife and daughters allowed a bit more freedom." In this period it also became more usual for married children to move away from their parents and for young women to hold jobs outside the home.[43]

By the 1950s these cultural patterns had become more clearly defined. Fewer adults expected to have their parents living with them during the latter's old age. About 80% of each generation "reported that they consulted with their wives before making important family decisions," and family arrangements appeared to have become "more equalitarian" between the generations. While the incidence of Mexican juvenile delinquency remained below that of other depressed areas, "changes in reference groups" were listed. The children were stated to be "more assertive" and less eager to accept traditional (usually paternal) authority. One researcher commented on a general trend among young Minnesota Mexican Americans in the 1950s "toward assimilating 'Anglo' styles of behavior and rejecting old Mexican traditions and the Spanish language." Unlike some other ethnic groups, however, this trend toward acculturation by Mexican Americans did not often include changing their names "to make them sound more Anglo-Saxon."[44]

A 1958–59 sample of the St. Paul colony found many indications of the second generation's further assimilation. Labor unions were the principal Anglo organization in which the first generation reported participation, but the second generation was active in a variety of community programs and groups. The use of Spanish had continued to decline. Language differences among generations were graphically summarized by an older Mexican-American woman interviewed in 1975. "I still don't speak English. . . . My children, too, learned to speak Spanish," she said. "I told them they could learn English but in the home they had to speak Spanish. My grandchildren come and they call me 'grandma,' and I tell them 'not grandma, it's abuela,' [and] they just laugh."[45]

Participation in church affairs also declined somewhat beginning in the 1950s — 41% of the first generation and 71% of the second reported attending church less often than did their respective parents. (As had always been the case, more women and children than men attended church and were involved in its affairs.) A Mexican American active in the pentacostal movement in Guckeen, six miles west of Blue Earth, told interviewers in 1976 that he and three other families there started a church during the early 1960s which was still in operation in the 1970s as the only one in the area holding Spanish services. This man, who was admittedly a biased observer, felt that the central reason for Mexican Americans leaving the Catholic church was "discrimination." Services were seldom held in the Spanish language, he said. Despite the fact, however, that the pentacostal churches in Guckeen and the Latin-American Gospel Mission in St. Paul offered Spanish services, most Mexican Americans in Minnesota in the 1970s remained Catholics, at least nominally.[46]

It is also clear that successive generations of mid-20th-century Mexican Americans increasingly realized "the important role of education, especially in obtaining better employment." A series of interviews in 1958–59 with 25 male respondents representing two generations supported this view. They also revealed that first-generation urban workers were "occupationally downgraded in comparison to their fathers who had remained in Mexico." While only 54% of the "grandfather" generation had been menial laborers, 83% of the "fathers" but only 32% of the "sons" were so classified. The fathers had frequently "surrendered better positions in Mexico for menial employment" in the United States. They had usually remained in this category, while their sons, in turn, became "occupationally diversified and upwardly mobile." Although often beginning at the bottom of the urban economic hierarchy — as interviews conducted in 1975 confirmed — the sons were able through training to elevate themselves occupationally. The mean yearly income for the "fathers" was about $3,620; for the "sons," $5,200. The sons owned newer and somewhat more expensive cars and lived in more valuable homes. The 1958–59 study indicated that fewer sons owned their homes, but a 1953 report cited a 37% increase in homeownership between 1946 and 1953.[47]

The two generations were also found to hold significantly different attitudes toward work. Of the fathers' generation 64% had "educational and professional aspirations for their sons," and 84% of the sons shared these expectations. The fathers, however, recalled no such aspirations on the part of the grandfathers. The fathers' "major concern was with security and length of employment," but the sons were more often "concerned with how much satisfaction the job would bring."[48]

The study also pointed to "important reflections of differential acculturation between the generations" as seen in the average lengths of school attendance; the sons completed an average of 9 grades, 2.9 for the fathers, 1.6 for the grandfathers. By 1952 many more Mexican Americans were graduating from high school, and a few more (5 from the St. Paul colony alone) were or had recently attended college. They were also to be found in trade and vocational schools. The study concluded that "American educational institutions have been the primary acculturative agency for the second generation immigrant (with resulting feedback to the first generation)," and that the sons' experience in the Anglo school system served as "one of the primary modes for social and economic ascent in an urban-industrial society."

A marked decline in family size was evident by the 1950s. Of the sons 71% had between one and three children; 48% of the fathers had from five to seven children and an additional 40% had sired from 10 to 12. It was noted that "Whereas large families were an asset to the migrant," they were "a hindrance in the industrial setting where the family consumes rather than produces." Later marriages affected family size. Although the Mexican American in St. Paul still married at an average age of 16 to 20 for girls and 18 to 23 for boys — earlier than other young people in the United States — the general tendency was toward later marriage.[49]

All of these factors as well as increased prosperity prompted some Mexican Americans to seek better housing. Some "of the even more successful" moved into the Minneapolis suburbs of Edina and Robbinsdale. Others left St. Paul's Lower West Side "both physically and socially." Mississippi River floods in the spring of 1951 and 1952 put much of the "flats" under water, and many residents began to look for housing elsewhere in the city. The Mexican Americans moved up onto the bluffs as had the Jews before them. The less upwardly mobile "moved into other Jewish neighborhoods . . . North and East of the Capitol Building."[50]

The 1960s to 1980

In the early 1960s the flats on St. Paul's West Side, which had long been subject to floods, were cleared and diked for industrial improvement. At the end of 1962 "about two-thirds of the people on the Lower West Side had been relocated." The last family moved in 1964. Approximately half of them resettled elsewhere on the West Side, mostly near Roosevelt School. Some Mexican-American families moved up to Concord Terrace, an area then slated for urban renewal. In 1968 Torre de San Miguel Homes, Inc., under the auspices of Neighborhood House, sponsored quality housing for low- to moderate-income families in the old area of Robert, Wabasha, and Concord streets. Eventually about 142 family-dwelling units were built, serving primarily Mexican Americans.[51]

Although young adults in the Roosevelt School area and other parts of the West Side reported three times as much discrimination as their parents, one researcher observed that the Mexican-American community of St. Paul's Lower West Side successfully retained "its identity and cohesiveness as a neighborhood in spite of its physical relocation." This was due in part to the strong influences of Neighborhood House and Our Lady of Guadalupe Church. The former offered English classes two nights per week, vocational classes, and such other services as a nursery school. In the mid-1960s the house erected a new facility in the Roosevelt School area, following in the footsteps of Guadalupe, which dedicated a new church and a school at 4th Avenue and Concord Street in 1961. To accommodate parishioners who had not moved, services were also continued in the old church until 1962.[52]

Other Mexican-American organizations were formed for definite purposes. The Mexican Independence Celebration Committee, originally established in the 1930s, was reorganized in 1969 to continue celebrating the anniversary on September 15 and 16, an event that had been observed in St. Paul since 1937. Azteca, a Mexican-American soccer team started in the 1960s, produced several professional players over the years. A local chapter of the American GI Forum was active on the West Side from the late 1940s to the early 1960s. And two older organizations merged in 1948 — the Anahuac Society, incorporated in 1922, and the Comité de Reconstrucción, formed in 1939. The latter had been created to purchase and refurbish the building at 186 East Fairfield for use by Our Lady of Guadalupe Church, while Anahuac had as its purposes providing the Spanish-speaking community of the Twin Cities with financial assistance, organizing social functions, and maintaining contact with other Mexican-American groups throughout the region. In 1958 Anahuac merged with El Comité Patriótico and assumed that name.[53]

By the end of the 1960s, the St. Paul colony was demographically centered in the Roosevelt School neighborhood.

In 1971 a Neighborhood House committee described some of the changes in the Lower West Side. It found that the movement out of the area by Mexican Americans was partially offset by religious, cultural, and social services, and by recreational activities "that focus on — or bring people back to — the lower West Side." The committee also stated that about "half the housing on the West Side" was built before 1900, and that the juvenile delinquency and welfare rates in the Concord Terrace-Roosevelt School area were high. The former was nearly three times that of the city as a whole (12.32% in Concord Terrace, 4.53% in St. Paul), and about a third of the people were on welfare. These findings represented a considerable change from earlier decades when the Mexican-American colony had relatively low crime and relief rates.[54]

Education continued to be an area of concern. In 1971 bilingual kindergartens were inaugurated in two West Side schools. The effort was extended the following year to include first grade and enlarged in 1974–75 to offer a bilingual-bicultural program at three public schools and one parochial school. The program quickly revealed that the number of English-deficient Mexican-American children in the attendance area of the four schools was constantly increasing, probably because migrant families continued to "settle out" in St. Paul each year. In Minneapolis, where the Hispanic school enrollment has remained the same for a decade, a bilingual-bicultural effort was begun in 1978, affecting some 40 children during the first semester.[55]

In 1970 fewer than a hundred Mexican Americans were enrolled at the University of Minnesota. A Department of Chicano Studies was established there in 1971, but enrollment figures for 1974–76 showed that "most of the students were, in fact, non-Chicanos." Nevertheless by 1974 approximately 300 Mexican-American undergraduates were attending the university, with 40 more in graduate and professional schools (medicine was the highest with 24). A university official put the undergraduate figures for 1977–78 at 358, and in that academic year the university had a director for the Office of Minority and Special Student Affairs as well as a Chicano/Latino co-ordinator; by autumn of 1980 Hispanic enrollment rose to 435. As one student said, "It's so different now. We have counselors that can speak two languages."[56]

These statistics, however, failed to tell the whole story of the Mexican-American community in the 1970s. That decade also witnessed the development of a growing interest in the preservation of the Mexican heritage — an apparent reversal of the earlier trend toward acculturation. In 1974 the governor established a state Office of Migrant Affairs, superseded in 1977 by the Office of Spanish-Speaking People and in 1978 by the Council on Affairs of Spanish-Speaking People. The increased emphasis on the retention of ethnicity was shown in several linguistic studies of the St. Paul colony. One conducted in 1959 indicated that 88% of first-generation Mexican Americans and 68% of their children spoke Spanish in their homes. On their jobs 76% of the first generation and 48% of the second used Spanish. Between parents and their children, both languages were used; usually the parents spoke Spanish and the children answered in

SURROUNDED by flags and pictures of Mexican and American heroes, a choir performed at the annual Mexican Independence Day celebration, May 5, 1940, at St. Paul's Neighborhood House.

English. Of the second-generation Mexican-American parents, however, 92% thought that their children should learn Spanish.[57]

Researchers in 1959 and 1971 found that "among West Side Mexican-Americans, it took three to four generations to lose the ability to use the Spanish language." In contrast, European immigrants often lost the use of a native language within the first two generations. Both researchers commented that "Spanish was rarely heard at dances and other social events; it was almost never used in community meetings."[58]

During the 1970s, however, use of the Spanish language increased in St. Paul. One former Minneapolis resident moved to St. Paul because, she said, "I don't feel strange about speaking my language. . . . In Minneapolis, I never dared." Community meetings which had been conducted solely in English became bilingual or were sometimes carried on in Spanish only. At least two more churches offered bilingual services — Faith Temple (Assembly of God) on the East Side and Zion Lutheran Church near downtown. The *West Side Voice,* a neighborhood St. Paul newspaper, published occasional articles in both English and Spanish; in Minneapolis *La Voz* (The Voice), a monthly bilingual paper begun in 1970, was still appearing in the 1980s; and at least two radio stations offered some Spanish broadcasts. Music for regularly held dances was provided by both local and imported Mexican-American musicians. The Mexican American Cultural Resource Center, sponsored by the St. Paul school board, became a focal point for numerous activities, meetings, and classes. A school-district-sponsored survey of parents or guardians of West Side Mexican-American children in 1975 revealed that 84.8% were either "Spanish-dominant or bilingual and use Spanish often in the homes."[59]

Although there is more information from a variety of sources about both the permanent Mexican-American community in Minnesota and the migrant workers in the 1970s, much of the data are contradictory. According to the 1970 census, the total Mexican population of the state was 4,575, including foreign born and native born of foreign and mixed parentage (see Table 5.1). The total number of Spanish-speaking persons counted was 23,198, making this group the second largest non-Anglo ethnic minority in the state at that time. By 1980 Spanish and Hispanic people were said by the census to number 22,124, and they had dropped to the fourth largest non-Anglo minority, exceeded by Asians, Blacks, and Indian peoples. While the 1970 and 1980 census figures included persons whose ancestors traced back to Spain, Mexico, South and Central America, the Caribbean, and the Philippines, one source reported that the majority were Mexican Americans.[60]

Other counts were significantly higher. In 1973 Migrants In Action (renamed Hispanos Minnesota in 1980), which served the seven-county Twin Cities metropolitan area, reported approximately 23,000 Mexican Americans there with 10,000 residing on St. Paul's West Side, where about 110 families (685 persons) attempted to "settle out." In 1975 a Mexican-American spokesman reported that there were "35,000 to 37,590 Spanish-speaking persons in Minnesota most of the time and about 46,000 during the summer months because of the influx of migrant farm workers." Interviews conducted in 1975–76 also suggested larger numbers than the census reported. "The way we figure," said one knowledgeable interviewee, "there are probably about 20,000 Mexican Americans living in the state of Minnesota, outside of the Twin Cities. . . . and maybe another 10,000 or 12,000 in the Twin Cities."[61]

By 1978 a University of Minnesota official estimated the number to be between 49,000 and 50,000. Two years later the Council on Spanish-Speaking Affairs reported about 50,000 persons, with 36,000 in the Twin Cities metropolitan area — 20,000 in Ramsey County alone. In contrast, the 1980 census counted 7,864 Spanish and Hispanic people in St. Paul and 4,684 in Minneapolis. To all these figures must be added an unknown number of illegal aliens. Immigration department officials hazarded that there may have been from 1,500 to 5,000 such persons in Minnesota in 1980.

Although some of these estimates may be too high, it is probable that the census figures were too low. Various sources indicated that migrants were employed in 10 to 13 counties in the 1970s (see Table 5.1). Those named were not always the same, but they were all in the Red River Valley and southern Minnesota. American Crystal Sugar Company (East Grand Forks), Owatonna Canning Company, and Libby, McNeill and Libby (Rochester) were major employers of migrants in the 1970s. Still others worked for local farmers, as in Freeborn County, who in turn sold their produce to the canning companies. Migrants In Action figured that about half of the estimated 10,000 to 18,000 migrants in Minnesota in 1975 did not have work orders before they arrived and "came with nothing but hope and willingness to work." Two years later the migrant population was estimated at 10,000 in the Red River Valley and over 4,000 in southeastern Minnesota.[62]

Although it is difficult to get an accurate count of migrant workers, it is known that about 95% of those in Minnesota in the 1970s originated in several parts of Texas. Those in southeast Minnesota were from west Texas (Llano Estacado), Bexar County (San Antonio), and the Sonora areas. In northwestern Minnesota they were from the Rio Grande Valley and Webb County areas. Year-round jobs were obtained largely by migrants from the border cities stretching from El Paso to Brownsville (see Map 5.1).[63]

Many Minnesota communities seemed to exhibit little intermingling of Anglo residents and Mexican-American migrant workers. According to one reporter, the "life of a migrant isn't just working in the fields 6 or 7 days a week. It's living in dilapidated shacks, courtesy of the farmer for whom you work. It's getting water from the farmer's outside hose because your house doesn't have running water. It's being stared at when you are inside a store and ignored when you are outside. An invisible barrier exists between the permanent residents of the Red River Valley and their migrant neighbors. It is lifted for a few hours every June when local citizens' committees welcome the migrants back with 'fiestas,' but it falls back in place as soon as the fiestas end."[64]

Conditions have improved slowly for the migrants since

the 1940s. In 1978 migrant workers in Minnesota were not unionized. An attempt was made in the state legislature to provide for collective bargaining for seasonal agricultural laborers, but the measure did not get out of committee and failed again in 1979 and 1980.[65]

As far back as 1953, Minnesota was among the few states which had laws pertaining to health and sanitation in migrant camps, even though they were not always well enforced. In the 1970s the state enacted three laws which offered some additional protection in labor conditions. The minimum wage law was extended to cover seasonal farm workers in 1973; the following year legislation was passed to ensure that children under 14 years of age did not work in the fields unless employed by their parents. (Migrant families found it easy to get around this law, and the age has since been lowered to 12.) A third measure, also effective in 1974, provided that migrants were to be covered by workers' compensation. The same year an office for migrant affairs to co-ordinate state services was established.

In addition, there has been increased awareness of the special needs of migrant seasonal farm workers in job placement, education, and health services. Since the Minnesota Department of Agriculture estimated that 15,000 migrants would work in the state during 1978, such programs were essential. Studies comparing job placements in a number of states showed, however, that much remained to be done to improve the migrant worker's lot. Minnesota still had a disproportionate number of such workers in short-term jobs in 1975. Compared to a national norm of 20.4%, Minnesota referred 37.4% of its migrant seasonal workers to such jobs. It also had a disproportionately low number of long-term (150 days) nonagricultural placements for migrant workers — 24.2% against a national average of 43.7% — and paid them less per hour. The national average wage rate was reported to be $2.50 an hour, but Minnesota workers were earning only an average of $2.19 an hour in 1975. A whopping 51.3% were reportedly placed in jobs paying $2.10 or less per hour.[66]

In the area of health services, the Minnesota migrant worker has been more fortunate. Since 1973 Migrant Health Services, Inc., has been active in the Red River Valley of both Minnesota and North Dakota, the Renville area, the sugar beet region in the Minnesota River Valley, and southeastern Minnesota. By 1976 the agency had received state funds to expand its services to migrants in southern Minnesota by means of a mobile unit. Located in Moorhead, the organization had field sites at Breckenridge, Hallock, Crookston, Halstad, Montevideo, Olivia, Clara City, Owatonna, and Blooming Prairie. It has determined that migrants remained a high-risk population. In 1975–76 infant mortality was about four times the national average, and life expectancy was only about 49 years.[67]

The state has also become involved in migrant education. Using the personnel and facilities of local school districts, the Migrant Education Program was established in 1967 to provide special academic instruction, enrichment activities, nutritional information, and medical and dental care for migrant children. By 1975, 17 districts offered the program: Argyle, Barnesville, Bird Island, Blooming Prairie, Brecken-

ridge, Campbell-Tintah, Clara City, Crookston, East Grand Forks, Hallock, Halstad, Kennedy, Montevideo, Moorhead, Oslo, Owatonna, and Renville. The program also provided assistance to children whose families had "settled out" at Owatonna, Litchfield, Kennedy, and St. Paul. In St. Paul 167 Mexican-American children whose families had "settled out" between 1975 and 1976 were identified as needing help — either with language problems or with "culture shock." A total of about 2,575 migrant children were included in the program in 1974, 4,333 in 1975, 4,500 in 1976, and 4,944 in 1977. Since then the numbers have dropped slightly; in 1979 they were 4,532, and in 1980 they were 3,392.[68]

Migrants who did not find work after they arrived in Minnesota are of concern to several agencies. Migrants In Action, organized in 1969 and funded by state and federal moneys, is a Twin Cities-based organization that deals with crisis situations. It gives assistance to the "family that shows up . . . at 5 p.m., 12 people in the family, no food and no shelter." Such emergencies force hundreds of people every summer to "settle out." "The job may end sooner than expected or not be had at all, or there is an accident or sickness or they run out of gas or food" or the car breaks down because "Coca-Cola cans around the tail pipes don't work in Minnesota." The chances are that the newly "settled-out" migrant does not speak English well and probably has not had a chance to learn a trade. "That usually means some kind of vocational training and some welfare aid to tide the family over."[69]

Another agency working directly with migrant workers and their families is the Minnesota Migrant Council, which is supported by substantial state and federal funds. Headquartered in St. Cloud, it operates through five area offices in Blooming Prairie, Crookston, Litchfield, Moorhead, and St. James. Its services include funds for emergency expenses, job information, health services, and classroom training.[70]

According to estimates released by three groups in 1975 and 1976, migrant workers in the following numbers were employed:[71]

County	Sugar Beets		Canning		Vegetables	
	1975	1976	1975	1976	1975	1976
Anoka					5	
Big Stone	10		25			
Chippewa	585	1,200				
Clay	1,310	2,000			*	
Dodge				800	510	1,175
Faribault			40		150**	
Freeborn					65	250
Grant	140					
Hennepin					10	
Kandiyohi	70					
Kittson	390	650			*	
Lac qui Parle	35					
Le Sueur			280			
McLeod			425			
Marshall	680	420			*	
Martin			10	30		
Meeker			55			
Nobles			5	10		
Norman	565	1,100			*	
Otter Tail	10		150			
Polk	2,000	3,000			*	
Redwood	90					
Renville	900	1,700	5			

County	Sugar Beets		Canning		Vegetables	
	1975	1976	1975	1976	1975	1976
Rice			35			
Sherburne					25	
Sibley	30		20		50	
Steele			125		90	700
Stevens	15					
Swift	250					
Traverse	170					
Watonwan			150	200		
Wilkin	720	950				
Wright			35			
Yellow Medicine	30					
Total	8,000	1,020	1,360	1,040	905	2,125

*Some workers in potato harvesting   **Includes beets

One further group of statistics indicated that the Mexican-American migrants were a community of young people and that 70% of them had less than eight years of education in 1975. The Minnesota Migrant Council reported that its clients fell into the following age groups: [72]

Age:	18 and below	2,858
	19–21	853
	22–44	2,466
	45–54	717
	55–64	241
	65 and over	49

Among Mexican Americans "Minnesota has gained a reputation . . . for offering a good quality of life to those who live here and a high level of services to assist those who wish to settle." [73] It is logical to assume that acculturation will continue among members of the Mexican-American community in the state, occurring perhaps more rapidly among young out-state residents relatively isolated from the larger community and consequently under greater pressure to adapt to Anglo ways. The St. Paul colony, on the other hand, some 60 years after its beginnings has already adopted many of the characteristics of an urban-industrialized society. But, as we have seen, a new trend emerged in the 1970s toward a systematic preservation of certain facets of Mexican culture and the Spanish language. Thus the St. Paul Mexican-American community in the 1980s is preserving aspects of its ethnic heritage even as it continues to demonstrate many of the general socioeconomic traits of Anglo society in Minnesota.

Reference notes

[1] United States, Census, 1860, Population, 262; 1880, 495; 1900, cxl, 606. On Garzón, see [A. Hermina Poatgieter], "Minnesotans of Mexican Heritage," in Gopher Historian, Fall, 1971, p. 5; Minneapolis Sunday Tribune, August 5, 1973, Picture Magazine, 10. The author and the editor wish to acknowledge the helpful suggestions received during the preparation of this chapter from Ramedo J. Saucedo of Mendota Heights.

[2] Information on places of origin was gleaned from marriage records, 1931–51, in Our Lady of Guadalupe Church Papers, MHS. It correlates with a list compiled by Norman S. Goldner, in The Mexican in the Northern Urban Area: A Comparison of Two Generations, 37 (San Francisco, 1972). A map of migrant travel patterns is in Neal R. Peirce, The Great Plains States of America, 363 (New York, 1973).

[3] Governor's Interracial Commission, The Mexican in Minnesota, 8, 13 ([St. Paul], 1948); Goldner, Northern Urban Area, 16, 17. The Minnesota Beet Sugar Manufacturing Co. is listed for the first time in Minneapolis City Directory, 1898, 1492.

[4] [Poatgieter], in Gopher Historian, Fall, 1971, p. 5; the 1912 figure is from Goldner, Northern Urban Area, 17; U.S., Census, 1900, Population, 1:734; 1910, 1:837; 1920, 3:49. If the census was taken in summer, these figures might reflect migrant residents.

[5] Governor's Commission, Mexican in Minnesota, 8; Alice L. Sickels, "The Mexican Nationality Community in St. Paul," 4, 6, a mimeographed report compiled in 1936 by Neighborhood House and the International Institute of St. Paul, copy in MHS; Goldner, Northern Urban Area, 11. In 1921–22 when the U.S. Steel plant in Duluth needed more workers, the company brought in about 400 Mexicans and built special housing for them. But the Mexicans could not get used to the cold weather and very few stayed, according to interview of George Orescanin by Marjorie Hoover, April 25, 1980, notes in MEHP Papers.

[6] Here and two paragraphs below, see Sickels, "Mexican Nationality Community," 6; Lorraine E. Pierce, "Mexican Americans on St. Paul's Lower West Side," in Journal of Mexican American History, 4:1 (1974); Goldner, Northern Urban Area, 17; oral history transcript, Crecencia O. Rangel, 1, 9; Lorraine E. Pierce, "St. Paul's Lower West Side," 37, 44, 47, 48, master's thesis, University of Minnesota, 1971, copy in MHS; Neighborhood House, "Annual Report, 1931," p. 2, Neighborhood House Association Records, MHS. On employment with the railroads see, for example, oral history transcripts, Ester M. Avaloz, 9, Guadalupe J. Cruz, 4, Alfonso Galván, 5, Francisco Guzmán, 7, Sebastián Jara, 8, David B. Limon, 4, 7, C. Rangel, 4, and Marcelina Urvina, 2. All oral history transcripts cited here and below were produced by the Mexican-American History Project, 1975–76; transcripts and taped interviews are in MHS.

[7] Sickels, "Mexican Nationality Community," 4; U.S., Census, 1920, Population, 3:49; 1930, 3:63. The 1930 census gives other figures on Mexicans in 2:250. See also oral history transcripts, Frank Guzmán, 3; Tony Martínez, 11, 12, and Cruz, 4.

[8] Pierce, in Journal of Mexican American History, 4:1; Martínez transcript, 10–12; "Report of the Migrant Worker Sub-Committee of the Governor's Human Rights Commission," 4 (1957), in Public Welfare Dept. Records, Minnesota State Archives, MHS. By 1976 there were regulations concerning living conditions for migrant workers that were enforced by the state division of occupational safety and health. See Minnesota Dept. of Administration, "Addendum for Directory of Services for the Migrant and Seasonal Farm Worker," June, 1976, copy in MHS.

[9] Goldner, Northern Urban Area, 18, 19, quoting Viola Battey, "The Mexican Situation in St. Paul," a report prepared in 1925. No extant copy of the latter has been located. See also oral history transcript, Henry T. Capiz, 4.

[10] Here and below, see Governor's Commission, Mexican in Minnesota, 8, 9; William Hoffman, Neighborhood House: A Brief History of the First 75 Years, [8] ([St. Paul], 1972); Pierce, in Journal of Mexican American History, 4:2; Goldner, Northern Urban Area, 19, 21. An interesting contemporary account of the St. Paul community is Louisa Lambert, "Tank Town: Mexicans in Minnesota," in Hamline Piper, May, 1935, pp. 24–31.

[11] Here and below, see Frank Guzmán transcript, 5.

[12] Governor's Commission, Mexican in Minnesota, 41; Goldner, Northern Urban Area, 20; C. O. Jenks to J. R. W. Davis, June 20, 1930, and O. B. Holton to W. P. Kenney, April 23, 1931, in Vice President Operating files, Great Northern Railway Company Records, MHS.

[13] Governor's Commission, *Mexican in Minnesota*, 40; oral history transcript, Cruz, 4; Sickels, "Mexican Nationality Community," 20; Goldner, *Northern Urban Area*, 21, gives slightly higher relief figures for 1936.

[14] Governor's Commission, *Mexican in Minnesota*, 40; oral history transcript, Leonard López, 2.

[15] Goldner, *Northern Urban Area*, 20, 21; Cruz transcript, 5.

[16] Pierce, in *Journal of Mexican American History*, 4:3; Goldner, *Northern Urban Area*, 21; Alice L. Sickels, *Around the World in St. Paul*, 75 (Minneapolis, 1945).

[17] Oral history transcript, Sebastián J. Hernández, 5; Goldner, *Northern Urban Area*, 26–29.

[18] Oral history transcripts, Cruz, 4, and Esiquia Monita, 5; U.S., *Census, 1930, Population*, 2:68, 70.

[19] Our Lady of Guadalupe Church Papers, in MHS; Goldner, *Northern Urban Area*, 31–33; oral history transcript, Joseph E. Anaya, 5–7; Our Lady of Guadalupe Parish Credit Union Records, MHS.

[20] Oral history transcripts, Matthew Casillas, 13, María J. Bósquez, 11, and Urvina, 12. See also Frank J. Rodríguez transcript, 9, 10, 12. Although most Mexican Americans were Roman Catholic, a few Protestants attended the First Baptist Church at 9th and Canada sts. which had Spanish-speaking clergy. Other non-Catholic Mexicans attended the Latin-American Gospel Mission, a Spanish-speaking pentecostal congregation numbering some 15 to 20 persons, which met at 223 Concord St. Oral history transcript, Rev. Juan L. Ríos, 3, 5; Goldner, *Northern Urban Area*, 31. Statistics on religion on the Lower West Side appear in *Neighborhood House*, 1936, unpaged pamphlet, in MHS.

[21] Here and below, see background folder and "Report," 1938, pp. 8, 14, in Neighborhood House Papers, MHS; wedding and baptismal invitations in Our Lady of Guadalupe Church Papers; Goldner, *Northern Urban Area*, 29; Governor's Commission, *Mexican in Minnesota*, 51; Neighborhood House, *The Neighbors Speak*, 8 (St. Paul, 1938). See also Chapter 26.

[22] Sickels, "Mexican Nationality Community," 8–14; Herman E. Olson, *The Minneapolis Property and Housing Survey*, n.p., June, 1934.

[23] Here and below, see Governor's Commission, *Mexican in Minnesota*, 11, 18, 21; *Our Northland Diocese* (Crookston), September, 1960, pp. 1, 20; Dr. and Mrs. David E. Henley, *Minnesota and Her Migratory Workers*, 8 (Minneapolis, 1950); M. J. Wegener, memorandum, May 5, 1943, in Vice President Operating files, Great Northern Railway Records; *Minnesota Migrant Neighbors*, March, 1943, a pamphlet in Minnesota Council of Churches Records, MHS.

[24] Minnesota Council of Religious Education, *Minnesota Migrant Service: A United Christian Ministry to Migrant Workers*, undated pamphlet in MHS; "Notes on Migrant Summer Employees of the Minnesota Valley Canning Company," 1947, p. 2 — typescript of an interview, copy in MHS.

[25] Council of Religious Education, *Minnesota Migrant Service*; Henley, *Migratory Workers*, 12.

[26] Oral history transcripts, Leo V. Castillo, 6, Teresa M. Muñoz, 8, Frank Guzmán, 9. Guzmán also indicated that St. Paul Mexican Americans who worked outstate in the summer months found the migrant workers in Hollandale rather alien. They "spoke Spanish," he said, and acted "peculiar . . . compared to people living around here."

[27] Here and below, see Council of Religious Education, *Minnesota Migrant Service*; Governor's Commission, *Mexican in Minnesota*, 50, and revised ed., (1953), p. 57; Hayden L. Stright, *Together: The Story of Church Cooperation in Minnesota*, 136, 138, 139, 147, 179 (Minneapolis, 1971); Minnesota Council of Churches, "A Summary Staff Report," Spring, 1957, p. 2, mimeographed pamphlet, in MHS; "Our Agricultural Migrants — Strangers or Neighbors?" a

mimeographed pamphlet [1962], in Minnesota Council of Churches Records.

[28] Governor's Commission, *Mexican in Minnesota, Revised*, 14–17; oral history transcript, Juan Rodríguez, 5, Frank Guzmán, 8; *Minnesota Daily*, May 31, 1978, p. 10.

[29] International Institute, Inc., "A Study of the Mexican Community in St. Paul, 1946," 2, a mimeographed booklet issued in co-operation with Neighborhood House, copy in MHS; Pierce, in *Journal of Mexican American History*, 4:6; Governor's Commission, *Mexican in Minnesota*, 19, 21, 26, 47; Minnesota Farm Employment Advisory Council, Minutes, November 29, 1951, in Public Welfare Dept. Records.

[30] Pierce, in *Journal of Mexican American History*, 4:9; Governor's Commission, *Mexican in Minnesota*, 41.

[31] International Institute, Inc., "Mexican Community in St. Paul, 1946," 2–4. Marriage records, 1931–51, in Our Lady of Guadalupe Church Papers show the same pattern of mixed marriages. According to the director of Migrants In Action, a St. Paul agency, there was still a definite feeling in the 1970s, especially among first-generation parents, that their children should not marry non-Mexican Americans. See Frank Guzmán transcript, 12.

[32] Minnesota Council of Churches, *Minnesota Migrant Neighbors*; International Institute, Inc., "Mexican Community in St. Paul, 1946," p. 5; Governor's Commission, *Mexican in Minnesota*, 35.

[33] Governor's Commission, *Mexican in Minnesota*, 27; Muñoz transcript, 6.

[34] Governor's Commission, *Mexican in Minnesota*, 27, 31; Casillas transcript, 4.

[35] Oral history transcripts, Casillas, 6; Dionisa C. Coates, 14, 15.

[36] Pierce, in *Journal of Mexican American History*, 4:10; International Institute, Inc., "Mexican Community in St. Paul, 1946," p. 8.

[37] Governor's Commission, *Mexican in Minnesota*, 37–39; "Notes on Migrant Summer Employment," 1947, p. 1; *Sunday Pioneer Press* (St. Paul), February 3, 1980, Focus sec., p. 4; information from police official, November 24, 1980.

[38] Here and below, International Institute, Inc., "Mexican Community in St. Paul, 1946," p. 5, 6; Frank Guzmán transcript, 9; United States, *Statutes at Large*, 43:153, 54:670.

[39] International Institute, Inc., "Mexican Community in St. Paul, 1946," 6; Governor's Commission, *Mexican in Minnesota*, 18, 47, 48, 49.

[40] Governor's Commission, *Mexican in Minnesota, Revised*, 43–46; Council on Religious Education, *Minnesota Migrant Service*.

[41] Governor's Commission, *Mexican in Minnesota, Revised*, 5; U.S., *Census, 1950, Population*, vol. 2, part 23, pp. 52, 66; 1960, vol. 1, part 25, pp. 340–342. The outstate figure of about 300 given by the 1950 federal census may be misleading, because persons who were not definitely of Indian or other nonwhite races were classified as white. The following quotation offers an example of the confusion arising from such an arbitrary decision (it would be interesting to know how this man was classified by the census takers): "My father was an Indian from Oklahoma. My mother was mostly Spanish. . . . Her father was a full-blooded Spaniard. . . . We had the opportunity to know some of her brothers before she died. They were really white, and had blue and green eyes." Oral history transcript, Ben P. Gonsález, 1.

[42] Oral history transcripts, Luis Martínez, 4, Castillo, 3, José A. Valdez, 3, Antonio Morales, 2, Angel García, 2.

[43] Oral history transcripts, Frank Chávez, 3, Casillas, 5; Franklin A. Hijikata, "The Mexicans in St. Paul," 1–3, a mimeographed paper, 1960, copy in MHS; Pierce, in *Journal of Mexican American History*, 4:3, 9; Goldner, *Northern Urban Area*, 46.

[44] Goldner, *Northern Urban Area*, 49, 60, 87, and "The Mexican in a Northern Urban Area: The Profile of an Ethnic Community," in

Minnesota Academy of Science, *Proceedings*, 29:108 (December, 1961); Pierce, in *Journal of Mexican American History*, 4:12; Governor's Commission, *Mexican in Minnesota, Revised*, 37.

[45] Goldner, *Northern Urban Area*, 52, 90; Hijikata, "Mexicans in St. Paul," 7; Cruz transcript, 5.

[46] Goldner, *Northern Urban Area*, 51, 82; Hijikata, "Mexicans in St. Paul," 6; González transcript, 9–11.

[47] Hijikata, "Mexicans in St. Paul," 5; oral history transcripts, Anaya, 10, Capiz, 10, Casillas, 10; Governor's Commission, *Mexican in Minnesota, Revised*, 30. Here and below, see Goldner, *Northern Urban Area*, 39, 40, 42, 45, 78, 79; Goldner conducted the 1958–59 interviews.

[48] Here and below, see Goldner, *Northern Urban Area*, 45, 54, 55, and in Minnesota Academy of Science, *Proceedings*, 29:108, 109.

[49] Goldner, in Minnesota Academy of Science, *Proceedings*, 29:107; Governor's Commission, *Mexican in Minnesota, Revised*, 36.

[50] T. Allen Caine, *Social Life in a Mexican-American Community*, 32, (San Francisco, 1974).

[51] Torre de San Miguel Homes Inc., Papers, 1969–75, in MHS; *St. Paul Pioneer Press*, December 27, 1970, sec. 3, p. 4; "Housing: Getting It Together in St. Paul," in National Federation of Settlements and Neighborhood Centers, *Annual Report*, n.p., 1972, copy in MHS; Pierce, in *Journal of Mexican American History*, 4:13–15.

[52] Pierce, in *Journal of Mexican American History*, 4:13, 15. The increased discrimination had been predicted by the Governor's Commission in 1948; see *Mexican in Minnesota*, 61.

[53] Mexican-American History Project Papers, MHS. Unlike most others, the records of the Comité de Reconstrucción and the Anahuac Society are almost entirely in Spanish.

[54] Hoffman, *Neighborhood House*, [16].

[55] St. Paul Independent School District 625, *A Proposal: A Bilingual Bicultural Program of Education*, 1 (St. Paul, 1974); *St. Paul Dispatch*, January 10, 1973, p. 1. Two other West Side efforts created in response to pressure from the Mexican-American community were the Migrant Tutorial Program, which used college students and Mexican Americans to teach children who had trouble in school, and Mi Cultura, a low-cost, day-care facility, where Mexican-American children learned cultural traditions and two languages. On Minneapolis schools, see *Minneapolis Tribune*, December 5, 1980, p. 1A.

[56] University of Minnesota, Department of Chicano Studies, "Proposal," 1, 2 (1976), copy in Mexican-American History Project Papers; *Minnesota Daily*, July 14, 1978, p. 9, August 4, 1978, p. 16; University of Minnesota, Office of Admissions and Records, *Minority Enrollment Report*, 5 (Minneapolis, 1980). Chicano is a term of recent origin used by 20th-century Mexican-American activists to describe themselves. Various explanations of its meaning have been offered. Popular mainly with younger people, the term has met with no small resistance from the older generations of Mexican Americans who variously find it to imply: (1) "an unwillingness to identify clearly with their ancestral country"; (2) "a spirit . . . of militancy and/or an attitude of . . . defiance toward the establishment of U.S. society"; (3) "an intimate and somewhat vulgar attempt to classify all people of Mexican descent." See Grant Moosbrugger, "Meaning of the Word Chicano," a paper dated August 18, 1976, in the Mexican-American History Project Papers; *Minneapolis Sunday Tribune*, August 5, 1973, Picture Magazine, pp. 10–17; Casillas transcript, 9.

[57] Goldner, *Northern Urban Area*, 65, 67; St. Paul School District 625, *Bilingual Bicultural Program*, 4; *St. Paul Dispatch*, October 12, 1970, p. 1; State of Minnesota, "Capsule," June 13, 1978, p. 1.

[58] St. Paul School District 625, *Bilingual Bicultural Program*, 4. This is borne out by the fact that few of the papers collected by the Mexican American Project were in Spanish.

[59] St. Paul School District 625, *Bilingual Bicultural Program*, 5; oral history transcript, Frank Rangel, 12–15. See also Mexican American Cultural Resource Center Papers, in MHS. On language use in the Twin Cities, see *Minnesota Monthly*, July, 1978, p. 7. Throughout the state, 25% of schoolchildren who were not proficient in English came from Spanish-speaking homes; *Minneapolis Tribune*, January 15, 1980, p. 1B.

[60] U.S., *Census*, 1970, *Population*, vol. 1, part 25, pp. 357–360, 405–412, 512, tables 102, 119, 141; St. Paul Human Resources Planning Council, *Migrants In Action Study Committee Report*, 5 ([St. Paul], 1975), copy in MHS. Minnesota Analysis and Planning System (MAPS), "Final Report of the 1980 Census," telephone information, April 10, 1981.

[61] Here and below, see Migrants In Action, *Annual Report*, 1973, pp. 7, 8, copy in MHS; *St. Paul Dispatch*, January 10, 1973, p. 1, September 25, 1975, p. 6; González transcript, 15; MAPS, "Final Report of the 1980 Census," telephone information, April 10, 1981; conversations with J. A. Cortez, June 7, 1978, José Trejo, November 19, 1980. Estimates of illegal aliens assayed by immigration officials were provided by Tony R. Vignieri, November 20, 1980.

[62] Joyceann Dulas, "The Migrant Situation in Minnesota," 1, 2, paper, 1976, College of St. Teresa, Winona, which conflicts with "the most dependable findings" of the Mexican-American History Project, copy in MHS; *St. Paul Dispatch*, May 7, 1976, p. 11; *Minnesota Daily*, May 31, 1978, pp. 9–12; *Minneapolis Tribune*, April 25, 1978, p. 2B.

[63] Minnesota Migrant Council, *MMC–75–76: Progress in Review*, 4, a biannual report, copy in MHS.

[64] *Minneapolis Tribune*, June 22, 1969, pp. 1B, 6B, August 8, 1971, p. 2.

[65] Here and below, see Minnesota Legislature, 70th session, 1977, Senate File 1541, 72nd session, 1979, Senate File 35; Dulas, "The Migrant Situation," 5, 8; Minnesota, *Laws*, 1953, p. 187; 1973, p. 2066; 1974, pp. 440, 924; Executive Order No. 92, November 27, 1974.

[66] *Minnesota Daily*, May 31, 1978, p. 9; "State Analysis Report, 1976," pp. 1–4, a mimeographed paper in Mexican-American History Project Papers, MHS.

[67] Migrant Health Services, *Project Proposal, 1976–1977*, 65; oral history transcript, Ann Zuvekas, 1, 2, 5.

[68] Sallie Kyle, "Children of Migrants to Have Summer School," in Minnesota State Dept. of Education, *Education Update*, May, 1975, p. 17, and "Education Unit to Aid Migrant Children," September, 1975, p. 3; oral history transcript, Peter Moreno, 5, 6, 7, 10, 11; information from Moreno, November 21, 1980.

[69] *St. Paul Dispatch*, May 7, 1976, p. 11; Frank Guzmán transcript, 16.

[70] *St. Cloud Daily Times*, February 12, 1975, p. 1.

[71] Minnesota Migrant Council, *Progress in Review*, 1975–76, p. 5; Winona Diocese, "Research Study of Migrants, 1975," p. 1, and Migrant Health Services, *Project Proposal, 1976–1977*, 28. The three sets of figures have been combined in this table. Those of the health service in 1976 are higher, perhaps because that agency served all family members, not just workers. None of the figures was broken down by ethnic group. The council, however, reported that 99.7% of its program participants were Mexican Americans. Thus it seems safe to assume that the statistics reflect the number of Mexican Americans in the state.

[72] Minnesota Migrant Council, *Progress in Review*, 9.

[73] St. Paul Planning Council, *Migrants In Action Report*, 5.

NORTHERN
AND
WESTERN
EUROPEANS

CHAPTER 6

The British

ENGLISH, SCOTS, WELSH, AND BRITISH CANADIANS

Sarah P. Rubinstein

ONE OF THE FAVORITE MYTHS of American history posited the existence of a monolithic Anglo-Saxon society. The Anglo-Saxons were depicted as members of a single group united by a common language, religion, and political philosophy. Even a cursory examination of Great Britain, however, reveals a political entity with considerable diversity. The British Isles were home to descendants of Celts, Angles and Saxons, Danes and Norsemen, and Norman French. Though the English language was dominant, Gaelic and Cymric were spoken in the Highlands of Scotland and the villages of Wales. Anglicanism was the official religion in England and Presbyterianism in Scotland, but other Protestant denominations, Catholicism, and Judaism gained official tolerance by the mid-19th century. In politics the entire political spectrum, from arch conservatism to pure communism, was present in some degree, and through all political, economic, and cultural intercourse threaded an intricate social structure divided into several broad classes.[1]

The English (including Cornish and Manx), Scots, Welsh, Scotch-Irish, and British Canadians exhibited certain shared characteristics as well as marked differences. In addition to using the English language as their official common tongue, residents of the British Isles had for centuries been free to migrate within the realm, intermingling and intermarrying. Most of the Canadians, who were only one or two generations removed from the homeland, regarded themselves as British. Finally, both Americans and Europeans viewed Canadians and island residents as a single people, often referring to them collectively as "the British," much to their distress.

How many British immigrants made their way to the United States and Minnesota cannot be accurately determined because of imprecise accounting procedures on both sides of the Atlantic. Americans, ignoring the fact that many British immigrants traveled first or second class, enumerated only steerage passengers. British officials counted everyone who departed, including vacationers and businessmen who intended to return. Thus the American total was too low and the British too high. Complicating the entire process was the

Canadian immigrant; neither the United States nor Canada kept track of such persons until 1908.[2]

Nevertheless, some trends can be suggested. In the 160 years (1820–1980) that immigration statistics of any kind have been recorded, approximately 8,000,000 British settled permanently in the United States. The figures indicated an almost continual drain upon Great Britain as its citizens moved to the United States, Canada, and all parts of the Empire. After permanent British settlement in North America began in 1607, the transatlantic stream continued for the next two and a half centuries, but the heaviest migration has been relatively recent. Taking the number of immigrants arriving between 1890 and 1950 as a percentage of the 1820–1950 total, then 42% of the English, 57% of the Scottish, and an amazing 65% of the Welsh and 67% of the Canadians reached the United States in the years from 1890 to 1950.[3]

The peak year of foreign-born British population in the United States was 1930 with 2,163,608, due mostly to the heavy Scottish and Canadian immigration in the preceding decade. The previous high point occurred in 1910 with 2,045,917, following heavy English and Welsh migration.

For Minnesota the peak occurred earlier, a statistic probably influenced by the preference of highly skilled 20th-century arrivals for the industrial eastern states. The British were among the first Europeans to migrate to Minnesota, and eventually they were to be found in every county. The 1850 census listed 119 natives of Great Britain and 1,379 Canadian born, but roughly three-fourths of the latter were French Canadian. The high point (21,515) for residents born in Britain was registered by 1890 and for Canadian born (35,515) in 1900, while the peak for native born of British and Canadian parents (87,092) followed 20 years later.

Who emigrated and why must also be answered on the basis of sparse information often inferred from fragments of lists. Two reasons for emigrating can be eliminated immediately; the Puritans notwithstanding, few people left Great Britain or Canada to gain religious freedom or because of political persecution. While the social system was not par-

111

ticularly flexible, neither was it unduly oppressive. The primary motive for British emigration was economic, as it was for many other groups.[4]

Those who arrived before the Civil War were for the most part from agricultural backgrounds. Once in the United States they stayed in farming and clustered in family groups. After the Civil War an increasing number of skilled laborers, many of them single men, began seeking jobs in the United States. The gradual emigrational shift from family farmers to single skilled laborers meant that Great Britain, then the most highly industrialized country in the world, was exporting workers.

In seeking reasons for this surplus of laborers, historians have noted the unremitting high rate of population growth coupled with a removal from farm to city that left many rural areas depopulated. Most immigrants listed their last place of residence as a town or city, suggesting that marginally employed persons followed a pattern of staged migration from farm to city to America.

Historian Brinley Thomas has argued that British decisions to emigrate were based on employment prospects. Viewing the countries bordering both sides of the Atlantic Ocean as a single economic entity, he observed that alternating cycles could be traced in Britain and the United States in the 19th century. When the United States experienced a period of economic growth, Great Britain entered a slump and lost workers at a rapid rate. Correspondingly, as the pace of building and investment picked up in Britain in the 1870s and 1890s, the United States weathered the depressions of 1873 and 1893, and British emigration slowed.[5]

Just as Great Britain and the United States can be viewed as part of a unified economic community, Canada and the United States can be considered together for purposes of discussion. The same forces which drew English, Scots, and Welsh to the United States also induced them to migrate to Canada. Perhaps a year or a generation later many turned

south and resumed their journeys. For all practical purposes, job and home seekers acted as though the border were nonexistent, moving freely north or south to economically or climatically desirable areas. For instance, after World War II, Florida grew in popularity while Michigan and New York lost favor. By 1968 California, with its mild winters and many business opportunities, was attracting one-fourth of all the Canadian migrants to the United States.[6]

Assimilation for the British should have been easy, because they did not face many of the obstacles confronting other immigrants. They had no new language to learn (the Welsh excepted) and most were literate. Indeed, parts of the American landscape were similar to the British Isles, churches of the same denomination were available, similar philosophies of hard work and egalitarianism were prevalent, discrimination and name-calling were not problems, and intermarriage was fairly easy.[7]

But these similarities masked difficulties in cultural adjustment. The English language in the United States had developed unfamiliar regional dialects and Americanisms, the climatic extremes were a shock, the foods strange, and the class structure uncomfortably democratic. The British found their beloved royal family ignored, their fondness for a pint of bitter beer condemned, their holidays (such as Boxing Day) unobserved, and their favorite sports unknown.

The middle and upper-middle classes often established colonies with the intention of avoiding social contact with Americans who failed to recognize the subtleties of class distinctions. Women especially felt isolated as strangers in a strange land. British immigrants founded few ethnic organizations to ease their adjustment. Those who adapted settled in family or kin groups where they could "find resources within themselves to withstand their transplantation."

Of the British groups in Minnesota, Anglo-Canadians (see Table 6.1) were the most numerous (as they were in the United States as a whole), followed by English, Scots,

Table 6.1. Canadians in Minnesota by County, 1860–1970

County	1860 foreign born	1880 fb	1890 fb	1910 fb	1910 foreign mixed	1930 fb	1930 fm	1970 fb	1970 fm
Aitkin		76	418	207	139	94	308	25	210
Anoka	344	703	733	314	141	218	483	283	1,605
Becker	84	362	384	220	136	141	335	14	309
Beltrami		3	25	716	319	243	502	101	610
Benton	25	148	270	126	106	76	207	8	151
Big Stone		153	187	103	62	46	168	20	81
Blue Earth	103	508	417	218	127	114	390	32	279
Brown	42	161	131	66	53	30	120	14	107
Carlton		143	846	474	300	275	690	88	697
Carver	57	91	32	41	9	21	79	11	60
Cass	5	60	124	250	137	133	324	30	191
Chippewa		131	102	84	41	38	149	13	119
Chisago	59	171	118	57	15	41	91	16	139
Clay		340	328	324	172	196	454	96	486
Clearwater				56	26	40	121	36	87
Cook		7	1	43	21	57	88	7	141
Cottonwood		95	79	63	19	53	131	10	88
Crow Wing	46	263	644	410	186	256	701	81	578
Dakota	445	474	551	201	82	220	410	309	1,407
Dodge	85	180	94	66	22	39	129		45
Douglas		139	145	106	85	63	184	79	166
Faribault	29	316	309	100	72	54	189	16	189

Table 6.1. Canadians in Minnesota by County, 1860–1970 (*continued*)

County	1860 foreign born	1880 fb	1890 fb	1910 fb	1910 foreign mixed	1930 fb	1930 fm	1970 fb	1970 fm
Fillmore	166	565	355	177	92	83	351		133
Freeborn	30	211	158	50	28	43	152	23	137
Goodhue	176	358	161	126	57	55	229	28	155
Grant		43	37	34	19	32	83	17	65
Hennepin	978	4,086	8,595	6,265	2,575	5,826	11,659	3,694	14,085
Minneapolis				5,877	2,423	5,358	10,588		
Houston	171	185	118	57	25	32	115		95
Hubbard			96	168	87	80	234	19	202
Isanti	8	49	40	34	14	30	73	28	96
Itasca		14	121	572	297	316	728	66	798
Jackson	10	90	57	44	17	23	78		42
Kanabec	5	14	9	72	55	46	98	12	118
Kandiyohi	21	201	153	111	59	84	181	64	212
Kittson	429	418	730	537	432	330	573	85	420
Koochiching				389	115	419	598	446	1,279
Lac qui Parle	1	310	91	54	25	22	66		21
Lake	24	10	176	317	130	113	173	28	278
Lake of the Woods						98	201	68	131
Le Sueur	173	366	246	90	47	54	204		65
Lincoln		75	58	31	14	11	60		59
Lyon		205	264	134	59	77	272	9	178
McLeod	116	303	213	61	33	30	115		144
Mahnomen	6			25	19	35	50	15	87
Marshall		240	529	151	115	130	273	25	337
Martin	8	167	125	94	50	63	234	7	104
Meeker	52	320	286	145	84	63	219	31	136
Mille Lacs	1	95	155	115	90	68	223	37	126
Morrison	155	711	930	197	98	84	261	35	356
Mower	50	413	313	143	81	68	326	37	266
Murray		90	152	66	16	42	155		29
Nicollet	105	170	134	58	24	38	138	23	144
Nobles		96	135	66	39	29	140		94
Norman			103	62	36	30	56	8	85
Olmsted	254	415	284	181	74	213	565	272	761
Otter Tail	27	452	541	295	156	215	497	59	363
Pennington				77	62	64	118	31	196
Pine	4	180	272	191	86	133	298	26	209
Pipestone		72	153	62	40	35	122		42
Polk	65	2,132	3,488	802	742	441	1,088	146	1,015
Pope		179	318	155	91	82	205	31	179
Ramsey	722	1,757	5,097	3,425	1,447	2,899	5,552	1,487	6,491
St. Paul				3,302	1,408	2,741	5,261		
Red Lake				50	45	30	112	27	552
Redwood		347	296	184	118	90	248		119
Renville	19	327	225	154	89	83	227	10	139
Rice	453	1,274	1,025	372	200	185	567	51	424
Rock		114	140	45	16	19	53		44
Roseau				212	120	133	244	106	440
St. Louis	27	387	5,052	6,308	2,867	3,677	7,039	853	4,866
Duluth				4,418	1,994	2,607	4,748		
Scott	144	240	125	80	35	27	103	50	208
Sherburne	67	241	209	88	58	57	166	55	233
Sibley	268	216	140	40	47	38	100	22	33
Stearns	123	532	636	302	178	220	652	115	529
Steele	102	268	172	88	48	47	167	12	156
Stevens		147	152	74	36	40	156		100
Swift		307	222	65	54	55	209	16	109
Todd	37	179	302	190	108	110	393	31	228
Traverse	5	88	77	69	33	49	126	8	35
Wabasha	252	391	243	113	46	54	180		74
Wadena		109	130	70	36	57	175	15	75
Waseca	59	229	146	66	25	20	116		33
Washington	556	1,751	1,951	681	547	278	773	179	962
Watonwan		137	105	52	21	31	97	10	25
Wilkin		74	90	82	39	38	126	6	141
Winona	308	558	421	224	97	115	366	40	283
Wright	172	946	1,000	308	213	151	408	58	419
Yellow Medicine		85	90	61	24	30	114	5	84
Total	7,673*	28,463*	43,580*	29,856	14,900	20,618	45,933	9,815*	47,789*
Published census figures	(8,023)	(29,631)	(43,580)	(29,856)	(14,900)	(20,618)	(45,933)	(9,815)	(47,789)

Source: See Appendix
*French Canadians are included; they constitute about 33%.

Welsh, and Scotch-Irish (see Table 6.2). (Figures for the Scotch-Irish exist for only a few years. There are no separate national or state statistics for the Cornish or Manx.) All five groups lived in the state's major cities of Minneapolis, St. Paul, and Duluth and on the iron ranges of northeastern Minnesota. Rural enclaves composed of a particular British group or groups were scattered throughout the state.

Perhaps a closer look at some persistent rural and urban communities will suggest in broad strokes something of the diversity of the elusive, often invisible, British immigrants in Minnesota.

BRITISH IN RURAL MINNESOTA

Welsh and Scots

In the 1850s Welsh and Scottish farmers founded enduring concentrations in the Minnesota River Valley, especially in Blue Earth County, and Scotch-Irish settlers began to create a similar cluster at Eden Prairie in Hennepin County. In the 1860s other Scotch-Irish farmers trekked from Indiana to Long Prairie Township in Todd County, and in the next decade both Welsh and Scots developed some of the first farms on the prairies of Lyon County; the English planted

Table 6.2. English, Scots, and Welsh in Minnesota by County and Major Urban Areas, 1860–1970

County	1860 foreign born	1860 foreign mixed	1880 fb	1880 fm	1895 fb	1905 fb	1905 fm	1930 fb	1930 fm	1970 fb	1970 fm
Aitkin			10	15	46	62	203	47	177	12	77
Anoka	56	27	162	244	156	123	459	92	306	100	709
Becker	3	4	115	112	123	104	344	38	183	25	112
Beltrami					8	93	288	49	265	19	144
Benton	44	28	48	117	86	76	179	24	101	7	43
Big Stone			89	137	77	71	227	25	119		6
Blue Earth	342	268	792	1,421	743	591	2,103	102	495	34	398
Brown	29	10	74	185	51	54	123	33	117		64
Carlton	4	1	33	36	64	63	283	61	196	13	107
Carver	73	40	59	88	20	24	85	4	41	11	60
Cass			13	3	31	60	299	38	243	25	43
Chippewa			36	63	45	47	218	17	116		60
Chisago	36	16	61	51	42	30	147	12	82	10	105
Clay			273	198	267	228	506	84	319	39	238
Clearwater						7	51	15	76	22	65
Cook			1		4	18	60	7	28	9	18
Cottonwood			39	57	103	37	184	20	108	8	52
Crow Wing	4	4	119	91	241	200	642	110	388	35	226
Dakota	252	164	311	437	319	246	629	113	491	119	711
Dodge	57	41	232	461	153	109	487	40	282	8	56
Douglas			99	303	85	70	318	24	133	8	51
Faribault	45	36	242	495	222	166	681	46	326	4	89
Fillmore	126	51	501	941	378	228	910	67	373	21	81
Freeborn	69	54	151	396	109	79	318	67	298	35	163
Goodhue	145	102	256	544	171	111	459	41	273	26	140
Grant			11	30	31	38	150	17	84		17
Hennepin	276	192	1,522	2,210	3,708	3,797	10,472	3,897	9,725	1,896	6,313
Minneapolis			953		3,409			3,704	4,062	931	2,723
Houston	149	131	198	295	83	53	202	5	78		41
Hubbard					37	49	222	29	150	39	128
Isanti	6		34	35	27	16	73	15	63	7	38
Itasca			1		73	138	360	89	427	36	302
Jackson	2		73	129	133	87	341	44	191		96
Kanabec			2	1	3	9	83	14	79	6	80
Kandiyohi	19	10	69	135	66	75	263	26	173	7	87
Kittson	4	11	95	142	150	105	404	52	125	6	30
Koochiching								77	209	52	160
Lac qui Parle			47	116	30	35	98	17	89		11
Lake	4	10			40	97	230	39	101	28	147
Lake of the Woods								43	124	22	50
Le Sueur	152	86	241	416	167	110	439	30	176	7	130
Lincoln			45	107	40	43	166	17	106	7	31
Lyon			247	446	291	247	678	73	303	25	92
McLeod	67	24	117	257	83	46	207	9	97		46
Mahnomen	5	2						1	19		
Marshall			31	36	192	109	261	53	144	14	77
Martin	1	4	243	330	207	141	454	63	352	13	100
Meeker	17	7	106	139	79	56	214	35	98		47
Mille Lacs			18	39	44	44	165	23	116	6	69
Morrison	19	20	70	160	95	87	455	27	137	22	79
Mower	92	85	240	628	246	187	760	87	479	57	197
Murray			66	115	173	111	290	40	154		74
Nicollet	124	85	111	175	52	51	192	41	161	21	55
Nobles			145	256	220	168	571	53	243	15	59
Norman					24	25	114	16	79		19
Olmsted	334	253	462	1,018	317	234	724	163	709	216	536
Otter Tail	7	11	217	342	234	206	721	101	400	26	158

Table 6.2. English, Scots, and Welsh in Minnesota by County and Major Urban Areas, 1860–1970 (*continued*)

County	1860 foreign born	1860 foreign mixed	1880 fb	1880 fm	1895 fb	1905 fb	1905 fm	1930 fb	1930 fm	1970 fb	1970 fm
Pennington								23	104	7	77
Pine			14	48	72	107	230	63	226	27	183
Pipestone	8	2	38	108	167	122	435	48	177	8	43
Polk	8		175	190	274	201	679	88	323	14	106
Pope			44	120	75	75	335	23	130	18	40
Ramsey	453	285	982	1,376	3,198	3,119	7,433	2,189	5,312	780	3,169
St. Paul			907		3,094			2,152	2,392	544	2,167
Red Lake						54	234	11	27	7	26
Redwood			98	315	190	162	622	59	298		110
Renville	4		72	206	109	66	200	19	153	7	54
Rice	191	147	250	558	204	144	580	64	360	32	201
Rock			78	130	88	86	277	34	157		43
Roseau					11	49	160	29	83		41
St. Louis	16	12	174	247	2,438	2,081	6,100	1,884	4,093	536	1,954
Duluth					1,601			1,114	1,287	335	927
Scott	116	112	108	323	84	53	176	14	64	7	77
Sherburne	12	19	108	125	97	92	320	49	172	7	84
Sibley	66	46	54	99	30	16	97	15	44	8	24
Stearns	57	57	152	232	261	180	528	106	387	20	195
Steele	124	141	192	332	120	97	350	54	213	14	117
Stevens			69	103	62	46	229	20	109		31
Swift			67	100	62	67	307	24	124	12	64
Todd	19	7	91	158	115	111	325	49	270	14	53
Traverse	4	3	27	47	51	29	145	23	89		31
Wabasha	189	98	319	502	202	140	480	45	239	17	71
Wadena			74	98	77	83	357	29	149	22	51
Waseca	77	60	150	382	96	69	240	34	160	25	86
Washington	217	147	283	563	223	174	535	96	358	104	326
Watonwan			52	151	70	67	199	26	127		62
Wilkin			35	88	73	81	277	20	123		37
Winona	349	319	585	1,040	387	297	904	101	567	37	137
Wright	96	60	139	321	141	88	388	47	208	27	147
Yellow Medicine			69	130	66	63	296	28	144		71
Total	4,569	3,292	12,626	22,044	19,432	17,280	52,950	11,686	35,917	4,868	20,804
Published census figures	(4,967)		(12,562)		(19,531)	(17,280)	(53,773)	(12,268)	(38,616)	(4,868)	(20,804)

Source: See Appendix

three rural colonies in the state, and English-speaking Canadians followed the railroad to farm in Kittson County on the Minnesota-Manitoba border. Descendants of these pioneer settlers can be found in the state in the 1980s.

Although some had worked in the mines of Wales, most Welsh seem to have emigrated from central and northern Wales because of agricultural depression, high rents and taxes, and the lure of owning their own land. They reached the Minnesota frontier after brief stopovers in Pennsylvania, Ohio, Illinois, New York, and Wisconsin, arriving with some capital, possibly earned in previous sojourns in the states to the east.[8]

As early as 1852 four families took up land near Little Canada northeast of St. Paul, but finding the soil too poor for their liking, they moved the following year to Le Sueur County in the Minnesota River Valley. Adjoining Blue Earth County also received its first Welsh in 1853. More soon followed. In May, 1856, a colony of 121 persons from Cardiganshire, Wales (see Map 6.1), who had lived for a time in Ohio, claimed land in two Blue Earth townships (Cambria and South Bend) as well as in two townships in Le Sueur (Sharon and Cleveland). By 1857, when the creation of the state of Minnesota was under consideration, there were enough of them to warrant translating the proposed state constitution into Welsh as well as into German. In 1859–60 after Minnesota was admitted to the Union as the 32nd state, David C.

Evans was elected to represent Blue Earth County in the state legislature, the first Welshman to serve there.[9]

From their bases in Blue Earth and Le Sueur counties, the Welsh spread westward to Brown County in an arc of farms stretching around the great bend of the Minnesota River. The 1860 census recorded a total of 251 persons of Welsh birth and 238 native born of Welsh parentage in this region. The *Mankato Semi-Weekly Record* of May 21, 1861, estimated that by fall the Welsh in Blue Earth County would "number about one-third of the population."

Their decision to locate in the Minnesota River Valley involved these settlers in the Dakota War of 1862, a brief but bloody encounter with the Indians which forced the Welsh and other whites to evacuate their homes. Many of the men took part in the fighting, and a few lost their lives. But because their farms were not situated in areas of major battles, the Welsh dislocation was temporary and they returned to their homes.[10]

The Minnesota Valley concentration, the heaviest in the state, retained considerable loyalty to Welsh traditions and language, although the people spoke English for public purposes. They were characterized as literate and hard-working Calvinists, affiliated largely with the Calvinistic Methodist, Congregational, and Presbyterian faiths. One writer claimed that as a people they were theologically argumentative and politically Republican. They were also regarded as careful

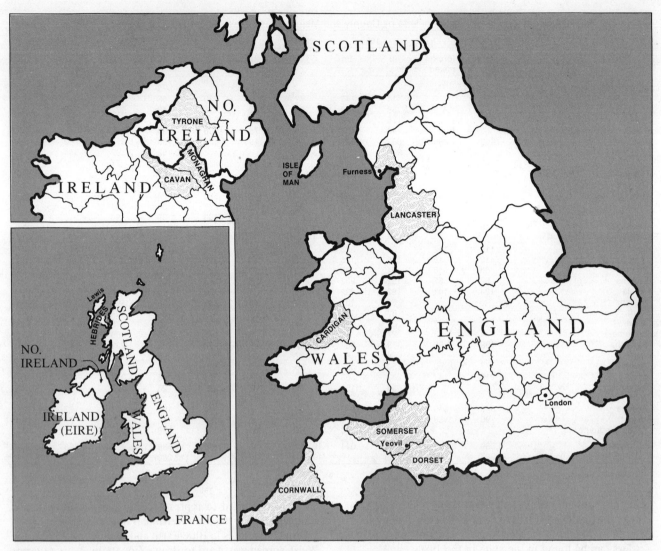

Map 6.1. Principal Counties of 19th-Century British Emigration to Minnesota

with money, ambitious for their children, and fond of sing-ing. The *eisteddfod* festivals, featuring recitations of literary compositions and the four-part singing for which the Welsh have become famous, were said to have started as early as 1855 at Mankato.[11]

Religion played an important role in the lives of the Welsh, for in Great Britain the retention of their culture had been inextricably intertwined with the Calvinistic Methodist church. The first Welsh church in Minnesota was erected by the Sharon Calvinistic Methodist congregation in Ottawa Township, Le Sueur County, in 1857. Five years later it was joined by a second Welsh church (Elim) in the same township. From 1856 to 1870 the Welsh founded seven more Calvinistic Methodist churches in Blue Earth County — three in Judson, two in Butternut Valley, and one each in Cambria and Mankato — as well as two Congregational churches at South Bend and Cambria, respectively.[12]

For purposes of governing the Calvinistic Methodist churches, the Minnesota Welsh set up a *gymanva*, or as-sembly, in 1858. It affiliated with the General Assembly of

all *gymanvas* in 1869 and outlasted the Calvinistic Method-ist-Presbyterian merger of 1920, finally disbanding in 1935. It never had complete control of the individual churches but rather acted in an advisory capacity and made recommenda-tions in such matters as acceptance of ministers to preach in Minnesota. Welsh would come from all member churches for the *gymanva* to hear the sermons which formed part of the meeting.

The Blue Earth congregations conducted services in Welsh until the early 20th century. The Calvinistic Method-ists began the transition to English in 1920, but some Welsh was used for the next two decades. Only the Mankato Cal-vinistic Methodist Church survived into the 1970s but dis-banded in 1971.

Although reduced in numbers, Welsh families still clus-tered near the old Welsh churches in the 1970s. Only Cotton-wood Township in Brown County had lost all of its Welsh population. Most of the decline can be explained by the out-migration of children, who tended to move to Lake Crys-tal, Mankato, or Minneapolis and St. Paul. At the Lake

Crystal Presbyterian Church in 1970, for example, the Welsh gathered as they had many times before for a *gymanfa ganu* (hymn singing) in celebration of the festal day of St. David, the patron saint of Wales. The 47th Welsh national *gymanfa ganu* was held in Minneapolis in 1978.[13]

The Scots were well represented among the fur traders who were the first group of Europeans in Minnesota, but they did not remain to farm or to found towns and cities in the mid-19th century. Like the French Canadians, they mingled easily with the Dakota and Ojibway people, often taking wives and acting as traders and interpreters for British and American fur companies. As the line of white settlement advanced across Minnesota, the Scottish fur trader retreated with his Indian in-laws and mixed-blood children.[14]

A group of Scots, notable for retaining their ethnic identity over 120 years, may be found, however, not far from the Welsh in Blue Earth County. Their story began in New York City in 1854 with a newspaper advertisement seeking persons interested in owning farms in the West. The people answering this call organized the Minnesota Settlement Association and paid membership fees. In return, each household received a guarantee of transportation to the West, 160 acres of farmland, and access to a townsite. Deciding that southern Minnesota offered the best opportunities, the founders sent a member already familiar with the area to select a specific location. By this time 239 persons had signed up; almost all had English or Scottish surnames.[15]

These families, calling themselves the Mapleton colony, arrived at their new homes in May, 1856. They found that only 65 claims had been laid out for 139 people. To solve the dilemma, the settlers drew lots, a process which left many of them dissatisfied. Some of the disenchanted found farms elsewhere in Minnesota; others returned to the East.

No concerted effort by any person or agency at any time seemed to have been made to induce Scots to settle in Blue Earth County, but they continued to arrive throughout the remainder of the 19th century. Many had gone from Scotland to Canada and from there either to New England or Wisconsin before arriving in Minnesota. Two of them opened the first stores in Mapleton, but when a church was organized in 1863, Scots were not numerous enough to insist that it be Presbyterian. Instead they compromised with other Protestants on the establishment of a Congregational church. Population figures for Scots in Blue Earth County showed a slow, steady growth. In 1860 after the arrival of the Mapleton colony, there were 17 foreign born and 7 native born there. Twenty years later the figures were 76 and 159, and by 1905, 62 and 275, respectively.[16]

An indication of the strong Scottish sentiment in the area was the founding of the Burns Club in Sterling Township in 1866, for "social, moral, intellectual and physical improvement and for benevolent purposes." The club was to meet twice a year — on January 25, Robert Burns's birthday, and again in June. Sometime in the 1870s, the June meetings were dropped, but the January celebrations continued. The 104th meeting took place in 1980. The club met in the homes of members until 1894, when it moved to the Mapleton Opera House in order to accommodate the large number attend-

SO SUCCESSFUL that it inspired the formation of a second Welsh band in Blue Earth County, the Cambria Philharmonic began lessons in April for its debut on July 4, 1890.

ing. Meetings featured games, Scottish dances and songs, and a pipe band.[17]

A hundred years after the club's founding a few new features had been added — a "Clan Gathering," or reunion, and the crowning of a "Bonnie Lass" queen wearing a royal Stewart shoulder scarf. The Heather Curling Club, which had been started in 1905, was still holding bonspiels in connection with the Burns's Day celebration. And of the early settlers who had been present when the Burns Club was founded, eight had descendants still living in the county.[18]

Some of the Mapleton colony members who were unable to obtain claims there moved just over the line to Delavan Township in Faribault County. Another long-lived community in that county, apparently unrelated to the Mapleton group, began farther south in Pilot Grove Township in 1856 when two brothers from Scotland began farming and making bricks. Population records indicated sizable groups of Scots in Faribault County by 1880. Among those who organized their own Presbyterian church in Pilot Grove in 1895 were early Scottish settlers, whose names were still present among the landowners in 1967.[19]

Farther west both Scots and Welsh were well represented in Lyon County, where settlement was spurred by completion of a railroad through the area in 1873. Among the influx of settlers were English and Canadian immigrants, who tended to settle together amid German or Old-Stock American neighbors.[20]

Few British had traveled directly to Lyon County; rather they followed a pattern of staged migration. Their routes varied widely. English and Scots traveled through Canada or migrated after stops in New Jersey, Pennsylvania, and eastern Minnesota. Anglo-Canadians were from Ontario, Michigan, and Illinois. The Welsh did not use Canadian routes, but instead stopped off in New York, Pennsylvania, Wisconsin, and Blue Earth County. So far as is known, no organized effort induced British to settle in Lyon County. But with acres of government land available for homesteading and with no known previous ties among them, these people selected claims on adjoining plots.[21]

A sample of British there in 1880 found 226 persons in 48 households living in Stanley, Lucas, and Sodus townships. Among the adults 90% of the males and 72% of the females were of foreign birth. Of the 13 native-born adult women, nine were of foreign or mixed parentage. The children, however, were overwhelmingly American, only 23% having been born abroad. These people showed virtually no evidence of intermarriage with other groups; all, with the possible exception of one Irish woman, were of British stock. Only five males and no females lived alone. The heads of households listed themselves as farmers; 34 had homesteaded rather than bought land. Some men added other businesses such as banking, grain buying, or keeping a store to their farming interests (see Table 6.3).

Twenty-two years later in 1902 about half of the families were still represented in the three townships. By 1952 only a half dozen were left. For the most part, they had sold out to prosperous Belgian farmers. While the British pioneers left no letters or diaries conveying their reactions to western Minnesota, one enduring institution remained. Built on the border of Stanley and Lucas townships in 1872, Swan Lake Presbyterian Church was organized by Scots immigrants and initially was named Argyle Presbyterian Church in honor of someone's hometown. Of the 34 families studied in these two townships, 18 belonged to the Swan Lake Church. Its records revealed that many were received by letter from the Presbyterian church of Canada.[22]

The Welsh, who chose land in Lyon County's Custer Township, maintained a community separate from but near the British cluster. They organized a Congregational church (1875 to 1928) and a singing school. In 1893 a second church was founded by 36 dissident Congregationalists who objected to services in English. Two years later it affiliated with the Calvinistic Methodists and continued to hold services until 1932, some in Welsh.[23]

At the turn of the century, Welsh farmers, many of whom had roots in Blue Earth County, were to be found throughout Custer Township. But by 1950 this rural population had vanished. Garvin, a small town in Custer Township, had increased its Welsh contingent and opened a Welsh Congregational Church in 1891. Meanwhile, Tracy, a nearby railroad center, recorded 37 Welsh attending the Presbyterian church there in 1895. Thus the rural Welsh of Lyon County exhibited a pattern characteristic of this group elsewhere in Minnesota — the children of Welsh farmers acquired an education and left the family farm to become town dwellers.

Scotch-Irish Farmers

Little has been said so far about the Scotch-Irish. They are a particularly difficult group to trace because separate statistics were not kept for various Irish groups until after the creation of the Irish Free State in 1922. Furthermore most of those who emigrated did so before the American Revolution, and by the time Minnesota opened for settlement, they had been absorbed into the Old-Stock American population. Nevertheless there are two groups in Minnesota who were specifically identified as Scotch-Irish. One group farmed in Eden Prairie Township (Hennepin County) and the other in Long Prairie Township (Todd County).[24]

Scotch-Irish settlers began arriving in Eden Prairie in 1853, migrating principally from the counties of Tyrone, Monaghan, and Cavan in northern Ireland (see Map 6.1). Their reasons for leaving were not directly attributable to the famines, which touched them very little, but rather to the ensuing changes in land laws which prohibited further division of farms, a process that left younger sons no option but to abandon their homes. Thus many single young men or recently married couples sailed for New York, moving westward to Minnesota in stages with brief stops in Ohio and Illinois. Others took the southern route via New Orleans and the Mississippi River or reached Minnesota via a northern approach through eastern Canada.[25]

Whatever the route, their destination in Minnesota was the same — the southeastern section of Eden Prairie Township. Their neighbors were Old-Stock Americans, a few English and Scots, a German community to the west, and a Bohemian one to the north. But the Scotch-Irish intentionally stuck together. The first arrivals staked claims to as much land as possible and held it for other family members.

Most Eden Prairie settlers acquired Minnesota land by pre-emption and began the business of farming. The initial job of clearing the land was a task for which they had little training since their agricultural experience had been limited to the intensive cultivation of a few acres. The sprinkling of millers, carpenters, and blacksmiths among them were even less prepared for farm life on the American frontier.

The census of 1880 indicated the cohesiveness of this community. Eden Prairie Township's population of 749 included 264 (47 households) of British birth or parentage. By far the largest contingent was Scotch-Irish: 49 Irish born and 192 born elsewhere in the United States of Irish parents. Thus 73% of the British and 26% of the township were of Irish stock. Furthermore of the 47 British households, 25 (53%) were represented by nine surnames, indicating that these families constituted a substantial kin group.[26]

The Scotch-Irish placed heavy emphasis on education. The 1880 census showed a number of both male and female adolescent children, even in large families, as having attended school within the past year. One family, acknowledging the insufficiencies of rural schools, managed to send each child to public schools in Minneapolis and to the University of Minnesota. Thus the children acquired the classic

Table 6.3. Lyon County British, 1880

	Children			Adults			Total
	M	F	Total	M	F	Total	
England	0	1	1	7	5	12	13
Scotland	1	0	1	22	8	30	31
Wales	0	3	3	7	5	12	15
Canada	15	7	22	18	15	33	55
United States	11	13	24	5	13	18	42
Minnesota	28	40	68	1	0	1	69
Total	55	64	119	60	46*	106	225*

Source: U.S. manuscript census, 1880.
*One additional adult female was born in Ireland.

tool for assimilation and moved easily into American society. Not one son or daughter of this family stayed on the family farm.[27]

Both the family and the church gave support to the individual in the process of adapting to the American frontier. One woman commented that it was an act of God that she was able to be with a kinswoman rather than strangers when her first child was born during the trip to Minnesota. The old attitudes, however, did not die. An aged man wanted no misunderstandings in the new land about his sympathies; he was an ardent Orangeman who requested that he "be buried with orange blossoms on his breast so there would be no question about his loyalties."[28]

These Scotch-Irish were, of course, Protestants; some were Episcopalians but most were uncompromising Presbyterians. At first their closest religious services were offered by the Pond brothers' Dakota mission at Bloomington, a long six miles away. By 1856 they had organized their own Presbyterian congregation, erected a building in 1869, and were still in existence in 1980 as the Eden Prairie Presbyterian Church. The Episcopalians also organized and built but lost members to other denominations and disbanded before the end of the century.[29]

The Todd County Scotch-Irish community, while similar to the Eden Prairie group, represented a different aspect of Minnesota settlement. It consisted of about a half dozen interrelated families, all of whom were members of a strict Presbyterian sect called Covenanters. Some, especially the adult males, were natives of Scotland or Ireland; others were born in Pennsylvania, Ohio, and Indiana. Their family relationships and their fundamental religious beliefs bound them together.[30]

In 1866 they sold their farms in Indiana and moved together to Long Prairie, Round Prairie, and Reynolds townships in Todd County. Their reasons for seeking new homes are not entirely clear, but whole families from grandfather to infant trekked by wagon caravan six days a week (they rested on the Sabbath) to reach Minnesota.

In Todd County, they settled among a few French and many Old-Stock Americans, and they were referred to by their neighbors as the Scotch-Irish Covenanters. The men farmed and also did some logging, surveying, and teaching. Religion continued to be a unifying force, but they did not organize the Round Prairie congregation of the Reformed Presbyterian church until 1873. Because the schoolhouse provided adequate meeting space, they never bothered to build a church.

Gradually the children and grandchildren moved away. Many went to the Twin Cities or to the Pacific Northwest, but others moved to Kansas, where there appears to have been a similar settlement. By World War II, only a few descendants of the Scotch-Irish Covenanters still lived in central Todd County.

The English Colonies

The English took part in three agricultural colonization efforts — in Martin County at Fairmont, in Wadena County at Furness, and in Clay County at New Yeovil. All three were undertaken in the 1870s in response to railroads' pro-

motions to sell land along their lines to farmers. None of the colonies had adequate planning, each encountered insurmountable obstacles, and all failed within ten years.

The Fairmont colony in southern Minnesota has long fascinated students because of the liveliness of its members, a mixed group of upper-middle-class families and single men, many of whom were younger sons who had no future on the family lands at home. Most were educated and all had sound financial backing. They paid cash for their farms, which they bought from an agent of the St. Paul and Sioux City Railroad, as well as for animals, equipment, and hired labor, thereby creating an awesome impression among their neighbors.[31]

In the first two years, 1873 and 1874, the colonists planted beans, 1,000 acres in 1873 alone, but lost their crops to invasions of locusts. Still the colony continued to grow as more people and cash flowed in from England. Other early Martin County settlers "were under great obligations to our English friends for the aid and assistance given them during the dark times of the locust devastations," wrote a local historian. "The English courage and pluck never let up, and while their loss was heavy, a benefit was derived by the settlers to whom they gave employment and kept money in circulation in buying horses and cattle and putting up buildings and making other improvements."[32]

The impact of the Fairmont colonists on Martin County was out of all proportion to their numbers. At their peak in 1880 only 219 British (English and Welsh) lived in the area, representing a mere 4% of the county's total population. But the English bought land in contiguous parcels near the lakes, rather than scattering on the prairie, and built some of the finest houses in the region.

Living in a compact group, they were able to continue "the habits and customs of England." Frontier Minnesota thus became the unlikely scene of fox hunts complete with red coats and hounds, horse races, boat club outings, and football (rugby) matches. The colonists also established the town's first library and church (Episcopal) and poured money into stores, banks, mills, a brewery to produce "genuine English ale and porter," and a saloon. Many caught the Yankee spirit and ran for local political office. Their activities were faithfully reported by the *Martin County Sentinel*, a newspaper started at Fairmont in 1874. Since many of the colonists returned to London for the winter, the newspaper also carried news of English politics and society so that all could keep in touch.

The Fairmont colony, however, was short-lived. Although their previous careers had been varied (military service, journalism, stock brokerage), its members attempted to become farmers — gentleman farmers, that is. But they had too little practical farming experience, indulged in too much high living, and encountered too many locusts to succeed. By the early 1880s many sold out and moved to St. Paul, St. Louis, Australia, or back to England. The few who remained continued to occupy positions of community leadership, however, until the last of the Fairmont colonists died in Martin County in 1940.[33]

North of Fairmont about 300 miles the Furness and New Yeovil colonies were started in 1872 on Northern Pacific

Railway Company lands. Railroad officials believed that organized colonies, by virtue of their unity of aims and purposes, would have a greater chance of enduring the difficult initial years of homesteading in Minnesota. Moreover the company seems to have decided that the English were peculiarly suited for such ventures, a hope in which they were to be disappointed in spite of the fact that 64% of the Northern Pacific's 1872–73 budget for the promotion of European emigration was spent in Great Britain.[34]

Recruiting among the laboring classes in the English counties of Dorset, Somerset, and Lancaster in 1872 (see Map 6.1), promoters insisted that prospective colonists have sufficient funds to cover travel and living expenses in Minnesota until their farms were paying propositions. These stipulations eliminated participation by the very poorest elements of society. Further it was made clear that participants should be young, willing to work, and experienced in agriculture. Each colony also forbade the use of liquor.[35]

Advance parties set out from Dorset in 1872 and from Lancaster in 1873 to inspect sites along the railroad and choose locations for town and farm development. The Dorset group selected Northern Pacific lands in Clay County near an already-established group of New Englanders. The Lancaster men found the Wadena region attractive for its mixed timberlands, luxuriant meadows, and ample supplies of sweet water. Named for the colonists' hometowns in England, New Yeovil in Clay County and Furness in Wadena County came into being in 1873.[36]

The first wave of colonists to arrive immediately expressed extreme dissatisfaction with nearly everything. At New Yeovil they were met by an April snowstorm, which dismayed those used to mild English springs, and by the news that the Lake Superior and Puget Sound Land Company, the colonizing organization, had changed the selected townsite to nearby Hawley, which already had a few settlers. Furthermore the town lots were much smaller than had been represented, no plat had been filed with the state

so no titles could be conveyed to them, Victoria Park and Albert Square (added to the promotional literature to "please the Johnny Bulls") were figments of an advertiser's imagination, and speculators had already taken up all the good land surrounding Hawley.[37]

Deceived and disgruntled, the colonists complained to the Northern Pacific. Acting in its capacity as the parent of the colonizing company, the railroad stepped in and attempted to satisfy their demands, offering to change the name of Hawley to Yeovil to make them happy and to sell them other railroad land. By the fall of 1873, however, as a period of economic stringency descended upon the country, the Northern Pacific fell into receivership and was no longer able to give the colony support of any kind. Many Englishmen abandoned the venture to seek their fortunes elsewhere in the state, move to Dakota Territory, or return to England. New Yeovil as a colony ceased to exist.

A remarkable remnant, numbering about 200 persons who had been recruited from many parts of England, decided to remain in Clay County. Despite bitterly cold winters, mosquito-filled summers, drought, prairie fires, and invasions of locusts, they settled on land in the vicinity of Glyndon and Hawley. Notwithstanding the supposed provisions for colony membership, none had any previous farming experience. Among their numbers were a mason, a toy manufacturer, a locksmith, a carpenter, a tailor, a piano tuner, a sea captain, and a cavalry officer whose brother was the British ambassador to Spain. Three had been in the service of Queen Victoria. They were men and women used to the comforts of life. Having determined to stay, the colonists devoted their energies to getting in a crop, in one case carefully planting wheat a single grain at a time.[38]

The women were as ill-prepared as their husbands. Many had never done any housework. One, a former music and French teacher, took lessons in breadmaking from her maid. Others could not cope with the hardships and isolation of homesteading. A young mother of six committed suicide on

AN ENGLISH FAMILY suitably attired for lemonade on its well-tended lawn in Lac qui Parle County, around 1890.

her second day in Hawley; three more women died within the year.[39]

According to their closest neighbors, the New Englanders of the Red River colony centered at Glyndon, the English were welcomed as men of substance and good moral character. But social contact between the two groups was not always smooth. The Yankees remarked upon the strange nasal tones of the British voices and commented disparagingly that the English seemed to think they were "better than Americans," and that, contrary to expectation, a Yankee woman was going to have to dress quite nicely on the frontier just to keep up with her English neighbors.[40]

Some English ways persisted among the settlers. At least in the early years, the Union Jack flew alongside the Stars and Stripes. The women continued to serve fruit sauce with pies and to make a heavy cake flavored with currants or caraway seeds. Yankee and Scandinavian neighbors enthusiastically adopted the English custom of a semiannual fair. Held at Hawley, the event at first resembled an English country fair. In times of crisis the emigrants showed their support for former countrymen. After Hawley women staged a fund-raiser and forwarded money to help widows and orphans of British Boer War casualties, the Lord Mayor of London returned his personal thanks.[41]

As Clay County's population slowly increased, some of the Englishmen found opportunities to follow their previous trades, opening stores, a pharmacy, a real estate office, and a saloon. (Despite the original temperance convictions of the Yeovil colonists, five men were saloon owners in 1885.) They joined both major political parties, and many of them held local political office. In a major co-operative effort with the Yankees they organized the Union Church in 1873 and erected a house of worship 14 years later.[42]

The settlement continued to attract other English and Canadian immigrants until the end of the 19th century. Within the British group there was a high degree of intramarriage as well as intermarriage with the Yankees. Children of the immigrants tended to continue the westward movement, and many of them made their homes in the Pacific Coast states. Representatives of five English families remained in the predominantly Scandinavian Hawley area in 1972.[43]

The Furness colony also disintegrated rapidly but for slightly different reasons. Before leaving Great Britain its ranks had been boosted by the addition of several Scots. The number of colonists totaled approximately 200 men, women, and children. Once in Minnesota the English and Scots found it impossible to agree upon how to divide the land. The Scots then left the colony and settled farther west at Compton Prairie in Otter Tail County while the English remained east and south of Wadena. By the end of the summer of 1873 many discouraged colonists had abandoned the effort to farm in Minnesota. Only 130 members were left in 1880.[44]

In order to file a claim for farmland, immigrants had to swear an oath whereby they relinquished allegiance to any and all foreign powers. A Furness colony Scot, when reminiscing about the process of repeating the oath and tendering the filing fee, commented that he "felt as if I wis sellin' mi queen an' country fur eighty acres o' land." His compan-

ion, also a Scot, replied, "That didna gang doon very weel wi' mi either. I mean ti be a guid American citizen, but I must say that in the meantime, the auld love [was] stronger then the new." These two men and their families were among the ones who stayed in Minnesota. By 1924, however, all of the original colonists had either died or moved away except for one old-timer.[45]

Another group of English, although not formally a colony, made their contribution in an industrial rather than agricultural setting. These people were immigrants from the peninsula of Cornwall in the southwest of England. Cornish miners, driven from home by economic depression caused by plummeting prices for tin ore, spearheaded the development of the iron and tin mining industry in Michigan, Wisconsin, and Minnesota. In 1884 after iron had been discovered on Minnesota's Vermilion Range, mining captain Elisha Morcom organized two train carloads of fellow Cornish miners and a few families and transferred them from Quinnesec, Michigan, to Tower, Minnesota.[46]

The census is of no help in identifying Minnesota's Cornish, who listed their place of birth as England. But the Cornish do have distinctive surnames, frequently using the prefixes Tre-, Pen-, or Pol-. Thus a scan of the manuscript census of range towns for 1885 and 1895 can reveal something about the Cornish, specifically, that they were grouped in only a few towns. Their location indicated that their mining skills were useful in the shaft mining of the Vermilion but not in the open pit system of the Mesabi. Gradually, as hundreds of Finns and Slavs became miners, the Cornish either were promoted into managerial positions or moved on to other mining districts in the western states. Few Cornish remained on the iron ranges by the late 1970s, but their homey, practical miners' noon meal, the pasty, a meat-and-potato-filled pastry envelope, remained a popular item in range town bakeries.[47]

An Anglo-Canadian Rural Settlement

Kittson, the most northwest of Minnesota's counties, contained one of the few rural concentrations of English-speaking Canadians in the United States. While no complete record of their origins was compiled, many hailed from Ontario and from Prince Edward Island. In a listing made in 1880, for example, 99 of 113 persons (87.6%) were natives of Ontario. In general, emigrants from both areas left for the same reason — lack of opportunity at home. After the economic panic of 1873, Canada recovered slowly. Shipbuilding in the Maritime Provinces was depressed, and the settled part of southern Ontario was becoming relatively overpopulated.[48]

The rush for land in Kittson County was part of a larger movement into northwestern Minnesota, eastern North Dakota, and southern Manitoba. Many homesteaders, whether they were Americans, Canadians, or Europeans, seemed unconcerned about what state or even which country their land lay in, so long as they could get title to a farm of their own. Along the unmarked United States-Canada boundary, families often did not know. Communities and church congregations were bisected by the international border. The fact that the land lay in Kittson County was unimportant to the settler; what mattered in 1878 was that the county contained rich farmland which had full rail service.[49]

Once the railroad was built to the Red River Valley, Canadians had a fairly easy rail and water route to the Minnesota northwest. A train ride to either Buffalo, New York, or Detroit, Michigan, followed by a boat trip on the Great Lakes to Chicago, Milwaukee, or Duluth, could now be climaxed by another train journey to Kittson County. After the Canadian Pacific Railroad reached Winnipeg in 1885, an all-Canada route was open as far as the Red River, which could then be followed upstream to Kittson County by steamboat, train, or wagon.[50]

Although the western part of Kittson County was well known to Canadians who had been active in the fur trade, only St. Vincent had the appearance of a permanent settlement in the mid-1870s. Its population was made up primarily of French Canadians and métis. But beginning in 1878 a rapid influx of homeseekers quickly filed claims on the available farmland. Settlers continued to arrive until World War I, but for the most part the later ones bought already-established farms. Often, however, such farms boasted only a small house and barn and a few acres of broken land.

Using St. Vincent as a jumping-off point, Canadians (as well as some English and Scots) moved east from the Red River principally into the townships of St. Vincent, Hill, Clow, Richardville, Hampden, Granville, Hallock, and Thompson, while the Swedes, who were the county's largest foreign-born group, favored Deadwood, Jupiter, and Poppleton townships.[51]

A profile of the British group in these Kittson County townships in 1880, obtained by analyzing the manuscript census, showed 424 individuals, 269 males and 155 females. Of those, 185 males and 82 females were adults (aged 18 or over), and 88 men (48% of adult males) and 69 women (84% of adult females) were married. As was usual on the frontier, there was a preponderance of young males, some of whom had left wives and children behind while searching for new homes. Among the 110 unmarried adults, only 13 were women, a not uncommon male-female ratio in newly settled areas (see Table 6.4).[52]

Nearly three-fourths of the British group were of Canadian birth. Scots outnumbered the English by a third. Their children were almost all of foreign birth, indicating that both newly married couples and those with growing families were entering the United States for the first time. (The youngest child was only three months old.) Of the large number of

very young children in the sample, only 12 (7%) had been born in the United States, 7 of them in Minnesota.

Among the 121 Canadian-born children, nearly half (56) had both parents born in Canada. Another 22 had one Canadian and one British parent, while a like number (26) had two parents born in Great Britain. The others had one Canadian and either an American or a European parent.

Interestingly the adults showed similar parentage patterns. Of those born in Canada (182), nearly a third (56) themselves had Canadian-born parents, including the oldest person in the group, a 63-year-old widow. The parents of over a fourth (50) were an English-Scottish combination, and a fifth (35) were Canadian-British. Only two Canadian adults in the sample did not have at least one Canadian or one British parent. Thus the 1880 census depicted a staged migration from the British Isles through Canada to Minnesota, carried out by a mixture of Canadian and British families.

Once in Minnesota, over half of the immigrants engaged in farm-related jobs. Town dwellers owned their own stores or other businesses (11), worked in the building trades (14), ran hotels (7), or were general laborers (16). Two were physicians, four clerks, three in steamboating, and eight in railroading. A cook and seven servants were all females.

By the end of the 19th century these people had established seven churches in Kittson County. Four were Presbyterian, two were Episcopal, and one was Methodist. Of 52 church affiliations specifically mentioned in biographical sketches, half were Presbyterian and the remainder were about evenly divided between Episcopal and Methodist. Most of the Presbyterians had emigrated from Scotland or from Canada's Maritime Provinces.[53]

Unfortunately, about those other two great assemblers of men — politics and clubs — the county histories were silent. While a number of men held local political offices, no indication of party affiliation was recorded. A few were listed as Masons and several later belonged to veterans' groups, but no identifiably British ethnic organizations appeared to have existed in the county.

Of the 80 British families for whom later information was located, at least 68 had descendants still living in Kittson County in the mid-1970s. Other members of succeeding generations moved to North Dakota, the Pacific Coast, Canada, or elsewhere in Minnesota. In the second generation, the process of out-marriage began, with the more numerous Swedes and Norwegians in the county as the usual partners. Fifteen members of one family, who emigrated from New Brunswick in 1880, were said to have spoken Gaelic and to

Table 6.4. Kittson County British, 1880

	Children			Adults			Total	% of British
	M	F	Total	M	F	Total		
Canada	67	54	121	128	54	182	303	71.5%
England	4	1	5	20	9	29	34	8.0%
Scotland	6	13	19	24	13	37	56	13.2%
Other	7	5	12	13	6	19	31	7.3%
Total	84	73	157	185	82	267	424	
% of Total	19.8%	17.2%	37.0%	43.6%	19.3%	63.0%		100.0%

Source: U.S. manuscript census, 1880.

have known no English when they arrived. They were followed by numerous relatives, bearing family names still prominent in Kittson County.

British Land Development

In addition to exporting people to the United States in the 1870s and 1880s, Great Britain exported an enormous number of pounds sterling. The reasons were threefold: railroads needed capital to reorganize after the panic of 1873, land could be bought cheaply, and interest rates were high (as much as four times higher) as American farmers borrowed the cash necessary to bring their land under cultivation. Nationwide, for example, British investment ranged from 15% to 20% of American railroad capitalization, a sum which represented about 18% of the total British investment abroad. British interests in Minnesota railroads were confined to the Northern Pacific and the Chicago, Milwaukee and St. Paul railroads and chiefly through middlemen and land sales.[54]

The pre-eminent English firms active in Minnesota were Close Brothers and Company and a related firm, the Western Land Company. Beginning in 1881 and continuing until the end of the century, the four Close brothers bought 48,400 acres in Pipestone, Rock, Nobles, Murray, and Jackson counties. In addition, they managed 110,000 acres in Pipestone County for other buyers.[55]

At least five Scottish corporations entered the Minnesota investment field after 1873 — the Scottish-American Mortgage Company, the Dundee Mortgage and Trust Investment Company, the Edinburgh American Land Mortgage Company, the (incongruously named) Oregon Mortgage Company, and the American Land and Colonization Company. Generally these companies operated in southwestern Minnesota. The first-named firm retained a local agent at Sleepy Eye (Brown County). The Dundee company bought, improved, and named the towns of Airlie and Dundee in Nobles County.[56]

The Close Brothers and the American Land and Colonization Company intended to recruit British colonists. The Scottish venture, as one historian stated, was founded "to help emigrants [*farmers from the Scottish Lowlands*] in their selection of a new home, to arrange for their transit by sea and by land, to offer them farms of an extent and description suitable to their means and tastes, to aid in the erection of their homesteads, and to permit payments in yearly installments." The firm was incorporated in 1881, capitalized at £500,000 in £10 shares, bought 84,000 acres in Pipestone and Murray counties and a half interest in the town of Woodstock, where they built a hotel and offices. Two years later they had sold or leased 43,000 acres, but profits were not as great as expected (a 40% return tapered off to less than 8%), and the stock was liquidated in 1895. The Close Brothers also advertised widely for British and American settlers, and, like the Scots, offered farms with essential buildings already constructed and a few acres broken and prepared for seeding.[57]

The American Land and Colonization Company sent David Maxwell Fyffe from Scotland to Woodstock as their local agent. His reminiscences reveal some reasons for the failure of the colonization enterprise. Many, especially the English in his opinion, were not suited to farming in the harsh frontier style. He hinted that other settlers did not accept the English: "at that time [*1886*] the Britisher was not altogether so well thought of in that country [*Pipestone County*] unless for his money." Though the individual schemes failed, Scottish and English capital provided a major portion of the money needed for western railroad development through buying railroad lands, but their greatest contribution was in loans to farmers to bring land under cultivation.[58]

BRITISH IN URBAN MINNESOTA

English, Scots, Welsh, and British Canadians were present in the Twin Cities area from early territorial days. Taken together, they also formed one of the largest segments of the foreign-born population of Duluth. But information about their urban occupations, religious affiliations, problems of adaptation, political activity, and social life is scanty. Census statistics on their numbers from 1890 to 1960 showed that British groups peaked in St. Paul and Minneapolis by 1920, and in Duluth probably at about the same time (see Tables 6.1 and 6.2).

By 1920 they had spread throughout the Twin Cities, forming no tightly knit ethnic communities but concentrating in Wards 8 and 13 in Minneapolis, between Lake of the Isles and the southern city limits, and Wards 7 and 11 in St. Paul, west of the cathedral and south of Marshall Avenue — the same wards in which native-born whites with native parents were concentrated in each city. In Duluth in 1910 the British, more than any other group of foreign born, had more of their number (16.4%) living in Ward 1, the largely residential eastern section which was inhabited by 24% of the native-born whites of native parents. Two subdivisions in this area — Hunter's Park and Glen Avon — had been named, platted in 1891, and settled by Scots. Based on these coincidences, one might suggest that the urban British were easily assimilated.[59]

In order to gain some insight into British urban migration, data were collected on 127 men living in St. Louis County in about 1910; 69 were of English, Scottish, or Welsh birth or descent and 58 of Canadian. Whether the immigrant was from Great Britain or from Canada, little significant difference appeared among them in regard to dates of migration, age and marital status at emigration, or route traveled. About two-thirds (65.5%) arrived between 1880 and 1900. For the most part they were young (less than 10% were over the age of 30), had not yet married, and followed the Great Lakes route to Duluth. Not uncommonly they had spent several years in Michigan or Wisconsin. Some, especially the adolescent boys, left home to join an older, settled relative, indicating the importance of family connections in the immigrants' choice of Duluth.[60]

Men in this group were remarkably successful in business and doubtless were not typical of all Duluth immigrants. Nevertheless, chiefly because of their youth and lack of experience, these men entered various occupational fields at the lowest levels. Nearly one-third succeeded in becoming

SCOTS of all ages turned out for a gathering of Clan Stewart in Duluth, around 1920.

company managers or owners of their own stores. About 10% entered the professions of law and medicine. The remainder were either in public service or self-employed as building contractors, real-estate brokers, or automobile agency owners.[61]

While men from the British Isles and Canada appeared in equal numbers in the above occupations, English, Scots, and Welsh outnumbered the Canadians three to one in mining. Moreover nearly one-third of the men from the British Isles were Cornish, who as members of mining families chose a time-honored Cornish occupation.

The most visible of the British in Duluth were the Scots. They were founders of banks, wholesalers of groceries and fish, organizers of the Chamber of Commerce and the Duluth Board of Trade, and promoters of the Duluth Life Saving Station (forerunner of the Coast Guard). Scots designed and built railroads, grain elevators, office blocks, churches, and houses. They developed iron mines and Great Lakes shipping; one of them, Alexander McDougall, invented the famous whaleback ore carrier. A Scot was a trustee of the Duluth Federated Trades Council when the American Federation of Labor granted it a charter in 1889. William McEwen, son of Scottish immigrant parents, was editor of the *Labor World* (Duluth) and active in the organized labor movement for more than 40 years. Not surprisingly, the Scots were staunch supporters of two Presbyterian churches in Duluth — First Presbyterian, founded in 1869 and the first organized church in Duluth, and Glen Avon Presbyterian started in 1893.[62]

Of those in the survey of British immigrants for whom religious affiliations were given, two-thirds were either Methodist or Presbyterian. Canadians tended to be Presbyterian (many had Scottish backgrounds) and the British Islanders were more strongly Methodist (testifying to the Cornish influence). Only one was Catholic. In politics 63 of the 70 who listed a party preference specified Republican. About 70% claimed membership in other organizations, especially the Masons.[63]

The urban British formed societies for the purposes of social exchange and assistance to fellow countrymen. The English established a mutual benefit organization known as the Sons of St. George and its auxiliary, the Daughters of St. George. The men's society was active in St. Paul by 1873 when it entertained English colonists who were on their way to the New Yeovil colony at Hawley. Some time before World War II these two groups were joined by the English-Speaking Union of the Twin Cities. Its membership was open to anyone interested in England; and its programs, all related to England, covered a wide variety of topics. For a brief time after World War II, groups known as British Clubs, their membership boosted by servicemen's brides, existed in both Minneapolis and St. Paul. By mid-century the assistance aspect had been replaced by cultural exchange. Of these various associations, only the English-Speaking Union was active in the Twin Cities in the 1980s. It was, however, joined in 1979 by the Manx Society of Minnesota, a cultural organization formed for Manxmen, their descendants, and anyone interested in the Isle of Man.[64]

The most enduring of the urban societies have been Scottish associations. The St. Andrew's Society, which was founded three separate times, made its first appearance in 1859 when several St. Paul men drafted a constitution for a benevolent society to provide for needy Scots and their children. They also planned to promote Scottish immigration to Minnesota and to hold an annual St. Andrew's Day dinner on November 30. Twenty years later another group of St. Paul Scots re-established the society. Their efforts, which lasted into the 20th century, included sponsoring celebrations of St. Andrew's Day as well as a gathering of the clans in 1892.[65]

A third St. Andrew's Society was chartered in Minnesota by Scots in 1976. Like its predecessors, it affiliated with the international St. Andrew's Society. In addition to gathering on St. Andrew's Day and Robert Burns's birthday, members revived the festival of Hogmanay, as the Scottish New Year's Eve celebration is known. Each year the society also

provided a scholarship for a student of Scottish studies, published a monthly newsletter, sponsored a Scottish ball, and took part in the Macalester College Scottish Country Fair. In 1978 the group held a Kirkin' O' the Tartan at St. Stephen the Martyr Episcopal Church, Edina, where each Scot could present a swatch of clan tartan to be blessed.[66]

Other Scots in the Twin Cities over the years have been active in the Caledonian Club (late 1880s), the Order of Scottish Clans with ladies' auxiliary (Clan Gordon in Minneapolis and Clan Campbell in St. Paul, about 1900–40), the Twin Cities Scottish Club and the Royal Scottish Country Dancers of the Twin Cities (1970s), and the Brian Boru Pipe Band (1970s). The Scotch-Irish probably were the supporters of Minneapolis and St. Paul chapters of the Loyal Orange Association, a national Protestant order. While the group had some fraternal functions, its main purpose was to counteract the self-perceived political and economic influence of the Catholic Irish.[67]

As early as 1870 Duluth Scotsmen had organized a local chapter of the St. Andrew's Society and a Caledonian Club. Little more is known about these groups; possibly they did not survive the panic of 1873. In 1888 Scots, by then more numerous, met to celebrate Robert Burns's birthday. The idea of forming a permanent group appealed to them, and by the end of the year they had received a charter as Clan Stewart No. 50 of the Order of Scottish Clans. Like most such groups it had both social and mutual benefit functions, as well as a ladies' auxiliary added in 1922. Four celebrations highlighted their year — Burns's birthday, the Battle of Bannockburn anniversary on June 24, St. Andrew's Day, and Hogmanay. But perhaps the most memorable occasion was the annual summer picnic. Upwards of 1,000 people would assemble and follow about a dozen kilted pipers down to a boat which conveyed them to their picnic spot. There followed a day of highland games, dancing, and bagpipe playing. After 74 active years the clan disbanded because the younger generations were no longer interested.[68]

With the nation's 200th birthday in the offing, Duluth Scots organized the Scottish Heritage Committee, which sponsored a festival, exhibit, and a publication on the Scottish legacy to the United States and to the Duluth area. Children of Scottish immigrants made many of the arrangements. This renewed interest continued through St. Andrew's Day, 1980, with a Kirkin' O' the Tartan at St. Paul's Episcopal Church. About 30 tartans were presented before a congregation of nearly 300; a Scottish tea, dancing, and piping followed.[69]

The Lewis Society was founded in 1911 in Duluth by several natives of the Isle of Lewis, an island in the Hebrides off the northwest coast of Scotland. An unusual feature of the Lewismen was their language; they were Gaelic speakers who made a conscious effort to maintain the traditions and language of the homeland. All society meetings were conducted in Gaelic, which was also used at home. By 1955 interest had lapsed and the society disappeared.[70]

Of the British groups in the Twin Cities, only the Welsh formed an identifiable urban, ethnic community, just as they had in the state at large. Though there were Welsh in St. Paul by 1850, the first settler on record in Minneapolis did not arrive until 1865. From then on the Welsh showed a preference for Minneapolis. By 1881 their population had increased sufficiently for 25 of them to found a Calvinistic Methodist Church. Two years later they built a church at 17th Avenue South near Franklin Avenue. Subsequently the center of the community shifted southward, and in 1911 they relocated their church at 15th Avenue South near Lake Street. At least some services continued to be held in the Welsh language until the late 1930s in order to please the older generation of the 200-member congregation. In 1947, however, so few people were attending regularly that the church disbanded.[71]

The assembly which drew Welsh from throughout the state was the *eisteddfod*. Whereas in Wales it had principally involved literature and allied fields, in the United States it divided evenly between spoken and musical performances. Minneapolis held its first *eisteddfod* in 1885. Others followed in 1888, 1894, and 1895, and Mankato was host in 1891 and 1905. As part of the Americanization movement in the early

20th century, the *eisteddfod* was replaced by the *gymanfa ganu*, a Welsh singing festival. The latter was especially popular among people of Welsh stock who could not speak the language but remembered the hymns of their childhood. In addition the *gymanfa ganu* was not associated with any religious denomination but rather was designed to appeal to all Welsh.[72]

The musical people also founded a Welsh Philharmonic Society in Minneapolis in 1889. In the early years of the 20th century they supported the Cambro-American Society and gathered at the annual St. David's Day banquet on March 1. When the International Institute began to sponsor its Festival of Nations in the 1930s, a Welsh choir took part and treated the audience to such selections in Welsh as the national anthem of Wales and a hymn, "Cwm Rhondda" ("Guide Me, O Thou Great Jehovah").[73]

After 1947, when the Minneapolis church closed its doors, the Welsh community depended on the St. David's Society, founded in 1910, to fill the ethnic void. In an effort to interest young people in their Welsh heritage, the society invited the national *gymanfa ganu* to hold its 1978 song fest in Minneapolis. The success of this meeting surprised many old-timers and generated fresh enthusiasm. In 1980 over 40 people attended the monthly meetings to practice singing in Welsh and learn about the land of their fathers.[74]

British Canadians in the Twin Cities often have joined societies associated with their parents' ethnic group. Scottish Canadians, especially, affiliated with Scottish groups. But during World War I St. Paul Canadian women got together for war work, calling themselves the Canadian Club. As a historian of the group said, "In 1918, members of the Canadian Club (there being no further need for war work) formed a chapter of the Daughters of the British Empire, known as the Bon Accord Chapter, its object being to maintain old associations, to bring British women together and to keep them in touch with their American neighbors." By 1952 St. Paul had nine chapters and Minneapolis, seven. Their activities over a 50-year period included charity to disaster-stricken areas of Canada, relief to Canadians in distress in the Twin Cities, further war work during World War II, and assistance to servicemen's brides in the early 1950s. They also sponsored Empire Day celebrations, an annual Magna Carta Day service at St. Mark's Episcopal Cathedral in Minneapolis, and the British Market Day Fair, complete with high tea, also in Minneapolis.[75]

A Canada Club re-emerged in the Twin Cities in the early 1970s and affiliated with the International Institute. In 1973 it had a membership of 125 families and celebrated the official Canadian Thanksgiving holiday, an October event.[76]

The urban British maintained a keen interest in at least two sports of their homeland. Curling and cricket had sufficient fans to form clubs in Minneapolis by 1887. The St. Paul Cricket and Curling clubs organized at about the same time. Duluth Scots joined the competition with their curling club in 1891. Enthusiasm for cricket appeared to have flagged before World War I, but curling continued to draw members for the clubs and spectators for the bonspiels. The urban clubs played each other as well as entertaining challenges from Canadian and Scottish teams. Both St. Paul and

Duluth built large indoor rinks for their curlers, who were still active in 1980.[77]

Evidently the Twin Cities British liked their ale and porter. From early statehood days until Prohibition, English native Edward Drewry and his sons found a ready market for ale, porter, stout, and beer produced by their St. Paul brewery. After the turn of the century the Minneapolis-based Imperial Brewing Company, headed by Hunter, Mackay, and Werth, offered a full range of English light-alcoholic beverages.[78]

The memberships of all the Twin Cities societies have been boosted in recent years by new immigrants. From 1956 to 1976 the British formed the largest group of immigrants in Minnesota, numbering about 10,000. Two-thirds or 6,543 of those were Canadians. The next largest group was the Germans with 5,545. As great as these numbers seem, they are only about 1% of the total for the post-World War II British in the United States.[79]

Over the past two decades controversy over these immigrants has given rise to such euphonious terms as "brain drain." More politely the movement has been called "professional elite migration." American studies indicated that a high percentage of professional and technical occupations were represented among the immigrants. A Canadian survey covering the 1955–68 period revealed that about one-fourth of the Canadian-born immigrants employed in the United States were professional or technical workers. Another study stated that Canada by 1961 was losing nearly 30% of its first-degree earners. One variable impossible to estimate was the extent of staged migration from other countries through Canada to the United States. Another was the extent of remigration to Canada, although it is known that the movement increased through the 1970s.[80]

While acknowledging that British of the professional and technical class have emigrated to the United States because of greater economic opportunities, no one has accurately determined how many chose Minnesota, though an amazing number seem to have settled in the state. One study indicated that they often had at least one degree from a foreign university; some had completed advanced degrees before emigrating. They taught at the University of Minnesota and at Mayo Graduate School of Medicine, did research at Honeywell, General Mills, and Control Data, and were company officers in such firms as Northwest Orient Airlines, Longyear Company, Tennant Company, and Minnesota Mutual Life Insurance Company.[81]

Mid-20th century British immigrants, whether part of a brain drain or not, were carrying on a tradition of making significant contributions to their adopted state and country. In this they joined such 19th-century arrivals as James J. Hill, founder of the Great Northern Railroad (Canadian); George D. Munsing, creator of the "union suit" (Scottish); William MacPhail, founder of the Minneapolis school of music named for him (Scottish); Dr. Walter R. Ramsey, founder of the St. Paul Children's Hospital (Canadian); Everett Fraser, dean of the University of Minnesota Law School (Canadian); Dr. Helen Hughes Hielscher, founder of the American Legion Auxiliary (Canadian); and Louis Nash, labor leader, editor, and father of the 6 o'clock closing (English).

The experiences of the British immigrants in Minnesota, on the whole, were paralleled throughout the nation. As immigrants the British have been called invisible. They faced no practical barriers to intermarriage or to advancement to managerial positions in business. Nevertheless the English, Scots, and Welsh, especially, struggled to cope with the vastness of the landscape and the extremes of temperature. They hungered for familiar foods and beverages and longed for the sociability of the holidays, sports, and games they had known in Great Britain. In times of need or crisis, it was to a compatriot and not a stranger that they turned. As one English journalist commented, they found not "Sheffield with an American accent . . . but . . . a new and terrifying civilization."[82]

The children of the British immigrants, however, seem to have encountered almost none of their parents' difficulties in adjustment. Having no memories of a different social and political system, they were totally assimilated culturally. The second generation truly was invisible.

Reference notes

[1] For an overview of British background, here and below, see Rowland T. Berthoff, *British Immigrants in Industrial America*, 1–4 (Cambridge, Mass., 1953).

[2] Berthoff, *British Immigrants*, 5–11.

[3] N. H. Carrier and J. R. Jeffery, *External Migration: A Study of the Available Statistics, 1815–1950*, 14 (General Register Office, *Studies on Medical and Population Subjects*, No. 6 — London, 1953). One can arrive at an annual rate per 10,000 mean population of gain or loss by emigration by using census figures, projecting population increase based on birth and death records, and then comparing that estimate to the actual census totals over 10-year periods.

[4] Here and below, see C[harlotte] J. Erickson, "Who were the English and Scots emigrants to the United States in the late nineteenth century?" in D. V. Glass and Roger Revelle, eds., *Population and Social Change*, 347–381 (London, 1972). There are statistics on what jobs immigrants entered after coming to the U.S., but none on what they did before leaving home. Ship lists are of some help if the captain took the time to do more than write "laborer" at the head of a column and follow it with a series of ditto marks. Great Britain and Canada did not record who left. An examination of ship lists, census data to check depopulated areas, immigrant letters and diaries, parish files, and union records, however, can lead to some valid conclusions.

[5] Brinley Thomas, *Migration and Economic Growth: A Study of Great Britain and the Atlantic Economy*, 87, 96, 111 (Cambridge, Eng., 1954).

[6] Marcus L. Hansen, *The Mingling of the Canadian and American Peoples*, 1–3 (New Haven, Conn., 1940); T. J. Samuel, *The Migration of Canadian-Born between Canada and United States of America 1955 to 1968*, 26 (Ottawa, 1970).

[7] Here and two paragraphs below, see Berthoff, *British Immigrants*, 126–154; Charlotte Erickson, *Invisible Immigrants: The Adaptation of English and Scottish Immigrants in Nineteenth-Century America*, 3–5, 64–73 (Coral Gables, Fla., 1972).

[8] For general background on this group in the U.S., see Edward G. Hartmann, *Americans from Wales* (Boston, 1967); Alan Conway, ed., *The Welsh in America: Letters from the Immigrants* (Minneapolis, 1961).

[9] Daniel J. Williams, *One Hundred Years of Welsh Calvinistic Methodism in America*, 207 (Philadelphia, 1937); Thomas E. Hughes et al., eds., *History of the Welsh in Minnesota, Foreston and Lime Springs, Ia.*, 13–41, 237 (n.p., 1895); Thomas Hughes, *History of Blue Earth County*, 62, 73 (Chicago, [1909]); Evan Jones, *The Minnesota: Forgotten River*, 134–137 (New York, 1962).

[10] Hartmann, *Americans from Wales*, 72; Hughes, *Welsh in Minnesota*, 61–110. The exception is the few Welsh who lived at Courtland, Nicollet County; they seem not to have returned after the war. See *Plat Book of Nicollet County, Minnesota* (n.p., 1899).

[11] Thomas Hughes, "History of the Welsh Settlements in the Minnesota Valley," in *Cambrian* (Cincinnati), 4:308, 333–338; 5:6–13, 73–78, 109–112, 137–141 (November, 1884–May, 1885); Essye P. Flaten, "Welsh Pioneers in Southern Minnesota: Their Contribution to the Culture," unpublished manuscript, 1969, copy in MHS. Calvinistic Methodism is peculiar to Wales. It is Calvinist in theology and akin to Presbyterianism in the form of its church government.

[12] Here and two paragraphs below, see U.S. Works Projects Administration, Minnesota, Historical Records Survey: Churches, 1936–41, Blue Earth County, Le Sueur County, in MHS, hereafter cited as WPA, Church Records; Williams, *Welsh Calvinistic Methodism*, 214–219; Hughes, *Welsh in Minnesota*, 26–61, 305; Hughes, *Blue Earth County*, 216, 292; Edward G. Hartmann, *Some Data on the Welsh Churches of Minnesota*, 1 (Boston, 1978).

[13] *Standard Atlas of Blue Earth County, Minnesota* (Chicago, 1914); *Atlas of Blue Earth County, Minnesota* (Fergus Falls, 1962); *Plat Book of Le Sueur County, Minnesota* (n.p., 1898); *Atlas of Le Sueur County, Minnesota* (Fergus Falls, 1963); *The County of Brown, Minnesota, 1905* (St. Paul, 1905); *Atlas of Brown County, Minnesota* (Fergus Falls, 1953); Hartmann, *Americans from Wales*, 89; First Presbyterian Church, *Gymanfa Ganu*, program, September 27, 1970, copy in MEHP Papers; program of *The 47th Welsh National Gymanfa Ganu*, September 1–3, 1978, copy in MHS.

Elsewhere in southern Minnesota there were scattered settlements to be found in Fillmore County, mostly in Bristol, Beaver, and York townships, in what was known as the Lime Springs settlement. All of these people took up farming, mostly of wheat, but after the depression of the 1870s, those who survived began to diversify and turn their attention to dairying and stock raising. By 1867 the people of Bristol had organized a church, though even before this, on Christmas Day, 1866, the settlement held its first *eisteddfod*. At the end of the century, the Welsh language was still used extensively. Fifty years later, very few Welsh remained and those only in Bristol and York townships. The church disbanded in the mid-1930s. Daniel Williams, "The Welsh Settlement of Lime Springs, Iowa," in *Welsh in Minnesota*, 138–158; Franklyn Curtiss-Wedge, *History of Fillmore County, Minnesota*, 1:338, 348; 2:555, 590, 690, 747, 749 (Chicago, 1912); *Standard Atlas of Fillmore County, Minnesota* (Chicago, 1896); *Atlas of Fillmore County, Minnesota* (Fergus Falls, 1956); Williams, *Welsh Calvinistic Methodism*, 223.

[14] M. M. Hoffmann, "New Light on Old St. Peter's and Early St. Paul," in *Minnesota History*, 8:43 (March, 1927); "Reminiscence of Thomas A. Robertson," in *South Dakota Historical Collections*, 20:599–601 (1940); Rollo C. Keithahn, "The American Fur Company in the Upper Mississippi Valley," 41–45, master's thesis, University of Minnesota, 1929.

[15] Here and below, see Hughes, *History of Blue Earth County*, 70–73; Ronald J. Newell, *Where the Winding Maple Flows: A History of Mapleton, Minnesota, and Surrounding Area*, 9 (n.p., 1978).

[16] Hughes, *History of Blue Earth County*, 354, 373, 386, 416, 487, 533; *Blue Earth County Enterprise* (Mapleton), August 17, 1928, sec. 1, p. 2, sec. 2, p. 3; *Enterprise-Herald* (Mapleton), January 30, 1980, p. 1.

[17] Here and below, see Hughes, *History of Blue Earth County*,

296, 588; *Blue Earth County Enterprise*, August 17, 1928, sec. 1, p. 8; *Enterprise* (Mapleton), January 19, 1967, p. 1; Newell, *Where the Winding Maple Flows*, 103, 110–112.

[18] Hughes, *History of Blue Earth County*, 373, 382, 413, 439, 487, 490, 589, 611; *Enterprise*, January 19, 1967, p. 1; *Atlas of Blue Earth County, Minnesota* (1962).

[19] *Blue Earth County Enterprise*, September 9, 1943, p. 1; *Memorial Records of the Counties of Faribault, Martin, Watonwan and Jackson, Minnesota*, 237, 333, 356 (Chicago, 1895); J. A. Kiester, *The History of Faribault County, Minnesota*, 598–603 (Minneapolis, 1896); "Local History Items," in *Minnesota History*, 14:456 (December, 1933); WPA, Church Records, Faribault County; *Atlas of Faribault County, Minnesota* (Fergus Falls, 1967).

[20] Here and two paragraphs below, see 1880 U.S. manuscript census schedules, tabulation MEHP Papers; Torgny Anderson, *The Centennial History of Lyon County Minnesota*, 9 (Marshall, 1970).

[21] Hughes, *Welsh in Minnesota*, 305. Agents of the Northern Pacific Railroad made unsuccessful attempts to attract Welsh immigrants to railroad lands in Minnesota, particularly through the Welsh Land and Emigration Society whose agent, Rev. R. G. Jones, had established a Welsh colony in Kansas in 1871. See John L. Loomis to R. G. Jones, July 25, 1871, in Letters Sent, Land Dept., Northern Pacific Railway Papers, MHS.

[22] Arthur P. Rose, *An Illustrated History of Lyon County*, 59, 60 (Marshall, 1912); *Plat Book of Lyon County, Minnesota* (Minneapolis, 1902); *Atlas of Lyon County, Minnesota* (Fergus Falls, 1952); Swan Lake Presbyterian Church, Parish Records, in Presbyterian Churches in Lyon and Yellow Medicine Counties Papers (hereafter cited as Presbyterian Churches Papers), copies in MHS.

[23] Here and below, see Rose, *Lyon County*, 58, 169, 224; Salem Calvinistic Methodist Church, Parish Records, in Presbyterian Churches Papers; *Atlas of Lyon County* (1952); Hartmann, "Data on the Welsh Churches."

[24] For background on the Scotch-Irish, see James G. Leyburn, *The Scotch-Irish: A Social History* (Chapel Hill, N.C., 1962). The Scotch-Irish were descendants of Scottish Presbyterians who had migrated from Scotland to northern Ireland (Ulster) in the 17th century.

About a dozen Manx families settled in southern Dakota County in the mid-1850s. Some of the men had mining experience and worked nearly 10 years in the lead mines in Illinois before becoming farmers in Minnesota. Thomas C. Hodgson, *Pioneer Experiences of Four Manxman and A Boy* (n.p., 1980).

[25] Here and two paragraphs below, see Helen H. Anderson, *Eden Prairie: the First 100 Years*, 21, 22, 89 (Eden Prairie, 1979); Mary Jane Hill Anderson, *Autobiography of Mary Jane Hill Anderson, wife of Robert Anderson, 1827–1924*, 3–17 (Minneapolis, 1934).

[26] 1880 U.S. manuscript census schedules, tabulation in MEHP Papers.

[27] 1880 U.S. manuscript census schedules, tabulation in MEHP Papers; Anderson, *Autobiography*, 35, 36.

[28] Anderson, *Autobiography*, 15; Anderson, *Eden Prairie*, 28. The color orange identified the Scotch-Irish and green the Catholic Irish.

[29] Anderson, *Eden Prairie*, 76–84; Anderson, *Autobiography*, 29–34.

[30] Here and three paragraphs below, see Todd County Bicentennial Committee, *Todd County Histories*, 390–395 (Long Prairie, 1976).

[31] Here and three paragraphs below, see Newman E. Olson, "An English Colony in the Middle West: A Study of the Fairmont Settlement in Southern Minnesota," undated typed paper, copy in MHS; William H. Budd, *Martin County Before 1880*, 77–94 (n.p., 1897); Maurice Farrar, *Five Years in Minnesota: Sketches of Life in a Western State*, 80–90 (London, 1880); Arthur R. Moro, "The Eng-

lish Colony at Fairmont in the Seventies," in *Minnesota History*, 8:140–149 (June, 1927).

[32] Budd, *Martin County*, 83.

[33] "Calendar of Events through the Years," undated typescript, in Walter W. Carlson Papers, Southern Minnesota Historical Center, Mankato.

[34] Bryn Trescatheric, "Furness Colony in England and Minnesota, 1872–1880," in *Minnesota History*, 47:17 (Spring, 1980); George Sheppard, "Accounts, March, 1872–June, 1873," in Letters Received, Land Dept., Northern Pacific Railway Papers, tabulation in MEHP Papers.

[35] Trescatheric, in *Minnesota History*, 47:19; Robert A. Brekken, ed., *Journey Back to Hawley*, 41 (Hawley, 1972); John L. Harnsberger and Robert P. Wilkins, "New Yeovil, Minnesota: A Northern Pacific Colony in 1873," in *Arizona and the West*, 12:5, 7, 15, 19 (Spring, 1970); handbill, 1872, in Furness Colony Papers, MHS.

[36] Trescatheric, in *Minnesota History*, 47:19, 20; *Wadena Pioneer Journal*, January 17, 1924, p. 6; Harnsberger and Wilkins, in *Arizona and the West*, 12:9; Brekken, ed., *Hawley*, 50, 55, 71.

[37] Here and below, see Harnsberger and Wilkins, in *Arizona and the West*, 12:18–20; Brekken, ed., *Hawley*, 43, 44, 55, 70, 75, 77, 81, 86.

[38] Harnsberger and Wilkins, in *Arizona and the West*, 12:21; Brekken, ed., *Hawley*, 47, 48, 83, 84, 88, 93, 95, 166, 173–175, 282.

[39] Brekken, ed., *Hawley*, 91, 95, 145–147, 231. For hardships experienced by women in the Furness Colony, see Margaret C. Kerr to Mrs. Arthur P. Stacy, January 31, 1892, in Robert Kerr and Family Papers, MHS.

[40] Brekken, ed., *Hawley*, 73, 147.

[41] Brekken, ed., *Hawley*, 86, 138, 231, 251, 340, 343.

[42] Brekken, ed., *Hawley*, 45, 157, 166, 173–175, 180, 198, 214, 215, 231.

[43] Brekken, ed., *Hawley*, 70, 77, 93, 166, 173–175, 180, 198, 205, 208, 231, 236, 243, 277, 282.

[44] Trescatheric, in *Minnesota History*, 47:16–25; *Wadena Pioneer Journal*, January 17, p. 6, January 31, p. 4, February 7, p. 4, 1924; John Stewart, *Building Up the Country on the Northwest Frontier* (n.p., [1967?]); East Otter Tail County Historical Society, *East Otter Tail County History*, 7, 18, 24, 69, 308, 312 (Dallas, 1978); *Ulverston* (Eng.) *Mirror*, May 31, October ?, 1873, photocopies, Newspaper Clippings and Related Data in Furness Colony Papers.

[45] *Wadena Pioneer Journal*, February 7, 1924, p. 4; Stewart, *Building Up the Country*, 45.

[46] William Blamey, "Reminiscences," July 27, 1928, unpublished manuscripts, in Northeast Minnesota Historical Center (NMHC), Duluth; Lake Superior Mining Institute, *Proceedings*, 14:197–199 (Duluth, 1909); *Tower News*, October 9, 1964, p. 1.

[47] John Syrjamaki, "Mesabi Communities: A Study of Their Development," 115, 118, 133, Ph.D. thesis, Yale University, 1940; Ely Historical Committee, *A Souvenir Booklet, 1888–1958*, 31, 36, 46 ([Ely, 1958?]); *Mesabi Daily News* (Virginia), February 14, 1964, p. 2; A[lfred] L. Rowse, *The Cousin Jacks: The Cornish in America*, 427–438 (New York, 1969). On word usage of Cornish miners in Minnesota, see Meridel Le Sueur, "Notes on North Country Folkways," in *Minnesota History*, 25:219 (September, 1944).

[48] 1880 U.S. manuscript census schedules, tabulation in MEHP Papers.

[49] Hansen, *Canadian and American Peoples*, 190.

[50] Here and below, see Kittson County Historical Society, *Our Northwest Corner: Histories of Kittson County, Minnesota* (Dallas, 1976), and *Our Northwest Corner: Histories of Kittson County, Minnesota* (Lake Bronson, 1979), two separate and distinct works.

[51] 1895 Minnesota manuscript census schedules, tabulation in MEHP Papers.

[52] Here and four paragraphs below, see 1880 U.S. manuscript census schedules, tabulation in MEHP Papers.

[53] Here and two paragraphs below, see Kittson County Historical Society, *Our Northwest Corner* (1976 and 1979).

[54] Dorothy R. Adler, *British Investment in American Railways, 1834–1898*, vi, xiii, 193n, 199 (Charlottesville, Va., 1970); W. Turrentine Jackson, *The Enterprising Scot: Investors in the American West after 1873*, 11 (Edinburgh, 1968).

[55] James P. Reed, "The Role of an English Land Company in the Settlement of Northwestern Iowa and Southwestern Minnesota: A Study in Historical Geography," 20, 75, 145–150, master's thesis, University of Nebraska at Omaha, 1974.

[56] Jackson, *Enterprising Scot*, 31, 37, 38, 41, 218.

[57] Reed, "English Land Company," 158; Jackson, *Enterprising Scot*, 218, 265.

[58] David Maxwell Fyffe, "Reminiscences," 1, 26, 28, 74, in David M. Fyffe Papers, MHS; Jackson, *Enterprising Scot*, 316.

[59] U.S., *Census, 1910, Population*, 2:1017; 1920, 3:523, 524. See also Herman E. Olson, *The Minneapolis Property and Housing Survey* (Minneapolis, 1934); Calvin F. Schmid, *Social Saga of Two Cities: An Ecological and Statistical Study*, 129–171 (Minneapolis, 1937); Jean M. Macrae, "Development of the Glen Avon-Hunter's Park Area," typed paper, University of Minnesota-Duluth, 1960, copy in MEHP Papers. Hunter's Park and Glen Avon had streets named St. Andrew's, Lewis, Stornaway, Abbotsford, Waverly, Melrose, Bruce, Laurie, Wallace, and Carlisle — all connected with Scottish history or literature. The area also bore the nickname of "Oatmeal Hill" for the frequent breakfast item of the Scots. *Duluth Herald*, October 21, 1980, p. 1B.

[60] Here and two paragraphs below, see Walter Van Brunt, *Duluth and St. Louis County, Minnesota*, 739–1247 (Chicago, 1921); Dwight E. Woodbridge and John S. Pardee, *History of Duluth and St. Louis County, Past and Present*, 777–893 (Chicago, 1910).

[61] Statistics for the British occupational distribution nationally show a similar range. See E. P. Hutchinson, *Immigrants and Their Children, 1850–1950*, 175, 177, 180 (New York, 1956).

[62] Jean M. Macrae, *Scots Wha Ha'e: The Scottish legacy to the United States and to the Duluth area*, n.p. (Duluth, 1976); *Labor World* (Duluth), June 7, 1924, p. 1, February 18, 1933, p. 1; Duluth First Presbyterian Church, *One Hundredth Anniversary, 1869–1969*, 3–6 (Duluth, 1969).

[63] Van Brunt, *Duluth*, 739–1247; Woodbridge and Pardee, *Duluth*, 777–893.

[64] National Groups folder, in International Institute of Minnesota Papers, IHRC; Brekken, ed., *Hawley*, 82; interview of Stanford E. Lehmberg by author, June 23, 1980, notes in MEHP Papers; Hodgson, *Pioneer Experiences*, i. The Sons and Daughters of St. George and the English-Speaking Union were chapters of national groups. A Canadian with a Scottish name, James W. Hamilton, while a resident of St. Paul, founded the International Magna Carta Day Association; *Who's Who in America*, 13:1436.

[65] *Constitution of the Saint Andrew's Society of the State of Minnesota* (St. Paul, 1859); St. Andrew's Society, *Souvenir: Gathering of the Clans* (St. Paul, 1892); *Daily Minnesotian* (St. Paul), February 26, 1859; Record book, in St. Andrew's Society Papers, MHS.

[66] *St. Andrew's Society News*, April, 1978, June–December, 1980; interview of William E. MacGregor, Jr., by author, July 1, 1980, notes in MEHP Papers.

[67] *St. Paul Daily Globe*, August 19, 1889; National Groups folder, in International Institute of Minnesota Papers; *Twin Cities Scottish Club Newsletter*, March, 1978; *Minneapolis City Directory, 1893–1905*; *St. Paul City Directory, 1892–1905*; Berthoff, *British Immigrants*, 191.

[68] Matti Kaups, "Europeans in Duluth," in Ryck Lydecker and Lawrence J. Sommer, eds., *Duluth: Sketches of the Past*, 77 (Duluth, 1976); Clan Stewart No. 50, Order of Scottish Clans, *Fiftieth Anniversary* (Duluth, 1938); *Duluth Herald*, August 8, 1924, p. 1, June 20, 1927, p. 1, August 12, 1927, p. 1, January 19, 1928, p. 8, January 24, 1929, p. 11, July 17, 1944, p. 4; *Duluth News-Tribune*, January 9, 1949, sec. 2, p. 7; Gertrude Anderson, "Scotch Folk Customs," Scot Activities Papers, NMHC; interview of Jean Macrae by Marjorie Hoover, November, 1980, notes in MEHP Papers. The Battle of Bannockburn, fought in 1314, ensured Scotland's independence from England for another 400 years. For a few years after 1890 Clan Matheson, No. 73, and Clan Forbes, No. 237, existed in West Duluth. The members transferred to Clan Stewart.

[69] *Duluth Herald*, January 20, 1976, p. 1B; Macrae, *Scots Wha Ha'e*; [Marjorie Hoover] to the author, undated letters, in MEHP Papers.

[70] "A Brief History of the Lewis Settlement in Duluth," copy in Scot Activities Papers, NMHC; Marjorie Hoover, notes on Scots in Duluth, in MEHP Papers.

[71] Williams, *Welsh Calvinistic Methodism*, 210, 225; Hughes, *Welsh in Minnesota*, 121–137.

[72] Hartmann, *Americans From Wales*, 101, 119–122, 146, 151; Hughes, *Welsh in Minnesota*, 111, 131–133; Hughes, *Blue Earth County*, 221.

[73] "Scrapbook Relating to David E. Jones and Welsh Choral Organizations, 1899–1919," in MHS; *Minneapolis Journal*, March 3, 1918, sec. 1, p. 11; National Groups folder, in International Institute of Minnesota Papers.

[74] Author's interviews of Mrs. Everett O. Thomas, May 8, 1978, Rev. Neal Lloyd, June 11, 1980, and Mary M. Merganthal, February 26, 1981 — notes in MEHP Papers.

[75] Daughters of the British Empire Papers, in MHS; *Minneapolis Tribune*, October 18, 1978, p. 3B.

[76] International Institute, *Newsletter*, October, 1973.

[77] *St. Paul City Directory, 1884–1942*; *Minneapolis City Directory, 1887–1912*; Alexander Macrae, *Reminiscences of the Curling Game in Duluth* ([Duluth, 1924?]); *St. Paul Pioneer Press*, February 5, 1888.

[78] *St. Paul City Directory, 1898*, 468; *St. Paul Pioneer Press*, December 17, 1926, p. 1; Sonja and Will Anderson, *One Hundred Years of Brewing*, 515 (Reprint ed., Newtown, Conn., 1973).

[79] U.S. British and Canadian statistics, in MEHP Papers, compiled by Jon A. Gjerde from U.S. Justice Dept., Immigration and Naturalization Service, *Annual Reports*, 1940–75.

[80] Walter Adams, ed., *The Brain Drain*, 33 (New York, 1968); Samuel, *Migration of Canadian-Born*; H. G. Grubel and A. D. Scott, "The Immigration of Scientists and Engineers to the United States, 1949–61," in *Journal of Political Economy*, 74:373, 376 (August, 1966); Robert C. Cook, "World Migration, 1946, 1955," in *Population Bulletin*, 77–95 (August, 1957); National Science Foundation, *Scientists and Engineers from Abroad, 1962–64*, 4–9 (Surveys of Science Resources Series — Washington, D.C., [1964?]).

[81] Here and below, see Biography cards, in MEHP Papers.

[82] Kenneth Lines, *British and Canadian Immigration to the United States Since 1920*, 30 (San Francisco, 1978).

CHAPTER 7

The Irish

Ann Regan

THE IRISH IN MINNESOTA performed two surprising feats. One was unusual for the group's behavior in the United States: in the early years of the state's history they established themselves as successful farmers in the southeastern counties on the Mississippi and Minnesota rivers and in settlements scattered across the state. The other was a more typical but still impressive achievement. Although outnumbered by their German neighbors, they stamped St. Paul, the state's capital, with an Irish label that was still attached in the 1980s.[1]

Minnesota's Irish formed only a small part of the group's total immigrant presence in the United States. From 1870 to its peak in 1890 the country's Irish-born population, most of which lived in the North Atlantic states, remained above 1,850,000. Throughout this period, one-fourth lived in the north-central region stretching from Ohio to the Dakotas. Within that area half of them were to be found in northern and western Illinois, eastern Iowa, southern Wisconsin, and southeastern Minnesota. The Irish-born population of Minnesota was by far the smallest of the four states, averaging only about 10% of the midwestern and 1.4% of the United States totals.[2]

These numbers disguise the relative size of the group in the state's early years. In 1860 Minnesota's 11,838 Irish-born residents constituted 20.2% of its entire foreign-born population. With those born of Irish parents, they made up 12% of the state's total population — a sizable minority, second only to the Germans. Most lived in southeastern and central Minnesota and the Twin Cities of Minneapolis and St. Paul. But the masses of arriving German and Scandinavian immigrants soon lowered the Irish profile. In 1870 the 21,746 Irish born constituted 13.5% of the foreign born; by 1890, the peak year for Irish immigrants in Minnesota as well as in the United States, there were 28,011, forming just 6% of the state's total foreign-born population. As political and economic conditions in Ireland improved, emigration to the United States slowed. The aging of Minnesota's first- and second-generation Irish further decreased their numbers. By 1940 only 4,219 natives of Northern Ireland and the Irish Free State lived in Minnesota; in 1970 the number had dropped to 1,003 (see Table 7.1).[3]

Why did so few Irish move west from the eastern seaports where they landed? The reasons are rooted in the conditions of Irish Catholic emigration, an outpouring that began in earnest after the War of 1812. Six centuries of British conquest had beaten the Irish into poverty and subjugation. Both English landlords and Irish tenants abused a land system that was inadequate in any case. Roman Catholicism, the mainstay of Irish nationalism, was the focal point of discrimination. From 1695 to 1829 Catholics were stripped of various property, civil, and religious rights. For some of these years a bounty was set on the heads of priests, and religious services had to be held secretly. Overpopulation, grinding poverty, high rents, excessive land subdivision, unemployment, agrarian violence, periodic crop failures, typhus epidemics, and political and religious disputes made Ireland a country of little opportunity and great despair.[4]

The failures of the potato crops between 1845 and 1851 added famine to the list and precipitated heavy emigration. A nutritious, high-yielding, and easily tilled vegetable, the potato had supported the overwhelmingly agricultural population of Ireland, had made excessive subdivision possible, and was essentially the only foodstuff for most of the people. With its failure, the nation of some 8.5 million endured the starvation and death by typhus of as many as a million people and the greatest population movement (relatively speaking) of any country in the 19th century. Between 1841 and 1854, at least 2,088,000 people left Ireland; more than 75% of them immigrated to the United States, an English-speaking country not under British rule. Letters and remittances from earlier arrivals established America's reputation for opportunity and high wages, and those in the vanguard then helped finance the trip for relatives who followed. Remittances from North America to the United Kingdom grew from $2,300,000 in 1848 to $8,650,000 in 1854; one scholar estimated that more than 90% of them went to Ireland.[5]

Although famine brought great numbers of Irish to the United States, only a small proportion of them reached the far-off frontier in Minnesota. Unlike earlier arrivals, many of whom had capital or ambitious plans, most of the famine Irish emigrated reluctantly, carrying cultural baggage which made them ill-suited to take advantage of agricultural opportunities in the United States in that period. Because of their experience with crop failures, their unfamiliarity with large-scale farming methods, their lack of capital, and their desire to remain close to countrymen and church, the Irish pre-

130

Table 7.1. Irish in Minnesota by County, 1860–1970

County	1860		1870	1880		1890	1905		1930*		1970**	
	foreign born	foreign mixed	fb	fb	fm	fb	fb	fm	fb	fm	fb	fm
Aitkin				11	17	28	23	177	9	101		6
Anoka	145	122	194	233	509	222	133	573	56	327	40	265
Becker	1	3	1	60	94	65	60	282	25	142		39
Beltrami						2	70	437	27	207		54
Benton	35	19	83	89	294	129	70	313	17	163		62
Big Stone				186	366	292	218	878	56	299		90
Blue Earth	180	101	523	491	1,129	406	252	1,142	51	543	6	116
Brown	8	1	83	109	322	97	40	438	8	91		26
Carlton	7	3	25	41	71	275	94	407	29	127	17	14
Carver	181	135	256	240	479	183	71	350	8	153	16	44
Cass	4	1	1	10	16	6	51	614	16	136	8	30
Chippewa				71	145	56	39	215	7	94		21
Chisago	52	44	106	150	206	90	56	221	10	69		29
Clay			1	130	167	117	99	423	17	229		46
Clearwater							4	31	2	36		7
Cook						1	7	47	3	22		
Cottonwood			7	76	93	44	35	207	19	87		18
Crow Wing	2		4	84	85	167	138	587	49	285		76
Dakota	1,153	815	1,699	1,557	2,579	983	575	2,352	123	1,076	39	530
Dodge	29	30	153	188	394	126	64	331	11	133		12
Douglas			68	95	253	81	56	306	8	121		27
Faribault	14	11	191	245	506	163	133	730	37	315	4	27
Fillmore	232	70	969	891	1,948	553	310	1,377	29	545		79
Freeborn	72	55	391	488	1,056	316	180	872	32	366	7	110
Goodhue	182	150	506	448	1,078	318	168	766	59	425		65
Grant			1	13	24	16	21	98	6	48		
Hennepin	955	737	1,896	1,765	3,454	4,275	3,547	13,818	1,564	11,310	233	2,881
Houston	694	574	1,053	863	1,727	589	245	995	30	426	9	73
Hubbard						10	30	121	8	93		17
Isanti	15	8	14	21	31	14	10	42	3	34		6
Itasca			1	1		24	86	463	48	257	8	71
Jackson	2		20	40	56	30	26	141	7	88		25
Kanabec					2	3	7	69	7	31		
Kandiyohi	18	11	85	88	266	68	36	390	16	133	16	25
Kittson	3	7		53	98	69	39	232	9	47		7
Koochiching									40	216	6	79
Lac qui Parle			5	21	75	22	13	78	2	57		15
Lake	3			3		31	54	209	5	90		19
Lake of the Woods									13	38	6	
Le Sueur	660	460	930	964	2,244	717	360	1,901	42	664		46
Lincoln				40	103	43	27	164	8	66		34
Lyon				95	197	118	84	587	26	305	5	97
McLeod	59	38	110	151	330	109	72	348	4	144	7	23
Mahnomen	13	4							5	38		12
Marshall				25	21	32	32	165	14	60		14
Martin			86	87	188	111	89	247	22	216		40
Meeker	100	59	326	382	750	333	151	871	20	301		8
Mille Lacs			37	28	54	31	31	194	10	91		13
Morrison	9		48	58	79	72	61	336	23	142	14	33
Mower	114	99	416	514	1,282	385	236	1,192	52	571		135
Murray			1	164	254	313	195	627	54	324		38
Nicollet	240	126	249	372	462	203	82	410	39	268		43
Nobles			1	178	288	197	145	581	25	296		77
Norman						32	34	107	13	55		21
Olmsted	574	359	1,128	1,057	2,403	818	465	1,618	131	1,322	56	295
Otter Tail	11	8	3	151	292	112	76	480	33	250		45
Pennington									3	55		19
Pine			91	73	110	78	93	252	22	131	6	20
Pipestone				81	151	134	85	414	22	191		6
Polk	6			190	236	239	174	666	29	289		65
Pope			68	79	167	92	54	274	16	118		30
Ramsey	1,903	949	2,276	3,085	5,198	6,235	5,195	15,120	2,310	11,126	393	3,113
Red Lake							47	220	10	50		
Redwood			32	100	237	126	70	429	29	239		7
Renville	9	19	146	284	942	261	152	725	13	279	5	34
Rice	732	440	1,167	983	2,413	775	325	1,346	64	835	25	86
Rock			5	124	260	94	59	273	8	118		45
Roseau							89	125	3	39		19
St. Louis	8	9	408	111	214	983	997	4,057	469	2,552	55	552
Scott	421	420	969	811	1,688	568	270	1,137	34	473		104
Sherburne	39	35	72	77	151	63	52	140	6	94		53
Sibley	595	639	608	610	1,353	488	183	920	8	310		8
Stearns	81	70	238	397	657	380	196	833	60	504	5	155

Table 7.1. Irish in Minnesota by County, 1860–1970 *(continued)*

County	1860		1870	1880		1890	1905		1930*		1970**	
	foreign born	foreign mixed	fb	fb	fm	fb	fb	fm	fb	fm	fb	fm
Steele	103	99	310	278	701	184	102	624	12	265		30
Stevens				245	526	203	139	481	27	230		39
Swift				571	982	348	254	1,146	54	409		35
Todd	57	3	22	48	128	92	73	301	15	177		25
Traverse	6			141	228	221	117	579	21	178		14
Wabasha	550	363	965	847	1,725	582	309	1,413	49	506		71
Wadena				23	70	27	31	162	10	94		17
Waseca	288	257	619	648	1,701	547	238	1,229	35	531	11	50
Washington	533	401	602	696	1,801	504	257	822	46	525		87
Watonwan			59	98	284	86	55	269	23	150		18
Wilkin			11	74	95	36	59	361	6	110		37
Winona	505	403	983	872	1,741	713	384	1,348	66	694	6	124
Wright	235	165	424	528	1,028	430	254	985	31	374		29
Yellow Medicine				33	67	45	18	128	10	78		20
Total	11,838	8,322	21,746	25,134	51,341	28,011	19,531	77,339	6,498	45,797	1,003	10,897
Published census figures	(12,831)		(21,746)	(25,942)		(28,011)	(19,531)	(77,239)	(6,498)	(45,797)	(1,003)	(10,897)

Source: See Appendix
*Includes both Irish Free State and Northern Ireland
**Republic of Ireland

ferred low-paying city jobs on the eastern seaboard (with wages six times the rate in Ireland) to risky farming farther west.[6]

They were, as one scholar has written, the "pioneers of the American urban ghetto." Characteristics stereotyped as Irish — rough manners, impulsive generosity, ready wit, heavy drinking — offered defense against, or respite from, brutal conditions both in Ireland and in American slums. Catholicism, which had been the symbol of Irish resistance to British domination, remained central to Irish-American ethnicity. Because of their "popery" and their intense and continuing interest in Ireland's struggle, the immigrant Irish seemed especially alien and unassimilable. The mistrust was mutual. The Irish blamed the British for all of their homeland's troubles, including the famine, and they carried over this prejudice in the form of distrust of the unsympathetic Protestant Anglo-American establishment.

Efforts to lure these people from city slums to farms in what was then the West constantly preoccupied Irish leaders in the United States, especially the western clergy. Some families moved to small Irish settlements in New York, Pennsylvania, Indiana, Illinois, Iowa, and Missouri, but organized colonization was less successful than the decisions of individuals in promoting westward migration. Jobs on building projects and farms and work in mines drew Irish laborers to Ohio, Indiana, Illinois, Wisconsin, and Iowa, and some of them stayed. Some midwestern Irish farmers probably left Ireland with capital and purchased land from Yankees who were moving farther west.[7]

It was from these states in the East and from Canada that Minnesota drew its early rural Irish settlers. Church histories, census records, and individual biographies suggest a staged migration in which typical patterns included arrival in New York or Canada and one or two subsequent moves over a period of years to Pennsylvania, Ohio, Illinois, Indiana, or Wisconsin, and then to Minnesota. Nor did these people cease moving after reaching Minnesota. From the Irish settlement in and near Faribault, for example, both the original settlers and members of the second generation were attracted to the Twin Cities and to such western states as Washington and California. Small towns across Minnesota also received many members of the second generation.[8]

Little information has thus far been accumulated on the counties in Ireland from which these people emigrated. An exception is the community of Belle Plaine in Scott County, where backgrounds of 233 persons, most of whom arrived as couples between 1853 and the early 1870s, have been traced. Virtually every region in Ireland was represented, with Cork and Kerry, the southwesternmost counties, each contributing about a fifth of the sample and the western counties of Clare, Galway, Mayo, and Sligo more heavily represented than the eastern areas (see Map 7.1).[9]

Patterns of Settlement

Minnesota's earliest Irish arrivals were probably lumberjacks who immigrated by way of the Canadian Maritime Provinces and Maine. Timber vessels, sailing regularly between Canada and Ireland's shipbuilding ports during the 1820s and 1830s, carried immigrants on the westbound voyage. Irish loggers from New Brunswick and Maine seem to have followed their bosses to the rich timberlands of Minnesota's St. Croix Valley in the 1840s.[10]

By 1850, 263 people of Irish birth were counted in Minnesota Territory. More than one-third of the men were soldiers at Forts Snelling and Gaines (later renamed Ripley), and three of these soldiers had been the first to claim land in what would become St. Paul. Many others were laborers in that city and in new communities in Dakota, Hennepin, Ramsey, and Washington counties. Stillwater's first Catholic settlers, "some 350 souls, mostly Irish laboring men from New Brunswick," built a church there in 1853. Some stayed to become farmers in Washington County. Others moved north

Map 7.1. Principal Counties of Irish Emigration to Minnesota

with the logging frontier or became craftsmen and small tradesmen in and near the new towns. Most of the women were wives and mothers, but a few worked for Yankee families as nursemaids or domestics. These Irish had been in North America for several years, and their children had been born in the East, predominantly in New Brunswick, Maine, and New York.[11]

Southeastern Minnesota, especially the counties along the Mississippi and Minnesota rivers, became the first major Irish concentration in the state (see Maps 7.2 and 7.3). Jessenland Township in Sibley County attracted in 1852 what was apparently the first Irish farming group in the state. By 1860 Dakota County had the greatest number of rural Irish, especially in its northwestern townships along the Minnesota River. This concentration extended westward into Glendale, Eagle Creek, Cedar Lake, New Market, and Credit River townships of Scott County. Farther up the Minnesota River early Irish communities were to be found in Belle Plaine Township of western Scott County, San Francisco and Hollywood townships of Carver County, Derrynane and Tyrone townships of Le Sueur County, and Jessenland, Green Isle, Washington Lake, and Faxon townships of Sibley County.[12]

In the Mississippi Valley farther south, smaller Irish farming settlements were located near such villages as Browns-

ville and Caledonia in Houston County, Chatfield in Fillmore County, and Rochester in Olmsted County. The valleys of the Zumbro River in Wabasha County and Winnebago Creek in Houston County also held Irish farms. Several river towns such as Winona, Lake City, and Hastings attracted Irish laborers as well as skilled craftsmen during the 1850s and 1860s. Hastings' male labor force, for example, was one-fifth Irish in 1860.[13]

The Irish population of southeastern Minnesota peaked in 1870 at over 14,085 (see Table 7.2). This represented 65% of the state's total Irish-born population that year. More than half (58%) of Minnesota's Irish listed as employed in 1870 were farm workers and owners; only Wisconsin and Iowa had similarly high proportions of Irish farmers, perhaps because these were the states where new land was available. But for the next 40 years the percentage of Irish working on Minnesota farms remained slightly higher than the average for all groups in the state (which fluctuated between 45% and 57%), and most of these Irish were listed as farm owners rather than farm laborers.[14]

Among those in Le Sueur and Rice counties were the residents of the state's first organized Irish colony. General James Shields, a nationally known Irish soldier, lawyer, statesman, and entrepreneur, purchased an interest in the townsite of Faribault in 1855 and selected lands in what became Shieldsville and Erin townships for an Irish Catholic colony. He laid out the townsite of Shieldsville, brought seven Irishmen from St. Paul to settle, and began to promote the colony.[15]

By advertising in the Catholic press he attracted from states to the east Irish farmers who virtually filled Shieldsville and Erin as well as parts of Webster and Wheatland townships. In 1856 St. Patrick's Church was erected at Shieldsville for the 460 Irish-born Catholics in the area. By 1860 Rice County had 732 residents from Ireland and 440 born of Irish parents (see Table 7.1). Of these, 215 families had pre-empted farms in Shieldsville, Erin, Wells, and Forest townships. Others lived in Shieldsville, and by the mid-1860s they were the predominant group in Faribault as well. They also moved to adjoining Kilkenny and Montgomery townships of Le Sueur County. This Irish concentration apparently functioned as a community. The 1860 census showed only 93 adult males in Shieldsville Township, but just months earlier 173 votes were cast there in the 1859 congressional election. "Wagonloads of Irish" were said to have crossed the line from Le Sueur County to make up the difference.[16]

Shields himself quickly became involved in other ventures. He was elected to the United States Senate in 1857 as a compromise candidate and served for three years. The colonists, who felt he neglected their interests for his investments in Faribault, quarreled with him over an extra fee he charged on deeds to the land. When a Republican state senate refused Shields reappointment in 1859, he moved to California to seek new opportunities.[17]

Census figures (see Table 7.1) demonstrate that while many Irish subsequently left Rice County and other areas of southeastern Minnesota, a fair number remained. The counties that had shown the highest numbers in 1870 still con-

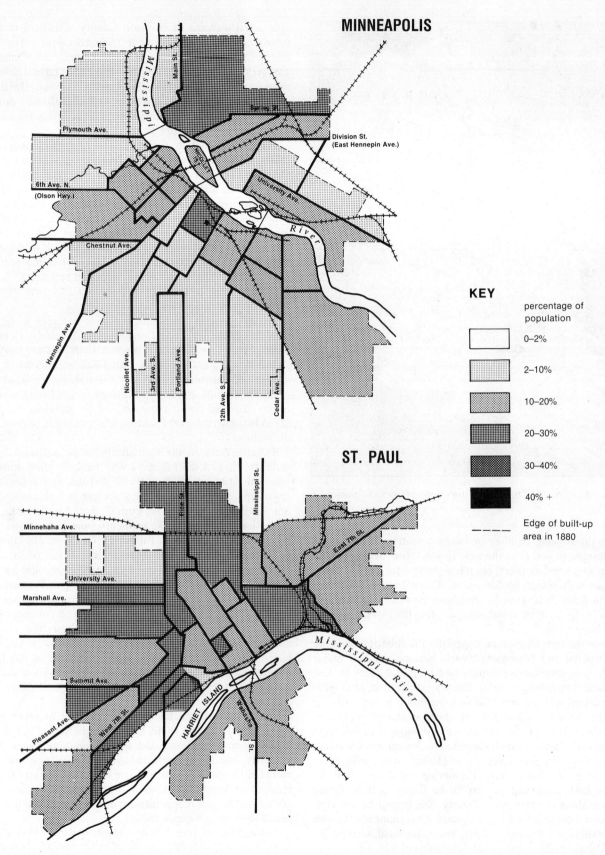

Map 7.2. Irish in the Twin Cities, 1880

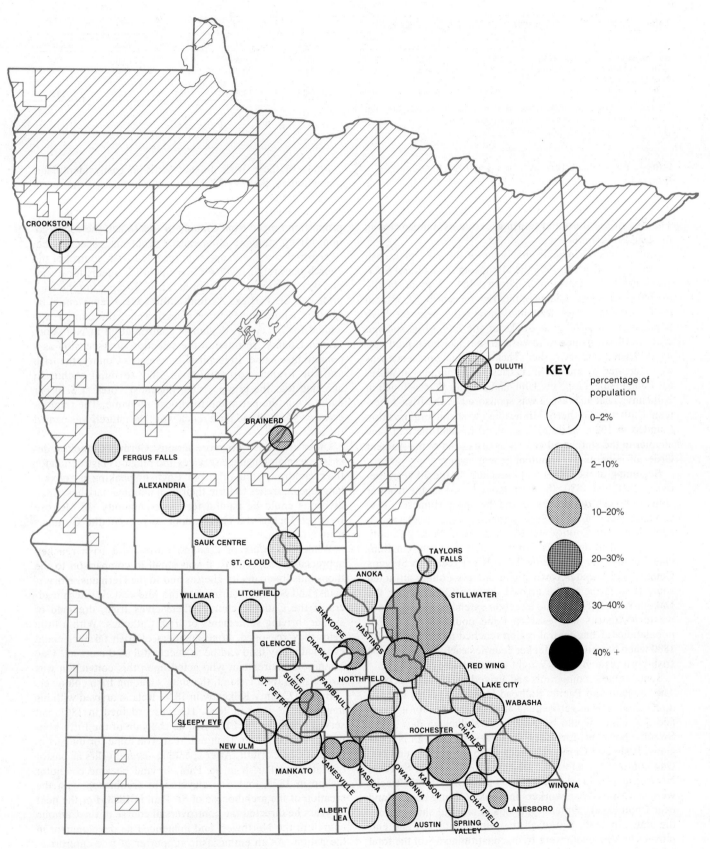

CROOKSTON

DULUTH

KEY

percentage of population

0–2%

2–10%

10–20%

20–30%

30–40%

40% +

BRAINERD

FERGUS FALLS

ALEXANDRIA

SAUK CENTRE

ST. CLOUD

TAYLORS FALLS

WILLMAR

LITCHFIELD

ANOKA

STILLWATER

SHAKOPEE

HASTINGS

GLENCOE

CHASKA

RED WING

LE SUEUR

FARIBAULT

NORTHFIELD

LAKE CITY

ST. PETER

WABASHA

SLEEPY EYE

ROCHESTER

ST. CHARLES

NEW ULM

MANKATO

JANESVILLE

WASECA

OWATONNA

KASSON

WINONA

ALBERT LEA

AUSTIN

SPRING VALLEY

CHATFIELD

LANESBORO

Map 7.3. Irish in Minnesota Towns, 1880

Map shows towns over 1,000 population in 1880.   The size of the circles is proportional to the population.

Table 7.2. Irish Born in Southeastern Minnesota, 1860–1970*

	1860	1870	1880	1890	1900	1910	1920	1930**
Southeast Minnesota Irish born	7,519	14,085	13,367	9,617	6,825	3,367	1,866	1,108
% of total Minnesota Irish born	58.6	64.8	51.5	34.3	30.4	21.2	18.1	17.0
% of total foreign born in SE Minnesota	65.0	60.0	41.9	24.5	19.9	15.1	12.4	11.4

Source: U.S. manuscript census, 1860, 1880; U.S., *Census,* 1870, 1890, 1900, 1910, 1920, 1930.
*See footnote 12 for the area defined as southeastern Minnesota
**Includes both Irish Free State and Northern Ireland

tained, by 1905, a few hundred Irish born and about a thousand second-generation Irish (see Map 7.4). But as immigration from Ireland slowed and the older generation died off, the Irish-born population of the area decreased. The size of the third and fourth generations, unrecorded in the census, is unknown.

Several factors indicate that some of these farming Irish stayed on the land. In 1976 the Minnesota Agricultural Society began to list farms that had been held by the same family for 100 years. Descendants of the Irish owned 13.7% of them in the nine counties that had shown the heaviest Irish populations in 1870. Plat books of the late 1970s showed scattered Irish names in townships that had been predominantly Irish a century earlier. Their continuing presence was also indicated by annual St. Patrick's Day parades in Waseca, Belle Plaine, and New Ulm, and a mulligan stew lunch in Kilkenny. That at Waseca was sponsored by the Irish American Club of Southern Minnesota, a social organization founded in 1969, while at Jessenland in 1980 the first new chapter in the state in 50 years was organized of the Ancient Order of Hibernians, a mutual benefit society.[18]

Beginning in the 1850s and especially in the 20 years between 1860 and 1880, the Irish moved west as the frontier shifted into central Minnesota and the upper Minnesota River Valley (see Map 7.3). Early settlements such as Darwin in central Meeker County and Maple Lake in Wright County were started in the 1850s. Birch Cooley Township in Renville County, the Pomme de Terre River region in Stevens County, and Wendel Township in Stearns County attracted some Irish farmers who arrived through Canada after the Dakota War of 1862, as did a section extending across northwestern Stearns and eastern Pope counties. The Irish populations of the central region reached modest peaks by 1880 when Stearns and Meeker counties each had nearly 400 Irish-born residents and Wright County had over 500.[19]

Some of these immigrants had arrived as railroad workers. The St. Paul and Pacific Railroad Company seems to have directed an 1862 advertisement at Irish laborers, for it specified that hands would be paid "nine shillings a day." The Swedes, however, furnished the largest force, with Norwegians, Irish, and Germans joining them in smaller numbers. One contractor preferred "Irishmen for the rock; Swedes, Norwegians &c for the shovel and barrow." After the tracks were laid, some Irish workers in Anoka County bought land near Coon Creek. Others took jobs in railroad shops across the state. In 1880, 870 of all the railroad officials and employees in Minnesota were Irish, constituting 6% of the total Irish labor force as well as 13.6% of the state's railroad employees.[20]

Many of these Irish did not settle in easily identifiable communities. Scores of Catholic churches across the southeastern and central parts of the state listed mixed German, French, and Irish settlers among their founders. The Irish proportion ranged from a family or two to half the congregation. Mixed ethnicity often caused problems, especially between Irish and Germans, who resented Irish control of the church hierarchy. In 1864 Germans in Le Sueur, for example, wanted to name the church for St. Joseph, but the Irish preferred St. Patrick. As both groups were represented by trustees whose wives were named Anne, the church was named for St. Anne. A similar confrontation in Norwood, Carver County, resulted in the selection of Ascension as a compromise name. In Paynesville, Stearns County, the Irish and the French co-operated in 1899 to build a church, agreeing that the group selling the most votes at $.10 per ballot would be permitted to choose its name. The total income was $85.00 and the French won; the church was named for St. Louis.[21]

Other divisions were more serious. German Catholics, desiring German-language services and religious instruction for their children, split off from English-speaking or mixed-language churches to form their own national parishes. Such divisions could be painful for the community. In Melrose Irishmen locked the church door to prevent the Germans from attending.[22]

While the influx of predominantly rural Irish reached appreciable proportions, it was small in comparison to the thousands living in city ghettos and to the Germans, Norwegians, and Swedes pouring into the Midwest. Western leaders of the Catholic church, themselves Irish, dreamed of similar thriving settlements of Irish Catholics. With a little help, they reasoned, large numbers of Irish farmers could eventually buy land and be as successful as the others. One Minnesota churchman who acted upon this conviction was Archbishop John Ireland, the state's leading Irish colonizer.

Born in County Kilkenny in 1838, Ireland arrived with his family in St. Paul in 1852. He was ordained in 1861 and served briefly in the Civil War as chaplain of the Fifth Minnesota Regiment, an Irish unit that won fame for its part in the battle of Corinth. After spending several years as pastor of Cathedral Parish in St. Paul, Ireland became coadjutor bishop in 1875, and was elevated to archbishop with the creation of the archdiocese of St. Paul in 1888. For the next 30 years he directed the controversial course of the Catholic church in the Northwest and influenced its development in the nation. As an enthusiastic supporter of free enterprise, he campaigned for the Republican party and was a friend of Republicans Cushman K. Davis, James G. Blaine, William

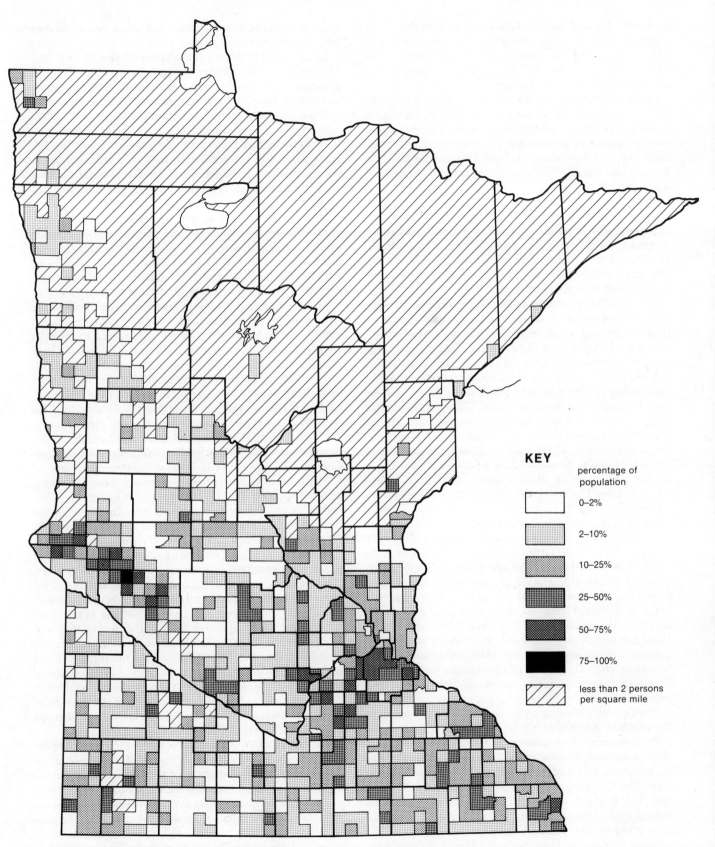

Map 7.4. Irish in Minnesota Rural Areas, 1880

KEY

percentage of
population

0–2%

2–10%

10–25%

25–50%

50–75%

75–100%

less than 2 persons
per square mile

McKinley, William Howard Taft, and Theodore Roosevelt. A man of strong opinions, strong will, and unbounded energy — he was called the "consecrated blizzard of the Northwest" by the archbishop of Philadelphia — his importance to the Minnesota Irish is considerable.[23]

Ireland's lieutenant in the colonizing effort was Dillon O'Brien, editor of the *Northwestern Chronicle*, the weekly diocesan newspaper, who used its pages to promote such favorite causes as immigration to Minnesota and temperance. The state legislature, apparently recognizing his effectiveness, appointed O'Brien to the Minnesota Immigration Board in 1879.[24]

Ireland's and O'Brien's first colonization attempts were faltering. They formed the Minnesota Irish Immigration Society in 1864 to promote immigrant aid and colonization programs on a national scale, but little came of these efforts. In 1876, within a month after he became a bishop, Ireland tried again, establishing the Catholic Colonization Bureau of St. Paul with O'Brien as its head.[25]

The new bishop avoided problems encountered by other colonizers by becoming an agent of the St. Paul and Pacific Railroad. Because he never bought land from the railroads, he assumed little risk, and he did not need to raise huge amounts of capital to finance the venture. And since he was the sole agent for these tracts, he could prevent speculators from buying up land within the colony and selling it for more than bona fide colonists could afford. During the next three years, from 1876 to 1879, Ireland contracted for a total of 369,000 acres in southwestern and west-central Minnesota. The towns of De Graff and Clontarf in Swift County, Adrian in Nobles County, Avoca, Iona, and Fulda in Murray County, Graceville in Big Stone County, and Minneota and Ghent in Lyon County became the business centers for his colonies.[26]

The total number of Irish in them was relatively small. In 1870 virtually none lived in the counties that were to contain the colonies; by 1880, 1,194 Irish born and 2,087 born in the United States of Irish parents lived there out of a total five-county population of 25,457. The number of foreign-born Irish increased slightly by the turn of the century, but then began to decline. Figures for the second generation do not appear in the census until 1905, when 3,819 persons with Irish-born fathers were recorded. While these were not all colonists (examination of the 1880 census shows that townships other than those of the colonies had Irish residents), the number suggests the size of the colonies' Irish population.[27]

The Catholic Colonization Bureau did not, however, have the satisfaction of knowing it was saving Irishmen from the evils of the cities. Poor laborers did not have the $400 minimum stake needed to see a family through its first year on a western farm. Those who took the archbishop up on his offer were, like Irish farmers across the state, from the Midwest and New England. Some left farms in eastern Minnesota. Others who immigrated directly from Ireland had enough money to pay their passages and expenses for a year. The colonies were largely Irish at first, but French, Belgian, German, and English Catholics also moved to the prairies. They had experience, capital, and the knowledge that after several years of work the farms — richer and larger than those they left — would be theirs.[28]

Ireland's and O'Brien's colonization scheme was satisfactory to all parties. Settlers bought fertile farms close to churches at reasonable rates. The railroads gained the money from the land sales and customers for their services. The Catholic Colonization Bureau earned the usual agent's fee of 10% on all sales and the satisfaction of seeing Catholic settlers do as well as Protestants. The importance of the colonies lies not in the number of Irish they attracted but in their status as the "largest and most successful Catholic colonization program ever undertaken in the United States," as historian James Shannon described them.[29]

Neither the Catholic bureau nor others were uniformly successful Irish colonizers. The Minnesota Colonization Company, organized in 1877 by William O'Mulcahy, a prominent Irishman from Rochester, failed for lack of financial backing, for the American Irish consistently refused to invest in colonization ventures, preferring to send money to family members in Ireland or to donate to groups working for Irish political and economic reform. Other colonizers found that the backgrounds of the immigrants as well as financial backing were important to the success of a project. Irish families sent with assistance from Boston to the Adrian colony in 1880 were markedly less successful than nonassisted immigrants. So also was a group imported in 1881 from Ireland to a colony near Currie in Murray County by John Sweetman, a wealthy Irishman from County Meath.[30]

To his dismay, Bishop Ireland was himself caught up in a purely benevolent settlement effort that failed more dramatically than all the rest. In 1880 he accepted responsibility for 309 Irish-speaking people from Connemara, County Galway, an area especially hard hit by crop failures in the late 1870s, and he placed them on colony land near Graceville in Big Stone County. Unfortunately, these former subsistence fishermen and garden farmers had no experience with large-scale wheat cultivation, no desire to invest labor one year for a return the next, and little energy to work for themselves. Contemporary newspaper accounts also indicated that some of the Connemaras had been professional beggars. Winter found them unprepared, and the St. Paul and Minneapolis newspapers made a great sensation of the story of their suffering. Realizing that the Connemaras would never become productive farmers, Ireland found jobs for them with the railroad companies in St. Paul. They lived in "Connemara Patch," a shantytown under Dayton's Bluff on Phalen Creek, and on the Mississippi River flats of the West Side. Some also moved to what later became known as Bohemian Flats along the river in Southeast Minneapolis.[31]

The failure of the Connemaras had a far greater impact than the incident would seem to warrant. Ireland recognized immediately the consequences of the extensive bad publicity. "The Connemara families are twenty-four in number," he wrote the *St. Paul Pioneer Press*. "Around Graceville are 400 other Catholic families, mostly Irish, and I beg the public, when Graceville is mentioned, to remember the latter rather than the former." Unfortunately for Irish colonization efforts, this was not to be. The story retarded the efforts of at least one recruiter in the East, and created the erroneous impression that the Irish were not competent farmers. It left its mark, too, on the sponsors. Dillon O'Brien's son wrote that the strain of these events contributed to his father's sudden death in 1882. One of Ireland's biographers reported that the archbishop characterized the incident as "the greatest grief of his life."[32]

As the 19th century waned, smaller groups of Irish were to be found in the Red River Valley and in the mines and logging camps of northern Minnesota. Those in the Red River Valley were farmers. Kittson County's first Irish settlers migrated from Canada in the 1870s. Tynsid Township near Fisher in Polk County was known as the "Irish Settlement" in 1872 because of its Irish squatters. Others later worked the vast wheat fields of the bonanza farms in summer and the lumber camps of northeastern Minnesota in winter. The St. Paul, Minneapolis, and Manitoba (later the Great Northern) Railroad, built in 1878, brought more Irish laborers. Those working at Hallock attended services in homes from 1879 until 1897 when James J. Hill donated two sections of land and $200 for a church.[33]

Some movement in the state between western wheat fields and eastern lumber camps occurred during periods of unemployment, but the Irish largely missed the next great employment opportunity in northern Minnesota. Irish immigration to Minnesota had slowed drastically by the time the iron ranges opened in the 1880s and 1890s. In 1885, as mining began, 44 Irish born comprised only 3.1% of the total population, or 4.8% of the foreign born, on the Vermilion Range. Three-quarters of them were working-age males. Ten years later 187 Irish born formed 1.2% of the area's population. They were employed as skilled laborers (craftsmen and heavy-equipment operators) and office workers. In 1907 a breakdown of the Oliver Iron Mining Company's work force showed that most (87.7%) of the 81 foreign-born Irish had been in the United States for 10 years or more and were naturalized citizens. Many had migrated from the iron districts of Michigan.[34]

For the first two decades of the 20th century, the Irish, who had the advantage of English as a native language, often became the political leaders of the more recently arrived Slavic and Italian miners on the ranges. Victor L. Power, the son of a Michigan Irish politician, became the first non-company mayor of Hibbing in 1913. For the next 20 years he taxed the mining companies to finance public improvements that made Hibbing the "richest little village in the world." Other elected officials in Virginia and Eveleth followed suit. One scholar has compared the towns' Irish-controlled political parties of that period to New York's Tammany Hall.[35]

In 1895 the Irish population of Duluth, the largest city of the northern region, peaked with 811 foreign-born Irish residents scattered throughout its wards. They formed only 3.2% of the city's foreign born and 1.4% of the total population and held a variety of jobs in Duluth's rapidly expanding economy. An analysis of the occupations of 671 male, Irish-surnamed Catholic parishioners in 1892 showed that over half were laborers: 28.9% unskilled, 16.2% skilled in building trades, and 10.1% skilled in industrial trades. Another 24.2% worked for the city (policemen and firemen), in traditional trades such as blacksmithing and printing, or in small businesses, especially those that supplied services — almost 10% of those listed were teamsters. The remaining 20% held white-collar jobs, a few as professionals but most as office workers. Of the 91 Irish-surnamed women working outside the home, 42.9% were domestics and 28.6% were dressmakers. The others were employed as office workers, teachers, and laundresses.[36]

Perhaps because of its small size, the group formed few organizations. The Duluth branch of the Society of United Irishmen held a "gay and festive occasion at Capt. Farrell's Continental Restaurant" in 1871. Four chapters of the Ancient Order of Hibernians were functioning in 1892, when they celebrated St. Patrick's Day with the help of such other Catholic ethnic organizations as the St. Jean Baptiste Society, the Polish National Benevolent Society, and the St. Boniface Society. By 1915 the *Irish Standard,* a newspaper published in Minneapolis by the Hibernians, carried a column of "Duluth News," reporting meetings and celebrations in that city as well as in towns on the iron ranges. From about 1900 to 1918 the group faced the anti-Catholic prejudice of the American Protective Association and the Ku Klux Klan.[37]

In the 1970s interest in folk dancing brought some ceilis (traditional Irish dances) to the city, but the sponsors were a political interest group, a neighborhood association, and food co-operatives rather than Irish organizations. The dances, held in the Sons of Norway Hall, drew many Finnish-American participants. A St. Patrick's Day parade, revived in 1970, continued the tradition of ethnic co-operation. One of the founders was Jewish, and the participants included the Italian-American Club.[38]

NOSTALGIA and pride probably mingled in the name ("Ireland Forever") of this Duluth saloon, pictured in 1875.

After the turn of the century, with the end of large-scale Irish immigration, the declining Irish-born population of the state became progressively more urban. In 1910, 60% lived in cities of more than 2,500. But even as their numbers in rural areas fell, Minnesota's Irish departed from the pattern in the United States. In 1920, when 17% of the nation's first- and second-generation Irish lived in rural areas and in towns of less than 2,500, more than twice that proportion — 38% — of Minnesota's Irish did so.[39]

St. Paul and Minneapolis

Throughout the state's history, however, the scattered rural Irish received less attention than those concentrated in St. Paul and Minneapolis. In 1890, when the Irish population reached its peak, 9,796 Irish born, or 35% of the Minnesota total, lived in the two cities (see Table 7.3). Moreover St. Paul, as the state capital, the center of the Democratic party for many years, and the seat of a large Catholic archdiocese, became the political, religious, and social center of Irish activity in the state.[40]

How did St. Paul, which was in truth a preponderantly German town, acquire its Irish image? The answer may lie in the downtown businessmen's vigorous promotion of the city's St. Patrick's Day parade, or in the forces that drove St. Paul and Minneapolis to prove they were fraternal rather than identical twins. Minneapolis found an obvious symbol in its predominantly Scandinavian population; that St. Paul chose an Irish rather than a German image, however, probably derives from the high Irish profile in the city's political history.

This characterization grew from modest beginnings. The Irish who migrated to St. Paul in the 1850s found many of the same problems that faced their countrymen in the East. In 1850 over half of them, a larger proportion than in any other group, were unskilled laborers. "The Catholics are very poor here — and what is worse very irreligious and indifferent," wrote a seminarian in 1852, "they are Half breeds, Canadians, and Irish — The Yankees have all the influence, the wealth and the power, although they are not near as numerous as the others." But even this churchman was not entirely sympathetic. "My mission is among the dirty little ragged Canadian and Irish boys. . . . To take the charge of these impudent and insulting children of unthankful parents was the greatest mortification I ever underwent."[41]

Yankee historians of the time took little notice of the Irish among them, but St. Paul newspapers offered some hints of their activities. The *Minnesota Democrat,* a sympathetic paper, noted on July 15, 1851, that 24 Irishmen donated their labor to construct the first Catholic school in downtown St. Paul. On May 19, 1852, it welcomed "two respectable and intelligent Irish families," who predicted "a considerable immigration of the most substantial class of Irish farmers, within the present season." The *Minnesota Pioneer* reported the first sermon in the Irish language in Minnesota on November 21, 1854.

Other frontier newspapers of opposing political views noted more sensational and less flattering activities. The *Daily Minnesotian* (St. Paul) was especially interested in the uses and abuses of the Irish vote. In 1857 it reported heavy emigration from Ireland with the comment, "We hope to gracious none of the Paddies will hear where St. Paul is. We consider that those now here can poll a large enough vote, provided they vote often enough apiece." On June 6 of that year the *Minnesota Weekly Times* (St. Paul) reported a riot of Irish angered by political defeat in which they "acted as if they were possessed of seven devils apiece." St. Anthony's *Minnesota Republican* printed a lively description of a disturbance in Minneapolis on St. Patrick's Day, 1858. The trouble started when pranksters hanged St. Patrick in effigy with a string of potatoes around his neck. The editor chastised both the culprits and the Irishmen who took bloody revenge.[42]

The Irish began to organize early. St. Patrick's Day celebrations (discussed below) began in 1851, and associations such as the St. Patrick's Day Society and the Benevolent Society of the Sons of Erin, were formed in the mid-1850s. The Shields Guards, a 52-member volunteer militia organized in 1856 and named for General James Shields, was the Irish answer to the Yankees' Pioneer Guard.[43]

St. Paul's Irish spread throughout the city (see Map 7.5), as the locations of their churches indicated. The first-comers attended the Cathedral of St. Paul with French and German Catholics. Bishop Joseph Cretin, a Frenchman, found it a "strange thing!" that they wished "to celebrate pompously the day of St. Patrick" in 1853, but he was pleased that "No one complains about the sermons in French and English." In 1867 wealthy English-speaking Catholics, several of whom were Irish, built the Church of St. Mary at 261 East 8th Street in Lowertown. The next year poorer Irish on the West Side formed St. Michael's Church so they could attend services without having to pay the toll to cross the bridge to the cathedral. Parishes organized in the following years in middle-class neighborhoods were St.Mark's (organized in 1877 and built in 1889 near the new St. Thomas Seminary on Dayton Avenue), St. Patrick's (built in 1884 near the railroad yards of upper Payne Avenue), St. John's (built in 1886 on

Table 7.3. Irish Born in St. Paul and Minneapolis, 1860–1930

	1860	1870	1880	1890	1900	1910	1920	1930*
St. Paul Irish born	1,903**	2,276**	3,013	6,040	4,892	4,184	3,053	2,242
% of total Minn. Irish born	14.8	10.5	12.0	21.6	21.8	26.4	29.7	34.5
Minneapolis Irish born	955***	1,896***	1,783	3,756	3,213	2,867	2,066	1,462
% of total Minn. Irish born	7.4	8.7	7.1	13.4	14.3	18.1	20.1	22.5

Source: U.S. manuscript census, 1860, 1880; U.S., *Census,* 1870, 1890, 1900, 1910, 1920, 1930.
*Includes both Irish Free State and Northern Ireland
**Includes Ramsey County
***Includes Hennepin County

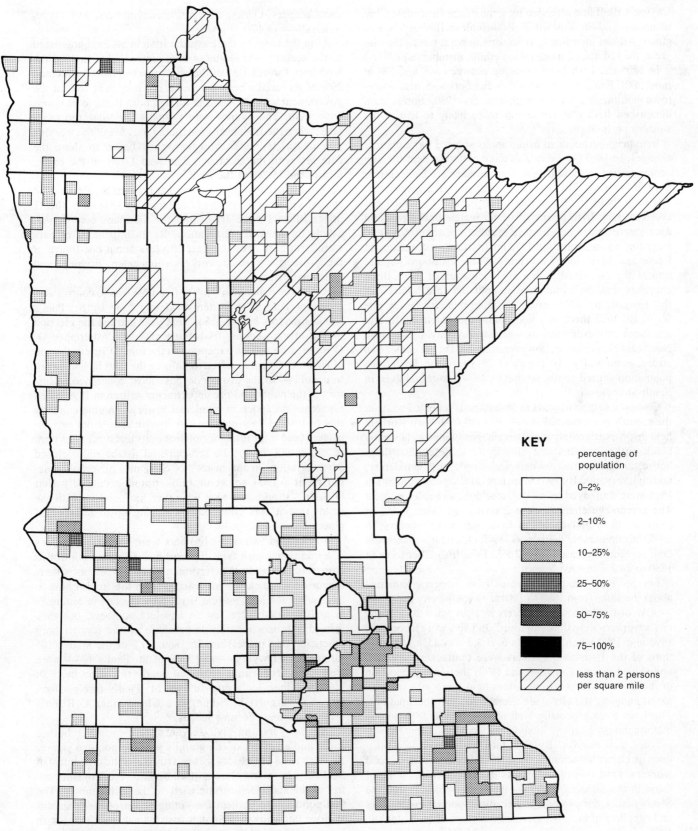

Map 7.5. Irish in Minnesota Rural Areas, 1905

KEY

percentage of
population

0–2%

2–10%

10–25%

25–50%

50–75%

75–100%

less than 2 persons
per square mile

Dayton's Bluff and attended by some of the Graceville Connemaras), and St. Vincent de Paul (built in 1888 at 651 Virginia). All had identifiably Irish parishioners, but as the city grew, they acquired more mixed ethnic memberships.[44]

In 1895 the Irish born made up between 3% and 5% of most of St. Paul's wards, with the neighborhoods near downtown holding the largest numbers. By 1930, however, a diminished Irish population was more likely to live in the western parts of the city.[45]

Irish neighborhoods in Minneapolis showed more distinct changes. In 1880 (see Map 7.2) three churches near the city center served Irish congregations: Immaculate Conception, built in 1868 at 3rd Avenue North and 3rd Street; St. Anthony, built in St. Anthony for French Catholics but taken over by Irish (many of whom were stonecutters and quarrymen) and other English speakers in the 1860s; and Holy Rosary, organized in 1878 for Irish railroad workers at Cedar and Riverside. Two-thirds of the Irish-born population of the city lived within six-block radii of these three churches, but the areas were so split by ward boundaries that they did not show up as a sizable minority in any one ward. By 1905 there had been some movement north and south out of the downtown area. St. Anthony's Church in Northeast Minneapolis, however, remained at the center of a strong community. In the next 25 years the Irish-born population shifted south, so that by 1934 two-thirds lived in South Minneapolis.[46]

Changing neighborhoods in Minneapolis reflected shifts in the group's occupational status. In 1880 Irish-born workers held disproportionately high percentages of jobs as laborers, blacksmiths, masons and stonecutters, hotel, boarding-house, and restaurant owners and employees, launderers, and civil servants. By 1905 more first- and second-generation Irish were employed as clerks, teachers, and sales people. The percentage changes were dramatic. In 1880, 36.8% of those living in households of Irish born were laborers; in 1905 the comparable figure was 18.4%. Clerical workers and civil servants increased from 7.5% of the Irish labor force in 1880 to 24.7% in 1905.[47]

For St. Paul the proportion of Irish laborers remained about the same from 1880 to 1900 at twice the city's average — 43% of the Irish were laborers in 1880 when 20% of the city's workers were thus employed, and 30% were laborers in 1890 and 1900 when the city's average was 15%. About a third of the Irish-born workers were craftsmen, foremen, and skilled laborers in 1880 and 1890; the same proportion of the first and second generations held these jobs in 1900, about equaling the city-wide average for such occupations. The Irish were especially well represented in 1880 among boardinghouse keepers, launderers, express company employees, and masons. By 1900 they had moved into positions as clerks, watchmen, firemen, policemen, and railroad workers. Like their counterparts in eastern cities, some of those in the building trades — the Butler brothers and the Shiely family, for example — became important contractors and suppliers of building materials. Women of Irish stock in 1900 were servants and waitresses (25.7%), dressmakers, seamstresses, and milliners (19.1%), and office workers (bookkeepers, clerks, copyists, stenographers, and "typewriters" — 15.1%).[48]

As in the cities of the East, the Irish in St. Paul gravitated to the security and status of civil service jobs. In 1880 the Irish born formed 10% of the city's working population (and 20% of its foreign-born workers), but they held 16% of the government jobs; 39% of the foreign born in these positions were Irish. The figures were virtually the same ten years later, when the Irish born constituted only 6% of the working population. By 1900, however, they began to share the category with the Germans, who held 17.7% of the public jobs to the 15.2% of the Irish.

Of these occupations the one that brought St. Paul's Irish special visibility was the police force. In 1858, 6 of the 11 police officers were Irish, and the Germans complained, asking for more representation. By 1878, 9 of 27 officers were Irish born. For the next 20 years about one-fourth of the protective service workers (policemen, firemen, and watchmen) were Irish.[49]

Part of the policeman's job at that time was to control vice by supervising it, a system evidently used by St. Paul's Yankee mayors before 1884. That year marked the election of the city's second Irish-born mayor, Christopher D. O'Brien, who was an exception to the rule. O'Brien, the son of Dillon O'Brien, resolved to enforce the laws he had sworn to uphold — to the dismay of those most concerned. A history of the police and fire departments written in 1899 called his term "an epoch in municipal history," noting candidly that he proved "a great city can flourish apart from periodical fees paid it for tolerance of vice in its midst. . . . His term of office will always be remembered as the only 'closed administration' in the history of St. Paul." The police department's 1904 souvenir book noted cryptically that O'Brien "suppressed vice wherever he found it, with the result that it was continually cropping up in unexpected places."[50]

O'Brien and two of his brothers were lawyers, examples of a traditional Irish type. Trained in the English-controlled courts of Ireland, the Irishman (stereotyped as silver-tongued and quick-witted) learned from the British how to manipulate the legal system. Irish-born lawyers in Minnesota and St. Paul were few in absolute numbers, but they formed a proportionately large share of the foreign born practicing that profession. In 1880, 20% of the state's 105 foreign-born lawyers — and 35% of St. Paul's 17 — were Irish. The proportions remained nearly the same in 1900: 21% of Minnesota's and 30% of St. Paul's foreign-stock lawyers were Irish. Some, like Christopher O'Brien's brother Thomas, became judges.[51]

Irish lawyers and civil servants were probably both a cause and an effect of the group's growing political power. Because rural Minnesota was heavily Republican, control of St. Paul's Irish and German Democratic voters meant control of the state Democratic party in the 19th century. The first politician to harness the voting power of the Irish was William Pitt Murray, a Scotch-Irish lawyer. In alliance with Louis Robert, who controlled the French vote, Murray directed the city's Democratic politics, holding various municipal and state offices from the 1850s until 1889. In the mid-1880s the big guns of the state Democratic party were Patrick H. Kelly, a wholesale grocer, and Michael Doran, a banker and merchant, who allied themselves with railroad magnate James J. Hill. Both were Bourbon Democrats, well-to-do men, whose primary goal was to keep agrarian radicals out of power. Kelly and Doran were known as "Me and Mike" by Republicans when they began to dispense patronage after President Grover Cleveland's election in 1884. Hill was a silent partner, described as "the *deus ex machina*" by Ignatius L. Donnelly, perhaps Minnesota's best-known 19th-century Irishman after Hill himself.[52]

Their successors were Richard T. ("The Cardinal") O'Connor and his brother James J. ("The Big Fellow"), sons of a boardinghouse operator and local politician. Richard, who had clerked for Hill's Minneapolis, Manitoba, and Pacific Railroad as a young man, became deputy city clerk in 1880 and served his political internship under the Irish leadership in City Hall. He took over direction of the party in 1889 when the older leaders bungled an election by nominating a ticket top-heavy with Irishmen. Richard, in alliance with William Hamm, Sr., a German brewer, rebuilt the party. Like Kelly and Doran, O'Connor was closely associated with Hill, and he became one of the most influential Democrats in the country after 1904. His brother James had worked in Patrick Kelly's grocery house before joining the police force in 1881. He became police chief in 1901 and held the position for 19 years.[53]

The brothers were the originators of the "O'Connor System," a scheme by which criminals across the country were told that they would not be arrested in St. Paul as long as they obeyed the law while within the city. The O'Connors oversaw the heyday of prostitution, including the operations of Nina Clifford, a famous madame whose house was around the corner from the police station. But when the O'Connors left St. Paul politics (James retired in 1920 and Richard became more involved in national politics), the system began to break down — with disastrous consequences for the peace of the city.[54]

More liberal Irish politicians opposed these conservative officials. Their best-known challenger was Ignatius Donnelly, politician, writer, and Populist philosopher who was born in Philadelphia in 1831 to an Irish immigrant father and a second-generation Irish mother. He moved in 1857 to Minnesota, where he entered territorial politics, helped found the townsite of Nininger on the Mississippi River in Dakota County, and wrote a number of literary, scientific, and political books of enduring interest. During the next 43 years, Donnelly was associated with many parties — Democrat, Republican, Granger, Anti-Monopolist, Greenback, Farmers' Alliance, People's, and Populist — and he battled with the leaders of each. He was lieutenant governor when the Civil War broke out and a representative in Congress from 1863 to 1869. Although he failed in five tries to regain a congressional seat, he became a favorite of Dakota County's Irish and Populist voters, who elected him to the state legislature six times. Donnelly was a talented, humorous, and popular speaker, a perennial favorite who addressed Irish

DOING BUSINESS AT THE SAME OLD STAND.

THE IRISH control of St. Paul politics was criticized in this cartoon in the Minneapolis Journal *of November 14, 1893.*

gatherings and St. Patrick's Day functions to loud and prolonged cheers.[55]

Another opponent of the O'Connor-Hill machine and the man who introduced Donnelly to the more successful national Populist of his day, William Jennings Bryan, was James Manahan. An Irish lawyer born in Chatfield in 1866, Manahan made his reputation as a Populist by arguing various lawsuits to lower the railroads' shipping, Pullman, and express rates, and to break the monopoly of the Minneapolis and Chicago grain exchanges. A Bryan Democrat, a Progressive Republican, and a leader of the Nonpartisan League, he served one term in Congress from 1913 to 1915.[56]

Even as they pursued jobs and political power in the cities and around the state, Minnesota's Irish maintained ties with the homeland. Two major Irish newspapers served both aims. The *Northwestern Chronicle*, official paper of the Catholic archdiocese, was printed in St. Paul from 1866 to 1900. The *Irish Standard*, founded in 1885 in Minneapolis as the *Northwest Standard*, was a semiofficial and, from 1915 to its demise in 1920, official paper of the Ancient Order of Hibernians. Both carried Catholic, Irish, and Minnesota news, anti-British editorials, columns on Irish history and politics, agricultural reports, serialized fiction, and social items. They printed news, notes, and advertisements from Irish communities throughout the state and, to a lesser extent, the region.[57]

One of the earliest and most active of the many organizations to demonstrate an interest in the homeland was the Fenian Brotherhood, which was organized in New York in 1859 to give political, financial, and military aid to revolutionaries in Ireland. Minnesota's circles seem to have been formed after eastern Fenians invaded Canada in 1866. The groups' activities aroused speculation in local newspapers, especially with regard to gunrunning. Although the eastern leadership disavowed the idea, St. Paul Fenians helped organize an attack on Canada in 1871, the plans for which were "hatched and matured" in St. Paul with the ardent support of Minnesota expansionists. Led by ex-Fenians General John O'Neill and William B. O'Donoghue, a force of about 35 made for Canada, where they hoped to unite with Louis Riel's métis and march on Winnipeg to strike a blow against the British. On October 5 they captured the Hudson's Bay Company post just north of the international border at Pembina, North Dakota, before being taken by United States soldiers.[58]

Irish patriotic groups formed in subsequent years proposed to work more peacefully for the political freedom and economic improvement of Ireland. For example, the constitution of the Friends of Ireland, organized in St. Paul in August, 1877, stated, "We hold that Ireland belongs to the Irish people, in Ireland; that they are the nation; that it is for them to select their form of government; for them to speak, to act; for us, their friends, to assist."[59]

Direct assistance was forthcoming in the late 1870s, when yet another famine struck Ireland. Chapters of the Irish National Land League were formed to help dispossessed farmers buy back their land. Charles Stewart Parnell, the Irish Protestant founder of the movement, traveled throughout the United States soliciting funds. He visited Minnesota in February, 1880, speaking to wildly enthusiastic crowds in Winona, Lake City, St. Paul, and Minneapolis. In St. Paul Coadjutor Bishop Ireland and a group of politicians received Parnell, who remarked that he thought land reform, rather than emigration, was the solution to his homeland's problems. The bishop asked nonetheless for Parnell's support of the Catholic Colonization Bureau. "A word from you will do a thousand times more than pamphlets or articles on the subject," said Ireland. The Land Leaguer's speech in St. Paul raised $1,700; he addressed a similar rally in Minneapolis later that evening. Irish from other parts of the state also contributed hundreds of dollars in the following weeks and months.[60]

Many of the Irish organizations that joined in these relief efforts were oriented primarily toward social life in the Twin Cities. Among them were drill teams (such as the Wolfe Tone Rifles of Minneapolis and the Emmet Light Artillery of St. Paul), literary societies, and social clubs. Irish drama, music, and comedy were presented in the 1870s in performances called Hibernicons, and festivals were held honoring such famous Irishmen as Robert Emmet and Thomas Moore.[61]

More prominent and longer lived was the Ancient Order of Hibernians (AOH), organized in the state in 1879, and its women's auxiliary, formed in 1894. Both groups functioned as mutual benefit societies and as organizers of such Irish celebrations as St. Patrick's Day. By 1912 there were 82 divisions in the state. The Ladies' Auxiliary, which had 68 divisions in 1949, also contributed to civic and Catholic projects. The men's fund failed in the 1940s, so the women allowed them to purchase policies — but male members were still not allowed voting representation in 1980.[62]

A great number of the organizations that donated to Irish relief were chapters of temperance or total abstinence societies. The Catholic church led the way in this effort, beginning as early as 1852 when Bishop Cretin organized the Catholic Temperance Society of St. Paul. The movement did not take hold, however, until after the Civil War. Then the Father Mathew Temperance Society, organized in 1868 at Belle Plaine, enrolled 170 members in less than a month. The movement received greater impetus in January, 1869, when a group of Irish drinkers in a St. Paul saloon decided to reform. Several of them (including the tavern's owner) signed a petition that read, by one account, "For God's sake organize a Temperance Society." An apparently inebriated member of the group set off to deliver the petition to the pastor of the Cathedral parish, John Ireland, who immediately agreed to the request.[63]

From these humble beginnings the movement grew rapidly. The Father Mathew Temperance Society of Cathedral parish set an example that was touted far and wide by the *Northwestern Chronicle* and the considerable energies of John Ireland. The greatest boom in membership occurred in 1875, when Paulist missionaries lectured throughout the diocese, gaining hundreds of recruits. In that year, too, Ireland became a bishop, a position that gave him a wider platform from which to urge the cause. By 1882 there were 62 branches throughout the state.[64]

Early temperance efforts emphasized setting up branches and recruiting members, but many who took the pledge did not keep it. Thus the societies developed additional ways of retaining members. In the early 1870s they sponsored social functions and, in some cases, offered libraries, marching bands, and glee clubs to replace the delights of the saloons. Such societies marched in St. Patrick's Day parades and at church celebrations. Some provided mutual benefit assistance. After 1873 many parishes started Cadet or Crusader groups for young men, in order to reduce the friction that developed among members of different ages. A state-wide temperance union formed in 1872 held annual conventions. Women's groups were belatedly initiated in 1876.[65]

Although these groups were called temperance societies, they really advocated total abstinence. Members were fined or expelled for imbibing. A major element of Bishop Ireland's effort aimed to force Irish saloonkeepers out of business. He led a successful campaign in 1886 to raise drastically the cost of liquor licenses in Minnesota, thereby reducing the number of taverns. The Democratic party, closely tied to the saloon interests, opposed the effort.[66]

It is difficult to judge the success of temperance organizations in reforming chronic drinkers. Church accounts are uniformly laudatory. The *St. Paul Pioneer Press*, a less biased observer, commented in 1882, "It was not many years ago that the Catholic Irish of St. Paul contributed a large proportion of the drunken, disorderly, and rowdy elements of the community. . . . From the most intemperate, disorderly, and unthrifty, they have, as a rule, become among the most temperate, orderly, industrious, thrifty and moral classes of the community." The transformation was credited to the temperance work of Ireland.[67]

Ireland's influence on Catholics of other nationalities was often equally dramatic. He and other church leaders, most of them Irish, wanted to produce a distinctly American Catholic church that would be acceptable to the country's Protes-

KILKENNY chapter of the Ancient Order of Hibernians around 1915. There is an Irish harp barely visible on the group's banner.

tant majority. In attempting to show critics that Catholics were patriotic Americans whose duties and devotion to the state matched those of other groups, Ireland assumed the task of mediating between Old-Stock Americans and new immigrants. In that role, he made few friends among the latter group.[68]

A particularly painful stricture for many of Minnesota's immigrant Catholics was the archbishop's insistence that national parishes use some English. Although he often assigned priests who spoke the language of the members to non-English-speaking congregations and permitted national churches to be built within a few blocks of English-speaking ones, he was not particularly sensitive to many of the problems faced by Catholics of other cultures.[69]

The Irish who took upon themselves the task of Americanization inevitably based their concept of Catholicism on what they had known in Ireland. Relegated to the hedges by British persecution, Catholic practice in Ireland emphasized respect for the priest rather than lay leadership or community worship. After the Great Famine, the Irish emphasized devotions (such as novenas, rosaries, and regular church attendance). For many European Catholics, in contrast, the church was the center of community social life. Thus when the archbishop closed the beer gardens and bazaars and began to discourage the use of native languages, he was threatening the religious as well as the ethnic identity of communities already struggling for survival in an alien land. He was accused of imposing Irish Catholicism, and he met resistance from the Germans and other ethnic groups. Glimpses of the conflicts appear in other chapters of this book.[70]

A more acceptable form of the Hibernicization of Minnesotans began to operate in the early 1850s. St. Patrick's Day,

the Irish-American national holiday, assumed a special role in Minnesota as the beginning of the end of the long winter. The *Minnesota Democrat* of March 17, 1852, announced that the day would be celebrated with a procession and a supper, "a pleasant and joyous gathering of the warm hearted sons of Erin, *and their countrymen of all nations.*" Two years later the festivities included some 18 toasts in honor of various dignitaries and institutions; elected officials of the United States and Minnesota, the press, the legal profession, women, and England's enemy in the Crimean War, "The Russian Bear; So fond of Honey, may she soon get her fill of Turkey." The group also drank to their fellow immigrants and guests, "the Natives of Foreign Countries; Naturalized citizens of the United States now celebrating the day with us."[71]

Festivities became more elaborate in the 1860s, setting a pattern followed for many years. The day began with a High Mass at the Cathedral, which usually included a sermon mourning the oppression of Ireland, praising the faith of the Irish, and extolling the virtues of temperance. After the service, such organizations as the temperance society and the Knights of St. Paul paraded with lavish green-silk and gold-braided banners, marching behind the Great Western Band to the bishop's house, where they heard a second address. For many years the speaker was John Ireland, who used the occasion to arouse pride and anger in his audience, and to channel those emotions into resolutions for self-improvement. Sometimes the marchers stopped at the Sisters of St. Joseph convent and orphanage to pay their respects and play music for the children. The procession would then call upon the governor or the mayor for speeches as well.[72]

After that the participants adjourned until evening, when

various entertainments were scheduled. In the early years one hall held all, but later several parishes sponsored separate observances. The programs featured sketches, music, dances, and recitations. A typical event at Mozart Hall in 1869 included the tableaux, "The Emigrant Boy Leaving His Father's Cot," "Erin," and "Emmet's Trial"; for musical entertainment, lyrically announced the *Northwestern Chronicle*, "One of our amateurs will sing 'Soggarth Aroon' [Beloved Priest], 'Kathleen Mavourneen,' and after having melted us to tears by the suavity of those lyrics, will set us in high glee by his rendering of 'The Irish Schoolmaster.'"[73]

Minnesota politicians even then were quick to recognize the opportunities inherent in such a holiday. So many turned out in 1860 that the *Pioneer and Democrat* was moved to complain. Such celebrations, it said, "should be made more truly representative of the nation participating in them, by addresses from their own speakers, their national and characteristic music, &c., especially where, as in this instance, the requisite talent can be found, without going out of their own ranks."[74]

These celebrations were occasions for much visiting among Minnesota's Irish communities. Seven hundred Irishmen gathered in Rochester in 1867 for speeches, supper, song, and the viewing of "eight pyramidal cakes, from three to four feet high." In 1875 seven temperance societies from Goodhue and Wabasha counties met at Lake City to mark the day. The Ancient Order of Hibernians arranged special railroad rates for those who wished to travel to St. Paul for the festivities in 1901, when 4,000 men marched in the parade. The occasion could also renew contact with Ireland, as it did for Winonans who received shamrocks from the Old Country to wear on St. Patrick's Day in 1909.[75]

The parade in 1901 may have been the last of its kind. None was reported in 1902, but in 1903 a newspaper discreetly noted that "St. Patrick's Day was celebrated very quietly and religiously in St. Paul." Tradition has it that Archbishop Ireland was responsible for the cessation. Observances continued in church halls, and the Ancient Order of Hibernians and its auxiliary sponsored open houses, dances, and dinners throughout the next several decades. Many of these were held at the Hibernian Hall, located at 72 West 7th Street until 1923, when the lodges purchased 435 Summit Avenue.[76]

Before and during World War I the Irish in Minnesota again worked to promote causes in the homeland. Various groups passed resolutions in support of an Irish republic and sponsored lectures by Irish politicians. Minnesotans bought bonds of the new republic in the 1920s. The *Irish Standard* vilified Britain and printed pro-German articles during the war. By the 1930s, with the republic a reality, the activity in Minnesota died down.[77]

Irish participation in Minnesota politics, however, did not slow. In 1920, when 11 of the 12 members of the State Democratic Executive Committee were Irish, the *St. Paul Pioneer Press* commented that there were "enough Irishmen in the list to make up a creditable ball team" and suggested that the single non-Irishman should be the umpire. Between 1932 and 1972 all but one of the 10 men who served as mayors of St. Paul — some of them Republicans — had Irish surnames.[78]

The control these conservative Democrats had over the party was responsible for its weakness in the state. Apparently forgetting the earlier examples of William Pitt Murray and Dick O'Connor, they ran heavily Irish tickets that one scholar has characterized as "appropriate for Boston politics." The party was split, with Irish names on both sides. But in 1940 a coalition of labor, more moderate Farmer-Laborites, and Catholic Democrats, backing John J. McDonough for mayor, won an impressive victory that foreshadowed the parties' merger four years later. St. Paul Irish names figured prominently in the formation of the Democratic-Farmer-Labor party in 1944.[79]

Within the city, however, ethnic and religious identities apparently remained important. In the early 1950s an Irishman with good connections downtown could get a city job for an immigrant friend. As late as 1957 a political study judged that being Catholic was "almost essential for political success in St. Paul," and that the Irish were the predominant Catholic group. This trend slowed, however, as affirmative action and civil service legislation diminished patronage hiring and the Irish became less prominent in city politics.[80]

By the late 1970s the number of St. Paul residents of Irish ancestry was estimated at 45,000 or about 15% of the city's population. A relatively small fraction of them belonged to the organized groups of the Twin Cities Irish community which, spurred by the renewed troubles in Ireland, reflected the diverse political, social, and cultural interests of Irish Americans. Several sponsored lectures by Irish politicians of various opinions. Minnesota Irish Northern Aid, active since 1970, issued calls for peace and sent money to the dependents of Catholic political prisoners in Northern Ireland. The Minnesota Irish National Caucus, formed in 1975, promoted education on Irish issues to create a politically aware and powerful Irish-American community. It hosted speakers representing both sides of the conflict in Ireland and sponsored plays and programs by contemporary Irish literary figures. The Liam Mellows Irish Republican Club (IRC), also established in 1975, was a Socialist group affiliated with the Irish Republican Clubs of North America. It called for peaceful reunification and worker control of Ireland, holding that the country's problems arose from economic rather than religious divisions. The various political groups retained some degree of autonomy from their national counterparts, the first two by choosing not to affiliate and the third by a schism. In March, 1980, several members of the Liam Mellows IRC formed the Irish Progressive League, protesting what they felt was a rightward swing by the national group.[81]

Other social and cultural groups generally avoided political issues. The Twin Cities Irish-American Club, founded after World War II by Irish immigrants, at first helped its members find jobs and then became primarily a social organization. Many of its members also belonged to the Ancient Order of Hibernians and its Ladies Auxiliary, groups that maintained close ties to the Roman Catholic church. The Hibernians offered scholarships for members' children attending parochial schools, helped endow a chair in Irish history at Notre Dame University, and organized the Irish exhibit at the St. Paul Festival of Nations. The Minneapolis

Irish Study Club, a group of about 200 second- and third-generation Irish Minnesotans, most of whom lived in the southern suburbs, began monthly meetings in 1973 to hear lectures on Irish culture and arts. St. Paul's chapter of Comhaltus Ceoltoiri Eireann, an Irish cultural organization, operated from 1977 to 1980, when its members dropped their affiliation with the Dublin main office and formed the Irish Music and Dance Association of Minnesota. Most of the group's 80 members were young. They espoused a nonpolitical position and sponsored appearances of touring Irish musicians and dancers in the cities.[82]

The largest Irish cultural organization in the United States, the Irish American Cultural Institute, was started in Minnesota in 1962 by Eoin McKiernan, a second-generation Irishman from upstate New York. In 1980 it had 78,000 members in the United States and in more than 20 other countries. The institute published *Éire-Ireland*, the most widely circulated scholarly periodical of Irish history and culture in the world. It also made grants to Irish artists, musicians, and writers, produced special programs for television, and sponsored projects such as the "Irish Way," which sent high school students to Ireland for study and travel. In 1969 the institute began to produce the "Irish Fortnight," an annual tour of artists, scholars, and musicians from Ireland who lectured on Irish culture and performed traditional arts in a series of evening programs. The 1980 tour appeared in 12 American cities. McKiernan attributed the phenomenal success of the institute to two major factors: (1) the sympathy of potential benefactors and the comparative ease with which they could be approached in the Twin Cities' loosely structured social world, and (2) the skills and continuity provided by the institute's paid professional staff — an advantage shared by no other Irish-American cultural organization in the United States.[83]

Many of the younger members of these groups attempted a revival of Irish music and dancing in St. Paul in the mid-1970s. By 1980 several organizations sponsored traditional Irish dances, perhaps two or three times a month. The Northern Stars Ceili Band and the Blackthorn Band usually provided the music. Teaching sessions preceded the dances and the large number of regular participants kept relative order on the floor. More formal instruction was available at the Crossroads School of Irish Dance. The Mooncoin Dancers, a local troupe that performed across the state, traveled in 1980 to Ireland for three weeks of instruction. The Brian Boru Pipe Band, established in 1961, played Irish and Scottish pipe music in parades and competitions throughout the Midwest.[84]

The observance of St. Patrick's Day in 1980 was as diverse as the groups themselves. About 500 persons attended the special St. Patrick's Day Mass at the Cathedral of St. Paul. Among them were the Hibernians, who marched into the church together in full regalia. Several groups sponsored ceilis during the month, and a local sporting goods store sponsored a 10-kilometer St. Patrick's Day run to inaugurate the jogging season. The St. Patrick's Day parade in St. Paul had been revived in 1967 with a new format by an organization of downtown businessmen. Most of the marchers in 1980 were family groups who carried identifying banners,

THE MOONCOIN Ceili Dancers in a three-hand reel at the Clontarf Centennial Celebration in 1978.

THRONGS of marchers, Irish and otherwise, in the 1972 St. Patrick's Day parade, St. Paul.

some from Irish rural communities. Green clothing was the fashion of the day; green faces, hair, and dogs were not uncommon. Joining them were a large contingent of politicians and several entries advertising businesses. The St. Paul Winter Carnival contributed floats and its representatives, the Vulcan Guards (who were equipped with green soot to smear on the unwary). A green stripe painted down 5th Street marked the route, which was lined by thousands of onlookers, many of whom were inebriated. After the parade, crowds of revelers, mostly young, flocked to downtown bars.[85]

Organizers of this essentially civic function carried on the tradition of inviting non-Irish to join, and the non-Irish obliged. The day became a springtime bacchanal, a northern Mardi Gras, with heavy participation by those who otherwise had no interest in Irish events. Raymond MacCafferty, owner of one of the most popular Irish bars in the city, voiced the sentiments of many when he explained the exuberance of the celebration in purely Minnesota terms. "St. Patrick's Day happens to fall just at the end of the winter. . . . They would have that day no matter who the saint was, whether it was Irish, German, Swedish, or . . ." — words failed him.[86]

St. Paul's Irish were of two minds about the parade. Many of those who belonged to the organizations described above scrupulously avoided the revelry, disliking the identification of Irishness with drunkenness and of Irish culture with green paint, shamrocks, and shillelaghs. Those who marched in the parade seemed to take a more casual view, enjoying the opportunity to identify themselves with their extended families and their heritage.

Why did this difference of opinion exist and why did some descendants of the Irish fail to take sides in the debate? The bulk of Irish immigration occurred over a century ago, and most Minnesotans of Irish heritage in 1980 were in the third, fourth, and fifth generations. They, like many Americans, grew up outside their ancestral culture. The versions of Irishness that they learned from their families or sought for themselves varied. Some accepted a convenient stereotype as a model Irishman: the hard-drinking, cheerful boaster, who generously provided an excuse for other Minnesotans to celebrate the winter's end. Others took great satisfaction in learning about the country's history, culture, and traditions. Still others accepted both or identified with neither. They all demonstrated that ethnicity and its manifestations were matters of choice.

Reference notes

[1] This chapter tells the story of the Irish who were predominantly Catholic and whose ancestors spoke Irish. For those who descended from Scottish settlers in Ireland and called themselves Scotch-Irish, see Chapter 6. For examples of St. Paul's Irish label, see Gareth Hiebert, *St. Paul Is My Beat*, 149 (St. Paul, 1958); Harrison Salisbury, "The Victorian City in the Midwest," in *Growing Up in Minnesota*, 51 (Minneapolis, 1976); Jim Klobuchar, "If You Like Barnacles and Moss, You'll Like St. Paul," in *Mpls./St. Paul*, June, 1978, p. 54; Joanna Baymiller, "Beware & Begorrah! St. Patrick's Day in St. Paul," in *Twin Cities*, March, 1979, pp. 34, 36.

[2] United States, *Census*, 1860, *Population*, 621; 1870, 340; 1880, 494; 1890, 607.

[3] U.S., *Census*, 1940, *Population*, vol. 2, part 1, p. 43, part 4, p. 31. The 1940 census gives total Irish populations for Minnesota and the U.S. from 1850 to 1940. Figures for second-generation Minnesota Irish in 1860 are from the U.S. manuscript census schedules, tabulations in MEHP Papers, MHS. For a map showing the distribution of the Irish in the U.S. in 1890, see U.S., *Census*, 1890, *Population*, vol. 1, map 11.

[4] K. H. Connell, "Land and Population in Ireland, 1780–1845," in *Economic History Review*, 2nd series, 2:282–284 (1950); William F. Adams, *Ireland and Irish Emigration to the New World from 1815 to the Famine*, 3–12, 16–26, 34–36, 69, 111, 117 (New Haven, Conn., 1932); Cecil Woodham-Smith, *The Great Hunger*, 18–24, 27–35 (London, 1962). See also R. B. McDowell, "Ireland on the Eve of the Famine," in R. Dudley Edwards and T. Desmond Williams, eds., *The Great Famine: Studies in Irish History 1845–52*, 3–86 (New York, 1957).

[5] Connell, in *Economic History Review*, 2:285–289; E. R. R. Green, "Agriculture," William P. MacArthur, "Medical History of the Famine," and Oliver MacDonagh, "Irish Emigration to the United States of America and the British Colonies During the Famine," all in Edwards and Williams, eds., *The Great Famine*, 89, 121, 329, 388; Woodham-Smith, *The Great Hunger*, 35, 411; Arnold Schrier, *Ireland and the American Emigration, 1850–1900*, 18–42, 105–109, 167 (Minneapolis, 1958). Connell (p. 288) gives astounding figures on the Irish diet of potatoes: in good years, an adult male consumed a pint of buttermilk and between 10 and 12 pounds of potatoes per day. This provided virtually all the nutrients he needed.

Irish mortality and emigration figures are by no means exact. For other estimates, see Schrier, *Ireland and the American Emigration*, 157; Francis Moorehouse, "Irish Migration of the Forties," in *American Historical Review*, 33:591 (April, 1928); Stanley C. Johnson, *A History of Emigration from the United Kingdom to North America 1763–1912*, 350 (New York, 1969).

[6] Here and below, see Carl Wittke, *The Irish in America*, 62, 114–124 (Baton Rouge, 1956); Lawrence J. McCaffrey, *The Irish Diaspora in America*, 6, 58, 63, 65, 81, 85 (Bloomington, Ind., 1976).

[7] On Irish migration through and occupations in the Midwest, see Sister Mary Gilbert Kelly, *Catholic Immigrant Colonization Projects in the United States, 1815–1860*, 26, 31, 106, 147–150, 179, 204–206 (United States Catholic Historical Society, Monograph Series XVII — New York, 1939); George Potter, *To the Golden Door: The Story of the Irish in Ireland and America*, 199, 201, 324, 535–537, 549; Sister Mary Evangela Henthorne, *The Irish Catholic Colonization Association of the United States*, 31 (Champaign, Ill., 1932); David E. Schob, *Hired Hands and Plowboys: Farm Labor in the Midwest, 1815–60*, 117 (Urbana, Ill., 1975); Wittke, *Irish in America*, 64; Sister M. Justille McDonald, *History of the Irish in Wisconsin in the Nineteenth Century*, 47 (Washington, D.C., 1954). In the 1850s the *Boston Pilot*, a widely circulated Irish paper, printed many stories about Irish settlers in Minnesota, Wisconsin, and Iowa. A list of the articles is enclosed in A. F. Mace to Most Rev. John Ireland, March 5, 1897, MHS.

[8] For examples of staged migration, see biographies in Mary L. Hagerty, *Meet Shieldsville: The Story of St. Patrick's Parish Shieldsville, Minnesota*, 77–167 ([Shieldsville, 1940]); James E. Child, *Child's History of Waseca County, Minnesota*, 669–808 (Owatonna, 1905); *Belle Plaine Herald*, March 26, 1931, p. 1; Johanna M. O'Leary, *Historical Sketch of the Parish of the Immaculate Conception Faribault, Minnesota*, 20–90 (Faribault, 1938). On migration through Canada, see Woodham-Smith, *The Great Hunger*, 211–217; Adams, *Ireland and Emigration to the New World*, 199, 219.

The U.S. manuscript census schedules also reflect these migration patterns. For example, in 1870 about half of the Irish families in Eagan and Burnsville townships, Dakota County, and Credit River and Cedar Lake townships, Scott County, had children who were born in Canada or states other than Minnesota.

[9] Harold Albrecht, *This Is Our Town*, 579, 580, 583 ([Belle Plaine, 1977]). The exact percentages are: Kerry, 22.3; Cork, 17.2; Clare, 9.9; Mayo and Galway, 5.6; Westmeath, Waterford, Meath, Roscommon, Sligo, Kilkenny, Tipperary, Tyrone, Longford, Cavan, Kings, Queens, Donegal, Antrim, Dublin, less than 5. Five per cent were from other places in the British Empire and the U.S. census takers recorded only the country of birth, and too few Irishmen were written up in county histories to give a statistically reliable picture. If the records exist, future researchers may find them in parishes, cemeteries, and naturalization files across the state.

[10] Hand count of Minnesota manuscript census schedules, 1850, in MEHP Papers; Kelly, *Catholic Immigrant Colonization Projects*, 35; Agnes M. Larson, *Lumbering in the Last of the White Pine States*, 76 (Minneapolis, 1949).

[11] Patricia C. Harpole and Mary D. Nagle, *Minnesota Territorial Census, 1850* (St. Paul, 1972) lists names and occupations for the Irish. A German soldier, writing home in 1849, complained about the Irish soldiers: "Then we have many Irish in our company, from whom we have to bear much; when they are intoxicated, they knock everything down and want to do nothing but fight; the guardhouse is always full of them." See Francis P. Prucha, "An Army Private at Old Fort Snelling in 1849," in *Minnesota History*, 36:17 (March, 1958). The first to settle in what became St. Paul were Edward Phelan, John Hays, and William Evans; Virginia B. Kunz, *St. Paul: Saga of an American City*, 8 (Woodland Hills, Calif., 1977). On lumbering, see Catholic Archdiocese of St. Paul and Minneapolis, Parish Questionnaires, Stillwater (St. Michael) and Mora (St. Mary), 1948, originals in the Catholic Historical Society, St. Paul Seminary, microfilm in MHS, hereafter cited as Parish Questionnaires. For examples of Irish farmers from New Brunswick in Washington County, see Augustus B. Easton, *History of the St. Croix Valley*, 1:294, 373, 414, 436, 480 (Chicago, 1909).

[12] Here and below, see 1860 U.S. manuscript census schedules, tabulations in MEHP Papers. "Southeastern Minnesota" here consists of Blue Earth, Carver, Dakota, Dodge, Faribault, Fillmore, Freeborn, Goodhue, Houston, Le Sueur, Mower, Nicollet, Olmsted, Rice, Scott, Sibley, Steele, Wabasha, Waseca, and Winona counties. For more on these communities, see William J. Casey, *A History of Cedar Lake Township Scott County Minnesota* ([Jordan], 1939); Albrecht, *This Is Our Town*, 573–583; John D. O'Connell, *The Log Church in Derrynane* ([Shakopee, 1946]); John G. Berger, *A History of St. Brendan's Parish, the Village of Green Isle, and Minnesota's First Irish Settlement* (n.p., 1968); Sister Mary Zaccheus Ryan, *Irish Roots*, 9 (Faribault, 1980).

[13] Parish Questionnaires; 1860 U.S. manuscript census schedules, tabulations in MEHP Papers; Carol Walhovd and Fern Heller, *The Brownsville Story*, 58 (Winona, 1976); Joel Sobel, "The Urban Frontier Labor Force: Structure and Persistence in Three Nineteenth Century Minnesota Towns," 19, 136, 171, Ph.D. thesis, University of Minnesota, 1978. For its size, Hastings' Irish population was overrepresented in the unskilled labor force.

[14] U.S., *Census*, 1870, *Population*, 719–765; 1880, 808–854; 1890, 2:530–627; 1900, *Special Reports: Occupations*, 220–422. By 1890 the Irish populations of Minnesota, Wisconsin, Iowa, Kansas, Nebraska, North Dakota, South Dakota, and Oklahoma were nearly or more than 50% agricultural. In absolute terms, however, the numbers were small; agricultural workers in those states totaled 35,701, only 2% of the nation's Irish population.

The 1900 census for Minnesota contains an interesting aberration, showing 19.8% of the American- and foreign-born Irish as farm owners, while 29.7% were farm laborers, compared to a mere 4% of the first generation who were laborers in 1890. It may be that, as in Ireland, the parents held title to the land until very late in order to

control their children far into maturity. No other group in that year showed such a discrepancy.

[15] Henry A. Castle, "General James Shields," in *Minnesota Historical Collections*, 15:719 (St. Paul, 1915); Hagerty, *Meet Shieldsville*, 9.

[16] Hagerty, *Meet Shieldsville*, 10, 18; Kelly, *Catholic Immigrant Colonization Projects*, 199, 201; O'Leary, *Historical Sketch of Immaculate Conception*, 11; L. E. Swanberg, *Then & Now: A History of Rice County, Faribault & Communities*, 248, 261–268, 285 ([Faribault, 1976]); *Northfield News*, May 19, 1933, p. 3. On Kilkenny and Montgomery townships, see Mae Z. Mach, *Remember When: A History of Kilkenny, Minnesota* ([Kilkenny, 1979]); Montgomery Bicentennial Committee, *Montgomery: From the "Big Woods" to the Kolacky Capital, 1856–1976* (Montgomery, 1976).

[17] Castle, in *Minnesota Historical Collections*, 15:719, 721; Edward D. Neill, *History of Rice County*, 576 (Minneapolis, 1882).

[18] Agricultural Society, Century Farms Project, Application Forms, 1976, in Minnesota State Archives, MHS; Rockford Map Publishers, *Land Atlas & Plat Book Dakota County Minnesota, 1976*, 15, 23, 27, *Houston County Minnesota, 1977*, 19, *Le Sueur County Minnesota, 1963*, 3, 7, 14, *Rice County Minnesota, 1976*, 24, *Scott County Minnesota, 1977*, 9, 17, 20, *Sibley County Minnesota, 1978*, 29, 34 ([Rockford, Ill., various dates]); *The Shamrock* (supplement to the *Waseca Daily Journal*), March 12, 1975, pp. 1–5, March 9, 1980, p. 4; *St. Paul Dispatch*, March 16, p. 21, March 26, p. 10, 1979; *Catholic Bulletin* (St. Paul), April 18, 1980, p. 3.

[19] Frank B. Lamson, comp., *Condensed History of Meeker County 1855–1939*, 90 ([Litchfield, 1939]); Parish Questionnaires, Maple Lake, Birch Cooley, Bird Island, Fairfax, Franklin; Franklyn Curtiss-Wedge, *The History of Renville County Minnesota*, 2:1292 (Chicago, 1916); Edna M. Busch, *History of Stevens Co.*, 5 (n.p., 1976); Alexius Hoffman, "Natural History of Stearns County," 115, typed manuscript, 1934, in St. John's Abbey Archives, Collegeville; "Past to Present: A History of the Church of St. Donatus, Brooten, Minnesota," undated photocopy in Stearns County Historical Society, St. Cloud; Daisy E. Hughes, *Builders of Pope County*, 26 ([Glenwood], 1930); 1870 and 1880 U.S. manuscript census schedules, Westline Township, Redwood County, Birch Cooley Township, Renville County. See also Table 7.1.

[20] *St. Paul Daily Press*, September 28, 1862; *Duluth Minnesotian*, May 8, 1869; Irving Caswell, "Pioneer Days at Coon Creek," in *Anoka County Union*, January 1, 1941, p. 7; Vincent A. Yzermans, *The Mel and the Rose*, 299 (Melrose, 1972); U.S., *Census*, 1880, *Population*, 715. The 1880 U.S. manuscript census showed several crews at work in Lime, Leray, and Lake Crystal townships and Mankato in Blue Earth County. The ethnic breakdown for these 522 workers was 49% Swedish, 19% Norwegian, 16% Irish, 5% American, 4% German, and 4% other European. Another camp at Fond du Lac, St. Louis County, showed a similar composition. According to the *St. Paul Pioneer*, September 21, 1867, the crews worked in gangs divided by nationality. Payrolls in the Great Northern Railway Company Records, St. Paul and Pacific Railroad Company, Dept. 0103, MHS, support the observation. For examples of Irish working in railroad shops, see Parish Questionnaires, Albertville, Cass Lake, Melrose, Morris, St. Joseph, and Tracy. Irish contractors who started with railroad work included the Foley Brothers of St. Paul.

[21] Le Sueur Bicentennial Book Committee, *Le Sueur: Town on the River*, 179 ([Le Sueur], 1977); Parish Questionnaires; Charles Zopf, "The History of the Church of St. Louis, Paynesville, Minnesota," [1], (1964), copy in Central Minnesota Historical Center, St. Cloud State University.

[22] Yzermans, *The Mel and the Rose*, 302. While Latin was used for Masses, the congregation's native tongue was used for other functions — sermons, confessions, and religious instruction, for in-

stance. Parish Questionnaires give examples of churches that split in this manner. See, for example, Melrose (St. Boniface), Glencoe (St. George and Sts. Peter and Paul), Mankato (St. John the Baptist), Hastings (Guardian Angel). For a description of the difficulty in reuniting a split congregation in Caledonia, see *Minneapolis Tribune*, June 11, 1979, p. 2B. For more on conflict between Germans and the Irish clergy, see p. 145, below.

On the other hand, the Czechs and the Irish near Shieldsville showed some startling examples of co-operation. By St. Patrick's Day, 1938, as the Czech settlement grew onto formerly Irish land, the Czechs of Lonsdale produced a performance entitled "My Wild Irish Rose" — in Czech. In 1979 a visitor was casually directed across "McGinnis Most" (*most* being the Czech word for bridge). Hagerty, *Meet Shieldsville*, 169; conversation of author with Winston Chrislock, October 11, 1979, notes in MEHP Papers.

[23] James H. Moynihan, *The Life of Archbishop John Ireland*, 1–9, 13, 363 (New York, 1953); Robert D. Cross, *The Emergence of Liberal Catholicism in America*, 38–40 (Cambridge, Mass., 1967); Philip H. Des Marais, "John Ireland in American Politics, 1886–1906," 30, 53, 77, 79, master's thesis, Georgetown University, 1950; Sister Helen Angela Hurley, *On Good Ground: The Story of the Sisters of St. Joseph in St. Paul*, 199 (Minneapolis, 1951). On the Minnesota 5th Regiment and Ireland's service in it, see William B. McGrorty to Mrs. William B. McGrorty, June 6, July 8, December 2, 1862, March 15, April 23, 1863, in William B. McGrorty Papers, MHS. McGrorty was a captain who shared a tent with Ireland.

[24] Thomas D. O'Brien, "Dillon O'Brien," in *Acta et Dicta*, 6:38, 41 (October, 1941).

[25] James P. Shannon, *Catholic Colonization on the Western Frontier*, 24, 44, 54 (New Haven, Conn., 1957), compares the Minnesota colonies to other western colonization projects. Howard E. Egan, "Irish Immigration to Minnesota," in *Mid-America*, 12:133–166, 223–245 (October, 1929, January, 1930) covers the same material in a much less critical fashion. Despite its title, Egan's work does not deal with total Irish settlement. The only surviving copy of the Minnesota Irish Immigration Society's founding circular is enclosed in A. D. McSweeney to Ignatius Donnelly, October 11, 1864, in Ignatius Donnelly Papers, MHS.

The failures of this group were intensely frustrating to those who believed in colonization. A correspondent of the *Northwestern Chronicle*, who signed himself as "The emerald Gem" in the issue of January 1, 1870, stated the case for them all, fulminating, "It appears . . . that the gentlemen who assembled, were only beginning to think, of thinking, to set about, to try to ameliorate the condition of the Irish. . . . The Germans can be unanimous when the welfare of their people is at stake — the Swedes have a well concerted plan by which their poor are settled down on land, and are fast taking poss[ess]ions of the best portions of Minnesota, but, are our Irish people, through *deceit, supineness*, and want of energy to be deprived of every opportunity of bettering their condition both at home and abroad."

[26] Shannon, *Catholic Colonization*, 47, 54, 59.

[27] Table 7.1; Shannon, *Catholic Colonization*, 264.

[28] Shannon, *Catholic Colonization*, 52, 135, 151. For example, St. Mary's Church in Lake City was greatly depleted in 1878 when many parishioners left for lands in western Minnesota; Parish Questionnaires.

[29] Shannon, *Catholic Colonization*, 88–91, 264.

[30] Shannon, *Catholic Colonization*, 81, 108–114, 182; John Sweetman, "The Sweetman Catholic Colony of Currie, Minnesota: A Memoir," in *Acta et Dicta*, 3:61–65 (July, 1911); Alice E. Smith, "The Sweetman Irish Colony," in *Minnesota History*, 9:331–346 (December, 1929). The Adrian Colony Papers are in the St. Paul Seminary Archives; Sweetman's Irish-Catholic Colonization Company, Ltd., Papers are in MHS.

[31] Shannon, *Catholic Colonization*, 155–165; *St. Paul Globe*, April 4, 1881, March 16, 1902, p. 7; Richard Berg, *The History of St. Michael's Parish*, 15 ([St. Paul, 1966]); Works Projects Administration, Writers' Program, *The Bohemian Flats*, 13 (Minneapolis, [1941]). Connemara Patch is depicted in Sanborn Map and Publishing Co., *St. Paul 1885*, map 7 (New York, 1885). Some of the Connemaras also settled in Swede Hollow; Nels M. Hokanson, "I Remember St. Paul's Swede Hollow," in *Minnesota History*, 41:365, 369 (Winter, 1969).

[32] *St. Paul Pioneer Press*, December 22, 1880; Shannon, *Catholic Colonization*, 165; O'Brien, "Dillon O'Brien," and Humphrey Moynihan, "Archbishop Ireland's Colonies," in *Acta et Dicta*, 6:51, 222 (October, 1933, October, 1934).

[33] Kittson County Historical Society, *Our Northwest Corner: History of Kittson County, Minnesota*, 4, 495, 588 (Dallas, 1976); *Our Northland Diocese* (Crookston), Golden Jubilee edition, September, 1960, p. 13; Hiram M. Drache, *The Day of the Bonanza: A History of Bonanza Farming in the Red River Valley of the North*, 113 (Fargo, 1964); Knut Hamsun, "On the Prairie, A Sketch of the Red River Valley," in *Minnesota History*, 37:266 (September, 1961). About half of the 20 men in the bonanza farm crew Hamsun described were Irish.

[34] Joseph Stipanovich, "The Report of the Iron Range Historical-Cultural Survey," 168, 173, 205 (September, 1979), copy in MHS; John Sirjamaki, "The People of the Mesabi Range," in *Minnesota History*, 27:205, 208, 210 (September, 1946); George O. Virtue, *The Minnesota Iron Ranges*, 345, 353 (United States Bureau of Labor, *Bulletin*, no. 84 — Washington, D.C., 1909). For ties to Michigan see Parish Questionnaires for St. Joseph's, Chisholm; Sacred Heart Cathedral, Duluth; St. Patrick's, Eveleth; St. Rose of Lima, Proctor.

[35] *Eveleth News-Clarion*, July 31, 1947, sec. 1, p. 8; Clarke A. Chambers, "Social Welfare Policies and Programs on the Minnesota Iron Range, 1880–1930," 18–22, typed paper, 1963, copy in MHS.

[36] Minnesota, *Census, 1895*, 192; author's analysis of Sacred Heart Cathedral and St. Clement's parishes, from *Catholic Directory of Duluth and Almanac for 1892*, 1–58, 73–84 (Duluth, 1892), in MEHP Papers. No occupations were given for 107 males and 24 single females; only 186 married females were listed. Irish surnames were identified with the help of Edward MacLysaght, *A Guide to Irish Surnames* (Baltimore, 1964). A separate tabulation for 358 parishioners with Scottish and English names, some of whom were undoubtedly Irish, revealed a lower proportion of unskilled laborers (23.6%) and correspondingly higher proportions of white-collar workers (24.3%) among males and a higher proportion (32.1%) of office workers among females.

[37] Minnesota, *Census, 1895*, 192; *Duluth Minnesotian*, January 21, 1871; *Irish Standard* (Minneapolis), March 19, 1892, March 27, 1915, p. 8; *Duluth Daily News*, March 18, 1892.

[38] Interview of Michael Whalen by author, November 2, 1980, notes in MEHP Papers; *Duluth News Tribune*, March 18, 1978, p. 6A.

[39] U.S., *Census, 1910, Population*, 1:841; 1920, 2:959, 961.

[40] U.S., *Census, 1890, Population*, 1:607, 671. St. Paul's German-born population was more than twice as numerous as its Irish born in 1890.

[41] James K. Benson, "New England of the West: The Emergence of American Mind in Early St. Paul, Minnesota, 1849–1850," 60, master's thesis, University of Minnesota, 1970; Daniel J. Fisher to B. J. McQuaid, [1852], in *Acta et Dicta*, 1:45 (July, 1907).

[42] *Daily Minnesotian*, June 5, 1857; *Minnesota Republican*, March 19, 1858. For other notes of irregularity at the polls, see *Daily Minnesotian*, May 7, 1857, *Minnesota Weekly Times*, May 6, 1857.

[43] *Minnesota Democrat* (St. Paul), March 21, 1855; *St. Paul City Directory, 1856–1857*, 22, 23; Benson, "New England of the West," 77; *St. Paul Pioneer Press*, July 17, 1856.

[44] Cretin to Bishop Mathias Loras, March 10, 1853, quoted in M. M. Hoffman, *The Church Founders of the Northwest*, 333 (Milwaukee, 1937); Parish Questionnaires.

[45] Calvin Schmid, *Social Saga of Two Cities: An Ecological and Statistical Study*, chart 88 (Minneapolis, 1937); Minnesota Emergency Relief Administration, *Foreign Born Population Studies: St. Paul, Minnesota*, [29] (St. Paul, 1934); Minnesota, *Census, 1895*, 187, *1905*, 171. The second and third generations, many of whom may have moved to the cities from farming areas, disappear in these statistics. It is thus impossible to measure the size of the group that was identified by surname as Irish in later years.

[46] Kathleen O'Brien, "Irish in Minneapolis," [12–16], typed paper, 1973, copy in MEHP Papers; Herman E. Olson, *The Minneapolis Property and Housing Survey*, p. 1 of sections on Wards 1–13 (Minneapolis, 1934); Parish Questionnaires. Cahill (now Edina) and Corcoran townships were early Irish settlements in Hennepin County. The author wishes to acknowledge the helpful suggestions she received from Ms. O'Brien.

[47] U.S., *Census, 1880, Population*, 887; O'Brien, "Irish in Minneapolis," [26, 68]. O'Brien's figures are based on a random sample of households with Irish-born members. The 1880 census, which counted only Irish born, gave 31% of that population as laborers. For other figures on Minneapolis Irish occupations, see U.S., *Census, 1890, Population*, part 2, p. 694; *1900, Special Reports: Occupations*, 614–617. Those for 1880 and 1890 included only first generation; for 1900 total foreign stock was given, listing each sex separately. Some Minneapolis Swedes resented Irish domination of public jobs. See *Svenska Amerikanska Posten* (Minneapolis), February 7, May 9, December 26, 1893.

[48] Here and below, see U.S., *Census, 1880, Population*, 901; *1890*, part 2, p. 726; *1900, Special Reports: Occupations*, 710–715. The Butlers were the general contractors for Minnesota's state Capitol built in 1905, and the Shielys were subcontractors. See Neil B. Thompson, *Minnesota's State Capitol: The Art and Politics of a Public Building*, 31, 39 (St. Paul, 1974). On the Butler family, which became deeply involved in contracting and iron mining and also produced several lawyers and a U.S. Supreme Court justice, see *Northwest Life*, January 29, 1946, pp. 18–20; on other Irish contractors, see Joseph L. Shiely, "Giants with the Earth," 1, 10, 14, 16–19, typed manuscript, 1958, in MHS.

[49] [Alix J. Muller and Frank J. Meade], *History of the Police and Fire Departments of the Twin Cities*, St. Paul, 46, 58 (Minneapolis and St. Paul, [1899]); Kieran D. Flanagan, "Immigration, Assimilation, and Occupational Patterns of the St. Paul Irish," 246, 250, master's thesis, University of Minnesota, 1969. In Minneapolis early proportions of Irish policemen were lower, but by 1900 25% of the city's protective service workers were Irish; U.S., *Census, 1900, Special Reports: Occupations*, 614.

[50] Minneapolis Mayor A. C. Rand defended a similar system in his city in 1881, noting that two-thirds of the fines levied upon Minneapolis' disorderly houses went to support Bethany Home, a private charity. [Muller and Meade], *History of the Police and Fire Departments*, St. Paul, 62, Minneapolis, 47; *Souvenir Book of the Saint Paul Police Department*, [25] (St. Paul, 1904).

St. Paul's first Irish mayor was William Dawson, who served from 1878 to 1881; Warren Upham and Rose B. Dunlap, eds., *Minnesota Biographies, 1655–1912*, 167 (St. Paul, 1912). On Christopher O'Brien, see Thomas D. O'Brien, *There Were Four of Us or, Was It Five*, 19 (St. Paul, 1936); *St. Paul Daily News*, January 10, 1933, p. 2.

[51] Wittke, *Irish in America*, 233; William V. Shannon, *The American Irish*, 11 (New York, 1963); U.S., *Census, 1880, Population*, 901, and *Special Reports: Occupations*, 710–715. On the O'Brien family, see O'Brien, *There Were Four of Us*.

[52] Horace S. Merrill, "Ignatius Donnelly, James J. Hill, and Cleveland Administration Patronage," in *Mississippi Valley Historical Review*, 39:508, 515 (December, 1952); *St. Paul Pioneer Press*, May 2, 1894; Upham and Dunlap, eds., *Minnesota Biographies*, 535; Horace S. Merrill, *Bourbon Democracy of the Middle West*, 2 (Baton Rouge, 1953). On Murray, see Thomas M. Newson, *Pen Pictures of St. Paul*, 149 (St. Paul, 1886; on Kelly, see *St. Paul Pioneer Press*, October 24, 1900, p. 1; on Doran, see *Belle Plaine Herald*, February 25, 1915, p. 1. On the Irish in Democratic machine politics, see McCaffrey, *Irish Diaspora*, 139–151; Elmer E. Cornwell, "Bosses, Machines, and Ethnic Groups," in American Academy of Political and Social Sciences, *Annals*, 353:27–39 (May, 1964); Terry N. Clark, "The Irish Ethnic and the Spirit of Patronage," in *Ethnicity*, 2:305–359 (1975).

[53] *St. Paul Pioneer Press*, August 11, 1930, p. 1, October 18, 1953 (on aperture card 10734, reference room, St. Paul Public Library); *St. Paul Daily News*, January 9, p. 1; 10, p. 1; 11, p. 7; 12, p. 5; 13, p. 2; 22, sec. 1, p. 5 — all 1933; *St. Paul Dispatch*, July 4, 1924, p. 1; W. B. Hennessy, *Past and Present of St. Paul, Minnesota*, 579, 753 (Chicago, 1909). The *Daily News* articles were part of "The Life of Dick O'Connor," by George C. Rogers, printed serially from January 9 to February 2, 1933.

[54] Nate N. Bromberg, "St. Paul and the Federal Building in the Twenties and Thirties," in Eileen Michels, *A Landmark Reclaimed*, 52, 58 ([St. Paul?], 1977); Jim Toland, *The Dillinger Days*, 42 (New York, 1963); Kunz, *St. Paul*, 132. The kidnapings in 1933 and 1934 of William Hamm, Jr., and Edward Bremer, whose families had originally supported the O'Connor system, were the most dramatic signals of the breakdown. Powerful St. Paulites, fearing they might be the next victims, called in help from Washington. An exposé of the collapsing system was printed in the *St. Paul Daily News*, June 24 to July 20, 1935.

[55] On Donnelly, see Martin Ridge, *Ignatius Donnelly: The Portrait of a Politician* (Chicago, 1962). For an example of Irish orations, see *The Irish-American Banquet to the Earl of Aberdeen*, 21–31 ([St. Paul], 1887), copy in MHS.

[56] On Manahan, see James Manahan, *Trials of a Lawyer* ([St. Paul, 1933]); Carl H. Chrislock, *The Progressive Era in Minnesota, 1899–1918*, 19, 51, 149 (St. Paul, 1971). Manahan's papers, containing personal, professional, and political correspondence, are in MHS. Many letters demonstrate the interconnections among St. Paul's Irish politicians.

[57] Eugene P. Willging and Herta Hatzfeld, *Catholic Serials of the Nineteenth Century in the United States: A Descriptive Bibliography and Union List*, 24, 41–43 (2nd series, part 1 — Washington, D.C., 1959). Other Irish Catholic papers printed in Minnesota were the *Irish Times* (St. Paul, 1872–?), *Western Times* (St. Paul, 1872–74), *Celtic World* (Minneapolis, 1881–82), and *National Hibernian* (St. Paul, 1892–95). MHS has some issues of all but the last of these.

[58] William D'Arcy, *The Fenian Movement in the United States: 1858–1886*, 15 (Washington, D.C., 1947); Joseph K. Howard, *Strange Empire: A Narrative of the Northwest*, 217–221 (New York, 1952); *St. Paul Press*, June 7, 1866; John P. Pritchett, "The Origin of the So-Called Fenian Raid on Manitoba in 1871," in *Canadian Historical Review*, 10:32–42 (March, 1929); *St. Paul Pioneer*, October 12, 1871; *St. Paul Globe*, November 18, 1871, December 7, 1902, p. 24. For newspaper reaction to the rumors, see *Minneapolis Tribune*, May 19, 1870; *St. Paul Dispatch*, May 28, 1870; *St. Cloud Journal*, June 16, 1870.

[59] *St. Paul Pioneer Press*, August 3, 1877.

[60] *St. Paul Globe*, February 27, 1880; *Northwestern Chronicle*, February 21, 28, 1880. Bishop Grace decreed that the collections from the services of February 29, 1880, were to be sent for Irish relief. A benefit in Stillwater on March 13 brought pledges of $800; Minneapolis Irish canceled their St. Patrick's Day parade "on

account of the distress across the water." See *St. Paul Dispatch*, February 27, 1880; *St. Paul Globe*, March 13, 1880; *Minneapolis Tribune*, March 6, 1880. Records of pledges from Irish communities in southern Minnesota are printed in *Northwestern Chronicle*, February 28, 1880. See also William G. Van Horn and the Irish National Land League to S. Freidlander, July 9, 1880, MHS, signed by Parnell and six other Land League officials.

[61] *Northwestern Chronicle*, November 22, 1883; *St. Paul Daily Pioneer*, January 11, 1874; *Stillwater Gazette*, January 20, 1875; *St. Paul Globe*, March 3, 1878, June 1, 1880.

[62] Ancient Order of Hibernians and Ladies Auxiliary of America in Minnesota, *Official Souvenir Program, Irish and Irish-American Centennial Celebration Day for Minnesota*, [21, 27] (St. Paul, 1949), copy in MHS; interview of Leah Curtin by author, January 24, 1980, notes in MEHP Papers. A Minnesotan, James J. Regan, served as national president of the AOH from 1908 to 1914.

[63] James M. Reardon, "The Catholic Total Abstinence Movement in Minnesota," in *Acta et Dicta*, 2:46, 48 (July, 1909); *Minneapolis Tribune*, September 26, 1918, p. 8; Charles J. Carmody, "Rechabites in Purple: A History of the Catholic Temperance Movement in the Northwest," 60, master's thesis, 1953, St. Paul Seminary.

[64] Reardon, in *Acta et Dicta*, 2:55, 85; Carmody, "Rechabites in Purple," 171; *St. Paul Pioneer Press*, August 2, 1882. Ireland lectured on temperance across the United States, earning for himself the title "Father Mathew of the Northwest." For examples of his temperance rhetoric, see *St. Paul Pioneer*, April 23, 1869, August 3, 1882; "Intemperance and Law," in John Ireland, *The Church and Modern Society*, 1:259–308 (St. Paul, 1904).

[65] Carmody, "Rechabites in Purple," 99, 134, 144, 162; Reardon, in *Acta et Dicta*, 2:58, 71, 83, 85, 91.

[66] Sister Joan Bland, *Hibernian Crusade: The Story of the Catholic Total Abstinence Union of America*, 8 (Washington, D.C., 1951); Reardon, in *Acta et Dicta*, 2:50; William W. Folwell, *A History of Minnesota*, 3:175, 178 (Reprint ed., St. Paul, 1969); Carmody, "Rechabites in Purple," 120, 157, 174; *Minneapolis Tribune*, September 26, 1918, p. 7; "The Catholic Church and the Saloon," in Ireland, *Church and Modern Society*, 1:309–325.

[67] *St. Paul Pioneer Press*, August 4, 1882. For other evaluations, see Reardon, in *Acta et Dicta*, 2:85, 92; Carmody, "Rechabites in Purple," 155; Folwell, *Minnesota*, 2:98 (Reprint ed., St. Paul, 1961); *St. Paul Daily Press*, May 2, 1873. All are laudatory.

[68] Cross, *Emergence of Liberal Catholicism*, 88–94; William Shannon, *American Irish*, 136. For an example of Ireland's rhetoric on Americanization, see "American Citizenship," in Ireland, *Church and Modern Society*, 1:183–214.

[69] Colman J. Barry, *The Catholic Church and German Americans*, 118 (Milwaukee, 1953); Daniel P. O'Neill, "St. Paul Priests, 1851–1930: Recruitment, Formation, and Mobility," 138, Ph.D. thesis, University of Minnesota, 1979.

[70] Thomas T. McAvoy, *A History of the Catholic Church in the United States*, 270–272 (Notre Dame, 1969); Emmet Larkin, "The Devotional Revolution in Ireland, 1850–75," in *American Historical Review*, 77:644 (June, 1972); Aloysius J. Wycislo, "The Polish Catholic Immigrant," Colman J. Barry, "The German Catholic Immigrant," and James Shannon, "The Irish Catholic Immigrant" — all in Thomas T. McAvoy, *Roman Catholicism and the American Way of Life*, 181, 191, 208 (Notre Dame, 1960). For a vivid example of one such conflict, see correspondence in Parish Questionnaires for St. Francis de Sales Church, St. Paul.

[71] *Minnesota Democrat*, March 22, 1854. For the first notice of a St. Patrick's Day celebration in St. Paul, see *St. Paul Pioneer*, March 20, 1851.

[72] See, for example, *Northwestern Chronicle*, March 21, 1868, March 20, 1869; *St. Paul Daily Press*, March 19, 1861; *St. Paul Globe*, March 18, 1880. On Ireland's speeches, see Charles J. O'Fahey, "John Ireland's Rhetorical Vision of the Irish in America," 44–47, master's thesis, University of Minnesota, 1973, and "Reflections on the St. Patrick's Day Orations of John Ireland," in *Ethnicity*, 2:249–254 (1975).

[73] *Northwestern Chronicle*, March 13, 1869; *St. Paul Daily Globe*, March 17, 1880.

[74] *St. Paul Pioneer and Democrat*, March 20, 1860.

[75] *Northwestern Chronicle*, March 23, 1867, March 13, 1875; *Irish Standard*, March 23, 1901, p. 1; *Winona Independent*, March 17, 1909, p. 4.

[76] *Irish Standard*, March 21, 1903, p. 5; *St. Paul City Directory, 1920*, 661, *1923*, 597; *St. Paul Dispatch*, August 30, 1922, p. 1. Examples of Irish groups mentioned in the *St. Paul Pioneer Press* were the Irish Benevolent Association of St. Paul (March 12, 1910, p. 12), Shamrock Club (March 17, 1911, p. 7), Minneapolis Sinn Fein Club (May 22, 1911, p. 8), Loyal Sons of Erin (March 18, 1932, p. 1), and Friendly Sons of St. Patrick (September 4, 1949, sec. 1, p. 3).

[77] *St. Paul Pioneer Press*, March 12, 1910, p. 12; interview of John Curtin by author, November 1, 1980, notes in MEHP Papers. For an example of a bond in the Irish Republic, see Miscellaneous Printed Materials, William Mahoney Papers, MHS. For examples of visiting Irish nationalist speakers, see *St. Paul Pioneer Press*, May 23, 1911, p. 10; *Minneapolis Journal*, March 3, 1918, p. 10.

[78] *St. Paul Pioneer Press*, March 17, 1920, p. 6; "Mayors of St. Paul," reference aid, MHS library.

[79] Millard L. Gieske, *Minnesota Farmer-Laborism: The Third-Party Alternative*, 224, 287, 291, 296, 325 (Minneapolis, 1979).

[80] John Curtin interview, November 1, 1980; Alan Altshuler, *A Report on Politics in St. Paul*, part 1, p. 5 (Cambridge, Mass., 1959).

[81] Baymiller, in *Twin Cities*, March, 1979, p. 35; interview of Charles McCafferty by author, October 30, 1980, notes in MEHP Papers; Whalen interview, November 2, 1980. For examples of some LMIRC and MINC activities, see *Minneapolis Tribune*, November 1, 1978, p. 15A, June 5, 1979, p. 6A; *Minnesota Daily* (Minneapolis), November 6, 1978, p. 1.

[82] Author's interviews of John Curtin, November 1, 1980, Leah Curtin, January 24, November 5, 1980, Donald H. Lamm, November 4, 1980, Sister Marie Clotilde, November 4, 1980, and Mary Hedlund, November 2, 1980 — notes in MEHP Papers. For examples of AOH and Comhaltus activities, see *St. Paul Pioneer Press*, April 15, 1979, sec. 3, p. 15; *Minnesota Daily*, October 20, 1978, p. 21AE.

[83] J. Herrnsohn, "The 'Professional' Irish," in *Twin Citian*, August, 1968, p. 15; Dixie Berg, "The Irish Way," in *Mpls./St. Paul*, March, 1979, p. 100; interview of Eoin McKiernan by author, November 4, 1980, notes in MEHP Papers. Irish Books and Media, founded by McKiernan in 1970, was one of two major distributors of Irish books in the U.S. in 1980; *Publisher's Weekly*, January 23, 1981, p. 95.

Almost all of the organizations named above took part in the First Annual Minnesota Irish Festival, an exposition held at the St. Paul Civic Center on November 23, 1980, that drew 5,000 people, many from southeastern Minnesota.

[84] Sam Dillon, "Pumping Irish in St. Paul," in *Sweet Potato* (Minneapolis), May, 1980, p. 13; Hedlund interview, November 2, 1980; interview of Peg Birse by author, November 20, 1980, notes in MEHP Papers.

[85] Interview of Msgr. Ambrose Hayden by author, March 20, 1980, notes in MEHP Papers; *St. Paul Area Downtowner*, March 6, 1980, p. 1; Baymiller, in *Twin Cities*, March, 1979, p. 34; observations of the author, who was present at the event.

[86] "Irish Immigrants in Minnesota," Minnesota Public Radio broadcast, March 17, 1979, tape in MHS.

CHAPTER 8

The Germans

Hildegard Binder Johnson

GERMAN-SPEAKING PEOPLES constituted the largest single foreign-born group in Minnesota from 1860 until 1905 when the Swedes took over first place. To outnumber those of German stock as recently as 1970, however, the figures for Swedes and Norwegians must be combined. Yet Minnesota has come to be regarded as a Scandinavian state, while Wisconsin, its neighbor to the east, is usually thought of as German.[1]

The term "German" presents difficult problems of definition, for the shifting boundaries of Germany and the widespread homelands of German-speaking peoples preclude a simple areal identification. Prussia finally succeeded in uniting the German states as a nation when under Otto von Bismarck it defeated France in 1870–71 (see Map 8.1). In the 20th century World Wars I and II brought drastic boundary changes in Bismarck's Second and Hitler's Third German Reich. So who were the Germans? For the purposes of this study, Germans will be considered any of those people who spoke different but mutually intelligible dialects and, if literate, read High German in a conglomerate of countries in central Europe. At various times they have included not only the two modern German states but also Luxembourg, the Alsace, parts of Switzerland and Poland, Austria, the rimland of Bohemia, local regions in Hungary, Yugoslavia, and other southeastern European countries, as well as the Black Sea and central Volga regions in European Russia. On some of these areas, additional information may be found in other chapters of this book.[2]

It should be apparent from this listing that Germans are not simple to define. Moreover their sheer numbers present a further problem, for German-speaking people contributed the second greatest number of immigrants to the United States over a span of more than three centuries. Outranked only by the British, they spread from the Atlantic seaboard to the Pacific, beginning with the 1683 settlement of Germantown near Philadelphia. Increased immigration in the 18th century gave rise to the only cohesive German cultural region of the United States in nearby southeastern Pennsylvania. From there German settlements extended south to the frontier of Georgia and north to the Mohawk Valley of New York.[3]

Between 1820 and 1900 at least 5,000,000 German immigrants arrived in the United States; they settled in Ohio, Texas, Missouri, Illinois, Wisconsin, and Minnesota, giving such cities as Cincinnati, Milwaukee, St. Louis, and early St. Paul a distinctly German atmosphere. By far the greatest number settled in the northeastern industrial region and in the Middle West, including Missouri. For the Germans in the westward movement during the first decades of Minnesota settlement, the state's location made it a terminal point. To reach it they bypassed completely, or stopped only temporarily to enjoy, opportunities afforded them by the presence of earlier countrymen already established along the routes to the Northwest.

Aside from their sheer numbers, Germans stand out among immigrant groups for their religious diversity. Not only were they divided between Catholics and Protestants, they also displayed an affinity for dissent that resulted in the formation of many sects which fully matured on American soil. Religious division was exacerbated in the homeland by its regional identification — Catholicism with southern Germany and the Rhineland, and Protestantism with Germany north and east of the Rhine-Main line. After 1555 one could assume a Bavarian to be Catholic, for example, and a Saxonian to be Lutheran. But one could not expect a German-speaking immigrant to be either as consistently Protestant as the Scandinavians or as reliably Catholic as the Polish and Irish. There were also articulate groups of German freethinkers in America in the last half of the 19th century, as well as many Jewish immigrants associated with German culture and language. In the 1930s and after World War II German Jews contributed another numerically small but culturally very special segment to American life.[4]

In the complexity and size of German immigration, Minnesota may be said to mirror the general picture in the United States. Its Germans were drawn not only from a wide spectrum of religious affiliations but also from all walks of life. They were not overwhelmingly of rural backgrounds as were the Irish, for example, and they were usually literate. It is difficult to ascertain the true reasons for the emigration of any large population. In each case it was a personal decision, often prompted by rarely revealed incidental experiences. Nevertheless, like most other migrants, the Germans' motives were largely economic, although in general they were better off economically than many northern Europeans. Some small groups, who left for political or religious reasons, brought a particular zest, if not a feeling of outright superiority, to the challenges of the new country.[5]

Map 8.1. Historic Principalities of German Emigration to Minnesota

Many aspects of the story of Minnesota's Germans can be encountered elsewhere, but a few are unique to the state — for instance, the persistence of the original German core region in the Minnesota Valley and the concentration of Catholic Germans in Stearns County (see Maps 8.2, 8.3, 8.4).

Minnesota's Germans shared the 20th-century traumas of two world wars with their homeland. But those in Minnesota during World War I were especially affected by the near-dictatorial tactics and abuse of the Minnesota Commission of Public Safety (see Introduction). After World War II the German state was divided by its former enemies into the Federal Republic of Germany and the German Democratic

Republic, popularly called West and East Germany, separated by the Iron Curtain. A mass exodus of German-speaking peoples took place from many regions east of the Iron Curtain. Today Americans of German background have to deal with at least two very different homelands when they attempt to trace their family trees or to visit ancestral places. Towns and villages from which grandparents emigrated are no longer to be found on modern maps, having been given new names in Poland, Czechoslovakia, Yugoslavia, and Russia.

While the numbers of Germans emigrating to Minnesota are roughly known, their points of origin are less clear cut. In 1850 Minnesota Territory had 6,077 inhabitants, 32.5% of

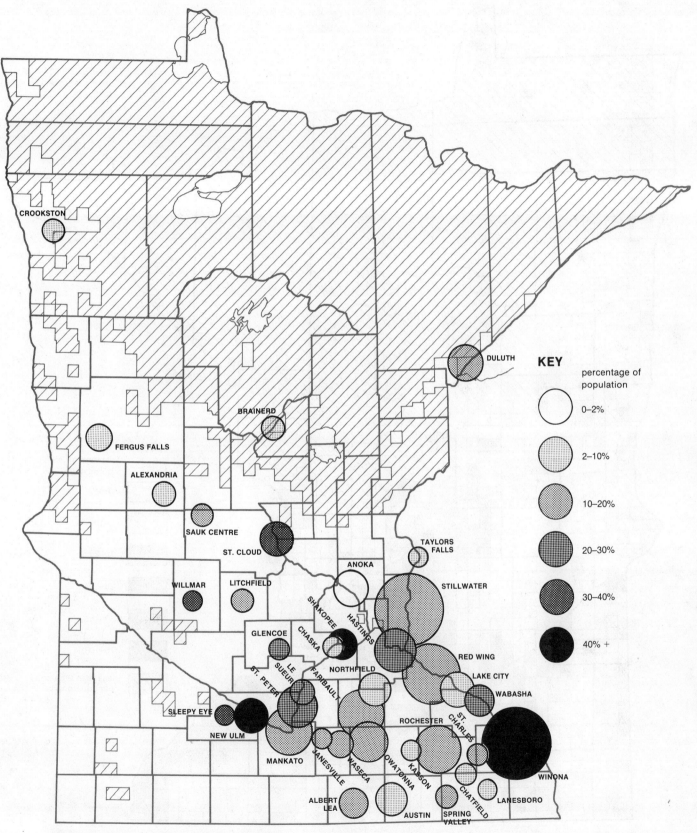

KEY

percentage of
population

0–2%

2–10%

10–20%

20–30%

30–40%

40% +

CROOKSTON

DULUTH

BRAINERD

FERGUS FALLS

ALEXANDRIA

SAUK CENTRE

ST. CLOUD

TAYLORS
FALLS

ANOKA

WILLMAR

LITCHFIELD

STILLWATER

SHAKOPEE

HASTINGS

GLENCOE

CHASKA

RED WING

ST. PETER

LE
SUEUR

FARIBAULT

NORTHFIELD

LAKE CITY

WABASHA

SLEEPY EYE

NEW ULM

ROCHESTER

ST.
CHARLES

WINONA

MANKATO

JANESVILLE

WASECA

OWATONNA

KASSON

ALBERT
LEA

AUSTIN

SPRING
VALLEY

CHATFIELD

LANESBORO

Map 8.2. Germans in Minnesota Towns, 1880

Map shows towns over 1,000 population in 1880.   The size of the circles is proportional to the population.

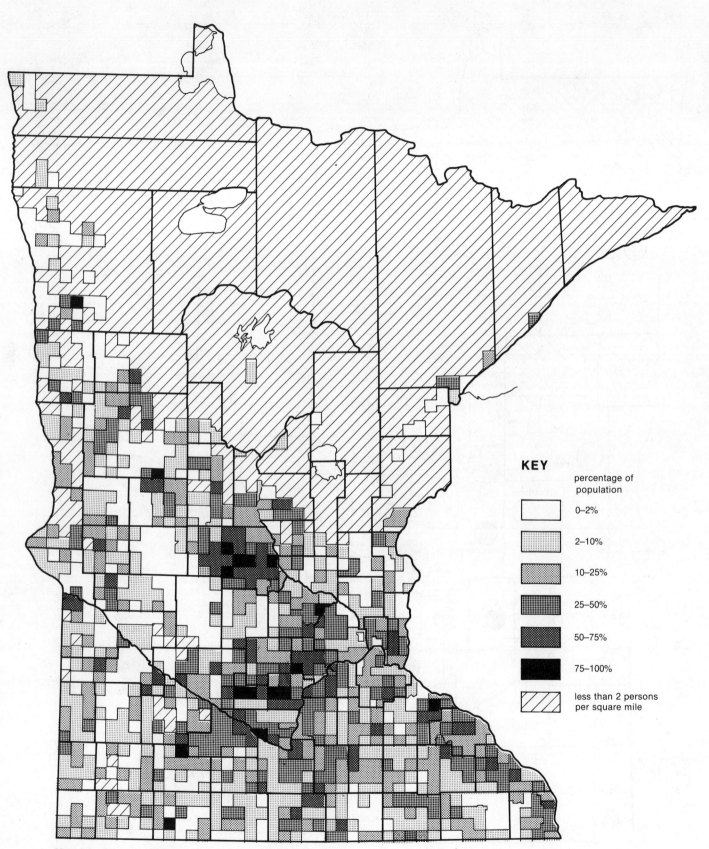

KEY

percentage of
population

0–2%

2–10%

10–25%

25–50%

50–75%

75–100%

less than 2 persons
per square mile

Map 8.3. Germans in Minnesota Rural Areas, 1880

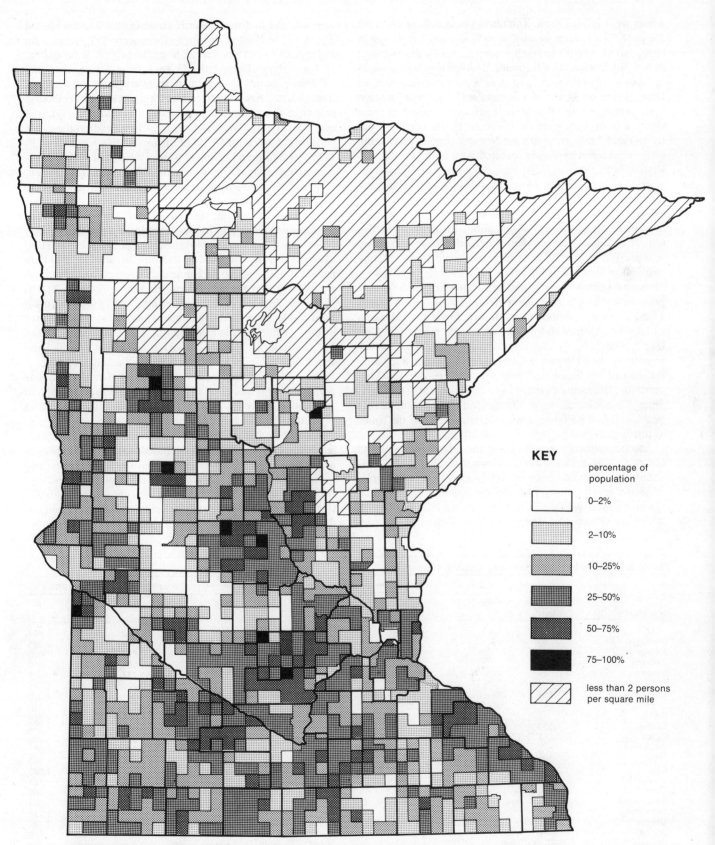

Map 8.4. Germans in Minnesota Rural Areas, 1905

KEY

percentage of
population

0–2%

2–10%

10–25%

25–50%

50–75%

75–100%

less than 2 persons
per square mile

whom were foreign born. The territorial census of 1849 and the published federal census of 1850 did not list places of birth, but the 1850 manuscript census, which did, showed that of 161 foreign-born Germans, 24 lived in Blue Earth, 23 in Dakota, 27 in Ramsey, and 69 in Washington counties. In 1860, 58,728 or 34.1% of the state's 172,023 were foreign born. Among them, 15,000 to 19,000 (see Table 8.1) were German born, compared to 11,000 to 13,000 persons from Ireland and 7,000 to 9,000 from Norway. But a study of the early manuscript censuses revealed why no figure for persons born in Germany can be quite precise. The assistant marshal of each county went from dwelling to dwelling and listed the state or country of birth of each resident as he heard it. Thus a Bavarian may be recorded as having been born in Bevaria, Bayern, Biron, Bion, Bien, Baen, or Byron. A Saxonian, whose dialect extended beyond Saxony into pre-World War II Prussia, pronounced the diphthong "eu" (as in *Deutsch* or Freud) as "ei" (as in *Reich* or prize). Thus the census taker's phonetic rendering of Saxonian pronunciation indicated that a group of Prussians in Wards 1 and 2 of St. Anthony came from "Prison." In Dakota County one German-born resident was rechristened "Gotleap" (Gottlieb) by the enumerator. Numerous "new" hometowns and regions in Germany were invented by well-intentioned but linguistically inept census recorders — Detmert for Detmold, perhaps, and Deering for Thuringia. Since the adding clerks in Washington, D.C., could hardly be expected to be familiar with German dialects, the totals as attributed must be regarded with suspicion.[6]

Another difficulty in pinpointing the origins of Minnesota Germans was created by the changing political divisions within the fatherland between 1860 and 1870. For example, in 1860 Carver County had already acquired a substantial German population (see Table 8.1). (Among its residents was Wendelin Grimm, an immigrant from Külsheim who de-

veloped "the first winter-hardy strain of alfalfa in the United States.")[7] In Benton Township there were 135 people from Prussia, 43 from Hanover, 26 from Bavaria, 18 from Baden, 16 from Hesse-Darmstadt, 11 each from Switzerland and "France" (doubtless German speakers from Alsace), six from Saxony, five each from Mecklenburg and Luxembourg, two each from Hesse and Brunswick (*Braunschweig*), and one from Austria. With their native-born children these 444 people accounted for 83.1% of the township's population. In 1870 this figure had dropped to 66.5%. By then of 452 foreign-born Germans, 348 were from Prussia, 20 from Baden, 19 from France, 18 from Bavaria, 12 from Württemberg, 10 from Switzerland, nine from Saxony, five from Hesse, four from Hesse-Darmstadt, three from Mecklenburg, two each from Saxe-Weimer and Lippe-Detmold, and one from Tyrol. None was listed from Hanover (although many of the Hanoverians of 1860 still lived in Benton), because in 1870 they named Prussia, which had annexed Hanover, as their country of birth. On the other hand, in Young America Township, also located in Carver County, 113 of 346 German-born residents in 1870 still named Hanover as their country of birth, while 161 claimed Prussia. In Scott County 111 of 247 Germans in Helena Township and 84 ot 354 in Sand Creek Township gave "Rhine" as their country of birth in 1870 — meaning, one may assume, Rhineland, which was politically Prussia. Thus it is obvious that any attempt to summarize Germans by the geographical origins given in the census cannot be very meaningful.[8]

A count by the writer, in which understatement was preferred in all doubtful cases, concluded that every fifth person in Minnesota in 1870 was of German stock. The most impressive increase of German-born residents occurred between 1880 and 1885. At the turn of the century, with 116,973 German born, they were still the leading single nationality in the state. By 1905, when they dropped to second place be-

Table 8.1. Germans in Minnesota by County, 1860–1970

County	1860 foreign born	1860 foreign mixed	1870 fb	1880 fb	1880 fm	1900 fb	1905 fb	1905 fm	1930 fb	1930 fm	1970 fb	1970 fm
Aitkin				5		160	217	607	243	872	31	444
Anoka	55	36	96	167	197	369	336	1,155	326	1,305	369	2,285
Becker				180	240	777**	776	2,289	449	1,924	38	920
Beltrami						209	322	1,011	236	1,053	40	519
Benton	17	11	78	267	299	1,112	1,420	4,404	631	2,744	64	973
Big Stone				95	162	396	467	1,490	269	1,228	64	621
Blue Earth	464	275	1,579	2,538	3,365	3,599	3,028	7,562	1,394	5,822	214	2,429
Brown	847	339	1,396	2,204	2,411	3,326	3,374	9,997	1,430	5,859	152	2,443
Carlton	8	3	11	40	36	269	353	824	184	830	11	458
Carver	1,530	708	3,108	3,407	4,526	3,198	2,736	9,182	947	4,473	90	1,364
Cass	1		1	5	14	169	244	764	185	959	40	512
Chippewa			11	107	129	848	794	2,488	556	2,059	81	1,007
Chisago	100	34	202	317	332	390	351	1,088	133	596	52	483
Clay			5	203	255	687	738	1,950	383	1,561	46	1,003
Clearwater							46	168	62	310		161
Cook						3	4	25	10	39		32
Cottonwood			6	256	224	645	734	2,339	411	1,740	93	1,004
Crow Wing	1		1	108	44	610	724	2,172	359	1,776	56	1,199
Dakota	190	83	1,263	1,737	2,173	2,621	2,699	7,607	1,363	5,278	522	3,788
Dodge	15	7	191	353	553	552	522	1,591	244	964	29	446
Douglas			257	576	662	907	890	2,890	469	2,028	6	1,079
Faribault	13	6	660	1,080	1,306	1,942	1,647	5,469	731	3,198	38	1,372
Fillmore	83	23	577	901	1,114	920	807	2,533	390	1,695	50	670
Freeborn	65	47	240	686	762	686	616	1,891	334	1,813	65	887

Table 8.1. Germans in Minnesota by County, 1860–1970 (*continued*)

County	1860 foreign born	1860 foreign mixed	1870 fb	1880 fb	1880 fm	1900 fb	1905 fb	1905 fm	1930 fb	1930 fm	1970 fb	1970 fm
Goodhue	472	253	1,564	2,330	2,603	1,926	1,757	5,259	795	3,927	124	1,475
Grant			1	61	102	192	260	924	159	896	14	345
Hennepin	1,180	621	2,906	4,418	6,082	9,287	10,987	30,696	6,958	34,971	2,897	19,945
Minneapolis				2,334		7,335	9,074	24,638	5,969	29,570	1,508	10,839
Houston	549	270	1,261	1,319	1,628	1,269	1,089	3,536	347	1,937	20	702
Hubbard						267	333	885	183	729	39	352
Isanti	23	4	71	193	166	323	330	1,008	204	647	66	459
Itasca				1		74	254	554	183	1,023	82	811
Jackson	5	5	47	201	227	1,426	1,317	4,034	676	2,870	55	1,087
Kanabec				7	10	136	193	600	160	638	40	345
Kandiyohi*	3	1	13	139	75	314	348	1,124	255	1,257	63	837
Kittson				12	30	55	116	387	60	282		91
Koochiching									196	656	49	289
Lac qui Parle			5	281	301	936	951	2,783	442	1,803	12	679
Lake	25	16	10	19	29	72	87	231	40	171	19	212
Lake of the Woods									57	182	20	98
Le Sueur	704	409	1,288	1,561	2,196	1,743	1,537	4,862	555	2,786	67	891
Lincoln				131	215	488	533	1,618	258	1,166	38	403
Lyon				141	119	523	645	2,032	334	1,608	42	882
McLeod	145	38	774	1,984	2,249	2,588	2,228	7,766	1,157	4,914	95	1,999
Mahnomen	4								93	515	37	266
Marshall				28	27	306	325	827	150	556	20	147
Martin			61	179	265	1,728	1,664	5,550	960	4,184	146	1,835
Meeker	32	6	162	489	582	781	752	2,559	356	1,995	61	810
Mille Lacs	20	8	18	27	35	358	391	996	291	1,150	72	593
Morrison			173	617	837	1,773	2,439	7,452	970	4,131	108	1,793
Mower	77	42	300	976	1,088	1,263	1,157	3,801	633	3,152	72	1,467
Murray	1			155	123	783	698	2,448	376	1,761	54	721
Nicollet	702	251	1,489	1,783	2,390	1,497	1,237	4,240	551	2,880	134	1,148
Nobles		2		184	256	1,377	1,311	4,390	835	3,725	103	2,245
Norman						405	416	1,451	185	830	24	349
Olmsted	205	105	1,025	1,432	1,660	1,691	1,477	4,326	823	4,496	288	2,674
Otter Tail	10	1	118	1,158	1,381	2,833	2,666	8,602	1,486	6,003	249	2,592
Pennington									77	428	31	285
Pine	28	7	34	85	75	547	782	2,029	397	1,433	46	722
Pipestone				65	117	683	721	2,023	472	1,867	125	841
Polk	11	4		317	419	679	845	2,848	349	1,515	39	721
Pope			31	43	74	150	206	689	115	569	37	326
Ramsey	1,851	860	3,644	5,420	6,751	13,772	16,672	41,024	8,033	32,048	1,740	14,609
St. Paul				4,956		12,935	15,868	38,815	7,478	30,160	1,333	11,217
Red Lake						286	371	1,305	102	445	15	105
Redwood			62	401	433	1,686	1,897	6,261	843	4,041	50	1,465
Renville	13	2	248	1,021	1,286	2,282	2,230	7,209	936	4,318	56	1,695
Rice	455	208	1,017	1,352	1,814	1,805	1,585	4,952	828	3,788	84	1,424
Rock			1	111	155	814	882	2,342	548	1,809	80	846
Roseau						55	246	787	121	477	9	141
St. Louis	17	3	327	397	388	2,167	2,672	7,605	1,563	6,667	498	3,281
Duluth						1,685	1,902	5,213	1,070	4,303	358	1,769
Scott	870	572	1,690	2,105	3,051	1,959	1,706	5,932	579	2,711	61	1,272
Sherburne	14	12	19	84	132	263	312	1,001	199	915	7	544
Sibley	822	368	1,616	2,340	2,888	2,634	2,280	7,676	829	4,425	43	1,450
Stearns	1,352	868	3,053	4,138	6,352	5,980	5,876	20,998	2,781	14,309	294	5,327
Steele	156	64	655	1,002	1,272	1,359	1,285	3,599	538	2,380	55	1,023
Stevens			8	187	229	532	635	2,181	325	1,607	42	564
Swift				368	385	780	613	1,968	315	1,444	62	718
Todd	40	3	208	545	650	1,419	1,557	4,711	885	3,003	71	1,609
Traverse				107	116	499	534	1,967	323	1,376	62	642
Wabasha	530	263	1,573	2,033	2,456	2,370	2,174	7,055	884	3,963	124	1,406
Wadena				56	87	483	490	1,582	274	1,143	33	572
Waseca	159	92	658	1,423	1,814	1,781	1,449	4,578	682	2,938	77	1,195
Washington	687	315	1,382	1,914	2,260	2,412	2,171	5,830	881	3,479	196	2,080
Watonwan				123	223	295	719	673	2,210	341	1,568	31	658
Wilkin			8	93	109	504	567	2,078	263	1,314	9	486
Winona	907	459	3,230	4,309	5,410	4,323	4,015	12,141	1,642	6,822	200	2,671
Wright	470	189	796	1,744	2,288	2,247	2,218	6,916	958	4,078	79	1,766
Yellow Medicine				196	215	974	861	3,166	443	2,045	84	756
Total	15,928	7,891	41,353	67,137	85,001	116,973	119,868	361,000	59,993	266,262	11,601	125,841
Published census figures	(18,400)		(41,364)	(66,592)		(117,007)	(119,868)	(361,099)	(59,993)	(267,792)	(11,601)	(125,841)

Source: See Appendix

*In 1870 part of present Kandiyohi County was named Monongalia; it had 11 German-born residents.

**In 1900 White Earth Reservation was counted with 34 German-born persons.

hind the Swedes, many people of German descent in the third generation could no longer be traced through the census; the nativity of grandparents was never recorded there.[9]

Travel Routes

After the Napoleonic Wars (1796–1815), bad harvests and high food prices in Baden, Württemberg, and the Palatinate gave impetus to the first 19th-century peak of German emigration in 1817. People were said to be afflicted with *Auswanderungsfieber* (emigration fever). Agents, operating illegally in the service of ship captains, solicited cargoes of poor passengers who were to pay off their passages through indentured servitude in America. This practice, common in the 18th century, was strongly protested by American port authorities and the German Society of Maryland in Baltimore; it ceased about 1820. But high taxation and inheritance laws dividing landholdings equally among heirs led to scattered small plots and *Zwergwirtschaft* (dwarf economy), which continued to oppress peasants in southwestern Germany, the main region of emigration through the 1820s and 1830s. In 1836 when 22,800 Germans took ship, Baden, Württemberg, and the Palatinate still provided 98.8% of those emigrating to America.[10]

As regions of heavy emigration shifted in the 19th century, so did the routes and ports of departure in use. American shippers favored the French port of Le Havre as the cheapest route because they secured lower rates there for transporting emigrants through France. Antwerp, Rotterdam, and Amsterdam in the Netherlands competed successfully for emigrants who departed from areas east of, and close to, the Rhine. All the ports, but particularly the Dutch ones, acquired a bad reputation for exploiting German emigrants by forcing them to exhaust their remaining resources while waiting for passages. Many had to turn back, and these returning paupers created new problems for government authorities and communities. Yet German officials did nothing to hinder emigration, which was generally regarded as a solution for impoverished surplus population and a subject of increasing interest to political scientists such as Friedrich List. In fact, between 1833 and 1850 alone there were at least 27 societies — headed by the *Nationalverein für deutsche Auswanderung und Ansiedlung* (National Association for Emigration and Resettling) — which encouraged and aided German emigrants.

On New Year's night, 1834, the toll barriers between the numerous German territories were lowered permanently. The *Zollverein* (tariff union) made the harbors of Bremen and Hamburg accessible from all parts of Germany. Bremen was the favored port; by 1836 it derived as much income from passenger transportation as it did from the tobacco trade. Rhineland, Westphalia, and Oldenburg contributed 12.5% compared to southwestern Germany's 28.8% of German emigrants between 1845 and 1849. The eastern regions of Prussia and Mecklenburg, previously recipients rather than losers of population, also began to send people to the United States. By 1850 German emigration was no longer regional; it had become a national phenomenon.[11]

With the diversification of regions of origin, a change occurred in the socioeconomic status of emigrants. In northern sections, farmsteads and shops could be passed intact to one heir without division. Small farmers, merchants, and craftsmen could still make a living, but since they did not have capital to expand with the changing agricultural and industrial economy, they saw no better future for their children. After selling their property, they could pay for passage and have some money left for a start in the New World. In addition, some of the most reputable German emigrant groups, such as the *Giessener Auswanderungs-Gesellschaft* (Giessen Emigration Society) and the Saxonian Lutherans, were part of the emigration between 1830 and 1845, which "probably included a higher proportion of prosperous and skilled, educated people than that of any other time."[12]

In the 1830s travel to Bremen from Osnabrück, Hanover, and Oldenburg was still more expensive than the Rhine route to the Netherlands. By 1843 a steamship company on the Weser River brought passengers on a regular schedule from Hanoversch-Münden and Hameln to Bremen. Four years later Bremen subsidized railway travel from as far away as Cologne to divert emigration from the Rhine corridor, and by 1850 trains were chartered from Berlin and Leipzig. On the average, passengers waited only three or four days before going aboard the ships; good hotels and many low-priced hostelries were available. Shipping companies financed a reference bureau for emigrants, which posted prices for hotels, food, liquor, and other items frequently purchased for the journey. They also tried to control the frequently fraudulent money exchanges. John W. Tubbesing and his family, who farmed from 1858 to 1866 near Red Wing, left Westphalia in September, 1852, and went by train to Bremen, where after an eight-hour wait a city agent took them to a lodging house. There Tubbesing purchased passages on a steamship sailing the next day, and departed from Bremerhaven for New Orleans, where he arrived on December 1.[13]

Some families carried large sums of money, the average being between 1,000 and 2,000 thalers. Albert Wolff, a "forty-eighter" who was Minnesota's commissioner of emigration for Germans from 1869 to 1871, reported from Bremen in the fall of 1870 that the city was "alive with emigrants," many of them Bohemians. He added that shippers, who according to contract had to pay the board of those waiting in Bremen, were unable to dispatch them promptly even though cabin passenger ships left for New York twice a week. Many passengers seemed to know their destination in America, but "whole *groups* of them," Wolff reported, "belonging sometimes to the best class too, were perfectly free yet, to go where they pleased, having no relatives or friends in America." The threat of war between Prussia and France frightened these "thousands of well to do and peaceable people of all ages, sexes and social classes away from pleasant and happy homes . . . never before [have] I beheld such crowds of emigrants whose wealth shone forth in their dress and baggage and whose good education in their fine bearing," Wolff wrote. He added that the boardinghouses, where people could lodge and eat well for $.40 a day, had "as good an array of fine looking and well behaving people as the hotels," which charged much more. As early as 1859 Bremen's *Syndicus* (physician general) had observed that any talk about emigrants from Germany being poor was no longer valid.[14]

Hamburg tried to follow Bremen's lead in caring for emigrants, but in 1851 it was still far behind. Those from southwestern Germany continued to prefer Le Havre, Antwerp, and Rotterdam to Hamburg and Bremen even when passages from the former became more expensive, due to American insistence on better conditions on shipboard. Rules to serve cooked food during the voyage were enforced, and crossing time was shortened as steam began to replace sails in the 1850s.[15]

Although various states employed commissioners like Minnesota's Albert Wolff to attract emigrants, letters to the homeland from earlier arrivals were probably the most important of the increasing sources of information about America. But not all of the news such letters contained was accurate. Contemporaries rightly advised against trusting their glowing descriptions. "Truth is from selfish motives very often trifled [with] in a manner, which made it the paramount duty of your agent . . . to denounce such extravagant and sometimes absurd statements," Wolff commented. One scholar of emigration believed that nostalgia and loneliness prompted early settlers to persuade relatives and friends to join them. On the other hand, many writers offered useful, practical advice. Writing from Stillwater in 1858–59 to his relatives in Blankenheimersdorf, a Washington County farmer discussed wages and the prices of land, food, clothing, and farm implements. He also realistically described opportunities for the industrious and compared Minnesota's winters to those in Germany.[16]

The state had another forceful and well-intentioned advocate in Eduard Pelz, a forty-eighter who had represented Silesia in the German parliament at Frankfurt. His voyage to America in 1850 as a steerage passenger was an unpleasant experience that inspired him to provide others with better information. After some years in New York he was persuaded to visit Chengwatana in Pine County. Impressed, he published in Germany in 1858 a popular book describing Minnesota. It included advice for immigrants by Hermann Trott, a land agent for the St. Paul and Pacific Railroad Company, and Daniel A. Robertson, a St. Paul newspaperman.[17]

Both Pelz and his friend Albert Wolff were intent on "a humanistic and public-minded effort" to inform Germans about Minnesota. To that end, on his return to Germany in 1866, Pelz published a translation of a pamphlet on the state; four years later, when the Northern Pacific Railway intensified its campaign to attract settlers, he established a monthly journal, *Der Pfadfinder* (The Pathfinder). Issued in Gotha, the publication contained articles about both North and South America, but particularly about Minnesota, with advertisements for the Northern Pacific Railway. Pelz regularly answered inquiries from correspondents, whose addresses revealed that his journal was read throughout Germany. Like many promoters of Minnesota, he defended its climate as healthful, described its location in the temperate zone as particularly suitable for Germans, and emphasized its location in the center of North America as advantageous — an argument that also appeared in pamphlets written by others. Pelz believed in Minnesota. He gave many details about various places in the state, but he expected a particularly great future for Duluth. Living in comfortable circumstances after his return to Germany, he was able to finance a wide information service addressed to interested countrymen. Pelz did not mean to persuade Germans to emigrate, he said, but "If somebody for one reason or another wants to change countries I say without hesitation 'Nach Minnesota!'"

Albert Wolff, Pelz's fellow forty-eighter, was responsible for translating in 1866 the state's official emigration pamphlet into German. As Minnesota's representative in Germany, he was able to spread information about the state among 57 emigrant boardinghouses and 23 ships' officers in 1870. He also found a ready audience among 13,000 Prussian soldiers and a troop contingent from the Rhineland quartered in Bremen on the eve of the 1870 war with France. Wolff's translation was objective; it was not particularly addressed to Germans in Germany, although the author pointed out that "Minnesota receives annually thousands of German immigrants. To those who want to part with Germany we recommend the beautiful healthy German Minnesota, the most faithful likeness of the old homeland that this continent can offer, as a home." The first pamphlet had no illustrations as had some Wisconsin publications, but the 1870 edition provided a map of Minnesota with an explanation in German of the "simple and admirable system" of the United States land survey. Nevertheless it is doubtful that Wolff's references to a *Viertelsektion* (a quarter section of land) were meaningful to European readers.[18]

The Northern Pacific Railway Company also advertised the Minnesota region through thousands of leaflets distributed by agents in southwestern and northeastern Germany. During the 1870s more and more Germans left home ports with specific destinations in mind, including Minnesota. Undesirable exploitation decreased. For the journey to Minnesota from New York or Boston, immigrants were advised to take the railroad to Buffalo, a boat across the Great Lakes to Milwaukee, the railroad to La Crosse on the Mississippi in western Wisconsin, and finally a steamboat up that river to Winona or St. Paul (see Map 0.1). After 1867 an alternate route was available by railroad all the way via Cleveland and Chicago. Travelers were admonished to be cautious and to check with the passenger agent of the Milwaukee and St. Paul Railroad in Milwaukee.[19]

To verify the immigrant's route from Germany to Minnesota can often be difficult. In order to utilize shipping lists to check the ports of departure and entry, it is necessary to know not only the emigrant's name but also the name of the ship, the port, and the approximate dates. Unfortunately, such information obtained from obituaries or personal memories is not always reliable.[20] Furthermore, data about migration routes, often obtained from the census via the ladder method of analyzing the states where children were born, can only be approximate rather than exact. To make matters worse, if there were no German-born children, par-

WILLIAM (Wilhelm) Pfaender enumerated his own family along with other Brown County residents in the 1870 manuscript census schedules.

ents may appear to have immigrated directly to Minnesota as adults when, in fact, they had arrived as children.

To identify the overland routes Germans followed to Minnesota with the help of census records looks promising initially but also presents problems. Consider the case of a New Ulm family in 1870. In the census the father was shown to have been from Württemberg, the mother from Bavaria. One child of 15 years had been born in Ohio, two in Kentucky of 16 and 14, and seven in Minnesota, ranging in age from 12 years to three months. This is the family of Wilhelm Pfaender, who was born in Heilbronn on July 6, 1826; his wife, Catherine Pfau Pfaender, born in Minfeld, "Rheinbayern," emigrated to Cincinnati as a small child. Pfaender stopped over in London, then crossed to New York with letters of recommendation to Friedrich K. F. Hecker, a famous political refugee of 1848. Hecker had moved west to Cincinnati, well known as a city of Germans, and Pfaender followed him. In Cincinnati, where he worked for Catherine's father, their first child was born; two others were born in Newport, Kentucky, across the Ohio River from Cincinnati. Using only census data one could deduce — incorrectly — that this couple married in Germany, traveled directly to Ohio, and moved with their children in stages to Kentucky and Minnesota.[21]

Such information about immigrant families in the United States is valuable, even if only approximate, for it suggests the stages and timing of their westward migration. In Stearns County, for example, 464 families (38.6% of all German families) had children born in the United States outside Minnesota by 1870. The places of birth ranged from Canada to Louisiana, Delaware to Missouri, and Connecticut to Iowa. More than half of these families had pre-Minnesota experiences in Illinois, Ohio, and Wisconsin (see Table 8.2). About two-thirds had more than one child in these states, giving

some indication of the intervening opportunities and the length of time a family spent before settling in Stearns County.[22]

For comparison, Wards 3 and 4 in St. Paul — its "German wards" — and the three wards of Winona were investigated. Of 146 (23.9%) German families in St. Paul in 1870, 26 had lived in New York, 26 in Wisconsin, and 25 in Illinois. (The remainder was scattered among Ohio, Indiana, Michigan, and Maryland.) In Winona 133 (31.4%) of all German families had pre-Minnesota American experiences; of those, 54 families had lived in Wisconsin. This large number may be due in part to Winona's location just across the Mississippi River from Wisconsin's western border.

Notices in Minnesota newspapers also provided clues to the places of origin of arriving Germans. On June 14, 1862, the *Mankato Semi-Weekly Record*, for example, noticed "a number of Immigrants in town, purchasing plows and other implements. This immigration is mostly well-to-do Germans, from Wisconsin — a class of people accustomed to pioneer life." Another paper, the *St. Paul Daily Press*, reported that a group of the "best class of mechanics, farmers and laborers" who moved west in 1858 were members of the *Turnver-*

Table 8.2. German Families in Stearns County, 1870, with Children Born in Wisconsin, Ohio, and Illinois

birthplace state	number of families	number of children	
		1	2 or more
Wisconsin	127	35.4%	64.5%
Ohio	75	32.0%	68.0%
Illinois	64	43.7%	56.2%
Total	266	36.5%	63.7%

Sources: Calculated from U.S. manuscript census, 1870.
Note: Failure to add up to 100% is due to rounding of figures.

ein in Cincinnati. The German Emigration Society in St. Paul, in addition to sending letters to all parts of the fatherland, attracted many Germans from eastern states, according to the *St. Paul Weekly Pioneer and Democrat* of April 15, 1858.[23]

As Minnesota developed a diversified economy, while still offering unoccupied accessible land in its western parts, a large number of Germans also moved directly there. The state agent at Milwaukee reported in 1869 that roughly 1,600 Germans went through that city between May 24 and July 14 en route to Minnesota; the next year 2,530 arrived via Chicago. Ten years later 12,640 Germans passed through New York City bound for the North Star State. During the last peak of German immigration from 1879 to 1882 — with 250,630 arriving in 1882 alone — comparatively fewer settled as farmers in the German pioneer region of the Minnesota Valley. More went to the cities of St. Paul, Minneapolis, and Duluth (see Map 8.2, Table 8.1).[24]

The immigrants who made the trek west to Minnesota benefited from the social, cultural, religious, and business contacts they made with German enclaves along the various routes. Rudolph Leonhart, for example, who taught school in New Ulm between 1860 and 1862, needed money to travel to Pennsylvania, where his wife "had all her relatives." Because he had a well-to-do brother-in-law in Wheeling, West Virginia, and because he was vouched for by a New Ulm resident formerly of Wheeling, a German banker in St. Paul loaned Leonhart $50.00. These funds enabled him to take his family via La Crosse, Chicago, and Rochester to waiting kin in Pennsylvania.[25]

The Core Regions

In 1860 the frontier line in Minnesota ran parallel to but west of the Mississippi in the southeastern counties of Fillmore, Dodge, and Rice. Then it formed a loop just west of New Ulm and across the Minnesota River, and continued in a northern direction through Nicollet, Sibley, Carver, Wright, and Stearns counties running along the Mississippi to St. Paul, but included southern Washington County. Whether German pioneers traveled via a northern Great Lakes route, the Ohio River, or later by railroad to Rock Island, Illinois, and La Crosse, the Mississippi corridor was usually their entryway. Persons of German stock in southeastern Minnesota comprised between 40% and 60% of the population behind the frontier line in some townships of Houston, Winona, Wabasha, and Goodhue counties by 1860. They reached 80% in Hay Creek Township, Goodhue County, a decade later. In the Minnesota Valley initial percentages of German settlers were much larger; Milford Township in Brown County and Courtland and Lafayette townships in Nicollet County were 80% to 99% German in 1860. The comparatively greater increase between 1860 and 1870 in farming areas rather than in such county seats as Shakopee, Chaska, Henderson, Le Sueur, St. Peter, Mankato, and New Ulm indicates that these river towns no longer offered the same opportunities to later arrivals. The subsequent proportionally larger rural settlement was comparable to the development that had earlier taken place around Mississippi River towns, for instance, in Iowa.[26]

By 1880 the German born were well represented in both Mississippi and Minnesota River towns (see Map 8.2). While Germans did not found these landing sites, many of which dated back to fur trading days, they contributed to their early growth. For example, Hastings in Dakota County, with 1,642 persons, of whom 132 were German born and 194 German stock, had 64 employed Germans in 1860. Most were craftsmen; 14 were laborers; there were also a physician, a hotelkeeper, a musician, and a merchant. Ten years later Hastings' population of 3,458 included 308 German-born persons and 662 of German stock (not including 37 children from mixed marriages). While the population had increased 110.1%, the number employed had risen by only 85.9% to 119. Six laborers worked in the shingle, saw, and flour mills; there were no domestic servants; and new occupations listed included a veterinary surgeon, the register of deeds, two lumber dealers, a wheat buyer, seven coopers, and seven brewers.[27]

While the number of gainfully employed Germans in Hastings did not increase proportionately with the town's growth between 1860 and 1870, the nature of their employment reflected upward mobility for the group as a whole. In Winona the occupations of Germans were similar to those in Hastings, which was half Winona's size, except that the number of laborers was proportionally much greater. Aside from the additional opportunities a bigger town offered to unskilled labor and the possibility that some men listed as "laborers" may have been skilled craftsmen, it is still probable that an urban place of Winona's ethnic variety and larger size could support only a limited number of professionals, semiprofessionals, tradesmen, and skilled laborers of one specific non-English-speaking ethnic group. It could, however, absorb proportionately more of them in low-level jobs than could a smaller town like Hastings.

Farther upstream along the Mississippi corridor north of St. Paul, another core region developed in and around Stearns County. By 1870 that area had the highest concentration of Minnesota townships in which Germans comprised 80% to 100% of the people. These enclaves spread across the Mississippi into Benton County and north to Morrison County, where Pierz Township was an outlier with 22 German households in 1870. Eleven of these families, each with more than one child born in Wisconsin, formed the core of the settlement founded in 1865 at Rich Prairie (now Pierz), under the care of Father Francis X. Pierz. Five years later it was 100% German. By 1898 it had 245 Catholic families, still mostly German, and two non-Catholics. Wright County, southeast of and adjacent to Stearns, became the link between the core regions of Stearns County and the Minnesota Valley — the areas still perceived as "German Minnesota." Landownership by persons of German stock there stood at 3% in 1858 and 39.4% in 1948.[28]

The location of "German Minnesota" cannot be explained by the assumption that Germans (as well as other European immigrants) sought places to settle that reminded them of their homeland. Such a myth may have developed from letters by settlers who wrote, after several years of clearing and building, that the environment reminded them of home. The myth was encouraged by immigration pamphlets, which de-

MOUNTAIN LAKE, the hub of the state's Russian-born, German-speaking Mennonite population, about 1920.

scribed climate, vegetation, and crops as similar to those of the homeland. Since Germans emigrated from many geographically very different regions, it would be difficult to match a specific American place with the one left behind. Only one group invites such matching — the German-speaking Mennonites from Russia's steppes who settled on America's prairies, including the group still to be found in the 1980s at Mountain Lake in Cottonwood County.[29]

One frequent comparison was that of the Upper Mississippi with the Rhine. It was often made in the 1850s by Americans who took the "Fashionable Tour" up the Mississippi and looked for romantic landscapes as beautiful as those of Europe. Even the noted German-American journalist and politician, Carl Schurz, campaigning in Minnesota for Abraham Lincoln in 1859, wrote to his wife that the Mississippi near Fort Snelling reminded him of the Rhine. Nevertheless this investigator has failed to find a German immigrant-settler who recorded in diaries or letters that he was reminded of his homeland or the Rhine when he traveled along the Mississippi from Brownsville to Hastings or along the Minnesota River from St. Paul to New Ulm.[30]

One plausible explanation for the German and Scandinavian occupation of much of the hardwood belt of south-central Minnesota can be found in the availability and accessibility of the Minnesota Valley to settlement at the time of their arrival. Another reason, of course, was the fact that they possessed capital for purchasing farms. River transportation was important in the pioneer years. Mississippi River steamboat arrivals at St. Paul increased from 95 in 1849 to over 1,000 in 1857, 1858, and 1862. Only four steamboat trips up the Minnesota River as far as Mankato were recorded in 1850; the number increased to a peak of 413 in 1862 before being supplanted by railroad service. The Minnesota's channel, narrow at all times, soon silted up, but it served long enough to contribute to the unparalleled speed with which Germans and other settlers occupied the valley.

Indeed the German concentration in central Minnesota — from Scott and Carver counties south and west to Nicollet, Brown, Sibley, and Renville and northwest to McLeod, Meeker, Wright, and Stearns — became the largest area in the state occupied "predominantly" by a single ethnic group (see Maps 8.3, 8.4). Since German-speaking people later participated in the westward movement of the frontier, other concentrations (having a minimum size of one township) can be found in the Red River Valley, in Otter Tail County, and in the nine counties along the Iowa border, but they lack the cohesiveness of "German Minnesota."[31]

The New Ulm Area

It is not possible to discuss each of the places in Minnesota where Germans settled, for by 1900 they lived in all of the state's counties, only 15 of which had fewer than 300 German-born persons.[32] An overview of towns in the two German frontier regions, New Ulm and St. Cloud, and of the Twin Cities — especially St. Paul — will allow us to present in more detail some significant aspects of Minnesota's German settlement (see Table 8.3).

New Ulm deserves attention because of its image as Minnesota's most German city and its importance for German occupation of the Minnesota Valley. Its beginnings gave it a reputation as a semiutopia through its association with the socialistic *Turnerbund* (athletic league) of North America. When Ferdinand Beinhorn arrived in New York from Brunswick in 1852, he planned to establish a German colony in the West. Proceeding to Chicago where more experienced countrymen discouraged his grandiose designs, Beinhorn decided "to buy a few sections of government land, plat a city, divide it into lots and then push these lots on the market." (This sounds more like a typical townsite speculation than a utopia.) With fellow students of English at an evening school in Chicago, he founded the Chicago *Land Verein* (Land Society) on August 10, 1853, and was elected its president. Membership, which cost only $.10, increased after the distribution of 500 copies of a small pamphlet and a notice in the *Illinois Staatszeitung* (State Journal) in November, 1853. A ball given by the organization in February, 1854, netted $300 for the project, and in March a second newspaper notice announced an initiation fee of $3.00 to be followed by the payment of $5.00 a week later. Membership in the Chicago group rose to about 800 by April. A cholera epidemic in the

---

Table 8.3. Towns with Greatest Concentrations of German Born, 1905

Metropolitan Areas*	% German	Service Centers in German Farming Regions	% German
South St. Paul	18.7	New Ulm	22.4
St. Paul	8.0	Mankato	10.4
		Faribault	10.2
River Towns		St. Cloud	9.7
Winona	9.8	Owatonna	8.5
Hastings	9.7	Rochester	7.8
Stillwater	7.2		

Source: Calculated from Minnesota, *Census, 1905*, for towns of 3,000 or over with concentrations of at least 7%.

*Minneapolis had only 3.4%; Duluth had only 2.9%; West St. Paul (pop. 2,100) had 20.7%.

summer of that year made the members — mostly working-men — eager to move west.[33]

The Minnesota Valley had been opened for settlement as a result of treaties signed with the Dakota Indians at Mendota and Traverse des Sioux in 1851. Thus when sites in Michigan and Iowa proved unsatisfactory, two scouts for the would-be settlers went to Minnesota Territory in June, 1854. They were joined by others during the summer and, dividing into search parties, investigated a number of locations along the lower Minnesota River. Continuing upriver toward Fort Ridgely late in the fall, four of the men met Joseph Laframboise, a trader, who recommended a site above the mouth of the Cottonwood River. Impressed by its scenery and water-power possibilities, the men brought the rest of the group from Traverse des Sioux for an inspection.[34]

They wintered near a heavily wooded creek about eight miles north of present New Ulm in an apparently abandoned Dakota Indian village. Difficulties ensued when the Indians returned to the site. If the immigrants were trespassing on reservation lands, they would have to move, according to the treaties signed at Traverse des Sioux. Since the land had not yet been surveyed, the reservation boundaries could not have been clear to either the Dakota or the Germans — "all fresh immigrants . . . not in the slightest degree familiar with frontier life."[35]

The following spring, after three surveyors had submitted differing reports, the settlers — joined by President Beinhorn — opted for the present New Ulm location. They obtained legal advice from Charles E. Flandrau, a New York-born lawyer of French and Irish extraction, who resided at Traverse des Sioux. He advised Beinhorn that he could pre-empt a townsite of only 320 acres; the latter had wanted a much larger area which would include farmland needed to support the townspeople. A total of 16 quarter sections was pre-empted on June 26, 1855, at Winona, the nearest land office. Each member of the organization was to be assigned 12 town lots and an additional nine (later changed to six) acres outside the village. In May, 1855, a plat fronting the river was staked out in a grid pattern that left several squares open for public use, and the name of Neu (later New) Ulm was adopted for the newly platted town at the suggestion of an emigrant from Ulm in Württemberg.[36]

No lots had been legally assigned when Wilhelm Pfaender, a member of the Turner movement in Germany and Cincinnati, arrived in St. Paul the following spring in search of a site for a Turner settlement. Learning of the German colony, Pfaender and his two companions, who represented a well-financed group of about 1,300 members, traveled to New Ulm where they met Beinhorn of the Chicago Land Society. Their mutual desire to establish a German town resulted in a merger as the German Land Association of Minnesota, which was incorporated a year later on March 4, 1857, and capitalized at $100,000.[37]

On August 17, 1856, a St. Paul surveyor was employed to complete the exact measurements of lots. (This was the fourth surveyor employed at New Ulm; Americans, as a rule, merely paced off their pre-emption claims.) Altogether 4,836 21/100 acres were purchased by the land association. "About 100 out of 200 acres . . . I secured are good wood-land," Pfaender wrote, adding "our all-too-anxious members can see they do not have to fear lack of wood in the future." Pfaender's report and the Chicagoans' tenacious search for a timbered site illustrate how essential wood for fuel, building, and fencing was for survival.[38]

Pfaender went on to inform the Cincinnati society that a steam-powered sawmill, a hotel, and a warehouse were planned, adding that three times the number of houses could have been built had the existing unfinished sawmill not been booked at least three months in advance. He warned would-be migrants that choice claims were becoming scarce and reminded future settlers to bring sturdy clothing, a few tools, and proof of citizenship or intent thereof in order to acquire 160 acres of government land at $1.25 per acre. Since steamers on the Minnesota could go only as far upriver as Traverse des Sioux in times of low water, settlers with light luggage were advised to take the boat to Shakopee and proceed by wagon to the Traverse. A Cincinnati Turner added to Pfaender's report the information that fellow Germans were available to assist the migrants at St. Paul and Traverse des Sioux.[39]

In spite of Pfaender's business acumen, the financial affairs of the New Ulm colony worsened as the effects of the 1857 panic reached Minnesota. The new sawmill was heavily in debt by 1858 and was sold four years later; the *Neu Ulm Pionier*, a bilingual, fiercely anticlerical, Turner newspaper published from January, 1858, to August 16, 1862, was sold in January, 1859; and the communal store was overtaxed by newcomers without money to pay for essentials. Poor harvests in 1856 and 1857, coupled with many settlers' distaste for farming, were also deterrent factors.

The German Land Association dissolved in 1859 and wound up its business affairs in 1862, giving 24 town lots, $5,594.25, and 320 additional lots to the school district; four acres were allotted for a hospital and a fire station, and several acres of river bottom land were reserved for a public beach. In 1871 leftover lots were still being sold. Readers of the *New Ulm Post* were asked on June 23 to buy and donate those adjacent to the spot where a New Ulm Academy, incorporated on May 1, 1871, was to be built.

Before the land association was dissolved, however, New Ulm's *Turnverein*, the first in Minnesota, was organized with 13 members on November 11, 1856. Volunteering their labor, its members erected a *Turnhalle* (Turner Hall). Measuring about 40 by 75 feet, the structure was built of wood taken from unclaimed land north of the town and cut into boards at the sawmill, which was borrowed on Sundays for the purpose. Dedicated on December 25, 1857, the *Turnhalle* was one of the town's most German-looking buildings, with a gable facing the street, two turrets, and slightly arched windows. It burned, along with more than 185 other New Ulm structures, during the Dakota War that took place in the summer of 1862.[40]

Rebuilt in 1866, the hall served for many years as the community center. Town meetings, concerts, lectures, dances, and court proceedings were held there. Sunday school classes in morality and humanity — typical of the anticlerical Turner philosophy — were taught by salaried freethinking teachers, and gymnastic classes for boys and

NEW ULM'S first Turner House completed in 1858 and burned in 1862.

girls fared well. Its theater was well known in the state. Light drama was the usual fare, for in 1873 the *Turnverein* ruled that the stage could be used only by amateurs, thus discouraging touring German artists. Lectures by visiting forty-eighters and nationally known freethinkers were frequent but less popular than the social gatherings held in the hall. Apparently, traditional disagreements among Turners, who favored Socialism and intellectualism on the one hand and physical training on the other, existed in New Ulm as elsewhere. But Pfaender, commenting on whether the *Turnerbund* had lost or gained through its settlement project, wrote in 1881 that New Ulm "had the reputation of an orderly and pleasant place, where the adherents of religious confessions and freethinkers lived in harmony, and the enforcement of rest on Sabbath and temperance were unknown."

Pfaender's dream of "a German settlement [with] avoidance of speculation, [and with] educational opportunities for the children of liberals and freethinkers" reflected a typical Turner position. While part of the *Turnverein* philosophy

was rooted in anticlericalism, there was also a strong trend toward accommodation to the religious life-style of the new homeland. As early as 1858 a German Methodist congregation was organized in New Ulm, followed by an Evangelical Lutheran church seven years later. Catholics in the town were served by a missionary priest from Mankato in 1857, and before the Civil War they built a small chapel which was a casualty of the Dakota War of 1862. Finally in the winter of 1868–69 Father Alexander Berghold, a native of Styria, Austria, recruited by Father Pierz, moved to New Ulm. He supervised the building of a Roman Catholic church and a school operated by the Sisters of Charity which was open to all denominations. A promoter of Minnesota, Berghold also published a guide for German-speaking immigrants, which drew a number of families directly from Bohemia (now Czechoslovakia) to New Ulm. By 1905 the original freethinking Turners were outnumbered, and Berghold's successor was able to pronounce New Ulm "a center of Catholicity."[41]

Lutheran settlers, who erected St. Paul's Church in 1865–66, were served by itinerant ministers until 1870 when a resident pastor arrived. As the congregation grew, it decided to build a grammar school. Then in 1884 Pastor C. J. Albrecht mustered support from church organizations to found Dr. Martin Luther College. Erected on a wooded bluff southwest of the city, the institution trained male students from Minnesota Valley towns. At first Martin Luther offered theological courses, but it became basically a teachers' college to supply German Lutheran parochial schools. Despite reverses suffered during World War I, the college grew, becoming coeducational in 1920. Early attempts to relocate it failed, and the Turner city thus remained a nodal point of German Lutheran education.[42]

The history of New Ulm is remarkable for the coexistence of three main streams among German Americans — Protestant, Catholic, and freethinker. The city remains perhaps the most "German" of the state's communities, offering visible symbols of its German diversity and American adaptations. Dominating the bluff above the town since its unveiling by the Sons of Hermann Lodge in 1897 is the Hermann Monument, modeled on one in Detmold, Germany. The former

THE SCHELL BREWERY in New Ulm as it looked in 1865.

post office, a hybrid of styles built in 1910 supposedly to resemble the town hall in Ulm, Germany, became the home of the Brown County Historical Society in 1976. Notable as examples of Germanic architecture are the brewery and home of August Schell; the earliest buildings were erected in 1861, and the brewery was still in operation in 1980. The present Holy Trinity Roman Catholic Cathedral, a large brick structure, was completed in 1905.

In 1860 New Ulm's population of 635 contained only two non-German persons. By the turn of the century 919 of its 5,403 citizens (nearly 20%) had been born in Germany. In 1970, 8.3% of the population of Minnesota as a whole claimed German as a mother tongue; in New Ulm the figure was a whopping 41% — an interesting indication of the community's lingering Germanness.[43]

St. Cloud and Stearns County

In 1850 Dahkotah and Wahnahta, the original territorial counties from which Stearns County was carved five years later, contained a total of 20 German-born persons. In 1860 Germans comprised 68.2% of its foreign born, and from 1870 through 1920 the figure remained well above 50%. As recently as 1970 German-born residents of Stearns County constituted 32.6% of the foreign-born population there.[44]

Much of the early attraction of German emigrants to this area can be traced to the Catholic church and particularly to Father Pierz, the Slovenian-born, German-speaking priest who had worked as a missionary among the Indians of northern Michigan, Wisconsin, and Minnesota since 1838. Writing in the *Wahrheitsfreund* (Friend of Truth), a German-Catholic weekly published in Cincinnati, on March 1, 1854, Pierz stressed Minnesota's mild climate, good soil, high wages, and economic opportunities for merchants, manufacturers, and tradesmen. Urging "Germans who live in overpopulated cities and are becoming too anglicized in the employ of Americans and Protestants" to take up farming in Minnesota, Pierz added: "I do wish, however, that the choicest pieces of land in this delightful Territory would become the property of thrifty Catholics who would make an earthly paradise of this Minnesota which Heaven has so richly blessed, and who would bear out the opinion that Germans prove to be the best farmers and the best Christians in America. I am sure that you will likewise do credit to your faith here in Minnesota, but to prove yourselves good Catholics do not bring with you any freethinkers, red republicans, atheists or agitators." As a result of Pierz's "facile pen," wrote Archbishop John Ireland many years later, "came crowds of settlers, sturdy sons of the Rheinland, Westphalia and Bavaria, until a new Germany rose in Stearns County."

At the request of Pierz, Bishop Joseph Cretin of St. Paul sought support from the Order of St. Benedict to meet Minnesota Territory's expanding need for German-speaking priests and teaching nuns. As a result, three priests — two of whom were consecrated at St. Paul — and two lay brothers led by Father Demetrius di Marogna, an Italian-born cleric who had studied at Mainz, arrived in 1856. They were welcomed at Sauk Rapids (where Pierz had already established a church) and St. Cloud by German Catholics who had been attracted to Stearns County by Pierz's glowing accounts.[45]

Two earlier settlers offered the Benedictines 320 acres along the Mississippi River on which to erect a monastery. With a site seemingly assured, the priests in 1857 acted to incorporate their order in Minnesota and to gain a charter for the school they named St. John's Seminary. They were assisted in doing so by John L. Wilson, a territorial legislator from Maine who is known as the "father of St. Cloud."

As it turned out, the original 320-acre site was not legally held by the donors, so after six years of litigation a 1,280-acre tract around Sagatagan Lake, four miles from St. Joseph, was secured in 1864. There the monks began the construction of their abbey and what became St. John's University.

Meanwhile four Benedictine sisters and two postulants had arrived at St. Cloud in July, 1857, a little prematurely, perhaps, considering that quarters for them did not as yet exist. Three of them had been born in Germany. They had responded to an appeal for teachers to educate the German Catholic children in the St. Cloud area, and they opened the first parochial school there in 1858. Five years later, when a public school was built in St. Cloud, the sisters accepted an invitation from St. Joseph parish, the largest and most prosperous in Stearns County, to conduct a school there. Thus the sisters established a permanent home, where they founded St. Benedict, which became a four-year liberal arts women's college as well as the largest community of Benedictine sisters in the world. By 1875 St. John's — which had been started with the help of a Slovenian missionary, a French bishop, a Bavarian abbot, an Italian priest, and a New England businessman — was on its way to becoming a university.

Throughout the county in which these institutions flourished, Germans, invited through the pages of *Wahrheitsfreund* and *Katholische Volkszeitung* (Catholic People's News) of Baltimore, migrated in groups from eastern states and from Wisconsin. Along with those directly from the fatherland, they — like other ethnic groups — often selected their claims in a way which allowed later arrivals to occupy leftover tracts in between, forming areas of kinship and regional groups. Among these were Bavarians at Cold Spring, Jacob's Prairie, and Collegeville; Lower Bavarians around Albany; Westphalians at St. Augusta; Low-German-speaking people at Freeport and Meire Grove; and Luxembourgers in Luxemburg Township. Twenty-one contiguous townships in eastern Stearns County, including rural St. Cloud Township, had German populations of over 60% in 1870; nine of them were more than 80% German. A circular issued in 1887 to land agents of the St. Paul, Minneapolis & Manitoba Railway Company indicated that the "predominating nationality" in Stearns County, where the railroad had land for sale, was German — especially in the central, eastern, and southern sections. Ten years later German-born settlers made up 58.3% of the county's foreign born, and the percentage rose to 67% in 1905. The area's attraction for German immigrants persisted in the 20th century; in 1940 they comprised 52.3% of the foreign born, and as recently as 1970 persons of German stock constituted over 50% of Stearns County's population. In that year 13% of St. Cloud residents claimed German as a mother tongue.[46]

SCHMIDT BROTHERS Meat Market in St. Cloud about 1887. Note the carcass hanging to the left of the door.

The stability of family names through three generations can be seen on cemetery markers, in census records and plat books, and on merchants' store fronts. An 1861 report of a German-Catholic mission society pointed out that "Whoever wants to own land can choose here after his liking, can claim or buy particularly from the Yankees, who all move away from the Catholic environment." [47]

The role played by the Catholic church in attracting German immigrants to Stearns County was a large one, but in 1870 there were also small numbers of Baptists, Congregationalists, Episcopalians, Lutherans, Methodists, and Presbyterians. By 1906, when only 47.6% of the state's population claimed religious affiliation, 73.8% of those in Stearns County did so — and 85.9% of these were Catholic. Twenty

years later 81.9% of the county's church members were Catholic, and the figure rose 10 years later to 83.5%. A 1957 survey of church membership revealed that, while 38.4% of the state was Catholic, in Stearns County Catholics comprised 68.5% of the church-affiliated population. [48]

The sizable numbers of German-speaking persons who wanted sermons and schools conducted in their native tongue led to a nationwide controversy during the last quarter of the 19th century. In 1878 Abbot Alexius Edelbrock of St. John's Abbey declared that persons "best acquainted with a foreign tongue should have the advantage of hearing the Gospel read, and sermons preached to them, in their own language." Other leaders, notably Archbishop Ireland of St. Paul, wanted to "Americanize" the church and thus defend it from what came to be called Cahenslyism, a plan proposed to Pope Leo XIII in 1891 by Peter Paul Cahensly, which would have organized foreign-born Catholics in the United States into congregations of like nationality served by priests of the same mother tongue. In his Americanization efforts Ireland initiated a takeover by public school boards of parochial schools in Faribault and Stillwater, perpetrating a dispute that reached all the way to Rome and persisted for many years in various forms. The archbishop insisted that, while German could be taught in parochial schools, English should be spoken in general so that the faith of the children was not restricted to the non-English tongue of their parents.

The fight was also seen as one between liberals and conservatives. In Minnesota it widened the rift between Irish and German Catholics. In Stearns County the opposition to English in churches and parochial schools was stronger in rural areas than it was in St. Cloud. In the church schools children were taught half in German and half in English, usually by sisters of German birth or descent. The readers used were printed in High German, as were such newspapers as *Der Nordstern* (The North Star) of St. Cloud and *Der Wanderer* (The Migrant) of St. Paul, which many parents read. The problem was further complicated by the various dialects spoken in extended families and by the children who in turn developed their own, as in "make the light out" or "make the door shut." The use of family dialects was pro-

HARVEST TIME on the Meyer farm near St. Joseph in Stearns County in 1890. The stability of German land ownership in the area is demonstrated by the Roman Landwehr family (right) whose farm near St. Augusta, like others in the county, had been in the family for well over a century in 1980.

longed by visiting relatives, former neighbors, and immigrants from the same regions in the fatherland, over 1,000 of whom were attracted by the Sauk Valley Immigration Society in 1866 alone, according to the *St. Paul Pioneer Press* of June 14.

Americanization was not served by premature insistence on having German Catholics listen to sermons in German or in English so poorly spoken that neither parents nor children understood. A survey revealed that a majority of the Catholic churches held services in German at least until 1917 and half in German, half in English into the late 1930s. In eastern and central Stearns County outside of St. Cloud, many Germans had little opportunity to use English for miles around; such areal coherence distinguished them from the Germans in southeastern Minnesota.[49]

Stearns County's Germanness was still vaguely discernible in 1980 in the persistence of certain architectural details. Its massive churches, supported by the surrounding rural areas, seemed outsized compared to those in the towns; some, like that at St. Joseph, were more remarkable for their building materials — fieldstone and native granite — than for their Rhineland Gothic architectural style. Houses, whether built of stone, brick, or wood, often displayed one distinctly German detail — curved upper window frames. As a whole, however, the region exhibited an attractive American rural landscape with virtually no visual evidences of Germanness.

The Twin Cities

In St. Paul and Minneapolis, both more ethnically mixed, the Germans did not dominate as in New Ulm and Stearns County. In 1850 only 27 German-born persons appeared in the Ramsey County census figures, and at that date the county included both St. Paul and St. Anthony (later part of Minneapolis). Among these immigrants were three carpenters, four farmers, seven laborers, two cabinetmakers, two stonemasons, and only one butcher, merchant, and cigarmaker. From this small beginning the German population grew to more than 2,000 a decade later — nearly two-thirds of whom lived in Ramsey County. By 1870 Germans constituted 28% of Hennepin County's foreign born (including Minneapolis) and 37% of Ramsey's (including St. Paul).[50]

The percentage of German-born residents remained higher in St. Paul than in Minneapolis; at the turn of the century only 13.8% of the foreign-born residents of Hennepin County were German, while the figure for Ramsey County was 28%. In the decade between 1910 and 1920, however, St. Paul's German-born population decreased by almost 6,000. By 1930 nearly 7,500 (17%) of St. Paul foreign-born residents were German; 40 years later the figure was 1,333 (11%), but an additional 11,217 (20%) of foreign or mixed parentage were German.

St. Paul in 1850 was the head of navigation on the Upper Mississippi and the jumping-off place for the untapped hinterland of the rich Minnesota River Valley. Among the influx of landseekers during the 1850s were many Germans, a great number of whom remained in the urban area. In St. Paul they settled near West 7th Street, along the Upper Levee, and across the Mississippi on the lower West Side, an area that has been something of an Ellis Island for immi-

THE CHURCH of St. Joseph in the Stearns County town of the same name, around 1959.

grants to the city. Others, largely Catholic families from Austria and the Sudetenland, lived near Dale and Thomas streets in an area called *Froschburg* or Frogtown. In Minneapolis the earliest area of German settlement was in St. Anthony on the east side of the Mississippi near the Falls of St. Anthony; by 1855 the Seven Corners section on the west bank of the Mississippi and south and east along Cedar Avenue attracted Germans. By the 1890s they were also to be found in the Camden neighborhood in North Minneapolis.

In their daily lives Twin Cities German Americans worked in a great variety of jobs. The earliest information we have is from 1850 when only 17% of St. Paul's Germans were unskilled laborers, as compared with 49% of French Canadians and 55% of Irish. Like the English and the Scots, twice as many Germans there were employed in nonmanual work as were French Canadians and Irish. During the 1850s there were German bankers, grocers, wagonmakers, a lumberman, a bar and restaurant owner, a candy manufacturer, a shoemaker, merchants of various kinds, and brewers.

Twin Cities Germans, like those in Winona, New Ulm, and elsewhere, had an affinity for beer. Not only were the major breweries German owned, but a large number of saloons were also German. In the 1870s the St. Paul group took out 121 of the 187 liquor licenses issued to foreign-born residents. During a five-month period in 1878 Germans held 54 of the city's 57 brewers' licenses. In Minneapolis one German-owned establishment, the Glueck Brewing Company founded in 1865, was the oldest existing business in the city by 1958.[51]

The diversity among Twin Cities Germans was evident in their early religious institutions, which included Catholics, several varieties of Lutherans, other Protestant denominations, Jews, and the freethinking Turners. As early as 1855 the first of six German Catholic national parishes in St. Paul (Minneapolis had only three), the Church of the Assumption, was organized on Exchange Street with 30 families as members. The need for a larger edifice to house its burgeoning congregation gave rise in 1871 to the twin-towered Romanesque stone building on 9th Street that still graces the St. Paul skyline. By that time the parish supported a number of organizations, such as a sodality to promote school attendance and a mutual benefit society. A Kolping Society, or workmen's union, modeled on similar European groups, was established in 1885; one of its services was to operate a boardinghouse for homeless laborers.[52]

Assumption grew to 450 families by the turn of the century, but by that time its members were moving away from the downtown neighborhood. A church historian remarked in 1906 that it was "already evident . . . that Assumption parish could no longer grow in the matter of families. For, with the speedy growth of the business section of the city invading the old Assumption parish, the locality must of necessity lose its attraction for persons who desire homes in a quiet district; the majority of people settle in the newer residential sections."

The locations of the other five German Catholic national parishes suggest the distribution of this ethnic group throughout St. Paul (see Map 8.5). Sacred Heart, established by 80 families in 1881, served the Dayton's Bluff area east of downtown. Three years later St. Francis de Sales offered a spiritual home in the West 7th Street community. Across the Mississippi from the downtown section, St. Matthew's was organized on the West Side in 1886 by 140 families from Austria, Germany, Switzerland, and the Netherlands. St. Agnes was founded the following year by German-speaking, working-class families who had moved from Assumption parish to Frogtown north and west of University Avenue and Rice Street. The growth of St. Agnes and the mobility of its parishioners resulted in 1890 in the establishment farther north at Rose and Albemarle streets of St. Bernard's, which served a number of Austro-Hungarian settlers.

Early German Lutheran congregations in the Twin Cities followed roughly the same geographic pattern as did the Catholic parishes. In St. Paul the German Evangelical Lutheran Trinity Church, the first Lutheran church in Minnesota, incorporated in 1855 and erected its first house of worship at 10th and Wabasha in the downtown area near Assumption. A splinter group formed St. John's in Lowertown, but as the membership grew it moved east to Dayton's Bluff in order to accommodate the Germans settling in that part of St. Paul. In 1873 seven Germans on the West Side established Emanuel Evangelical Lutheran Church, and by 1890 German Lutherans in both the West 7th Street and Frogtown areas had founded churches.[53]

By 1856 in Minneapolis the German Lutherans founded another Trinity Church — the oldest Missouri Synod congregation in the state — in St. Anthony. Like its St. Paul namesake, this Trinity spawned other congregations, Immanuel (1889) in North Minneapolis and then Mount Olive (1909) in the south section of the city. The relatively slower growth of Minneapolis Trinity was later explained as being due to the Scandinavian character of the city and to "the presence of other atheistic organizations" such as the *Turnverein*, which "worked an unwholesome leaven among the German immigrants."

The theological differences reflected in various synods perpetuated controversies that went back to the so-called Prussian Union of 1817 during the reign of King Friedrich Wilhelm II. In Minnesota, as in other parts of the United States, these differences led to the construction of churches to accommodate the divergent views. St. Paul Trinity Lutheran and most of its daughter churches, for example, were originally members of the Minnesota Synod; Zion, on the other hand, formed by dissident members of Trinity, represented the Missouri Synod, which was to become the largest group ministering to the spiritual needs of Minnesota's German Lutherans. In 1890 both the Minnesota and Missouri synods had 62 pastors working in the state, but after that date the Missourians drew farther and farther ahead, so that by 1977 they had 333 pastors and more than 168,000 communicant members.

Though fewer in number than the Lutherans, other German Protestants were to be found in the Twin Cities. German Methodists in St. Paul formed a congregation in 1851 and erected a church at Broadway and 6th streets two years later. Others of this denomination were built near Dayton's Bluff (1875), the West Side (1885), and Frogtown (1900). The earliest Minneapolis German Methodist church, established in 1870, was erected in the northeast section of the city; two others were organized — one in the north and one in the southeast part of town — before 1890. German Methodism made slower advances in Minnesota after a part of the German core region in the southeast area of the state had been successfully covered in the 1870s and 1880s because, said one Methodist minister, the Lutherans were now "looking after their stray sheep much more faithfully."[54]

By 1885 there were 67 such churches in the state (four in St. Paul and three in Minneapolis) with 4,200 members. If the membership of the Evangelical Association were added, the German Methodist population would total 25,000, according to the church historian, who added: "Certainly there can be no other means by which so much can be done for the temperance cause as by making true Methodists of the Germans." Since temperance was a key tenet of Methodism in the 19th century, its success among Germans (not all of whom were habitual beer drinkers) was partially due to the early frontier arrival of its wide-ranging circuit riders who preceded other Protestant missionaries. One minister recalled that his grandparents, "who had never heard of a Methodist," were approached by a circuit-riding preacher asking if he might hold services in their log cabin. It was the first church service the German immigrants had heard in three years, and it was the beginning of three Methodist churches in the Blooming Grove area of Waseca County. Another appeal of Methodism, which began among the Germans of Cincinnati, was the accurate perception of it as an American church. German Methodists, in fact, exported Methodism back to the Old Country, while American Methodists welcomed and supported the new German parishes in the United States.

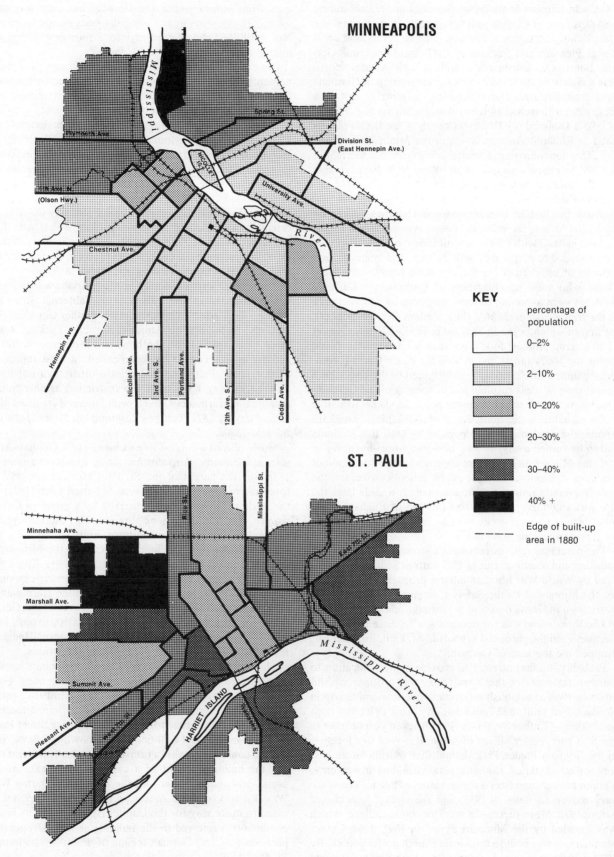

MINNEAPOLIS

Mississippi

Plymouth Ave.

Sixth St.

Division St.
(East Hennepin Ave.)

NICOLLET IS.

University Ave.

6th Ave. N.
(Olson Hwy.)

River

Chestnut Ave.

Hennepin Ave.

Nicollet Ave.

3rd Ave. S.

Portland Ave.

12th Ave. S.

Cedar Ave.

KEY

percentage of
population

0–2%

2–10%

10–20%

20–30%

30–40%

40% +

Edge of built-up
area in 1880

ST. PAUL

Mississippi St.

Minnehaha Ave.

Marshall Ave.

Summit Ave.

HARRIET ISLAND

Pleasant Ave.

St.

Mississippi River

Map 8.5. Germans in the Twin Cities, 1880

German Baptists formed two churches in St. Paul during the 1880s (one at Canada and 13th streets, the other on the West Side), and German Presbyterians began to hold services at Pleasant and Ramsey in 1887. In Minneapolis German Baptists established a church at 20th Avenue North near Lyndale in 1885; four years earlier a group of Germans formed an Evangelical congregation, meeting at first in a Presbyterian church at 14th and Washington avenues North. In 1905 a Dunkard (or Dunker) Church of the Brethren was listed at Fremont Avenue North in the Minneapolis directory. This denomination, founded in Wittgenstein, Germany, in 1708, had spread to the Middle West from Pennsylvania with the Mennonites. As early as 1873 Mennonites had visited the Twin Cities area; not until 1957, however, did they establish the first of two Minneapolis churches — one on East 22nd Street, the other on Boone Avenue North.

Hand in hand with religious institutions, parochial schools were founded to perpetuate faith, culture, and language, and virtually all children of German-speaking families attended. Those who were not members of Lutheran or Catholic churches went to private German nonsectarian schools, such as the *freie deutsche Schule* (Independent German School), the first of which began in St. Paul in 1858 with tuition set at $3.00 a term. At least four more such schools mushroomed during the 1860s and 1870s. In 1866 St. Paul's German community united to elect fellow countrymen to the city school board; their success resulted in the opening of the German-English Academy, which received public funds not available to the parochial institutions. Located at Washington and 5th streets, the academy was so popular by 1869 that students had to be turned away. It was, however, short-lived, for in 1867 the Minnesota legislature approved the introduction of the German language into the public school curriculum, the state university, and the normal school. A decade later the law was amended to emphasize the use of English, while other languages were to be used to facilitate understanding for foreign-speaking students.[55]

The parochial schools remained a stronghold for German speaking and teaching. But in 1917 nativist sentiments, fertilized by World War I and an intense propaganda campaign, led the Minnesota Public Safety Commission to discourage instruction in German except in language and religion classes. So threatening was the commission's stance that all five German Catholic parochial schools in St. Paul, for example, dropped the teaching of German.

Probably the first attempt to provide higher education to German residents of the Twin Cities was an unsuccessful effort in 1868 to establish a German-American university in St. Paul. Not until 1892 could that city boast of its first such institution — Luther Seminary. Begun seven years earlier in the St. Croix Valley village of Afton, it moved to a location in the city near Phalen Park. Established to train future pastors and missionaries, Luther expanded, adding an academy, a junior college, and later a conservatory of music. The seminary moved to Iowa in 1932, and the college was closed before 1938. More successful was Concordia College, which was founded by the Missouri Synod in 1892. Like Luther Seminary, it was built to train male church professionals. By 1920 it was a recognized junior college with "many students

. . . from homes where the German language was often used." Thirty years later Concordia became coeducational. Not until 1962 did it expand into a four-year liberal arts institution, still operating in St. Paul.[56]

Love of the German language and traditions gave rise to numerous societies — many of them devoted to furthering the arts as well as a sense of *Deutschtum* (Germanness). Probably the earliest such group in the state was *Der deutsche Lese- und Bildungsverein* (German Reading and Educational Society), founded in 1852 in St. Paul "for the advancement of culture, enlightenment, and freedom of thought." Incorporated by the territorial legislature two years later as the German Reading Society, this organization included choral, dramatic, and gymnastic divisions. Indeed the St. Paul *Turnverein*, formed officially in 1858, was originally a section of the reading club. The Thalia *Liebhabertheaterverein* (Amateur Stage Association), founded in 1857 to promote the cultural values of the German theater, joined forces with the reading society in 1859.[57]

The oldest German society in Minneapolis was the *Turnverein*, founded in 1857. Its hall on California Street was used by the Turner singing society and other German organizations, including the Amateur German Theater, one of three such groups in St. Anthony and Minneapolis. But the activity in Minneapolis has been called "a weak reflection" of that in St. Paul, and one reason other than population differences may have been the restriction against Sunday theatrical performances. Such prohibitions were lifted in the capital city by 1871, but they continued in Minneapolis until the mid-1880s.

Music played a central role in many early German-American associations. An informal string quartet organized in 1858 was the parent of the St. Paul Musical Society. The forerunner of that city's still vital Schubert Club (1891) was the Ladies' Musicale begun in 1882 by a group of German women. Early in its existence the Schubert Club enjoyed the musical talents of Bavarian-born Emil Oberhoffer, who went on to become the first conductor of the Minneapolis (now Minnesota) Symphony Orchestra in 1903. There were also many singing clubs, the best known perhaps being the Germania Choral Society in St. Paul and the Harmonia Society across the river in Minneapolis. By 1890 the German talent for organization had created about 100 groups in St. Paul alone, including chapters of such fraternal lodges as the Sons of Hermann and the Order of the Druids.

The proliferation, in turn, created a concomitant need for a building to house the activities of all these groups. For 30 years such a project was discussed. At last in 1920 a total of 51 German-American societies and lodges joined forces to build a $180,000, three-story structure on Rice Street known as German House. Equipped with bowling alleys, poolrooms, conference halls, a rathskeller, and a 1,000-seat theater, the building served as a cultural, theatrical, musical, social, and sports center into the late 1940s. During World War II it was renamed American House, and in 1958 it was razed to make way for the Capitol Approach. In its heyday one historian referred to the building as the "strongest expression . . . [of] German feeling of origin" to be found in St. Paul.

THE 50TH ANNIVERSARY of the Minnesota chapter of the Sons of Hermann, celebrated in St. Paul in 1890.

More recently, social affairs are served by the present-day Volksfest Kultur Haus operated by the Volksfest Association on Summit Avenue. (A Minneapolis counterpart, Old Heidelberg Club, had sponsored large picnics in the 1930s and early 1940s but disbanded with the onset of World War II.) But little German is spoken there, and ethnic indicators seem to have faded. Half of the 24 new members of the Volksfest Association listed in its April, 1979, newsletter did not have German names, and only four of 15 persons on its board could speak German. Its uncatalogued library was little used, and English and German newsletters produced by the German Information Service seemed to attract scant attention. The association's membership increased after it began to sponsor annual charter flights to Germany in 1968, but dropped from 3,000 to about 2,000 when membership in the organization was no longer required to obtain charter-flight rates. The big annual event is the Volksfest, begun in 1958 on Whitsunday. Held for some years in Minnehaha Park, the event later took place during the 1970s and in 1980 at Highland Park, St. Paul.[58]

Press, Politics, and Nationalism

St. Paul was the headquarters over the years for more than 20 German-language newspapers, the largest number produced by any Minnesota community and an important element in the life of both urban and rural German Americans in the state. Like those of other ethnic groups, these newspapers served as links between the immigrants and their homeland and as stabilizing factors for the immigrant in a new country. Of foreign-language papers in the United States, those in German constituted 79% in 1885, and they totaled nearly 800 papers nationally in 1893–94. Minnesota by 1860 had more than 50 English-language papers as well as seven published in German — five of these in St. Paul, one in New Ulm, and one in Carver. Over the next century at least 100 German-language newspapers were founded in the state, most of them short-lived.[59]

The earliest of those started in St. Paul were *Minnehaha*, an early Sunday edition of *Minnesota Volksblatt* (People's Newspaper), and *Minnesota Deutsche Zeitung* (German Times), all founded in 1855. The latter was edited and pub-

ST. PAUL Turnverein in the 1920s: female and male drill teams.

lished by Albert Wolff and Friedrich Orthwein, who two years later established the *Minnesota National-Demokrat*, a Democratic weekly. Under the leadership of freethinking Samuel Ludvigh, the *Deutsche Zeitung* then became the *Minnesota Staatszeitung*, which was at first politically independent. From 1858 to 1877 it was edited chiefly by Wolff, largely as a Republican paper. In the secular German press, the daily *Volkszeitung*, edited by Wolff for nearly 20 years, lasted until 1941; it was formed in 1877 by a union of earlier papers. Various religious bodies also published German-language periodicals, including the Missouri Synod, the Evangelical Lutheran Synod, and the Catholic church. The latter's conservative weekly newspaper, *Der Wanderer*, was started in 1867. It was still being published in the 1980s, although the last German-language edition appeared in 1957.

While St. Paul had the greatest number of newspapers over the years, Winona with 22 and New Ulm and Minneapolis with 10 each accounted for a sizable proportion of the state's German press. The *Neu Ulm Pionier*, established by the Turners as "an organ for the propagation of radical principles," had a circulation of 1,200 in 1860; its publication was interrupted by the Dakota War of 1862, but it continued as the *New Ulm Post* from 1864 to 1933. Winona's earliest German-language weeklies, the *Winona Banner* (1866) and the *Mississippi Bote* (Messenger, 1870–71), were of brief duration, but the Leicht press endured. Its founder, Bavarian-born Joseph Leicht, began his newspaper career in St. Louis, moved in 1869 to Fountain City, Wisconsin, across the Mississippi from Winona, and in 1881 started the *Westlicher Herold* (Western Herald, 1881–1924), a Democratic weekly that absorbed the *Winona Adler* (Eagle, 1873–89) eight years later. Through a series of consolidations with 22 German papers in Wisconsin, 10 in Minnesota, and others in Nebraska, Montana, and Pennsylvania, the Leicht enterprise became National Weeklies, Inc., boasting in 1940 a circulation of 250,000 for 11 of its publications. Only one Minneapolis publication survived for long; the *Freie Presse-Herold* (1869–1924) became part of the Leicht newspapers in 1919. For 17 years, however, the German community in Minneapolis enjoyed a weekly humorous paper, *Der Lustige Bruder* (Jolly Fellow), founded in 1890.[60]

Twenty-six communities in Minnesota have at some time supported German-language publications. In 1910 they served an estimated 8,000 to 10,000 families in the core region of the Minnesota River Valley. Two with some longevity were the weekly *Duluth-Superior Volksfreund* (People's Friend, 1886–1901) and the *Unser Besucher* (Our Visitor, 1901–22) in the Mennonite stronghold of Mountain Lake. But periodicals from beyond the state — especially from St. Louis, Milwaukee, and Cincinnati — also circulated. The Carver County German Reading Society, for example, subscribed to newspapers from Baltimore, Chicago, and San Francisco. Church members could choose from a variety of national publications, including *Der Lutheraner*, *Die Abendschule* (Night School), *Der Friedensbote* (Messenger of Peace), and *Wahrheitsfreund* (Friend of Truth), to name a few, while freethinking families took the *Freidenker* (Freethinker, 1872–1942) and the *Amerikanische Turnzeitung* (American Turner Journal, 1885–1943), both published in Milwaukee.

As the state's German-born population decreased, so did the newspapers that served it during the years of assimilation. One scholar maintained that the effect of World War I on the German-language press was "catastrophic," but it can be argued that with seven papers still publishing in 1920, Minnesota did not follow the national pattern. Of the one daily and 18 weekly German newspapers in the state, only four ceased publication during 1917–18, although at least 20 German-language journals went out of circulation during the 1890s and the first decade of the 20th century.

Newspapers have long served as political forums. During the 1850s and 1860s the national issues that engaged the attention of German immigrants were nativism (an ideology that advocated favoring native citizens over the foreign born), prohibition, slavery, homestead legislation, and enfranchisement. Until late in the 1850s, German settlers (who could vote after four months' residence) tended to cast their ballots for Democrats, largely because of the nativist attitude of the Republicans. The state Republican convention in 1859 adopted an antinativist plank similar to the "Dutch plank" in the national platform. And German Americans were also disgruntled by the failure of the Democrats to enact a homestead bill. Thus when the Republican party included a homestead plank in its 1860 platform, the move was acclaimed in Minnesota's German press.[61]

The election of 1860 may be said to mark the entrance of the so-called German vote in national politics. It was wooed by both major parties, each of which named a German as one of the four electors on its state slate. This made good political sense in Minnesota, where one out of every seven potential voters was German. A number of scholars have pointed out the effect of German votes in the election of Abraham Lincoln as president, but in Minnesota it has not been established that these were crucial to his victory. In 1860 the Minnesota counties with the largest German populations were Brown, Carver, Hennepin, Le Sueur, Nicollet, Ramsey, Scott, Sibley, Stearns, and Winona. Only Scott and Stearns returned Democratic majorities. Nevertheless the county vote totals cannot be attributed to any one ethnic group, since Minnesota counties are large and election results at the township level are not uniformly obtainable for the state. It is still more difficult to identify the religious faiths of voters and to explain voting majorities when German Lutherans, Catholics, Methodists, and freethinkers are intersettled. In general, however, Democratic majorities in 1860 coincided with prevailing Catholic populations, while Republicans were more numerous in Lutheran areas of Minnesota.

On the issue of slavery, Minnesota Germans were generally in favor of gradual abolition — an attitude prevalent among most of their countrymen in the northern states. Indeed, the abolition question was tailor-made for the forty-eighters, many of whom were influential with the German-language press of the nation. Minnesota's most prominent forty-eighters, Albert Wolff and Samuel Ludvigh, both opposed slavery. In the Turner colony of New Ulm denunciation of the institution could be taken for granted, because the national Turner organization was committed to antislavery. On April 21, 1860, the *Neu Ulm Pionier*, whose motto was "Free men, free labor, free press," described slavery as "the most ruinous curse." A number of German churches — notably the Catholic and those of the Missouri Lutheran Synod — either took no stand or were split on the issue, but German Methodists, Moravians, and most freethinkers were strongly antislavery. Interestingly, at the end of the Civil War, the New Ulm paper moderated its opinion and advocated that the solution of Black enfranchisement might vary from state to state.[62]

Another political issue on which Minnesota Germans had strong feelings was prohibition. Measures associated with opposition to the sale of liquor to the Indians as early as 1855 were not popular among Minnesota Germans, although German Methodists consistently favored temperance. Most others regarded prohibition and Sunday observance as worse for the breweries, which were generally German owned, than for the whiskey trade, which was largely controlled by Old-Stock Americans. Many felt such laws denied their right to continue the cultural tradition of a Sunday family outing to beer gardens, parks, and picnic grounds, preferably with music. When the Republican party relaxed its 1857 stand on Sunday laws and prohibition, the Germans approved. In the early 20th century, county option, which allowed its voters to decide whether each county would be "wet" or "dry," set many Minnesota Germans against the Progressive movement and thus helped the Republicans retain them. One journalist claimed that the "records of state legislators representing German-American areas were often reactionary," reflecting their attitude on the liquor question. However, to identify legislators as German born or of German descent is difficult after the pioneer period since names can be misleading. For example, the Democratic gubernatorial candidate in 1883, Adolph Biermann, was born in Norway.

The homestead plank of the 1860 Republican platform was supported by German Republican papers, but as an issue it was perhaps of less significance to individual Germans in the core region than is generally assumed. The Homestead Act of 1862 was, however, a key factor in the expansion of German settlers into western Minnesota. German Republican newspapers greeted its passage as a victory for justice and humanity, even as a triumph of free labor.[63]

In the 1870s renewed indications of support for the Democratic party surfaced among Germans. In German-Catholic Stearns County, for example, the incumbent Republican president, Ulysses S. Grant, lost to the Democratic challenger in 1872; four years later the county again backed the Democratic candidate for president. During the 1890s and through the first decade of the 20th century, its voters were largely loyal to the Democrats, but the onset of World War I generated great hostility to Woodrow Wilson and his party. In 1916 the predominantly German residents there voted Republican by almost seven to one. One political analyst has stated that Stearns County "cost Wilson Minnesota in 1916"; another authority believed that German-American political influence in that election reached a degree "never before nor since achieved by a non-English ethnic group in

the United States." State-wide, however, the actions of the Minnesota Commission of Public Safety against German Americans during United States involvement in the war were inextricably associated with the Republican administration of Governor Joseph A. A. Burnquist, an association that "unwittingly encouraged the alienation of German-Americans from the conservative wing of the Minnesota Republican party" and aligned them with the more radical Nonpartisan League and the emerging Farmer-Labor coalition. By 1927 the Stearns County electorate chose the new Farmer-Labor party over the Republicans, while the Democrats ran a poor third.[64]

World War I

During the decades before World War I editorial opinion in German weeklies regarding foreign policy issues was fairly united. The papers opposed protective tariffs more strongly in Minnesota than in the German press as a whole; most, however, were unenthusiastic about the antitrust actions of Theodore Roosevelt's administration. On foreign affairs, the journals did not look with favor upon United States imperialism in the Philippines following the Spanish-American War of 1898. Nor did they regard as desirable the application of the Monroe Doctrine to the Panamanian revolution in 1903 or to other Latin American interventions in the early years of the 20th century. By and large the state German-language press was nonpartisan on most foreign policy issues, expressing more concern with domestic matters such as the tariff and prohibition.[65]

In their attitude toward Germany before World War I, German Americans in Minnesota and elsewhere took pride in the unification of the Reich and in its imperial achievements. As American popular feeling against Germany increased in the spring of 1915, lecturers and the state's German-language press, which had an estimated circulation of 125,000, seemed to become more stridently pro-German as they attempted to "mobilize the political and economic power of their own constituency on the side of American neutrality." On May 13, 1915, six days after the sinking of the "Lusitania," *Der Wanderer* (St. Paul) carried a lengthy front-page editorial hailing the event as a proof of the effectiveness of Germany's undersea campaign against the "inhuman" British blockade and censuring Theodore Roosevelt and the "Anglophile" American press for their condemnation of the "atrocity." In October Eugene Kuehnemann, professor of German at Breslau University, gave an inflammatory lecture before a full house at New Ulm in which he touted Germany as "the greatest democratic state in the world" and insisted that it had not been responsible for the outbreak of World War I. The following year, while war clouds drew ever closer to the United States, Joseph Matt, longtime editor of *Der Wanderer*, defended German *Kultur* against that of "decadent" France.

In March, 1916, when the entire Minnesota delegation in the House of Representatives, as well as one of its United States senators, seemed to favor the Gore-McLemore resolutions warning Americans against taking passage on belligerent ships, the *New York Times* declared that the congressmen were pro-German. The Minnesota delegation, said the paper on March 22, 1916, consisted of "eleven Kaiserists and one American" (Knute Nelson, who had been born in Norway). That they faithfully represented the German-American point of view is suggested by the fact that the German-American Alliance, a loose federation of organizations with over 3,000,000 members in 40 states, had urged them to vote for tabling the resolution. A year later three Minnesota congressmen from St. Paul, St. Peter, and St. Cloud — all of which had substantial German populations — and a fourth from Minneapolis voted against President Woodrow Wilson's declaration of war.[66]

The Alliance, which had come into being in 1902 as a defense against the Anti-Saloon League, was the leading German-American organization in the state at the outset of World War I. In 1916 it raised money for the German and Austro-Hungarian Red Cross by holding a three-day *Volksfest des Nordwestens* in the St. Paul Auditorium. Early in 1917 the Alliance petitioned Senator Moses Clapp to exert himself against the war; at the same time, the organization's president reminded members of their duty to support actions of the government — be they right or wrong. By 1918, however, the German-American Alliance was a shadow of its prewar membership, for many state chapters had either disbanded or assumed new names.[67]

The demise of the Alliance was but one manifestation of the difficulties faced by German Americans and other immigrants during World War I. Their loyalty was seriously questioned by both federal and state governments. Under the guise of an excessive patriotism, Minnesota was especially severe. Soon after the United States declared war on Germany, the legislature on April 16, 1917, created the Minnesota Commission of Public Safety and ordered it to protect life and property and to aid the prosecution of the war. In a move unusual even in wartime, the lawmakers invested the commission with sweeping powers which it used energetically to harass non-English-speaking immigrants, especially Germans, and members of the Nonpartisan League, a supposedly radical farmer-labor movement which had begun in North Dakota and spread to Minnesota. To carry out its overly zealous aim of achieving what it regarded as nothing less than 100% patriotism, the commission employed a network of spies, undue use of its investigatory powers, the encouragement of denunciations often made out of personal spite, and the deplorable compliance of Minnesotans, including German-born citizens, many of whom hastened to express their loyalty. During 1917 and 1918 there were 1,739 complaints made to the commission, and 974 (56%) were directed against Germans.[68]

The commission's attention was quickly attracted to a rally, held at New Ulm on July 25, 1917, under the auspices of the People's Council of America. This organization did not believe any war was justified, except in self-defense and then only by a referendum; it also opposed compulsory sending of troops overseas. The New Ulm rally was attended by a crowd estimated at between 6,000 and 10,000; the main speaker, New Ulm's city attorney and the son of city founder and Civil War hero Wilhelm Pfaender, was Albert E. Pfaender. He advised draftees to abide by the law but urged those still at home to petition Congress for a constitutional

RESIDENTS OF New Ulm gathered to watch Brown County men march off to war in 1917.

amendment that would provide for a referendum on the question of war.

The Safety Commission's reaction to the meeting was swift. Calling the gathering "unpatriotic and un-American," Burnquist suspended three of New Ulm's officials — Louis A. Fritsche, Pfaender, and Louis G. Vogel, Brown County auditor — and the commission launched an investigation. Pfaender was accused of sedition and of violating his oath as an attorney. The state bar association was asked to investigate and disbar him if he were proved disloyal. The commission sustained Pfaender's removal from office and exacted from him a promise to stump the state making loyalty speeches. Fritsche, a physician who was the son of native-born parents, was investigated by the commission and by the state medical society. At the hearing, held before the Brown-Redwood County Medical Society, five of seven members found him not guilty. Vogel, the third official, was exonerated.

Another commission victim was Wisconsin-born William A. Schaper, for 15 years a professor of political science at the University of Minnesota who had done graduate work in Berlin. As a result of a letter from the commission charging him with disloyalty, Schaper was dismissed by the board of regents in September, 1917, as a "rabid pro-German." A member of the board compared the professor to Albert Pfaender, whose loyalty, he said, was the "kind that hurts the cause of America." Schaper vehemently denied the charges, asked for a hearing, and maintained that he had advised students to abide by the law and register for the draft, but his protests were unavailing. Ultimately he left Minnesota to join the faculty of the University of Oklahoma.[69]

Despite mounting war fever, the Minneapolis Board of Education on September 19, 1917, found absolute abolishment of the teaching of German in public schools not yet advisable. Nevertheless the commission published lists of permissible and unsuitable books; 30 were banned entirely; some among those permitted needed corrections. By the following May, 119 of 222 state high schools reporting to the commission had used blacklisted books; 93 discarded them; 23 eliminated objectionable parts; and three used the latter to discuss German fallacies. Twenty-five schools had discontinued German-language classes, and 34 more planned to do so by the end of the school year.

The commission received many letters from people who wished to see the speaking and writing of German outlawed entirely. Among them were the pastor of a Lutheran church in Chaska who complained that he had been forced to resign because he was "too patriotic" and who told the commission he felt "that people should have lived thirty to forty years in Carver Co. without being able to write a single English character and to speak but a few words is a shame, to bring up our children that way is a crime"; a doctor from Arlington who wanted to "cut out [all] the foreign language" from schools and churches and who signed himself "neither Catholic nor a German Lutheran but an American"; and an attorney in Ortonville who wanted "Minnesota to follow South Dakota's example" and forbid the use of German completely. One man who worked for a construction company thought that speaking German should be prohibited on the telephone because "line crews in Stearns County said they never heard a word of English." Similarly a woman from Brownton complained that she "heard nothing but German on the telephone lines." While the records showed all social classes participated in voluntary anti-German activities, one excellent study of Stearns County revealed that educated professional people were more often the denunciators than were blue-collar workers.[70]

Lutheran pastors were divided; some assured the commission of parishional loyalties, others were "stubborn," and still others inquired what they were supposed to do. One parish was reprimanded for holding a dedication ceremony with German and English sermons. A Le Sueur County jeweler, who served as a justice of the peace, said "I am a German born, like the German people but hate the German Government." He asked the commission to "take some steps to check the Pro-German activities in and about Le Sueur," reporting a list of suspects with the request: "Please do not expose my name at pre[se]nt at least."[71]

But the commission did not wait for people to come to it. Its efforts were especially directed toward the control of immigrants and labor unions. It required the registration of all aliens in the state, producing a set of records which offer a wealth of data on immigrant patterns in 1917–18, outlawed strikes and further efforts to unionize workers, authorized a Home Guard, organized local councils throughout the state in which women's groups were enlisted to help sell some $450,000,000 worth of Liberty Bonds in Minnesota, commissioned over 600 temporary constables, operated a publicity bureau which "flooded the state with informational bulletins, news, and reports," and maintained a censorship division to which foreign-language newspapers were regularly required to send English translations of their issues. The division received frequent reports on the *St. Paul Volkszeitung*, for example, from a self-appointed spy. The commission further augmented its manpower in 1917–18 by employing 60 men of the Pinkerton Detective Agency and a

number of "special employees" who toured the state checking on suspects.

One special employee in the Wilton area wrote that "we have some bad ones we must reach and the only way I know to reach them is to send a detective this way or else get up some kind of a pledge card that they must sign or go to prison." In most instances no serious offenses were uncovered. A commission man who was able to get German-speaking telephone operators "into the inner circle" might find a "radical" German Lutheran minister at Buffalo Lake, but he could discover "absolutely no organized attempt to combat the government."

Attempts to promote loyalty among German Americans through lectures were handicapped because not many German-speaking lecturers were available. One F. Osten-Sacken who lectured commercially on the "Highways and Byways of Life," according to his letterhead, offered his services as a patriot and a member of the German royal family but was turned down. A reporter from Paynesville informed the commission that "Germans won't go to hear any Lecture." In St. Paul "Patriotic Americans of German Origin" was organized on April 2, 1918, to bring "citizens of German lineage . . . to see their patriotic duty, especially in purchasing Liberty bonds."[72]

The local councils tracked down persons suspected of disloyalty and harassed others who did not buy what they deemed a fair share of Liberty Bonds. In Cottonwood County, for example, two Russian-born Mennonites, both of whom had lived in the United States since 1875, appeared before a county Safety Commission hearing to respond to such charges. One explained that he had come to America "to get away from war. Our religion does not allow war." His questioners responded that he had "too much property" to refuse to buy an $800 bond, and they concluded his hearing by asking who he wanted to see win the war. "I don't care," he replied. "I would like to see it stopped, that's all. I am for America." His fellow Mennonite, who had also refused to buy bonds, was threatened with jail and called an enemy of the country. He replied that while President Wilson merely asked people to purchase, "You say, 'You have to.'" Pressured further he pointed out that he was "sworn to this country and not to British and France and Russia," adding "I do not believe in war. I believe in peace. . . . You are my brother." The fortitude of the German-speaking Mennonite "Russlaenders" is an important aspect of the Mennonite folk culture in Cottonwood County.[73]

Language and Culture

World War I accelerated the transition in parochial schools and elsewhere from German to English. Before 1917 nearly two-thirds of the state's church schools had used German as a language of instruction. Among Lutheran schools, bilingual teaching by 1931 continued in just over one-fourth of them, and one authority stated that by the mid-20th century "Catholics and Lutherans had abandoned German entirely," leaving its preservation in parochial teaching to groups such as the Amish and the Mennonites. The decline in the number of German-language newspapers also continued. While restrictions placed on them by World War I dealt the initial blow, the Depression years of the 1930s and the emergence of radio as a competitor probably administered the *coup de grace* to those papers that had survived the war. Nationally 433 German-language weeklies, for example, were published in 1910; by 1960 the number had dropped to 29. In Minnesota the last one disappeared in 1957. As this was being written, the *Volkszeitung Tribune* was still being published in Omaha, although it was edited in Minneapolis.[74]

While the transition from German to English in schools, churches, and other organizations proceeded, not all middle-class Germans in Minnesota lost their ethnic self-consciousness. In the 1940s some German-American homes still revealed much about the family's social status and period of emigration through memorabilia, furnishings, and manner of speech. World War II produced a campaign against the Japanese but no "routing the hun" — a phrase used by the Public Safety Commission. German prisoners of war were sought after as farm laborers, work for which they volunteered. Farmers in Minnesota's Red River Valley obtained such help from army headquarters in Omaha. Interviews with some farmers who used prisoners from a camp at Ortonville showed that the hosts corresponded with the prisoners after the war and sent them packages. One farmer described difficulties at first with "arrogant" stormtroopers; another was almost proud to have employed the "élite of all the German army" — some men of the Rommel Corps.[75]

It has been estimated that there were some 9,000,000 German-speaking people in the United States in 1910. By 1940 the figure had fallen to 4,950,000, but in 1970 it was reported at 6,093,054. By the latter year 17.4% of the state's foreign born spoke German. In the metropolitan Twin Cities area of over 1,800,000 people, more than 116,000 persons spoke German — a larger number of them in St. Paul than in Minneapolis. The dialects of parents could still be discerned from time to time in the little German spoken by 1980. The number of churches offering German-language services dwindled, until by 1975 only 12 Lutheran churches in the state, for example, offered sermons in German. None of the German Catholic national parishes in St. Paul provided homilies in that language in 1981.[76]

Among German-American organizations one could find as recently as 1975 evidence of German language and customs being fostered. There were such groups as the German-American National Congress, the Volksfest Association of Minnesota, the Catholic Aid Society, and the Turners in St. Paul; the German Club and a theater offering one German film each month in Minneapolis; the Schuhplattlers, a dancing group, in Excelsior; and singing and athletic societies in New Ulm and in Stearns County. Six radio stations provided some German-language programs, and an educational television station presented classes in the language. Despite these activities, one student of German ethnic culture pointed out that as a living language, German, for all practical purposes, did not exist in Minnesota. Rather, it belonged to the "romanticism of memory" — nostalgia among persons of German immigrant stock.

The later generations of German Americans among Minnesota's people no longer harbor much nostalgia for the homeland overseas, nor do they evince great interest in things German. The idol of the forty-eighters, Friedrich von Schiller, has a monument in heavily used Como Park in St. Paul, but one wonders how many passersby find it meaningful. Like other Americans, those of German descent have become more eager to investigate their family backgrounds since the upsurge of interest in genealogy that occurred in the 1970s. In so doing some have procured recently published books, painstakingly compiled by a *Heimat Verein* (Hometown Society) in West Germany, about a single district, parish, or village now beyond Germany's borders, or boarded chartered planes to Europe to satisfy their curiosity. But thus far neither in the United States nor in Minnesota has the German immigrant experience attracted the scholarly attention lavished on many other groups in recent decades.[77]

When one recalls that there were no fewer than 9,000,000 German-speaking people in the United States in 1910, their seemingly thorough assimilation represents a feat of staggering proportions — "the most striking event of its kind in the annals of modern history," wrote Heinz Kloss in 1966. "No other nationality group of equal numerical strength and living in one country has ever been so well nigh completely assimilated." Another observer wrote in 1873 that "in ceasing to be German," the immigrants "become American; but, on the other hand, not American in precisely the signification that word bears today; for America, even, is not exempt from the laws which produce . . . the constant variation of national character."[78]

The nuances of that transition remain to be explored. Surprisingly few have as yet been studied. The myth that Germans are or were "the best farmers with small houses and big barns" has been modified by modern comparative investigations, which indicated that other ethnic groups scored higher on several points. Many other aspects of the assimilation story remain untouched. It could be suggested that as Minnesota's German settlers shifted from a traditional, communal attitude to a capitalistic, contractual one — from *Gemeinschaft* to *Gesellschaft* — ethnic differences faded. How that phenomenon took place within the state at various times and places is a topic deserving of considerable further research.

Reference notes

[1] United States, *Census, 1860, Population,* 621; 1970, vol. 1, part 25, pp. 226, 252; State of Minnesota, *Census, 1905,* 120–122. In 1860 a large number of immigrants from Alsace and Lorraine were counted as French, although they were of German descent and language; U.S., *Census, 1860,* xxix. The manner of counting these groups continued to be complicated from 1871 until after the Treaty of Versailles in 1919. In 1870 combined Swedish and Norwegian immigrants outnumbered the Germans for the first time; *Census, 1870,* p. 360.

[2] Hildegard Binder Johnson, "Distribution of German Pioneer Population in Minnesota," in *Rural Sociology,* 6:1, 16–34 (March, 1941), and "The Location of German Immigrants in the Middle West," in Association of American Geographers, *Annals,* 41:1–41 (March, 1951). The Mennonites from the Crimea, who settled in Cottonwood and Watonwan counties in the 1870s and 1880s, are a Minnesota example of the tenacity with which German minorities have maintained their cultural and linguistic traditions for over 100

years; see note 29, below. For information on the location of ethnic Germans in Europe between 1939 and 1952, see Malcolm J. Proudfoot, *European Refugees: A Study in Forced Population Movement* (Evanston, Ill., 1956), especially table on p. 370.

[3] On distribution of Germans, here and below, see U.S., *Census, 1910, Population,* 1:791, 792, 2:996; Johnson, in Association of American Geographers, *Annals,* 41:2, 10–12. Minnesota's first territorial governor, Alexander Ramsey, was a Pennsylvanian of half-German stock who "spoke as well in German as in English." James H. Baker, *Lives of the Governors of Minnesota,* 28 (*Minnesota Historical Collections,* vol. 13 — St. Paul, 1908). Ramsey's first message to the territorial legislature, September 4, 1849, was published in German as *Botschaft vom Gouverneur des Territoriums Minnesota an die beiden Häuser der Gesetzgebenden Versammlung.*

[4] The peace of Augsburg signed in 1555 divided church lands between Lutheran and Roman Catholic and gave the ruling prince the right to determine which religion was to be official within his domain. The division of religion by geographical region given here, however, is a simplification, because many clerical and secular territories dating from the 15th century were incorporated into larger political units during the 19th century — the diocese of Münster into Prussia and the free city of Nuremburg into Bavaria, for example. The first question on the *Ausreisepass,* a document needed for permission to emigrate, concerned religion. See, for example, Paulin Blecker, *Deep Roots,* 26 (St. Cloud, 1958). On other groups, see Berenice Cooper, "Die Freie Gemeinde: Freethinkers on the Frontier," in *Minnesota History,* 41:53–60 (Summer, 1968); Eric E. Hirshler, ed., *Jews from Germany in the United States,* 162–168 (New York, 1955) and Chapter 26, below.

[5] In view of the subject's complexity, it is understandable that a definitive history of Germans in America is not yet available. Albert Bernhard Faust, *The German Element in the United States* (Reprint ed., New York, 1927) has a eulogistic approach which is outdated; La Vern J. Rippley, *The German-Americans* (Boston, 1976) is a readable overview and includes World War II. See also Clarence A. Glasrud, ed., *A Heritage Deferred: The German-Americans in Minnesota* (Moorhead, 1981).

[6] Patricia C. Harpole and Mary D. Nagle, eds., *Minnesota Territorial Census, 1850,* vii, 15, 40–59, 75–91 (St. Paul, 1972); U.S., *Census, 1860, Population,* 253, 262; Johnson, in *Rural Sociology,* 6:24.

[7] On Grimm, who lived in Laketown Township, see June D. Holmquist and Jean A. Brookins, *Minnesota's Major Historic Sites: A Guide,* 56 (St. Paul, 1972); Everett E. Edwards and Horace H. Russell, "Wendelin Grimm and Alfalfa," in *Minnesota History,* 19:21–33 (March, 1938).

[8] Of a total of 41,353 Germans in the state in 1870, 23,688 were from Prussia and 5,191 from Germany (69.8%); in 1880 of 67,137 Germans, 38,067 were from Prussia and 13,652 from Germany (77%). Fourteen German states were listed in U.S., *Census, 1860, Population,* 262; 1870, p. 338; 1880, pp. 461–464. Germans emigrated from all parts of the former Holy Roman Empire. After its unification under Prussia in 1871, Germany continued to issue emigration statistics that distinguished among 13 Prussian provinces and 25 political divisions such as Bavaria. This differentiation cannot be made for U.S. or Minnesota statistics. See John C. Massmann, "German Immigration to Minnesota, 1850–1890," 228, Ph.D. thesis, University of Minnesota, 1966; Wolfgang Köllmann and Peter Marschalck, "German Emigration to the United States," in *Perspectives in American History,* 7:499–554 (1973). Austrians present a special problem; census statistics offer inexact information since the term "Austrian" when used on the iron ranges meant all Slavs, but in Jackson County, for example, the names are clearly Czech. It is probable that in heavily German counties those listed as Aus-

trian were actually German speakers from Austria, although they could have been Hungarian or members of other ethnic groups within the Austro-Hungarian Empire. For maps of Germany, see F. W. Putzger, *Historischer Schulatlas* (Leipzig, 1918) and *Historischer Weltatlas* (98th ed., Berlin and Bielefeld, 1974).

[9] Here and below, see Johnson, in *Rural Sociology,* 6:1, 29–31; U.S., *Census, 1880, Population,* 493; 1900, clxxiii; Minnesota Commissioner of Statistics, *Seventeenth Annual Report,* 457 (1886); State of Minnesota, *Census, 1905,* 122. See also A. E. Zucker, ed., *The Forty-Eighters: Political Refugees of the German Revolution of 1848* (Philadelphia, 1952).

[10] Here and below, see Peter Marschalck, *Deutsche Überseewanderung im 19. Jahrhundert,* 21, 34–43 (Stuttgart, 1973); Harald Focke, "Friedrich List und die Südwestdeutsche Amerikaauswanderung 1817–1846," cited in Günther Moltmann, "Deutsche Amerikaauswanderung im 19. Jahrhundert," in *Amerika Studien,* 44:73 (Stuttgart, 1976); Rippley, *German-Americans,* 78. The term "dwarf economy" was introduced by List. Some Germans who found their way to Minnesota by the 1850s had participated in the emigration of the first three decades of the 19th century. For an example see the headstone of Henry Marshall in New Trier cemetery, Dakota County.

[11] Rolf Engelsing, *Bremen als Auswanderungshafen 1683–1880,* 26 (Publications of the State Archives of the Free City of Bremen, Paper 29 — Bremen, 1961); Walter F. Willcox, ed., *International Migrations,* 1:686–709 (Reprint ed., New York, 1969). After 1866 "Prussia" could mean the area west to Aachen, east to Tilsit, south to Saarbrücken, or north to Flensburg. With the exception of a few small enclaves, Prussia at one time or another consisted of all of Germany north of Bavaria, Baden, and the Palatinate.

[12] Mack Walker, *Germany and the Emigration, 1816–1885,* 49–51 (Cambridge, Mass., 1964).

[13] John W. Tubbesing Papers, originals in possession of Mrs. C. J. Thiseth, Red Wing, translation in MHS; Franklyn Curtiss-Wedge, ed., *History of Goodhue County,* 680 (Chicago, 1909); Elizabeth Marshall and Dorothy Beattie, "Immigration," unpublished manuscript, 1976, in Goodhue County Historical Society, copy in MEHP Papers, MHS.

[14] Engelsing, *Bremen als Auswanderungshafen,* 148, 149; Albert Wolff to Horace Austin, September 7, 1870, Governors' files, Minnesota State Archives, MHS. In 1873 a thaler was worth $.71. The term "forty-eighter" refers to a relatively small group of German-speaking immigrants whose move to the United States was a direct result of their participation in the German political upheavals of 1848 and whose influence was disproportionately greater than their numbers. The term does not include the majority of Germans who emigrated at that time for economic reasons. Carl Wittke, *Refugees of Revolution: The German Forty-Eighters in America,* 58–60 (Philadelphia, 1952); Zucker, *The Forty-Eighters,* vii–ix, 22.

[15] Walker, *Germany and the Emigration,* 90–92, 160; Günter Moltmann, "Die Transportation von Sträflingen im Rahmen der deutschen Amerikaauswanderung des 19. Jahrhunderts," in *Amerika Studien,* 44:150–155, 175; Philip Taylor, *The Distant Magnet: European Emigration to the U.S.A.,* chapters 7 and 8 (London, 1971).

[16] Wolff to Austin, September 7, 1870, Governors' files, State Archives; Walter Diener, "Die Auswanderung aus dem Amte Gemünden (Hunsrück) im 19. Jahrhundert. Nach den Bürgermeisterakten," in *Rheinische Vierteljahrsblätter* (Quarterly), 5:195, 200, 213 (April, July, 1935); Friedrich Schmitz to "Well beloved Parents and Brothers and Sisters," April 4, 1858, March 13, 1859, in Joseph Scheben, "Letters from Minnesota Immigrants to Relatives in Germany, 1858–1931," originals privately owned, copies in MHS.

[17] Here and below, see Hildegard B. Johnson, "Eduard Pelz and German Emigration," in *Minnesota History,* 31:222–230 (December

1950); Eduard Pelz, *Nachrichten über Minnesota* (Bamberg, Ger., 1858), three editions of which were published. See also Thomas Rawlings, *Die Auswanderung mit besonderer Beziehung auf Minnesota und Britisch Columbia*, trans. and introduction by Pelz (Hamburg, 1866). For examples of German geographic literature about Minnesota, see Karl Andree, *Geographische Wanderungen*, 227–242 (Dresden, 1859); Traugott Bromme, *Handbuch für Auswanderer und Reisende nach Nord-, Mittel- und Süd-Amerika* (Bamberg, Ger., 1854); Carl L. Fleischmann, *Der Nordamerikanische Landwirth: Ein Handbuch für Ansiedler in den Vereinigten Staaten* (Frankfurt, Ger., 1848).

[18] See Wolff's translation, *Minnesota als eine Heimath für Auswanderer*, 29, 30 (St. Paul, 1866). The English edition entitled *Minnesota as a Home for Immigrants* was commissioned by the legislature to set "forth the advantages which this State offers to immigrants"; Johnson, in *Minnesota History*, 31:226. On encouragement of emigration, below, see, for example, Livia Appel and Theodore C. Blegen, "Official Encouragement of Immigration to Minnesota during the Territorial Period," Harold F. Peterson, "Early Minnesota Railroads and the Quest for Settlers," and Carlton C. Qualey, "A New El Dorado: Guides to Minnesota" — all in *Minnesota History*, 5:167–203 (August, 1923), 13:25–44 (March, 1932), 42:215–224 (Summer, 1971).

[19] Promotional activities of the St. Paul and Pacific and the Northern Pacific Railway companies are discussed in detail in Massmann, "German Immigration to Minnesota," 98–134; Harold F. Peterson, "Some Colonization Projects of the Northern Pacific Railroad," in *Minnesota History*, 10:127–144 (June, 1929).

[20] The author is indebted to John Hickey, Ph.D. candidate in the Dept. of Geography, University of Minnesota, for information about the difficulties in using shipping lists in the National Archives.

[21] Grace Lovel May and Wilhelmina Pfaender Loenholdt, *Memory's Trail*, 9–14 (New Ulm, 1954). On Hecker, see Dumas Malone, ed., *Dictionary of American Biography*, 8:493 (New York, 1932). For other examples of immigration routes, see Introduction, above, and 1870 U.S. manuscript census schedules, microfilm in MHS.

[22] Here and below, see 1870 U.S. manuscript census schedules, tabulation in MEHP Papers.

[23] *Daily Minnesotian*, April 3, 1858; *St. Paul Daily Press*, June 4, 1861; *Goodhue County Republican* (Red Wing), May 11, 1860. See also map showing the density per square mile of "natives of the German Empire," in U.S., *Census*, 1880, *Population*, 609. A *Turnverein* was an association devoted to physical and intellectual development.

[24] William Abell to State Board of Immigration, Governors' files, State Archives; *Wochenblatt der New York Staatszeitung*, January 29, 1881.

[25] Rudolph Leonhart, *Erinnerungen an Neu Ulm, Erlebnisse aus dem Indianer-Gemetzel in Minnesota 1862*, 44 (Pittsburg[h], 1880).

[26] See 1870 U.S. manuscript census schedules, microfilm in MHS, for township data in the above-named counties; Neil A. Markus, "Areal Patterns of Religious Denominationalism in Minnesota," 56, master's thesis, University of Minnesota, 1961; Marian Deininger and Douglas Marshall, "A Study of Land Ownership by Ethnic Groups from Frontier Times to the Present in a Marginal Farming Area in Minnesota," in *Land Economics*, 31:357 (November, 1955). For maps and tables on German population and growth, see Hildegard B. Johnson, "Factors Influencing the Distribution of the German Pioneer Population in Minnesota," in *Agricultural History*, 19:42, 44, 47 (January, 1945); Johnson, in Association of American Geographers, *Annals*, 41:21–23, and in *Rural Sociology*, 6:1. On frontier lines and ethnic distribution, see also John R. Borchert and Donald P. Yaeger, *Atlas of Minnesota Resources and Settlement*, 38 (Revised ed., St. Paul, 1969).

[27] Here and below, see 1860 and 1870 U.S. manuscript census

schedules, data in MEHP Papers. See also Ralph H. Brown, *Historical Geography of the United States*, 340 (Reprint ed., New York, 1976).

[28] Robert J. Voigt, *Pierzana, 1865–1965: The Religious and Secular History of the Community at Pierz, Minnesota*, 12–18 (St. Cloud, 1965); Kathleen Neils Conzen, "Foundation of a Rural German-Catholic Culture: Farm and Family in St. Martin, Minn., 1857–1915," 1–29, in University of Notre Dame, *Working Paper Series*, No. 2 (Spring, 1977). For more information on Father Pierz, see note 44, and Chapter 20, below.

[29] On the Mennonites in Minnesota, see Richard Sallet, trans. by La Vern J. Rippley and Armand Bauer, *Russian-German Settlements in the United States*, 53, 113 (Fargo, N. Dak., 1974); Ferdinand P. Schultz, *A History of the Settlement of German Mennonites from Russia at Mountain Lake, Minnesota* (Minneapolis, 1938). Another small, German-speaking religious group, the Hutterites, established a colony near Graceville, Big Stone County, in 1956. Victor Peters, *All Things Common: The Hutterian Way of Life*, 210 (Minneapolis, 1965); *Minneapolis Star*, September 6, 1956, p. 6A. One Amish settlement was established in Winona County in 1974; others are located in Fillmore and Todd counties. *Minneapolis Sunday Tribune*, March 16, 1975, p. 1B; *Winona Daily News*, February 24, 1977, p. 8A; Christiane Buchinger-Heringman, *Wegweiser zur Wandertour: A Guide to the Historical and Cultural Background of Die Wandertour Durch Deutsch-Minnesota*, 40 (Moorhead, 1979).

[30] Carl Schurz to Margarethe Schurz, September 21, 1859, in Joseph Schaefer, trans. and ed., *Intimate Letters of Carl Schurz, 1841–1869*, 194 (*Wisconsin Historical Collections*, vol. 30 — Madison, 1928). See also Theodore C. Blegen, "The 'Fashionable Tour' on the Upper Mississippi," in *Minnesota History*, 20:377–396 (December, 1939).

[31] Thomas Hughes, "History of Steamboating on the Minnesota River," in *Minnesota Historical Collections*, vol. 10, part 1, pp. 134–137, 150 (St. Paul, 1905); William J. Petersen, "The Early History of Steamboating on the Minnesota River," in *Minnesota History*, 11:126 (June, 1930). See also *Minneapolis Sunday Tribune*, Centennial ed., August 28, 1949, p. 1, a map based on a survey of 1947–48 made by University of Minnesota graduate students under sociologist Douglas Marshall and by county agricultural agents; U.S., *Census*, 1900, *Population*, 762. The term "German Minnesota" was used for the *Wandertour* conducted in 1978 by Concordia College, Moorhead, which was routed through Waconia, Hamburg, Cologne, Arlington, New Ulm, Hutchinson, Collegeville, New Munich, Sauk Centre, and north to Bemidji. See note 29, above.

[32] For example, two northern Minnesota areas separated from the core regions were founded by Germans — Beaver Bay on the north shore of Lake Superior in Lake County and Hibbing on the Mesabi Iron Range in St. Louis County. Beaver Bay was founded by Christian and Henry Wieland, whose father was a well-to-do tanner in Neuenstadt am Kocher, Württemberg, and a forty-eighter. His sons reached Beaver Bay in 1856 with a group of 25 persons, including some Swiss. The area was still predominantly German in 1949. Franz Dietrich von Ahlen, better known as Frank Hibbing, emigrated from Kirchboitzen, Hanover, at the age of 18. An explorer of the Mesabi Range, he platted the town of Hibbing in 1893. See J. William Trygg, *Composite Maps (based on) Land Surveyors' Original Plats and Field Notes*, sheets 15, 17 (Ely, 1966), originals in MHS; Helen Wieland Skillings, *We're Standing on Iron! The Story of the Five Wieland Brothers, 1856–1883*, 3–8, 13, 49, 55 (Duluth, 1972); Walter Van Brunt, *Duluth and St. Louis County, Minnesota*, 1:124, 3:32–34 (Chicago, 1921); Jessie C. Davis, *Beaver Bay: Original North Shore Village*, 15, 17, 21 (Duluth, 1968).

[33] Eduard Petry, *Turnverein New Ulm, 1856–1906*, 9 (New Ulm, 1906); Hildegard B. Johnson, "The Founding of New Ulm, Minne-

sota," in *American-German Review*, June, 1946, p. 8; Fred W. Johnson, "The Acquisition of a Townsite," typewritten manuscript in Brown County Historical Society, New Ulm. Beinhorn's account of founding New Ulm was translated and published in the *New Ulm Review*, August 15, 1938, p. 4. On New Ulm as a utopia, see Alice Felt Tyler, "William Pfaender and the Founding of New Ulm," in *Minnesota History*, 30:32 (March, 1949); Noel Iverson, *Germania, U.S.A.: Social Change in New Ulm Minnesota*, 6 (Minneapolis, 1966).

[34] Willoughby M. Babcock, "Up the Minnesota Valley in 1853," in *Minnesota History*, 11:161, 162, 167 (June, 1930). Two general accounts of the region are Louis A. Fritsche, *History of Brown County, Minnesota*, 2 vols. (Reprint ed., Marceline, Mo., 1976), and Edward D. Neill, *History of the Minnesota Valley* (Minneapolis, 1882). The number of searchers varies as do the names of the four who continued toward Fort Ridgely. See Elroy E. Ubl, trans., *A Chronology of New Ulm, Minnesota, 1853–1899*, 1 (New Ulm, 1978); Alexander Berghold, "Geschichte von New Ulm," in *Der Deutsche Pionier* (Cincinnati), 4:124 (June, 1872); Leota M. Kellett, *Early Brown County*, 6 (New Ulm, 1966); Warren Upham, *Minnesota Geographic Names*, 67 (Reprint ed., St. Paul, 1969).

[35] Berghold, in *Der Deutsche Pionier*, 4:163; Russell W. Fridley, Leota M. Kellett, and June D. Holmquist, eds., *Charles E. Flandrau and the Defense of New Ulm*, end sheet map (New Ulm, 1962). The Indian village was probably the Sisseton settlement of Sleepy Eyes; his band is known to have had camps at the mouth of the Cottonwood River as early as 1838; see Edmund C. Bray and Martha Coleman Bray, *Joseph N. Nicollet on the Plains and Prairies: The Expeditions of 1838–39 with Journals, Letters, and Notes on the Dakota Indians*, 55, 255 (St. Paul, 1976). The Indians disputed the rights of the Germans to use their village, and the case was settled by a ruling from the commandant at Fort Snelling. See *New Ulm Journal*, August 13, 1954, p. 4.

[36] Here and two paragraphs below, see Berghold, in *Der Deutsche Pionier*, 4:163; Tyler, in *Minnesota History*, 30:30; Fridley *et al.*, eds., *Flandrau and the Defense of New Ulm*, 13–15. For a good reproduction of the original plat, see Alfred T. Andreas, *Illustrated Historical Atlas of the State of Minnesota*, 91 (Chicago, 1874).

[37] Tyler, in *Minnesota History*, 30:26–28; Minnesota, *Territorial Laws*, 1857, chapter 35, p. 147. Pfaender's letter proposed a settlement where the physical and mental aspects of Turnerism could be "practiced" without interference from American nativists. The Cincinnati *Turnverein* approved a committee to investigate a joint stock company, and eventually the project was submitted to the national meeting of the Turners. Heinrich Huhn, "Sonst und jetzt," in *Amerikanischer Turnkalender*, 28 ([Milwaukee?], 1893). For a general account of the movement, see Augustus C. Prahl, "The Turner," in Zucker, ed., *The Forty-Eighters*, 79–110. For an evaluation of the tension between "old" German immigrants and the forty-eighters and the latter's clash with nativism, see Iverson, *Germania*, 40–52. See also Emil Klapprecht, *Deutsche Chronik in der Geschichte des Ohio-Thales und seiner Hauptstadt Cincinnati*, chapter 28 (Cincinnati, 1864), for a contemporary account of struggles between anti-Catholic liberal Germans and Catholic forces.

[38] Here and below, see "Report of Agent Pfaender to the Administration," and "A Statement of the Aims and Purposes of the Turner Colonization Society," in Turner Colonization Society of Cincinnati file, Brown County Historical Society, New Ulm.

[39] Here and below, see Henry D. Dyck, "The Neu Ulm Pionier," in *American German Review*, February, 1952, pp. 35–38; Iverson, *Germania*, 63–65.

[40] Here and below, see Ubl, *Chronology*, 4, 21; Petry, *Turnverein*, 11, 12, 20, 27; Kenneth Carley, *The Sioux Uprising of 1862*, 32–39 (Revised ed., St. Paul, 1976); Hermann E. Rothfuss, "The Early German Theater in Minnesota," in *Minnesota History*, 32:168–172

(September, 1951), and "Criticism of the German-American Theater in Minnesota," in *Germanic Review*, 27:124–130 (April, 1952); William Pfaender, "Die Pioniere von Neu Ulm," in *Amerikanischer Turnkalender*, 65–68 (1881). On relations between German settlers and the Indians, see Johnson, in Association of American Geographers, *Annals*, 41:24, 30, 31, 40; Hugh Honor, *The New Golden Land: European Images of America from the Discoveries to the Present Time*, 232–242 (New York, 1975). Disagreements among New Ulm Turners appear in articles published in *Das Nordlicht* (New Ulm), a biweekly, four-page paper published between February 1, 1885, and January 16, 1887.

[41] Berghold's guide was entitled *Führer für Einwanderer deutscher Zunge nach Minnesota* (1876). See also *New Ulm Daily Journal*, June 26, 1962, p. 2; Iverson, *Germania*, 44, 45n, 92; Ubl, *Chronology*, 7, 21, 26, 79; Fritsche, ed., *History of Brown County*, 380, 388, 395; Alexander Berghold and Robert Schlinkert, *Geschichte der Hl. Dreifaltigkeits Gemeinde New Ulm*, 79 (New Ulm, 1919). Berghold acted as secretary of the New Ulm Citizens' Relief Committee which raised funds to rebuild the town following the tornado of July 15, 1881; Germans in the U.S. donated $40,000 — $1,500 of which was from Henry Villard (born Hilgard) of the Northern Pacific Railway; La Vern J. Rippley, "Alexander Berghold, Pioneer Priest and Prairie Poet," in *Currents*, Fall, 1979, pp. 18–22. As recently as 1961 a Methodist description of New Ulm stated that it was "founded by a group of German beer drinkers" whose "religion was found in athletics." Ernest C. Reineke, "Ad[d]enda," 3, typed manuscript, 1961, original in Archives of the Minnesota Conference, United Methodist Church, Minneapolis, copy in MHS.

[42] E. R. Bliefernicht, *A Brief History of Dr. Martin Luther College*, 12, 17, 19, 23, 30, 53, 59 (New Ulm, 1934); Louis Lange Publishing Company, *Geschichte der Minnesota-Synode und ihrer einzelnen Gemeinden*, 163–166 (St. Louis, [1910]). Below see Ubl, *Chronology*, 112.

[43] Here and below, see Johnson, in *American-German Review*, June, 1946, pp. 8, 12; Ubl, *Chronology*, 60, 63, 68, 112; *Minneapolis Sunday Tribune*, August 15, 1954, Picture Magazine, p. 17; U.S., *Census*, 1860, *Population*, 255; 1900, pp. 216, 588, 762; 1970, vol. 1, part 25, pp. 252, 359. Only 2% of the people in the U.S. claimed German as a mother tongue in 1970.

[44] Here and below, see Harpole and Nagle, eds., *Minnesota Territorial Census*, 14–17, 94–96; U.S., *Census*, 1860, *Population*, 262; 1870, p. 360; 1900, p. 589; 1920, p. 521; 1970, vol. 1, part 25, p. 411, table 119; William B. Mitchell, *History of Stearns County, Minnesota*, 43, 44 (Chicago, 1915). On Pierz, see August C. Krey, "Monte Cassino, Metten, and Minnesota," in *Minnesota History*, 8:225 (September, 1927); William P. Furlan, *In Charity Unfeigned: The Life of Father Francis Xavier Pierz*, 26, 38, 144, 214 (St. Cloud, 1952); J. B. Tennelly, trans., "Father Pierz, Missionary and Colonizer," in *Acta et Dicta*, 7:129 (October, 1935). "A Brief Description of Minnesota Territory," an appendix to Pierz's *Die Indianer in Nord Amerika, ihre Lebensweise, Sitten und Gebräuche* (St. Louis, 1855) may be found in *Social Justice Review*, 41:98 (June, 1948). Ireland's assessment appears in *Acta et Dicta*, 2:278 (July, 1910).

[45] Here and three paragraphs below, see Colman J. Barry, *The Catholic Church and German Americans*, 11, 13 (Milwaukee, 1953); Mitchell, *Stearns County*, 645; Tennelly, in *Acta et Dicta*, 7:129; Vincent Tegeder, "The Benedictines in Frontier Minnesota," and Sister Grace McDonald, "Pioneer Teachers: The Benedictine Sisters of St. Cloud," in *Minnesota History*, 32:37–42 (Spring, 1951), 35:264, 266, 268 (June, 1957). For a comprehensive account of early Benedictine settlement, see Colman J. Barry, *Worship and Work*, 28, 32, 35, 45–53 (Collegeville, 1956); Alexius Hoffmann, O.S.B., "Natural History of Collegeville," manuscript, 1926–34, original in St. John's Abbey Archives, Collegeville, excerpts in MEHP Papers.

[46] From north to south and east to west the townships were Millwood, Krain, Grove, Oak, Albany, Avon, St. Wendel, Spring Hill, St. Martin, Farming, Collegeville, St. Joseph, St. Cloud, Lake Henry, Zion, Munson, Wakefield, Rockville, St. Augusta, Luxemburg. See map, in Johnson, *Rural Sociology*, 6:1. See also U.S., *Census, 1880, Population*, 515; 1940, vol. 2, part 4, p. 74; 1970, vol. 1, part 25, pp. 360, 411; Circular No. 1, January 15, 1887, in Great Northern Railway Company Records, MHS.

[47] *Berichte der Leopoldinen-Stiftung*, 31:40–44 (Vienna, 1861); [Colman J. Barry], *Catholic Minnesota: Historic Places and Tours*, 2 ([St. Cloud, 1958]). The St. Cloud Area Genealogists have compiled an index to all cemeteries in Stearns County; it is on file in their library in St. Cloud.

[48] Here and two paragraphs below, see Barry, *Catholic Church*, 100, 105, 185, 199, 217, 245; U.S., *Census, 1870, Population*, 544; U.S. Census Bureau, *Special Reports, Religious Bodies: 1906*, 1:327–329; *1926*, 1:628–631; *1936*, 772, 773; National Council of Churches of Christ in America, *Churches and Church Membership in the United States*, tables 50, 52 (New York, 1957). For 1950, see Markus, "Areal Patterns," 44. Earlier data may be found in Heinz Kloss, *Atlas of 19th and 20th Century German-American Settlements*, G12 (Marburg, Ger., 1974). Cahensly, a leading lay Catholic in Germany, had a genuine concern for emigrating fellow church members, but his activities became associated by some with the rise of nationalism in the fatherland.

[49] *Northwestern Chronicle* (St. Paul), August 18, 1887; Barry, *Catholic Church*, 116, 177–182. For a study of the language problem, see Vincent A. Yzermans, *The Mel and the Rose*, 305–310 (Melrose, 1972); La Vern J. Rippley, "Archbishop Ireland and the School Language Controversy," in *U.S. Catholic Historian*, Fall, 1980, pp. 1–16. Joseph Matt, editor of the weekly *Der Wanderer* (St. Paul) from 1900 to 1944, spoke of the division among Catholics in an interview by the author on February 13, 1941, and quoted one priest as saying, "We had to fight three sides: The environment, that is, Americanization, the freethinkers . . . and our own authorities." On parochial schools, see Mitchell, *Stearns County*, 188, 287. See also Don H. Tolzmann, "The German Language Press in Minnesota, 1855–1955," in *German-American Studies*, 5:169–178 (1972); Karl J. Arndt and May E. Olson, *German-American Newspapers and Periodicals, 1732–1955*, 226 (Heidelberg, 1961). For information on use of language, see U.S. Works Projects Administration, Minnesota, Historical Records Survey: Churches, 1936–41, Stearns County, in MHS, hereafter cited as WPA, Church Records.

[50] Here and two paragraphs below, see Harpole and Nagle, eds., *Minnesota Territorial Census*, 38–70; William W. Folwell, *A History of Minnesota*, 1:352 (Reprint ed., St. Paul, 1956); U.S., *Census, 1870, Population*, 360; 1880, p. 515; 1890, p. 635; 1900, vol. 1, p. 762; 1970, vol. 1, part 25, pp. 519, 520; data compiled from Minnesota manuscript census schedules, in MEHP Papers; St. Paul City Planning Board, *Foreign-Born Population Studies, Saint Paul, Minnesota*, 7 (St. Paul, 1934); Calvin S. Schmid, *Social Saga of Two Cities: An Ecological and Statistical Study*, 132 (Minneapolis, 1937).

On Minneapolis neighborhoods, see Theodore Guminga, "Some Aspects of the Catholic Immigration of the 19th Century with Reference to Minnesota," 90, master's thesis, St. Paul Seminary, 1958; City Planning Commission, *Riverside: Challenge and Opportunity*, 1, and *Camden Community*, 10 (Community Improvement Program, Series 12 — Minneapolis, 1965); Grace E. Pratt, *A Study of Community Conditions*, 15 (North District Women's Co-operative Alliance, *Publication 68*, series 1 — Minneapolis, 1925).

[51] James K. Benson, "New England of the West: The Emergence of the American Mind in Early St. Paul, 1849–1855," 77, master's thesis, University of Minnesota, 1970; O. H. Rudnick, *Das Deutschtum St. Paul's in Wort und Bild*, 7–17 (St. Paul, 1924); Sis-

ter John Christine Wolkerstorfer, "Ramsey County's German Americans," in *Ramsey County History*, 5:8 (Spring, 1968); *St. Paul Daily Press*, July 2, 1861; *St. Paul Daily Dispatch*, March 12, 1876; *St. Paul Daily Globe*, October 6, 1878; Guminga, "Aspects of Catholic Immigration," 90; Dan Armitage, "The Curling Waters: A West Bank History," in *Minnesota Daily*, August, 1973, pp. 13–15.

[52] Here and two paragraphs below, see Church of the Assumption, *A History of the Assumption Parish*, 8, 16, 18, 22, 31, 39 (St. Paul, [1931]); Catholic Archdiocese of St. Paul and Minneapolis, Parish Questionnaires, 1948, Sacred Heart, St. Francis de Sales, St. Matthews, St. Agnes, and St. Bernard's, originals in the Catholic Historical Society, St. Paul Seminary, St. Paul, microfilm in MHS (hereafter cited as Parish Questionnaires); Church of St. Matthew, *Golden Jubilee, 1886–1936*, 4, 14 (St. Paul, 1936); James J. Byrne, *A History of St. Agnes: A Condensed Chronicle*, 15 ([St. Paul, 1953]); St. Bernard's Church, *Golden Jubilee, 1890–1940*, 13, 15 ([St. Paul, 1940]). Of the pastors who served Assumption during its first 70 years three were German born, two Alsatian, four Austrian, one each Swiss and Luxembourger; Parish Questionnaires, Assumption, 1948. The national parishes in Minneapolis were St. Boniface in St. Anthony, St. Joseph's on the near North Side, and St. Elizabeth's near Cedar-Riverside; Isaac Atwater, ed., *History of the City of Minneapolis*, 218 (New York, 1893).

It seems likely that Germans who left St. Paul's downtown neighborhood in the 1880s and 1890s also moved to West St. Paul and South St. Paul. See Table 8.3.

[53] Here and two paragraphs below, see Esther A. Selke, "The Beginnings of the German Lutheran Churches in Minnesota," in *Concordia Institute Historical Quarterly*, 2:75–81, 108–115 (October, 1929, January, 1930); *Dedication Memorial of Trinity Lutheran Church, U.A.C.*, 11 (St. Paul, 1951); *Die Evangelisch-Lutherische St. Johannes-Gemeinde, 1871–1921*, 21 (St. Paul, 1921). On various synods, see H. Meyer, *The Planting Story of the Minnesota District of the Evangelical Lutheran Synod of Missouri, Ohio and Other States*, 14, 19, 32, 35, 51, 56, 63, 77 (Minneapolis, 1932); *Geschichte der Minnesota-Synode und ihrer einzelnen Gemeinden*, 4, 221–238 (St. Louis, 1910); Trinity First Lutheran Church, *The Ninetieth Anniversary, 1856–1946*, 7, 15, 23, 24, 25 (Minneapolis, 1946). In 1921 the Missouri Synod had 337 pastors in Minnesota; the Wisconsin Synod, which absorbed the Minnesota Synod in 1918, had 84. In 1953 the Missourians were second in national membership only to the United Lutheran Church in America; they claimed over 220,000 baptized members in Minnesota by 1977 — many of whom were of German stock. *Amerikanischer Kalender für deutsche Lutheraner, 1921*, 90–93 (St. Louis, 1920); *Lutheran Annual, 1979*, 20, 98–108 (St. Louis, 1978).

[54] Here and two paragraphs below, see Christopher C. Andrews, ed., *History of St. Paul, Minn., with Illustrations and Biographical Sketches*, 491–493, 508 (Syracuse, N.Y., 1890); Chauncey Hobart, ed., *History of Methodism in Minnesota*, 335, 339 (Red Wing, 1887); Atwater, *Minneapolis*, 177, 208; Dayton's Bluff Methodist Episcopal Church, *Golden Jubilee, 1886–1936*, n.p. ([St. Paul, 1936]); Reineke, "Ad[d]enda," 3, 5; Carl Wittke, *William Nast: Patriarch of German Methodism*, 34–36, 175–190 (Detroit, 1959). On German Evangelical churches, see *Der Volksbote*, a monthly religious newsletter published in German in St. Paul, 1889–95; Carl E. Schneider, *The German Church on the American Frontier: A Study in the Rise of Religion among Germans of the West*, vi, 27, 41, 108n, 438–444 (St. Louis, 1939). Although the Moravians were not represented in the Twin Cities, they were well established in nearby Carver County as well as in southeastern Minnesota. See Estella L. Elke, "The Moravians in Carver County, Minnesota," term paper, University of Minnesota, 1933, copy in MHS; [H. H. Hill Co.], *History of Winona and Olmsted Counties*, 598 (Chicago, 1883).

55 Here and below, see Margaret Mussgang, "The Germans in St. Paul," 73, 75, 79, 80, 87–89, 91, master's thesis, University of Minnesota, 1932; Minnesota, *Laws*, 1867, p. 1, 1877, p. 125; Sister John Christine Wolkerstorfer, "Nativism in Minnesota in World War I: A Comparative Study of Brown, Ramsey, and Stearns Counties, 1914–1918," 154, Ph.D. thesis, University of Minnesota, 1973; Heinz Kloss, *The American Bilingual Tradition*, 87, 89–91, 97 (Rowley, Mass., 1977).

56 Mussgang, "Germans in St. Paul," 67; Luther College (St. Paul), *Catalog*, April, 1933, p. 10, April, 1934, p. 11; Oswald B. Overn, *A History of Concordia College, St. Paul*, 6–8, 24, 30 (St. Paul, [1968]); Fred Wahlers, *A Short History of Concordia at St. Paul*, [19] ([St. Paul, 1953?]). A statue of Martin Luther, copied from the Luther monument at Worms, Germany, stands in front of Concordia as a symbol of the school, the synod, and the fatherland. Neither Overn nor Wahlers discussed language problems at Concordia during World War I, but in September, 1925, its Board of Control began to record its minutes in English; Glenn W. Offerman to Mary Cannon, June 6, 1980, MEHP Papers; La Vern J. Rippley, "The German-American Normal Schools," in Erich A. Albrecht and J. Anthony Burzle, eds., *Germanica Americana 1976*, 63–71 (Lawrence, Kans., 1977).

57 Here and three paragraphs below, see Wolkerstorfer, in *Ramsey County History*, 5:8; Mussgang, "Germans in St. Paul," 33, 36–39, 56, 59, 62; Rothfuss, in *Minnesota History*, 32:100–105, 164–173. Two early St. Paul buildings were the Athenaeum (1857), which burned in 1886, and the Turner Hall (1870) at 7th and Franklin. On German House, designed by local German architects Peter J. Linhoff and Rudolph Zelzer, see Rudnick, *Das Deutschtum St. Paul's*, 40–45; Guminga, "Aspects of Catholic Immigration," 94. On the Schubert Club, see James T. Dunn, "St. Paul's Schubert Club: Musical Mentor of the Northwest," in *Minnesota History*, 39:51–64 (Winter, 1964). On the Minneapolis Symphony, see John K. Sherman, "The Birth of a Symphony Orchestra," in *Minnesota History*, 33:95 (Autumn, 1952).

58 Georg Mann, "The Furor Teutonicus; Upper Mississippi Abteilung," in *Yale Review*, Winter, 1971, p. 320; Hildegard B. Johnson, "The Volksfest Association of Minnesota," in *American-German Review*, April–May, 1959, p. 31. One member of the Volksfest Assn. recalled that it began shortly after the *Deutsche Haus* was razed and that for a time the member organizations of the latter met in the Turner Hall at Ohio and Baker sts.; information from Alfred C. Grossmann, June 19, 1980.

59 Here and below, see Arndt and Olson, *German-American Newspapers*, 224–226, 233. On Orthwein and other St. Paul papers, see Hildegard B. Johnson, "The Election of 1860 and the Germans," in *Minnesota History*, 28:22–24 (March, 1947); John C. Massmann, "Friedrich Orthwein, Minnesota's First German Editor," in *American-German Review*, April–May, 1960, pp. 16, 17, 38.

60 Here and two paragraphs below, see Arndt and Olson, *German-American Newspapers*, 221, 224, 247, 255, 262, 457, 670, 680; Wittke, *German-Language Press*, 234; La Vern J. Rippley, "Notes about the German Press in the Minnesota River Valley," in *The Report: A Journal of German-American History*, 35:41–43 (1972); William L. Crozier, "A Social History of Winona, Minnesota, 1880–1905," 9, 198, Ph.D. thesis, University of Nebraska, 1975; interview of Emil Leicht by author, November 10, 1940; La Vern J. Rippley, "A History of the *Dakota Freie Presse*," in *Heritage Review* (Bismarck, N. Dak.), December, 1973, pp. 9–17; Hildegard B. Johnson, "The Carver County German Reading Society," in *Minnesota History*, 24:222 (September, 1943); Carol Ann Mayer, "Editorial Opinion in Minnesota's German Language Weeklies, 1890–1920," 159, master's thesis, St. Cloud State College, 1974.

61 Here and below, see Johnson, in *Minnesota History*, 28:20–36; Minnesota Constitution, Article 7, sec. 1. For various views on the election issue, see Frederick C. Luebke, ed., *Ethnic Voters and the Election of Lincoln* (Lincoln, Neb., 1971).

62 Here and below, see Rippley, *German-Americans*, 58; Zucker, *Forty-Eighters*, 183; Dorothy E. Johnson, "Attitude of the Germans in Minnesota toward the Republican Party to 1865," 46, 50, 51, 56, 66–73, master's thesis, University of Minnesota, 1945; *New Ulm Post*, January 20, February 10, 1865. On opposition to prohibition, see Folwell, *Minnesota*, 1:307, 376; Rippley, *German-Americans*, 55, 109; Wittke, *German-Language Press*, 134, 140; Lynn Haines, quoted in Carl H. Chrislock, *The Progressive Era in Minnesota, 1899–1918*, 34 (St. Paul, 1971).

63 On the Homestead Act, see *Minnesota Staats-Zeitung*, May 15, 1862; *Neu Ulm Pionier*, June 7, 1862; Folwell, *Minnesota*, 2:341–343 (Reprint ed., St. Paul, 1961). Early claims to land could make it difficult for later arrivals to take full advantage of the Homestead Act; Hildegard B. Johnson, *Order Upon the Land: The U.S. Rectangular Land Survey and the Upper Mississippi Country*, 66–72 (New York, 1976).

64 Minnesota, *Legislative Manual, 1873*, 122, *1877*, 114, *1893*, 446, *1895*, 448, *1917*, 332, *1921*, 500, *1927*, 328; Mayer, "Editorial Opinion," 186–188; Chrislock, *Progressive Era*, 124, 144, 179–181; Samuel Lubell, *The Future of American Politics*, 131, 148–151 (Revised ed., New York, 1965); Heinz Kloss, "German-American Language Maintenance Efforts," in Joshua A. Fishman *et al.*, *Language Loyalty in the United States*, 238 (The Hague, 1966); Carl H. Chrislock, "The German-American Role in Minnesota Politics, 1850–1950," in Glasrud, ed., *Heritage Deferred*, 109–113.

65 Here and below, see Mayer, "Editorial Opinion," iii, 27, 61, 64, 115–117, 185, 188; Wittke, *German-Language Press*, 162, 163; Chrislock, *Progressive Era*, 95–98, 104, 135. On Matt's position, see George Pfeilschrifter, ed., *German Culture, Catholicism and the World War: A Defense against the Book La Guerre Allemande et le Catholicisme*, 3–8 (St. Paul, 1916); Franklin F. Holbrook and Livia Appel, *Minnesota in the War with Germany*, 1:52 (St. Paul, 1928).

66 Chrislock, *Progressive Era*, 135. For a detailed account of the German-American Alliance, see Clifton J. Child, *The German-Americans in Politics, 1914–1917* (Madison, Wis., 1939).

67 The fund-raising event included such divergent personalities as banker Otto Bremer, clergyman Theodore Buenger, and lumberman Frederick Weyerhaeuser; among the participants were dance troupes, singers, churches, and representatives of Irish, Polish, Hungarian, and Swedish ethnic groups. Joseph Matt, "The Catholic City Federation of St. Paul," in *Acta et Dicta*, 7:95–103 (1935); Holbrook and Appel, *Minnesota in the War*, 1:15, 22, 49, 50; *Volksfest des Nordwestens: Souvenir Program*, 18, 19, 20 (St. Paul, 1916); Rippley, *German-Americans*, 190, 191; Chrislock, *Progressive Era*, 98.

68 Here and two paragraphs below, see Holbrook and Appel, *Minnesota in the War*, 2:256; Minnesota, *Laws*, 1917, p. 256; Carol Jenson, "Loyalty as a Political Weapon: The 1918 Campaign in Minnesota," and La Vern J. Rippley, "Conflict in the Classroom: Anti-Germanism in Minnesota Schools, 1917–19," both in *Minnesota History*, 43:42–57, 47:171–183 (Summer, 1972, Spring, 1981); Chrislock, *Progressive Era*, 131, 141–144. On the New Ulm antiwar rally, see Wolkerstorfer, "Nativism in Minnesota," 54–58, 70; *New Ulm Review*, July 25, p. 1, August 1, p. 1, 1917. Both Pfaender and Fritsche were later re-elected to public office in New Ulm. See also Willis H. Raff, "Civil Liberties in Minnesota: World War I Period," master's thesis, University of Minnesota, 1950; Martin H. Steffel, "New Ulm and World War I," master's thesis, Mankato State University, 1966.

69 Here and below, see Correspondence with Counties file, Hennepin County, September 15, 1917, and Minneapolis Board of Education, special meeting, September 19, 1917, file no. 184, both in Minnesota Commission of Public Safety (PSC) Records, State

Archives; Folwell, *Minnesota*, 3:567n (Reprint ed., St. Paul, 1969). Shaper's stirring defense appeared in full in *Minneapolis Tribune*, September 18, 1918, p. 8. German had been taught in all but 23 public and 307 parochial schools during the academic year 1914–15; Rippley, in *Minnesota History*, 47:176.

[70] Dr. M. E. Bushey to J. A. A. Burnquist, December 18, 1917, file no. 68; Charles E. Chrisman to PSC, August 24, 1918, file no. 213; W. C. Rehwaldt to Charles W. Henke, December 13, 1918; Andrew Nordby to Department of Justice, July 19, 1918; Mrs. Ed. Preston to Senator Knute Nelson, December 18, 1918, all in file no. 184 — all in PSC Records. See also Wolkerstorfer, "Nativism in Minnesota," 113–115.

[71] Here and two paragraphs below, see E. N. Prentice to J. A. A. Burnquist, August 16, 1918, file no. 213; PSC Publicity Director to Volkszeitung Printing Co., April 1, 1918, Correspondence with Counties file, Ramsey County; Max Distel to John S. Pardee, August 8, 1917, Correspondence with Counties file, Le Sueur County; Charles W. Farnham to C. W. Ames, July 2, 1917, file no. 68; T. G. Winter to Pardee, September 4, 1917, file no. 153; J. L. Coy to H. W. Libby, January 12, 1918, Publicity file — all in PSC Records; Chrislock, *Progressive Era*, 131–133; Theodore C. Blegen, *Minnesota: A History*, 471 (Minneapolis, 1963).

[72] F. Osten-Sachen to I. A. Caswell, August 18, 1917, Speakers Bureau file; J. G. Nehring to C. W. Henke, May 20, 1918, Publicity file; pamphlet in Winona County historical files, Germans, copy in Publicity file — all in PSC Records.

[73] Undated transcripts of hearings, County Branches file, Cottonwood County, in PSC Records.

[74] Rippley, *German-Americans*, 127; Joshua A. Fishman *et al.*, "The Non-English and the Ethnic Group Press, 1910–1960," and Kloss, both in Fishman *et al.*, *Language Loyalty*, 55, 241; R. Klietsch and W. Nelson, "The Ethnic Newspaper," 23, term paper, [University of Minnesota, 1963?], copy in MHS; Arndt and Olson, *German-American Newspapers*, 232.

[75] Wolkerstorfer, "Nativism in Minnesota," 178; taped interviews of Hank Peterson, Paul Horn, and Loren Clark, December 30, 1973, January 11, 1974, transcripts in Northwest Minnesota Historical Center, Moorhead; Edward J. Pluth, "Prisoner of War Employment in Minnesota during World War II," in *Minnesota History*, 44:290–299 (Winter, 1975).

[76] Here and below, see U.S., *Census*, 1970, *Population*, vol. 1, part 1, p. 382, part 25, pp. 252, 514; John E. Hofman, "Mother Tongue Retentiveness in Ethnic Parishes," and Kloss, both in Fishman *et al.*, *Language Loyalty*, 145, 209, 213, 214; La Vern J. Rippley, "Deutsche Sprache in Minnesota," in Leopold Auburger *et al.*, eds., *Deutsch als Muttersprache*, vol. 4, part 1, pp. 84, 87, 88 (Wiesbaden, 1979). The Minnesota State Board of Education reported in 1980 that of 17,000 students from non-English-speaking homes in Minnesota, 21% spoke German; *Minneapolis Tribune*, January 15, 1980, p. 1B.

[77] One example of such books is Johann Gröbner *et al.*, *Chronik der Pfarrgemeinde Berg* (Furth im Wald, Ger., 1976), a documented history of a seven-hamlet parish in Czechoslovakia, with data on every family and its property. See also Ernst Feise, "Colonial Petrification — A Neglected Field for Research," in *German Quarterly*, 13:117–124 (May, 1940).

[78] Here and below, see Kloss, in Fishman *et al.*, *Language Loyalty*, 249; J. J. Lalor, "The Germans in the West," in *Atlantic Monthly*, 32:470 (October, 1873); Marian N. Deininger, "Some Differential Characteristics of Minnesota's Ethnic Groups in Selected Rural Townships," 205, 211, 228, Ph.D. thesis, University of Minnesota, 1958. On the concept of community and society, see Ferdinand Tönnies, *Gemeinschaft und Gesellschaft* (Leipzig, 1887).

CHAPTER 9

The Low Countries

BELGIANS, NETHERLANDERS, AND LUXEMBOURGERS

Louis M. deGryse

THE NAME LOW COUNTRIES or Lowlands has been applied to the present kingdoms of the Netherlands and Belgium and the Grand Duchy of Luxembourg. They are called "low" or "nether" lands because they lie largely within the westernmost extension of the great north European plain. The real basis of the grouping is, however, historical and political, for these were the lands gathered together in the 15th and 16th centuries by the dukes of Burgundy and their Habsburg successors as the forerunners of the first Netherlandish state.

Belgians, Netherlanders, and Luxembourgers form long-established but small elements in the population of Minnesota. The first portion of this chapter will treat Belgians and Netherlanders. Luxembourgers will be discussed in the following section.

Belgians and Netherlanders

Belgians and Netherlanders in the United States and Minnesota have colonized in cycles as conditions in the Lowlands deteriorated or those in North America made immigration inviting. After early settlements by Protestant French-speaking Walloons and Protestant Dutch who reached New York in the 17th century, the high cycles occurred in the late 19th and early 20th centuries. Nationally the peak year for Dutch arrivals was 1882, when 9,517 emigrants moved to the United States. Thirty-one years later the Belgians reached their national peak with 7,405. During the second cycle, lasting roughly from 1882 to 1924, 179,258 Dutch and 111,864 largely Flemish-speaking Belgians moved to America, totaling about 3.5% of the home country's turn-of-the-century population for the former and 1.6% for the latter.[1]

A third cycle occurred in the mid-20th century occasioned partly by overpopulation, the devastation of World War II, and severe coastal floods in 1956. From 1951 to 1960 a total of 18,575 Belgians and 52,277 Netherlanders emigrated to the United States. Among them were many professionals — the engineers, technicians, and doctors of the so-called brain drain. The figures then dropped to 30,606 Netherlanders and 9,192 Belgians in the years from 1961 to 1970.

The smaller Minnesota migration differed somewhat from the national pattern. Overwhelmingly rural in character, its Dutch and Belgian colonization took the form of two cycles closely related to the founding of farming settlements in southern Minnesota. In the first both Catholic and Protestant Belgians and Dutch arrived from 1850 to about 1870, settling initially in Rice, Wright, Carver, and Fillmore counties.[2]

After 10 years of stagnation, a second cycle of Lowland settlement began to flower in 1880 with the most important colonizing activities. The Ghent colony, founded in Lyon County in 1880, would grow to over 1,100 people of Dutch and Belgian descent by 1905. Other settlements planned by a Dutch entrepreneur spurred colonization in the same period. After 1905 new Dutch-Flemish immigrant colonies were founded under the auspices of the missionary order of Crosier fathers at Butler and Onamia in Otter Tail and Mille Lacs counties, respectively. The last major area of Lowland settlement took form in the 1920s at Hollandale in Freeborn County. By 1920 the state peak had been reached with 5,420 Dutch and 2,089 Belgians, about 1.4% of the foreign-born population of Minnesota.[3]

Both the Belgians and Dutch in the state remained preponderantly rural and agrarian. In 1970 the census reported 3,979 persons of Belgian stock in Minnesota, of whom 3,378 lived in rural areas and small towns and 601 in the metropolitan centers of Minneapolis, St. Paul, and Duluth. As for Netherlanders, the 1970 census counted 13,453 foreign born or of foreign or mixed parentage living in all but five northern counties, with the largest numbers in Hennepin, Pipestone, Nobles, Ramsey, Rock, Kandiyohi, Murray, Freeborn, Lyon, and Mille Lacs counties. (See Table 9.1).[4]

Table 9.1. Dutch in Minnesota by County, 1860–1970

County	1860 foreign born	1860 foreign mixed	1880 fb	1880 fm	1900 fb	1930 fb	1930 fm	1970 fb	1970 fm
Aitkin					12	27	66	61	263
Anoka			14	11	6	16	24	30	175
Becker			3	4	3	12	40	8	25
Beltrami					4	9	40	8	65
Benton	5	8	17	3	8	14	63		40
Big Stone			1		14	15	75		27
Blue Earth	36	14	5	10	17	52	87	46	141
Brown	1		4	4	7	19	57	8	71
Carlton					7	3	16	11	35
Carver	17	2	419	368	161	36	237	5	73
Cass					2	15	61	10	22
Chippewa					153	62	160	23	114
Chisago			1	1	1	5	10		47
Clay			8	1	13	21	33		80
Clearwater						4	7		
Cottonwood					2	31	103	6	66
Crow Wing	1			1	21	29	66	8	31
Dakota			17	21	16	62	109	50	208
Dodge	8	2	55	87	34	9	54		45
Douglas			20	10	34	19	79	9	66
Faribault	1		9	14	8	3	31		32
Fillmore	62	8	209	350	147	52	385	7	166
Freeborn			2		3	211	327	126	387
Goodhue	3		10	21	3	2	22		25
Grant					1	15	35		22
Hennepin	4	6	138	106	133	443	1,148	523	1,514
Minneapolis			91			355		190	548
Houston	62	27	13	19	14	10	18		5
Hubbard					10	9	41		39
Isanti			5	16	1		8	9	40
Itasca					1	4	25		24
Jackson				3	2	28	47		75
Kanabec					14	63	118	60	174
Kandiyohi			4	6	207	240	741	97	543
Kittson			1	1	8	3	13		8
Koochiching						7	17		
Lac qui Parle			1	6	3	2	8		11
Lake					1	2	7		10
Lake of the Woods						2	3		
Le Sueur	7		11	8	7	5	19		21
Lincoln			2		2	30	70	4	118
Lyon			4		188	191	513	28	417
McLeod			60	68	27	14	42		30
Mahnomen						39	74	5	45
Marshall					1	1	5		20
Martin			3	9	8	26	66		82
Meeker			35	35	5	14	46		26
Mille Lacs	1	4	1	6	69	204	529	38	262
Morrison	1	5	7	12	1	8	57		57
Mower			17	35	21	37	116		121
Murray			1		87	259	656	103	552
Nicollet	20	16	8	13	5	11	31	15	23
Nobles			3	10	185	456	902	213	689
Norman					1	25	50		22
Olmsted			12	10	3	29	79	27	139
Otter Tail			16	33	19	117	182	28	163
Pennington						7	12		17
Pine			2	2	136	88	152	15	51
Pipestone			1	2	154	409	996	191	816
Polk	3	2	3	10	5	128	167	21	61
Pope					5	39	80	13	74
Ramsey	4	5	81	85	126	187	610	206	588
St. Paul			79			181		112	370
Red Lake						3	10		13
Redwood					9	10	28		20
Renville			3	1	141	72	201		83
Rice	5		6	16	55	113	249	43	144
Rock			4	5	57	359	586	114	647
Roseau					3	4	23		6
St. Louis			9	3	26	64	157	64	176
Duluth						44		34	53
Scott	2	3	72	94	33	13	71	7	94
Sherburne	1		3	1	3	5	23	8	30
Sibley			2	8	3	1	12		8

Table 9.1. Dutch in Minnesota by County, 1860–1970 (*continued*)

County	1860 foreign born	1860 foreign mixed	1880 fb	1880 fm	1900 fb	1930 fb	1930 fm	1970 fb	1970 fm
Stearns	30	12	101	113	87	100	383	27	182
Steele			1	7	2	7	34		47
Stevens			8	3	4	33	110	7	40
Swift			10	7	6	12	59	5	31
Todd			11	1	8	13	62	6	69
Traverse			5	4	26	12	36	7	21
Wabasha	42	11	11	24	1	1	14		7
Wadena					8	6	24	19	4
Waseca			7	15	5	1	10	8	32
Washington	8	9	9	5	7	5	26	35	59
Watonwan				2	2	3	12	31	9
Wilkin			2	7	1	12	15		19
Winona	26	7	35	58	40	10	65	7	59
Wright			50	19	40	80	243	7	137
Yellow Medicine					4	13	42		46
Total	350	141	1,572	1,794	2,697	4,832	12,330	2,407	11,046
Published census figures	(391)		(1,581)		(2,717)			(2,354)	(10,812)

Source: See Appendix

European Backgrounds

Ethnically and culturally the Low Countries were and are diverse. Their past and present religious divisions and linguistic cleavages have little to do with natural barriers or modern political frontiers, for during most of their history the Low Countries have been a borderland.[5] They lie athwart the great division line between the Germanic and Latin peoples of Europe. This linguistic frontier has remained razor sharp and remarkably stable for almost 1,000 years, a puzzlement and fascination to geographers, sociologists, and historians alike. North and east of the line, the Germanic region includes a small area in northern France, northern or Flemish Belgium, a few small areas hugging the borders in eastern Belgium, the entire kingdom of the Netherlands, and Luxembourg except for two small Walloon villages. To the south and west of the line, the dialect of French called "Walloon" prevails (see Map 9.1).[6]

Within the Germanic area, there are several important dialect frontiers and two or three distinct Germanic languages: Low German, including Dutch and Flemish; Middle German, including the Luxembourg dialect; and Friesian, a Germanic, but non-German, language closely akin to Anglo-Saxon, now spoken only in the Dutch province of Friesland and on a few North Sea islands.[7]

French has been favored by the social elites in Belgium and Luxembourg. In the historic past this has been a disadvantage and often a hardship for Germanic monoglots, creating a tense political-linguistic situation with strong social and economic overtones, particularly in Belgium.

The Low Countries are also sharply divided along religious lines (see Map 9.1). Belgium and Luxembourg may be considered strongly Roman Catholic, while the Netherlands long had a Calvinist Protestant majority with a large Catholic minority. The Catholic region of the Low Countries is thus a continuous area extending northward to the Rhine and sometimes even beyond. Some are to be found in all provinces, but Catholics predominate in the southern areas which remained longer under Spanish control. Catholic Dutch and Dutch-speaking Belgian Catholics (Flemings) mingled in both the Old World and the New.[8]

The Friesians are largely Calvinists who coalesced with other Protestant Dutch while remaining conscious of their Friesian identity. The East Friesians, a group living in the extreme northwestern corner of Germany, traditionally looked to Holland for religious and moral sustenance, although they were never politically attached to it. Nor do they speak the Friesian language, which they gave up long ago for a dialect of Low Saxon. But they use Dutch as a liturgical language and High German for other official purposes. In America, they were often to be found in association with Calvinist Netherlanders.

Thus Netherlanders can be said to include parts of two linguistically mixed culture groups: Protestant Dutch and Friesians, and Catholic Dutch. Belgians are divided among three groups: (1) Catholic Germanic-speaking Flemings often in association with Catholic Dutch, (2) Catholic French-speaking Walloons, and (3) Catholic Germanic-speaking Belgian Luxembourgers, who form a single group with the Luxembourgers of the Grand Duchy.

Three primary motivating factors in the 19th-century Lowland migrations were overpopulation, economic conditions, and religious dissent. The Netherlands and the Flemish regions of Belgium, which were overwhelmingly agricultural, could not absorb the burgeoning population. Nor could Dutch and Belgian farmers compete with the cheap grain produced in ever-increasing quantities in Russia and North America. Moreover, despite old traditions of industry and commerce in Holland and Flanders, these sectors of the economy were relatively stagnant in the 19th century, providing little outlet for the surplus rural population. Wallonia, by contrast, was the first region on the European continent to feel the effects of the Industrial Revolution. In consequence, Walloon emigration, though it began early, never reached the dimensions of the Flemish or Dutch. By the opening of the 20th century (1901 through 1910), only 21% of the Belgians arriving annually in the United States were French-speaking.[9]

Dissent within the Dutch Reformed church was a third motivating factor for Protestant Dutch emigration. After the fall of Napoleon, William I, king of the newly created Netherlands, which then included Holland, Belgium, and Luxembourg, undertook certain reforms in the Dutch Calvinist church. His efforts were profoundly repugnant to rigid Calvinists, who seceded from the official state church in 1834. Among the early emigrants were many Seceders, who, although they again split in the United States, founded several key Dutch settlements in the New World.[10]

Religious motives and agricultural conditions, however, do not account for the total out-migration. Although many people emigrated directly from the farm, a wide diversity of occupations was represented among the others. In general, they were people of fairly limited means seeking to avoid the decline in status which would almost surely result from the increasingly restricted opportunities in their own countries.

Map 9.1. The Netherlands, Belgium, and Luxembourg

Nevertheless no crisis of magnitude occurred in the Lowlands, and their loss of population to the New World was modest compared with that from Ireland or Scandinavia.

It should be observed that the vast majority of Lowlanders did not emigrate, although they were exposed to the same conditions. It is often suggested that those who did were among the more affluent and successful with the capital necessary for the passage as well as to make a fresh start. From this image it is an easy step to the self-flattering American stereotype of the intelligent, ambitious, and venturesome as the archetypal immigrant. Much more probable is the view that immigrants were individuals, each with his or her own reasons. Some Lowlanders were prosperous farmers, some poor common laborers, and some went to the United States only to return. Lowland returnees have not been extensively studied. Though their numbers seem to have been small, they, too, must have varied from the successful to the disillusioned.[11]

Catholic Walloon, Flemish, and Dutch Settlements

In the 19th century the Dutch and Belgian settlements in Wisconsin were among the earliest in the United States. Dutch immigrants were attracted to Milwaukee, Sheboygan, Alto, Waupun, and the Fox River Valley in the 1840s, while Belgian Walloons from southern Brabant appeared at Green Bay in the 1850s. Soon neighboring Door County, already occupied by French Canadians, was filled with Belgians, a pattern of Walloon-French Canadian association also to be found in Minnesota, where the immigrants shared a common language and French-speaking priests. Also important in the 1840s were three Calvinist Seceder organizations which laid the Dutch foundations at Holland and Zeeland, Michigan, and at Pella, Iowa. These early colonies served as springboards from which Dutch pioneers made the trek to Minnesota, beginning in the 1850s.[12]

Belgians also arrived in the 1850s, some perhaps in response to the largely ineffectual efforts in 1856 of the territory's first emigration commissioner, Eugene Burnand, who envisioned a colony in Pine County. The oldest and largest Walloon settlement in Minnesota, however, occurred in the late 1850s in Wells and Shieldsville townships of Rice County in the southeastern part of the state. Once established, these Walloons then attracted a continuing flow of their countrymen, most of whom appear to have emigrated directly from Belgium. Although this little-known colony was almost as old as that at Green Bay, there is little indication of secondary migration from Wisconsin. By 1885 the census showed 195 foreign-born Belgians and 121 American born of Belgian or mixed parentage living in Rice County. Not all were Walloons, for by then the city of Faribault and Walcott Township seem to have contained a few Flemish immigrants. In the 1880s the Rice County area was second in size only to Ghent in Lyon County as a Belgian concentration in Minnesota (see Table 9.2). Most of the people living in the two core townships were Walloons. Subsequent censuses showed declining numbers, indicating that fresh immigration did not keep pace with the attrition caused by death and out-migration.[13]

More typical of the small, rural concentrations of Wal-

loons in Minnesota was that in Wright County. Like the Rice County group farther south, it too took form in the 1850s and was closely associated with French Canadians. Unlike the larger colony, however, some of the earliest Wright County families moved from Wisconsin, and it is tempting to see this group as an extension of the same migration flow that peopled Green Bay in the 1850s and 1860s. The settlement remained very small, never spreading beyond the limits of Albion and French Lake townships, the latter of which was named by the Walloons. By 1885 there were only six or seven families totaling 18 foreign born and 42 native born of Belgian or mixed parentage in the community. A sense of ethnic identity was unlikely to persist in such a situation, where exogamy was almost mandatory. Also working against it was the fact that French Lake never developed a Catholic parish of its own.[14]

Table 9.2. Belgians in Minnesota by County, 1860–1900

County	1860 foreign born	1860 foreign mixed	1880 fb	1880 fm	1900 fb
Aitkin					5
Beltrami					2
Benton			6	20	35
Blue Earth	5	7	5	20	23
Brown			4	1	3
Carlton			1	2	7
Carver	1		44	45	28
Chippewa				1	2
Chisago			2	2	3
Clay			2	2	
Cottonwood			1	1	1
Crow Wing					22
Dakota	1		10	14	7
Dodge	1		2		2
Douglas			1	8	26
Faribault			1	3	2
Fillmore			4	6	2
Freeborn			1		1
Goodhue	5	5	38	57	12
Hennepin	2	1	27	22	41
Minneapolis			10		32
Houston	3		22	18	6
Hubbard					2
Jackson					6
Kandiyohi			4	6	1
Kittson					1
Lac qui Parle				1	2
Lake				1	1
Le Sueur			7	3	2
Lincoln			3	9	1
Lyon			3		311
McLeod				1	
Marshall					2
Martin			19	37	16
Morrison			1	8	1
Mower			1	1	1
Murray					4
Nicollet	7	9	12	42	10
Nobles			6	8	2
Norman					1
Olmsted			1	1	4
Otter Tail			3	3	2
Pine					1
Pipestone					1
Polk			5	13	8
Pope			1		1
Ramsey	2		18	17	41
St. Paul			15		40
Red Lake					4
Redwood					3

Table 9.2. Belgians in Minnesota by County, 1860–1900 (*continued*)

County	1860 foreign born	1860 foreign mixed	1880 fb	1880 fm	1900 fb
Renville					11
Rice	46	3	116	95	123
Rock					9
Roseau					8
St. Louis	1	1	4	4	46
Duluth					31
Scott			22	15	11
Sibley	1		3	4	
Stearns	1		38	71	15
Steele			1	2	1
Stevens					2
Swift			10	13	
Todd					1
Traverse					1
Wabasha	8	2	67	87	28
Wadena			3	7	
Waseca			1	8	1
Washington	4		2	8	2
Watonwan			1		
Wilkin					2
Winona	1	2	22	20	7
Wright	5		45	51	29
Yellow Medicine					1
Total	94	30	590	758	957
Published census figures	(94)		(615)		(957)

Source: See Appendix

The first settlement of Dutch Catholics, and possibly the oldest Dutch group in Minnesota, may have started in the 1850s in Chanhassen and Benton townships of Carver County. The *Minnesota Pioneer* of December 1, 1853, reported: "A Dutch Colony, of twenty-five families, has settled within ten miles of Minnetonka Lake, at a place called Bavaria Lake. They are direct from 'Faderland', and are industrious, temperate, and several of them quite wealthy." In 1866 a young Dutch investor visited Benton, where he found "a colony of Hollanders . . . from the province of Limburg: they are well-to-do people who came here with some capital and have prospered," he wrote.[15]

At least four Dutch farmers in Benton Township arrived directly in this period, traveling from the Netherlands to New York and then to Minnesota. They may have been attracted by Catholic churches started as early as 1858 at nearby Victoria and Chaska, and in the 1860s at Chanhassen and Carver, all of which Netherlanders are known to have attended. By 1880 the census recorded 787 people of Dutch stock in Carver County, most of whom lived in the two core townships. This little-known group has been virtually ignored in standard histories of Dutch immigration, probably because it blended into the strongly German Catholic social landscape.

By far the largest and most important Catholic settlement of Belgians and Dutch in Minnesota lies farther west in the Ghent-Marshall-Minneota cluster in Lyon County, one of the few planned Belgian colonies in the United States. It originated as a project of Bishop John Ireland's Catholic Colonization Bureau designed in the first instance to settle Irish on the land. Dutch and Belgians became involved because one of Ireland's agents in England distributed litera-

ture on the project to a fellow priest who happened to be a Belgian. In the spring of 1881 this man's brother led a contingent of 50 families to the selected site in western Minnesota. Discouraged by reports of the harsh winter of 1880, many had abandoned the agricultural colony to remain in the Belgian enclaves in Chicago and Moline, Illinois, but about a dozen families went on. A new recruiting drive was organized, which resulted in the arrival of 17 families from Belgium and the Netherlands in 1883. By this time the first settlers had petitioned in 1881 to have the name of the post office and Winona and St. Peter Railroad station changed from Grandview to Ghent in the hope of attracting more Flemish colonists. Two years later they founded a Catholic church named for St. Eloi, one of the apostles of Flanders.[16]

Much is made of the Belgian character of the Ghent colony, but the 1885 census showed 164 persons of Belgian stock to 182 of Dutch extraction living in the eight-township area around the villages of Marshall and Ghent. Although most accounts do not recognize this early preponderance of Dutch, it was a thoroughly mixed Dutch-Flemish colony from the beginning, and intermarriage between the two groups was common. While people living there in the 1970s retained a distinct memory of whether their family names were "Belgium" or "Holland," they were in many instances descended from mixed stock.[17]

The flow of immigrants, both Belgian and Dutch, into the Ghent colony was continuous, if uneven, between 1880 and 1930, with marked peaks in 1883, 1892, and 1903, and a generally rising curve from 1897 to 1905. A total of 501 foreign-born Belgians and Dutch in the Ghent colony reported in 1905 that they had entered the state in the preceding 20 years. Moreover the community itself appeared remarkably stable. Of the Belgian-Dutch immigrants present in 1885, 44.9% were still there in 1905. Sex ratios calculated for Belgian stock in Lyon County in 1905 were 120.4 males to 100 females and for Dutch stock 164.7 to 100. (National ratios in the United States in 1900 were 144.6 and 126.1, respectively.)[18]

The immigrants at Ghent hailed largely from three predominantly Catholic regions. Most of the Belgians derived from the province of West Flanders; considerable numbers of the Dutch originated in localities just across the border in Zeeuwsch-Vlaanderen within the same dialect region (see Map 9.1). The rest of the Dutch emigrated chiefly from Limburg and North Brabant. Only a scattering were from predominantly Protestant provinces. Kinship ties were undeniably a major factor in the peopling of the colony. When lists of immigrants over a period of years are reviewed, the same family names keep turning up. Although it cannot be shown that all these persons are related, there is evidence that the Ghent settlers, like other ethnic groups, sent remittances to relatives, thus stimulating further migration.[19]

A fact not often recognized in accounts of the colony, however, is that from the very beginning Belgian and Dutch migrants from other states and from localities in Minnesota were important. The Dutch seem to have moved particularly from Wisconsin and Iowa, the Belgians from Illinois and Indiana. Indeed, an examination of biographies and manuscript census materials suggests considerable movement among the various settlements of Catholic Dutch and Belgians in the United States. For the Ghent colony, especially strong ties can be demonstrated with Rock Island-Moline in Illinois, South Bend-Mishawaka in Indiana, and De Pere in Wisconsin. Within Minnesota there appear to have been links with the older Dutch Catholic colony in Carver County and the Belgian settlement at Faribault in Rice County.[20]

Relations between the Ghent settlers and neighboring ethnic groups have been varied. The Belgians and Dutch were preceded in northern Lyon County by Norwegians and Icelanders, who were mainly farmers, and by Yankees, who were generally town folk. As the colony grew, the Lowlanders often displaced the Scandinavians, who sold out and moved elsewhere. The settlement exhibited a marked pattern of territorial growth, uninterrupted since its foundation. Plat maps and rural directories from 1902 to 1967 show a steady extension of Dutch and Belgian land ownership and a strong tendency toward consolidation. In 1902 the colony was still confined largely to Grandview Township and the southern parts of neighboring Westerheim Township. By 1914 Belgian and Dutch land ownership in Grandview was considerably denser, and deep inroads were being made into Scandinavian areas in Westerheim, Vallers, and Eidsvold townships. By 1952 no township in the county was without landholders of Belgian or Dutch descent.[21]

Although a number of Lowlanders settled in nearby towns, the great majority have been farmers. Excellence in farming is a point of pride as well as a significant element in their sense of group identity. They rapidly acquired a reputation among the local Yankee businessmen as expert farmers and good credit risks. In fact, in Marshall the mainly Protestant businessmen contributed heavily to the building of the first Catholic church (Holy Redeemer) in that town in 1884 with the hope of attracting more Dutch and Belgians to the area. Relations with the Yankees, however, were not uniformly good. Like many immigrant groups, the Ghent settlers evidently felt that Old-Stock Americans exploited them, and they early sought the support of Henry M. Burchard of Marshall, a lawyer, railroad land agent, and state legislator, who looked out for their interests.[22]

The third major ethnic group with which the Ghent settlers had mixed relations were the French Canadians, who were attracted to the area by the presence of a French-speaking Belgian priest at St. Eloi. However, tensions mounted between the two groups, which were usually to be found on opposite sides of controversial parish issues. At one point, the French attempted unsuccessfully to have a Dutch priest removed. St. Clotilde's Catholic Church in Green Valley near Ghent was founded in 1912 by 33 French families who apparently had left St. Eloi. Differing customs about Sunday behavior seem to have especially aggravated divisions, for in 1898 Ghent was placed under interdict until the Belgians and Dutch agreed to close the tavern on Sundays. The net result of such tensions and conflicts was the out-migration of many French-Canadian farmers, although some remained and intermarried with the Ghent settlers. Not surprisingly, the 1978 Belgian-Dutch explanation for this out-migration was that the French could not compete with their neighbors who were better and more progressive farmers. True or not, there

is little doubt that the immigrants from the Low Countries, using intensive farming methods characteristic there, brought their Lyon County lands to a high level of productivity, and astutely reinvested their gains in capital improvements.[23]

For the most part, the Belgians and Dutch of Ghent have been politically active only at the very local level. After sharing it at first with the French Canadians, they eventually took over the Ghent village board, but they never made deep inroads into Lyon County administration. When asked in the 1970s why Scandinavians and Yankees had always been more prominent in county government, the Belgians and Dutch professed to be interested in politics only to the extent that they related to farm problems, claiming they did not seek public office because they were too busy working. They jestingly suggested that the Scandinavians devoted more of their efforts to politics but neglected to get their harvests in on time. In the 1970s relatively few of the group were to be found in professional positions in the towns. Even the Catholic church failed to attract them as priests. Their prime loyalty has been to the land.[24]

Bishop Ireland's colonization scheme and the Ghent colony in particular were the inspiration for several later efforts to establish Catholic Dutch and Flemish settlements. With Bishop James R. McGolrick of Duluth as president, the Minnesota Catholic Colonization Society was organized in St. Paul in 1909 for the purpose of keeping Flemish and Dutch Catholic immigrants from dispersing and losing their group identity. The society planned a Dutch-Belgian colony at Butler in Otter Tail County in an effort to sell 18,000 acres owned by the D. S. B. Johnston Land Company of St. Paul. Acting primarily as a front for the land company, the society met considerable resistance from clergy in the Low Countries on the ground that immigrants would not receive adequate spiritual ministration. For this reason the society's agent approached the Order of the Holy Cross (Crosiers), asking that it send priests for the new colony. As Dutch-speaking Catholic monks, known and trusted by the prospective emigrants, the Crosiers would be the ideal foil for such criticism.[25]

In the spring of 1910, three Crosiers and 68 immigrants, almost all from the Netherlands with a few from Belgium, arrived to take up their new homes. The land company had undertaken to provide them with a church, a parish house, and a creamery and had arranged for temporary shelter until the settlers could build houses. Although these obligations were honored "to the letter," the immigrants seem to have been bitterly disappointed in their new home. When they arrived, Butler consisted of no more than two or three farmhouses and a few tarpaper shacks. The spring rains turned the primitive roads into muddy tracks. The cutover lands provided no timber of sufficient size to build the substantial "block" houses they had known in the Netherlands, and the forests were devoid of big game for food. Intense heat, flies, and mosquitoes plagued the people throughout a dry summer. All of the women and some of the men wanted to return immediately. The Crosier fathers were similarly unfavorably impressed. As a result, they decided not to build the monastery they planned at Butler but rather to look for a more

SETTLERS bound for the Butler colony began the last stretch of their journey at a Chicago depot in 1910.

satisfactory place. Despite the early discontent, however, most of the settlers stayed on and eventually built a prosperous dairying community. Although the settlement remained small, land ownership maps in successive years revealed a steady influx of newcomers.[26]

Farther to the east the Crosiers began to take an interest in the Onamia area of Mille Lacs County, where the Johnston Land Company had large cutover holdings. Bolstered by this interest, the Minnesota Catholic Colonization Society undertook a new campaign to recruit people in the Low Countries. During the winter of 1910–11, a total of 77 prospective settlers were assembled in Belgium and the Netherlands. The group arrived in Minnesota in May, 1911, but complained that the land around Onamia was unsuitable for successful farming. Most of the Dutch settlers seem to have left shortly after arrival, and those who remained were hardly sufficiently numerous to constitute an ethnic settlement in the true sense.[27]

A similar effort by the society to establish a colony at Radium in Marshall County also proved to be a dismal failure. Finding it "nothing but a spot in the woods, miles from the nearest signs of civilization," the 34 immigrants "dispersed almost immediately." The chief interest of these experiments lay in the concern they demonstrated for preserving Catholic Dutch and Flemish culture in rural Minnesota. Onamia remains the site of the Crosier monastery and college, a continuing Dutch contribution to Catholic life in the state.

A fourth Flemish concentration at Proctor in northern Minnesota presents an interesting contrast to such rural settlements as Ghent. Located a few miles west of Duluth, Proctor forms part of a larger Belgian community, including Brimson, Wrenshall, Lakeville, and Hermantown, which sprawls across the Minnesota-Wisconsin border and has its center of gravity in Superior, Wisconsin. An industrial town dominated by the Duluth, Missabe, and Iron Range Railroad, Proctor got its start in 1895 when that railroad's predecessor, the Duluth, Missabe, and Northern, com-

pleted a sorting yard there. It was in 1980 still a key site on the line of the state's major ore-carrying railroad, located as it was at the point where the ore trains began the steep descent to the docks on Lake Superior. Meager available indications are that at least some Belgians, who arrived to work in the mines of the Mesabi Range in 1908, later settled at Proctor and that the community received additional post-World War I immigration.[28]

The majority of Belgians in the Duluth-Superior area were Flemings, although a few Walloons from Brabant lived there for a time. Proctor parish questionnaires as late as 1949 indicated the continuing presence of Belgians and some Catholic Dutch as well. In marked contrast to the situation at Ghent, there were suggestions of a secular and anticlerical orientation among them. Although most found industrial jobs, others were farmers and devoted churchgoers.

The Belgians were employed initially as miners on the Mesabi Range, in breweries and ironworks, on the ore and coal docks of Duluth-Superior, by roofing and streetcar companies, and, especially at Proctor, in the locomotive and car repair shops of the railroad. In the shops the Belgians did not stand very high in the informal pecking order, ranking after Swedes, Norwegians, and Danes but before Irish and Poles. They had an excellent reputation as hard workers, however, and were readily hired.

Many of the Belgians in the Proctor-Duluth community belonged to ethnic organizations in Superior, where a Belgian Hall and associated Belgian Club, for example, still flourished in the 1970s. Some contacts apparently also existed with such other Belgian centers as Detroit, Chicago, and Ghent, and letters and visits continued to be exchanged with relatives and friends in the Old Country. Exogamy, however, appeared to be common, with second- and third-generation Belgians becoming upwardly mobile and often moving into the professions. Some folkways persisted in the 1980s — beer drinking, baking honeycake (zoetekoek), rabbit raising and rabbit cookery, cards, darts, and accordion playing.

Protestant Dutch and Friesian Settlements

The history of Dutch ethnicity in the United States and in Minnesota is closely tied to the two national churches of the Netherlanders, which have worked to maintain ethnic identity and resist rapid assimilation into American society. The two churches — the Christian Reformed and the Reformed — were originally one, formed by Seceders who had broken away from the state church of the Netherlands. In 1857, after its arrival in America, the Seceder church in turn split asunder on a variety of issues. The Christian Reformed, which was the more conservative group, was determined to maintain separate schools, where instruction in the Dutch language was considered essential. (The first such school was established in the late 1880s.) In consequence, this group played a major role in preserving Dutch ethnic consciousness in the Middle West, and its churches are more numerous in Minnesota Protestant Dutch settlements than are those of the more moderate Reformed church. Both groups stressed the necessity of establishing exclusively Dutch village communities to avoid the contamination of urban life and alien ideas. Even the less conservative of the two preserved the use of Dutch as the liturgical language and encouraged its use by auxiliary organizations well into the 20th century.[29]

The first substantial Protestant Dutch settlement in Minnesota Territory was established in Fillmore County in 1856. The earliest settlers moved by ox-drawn wagons from the Alto colony in Wisconsin. They chose land at the meeting point of York, Bristol, Carimona, and Forestville townships, which together ultimately became the core of the Greenleafton settlement. Their enthusiastic letters to Alto and Waupun drew more Wisconsin Dutch and new arrivals from the Netherlands, principally from the province of Gelderland. In 1867 the first Reformed church in Minnesota was organized by 24 Dutch families at Greenleafton.[30]

The colony of farmers prospered and soon came to occupy most of the four townships of York, Forestville, Carimona, and Bristol. By 1880 there were 209 persons born in the Netherlands and 350 more of Dutch parentage living in Fillmore County. The settlers initially raised wheat and corn, which they marketed "as much as 70 miles" away at La Crosse, Wisconsin, on the Mississippi, where they also went by wagon to secure supplies. With the coming of the Chicago, Milwaukee, and St. Paul Railway in 1868, greater specialization became possible, and the breeding of Holstein-Friesian cattle was introduced after 1860.

That the Dutch stayed is indicated by a newly constructed Reformed church dedicated in August, 1914, with services in both Dutch and English. The transition to English was completed by the congregation by 1923, but as late as 1967 a commemorative booklet marking its 100th anniversary included several verses from Psalms printed in the Dutch language. The 1970 census recorded 173 persons of Dutch birth or ancestry in Fillmore County (see Table 9.1).

Sometime before 1860 a group of Zeelanders also seems to have settled in Dodge County, but very little is known of their history. At that time southeastern Minnesota was very much on the frontier of cultivation, but thereafter Dutch settlement followed the movement of that frontier at a much more respectful distance, usually advancing with the railroads.[31]

After the Civil War, Dutch businessmen began to invest heavily in the rapidly developing Minnesota railroad network and thus became interested in land speculation and colonization. In 1867 several Netherlands-based investors persuaded the St. Paul and Pacific Railroad Company to advertise 450,000 acres of land along its line. As a result, advertisements were placed in the Dutch-language newspaper, *De Hope*, of Holland, Michigan. Two years later the *St. Paul Daily Pioneer* of May 22, 1869, reported that "some of the Hollanders who recently arrived in Minnesota, have taken up their residence in Sauk Rapids; the balance are looking around for farming lands and improved farms." Subsequent pamphleteering urging the raising of sugar beets attracted small groups from the provinces of South Holland and North Brabant to Wright and Benton counties in 1870, and others, including a few Friesian families, settled at St. Joseph and St. Cloud in Stearns County.

In this period the state of Minnesota itself also participated in the effort to attract Netherlandish immigrants, publishing in 1868 a Dutch version of Girart Hewitt's *Minnesota: Its Advantages to Settlers* at state expense at Heerenveen in the Netherlands. A newspaper, *De Landverhuizer* (The Emigrant), also appeared there under its aegis in 1872. These efforts seem to have been no more successful than those initiated in 1856 to lure Belgians to Minnesota Territory. In the opinion of both contemporaries and later historians, many such efforts, both official and private, were enthusiastic but ill-conceived, producing disillusionment among the few settlers who heeded the call.[32]

An example of this phase in the history of Dutch colonization is provided by a projected colony at Audubon in Becker County in 1872. One of the first serious Dutch ventures in the Red River Valley, it was an attempt by the Northern Pacific Railway, working through J. P. Ittmann, a Dutch agent in Rotterdam, to attract settlers from the Netherlands.[33] Writing from Rotterdam in May, 1872, to the managing director of the Northern Pacific Land Department in New York, a railroad representative noted that Dutch emigration at that time was "composed principally of the small farming class and is derived from Zierickzee in the province of Zeeland, Haringvliet in the Province of South Holland, Nijmegen in Gelderland, Neden, and several other towns in North Brabant and Limburg. Harlingen in the province of Friesland has direct steam communication with Hull. From the other districts named, the emigrants have gone via Rotterdam to Hull, whence they are transported by rail to Liverpool . . . a very small percentage has gone to Minnesota. Michigan has perhaps absorbed the largest proportion, and Iowa comes next. Great reliance is placed by the officer here [*he is referring to the Netherlands Emigration Office, organized for the protection of emigrants*] upon the German societies in New York, all the emigrants going hence being advised to call there and to accept the Society's advice, particularly as to route and tickets. Destinations seem for the most part to be decided upon before the start is made.

"The prospect for future emigration seems brightest in connection with the farming class. Here, as in other parts of Europe, the value of land has increased so rapidly that the thrifty Hollander finds it impossible to provide as he would like to provide for his family, and emigration is regarded as the only mode of enabling them to acquire the coveted land.

"A line of steamers direct from Rotterdam to New York is in contemplation, and the expectation . . . is . . . that the bulk of the emigrants . . . may be brought this way in consequence of the cheapness of the route as compared with that via Bremen and Hamburg. The firm most prominently connected with the enterprise is that of van Es, Kambersie, Ruys & Co. . . . a gentleman actively connected with societies organised here for transferring to farming districts the unemployed poor of the towns and cities, came in with the view of ascertaining to what extent and in what way the Northern Pacific would be ready to cooperate with these Dutch societies, if a portion of those now sent to farms here were sent straight to Minnesota. The consideration naturally suggested is whether these colonising societies will be prepared to purchase land from the Northern Pacific, leaving our officers in Minnesota to superintend and some degree administer the trust, or whether the parties sent out are to be left in the first instance to seek employment. The gentleman referred to is Mr. Voorhoeven, banker, & he also spoke for Baron van den Berg & Heemstede. His impression is that the societies may ultimately be induced to purchase land for colonies, but as he had not full authority to say so, this matter also stands over until I return."

It is not clear whether these societies were directly involved in the troubled Audubon project, but it is known that in 1873 two spokesmen for a group contemplating emigration went to the United States to inspect lands in Iowa, Michigan, and Minnesota. They opted to purchase railroad lands in Audubon and Lakeside townships, evidently believing they

had reached a firm understanding as to price and conditions of sale. Bad faith on the part of some company officials and misunderstandings between the railroad and its Dutch agent led to considerable bitterness on the part of the approximately 40 immigrants who arrived in May, 1873, via Liverpool and Quebec aboard Allan Steamship Lines "Sarmatian" and "Nestorian" and the Cunard steamer "Samaria." No trace of Dutch names has been found on available land ownership maps of Becker County. Presumably the settlers did not remain and the projected colony failed.[34]

The period between the end of the Civil War and the Panic of 1873 saw little successful Dutch settlement in the state. By 1876, however, the economy took an upward turn, and the 1880s not only witnessed the establishment of the Catholic Ghent colony but also the state's single most impressive Protestant Dutch venture. The latter was the work of Theodore F. Koch, an outstanding Dutch entrepreneur. A Gelderlander, Koch was affiliated with the firm of Prins and Zwanenburg in Groningen, which served as land agent for several American railroads. In 1884 he made a trip to the United States and was given a grand tour by the Chicago, Milwaukee and St. Paul Railroad (formerly the St. Paul and Pacific) of its holdings in Iowa, Minnesota, and South Dakota. As a result, he purchased, in association with Prins and a Chicago Dane named Nils C. Frederickson, 34,000 acres in the west-central Minnesota counties of Kandiyohi, Renville, and Chippewa.[35]

Unlike the Seceder patriarchs, Koch did not seek to build a city of Christian refuge, nor was he moved by philanthropic or patriotic impulses to found colonies for the poor or build a New Netherland beyond the seas. He was a businessman. His connections and credit resources were international, and he organized colonies of several nationalities. If he is best remembered for his work with the Dutch, it is primarily because his connections with these groups were par-

CLARA CITY, one of Theodore F. Koch's successful promotions, about 1895.

ticularly good and his Dutch colonies were particularly successful. If Minnesota occupied his attentions longest, it was because he felt the state was a good field for investment; as soon as it ceased to be, he transferred his activities to Texas. He ended his days in California, although he left a brother and a son to carry on in St. Paul.[36]

Koch seems to have been a man of astute judgment, a shrewd evaluator of lands, and an expert in the techniques of colonization and public relations. He recognized the advantages of recruiting settlers from the experienced pioneers of older settlements in America. Some land he sold outright; some he rented or leased. In one case (Clara City), he built an entire prefabricated town under an agreement with a contractor and rented houses and land to settlers. When his colonists in Pine County in the east-central part of the state were discouraged by the problems of clearing their poor, burnt-over lands of stumps, he set up a turpentine factory to provide a profitable market for the stumps and an inducement to further clearing. A true professional, Koch was vastly more effective than his precursors of the 1860s and 1870s. During his 22 years in Minnesota, he is estimated to have "sold and colonized over one million acres in more than 20 counties."

His advertising campaign for his land holdings in Kandiyohi, Renville, and Chippewa counties began in earnest in 1885. Working through agents in all the key Dutch settlements in the United States and advertising in the columns of the three major Dutch-language newspapers, Koch offered land at $6.00 to $8.00 per acre, with a down payment of only $2.00 an acre. He also astutely promised to provide half the cost of a new church as soon as 20 settlers had taken up their abodes and conducted twice-monthly railroad excursions for prospective land seekers who gathered in Chicago.[37]

By early 1886, he had sold 30,000 acres to families in the Netherlands and the United States and had raised the price of land to $9.00 an acre. A colony in Kandiyohi County was to be named Prinsburg in honor of the firm of Prins and Zwanenburg. The campaign, which was a thorough success, was especially heavily subscribed by Dutch settlers in Nebraska and Kansas, who had been discouraged by recurrent droughts. Soon a second Kandiyohi County settlement developed at Roseland, east of Prinsburg, where the first Dutch settlers to locate in the township arrived late in 1884.

By 1887 a third settlement was founded at Clara City in Chippewa County. Adjacent to Prinsburg, it was named for Koch's new wife, Clara D. Hoeborn, whom he had married in Germany in the course of a visit to Europe that year. Clara City acquired a somewhat distinctive character by virtue of the East Friesians who moved there from various settlements in Illinois, as well as from Grundy Center and Breda in Iowa. The names of Rheiderland Township and the village of Bunde are also reminders of East Friesland.

By 1889 there were 150 Dutch and Friesian families in *De Kolonie*, as the Koch area came to be called. In 1905 the total membership of the Prinsburg and Roseland communities alone was 621. Both major Reformed sects were represented. Christian Reformed churches were built for the Dutch at Prinsburg and the Friesians at Emden and Bunde, while a Dutch Reformed church was erected at Roseland.[38]

These were not the only Minnesota colonies promoted from the late 1880s to the outbreak of World War I. During this period Protestant Dutch settlement was vigorously encouraged by Koch and by other Dutch land companies in the southwestern Minnesota counties of Pipestone, Nobles, Murray, Jackson, and Lincoln. A few Dutch families from Alto, Wisconsin, were to be found at Holland (Pipestone County) beginning in 1887. Other places to develop as Dutch centers before World War I were Luctor, Jasper, and Edgerton (Pipestone County), Leota (Nobles County), Chandler (Murray County), Alpha (Jackson County), and Hills (Rock County). Most of the landholders were migrants from Illinois, Iowa, and the plains states. By 1916 Norman County in the Red River Valley was also receiving an influx of Dutch secondary migrants from such older Minnesota settlements as Roseland as well as from Wisconsin, Iowa, Illinois, and South Dakota. With the Catholic colony at Ghent, the settlements in the southwest comprised the largest concentration of Lowlanders in the state, accounting for almost one-quarter of all Minnesota's foreign-stock Dutch in 1970.[39]

The hand of Theodore Koch may also be seen in the establishment of Dutch settlement in Pine County during the 1890s. Securing an agreement with the St. Paul and Duluth Railroad to act as its agent in disposing of a tract of burnt-over pineries, he mounted an advertising campaign in the American Dutch-language newspapers and by September, 1895, had managed to sell about 25,000 acres at $3.00 to $6.00 per acre to Netherlanders from many parts of the United States. Before a single colonist arrived, Koch, with characteristic shrewdness, named the two townsites Friesland and Groningen. By the spring of 1896 about 200 people had moved from Sioux County, Iowa, or directly from the Netherlands. Koch gave easy credit terms and provided the settlers with inexpensive livestock. The Friesland-Groningen colony, however, failed to grow to the extent Koch had originally hoped, perhaps because of the poor quality of the soil.[40]

Some Hollanders soon moved into nearby Hinckley and Sandstone, where both Reformed and Christian Reformed congregations were organized. Hinckley had earlier attracted a few Dutch from Colorado even before Koch became active in Pine County. A devastating forest fire there in 1894 apparently caused them to move west to Pease in Mille Lacs County. There in 1896 their ranks were swelled by eight families of refugees discouraged by the drought in Charles Mix County, South Dakota. By 1911 Pease numbered 50 families of Netherlanders; by 1917, 110 families had settled there and land values were appreciating rapidly. This successful Dutch settlement area eventually extended from Pease southward to the vicinity of Princeton. It was a considerable source of later out-migration to the Twin Cities.

As the Pease concentration continued to expand, a scattering of Protestant Dutch also moved to other Minnesota areas. They were to be found at Ogilvie and McGrath (Kanabec County), Hancock (Stevens County), Brooten (Stearns County), and Bejou (Mahnomen County). Just after World War I a totally new community took form at Hollandale north of Albert Lea in Freeborn County, where in 1919 the Albert Lea Farms Company of Omaha, Nebraska, decided to reclaim a tract of swamp and lake-bottom land and advertised for Dutch farmers experienced in such work. About 15 arrived from the Netherlands as well as from Iowa and reclamation began in 1922. The project was an immediate success. By 1924 Hollandale had 324 people, a hotel, an onion warehouse, a Reformed church, post office, telephone service, and substantial homes "with neat looking entrance arches" on which were printed farm names, some in Dutch. Specializing in truck farming, the Dutch in two years reclaimed about 2,300 acres and were raising celery, potatoes, onions, carrots, and cabbage, as well as timothy, soybeans, flax, clover, and sugar beets. By 1930 the colony numbered more than 500 persons and it has continued to thrive.[41]

The southwestern concentration also grew. Following World War II, descendants of Dutch immigrants moved in the 1950s from northwestern Iowa to the Slayton area of Murray County, ostensibly because of cheaper land prices, according to one informant. In the 1970s both Reformed and Christian Reformed congregations in Slayton still sang the old Dutch hymns, and everyone in the Dutch community knew everyone else.

Assimilation and Ethnicity

Urban groups with large ethnic populations have often successfully kept alive obvious elements of their culture. An example can be seen in the Belgians of Detroit, Michigan. Besides maintaining their own Catholic parish, they have founded a wide range of societies and clubs for both utilitarian and social purposes. The reinforcement they provided kept alive pride in traditions of Flemish art, music, and craftsmanship. In the 1970s a lively interest was shown in Belgian popular music; theater groups produced traditional and new Flemish plays; and a newspaper published articles in Flemish and English.[42]

By contrast no Belgian or Dutch community was visible in the Twin Cities. Of a total metropolitan population of about 1,814,000 in 1970, 346 persons of Belgian stock and 738 of Dutch were recorded in Minneapolis and 132 and 482 in St. Paul. A nationality census of Minneapolis in 1934 revealed 265 Dutch and 39 Belgian families scattered throughout the city. As for St. Paul, a study of that city's foreign born in the same year recorded 181 Dutch and did not deign to notice the number of Belgians. In 1980 the Twin Cities revealed no ethnic neighborhoods of Lowlanders and only two organizations designed to promote the national culture.[43]

In general Belgians and Dutch were simply too few and too scattered to form self-conscious communities in the Twin Cities. Many were migrants from rural portions of the state, and their ethnic ties, if maintained, were likely to be with their childhood homes. Some no doubt preferred to shed their ethnic identity and may have moved to the city for that very reason.

From the 1950s to the 1970s a few emigrated directly from the Netherlands and Belgium attracted by cultural institutions and the computer industry. A small number were to be found at the University of Minnesota in Minneapolis, where an interested group of faculty and students organized a Netherlands House as a social center and lecture forum. But this is not the stuff of which ethnic communities are made. The only apparent ethnic organization in the Twin Cities in 1980 was a Holland Club affiliated with the Dutch Immigrant Society of Grand Rapids, Michigan. Twice yearly it showed Dutch films and held fairs promoting Dutch products and cookery, a far cry from the varied activities of the Detroit Belgians.

In 1980 Dutch and Belgians in Minnesota lived largely on farms and in country towns. While attempts to carry on "high cultural" activities, such as the production of plays in Detroit, were largely lacking and while they made little concerted effort to keep specifically Belgian or Dutch traditions

THE TRADITIONAL Saint Nicholas and Black Piet put in an appearance at the Holland-America Club's Christmas party in Minneapolis, around 1924.

alive, these groups have perpetuated certain Old Country cultural values. The emergence of a sense of ethnic identity has taken place in a purely American cultural context. The people were Belgian or Dutch vis-à-vis their Norwegian, Icelandic, Polish, French-Canadian, or Yankee neighbors. There was little outward appearance of emigrant nostalgia in Ghent.[44]

Of the folkways which have survived, probably the most obvious is a popular Belgian sport known as *rolle bolle* or *krulbolling* or *prysbolling*, a form of bowling with disk-like bowls. Teams from the United States and Canada gathered regularly to hold competitions. Open air *rolle bolle* courts were distinctive features of Ghent and Marshall, and the game was much discussed in 1980. The phrase commonly heard, "When two men use the same *rolle bolle* ball they're probably related," showed an ethnic and family identification with the game. A card game called *bien*, still popular in Detroit, was also played but seemed to be declining. Pigeon racing used to be practiced at Ghent but had gone out of fashion. Nor did ethnic cookery seem to be a major item,

TRICYCLE RELAYS shared the program with rolle bolle *games in a mingling of the old and the new at this 1978 celebration in Ghent.*

although older persons recalled *zoetekoek*, a honeycake, and *hutsepot*, a hearty stew. Apart from thin Belgian cookies, which are homemade on special irons and seemed to be an authentic survival, other ethnic foods appeared only on holidays or such occasions as Belgian-American Day and were not really a part of everyday life. As one man expressed it, "We generally eat what we grow on the farm, which is the same as what everybody else eats."[45]

In 1978 Belgian-American Day itself was an unabashedly commercial operation devised by local businessmen in co-operation with the Belgian national airline (Sabena) and the consulate to attract business to the town. It began in 1953. The day was filled with games, including a *rolle bolle* tournament, and in the evening a beauty queen was chosen in the local hall. Ethnic cookery was not in evidence at the luncheon but was consigned to a garage behind the *rolle bolle* courts.[46]

The language, again in contrast to Detroit, had also gone by the wayside. By 1978 many older persons, monolingual in childhood, also spoke English, albeit with heavy accents. Much Flemish was still in use among middle-aged people, but the younger generations generally either dropped it or never learned it. No doubt part of the language persistence can be ascribed to the continuing flow of immigrants from the Low Countries. The last person who could speak no English, a long-time resident of Ghent, died in 1967.[47]

Yet despite the decline of language and some other cultural accoutrements, certain aspects of both the Dutch and Belgian ethnocultural background have remained vitally apparent. They may be observed by comparing the Dutch community in Prinsburg with the Belgian one in Ghent. In the Kandiyohi County settlement, the stern Calvinistic ethos has left a deep imprint on Reformed and Christian Reformed communities. Calvinist conceptions of morality, church polity, and social discipline bring heavy pressure on members to live exemplary lives, to avoid the corrupting influence of such worldly activities as gambling, dancing, theatergoing, and consuming alcoholic beverages. A journalist visiting Prinsburg in 1977 observed: "In Prinsburg, a west-central Minnesota community of 467, people are expected to keep homes in good repair and yards well-groomed. . . . There are no beer parlors, no liquor stores, no dance halls and no billiard parlors. The town has only one church — Christian Reformed — and the only school . . . is Central Minnesota Christian School. Miniature windmills spin on the lawns, and during the Fourth of July *Klompen* folk dances, wooden shoes and bonnets appear. But the traits of the people are what make Prinsburg different. . . .

"Work may be the major recreational activity, the mayor [Henry Duininck] said, although there is bowling and golfing and the card game Rook. School and church activities provide most of the community's social life. Some townspeople suggest 'Americanization' has gone too far. Many people discontinued use of the Dutch language during World War I, when the Dutch were wrongfully associated with the German enemy. Nowadays, Dutch is spoken in few homes.

"In religion, Mrs. [Nell] De Vries [a Prinsburg resident] believes the young don't take their faith as seriously as their forebears. Even she now washes pots and pans on Sundays, something that was considered a sin when she was a girl."[48]

This life-style, indeed this world view, contrasted strongly with that of the Catholic Dutch and Flemings, making a Dutch Calvinist village like Prinsburg a very different place from Ghent. A saloon in Prinsburg would be unthinkable; in Ghent the saloons were the first in the state to reopen after the repeal of Prohibition, a point of local pride.[49] These groups were united in their devotion to thrift, hard work, and good farming, but the same differences in social mores which kept them apart in the Old Country continued to separate them in the new.

Belgian and Dutch ethnicity in Minnesota is not to be discovered in outward behavior or in the preservation of quaint customs and folkways. Rather it appears in the form of persistent attitudes and values: devotion to the church, an obsession with hard work and good farming, thrift and pride in the meeting of financial obligations, and a general sociability and conviviality. Dutch and Belgian ethnicity must be seen in the behavior the people themselves deem important. Belgian plays and the Dutch language simply were not as important to them as the standards of morality transported from Europe and rigorously maintained by the two groups.[50]

The Luxembourgers

OF THE THREE LOWLAND NATIONALITIES, the Luxembourgers, including German-speaking Luxembourgers from Belgium, are proportionately more heavily represented in Minnesota than either the Dutch or the Belgians. The smallest of the three European nations, with a total area of about 999 square miles, the Grand Duchy of Luxembourg is not quite the size of Rhode Island. During the 19th century it is estimated to have yielded no fewer than one out of every five of its inhabitants to the United States. As late as the 1940s Luxembourg's population was estimated at 301,000 and the number of Americans of Luxembourg descent at about 100,000. By the 1970s, however, when Luxembourg had approximately 330,000 inhabitants, its foreign-stock population in the United States was presumably too insignificant to merit mention in the national census. Only for states such as Minnesota, which had sizable concentrations of Luxembourgers (2,315), were foreign-stock figures published after 1940.[1]

Minnesota was one of the four states which received the heaviest immigration, the others being Iowa, Illinois, and Wisconsin. Moreover Luxembourgers were among the early Minnesota arrivals, for the beginnings of most of their settlements antedated 1860. By 1870 at least 1,173 were to be found in the state, and 10 years later 7,069 foreign-born and American-born Luxembourgers were living largely along the Mississippi and Minnesota rivers (see Table 9.3). The heaviest concentrations in the Mississippi Valley occurred in the state's southeastern corner in Houston, Winona, Wabasha, and Goodhue counties and in central Minnesota in Stearns County. The metropolitan counties of Ramsey and Hennepin had sizable numbers, and these people were also to be found near the junction of the Mississippi and St. Croix rivers in Washington County. In the Minnesota Valley most of them settled in Dakota and Scott counties, with smaller clusters in Blue Earth, Brown, Carver, Nicollet, and Sibley counties.[2]

The Red River Valley and northeastern and southwestern Minnesota, on the other hand, harbored few Luxembourgers. Except for Stearns County, only a handful were

counted in central and southern Minnesota, and in 1880 none was recorded in 21 established counties — Aitkin, Beltrami, Benton, Cass, Cook, Crow Wing, Dodge, Faribault, Grant, Itasca, Isanti, Kanabec, Kittson, Lake, Martin, Mille Lacs, Pine, Sherburne, Stevens, Wilkin, and Yellow Medicine.

Except in Carver County, immigrants from Luxembourg rarely settled alongside Netherlanders or Belgian Walloons. When overlaps with Belgians were recorded — as in Houston, Wabasha, Goodhue, and Nicollet counties — most of the "Belgians" in question were actually German-speaking Belgian Luxembourgers, ethnically the same people as those from the Grand Duchy. The strongest correlation was registered between areas of Luxembourger concentration and those of Roman Catholic Germans in Blue Earth, Brown, Carver, Houston, Nicollet, Scott, Stearns, and Wabasha counties. The clustering of these people along the Mississippi — from Houston County north to the Twin Cities — was the result of migration from Dubuque on the river in northeastern Iowa.[3]

The regular association of immigrants from the Grand Duchy with those from the Belgian province of Luxembourg and with Roman Catholic Germans in Minnesota points up a difficult and delicate problem of ethnic and political history which has a distinct bearing on the affairs of these people in Minnesota and in the Middle West generally. Like many ethnic problems, this one had its roots almost entirely in Europe. It concerns the relations of Luxembourg and Germany and of ethnic Luxembourgers and ethnic Germans.

Luxembourg Ethnicity

From the mid-15th to the late-18th centuries the old duchy of Luxembourg was part of the dynastic-territorial complex long ruled from Brussels by governors and administrators serving the Spanish and Austrian Habsburgs. It was annexed to Revolutionary France in 1795, but after the fall of Napoleon in 1815, Luxembourg acquired strategic importance and complex ties to Prussia and the Netherlands. For security against France, a Prussian garrison was installed in the fortress on the Bock, an eminence on and around which the city

Table 9.3. Luxembourgers in Minnesota by County, 1860–1900

County	1860 foreign born	1860 foreign mixed	1880 fb	1880 fm	1900 fb
Anoka				2	6
Becker					1
Beltrami					3
Big Stone				1	
Blue Earth	3		40	84	1
Brown	32	12	117	165	27
Carlton	1		1	2	
Carver	39	23	41	78	1
Chippewa			4	8	1
Chisago			3	12	
Clay			8	10	
Cottonwood			9	8	
Dakota	23	268	427	475	23
Douglas			4		
Faribault					2
Fillmore			8	29	
Freeborn			2		
Goodhue	14	3	98	161	2
Hennepin	13	4	143	208	30
Minneapolis			87		24
Houston	42	11	426	511	2
Itasca					3
Jackson			6		
Kandiyohi			1		
Lac qui Parle				1	
Le Sueur	1		39	31	2
Lincoln				1	
Lyon			3	3	
McLeod			11	24	
Marshall				1	1
Meeker	1		9	25	
Mille Lacs					1
Morrison			1	4	1
Mower			45	25	10
Murray			3	4	13
Nicollet	85	18	115	133	1
Nobles			12	11	2
Norman					1
Olmsted			32	27	
Otter Tail			17	30	9
Pipestone			2	5	2
Polk	1	2	7	1	9
Pope			6	4	5
Ramsey	26	9	87	95	57
St. Paul			80		57
Redwood			1	8	1
Renville			7	16	1
Rice			22	29	
Rock			1		1
St. Louis	4		11	9	2
Duluth					2
Scott	97	42	251	467	8
Sibley	36	19	36	71	
Stearns	147	59	277	312	41
Steele			5	5	
Stevens					4
Swift			4	2	
Todd			5	4	1
Traverse			2		
Wabasha	7	3	264	340	26
Wadena			2	7	
Waseca			2	3	
Washington	20	12	52	89	2
Watonwan			21	53	
Winona			361	407	134
Wright	2		7	3	
Total	594	485	3,061	4,008	430
Published census figures				(2,949)	(430)

Source: See Appendix

of Luxembourg was built. The country was reorganized as a Grand Duchy with William I, king of the Netherlands, as its first grand duke. In 1815 it joined the German Confederation, a bond it maintained until the confederation was dissolved in the Austro-Prussian War of 1866. The Prussian garrison was evacuated from the Bock the following year.[4]

Luxembourg did not become a member of Bismarck's North German Confederation of 1866, or of the second German Empire proclaimed at Versailles in 1871. The chancellor's struggle to combat Roman Catholic church influence over educational and ecclesiastical appointments did not appeal to Luxembourgers either at home or abroad. Anti-Prussian sentiment was strong, and the new Germany was perceived as Prussian. German occupation of Luxembourg in World Wars I and II thoroughly embittered its people, completely alienating them from any idea or ideal of union with Germany.

In considering ethnicity, however, the German connection arises in another form. Are Luxembourgers *ethnically* Germans or not? Is the *Letzeburgesch* tongue a dialect of German or a separate language? What criteria ought to be applied in attempting answers to these questions? Given the heated political atmosphere in which present-day Luxembourg developed, dispassionate answers are not easily come by. Some distinctions may, however, be helpful.

First, a distinction should be made between an official language and the language of everyday speech, normally the realm of dialect. Any spoken idiom can become an official language by legislative act or some other form of legal recognition. From this point of view, Luxembourg since 1939 has had three official languages — French, German, and *Letzeburgesch*. Furthermore, *Letzeburgesch* is spoken in southeastern Belgian Luxembourg (see Map 9.1), in that part of French Lorraine just south of the Grand Duchy, and in the Bitburg-Prüm region of the Rhine Province (now in West Germany). Public authorities in these three areas usually regard it as a local German dialect. Linguistic scholarship, concerned purely with the scientific classification of spoken languages, places *Letzeburgesch* among the group of dialects called Moselle Frankish, a subgroup of the larger Middle German. Such classifications, however, have no political implications whatsoever, except to those who insist upon seeing them.[5]

For ethnicity, linguistic classifications are frequently less important than what people believe themselves to be, a perception which often varies over time. Luxembourgers in Europe and the United States seem to have evolved their sense of identity in relation to Germans and Germanness. According to recent scholarship, they were in the early 19th century intensely localistic with only a very dim sense of nationhood. Some immigrants, for example, reported their place of birth as "Luxemburg, Germany."[6]

This ambivalence was apparent in remarks by Father Michael Flammang appearing in the first issue of the *Luxemburger Gazette* published at Dubuque, Iowa, on August 4, 1871. The Luxembourgers "do not want to be anything other than German," he wrote. "With a great German power under Prussian leadership, however, they wanted nothing to do. If the various German states find their ideal in Prussia and have nothing more pressing to do than to deliver themselves with sack and pack into the Prussian army, then we have nothing to say against this . . . ; they have made use of a right of which they need offer no account to us. But the Luxemburgers also claim the same right for themselves. They see in Prussia a military state, and the misfortune of Germany."[7]

Nicholas Gonner, another opinion leader of his countrymen in the United States who was no whit less hostile to Prussianism, expressed himself in a somewhat different way 18 years later. After speaking of the animus raised against the Prussians in the 1870s, he commented that "Luxemburgers too must profit from the respect which through its victories Germany won in the eyes of the world, since in the view of the Americans and the Irish, not only the great Prussian but everyone who uses the German language counts as 'German.'"[8]

Thus in 1871 and 1889 some feelings of Germanness were still intact among immigrant Luxembourgers. Even though both men rejected Prussianism, Gonner was willing to borrow prestige from the Bismarck victories, which he regarded as reflecting favorably on the German people as a whole, including Luxembourgers. Ethnic consciousness among these immigrants had not yet reached an absolute breaking point with Germanness and, while ambivalent, still retained a considerable degree of identification with Germans in America, especially if they were Catholics. These attitudes become understandable when we realize that most Luxembourg immigrants of that period could speak or understand some German, but few of them seem to have been at ease in French. As a result they sought out settlements of German coreligionists with established parishes and German-speaking priests, especially in the crucial years of settlement before 1870.[9]

As for Belgian Luxembourgers, Gonner's authority may again be invoked. As a "fullfledged Luxemburger," he wrote, one "counts not only the man from the Grand Duchy, but also the German-speaking Luxemburger from the Belgian province of Luxemburg. Vis-a-vis the foreigner he calls himself first a Luxemburger, and only then makes the explanatory remark that he is from the province. The Walloon in contrast is a full Belgian."

Settlement Patterns

The basic pattern of Luxembourger settlement in Minnesota, Wisconsin, Iowa, and Illinois was established by 1860 (see Table 9.3). Although New York and Ohio had attracted these people earlier in the 19th century, the opening of the Middle West drew them steadily away from eastern centers, while direct immigrants also began to take up farms in the four states. Luxembourgers left their European homes because of poverty of the soil (especially in the Ardennes region of the northern Grand Duchy), crop failures and potato famines in the 1840s, aversion to military service, and lack of sufficient industry to absorb population growth before 1870.[10]

After 1870 the picture gradually changed with the discovery and development of the rich iron deposits of the Minette Basin, a portion of which intrudes into Luxembourg near Esch-sur-Alzette (Map 9.1). Although the duchy continued to export its citizens in considerable numbers during the 1870s, 1880s, and 1890s, it soon came to have an immigration rather than an emigration problem, a situation that still existed in the 1970s. Before 1858 the majority of emigrants were of the small-farmer class; after 1858 they were chiefly manual workers and landless rural proletarians.

Scholars have divided the movement into three parts or "waves." The first, extending from about 1828 to the early 1840s, was relatively small and chiefly affected western New York and Ohio. The larger second movement, from 1845 to 1860, reached Chicago, progressed along Lake Michigan in eastern Wisconsin, northwest to the Mississippi Valley in eastern Iowa at Dubuque and St. Donatus, and then north to southeastern Minnesota. The approximate chronology of these movements may be suggested by the occupation of the ridge area north of Chicago in 1845, of the eastern Wisconsin lake shore region between 1845 and 1858, and of the Mississippi Valley after 1846.

A few Luxembourgers reached Minnesota as early as 1846, although the territorial census of 1850 identified none as such. This discrepancy may be accounted for by the tendency of Luxembourgers in that period to give their place of birth as "Luxemburg, Germany," or it may simply be the result of inaccurate recording. In any event, at least eight are known to have been present in the 1850s: five in rural Oakdale Township in Washington County, one in New Ulm, and three in the Twin Cities. The last three were successful businessmen. Two operated hotels in St. Paul and the third "employed a large capital and enjoyed a large trade" in Minneapolis.[11]

Although the principal Luxembourger communities in Minnesota originated in the 1850s, appreciable numbers of settlers did not arrive until the 1860s — the opening of the third movement and the period of maximum emigration, which lasted until 1900. From 1860 to 1870 about 5,000 persons arrived in the United States; from 1870 to 1880 about 8,000; from 1880 to 1890 another 8,000; and from 1890 to 1900 about 6,000. The effects of the "third wave" were essentially different from the two preceding ones, for the later years also saw the children of earlier immigrants migrate from the older centers to locations farther west, especially in Kansas, Nebraska, and the Dakotas. These settlers tended to lose contact with the older, better-established centers, and most became lost in the American mass.[12]

The earliest Luxembourger settlements in Minnesota seem to have begun in 1853 along the Mississippi River in the southeastern corner of the state at Minnesota City in Winona County and at Lake City in Wabasha County. Antedating the railroad, these and other ventures along the rivers in the years immediately following were real pioneering experiences conducted under truly primitive conditions. For example, at Lake City and Minnesota City the first farmers lived in mud huts they called "gopher holes." By 1856 some settlers were pentrating the Indian country along the Minnesota River in Scott County. There Theodore Rosen settled among the Dakota Indians at New Market, while Nicholas Kranz and others began to take up land at Hastings and New Trier in Dakota County. Others could be found at Shakopee (Scott

County), Mankato (Blue Earth County), and Chanhassen (Carver County) before 1860.[13]

The second major place where Luxembourgers settled was Stearns County in central Minnesota, where migrants from the Grand Duchy began to appear from 1854 to 1859 at St. Cloud, St. Wendelin (now Luxemburg), Cold Spring, St. Nicholas, St. Augusta, and Maine Prairie. The most conspicuous common factor affecting these choices of locality seems to have been the presence of German Catholic churches. For example, St. John's Abbey, a Benedictine monastery which ministered to a whole cluster of German-speaking communities in the vicinity (including Luxembourgers), was a decisive influence. In other areas of the state, Luxembourgers settled with Irish or Bohemian Catholics, but their preference for German parishes was marked. Of nine Luxembourger settlements that contained over 35 families in 1889, seven were near German-language Roman Catholic parishes. "They are farmers," wrote Abbot Alexius Hoffmann of St. John's, "conservative, energetic and intelligent," who retained "their old usages . . . and insisted upon speaking German, spiced with French terms."[14]

Among these new Minnesotans were settlers from older Luxembourger communities in the United States as well as direct immigrants from he Grand Duchy and the Belgian province. Those at Belvidere in Goodhue County, for example, were chiefly families from Belgian Luxembourg, who had settled first in New York in the 1840s and migrated to Minnesota in the late 1850s and early 1860s. The large colony at Caledonia in Houston County was composed of various groups from upstate New York, Tiffin, Ohio, and St. Donatus, Iowa. Other centers such as Port Washington, Wisconsin, and Dubuque, Iowa, were represented in the Minnesota settlements. As for local provenance in the Old Country, every district and canton of the Grand Duchy and the German-speaking districts of the Belgian province were represented among the Minnesota settlers.[15]

These early Minnesota arrivals have been little chronicled. Given the dearth of sources, it may be useful to look briefly at Rollingstone in Winona County, one of the earliest as well as the most culturally retentive Luxembourger settlements in Minnesota. Visitors acquainted with both landscapes frequently profess to see a resemblance between the Rollingstone area and the Moselle River Valley in Luxembourg. They also find Rollingstone's Holy Trinity Church reminiscent of the stone edifices in the Grand Duchy. With neighboring Elba, Oak Ridge, and Altura, this Winona County area was undoubtedly the strongest Luxembourger concentration in the state.[16]

Although the Rollingstone colony got its start as a result of the activities of the Western Farm and Village Association organized in New York City in 1851, its first settler was Peter Stoos, who arrived in 1855 directly from Luxembourg. He purchased two sections of land (1,280 acres) from the United States General Land Office and began to farm, laboriously clearing an acre at a time. During the first few years provisions had to be hauled from Winona, some 10 miles away, a trip he attempted only about twice a year. His first dwelling, situated at the center of the future village, was a log cabin in which the first Mass was said by a Benedictine priest in 1857. Stoos donated land for the site of Holy Trinity Church. The first wooden building was replaced in 1881 with the stone church still in use a hundred years later.

Stoos was soon joined in the 1850s by other Luxembourgers, many of whom had also emigrated from the region between the Ernz and the Alzette rivers — the villages of Heffingen, Junglinster, Bettendorf, and Godbringen, for example. More arrived in the 1860s and 1870s from Iowa and Wisconsin as well as from the villages of Rosport and Greiweldingen in Luxembourg.

By 1860 Rollingstone had a one-room schoolhouse. A second school, built by the Catholic parish, made its appearance in 1886. Its records list 37 Luxembourger families (not including Stoos), but a historian in 1899 professed to know of 54 families at Rollingstone, 17 at Elba, and 24 at Oak Ridge. By the early 1870s the first of three hotels, the Schommer Hotel, was built complete with saloon. A second, erected by John Schuh, Sr., had not only a saloon but also a dance hall and stables. The Luxembourgers' love of music was well illustrated by the founding of a band in Rollingstone in 1876. In 1962 Schuh's son, John Jr., who is remembered as one of the town's more active musicians, could still perform music from Luxembourg which he had played in his youth.

A number of church-related organizations, some of them extant in 1980, were begun at Holy Trinity Church during this period. The first on record was a women's organization, the Rosary Society, founded in 1868. Next came the St. Nicholas Society (1884), a multipurpose male group dedicated to a favorite Luxembourg saint. It held an annual festival on December 6, St. Nicholas' Day, and served charity, insurance, and social functions. In 1891 a Young Ladies' Society was added, and in 1930, the St. Theresa Society, affiliated with the Catholic Aid Association, a midwestern group, was founded.[17]

THE INTERIOR of Holy Trinity Church, Rollingstone, about 1909. The church remained in use in 1981.

Other pioneer Luxembourgers found political and business success in communities where they were in the minority. Francis Baasen, an attorney, was elected to many local offices in New Ulm. He also served in the territorial legislature, was a delegate to the state constitutional convention in 1857, and was elected as a Democrat to the post of Minnesota's first secretary of state (1858–60). During the Civil War, Baasen also served with distinction in the famed First Minnesota Regiment.[18]

Jacob Ries, a Luxembourger who homesteaded in Scott County in 1857, combined politics with business. In 1872 he founded a soft drink and bottling factory in Shakopee that prospered for 104 years under the direction of three generations of the family. Its products, chiefly spring water and beverage mixes, were produced under the trade name "Rock Spring," which became nationally and even internationally known. Ries also served 12 years on the Shakopee council and was elected mayor in 1895 and 1897.[19]

The years between 1858 and 1862 saw some falling off of emigration from Luxembourg, perhaps inspired by the fear of Know-Nothing nativism on the one hand and of wandering into a country locked in Civil War on the other. But in the decades after passage of the Homestead Act in 1862, increasing numbers arrived. For the most part, this revival did not lead to the formation of many new Luxembourger settlements. Rather it augmented those which already existed. A partial exception might be the relatively small but new settlements in north-central Minnesota and the Red River Valley, where Otter Tail, Clay, and Polk counties registered a few Luxembourgers by 1880. Gonner, writing in 1889, spoke of knowing about two dozen families, including 13 in Polk County near Euclid and half a dozen in Crookston, which had a German Catholic parish.[20]

During this period, the Twin Cities began to attract larger proportions of the state's Luxembourger population. The foreign-stock population from the Grand Duchy in Hennepin and Ramsey counties jumped from 52 in 1869 to 533 in 1880. The earliest settlement was concentrated in Minneapolis, but by 1889 St. Paul was becoming the Luxembourger center. In that year, well over 100 families in addition to single individuals lived in the capital city, compared to 68 families and about 50 individuals in Minneapolis. By 1905 St. Paul had over two and a half times as many Luxembourgers as its sister city (261 of foreign and mixed stock compared to 105).[21]

As in the rural areas, those in the Twin Cities tended to settle near German neighborhoods. The center of the community in St. Paul, for example, was within Frogtown or Ward 8, the largest German concentration in the city. Nearly nine-tenths of the Luxembourgers (87% to be exact) lived in Frogtown, west of Rice Street and north of University Avenue. Within that area stood St. Agnes Roman Catholic Church, whose congregation was not only German and Austrian but Luxembourger as well. Although the population had decreased by 1930, the same German-Luxembourger concentrations maintained themselves. In Minneapolis the picture was similar, despite a smaller Luxembourger contingent. Eighty-three per cent of first- and second-generation immigrants from the Grand Duchy (87 out of 105) in 1905 lived in Northeast Minneapolis' Ward 1, the second largest German ward in the city.[22]

In rural sections of Ramsey and Hennepin counties in 1905, the largest number of Luxembourgers was to be found in the White Bear Lake area. The census of that village and township listed 56 Luxembourgers, both foreign born and second generation, and 169 foreign-born Germans. In rural Hennepin County, small numbers of Luxembourgers were scattered among Plymouth, Maple Grove, Hassan, and Crystal Lake townships and in Edina. A survey of the occupations of these rural Luxembourgers showed that most were farmers.[23]

Organizations, Politics, and Activities

The Twin Cities of St. Paul and Minneapolis were particularly important as scenes of Luxembourger attempts to respond to life in a new country by organizing for mutual aid and political action. Indeed, these attempts and the organizations they produced constitute the best-documented chapter in the story of the Luxembourgers in Minnesota from 1860 to 1900. The Civil War brought heavy pressures to bear upon the newly settled immigrants. As antimilitarists, Luxembourgers tended to oppose the war; as constitutionalists who were strongly antislavery and committed to the Union and to their adopted nation, they supported the war. Politically they tended to be conservative Democrats who temporarily became Republicans. As the beneficiaries of a more or less liberal constitution in the homeland, Luxembourgers were both antislavery and antiprotectionist, advocating both civil rights and free trade. These conflicting positions placed them on both sides of the American political fence in 1860 and under inveterate suspicion of being both pacifistic and pro-Southern.[24]

No such ambivalence was exhibited by Luxembourg immigrants toward the threatened annexation of the Grand Duchy by France and Germany in 1867–71 and the concurrent annexation of papal Rome by the new kingdom of Italy. In the face of these threats to homeland and church, patriotic and religious sentiment coalesced in a rising demand for a voice that could speak for Luxembourgers in American public affairs. In the preliminaries of this movement, which saw the creation of an ethnic press in the United States, those in Minnesota played an important part.[25]

On December 31, 1870, a Luxembourger named Jean-Pierre Michels protested the threatened annexation of the duchy by Prussia in the pages of *Der Wanderer* (The Migrant), a German-language paper published in St. Paul. On January 22, 1871, concerned like-minded persons met in Dominick Barthel's clothing shop. After some discussion of the German and Italian aggressions, Eugène Thein of New Trier expressed dissatisfaction with the local German press and offered to contribute substantially toward starting an ethnic newspaper. He found a warm supporter in Michels, and an attempt was made to found a Minnesota-based paper to be called the *Luxemburger Telegraph*.

Difficulties arose, however, in negotiations with a prospective editor. Thein tried to carry on alone, even to seeking subscriptions, but was finally induced by friends to approach Father Michael Flammang of St. Donatus, an energetic leader of the midwestern Luxembourger community, who succeeded in arousing the interest of Catholic diocesan authorities in Dubuque. The upshot was the founding in 1871 of the *Luxemburger Gazette* at Dubuque, with Thein as the sole Minnesota member of the board of directors.

By the 1880s Minnesota immigrants from Luxembourg had developed various other institutions. Rollingstone had a benevolent society as well as a musical band, and New Trier had a *Leseverein* (reading club). A group at first called *Luciliburgia*, from the medieval Latin name of Luxembourg, was organized in St. Paul. Later renamed the Luxembourger *Unterstützungs-Verein* (Benevolent Society), it offered collective entertainments and advice to immigrants and provided work disability payments to members ($5.00 per week for six months) and burial benefits of $25.00 to survivors. In addition, the group sponsored an annual feast on St. Nicholas' Day, December 6, to underscore the Catholic traditions of the homeland. Although it was based in St. Paul, the society's membership was said to have extended to countrymen in the surrounding area as well. In 1888 it had 68 members. In 1905 the society celebrated its 25th anniversary at the Church of St. Agnes in St. Paul's Frogtown. Less well known but having similar purposes was the Luxembourger *Bruderbund* or Brotherhood, a St. Paul chapter of an organization founded in Chicago in 1887. Minneapolis too had a group, known as the *Nationale*.[26]

In 1894 St. Paul demonstrated the strength of its organizations by hosting the annual gathering, or congress, of the Luxembourger societies in the United States, with delegates from 13 states attending. The two St. Paul groups at that time were said to have a combined membership of 1,200 and the Minneapolis *Nationale* sent 50 delegates to the conference. Several Minnesotans figured prominently as officers of the national congress, which was principally concerned with combating anti-immigrant nativism and with providing death-benefit insurance.

These ventures in organization did not long survive. Their

MEMBERS posed with the banner of the Luxembourger Benevolent Society in St. Paul about 1905.

demise was in part attributable to the very nativism the Luxembourgers so much feared and reprehended. The *Luxemburger Gazette* was an example. Although it originated in the reaction against triumphant Prussianism in the 1870s and strengthened its hostility to the German government in the Bismarck era, it nonetheless adopted a somewhat pro-German stance in 1914 at the outbreak of World War I, a position by no means unique among midwestern journals at the time. With the American entry into the war in 1917, public pressure on German-language newspapers, the playing of German music, and the teaching of German in the schools was so great that the *Gazette* quietly closed its doors in 1918. Both of the St. Paul societies also gradually disappeared, although the benevolent group led a shadowy existence until 1951, when it was dissolved by court decree, presumably for want of adequate membership to sustain its functions. In 1979 an attempt was under way to resuscitate *Luciliburgia*, not as an insurance group, but as a historical society concerned with the Luxembourger heritage in the state.[27]

One of the salient characteristics of Luxembourgers was the extent of their civic involvement in Minnesota affairs from the very beginning, the same impulse that led to the founding of the *Gazette*. The immigrants apparently had a high literacy rate and strong political and social consciousness. Many became active in politics, often attaining public office with the support of partly German constituencies.[28]

Of the numerous Luxembourgers who participated in local politics, two examples must suffice. John Ludwig, a Winona hotel proprietor and banker, emigrated first to Wisconsin from Canach in the Grand Duchy. He moved to Winona in 1866 where he served four years as mayor (1883–85, 1888–90) during which he was given much of the credit for the establishment of city-owned water works, an electric plant, and street railways. In 1925 and 1927 Elizabeth K. Ries, Jacob's daughter, was elected mayor of Shakopee, a position she resigned in 1928 to accept an appointment as postmaster.[29]

At least six Luxembourgers are known to have served in the Minnesota House of Representatives in the 1870s and 1880s; at least one more served in the state senate in the 20th century. Most of them were Democrats in a period in state politics dominated by Republicans. The constituencies they represented were, for the most part, areas of Luxembourger concentration, but in none of them did their fellow countrymen become numerous enough to dominate elections.[30]

In notable contrast to the Belgians, for example, a whole array of Luxembourger sheriffs, auditors, county commissioners, surveyors, postmasters, coroners, and other local officials can easily be adduced to demonstrate the civic involvement of this group at the county, town, and village levels in areas where they were most thickly settled. The support of Catholic Germans was probably an important factor in their political success. Luxembourgers in the 19th century had a saying that when four Germans gathered, there were five opinions. Not so with Luxembourgers, who tended to pull together, a trait that may have given them an advantage in mixed German-Luxembourger communities.[31]

Be that as it may, they made their mark in religion as well

as in politics, exhibiting notable devotion to the Roman Catholic faith of their fathers. Both sexes have entered the ranks of the religious in considerable numbers. Two immigrant priests of the 19th century, for example, were closely associated with the building of St. John's Abbey in Stearns County. In the 20th century three men of Luxembourger stock have thus far risen to the rank of bishop in the Minnesota Catholic hierarchy and a fourth held the post of archbishop of St. Paul.[32]

Mother Alfred (born Mary Josephine Moes in the Luxembourg canton of Remich), a Franciscan nun who emigrated in 1851, consulted Dr. William W. Mayo for help in planning a hospital in Rochester after that city was struck by a devastating tornado in 1883. St. Mary's Hospital opened its doors in 1889. In time its association with Dr. Mayo led to the organization of the internationally famous Mayo Clinic.[33]

Ethnicity in the 20th Century

Emigration from Luxembourg dwindled after the peak years in the 1870s and 1880s, but rose dramatically after World War I. The number of Luxembourgers in the state quadrupled from 1910 to 1920, increasing from 459 to 1,782.[34]

In Rollingstone this period was the heyday of ethnicity. The Holy Trinity Church, the combined general store and post office, the five hotel-saloons, and the barbershop were daily gathering places where *Letzeburgesch* was in regular use. Children, born around the turn of the 20th century and representing the third or fourth generation removed from Luxembourg, spoke *Letzeburgesch*, learned English as a second language, studied High German in the parochial

school, and received religious instruction in German in the primary grades as late as about 1915.[35]

It was a small, tightly knit community considerably dependent on its own social resources. The town band still played Luxembourg music. In an amusement hall adjacent to Schuh's Hotel dances were held and movies were shown. The local butcher shop produced such Luxembourg specialties as *Treipen* (blood sausage) and *Zôssis* (a hard, smoked sausage). In October there were quilting competitions and bazaars at which prize pieces were raffled in the Parish Hall, and in late May or early June, a special characteristically Luxembourger celebration — the Corpus Christi procession around the church and churchyard — was held.

A convivial people, Minnesota's Luxembourgers resembled their Belgian and German Catholic neighbors in their fondness for good food, social drinking, and tavern life. No Luxembourg settlement in Minnesota was without at least one *Salo'ne*, and it is interesting that a number of the Luxembourgers elected to become hotelkeepers. Ethnic retentions included home winemaking and the preparation of many food specialties such as the aforementioned *Treipen* and *Zôssis*, *Stertzelen* (a sort of buckwheat dumpling), homemade cottage cheese, pickled heart and tongue, Luxembourg dressing for poultry, Luxembourg Easter eggs, *Durchenaner* (similar to scrambled eggs), eggs over potatoes, wheat wine, and *Tortelen* (raised doughnuts). Another common rural practice was the building of stone houses and stone walls (for fencing fields) that were so finely joined they required no mortar.[36]

Lacking numerical reinforcements, it was virtually impossible for Minnesota's Luxembourgers to maintain a high

ROLLINGSTONE, about 1920.

level of ethnic activity through the Great Depression and World War II. The foreign-born population dwindled from 1,782 in 1920 to 1,032 in 1930 and 685 in 1940. There was no increase in emigration from Luxembourg after World War II comparable to the influx after World War I — an estimated 800 immigrants, including about 300 war brides reached the United States between 1947 and 1960. Figures were not given in the 1950 census, but in 1960 the number of foreign-born Luxembourgers in Minnesota was 295 and by 1970 it had dropped to 170. Total Luxembourg stock in the state for 1960 and 1970 was 3,028 and 2,315, respectively.[37]

Older residents of Rollingstone testified in 1979 both to the persistence of Luxembourg cultural traits and to their gradual decline. All had spoken *Letzeburgesch* as small children. In 1962 a visiting historian found 75 of the town's 300 inhabitants speaking the language in a less acculturated ethnic, religious, and social community than existed in 1979 when the number of *Letzeburgesch*-speakers in the community of 425 was probably no more than a dozen, and there were less than half a dozen in the Elba area.

Most older persons, however, said they could still speak the language but rarely had occasion to do so, considering it a former accomplishment now lost. Some contended that it was still widely spoken among older inhabitants in the mid-1960s, but they also admitted that it was dropping out of use as an everyday medium of communication as early as the 1920s. Likewise in St. Paul second-generation Luxembourgers who had spoken the language almost exclusively in childhood had lost fluency through long disuse. They still understood it, however, and spoke English with marked accents.[38]

The church and related associations — St. Nicholas and St. Theresa societies — remained the core of most surviving Luxembourg solidarities. Older residents of Rollingstone were able to throw some light on the relationships of the Roman Catholic Luxembourgers with other groups in the area. There were suggestions of rivalry, if not conflict, both with Irish Roman Catholics, who lived in a neighboring part of the Rollingstone Valley known as "Irish Valley," and with German Protestants, who occasionally married into Luxembourger families despite social and religious sanctions. Although a public school existed, it was not attended by Luxembourgers because of their monolithic Catholic adherence to the parochial school. Children of mixed Luxembourg and Protestant parentage therefore usually also attended the parochial school, where they felt the ostracism keenly.[39]

A 1979 example of Irish-Luxembourger conflict occurred in Caledonia in Houston County, another part of southeastern Minnesota where members of both groups settled. The two Roman Catholic churches in town were merged by directive from the church hierarchy, eliminating the one identified with the Irish in favor of the "German" church on a vote of the members of both parishes. Although popularly referred to as Germans, many of the German-speakers who settled in Caledonia were Luxembourgers. Despite their intermarriage and the increased use of English, some Germans and Irish continued to see unacceptable differences, which culminated in 1979 in a protest by some Irish people over the closing of "their" church.[40]

Thus, in 1980 most of the traditions and visible symbols of ethnicity had disappeared even in Rollingstone. The general store was defunct, the post office was a separate entity housed in its own building, only two saloons remained, the hotels had fallen into disuse, the amusement hall and the band had vanished, and the butcher shop which made Luxembourg specialties had been sold in the mid-1970s. Perhaps half of the 1980 population had no roots in the Luxembourg heritage, and ethnic delicacies had virtually disappeared from most Rollingstone tables. With a few notable exceptions, the younger generations seemed uninterested in such things. An annual Rollingstone Day of relatively recent origin had no specific ethnic associations.[41]

BELGIANS AND NETHERLANDERS — *Reference notes*

[1] Here and below, see Henry G. Bayer, *The Belgians: First Settlers in New York and in the Middle States* (New York, 1925); Joseph A. Griffin, *The Contribution of Belgium to the Catholic Church in America, 1523–1857* (Catholic University of America, *Studies in American Church History*, vol. 13 — Washington, D.C., 1932); Walter F. Willcox, ed., *International Migrations*, 1:96, 125, 377, 384–393 (Reprint ed., New York, 1969); Gerald F. De Jong, *The Dutch in America, 1609–1974*, 173–193, 262 (Boston, 1975). Ministry of Foreign Affairs, *Belgians in the United States*, 5 (Brussels, 1976) gave the following figures: "Altogether, Belgian immigration from 1820 to 1910 reached about 104,000; from 1910 to 1950, 62,000; and since 1950 [to 1976], about 10,000 — our present modest quota of 1,350 is usually never filled." For Dutch and Belgian examples, see Donald Fleming and Bernard Bailyn, *The Intellectual Migration, Europe and America, 1930–1960*, 683, 698 (Cambridge, Mass., 1969).

[2] By 1870 Minnesota had the fourth largest Belgian population (622), the leaders being Wisconsin (4,804), Illinois (1,071), and Michigan (832). It had the eighth largest Dutch population (1,855), with Michigan (12,559), New York (6,426), Wisconsin (5,990), Iowa (4,513), Illinois (4,180), New Jersey (2,994), and Ohio (2,018) well ahead; see United States, *Census, 1870, Population*, 337, 340. Samuel R. Van Sant, the descendant of a Dutch ancestor who reached New York in 1607, served as governor of Minnesota, 1901–05. Another governor of partial Dutch descent was Lucius F. Hubbard, 1882–87. See James H. Baker, *Lives of the Governors of Minnesota*, 254, 398, 402 (*Minnesota Historical Collections*, vol. 13 — St. Paul, 1908).

[3] State of Minnesota, *Census, 1905*, 197; U.S., *Census, 1920, Population*, 2:915; 1930, 2:295.

[4] U.S., *Census, 1970, Population*, vol. 1, part 25, p. 512. The five northern counties were Clearwater, Cook, Koochiching, Lake, and Roseau. These figures, however, do not necessarily include Dutch Americans beyond the second generation.

[5] On the general history of the Low Countries, the standard work is J. A. van Houtte *et al.*, *Algemene Geschiedenis der Nederlanden*, 12 vols. (Utrecht and Antwerp, 1949–58). Older but of value are Henri Pirenne, *Histoire de Belgique*, 7 vols. (3rd ed., Brussels, 1909), and Petrus J. Blok, *History of the People of the Netherlands*, 5 vols. (New York, 1898–1912). Useful manuals in English describ-

ing the countries and including historical reviews are Jan-Albert Goris, ed., *Belgium* (Berkeley, Calif., 1945) and Bartholomew Landheer, ed., *The Netherlands* (Berkeley, Calif., 1943), both in Robert J. Kerner, ed., *United Nations Series*.

[6] The linguistic frontier, here and below, is the subject of an enormous literature. Only in northern France has attrition occurred. There French gained at the expense of Flemish dialects, and Dunkirk is now the line's western anchor. For convenience and a map in English, see Leon Dominian, *Frontiers of Language and Nationality in Europe*, 19–34 (New York, 1917). For a recent review of scholarly controversies, see André Joris, "On the Edge of Two Worlds in the Heart of the New Empire: The Romance Regions of Northern Gaul During the Merovingian Period," in *Studies in Medieval and Renaissance History*, 3:9–21 (Lincoln, Neb., 1966).

[7] On the language problem, here and below, see Shepard B. Clough, *History of the Flemish Movement in Belgium* (New York, 1930).

[8] Here and below, see Henry S. Lucas, *Netherlanders in America: Dutch Immigration to the United States and Canada, 1789–1950*, 4, 5 (Ann Arbor, Mich., 1955).

[9] Clough, *Flemish Movement*, 54, 244–246; Henry Beets, *The Christian Reformed Church: Its Roots, History, Schools and Mission Work A.D. 1857 to 1946*, 46–48 (Grand Rapids, Mich., 1946); Willcox, ed., *International Migrations*, 1:485.

[10] Here and below, see De Jong, *Dutch in America*, 129–132; Henry Beets, *The Christian Reformed Church in North America*, 44–54 (Grand Rapids, Mich., 1923); Pieter R. D. Stokvis, "The Dutch America Trek, 1846–1847: A Reinterpretation," in *Immigration History Newsletter*, November, 1976, p. 3, and *De Nederlandse trek naar Amerika, 1846–1847* (The Hague, 1977).

[11] On the occupations of Dutch and Flemish immigrants, see Robert P. Swierenga, "The Dutch," in Stephan Thernstrom, ed., *Harvard Encyclopedia of American Ethnic Groups*, 284–286 (Cambridge, Mass., 1980); Willcox, ed., *International Migrations*, 1:452; Philemon D. Sabbe and Leon Buysse, *Belgians in America*, 104, 312 (Tielt and The Hague, 1960). A few Minnesota returnees are mentioned in Arthur P. Rose, *An Illustrated History of Lyon County*, 318, 381, 414, 480 (Marshall, 1912). See also Willcox, ed., 1:476, 479, for returnee figures, 1908–24.

[12] Recent research indicates some Dutch settlements in New York may have predated those in Wisconsin; see Robert P. Swierenga to the author, December 12, 1980, in MEHP Papers. The author acknowledges with thanks the helpful suggestions he received from Professor Swierenga. See also Lucas, *Netherlanders*, 40, 196–205, 223, 361; De Jong, *Dutch in America*, 135–148. For a guide to the extensive literature on the Belgians of Green Bay, see Dorothy L. Heinrich and Lynn C. McAuley, comps., *Belgian American Research Materials* (Green Bay, Wis., 1976); for a recent account, see Math S. Tlachac, *The History of the Belgian Settlements in Door, Kewaunee and Brown Counties* (Algoma, Wis., 1974).

[13] Burnand, a Swiss, evidently entered into negotiations with private associations in Belgium, with the Belgian chargé d'affaires in Washington, and with the Belgian consul at New York in an unsuccessful attempt to promote direct immigration to a projected colony at what is now Pine City in Pine County. Livia Appel and Theodore C. Blegen, "Official Encouragement of Immigration to Minnesota During the Territorial Period," in *Minnesota History*, 5:170, 177–180, 196–199 (August, 1923). Virtually the only information found on Walloons in Minnesota was in state and federal manuscript census schedules and in the "Books of Petition and Record" in county clerks' offices containing immigrant petitions for citizenship after the filing of first papers. As this book went to press, many of these county records were being transferred to the Minnesota State

Archives in MHS. For Rice County, see, for example, Minnesota manuscript census schedules, 1885, roll 40, microfilm in MHS; Minnesota, *Census, 1905*, 197. The evidence for in-migration is indirect: the absence of children of immigrants born in other states. Most intermarriages were with French Canadians. For family names in Faribault and Rice County and migrants from Wisconsin, see Johanna M. O'Leary, *Historical Sketch of the Parish of the Immaculate Conception, Faribault*, 11, 49, 55, 65, 68, 81, 82, 89 (Faribault, 1938); Louis M. deGryse, "The Belgians and the Catholic Netherlanders," 38–43, typescript and accompanying notes in MEHP Papers.

[14] On French Lake and Albion townships, see Minnesota manuscript census schedules, 1885, Rice County, roll 46, microfilm in MHS. Ernest Howard, a Belgian, moved from Wisconsin to Minnesota in 1856 as did Alexander Fashant in 1863. Thirty years later Peter J. Direcks, born in Carver County of Belgian immigrants who arrived in 1860, migrated to Wright County and bought land; Franklyn Curtiss-Wedge, *History of Wright County, Minnesota*, 1:279, 352, 2:749–752 (Chicago, 1915). For other family names, see deGryse, "Belgians and Catholic Netherlanders," 34–38. Another small Walloon group located in Jay Township, Martin County, in the 1870s; see Walter Carlson, ed., William H. Budd, *Martin County Before 1880*, 93 (Reprint ed., [Trimont?, 1974]); Minnesota manuscript census schedules, 1875, Martin County, roll 11, 1885, roll 33.

[15] Here and below, see Carver County, *Plat Book*, 10 ([Philadelphia?], 1898); Arthur H. Schrynemakers to MHS, December 19, 1974, copy in MEHP Papers, listing Carver County family names found in the Netherlands archives; William H. Bingham, ed., *Compendium of History and Biography of Carver and Hennepin Counties, Minnesota*, 312, 321 (Chicago, 1915). Minnesota manuscript census schedules, 1905, Carver County, roll 111, lists 22 foreign-born Hollanders and their dates of arrival in the Chanhassen area in the 1860s, but the 1860 manuscript schedules show no Hollanders there. On Benton Township, see Muriel E. Hidy, ed., "A Dutch Investor in Minnesota, 1866: The Diary of Claude August Crommelin," in *Minnesota History*, 37:160 (December, 1960); biographies of Pieter Jorissen, Lucas Dols, M. Sieben, and William Williams or Willems, in Edward D. Neill, *History of the Minnesota Valley*, 394–396 (Minneapolis, 1882).

It might be observed that such historians of Dutch settlement as Henry S. Lucas and J. van Hinte have been Protestants little interested in Catholic groups. On the churches — St. Victoria in Victoria, St. Nicholas in Carver, St. Hubert in Chanhassen, and Guardian Angels in Chaska — see Catholic Archdiocese of St. Paul and Minneapolis, Parish Questionnaires, 1948, originals in Catholic Historical Society, St. Paul Seminary, St. Paul, microfilm in MHS, hereafter cited as Parish Questionnaires.

[16] On the Ghent-Marshall-Minneota colony, see James P. Shannon, *Catholic Colonization on the Western Frontier*, 140–150 (New Haven, 1957); C. F. Case, *History and Description of Lyon County, Minnesota*, 24, 51–54 (Marshall, 1884); Rose, *History of Lyon County*, 211–215; Torgny Anderson, *Centennial History of Lyon County*, 110–113 (Marshall, 1970); Aletha M. Herwig, "The Belgians in Ghent," 3–7, term paper, University of Minnesota, 1927, copy in MHS. See also chapter 7.

[17] Tallies by the author from Minnesota manuscript census schedules, 1885, Lyon County, roll 32.

[18] Sex ratios were calculated from Minnesota manuscript census schedules, 1905, Lyon County, roll 133, which also noted the length of time an individual had lived in the state and the district in which he or she then lived. By figuring backward, one can roughly determine peak years of settlement. The rising curve from 1897 to 1905 can be partially attributed to the shorter period between immigration and the taking of this census, which allowed less time for the immi-

grants to move. Thereafter the sources are shakier, but Lyon County, *Atlas and Farmers' Directory* (St. Paul, 1914), giving dates of arrival of rural heads of households, suggested another peak about 1912. The persistence of the Ghent community members is more remarkable when one realizes that many of the 55.1% not present probably died. According to *Minneota Mascot*, June 16, 1933, p. 1, 20 original members of St. Eloi's Church were still living in Ghent 50 years after the parish was founded. For national sex ratios, see U.S., *Census*, 1910, *Population*, 1:830.

[19] Lyon County, "Books of Petition and Record," B, C, I, J, 1880–1930, in county clerk's office, Marshall, were sampled by the author. For lists and greater detail on these samples, see deGryse, "Belgians and Catholic Netherlanders," 48–50. Lyon County, *Atlas and Farmers' Directory* (1914) listed 18 family names with from two to four members arriving at different times. See also Shannon, *Catholic Colonization*, 149.

[20] For a detailed review of the evidence, see deGryse, "Belgians and Catholic Netherlanders," 56–62.

[21] Shannon, *Catholic Colonization*, 143, 145, 148–150.

[22] Author's interviews of Leonard Coequyt, St. Paul, July, 1978, Charles Lens, Ghent, August 8, 1978; Donald Rubertus, "History of Holy Redeemer Catholic Church, 1869–1916, Marshall," 9, 17–20, typescript, 1956, in Southwest Minnesota Historical Center, Marshall, copy in MEHP Papers; Herwig, "Belgians," 5.

[23] Local residents belonging to both groups in the 1970s have distinct memories of these tensions and conflicts. The paragraphs here and below are based on author's taped interview of Margaret Regnier, Ghent, August 8, 1978, in MHS; Lens interview, August 8, 1978; Parish Questionnaires. By the 1950s the Green Valley church also had Dutch and Belgians among its adherents, and additional Belgians arrived after World War II; *Dedication Church of St. Clotilde*, 46 (Marshall, 1956).

[24] For lists of elected Ghent officials, 1899–1912, see Rose, *History of Lyon County*, 213; Coequyt interview, July, 1978. The late Charles L. De Reu, a Marshall attorney, is an interesting exception. Born in Lyon County, he received his early education in Belgium, became a prominent figure in Farmer-Labor party politics and in the American Legion, and acted as a leader and protector of local Belgians. In the "Books of Petition and Record" for Lyon County he appears regularly as their lawyer. He is credited with having attempted to organize a Belgian Netherlandish Assn., and he was a mover in starting Belgian American Day in Ghent. See Rose, *History of Lyon County*, 477; Theodore Christianson, *Minnesota, the Land of Sky-tinted Waters*, 3:474 (Chicago and New York, 1935); Anderson, *History of Lyon County*, 112. According to a plaque in St. Eloi's Church, Ghent, only four local sons have become Catholic priests, although numerous women have entered its orders. See also *Minneota Mascot*, June 16, 1933, p. 1.

[25] The real mover behind the Butler project was Francis H. Murray, a well-known Catholic layman acting on behalf of the Johnston Land Company. See Jerome W. Rausch, O.S.C., *The Crosier Story: A History of the Crosier Fathers in the United States*, 140–147, 151–153, 167 (Onamia, 1960); John W. Mason, *History of Otter Tail County, Minnesota*, 1:393 (Indianapolis, 1916).

[26] Francis H. Murray, "The Arrival of the Crosier Fathers in America," 1, 2, undated typescript in Francis H. Murray Papers, MHS; reminiscences by Father Henry Yzermans and Jacques Hendrickx, both of whom arrived at Butler in 1910, in *Verndale Sun*, February 9, 1933, p. 1, and *Fergus Falls Daily Journal*, March 19, 1935, p. 3, respectively; Rausch, *Crosier Story*, 169, 173–188. Early names can be gleaned from these three printed accounts, and new Dutch-Flemish ones appeared on plat maps of 1925 and 1953 in the MHS collections. Altogether the landholdings represented no more than half a township in area. See Butler Township in Otter Tail

County, *Standard Atlas*, 89 (Chicago, 1912); *Plat Book*, 91 (St. Paul, 1925); *Atlas*, 7 (Fergus Falls, 1953).

[27] Here and below, see Rausch, *Crosier Story*, 158n, 189–192, 207–212.

[28] Parish Questionnaires; Frank A. King, *The Missabe Road: The Duluth, Missabe and Iron Range Railway*, 60, 79–81 (San Marino, Calif., 1972). Here and three paragraphs below, see also interview of Ferdinand Van Neste, Proctor, by Deborah Stultz, July 12, 1979, notes in MEHP Papers; Minnesota manuscript census schedules, 1905, St. Louis County, roll 154.

[29] Beets, *Christian Reformed Church: Its Roots*, 55–64; De Jong, *Dutch in America*, 203; Neil A. Markus, "Areal Patterns of Religious Denominationalism in Minnesota, 1950," 106, 111, master's thesis, University of Minnesota, 1961. On the Reformed and Christian Reformed churches in America, see Robert P. Swierenga, "Local-Cosmopolitan Theory and Immigrant Religion: The Social Bases of the Antebellum Dutch Reformed Schism," in *Journal of Social History*, 14:113–115 (Fall, 1980).

For a complete list of Reformed and Christian Reformed churches in Minnesota, see Peter N. Vandenberge, *Historical Directory of the Reformed Church in America* (Grand Rapids, Mich., 1978).

On the use of the Dutch language at Greenleafton, for example, a decision was made to hold Sunday school classes in English in 1888; in 1901 English services began on alternate Sundays; in 1903 hymns were first sung in English; after 1919 all consistory minutes were kept in English; since 1923 prayer meetings have been conducted in that language, and the transition to the exclusive use of English was completed before 1946. See Greenleafton Reformed Church, *One Hundredth Anniversary, 1867–1967*, 9–12 ([Preston?], 1967).

[30] Here and below, see Greenleafton Reformed Church, *One Hundredth Anniversary*, 4, 6, 12; Lucas, *Netherlanders*, 361; Henry S. Lucas, ed., Herman Borgers, "The Hollanders in Minnesota, 1856–97," in *Minnesota History*, 28:121–124 (June, 1947).

[31] Here and below, see Lucas, *Netherlanders*, 363–366.

[32] Appel and Blegen, in *Minnesota History*, 5:196–199, 201; Lucas, *Netherlanders*, 365.

[33] Here and two paragraphs below, see George Sheppard to Frederick Billings, May 13, 1872, in Land Dept., Letters Received Foreign Agents, Northern Pacific Railway Company Records, MHS. Sheppard was manager of the railroad's European Land Emigration Department; Billings was its New York manager.

[34] The two leaders were Gerrit Vander Meer and Renert Okma. For interesting comments on Dutch emigration and its origins, see George Sheppard to George B. Hibbard (Northern Pacific superintendent of emigration, New York), April 28, 1873; Ittmann to Hibbard, May 1, 1873; Sheppard to Billings, September 13, 1873 — all in Land Dept., Letters Received Foreign Agents, Northern Pacific Records.

In June, 1873, James B. Power, Brainerd agent, noted: "Ten men from Holland have at different times presented [Ittmann's] cards of introduction here, wanting nothing but work. This we cannot get for them. Dutch curses are not loud, but they are as emphatic as English ones. Every one of these men say they have been cruelly deceived by Ittmann's representations in this respect, and their letters home will do us harm. Our agents on the other side must be very careful of their representations, especially to the poor man." Power to Hibbard, June 23, 1873, in vol. B7, no. 77, in Land Dept. letter books, Northern Pacific Records.

[35] Borgers, in *Minnesota History*, 28:124–128; Shannon, *Catholic Colonization*, 11; Lucas, *Netherlanders*, 367; Theodore F. Koch, "A Brief Description of My Life," typescript, 1930, copy in MHS, partially printed on p. 2 of weekly issues of the *Clara City Herald* from June 27 to September 26, 1958. A hand-paginated copy of the

printed version is in the MHS library; see pp. 1–3 (hereafter cited as Koch, *Journal*).

[36] Here and below, see Koch, *Journal*, 5, 11, 13, 14.

[37] Koch advertised in *De Hope* (Holland, Mich.), *De Volksvriend* (Sioux City, Ia.), and *De Grondwet* (Grand Rapids, Mich.). Here and two paragraphs below, see Lucas, *Netherlanders*, 366–370; Koch, *Journal*, 4, 5; Kandiyohi County Centennial History Committee, *Centennial History of Kandiyohi County, 1870–1970*, 200 (Willmar, 1970). For an account of a visit to Minnesota by Prins, see *Minneapolis Tribune*, October 24, 1885. On the social and demographic aspects of the settlement, see John G. Rice, *Patterns of Ethnicity in a Minnesota County, 1880–1905* (Umeå, Swed., 1973).

[38] Minnesota, *Census, 1905*, 197; Borgers, in *Minnesota History*, 28:125–127.

[39] Parish Questionnaires; Lucas, *Netherlanders*, 371, 374; Borgers, in *Minnesota History*, 28:128–130; Arthur P. Rose, *Illustrated History of the Counties of Rock and Pipestone*, 365–375, 393 (Luverne, 1911); Minnesota Analysis and Planning Systems, *Minnesota Socio-Economic Characteristics From the 4th Count Summary Tape of the 1970 Census*, vol. 3, n.p. (St. Paul, 1972); Mrs. Gerald Olson and Mrs. Joel W. Johnson, eds., *In the Heart of the Red River Valley: A History of the People of Norman County*, 26, 82, 172, 218, 413, 431–433, 445 (Dallas, 1976); Sandra Beckering, *Edgerton, Minnesota: A History 1879–1979*, 94, 100–106 (Edgerton, 1979).

[40] Here and below, see Koch, *Journal*, 9; Van Hinte, *Nederlanders*, 1:122–124; Lucas, *Netherlanders*, 372–374; Borgers, in *Minnesota History*, 28:130.

[41] Here and below, see Edna Mae Busch, *The History of Stevens County*, 168 ([Morris?], 1976); Lucas, *Netherlanders*, 374–376. On Hollandale, see U.S., *Census, 1930, Population*, 3:1220, 1222; *St.

Paul Pioneer Press, August 24, 1924, sec. 2, p. 6, March 3, 1929, sec. 1, p. 1; *Albert Lea Tribune*, December 18, 1924, sec. 2, p. 2; *Minneapolis Tribune*, February 19, 1956, *Picture Magazine*, 19. Information on Slayton provided by Jay Fonkert, May 8, 1978, notes in MEHP Papers.

[42] Sabbe and Buysse, *Belgians in America*, chapters 13–16.

[43] U.S., *Census, 1970, Population*, vol. 1, part 25, p. 513; Herman E. Olson, *Minneapolis Property and Housing Survey* (Minneapolis, 1934); Katherine Spear, *Foreign Born Population Studies, Saint Paul, Minnesota*, n.p. (St. Paul, 1934). The two paragraphs below were based on conversations of the author with Margo de Wilde and Pierce Butler, St. Paul Netherlands consul, July, 1978, notes in MEHP Papers. An outstanding example of a Belgian musician was Henri A. Verbrugghen (1873–1934), conductor of the Minneapolis Symphony from 1923 to 1932 and subsequently chairman of the department of music in Carleton College, Northfield. See *Dictionary of American Biography*, 19:250 (1936).

[44] Author's taped interview of Arthur Vermeersch, in MHS, and interview of Frank Senden — both Ghent, August 8, 1978.

[45] Vermeersch and Lens interviews, August 8, 1978; Coequyt interview, July, 1978. A *rolle bolle* tournament was held at Marshall in 1978. See also *Minneapolis Tribune*, September 1, 1980, p. 3B.

[46] Anderson, *Centennial History of Lyon County*, 112.

[47] Vermeersch and Lens interviews, August 8, 1978; Coequyt interview, July, 1978.

[48] *Minneapolis Tribune*, December 9, 1977, p. 2B.

[49] Anderson, *Centennial History of Lyon County*, 112.

[50] Vermeersch and Lens interviews, August 8, 1978; Coequyt interview, July, 1978.

LUXEMBOURGERS — *Reference notes*

[1] General Consul of Luxembourg, Chicago, interview by author, May 7, 1979; *Luxemburger Bulletin*, June, 1943, p. 69, quoted in Sister Mary De Paul Faber, "The *Luxemburger Gazette*: A Catholic German Language Paper of the Middle West, 1872–1918," 19, master's thesis, Catholic University of America, 1948; *World Almanac and Book of Facts*, 247 ([New York], 1940); United States, *Census, 1970, Population*, vol. 1, part 25, p. 512.

The two standard works on these people are Nicholas Gonner, *Die Luxemburger in der neuen Welt* (Dubuque, Ia., 1889) and Roger Krieps, *Luxemburger in Amerika* (Luxembourg, 1962). The author wishes to acknowledge his dependence upon these books, neither of which is printed in English, as well as upon the private collection, including scrapbooks and notes, compiled by James Taylor Dunn and Mária Bach Dunn, to which he was graciously granted access. An excellent translation of Gonner's chapter on "The Luxemburger in Minnesota," prepared by Mrs. Dunn, a native of Esch-sur-Alzette, Luxembourg, is in MHS.

A word about the spelling of both the name of the country and the city of Luxembourg should be added. The older German spelling (Luxemburg) has been retained in quotations and titles; in all other instances the current gallicized spelling (Luxembourg) has been used. Unless otherwise indicated, translations in this chapter are by the author.

[2] For additional detail and county-by-county descriptions for the 1880s, here and below, see Gonner, *Die Luxemburger*, 302–312; Dunn, trans., "Luxemburger in Minnesota," 1–16.

[3] Map showing ethnic distributions of "Minnesota's People," based on studies by Douglass C. Marshall, in *Minneapolis Tribune*, August 28, 1949, Territorial Centennial Edition, part 4, p. 1; Gonner, *Die Luxemburger*, 306; A. T. Andreas, *An Illustrated Historical*

Atlas of the State of Minnesota, 371, 372, 376, 390 (Chicago, 1874). On the Iowa migration, see note 15, below.

[4] A handy reference for the historical outline here and below is A. H. Cooper-Prichard, trans., Arthur Herchen, *History of the Grand Duchy of Luxemburg* (Luxemburg, 1950).

[5] On the 1939 decree, see Royal British Admiralty, Naval Intelligence Division, *Luxembourg*, 43 (*Geographical Handbook Series*, B. R. 528 — 1944); J. P. Glaesener, *Le Grand-Duché de Luxembourg, Historique et Pittoresque*, 264–275 (Diekirch, Luxembourg, 1885); for more on the *Letzeburgesch* tongue, see James Taylor Dunn, "The Luxembourg Language, Birth of a Literary Tradition," in *Luxembourg News of America* (Chicago), April, 1979, pp. 2, 5, 6, 8.

[6] Krieps, *Luxemburger*, 41, 177.

[7] Quoted in Krieps, *Luxemburger*, 179. A file of the *Luxemburger Gazette*, 1871–1918, is in the Loras College Archives, Dubuque, Ia.

[8] Gonner, *Die Luxemburger*, 218. For background on Gonner's career, see Krieps, *Luxemburger*, 180.

[9] On some Luxembourgers' lack of fluency in French, see Glaesener, *Grand-Duché de Luxembourg*, 274. The quotation below is translated from Gonner, *Die Luxemburger*, 219.

[10] Here and two paragraphs below, see Krieps, *Luxemburger*, 27–33; Gonner, *Die Luxemburger*, 74–83, 91–93.

[11] The eight were John Wilhelm and George Berschens, Michael S. Clessen or Claessen, and J. H. Cram in Oakdale Township; Martin Peiming or Penning in New Ulm; Paul Faber and Michael Martin in St. Paul; and Martin Ferrant in Minneapolis. See Andreas, *Atlas*, 365, 383, 389; Augustus B. Eaton, ed., *History of the Saint Croix Valley*, 1:465 (Chicago, 1909); Willard E. Rosenfelt, ed., *Washington: A History of the Minnesota County*, 206 (Stillwater, 1977); *Plat*

Book of Washington County, 28 (Minneapolis, 1901); Patricia C. Harpole and Mary D. Nagle, *Minnesota Territorial Census, 1850*, 6 (St. Paul, 1972).

On Faber, Martin, and Ferrant, see Gonner, *Die Luxemburger*, 308, 425; Dunn, trans., "Luxemburger in Minnesota," 10; Krieps, *Luxemburger*, 157; John H. Stevens, *Personal Recollections of Minnesota and Its People and Early History of Minneapolis*, 289, 328 (Minneapolis, 1890); *St. Paul City Directory, 1856–57*, 88; Thomas M. Newson, *Pen Pictures of Old St. Paul*, 369 (St. Paul, 1886); *New Ulm Review*, October 17, 1917, p. 8; *New Ulm Journal*, February 23, 1923, p. 3; Lois M. Fawcett, MHS librarian, to Casper Schenk, August 20, 1947, January 30, 1948, copies in James Taylor Dunn, Scrapbook, vol. 2; *St. Paul Globe*, April 30, May 2, 3, 1894.

[12] Krieps, *Luxemburger*, 185–188.

[13] "Gopher holes" were crude huts used primarily as sleeping quarters. The roof was made of logs over which dry grass and turf were laid to help keep out rain. The dirt floor inside the hut was excavated a foot or more to increase the enclosed area. See *History of Wabasha County. . . . Also a History of Winona County*, 206 (Chicago, 1884); Dunn, trans., "Luxemburger in Minnesota," 10. The passage containing information on Rosen does not appear in the MHS copy of Gonner, *Die Luxemburger*; it is included, however, in Dunn, trans., "Luxemburger in Minnesota," 1.

[14] Colman J. Barry, *Worship and Work: Saint John's Abbey and University, 1856–1956*, 85–90 (2nd ed., Collegeville, 1980); William B. Mitchell, *History of Stearns County*, 1:195 (Chicago, 1915); Gonner, *Die Luxemburger*, 28, 303–307, 309–311; Dunn, trans., "Luxemburger in Minnesota," 2–14; Frederick Wiechmann, *A History of St. Wendelin's Parish, Luxemburg, Minn.*, 7 (n.p., 1935); Alexius Hoffmann, O.S.B., "Natural History of Collegeville," 78, 116, 123, manuscript, 1926–34, original in St. John's Abbey Archives, Collegeville, excerpts in MEHP Papers.

[15] Interview of Mrs. George W. Diepenbrock, Belvidere, by Frances T. Densmore, 1939, transcript in Frances Densmore Papers, MHS; Gonner, *Die Luxemburger*, 183, 303, 306; Dunn, trans., "Luxemburger in Minnesota," 3, 7; Krieps, *Luxemburger*, 27–30. An untitled manuscript by Lucia Beckius Johnson, in MHS, contains information on pioneers who moved via covered wagon from Dubuque to Jordan, Lakeville, St. Joseph, and St. Peter after 1855. Two settlers from Port Washington, Wis., were Peter Stemper, a resident of St. James who was sheriff of Watonwan County, 1866–70, and George Noesen, who emigrated first to Wisconsin and then moved to Hastings in 1879. For a list of the districts, cantons, and even communes in Luxembourg that contributed settlers, see MEHP Papers.

[16] Here and three paragraphs below, see *St. Paul Sunday Pioneer Press*, March 4, 1962, Pictorial sec., 5–7; Krieps, *Luxemburger*, 151–154, plates 50–52; Luella Guidinger, "History of Rollingstone," manuscript notes in Dunn, Scrapbook, vol. 1; Gonner, *Die Luxemburger*, 304; Dunn, trans., "Luxemburger in Minnesota," 4–6; Mary E. and Myron Nilles, "From the History of Rollingstone, Minn.," in *Luxembourg News of America*, October, 1977, p. 9.

[17] Catholic Archdiocese of St. Paul and Minneapolis, Parish Questionnaires, 1948, originals in Catholic Historical Society, St. Paul Seminary, St. Paul, microfilm in MHS.

[18] On Baasen, see Gonner, *Die Luxemburger*, 421; James Taylor Dunn, comp., Biographical Notes on Luxemburgers, in Dunn's possession; three misdated New Ulm newspaper clippings in the François (Francis) Baasen File, Brown County Historical Museum, New Ulm; L[ouis] A. Fritsche, *History of Brown County, Minnesota*, 1:442 (Reprint ed., Marceline, Mo., 1976). A small collection of Francis (Franz) Baasen Papers, consisting largely of school records and certificates, is in Minnesota State Archives, MHS.

[19] On the Jacob Ries family and the bottling works, see Julius A. Coller II, *The Shakopee Story*, 605–609 (Shakopee, 1969); *The Story of Jacob Ries Bottling Works* (n.p., [1947]), a pamphlet published for the company's 75th anniversary; Valdimar Bjornson, *The History of Minnesota*, 4:927 (West Palm Beach, Fla., 1969); author's interview of Hildegarde Ries Kopp, May 22, 1979.

[20] Krieps, *Luxemburger*, 143; Gonner, *Die Luxemburger*, 311; Dunn, trans., "Luxemburger in Minnesota," 14.

[21] Gonner, *Die Luxemburger*, 308; Dunn, trans., "Luxemburger in Minnesota," 10; tabulation sheets on Ramsey and Hennepin counties compiled from U.S. manuscript census schedules, 1860, 1880, in MEHP Papers.

[22] St. Paul and Minneapolis statistics were tabulated by the author from Minnesota manuscript census schedules, 1905, rolls 121–128, 144–149, microfilm in MHS. See also Calvin F. Schmid, *Social Saga of Two Cities: An Ecological and Statistical Study*, 142, 143, 162 (Minneapolis, 1937); author's interviews of Duane Galles, Minneapolis, Frank Thill, St. Paul, February, 1979; ward maps of Minneapolis (1899) and St. Paul (1892), in MHS. See also note 26, below.

[23] Minnesota manuscript census schedules, 1905, Hennepin County, rolls 119–120, Ramsey County, roll 144. No occupational pattern was discernible in the Twin Cities.

[24] Krieps, *Luxemburger*, 85–90.

[25] Here and two paragraphs below, see *Der Wanderer* (St. Paul), December 31, 1870; Krieps, *Luxemburger*, 177–179.

[26] Here and below, see *St. Paul Globe*, April 30, May 1, 1894; Gonner, *Die Luxemburger*, 206, 211; Krieps, *Luxemburger*, 306, 308. The annual conferences were of short duration. The first was held in Chicago in 1893, the sixth and last in Minneapolis in 1899. The membership figures given for St. Paul seem high. Alexander Ramsey, former Minnesota governor and U.S. senator, noted "A Luxemburg procession in the streets" in his diary for April 29, 1894; see Ramsey Papers, roll 45, frame 75, microfilm in MHS.

[27] Faber, "*Luxemburger Gazette*," 52, 64–66; Galles interview, February, 1979.

[28] Faber, "*Luxemburger Gazette*," 47.

[29] Lake City Publishing Company, *Portrait and Biographical Record of Winona County, Minnesota*, 257 (Chicago, 1895); Franklyn Curtiss-Wedge, *The History of Winona County, Minnesota*, 2:997 (Chicago, 1913). On Ries, see note 19, above.

[30] The six were Mathias Siebenaler (1876) Dakota County, E. Peter Bertrand (1877–80) Brown County, Peter Weinant or Weinand (1877) Hennepin County, Peter Barthel (1878) Carver County, Perry (Pierre) George (1879) Goodhue County, and Jacob Kummer (1887) Dakota County. J. Vincent Weber, long-time publisher of the *Murray County Herald* at Slayton, served in the state senate in 1930–45. Warren Upham and Rose B. Dunlap, eds., *Minnesota Biographies, 1655–1912*, 36, 532, 834 (St. Paul, 1912); Gonner, *Die Luxemburger*, 182, 422, 453, 456; W. F. Toensing, *Minnesota Congressmen, Legislators, and Other Elected State Officials: An Alphabetical Check List, 1849–1971*, 7, 10, 42, 67, 125, 126 (St. Paul, 1971).

[31] The saying is noted in *St. Paul Globe*, May 1, 1894. Hildegard B. Johnson, "The Election of 1860 and the Germans," in *Minnesota History*, 28:27 (March, 1947), pointed out that Baasen was the "German" candidate of the Democrats on the state ticket in 1857 and 1859 and that the Republicans often named another German candidate for the post of state treasurer.

[32] On the pioneer priests, Brothers Placid Brixius and Gregor (Gregory Steil), both from canton Echternach, see Dunn, Biographical Notes; Thomas Whitaker, O.S.B., "The Brothers of Saint John's Abbey: The Building Era," in *Scriptorium*, December, 1953, pp. 71–86; Gonner, *Die Luxemburger*, 411; Krieps, *Luxemburger*, 37; Barry, *Worship and Work*, 76, 141, 145, 153, 162.

The bishops were Peter W. Bartholomé (1953–68) and George H. Speltz (1968–) both of the St. Cloud diocese, and Raymond A. Lucker (1975–) of New Ulm. The archbishop of St. Paul, Leo

Binz (1962–75) was half Luxembourger. See Krieps, *Luxemburger*, 48, 49; A. N. Marquis, ed., *Who's Who in Religion*, 51, 352, 533 (Chicago, 1975); Catholic Bulletin, *Official Minnesota Catholic Directory*, 145 (St. Paul, 1978).

[33] Helen Clapesattle, *The Doctors Mayo*, 242–256 (Garden City, N.Y., 1943); Krieps, *Luxemburger*, 176.

[34] U.S., *Census*, 1940, *Population*, 2:31.

[35] Here and below, see Krieps, *Luxemburger*, 153; *St. Paul Sunday Pioneer Press*, March 4, 1962, Pictorial sec., 6; author's interviews of Richard E. Reiland, Luella E. Guidinger, Rollingstone, June 29, 1979; information on the use of *Letzeburgesch* from author's interviews of Hattie Nilles and Arnold Nilles, Rollingstone, notes in MEHP Papers, and Father Donald P. Schmitz, St. Anthony's Catholic Church, Altura, June 30, 1979, notes in MEHP Papers. See also *Rollingstone Record*, 1915–16, in Southeast Minnesota Historical Center, Winona.

[36] Mrs. A. G. (Lucille) Lackore, *Winona County Bicentennial Recipes of the Past* (Winona, 1976); A. Nilles interview, June 30, 1979; Guidinger interview, June 29, 1979.

[37] U.S., *Census*, 1940, *Population*, 2:31; 1960, vol. 1, part 25, p. 340; 1970, vol. 1, part 25, p. 512; Krieps, *Luxemburger*, 301.

[38] H. and A. Nilles, Schmitz interviews, June 30, 1979; Thill interview, February, 1979; Krieps, *Luxemburger*, 151.

[39] Author's interviews of Myrton Stoos, Rollingstone, A. Nilles, and Schmitz, June 30, 1979, notes in MEHP Papers.

[40] *Minneapolis Tribune*, June 11, 1979, p. 2B.

[41] A. Nilles, Schmitz interviews, June 30, 1979. On Luxembourgers in Dakota County, see *St. Paul Dispatch*, October 9, 1979, Extra/neighborhoods sec., p. 1; *Minneapolis Tribune*, February 22, 1981, p. 1B. *Luxembourg News of America* had a number of Minnesota subscribers in 1980 and was perhaps the strongest remaining source of American-Luxembourg identity.

CHAPTER 10

The Swiss

Louis M. deGryse

EMIGRANTS from Switzerland are known to have been in the English colonies of North America before 1710, and Swiss settlers were in Pennsylvania and the Carolinas early in the 18th century. Between 1850 and 1900, however, they moved to the United States in record numbers, and during the peak decade of the 1880s, about 80,000 Swiss migrated to the New World. After 1893, annual emigration figures never exceeded 5,000, except for a brief spurt following World War I. While the Swiss element in Minnesota has never been large, it has been present since the early 1820s.[1]

The land from which these emigrants came was one of great geographic diversity. Bounded on the northwest by the Jura Mountains, Switzerland straddles the highest Alps at several points, though a considerable part of the north and west also encompasses a plateau which reaches toward the Rhine and Lake Constance in the north and the Rhone and Lake Geneva in the southwest (see Map 10.1). Nearly 25% of the country is considered unproductive; the plateau is the richest area and also the most populous, although the birth rate of the Alpine region has traditionally been high. The geography of Switzerland provides the key to the nation's political existence, for domination of the major Alpine passes was vital to its economy, helpful to its neutrality, and critical to foreign powers in time of war. One export — Swiss mercenaries from the Alpine areas — was often of decisive importance to the military success of contending foreign powers, and the income derived from mercenary services bolstered the economy.

The Swiss emigrants left an ethnically plural nation that embraced four distinct languages and two major religions. About 72% were normally German speaking; 20% spoke French, 6% used Italian, and about 1% were Romansh or Ladin speaking. In 1970 the majority (52%) belonged to the Swiss Reformed Church, and 46% were Roman Catholics.[2]

The basic linguistic divisions of modern Switzerland may be traced from the time when the Roman Empire controlled all Switzerland to the barbarian invasions in the 5th century A.D. Many of the Latin-speaking people took refuge in the less accessible high valleys of the Grisons where a distinct Romance language, variously called Rhaeto-Roman, Romansh, Romonsch, or Ladin, emerged. The language of the Germanic Burgundians succumbed in time to that of the more numerous Romanized populace and became a dialect of French, which prevailed in the western cantons and in Valais to the south. The Alamanni preserved their linguistic heritage and were the direct ancestors of the present German Swiss in the large central region of Switzerland. South of the Alps, Latin became Italian — the language which still prevails in the southeastern canton of Ticino and the southern edge of Graubunden. Language divisions in Switzerland did not generate much friction due, perhaps, to the highly decentralized system of government and to the abundant physical barriers which tended to keep the linguistic groups geographically separated. On balance, there has not been a serious linguistic schism in Switzerland such as has occurred in Belgium, Alsace-Lorraine, and the Tyrol.

Religion, however, was an entirely different matter. Switzerland was profoundly affected by the Reformation, which at first divided Swiss Protestants into three groups — followers of Martin Luther, Huldreich Zwingli, and John Calvin. But in 1566, due chiefly to the conciliatory efforts of Heinrich Bullinger, a merger of the dissident groups into the Swiss Reformed Church was effected. The religious divisions followed cantonal lines to a certain extent; but very generally, it can be said that the major part of the plateau — the more prosperous and urbanized area of the country — is Protestant, and the poorer, more southerly region is Catholic.[3]

Deep religious divisions between Swiss Catholics and Protestants culminated during the 16th century in the battle of Kappel, after which religious unity was not possible. Cantons within the confederation made independent alliances with foreign powers, and frequently the mercenaries of one canton fought those of another during religious wars. The divisions persisted well into modern times, and in 1846 the Catholic cantons, opposing reform and a stronger federation, mounted a brief and unsuccessful war against the dominant Protestants. These antipathies lingered during the period of emigration to the United States in the 19th century.

Patterns of Emigration, 1800–1850

Historians of Swiss emigration point to three key periods of movement out of the country during the 19th century, a time when nearly 90% of the migration went to the United States. These were (1) the so-called hunger years of 1816–17 when bad harvests were complicated by economic changes after the Napoleonic Wars; (2) the decade of the 1840s when the introduction of machinery destroyed the livelihood of

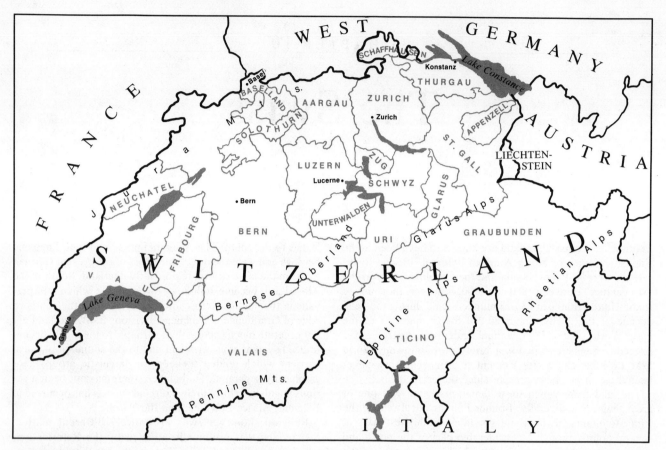

Map 10.1. Switzerland

small farmers who had grown increasingly dependent on cottage weaving; and (3) the 1880s when an agricultural depression affected all Europe. Like that of France, Swiss emigration was not a result of overpopulation; indeed, between 1871 and 1880 "every emigrating Swiss was replaced by a foreigner," and in the decade before the turn of the century "the influx of foreigners into Switzerland was even greater than the number of people leaving the country."[4]

Emigration was stimulated by "America letters," and the cantonal and federal governments frequently subsidized resettlers — sometimes as a method of reducing the poor rolls and removing undesirable persons. Occasionally a canton served as the parent figure for a specific colony and saw it through financially, as in the case of New Glarus, Wisconsin; usually emigrants either formed associations themselves or departed as individuals.[5]

The destinations of Swiss emigrants to the United States were chiefly New York, New Jersey, and Pennsylvania in the east; Ohio, Indiana, Illinois, Missouri, Wisconsin, and Iowa in the central region; and especially California, which since 1920 has attracted more Swiss than any other core region. The latter area drew principally from the Italian Swiss of the Ticino; most of the other centers were German Swiss, with a leavening of French, and there were also a few well-defined Romansh settlements.

While Minnesota was not the most favored destination of Swiss immigrants, it nonetheless received appreciable num-

bers, and although they were fewer than the Dutch, for example, they outranked the Belgians in the state. Census figures on Swiss stock are deceiving because of the length of time the Swiss have been in Minnesota. The story of the preterritorial Swiss immigrants is well documented and goes back to the venerable institution of the Swiss mercenary regiments.[6]

In the summer of 1817 Thomas Douglas, fifth Earl of Selkirk, recruited the services of two groups of mercenaries to defend his newly founded colony at the confluence of the Red and Assiniboine rivers in what is now Manitoba. The regiments were the De Meurons of Neuchatel and the De Wattevilles of Bern, and although many of these soldiers were not Swiss, there were a number among them. Selkirk appointed Captain Rodolphe de May d'Ubzenstorf to act as an immigration agent for the colony, particularly in Switzerland. De May met with hostility from the government in Bern, but by 1821 he had recruited 175 settlers who sailed from Rotterdam on a British ship which carried them to York Factory on Hudson Bay. From there they proceeded by Mackinaw boats via the Nelson River to the Red River Settlement. According to a report written by one of the new colonists, the group included 24 householders from Bern, 15 from Neuchatel, two each from Baden and Württemberg in Germany, and one from Geneva. The majority were French speaking, and few among them had farmed in Europe, a fact which ill-fitted them for their role in the new settlement.

Most of them were craftsmen such as clockmakers, locksmiths, and carpenters; a few were professionals and included a doctor, a pharmacist, a veterinarian, and a teacher. The report imputed bad character to 38 of the 81 new settlers, describing one as "crazy," another as "simple-minded," and others as "dissolute." (This may, in part, explain the failure of the Swiss colony.) Several of the women in the new group married De Meuron veterans, of whom at least two were Swiss born.[7]

The extravagant promises of the immigration agent brought early disillusionment to some of the Red River Swiss. By the fall of 1821 five families abandoned the colony and moved south over the Red River trails to Fort Snelling in what was to become Minnesota Territory. They were followed two years later by 13 more families who took the same route. The recurrent hardships of prairie life brought succeeding waves of migrants until, by 1826, no Swiss remained at the Selkirk colony.

The numbers of those who squatted at Fort Snelling are not known, and only three of the Swiss who stopped can be identified for certain. Two of these, Peter Rindisbacher and Barbara Anne Shadecker (or Scheidegger), exemplify the transitory element that was characteristic of most of the Swiss who passed through the Minnesota country in the pre-territorial period. Rindisbacher, the teen-aged son of a large Swiss Reformed family from canton Bern, became an important frontier artist and during the migration from the Selkirk settlement drew and painted a remarkable record of the Red River Swiss. Shadecker lived at Fort Snelling from 1823 to 1829 when she married Joseph Adams, a fort officer who later became one of the early settlers of Chicago. In 1981, however, returned descendants were living in Minnesota.[8]

The enduring element of the Swiss sojourn at Fort Snelling was personified by Abram Perret, who later called himself Abraham Perry. Members of his family were almost the only persons of Swiss stock in Ramsey County when the first territorial census was taken in 1850. His wife was an accomplished midwife, much in demand with wives of officers at the fort.[9]

A more deliberate Swiss initiative than the presence of the Red River Swiss was one inspired by Protestant missionary zeal. In 1834 the Evangelical Mission Society of Lausanne sent two men to work among the Dakota Indians. Their first station was at Trempealeau on the east side of the Mississippi River below present Winona. One of the missionaries, Samuel Dentan, established another station in 1836 or 1837 at Red Wing in Minnesota Indian country where his fellow countryman joined him briefly. For a time the two men did itinerant missionary work among the Indians near Fort Snelling. But the Swiss society's work at Red Wing was not notably successful, and in 1847 the mission was turned over to the Boston Missionary Society. Dentan remained in the area, establishing a farm at Kaposia (now within South St. Paul).[10]

There were a few other Swiss in Minnesota Territory in 1850. The greatest number was a group of nine in Stillwater, of whom the census showed four laborers, one waiter, and a family of four. County histories suggest that there were already other Swiss in the Stillwater area and indicate a flow of migration, probably from canton Glarus, that converged in the United States at St. Louis and thence up the Mississippi, arriving in the St. Croix area between 1848 and 1850.[11]

The Territorial and Early Statehood Period

A marked influx of Swiss settlers occurred in the 1850s, when the number of foreign-born Swiss in Minnesota grew from 17 in 1850 to 968 in 1860 (see Table 10.1). The areas of settlement correlated closely with those of the Germans, for a majority of the Swiss in the state were undoubtedly German speaking. There were a few Italian speakers, however, and a regular Romansh colony eventually developed in St. Henry the Emperor parish near Le Sueur Center. The French Swiss seem to have been the least numerous and least-known group, but one such family left a singular set of documents that spans the greater part of the period of Swiss immigration to Minnesota.[12]

Among the immigration agents appointed during Minnesota's infancy was Eugene Burnand, a native of canton Vaud, who moved to the new territory in 1854 as a teacher. In the post to which he was named by Governor Willis Gorman in 1855, Burnand allegedly "did much to encourage Swiss settlers to locate in Minnesota" during his two-year tenure. Writing from his New York office to Gorman in late spring of 1856, Burnand said that 106 persons had "lately called at . . . [his office] and left for Minnesota," and 16 of these were Swiss.[13]

It is not known where Burnand's recruits settled, but it is clear that several concentrations of Swiss had formed before his appointment was made. In addition to the group at Stillwater, there were Swiss in New Schwanden in Hennepin County, in Le Sueur, Helvetia in Carver County, and Berne in Dodge. By 1860 Brown County boasted 42 persons of Swiss birth or Swiss male parentage, including 15 in New Ulm. Several of the Minnesota settlements were peopled by secondary migrants from other states; two, for example, were founded chiefly by immigrants who had moved west from the New Glarus colony in Green County, Wisconsin.[14]

New Glarus, founded in 1845, became one of the most important Swiss settlements in the United States. As it prospered, land values rose and newer arrivals from Switzerland were tempted by cheaper land farther west — a familiar pattern in frontier history. The colony at Berne was founded, reportedly, by former residents of New Glarus, but it was a predominantly Bernese group. The 1860 census, which gives the cantonal origins for Milton Township in which Berne was located, showed that of 116 persons of Swiss stock (79 of whom were foreign born) only 6 were from Glarus; the rest, except for one person from Basel, were from Bern. Other evidence, however, suggests that many Berne residents had left Switzerland after the New Glarus colonizers of 1845; the names in the 1860 census, for example, are different from a compiled list of the first New Glarus settlers. A county history described at least four Swiss settlers as early as 1855 and pictured the settlement as thriving by 1858, with a harness shop, two breweries, a hotel, a sawmill, a blacksmith shop, a store, and a post office — named in that year no doubt to attract other immigrants. In 1872 the Zwingli German Reformed Church Society was organized with a membership of 25 families; in 1980 it was the only surviving trace of the village, although many farmers in the neighborhood bear the names of Swiss pioneers.

Like their counterparts in Wisconsin and elsewhere, the residents of Berne distinguished themselves in cheese making and brewing. They "wasted little time," stated one historian of the county, "in beginning to make either cheddar or Swiss-style cheese in their homes. . . . and later . . . agreed to pool their milk output and haul to the little one- or two-man [cheese] factories. Later these little factories combined to form the giant Minnesota Cheese Producers' Association at Pine Island (just across the county line in Goodhue County)."[15]

Biographical data on 20 early Swiss settlers in Dodge County indicated that most of them were members of the German Reformed church; only one was Catholic and two were Lutheran. Their cantons of origin were Bern, Glarus, Zurich, and St. Gall (see Map 10.1). Most of the first generation married other Swiss, but some wives' maiden names indicated that marriage with other groups occurred. A comparison of names in the 1860 census showed that later arrivals from Switzerland often bore the same patronym as did early settlers, and there was a small but continuing flow of new arrivals after the original nucleus was established.

Another early Minnesota Swiss settlement was that of New Schwanden in Hennepin County. Though numerically smaller than Berne, more is known about its origins. The first settlers emigrated from Switzerland in 1853, landing at New York and at New Orleans. They traveled first to New Glarus, but eventually sought land near St. Anthony (later Minneapolis), finally purchasing some near the village of Champlin on the Mississippi River in 1855. The colonists, who renamed the site New Schwanden for their old home in Glarus, consisted of six families, but their numbers increased as new arrivals filtered in during the years between 1860 and 1885. The families were interrelated and continued to marry within the group until the third generation when exogamy became more common. The patriarch of the community, Peter Blesi, donated four acres for the First German Evangelical Lutheran Church, which was dedicated in 1866 and renamed in 1893 German Evangelical St. Fridolin's Church for the patron saint of Glarus. (For a number of years the congregation was served by pastors from the St. Petri Evangelical Lutheran Church at 18th Street and Dupont Avenue North in Minneapolis.) Blesi's wife, Margaret, made cheese as early as 1858; it was reputedly the first Minnesota-made cheese to be sold in the market. The types of cheese were Schäbziger and a yellow brick, both made by hand at first. The village of New Schwanden no longer exists; its church and houses were razed in 1955 to make way for the Elm Creek Park Reserve.[16]

Other Swiss settlements in the early days of statehood appeared in Brown and Carver counties, near or mingled with German enclaves. Helvetia, for example, had a number of German-speaking natives of Bern; in New Ulm, as might be expected, the Swiss-born residents had German names. Far to the north in Lake County a colony of about 25 Swiss was located at Beaver Bay. And perhaps among the least-known settlements of Swiss were those of Le Sueur County.

ST. FRIDOLIN'S German Lutheran Evangelical Church, New Schwanden, in 1899.

There by 1860 were 203 residents, and their number grew to 323 two decades later (see Table 10.1). The predominantly Romansh parish of St. Henry the Emperor was established just outside Le Sueur Center in 1861, and Le Sueur itself apparently harbored numbers of Swiss, as did the nearby rural townships of Sharon, Tyrone, and Cleveland. Most of the names of known Swiss settlers appeared to be German, and each of the four communities built Evangelical churches which were known to have had Swiss members.[17]

Growth and Decline

The territorial census showed only 17 persons of Swiss birth in Minnesota. Ten years later there were over 1,000, with each of nine counties — Carver, Dakota, Dodge, Le Sueur, Nicollet, Ramsey, Stearns, Wabasha, and Washington — having more than 50 persons of Swiss stock. By 1880 all of the older settlements had grown and several new centers had appeared; Goodhue, Houston, McLeod, Otter Tail, Polk, Waseca, Winona, and Wright counties each had well over 100 Swiss, for example. The most striking change was the shift from rural to urban settlement, as the metropolitan counties of Hennepin and Ramsey increased significantly, with 537 and 448, respectively. (See Table 10.1.)

There is little doubt that at least some of the Swiss movement into Minnesota was secondary migration from states such as Ohio, Pennsylvania, and Missouri, as well as that previously mentioned from Wisconsin. But there was a continuing direct immigration to the established centers as well. In 1873, for example, the St. Paul Daily Pioneer for November 18 reported that a resident of Berne was to travel to Switzerland, and it was understood that he had been appointed as an immigration agent. As a result, the paper

Table 10.1. Swiss in Minnesota by County, 1860–1970

County	1860		1880		1900	1905	1930		1970		Concentrations
	foreign born	foreign mixed	fb	fm	fb	fm	fb	fm	fb	fm	
Aitkin					7		14	46		17	
Anoka	10	9	13	24	30	79	41	73	9	135	
Becker			5	12	10	27	12	47		55	
Beltrami					4		10	40	15	7	
Benton			7	13	5		12	33			
Big Stone			21	11	12		6	40		11	
Blue Earth	24	8	71	101	70	143	28	137		43	Mankato
Brown	36	6	103	114	55	124	19	83		15	New Ulm
Carlton					11	48	17	38		6	
Carver	102	59	128	154	47	164	10	84		34	Chaska, Helvetia, Waconia
Cass			1		3	19	10	40	6	58	
Chippewa			2	1	3	48	11	50		7	
Chisago	4	2	15	10	10	24	1	16		6	
Clay			1	6	31	14	14	64		28	
Clearwater						2	5	21		8	
Cook					1		1	2			
Cottonwood			4	3	4	14	2	27		7	
Crow Wing			5	2	17	61	16	56		18	
Dakota	34	18	47	38	57	173	51	157	12	142	Hastings, S. St. Paul
Dodge	79	37	201	281	248	658	82	294	13	57	Milton, Concord, Berne
Douglas			14	16	14	43	5	31		36	
Faribault			7	9	29	45	6	21		7	
Fillmore	2		23	38	19	66	5	41	6	11	
Freeborn	4		11		10	34	5	23		6	
Goodhue	6		72	147	58	152	40	165	6	91	Pine Island
Grant			1	2		11	2	9		12	
Hennepin	33	7	209	328	407	984	357	1,453	79	763	Minneapolis, Edina, New
Minneapolis			140		303	898	288	1,172	23	383	Schwanden
Houston			59	66	53	117	13	87		86	
Hubbard					7	26	3	23			
Isanti			4	10	2	7	5	14			
Itasca					1	18	8	51		15	
Jackson					27	51	10	33			
Kanabec					5	9	2	13	7	9	
Kandiyohi			2	5	3	18	4	30		12	
Kittson			1	7	2	13	4	11		9	
Koochiching							5	31		12	
Lac qui Parle			20	46	35	98	9	32		7	
Lake			2	8	3	6	1	13		8	Beaver Bay
Lake of the Woods							2	5			
Le Sueur	139	64	128	195	70	218	14	135		52	Sharon, Le Sueur, Le Sueur Center
Lincoln			1	5	1	24	3	20			
Lyon			21	12	10	14	2	25		19	
McLeod	3	1	42	86	35	118	9	67		6	
Mahnomen							1				
Marshall			4	6	7	14		10		5	
Martin			2	3	18	54	11	83		43	
Meeker	3	1	3	4	5	25	1	25			
Mille Lacs						25	5	33		13	
Morrison	1		13	21	23	45	9	25			
Mower	7	1	22	43	46	129	20	82		39	Austin
Murray			4	9	12		4	29			
Nicollet	34	17	45	71	37	61	12	62	7	14	
Nobles			10	34	12	74	9	43		11	
Norman					40	84	7	39			
Olmsted	23	2	69	89	50	82	37	210	10	190	Rochester
Otter Tail			60	118	46	88	20	95		33	Elizabeth, Fergus Falls
Pennington								5			
Pine	10	3	12	6	13	52	20	64		20	
Pipestone				3	8	36	4	23		23	
Polk			61	74	34	131	7	56		12	
Pope					3	9	5	11			
Ramsey	97	48	204	244	544	1,355	526	1,593	154	713	St. Paul, Roseville
St. Paul			185		492	1,203	421	1,396	69	495	
Red Lake					1	7		7			
Redwood			36	20	73	110	44	135	7	83	Redwood Falls
Renville	9	3	6	5	22	90	12	58		18	
Rice	16	4	43	48	29	39	20	98		48	
Rock			5	8	4	17	2	8		7	
Roseau					3	46	5	26		16	
St. Louis			10	17	60	154	86	286	8	125	Duluth
Duluth					41	107	56	192	8	71	
Scott	13	5	43	51	28	68	12	46	5	22	

Table 10.1. Swiss in Minnesota by County, 1860–1970 (continued)

County	1860 foreign born	1860 foreign mixed	1880 fb	1880 fm	1900 fb	1905 fm	1930 fb	1930 fm	1970 fb	1970 fm	Concentrations
Sherburne			6	1	4		11	26		28	
Sibley	5	11	13	35	14	47	8	41		8	
Stearns	42	27	114	151	108	323	43	211	14	95	St. Cloud, St. Augusta
Steele	5	3	60	79	22	94	8	83		27	
Stevens			6	1	23	87	16	78		6	
Swift			10	13	16	64	7	13		16	
Todd	3	1	14	21	49	113	23	111		18	
Traverse			7	1	13	41	6	29			
Wabasha	62	31	151	183	112	236	37	139	7	40	Wabasha, Lake City
Wadena			1		7	33	8	26		12	
Waseca			41	123	25	99	6	51		14	
Washington	147	44	215	280	141	243	39	223		161	Stillwater
Watonwan			7	15	15	51	6	45	18	67	Madelia
Wilkin			13	10	24	88	9	64		32	
Winona	18	21	118	135	101	244	41	195	8	72	Winona
Wright	15	5	72	102	41	123	17	61		38	Monticello
Yellow Medicine			2	7	10	33	1	22		7	
Total	968	419	2,744	3,781	3,258	8,385	2,041	8,251	391	3,891	
Published census figures	(1,085)		(2,828)								

Source: U.S. manuscript census, 1860, author's computation; for 1880–1970, see Appendix.

declared, he "will doubtless be accompanied on his return by a large number that he may induce to leave their native land." Later in the decade some settlements formed in the western part of the state. The *St. Paul Daily Globe* of April 15, 1878, mentioned "A Swiss colony of 200 families" that was to locate near Ada in Polk County.

One student of the Swiss in the United States during the years of the 1870s and 1880s indicated that to a large extent the economic history of the early Swiss in Minnesota was a story of cheese, beer, hotels, doctors, lawyers, millers, manufacturers, and musicians. A few gravitated to politics, but most Swiss seem to have been drawn to economically productive activities, the professions, and the arts. Cheese farming was perhaps the most distinctively Swiss culture trait to be introduced by immigrants to the state. As early as 1885 Swiss-born Minnesotans won prizes for Limburger and Swiss cheeses at an exposition in New Orleans. As a group they were instrumental in the organization of the Minnesota Butter, Cheese, and Livestock Association.[18]

Another skill fostered by Swiss immigrants was the brewing of beer and the manufacture of malt. An early Swiss brewery was that of Jakob Meili in Stillwater. Another early Swiss brewery existed in Rochester.

Swiss versatility was evident in the burgeoning economy of the Twin Cities. A partial list of Swiss in Minneapolis included two bankers, a barber, a tobacconist, a paper manufacturer, a mill owner, a factory superintendent, a doctor, a druggist, a lawyer, and an architect. The St. Paul roster contained a doctor, a lawyer, a notary public, a malting company president, several musicians including an organist, and an editor. Also in the capital city was a poet-writer-publicist of some note, Franz Xavier Fassbind, who wrote and published the Catholic German-language newspaper *Der Wanderer* (The Migrant) from 1869 to 1883. Similar lists for other localities suggest the diversity of economic endeavor among Minnesota's Swiss-born residents.[19]

Like other ethnic groups, the Swiss established a number of nationality-based organizations. As early as 1881 Minneapolis Swiss founded a *Grütli-Verein* (Grutli Society), and two authorities indicated the formation of a German and Swiss choral group, Harmonia, in either 1861 or the early 1870s. In any case, a music club was apparently the nucleus from which not only the *Grütli* but also the *Schweizer Kranken-Unterstützungsverein* (Swiss Health Assistance Society) sprang. There was, in addition, a dramatic society. With the choral unit it gave spring performances, but the important annual event was the *Novemberfest*, which commemorated the Swiss declaration of independence made on the field of Grütli in 1291. All of these clubs operated under the aegis of the national *Grütlibund* with which the Minnesota group affiliated in 1884; this was in accord with the parent organization's purpose "to unite into one alliance all the Swiss societies . . . in the United States. . . . [and] to promote among Swiss-Americans an active and cultural life, to treasure the love and affection for the old home country and to work in the new country for the respect of all that is Swiss." At the end of 1889 the Minneapolis *Grütli-Verein* boasted 46 members and a treasury of $550.00.[20]

In St. Paul the *Grütli-Verein*, established in 1884, had 70 members and a fund of $600. Like its counterpart across the river, the St. Paul group had a benevolent society, a *Gesang-Verein* (Glee Club), and a mixed chorus. When the Minneapolis *Grütli* held a ceremonial dedication of banners on November 24, 1888, St. Paul members contributed singers, thus establishing a tradition of co-operation and association between the two cities. Speeches, concerts, and balls seem to have attracted considerable numbers of the German community, and the co-operation of the St. Paul *Liederkranz* (Singing Society) ensured a basis for larger celebrations which virtually took on the form of German national festivals, pointing up the cordial relations between German Swiss and Germans and their common settlement patterns.

A PREPAID steerage ticket issued by the Rush City Bank in 1883, when $158.98 would bring three adults and one child there from Glarus, Switzerland.

The social activities of the *Grütli* were not limited to the Twin Cities. In Winona, for example, with a population of about 20,000 in 1889, the Swiss colony of about 100 persons organized a *Grütli-Verein* in 1885. Like the metropolitan groups, the Winona society had a glee club which gave concerts, particularly for the *Novemberfest*. Other Swiss singing clubs existed in Mound Prairie and Bush Valley. In Stillwater the Swiss tradition of marksmanship was upheld by some of the early residents. On August 2, 1876, the *Stillwater Gazette* reported that three local men, "all natives of Switzerland, a country noted for the skill and proficiency of its people with the rifle," were participants in a national shooting match in Philadelphia.

After 1880 when emigration peaked, the history of Swiss immigration and settlement in Minnesota is not well chronicled. The inflow diminished after the 1890s, and the second generation soon outnumbered the first. In rural centers, especially, the decline in the number of second-generation Swiss appeared to be a sign of an aging foreign-born population not being replaced by new immigrants and undoubtedly undergoing the process of assimilation. In 1905 the total Swiss stock was 8,385 (see Table 10.1), and only three counties — Hennepin (984), Ramsey (1,355), and Dodge (658) — had more than 500. Five counties had more than 200, and 13 numbered more than 100.[21]

Settlement patterns of all the counties with over 100 Swiss in 1905 fell into four distinct blocs. One lay along the Mississippi River from Houston County to Stearns; another extended upstream along the Minnesota River from Le Sueur to Redwood Falls; a third area was Duluth in St. Louis County; and the fourth region was Polk County in the Red River Valley. Census figures of the foreign-born Swiss remained nearly identical from 1910 to 1930 (between 2,000 and 3,000); the latter year showed 10,292 total Swiss stock, a number which had declined by more than 50% in 1970. Such figures, it must be remembered, take no account of the buildup of third, fourth, and even fifth generations in areas of older Swiss settlement and are in that way misleading.[22]

In the quarter century after 1905 there was a greater spread of Swiss throughout the state, with every county having at least a few (Table 10.1). The significant growth was in the metropolitan area of the Twin Cities and adjacent Dakota County, Rochester in Olmsted County, and Duluth — all essentially urban places. One rural area around Redwood Falls also showed some increase. But by the 1970 census only Watonwan County in southwestern Minnesota had an appreciable increase in Swiss residents, and the number involved was small — about 80.

Swiss social institutions reflected the decline shown in the census tables. Membership in various branches of the *Grütli-Verein* fell. In Minneapolis it dropped from 52 in 1926 to 16 in 1960; St. Paul's *Helvetia-Verein* went from one in 1926 to none in 1929 when the organization ceased; and the Winona *Grütli* suffered a similar fate. It seems possible that since the *Grütli* was a German-language organization, it may have experienced the hostility and discrimination visited on German groups during and after World War I.[23]

But Swiss organizations were not dead, particularly in St. Paul. Two of their groups, the men's and women's benevolent societies, emerged as English-language organizations and met in the German-sponsored *Deutsche Haus* on Rice Street. In 1979 the men numbered about 90 members, the women about 75, and younger members are currently drawn from the ranks of their children. The *Gesang-Verein* survived for a time as the Swiss Singing Society, and other Swiss have contributed to the Festival of Nations sponsored by the International Institute of St. Paul (now Minnesota) since 1932. The names that appeared in festival brochures showed a growing pattern of exogamy. In 1939 most of them were German, but by 1961 nearly half the names seemed to be English, Scottish, Scandinavian, or French Canadian.[24]

The Minneapolis-based Twin Cities Swiss-American

THE MINNEAPOLIS Grütli-Verein *celebrated the 600th anniversary of the confederation of Switzerland with song, symbol, and pageantry in 1891. Included in the historical tableau are representatives of the first three Swiss cantons, Wilhelm Tell, and the Swiss Club Choir. The motto above translates as "One for all, all for one."*

Association was founded in 1979 with 120 members who were either American born of Swiss ancestry or latecomers from Switzerland. Among them were many employees of a Swiss-owned engineering company in Minneapolis. The association has been helpful in furthering the Americanization of the newer arrivals, and it has provided a valuable link for American Swiss to their heritage and traditions.

Another Swiss-organized activity in 1980 was a so-called *Swissfest,* held annually since 1953 in Dodge County. Essentially an entertainment with promotional overtones, the affair drew thousands of Minnesotans and hundreds of Swiss from the Old Country and advertised Swiss products and tourism. It is ironic that the festival site is the vanished village of Berne.[25]

More expressive, perhaps, of the ongoing sense of ethnicity among progeny of early Swiss settlers has been an annual picnic held by descendants of New Schwanden pioneers for themselves alone. This group raised money for a monument to commemorate its vanished village. Perhaps the New Schwanden descendants may serve as a rough indication of what happened to the early Swiss stock of Minnesota. Since the village's original six families moved to the area in 1854, six generations and 115 families, now spread over several states, have sprung from those first settlers. Clearly the process of assimilation has been at work, but still, six generations later, a sense of pride in the heritage and traditions of their ancestors exists among Minnesota's Swiss.[26]

FRANK BRAND (right) in his newly established Swiss grocery store in New Duluth about 1895.

Reference notes

[1] Heinz K. Meier, *The United States and Switzerland in the Nineteenth Century*, 105 (The Hague, 1963); Walter F. Willcox, ed., *International Migrations*, vol. 1, *Statistics*, 769 (Reprint ed., New York, 1969); Stephan Thernstrom, ed., *Harvard Encyclopedia of American Ethnic Groups*, 983–985 (Cambridge, Mass., 1980).

Among the best standard one-volume treatments of Swiss history in English are William Martin, *Switzerland from Roman Times to the Present* (New York, 1971) and E. Bonjour, H. Offler, and G. R. Potter, *A Short History of Switzerland* (Oxford, 1952).

[2] Here and below, see Thernstrom, ed., *Harvard Encyclopedia*, 982; Bonjour *et al.*, *Short History*, 40, 303–306, 344. A good discus-

sion appears in Leon Dominian, *Frontiers of Language and Nationality in Europe* (New York, 1917); a more recent treatment of the linguistic frontier is Max Pfister, "Die Bedeutung des Germanischen Superstrates für die sprachliche Ausgliederung der Galloromania," in Helmut Beumann and Werner Schröder, eds., *Aspekte der Nationenbildung im Mittelalter*, 128–140 (Sigmaringen, Ger., 1978).

[3] Here and below, see G. R. Elton, *Reformation Europe, 1517–1559*, 73 (New York, 1966); Martin, *Switzerland*, 76–119.

[4] Meier, *United States and Switzerland*, 107; Leo Schelbert, ed., *New Glarus 1845–1970: The Making of a Swiss-American Town*, 10 (Glarus, Switz., 1970). The latter volume contains an outstanding classified and annotated bibliography, pp. 222–233; to it should be added Karl Lüönd, *Schweizer in Amerika* (Olten, Switz., 1979). The cantons with the highest emigration figures were Bern, Zurich, Ticino, St. Gall, and the town of Basel.

[5] Here and below, see Meier, *United States and Switzerland*, 106–118; John Paul von Grueningen, *The Swiss in the United States*, 17 (Madison, Wis., 1940). On the Italian Swiss, see Maurice Perret, *Les Colonies-Tessinoises en Californie* (Lausanne, 1950); on Romansh settlements, see Guglielm Gadola, "L'emigraziun Aujetschina ell'America," in *Societa Retrumantscha Annales*, 5:137–173 (1936), and Augustin Maissen, "Ils Romontschs ell'America," in *Radioscola*, 11:14–19 (Chur, Switz., 1966).

[6] For example, State of Minnesota, *Census, 1905*, 198, table 14, gives Swiss stock as 8,385, Dutch as 6,532, and Belgian as 2,038; figures from later years give the Dutch an edge over the Swiss, and figures on foreign born alone strengthen this picture.

[7] Here and below, see John Perry Pritchett, *The Red River Valley, 1811–1849: A Regional Study*, 182, 224 (New Haven, Conn., 1942); George F. G. Stanley, ed., "Documents Relating to the Swiss Immigration to Red River in 1821," in *Canadian Historical Review*, 22:42, 43, 45–47, 50 (March, 1941); J. Fletcher Williams, ed., "Early Days at Red River Settlement and Fort Snelling: Reminiscences of Mrs. Ann Adams," in *Minnesota Historical Collections*, 6:75–116 (St. Paul, 1894); William W. Folwell, *A History of Minnesota*, 1:213–217 (Reprint ed., St. Paul, 1956); Rhoda R. Gilman, Carolyn Gilman, and Deborah M. Stultz, *The Red River Trails: Oxcart Routes between St. Paul and the Red River Settlement, 1820–1870*, 6, 28 (St. Paul, 1979).

[8] Grace Lee Nute, "Peter Rindisbacher, Artist," in *Minnesota History*, 14:283–287 (September, 1933); Williams, ed., in *Minnesota Historical Collections*, 6:88. On Scheidegger descendants, see *Minnesota History News*, May, 1981.

[9] On the Perrets, see Henry A. Castle, *History of St. Paul and Vicinity*, 1:32 (Chicago, 1912); Thomas M. Newson, *Pen Pictures of St. Paul, Minnesota*, 20 (St. Paul, 1886); Stanley, ed., in *Canadian Historical Review*, 22:46, 47; Patricia C. Harpole and Mary D. Nagle, eds., *Minnesota Territorial Census, 1850*, 40, 44, 52, 68 (St. Paul, 1972).

[10] A. Grandjean, *La Mission Romande*, 1–30 (Lausanne, 1917).

[11] Harpole and Nagle, eds., *Territorial Census*, 59, 74, 85; Augustus B. Easton, *History of the St. Croix Valley*, 1:314 (Chicago, 1909); Edward D. Neill, *History of Washington County and the St. Croix Valley*, 425 (Minneapolis, 1881); Von Grueningen, *Swiss in the United States*, 28.

[12] United States, *Census, 1860, Population*, 262; Charles Marc Bost, ed., *Les derniers puritains: pionniers d'Amérique, 1851–1920*, 38, 351, 385, 426 (Paris, 1977), translated by Ralph H. Bowen as *A Frontier Family in Minnesota* (Minneapolis, 1981). The letters of Théodore Bost and his wife Sophie Bonjour described their life

on a farm near Chanhassen, relations with neighbors, local political and economic conditions, and other details of frontier life from 1855 to 1887. Later letters of the Bosts reflect their pro-French sentiments.

[13] Livia Appel and Theodore C. Blegen, "Official Encouragement of Immigration to Minnesota during the Territorial Period," in *Minnesota History Bulletin*, 5:170, 177–180, 201 (August, 1923).

[14] Here and below, see B[ertha] L. H[eilbron], "Swiss Settlement in Minnesota," in *Minnesota History*, 8:174 (June, 1927); figures compiled from Minnesota manuscript census schedules, 1860, in MEHP Papers, MHS; Schelbert, ed., *New Glarus*, 200–205; [H. H. Hill Co.], *History of Winona, Olmsted, and Dodge Counties*, 1030, 1244, 1245 (Chicago, 1884); *Land Atlas and Plat Book, 1978, Dodge County, Minnesota*, 26 (Rockford, Ill., 1978).

[15] Here and below, see Harold Severson, *Dodge County Profiles, 1960*, 5 ([Kenyon, 1960?]). See also biographies of Swiss settlers in Dodge County in [Hill Co.], *History of . . . Dodge*, 1020, 1030, 1042, 1059, 1105, 1106, 1110, 1132, 1138, 1139, 1165, 1166, 1184, 1186, 1216.

[16] Wayne C. Blesi, "Early Swiss Pioneers in Minnesota," in [Minnesota Territorial Pioneers], *Pioneer Chronicles*, 46–48 (Minneapolis, 1976); interviews of Wayne C. Blesi by author, October, 1979, notes in MEHP Papers.

[17] Adelrich Steinach, *Geschichte und Leben der Schweizer Kolonien in den Vereinigten Staaten von Nord-Amerika*, 312 (New York, 1879); Minnesota manuscript census schedules, 1860, Brown County, roll 1, microfilm in MHS; William G. Gresham, *History of Nicollet and Le Sueur Counties*, 1:515, 2:396 (Indianapolis, 1916); Catholic Archdiocese of St. Paul and Minneapolis, Parish Questionnaires, 1948, originals in Catholic Historical Society, St. Paul Seminary, St. Paul, microfilm in MHS; *St. Paul Dispatch*, April 17, 1975, p. 13.

[18] Here and below, see Steinach, *Schweizer Kolonien*, 306–312, which gives considerable information on Minnesota and is valuable because of the contemporary documents available to the author. See also Merrill E. Jarchow, *Economic History of Agriculture in Minnesota*, 139 (Minneapolis, 1941). Steinach erroneously listed German-born brewers August Schell and John Hauenstein as Swiss.

[19] Steinach, *Schweizer Kolonien*, 310, 359.

[20] Here and two paragraphs below, see Steinach, *Schweizer Kolonien*, 306, 307, 309, 310; *Minneapolis Tribune*, November 20, 1881; *St. Paul Daily Globe*, November 22, 1881; Horace B. Hudson, *A Half Century of Minneapolis*, 113 (Minneapolis, 1908). Wayne Blesi gives 1861 as the founding date of Harmonia; typed statements by Blesi, MEHP Papers.

[21] Minnesota, *Census, 1905*, 196–198. The five counties were Le Sueur, Stearns, Wabasha, Washington, and Winona; the 13 were Blue Earth, Brown, Carver, Dakota, Goodhue, Houston, McLeod, Mower, Polk, Redwood, St. Louis, Todd, and Wright.

[22] U.S., *Census, 1910, Population*, 2:601; 1920, 2:697; 1930, 3:1220; 1970, vol. 1, part 25, p. 231.

[23] Information on the *Grütli* is from *Der Schweizer*, later retitled *Swiss American*, a monthly publication of the Nord-Amerikanische Schweizer-Bund, copies from 1926 to 1960 in MHS.

[24] Author's interviews of Mrs. G. Harold Routier, October 9, 1979, Alfred Linder, October 10, 1979, Blesi interview notes, October, 1979. See also Chapter 8. On the Festival of Nations, see Alice L. Sickels, *Around the World in St. Paul*, 108 (Minneapolis, 1945).

[25] *Minneapolis Tribune*, August 9, 1978, p. 2B.

[26] Blesi interview, October, 1979. A flyer for the 1979 picnic is in the MEHP Papers.

CHAPTER 11

The Norwegians

Carlton C. Qualey and Jon A. Gjerde

AN ELDERLY NORWEGIAN AMERICAN living in Minneapolis in the 1950s pointed proudly to the fact that "no State in the Union and no American city of the first class have proportionately as many people of Norwegian blood. I was impressed by this back in the old homeland. . . . Even the school children . . . would talk about all those people going to America. Indelibly implanted in my mind even now is a remark made by one of my school mates . . . 'And they are all bound for Minnesota.' "[1]

Although the schoolmate exaggerated a bit, Minnesota attracted more of the approximately 850,000 Norwegians who immigrated between 1825 and 1928 than any other state. It became both a population and a cultural center for Norwegian Americans, and they became its third largest ethnic group (see Table 0.1). Norwegians began to arrive in the United States in large numbers in the late 1840s, rising in 1882 to 28,500 persons. The number of Norwegian born in Minnesota peaked in 1905 with 111,611; five years later the census counted 105,302, more than 26% of those in the entire United States and more than the next two leading states of Wisconsin and North Dakota combined. The Norwegian-American community in Minnesota has not only persisted, it has flourished. In 1970, 156,841 Minnesotans claimed Norwegian as their mother tongue — a number roughly equal to the combined populations of Edina, Mankato, Moorhead, and Rochester. It is no coincidence that one of the state's most prevalent late 20th-century symbols is the Viking.[2]

Why did Norwegians emigrate in such large numbers? In the 19th century only the famine-stricken Irish exceeded the emigration rate of the Norwegians. Like other European nations in the mid-19th century, Norway experienced wrenching economic changes and a doubling of its population from 1815 to 1865. The latter resulted primarily from a declining infant and child mortality rate. Per capita agricultural output rose 70% from 1800 to 1830, but the country was, and is, both mountainous and forested, with little arable land. Job opportunities in its agricultural, fishing, and lumbering economy were limited. Many young people were forced to seek day-laboring jobs on the farms of others, while a second, more diverse group called *husmenn* (cotters), whose rights and duties varied by region, formed a kind of intermediate rural class between the independent farm owners who were called *bønder*, and the day laborers. More inten-

sive cultivation and the colonization of northern Norway supported a 27% increase in the *bønder* between 1801 and 1855. But at the same time the number of *husmenn* nearly doubled and day laborers trebled.[3]

No massive emigration resulted, however, until the mid-1860s when a combination of overpopulation, food shortages, mechanization, and changing market structures led to farm foreclosures. Even worse, poor crops, coupled with the disappearance of the fickle spring herring run from the Norwegian coasts, resulted in actual starvation. Infant mortality rose, and there were reports of bread made from tree bark. The country's belated experience with mechanization worked to increase emigration. Between 1865 and 1900 the agricultural labor force was reduced by some 50,000 and the number of *husmenn* fell by half to less than 25,000 as many of them swelled the stream of emigrants. With the decline in the availability of cheap labor, farm owners began to invest in harvesting and sowing machines, potato diggers, and self-binders. Higher wages, increased production per man hour, and improved transportation would militate against further starving times, but many small *bønder* could not afford to mechanize and were forced to sell out. With the displaced farm laborers and cotters, they found their way to the slowly industrializing Norwegian cities. Information about America and the rich farmlands of its Midwest, however, opened another, more attractive option to these people and led them to consider emigrating.[4]

The rapid changes in Norwegian society were accompanied by a pietistic religious movement, inspired by the late 18th-century leadership of Hans Nielsen Hauge, and by a blossoming of romantic nationalism. The latter regarded rural society as truly Norwegian, while viewing the urban community as hopelessly compromised by its ties to Denmark and Sweden, which had successively ruled Norway for four centuries. The two movements introduced new ideas and contributed to the creation of an increasingly assertive and nationalistic peasant class (*bonde*), resentful of the pretensions of the official and clerical classes, distrustful of Danish language and customs, and dedicated to perpetuating Norwegian rural life and culture.[5]

Ironically, it may have been the conservatism of the Norwegian farmers that in part prompted them to make the radical decision to move to the New World rather than to Norway's cities, as Norwegian historian Ingrid Semmingsen contended. By emigrating, they believed, their rural way of life could be maintained without the overpopulation and socioeconomic problems existing at home. Although their motivation to migrate was primarily economic in nature, the rural Norwegians' desire to perpetuate rural life and their distrust of the city provided a cultural background important in the development of the 19th- and early 20th-century Norwegian-American community. In Minnesota Norwegians took land in rural areas, where they clung to traditions and patterns which provided some continuity with the homeland.[6] The parish church, for example, remained the central institution, and the rural immigrants, some of whom had been active participants in Norway's social reforms, quickly became involved in the Minnesota political scene.

Settlement Patterns

The earliest emigrants left Norway in 1825, settling ultimately in Illinois after a stay in New York. By the late 1830s Norwegians were to be found in the Wisconsin areas that would become mother settlements for the first influx to Minnesota in the 1850s. The best-known of the southeastern Wisconsin concentrations were located at Muskego in Waukesha County; Jefferson and Rock Prairie in Rock County; Koshkonong in Dane, Jefferson, and Rock counties; and Wiola, Spring Prairie, and Bonnet Prairie in Lafayette and Columbia counties.

These early immigrants had been the victims of "America fever," which reached epidemic proportions in the 1860s. Its spread throughout the mountains and valleys of Norway was fanned by the so-called America letters written by friends and relatives who had gone to the United States. Though some were negative in their accounts of the everyday conditions of American life, many enthusiastically described the abundance of land, the higher wages, and other wonders. Handed from neighbor to neighbor and from parish to parish, a single letter might be copied hundreds of times.[7]

One example of these influential and individualistic missives will perhaps suggest something of their fervor and flavor. Jens Grønbek wrote from Rice County, Minnesota, to his brother-in-law, Christian Heltzen of Hemnes in Nordland, Norway, in September, 1867: "You ask that I report to you concerning conditions here. . . . America is a naturally rich land, endowed with virtually everything, except to a dull-witted European who is disappointed not to find money in the streets or who expects to get things without moving his arms. . . .

"There are many thousand acres of available land here — government, school, and railroad land — although it is increasingly in the West. As for government or homestead land, one can take a quarter section or 160 acres free, except for payment of a registration fee of $14 per quarter, and this is almost all arable land. An acre is 4½ Norwegian *maal*. Schools and railroad companies have received large grants of land for their support, and they sell for 6 shillings American or 75 shillings Norwegian per acre. This land you can use as you wish and can sell when you will, and therefore it is most sought. On homesteads, you are obligated to establish a residence, build a house, and start cultivation. You must live on the claim for six months of each year, and you

may not sell it for five years, during which time it is free of taxes or further payments. It is this policy, of course, that makes the American government so generous and good for immigrants.

"Now then, if one has land, the most important items are horses or oxen, a wagon, a plow, and other things necessary for a farmer. . . . A beginner usually buys a pair of oxen and a wagon and makes out very well. . . .

"This year my employer got about 1,200 to 1,400 bushels of wheat. The price this spring was two specie dollars for No. 1 wheat, 1½ dollars for No. 2, and 1 specie dollar for No. 0. A bushel weighs about 60 pounds.

"Do you know what, my dear Christian? If you find farming in Norway unrewarding and your earnings at sea are poor, I advise you, as your friend and brother-in-law, to abandon everything, and — if you can raise $600 — to come to Minnesota. Do not believe that all is lies and fables in reports that in one year in America all will be well, for I can testify that it is true, despite the fact that, last fall when I came, I thought for a time I would starve. But an American came to me in friendly fashion and said, "Huad yuh want? Want yuh work? Will yuh have som ting to eat and trink?" That is, did I need anything, did I want work, and was I hungry? I did not understand him and continued hungry even though I had been offered all these good things.

"I have now worked for a Norwegian farmer since Christmas and will remain here until October. I have it very good here. Five meals each day of the best food in the world, so that I fear I have become choosy. . . .

"Now, dear Christian, if you consider selling and emigrating across the Atlantic Ocean, please write me. Do not be worried about the voyage, either for your wife or for the children. Neither should you be alarmed about Indians or other trolls in America, for the former are now chased away, and the Yankees, that is Americans, are as kind a folk toward a stranger as I can imagine.

". . . I have met no acquaintances from Norway since Christmas. Nearly all newcomers want to return to the homeland until they have become American citizens, and then hardly anyone wants to return."

Such letters not only determined patterns of emigration from the homeland, they also influenced Norwegian patterns of settlement in the United States. Those who emigrated wrote back to their home regions, and others then decided to follow. The Stavanger district on the west coast of Norway was an area of early emigration. America fever then moved north up the coast and into the mountains to the east. Well into the 1860s most emigrants left Norway's inner fjords and high mountain districts, but the whole nation was stricken at one time or another (see Map 11.1).[8]

Once in the United States, the immigrant often made his way to a settlement from which letters had been sent. In the beginning this process produced homogeneous rural communities in which only certain districts or parishes in Norway were represented. "A remarkable aspect of the tendency of the Norwegian immigrants to flock together was that it was not enough for them to seek out fellow Norwegians," wrote Theodore C. Blegen. "They went further and associated themselves with people who had come from the very valley'' they had left. Thus the Muskego colony in Wisconsin, for example, was at first made up largely of people from the Telemark area. As settlement continued, the groups became more heterogeneous, retaining, however, a common base of Norwegianness.

In the 1850s the attention of Norwegian immigrants shifted from Wisconsin to Minnesota Territory. The first permanent Norwegian colonies were begun in 1865 by groups of settlers

Map 11.1. Areas of Norway from which Emigrants Reached Minnesota

who migrated from Wisconsin to the oak-opening lands along the Mississippi River in southeastern Minnesota. By 1880 numerous settlements dotted a block of counties — Houston, Fillmore, Goodhue, Freeborn, Mower, Dodge, part of Olmsted, Rice, Faribault, Steele, and Waseca — which became the first major concentration of Norwegians in Minnesota (see Table 11.1, Maps 11.2, 11.3).[9]

The peopling of this area and other parts of the state where farming was the main occupation resulted from a three-stage chain migration, a process that was repeated many times as the immigrants moved westward. In the first stage, families sailed from Norway to form a new settlement in, say, Wisconsin. From their new homes they wrote back to friends and relatives in their old parishes, encouraging others to join them. With high birth rates and the arrival of more and more people, the first-stage settlement area soon became too crowded. Newcomers then stayed only a short time before moving on to cheaper lands farther west — thus creating a second settlement.

One Norwegian American in Wisconsin's Koshkonong settlement complained in 1869 that immigration had been at a standstill there for a dozen years. It was true, he said, that newcomers arrived, but they remained with friends and relatives only long enough ''to gain a little money and experience'' in American farming methods, ''after which they go west to purchase land.'' Thus when one traveled in Minnesota, ''he almost everywhere comes in contact with individuals who for a longer or shorter time have lived in Koshkonong.''[10]

The third stage in the migration pattern came into being as others were drawn to the second settlement directly from Norway by the need for workers on the frontier. Minnesota farmers received laborers they could trust by sending prepaid tickets to friends and relatives in Norway. Of the emi-

Table 11.1. Norwegians in Minnesota by County, 1860–1970

County	1860 foreign born	1860 foreign mixed	1880 fb	1880 fm	1895 fb	1905 fb	1905 fm	1930 fb	1930 fm	1970 fb	1970 fm
Aitkin			2		257	378	764	354	855	58	388
Anoka			133	80	315	248	623	444	893	157	2,091
Becker			897	686	1,616	1,684	4,557	967	2,705	98	1,371
Beltrami					225	1,381	2,660	1,009	2,463	129	1,130
Benton			27	16	127	184	465	131	421	41	251
Big Stone			297	176	607	584	1,292	281	833	18	320
Blue Earth	49	30	799	688	969	817	2,519	339	1,213	49	685
Brown	1	1	771	555	781	724	2,086	311	1,062	14	305
Carlton			30	14	295	907	1,577	597	1,135	68	777
Carver	125	60	84	98	53	58	130	22	87	12	200
Cass			11	2	133	536	1,096	389	1,039	88	428
Chippewa			1,417	1,106	2,054	1,766	4,688	898	2,908	50	1,183
Chisago	12	1	55	35	90	76	184	94	216	8	222
Clay			1,284	938	3,186	2,968	6,631	1,533	4,921	165	3,018
Clearwater						1,409	3,344	957	2,463	58	1,209
Cook			1		103	154	254	264	371	60	193
Cottonwood			547	432	931	900	2,564	437	1,396	34	477
Crow Wing			52	25	511	675	1,636	600	1,504	128	1,047
Dakota	148	45	487	353	398	373	772	335	918	105	1,380
Dodge	293	98	1,421	1,458	1,065	802	2,364	318	1,313	37	376
Douglas			1,048	962	1,434	1,179	3,177	544	1,777	40	978
Faribault	3		956	994	1,191	1,141	3,172	596	2,198	89	768
Fillmore	2,034	602	5,334	5,317	4,098	3,228	9,421	1,225	4,867	65	1,541
Freeborn	535	233	3,090	2,832	2,647	2,265	6,212	1,094	4,480	135	2,052
Goodhue	1,164	428	4,679	3,921	3,513	2,898	7,300	1,170	4,071	81	1,371
Grant			803	791	1,754	1,428	4,025	585	2,135	61	771
Hennepin	6		9,933	1,204	12,762	15,571	27,287	16,401	36,242	3,297	25,339
Houston	1,087	528	2,155	2,124	1,779	1,472	3,951	477	2,169	20	722
Hubbard					26	391	813	326	792	53	381
Isanti			12	8	52	72	172	88	244	16	342
Itasca					72	704	838	532	1,319	124	957
Jackson	26	8	1,006	910	1,194	1,071	2,481	400	1,434	49	451
Kanabec					35	154	475	155	450	19	300
Kandiyohi	61	21	1,967	1,716	2,452	2,299	6,032	1,352	3,822	188	1,788
Kittson			14	9	571	732	1,866	395	1,066	40	583
Koochiching								660	1,229	105	719
Lac qui Parle			1,511	1,148	2,873	2,607	6,874	1,142	3,782	74	1,251
Lake					143	479	2,015	543	756	187	584
Lake of the Woods								242	464	50	186
Le Sueur	4	2	69	45	66	71	319	40	141	6	153
Lincoln			451	277	590	494	1,497	263	999	20	407
Lyon			704	645	1,065	1,134	2,788	516	1,617	19	666
McLeod	70	24	250	256	155	117	332	46	209	6	160
Mahnomen								134	548	9	227
Marshall			68	32	1,907	2,519	5,969	1,292	3,526	59	1,333
Martin	27	4	143	79	243	234	732	153	610	29	424
Meeker	58	28	718	531	664	567	1,467	264	801	14	281
Mille Lacs			54	37	119	361	864	315	730	54	459
Morrison			20	18	376	328	832	150	421	21	193
Mower	339	138	2,059	1,871	1,874	1,503	4,236	788	2,966	77	1,592
Murray			439	293	852	799	2,089	332	1,109	28	366
Nicollet	159	87	836	655	491	514	987	226	709	14	338
Nobles			186	193	372	313	795	158	601		262
Norman					4,388	3,567	10,323	1,601	4,800	108	1,749
Olmsted	301	81	968	939	743	553	1,361	461	1,677	80	1,170
Otter Tail			3,490	2,586	5,740	5,140	13,541	2,685	7,788	171	3,549
Pennington								1,045	2,947	115	1,444
Pine			240	201	228	382	658	317	732	39	340
Pipestone	4	3	53	40	322	349	844	230	598	15	320
Polk			2,458	1,886	8,048	6,358	14,872	2,951	8,694	233	3,596
Pope			1,776	1,477	2,618	2,287	6,479	1,035	3,498	69	1,377
Ramsey	74	19	757	355	3,087	4,291	7,032	3,589	9,453	496	6,687
Red Lake						2,252	4,220	262	732	32	263
Redwood			295	219	568	508	1,449	282	1,013	31	437
Renville	1		1,814	1,602	1,820	1,491	3,868	581	2,033	52	697
Rice	299	139	1,416	922	1,399	1,031	2,642	530	1,841	53	1,078
Rock			520	463	1,137	1,046	2,361	646	1,457	94	611
Roseau					861	1,797	4,395	1,011	2,695	151	1,122
St. Louis	1		150	81	4,199	5,866	8,963	5,916	11,228	1,203	6,128
Scott	8	5	302	221	243	205	509	95	285	18	249
Sherburne	1		144	53	392	346	901	215	613	18	224
Sibley	22	11	142	77	135	104	338	52	193		107
Stearns	7	1	412	403	755	540	1,573	346	1,152	36	784
Steele	66	20	636	506	542	525	1,457	236	1,094	16	690
Stevens			404	316	800	641	1,689	321	981	17	452

Table 11.1. Norwegians in Minnesota by County, 1860–1970 (*continued*)

County	1860 foreign born	1860 foreign mixed	1880 fb	1880 fm	1895 fb	1905 fb	1905 fm	1930 fb	1930 fm	1970 fb	1970 fm
Swift			1,140	859	1,847	1,554	4,201	776	2,487	50	925
Todd	1		360	189	981	939	2,064	468	1,388	32	540
Traverse			8	2	185	173	481	96	303		101
Wabasha	52	31	236	162	129	110	278	68	230	35	127
Wadena			37	22	221	301	801	167	513	13	293
Waseca	190	106	741	772	634	493	1,428	188	737	19	337
Washington	24	7	223	117	461	499	745	244	597	20	763
Watonwan			787	603	1,168	1,015	2,135	553	1,592	31	579
Wilkin			214	138	851	661	1,652	296	1,058	24	485
Winona	199	77	609	557	514	432	1,050	228	881	16	557
Wright	8	2	237	149	346	293	631	163	504	33	313
Yellow Medicine			1,856	1,681	2,394	2,593	6,773	1,024	3,556	54	1,331
Total	7,738	2,840	69,255	51,128	106,842	111,611	260,938	71,562	196,350	9,800	104,421
Published census figures	(8,425)		(62,521)		(107,319)	(111,611)	(260,938)	(71,562)	(196,350)	(9,800)	(104,421)

Source: See Appendix

grants leaving Christiania (now Oslo) between 1872 and 1875, for example, 39% had received prepaid tickets.

Spring Grove Township in Houston County, an area within the first Minnesota concentration, illustrates this migration process and its lingering effects. Beginning in 1852, when it received some of "the first half-dozen permanent Norwegian settlers in all of Minnesota," Spring Grove Township went on to become "one of the most densely settled Norwegian-American colonies in the United States" and "one of the important distribution points for Norwegian settlement in the American Northwest." In 1870 Spring Grove had a total of 1,135 Norwegians and only a few dozen others. Many of its early settlers were born in Hallingdal, and they had spent some time in Rock County, Wisconsin, before moving to Minnesota in 1852. Plat maps of the area show that these Hallings tended to settle together in the township, where they were joined by immigrants who arrived directly from Hallingdal as well as from various other regions.[11]

In spite of the fact that people from throughout Norway could eventually be found in Spring Grove, it retained traces of the Halling subculture into the 1930s. For three to four generations the language lingered, along with some old Norwegian agricultural customs. Farms "among the trees were built little by little" until there was "a cluster of small buildings consisting of horse stable, cow barn, sheepfold, hog barn, doghouse, chicken house, wagon shed, granary, corncrib, hay sheds — merely a roof supported by four posts — even a smokehouse for meats, [and a] privy, in addition to the residence, which was the first erected. All of these were built and arranged somewhat like farm places in Norway." The grouping of friends and relatives from Hallingdal also made it easier to maintain the regional dialect. One resident in 1920 recalled a Halling "who left some fine talented boys who neither despise their mother tongue nor are ashamed of being of Norwegian descent. Furthermore one of them can both write and speak such genuine Halling dialect that it is as if he were raised in Hallingdal itself."

But the most visible manifestation of the bridges between the Norwegian and Norwegian-American cultures in Spring Grove and in Norwegian America as a whole was the Lutheran church. Still dotting the rural Minnesota landscape, these white spires once marked the undisputed social and religious centers of the rural communities. In Spring Grove the building of a church was preceded by the formation of a congregation in 1855 in a settler's home. Because of the chain migration pattern, congregations were usually formed by a group from a certain district in the homeland. The call to a pastor then went out, but because of the scarcity of ordained ministers, especially in the early years, several fledgling parishes were often served by a single Lutheran pastor. The thirst for his services is illustrated by the mission of one pioneer minister who visited a pastorless area of southeastern Minnesota in 1857. While there, he celebrated communion for 60 persons, churched 21 women after childbirth, christened 21 children, catechized eight and confirmed six youths, and performed services — all in the course of one day and two "wakeful nights."

THE SMALL CHURCH of the Norwegian Bö congregation on the prairies of the Red River Valley near Oslo in Marshall County about 1916.

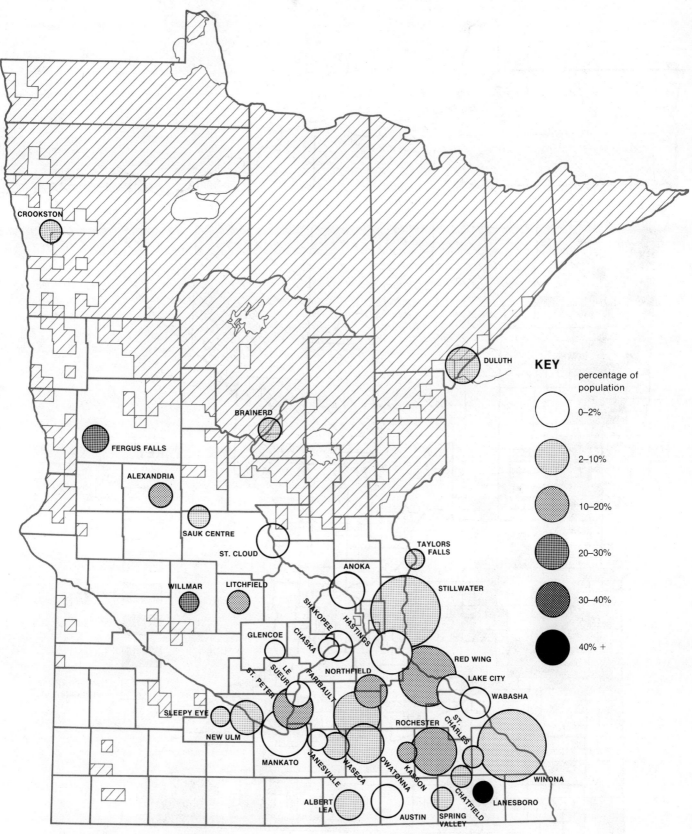

CROOKSTON

DULUTH

KEY

percentage of
population

0–2%

2–10%

10–20%

20–30%

30–40%

40% +

BRAINERD

FERGUS FALLS

ALEXANDRIA

SAUK CENTRE

ST. CLOUD

ANOKA

TAYLORS
FALLS

WILLMAR   LITCHFIELD

STILLWATER

SHAKOPEE

HASTINGS

RED WING

GLENCOE

CHASKA

LAKE CITY

ST. PETER

LE
SUEUR

FARIBAULT

NORTHFIELD

WABASHA

SLEEPY EYE

ROCHESTER

ST.
CHARLES

NEW ULM

MANKATO

JANESVILLE

WASECA

OWATONNA

KASSON

WINONA

ALBERT
LEA

AUSTIN

SPRING
VALLEY

CHATFIELD

LANESBORO

Map 11.2. Norwegians in Minnesota Towns, 1880

Map shows towns over 1,000 population in 1880.   The size of the circles is proportional to the population.

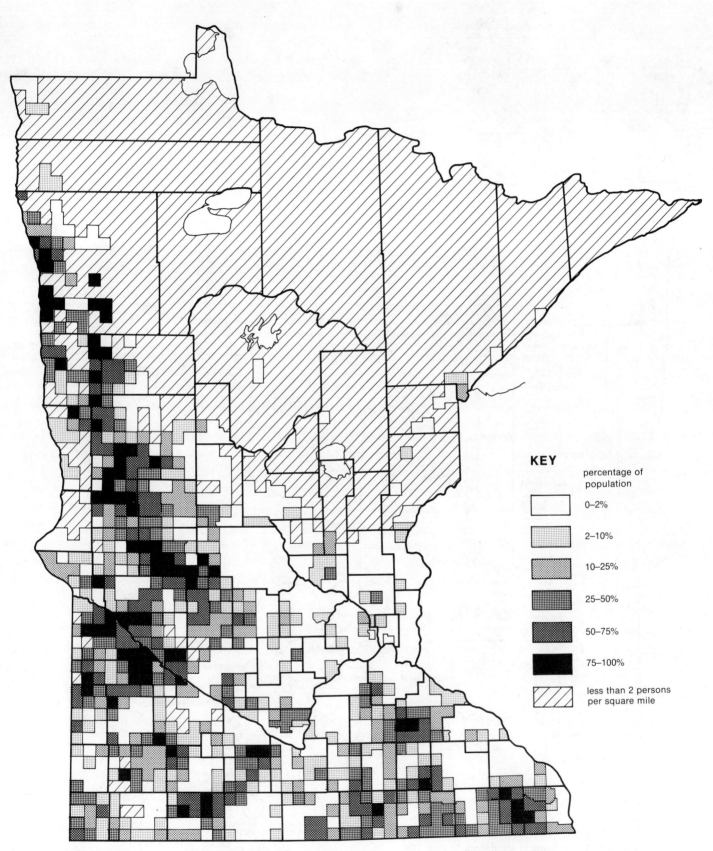

KEY

percentage of
population

0–2%

2–10%

10–25%

25–50%

50–75%

75–100%

less than 2 persons
per square mile

Map 11.3. Norwegians in Minnesota Rural Areas, 1880

Following the call to a minister, the congregation then set about the construction of a church and a parsonage. In Spring Grove the Norwegians erected a stone church in 1860, which was served by a minister who had emigrated directly from Norway three years before. Members contributed sizable sums for these structures, which were frequently built when money was scarce. At such times, the people resorted to another custom common in Norway — the payment of tithes in agricultural produce.[12]

Once built, the church quickly became the heart of the community. As one observer put it, "If one did not come to worship God, one might come for other purposes, such as trading horses, assigning road work, hiring thrashers, or hearing the latest news." Another immigrant recalled that the churchgoers usually gathered from long distances. "They usually walked. They left early and might stand outside the church to wait for each other. They were so happy to meet and find out if everything was well, and then they were so eager to find out if anyone had received a letter from Norway, because almost all of them longed to hear news from the home *bygd* [*district or rural community*]."[13]

Another factor that influenced Norwegian patterns of settlement as well as the retention of Norwegian rural cultural traits in the United States was the immigration of families. In the 1850s 32% of all Norwegian emigrants were children under 12 years of age. The ratio of males to females was at first unusually equal. In Spring Grove, for example, the 1870 sex ratio was 107.9 males for each 100 females, a far more balanced proportion than the 127.7 males per 100 females in the state as a whole. Many of the community's children had been born in Norway, and there were 628 young people under 19 as opposed to only 403 persons between 20 and 49.[14]

Given this preponderance of young people, it was not surprising that as the southeastern Minnesota communities grew older, overpopulation again acted as a push factor in the further migrations of young Norwegian Americans. As had been the case in Norway, some were able to take over the family farms, but many were forced to move to the cities or to less crowded lands farther west. "The America fever has raged in many places in old Norway . . . ," wrote a clergyman in 1885. "This fever is not always quieted by the establishment of a home in the New World. Those who live in the older settlements learn that great reaches of fertile and free lands are to be had to the westward, and so they again turn toward the new and the unseen."[15]

Some migrated to the so-called Linden settlement to the west in Blue Earth, Brown, and Watonwan counties, an area unique among pre-Civil War Norwegian settlements in Minnesota because it was located on the prairie. After 1865 many more chose the Park Region of west-central Minnesota, the second major Norwegian concentration in the state. Bordered on the west by the Red River Valley and on the northeast by pine forests, this rolling, well-watered, wooded region contained 6,175 Norwegians in 1870 and 15,859 in 1875 — 25% of its total population. By 1909 it featured "an almost unbroken series of Norwegian settlements" and not less than 100,000 Norwegians. One man wrote that nearly all of its thousands of lakes were surrounded by their homes.[16]

Many of these later settlements in western and central Minnesota were offshoots of those in the southeast. Just as land in Goodhue County had been taken up by Norwegians from Wisconsin, so were portions of Lac qui Parle County, in the upper Minnesota River Valley, the "daughters" of Goodhue. In the 1870s a "considerable migration" occurred when "no more land was available in Goodhue," wrote Olaf O. Stageberg. Many migrants then went to Lac qui Parle, so that "anyone who travels around in these two counties, as I have done, finds the same names in both places." As had been the case with the earlier Wisconsin colonies, the southeastern Minnesota areas became mother settlements, serving as jumping-off places for new emigrants from Norway. The first-stage Valdris settlement in Holden and Warsaw townships of Goodhue County, for example, "served for a long time as the destination" of numerous Norwegians who emigrated from the Valdres region in Norway. As the Goodhue County area filled up, the three-stage process was repeated. Most latecomers remained "there only a short while," wrote O. J. Flaten, before going farther west where open land was still available and where second-stage Valdris settlements were then created.[17]

The Spring Grove Norwegians also participated in this process. In 1865 six families that had originally emigrated from two parishes in Hallingdal moved from Spring Grove to a second-stage settlement that became known as Big Grove near Brooten in southwestern Stearns County. Others from Spring Grove and from Hallingdal followed, with Spring Grove acting as a mother settlement for Hallings who stopped there for a time before pushing farther west. Hallings made up nearly 70% of the foreign-born members of the Big Grove Norwegian Lutheran Church. Some 10% hailed from mountainous Telemark, whose earliest representatives had reached Spring Grove from Winnebago County, Wisconsin, about the same time as the Rock County Hallings, and about 20% had been born in other parts of Norway.[18]

The latter were frequently lured to the new settlements by notices in Norwegian-language newspapers praising their prospects. In 1860, for example, when an article in *Emigranten* (The Emigrant) praised Blue Earth County's attributes, subsequent issues contained inquiries about land there. The reply of a Linden settler undoubtedly influenced some to go to this region near the big bend of the Minnesota River. Thus, while the early communities remained heavily Norwegian, the addition of migrants from various places in Norway combined with newspapers and other pan-Norwegian agencies to bring about the gradual loss of Old Country regional exclusiveness.[19]

Big Grove and Spring Grove faced these changes with little overt conflict. Other communities were not so fortunate. In one, tensions developed between a group of Hallings, who were in the majority, and people from the Trondheim region, who constituted a tiny minority. It seemed to at least two Trønders that the Hallings "kind of liked to have the upper hand" and that the Halling kids in the parochial school asserted their "superiority" over the others. Such tensions were often tied to socioeconomic differences, since the regional group that arrived first frequently acquired greater wealth and status. Certain periods also involved bitter theological disputes among Norwegians, which led one scholar to assert that if rural travelers "saw two churches close together, preferably one on each side of the road, they were sure to be in the heart of a Norwegian settlement."[20]

During the early period such settlements were usually situated in or near wooded areas and on streams or lakes, for the Norwegians regarded the prairies as less fertile because they lacked trees. Moreover, since there were no trees, how would one build a house or secure fuel, and what would break the force of the winds to provide protection during storms? The myth of the Great Plains as a desert led Norwegians as well as other groups to fear the treeless areas. It remained for Paul Hjelm-Hansen to convince his fellow countrymen that the prairies were indeed desirable.[21]

Hjelm-Hansen arrived in the United States in 1867 at the age of 57. An experienced newspaperman, he went to work for *Fædrelandet og Emigranten* (The Fatherland and the Emigrant), a Norwegian-American journal published at La Crosse, Wisconsin. In a series of articles Hjelm-Hansen "emphasized the danger in so many of the emigrants remaining in the city to which their train ticket had taken them." Reflecting the Norwegian penchant for life on the soil, he argued that the surplus labor available in the cities would prevent workers from getting ahead and keep them forever poor. Life as a farmer in Minnesota, he said, was the best option. Lars K. Aaker of Alexandria, a legislator who was also president of the Scandinavian Emigrant Society, organized in 1869, was impressed by Hjelm-Hansen's warnings. Through Aaker the journalist was appointed by Governor William R. Marshall in 1869 as a special agent to encourage Norwegian settlement in Minnesota areas where government land was still available.[22]

Traveling about the state in the summer of 1869, Hjelm-Hansen became "particularly enthusiastic" about the lands of the Red River Valley, which he thought "were best for the Scandinavian immigrants." In dispatches carried by Norwegian-language papers in Minneapolis and La Crosse, he predicted accurately: "Concerning the problem of settlement, it is not only my opinion but that of all who have seen this part of the country, that it presents so many advantages for Scandinavian farmers that immigrants are likely to stream in here within the next year, that this tract of land will in ten years be built up and under cultivation, and that it then will become one of the richest and most beautiful regions in America. The soil is fertile to the highest degree and is exceptionally easy to cultivate, for there is not so much as a stone or a stump in the way of a plow." Hjelm-Hansen's advocacy, coupled with the penetration of the St. Paul and Pacific Railroad into the area in the early 1870s, was instrumental in encouraging the migration which made the Red River Valley the third major Norwegian settlement area in the state.[23]

Following the patterns already described for the southeast, groups from various earlier Norwegian regions took up land on the fertile prairies of the valley. In 1870, for example, people who had emigrated originally from Telemark read Hjelm-Hansen's reports, left Mound Prairie in Houston County, and traveled for two months to reach the Red River Valley. With the help of several earlier settlers, they found satisfactory land on the Buffalo River in Clay County northwest of Glyndon. The first winter was long, but life was brightened by one or two letters a week from neighbors and friends in Houston County as well as by the magazine *Ved Arnen* (By the Hearth) published at Decorah, Iowa. In 1871 news came from a former next-door neighbor in Houston County announcing that he was planning to move to the valley. By June, 1871, 34 more Telemarkings had arrived from Mound Prairie. "Now we had quite a settlement . . . ," one of them recalled, "and the funny part of it was that all of these settlers . . . here so far had emigrated from the same district in Old Norway, and that was the cause of . . . this Township being named after Moland Prestegjeld Fyresdal, Norway." To this day Moland Township is peopled by Norwegian Americans.[24]

Major settlement of the Red River Valley got under way in 1871 as wagon trains slowly moved to the open lands. Levi Thortvedt, one of the early Moland Township Norwegians, could remember the passing of as many as 20 trains of covered wagons a day, with cattle and sheep driven along behind. The 1875 state census reported that about 55% of the foreign-born residents and 30% of the total population of Polk and Clay counties had emigrated from Norway. Many of these people had moved from southeastern Minnesota, as had the Thortvedt party in 1870. In the next decade the Northern Pacific and Great Northern railroads became important, carrying thousands of immigrants throughout the valley and into the Dakotas. In Marshall County, for example, Norwegians followed the railroad rights of way to concentrate near Warren, Argyle, Stephen, and in New Folden Township, where the Marshall County Skandinaviske Mutual Fire Insurance Company had its headquarters. Later, about the turn of the century, more emigrated directly from Norway, until by 1905 some 57.5% of the people of Marshall, Clay, Norman, and Polk counties had either been born in Norway or were the children of those who had (see Map 11.4).[25]

The Red River Valley was the last Minnesota agricultural region to be developed as well as that most heavily settled by Norwegians. The four counties of Clay, Marshall, Norman, and Polk exhibited at least 84 Norwegian place names compared to only 19 in Fillmore and Goodhue counties in the southeast. Norman County in fact may have been named for the many Norse or "Norman" residents. Later they also spread into nearby Red Lake, Grant, Pennington, Kittson, and Roseau counties.

Because they were frequently the earliest and the most numerous group, Norwegians established the valley's churches and often dominated its businesses and local affairs. To the northeast in Badger, Roseau County, for example, the Norwegian-owned Scandinavian-American Bank served both Norwegians and Swedes. In Thief River Falls in Pennington County, the local chapter of the Sons of Norway was instrumental in convincing the school board to add a Scandinavian-language course in the high school. During the anti-immigrant hysteria of World War I, Sheriff Ole A. Rice of Roseau County, himself of Norwegian descent, assured all foreign-born residents that "they need not fear invasion of

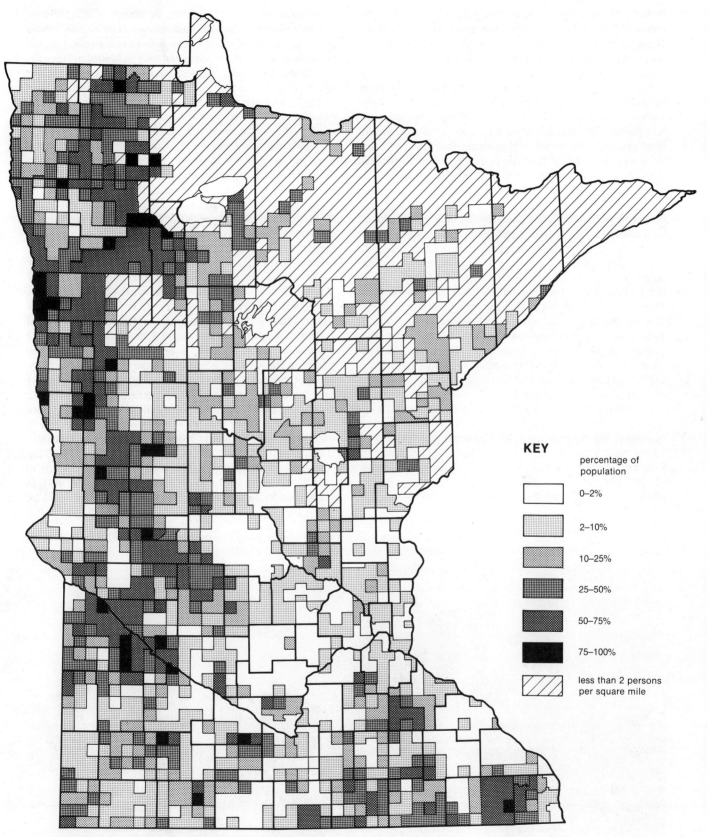

KEY

percentage of
population

☐ 0–2%

▨ 2–10%

▨ 10–25%

▨ 25–50%

■ 50–75%

■ 75–100%

▨ less than 2 persons
per square mile

Map 11.4. Norwegians in Minnesota Rural Areas, 1905

their rights" or confiscation of their property. The predominance of Norwegians permitted the maintenance of various Norwegian cultural elements and the persistence of the language in portions of the Red River Valley into the 1970s and 1980s.[26]

Norwegian Americans settled in all of Minnesota's major agricultural regions. Whether they took land in the hilly, wooded southeast, the lake-filled Park Region, the flat, treeless plains of the Red River Valley, or the rolling prairies of southern and southwestern Minnesota, they were fulfilling what was perceived at the time as a widespread Norwegian desire to farm. Speaking in 1916, Nicolay A. Grevstad, former editor of Chicago's influential newspaper *Skandinaven* (The Scandinavian), stressed the Norwegian immigrant's propensity to make "a bee-line from the little plot of ground on a hillside in Norway to the princely 160 acres waiting for him in the west," where he reaped "a rich reward." According to Grevstad, at that time foreign-born Norwegian-American farmers owned an estimated 11,000,000 acres in the United States worth about $650,000,000. One-third of them lived in Minnesota. And the well-known Norwegian love of the soil carried over to the second generation, for even more of its members (54.3%) farmed than did the first-comers. Moreover a larger percentage of them remained rural dwellers than of any other ethnic group. In 1920, 52% of the Norwegian born and 65.4% of their descendants resided in rural areas of the United States.[27]

As Minnesota's portion of the Red River Valley filled up, Norwegian farmers headed farther west to North Dakota, Montana, Washington, and the Canadian prairies. Spring Grove again reflected the general pattern, as 100 residents joined a colony that set out for North Dakota in the summer of 1886. The early Norwegian exodus had begun in part as an attempt to escape urbanizing Norway. So many Norwegian

immigrants flocked to the fertile farmlands of the Midwest that by 1910 they were the most agriculturally inclined ethnic group in the nation. Many were able to live a rural life that would have been denied them had they remained in Norway. Ironically, however, Norwegian immigrants saw greater urbanization in the new land than at home. While about half of the Norwegian born and 63% of their children lived in rural America in 1900, in Norway nearly two-thirds were still rural dwellers — a proportion made possible by the numbers who had emigrated from the Old Country in the 19th century. Even in Clay County in the heart of the Red River Valley, the number of Norwegians living in villages increased while those on farms declined between 1885 and 1895. By no means did all Norwegian immigrants to the state choose to farm. Urban areas — especially the Twin Cities for those in the Upper Midwest — began to offer more occupational opportunities as industries grew and good land for farming became scarcer.[28]

Norwegian Americans also worked as lumberjacks in the pine forests of northern Minnesota, where they might have earned $25 to $30 a month in the cold winter seasons of the 1880s. Others became part of the small community of Duluth, which in 1870 numbered 3,131 souls of whom 242 were Norwegians. By 1900, over 7,500 native-born and foreign-born Norwegians were listed in the city (see Table 11.2). Some of the men became fish merchants there, while others used their considerable skills, experience, and Norwegian methods to pioneer commercial fishing along the north shore of Lake Superior in the 1870s and 1880s. Concentrated in such small, predominantly Norwegian villages as Tofte and Hovland, Norwegians increased from nearly 50% of the commercial fishermen along the north shore and in Duluth in 1895 to between 80% and 90% of the 276 people in that occupation in 1920. Catching largely herring that could be

A HIGH PERCENTAGE of Norwegian settlers became farmers as did this family, who lived near Hendricks in Lincoln County about 1880. This photograph revealed the immigrants' success to folks in the Old Country.

Table 11.2. Norwegians in Minnesota's Three Major Cities, 1880–1970

	1880	1890	1895	1900	1905	1910	1920	1930	1940	1950	1970*
Minneapolis											
foreign born	2,651	12,624	12,275	11,532	14,953	16,401	16,389	15,492	11,777	8,568	2,219
foreign mixed		6,176		22,183		17,870	24,901	33,917			15,202
St. Paul											
fb	664	3,521	2,966	2,900	4,155	4,063	3,818	3,414	2,548	1,692	367
fm		2,228		6,144		5,321	6,732	9,023			4,741
Duluth											
fb			3,580	2,655	3,968	5,009	4,823	4,163	3,251	2,410	848
fm				4,909			6,106	7,569			3,838

Source: See Appendix

*Norwegian-language mother-tongue statistics for 1970 allow some distinction between second and third generation Norwegian Americans — one of the few ways in which the third generation is documented in the census. By that measure Minneapolis had 10,481 second generation and 5,967 third generation American-born people who had grown up hearing Norwegian spoken in their homes; St. Paul's equivalent figures were 2,814 second generation and 1,969 third generation.

sold to their countrymen throughout the Midwest, these immigrants subsisted on a combination of fishing and farming, maintaining a life-style that had its roots in the Old Country. Late in the 19th century and early in the 20th, other Norwegian immigrants arrived in northern Minnesota to work in the iron mines. There they found not only ready employment but also a chance to move up in the mining company hierarchies.[29]

Urbanization in Norway was reflected in altered emigration patterns. Beginning in the mid-1880s Norwegian emigration was no longer composed primarily of peasant families. Like the urban centers of the United States, Norway's cities were providing more work opportunities as industrialization raised the country's standard of living. Its gross national product increased by 150% in the 40 years before World War I, while its population grew only 35%. But Norwegian cities

not only received in-migrants, they also sent emigrants abroad: more than half the Norwegians who arrived in the United States between 1900 and 1910 were unmarried city dwellers. Nearly two-thirds were men between the ages of 15 and 25. Their reasons for emigrating were still largely economic, but fewer intended to become permanent residents of the New World. Where once the immigrants sailed aboard a creaking wooden ship on an Atlantic crossing that took months, they could now make the trip more swiftly, safely, and cheaply on comfortable steamships. Lower fares made the journey more affordable for larger numbers of people. They could go to Minneapolis for a few years, earn higher wages in Minnesota despite Norway's increasing standard of living, accumulate funds to invest in Norway, and then return as three-fourths of the remigrants to Norway did in 1920 after a stay of from two to nine years abroad. In short, the

PULLING IN a catch about 1923 along the north shore of Lake Superior, where many of the fishermen were of Norwegian birth or descent.

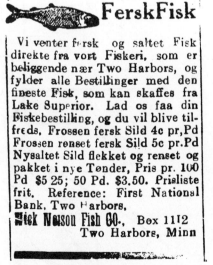

FerskFisk

Vi venter fersk og saltet Fisk direkte fra vort Fiskeri, som er beliggende nær Two Harbors, og fylder alle Bestillinger med den fineste Fisk, som kan skaffes fra Lake Superior. Lad os faa din Fiskebestilling, og du vil blive tilfreds. Frossen fersk Sild 4c pr.Pd Frossen renset fersk Sild 5c pr.Pd Nysaltet Sild flekket og renset og pakket i nye Tønder, Pris pr. 100 Pd $5 25; 50 Pd. $3.50. Prisliste frit. Reference: First National Bank, Two Harbors.

Nick Nelson Fish Co., Box 1112
Two Harbors, Minn

THE ADVERTISEMENT for "Fresh Fish" from Two Harbors on the north shore appeared in Folkets Röst, *a Norwegian-language newspaper published at Minneapolis on June 13, 1925.*

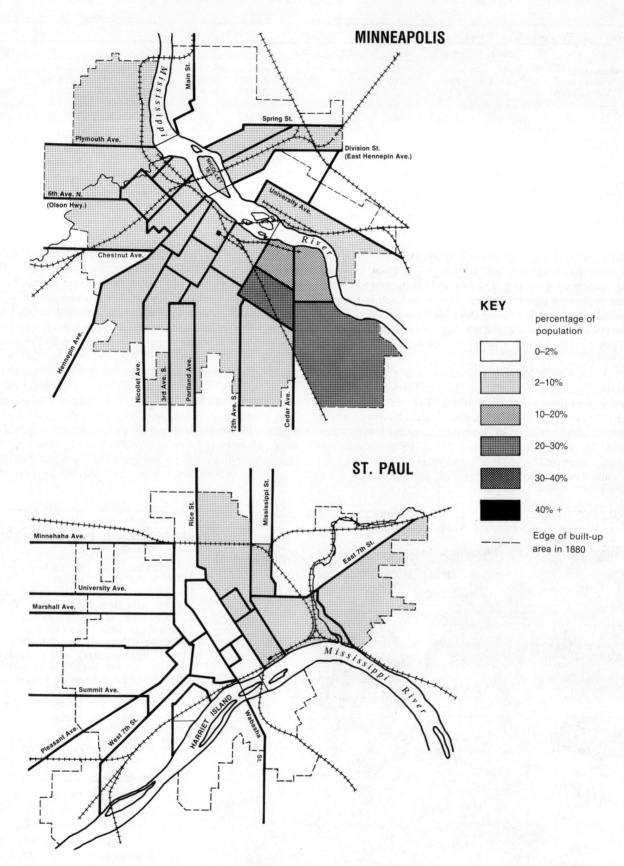

Map 11.5. Norwegians in the Twin Cities, 1880

KEY

percentage of population

0–2%

2–10%

10–20%

20–30%

30–40%

40% +

Edge of built-up area in 1880

later Norwegian immigrants, like those from southern and eastern Europe, did not intend to remain for life; they could more easily go back to the homeland, and many did.[30]

The Urbanization of Norwegian Americans

Once these immigrants arrived in the 1890s and early 1900s, they gravitated to the cities, where they joined migrating rural Norwegian Americans. It was in this period that Minneapolis assumed its pre-eminence as the country's major Norwegian metropolis. Calling it the second largest Scandinavian city in the world, Lincoln Steffens wrote in 1903 that Minneapolis consisted of "a Yankee with a round Puritan head, an open prairie heart, and a great, big Scandinavian body."[31]

Norwegian immigration to the Twin Cities of Minneapolis and St. Paul had occurred as early as the 1850s, but the major influx began between 1880 and 1890. In 1880, 11.3% of the state's total population but only 5.3% of its Norwegians lived in the Twin Cities (see Map 11.5). Soon, however, they constituted the third largest foreign-born group in Minneapolis after the Swedes and the British, increasing fivefold in ten years. By 1890 Minneapolis had replaced Chicago as the principal destination of Scandinavian immigrants to the United States. By then Minneapolis and St. Paul included almost 23% of all Minnesotans and 16% of the Norwegian born. The Norwegians were urbanizing rapidly, but their fellow Minnesotans continued to flock to the cities at a greater rate. In absolute numbers there were 3,315 foreign-born Norwegians in the Twin Cities in 1880; the figure was 16,145 ten years later. By 1910 Minneapolis alone had 16,401, nearly 16% of all the Norwegian born in the state (see Table 11.2).[32]

According to one author, Norwegians in 1914 controlled 4 of the city's 27 banks, 13 of 26 musical organizations, 15 of 100 newspapers and periodicals, and 23 of 195 churches, while several of the 110 hotels were Norwegian-run, and 37 of 500 doctors were Norwegian. Norwegian and other Scandinavian merchants in Minneapolis were centered on Washington Avenue South. About 1880 their grocery stores, undertaking parlors, and furniture showrooms were concentrated at or near the corner of 11th Avenue South and Washington Avenue, within walking distance of the Norwegian residential community. The latter included "Noah's Ark," a 60-apartment building covering an entire square block at 12th Avenue and 2nd Street South. As they did in rural Minnesota, new arrivals frequently lived with earlier immigrants until they found work, often in the nearby flour mills and sawmills. Thus, as one put it, "It sometimes happened that families which had been close neighbors in Norway became next door neighbors in Noah's Ark."[33]

During the 1880s the Norwegian enclave shifted farther up Washington Avenue to Cedar Avenue, later known as "Snoose Boulevard" because of the large consumption of snuff by its Scandinavian residents. This development was hastened by the establishment of the Scandia Bank in 1883 on the corner of Cedar and 4th Street South. To be near the new bank, many Norwegian merchants relocated in the Cedar-Riverside area, and soon nearly all the businesses there were operated by Scandinavians, many of them

Norwegians. The community continued its southward movement, so that in later years South Minneapolis, predominantly Swedish, also became the major domain of Norwegian Americans and their institutions, although some were also to be found in other sections of the city.[34]

Certain patterns of urban settlement were much like rural ones. Relatives and friends often lodged together in the same households, and remittances eased the cost of making the journey to Minnesota. But the Minneapolis Norwegian community differed in several important ways from its rural Minnesota counterparts. For one thing, even the most compact block of Norwegians in the city mingled with other nationalities, occupations, and classes. In the 1890s Ward 11, stretching along the Mississippi from 6th Street to 24th Street South, contained more Norwegians than any other. Nevertheless in 1895 they made up only 15.9% of the population. As a result, Norwegians were more likely to interact with other ethnic groups, particularly Swedes or Danes, than they were in a homogeneous rural settlement like Spring Grove.

In the 1880s and 1890s many Minneapolis secular organizations in which Norwegians took part were Scandinavian rather than exclusively Norwegian. Among those listed by a local historian were the Scandinavian Labor and Benefit Society, the Scandinavian Lutheran Temperance Society, the Scandinavian Old Settlers Society, the Scandinavian Brass Band, as well as numerous singing, athletic, and dramatic groups. Ethnic labels were often imprecise in urban areas; the same writer recalled a club, known as *Den Norske Gutteforening* (Norwegian Boys' Association), which flourished in his childhood neighborhood. To its members, he said, all non-Scandinavian children were referred to as "Irish," while members of the Norwegian club were regarded as "Swedes" by the non-Scandinavian residents.[35]

While the city seems to have blurred national origins in this instance, its greater occupational diversity was a powerful factor in creating more pronounced class differences. The duties of a farm owner and his hired hand were often similar,

URBAN NORWEGIANS were responsible for starting Lutheran Deaconess Hospital in Minneapolis. This photograph was taken about 1890.

but in the city a Norwegian might be a common laborer or a bank president. It is unlikely that the members of the Scandinavian Labor and Benefit Society, which published *Arbeidets Ridder* (Knights of Labor) in 1886–87 and became a unit of the national labor organization of the same name, associated regularly with members of the Scandia Club, an exclusive Scandinavian group formed in the mid-1880s. When singer Christina Nilsson visited the city from Europe in 1886, her reception was "an exclusive affair" attended by the Scandinavian "high life," who deliberately failed to invite large numbers of working-class Norwegians.[36]

Further diversity in the Norwegian community was provided in the 1880s and 1890s by a lively group of intellectuals in Minneapolis. Among them were Kristofer N. and Drude Janson and Knut Hamsun. Janson, author and Unitarian minister who founded several congregations during his 12 years in the state, was sympathetic to such then-radical ideas as Socialism and the "social gospel." His wife, Drude, was a novelist and an ardent feminist. Hamsun, who lived for a time with the Jansons in the 1880s, returned to Norway, where he, too, became a well-known author and the winner of a Nobel prize for literature. A frequent correspondent and mentor of the group was Bjørnstjerne Bjørnson, iconoclastic writer, poet, and champion of causes, whose career would bring him world fame. Bjørnson spent a short time lecturing in the United States in 1880–81 and came to know the Janson circle in Minneapolis.[37]

As in rural areas, factions of the Norwegian-American urban community violently disagreed over the course they should follow. The intellectuals, for example, were regarded with disdain by Lutheran church people because of the Unitarianism of the Jansons and their associates. Both of those groups, however, felt the "saloon element" to be disreputable and manipulable by machine politicians. In addition to ethical cleavages, regional differences split Twin Cities Norwegian Americans. The smaller North Minneapolis enclave, for example, regarded their countrymen in South Minneapolis as arrogant and elitist.[38]

One urban organization that crossed economic, class, and occupational lines and served various purposes over the years was the fraternal society. Like the Lutheran churches of rural areas, the fraternal society in the cities provided a place to meet and exchange news. Like the early churches, too, lodges were often formed by immigrants who hailed from the same region in Norway. Such was the case with the Sons of Norway, one of the largest and best-known Norwegian-American groups in the 1980s, which had its beginnings in a small Norwegian concentration in North Minneapolis in 1895. Of its 18 founders at least nine were born in the Trøndelag district of Norway and six were from the parish of Selbu there. Begun in a period of severe national financial panic, the group provided insurance and fostered Norwegian culture in the United States. As later lodges came into being in South Minneapolis near the core of the city's Norwegian settlement, the organization also spread to other communities. Both its fraternal and insurance purposes retained their importance.[39]

Nevertheless the Sons of Norway remained an urban institution. Distrust of "city slickers" selling insurance and of "secret societies" was so great a deterrent to securing a large following in the countryside that in 1903 its general secretary warned against organizing lodges in small places. Instead the rural counterparts of such secular organizations were the *bygdelag* (district societies) composed of immigrants from particular areas in Norway, such as Valdres or Sogn. These two parallel lines of development produced occasional clashes between those who wished to maintain the rural Norwegian culture represented by the *bygdelag*, and those who wished to become part of the more urbanized, pan-Norwegian heritage represented by the Sons of Norway. It should be noted, however, that the *bygdelag* were also active in the cities; they continued to function there and in rural areas in the 1980s.[40]

Institutional Development

The movement of Norwegian immigrants to the city not only changed occupational patterns and blurred regional and national identifications, it also influenced the social and cultural emphases of community development. The increasing numbers of Norwegian Americans demanded more efficient and often larger institutions, while improved standards of living made possible a more varied supply of goods and services. As a result, the Minnesota Norwegian-American community produced not only church synods and colleges, but newspapers, political organizations, literature, and art. The development of this cultural structure did not mean that organizational conflicts ended. Indeed disagreements among those with varying theological, class, occupational, and political viewpoints continued to occur within that structure.

A case in point can be found in the Norwegian Lutheran church. In 1914 Waldemar T. Ager, the editor of a Norwegian-language newspaper, maintained that the "large and affluent Norwegian-American family had only two children, and both were well nourished. The two were church and politics." Strong, sometimes violent, controversies frequently raged over the first "child," the church. Coming from an at least nominally united state church in Norway, Lutheran Norwegians in the United States quickly split into synods in what one scholar called "the first enterprise that can be called Norwegian-American."[41]

The synods reflected differing theological viewpoints rooted in both the Norwegian and American cultural landscapes. The Evangelical Lutheran Church in America, which emphasized the "low church," pietistic teachings of Hans Nielsen Hauge, was founded in 1846. The views of the state church of Norway were evident in the Norwegian Evangelical Church in America (later referred to as the Norwegian Synod), which was founded in 1853 by wealthier *bonde* immigrants. Later disagreements over the degree of "low church" tendencies, the relations of Norwegian Lutherans with other nationalities, and personal politics resulted in the creation of additional synods. By 1876 there were five in the United States, and "each charged the others with failure to represent the true teaching or spirit of Lutheranism." Nevertheless it is possible that the multiplication led to a stronger Lutheranism among Norwegians. The ability to join a church that reflected one's personal theological proclivities kept many in the fold who otherwise, like the Swedes, might have joined such churches as the Baptists or Methodists in greater numbers.[42]

The theological diversity can be suggested by the gigantic controversy over the doctrine of election that rocked the high-church Norwegian Evangelical Synod in the 1880s. Before it was over, 92 congregations in Minnesota alone were involved, and in the tumult 23 of them split to form new churches. The latter then united with two other synods to establish the United Norwegian Lutheran Church in 1890. The movement toward union culminated on June 9, 1917, when the pietistic Hauge Synod, the Norwegian Evangelical Synod, and the United Church officially merged to form the Norwegian Lutheran Church in America. In 1930 in Minneapolis the Norwegian church joined some other Lutheran groups to become the American Lutheran Church.[43]

With so many Norwegian congregations sprouting in the Midwest, early pastors decided that some means of educating a clergy were needed on American soil. Norwegian-American colleges, a second major institutional development, were thus given impetus by the various Lutheran groups. In 1857 the Norwegian Evangelical Synod endorsed a recommendation for the establishment of a Norwegian professorship at Concordia Seminary, a German-Lutheran school in St. Louis, Missouri. When the German Lutherans declined to take a stand against slavery, however, Norwegian Lutherans in 1861 formed their own seminary, which became Luther College in Decorah, Iowa.[44]

The numerous synods, each desiring a place where the "true" doctrine would be taught, went on to found four other surviving Norwegian-American schools in Minnesota. St. Olaf College in Northfield had its beginnings in 1874 as an academy under the leadership of the Reverend Bernt J. Muus. By 1886 it was being transformed into a college, eventually sponsored by the United Church. Augsburg Seminary moved from Marshall, Wisconsin, to Minneapolis in 1872; by 1897 in another of the many splits Norwegian Lutheranism was prey to, the Lutheran Free Church was organized with Augsburg College as its institution of learning. Concordia College in Moorhead began as an academy affiliated with the United Church in 1891. By 1914 it, too, had become a four-year college. Red Wing Seminary was founded in 1879 to serve the Hauge Synod. In 1903 it added a college, which merged with St. Olaf in 1917. The same year its seminary merged with Luther Theological Seminary, which had been started in St. Paul in 1900 by the United Church. Moreover, through the urging of Truls Paulson, a Norwegian serving in the legislature from Spring Grove, a Scandinavian department was started at the University of Minnesota in 1884.

Although many were founded to educate pastors, the church schools quickly evolved into colleges where Norwegian Americans, whether working toward the ministry or not, could find liberal educations. The desire of Norwegians to invest heavily in education spurred them in this direction. One Lutheran leader was amazed at how ready Norwegian parents were "to sacrifice and to suffer that their children may have an education." He "actually saw," he said, "large families living in sod shacks on the open prairie" who were sending a boy or girl to Concordia College at Moorhead.[45]

A third major institution developed by the early immigrants was the Norwegian-language press. Like the synods, the press functioned as a "steadying point . . . to weld these people together in common interests, to give reality to the geographically nebulous concept of a 'Norwegian America.'" Initially the founding of healthy newspapers among the Norwegians was difficult. The immigrants were poor, and few had regularly read papers in Norway. After the Civil War, however, their growth accelerated. Between 1865 and 1914 some 400 to 500 Norwegian-language newspapers and magazines existed at one time or another. The earliest one in the United States was *Nordlyset* (Northern Light), launched at Norway, Wisconsin, in 1847.[46]

The first of at least 115 such periodicals known to have been published in Minnesota was *Folkets Röst* (People's Voice) issued in St. Paul in 1857–58. The last of them, *Minnesota Posten* (Minnesota Post), ran from 1897 until it closed its doors in Minneapolis in 1979. At least 45 journals were headquartered in Minneapolis over the years, 10 in St. Paul, and 8 in Fergus Falls. Among the long-lived Minneapolis papers and magazines were: the weekly *Budstikken* (The Messenger) 1873–94, which then merged with *Fædrelandet og Emigranten* (The Fatherland and the Emigrant) to form *Minneapolis Tidende* (Times), which began as a daily in 1887 and continued into the 1930s; *Folkebladet* (People's Paper) 1880–1930, *Nye Normanden* (New Norseman) 1894–1922, *Skandinavisk Farmer Journal* 1883–1910, *Ugebladet* (Weekly Paper) 1886 or 1890 to 1929 or 1931, and *Ungdommens Ven* (Youth's Friend) 1890–1916. The last merged with *Kvindens* (Women's) *Magasin* in 1919 to form *Familiens* (Family's) *Magasin*, which ceased publication in 1928. St. Paul's *Nordvesten* (The Northwest) ran from 1881 to 1907, *Ugeblad* (Weekly Paper) of Fergus Falls, which was sometimes spelled *Ukeblad*, from 1882 to 1946, and *Duluth Skandinav* from 1887 to 1965.[47]

Over the century, newspapers and magazines served the Minnesota Norwegian community not only from these cities but also from bases of varying stability in Albert Lea (5), Crookston (4), Duluth (4), Madison (3), Moorhead (3), Northfield (3), Red Wing (4), Rochester (2), Sacred Heart (3), and St. Cloud (2). More than 20 additional Minnesota towns, including Spring Grove, had at least one Norwegian newspaper.

The immigrant press has been called a "clearing house for immigrant thought as well as a round-robin letter," for it provided both news of Norway and reports from American settlements. For the immigrants, the press helped preserve and even accentuate ties to the Old Country, while it also served as "a kind of composite America letter . . . for the common people of Norway." Articles about various settlements and the availability of land near them served as a link to tie the scattered communities together while at the same time drawing more immigrants to them. "Let them come — not only from the Old World but also from the East. There is room here for them all," trumpeted *Nordisk Folkeblad* (Nordic People's Paper, Minneapolis) on April 2, 1868, expressing an attitude frequently voiced in that period.[48]

The papers also acted as a forum for ideas. The Lutheran church used them to discuss moral and theological questions, including whether a wife owed complete obedience to her husband. As time went on, other topics such as temperance, the virtues of public schools versus Norwegian-language parochial schools, and the transition of immigrants to Americans continued to be debated. *Nordisk Folkeblad*, probably the earliest widely influential Norwegian paper in the state (1868–75), attempted to unite Scandinavians in various causes. As early as 1869 it led a campaign to elect Hans Mattson, a Swede, as Minnesota's first Scandinavian secretary of state. *The North*, an English-language paper published in Minneapolis from 1889 to 1894, was founded by Luth Jaeger, a Norwegian, to aid in Americanizing Scandinavians there. Other papers, such as *Minneapolis Tidende* and *Reform* (Eau Claire, Wis.) worked to maintain links with the homeland or to help develop a distinctive Norwegian-American culture.[49]

More noticeable in later years, however, was the papers' allegiance to the two major parties and to such third-party movements as the Populists or Prohibitionists. At election time political debates filled the pages, relegating other issues to the background. Norwegian editorials tended to support reform and the rights of labor and farmers. The *Fergus Falls Ugeblad*, a Populist journal, "declared that oil and coal lands should be nationalized." Socialist papers in Minneapolis such as *Gaa Paa!* (Forward) and Janson's *Saamanden* (The Sower) defended strikers, as did *Nordvesten*, a Republican, business-oriented paper based in St. Paul.[50]

Aided by an active press, politics — Norwegian America's second "child" — was particularly well nourished in Minnesota. That Norwegian Americans are assured a prominent place in the state's political pantheon is evident on the grounds of the Minnesota Capitol. Of the three political figures immortalized in statues there, two — Floyd B. Olson and Knute Nelson — were of Norwegian descent. The careers of these two men point up the diversity of the Norwegian political heritage. Knute Nelson served as a staid Republican congressman in the 1880s, governor in the 1890s, and United States senator from 1895 until his death in 1923, the longest Senate record of any Minnesotan thus far — becoming increasingly conservative throughout his career. In contrast, Olson, a popular three-term governor during the Great Depression, remarked in 1934, "I am frank to say I am what I want to be. I am a radical."[51]

One way to understand the success of Norwegian Americans as leaders of various parties is to look to the activism that was a part of their heritage. This explanation emphasizes the *bonde* movement, which represented the rural middle class in Norway, as one which lent itself well to political transplant to Minnesota's rural areas. Unlike many European peasant groups, Norway's freeholding *bønder* had never been serfs and "had remained defiantly independent through the centuries." They were represented in Norway's parliament, which they had helped to form, and they did not hesitate to raise their voices as leaders of various reform efforts there. Moreover in Norway they had also gained experience in working together in agricultural co-operatives and other rural communal groups.[52]

During the initial period of settlement following the Civil War, Norwegian voters in the United States were loyal to the Republican party — the party of "free land, free soil, and free men." By the 1880s, however, Norwegian communities in Minnesota were beginning to support Norwegian candidates and to object to the Yankee dominance of Republican politics, which reflected the urban capitalism of the era rather than communal rural values. In response, Norwegians throughout the Upper Midwest organized Viking leagues to obtain greater political impact. As the president of the Minnesota league put it in 1899, the immigrants needed "to teach the silk stocking, blue blood Yankees that the Scandinavians are not descendents of the lower conditions of nature."[53]

The first "great political clash" between the Norwegian and Yankee elements in the state's Republican party occurred in 1882 when Knute Nelson became the first person of Norwegian birth to be elected to the United States Congress. He represented the fifth district of western Minnesota in the House until 1889. Thereafter various political parties found it to their advantage to nominate Norwegian — or Scandinavian — candidates. By 1914 the power of Norwegians to draw votes was well established. From the 1850s to 1914 six from Minnesota had been elected to Congress, 68 had been elected or appointed to judgeships or various other state offices, 259 had served in the Minnesota legislature, and 893 had held county offices. Norwegians had proportionally higher representation in many Minnesota legislatures than did members of other large ethnic groups, such as Swedes and Germans.[54]

With the growth of the Viking leagues and hard times in the late 19th century, Norwegian allegiance to the Republican party began to splinter as the party adopted the garb of industrial capitalism and big business. Among the Norwegian farmers of southeastern Minnesota, this new image proved less threatening than it was for those in the Red River Valley. By the closing decades of the century southeastern farmers had shifted from one-crop agriculture to diversified corn, dairy, or livestock farming, which was more easily adaptable to changing economic conditions. For them the Republican emphasis on business was less uncomfortable, balanced as it was by what they viewed as the party's "correct" stand on such moral issues as temperance. For those in the Red River Valley, still largely tied to single-crop wheat farming, the situation was different. Unregulated grain prices and discriminatory railroad rates controlled the wheat farmer's income and his transportation costs.

Some were attracted to political groups such as the Prohibitionist party, which adopted Republican party moral stands but rejected its economic views. More, however, abandoned the Republicans to join first the Farmers' Alliance and later the Populist party. In 1890, for example, an estimated 25,000 Norwegian-born Minnesotans voted for Sidney M. Owen, the Farmers' Alliance candidate for governor. Explaining the defection, a Norman County man wrote that "The Republican party started with good principles and the farmers followed," but it had now "ruined us as a class of people, and by putting party before men they have been able to elect millionaires and railroad agents."[55]

To stem the tide, the Republicans in 1892 nominated

Norwegian-born Knute Nelson of Alexandria for governor — a tactic that did not set well with all of the voters. One of them wrote Nelson that "The silk stocking element in the Republican party has always opposed you until now. I do not think that they love you now." He added that Nelson had been "selected" to bring in the Norwegian vote, but the "most bitter opposition you will meet will be from Norwegians." But Nelson won, probably with significant Norwegian help. Republican dominance was, however, shattered in the Red River Valley. The Farmers' Alliance-Populist party remained strong among Norwegians there because many felt the Republican position was inimical to their way of life.[56]

Like the farmers, Norwegian urban dwellers in the Twin Cities also abandoned the Republican party. In the 1890s and early 1900s some switched to the Democrats, probably thanks to the influence of Norwegian-born Lars M. Rand, a Democratic machine politician and Minneapolis alderman from the Cedar-Riverside area. Others participated in the growth of "agrarian radicalism." In the 1890 election defections from the Republicans to the Farmers' Alliance were (with one exception) most obvious in the heavily Scandinavian wards of Minneapolis. A student of this political phenomenon concluded that "Populism, despite its constant appeals for labor support, apparently received, not a labor vote, but a Scandinavian vote, in Minneapolis and St. Paul — the largest cities in which the Populists made a strong showing."[57]

Norwegians in the Red River Valley and the Twin Cities retained their penchant for third-party movements, while those in the rural areas of southeastern Minnesota remained predominantly loyal Republicans. After the demise of the Populist party in 1896, Norwegian Americans in North Dakota and western Minnesota became active in the Nonpartisan League, a radical farmer-labor movement during World War I which led to the development of the Farmer-Labor party in the 1920s. Under its banners Floyd B. Olson, an urban, part-Norwegian American, and Elmer A. Benson, a rural one whose father and mother were both immigrants, became successive governors of the state from 1931 to 1939.[58]

The differing political preferences of Norwegian Americans in these three Minnesota regions can be explained in terms of their reactions to varying economic conditions. But the chronology of immigration and the background in Norway should also be acknowledged. Those in the southeast, who were satisfied with their farming operations, had immigrated earlier, had experienced a longer period to adapt to American economic and social conditions, and were loathe to leave the Republican party. Those in the west, on the other hand, saw similarities between the big business monopolies in the United States and the urban-class dominance they had known in Norway. Nurtured on the values of a rural Norwegian life-style, Norwegian Americans whose livelihood was threatened by monopoly capitalism revolted and aided in the creation of new grass-roots political parties.[59] Finally, the urban, working-class Norwegian, who was often a migrant from a Minnesota farm, voted for the party he thought best represented his interests. At times this

led him to support the forces of agrarian discontent even though he lived in an urban world.

Literature and Art

While emphasizing Norwegian-American political and religious contributions, Waldemar Ager went on to blame the "two children" — the church and politics — for depriving Norwegian-American literature. He noted that when fiction was mentioned, the answer was "nonsense. Sensible people knew that they had the church and politics — what would one do with books? . . . And so they smothered the brat [of literature], or nearly did."[60] Despite contentions that art and literature were stifled, Norwegian Americans pursued those callings, with Minnesota contributing some of the nation's best-known exponents.

The first novel of Norwegian-American life in the United States was written by Tellef Grundysen of Fillmore County in 1877. Like many others, it was put out in book form only after it had appeared as a newspaper serial. Such early works of fiction concentrated on church issues, temperance, or the rags-to-riches myth of Norwegians in America. Other authors attacked the rich, the Lutheran church, and the Jews. Lars A. Stenholt, for example, produced pulp stories in this vein so popular on trains and newsstands that he is said to have been the only writer of the Norwegian immigrant tradition who made a living from his pen. In time, colleges and literary societies such as the influential Ygdrasil in Madison, Wisconsin, and the Symra Society in Decorah, Iowa, attempted to bring about a flowering of Norwegian-American literature. In Duluth, for example, the enduring Aftenro Society promoted interest in Norwegian literature beginning in 1908; it was still functioning in the 1980s. Output multiplied so that by the mid-1960s about 250 large and small works of fiction and some 120 volumes of poetry had been produced by three generations of Norwegian-American authors, writing in Norwegian or in English.[61]

Two famous writers from Minnesota whose Norwegian backgrounds colored their work in diverse ways were Ole E. Rølvaag and Thorstein Veblen. They were born about 20 years apart on different continents, Veblen in Wisconsin in 1857 and Rølvaag in Norway in 1876. The son of a Norwegian immigrant farmer, Veblen was eight years old when the family moved to virgin land near present Nerstrand in Rice County, Minnesota. Rølvaag immigrated to the United States soon after his 20th birthday. By 1901 he was attending St. Olaf College in Northfield, where he would remain as a teacher for most of his life. Veblen had entered Carleton College, also in Northfield, 27 years earlier. His matriculation in that New England-oriented school launched a career closely tied to the Progressive movement of the early 20th century.[62]

From the publication of his first book, *The Theory of the Leisure Class*, in 1899 until his death 30 years later, Veblen remained an acidic critic of American capitalistic society. David Riesman has emphasized this author's "marginality as a second-generation Norwegian, put off and alienated from the parents' parochial culture but without the ability fully to assimilate and accept the available forms of Americanism."

A more convincing explanation, however, may be found in the influence of the Norwegian *bonde* culture of his father. The son's hatred of business, with its "parasitic" system of credit and distribution and its promotion of "conspicuous consumption," can be related to his dislike of the Norwegian urban classes instilled in him by his father. Despite his inability to fit into the Norwegian-American settlement at Nerstrand and his education at Carleton College and Yale University, Veblen's Norwegian cultural heritage influenced the development of the economic theory for which he is famous.

Rølvaag's career differed greatly from Veblen's. Educated in Norwegian-American academies in South Dakota and Minnesota, he never left Norwegian institutions of learning. Immersed in Norwegian-American culture, his novels and short stories dealt with the Norwegian immigrant and his or her difficulty integrating into American society. His most famous book, *Giants in the Earth*, considered by many to be the finest fictional account of the immigrant experience, was published in Norwegian in Oslo in 1924 and in English translation in the United States in 1927.[63]

Rølvaag believed it essential that the immigrants retain their Norwegian cultural backgrounds, for by leaving Norway, he said, they became strangers — "strangers to the people we forsook and strangers to the people we came to." Although he looked upon immigrants in America as "rootless," he was convinced that assimilation was not desirable. If they tried to become Americans, their strong but "hidden" Old Country cultural forms would give way to an emptier society, which, his biographer said, would resemble a "gilded shell." In Rølvaag's apocalyptic vision, denial or neglect of "the heritage of our fathers" would result in a culture without substance, and eventually America would destroy itself. On the other hand, if the immigrants retained their cultures in the new land, America would develop "a future rich in tradition and progressive in spirit."

The careers of Veblen and Rølvaag were in many ways as different as day and night. Veblen moved into the Ivy League academic world and did not explicitly write of his Norwegian heritage. Rølvaag devoted his life to the maintenance of that heritage. He celebrated his Norwegianness, while Veblen, though moving outside the Norwegian-American community, never escaped the assumptions of *bonde* culture passed on to him by his father. In the end, both men were heavily influenced by their immigrant backgrounds.

Similar forces were at work among notable Minnesotans of Norwegian descent who were active in painting, sculpture, and music. Herbjørn Gausta, "the first professional artist of Norwegian immigrant origin," left Norway when he was 13. Nevertheless his work drew upon his memories of his native Telemark, although he lived in Minneapolis and in rural Fillmore County for most of his life. Jacob H. Fjelde, a noted sculptor, whose son Paul followed in his footsteps, immigrated to Minneapolis in 1887. He brought with him the traditional craftsmanship of Norwegian wood carving augmented by study in Copenhagen and Rome. His final work was a statue of Ole Bull, famed Norwegian violinist, which stands in Loring Park, for many years the site of the annual Norwegian constitution day *syttende mai* (May 17) celebrations in Minneapolis.[64]

F. Melius Christiansen, who immigrated in 1888 as a boy

A SYTTENDE MAI *(May 17) gathering at Ole Bull's statue in Minneapolis' Loring Park in 1935.*

of 17, became head of the music department at St. Olaf College in 1903 and retained the post until his retirement in 1944. During his long career (carried on by his son Olaf), he developed the famous choirs that were largely responsible "for having started the a cappella movement in the United States." In his choral work and in the music he composed, Christiansen drew on the treasury of music within the Norwegian Lutheran church and made it accessible to the millions who heard his St. Olaf choirs on their numerous international tours.

Although such institutions as churches and newspapers, literature, and other arts were initially designed to serve a Norwegian-American audience, some developed a wider following. In so doing, their adaptations have varied greatly. As artists, for example, became less dependent on Norwegian-American patronage, the content of their work often changed so that the Norwegian immigrant experience was less emphasized. It is significant, however, that as the content changed, the basic assumptions frequently remained the same. Norwegian roots were usually apparent, whether they lay in the artistic depiction of religious forms or in the revival of Norwegian Lutheran music. Some, like newspaper editors or Lutheran ministers serving predominantly Norwegian-American audiences, accepted, as did Rølvaag, the necessity of maintaining the ancestral heritage. Others, perhaps politicians or artists with a more mixed clientele, often remained, like Veblen, so bound to unconscious Norwegian-American cultural beliefs and assumptions that their work reflected them even when it was not intended to do so.

Acculturation

From the days of settlement Minnesota Norwegians debated to what degree they should give up their European heritage and replace it with American forms and practices. Acculturation did not proceed in a straight line from an extremely retentive Norwegian group in the 1850s to one that valued assimilation in later years. In fact, the first arrivals expected their folkways to die very quickly. As early as 1845 one predicted that Norwegian-language usage would end "in the second generation."[65] Instead ethnic maintenance for a time became more pronounced as immigration continued, the community grew in wealth and influence, and institutions were founded to facilitate the development of a Norwegian-American culture. It was in the early 20th rather than in the mid-19th century that Norwegian ethnic consciousness seemed most pronounced. This high point was probably reached just before World War I, but ethnicity did not continually decline thereafter. Indeed, the Norwegian-American identity in Minnesota may have been more self-conscious in 1980 than it was in 1950.

The first quarter of the 20th century marked both the peak of Norwegian-American cultural forms and the beginning of their decline. In 1914 Minnesota's Norwegians vigorously celebrated the centennial of the Eidsvoll Constitution that had signaled Norway's independence. After parades in both of the Twin Cities, about 50,000 people — the largest known gathering of Norwegian Americans thus far — congregated at the Minnesota State Fairgrounds in St. Paul on May 17. The program featured music, fireworks, and many speakers, but its high light was Swedish-born Governor Adolph O. Eberhart's recitation of Norway's national anthem in Norwegian. Symbolically the celebration was important to Minnesota Norwegians as a milepost marking "their strength and also the fact of their acceptance as a part of the American nation."[66]

The year 1914 might be arbitrarily taken as a high-water mark of Norwegian-American activity in the state. The previous decade had been one of substantial immigration, and numerous organizations had been formed in response to the large influx. Not only were there the lodges of the Sons of Norway and the *bygdelag*, but *Det norske Selskap i Amerika* (The Norwegian Society of America) was founded in Minneapolis in 1903 for the purpose of preserving Norwegian culture in the United States. Furthermore enrollment in Norwegian-language classes was apparently on the upswing. One figure based on reports from 32 of Minnesota's 87 counties indicated that Norwegian was taught in 103 grade and country schools during the 1913–14 school year. But this activity was short-lived. Five years later the state's Norwegians would be much more timid about celebrating their ancestral heritage.[67]

A significant problem in its maintenance was the changing nature of the immigrant population. Later-arriving Norwegians were better educated and adapted more easily to urbanized America than those of the mid-19th century. More important, the first arrivals were dying off and the second and third generations were maturing. The greater prosperity and education of the immigrants' children pushed Norwegian-American institutions to improved intellectual and literary activity, but these young people lacked their parents' personal attachment to Norway. The English language they had been taught in the public schools seemed more natural to them than the Norwegian their parents often insisted on speaking at home. Painful cleavages between generations and breakdowns of communication between parent and child occurred when Norwegian questions received only English answers. Moreover geographical and social mobility worked against the maintenance of ethnic consciousness. Many of those who had achieved success in business after moving to the cities were not conspicuous advocates of an independent Norwegian-American culture. Instead they supported integration into the broader American society.

Although 1914 may be regarded as a high point for Norwegian-American community life in Minnesota, cracks in the edifice were evident as early as 1890 when the introduction of English-language preaching in the Lutheran church was anonymously suggested in a synod publication. Seven years later another proponent was criticized for addressing a church convention in English. No sermons were preached in English before 1900, but church leaders realized the question would not go away. Between 1905 and 1915 English sermons in the Norwegian Lutheran church rose from 5% to 22%. In 1913 Theodor H. Dahl, president of the United Norwegian Lutheran Church, encouraged "English work," for he feared that without it the churches would lose the third and fourth generations.

The slow, laborious transition from Norwegian to English would probably have been made more gradually had not

World War I with its 100% Americanism intervened painfully to speed it up. As they did among other ethnic groups, nosey "Americanizers" intruded upon Norwegian-American social, political, and religious life to denigrate hyphenated Americans. The Minnesota Commission of Public Safety, established by the legislature in April, 1917, was given near-dictatorial powers to impose conformity on ethnic groups. The agency required the registration of all aliens, resolved that English was to be the "exclusive medium of instruction" in all the state's schools, and banned meetings of any groups suspected of favoring the "idea of peace." Spies were sent to rallies and speeches, with instructions to report any Socialistic, antiwar, and anticonscription tendencies to their superiors.[68]

While Minnesota's Germans were more harshly repressed, suspicion also fell on Norwegians. In 1917 a spy reported on the activities of a speaker lecturing primarily to Scandinavian audiences, including many Norwegians, in such Red River Valley towns as Fertile, Climax, and Erskine. The Safety Commission also organized a Scandinavian Press Service to watch over the foreign-language press and to provide pro-America tracts for use in the newspapers. Nicolay Grevstad, chairman of the service, remarked that at its inception in August, 1917, some Scandinavian papers "were as little loyal as they found it safe to be." He added that "nearly all have wheeled into line, and some are now aggressively American." Nor was the Norwegian Lutheran church beyond reproach. When O. Morgan Norlie was asked to report on the church and its schools, he attempted to soothe the commission's suspicions by suggesting that the "Norwegian parochial schools are religious schools, not language schools," adding that English was gaining in influence within the church.[69]

World War I hysteria and its coincident militant Americanism put increasing pressure on ethnic communities in Minnesota to renounce their Old World ties. Norwegian Americans, most of whom backed the effort once war was declared, were forced to examine their institutions through the prism of magnified American perceptions, which now viewed any "foreign" activity as suspect. Responding to this pressure, the name of the Norwegian Lutheran Church in America was changed in 1918 to the United Lutheran Church, and Norwegian-language services dropped precipitously from 73.1% to 61.2% between 1917 and 1918. Many bygdelag gatherings were canceled in 1917, for as one of them (Nordhordlandslaget) cautiously explained, "we don't want to give anyone opportunity for misunderstanding, but prove that we are citizens of this country."[70]

The constant doubts thus cast on the virtues of Norwegianness accelerated the transition to American norms. That the period was an aberration in the speed of transition can be seen in the resumption of Norwegian-language church services, which rose from 61.2% in 1918 to 65.7% the following year before beginning a long decline averaging 2.3% a year to 1948. The Norwegian Lutheran Church resumed its original name in 1920, and the Sons of Norway prospered as did numerous other Norwegian groups. But such institutions as the bygdelag and the foreign-language press declined. Subscribers to the newspaper Minneapolis Tidende dropped from 32,931 in 1910 to 17,000 in 1925. Unless institutions maintained their utility for the changing needs of the Norwegian-American community in Minnesota, they appeared doomed to oblivion.

Some intellectual leaders believed that the period's extreme pressures to conform had sapped the strength of Norwegian-American culture. With others of similar mind, Ole Rølvaag in 1919 was instrumental in founding For Fedrearven (For the Ancestral Heritage), an organization whose aim was "To awaken . . . a deeper appreciation of and love for the great values we have received from our fathers." With Rølvaag as secretary and the Reverend Halvor Bjørnson of Kratka in the Red River Valley as vice-president, the society worked for ethnic maintenance. To insinuate that people of immigrant stock were not true Americans "wholly to be depended upon" in wartime, Rølvaag asserted in 1921, was "a virulent contagion" which destroyed their ideals and values. Once again he proclaimed the need to maintain ties to the past in order to create a strong culture in the present. His concern was not widely shared, however, and For Fedrearven folded only three years after its inception.[71]

The transition from a Norwegian-American culture to what might be called an American-Norwegian one affected different groups in varying degrees. After World War I the shift to English continued more gradually in the church and on the street until by 1925 the number of church services in English exceeded those in Norwegian for the first time. In compact rural parishes, the change-over took longer. In addition to the concern expressed by intellectuals like Rølvaag, Lutheran ministers feared the demise of the Norwegian language for both personal and cultural reasons. On the one hand, the prospect of speaking English, which was a foreign language to many of them, was daunting. As early as 1914 the Reverend Johan A. Bergh recorded that Norwegian pastors were "meeting with the unfortunate circumstance that their congregations are very critical with regard to their English." Youths who had attended public schools, he wrote, were prone to criticize "the pastor who uses a word incorrectly or puts an intonation in the wrong place." On the other hand, pastors and elderly church members had difficulty accepting a traditional ritual performed in English. "I have nothing against the English language," one man said, "I use it myself every day. But if we don't teach our children Norwegian, what will they do when they get to heaven?"[72]

As the passage of the Immigration Act of 1924 signaled the end of the era of free immigration, the year 1925, like 1914, was marked by a celebration that may serve as a second milepost for Norwegian Americans. To call attention to the centennial of the arrival of the first group of Norwegians in the United States, President Calvin Coolidge spoke to thousands, who again gathered at the Minnesota State Fairgrounds. But things had changed since 1914. Now the speeches were predominantly in English, and instead of a reading of the Norwegian anthem in Norwegian, the crowd heard a series of nostalgic addresses extolling the Norwegian-American past as well as an assimilationist future. In 1925, too, the Norwegian-American Historical Association

PRESIDENT Calvin Coolidge addressed Norwegians gathered at the Minnesota State Fairgrounds in June, 1925, to celebrate the centennial of the arrival of the first group of Norwegian immigrants to reach the United States.

was formed with headquarters at Northfield. Like the centennial celebration, its organization signaled to some the fact that Norwegian America would no longer make history but only write it — in English.[73]

The decades of the 1920s, 1930s, and 1940s saw further changes in the institutions of Americans of Norwegian descent. About 1935, during the Great Depression, both the Norwegian-American Historical Association and the Sons of Norway reached low points in membership as people failed to pay their dues. That this failure was attributable to poverty rather than disinterest is indicated by the increases recorded by both organizations after that date. In the 1940s American xenophobia during World War II focused upon the Japanese rather than the Europeans, so Norwegians escaped the discrimination they had experienced in World War I. In fact, Norway's bravery in the face of Nazi oppression gave added luster to the image of those in America and enlisted their support. In 1944 the Norwegian church voted to change its name to the Evangelical Lutheran Church, noting that the change was "not born of any wish to repudiate our Norwegian heritage." In 1942 the Sons of Norway decided that the time had come to issue that group's magazine in English rather than Norwegian in order to make the organization more effective. Apparently overwhelming numbers of Norwegian Americans now spoke only English.[74]

Not only had the children of immigrants stopped speaking Norwegian, but fewer and fewer new immigrants were arriving to help keep Norwegian cultural traits alive. Restrictive quotas on immigration, beginning in the 1920s, combined with the Great Depression and World War II to end the mass migrations that had characterized previous periods.

Despite dwindling numbers of immigrants, World War II provoked a flurry of activity in Norwegian America. Minneapolis Norwegians organized the Camp Little Norway

Association in 1941, named for the training school of the Royal Norwegian Air Force in Toronto. The national board of the organization was located in Minneapolis. Other groups such as the National Ski Association and the Supreme Lodge of the Sons of Norway joined as special chapters to aid Norway and Norwegians during the war.

When the fighting ended, the association gave way to another organization called American Relief for Norway. Money and clothing were collected by Minnesota Norwegian Relief, Inc., with 3,000 ladies' aid societies in the state participating in the work. Among the organizations which collected money were numerous *bygdelag*, temperance groups, churches, the Sons and the Daughters of Norway, singing and folk-dance groups, the Norwegian-American Athletic Club, and the Progressive Literary Club. From 1942 to 1945 a Service Center for Norway, run by Norwegian-American women's groups, also operated in Minneapolis. Through it some 82,000 pieces of clothing were sent to Norway.

Nor was Minneapolis the only place in the state where efforts to aid the Norwegians were organized. In Duluth the Women's Committee for Norwegian Relief, representing 1,000 Norwegian-American women in some 20 organizations, was formed to "raise money, buy and distribute materials to be made up for the Norwegian Armed Forces and civilians and to cooperate with other relief agencies." Women in such other northern Minnesota towns as Two Harbors, Cloquet, Barnum, Carlton, Hibbing, Virginia, International Falls, and Little Fork joined the effort. Women in Northfield also knitted, sewed, and raised money for Norwegian relief through their local branch of *Nordmanns-Forbundet* and the Nordic Arts Club.[75]

Post-World War II saw a changed pattern, as Norwegians and others emigrated as individuals or as families to take white-collar jobs, not always intending to stay for extended lengths of time. During that period emigration remained under 3,000 per year, dwindling to less than 1,000 in the late 1960s and 1970s. In the 30 years from 1946 to 1975, only 46,881 Norwegians moved to the United States and many of these returned. The so-called brain drain does not seem to have been a large component of the immigration in this period; scattered annual figures from the mid-1950s through much of the 1960s show a maximum of 176 scientists, engineers, and medical personnel. Nevertheless the migration was significant in Norwegian terms. Engineers represented a consistent percentage, perhaps following a tradition which brought many of them to the United States temporarily or permanently since 1879. A second large group represented in the 1950s and 1960s was made up of nurses; doctors were not numerous.[76]

The reasons these people had for coming to the United States were, as they had been in the 19th century, primarily economic. But unlike the *bønder* and *husmenn* of earlier years, few of these migrants were attracted to farming. Like the previous migration, however, the mid-20th-century one contained numerous family units with a "near balance between the sexes." Over 40% ranged in age from 15 to 29 years.

Relatively few chose Minnesota as their destination. The state ranked second only to New York in number of Norwegian aliens in 1940 with more than 12% of the United States total; nine years later a count of naturalized Norwegians dropped Minnesota behind California and Washington as well. A 1980 study of the postwar migration showed that in 1970 Minneapolis had a relatively large 20% of second-generation Norwegian Americans in the United States, but only 10% of those born in Norway.

By 1950 the Norwegian America of 1914 was no longer clearly visible in Minnesota. The third and fourth generations considered themselves Americans, spoke English, and increasingly married persons from other ethnic groups. A culture based on class, occupation, or region (such as the Midwest) seemed to have displaced Norwegianness. Like Veblen in his Yankee world, Norwegians may have exhibited certain characteristics — perhaps the cultural traditions of the home such as Lutheranism, a continued predilection for farming, a preference for the professions, or a fondness for certain ethnic foods. But it could be argued that some of these traits were midwestern rather than exclusively Norwegian. On the other hand, 1949 was the year that 5,000 people attended the unveiling of a statue of Leif Erikson on the grounds of the state Capitol in St. Paul.

In any case, an obituary for Norwegianness in Minnesota in 1950 would have proven premature. In the following decades a growing national interest in "roots" spurred a reemergence of emphasis on ethnic life.[77] Derived as was much of the so-called new ethnicity from the rising Black national consciousness, a new awareness of their Norwegian heritage began to appear among Norwegian Americans. The causes of this renaissance were at least twofold. First, the revivals of interest in the 1960s were based on a new awareness of the nation's unmelted ethnic diversity. Norwegians as well as other groups began to celebrate a past their parents had been persuaded to believe was undesirable. The

second factor was related: the pressures to conform to so-called American or Yankee values had diminished and were now muted. For some groups like the Norwegians the new maturity that recognized and applauded such diversity almost arrived too late. Much of their ethnic heritage had disappeared from everyday life.

The rebirth of awareness of ethnicity among Minnesota's Norwegian Americans differed from older forms of ethnicity. In the past, Norwegians lived their Norwegian folkways, speaking Norwegian on the street and in their churches. Today in a more complex society, Norwegian Americans may speak Norwegian perhaps only at the meeting of a fraternal organization or singing society, and they may participate in traditional folk dances as a diversion. Their interest in Norwegian-American culture is casual. They are Americans curious about their backgrounds, not Norwegian immigrants trying to become Americans.

The pursuit of Norwegianness in Minnesota in the late 20th century took various forms. In 1980, for example, 63 Norwegian groups co-operated in organizing the first statewide *syttende mai* celebration, which was held in Minneapolis. The parade, studded with Norwegian costumes and American and Norwegian flags, included representatives of several Sons of Norway lodges, at least two *bygdelag*, and an impressive Norwegian men's choral group, as well as the Macalester College Pipe Band of St. Paul in full Scottish regalia, Minneapolis Aquatennial and St. Paul Winter Carnival royalty, and Minnesota-based officials from several Nordic countries, among them the Swedish and Icelandic consuls.[78]

The trend toward the inclusion of non-Norwegians and even non-Scandinavians in traditionally Norwegian pursuits can also be seen in the proliferation of what might be called Norwegian eating clubs in the Twin Cities. The progenitor of such groups, *Torskeklubben* (The Codfish Club), which was founded in 1933, developed such a long waiting list of prospective members that six other clubs were organized to help meet the demand. Among them were *Saga Klubben*, started in 1973, which does not limit its membership to those of Norwegian descent, and *Norske Torske Klubben* of St. Paul, which is said to be the largest of the six. The original *Torskeklubben* consisted of a group of men (women were invited once a year) who gathered monthly at the Curtis Hotel for luncheons at which they spoke only Norwegian and ate only *torsk* and boiled potatoes with melted butter, followed by a chaser of aquavit. Although the language requirement is no longer in force, the menu has remained the same and has been adopted by the other clubs as well.[79]

Norwegian-language services were conducted every Sunday in 1980 at *Mindekirken*, the Norwegian Lutheran Memorial Church of Minneapolis, one of three such congregations in the United States to do so. This church had an official membership of 300, 75% of whom were born in Norway; it sponsored Norwegian classes and was proud to announce that "the kitchen in the basement is just as important as the pulpit upstairs." Language classes were also offered regularly by the Sons of Norway, whose Minnesota membership increased from 13,000 in 1970 to 30,000 eight years later. Not all of the increase was provided by people of Norwegian descent or interests; many others were attracted by the group's popular annual charter flights to Norway. Nevertheless the organization also experienced large enrollments in its language classes as well as those in *rosemaling* and folk dancing. Not only were individuals interested in Norwegian-American activities, but whole communities were organizing festivals to celebrate their immigrant heritage. Some, such as the Viking Sword and Turkey Barbeque Day at Ulen in the Red River Valley, reached back to a more ancient past, combining it with typically American food and parades.[80]

Seminars and symposia with titles such as "Norway Today" and "Contemporary Issues — Scandinavia and America" seemed to point to a trend suggested by the Sons of Norway charter flights — a growing interest in present-day Scandinavia which might have been supplementing the nostalgic search for a 19th-century heritage of Norwegian grandparents or great-grandparents. On the other hand, many Norwegian Americans in Minnesota were also taking advantage of the favorable climate for diversity to search for their roots in an ethnic past, adapting for their own use Ole Rølvaag's words from generations before: "We urge a cultural solidarity with the past because we desire that our people shall be made to feel at home in this new land of theirs. . . . We believe that this cultivation of love for home and heritage is the truest Americanization that any citizen may be taught."[81]

Reference notes

[1] Carl G. O. Hansen, *My Minneapolis: A Chronicle of What Has Been Learned and Observed About the Norwegians in Minneapolis Through One Hundred Years*, 11 (Minneapolis, 1956). The authors wish to acknowledge the helpful suggestions received during their work on this chapter from Professors Odd S. Lovoll and Carl H. Chrislock.

[2] Arlow W. Andersen, *The Norwegian-Americans*, 38 (Boston, 1975); United States, *Census*, 1910, *Population*, 2:991; 1970, vol. 1, part 25, pp. 12–15, 514; State of Minnesota, *Census, 1905*, 195. In some census calculations, Norwegians were counted with Swedes. The foreign-stock figures are too inconsistently presented to give a definitive picture of the changing numbers of native-born persons with Norway-born parents. According to a count of listings in 1979 telephone directories for Minneapolis and St. Paul, the National Football League team and 97 businesses in the Twin Cities alone carried the name Viking.

[3] Theodore C. Blegen, *Norwegian Migration to America 1825–1860*, 22 (Northfield, 1931), hereafter cited as vol. 1; Ingrid Semmingsen, *Norway to America: A History of the Migration*, 100–102 (Minneapolis, 1978); Semmingsen, "The Dissolution of Estate Society in Norway," in *Scandinavian Economic History Review*, 2:[166]–203 (1954); Michael Drake, *Population and Society in Norway 1735–1865* (Cambridge, Eng., 1969). For a more recent view of the Norwegian society which produced the emigrants, see Francis Sejersted, *Den Vanskelige Frihet, 1814–51*, especially 97, 103–109, 120–125 (*Norges Historie*, vol. 10 — Oslo, 1978).

At one time the falling death rate was linked by historians to the introduction of the potato and the increasing use of vaccines against smallpox, but those two causes have been questioned by recent research. See Kåre Lunden, "Potetdyrkinga og den raskare folketalsvoksteren i Noreg frå 1815," in *Historisk tidsskrift*, 54:4, pp. 275–313, English summary, 313–315 (1975); Edgar Hovland *et al.*, "Poteta og folkeveksten i Noreg etter 1815: Fire debattinnlegg," in *Historisk tidsskrift*, 57:3, pp. 251–299 (1978).

[4] It is debatable whether the new machinery pushed laborers off the land or the decline in the labor pool forced farmers to mechanize. Recent research suggests the latter, since mechanization occurred later than the rural emigration and in regions where emigration was less pronounced. See Semmingsen, *Norway to America*, 104, 108–110, and Kjell Haarstad, "Utvandrerne fra bygdene — presset eller lokket," in Arnfinn Engen *et al.*, *Utvandringa — det store oppbrotet*, 38–56 (Oslo, 1978), for differing interpretations.

[5] Semmingsen, *Norway to America*, 34–36, 40; Peter A. Munch, *A Study of Cultural Change: Rural-Urban Conflicts in Norway*, 41–46, 52, 59 (*Studia Norvegica: Ethnologica and Folkloristica*, no. 9 — Oslo, 1956).

[6] Ingrid Semmingsen, "Origin of Nordic Emigration," in *American Studies in Scandinavia*, 9:14 (1977); Andersen, *Norwegian-Americans*, 4, 59–71. Nicholas Tavuchis, *Pastors and Immigrants: The Role of a Religious Elite in the Absorption of Norwegian Immigrants*, 13–21 (The Hague, 1963), estimated that seven out of eight immigrants left from rural districts in the early stages of immigration up to 1865. See also George T. Flom, *A History of Norwegian Immigration to the United States From the Earliest Beginning down to the Year 1848*, 33 (Iowa City, Ia., 1909).

[7] Carlton C. Qualey, *Norwegian Settlement in the United States*, 17–75, 112 (Reprint ed., New York, 1970); Ingrid Semmingsen, *Veien Mot Vest: Utvandringen Fra Norge 1865–1915*, 2:74 (Oslo, 1950); Semmingsen, "Emigration and the Image of America in Europe," in Henry S. Commager, ed., *Immigration and American History: Essays in Honor of Theodore C. Blegen*, 26–54 (Minneapolis, 1961). For a complete translation of the letter below, see Carlton C. Qualey, trans. and ed., "Three America Letters to Lesja," in *Norwegian-American Studies*, 27:46–48 (Northfield, 1977); for a collection of these letters in English, see Theodore C. Blegen, *Land of Their Choice: The Immigrants Write Home* (Minneapolis, 1955).

[8] Here and below, on origins of the earliest emigrants and the geographical development of the migration itself, see Flom, *Norwegian Immigration*, 376–379; Semmingsen, *Norway to America*, 33; Semmingsen, *Veien Mot Vest*, 2:493; Theodore C. Blegen, *Norwegian Migration to America: The American Transition*, 74–77 (Northfield, 1940), hereafter cited as vol. 2; Odd S. Lovoll, *A Folk Epic: The Bygdelag in America*, 8–10 (Boston, 1975); Hjalmar R. Holand, *Norwegians in America: The Last Migration*, 31–40 (Sioux Falls, S. Dak., 1978), an English translation by Helmer M. Blegen of Holand's *Den Siste Folkevandring* published in Norwegian in 1930. The latter is a selective condensation with some additions of Holand's longer study, *De Norske Settlementers Historie* (Ephraim, Wis., 1909). An excellent series of maps showing the districts in all the Nordic countries from which emigrants left during five-year periods between 1865 and 1914 is in Harald Runblom and Hans Norman, eds., *From Sweden to America: A History of the Migration*, between pp. 128 and 129 (Stockholm and Minneapolis, 1976).

[9] For detailed discussions of Norwegian settlement in southeastern Minnesota, see Qualey, *Norwegian Settlement*, 97–119; Holand, *De Norske Settlementers Historie*, 358–501.

[10] Here and below, see *Billed-Magazin* (Madison, Wis.), August, 1869, p. 287, quoted in Theodore L. Nydahl, "The Early Norwegian Settlement of Goodhue County, Minnesota," 16, master's thesis, University of Minnesota, 1929; Semmingsen, *Veien Mot Vest*, 2:54, 57.

[11] Here and below, see Carlton C. Qualey, "A Typical Norwegian Settlement: Spring Grove, Minnesota," in *Norwegian-American Studies*, 9:54–66 (Northfield, 1936); Ole S. Johnson, *Nybyggerhistorie fra Spring Grove og omegn Minnesota*, 103, 123 (Minneapolis, 1920); *Plat Book of Houston County Minnesota*, 6 (Philadelphia, 1878); Franklyn Curtiss-Wedge, ed., *History of Houston County Minnesota*, 173–181 (Winona, 1919); U.S. manuscript census

schedules, 1870, Houston County, Spring Grove, roll 6, microfilm in MHS; Einar Haugen, *The Norwegian Language in America: A Study in Bilingual Behavior*, 2:337–360 (Philadelphia, 1953). Mixtures of Norwegian dialects in Minnesota settlements produced identifiable American Norwegian ones such as the "Spring Grove dialect"; Haugen, 2:351. On the church below, see Sydney L. Roppe and Blayne Onsgard, *History of Spring Grove*, [15–19] (Spring Grove, 1952).

[12] Jon A. Gjerde, "The Effect of Community on Migration: Three Minnesota Townships," in *Journal of Historical Geography*, 5:403–422 (October, 1979); Peter A. Munch, ed., *The Strange American Way: Letters of Caja Munch from Wiota Wisconsin, 1855–1859*, 118 (Carbondale, Ill., 1970). In one year, for example, members of the North Prairie Lutheran Church in Arendahl Township, Fillmore County, gave $762.50 toward the construction of a church erected 10 years after the first Norwegian settlers arrived. A year later in 1864, still heavily in debt, the congregation contributed $609 toward the building of Luther College of Decorah, Ia. See North Prairie Lutheran Church, *Eightieth Anniversary Year Book: A Brief Historical Sketch*, 7–9 (Minneapolis, [1936]).

[13] J. S. J[ohnson], *Valdris Helsing*, 7:80 (May, 1905), quoted in Haugen, *Norwegian Language in America*, 1:34; *Telesoga*, 33:30 (September, 1917), quoted in Lovoll, *A Folk Epic*, 13. On the Norwegian Lutheran Church, see p. 234, below.

[14] Statistics derived from a sampling of *Det statistiske Sentralbyrå* records, quoted in Semmingsen, *Veien Mot Vest*, 2:492; U.S. manuscript census schedules, 1870, Houston County, Spring Grove, roll 6; U.S., *Census*, 1870, *Population*, 606. Of the children born outside of Minnesota, 76.7% were born in Norway. Minnesota's foreign born as a whole had a ratio of 127.7 to 100 in 1870. Norwegian migration was more family centered than that of the British Isles and Ireland in which only 19% were children under 12.

[15] *Amerika* (Chicago), July 29, 1885, quoted in Qualey, *Norwegian Settlements*, 12.

[16] Qualey, *Norwegian Settlements*, 124–126; Holand, *De Norske Settlementers Historie*, 533. The Linden settlement occupied portions of southern Brown and western Blue Earth counties as well as most of Watonwan County. The Park Region is here defined as Becker, Otter Tail, Pope, Kandiyohi, Douglas, Swift, Todd, western Stearns and Meeker, and eastern Grant and Stevens counties.

[17] Holand, *De Norske Settlementers Historie*, 485, 509; Stageberg and Flaten, both quoted in Nydahl, "Early Norwegian Settlement of Goodhue County," 36, 37. Minnesota county histories provide impressionistic views of these strung-out communities. The earliest settlers in Freeborn, Kandiyohi, and Martin counties were largely from Rock Prairie. In Lincoln County, the Spring Grove settlement served as the mother colony. The earliest Redwood County Norwegian had lived in Fillmore County. The pattern suggests numerous parallel, northwesterly movements frequently with little contact among them in spite of the similarity of direction.

[18] [Gena Lee Gilbertson], *Big Grove Norwegian Lutheran Church 75th Anniversary 1867–1942*, 6–10, 80–89 (Grand Forks, N. Dak., 1942); Big Grove Norwegian Lutheran Church Records, microfilm roll 306, American Lutheran Church Archives, Dubuque, Ia., calculations in MEHP Papers. The actual figure was 69.1%. Because of its Halling background, Big Grove in 1911 was the site of a three-day convention of some 6,000 Halling-Americans who gathered from throughout the U.S.; Lovoll, *A Folk Epic*, 90.

[19] Qualey, *Norwegian Settlements*, 120.

[20] Taped interview of Mrs. Johanna Nelson Aune and Mrs. Gertie Nelson Holm, April 9, 1976, who grew up in Spring Prairie Township, Clay County, one of an extensive collection of oral history interviews of Red River Valley Scandinavians in Northwest Minnesota Historical Center, Moorhead; Peter A. Munch, "His-

tory and Sociology," in *Norwegian-American Studies*, 20:53 (Northfield, 1959). See also note 43, below.

[21] Qualey, *Norwegian Settlements*, 120.

[22] Lars Ljungmark, *For Sale — Minnesota: Organized Promotion of Scandinavian Immigration 1866–1873*, 61 (Chicago, 1971).

[23] *Nordisk Folkeblad* (Minneapolis), August 11, 1869; Ljungmark, *For Sale — Minnesota*, 62–64; Qualey, *Norwegian Settlements*, 127.

[24] Levi Thortvedt, "The Early History of the Red River Valley," 1–11, 29, 35, in Levi Thortvedt Papers, MHS, condensed as "A Journey across Minnesota in 1870," in *Gopher Historian*, Spring, 1965, pp. 15–20. See also Dora J. Gunderson, "The Settlement of Clay County, Minnesota, 1870–1900," 27–30, master's thesis, University of Minnesota, 1929; *Clay County Land Atlas & Plat Book*, 32 (Rockford, Ill., 1976).

[25] Thortvedt, "History," 36; calculated from Minnesota, *Census, 1875*, table facing p. 98, and *1905*, 134, 156, 163, 168–170; Gunderson, "Settlement of Clay County," 59.

[26] Martin Ulvestad, *Nordmændene i Amerika, deres Historie og Rekord*, 1:87, 90, 95, 102, 107, 112–114, 117–119, 121, 123 (Minneapolis, 1907); Mrs. Gerald Olson and Mrs. Joel W. Johnson, eds., *In the Heart of the Red River Valley: A History of the People of Norman County, Minnesota*, 2 ([Ada?], 1976); Hazel H. Wahlberg, *The North Land: A History of Roseau County*, 115, 126 (Roseau, 1975); *Pioneer Tales: A History of Pennington County*, 499 (Thief River Falls, 1976); interview of Hazel H. Wahlberg by Deborah Stultz, May 21, 1980, notes in MEHP Papers. Recently published county and local histories on the Red River Valley and elsewhere contain much information about Norwegian-American activities and organizations in rural and small-town Minnesota. See, for example, Roberta Olson, *Fertile — Hub of the Sand Hill Valley*, 11, 67 ([Fertile, 1975?]) on Polk County, and Blanche Iverson, *Buzzle Township, Pinewood, Minnesota, 1898–1976* (Pinewood, 1976) on Beltrami County.

[27] Nicolay A. Grevstad, "The Norwegians in America," in Martin Ulvestad, *Norsk-Amerikaneren Vikingesaga samt Pioneerhistorie, statistik og biografiske Oplysninger om Nordmænd i Amerika*, 215, 216 (Seattle, 1928); U.S., *Census*, 1909–10, *Agriculture*, 5:181; Torger A. Hoverstad, *The Norwegian Farmers in The United States*, 7, 11–13 (Fargo, N. Dak., 1915); Andersen, *Norwegian-Americans*, 87.

[28] Odd S. Lovoll and Kenneth O. Bjork, *The Norwegian-American Historical Association, 1925–1975*, 2 (Northfield, 1975); Stanley S. Guterman, "The Americanization of Norwegian Immigrants: A Study in Historical Sociology," in *Sociology and Social Research*, 52:252–270 (April, 1968); Hoverstad, *Norwegian Farmers*, 11; Aftenposten, *Facts about Norway*, 6 (Oslo, 1977); *Folkebladet*, May 5, 1886; Gunderson, "The Settlement of Clay County," 62. On the other hand, a study of population changes in Stevens County showed a decline of Norwegians in both the village of Morris and in Morris Township from 1885 to 1895; see Peggy Cottrell, "Immigration in Stevens County, 1870–1890," tables 2, 3, course paper, 1973, in West Central Minnesota Historical Center, Morris, copy in MEHP Papers.

[29] Semmingsen, *Veien Mot Vest*, 2:246; Matti Kaups, "Norwegian Immigrants and the Development of Commercial Fisheries Along the North Shore of Lake Superior: 1870–1895," in Harald S. Naess, ed., *Norwegian Influence on the Upper Midwest*, 21–34 (Duluth, 1976). Both the MHS and the Northeast Minnesota Historical Center in Duluth have excellent collections of taped and transcribed oral history interviews with north shore fishermen, including a number of Norwegians. The Norwegians on the range were largely from the southeastern regions of Akershus and Buskerud and the west coast from Bergen to Nordland. Although appreciable numbers worked in mining, they were not nearly as numerous as

the Swedes. John Sirjamaki, "The People of the Mesabi Range," in *Minnesota History*, 27:206–210, 212 (September, 1946).

[30] Semmingsen, *Norway to America*, 112–115; Lennart Jörberg, "The Industrial Revolution in the Nordic Countries," in Carlo M. Cipolla, ed., *The Emergence of Industrial Societies*, 377–380, 453 (*The Fontana Economic History of Europe*, vol. 4, part 2 — Reprint ed., New York, 1976); Ingrid Semmingsen, "Family Emigration from Bergen 1874–92," in Harald S. Naess and Sigmund Skard, eds., *Americana Norvegica: Studies in Scandinavian-American Interrelations Dedicated to Einar Haugen*, 3:38–63 (Oslo, 1971); Semmingsen, *Veien Mot Vest*, 460–470. Semmingsen saw the Norwegian city as a "stage" in the move to America. She also found that of the nearly 50,000 remigrants in Norway in 1920, many who had been industrial workers and miners in the U.S. returned to take up farming; 82% of the men returned to their home communities. Little has been published on urban emigration from Norway, but see, for example, Peter Rinnan and Rolf Kåre Østrem, "Utvandringen fra Kristiania 1880–1907. en studie i urbanutvandring," master's thesis, University of Oslo, 1979.

[31] Lincoln Steffens, *The Shame of the Cities*, 64 (New York, 1904).

[32] The general data were extracted from U.S., *Census*, 1880, *Population*, 451; 1890, part 1, pp. 2, 370.

[33] John S. Johnson, *Minnesota, En Kortfattet Historie av Nordmændenes Bebyggelse av Staten*, 160 (St. Paul, 1914); Hansen, *My Minneapolis*, 52–54. The Norwegians lived with some Danes and more Swedes in Minneapolis's West Bank and South Side neighborhoods; see Chapters 12 and 13.

[34] Hansen, *My Minneapolis*, 145–152. See also Dan Armitage, "The Curling Waters: A West Bank History," in *Minnesota Daily* (Minneapolis), September 27, 1973, pp. 15–25. Here and below, see Calvin F. Schmid, *Social Saga of Two Cities: An Ecological and Statistical Study*, 157–160 (Minneapolis, 1937). Norwegians were far less numerous in St. Paul; see Schmid, 135, 155. 155.

[35] For an elaboration of rural-urban differences, see Guterman, in *Sociology and Social Research*, 52:252–270; Hansen, *My Minneapolis*, 29, 54, 63–92. A similar co-operative situation existed in the Scandinavian community of Duluth, where the 1870 census counted 625 Swedes and 242 Norwegians. *Det Nordiske Forbund* was founded there in 1871 for social and other purposes, and the community supported *Duluth Skandinav*, a newspaper established in 1887 which lasted for 78 years. Jørgen Fuhr edited and later published the paper from 1915 until his death in 1930; Anna, his widow, then ran the Fuhr Publishing and Printing Co. for 25 years until illness forced her to sell in 1955. *Duluth City Directory, 1915, 1930, 1958; Duluth News-Tribune*, November 24, 1956, p. 6; Matti Kaups, "Europeans in Duluth: 1870," in Ryck Lydecker and Lawrence J. Sommer, eds., *Duluth: Sketches of the Past*, 74, 78 (Duluth, 1976).

[36] Hansen, *My Minneapolis*, 114, 118, 128.

[37] Nina Draxten, *Kristofer Janson in America*, 100, 197, 218 (Boston, 1976); Carl H. Chrislock, *From Fjord to Freeway: 100 Years. Augsburg College*, 43 (Minneapolis, 1969); Gerald Thorson, "Tinsel and Dust: Disenchantment in Two Minneapolis Novels from the 1880s," in *Minnesota History*, 45:210–222 (Summer, 1977); Hansen, *My Minneapolis*, 99–109; Arthur C. Paulson, "Bjørnson and the Norwegian-Americans," in *Norwegian-American Studies*, 5:84–109 (Northfield, 1930). The Nora Free Christian Church, founded by Janson at Hanska, Brown County, flourished in the 1980s, as did the Unitarian Church at Underwood, Otter Tail County, which he organized as the Underwood Free Christian Church, but the Nazareth Church in Minneapolis persisted only until 1906; Draxten, 56, 330; interview of Pastor Paul Johnson of the Nora Church by Deborah

Stultz, May 12, 1980, notes in MEHP Papers. For more on Bjørnson in the U.S., see Eva L. Haugen and Einar Haugen, eds. and trans., *Land of the Free: Bjørnstjerne Bjørnson's America Letters, 1880–1881* (Northfield, 1978).

[38] Chrislock, *From Fjord to Freeway*, 33; Carl H. Chrislock to Deborah Stultz, December 27, 1980, in MEHP Papers.

[39] Carl G. O. Hansen, *History of Sons of Norway*, 13–16 (Minneapolis, 1944).

[40] Hansen, *History of Sons of Norway*, 32; C. Sverre Norborg, *An American Saga*, 52 (Minneapolis, 1970); Lovoll, *A Folk Epic*, 22.

[41] Waldemar Ager, "Norsk-amerikansk skjønliteratur," in Johs. B. Wist, ed., *Norsk-Amerikanernes Festskrift 1914*, 294 (Decorah, Ia., 1914); Semmingsen, *Norway to America*, 83.

[42] E. Clifford Nelson and Eugene L. Fevold, *The Lutheran Church Among Norwegian-Americans: A History of the Evangelical Lutheran Church*, 1:123–125 (Minneapolis, 1960). Election is doctrinally similar to Calvinist predestination; for particulars, see Nelson and Fevold, 1:254. Some Norwegians did join Methodist and Baptist churches, often in association with Danes. On the Methodists, see Arlow W. Andersen, *The Salt of the Earth: A History of Norwegian-Danish Methodism in America* (Nashville, 1962); on the Baptists, see P. Stiansen, *History of the Norwegian Baptists in America* (Wheaton, Ill., 1939). The records of some Minnesota Norwegian Lutheran churches are available in MHS; see, for example, entries 2427, 2593, 2708 in Lydia A. Lucas, comp., *Manuscripts Collections of the Minnesota Historical Society, Guide Number 3* (St. Paul, 1977).

[43] Hansen, *My Minneapolis*, 94; Nelson and Fevold, *Lutheran Church Among Norwegian-Americans*, 2:4, 222, 305. Minnesota figures were calculated from O. M. Norlie, *Norsk Lutherske Menigheter i Amerika 1843–1916*, 436–840 (Minneapolis, 1918).

[44] Here and below, see Blegen, *Norwegian Migration to America*, 2:518, 530; Merrill E. Jarchow, *Private Liberal Arts Colleges in Minnesota: Their History and Contributions*, 25–33, 41–43, 77–88, 101–105, 185–199, 216–223 (St. Paul, 1973); Norlie, *Norsk Lutherske Menigheter*, 1:835; Andersen, *Norwegian-Americans*, 104, 130; Hansen, *My Minneapolis*, 302–318. It is interesting to note that Muskego Church, the first in the U.S. built by Norwegian immigrants in 1843–44, was moved from Wisconsin to the campus of Luther Seminary in 1904. It may still be seen there. Sue E. Holbert and June D. Holmquist, *A History Tour of 50 Twin City Landmarks*, 24 (St. Paul, 1966).

[45] Neil T. Eckstein, "The Social Criticism of Ole Edvart Rølvaag," in *Norwegian-American Studies*, 24:122 (Northfield, 1970).

[46] Blegen, *Norwegian Migration to America*, 2:281, 284, 289, 547; Semmingsen, *Norway to America*, 138; Arlow W. Andersen, *The Immigrant Takes His Stand: The Norwegian-American Press and Public Affairs, 1847–1872*, 12 (Northfield, 1953.)

[47] This paragraph and the one which follows were based on information compiled by the MHS Newspaper Department and on John A. Fagereng, "Norwegian Social and Cultural Life in Minnesota, 1868–1891: An Analysis of Typical Norwegian Newspapers," 1–11, master's thesis, University of Minnesota, 1932; interview of Jenny A. Johnson, editor of *Minnesota Posten*, by Deborah Stultz, May 22, 1980, notes in MEHP Papers. Many of the papers were printed in Norwegian, Danish, and/or English. For more on the Norwegian press in Minnesota, see Carl Hansen and Johs. B. Wist, "Den Norsk-Amerikanske Presse," in Wist, ed., *Norsk-Amerikanernes Festskrift*, 9–203.

[48] Richard B. Eide, comp., *Norse Immigrant Letters: Glimpses of Norse Immigrant Life in the Northwest in the Fifties*, 6 (Minneapolis, 1925); Blegen, *Norwegian Migration to America*, 2:327; Fagereng, "Norwegian Social and Cultural Life," 18, 43.

[49] On the content of various papers, see Fagereng, "Norwegian Social and Cultural Life," 16, 25, 62–97, 107–111, 114, 121–123; Wist, ed., *Norsk-Amerikanernes Festskrift*, 105, 119.

[50] Jon Wefald, *A Voice of Protest: Norwegians in American Politics, 1890–1917*, 32–44 (Northfield, 1971); *Gaa Paa!*, December 6, 1917, p. 1.

[51] The other statue depicts Swedish-born John A. Johnson. See George H. Mayer, *The Political Career of Floyd B. Olson*, 171 (Minneapolis, 1951). On Nelson's career, see Walter B. Evans, "The Early Political Career of Knute Nelson, 1867–1892," master's thesis, University of Minnesota, 1937; Millard L. Gieske, "The Politics of Knute Nelson, 1912–1920," Ph.D. thesis, University of Minnesota, 1965.

[52] Wefald, *Voice of Protest*, 4–7, 18–24, 30; Andersen, *Norwegian-Americans*, 4–8. No thorough investigations have been made, however, of the class backgrounds of Norwegian Americans active in politics in Minnesota or elsewhere.

[53] Wefald, *Voice of Protest*, 24.

[54] Here and below, see Laurence M. Larson, *The Changing West and Other Essays*, 76–78 (Northfield, 1937); Carl H. Chrislock, "The Norwegian-American Impact on Minnesota Politics: How Far 'Left-of-Center'?" in Naess, ed., *Norwegian Influence on the Upper Midwest*, 106–108, 111–116; Sten Carlsson, "Scandinavian Politicians in Minnesota Around the Turn of the Century," in Naess and Skard, eds., *Americana Norvegica*, 3:263–267. On the economic status of Norwegian wheat farmers in the Red River Valley, see Charles R. Lamb, "Up from the Wheat Fields: The Nonpartisan League's Expansion into Minnesota," 48, 49, Plan B paper, University of Minnesota, 1979, copy in MHS. Norwegians constituted 28.4% of the four ethnic groups, yet in 1893 there were 12 Norwegians compared to 12 of German, Swedish, and Danish birth or parentage; in 1901 there were 17 and 16; in 1917, 21 and 22; and in 1931, 30 compared to 28; Wefald, *Voice of Protest*, 24, 27.

[55] J. J. Skordalsvold editorial in *Heimdal* (St. Paul) and John M. Hetland letter to the editor, *Norman County Herald* (Ada), April 11, 1890, both quoted in Wefald, *Voice of Protest*, 47. Owen carried 24 Minnesota counties; Wefald, 47–52. See also Carl H. Chrislock, "The Politics of Protest in Minnesota, 1890–1901: From Populism to Progressivism," Ph.D. thesis, University of Minnesota, 1954.

[56] H. G. Stordock to Knute Nelson, March 19, 1892, in Knute Nelson Papers, MHS, quoted in Wefald, *Voice of Protest*, 49. This prediction proved true for Polk and Otter Tail counties; see Wefald, 47, 51.

[57] Chrislock, in Naess, ed., *Norwegian Influence*, 109, quoting Michael Barone, "The Social Basis of Urban Politics: Minneapolis and St. Paul, 1890–1905," honors paper, Harvard University, 1965.

[58] Chrislock, in Naess, ed., *Norwegian Influence*, 114; Bruce M. White et al., comps., *Minnesota Votes: Election Returns by County for Presidents, Senators, Congressmen, and Governors, 1857–1977*, 220, 224 (St. Paul, 1977); James M. Shields, *Mr. Progressive: A Biography of Elmer Austin Benson*, 14 (Minneapolis, 1971); Mayer, *Floyd B. Olson*, 7–9. On the Nonpartisan League and ethnic groups, see Lamb, "Up from the Wheat Fields," 45, 46.

[59] Wefald most successfully presented this point of view in *Voice of Protest*, 34–44, 55–72, but failed to examine the Norwegian Republican elements in the southeast.

[60] Ager, in Wist, ed., *Norsk-Amerikanernes Festskrift*, 294.

[61] Laurence M. Larson, "Tellef Grundysen and the Beginnings of Norwegian-American Fiction," in *Norwegian-American Studies*, 8:6 (Northfield, 1934); Dorothy B. Skårdal, *The Divided Heart: Scandinavian Immigrant Experience through Literary Sources*, 35–38 (Oslo, 1974); Ager, in Wist, ed., *Norsk-Amerikanernes Festskrift*, 296; Odd G. Andreassen, "Lars Andreas Stenholt: Norwegian-American Author," 1, 11–31, thesis paper, University of Oslo, 1977, copy in MHS; Andersen, *Norwegian-Americans*, 174; Sem-mingsen, *Norway to America*, 140–142; Harald Naess, "Ygdrasil Literary Society, 1896–1971," in Brita Seyersted, ed., *Americana Norvegica: Norwegian Contributions to American Studies Dedicated to Sigmund Skard*, 4:31–45 (Oslo, 1973). Aftenro Society Records may be found in Northeast Minnesota Historical Center, Duluth.

[62] Theodore Jorgenson and Nora O. Solum, *Ole Edvart Rölvaag: A Biography*, 18, 26, 54–58 (New York, 1939). Here and below, see David Riesman, *Thorstein Veblen: A Critical Interpretation*, 206 (New York, 1953); Joseph Dorfman, *Thorstein Veblen and His America*, 3–13, 174, 504 (New York, 1934); George M. Frederickson, "Thorstein Veblen: The Last Viking," in *American Quarterly*, 11:403–415 (Fall, 1959); Carlton C. Qualey, "Thorstein Bunde Veblen, 1857–1929," in Odd S. Lovoll, ed., *Makers of an American Immigrant Legacy: Essays in Honor of Kenneth O. Bjork*, 50–61 (Northfield, 1980).

[63] Here and below, see Jorgenson and Solum, *Rölvaag*, 46–55, 155–159, 293–297, 340, 371.

[64] Here and below, see Marion J. Nelson, "Herbjørn Gausta, Norwegian-American Painter," in Naess and Skard, eds., *Americana Norvegica*, 3:105–128; O. N. Nelson, comp., *History of the Scandinavians and Successful Scandinavians in the United States*, 1:404 (Minneapolis, 1893); Rena N. Coen, *Painting and Sculpture in Minnesota 1820–1914*, 71–74, 92 (Minneapolis, 1976); Hansen, *My Minneapolis*, 169–173; Luth Jaeger, "Two American Sculptors: Fjelde — Father and Son," in *American-Scandinavian Review*, 10:467–472 (August, 1922); Leola N. Bergmann, *Music Master of the Middle West: The Story of F. Melius Christiansen and the St. Olaf Choir*, 5, 21, 84, 114, 117, 131, 169, 195 (Minneapolis, 1944).

[65] Haugen, *Norwegian Language in America*, 1:240. For two of the standard works on the problem of assimilating or "Americanizing," see Milton M. Gordon, *Assimilation in American Life: The Role of Race, Religion, and National Origins* (New York, 1964); Joshua A. Fishman et al., *Language Loyalty in the United States* (The Hague, 1966).

[66] Lovoll, *A Folk Epic*, 120; Carl H. Chrislock, "Introduction: The Historical Context," in Odd S. Lovoll, ed., *Cultural Pluralism versus Assimilation: The Views of Waldemar Ager*, 5 (Northfield, 1977).

[67] Here and two paragraphs below, see Chrislock, "Introduction," and Kenneth Smemo, "Waldemar Theodore Ager," both in Lovoll, ed., *Cultural Pluralism*, 10–12, 16–18, 131; Einar Haugen, "The Struggle over Norwegian," in *Norwegian-American Studies*, 17:18, 19, 28 (Northfield, 1952); Skårdal, *Divided Heart*, 317–325. The Norwegian Society of America persisted until 1977; its publication, *Kvartalskrift*, ran from 1905 to 1922; Lovoll, ed., *Cultural Pluralism*, [i].

[68] Theodore C. Blegen, *Minnesota: A History of the State*, 470–473 (Minneapolis, 1963).

[69] "D.J.G." reports, June 18, 20, 21, 1917, in Correspondence and Miscellaneous Records, Woman's Committee, Council of National Defense, War Records Commission Records, Minnesota State Archives, MHS; "The Scandinavian Press Service," appended to Nicolay A. Grevstad to A. C. Weiss, October 30, 1917, File 117, and O. Morgan Norlie, "The Norwegian Parochial Schools," appended to Grevstad to C. W. Ames, November 26, 1917, File 68, both in Minnesota Commission of Public Safety Records, State Archives. See also Carl H. Chrislock, *Ethnicity Challenged: The Upper Midwest Norwegian-American Experience in World War I* (Northfield, 1981).

[70] Here and below, see Haugen, in *Norwegian-American Studies*, 17:29–31; Lovoll, *A Folk Epic*, 138; Chrislock, in Lovoll, ed., *Cultural Pluralism*, 34; Andersen, *Norwegian-Americans*, 193.

[71] Jorgenson and Solum, *Rölvaag*, 293–295; Haugen, in *Norwegian-American Studies*, 17:32–34.

[72] Haugen, *Norwegian Language in America*, 1:263, 264; Haugen, in *Norwegian-American Studies*, 17:5; Dorothy C. A. Pederson, "Pope County Area Lutheran Churches Shift from Norwegian to English," 20, term paper, University of Minnesota, Morris, 1976, copy in West Central Minnesota Historical Center, Morris; Peter A. Munch, "The Church as Complementary Identity," in Erik J. Friis, ed., *The Scandinavian Presence in North America*, 64 (New York, 1976).

[73] Lovoll, *A Folk Epic*, 164–171; Lovoll and Bjork, *Norwegian-American Historical Association*, 15; Haugen, in *Norwegian-American Studies*, 17:34. Inspired by the centennial of organized Norwegian immigration to the U.S., a filiopietistic work on Norwegian-American women, Alma A. Guttersen and Regina Hilleboe Christensen, eds., *Norse-American Women, 1825–1925* (St. Paul, 1926), reflected the attitudes of the elite women who wrote the articles in it as well as the general tone of ethnic celebratory volumes of that day. The Immigration Act of 1924 allotted an annual quota of 2,377 to Norway.

[74] Lovoll and Bjork, *Norwegian-American Historical Association*, 30–32; Norborg, *American Saga*, 141–144, 161, 191; A. N. Rygg, *American Relief for Norway*, 8 (Chicago, 1947); Andersen, *Norwegian-Americans*, 202; Haugen, *Norwegian Language in America*, 1:275, 277; Hansen, *History of Sons of Norway*, 371.

[75] Rygg, *American Relief for Norway*, 208–221. Many of the organizations were still functioning in 1980, including the Progressive Literary Club, "a group of women united to pursue mutual interests in their Norse heritage and to study the contributions of that nation to our culture," which dated from 1921; copy of organizational literature in MEHP Papers.

[76] Here and below, see Odd S. Lovoll, "From Norway to America: A Tradition of Immigration Fades," in Dennis L. Cuddy, ed., *Contemporary American Immigrations: Interpretive Essays*, vol. 1 (Boston, to be published); United States Scandinavian statistics in MEHP Papers, compiled by Jon A. Gjerde from U.S. Justice Dept., Immigration and Naturalization Service reports for those years (Minnesota figures are not available because Norwegians were counted with Danes and Swedes); 90 Congress, 1 session, House of Representatives, Committee on Government Operations, *The Brain Drain into the United States of Scientists, Engineers, and Physicians: A Staff Study*, 18, 28, 30, 40, 42, 52, 54, 64, 76, 78, 88 (Washington, D.C., 1967); Kenneth Bjork, *Saga in Steel and Concrete: Norwegian Engineers in America* (Northfield, 1947); Hugh Carter, "Social Characteristics of Naturalized Americans from Norway," in Immigration and Naturalization Service, *Monthly Review*, 9:59 (November, 1951). On the Leif Erikson statue, see *St. Paul Pioneer Press*, October 10, 1949, p. 1.

[77] Lovoll and Bjork, *Norwegian-American Historical Association*, 5–8.

[78] *Minneapolis Tribune*, May 4, 1980, p. 16F.

[79] Hansen, *My Minneapolis*, 301; *Minneapolis Tribune*, May 3, 1980, p. 1B; see also *Torske Klubben: The Norwegian Luncheon Club of Minneapolis, Minnesota* (Minneapolis, 1978), copy in MHS.

[80] On *Mindekirken*, see *Minneapolis Tribune*, March 22, 1980, p. 1B. Among a sample of Lutheran churches of Norwegian background in Iowa in 1972, pastors under the age of 50 were found to be using the Norwegian language in services more and more, and 90% reported growing interest in ethnic backgrounds on the part of their parishioners; see Duane R. Lindberg, "Ethnic Awareness Among Clergy and Parishioners," in Friis, ed., *Scandinavian Presence*, 70–76. On the Sons of Norway, see Harry Johnson to Jon Gjerde, September 24, 1979, in MEHP Papers. *Rosemaling* is the decorative art of flower painting as interior decoration or on wooden objects. The sword which inspired the Ulen festival was discussed in *The Forum* (Fargo-Moorhead), October 22, 1979, p. 1. A telling comment on the self-image some Twin Cities Norwegian Americans cultivated in the 1970s was the effort — an unsuccessful one — by Norwegian groups to move the statue of violinist Ole Bull from Loring Park, which they considered disreputable, to a close association with Minnesota's cultural elite on the Peavey Plaza next to Minneapolis' Orchestra Hall; *Minneapolis Tribune*, September 7, 1978, p. 9B.

[81] Brochures on the two conferences, which were held at St. Olaf College, Northfield, and Augsburg College, Minneapolis, respectively, are in MEHP Papers; Jorgenson and Solum, *Rölvaag*, 295.

CHAPTER 12

The Swedes

John G. Rice

FROM 1845, when the mass movement of people from Sweden to North America began, to 1930 after it ended, about 1,250,000 Swedes left their homes to settle in the New World. They constituted 20% to 25% of all the Swedes who were alive during those years. Only Ireland, Norway, and Iceland suffered greater percentage losses of population in the Great Atlantic Migration. More of these immigrating Swedes made their homes in Minnesota than in any other state. Minnesota became the center of Swedish America, and today, both in the United States and abroad, it is perceived as the most Scandinavian, and specifically the most Swedish, state in the union.[1]

The importance of Minnesota as a destination for Swedish immigrants resulted mainly from a coincidence in the timing of the emigration with the settling of the Minnesota country. The first Swedes to arrive seeking land for settlement reached what is now Scandia in Washington County in 1850.[2] In that year only slightly over 6,000 people lived in Minnesota Territory, which stretched beyond the boundaries of the present state to the Missouri River. By 1920 the population of the state had grown to almost 2,400,000, after which the decennial rate of growth fell below 10% for the first time. Of Minnesota's 486,164 recorded foreign-born whites in 1920, 23% were Swedes, about half of whom lived in the Twin Cities of Minneapolis and St. Paul. Significant in-migration ceased. The basic 19th-century composition of the state's population had been established and future increases would largely be the result of internal growth.[3]

By the middle of the 19th century not more than 5,000

people had left Sweden for the United States. During the 70 years of rapid population growth in Minnesota more than 1,000,000 Swedes emigrated to the country, about 90% of all who came. Table 12.1 depicts the relationship between Minnesota's population and Swedish emigration by decade from 1850 to 1920. The correspondence between the decades of greatest increase in the state and those of greatest emigration from Sweden is striking. In the 19th century Swedes were attracted to Minnesota in such large numbers because it was there, more than anywhere else in the country, that opportunities for land and employment presented themselves just when the immigrants needed them.

The stream of migrants from Sweden did not flow steadily, as the figures in Table 12.1 clearly show. In some years nearly 12 Swedes in every thousand left the homeland; in others the emigration dropped off to almost nothing. Although no complete agreement has been reached, there is general consensus among scholars that the causes of these fluctuations were related to changing economic conditions in Sweden and America. There were, of course, groups who left because of religious discrimination, while others clearly found the civil authorities too repressive. These motivations were, however, marginal. They may have reinforced the decision to emigrate, but they seldom initiated it. Rather most people were motivated to leave their homeland by economic considerations.[4]

In Minnesota the history of Swedish settlement may be divided into five distinct periods of heavy emigration separated from each other by years in which the flow of migrants

Table 12.1. Growth of Minnesota's Population and Swedish Emigration, 1850–1920*

Year	Minnesota Population	Increase	Increase as a % of 1920 Total	Swedish Emigrants Departed for the U.S.	Increase	Increase as a % of 1920 Total
1850	6			5		
1860	172	166	7.0	19**	15	1.4
1870	440	268	11.2	108**	89	8.6
1880	781	341	14.3	209***	101	9.8
1890	1,302	521	21.8	534	324	31.3
1900	1,751	450	18.8	734	201	19.4
1910	2,076	324	13.6	953	219	21.1
1920	2,387	311	13.0	1,035	82	7.9

Sources: U.S., *Census*, for years listed; calculations based on Sten Carlsson, "Chronology and Composition of Swedish Emigration to America," in Harald Runblom and Hans Norman, eds., *From Sweden to America: A History of the Migration*, 116–118 (Minneapolis and Uppsala, Swed., 1976).
*All figures in thousands
**Includes emigration to Canada and the rest of the Americas
***Includes emigration to Canada

248

was light. During each of these migration waves, the characteristics and the goals of the immigrants as well as the opportunities to be found in Minnesota differed. The interplay among these factors produced the Swedish settlement pattern in the state.

The Pioneer Period, 1845–54

By later standards, Swedish emigration in this period was modest. Only about 14,500 people crossed the Atlantic during the 10 years from 1845 through 1854. They were, however, more important than their numbers suggest because they established the first Swedish settlements in North America, thereby laying the groundwork for a national pattern which persists today. The early start in Illinois, rather than, say, Missouri, led to the development of the Upper Midwest as the major area of Swedish settlement. Many of these migrants traveled in large groups, and it was common for whole families to leave at once. Some, like the approximately 1,500 followers of Erik Jansson who founded the colony of Bishop Hill in Illinois in 1846, departed for religious reasons. But most of the migrants were probably attracted by the possibility of making profitable land investments on the advancing frontier. In other words, the pull of opportunity in America was greater than the push of discontent in Sweden, creating a movement one scholar has said was "characterized to some extent by a 'folk migration'" (that is, of families) in contrast to the "labor migration" of single people in later periods.[5]

At the time this migration began, the agricultural frontier in the United States stretched through northwestern Illinois and across the Mississippi River into southeastern Iowa, which attained statehood in 1846. There on the rich prairie lands between the Illinois and Mississippi rivers the first large Swedish agricultural settlements were made. Once established, they continued to attract immigrants and to serve as springboards for a second stage in the migration process—the founding of new settlements as the frontier moved west. By the early 1850s the outposts of agriculture were to be found in western Missouri and Iowa and in southeastern Minnesota. The Illinois settlements funneled Swedish immigrants primarily to the northern portion of this frontier. Significant colonies were also established to the south in Iowa, Nebraska, Kansas, and Texas, but their numbers were small compared to those that poured into Minnesota Territory.[6]

The Swedish preference for the north is often explained in terms of supposed environmental similarities. Apart from the fact that large areas in Minnesota where Swedes settled (the Red River Valley, for example) did not remotely resemble any part of Sweden, a simpler explanation may be found in the pattern of transportation routes. Most Swedish immigrants disembarked at Montreal or New York City and headed directly by train and boat for Chicago. Its proximity to the Illinois agricultural settlements early made that city a mecca for Swedes in America; by the end of the 19th century its Swedish-speaking population was second only to that of Stockholm. From Chicago the immigrant land seeker reached the Mississippi River at first by road and boat and after 1854 by rail. A relatively short journey by steamboat

then took him upriver to St. Paul at the practical head of navigation. No other land on the frontier was so accessible from Chicago, and it became even easier to reach with the completion of the first all-rail route to St. Paul in 1867. By then the size of Minnesota's Swedish population alone guaranteed that a lion's share of future immigrants from Sweden would follow their friends and relatives to the North Star State.[7]

The first sizable group of Swedes to settle in Minnesota arrived in the summer of 1851 in what is now the Chisago Lake-Center City-Lindstrom area in Chisago County (hereafter referred to as Chisago Lakes). They made the trip from Moline, Illinois, apparently in response to an enthusiastic letter from Erik U. Norberg, a Bishop Hill friend who had found his way to the St. Croix Valley the year before. The group was led by Per Andersson, a farmer from a remote forest district in the northern Swedish province of Hälsingland (see Map 12.1). The Reverend Eric Norelius, chronicler of early Swedish settlement in the state and a personal friend of Andersson's, attributed this move to the resemblance the Chisago Lakes region bore to Andersson's home district. "He was thus a peasant of the 'Finn forests,'" wrote the churchman. Such a person, he continued, "considers it almost an indispensable condition for this life to have plenty of space, a lot of forest, lakes, fish, game to hunt and an inexhaustible supply of fresh air; but on agricultural land he sets less value. Thus it was not strange that Per Anders-[s]on under no condition wanted to stay in Illinois." In his early letters to Norelius, Andersson remarked that "The land is forested, no dry prairies." He was also pleased by the snow cover, saying "I like the winter here much better than in Illinois."[8]

If Per Andersson was an example of a settler who placed a Swedish environment high on his priority list, most of his friends were not. In spite of his constant pleas to countrymen in Illinois to join him, only a few families settled at Chisago Lakes over the next two years. It was not until 1854, when land shortages began to be felt in Illinois and a railroad reached the shores of the Mississippi, that the stream of Swedish land seekers entering Minnesota from earlier colonies and directly from Sweden began to swell. In the spring of that year a large party of settlers appeared at Chisago Lakes after spending the winter in Illinois. The group, which included Andersson's brother, had sailed from Sweden the year before, but had landed too late in the autumn to make the boat trip north. Altogether about 200 Swedes arrived during 1854, setting off a boom that resulted in the sale of much of the land in Chisago County. Most of it had earlier fallen into the hands of native-born Americans, who profited substantially by reselling it to Swedish immigrants.[9]

The stream of Swedes flowing into the region continued well into the 1880s, after which the scarcity of land forced them to look elsewhere. The Chisago Lakes area became the largest and best-known Swedish settlement in the St. Croix Valley. Another notable one developed to the south at Scandia in Washington County, while a smaller cluster sprang up to the east around Taylors Falls. Scandia can rightfully lay claim to a slightly earlier start than Chisago Lakes, but development there was not continuous. It is probably most

Map 12.1. Provinces of Sweden from which Emigrants Reached Minnesota

reasonable to regard these three communities collectively as the earliest pioneers of Swedish settlement in Minnesota. Eventually they grew together and spread into adjoining Isanti County to form the core of the largest Swedish-speaking rural area outside of Sweden. Known today as "Swedeland, U.S.A.," this major concentration encompasses both the upper St. Croix and Rum River valleys. In fact, one Swedish scholar noted in 1943 that "In the whole

of America there are not two counties showing so compact a majority of Swedish stock as Chisago and Isanti Co[un-tie]s" (see Table 12.2).[10]

The dominance of a single ethnic group over so large a rural area is unusual in American settlement history. In this case it was possible because the region lay on the edge of the main path of settlement. Early pioneers in Minnesota were first attracted to the deciduous hardwood forests near the lower Mississippi and Minnesota River valleys. This broad-leaf woodland was an environment familiar both to Old-Stock Americans from the East and Lower Midwest and to newer immigrants from northern and western Europe. Although it was laborious to clear, the land was known to be agriculturally productive, and it provided shelter from the elements as well as wood for fuel and construction. This hardwood forest, known in its southern reaches as the Big Woods, followed the belt of hilly glacial moraine that stretches from southeastern Minnesota northwestward into Otter Tail and Becker counties. South and west of the forest lay the prairie, a vast open grassland unlike anything the immigrants had ever seen. Unfamiliarity, coupled with the scarcity of wood and the difficulty of breaking the thick sod, discouraged settlement on the prairies until the early 1870s when the completion of railroads provided cheap transportation for timber and heavy equipment. North and east of the belt of broadleaf woodland was the coniferous forest, rich in the eyes of the lumber barons, but poor for agriculture because of its stony, acid soils, leached of minerals and low in organic matter.

The Chisago Lakes region lay on the southern edge of the coniferous forest and on the northern edge of the hardwoods in a zone of transition called the mixed forest. Most settlers bypassed it to the south as they sought land in the Big Woods. Swedes who might otherwise have followed the main path chose the area because relatives and friends had gone there before. The development of "Swedeland" offers a dramatic illustration of the important role in the migration process played by America letters, the correspondence between the settlers and those they left behind. Given an early start in a peripheral area where competition for land was not severe, subsequent migration was not only stimulated by these letters but also given direction. The result was an almost exclusively Swedish settlement of impressive proportions.[11]

Within it the network of personal contacts also produced subconcentrations, enclaves of people from provinces, sub-provincial districts, and occasionally even parishes. A majority of the Swedes who poured into the Chisago Lakes region in the middle 1850s were from the province of Små-land, an early center of Swedish emigration. Once this pro-vincial stamp had been placed upon the area, it remained.

A detailed study of the origins of Chisago County's Swed-ish population has revealed that, even though emigration from other provinces was heavy, for decades most of the immigrants continued to be from Småland. Using the records of the county's nine Swedish Lutheran churches, the study plotted the birthplaces of members from 1850 to 1905. The five churches in the southern part of the county, the original settlement core, showed a compact pattern of births in the

Table 12.2. Swedes in Minnesota by County, 1860–1970

County	1860 foreign born	1860 foreign mixed	1880 fb	1880 fm	1895 fb	1905 fb	1905 fm*	1930 fb	1930 fm	1970 fb	1970 fm
Aitkin			1		963	1,323	2,116	876	1,406	247	656
Anoka	2		425	194	1,215	1,123	2,434	992	1,687	267	2,943
Becker			352	187	883	958	2,184	571	1,502	77	797
Beltrami					36	744	1,236	604	1,121	32	547
Benton	1		25	10	380	479	1,180	340	706	13	275
Big Stone			256	123	657	602	1,360	333	829	36	334
Blue Earth	45	26	414	221	951	783	1,828	342	864	60	566
Brown	2		109	67	187	182	484	99	301	13	253
Carlton	4	4	111	47	1,146	1,743	3,314	1,291	2,139	158	1,426
Carver	664	170	1,267	947	1,127	823	2,017	303	789	11	341
Cass			11		283	508	902	367	730	69	534
Chippewa			348	198	696	582	1,361	294	848	39	417
Chisago	528	159	3,157	1,819	4,780	4,252	9,737	2,319	4,899	220	1,970
Clay			355	99	1,341	1,182	2,406	633	1,555	73	918
Clearwater						530	1,118	417	903	7	333
Cook					52	153	268	176	248	83	226
Cottonwood			113	58	253	219	509	115	344		235
Crow Wing	6		94	32	850	1,092	2,194	950	1,992	131	1,159
Dakota	31	14	344	186	787	667	1,493	644	1,144	103	1,610
Dodge			91	43	81	37	104	66	191	8	80
Douglas			1,161	602	2,824	2,277	5,433	1,279	2,649	111	1,289
Faribault			32	15	228	163	344	107	309	14	160
Fillmore			67	62	57	45	110	44	127		91
Freeborn	12	6	100	57	365	290	633	192	514	49	392
Goodhue	238	76	4,296	2,571	3,731	3,013	6,536	1,214	3,236	115	1,345
Grant			282	135	922	702	1,804	327	880	7	221
Hennepin	18	8	3,524	1,432	22,480	27,126	49,501	26,869	49,248	5,068	32,413
Houston	44	19	213	89	238	190	430	83	230	12	75
Hubbard					55	408	723	275	450	25	257
Isanti	42	10	2,336	1,110	4,346	4,453	8,933	2,165	4,379	199	1,592
Itasca					210	967	1,475	874	1,652	161	1,075
Jackson			78	38	257	212	474	127	343	22	147
Kanabec	1		215	93	1,423	1,630	2,044	1,023	1,820	145	743
Kandiyohi	97	31	2,120	1,408	3,009	2,694	6,550	1,431	3,571	108	1,697
Kittson			57	28	1,851	2,120	5,317	1,184	2,446	95	927
Koochiching								713	966	133	617
Lac qui Parle			142	76	482	487	1,164	278	737	47	402
Lake	1				581	1,364	2,075	943	1,301	129	879
Lake of the Woods								288	425	76	168
Le Sueur	4	1	98	73	336	267	498	148	261	12	138
Lincoln			38	3	205	202	473	118	281	15	110
Lyon			87	32	478	543	1,009	292	692	32	407
McLeod	12	6	143	118	182	109	297	66	205	54	211
Mahnomen								54	119		55
Marshall			68	43	2,596	2,523	5,102	1,148	2,487	101	974
Martin			89	61	822	817	1,901	472	1,120	34	715
Meeker	101	17	1,878	1,214	3,311	2,790	6,439	1,274	2,973	124	1,139
Mille Lacs			3		877	1,437	3,272	1,292	2,204	161	1,116
Morrison			27	27	1,457	1,647	3,722	1,067	1,793	66	728
Mower	1		135	68	237	168	364	127	355	13	256
Murray			211	113	654	612	1,529	311	923	39	327
Nicollet	192	61	1,433	833	1,540	1,194	2,795	676	1,523	68	630
Nobles			173	119	781	576	1,160	340	825	29	393
Norman					317	321	597	157	413	6	178
Olmsted	9	3	55	53	86	75	184	220	549	31	492
Otter Tail	22	2	1,001	587	2,763	2,594	6,085	1,443	3,288	117	1,574
Pennington								386	868	45	602
Pine	1		67	32	1,951	1,904	3,549	1,287	2,333	90	921
Pipestone			22	8	123	136	264	83	216		93
Polk			217	123	2,625	1,707	3,449	913	2,050	54	907
Pope			383	279	721	609	1,603	280	788	12	321
Ramsey	96	26	2,009	554	10,665	12,365	23,336	8,888	17,902	1,317	10,557
Red Lake						884	1,540	66	178	8	68
Redwood			158	97	377	327	984	220	503	28	235
Renville			564	367	1,347	1,047	2,423	450	1,270	7	469
Rice	25	10	166	120	315	232	574	117	579	11	414
Rock			24	29	79	66	152	37	145		140
Roseau					676	1,327	2,369	862	1,730	114	752
St. Louis	14	5	398	129	9,013	11,146	17,067	10,115	16,558	1,558	8,507
Scott	22	5	171	113	124	81	195	44	142	7	238
Sherburne	1		224	98	720	564	1,465	365	734	26	462
Sibley	13	2	557	377	1,131	689	2,441	372	947	41	393
Stearns	12	4	165	101	559	424	1,020	369	832	53	680
Steele	12	9	38	31	45	47	212	51	174	21	207

Table 12.2. Swedes in Minnesota by County, 1860–1970 (*continued*)

County	1860 foreign born	1860 foreign mixed	1880 fb	1880 fm	1895 fb	1905 fb	1905 fm*	1930 fb	1930 fm	1970 fb	1970 fm
Stevens			140	57	411	340	869	131	418	35	226
Swift			478	277	840	741	1,827	374	938	54	434
Todd			108	59	923	973	2,309	620	1,493	32	613
Traverse			151	71	983	749	1,695	319	715	13	217
Wabasha	41	11	486	327	534	416	955	215	490	13	205
Wadena			13	11	213	281	652	199	518	16	383
Waseca	27	8	265	208	309	224	537	97	361	11	162
Washington	570	135	2,189	1,034	3,230	2,805	5,708	1,151	2,523	97	1,535
Watonwan			416	320	856	676	1,660	413	1,018	68	394
Wilkin			31	16	221	216	537	126	411	24	128
Winona	18	9	197	104	173	134	356	85	285	10	127
Wright	20	6	1,852	1,199	3,016	2,633	5,802	1,347	2,726	128	1,257
Yellow Medicine			214	127	503	542	1,317	288	783	20	334
Total	2,949	843	39,238	21,559	119,052	126,283	254,085	90,623	180,120	12,978	101,534
Published census figures	(3,178)		(39,176)		(119,554)	(126,283)	(253,885)	(90,623)	(180,150)	(12,978)	(101,534)

Source: See Appendix

heart of the province of Småland, while the four later churches in northern Chisago County drew immigrants with more diverse origins. The study also indicated a relationship between the compactness of the birthfields and the stability of the communities. In those with the most compact birthfields, there tended to be less movement in and out, suggesting that the immigrants may have been more comfortable in a setting which, in human terms at least, was familiar to them. Regional concentrations characterized most Swedish rural settlements in Minnesota, but they were especially well developed in Chisago County, where settlement proceeded rather slowly.[12]

Two smaller Swedish centers during the pioneer period lay in the main path of movement. In September, 1853, Hans

THE PIONEER Swedish Evangelical Lutheran Church at Center City in 1894. The church remained active in the 1980s and was often visited by Swedish tourists.

Mattson of Skåne, who was later to serve as a land agent for the state of Minnesota and for several railroad companies, arrived in St. Paul with a group of immigrants. He was advised that good land could be obtained near the newly founded city of Red Wing in Goodhue County, and, guided by a man who knew the area, the party searched the deep valleys of the Cannon River system for a suitable location there. We "were not satisfied," Mattson wrote, "until we came upon the large prairie where Vasa is now situated. On this prairie we found the best soil and saw good oak woods in all directions." By the summer of 1854 at least ten Swedish families were living in the Vasa colony; over the next few years it grew until it came to embrace parts of nine contiguous townships in north-central Goodhue County.[13] Competition from Germans to the east, Norwegians to the south, and a variety of groups to the west put an end to expansion of the settlement, however, and by the late 1850s new settlers attracted to the area were forced to seek land at some distance to the west (see Maps 8.4, 11.4).

The last of the three early Swedish centers had even less chance to spread. In the spring and summer of 1854 a handful of settlers staked claims in a forested spot on the left bank of the Minnesota River four miles from the newly planned town of Carver. Originally called Oscar's Settlement, it became known as the Union Colony and in 1858 was divided into the East and West Union Lutheran congregations. In the lower valley of the Minnesota River, however, land was in great demand, and the small colony, which also included Norwegians, was never able to expand over more than two townships.[14]

From the beginning the population contained a strong component from the province of Västergötland. The son of one of the colony's founders underscored the importance of the America letters in creating regional concentrations of this kind. In recounting the history of his family, he wrote that his "parents emigrated in the year 1852. . . . within five years my father's parents, my mother's mother — her father was already dead — all of my parents' brothers and sisters and a whole host of other relatives, enticed by my father's letters, had ended up in Minnesota, where my parents after a long search and many distressing experiences had finally found an idyllic place in which to live. In our community, about two Swedish miles long and one Swedish mile wide [*about 12 by 6 English miles*] and containing two congregations, most of the people probably belonged to our family and nearly all had come from the same district in Sweden. So completely had they transplanted a piece of Sweden to America that the names given to groves of trees and farmsteads were largely identical with those in the home district. This great emigration had been set in motion by a few personal letters.''

Expansion from the Early Cores

Emigration from Sweden to the United States dropped from 3,980 in 1854 to 586 in 1855, marking the end of the pioneer period. Throughout the late 1850s and early 1860s it remained low, discouraged in part by the financial panic of 1857 and the Civil War, events which also slowed development within the newly created state. Railroad construction, much discussed in Minnesota just before the panic, was delayed well into the 1860s and 1870s. With the insecurity caused by the Dakota War of 1862, this delay retarded the advance of the frontier. Despite the small numbers of new immigrants, however, a considerable expansion of Swedish settlement occurred. It was spurred by the population pressure that was beginning to be felt in settlements farther east, especially those in Illinois. Ten years had passed since these colonies were founded. Some of the original settlers who had fashioned farms from the prairie found they could sell at a nice profit, buy cheap land farther west, and begin again on a larger scale. Others had sons who were now grown and looking for land they could afford.[15]

Except for the Chisago Lakes region, the pioneer Minnesota settlements could not absorb many newcomers. In the spring of 1857, for example, a group of Swedes from the vicinity of Lafayette, Indiana, arrived in Goodhue County. They stayed the summer and autumn in Cannon Falls while searching for land to their liking. Failing to turn up anything nearby, they eventually located about 50 miles from Cannon Falls on the edge of the prairie in eastern Waseca County. They called their settlement Vista for the Småland parish from which most of them had emigrated. In this remote location, a week's journey from the closest markets in Hastings and Red Wing, they built their sod huts, tilled the prairie soil, and developed their community. It was years before a railroad reached them.[16]

Not all newcomers looked so far afield. With the Carver settlement already established in the lower Minnesota Valley, many other prospective Swedish settlers were drawn to that region. By the mid-1850s most land near the river had been taken, but only a few miles to the west much was still available. Four Swedish settlements sprang up there; all were founded by people from Illinois and Iowa.

The first was established in 1855 on the eastern shore of Clearwater Lake by groups from Burlington, Iowa, and Galesburg, Illinois. One pioneer, anxious to attract more of his countrymen, described the site for readers of *Hemlandet*

(The Homeland), a Swedish-language newspaper published in Chicago: "This place lies ten miles northwest of Carver and constitutes, in my opinion, the most beautiful and best part of Carver County, lying on one of the most beautiful, if not the most beautiful lake in this state. . . . The lake is twelve square miles in size and is surrounded by forest of the most fertile nature. The forest consists mostly of sugar maple, mixed with other common varieties."

The land around this settlement, which came to be called Scandia and then Waconia, was taken very quickly, and a year later, when more settlers arrived from Illinois, they were directed to another lake six miles to the north. There they started Götaholm on Swede Lake two miles south of Watertown — a Carver County area one described as "mostly forested with several kinds of broadleaf trees, except for an abundance of large and small meadows, some marshy, which carry a superb grass suitable for animal feed. We have forest in profusion, for building and other needs as well as for sale."

A third group from Princeton, Illinois, dissatisfied with the land they saw near Carver in 1855, secured a claim in Nicollet County seven miles northwest of St. Peter, a town that already contained the nucleus of what would become a substantial Swedish population. Known as Scandian Grove, or the Lake Prairie Township Settlement, the third community grew up on the edge of the prairie, but it was the forest the early settlers emphasized in their descriptions. Wrote one: "There are about 1,200 acres of forest in our colony. . . . Four miles west of this forest are several thousand acres of prairie land at the congressional price ($1.25 per acre). This prairie has between one and two feet of black loam on a clay base, is free of stones, and is bordered on the south by large forests. . . . one can be sure that here there will never be a lack of necessary forest." As the demand for land continued, the settlement spread westward, and in 1858 a fourth community, first called New Sweden and later renamed Bernadotte, came into being.

At times religious conflict was responsible for the establishment of new settlements. The mid-19th century had seen the advent in Sweden of numerous nonconformist ideas, many of them emanating from England. These ideas normally entered the country at Stockholm and then spread to the provinces, taking hold most strongly where a tradition of lay evangelism already existed within the Lutheran faith. The southern part of Norrland, particularly the province of Hälsingland, proved especially receptive to such ideas. The state church of Sweden had long tried to protect itself against such deviant doctrines by means of the so-called *konventikelplakatet* (1726–1858), which forbade any private gathering for religious purposes. Offenders were punished by fines and prison sentences. Not surprisingly nonconformists were abundantly represented among the earliest emigrants from Sweden.[17]

The intolerance of the Swedish church toward these groups was carried to the New World. In 1856, for example, a Swedish Baptist congregation was started at Center City in Chisago County by a group of emigrants from Hälsingland. It soon became apparent that the Swedish Lutheran majority did not intend to let it exist in peace. Before the year passed the Hälsingland congregation informed the Minnesota Baptist Convention that it was "surrounded with a great number of our own nation who are all greatly opposed to our principles."[18]

Not wishing to remain in such a hostile environment, two members set out in 1857 to investigate land advertised for sale near Princeton in Mille Lacs County. After looking at it, they decided that they preferred the Rum River Valley, where they had camped on their way to Princeton. A migration from Center City then began to what is now the Cambridge area in Isanti County. By 1860 the Center City Baptist Church had been closed, and a new congregation had been organized by 14 Hälsingland Baptists who had moved to southeastern Isanti County. Despite the in-migration of large numbers of Lutherans in the late 1860s and the building of the first Swedish Lutheran church in Cambridge in 1866, Isanti remains today the most Baptist of the state's 87 counties.

Exceeding religious conflict as an incentive to open up new areas in this period, however, was a provision in the Pre-emption Act of 1841 stipulating that an individual could stake a claim on government land *before* it was offered for sale. This meant that payment could be delayed until the government placed the land on the market. Many immigrants who arrived with little or no capital saw this opportunity to farm now and pay later as the best way to get a start in the New World. A number of the small Swedish settlements planted in 1856 and 1857 far from markets on the edge of the Minnesota prairies had their origins in this practice. Litchfield and Swede Grove townships in Meeker County and Kandiyohi and Eagle Lake farther west in Kandiyohi County are examples.[19]

A Meeker County Swede reported to *Hemlandet* in 1859: "Our farmers out here have been greatly troubled for a while now as a result of the anticipated land sale. Those who had animals reckoned they would have to part with their last cow to avoid becoming homeless; and those who didn't have any — well they were perhaps the most fortunate, at any rate the least concerned, for they consoled themselves with the thought that 60 or 100 miles farther west there is still a lot of land which isn't on the market; so they guessed they would have to go there and begin again hunting, fishing, and digging. But maybe we could get a generous government that wanted to give a poor man 160 acres for nothing, and then they would have their modest dream. . . . For the moment, since the land has been taken off the market again, things have calmed down, and the Democrats are beginning to want to assert their claims on the people's gratitude."[20]

Some of the wilderness settlements beyond the settled edge of the frontier were short-lived, not because the government offered the land for sale, but because in August, 1862, the Dakota Indians living on reservations along the Minnesota River began a war that caught the settlers completely off guard. Those fortunate enough to escape fled eastward to safer areas behind the frontier. The fighting was quickly ended, but people were slow to return. Some never did so; others, joined by emigrants of the second wave, gave some settlements renewed life by deciding to try again.[21]

Second Wave — The Flight from Hunger, 1863–77

According to the census of 1860 the 2,949 foreign-born Swedes living in Minnesota constituted 17% of those in the United States but less than half as many as there were in Illinois. Over the next two decades the Swedish population of the state would rise to just over 39,000, a fifth of the national total. Most of this growth was the result of a second emigration wave between 1863 and 1877 when nearly 135,000 Swedes left their homes for the United States. Forty per cent of them departed in the peak years of 1868 and 1869, fleeing the aftermath of severe crop failures and widespread hunger. In contrast to the first wave in the 1850s, most of these migrants were driven from Sweden by difficult, if not desperate, circumstances. Push factors in this period were much stronger than pull factors. Families were still prominent in the emigration, but there were more young, single people than earlier. Large group migration was far less common; religious motivations were completely overshadowed by economic ones. A majority of the emigrants were from rural areas, and they were still looking for land. Many were poor, however, and had little capital with which to make a start.[22]

The conditions these immigrants encountered in Minnesota were very different from those of the 1850s. By 1865 the Indian danger was past, most of the Dakota had been expelled from the state, and large expanses of virgin land were open for settlement. Millions of acres would be offered free to settlers under the Homestead Act passed in 1862. Millions more would be sold at reasonable prices by the railroads rapidly reaching out from the growing Twin Cities. The Swedish immigrant of the late 1860s found in Minnesota a spirit of optimism that must have contrasted sharply with the atmosphere of hopelessness he had left behind. The railroad would conquer the prairie. Where it led, the settler would follow, secure in the knowledge that the wilderness he planned to farm would no longer be inaccessible to markets. By 1860 only 15% of the land in Minnesota had been settled. In the next two decades an additional 34% of the state was peopled, the largest expansion in any 20-year period.[23]

Railroads were the key to the location of new Swedish settlements during what we may call the "period of expansion." As the tracks plunged across the prairies, communities sprang up at Sveadahl in Watonwan County (1868), Comfrey in Brown County, Dunnell in Martin County, Louriston in Chippewa County (all in 1869), Balaton in Lyon County, and Worthington in Nobles County (both in 1871). In addition to offering ease of access to unsettled prairie, the railroads provided work for newly arrived immigrants. Many a prospective settler selected the site of his future home while earning "seed capital" in the railroads' employ (see Maps 12.2, 12.3, 12.4).[24]

The pastor of the Swedish Baptist Church recalled the birth of such a Swedish cluster at Worthington when he wrote: "Attracted by reports of fertile prairie land in the southwestern part of Minnesota, after the Indian disturbance had been quelled, some Scandinavians were found among the early settlers about Worthington in the year 1870. . . . In 1871, when the railroad was projected through the regions, several Swedish railroadworkers who observed the fertility of the country and heard that there was land to be

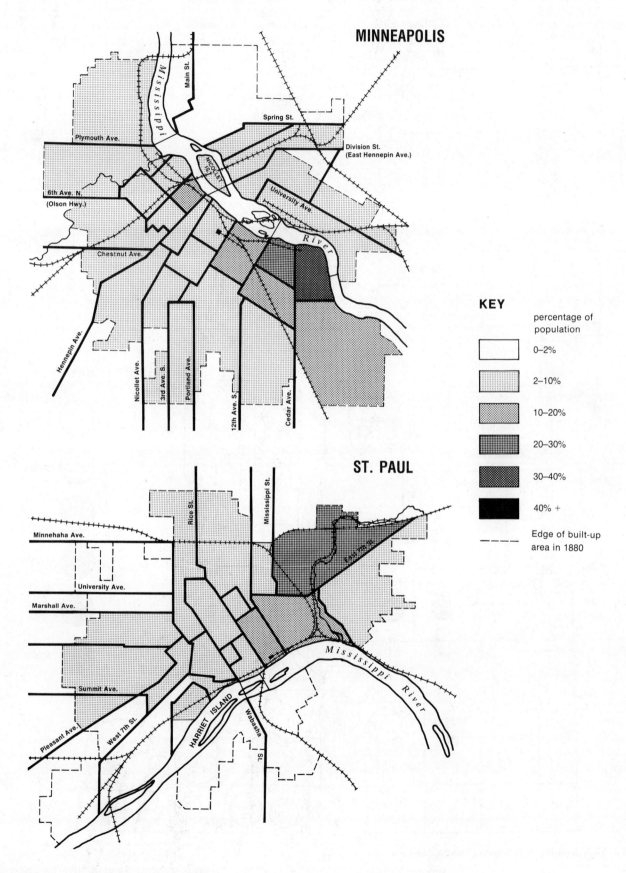

MINNEAPOLIS

ST. PAUL

KEY

percentage of
population

0–2%

2–10%

10–20%

20–30%

30–40%

40% +

Edge of built-up
area in 1880

Map 12.2. Swedes in the Twin Cities, 1880

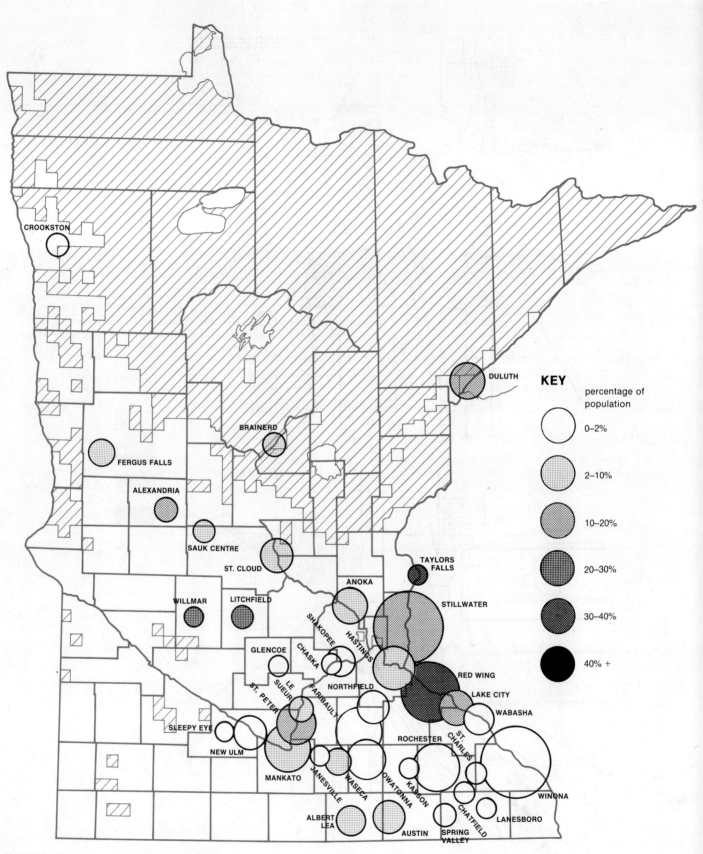

CROOKSTON

DULUTH

KEY

percentage of
population

0–2%

2–10%

10–20%

20–30%

30–40%

40% +

BRAINERD

FERGUS FALLS

ALEXANDRIA

SAUK CENTRE

ST. CLOUD

TAYLORS
FALLS

ANOKA

STILLWATER

WILLMAR   LITCHFIELD

SHAKOPEE

HASTINGS

RED WING

GLENCOE   CHASKA   LAKE CITY

LE
SUEUR   NORTHFIELD   WABASHA

ST. PETER   FARIBAULT

SLEEPY EYE   ROCHESTER   ST.
CHARLES

NEW ULM   WINONA

MANKATO   JANESVILLE   WASECA   OWATONNA   KASSON

CHATFIELD   LANESBORO

ALBERT
LEA   AUSTIN   SPRING
VALLEY

Map 12.3. Swedes in Minnesota Towns, 1880

Map shows towns over 1,000 population in 1880.   The size of the circles is proportional to the population.

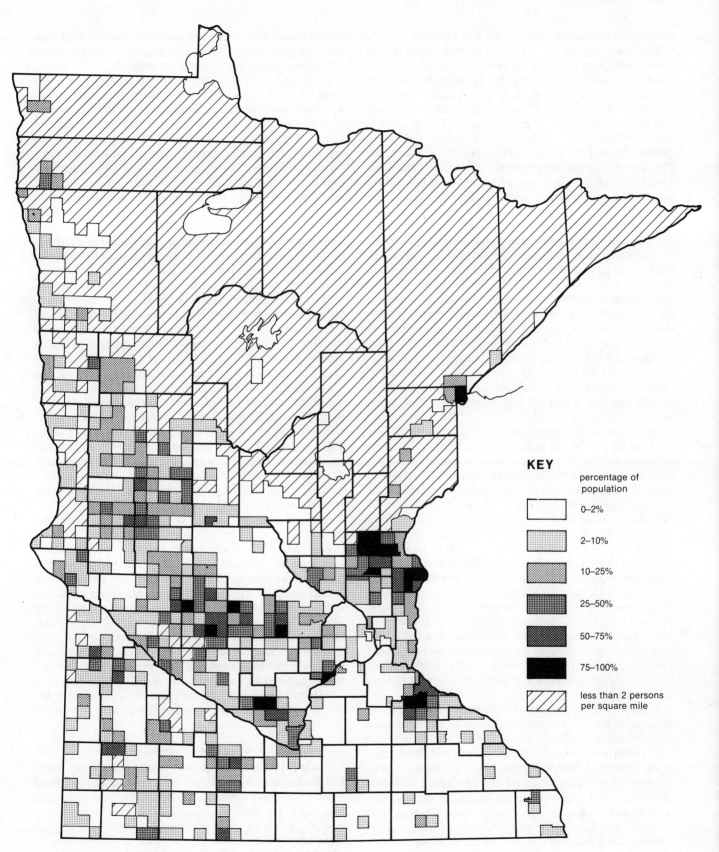

Map 12.4. Swedes in Minnesota Rural Areas, 1880

KEY

percentage of
population

0–2%

2–10%

10–25%

25–50%

50–75%

75–100%

less than 2 persons
per square mile

gotten took the opportunity to file for homesteads. . . . Others who had been made destitute by Indian raids farther North, came here to file on the land the same year.''

Like most settlers the Swedes had no experience with the prairie, but they accepted its challenges. A man who grew up near Sveadahl during the 1870s and 1880s remembered that ''all of the people were poor, and many of them lived in houses of turf. Most of them used hay as fuel, and I often admired the skill of the women in twining 'hay whisks.' . . . The hay cost nothing and produced a strong heat. The worst was the smoke and smell that permeated everything in the house. The neighborhood appeared desolate, since there were very few plantations of trees. The snowstorms of the winter, which usually lasted three days in succession, were a deadly peril. Our first winter in Sveadahl was 'the terrible snowwinter', when the snowdrifts reached as high as the roofs of the houses and stables. . . . Then, in the eighties, the locust period was past, but the population was still to a great extent destitute and hopeless. It almost seemed as if the earth were cursed since the invasions of the locusts. On the fields almost nothing but weeds grew. Many began to think that the land could not be used for farming. . . . My father, who was an old experienced farmer, tried to persuade them to plow both deeper and earlier and not to lose heart. It helped. And the land that then could be obtained for 5 dollars an acre can now [1920] not be bought at less than 200 an acre.''

Nevertheless the main thrust of Swedish settlement was not onto the prairie, but rather along the boundary between the prairie and the timber-clad moraine, a course followed by the main line of the St. Paul and Pacific Railroad. The great number of Swedish and other Scandinavian settlements which sprang up along this line owed their beginnings to the activities of Hans Mattson, a promoter of immigration for the state of Minnesota and a land agent for the railroad from 1866 to 1871. As one of the founders of Vasa, he not only influenced many Swedes from that colony to move to central Minnesota, he lured others directly from Sweden to the railroad lands in Meeker and Kandiyohi counties. In later years he continued his activities in the employ of the Lake Superior and Mississippi Railroad, the Canadian government, and as editor and owner of *Minnesota Stats Tidning* (Minnesota State Times), capping a career that would be the envy of any modern promoter. Probably no other single individual had so great an influence on Swedish settlement patterns in Minnesota.[25]

A number of the main-line settlements encouraged by Mattson in the late 1860s were located on the abandoned sites of ''squatter'' claims which predated the Dakota War. They began in southwestern Wright County with Stockholm-Cokato (formerly Mooers Prairie), which the tracks reached in 1869, and stretched westward through Dassel, platted by the railroad that year and peopled by Swedes from Västergötland and Värmland. They continued to Litchfield and Swede Grove (now Grove City) in Meeker County, and to Atwater, Lake Elizabeth, New London, and Mamre in Kandiyohi County. West of these areas Norwegians predominated and Swedish clusters became more scattered. But Swedes were also attracted to lands along the St. Paul and

Pacific branch line, which ran northwest through St. Cloud and Alexandria to Moorhead, giving rise to a large number of settlements, especially in Douglas County.[26]

By the end of the 1860s public and railroad land alike was being taken up very rapidly, not an optimal situation for the development of strongly national or provincial communities of any size. Yet a study has shown that around each of Kandiyohi County's seven Swedish Lutheran churches the first farms were usually developed by people from the same Swedish province. These core areas were still clearly evident in 1905, the last date for which they can accurately be reconstructed (see Map 12.5). In one of the communities, the dominant group emigrated from the single parish of Gagnef in Dalarna or Dalecarlia. These clusters of Swedes, formed amidst a veritable land rush by people of many nationalities, attested not only to the competence of railroad agents like Mattson, but also to the efficacy of the network of personal ties operating through the America letters.[27]

Most of the second-wave Swedes who were not drawn to the railroad lands headed for the expanding settlements in the St. Croix and Rum River valleys. The Småland flavor of the core Chisago Lakes communities was maintained as more immigrants followed friends and relatives who had left during the first wave, but the newer settlements, especially those in northern Chisago County, tended to be more mixed. In adjacent Isanti County the Hälsingland Baptists, who had sought refuge from the Lutherans a decade earlier, were invaded by a flood of immigrants from upper Dalarna. This emigration began in 1862 with the Baptists of Orsa parish, who had close ties with those of nearby Hälsingland. The idea of emigrating spread from parish to parish, and by the famine year of 1868 nonconformists and Lutherans alike were streaming out of Dalarna.[28]

Although their destinations in America were varied, the early Isanti connection led many to Minnesota. The first large group reached the Rum River Valley near Cambridge in 1866 from the parish of Rättvik; large numbers from other parishes followed. Lack of competition for land in Isanti County allowed some to establish what practically amounted to daughter parishes. A study of the Rättvik group, whose center was the Cambridge Lutheran Church, found that certain organizational features of the homeland parish were transplanted and consciously perpetuated. So completely did immigrants from upper Dalarna dominate Isanti County that it came to be called ''the Dalecarlia of America'' or ''America's Dalarna,'' and well into the 20th century the distinctive dialects of that province could be widely heard there.[29]

Third Wave — The Mass Emigration, 1880–93

Toward the end of the 1870s Swedish emigration, which had been slowed by the depressed economy in the United States, began to pick up again. By 1880 it reached 36,263, ushering in the third wave and a 14-year era of mass emigration. In five of those years annual emigration reached more than 40,000, and over the period it totaled close to 475,000 Swedes.[30]

During the third wave, emigration characteristics changed markedly. In its early stages the migration was prompted by

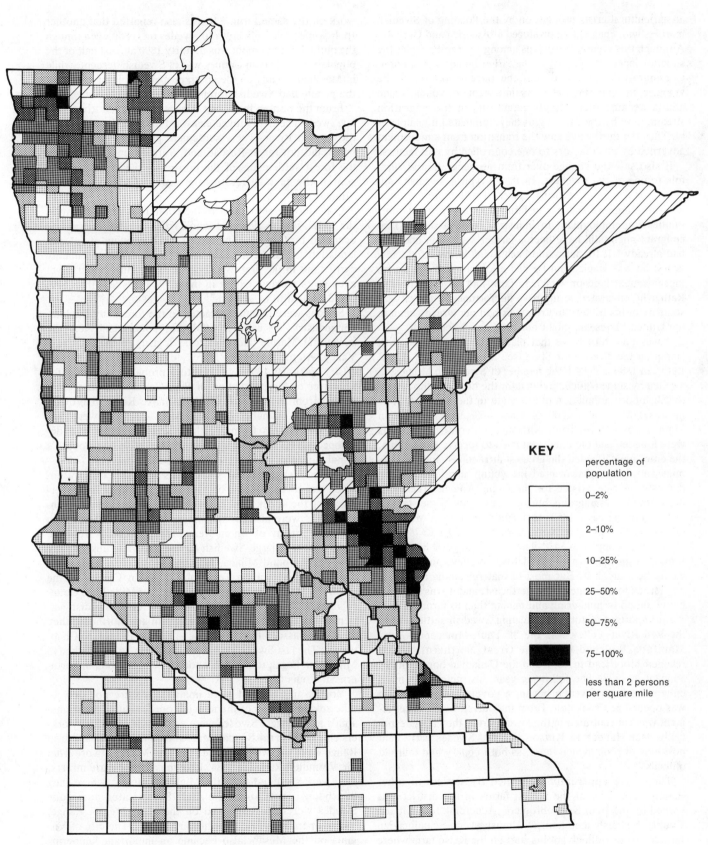

Map 12.5. Swedes in Minnesota Rural Areas, 1905

KEY

percentage of
population

0–2%

2–10%

10–25%

25–50%

50–75%

75–100%

less than 2 persons
per square mile

an agricultural crisis brought on by the flooding of Swedish markets with cheap grain produced in America and Ukraine. Although this created hardships among the rural people, the situation lacked the gravity of the earlier famine years. Family emigration continued, but the parents tended to be younger, the children fewer. As time went on, young, single adults became increasingly numerous in the migration stream, until by the early 1890s they dominated it completely. Thus the third wave saw the transition from a movement governed by push factors to one controlled by pull factors.

It also saw the change-over from an emigration of rural folk to one of city dwellers. In 1880 a typical Swedish emigrant was the son of a farmer, married with a child or two, with little hope of success in farming and with few opportunities for employment in industry. In 1893 that typical emigrant might still have been a farmer's son, but one who had already left the farm and been living in town for a few years; he was single, and he had a job. In America he no longer sought land on which to farm and raise his family. Rather he emigrated to improve his fortunes in the city. If so many of his friends and relatives had not already been in the United States, he might not have emigrated at all.

It was this third wave that placed the heaviest Swedish stamp on the North Star State (see Maps 12.2, 12.3, 12.4). Between 1880 and 1890 the number of Swedes in Minnesota swelled by some 60,000, giving it for the first time the largest Swedish-born population of any state in the nation. Of this increase, more than 26,000, or almost 45%, were recorded in Minneapolis and St. Paul. Although new rural settlements were founded and old ones continued to receive immigrants, the cities now afforded the greatest attractions. Jobs in sawmills and flour mills awaited the young men; positions in domestic service existed for the young women. The cities drew not only immigrants but rural residents of the state as well. From the early 1850s to 1880 the portion of Minnesota's population living on farms varied from 70% to 75%; by 1890 it had dropped to 54%. There was still good land to be broken, especially in the Red River Valley, and Swedes would help break it. But most of that remaining lay in the coniferous forest zone of the northeast, and it was to prove better suited to lumbering and mining than to farming.[31]

An important factor in stimulating Swedish settlement in the Red River Valley was the St. Paul, Minneapolis, and Manitoba Railroad (later the Great Northern), which reached Moorhead in 1871 and the Canadian border at St. Vincent in 1878. The following year, just before the mass emigration from Sweden began, a government land office was opened at Crookston. From the outset, Swedish settlement was concentrated in the lower part of the valley, especially near Hallock in Kittson County. Swedes early held positions of prominence there, as both county and railroad officials.[32]

They were apparently welcomed by settlers of other nationalities. One of the largest farms in the district was owned by the Irish Kelso brothers. According to a Kittson County Swedish merchant, "Almost every Scandinavian farmer east of Hallock got his start on the Kelso farm where they usually worked a few years until they had saved enough to buy a bit of land, and their wives, too, often had their first

work on the same farm." It was also reported that another Irish farmer sold milk cows to Swedes on credit even though the outlook for payment was dim. By 1890 at least half of the population of Kittson County was of Swedish descent, while in Marshall County to the south probably at least a third of the people had Swedish forebears.

From the bottom lands and terraces of the Red River Valley Swedish settlers moved eastward into the upper basin of the Roseau River. There settlement preceded the railroad, which did not reach Roseau and Warroad until 1908. With the forest settlements of the northeast, this district represented the last agricultural frontier of the Swedes in Minnesota.[33]

Considerable settlement of the coniferous forest began in the 1880s, but by 1900 less than 25% of the vast region was occupied by farmers. The clearing and plowing of cutover lands left by lumbering and mining companies was mainly carried out in the first two decades of the 20th century, yet even at its greatest extent in the early 1920s less than 60% could be said to be settled.[34]

Swedes were initially attracted to the forests by the lumber industry. As early as 1853 they bought land near the sawmill at Marine and worked as loggers in the St. Croix Valley. As their numbers increased, many followed the industry north. By 1890 Swedish stock probably accounted for a quarter of the population of Pine County. As lumbering moved from the St. Croix up the Snake River, it brought Swedes into Kanabec County. After the trees were cut, many immigrants from Jämtland and Ångermanland developed farms there, and even in the 1970s the county's population was predominantly of Swedish descent.[35]

The early agricultural settlements in Isanti County ensured that Swedes would be especially prominent in lumbering along the upper Rum River. In Mille Lacs County extensive areas were also brought under the plow by Swedes in the 1890s, many of whom were sawmill workers from the Twin Cities. A large Swedish farming district subsequently developed around Milaca, Isle, and Opstead in Mille Lacs County and in Malmo Township in Aitkin County to the north. By 1930 Swedes constituted 53% of Mille Lacs County's foreign born. Elsewhere in the pine forest Swedish settlements were small and scattered. In the northeast they were often associated with those of Swede-Finns (see Chapter 15). The last Swedish rural settlement to be established in Minnesota began to develop about 1900 near Cook in northern St. Louis County.[36]

Young, single, third-wave immigrants were not slow to take advantage also of the new job opportunities on Minnesota's iron ranges. Swedes were among the very first workers employed in the Soudan Mine and on the Duluth and Iron Range Railroad, which shipped the first Minnesota ore from the Vermilion Range in 1884. Like most of the early miners, they were recruited from the Michigan ranges, where they had been active since the mid-1860s. Later numerous Swedes were also employed on the giant Mesabi Range, where operations began in the early 1890s. The city of Virginia on the Mesabi also became an important lumbering center at the end of the century, and the chance to earn better wages probably drew some woodsmen, especially marginal laborers who tended to be recent immigrants, to the nearby mines. Swedes rose quickly in the mining hierarchy; by 1900, with the Finns, they had largely replaced the Cornishmen as skilled workers and mine bosses. After the turn of the century the number of Swedish laborers declined as southern and eastern Europeans replaced them in the mines. Though they left the mines, for the most part they did not leave the Minnesota ranges to find other mining opportunities as the Cornish workers had. Rather they stayed on as mining company officials or learned new trades and became the carpenters, masons, plumbers, and plasterers of the iron range cities.[37]

In 1905, 7.6% of the population of all Minnesota towns with more than 3,000 people had been born in Sweden. Table 12.3 lists those towns in which the Swedish-born population reached at least 7%. The withdrawal of the Swedes from the mines was reflected in the fact that of the five iron range towns in this class, only the two main service centers, Virginia and Hibbing, are listed. Swedes were particularly numerous in such important lumbering towns as Stillwater, which was close to the early rural Swedish settlements in the St. Croix Valley, as well as in Brainerd and Cloquet. The Minnesota town with the highest percentage of Swedes was Two Harbors, to which the Duluth, Missabe, and Iron Range Railroad carried ore for shipment east across the Great Lakes. Outstate the largest number (6,920) of Swedes, however, was to be found in Duluth, the major iron- and grain-shipping port at the western end of Lake Superior, where a significant Swedish community had existed almost from the city's beginnings. As early as 1870, more than a decade before iron mining got under way, Swedes comprised a fifth of Duluth's population.[38]

Table 12.3. Towns with Greatest Concentrations of Swedish Born, 1905

	% Swedish		% Swedish
Metropolitan Minnesota		Iron Range Towns	
Minneapolis	9.8	Hibbing	7.9
Service Centers in		Virginia	9.2
Swedish Farming Regions		Iron Ore Ports	
Alexandria	8.9	Duluth	10.7
Moorhead	8.6	Two Harbors	27.2
Red Wing	12.9	Lumber Towns	
St. Peter	9.3	Brainerd	7.3
Willmar	13.3	Cloquet	11.7
		Stillwater	9.6

Source: Minnesota, *Census, 1905.*
Note: Only 6% of St. Paul's population was Swedish born in 1905.

Five places on the list were agricultural service centers in areas of heavy Swedish rural settlement. Like other country towns in the state that began as Yankee enclaves, Alexandria, Moorhead, Red Wing, St. Peter, and Willmar eventually took on the ethnic flavor of their trade areas as retired farmers moved in and their children sought opportunities outside of farming. Red Wing served Goodhue County, including Vasa, and, as a steamboat stop on the Mississippi River, was long a destination for immigrant Swedes. Willmar and Alexandria were centers for the clusters that developed along the St. Paul and Pacific routes to the west. Moorhead,

as the first rail hub in the Red River Valley, attracted a considerable number of Swedes to its hinterland. St. Peter was somewhat unusual. It served the Swedish agricultural settlements of Scandian Grove and Bernadotte, but it also became the home in 1876 of Gustavus Adolphus College, Minnesota's only Swedish Lutheran institution of higher education.[39]

In 1905 cities of over 3,000 people contained 44% of Minnesota's Swedish born but only 32.7% of the state's total population. By that time Swedes were clearly more urban than the population as a whole. And more than half of the urban-dwelling 44% lived in the Twin Cities (29.7% of the foreign-born Swedes as against 23.2% of the total population). The third wave of emigration from Sweden placed a special stamp on the Twin Cities, particularly Minneapolis, that survives to this day.

Fourth Wave — The Fortune Seekers, 1900–13

After the severe depression of 1893, annual Swedish emigration to the United States rose above 15,000 for the first time in 1900. This level was exceeded in every year but two through 1913, rising to 35,439 in 1903. Altogether just over 280,000 people joined the fourth wave, only 60% of the volume of the third wave, which covered the same number of years. The movement was overwhelmingly one of young, single adults, attracted in part by the strong pull of the American labor market's higher pay and in part by the encouragement of a large Swedish-American community. By this period almost every young Swede had a relative somewhere in the United States whose tales of instant success were hard

OLD MAIN at Gustavus Adolphus College in St. Peter, a Swedish center, about 1915.

SWEDE HOLLOW in 1915, half a century after it earned its name.

to resist. But industrialization was moving ahead in Sweden, creating many job opportunities, and this surge of departures produced the first large-scale public opposition to emigration within Sweden.[40]

Minnesota, with its already large Swedish population, inevitably received a significant portion of the surge, much of which settled in the Twin Cities. The distribution of rural Swedes in the state in 1905 may be seen in Map 12.5. The Swedish-born population of the state peaked in 1905 at just over 126,000. At that time almost 38,000 Swedes lived in Minneapolis and St. Paul, making them the second largest urban concentration in the United States after Chicago with 63,000. Almost 7.5% of the Twin Cities' population was Swedish born, a proportion far larger than that of any other city of more than 100,000 people in the nation.[41]

As they did in the countryside, Swedes in the Twin Cities tended to settle in clusters. Because of the much greater population density, however, these urban groupings were usually less homogeneous than those in rural areas. In both Minneapolis and St. Paul, Swedes often intermingled with Norwegians and Danes, and in many ways it is more accurate to speak of Scandinavian clusters than of strictly Swedish ones. Nonetheless it should be remembered that in 1910 Swedes constituted 61% of the Scandinavian born in the Twin Cities.

St. Paul, the older of the two cities, was the first to attract them in numbers. In the late 1850s Swedes began to move into the shacktown that had sprung up a decade earlier in the steep-sided valley carrying Phalen Creek to its junction with the Mississippi River. This valley early attracted the milling and brewing industries with their high demands for unskilled and semiskilled labor. The Swedes provided some of that labor. Most of the few first-wave emigrants to the city were the rural poor who lacked the capital to farm. The Swedish community in St. Paul had its roots in their search for a path out of poverty. The squalid cluster of wooden huts spreading along the valley was to be a stepping stone to better things.

For almost half a century the Phalen Creek community, which became known as *Svenska Dalen* or Swede Hollow, served as a funnel for newly arrived Swedish immigrants. So strongly were they associated with the valley that even after the Italians and the Mexicans succeeded them there, the name lived on.[42]

As success came to the early Swedes of the hollow, they spread north along Payne Avenue and up the bluff into Arlington Hills, where they were joined by second- and third-wave emigrants. There on the East Side, the city's largest Swedish community developed. At its height it stretched from the Mississippi River bluff north to Lake Phalen and the city's boundary with Maplewood. Its nerve center was Payne Avenue, the neighborhood shopping street and the stage for community celebrations. One former merchant has been quoted as saying that if you didn't speak Swedish you had no business on Payne Avenue.

The East Side community offered variety in job opportunities and residential areas. Hamm's Brewery was the largest single employer; retailing, crafts, a variety of small businesses, and the professions were present. Property values rose as one moved toward the city limits, so it was possible to move up the social ladder without leaving the community. As transportation methods changed and people became more mobile, however, the distinctive Swedishness of the East Side declined. The automobile permitted people to live farther from work. It also allowed friendship circles to expand beyond the limits of a single city neighborhood. The result was a dispersion of Swedish stock throughout St. Paul and the entire metropolitan area. In 1980 the East Side still contained a sizable population of Swedish ancestry, but it was no longer the clearly discernible Swedish heart of the city that it had been before World War II.

Although Minneapolis could not boast the earliest Swedish settlement, by 1910 it contained 70% of all the Swedes living in the Twin Cities. Their preference for Minneapolis was probably twofold: (1) they encountered no serious competition from other established groups, such as they did with the Germans and the Irish in St. Paul; (2) the city's extensive trade area contained a large part of the considerable Swedish rural settlement in Minnesota and the Dakotas. In 1930 Swedes were the largest foreign-born group in every section of the city except heavily eastern European Wards 1 and 3.[43]

The substantial Swedish influx into Minneapolis began with the second-wave emigrants of the late 1860s. The first nucleus took shape near the corner of South Washington and 2nd avenues, from which the Scandinavian neighborhood spread eastward toward Cedar Avenue and Seven Corners. The third and fourth waves — the mass emigration and the fortune seekers of the period from 1880 to 1910 — established Cedar-Riverside as the largest Scandinavian cluster in Minneapolis. A wide variety of life-styles could be found there, from the down-and-outers who frequented the stretch of Washington Avenue known as Snoose Boulevard (Swedish *snus* = snuff) to the middle-class pillars of the Augustana Lutheran Church at 7th Street South and 11th Avenue. The community also had its shacktown, located on a low terrace along the Mississippi River and known as Bohemian Flats, which was shared by Czechs and Irish among other groups.

Like St. Paul's East Side, Cedar-Riverside was a self-contained neighborhood, offering residences, employment, shopping, and entertainment within walking distance. Cedar Avenue was the main street, and along it could be found Scandinavian bars, hotels, rooming houses, banks, and bookstores. In the late 1880s Dania Hall was built. The offerings of its upstairs theater and the nearby Southern Theater ranged from Strindberg to vaudeville comedy. In the 1890s Pillsbury Settlement House was built in the area as a community center.

By the 1890s population pressure was pushing Scandinavians south of Franklin Avenue into the Powderhorn Park area, a middle-class neighborhood containing working-class

sections like that along Milwaukee Avenue. At the same time, Scandinavians were also moving along the river into the Seward and Longfellow neighborhoods as far southeast as Minnehaha Park, where the annual Swedish midsummer festival, *Svenskarnas Dag*, is still held. After Cedar-Riverside, the old core, began to decline in the 1920s when Prohibition put a damper on its vital entertainment district, South Minneapolis became the 20th-century heart of the city's Scandinavian community with Riverside Avenue as its northern boundary. In that decade Blacks began to move eastward along Washington Avenue South as the Scandinavians had done earlier, but the two groups "remained largely aloof from each other." Since the 1950s the expansion of the University of Minnesota to the west bank of the river, the destruction of part of the area to construct Interstate 35W, and the block-busting tactics of Heller-Segal Associates, a real estate firm which placed long-haired students in houses on predominantly Scandinavian blocks, dealt the final death blow to the old neighborhood.[44]

Another large Scandinavian settlement grew up in Northeast Minneapolis, where a concentration of flour mills, breweries, foundries, railroad repair shops, and small industries led to the development of a distinctive blue-collar community. In the early 20th century the boundary between the area's Scandinavian and Polish and Ukrainian people followed 5th Street, with the Scandinavians living to the east and the Slavs to the west. As late as 1930 Swedes were the largest single foreign-born group in Ward 9, the larger of the two Northeast wards. They dominated the Maple Hill-Columbia region, stretching from Broadway on the south to Columbia Park on the north, and the small Dogtown neighborhood south of Broadway. A stretch of Pierce Street was referred to as "Swede Alley." But even then they were beginning to move to South Minneapolis. After World War II others doubtless joined the exodus to the suburbs. Today in

SAMUELSON'S CONFECTIONERY in the Minneapolis Seven Corners area about 1890. The shop sold items ranging from fresh fruit to candy and cigars well into the 1940s.

A CROWD of adults and children spilled out of the Southern Theater on Washington Avenue in Minneapolis in 1910. By 1980 the face of the Seven Corners neighborhood had changed considerably, but the building once again served as a theater.

Northeast, Scandinavian neighborhoods are confined largely to an area east of Fillmore and north of 18th Avenue. They have been replaced west of Central Avenue mainly by the eastward-moving Slavs; in Dogtown they have been supplanted by the Italians.[45]

Across the river from Northeast a third major Scandinavian community developed in the Camden district, where a settlement had grown up around a shingle factory at the mouth of what came to be called Shingle Creek. Originally a Yankee enclave, it attracted Scandinavians and other immigrants who found jobs during the latter part of the 19th century in its lumberyards and brickworks. By 1920 a heavily Scandinavian settlement extended from North 26th to 44th avenues. From Lyndale Avenue to the river the neighborhoods had a distinctly working-class flavor; to the west most residents owned their own homes and were comfortably well off. North of 44th Avenue, the landscape was still almost rural. Houses were small with big gardens, and the largely Scandinavian residents were young. In 1905 Camden (Ward 10) had a higher percentage of Swedish born than any other part of the city except the old Cedar-Riverside core. A substantial Scandinavian concentration, Camden has been surprisingly neglected in accounts of those groups in Minneapolis.[46]

Two other small clusters in Minneapolis are worthy of mention. Both developed on the near North Side in the midst of mainly Jewish neighborhoods. One was located from 6th Avenue north to Broadway and between Knox and Lyndale avenues. By 1980 both the Jewish and Scandinavian communities had disappeared, replaced by Blacks who began to move there in the 1920s. The other cluster lay immediately southwest from Knox west to Xerxes and from Chestnut south to Cedar Lake in an area known as Bryn Mawr. There the Scandinavian element had weakened considerably by 1980, and the area was racially mixed.[47]

Fifth Wave — The End of an Era, 1920–30

By 1913 the basic pattern of Scandinavian settlement in the Twin Cities and in Minnesota as a whole had been established. Following a lull caused by World War I, Swedish emigration rose briefly once again, but only about 100,000 people arrived during this fifth and final wave in the 1920s. In Minnesota these immigrants were not sufficiently numerous to replace the losses by death in the state's Swedish-born population. The 1930 census recorded only 90,623 Swedes, less than three-quarters of the peak population in Minnesota two decades earlier. Thereafter emigration remained small; those who left were exceeded in some years by those who decided to return. In the second half of the 20th century emigration to the United States continued to be inconsiderable. For the most part, Swedes did not participate heavily in the so-called brain drain of professionals who were for a time drawn to the United States by the high salaries of the 1950s and 1960s. Most of those who immigrated then were engineers or nurses. The few who did arrive in Minnesota tended not to identify with the long-established Swedish-American community. They cannot be said to have altered the imprint placed on the state by the great migration of the late 19th and early 20th centuries.[48]

Assimilation

So far Swedish immigrants to Minnesota have been identified in terms of their place of birth (national origin), and a group identity has been assumed on the basis of a common language albeit with marked dialectal variations. Associated with the Swedish language was a common historical tradition, written and oral, and a background of Lutheranism extending over 300 years. Now it is time to consider definitions. Shall we regard the Minnesota Swedes of the 19th century as an ethnic group? Or is there a better term that might be employed?

Orlando Patterson has offered a useful distinction between an ethnic group, which *chooses* to emphasize common cultural traits "as their most meaningful basis of primary, extrafamilial identity" and a culture group, which shares, consciously or unconsciously, an "identifiable complex of meanings, symbols, values, and norms."[49] Swedish immigrants arriving in America formed a minority culture group. At some times and in some places they doubtless also constituted an ethnic group, as Patterson defined it. Some quickly lost the cultural baggage they carried from the Old World and melted into American society. Others strove to retain a sense of Swedishness, establishing institutions that enabled them to do so, and thereby creating, in Patterson's sense, a Swedish ethnic group in the United States. Not all Swedish Americans belonged to this ethnic group just as individual Swedes were not always conscious of belonging to the cultural group. Those who did exhibited a wide range of commitments.

Patterson argued that the degree of commitment an individual makes to an ethnic group depends on his or her socioeconomic context. Thus ethnic identity is likely to occur (1) only where it does not conflict with other group identities such as profession or class, and (2) only where the best interests of the individual are served by emphasizing ethnic identity in cases where conflict does exist. If we accept this analysis, we should not expect the assimilation of Swedes to have proceeded at the same pace everywhere in the state. It should be slow, for example, in Chisago and Isanti counties, where almost everyone was a farmer and Swedes constituted a substantial majority. There ethnicity did not conflict with status. Indeed membership in the ethnic group was an advantage since Swedes usually dominated local society. In Minneapolis, on the other hand, even though the Swedish population was large, it shared the city with many other culture groups, the host society was in much firmer control, and the range of occupations and other sources of group identification was considerably wider. In such a situation strong ethnic identity might well conflict with socioeconomic aspirations, thus weakening the individual's commitment to the ethnic group and hastening assimilation.

And how shall we define assimilation? Milton M. Gordon described two aspects of the assimilation process, which he called cultural assimilation (or acculturation) and structural assimilation (or amalgamation). In the first process the immigrant adopts the cultural trappings of the host society — its language, belief systems, values, norms, patterns of consumption, etc. The Swede begins to *look* like an American. In the second process the immigrant becomes integrated into the host society, first through its schools, work places, and community organizations, then by means of its private clubs, social organizations, and friendship groups, and finally through intermarriage. The Swede begins to *act* like an American. The assimilation process is complete when the immigrant no longer thinks of himself as a hyphenated American and is unwilling to support a special interest position that conflicts with the values and interests of the host society, a process Gordon called civic assimilation. The Swede begins to *think* like an American.[50]

Cultural Assimilation

During his tour of America in 1872–74, Hugo Nisbeth, a Swedish traveler, was invited to celebrate the traditional Swedish Midsummer Day in the Vasa community. He attended services in the newly finished Lutheran church, where he "looked in vain . . . for something of the Swedish folk dress, but not a trace of it was to be seen. The men were dressed in neat, light-weight American suits, and to judge from the women's apparel one would have thought one was at a performance in Stockholm instead of in a Swedish rural church on the westernmost outskirts of American civilization. . . . Not just here but everywhere else I have been in America I have found that no one so quickly and willingly adopts the American's weaknesses for dressing his women well as the Swede. . . . And this weakness for clothing has spread to all classes, and one must be a sharp and well-trained observer if one is to tell the servant girl from her mistress out here in the West."[51]

The abandonment of such outward appearances of foreignness proceeded rapidly among the Swedes, who soon came to look like their other American neighbors. Their homes, too, save for a few precious items borne from Sweden, resembled everyone else's. Nisbeth observed as unusual a Swedish flag flying over a house in Litchfield on the 4th of July and a portrait of Charles XV hanging over the table in a sod hut on the prairie.

Eating and drinking customs were even harder to maintain in a land where the agricultural system was so different. Thus traditional dishes quickly came to be associated mainly with the major holidays, especially Christmas, where they have tenaciously persisted to the present. Nisbeth remarked that while in Breckenridge he stayed at the best hotel, which was operated by Swedes, and was served as a special favor "as Swedish a supper as could be produced." In Minneapolis and St. Paul, where customers were more numerous, specialty food shops could and did develop, but the everyday cuisine nonetheless became Americanized. At Christmas, however, supermarkets in the 1980s advertised lutfisk (lye-treated cod) and lingonberries, and spritz and other sweets suddenly appeared in many homes. Moreover it was still possible to buy locally made *korv* (sausage) throughout the year, although specialty butcher shops had for the most part disappeared.

Traditional foods were not the only evidence of Swedishness to persist. Swedes in Minnesota retained for some time one of the most important aspects of culture — their language. The so-called language question long held the attention of many persons in the Swedish community. From the outset it was clear that if the Swedish language were to continue to be used by future generations it would have to be supplemented by English. Nowhere in Minnesota, or anywhere else in the United States for that matter, was there a Swedish settlement so large and diverse that all the affairs of daily life could be conducted in Swedish. Even in the Chisago-Isanti region, many merchants in the towns were Old-Stock Americans. Dealings with them and with most state and local government officials had to be conducted in English. Thus Swedish immigrants did not question the need to know English. It is significant that, unlike some German groups, they made no attempt to establish full-time Swedish primary schools.

It was in the churches that the greatest effort was made to preserve Swedish as the spoken language of the home and local community. The principal religious bodies to which Swedish Americans belonged were the Augustana Lutheran Synod and the Mission Covenant, Swedish Baptist, and Swedish Methodist churches. All initially retained Swedish as the working language of the church. It is hard to overestimate the importance of the church as a community center, especially in rural areas of 19th-century Minnesota, where it forged the basic friendship circles in the society.[52] By keeping Swedish not only as its liturgical language but as its social language as well, the church created an atmosphere in which Swedish was able to flourish, something individual families would have found very difficult to do.

A major problem faced by the churches concerned the children, who were receiving their educations entirely in English-language public schools. The effort to pass the Swedish language along to them fell to the Sunday schools, although the Augustana Synod also established summer "week-day schools," sometimes known as "Swede schools." Patterned after the Swedish *folkskola*, they taught children to read the Bible and the catechism, using ABC books, Luther's Bible history, and native songs to carry out instruction entirely in Swedish.[53]

The churches also concerned themselves with higher education. Secondary schools (then called academies) were established at St. Peter by the Augustana Synod (Gustavus Adolphus), in St. Paul by the Swedish Baptist Church (Bethel), and in Minneapolis by the Mission Covenant Church (Minnehaha Academy). At Gustavus Adolphus and Bethel the academies were associated with colleges. Originally designed to train ministers, these institutions gradually acquired more general educational functions, and helped keep an interest in Swedish language and culture alive among the intellectuals of the community.[54]

In the realm of public education, the legislature in 1883 passed a bill requiring that a professorship in Scandinavian languages and literature be established at the University of Minnesota. Secondary schools, however, were slow to follow this lead. Not until 1910, with the introduction of a course at South High School in Minneapolis, was instruction in the Swedish language available at that level. By 1913, 10 high schools in the state offered Swedish, while in the rest of the country there were only four. This rising interest in teaching Swedish to the young coincided with the peaking of the Swedish-speaking population of the state, but it was brought to an abrupt halt by the antiforeign reaction which accompanied World War I.[55]

While the churches strove to preserve Swedish as the living language of the local communities, the Swedish-American press reinforced this effort by providing a wide range of reading material in Swedish. Many newspapers were organs of various churches; others represented political organizations, and some were purely literary in content. One survey has revealed that at one time or another 106 Swedish-language papers were published in Minnesota. Most were short-lived, however, and many never got beyond their first issue.[56]

Three newspapers stand out as the most important in terms of their circulation and length of publication. *Vecko-bladet* (Weekly Blade), published by the Mission Covenant Church from 1884 to 1935, began as *Svenska Kristna Härolden* (Swedish Christian Herald) and was also known for a time as *Minneapolis Weckoblad*. *Minnesota Stats Tidning*, founded by Hans Mattson in 1877, continued in print until 1939. It was always closely associated with the Augustana Synod. By far the most widely read of the three was *Svenska Amerikanska Posten*, begun in 1885 by the Swedish temperance movement. It was later purchased by Swan J. Turnblad, who built the annual circulation to more than 56,000 in 1915. The paper's success is visible today in Turnblad's elaborate mansion, erected in 1905 at the corner of Park Avenue and 26th Street in Minneapolis. It now houses the American Swedish Institute, founded by Turnblad in 1929.

In spite of the efforts of the churches and the press, the use of Swedish in Minnesota declined, partly as a natural outcome of the cessation of immigration upon the outbreak of World War I. An ever-increasing number of Swedish Americans who had received their education in the English language regarded it as their mother tongue. Without the reinforcement of new immigrants, the older generations had a more and more difficult time convincing the younger ones that preservation of the language and a distinctive Swedishness was important. Their task was made much harder by the entry of the United States into World War I in 1917. The hostile attitude adopted by many native Americans toward anything foreign not only ended Swedish-language instruction in the schools but also severely weakened its position in the home and church.

It is significant that the golden era of Swedish-language publication in the United States was the period from 1910 to 1915, just before the war. By 1918 only seven or eight Swedish-language papers were being published in Minnesota, and of these just three survived into the 1930s. The last to go was *Svenska Amerikanska Posten*, which merged with the Chicago-based *Svenska Amerikanaren Tribunen*. In its final issue of September 11, 1940, *Posten* called attention to the fact that Minnesota was losing its only Swedish-language newspaper, pointing out that its purposes, as established and defined by Swan Turnblad, had been to promote "God's work, Prohibition, the advancement of the 'people,'" as well as "to foster Swedish culture in America and to spread the news."

The interwar decline of the Swedish-language press was paralleled by a more gradual discontinuation of the use of Swedish in the churches. As early as 1880 the exclusive use of Swedish within the Augustana Synod had been questioned. The Reverend Eric Norelius, pastor of the congregations at Vasa and Red Wing, noted that "English missions" had begun to attract Minnesota Swedes away from the Augustana churches. He launched a campaign that ultimately led to the adoption by the synod of a policy of gradual transition to English. Little change occurred, however, for many years. The minutes of the synod continued to be printed in Swedish; not until 1919 did they also become available in an English version. In 1921, even after the bitter attacks on foreign-language use fostered by World War I, 85% of all sermons in synod churches were reportedly in Swedish. The first complete English order of service was not drawn up until 1925.[57]

Nils Hasselmo, a Minnesota scholar who has made an extensive study of the use of Swedish in the Chisago Lakes community, found that before 1915 all church activities were conducted in Swedish and all records were kept in Swedish. By the middle 1920s occasional services were being held in English, while Sunday school classes were carried on in both Swedish and English. Summer "Swede schools" were still being held on a regular basis. A decade later English and Swedish services were featured on a regular basis, Sunday school classes were principally in English, and summer language schools were a thing of the past. By 1945 all regular services were conducted in English; the language transition was complete.[58]

The demise of the Swedish language in America did not occur without protest. In a booklet entitled *Hvarför böra vi bibehålla och bevara, vårda och bruka svenska språket i Amerika?* (Why should we maintain and preserve, cultivate and use the Swedish language in America?), published in Minneapolis in 1923, J. S. Carlson asserted that "the spirit of a people dwells in the language of that people." In a tone characteristic of romantic nationalism, he argued that values were expressed through language; if the language were lost, then these values were also lost. If Swedes were to be able to contribute fully to American culture, they must preserve their language. The argument was doubtless a reaction against 100% Americanism, which labeled any use of a foreign language un-American. Carlson went so far as to claim that among all foreign languages, Swedish was especially compatible with American ideals because "True popular freedom had its origin in Sweden."[59]

The degree to which such idealistic notions may have influenced the average Swedish American is difficult to assess. It is clear, however, that a close connection existed in the minds of many Swedes between their language and their religion. They considered the language sacred, and they could not conceive of worshiping in another tongue. As scholars of the language transition have pointed out, "They had received their religious upbringing by reading the *Bible* in Swedish, by memorizing their catechism in Swedish, and by attending services in Swedish. For many it was difficult to translate their faith into English." Thus it is not surprising that the pastor of the Chisago Lakes church cautioned as late as 1931, "This community is an ultra-Swedish [*ultrasvenskt*] one. Therefore, we do not wish to speed up an inappropriate

Americanization and thereby harm the sensitive plant of the spiritual life. We ought to move cautiously in these sacred areas."[60]

Protests and pleas for caution notwithstanding, the Swedish language in Minnesota slowly died. One scholar estimated that the largest number of Minnesotans ever to have some knowledge of Swedish was about 300,000, or 15% of the state's population, in the years just preceding World War I. This amounted to about 20% of all the Swedish speakers in the United States. Their maximum numbers thus coincided with the heyday of Swedish-language publishing. By 1940 there could hardly have been more than 165,000 Swedish-speaking persons in the state, for this figure represented the total of the first-, second-, and third-generation Swedish Americans. The 1970 census enumerated 105,472 Minnesotans who spoke Swedish; almost half of them lived in the seven-county Twin Cities metropolitan area.

By then Swedish as a second language had come to be used more as a medium for the exchange of pleasantries, a badge of the speakers' Swedishness, than as a vehicle in which people felt comfortable carrying on a serious conversation. In the late 1960s well over 40% of the residents of Chisago Lake Township born between 1890 and 1909 felt they could speak Swedish "without difficulty." Of those born between 1910 and 1929, however, less than 15% reported that level of proficiency, while for those born since 1929, the figure was only 2%. The impact of World War I on deterring its usage is clear.

Lack of similar detailed studies prevents a comparison of language retention in the highly Swedish Chisago County rural area with less concentrated places, either urban or rural. With the passing of the first generation, however, it seems likely that the Swedish language lost its function as a primary means of communication, except in areas like Chisago County, where the density of Swedish Americans was so great that few daily conversations were likely to take place with members of any other national group. Some visitors from a rural Småland parish observed as late as 1963 that a German used-car salesman in that county could also speak the Småland dialect, claiming that he would not be able to sell cars there if he could not. So all-pervasive were the Swedes there that third-generation Swedish Americans could still be found speaking the same Småland dialect in 1980. Their numbers were declining, however. Even in Swedeland, U.S.A., conditions changed between the 1960s and the 1980s as new people moved to what had become a popular exurbia for commuters working in the Twin Cities, and the influence of television made itself increasingly felt. In Patterson's terms, the language no longer served the best interests of the individual and, except in a symbolic sense, it had fallen into disuse.[61]

Structural Assimilation

The course of Swedish structural integration into American society is difficult to follow because the phenomenon has not yet been subjected to sufficient critical study. At the level of the individual's friendship circle, virtually nothing is known about assimilation. Even the question of intermarriage has been overlooked to a remarkable extent. Thus this discussion will focus on the degree to which Swedes have maintained their own separate organizations. A look at the persistence, or lack of it, of purely Swedish institutions should tell us something. People have only so much time to give to organizations. A large number of them composed along ethnic lines would suggest that many persons are finding social outlets in them rather than in nonethnic groups. A decline in the success or strength of such groups might indicate a weakening of the ethnic pull and a tendency to assimilate into the larger society.[62]

The early maintenance of separate churches offers perhaps the best evidence of Swedish resistance to structural assimilation. Since the 16th century the Swedish state church had been Lutheran, and in the 19th century most Swedes were members of it. From the end of the 18th century pietistic movements had begun to influence Swedish religious life. Some, like the Baptist and Methodist, came from England. Others, like the Mormon, originated in the United States, and still others were evangelical reform movements within the Swedish church itself. In America the immigrants found a diverse society in which virtually every religious persuasion was represented. They could have joined American churches whose doctrines were compatible with their own beliefs. Many chose not to do so.[63]

Although they received no help or encouragement from the church at home, one of the first things Swedish settlers in Minnesota did was to establish Lutheran congregations in their new communities. In 1854 congregations existed in St. Paul, Center City, and Scandia. In the next year two more were founded in Vasa and Red Wing, and by 1858 a total of 12 were functioning in the new state. In that year these 12, with the congregation at Stockholm, Wisconsin, founded the Minnesota Conference. Originally it affiliated with the synod of Northern Illinois, a body that also included Norwegian, German, and American elements. Significantly the two Scandinavian groups withdrew in 1860 to establish the Scandinavian Lutheran Augustana Synod. This move was not enough to satisfy the urge for cultural separatism, however, and in 1870 the Swedes and Norwegians parted ways. The former reorganized Augustana as an exclusively Swedish-American Lutheran body which succeeded in attracting more immigrants to its fold than any other Swedish group. Even so its success was not spectacular. It has been estimated that in 1890 the Minnesota Conference had achieved only 27% of its potential membership in Minnesota and less than 10% in the Twin Cities and Duluth.[64]

The pietist movement within the Lutheran church in Sweden had produced by the middle of the 19th century many groups that, although they continued to attend regular services and to consider themselves Lutherans, held additional meetings led by evangelical lay preachers. Most of the immigrants who had been active in these "Mission Friends" movements at home did not feel comfortable in the Augustana Synod, even though from the beginning it had assumed a more pietistic flavor than the state church. In the 1870s two Mission synods were founded in the United States, and in 1885 they joined to form the Swedish Evangelical Mission Covenant of America. By 1906, 80 Mission Covenant congregations existed in Minnesota with a membership of 5,017, making it the second largest Swedish church body but far smaller than Augustana.[65]

Swedish pietists were also present in the Baptist and Methodist churches. In the 1850s the Baptist movement had taken hold strongly in some areas of Sweden, where a number of emigrants had been converted before they left. Methodism never gained as large a following in Sweden, but it was an attractive alternative in the United States for those who preferred a more evangelical approach to religion than the Augustana Synod provided. In Minnesota the Baptists were more numerous than the Methodists, having established 49 congregations with a membership of 3,542 by 1892. In both churches Swedish congregations were given considerable control over their own affairs through membership in special Swedish conferences.[66]

The preference among many Swedish immigrants, even those who remained Lutherans, for less formal worship services and more participation by the congregation in church government made them an attractive target for missionary work by the Yankee Congregationalists. In 1882 the Minnesota Congregational Conference, alarmed no doubt at the speed with which Scandinavians were overrunning their "New England of the West," decided to try to familiarize them with the Congregational church. The conference resolved that "wherever they are sufficiently numerous, Sabbath-schools be organized among them, to be conducted in English; and that as a denomination we send official representatives to their synods, both to assure them of our interest and fellowship, and have a warm and intelligent interest in their progress."[67]

The nonconformist Mission Covenant congregations benefited most from the attentions of the Congregationalists, both in spiritual encouragement and financial aid. In spite of their work, however, the Congregationalists made few converts among the Swedes. The church's high social prestige did not make it attractive to a foreign immigrant population, and only about two dozen Swedish Congregational churches were established in Minnesota between 1880 and 1920. None existed by 1950.[68]

Two other Protestant denominations, Presbyterian and Episcopal, carried on mission work among the Swedes in Minnesota. Like the Congregationalists, both churches had strongly middle- and upper-middle-class memberships and thus would not appear to have been attractive to recent immigrants. This was certainly true of the Presbyterians, whose strongly Calvinistic beliefs were foreign to the Swedes. The Protestant Episcopal church, on the other hand, had an appeal for some Swedes, in that its hierarchical organization more closely resembled that of the Swedish state church than did that of the Augustana Synod. Realizing this, the Episcopalians began missionary work among Minnesota Swedes in the late 19th century, attracting several congregations which switched over from the Augustana Synod. By 1910 eight Swedish Episcopal churches existed in the state.[69]

It is significant, in my opinion, that from the beginning these religious groups recognized a need for distinctively Swedish congregations and, where those congregations were numerous enough, for a separate Swedish organization within the American church. Convenience was, of course, a factor, but the close association among language, religion, and other aspects of culture also played an important role. For many Swedes and their American children, it took a long time for their feeling of ethnicity to weaken to the point where they were ready to deny the sacredness of the Swedish language. Particularly in rural areas, where the church was the dominant social institution, this attitude was a major hindrance to the rapid structural integration of Swedish Americans into the larger society. For such integration to occur a successful transition from Swedish to English was a primary precondition, since it allowed people of non-Swedish ancestry to join the congregations.

The course of the language transition within the Augustana Synod has already been briefly traced. It was even more important for the Baptists and Methodists to preserve the language than it was for the Lutherans or Covenanters. "When so-called 'reformed' congregations became English, they were absorbed into the American synods and conferences, and it was thus a matter of self-preservation for them to retain the Swedish language." For this reason, and because later immigrants tended to be closer to the "free church" movements, one would expect the transition to have proceeded more slowly in the nonconformist churches. In fact there does not seem to have been much difference. In 1928 Swedish Methodists lost their separate identity, and about the same time Swedish Baptist congregations began gradually to Americanize. In 1945 the term "Swedish" was dropped from the Baptist conference title. English became the official language of the Swedish Evangelical Mission Covenant Church in 1929, and today it is known simply as the Evangelical Covenant Church. Even the Swedish origins of the Augustana Synod were submerged when it joined three other groups in 1962 to form the Lutheran Church in America.[70]

By the end of World War II, Swedish Americans were well integrated into American society in terms of their religious life, although many congregations still remembered and took pride in their Swedish beginnings. In recent years some have reinstated Swedish-language services on special days, such as Christmas and Midsummer. Others never gave them up completely, scheduling annual events that became traditions. But they are a celebration of the past, not a part of the reality of the present. A century after the first Swedish settlers reached Minnesota religious assimilation had become a fact.

Outside of the churches, to which probably fewer than half of the immigrants belonged, Swedes in Minnesota could find ethnic homes in a bewildering variety of secular organizations. They were particularly important in the larger urban areas where large concentrations of people ensured a wide variety of interests and church membership was low. The aims of these organizations ranged from moral missions in the case of the International Order of Good Templars temperance lodges, through the provision of insurance benefits in mutual aid societies such as the Vasa Order of America, the Society Norden, *Svenska Bröderna* (the Swedish Brothers), and the Gustaf II Adolph Society, to preserving Swedish culture via uncounted numbers of choral groups

OLLE SKRATTHULT'S ORCHESTRA, a popular Swedish group from Princeton, was especially noted for its instrumental dance music in the 1920s.

and drama clubs. All provided the fellowship of compatriots. Some were organized as early as the late 1860s, but the bulk seem to have appeared during the three decades preceding World War I in the period when Swedish language and culture were strongest in Minnesota. Their flourishing numbers show that Swedes, even in the cities, possessed a vigorous sense of ethnicity at that time.[71]

The disruptive influence of World War I, noted earlier in connection with language and religious life, was also felt by secular organizations. Interest waned in the 1920s as the older generations persisted in using a language the young did not understand, and by the end of the decade the ethnic club appeared to be out of date. In the 1930s, however, Swedish secular organizations received renewed attention, stimulated in part by the Depression. But the effects of the Depression were mixed. Some students argue that the unprecedented hard times hastened assimilation while at the same time pushing Swedes and other national groups to band together for security in a trying time.[72] The banding together may suggest strong latent ethnicity in spite of the progress structural assimilation had made, or it may be seen as a reaction against the assimilation that had been taking place. Action was needed if the memory of the homeland and its culture was not to fade forever.

Perhaps all of these factors were at work in the formation of the American Swedish Institute, the most notable organization to arise in Minnesota in this period. With thousands of members in 1981, it remained the single most important institution in the state dedicated to fostering an understanding of both Sweden and Swedish America. Its functions, however, were very different from those of the clubs and societies of the early 20th century. Then such organizations were essential to the well-being of their members, often pro-

viding the only place where urban Swedish Americans could find companionship. They were the institutions of a truly ethnic society. Although the institute also provided companionship, it was only one of many places to serve that function for Minnesotans in the 1980s. Rather its primary purpose has become education — the education of an assimilated group of people about their past and about the land their forefathers left.[73]

Civic Assimilation

For Swedish Americans the first real test of civic assimilation — whether they would support a position in conflict with the values and interests of American society at large — came during World War I. Then as never before the hyphenated American was subjected to pressures to reject his native culture. The situation was far worse for German Americans, but the Scandinavians, too, were watched very closely.[74]

At the opening of the war Swedish-American sympathy for the Central Powers was apparent. On July 22, 1914, Minneapolis-based *Svenska Amerikanska Posten* expressed the view that the brewing crisis was just another example of the classic struggle between the Germanic and Slavic peoples. Russia, Sweden's traditional enemy, was viewed as the villain, and the plight of Finland, which had by then been under Russian rule for a century, was pointed out. "The question boils down to whether or not the ancient German culture, with its free and ordered social system will be destroyed. . . . It is not difficult to decide which side to take in this conflict," the paper concluded. Reiterating this theme on August 5, *Posten* said, "What this struggle really involves is not Austria's Balkan interests, but the question of hegemony in Europe, nothing more and nothing less. The question is whether Germans or Slavs will dictate its future development."

Three days later Sweden and Norway issued a joint declaration of neutrality. Disappointed by their stand, *Posten* on August 12 hoped that Sweden might yet see its way clear to do its Germanic duty in the struggle with the Slavs, noting that if the German people lost, the cost would be enormous, for the conflict was a holy war, an effort by "Greek Catholicism" to dominate the world.

The editorials of a single newspaper, however large and influential, do not, of course, reflect the attitudes of the entire Swedish-American community. Only a minority of Swedish-language newspapers in the United States wholeheartedly supported Germany. According to one scholar, most of those "in Illinois and Minnesota assumed a more cautious and impartial attitude which on the whole agreed with official American foreign policy." Nonetheless the evidence from *Veckobladet* and *Minnesota Stats Tidning* as well as from *Svenska Amerikanska Posten* suggests that in 1914 there was considerable pro-German feeling within the Minnesota Swedish community, especially in Minneapolis. As German submarines became more active in the Atlantic in 1916, the Swedish-American press turned from arguments about who was responsible for the war and condemnations of American arms shipments to the Allies to an almost unanimous plea for the maintenance of American neutrality. As late as February 14, 1917, *Posten*, while urging that President Woodrow Wilson should receive bipartisan support in his policy against Germany, also expressed the hope that the United States would be able to avoid entering the fighting. In Chicago *Missionsvännen* put it even more strongly. "Why," it asked, "cannot the United States on this side of the globe maintain its neutrality when little Sweden can do it even when fires of war surround it close to its borders?"[75]

The early pro-German and the later strict neutrality stances of Minnesota's leading Swedish-language newspapers were also mirrored in the opinions expressed by many of the state's prominent elected officials of Swedish descent. Most vocal in their opposition to American involvement were Charles A. Lindbergh, Sr., who represented Minnesota in the House of Representatives from 1907 to 1917, and Ernest Lundeen, who served in the same body from 1917 to 1919. When the debate over American entry reached its climax on the House floor, Lundeen voiced his belief that the American people did not want war. He insisted that war should not be declared without a national plebiscite. To demonstrate what the results of such a vote would be, he said, he was polling 54,000 people in his home district. Although he did not yet have all the results, he noted that they were then running 10 to 1 against entry. Lindbergh opposed American involvement on the grounds that the war would benefit "professional speculators" and " 'the lords of special privilege' who 'in their selfish glee [were] coining billions of profit from the rage of war.' "[76]

When Congress at last declared war in April, 1917, public expressions of antiwar opinion by Swedish Americans in Minnesota ceased. On May 9, 1917, *Posten* placed the blame for starting the war squarely on the shoulders of Kaiser Wilhelm and called for his abdication so that peace could be made with a democratic Germany. On July 25 an editorial compared the political philosophies of Gladstone and Bismarck, deriving the current policies of England and Germany from them. On November 21 the paper began reprinting in English a book by K. G. Ossian Nilsson entitled *Who Is Right in the World-War?*, which unequivocally found Germany guilty and England, France, and Russia innocent, and called upon a somnolent Sweden to rise up against Germany. Meanwhile some Minnesota political leaders of Swedish descent campaigned to rally Swedish-American opinion to the cause. On a swing through the state to promote draft registration, Governor John Lind, who had been born in Sweden, emphasized that no one nation had been totally responsible for starting the war. As for ending it, he asked his listeners to consider how long it would "be before they dominate us" if the Prussians come to dominate Europe. "This is a just war and a holy war," he said, "And to the young people who will take part in it I say, 'God be with you for you are the protectors of humanity.' "[77]

Resistance to the draft was not uncommon among recent immigrants. Deservedly or not Swedes acquired a reputation for being especially reticent, probably because of some early incidents in Illinois, where Swedes were arrested for refusing to register. The incidents provoked severe criticism in the Swedish-American press, which may, in fact, have blown the problem out of proportion. In Minnesota the Commission of Public Safety was aware that many Swedes and

other Scandinavians opposed the war. Created in April, 1917, when the United States entered the war, the commission was given unusually wide-ranging powers to distribute prowar propaganda and to restrict activities it regarded as inimical to the public interest. It endeavored to approach leading members of ethnic groups whose loyalty might be doubted and enlist their aid in planning an "educational campaign." In a letter dated August 8, 1917, one of those approached in the Minneapolis Scandinavian community informed the commission that "Misinformation and misunderstandings are more or less prevalent among Scandinavians as among other groups of citizens. On account of their economic and political strength it is of the utmost importance that the full weight of their influence should be on the side of the government in this crisis."[78]

The Public Safety Commission, which had virtually dictatorial powers, hired agents to travel about the state, attend rallies and meetings of many kinds, and send to the commission any information they gathered from or about the activities of "foreigners," "radicals," "slackers," and any others suspected of lack of enthusiasm for the war effort. A letter dated May 31, 1917, and headed "C. H. reports," told of a visit to the shoe repair shop of a man he described as a known German Socialist, who purportedly said "that a good many are against conscription, especially among the socialists; that if the socialists refuse to register, he believes many of this number will be Swedes, and that this is because they do not like Russia and the socialist movement is strong among the Swedes; and the fact that Russia is an old enemy of Sweden, would tend to keep them from registering. . . . I judge from what he said that they are using this argument about Russia, in an effort to influence the Swedes against enlisting."[79]

Agents C. U. P. and C. H. were apparently assigned to look into the activities of supposed Socialists among the Swedes of Chisago County in June. They seem to have had no difficulty in locating a local informant who obligingly joined the witch hunt by identifying some Socialists "who are stirring up the people of that locality to such an extent that he is afraid they will cause considerable trouble." The agents reported hearsay evidence of several Socialist meetings, naming the supposed ringleaders and stating that "the people who attended the meeting . . . were all Swedish Lutherans" except one, who was a German. C. U. P. quoted the informant concerning the refusal of several farmers to buy Liberty Bonds. Connecting two not necessarily related things, the alarmist informer leaped to the conclusion that the refusal of these farmers meant they were Socialists. He told the agent that he "hoped the Governor would inform these men . . . that their views were known to him and that any attempt on their part to agitate the people against the Government in this crisis would cause them severe punishment. This he felt would put a stop to this socialism, which he felt is at present growing hourly . . . and would 'blot out the stain now placed on the fair name of the Swedish people of this community.' "

In September, 1917, the director of the neighboring Pine County Public Safety Association volunteered to rescue the citizens of Chisago County who were reportedly "afraid to sleep nights for fear of fire or personal violence from the anti[war] element. . . . Evidence could be gotten on these people and plenty of it,'' he wrote to a superior in Minneapolis, ''if you could get some fellow who could pitch bundles, dig potatoes and drink a little beer and mix among them. . . . Unless something is done, you need not be surprised to hear of bloodshed in that locality.''[80]

An unsigned reply assured the director: ''I can send a man to dig potatoes and drink beer. Now where shall I send him, and to whom shall he first apply for work, and should he be able to talk Swedish or German, I have both in my employ. . . . Let me know as soon as you can how best to go about this, and send me a list of your worst actors and where they live.''

Relieved, the director responded, ''Thank God for your letter of September 22nd! Send both a Swede and a German, and let them attend their Sunday beer parties and things of that kind, and if they can't get them it is their fault.'' He included a long list of people he termed ''Kaiserites'' and concluded, ''If these fellows were prairie chickens in that locality, the hunters of the State could have excellent hunting, because there are more of them than there are of prairie chickens in the State.''

The evidence would seem to suggest that in this period civic assimilation among Swedish Americans was not yet complete. It must be remembered that a large immigration from Sweden had continued right up to the beginning of the fighting and that many of those who opposed the war most vigorously were recent immigrants. They had left a country in which rapid industrialization was bringing with it increasing social reform. The world-wide Socialist movement had far more appeal for these people than it had for their countrymen who had emigrated from rural Sweden 50 or 60 years earlier. While it is fair to say that Swedish Americans in 1914 expressed opinions about the war based on cultural biases peculiar to their group, when the crunch came and their new country went to war in 1917, the vast majority put aside these biases, however reluctantly, and behaved as loyal Americans. Nevertheless, the perception of Swedes as a group containing an especially large number of dangerous elements persisted throughout the war, particularly in the minds of advocates of 100% Americanism. It is significant that when World War II broke out, Minnesota felt no need to establish another Public Safety Commission. In 20 years the supposed threat of the hyphenated American had diminished.[81]

The Swedes: An Ethnic Group Today?

In 1980 the large Minnesota population that traced its ancestry to Sweden did not meet Patterson's definition of an ethnic group. Few individuals regarded the Swedish cultural heritage as the basis of their most important group identity outside the family. By every measure in Gordon's assimilation model, Swedish Americans have melted into American life. Identification with religion, profession, class, and neighborhood were probably all more important than ethnicity.[82] This is not to say they had no awareness of, or interest in, their Swedish backgrounds. Organizations such as the American Swedish Institute and the local chapter of the American Scandinavian Foundation actively kept memories of the Swedish heritage alive. In 1933, only a few years after immigration ceased, the first *Svenskarnas Dag* celebration was held in Minnehaha Park near the large Scandinavian neighborhood in South Minneapolis. The event, scheduled close to the date of the traditional Swedish Midsummer Day festival, became an annual one and has continued to attract thousands from all over the state. In 1981 the festivities included instrumental and vocal music by groups from both Sweden and Minnesota. A midsummer queen was chosen and the traditional Maypole dance was performed. Among the trees hung the banners of the remaining provincial associations (*hembygdsföreningar*), but those who sat under them were few and for the most part well advanced in years. For many Minnesota Swedes *Svenskarnas Dag* is happily anticipated and thoroughly enjoyed. It reminds them that they have roots in another culture, and it helps them to retain contact with that culture. But it is not essential to their well-being. They can function successfully in society without reference to their Swedish heritage.

In recent years many local celebrations emphasizing cultural origins have sprung up in Minnesota towns where Swedish settlement was important. Winthrop has its Swedish Midsummer Festival, Willmar its Kaffefest, and Lind-

THE 1981 POSTER for Minnesota Day in Växjö used Swedish and American colors — yellow, blue, white, and red — to promote a varied program which included honoring Swedish American of the year, Curtis L. Carlson of Minneapolis.

strom its Karl Oskar Days. Nor is the phenomenon limited to Swedish areas. Perhaps the search by Black Americans for their African roots has triggered a similar interest among descendants of the hyphenated Americans. For Swedes, however, this search lacks the deep meaning it has for Blacks. Self-esteem and equality are not issues here. The Swedish American is only curious about his past. An understanding of it is not essential to his present or future happiness.

Paralleling and reinforcing the increased curiosity of Minnesotans about their Swedish heritage has been a corresponding growth of interest by Swedes in the great migration to America and particularly to Minnesota. Novelist Vilhelm Moberg's saga about Karl Oskar Nilsson and his Swedish family's flight from poverty and hunger to a new life on the shores of Chisago Lake and the two full-length films based on it have done much to fan the flames of interest. In 1962 an ongoing research project called "Sweden and America after 1860: Emigration, Remigration, Social and Political Debate" was established in the Department of History at Uppsala University. Three years later another research organization, the Emigrant Institute, was founded in Växjö in the heart of one of the earliest areas of out-migration. In 1968 a celebration called Minnesota Day was held for the first time in the park adjoining the institute. It has been held annually since then and bears a striking resemblance to *Svenskarnas Dag* in Minneapolis. The Växjö museum has become a popular mecca for Swedish Americans visiting the Old Country. The increased exchange of people and ideas between Minnesota and Sweden over the past two decades has done much to heighten public awareness of the distinctive cultural contribution these immigrants have made to this state. One cannot say, however, that these events signal the reawakening of a true ethnic consciousness in the sense we have defined it in this chapter.[83]

Reference notes

[1] The author wishes to thank Nils Hasselmo, University of Minnesota, Minneapolis, for his helpful suggestions on this chapter. Sten Carlsson, "Chronology and Composition of Swedish Emigration to America," and Hans Norman, "Swedes in North America," in Harald Runblom and Hans Norman, eds., *From Sweden to America: A History of the Migration*, 119, 245–247 (Minneapolis and Uppsala, Swed., 1976); Lars Ljungmark, *Swedish Exodus*, 10 (Carbondale, Ill., 1979).

[2] Jacob Falstrom, who found his way to the Minnesota country in the early 1800s, has been generally regarded as the first Swede in the area. He pursued a varied career as a fur trader and farmer, but there is no clear link between his early presence and the subsequent migration of the first three known Swedish settlers — Oscar Roos, Carl A. Fernstrom, and August Sandahl of Vastergötland. See Anna Engquist, *Scandia: Then and Now*, 9 (Stillwater, 1974); Robert Gronberger, "Historical Account of the Swedish Settlement . . . in Washington County," in Swedish Historical Society of America, *Year-Book*, 10:55–57 (St. Paul, 1925); Theodore A. Norelius, "The First Swede in Minnesota," in *Swedish Pioneer Historical Quarterly*, 8:107–115 (January, 1957).

[3] Here and below, see Patricia C. Harpole and Mary D. Nagle, eds., *Minnesota Territorial Census, 1850*, viii (St. Paul, 1972); Axel Friman, "Swedish Emigration to North America, 1825–1850," in

Swedish Pioneer Historical Quarterly, 27:153–177 (July, 1976); Walter F. Willcox. ed., *International Migrations*, 1:756 (Reprint ed., New York, 1969); United States, *Census*, 1920, *Population*, 3:15, 504, 507, 509; U.S. Scandinavian statistics, in MEHP Papers, MHS, compiled by Jon A. Gjerde from U.S. Dept. of Labor, Bureau of Immigration, *Annual Reports*, 1909–39, and U.S. Justice Dept., Immigration and Naturalization Service, *Annual Reports*, 1940–75, hereafter cited as Gjerde, Scandinavian statistics.

[4] Dorothy S. Thomas, *Social and Economic Aspects of Swedish Population Movements, 1750–1933*, 304 (New York, 1941); Hans Norman, "The Causes of Emigration: An Attempt at a Multivariate Analysis," in Runblom and Norman, eds., *From Sweden to America*, 150–153.

[5] Carlsson, in Runblom and Norman, eds., *From Sweden to America*, 116–120, 132. After Jansson was murdered in 1850, internal strife developed at Bishop Hill. The colony was disbanded in 1860, and some of its members went to Chisago County, Minnesota. See Olov Isaksson, *Bishop Hill, Ill.: A Utopia on the Prairie*, 128, 141 (Stockholm, 1969) with a text in both English and Swedish.

[6] For a state-by-state overview, see Helge Nelson, *Swedes and the Swedish Settlements in North America*, 138–174, 248–292, 301–309.

[7] On the routes to Minnesota, see Introduction, above. On Swedish Chicago and its remnants, see Ulf Beijbom, *Swedes in Chicago: A Demographic and Social Study of the 1846–1880 Immigration* (Chicago, 1971).

[8] On the man whose letter drew the first group of Swedes, see Emeroy Johnson, "Norberg — First Swede at Chisago Lake," in *Arkivfynd*, May, 1979, pp. 1–31, published by Gustavus Adolphus College, St. Peter. See also E[ric] Norelius, *De Svenska Luterska Församlingarnas och Svenskarnes Historia i Amerika*, 1:541, 543, 545 (Rock Island, Ill., 1890) and the same author's second volume published in 1916 which carries the story of the Chisago settlements to 1911. The letters quoted were dated September 1, 1851, and January 18, 1852. For English translations, see Emeroy Johnson, "Per Andersson's Letters from Chisago Lake," in *Swedish Pioneer Historical Quarterly*, 24:9, 15 (January, 1973). The Norelius translation and others in this chapter not otherwise acknowledged were made by the author.

[9] Norelius, *De Svenska Luterska Historia*, 1:544, 549, 550; Robert C. Ostergren, "Cultural Homogeneity and Population Stability Among Swedish Immigrants in Chisago County," in *Minnesota History*, 43:257 (Fall, 1973).

[10] George M. Stephenson, "Sidelights on the History of the Swedes in the St. Croix Valley," in *Minnesota History*, 17:396–405 (December, 1936); James T. Dunn, *The St. Croix: Midwest Border River*, 161–171 (Reprint ed., St. Paul, 1979); Jim Cordes, *Reflections of Amador* (North Branch, 1976); Theodore A. Norelius, *In the Land of Kichi Saga* (North Branch, 1973); Alfred Bergin, "Dalarna in America," translation of a 1903 article, copy in MHS; Gareth Hiebert, "Swedeland," in *St. Paul Sunday Pioneer Press*, February 18, 1962, *Pictorial Magazine*, 6–8. For a map showing the state's vegetation zones, discussed below, see Francis J. Marschner, comp., *The Original Vegetation of Minnesota* (Reprint ed., St. Paul, 1974), copy in MHS.

[11] For a collection of America letters, see H. Arnold Barton, *Letters From The Promised Land: Swedes in America, 1840–1914* (Minneapolis, 1975). On the Chisago area, see Conrad Peterson, comp. and ed., "Letters from Pioneer Days," in Swedish Historical Society, *Year-Book*, 9:74–76, 80, 81 (St. Paul, 1924).

[12] Ostergren, in *Minnesota History*, 43:263–269. The term "birthfield" refers to the spatial distribution of the birthplaces of a given population. For a detailed study of the members of one Swedish parish who emigrated to Chisago County, see Långasjö Emigrantcirkel, *En Smålandssocken Emigrerar: En Bok om Emigration en till*

Amerika från Långasjö Socken i Kronobergs Län, 561–768 (Långasjö, Swed., 1967). A Chisago County native recounted the history of wandering Smålanders in Irving J. Olson, *Smolenning Slekt* (Stillwater, 1973).

[13] Norelius, *De Svenska Luterska Historia*, 1:624, 628; Carl Roos, "Vasa, Goodhue County," in Swedish Historical Society, *Year-Book*, 10:88–113. The papers of Roos, one of the original settlers, are in the Goodhue County Historical Society, Red Wing, microfilm in MHS.

[14] Emeroy Johnson, *A Church Is Planted: The Story of the Lutheran Minnesota Conference, 1851–1876*, 85–97 (Minneapolis, 1948); West Union Lutheran Church, *Anniversary Album 1858–1958*, 8–16 (Carver, 1958); East Union Evangelical Lutheran Church, *A Century of God's Grace, 1858–1958*, 6–9 (Carver, 1958). A series of letters from Pehr and Catharina Carlson, 1850s immigrants to East Union, may be found in MHS. For the quotation below, see A. A. Stomberg, *Den Svenska Folkstammen i Amerika: Några Synpunkter*, 19 (Stockholm, Swed., 1928).

[15] Carlsson, in Runblom and Norman, eds., *From Sweden to America*, 117. Although the Illinois and Iowa settlements were the principal American contributors to Minnesota's Swedes, early colonies near Jamestown, N.Y., and in northern Pennsylvania also provided sizable numbers. The Chisago Lakes Church records revealed many people born in Illinois, for families frequently had more sons than they could find land for nearby. The phenomenon was a common one in the settlement history of the country.

[16] On the various settlements discussed here and four paragraphs below, see Norelius, *De Svenska Luterska Historia*, 1:708–711, 740, 750, 755; Nelson, *Swedes and Swedish Settlements*, 216; Johnson, *A Church Is Planted*, 98–117, 121, 138–141, 204–207; Ronald J. Johnson, *Vista '76: 120 Years of a Scandinavian-American Community* (New Richland, 1976). On the records dating from 1858 of the Swedish Lutheran Church at Scandian Grove, see Emeroy Johnson, "What An Old Minnesota Church Register Reveals," in *Swedish Pioneer Historical Quarterly*, 18:157–168 (July, 1967).

[17] Florence E. Janson, *The Background of Swedish Immigration, 1840–1930*, 169–221 (Chicago, 1931).

[18] Here and below, see P[eter] Ryden, *Svenska Baptisternas i Minnesota Historia*, 241 (Minneapolis, 1918); Bergin, "Darlarna in America," 2, 6; Neil A. Markus, "Areal Patterns of Religious Denominationalism in Minnesota, 1950," 148, master's thesis, University of Minnesota, 1961.

[19] *Album of History and Biography of Meeker County, Minnesota*, 561, 571 (Chicago, 1888); Victor E. Lawson, "The First Settlements in the Kandiyohi Region," in Swedish Historical Society, *Year-Book*, 10:19–31; Victor E. Lawson, *Illustrated History . . . of Kandiyohi County*, 253–256, 302, 317, 373, 383, 436 (St. Paul, 1905); Nelson, *Swedes and Swedish Settlements*, 221. For more on Swedes in Meeker County, see Svenska Evangeliskt Lutherska Beckville-Församlingen, *Minnesalbum, 1869–1919* (Rock Island, Ill., 1919); see also note 26, below. On the Pre-emption Act, see Paul W. Gates, *History of Public Land Law Development*, 238 (Washington, D.C., 1968).

[20] Norelius, *De Svenska Luterska Historia*, 1:762.

[21] For a view of the war through Swedish eyes, see Albin Widén, *Svenskarna och Siouxupproret* (Stockholm, 1965). A good overview in English is Kenneth Carley, *The Sioux Uprising of 1862* (2nd ed., St. Paul, 1976).

[22] U.S., *Census, 1860, Population*, xviii, 104, 262; 1880, p. 495; Carlsson, in Runblom and Norman, eds., *From Sweden to America*, 117, 120–123, 130, 140–148.

[23] Harold F. Peterson, "Early Minnesota Railroads and the Quest for Settlers," in *Minnesota History*, 13:25–44 (March, 1932). In deriving these figures from federal decennial census rolls, land was considered settled when the population of a township reached 72, or

a density of 2 persons per square mile. See also map of railroads and Swedish settlements in Minnesota in Nelson, *Swedes and Swedish Settlements*, 1:46.

[24] Here and two paragraphs below, see Nelson, *Swedes and Swedish Settlements*, 213–217, 226. On Comfrey, where the main group of Swedish settlers arrived in 1871 after moving west from Houston County, see First Lutheran Church, *Golden Jubilee Memorial Booklet*, 9 (Comfrey, 1923).

[25] Lars Ljungmark, *For Sale — Minnesota: Organized Promotion of Scandinavian Immigration 1866–1873*, 9–11, 267 (Chicago, 1971).

[26] On Wright, Meeker, and Kandiyohi counties, see Carlton R. Lee, *Cokato Centennial Scrapbook*, 18 (Cokato, 1978); Oscar E. Linquist, *Dassel, Minnesota: Those Were The Days, 1869–1904*, 1 ([Dassel], 1904); and note 19 above. The unusually large concentration of Swedes and Norwegians in Douglas County may be related in part to the fact that Lars K. Aaker, the federal land agent in Alexandria from 1869 to 1875, was also president of the Scandinavian Immigration Society in Minneapolis, according to Markus, "Areal Patterns," 49. See also Douglas County Historical Society, *Douglas County Album of the Ages* ([Alexandria, 1979?]).

[27] John G. Rice, *Patterns of Ethnicity in a Minnesota County, 1880–1905*, 31–35 (University of Umeå, *Geographical Reports*, no. 4, 1973), copy in MHS. For the story of the parish of Gagnef and its move to southern Kandiyohi County, see Rice, "The Effect of Land Alienation on Settlement," in Association of American Geographers, *Annals*, 68:70–74 (March, 1978).

[28] Ostergren, in *Minnesota History*, 43:258, 261, 263–268; Ostergren, "Rättvik to Isanti: A Community Transplanted," 66, 91, 96, Ph.D. thesis, University of Minnesota, 1976; John G. Rice and Robert C. Ostergren, "The Decision to Emigrate: A Study in Diffusion," in *Geografiska Annaler*, 60:1–15, series B (1978).

[29] Robert [C.] Ostergren, "A Community Transplanted: The Formative Experience of a Swedish Immigrant Community in the Upper Middle West," in *Journal of Historical Geography*, 5:189–212 (April, 1979). On the retention of Dalarna dialects in the area, see Folke Hedblom and Gunnar Nyström, "Från Älvdalen i Mellanvästern," in *Darlarnas Hembygdsbok 1966*, 97–106 (Falun, Swed., 1968) and Folke Hedblom, "Svenska dialekter i Amerika: Några erfarenheter och problem," in *Kungl. Humanistiska Vetenskaps-Samfundet i Uppsala, Årsbok 1973–1974* (Uppsala, 1974). Nelson, *Swedes and Swedish Settlements*, 196, observed in 1921 that not only were the dialects of Lake Siljan and Västerdalarna well preserved in the area but that Swedes from other provinces had also learned to speak them.

[30] Here and below, see Carlsson, in Runblom and Norman, eds., *From Sweden to America*, 117, 130–140; Rice and Ostergren, in *Geografiska Annaler*, 60:6–9. For more on working-class life in Minneapolis during this period, see the papers of the Minneapolis Scandinavian Workingmen's Society, 1885–1901, in MHS.

[31] U.S., *Census, 1880, Population*, 541; 1890, part 1, pp. 607, 671; Edward Van Dyke Robinson, *Early Economic Conditions and the Development of Agriculture in Minnesota*, 56, 102, 104, 164 (University of Minnesota, *Studies in the Social Sciences*, no. 3 — Minneapolis, 1915).

[32] Here and below, see Nelson, *Swedes and Swedish Settlements*, 239–241; Ernst Skarstedt, *Svensk-Amerikanska Folket i Helg och Söcken*, 61 (Stockholm, 1917); Kittson County Historical Society, *Our Northwest Corner: Histories of Kittson County, Minnesota*, 4 (Lake Bronson, 1979); *History of the Red River Valley, Past and Present*, 2:875 (Chicago, 1909). Some credit for the large number of Swedes in the Red River Valley must be given to S. J. Kronberg and A. P. Montén, Augustana Synod ministers. The former "probably organized more congregations in this region than any other pastor," while the latter was instrumental in founding the Swedish Colonization Bureau in St. Paul in 1881, an agency which co-operated with

the Great Northern Railroad. See John O. Anders, *The Origin and History of Swedish Religious Organizations in Minnesota, 1853–1885*, 80–83 (Rock Island, Ill., 1932).

[33] Hazel H. Wahlberg, *The North Land: A History of Roseau County*, 72 (Roseau, 1975).

[34] W. A. Hartman and J. D. Black, *Economic Aspects of Land Settlement in the Cut-over Region of the Great Lakes States*, 3–6, 84 (U.S. Dept. of Agriculture, *Circular*, no. 160 — Washington, D.C., 1931).

[35] Agnes M. Larson, *History of the White Pine Industry in Minnesota*, 62, 76, 174 (Minneapolis, 1949); Nelson, *Swedes and Swedish Settlements*, 200; Minnesota Analysis and Planning System (MAPS), *Minnesota Socio-Economic Characteristics*, from the 4th Count Summary Tape of the 1970 Census, Vol. 3, Education and General Characteristics, n.p. ([St. Paul], 1972). For more on Swedes in Pine County, see Centennial History Committee, *One Hundred Years in Pine County*, 33, 49, 51, 72, 88, 92, 131–133, 144, 145 ([Pine City, 1949?]), in which a Mr. Wahlberg is quoted (p. 133) as reassuring his family about the many Indians in the area in the 1880s, "They are just like the Laplanders we used to see in Sweden." See also O. Bernard Johnson, *The Homesteaders: The Experiences of Early Settlers in Pine County, Minnesota* (Staples, 1973), and a novel by Lillian K. Anderson, *Father Hollis of Long Shot, Minnesota* (New York, 1951).

[36] Nelson, *Swedes and Swedish Settlements*, 190, 202, 227, 233–238; Mary Olson Norlander, "Reminiscences of Swedish Pioneer Life in Mille Lacs County," 1950, a manuscript in MHS by a woman who arrived in the county in 1891; Gerald D. Larson, "Ethnic and Cultural Homogeneity of Kanabec County, Minnesota, in 1895," 1–21, course paper, 1977, University of Minnesota, copy in MHS. For more on Mille Lacs County Swedes, see Herman Nelson, *The Axe and the Plow: Stories of Mille Lacs* (Princeton, 1974); on Aitkin County, see Tolleif G. Thomsen, *Memories from Bear Lake* (Seattle, Wash., 1968) and Kenneth W. Sheeks, "Selected Aspects of the Economic History of Aitkin County, Minnesota," 37–44, Plan B paper, University of Minnesota-Duluth, 1966, copy in MHS.

[37] David A. Walker, *Iron Frontier: The Discovery and Early Development of Minnesota's Three Ranges*, 55, 61n, 90, 96, 234 (St. Paul, 1979); John Sirjamaki, "The People of the Mesabi Range," in *Minnesota History*, 27:203–215 (September, 1946). Employment records of the Duluth, Missabe, and Northern Railroad have been preserved in the company's headquarters in Duluth.

[38] State of Minnesota, *Census, 1905*, 122, 124–192; Matti Kaups, "Swedish Immigrants in Duluth, 1856–1870," in Nils Hasselmo, ed., *Perspectives on Swedish Immigration*, 168, 180 (Chicago and Duluth, 1978).

[39] Here and below, see notes 19 and 26, above; Madeline Angell, *Red Wing, Minnesota: Saga of a River Town* (Minneapolis, 1977); Richard J. Jobes, "Saint Peter, Minnesota: The History of a Frontier Community, 1851–1905," master's thesis, University of North Dakota, 1956; Fargo-Moorhead Centennial Corporation, *A Century Together: A History of Fargo, North Dakota and Moorhead, Minnesota*, 174, 188, 194 ([Fargo-Moorhead], 1975); Minnesota, *Census, 1905*, xiii, 122, 124–192.

[40] Carlsson, in Runblom and Norman, eds., *From Sweden to America*, 118, 126–128. On the Swedish reaction, see Ann-Sofie Kälvemark, *Reaktionen mot utvandringen: Emigrationsfrågan i svensk debatt och politik 1901–1904* (*Studia Historica Upsaliensia*, no. 41 — Uppsala, 1972); for a brief account in English, see Kälvemark, "Swedish Emigration Policy in an International Perspective," in Runblom and Norman, eds., *From Sweden to America*, 106–112. For the story of one Swedish woman's work experiences in Minneapolis just after the turn of the century, see Byron J. Nordstrom, "Evelina Månsson and the Memoir of an Urban Labor Mi-

grant," in *Swedish Pioneer Historical Quarterly*, 31:182–195 (July, 1980).

[41] Here and below, see U.S., *Census, 1910, Population*, 2:512, 996, 1018; Minnesota, *Census, 1905*, 120. On the other Scandinavian groups with which Twin Cities Swedes settled, see Chapters 11 and 13. Many fourth-wave emigrants, especially those from the forest districts of Sweden, followed the lumber industry to the Pacific Northwest, where Washington's Swedish-born population rose from not quite 13,000 to more than 32,000 between 1900 and 1910. See Allan Kastrup, *The Swedish Heritage in America*, 481–490 (St. Paul, 1975); U.S., *Census, 1920, Population*, 2:725.

[42] On St. Paul's Swedish settlement here and two paragraphs below, see Byron Nordstrom, ed., *The Swedes in Minnesota*, 29–31 (Minneapolis, 1976); Calvin F. Schmid, *Social Saga of Two Cities: An Ecological and Statistical Study*, 129–171 (Minneapolis, 1937). On Swede Hollow, see Nels M. Hokanson, "I Remember St. Paul's Swede Hollow," in *Minnesota History*, 41:362–371 (Winter, 1969); tape of Arthur E. Sundberg, 1976, and taped interview of Hokanson by Steve Trimble, 1977, both in MHS. On the Italian and Mexican succession in the Hollow, see Chapters 24 and 5.

[43] Here and two paragraphs below, see U.S., *Census, 1910, Population*, 2:1018; Schmid, *Social Saga of Two Cities*, chart 76, [p. 147]; Nordstrom, ed., *Swedes in Minnesota*, 32–38; Byron J. Nordstrom, "The Sixth Ward: A Minneapolis Swede Town in 1905," in Hasselmo, ed., *Perspectives on Swedish Immigration*, 151–165; Dan Armitage and the West Bank Historical Collective, "The Curling Waters: A West Bank history," in *Minnesota Daily*, September 27, 1973, pp. 15–25. See also Alfred Söderström, *Minneapolis Minnen: Kulturhistorisk Axplockning Från qvarnstaden vid Mississippi* (Minneapolis, 1899), which interspersed general information about Minneapolis with details on its Swedish community. On the Bohemian Flats, see Work Projects Administration, Writers Program, *The Bohemian Flats* (Minneapolis, [1941]).

[44] Minneapolis Planning Commission and City Council, *Powderhorn Community: Analysis and Action Recommendations*, 6, 9, 12 (*Community Improvement Series*, no. 12 — Minneapolis, 1965); Minneapolis Planning Commission and City Council, *Longfellow Community: Analysis and Action Recommendations*, 5, 11 (*Community Improvement Series*, no. 14 — Minneapolis, 1965); Jerry Ravenhorst and Peggy Boyer, "Seward West — Milwaukee Avenue in History?" and Armitage and the West Bank Historical Collective, "The Curling Waters: A West Bank History," both in *Common Ground* (Minneapolis), 1:49, 50, 59 (Spring, 1974). The Powderhorn Park area in present-day terms is bounded on the north by Franklin Ave., on the east by Hiawatha Ave., on the south by East 42nd St., and on the west by Interstate 35W and Lyndale Ave. South. Milwaukee Ave. is also part of the Seward neighborhood.

[45] Richard Wolniewicz, "Northeast Minneapolis: Location and Movement in an Ethnic Community," 57, 178–184, 216, Ph.D. thesis, University of Minnesota, 1979; Lisa Knazan, "The Maple Hill Community, 1919–1940," 21–31, 39, *summa* paper, University of Minnesota, 1973, copy in MHS; Erma Robertson, *A Study of Community Conditions, East District*, 6 (Women's Co-operative Alliance, *Publication 68*, series 2 — Minneapolis, ca. 1925).

[46] Gail Andersen, "The Neighborhoods of Minneapolis: Camden," in *Greater Minneapolis*, July, 1974, p. 48; Minneapolis Planning Commission and City Council, *Camden Community: Analysis and Action Recommendations*, 8–10 (*Community Improvement Series*, no. 21 — Minneapolis, 1965); Schmid, *Social Saga of Two Cities*, chart 83, [p. 158]; Grace E. Pratt, *A Study of Community Conditions, North District*, 15 (Women's Co-operative Alliance, *Publication 68*, series 1 — Minneapolis, 1925).

[47] Abe Altrowitz, in *Minneapolis Star*, February 21, 1956, p. 3B, February 23, 1956, p. 4B.

[48] U.S., *Census, 1910, Population*, 2:122, 427, 996; 1920, 3:112,

117, 521; Carlsson, in Runblom and Norman, eds., *From Sweden to America*, 129; Gjerde, Scandinavian statistics; 90 Congress, 1 session, House of Representatives, Committee on Government Operations, *The Brain Drain into the United States of Scientists, Engineers, and Physicians: A Staff Study*, 18, 20, 22, 26, 28, 34, 38, 40, 42, 46, 50, 52, 54, 58, 62, 64, 68, 70, 74, 76, 78, 82, 84, 88 (Washington, D.C., 1967). On the remigration of Swedish Americans to Sweden and its role in Americanizing Swedish society, see Janson, *Background of Swedish Immigration*, 433; Lars-Göran Tedebrand, "Remigration from America to Sweden," in Runblom and Norman, eds., *From Sweden to America*, 201–227.

[49] Here and below, see Orlando Patterson, "Context and Choice in Ethnic Allegiance: A Theoretical Framework and Caribbean Case Study," in Nathan Glazer and Daniel P. Moynihan, eds., *Ethnicity: Theory and Experience*, 308, 309, 311–313 (Cambridge, Mass., 1975).

[50] Milton M. Gordon, *Assimilation in American Life: The Role of Race, Religion, and National Origins*, 70–83 (New York, 1964).

[51] Here and two paragraphs below, see Hugo Nisbeth, *Två år i Amerika, 1872–1874: Reseskildringar*, 39, 58, 65, 67 (Stockholm, 1874). On the "language question," see, for example, Sture Lindmark, "The Language Question and Its Resolution," in *Swedish Pioneer Historical Quarterly*, 23:71–95 (April, 1972).

[52] Rice, *Patterns of Ethnicity*, 37–39.

[53] Randolph E. Johnson, "Rural 'Swede Schools' of Isanti County, Minnesota," in *Swedish Pioneer Historical Quarterly*, 23:110–112 (April, 1972).

[54] Gustavus Adolphus was founded by Eric Norelius in 1862 at Red Wing. It was moved to the East Union Church at Carver in 1863 and named St. Ansgar's Academy, and then to St. Peter in 1876, where it was renamed Gustavus Adolphus College. Bethel Academy, which had its beginnings in St. Paul in 1905, merged with a Baptist seminary in Illinois in 1914; since 1945 the institution has been known as Bethel College and Seminary. Minnehaha Academy, a private high school in Minneapolis, was created in 1905 out of Northwestern Collegiate and Business Institute. See Merrill E. Jarchow, *Private Liberal Arts Colleges in Minnesota: Their History and Contributions*, 17–19, 271–275 (St. Paul, 1973); Nordstrom, ed., *Swedes in Minnesota*, 74; Swedish Evangelical Mission Covenant, *Covenant Memories: Golden Jubilee, 1885–1935*, 451–459 (Chicago, [1935]).

[55] Nordstrom, ed., *Swedes in Minnesota*, 74.

[56] Here and three paragraphs below, see Nordstrom, ed., *Swedes in Minnesota*, 64, 75; Sture Lindmark, *Swedish America, 1914–1932: Studies in Ethnicity with Emphasis on Illinois and Minnesota*, 218, 331 (Uppsala, 1971). On Turnblad, see J. Oscar Backlund, *A Century of the Swedish American Press*, 63 (Chicago, 1952); Mabel D. Abramson, "Swan J. Turnblad and His Swedish Castle," in American Swedish Institute, *Bulletin*, September, 1949, pp. 3–8. The papers published as semimonthlies or weeklies in 1918 included four in Minneapolis and one each in St. Paul, St. Peter, Duluth, and Red Wing. In the 1930s only Minneapolis' *Svenska Amerikanska Posten* and *Missions Tidninger* and St. Paul's *Minnesota Stats Tidning* remained; Brigid Shields, comp., preliminary Minnesota newspaper bibliography on file in MHS newspaper department.

[57] Nordstrom, ed., *Swedes in Minnesota*, 71.

[58] Nordstrom, ed., *Swedes in Minnesota*, 72; Nils Hasselmo, *Swedish America: An Introduction*, 40 (New York, 1976) and "The Language Question," in Hasselmo, ed., *Perspectives on Swedish Immigration*, 225–243. Other published work by Hasselmo bearing on this question may be found in "Language Displacement and Language Influence in Swedish America," in *Swedish Pioneer Historical Quarterly*, 14:62–84 (April, 1963); "Language in Exile," in J. Iverne Dowie and Ernest M. Espelie, eds., *The Swedish Immigrant Community in Transition; Essays in Honor of Dr. Conrad*

Bergendoff, 121–146 (Rock Island, Ill., 1963); *Amerikasvenska: En bok om språkutvecklingen i Svensk-Amerika* (Lund, Swed., 1974).

[59] Hasselmo, *Amerikasvenska*, 40; Nordstrom, ed., *Swedes in Minnesota*, 69.

[60] Here and two paragraphs below, see Lindmark, *Swedish America*, 259; Nordstrom, ed., *Swedes in Minnesota*, 67, 68, 70, 72; MAPS, *Minnesota Socio-Economic Characteristics*, 1970 census, vol. 3, n.p.

[61] Långasjö, *En Smålandssocken Emigrerar*, 666; Patterson, in Glazer and Moynihan, eds., *Ethnicity: Theory and Experience*, 348.

[62] Only one study of Scandinavians at the friendship level has been made in the Upper Midwest; see Peter A. Munch, "Segregation and Assimilation of Norwegian Settlements in Wisconsin," in *Norwegian-American Studies*, 18:102–140 (Northfield, 1954). Two studies of marriage behavior among Swedish Americans in Minnesota are: Lowry Nelson, "Intermarriage among Nationality Groups in a Rural Area of Minnesota," in *American Journal of Sociology*, 48: 585–592 (March, 1943); John G. Rice, "Marriage Behavior and the Persistence of Swedish Communities in Rural Minnesota," in Hasselmo, ed., *Perspectives on Swedish Immigration*, 136–150. Nelson found that the numerical importance of the group in the population, residential propinquity, and religious differences were the main influences in intermarriage and that between 60% and 70% of the husbands and wives who identified themselves as Swedish married others of Swedish descent. In Rice's study the marriage behavior of groups from the same parish, the same province, and from diverse parts of Sweden was compared. The hypothesis that endogamy would be greater the more restricted the home area in Sweden was borne out, although the small numbers involved make generalization hazardous.

[63] For more on the religious background of Swedish Americans, see Janson, *Background of Swedish Emigration*, 167–221.

[64] Nordstrom, ed., *Swedes in Minnesota*, 48–52; for details on the organization of the Minnesota Conference, see Anders, *Swedish Religious Organizations*, 23, 25.

[65] U.S. Census Bureau, *Special Reports, Religious Bodies: 1906*, 2:631, 632; George M. Stephenson, *The Religious Aspects of Swedish Immigration: A Study of Immigrant Churches*, 110, 264–266, 271–273 (Minneapolis, 1932). Religious censuses of the U.S. were also published in 1916, 1926, and 1936 by the Census Bureau.

[66] Stephenson, *Religious Aspects*, 85–87, 123n, 246–263; Nordstrom, ed., *Swedes in Minnesota*, 56.

[67] Arvel M. Steece, "A Century of Minnesota Congregationalism," 170, 171, Ph.D. thesis, Harvard University, 1957.

[68] Archibald Hadden, *Congregationalism in Minnesota, 1851–1891*, 14 (Minneapolis, 1891); Steece, "Minnesota Congregationalism," 171–178, 338.

[69] Maurice D. Edwards, *History of the Synod of Minnesota, Presbyterian Church, U.S.A.*, 248 (St. Paul, 1927); Markus, "Areal Patterns," 130. Unlike other Lutherans, the Swedish church from the time of the Reformation onward preserved the idea of the succession of bishops beginning with Peter. Since this was true also of the Church of England and because the Augustana Synod was colored by pietism, some Swedes felt that the Episcopal church provided a more congenial home. See Stephenson, *Religious Aspects*, 200–222. On the Episcopal mission efforts, see George C. Tanner, *Fifty Years of Church Work in the Diocese of Minnesota, 1857–1907*, 490, 503 (St. Paul, 1909).

[70] Stephenson, *Religious Aspects*, 424; Nordstrom, ed., *Swedes in Minnesota*, 52, 54, 73.

[71] For a more complete discussion, see Nordstrom, ed., *Swedes in Minnesota*, 60–65; Söderström, *Minneapolis Minnen*, 262–304.

[72] Lindmark, *Swedish America*, 179–190, detailed the reaction of the Chicago Swedish community to the Depression and mentioned

that Minneapolis Swedish-language newspapers of the 1930s would be potential sources of information on that city.

[73] On the institute, see Lilly E. Lorenzen, "The Institute: A Short History," in American Swedish Institute, *Bulletin*, Autumn, 1954, pp. 3–11; John Z. Lofgren, *The American Swedish Institute: Collections and Swan J. Turnblad Mansion* (Minneapolis, 1979).

[74] Here and two paragraphs below, see Lindmark, *Swedish America*, 64–69; *Svenska Amerikanska Posten*, August 12, 1914, p. 6.

[75] Lindmark, *Swedish America*, 70, 75, 77; Finis H. Capps, *From Isolationism to Involvement: The Swedish Immigrant Press in America, 1914–1945*, 37 (Chicago, 1966).

[76] Lindmark, *Swedish America*, 90, 91, 95.

[77] *Svenska Amerikanska Posten*, September 19, 1917, p. 2.

[78] Lindmark, *Swedish America*, 124–126; N. A. Grevstad to Public Safety Commission, in file 117, Main Subject Files, Minnesota Commission of Public Safety Records, Minnesota State Archives, MHS.

[79] Here and below, see Theodore C. Blegen, *Minnesota: A History of the State*, 470 (Minneapolis, 1963); "C.H. Reports," May 31, June 15, 1917; "C.U.P. Reports," June 10, 1917 — all in Correspondence and Miscellaneous Records, Woman's Committee, Council of National Defense, War Records Commission (WRC) Records, Minnesota State Archives.

[80] Here and two paragraphs below, see F. R. Duxbury to T. G. Winter, September 13, 24, 1917; unsigned to F. R. Duxbury, September 22, 1917 — all in Correspondence and Miscellaneous Records, Woman's Committee, Council of National Defense, WRC Records.

[81] Lindmark, *Swedish America*, 130.

[82] Nordstrom, ed., *Swedes in Minnesota*, 65. The triumph of neighborhood over ethnic identity was well illustrated by the emergence in 1973 of a folk hero in the distinctive mixed-ethnic, blue-collar community of Northeast Minneapolis. His name was Swen Ivan O'Myron Wisniewski. He had shoulders two ax handles wide and a 22-inch waist, chugged beer by the keg, and stole the girl friend of an affluent resident of Edina. Swen's name indicates that he was part Swedish, but what is more important about him is the class and the community he represented. See Wolniewicz, "Northeast Minneapolis," 98.

[83] Moberg's epic includes four novels: *Utvandrarna* (Stockholm, 1949) translated as *The Emigrants* (New York, 1951), *Invandrarna* (Stockholm, 1954) as *Unto a Good Land* (New York, 1954), *Nybyggarna* (Stockholm, 1956) as *The Settlers* (New York, 1978), and *Sista Brevet till Sverige* (Stockholm, 1959) as *The Last Letter Home* (London, 1961).

Other products of the Uppsala project of interest to researchers of Minnesota Swedes — in addition to those already cited in earlier notes — are Nils Runeby, *Den nya världen och den gamla: Amerikabild och emigrationsuppfattning i Sverige, 1820–1860* (Stockholm, 1969); Fred Nilsson, *Emigrationen från Stockholm till Nordamerika, 1880–1893: En studie i urban utvandring* (Stockholm, 1970; Sune Åkerman et al., *Aristocrats, Farmers and Proletarians: Essays in Swedish Demographic History* (Stockholm, 1973); Berit Brattne, *Bröderna Larsson: En studie i svensk emigrantagentverksamhet under 1800-talet* (Stockholm, 1973), plus several more which focus on such specific areas in Sweden as Västernorrland, Bergslagen, and Halmstad.

See also Runblom and Norman, eds., *From Sweden to America*, 11, 14; *Chisago County Press* (Lindstrom), July 23, 1980, pp. 1, 12. For Swedish places of interest all over the state, see Minnesota American Swedish Bicentennial Council, Heritage Task Force, *A Guide to Swedish Minnesota* ([Minneapolis, 1976?]).

CHAPTER 13

The Danes

Ann Regan

MINNESOTA is known as a Scandinavian state on the strength of its large Swedish and Norwegian populations. The third largest Scandinavian group, the Danes, scattered more widely across the country, but they also contributed a relatively large fraction to Minnesota. The states with the greatest Danish populations in 1910 each had about a tenth of the national total: Iowa 10.4%, Wisconsin 9.6%, and Minnesota 9.4%. When Minnesota's Danish population peaked in 1920, the state had 16,904 Danish-born residents.[1]

Other patterns of Danish immigration differed markedly from those of the Swedes and Norwegians. Danes emigrated later and in much smaller numbers: about 309,000 left their homeland between 1840 and 1914, in comparison to the 1,105,000 Swedes and 754,000 Norwegians who departed during the same years. Although Swedes and Norwegians formed colonies in the United States beginning in the 1830s, Danes joined them in considerable numbers only after the Civil War. In the 1880s emigration from Denmark, like that from Norway and Sweden, was at its highest sustained levels.[2]

The flow of Danes into the United States fell off during the decade of World War I. The Immigration Act of 1921 set a quota roughly equal to the increased postwar level of Danish immigration, but modifications of the law in 1924 and 1927 reduced the numbers to less than one-fifth of the 1920 level. Danish emigration then turned to Canada, Argentina, Australia, New Zealand, and South Africa. The Depression and World War II further cut immigration to the United States. The country's Danish-born population declined as the immigrants of the late 19th century aged and died. From a peak of 189,154 in 1920, the nation's foreign-born Danish population dropped to 61,410 in 1970.[3]

Kristian Hvidt, a prominent historian of Danish emigration, has pointed to two major factors that delayed and discouraged migration from Denmark. Because Danish towns were more numerous and more industrialized than those in Sweden and Norway, they offered more jobs to migrant Danes from rural areas. In addition, Danish agriculture was better able to provide for those who wanted to stay in the country. The subdivision of Danish farms was not as excessive as in Sweden, for example, and a massive land reclamation project in Jutland (see Map 13.1) from the 1860s through the 1880s provided new farms for some of the landless. Hvidt has also suggested that the Swedish and Norwegian colonies

established in the United States by 1850 may have further stimulated the large-scale emigration that began in Scandinavia in the 1860s. The Danes lacked such concentrated magnet settlements. But, as in the other Scandinavian countries, many farmers' children in overcrowded rural areas contracted "America fever" and chose to seek a new life across the Atlantic. Of the Danes who arrived in Minnesota between 1868 and 1900, 70% were from Denmark's rural areas.[4]

Their reasons for emigrating were varied. Some expressed dissatisfaction with Denmark's future prospects after it lost the provinces of Schleswig and Holstein to Prussia in 1864. Thousands were persuaded to make the voyage by ubiquitous shipping agents or by Mormon missionaries who attracted Danes to Utah. Later Lutheran immigrants moved to religious colonies like those at Tyler and Askov in Minnesota, established by the Danish Evangelical Lutheran Church and the *Dansk Folkesamfund* (Danish Folk Society). In 1879 Denmark established its own national shipping company, the Thingvalla Line, which offered direct transportation to the United States to many who distrusted German and English ships. And after steamship ticket prices fell in the 1880s, more people could afford the journey.[5]

Probably the greatest factors in later years were prepaid tickets and remittances sent by relatives already in the United States. Although the total amount of prepaid emigration was much less than in Sweden, for example, about one-fourth of Danish emigration from 1877 to 1895 was by prepaid tickets. Hvidt estimated that these personal contacts motivated at least 55% of the emigration from 1868 to 1914.

Danish settlement in the United States followed several patterns. Some Danes moved to Scandinavian neighborhoods in large cities, while others immigrated to several planned colonies built by Danish Lutherans in Minnesota, Texas, Wisconsin, Montana, and California. Dissent within the church over these colonies, and the lateness of their founding (after 1878) prevented them from attaining any large-scale success.[6]

Two other factors lowered the Danes' visibility in the United States. Many of the men married non-Danish women, perhaps because before 1900 there were two Danish immigrant males to each female. In contrast, a nearly even balance prevailed among the Swedes. Danes were also less likely than Swedes and Norwegians to retain membership

Map 13.1. Denmark

in the Lutheran church. Only 25% of the Danes were registered members in 1906, compared to 75% of the Norwegians and 40% of the Swedes. Other less ethnically identified churches — Mormon, Baptist, Methodist, and Seventh-Day Adventist — attracted some Danish members.

Settlement Patterns

Danish settlement in Minnesota (see Map 13.2) paralleled patterns set by Danes elsewhere in the United States. Early immigrants were few and widely dispersed. The only Dane listed in the 1850 territorial census was Charles W. W. Borup, a physician and fur trader who settled in St. Paul in 1848 and became one of the city's first bankers. By 1860, 216 persons of Danish stock were counted, scattered across southern Minnesota (see Table 13.1).[7]

Many of Minnesota's Danes disappeared into the communities of Norwegians with whom they settled. There were several reasons for this. Their spoken languages were similar, and their written languages were virtually the same. Denmark had dominated Norway for 400 years, establishing traditions of religious and political co-operation. The two countries had often united to fight the Swedes.[8]

The three major rural settlements that Minnesota Danes formed, however, were closely identified with their churches. The Baptists founded the first in 1863. Led by the Reverend Lars Jørgensen Hauge, six Danish Baptists moved from Raymond, Wisconsin, to the area near Geneva Lake in Freeborn County that later became Clarks Grove. Although they had planned to travel farther west to homestead, they found reasonably priced land near several Baptist families from Waushara, Wisconsin, and decided to stay. Other Danes from Wisconsin (some attracted by Hauge) and from Denmark joined them in Bath, Bancroft, Riceland, Alden, and Geneva townships and in the village of Albert Lea during the next few years. By 1880 Freeborn County had 1,107 Danish-born residents and 535 born of Danish parents. Most

Table 13.1. Danes in Minnesota by County, 1860–1970

County	1860 foreign born	1860 foreign mixed	1880 fb	1880 fm	1895 fb	1905 fb	1905 fm	1930 fb	1930 fm	1970 fb	1970 fm
Aitkin					13	52	80	61	156	22	71
Anoka	1		18	5	99	100	216	112	220	33	432
Becker			36	19	85	118	196	59	174	14	178
Beltrami					8	99	179	87	219	28	134
Benton				1	14	23	69	15	63	6	93
Big Stone			34	11	99	84	204	44	140		63
Blue Earth	6	1	88	43	253	220	452	182	420	49	209
Brown			392	305	392	318	1,069	199	468	4	125
Carlton			2	1	41	56	116	59	146		148
Carver	3	3	16	8	10	18	40	19	34		62
Cass			3	5	21	65	167	63	177	11	60
Chippewa			27	25	70	109	271	74	222	21	84
Chisago			59	28	48	63	121	41	113	6	87
Clay			27	17	83	110	232	81	244	9	183
Clearwater						47	104	26	112	6	65
Cook						2	3	6	14	5	24
Cottonwood			59	37	242	213	553	176	440	27	219
Crow Wing	1		18	7	157	184	505	126	350	80	228
Dakota			53	25	211	246	545	211	430	32	480
Dodge	4		195	107	267	195	517	115	354	31	168
Douglas			96	81	258	242	608	121	214		131

Table 13.1. Danes in Minnesota by County, 1860–1970 (*continued*)

County	1860 foreign born	1860 foreign mixed	1880 fb	1880 fm	1895 fb	1905 fb	1905 fm	1930 fb	1930 fm	1970 fb	1970 fm
Faribault			45	9	209	167	358	106	285	6	147
Fillmore			98	59	60	49	130	35	105	11	50
Freeborn	2	1	1,107	535	1,945	1,758	3,931	1,115	2,648	234	1,140
Goodhue	16	3	56	45	116	114	217	74	192	40	171
Grant			16	7	46	28	81	24	88	9	77
Hennepin	1		261	126	1,917	2,369	4,738	2,874	5,823	684	4,568
Minneapolis			206		1,515	1,904	3,829	2,418	4,998	396	2,238
Houston	3	3	14	22	7	7	18	5	24		24
Hubbard					5	16	72	34	97	7	41
Isanti			14	13	12	16	52	37	89	10	75
Itasca					10	64	163	62	163	6	104
Jackson			35	37	250	225	581	144	329	22	145
Kanabec	1				3	30	73	45	105	15	39
Kandiyohi			202	101	328	253	584	182	445	8	263
Kittson					36	43	138	33	75		31
Koochiching								58	158		157
Lac qui Parle			6		71	111	160	79	199	25	110
Lake					19	21	31	19	46		33
Lake of the Woods								25	57		30
Le Sueur	4	7	4	18	8	12	28	13	43		57
Lincoln			54	17	820	800	2,384	648	1,438	95	514
Lyon			18	10	196	168	468	156	371	9	264
McLeod	1		179	66	610	475	1,148	291	540	35	229
Mahnomen								18	40		38
Marshall			68	32	73	82	192	59	201		42
Martin			37	37	148	158	392	162	377	23	173
Meeker			162	120	268	273	575	125	372	31	163
Mille Lacs			16	15	27	71	163	70	168	18	128
Morrison	2	1	111	75	172	158	630	75	208	6	119
Mower			214	194	370	261	567	254	632	60	504
Murray			12	9	78	102	227	61	210	6	122
Nicollet	6	4	15	4	61	49	90	70	136		64
Nobles			5	17	61	92	238	67	177	14	82
Norman					18	51	80	25	126		28
Olmsted	5	2	208	105	302	241	569	225	610	30	535
Otter Tail			201	197	321	346	1,026	237	684	41	319
Pennington								51	125	15	85
Pine			15	4	44	41	125	507	861	56	251
Pipestone			4	2	116	154	340	127	264	23	146
Polk			51	46	257	205	452	101	268	24	135
Pope			5	5	64	58	137	28	111	13	104
Ramsey	18	3	254	101	1,412	1,423	2,577	1,261	2,868	260	2,101
St. Paul			218		1,350	1,344	2,453	1,164	2,657	206	1,482
Red Lake						85	171	17	50		39
Redwood			134	89	509	569	1,253	276	813	15	335
Renville	2		50	15	158	103	244	81	218	5	114
Rice	1		52	24	182	144	297	134	321	48	218
Rock			25	9	65	67	164	32	136	7	103
Roseau					1	36	94	48	122		55
St. Louis			64	27	372	409	1,689	459	948	95	652
Duluth					332	297	1,476	324	628	81	385
Scott	4	2	10	1	37	23	52	26	88		72
Sherburne			87	21	183	156	365	106	184	21	133
Sibley	3	1	13	26	37	27	58	19	60		85
Stearns			45	25	154	71	255	83	279	16	170
Steele	3		419	196	755	598	1,296	329	724	54	408
Stevens			12	8	35	71	132	62	160	18	90
Swift			15	17	56	54	165	70	159		50
Todd	1		8	7	48	50	153	73	217		107
Traverse			8	4	26	45	140	19	50		14
Wabasha	50	16	15	20	11	19	49	20	54		33
Wadena			2	1	13	82	162	52	162	18	32
Waseca			31	35	43	49	107	38	114	11	46
Washington	13	2	115	49	296	241	468	175	334	22	259
Watonwan			21	14	57	73	187	32	114	12	43
Wilkin			30	15	32	40	85	42	130	10	31
Winona	12	3	74	45	116	88	294	54	174	34	169
Wright	1		29	29	40	53	95	40	113	15	108
Yellow Medicine			9	14	43	58	164	85	197		123
Total	164	52	5,878	3,444	16,100	16,266	38,121	13,831	32,389	2,621	20,141
Published census figures	(170)		(6,071)		(16,143)	(16,266)	(37,540)	(13,831)	(32,389)	(2,621)	(20,141)

Source: See Appendix

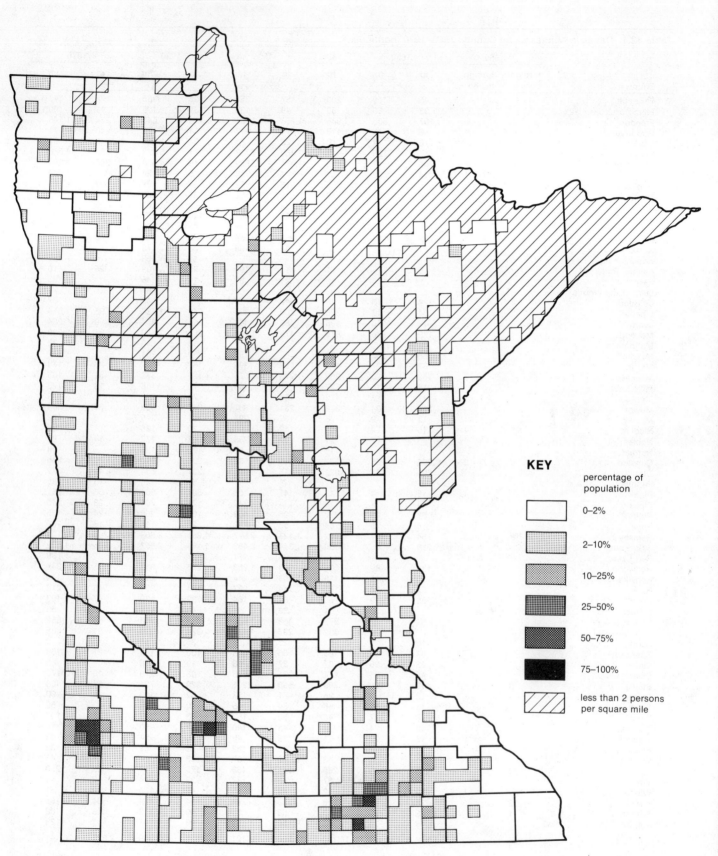

KEY

percentage of
population

0–2%

2–10%

10–25%

25–50%

50–75%

75–100%

less than 2 persons
per square mile

Map 13.2. Danes in Minnesota Rural Areas, 1905

DANES helped pioneer the establishment of co-operative creameries in Minnesota. That at Clarks Grove was still in operation in 1980.

were farmers, who first grew wheat and then raised livestock as well.[9]

The strict rules of Clarks Grove's First Danish Baptist Church, built in 1866, were of "a kind unknown to Danes in the mother country," according to one historian. Work and travel on Sundays, drinking, card playing, ball playing, and marriage outside the church were all forbidden, as was cutting timber on another's land. (The homemade Danish beer drunk at haying and harvest times was not included in the ban on alcohol.) Their hard work paid off in material terms. The congregation's fourth church, built in 1915 for $22,574, was free of debt at its dedication.[10]

Some of this success grew from practices and theories imported from Denmark. In 1884 one of the Freeborn County settlers, Hans Peter Jensen, returned to Denmark for a visit. He was struck by the changes he saw in Danish agriculture. Impoverished farmers, who had been working exhausted soils when he emigrated, were now enjoying the advantages of the newly invented cream separator and good herds of purebred cattle. Co-operatives, which enabled the farmers to combine their resources, had produced these startling improvements, and Denmark had begun to export fine butter.[11]

Jensen quickly recognized the potential that the co-operative idea could have for the Danes of Freeborn County. Each farm wife there made butter and sold it in small quantities to local stores, but because of its widely varying quality it generally commanded a low price. When he returned to Minnesota, Jensen trumpeted the success of co-operatives to all his neighbors who would listen. Many of them were interested, but six years went by before they acted. During that time the opening of the prairies farther west began to flood the market with wheat.

In 1889, after a visitor reported favorably on co-operative creameries in Iowa, the farmers near Geneva Lake held their first organizational meetings. Then they made a careful study of the successful co-operatives at Oran and Fremont, Iowa. In January, 1890, they formed the Clarks Grove Co-operative Creamery Association. Their first building was designed according to the plans of the Fremont co-op, and their constitution and bylaws, written in Danish, were based on those used at Oran. They called the new organization Clarks Grove after a stand of trees (named for an early postmaster) that grew near the new creamery.

While the Clarks Grove co-operative is sometimes referred to as the first in Minnesota, its claim to that distinction is disputed. Three other dairy co-ops started by German and Norwegian farmers at Biscay, Vernon, and Zumbro had begun operations a few months earlier in 1889. But Clarks Grove was the most successful. It paid off its building debt within three years and erected a new and larger creamery in 1905. Its prosperity also inspired the farmers to form mercantile, lumber and fuel, and hardware co-operatives during the next 20 years. Non-Danes and non-Baptists were welcome to join, and did, but the Clarks Grove farmers were generally united by language and religion.[12]

The influence of the dairy co-operative was spread throughout the state largely by the work of Theophilus L. Haecker, father of Minnesota dairying and professor of dairy husbandry at the University of Minnesota from 1891 to 1918. Haecker, who first visited the creamery in 1892, wrote a pamphlet on how to organize a co-operative which included a proposed constitution and bylaws based on those of Clarks Grove. By 1918, at the end of Haecker's career, there were 630 co-operative creameries in Minnesota, many of them modeled on the example set at Clarks Grove.[13]

In 1980 the creamery still did business, but the center of Danish activity in Freeborn County was Albert Lea. An evening class in the Danish language, sponsored by the public school district, drew 25 students. Lodges of the Danish Brotherhood and Sisterhood (fraternal insurance organizations) held monthly meetings, including an annual St. Hans Picnic on Midsummer Day, at which they continued the custom of burning a straw witch to drive away evil spirits. The groups planned to dedicate in 1981 a lighted fountain with a bronze statue of a young Danish immigrant and place it in a park on the north side of the city, a section once known as New Denmark. The project received contributions from Danes throughout the state and across the country.[14]

The Danish Baptists of Freeborn County spread their influence in a more traditional way as well. Missionary work, an important aspect of their religion, took them into the growing Danish settlements in their own and other counties. Immigration to the area continued through the 1880s and 1890s, as Danes moved north to Steele County (Ellendale, Lemond Township, Blooming Prairie, and Owatonna) and east to Dodge County (Hayfield Township and Kasson village) and Olmsted County (Salem Township and the city of Rochester).[15]

In the late 1860s, Danes from Freeborn County moved west to Sleepy Eye, Linden, and Prairieville townships in Brown County, where they were joined by migrants from Wisconsin and Denmark. In 1883 migrants and immigrants representing Lutheran, Baptist, and Seventh-Day Adventist faiths combined forces to erect a union church in Prairieville Township. They shared the building until 1894, when the Lutherans built their own church. Offshoots of this group expanded southwest into Cottonwood County and northwest into Sundown and Brookville townships in Redwood County. As in Brown County, Baptists, Lutherans, and Seventh-Day Adventists in Brookville Township together built a church.

Lutheran Colonies

Many of the Danes in these settlements belonged to the Danish Evangelical Lutheran Church in America, founded in 1872. This body contained two major factions, Grundtvigian and Inner Mission. The first was started by Nikolai Frederik Severin Grundtvig, a 19th-century bishop in Denmark who rejected what he regarded as narrow pietism in the established church. He believed that people must be fully aware of their humanity before they could make a total Christian commitment and that this awareness could be gained and fostered by educational and cultural activities. His followers carried this Danish tradition to America.[16]

Grundtvig's favored method of promoting education was through folk high schools, which he initiated in Denmark in 1844. These institutions taught Danish adults their country's history and literature and offered some scientific and vocational instruction. The schools became very popular in Denmark after 1864, when their patriotic curriculum helped renew national pride damaged by the loss of Schleswig and Holstein. The folk high schools later provided trained managers for Denmark's co-operative businesses.

The Inner Mission group, larger and more pietistic than the Grundtvigians, also rejected the established church in Denmark in the 19th century. But they objected to the secular emphasis of the Grundtvigians, arguing that conscious efforts to retain Danish language and culture held back their children's progress in the new land.[17]

In the 1890s the differences between these factions brought schisms and mergers that produced two bodies, the Danish Evangelical Lutheran Church in North America (the Grundtvigians, or "happy Danes") and the United Danish Lutheran Church in America (the Inner Mission people, or "holy Danes"). In Minnesota, as in the rest of the country, the latter had the larger official membership. In 1906 there were 20 Inner Mission churches and 2,376 communicants throughout the state. The Grundtvigians had 9 churches and 1,081 registered members. By 1916 Steele County alone had six Inner Mission congregations. Ten years later the two groups' memberships were each close to 2,800, but the more scattered Inner Mission church had three times as many buildings (21) as the Grundtvigians (7). The mergers among American Lutheran churches in the 20th century eventually put the Inner Mission group in the American Lutheran Church and the Grundtvigians in the more liberal Lutheran Church in America.

In spite of their smaller numbers, the Grundtvigian immigrants, with their folk school emphasis on Danish patriotism and mass education, became much more visible in Minnesota than their Inner Mission counterparts. Reacting to the scattering of Danes in the Midwest, they began to gather their followers into settlements where Danish language and culture could be reinforced and promoted. They founded colonies in two widely separated areas of the state — Tyler on the western border and Askov on the eastern — that retained a Danish awareness through 1980.[18]

The Danish Evangelical Lutheran Church officially founded the Tyler colony. A convention at Clinton, Iowa, in 1884 appointed a committee led by Frederik L. Grundtvig, the bishop's youngest son, to find land for a colony that would aid "poor people in the cities who wish to live on a farm." From the Winona and St. Peter Railroad the group secured an option on 35,000 acres of land in Lincoln County, north, east, and south of Lake Benton and near the village of Tyler, which became the area's trade center. For three years the land was to be sold only to Danes; the railroad agreed to donate 240 acres for a church and a folk high school.

In June, 1885, the first 70 settlers proceeded in a caravan to the lands selected. After that the colony grew quickly. Other Danes, including non-Lutherans, were attracted from Illinois (especially Chicago), Iowa, and South Dakota, as well as from other parts of Minnesota. A few emigrated directly from Denmark. By 1905 there were 800 foreign-born and 2,384 American-born Danes in Lincoln County, and they had spilled over into Lyon and Pipestone counties.

Like their countrymen at Clarks Grove, the Lincoln County Danes organized co-operative dairies — at Tyler (1894), Ruthton (1895), Lake Benton (1897), and Arco (1910). By 1916 the four co-ops were producing about 1,000,000 pounds of butter a year. Soon after the turn of the century, the farmers established other co-operatives, including a fire-insurance company, a lumber company, a grain elevator, a bank, a telephone company, and a shipping firm for marketing farm animals.[19]

But the Tyler colony's most distinctive institution was Danebod, a church and folk high school complex at the heart of the community. The name, which means "one who mends or saves the Danes," was first given to a 10th-century Danish queen who united her people against invaders. The congregation was organized in 1886 and called Hans J. Pedersen, a minister from Michigan, in 1888. His enthusiastic building program included a folk high school (1888), a

TWO of the buildings which comprised the church and folk high school complex known as Danebod at Tyler in 1910. The stone structure on the left served as both meetinghouse and gymnasium beginning in 1889.

stone meetinghouse and gymnasium (1889), a parochial school (1892), and finally a church (1895). Pedersen put off the construction of the last, arguing that "a gym hall can be used temporarily as a church; a church cannot be used as a gym hall." An orphanage built in 1909 became a home for the aged in 1935.[20]

Tyler's Danebod, a center for religious, educational, and cultural activities, functioned as a unifying force. Speakers lectured in Danish on literature and history; reading groups discussed books written in both Danish and English. Concerts, plays, readings, folk dances, and harvest festivals were held there, as well as weddings, funerals, baptisms, and Sunday school classes.

In the classes, Danish began to give way to English in the 1920s, but the church did not offer any English-language services until 1943. A weekly Danish service continued until at least 1961. The pastor's notes for 1965 recorded the end of regular Danish-language worship: "Christmas, 1964 and Easter, 1965 — *no* Danish services — and no repercussions." The folk high school closed in 1940, but was revived in 1946 by the Folk School Association, which offered week-long Danish Folk Meetings. These sessions, which were later shortened to four days, featured singing, Bible study, and lectures in Danish and English. Two-thirds of the 145 participants in 1980 were from outside the town. Askov, the Twin Cities, and nine midwestern and west coast states were represented. The use of Danish was limited to a church service and Danish songs in order to encourage participation. "We want to continue in the Danish spirit, but not necessarily in the language," explained one organizer who had lived in Tyler for 36 years.[21]

Danebod was also used by the Family Recreation Camp, a nondenominational organization started in 1948 by the Folk School Association and later managed by an independent board. Over 200 people attended the sessions in June and August, 1977, participating in folk dancing, singing, craft classes, and discussion groups.[22]

The town of Tyler celebrated its Danish heritage in an annual midsummer festival known as Æbleskiver Days. Service organizations sold *æbleskiver* (Danish apple pastries) and *smørrebrød* (open-faced sandwiches on thin rye bread), and local merchants decorated their shops with plywood figures of *nissemænd* (Danish elves) during the three-day celebration. The program in 1980 included Danish food and folk dancing as well as more traditional American activities such as a parade, a foot race, a queen contest, and an art fair.[23]

The third major Danish colony in Minnesota was established in 1906 in Pine County by the *Dansk Folkesamfund* (Danish Folk Society). This nonsectarian organization, formed in 1887 by members of the Danish Evangelical Lutheran Church, proposed to establish colonies where Danish language and culture could be preserved. Acting as the society's agents, men from the Tyler colony purchased 20,000 acres of cutover and burned-over land in Pine County. Stripped of its forests, the area was not appealing, and it had remained sparsely settled. Heavy brush had grown up between the stumps after the devastating Hinckley fire in 1894, and the soil was full of rocks. Earlier German settlers had cleared some land, built roads, and founded the town of Partridge, but most of them had left the area in search of better farms. In 1908 the Danes, undaunted, renamed the town in honor of the Askov Folk High School in Denmark, where young men were trained for the Danish-American ministry.[24]

By 1910, 193 first-generation and 162 second-generation Danes lived in Pine County; 10 years later 520 foreign-born Danes lived there. Using tons of explosives, they had blasted out the tree stumps and planted potatoes in the rocky, cleared lands. Ludwig Mosbaek, one of the first settlers, grew rutabagas from seeds sent by a friend in Denmark in 1890. Others followed his example with great success. By the 1950s farmers around Askov were growing 3,000 tons of rutabagas annually, or one-fourth of the national crop, and the town was billing itself as the "Rutabaga Capital of America."[25]

These farmers, like those of Clarks Grove and Tyler, put co-operatives to work for them. Because fire hazards were great in the cutover lands of northern Minnesota, commercial insurance companies charged high rates, so in 1908 the Danish farmers formed a fire-insurance co-operative. They also established both producers' and consumers' co-operatives, a creamery, a livestock-shipping association, oil and mercantile associations, a potato warehouse, a feed mill, and a credit union.[26]

The colonists strove to preserve their Danish heritage.

ASKOV in Pine County was established in the early 20th century among the cutover stumps left by lumbering.

"We have worked hard to gather our own people here," claimed Askov's promotional literature in 1926, "not in order to segregate them from America and American ideals, but in order to have a place where all the good we have brought with us from the mother country may thrive and bear fruit and where we may, in some degree, inculcate some of these ideals into our friends who came from other lands to found homes in America."[27]

Both church activities and daily life served this goal. In 1926 a study of 287 families showed that about 80% of the children spoke Danish to their parents. The language and the history of Denmark were taught for an hour each day in the public schools until 1942. The church-sponsored Young People's Society and Danish Ladies' Aid, a chapter of the Danish Folk Society, and a Danish Brotherhood lodge provided the framework of community social life. Although Askov did not have a folk high school, the church offered preparatory courses for those who planned to attend folk schools elsewhere.[28]

While the community did not remain exclusively Danish, the town still identified with that heritage in the 1980s. The basketball team was named the Askov Danes, merchants decorated their stores with plywood *nissemænd* at Christmas, and the town held a Rutabaga Festival and Danish Days celebration every summer. The local bicentennial project in 1976 was the erection of Danish-language street signs, an idea supported by some non-Danes and opposed by some Danes. A Danish Brotherhood lodge and Danish Folk Dancers also still met.[29]

Danes who did not join a self-defined colony settled in almost all Minnesota counties (see Table 13.1). The largest nonmetropolitan numbers outside the areas already described were in the central counties of Meeker (Danielson and Litchfield townships), Kandiyohi (Willmar), Otter Tail (Fergus Falls), and McLeod (Lynn Township and Hutchinson).[30]

Most of the Danes at Hutchinson, including several families who arrived directly from Denmark in 1867, were from Vejle, a region in Jutland. They worshiped in Lutheran, Baptist, Methodist, and Adventist churches and formed lodges of the Danish Brotherhood and Sisterhood. Lutherans built Ansgar College there in 1902, but the school failed after a few years. In 1909 a committee of Seventh-Day Adventists bought the empty buildings and established the Danish-Norwegian Seminary, later known as the Hutchinson Theological Seminary, which became Maplewood Academy in 1928.[31]

In 1895 Duluth's small Danish-born population numbered 332; 10 years later St. Louis County listed 409 first-generation and 1,689 second-generation Danes. By 1916 those in Duluth had a Lutheran church and supported Danish Brotherhood and Sisterhood lodges.[32]

The Twin Cities

Although more than half the state's Danes remained in rural areas through 1920, a substantial number moved to Minneapolis and St. Paul (see Table 13.1). Between 1880 and 1890 the cities' Danish population grew by over 700%, while their total population increased at half that rate. By 1920, 23% of the state's Danes lived in the Twin Cities, with about two-thirds of them in Minneapolis.[33]

Housing patterns among the Minneapolis Danes suggest that they initially found work as laborers and artisans. They settled in the 1870s on the Danish Flats, later known as the Bohemian Flats, along the Mississippi River in South Minneapolis. From there they climbed the hill to Cedar and Riverside avenues and Seven Corners, and they followed the Norwegians to the south and east along the river. With the Swedes and Norwegians, they clustered for a time on Milwaukee Avenue, which was briefly known as Copenhagen Avenue. The Scandinavians worked in the flour mills, the breweries, and small factories nearby. The west river area as far south as Minnehaha Park continued to be the principal concentration in Minneapolis until at least 1930. The Danes supported Norwegian-Danish Methodist and Baptist churches and two Danish Lutheran churches in the neighborhood.[34]

In the 1880s many of St. Paul's Danes lived on the West Side, where they built a Lutheran church. Later they scattered throughout the city. Between 1910 and 1930 no ward had more than 200 Danish-born residents. They established a second Lutheran church in 1909 and worshiped with Norwegians in Baptist, Methodist Episcopal, and Presbyterian churches.[35]

The Danes' interest in their culture and their love of celebration found expression through several social and cultural organizations. Minneapolis had men's and women's athletic clubs, a literary club, and several organizations for young people. The Danish Brotherhood and Sisterhood had lodges in both cities that promoted Danish activities and contributed to Danish charities. The Sons and Daughters of Denmark, similar organizations, had lodges in St. Paul.[36]

An example of an early Danish celebration in St. Paul was the Hans Christian Andersen Festival and Bazaar, held April 27–29, 1892, to raise funds for the erection of a monument in the United States "to the memory of the far-famed writer and author of Fairy Tales." The entertainment included speeches by Minnesota politicians, music, "Roller Skating by an expert on the stage," "the Tableau 'Denmark,' represented by a bevy of beautiful ladies dressed in national costumes," and "the bold Sir Knights, Lars and Svend in a Danish Tournament (as they did it in the 14th century)."[37]

The Minneapolis community, larger and more organized than that of St. Paul, used several buildings as gathering places. The most important was Dania Hall, built in 1886 at the corner of 5th Street and Cedar Avenue by the Society Dania. The society was formed in 1875 when the Danes withdrew from Norden, a Scandinavian group, "because they thought there were entirely too many Norwegians in it." The planners declared, "We are about to erect a home, not alone for those Danish people who have homes here, but also a home for those of our fellow-countrymen who are to come hereafter. We desire that when they come as strangers in this great city they can come to our hall and enjoy themselves, and not be compelled to go to saloons and worse places." The speech "was applauded to the echo."[38]

Dania Hall served as a center for Danish and Scandinavian activities for decades. It housed a library and provided facilities for plays, reading groups, dances, weddings, funerals, and political meetings. In 1926 the society had between 300 and 400 members, and it survived until the 1950s.

The Danish Young People's Home, a nonprofit boardinghouse, opened in 1917 at 3010 20th Avenue South in Minneapolis. It was a gathering place for young Danes who belonged to *Dansk Samensluttet Ungdom* (Danish United Youth, associated with St. Peder's Danish Lutheran Church) or to *Ungdomsforeningen af 1905* (Young People's Society of 1905). The latter, which bought the building from the former in 1922, produced dozens of plays and held many parties there. A total of 660 people joined in its first 21 years, but because the society served Danish families that were passing through the Twin Cities, its membership in 1926 was only 109. The home, which also operated an employment bureau, was moved in 1933 to 3620 East 42nd Street, where it remained until its closing in 1970.[39]

MINNEAPOLIS DANES performed Bro over Havet (Bridge over the Sea) *at Cedar-Riverside's Dania Hall in 1933. The stage curtain behind the actors depicts the town of Odense, on the Danish island of Fyn. At left, Dania Hall, with its Danish and American flags flying, dominated the neighborhood about 1906.*

Concern for the elderly balanced these efforts for the young. In 1924 a group of 18 Danish churches, societies, and lodges from Minneapolis and St. Paul built Danebo, a Danish retirement home, on West River Boulevard. Support from rural Minnesota and Wisconsin Danes made the home a regional institution. Supporting organizations called Danebo Circles, of which there were 17 in 1974, contributed to its operation. In 1980 Danebo was occupied by people of various Scandinavian descents.[40]

By 1980 the state's largest Danish organization was the Danish American Fellowship, established in 1948 and reincorporated in 1979 "to engage in developing, promoting, and sponsoring cultural, educational, charitable, social, and recreational activities so as to gain a fuller understanding of and appreciation for our Danish heritage and its impact on the Danish-American experience." The group bought the Danish Young People's Home in 1966 and operated it as a rooming house and clubhouse until 1970. The Danish American Center at 4200 Cedar Avenue was purchased that same year. In 1980, with about 800 members, the fellowship sponsored classes in Danish folk dancing, folk costumes, *smørrebrød* preparation (with beginning, advanced, and expert levels), embroidery, gymnastics, and language. Its cultural outreach activities included performances throughout the Midwest by the Danebrog Folkdancers, participation in St. Paul's Festival of Nations, and cosponsorship, with other arts organizations, of Danish performers.[41]

Between 1,000 and 1,400 people usually attended Danish Day, a festival sponsored since 1960 by the fellowship on the Sunday nearest June 5, Danish Constitution Day. The 1980 celebration in Minneapolis' Minnehaha Park began with an open-air Lutheran church service. The picnic featured 3,000 pieces of *smørrebrød* with *kringle* and *kransekage* (Danish pastries). Danish people from across the state journeyed to Minneapolis to visit with old friends and relatives. An afternoon program with a speaker, a folk dance performance, and music completed the celebration.

The diffused Danish population in the United States kept informed of events in the homeland and in the Danish-American community through their own press. Minnesota was the home of two of the important Danish publishers. Christian Rasmussen, who moved his business from Chicago to Minneapolis in 1887, established an operation that was known locally as *Bladfabrikken* (the newspaper factory). He printed as many as 16 Danish- and Norwegian-language papers, including *St. Paul Tidende* (St. Paul Times), published from 1903 to at least 1927 as a successor to *Heimdal* (Home Valley) begun in 1891 by a Norwegian, and *Ugebladet* (Weekly Blade). The latter, which first appeared in 1890, was in 1942 one of seven surviving Danish-language newspapers in the United States. It became the *Midwest Scandinavian* in 1945 and was produced in English until its demise in 1959. C. Rasmussen Company also published books and printed pamphlets and advertising for Danish organizations.[42]

Another important Danish newspaperman was Hjalmar Petersen, perhaps better known as the man who filled out Governor Floyd B. Olson's term as governor after Olson's death in 1936. Born in 1890 in Denmark, Petersen immi-

grated with his parents to Lincoln County by way of Chicago. He worked on the *Tyler Journal* before moving to Askov in 1914 and founding the *Askov American*. The newspaper, printed in English, claimed to have the largest circulation in the United States of any originating in a town of Askov's size. No one disputed the boast. Petersen also founded the American Publishing Company, which printed the national magazine of the Danish Brotherhood from its second issue in March, 1928, as well as many books on Danish-American topics.[43]

While these publishers were finding works printed in English more successful, Danish churches were also undergoing language changes. Danish gave way to English as early as 1900 in some Baptist and Seventh-Day Adventist congregations, but most churches began to change in the middle and late 1920s. Many still offered Danish services in the middle 1930s. The shift to English occurred somewhat later in the state's major colonies, as might be expected. Six of the nine Danish churches in Freeborn County offered regular services in the mother tongue in 1936. Lutherans in Pine County held some Danish services until at least 1949, and those at Tyler's Danebod did so until 1965. Not surprisingly, church records show that Grundtvigian churches used the mother tongue longer than Inner Mission ones. Immanuel Danish Evangelical Lutheran Church (Inner Mission) in Minneapolis changed completely to English services in 1932, while St. Peder's Danish Evangelical Church (Grundtvigian), a few blocks away, held half its services in the mother tongue until at least 1936. The Inner Mission church at Hutchinson converted to almost fully English services in 1900, but the Grundtvigian church there used Danish in half its services until 1932.[44]

The histories of these two denominations demonstrate an ironic twist in the role of the immigrant church as outlined in other chapters of this book. The Grundtvigians were both more socially liberal and more conservative of the values of the Old Country. The Inner Mission faction was both more socially conservative and more willing to adopt American ways in order to succeed. The Grundtvigians maintained their Danish self-awareness much longer, in part by hiring ministers trained in Denmark. The Inner Mission churches apparently succeeded in their goal of assimilation. Their diffused settlements did not demonstrate the intensity of ethnic activity evident in Tyler and Askov in 1980. The Minneapolis churches offered an urban example. Immanuel (Inner Mission) disbanded in 1960. St. Peder's (Grundtvigian) was only about 30% Danish in 1980, but some members of the congregation retained ties to Denmark, visiting the Old Country on flights sponsored by the Danish American Fellowship.[45]

But the Grundtvigians, too, have felt the impact of time and the change in their church's independent status. As Tyler's Danebod received pastors not of Danish background, says one long-time member, the relationship between the church and its people changed. The liberal and social Grundtvigian tradition faded into the more homogeneous Lutheran Church in America. But older Minnesota "happy Danes" fought back by adding a stage to their parents' migration. Many from Tyler, Askov, and the Twin Cities retired to Solvang, California, which was founded in 1911 as a Danish colony. "I think the town was made up of [Danish] people from the Middle West who retired there," speculated a woman who had many friends in Solvang. "It's a mecca for retired [Danish Lutheran] ministers." And in yet another phase of Danish immigration to America, the former Minnesotans in California began to attract new arrivals from Denmark.[46]

Reference notes

[1] United States, *Census*, 1910, *Population*, 1:898; 1920, 3:507; 1970, vol. 1, part 1, p. 598, part 25, p. 232. The author wishes to acknowledge the helpful suggestions she received on this chapter from Reverend Enok Mortensen and Professor Harold Jensen.

[2] Kristian Hvidt, *Flight to America: The Social Background of 300,000 Danish Emigrants*, 3, 9, 49 (New York, 1975), an abridged translation of *Flugen til Amerika eller Drivkræfter i masseudvandringen fra Danmark 1868–1914* (Copenhagen, 1971); Albert Kamp, "Danish Emigration to North America," in *Le Nord*, 1:8 (1942). Danish emigration was smaller than that of Sweden and Norway in relative terms, as well. Between 1861 and 1908, for each 100,000 of population, an average of 242 Danes, 401 Swedes, and 665 Norwegians left their countries.

Danish immigration statistics have minor inaccuracies. After the transfer of Schleswig-Holstein to Prussia in 1864, Germans from north Schleswig could escape enforced service in the Prussian army by emigrating to America via Denmark. It is not known how many did so. Icelanders, as subjects of Denmark until 1918, were counted as Danes in the U.S. census through 1930. Danes emigrating from Schleswig-Holstein after 1864 would have been counted as Germans.

[3] Kamp, *Danish Emigration*, 11; Press and Cultural Relations Dept. Ministry of Foreign Affairs, *Denmark: An Official Handbook*, 116 (Copenhagen, 1974); U.S., *Census*, 1920, *Population*, 2:897, 1970, vol. 1, part 1, p. 598.

[4] Hvidt, *Flight to America*, 39, 88, 127, 129, 173, 198. See also W. Glyn Jones, *Denmark*, 40 (London, 1970); Stewart Oakley, *The Story of Denmark*, 158 (London, 1972). Although statistics also show higher urban Danish emigration than was the case from Norway and Sweden, many people who departed from Denmark's cities had stopped there only temporarily after leaving their homes in the countryside. Thus, while the statistics listed urban emigrants, many of them were undoubtedly people in a second or third stage of migration. See Hvidt, *Flight to America*, 47.

[5] Here and below, see Kristian Hvidt, *Flight to America*, 37, 141, 148, 172, 191, 194, 201, and "Danish Emigration Prior to 1914: Trends and Problems," in *Scandinavian Economic History Review*, 14:175 (1966).

[6] Here and below, see Hvidt, *Flight to America*, 83, 166, 169–172, 198; Enok Mortensen, *The Danish Lutheran Church in America: The History and Heritage of the American Evangelical Lutheran Church*, 76, 148 (University of Copenhagen, *Studies in Church History*, series 2, no. 25 — Philadelphia, 1967); John M. Jensen, *The United Evangelical Lutheran Church: An Interpretation*, 32–36 (Minneapolis, 1964).

[7] Nancy L. Woolworth, "Charles Borup: Fur Trader, Banker, Lumberman, and Minnesota's First Danish Consul," in *Ramsey County History*, Fall, 1967, pp. 13, 17; Patricia C. Harpole and Mary D. Nagle, eds., *Minnesota Territorial Census, 1850*, 43 (St. Paul, 1972). In 1859, with the establishment of the first Scandinavian consulate in Minnesota, Borup was appointed vice-consul for Denmark in St. Paul.

[8] Einar Haugen, *Norsk i Amerika*, 80 (Oslo, 1939), and *The Norwegian Language in America*, 1:104 (Philadelphia, 1953); Thomas P. Christensen, "Danish Settlement in Minnesota," in *Minnesota History*, 8:374 (December, 1927); Johannes Knudsen and Enok Mortensen, *The Danish-American Immigrant: Phases of His Religion and Culture*, 8 (Des Moines, Ia., 1950). In 1903 the Norwegian Synod had 24 Danish pastors and about 48 Danish congregations. See Olaf M. Norlie, *History of the Norwegian People in America*, 268 (Minneapolis, 1925).

[9] On the Clarks Grove settlement, here and below, see Franklyn Curtiss-Wedge, comp., *History of Freeborn County Minnesota*, 443 (Chicago, [1911]); Thomas P. Christensen, "De Danske Baptister i Clarks Grove, Freeborn County, Minn.," in C. Rasmussen Publishing Co., *Danske i Amerika*, 271–286 (Minneapolis, 1916), and in *Minnesota History*, 8:366–371; Danish Baptist General Conference of America, *Seventy-Five Years of Danish Baptist Missionary Work in America*, 9 (Philadelphia, 1931).

[10] Christensen, in *Minnesota History*, 8:369–371; A. W. Warren, comp., *A Brief Historical Sketch of the First Danish Baptist Church, Clark's Grove*, 17 (Clarks Grove, 1923).

[11] On Jensen's impressions and the founding of the Clarks Grove creamery, here and below, see Floyd Sorensen, "The Development of a Cooperative Community: Clarks Grove, 1863–1912," in *Albert Lea Evening Tribune*, July 6, p. 7; 7, p. 6; 9, p. 10; 10, p. 12; 11, p. 12 — all 1934; *Freeborn County Times* (Albert Lea), February 9, 1900, p. 1. See also F. E. Balmer, "The Cooperative Movement in the Minnesota Dairy Industry," 1930, and T. L. Haecker, "The Story of Clarks Grove," 1913, typescripts in MHS.

[12] On the other three co-operatives, see "Biscay, the Cradle of Cooperation," in *The Farmer*, 43:727 (May 16, 1925); J. A. Vye, "Little Journeys Here and There," in *St. Cloud Daily Journal-Press*, January 12, 1928, p. 10. The farmers' unity forced the relocation of the Dorwart railroad station, which was built in 1900 a mile south of Clarks Grove on land owned by speculators. They refused to patronize the railroad even when the depot was moved to Clarks Grove several years later, preferring to haul their produce to Albert Lea until the depot's name was changed from James to Clarks Grove.

[13] Everett E. Edwards, "T. L. Haecker, the Father of Dairying in Minnesota," in *Minnesota History*, 19:152, 155–157 (June, 1938).

[14] Interview of Arnold Levison by the author, February 18, 1981, notes in MEHP Papers.

[15] Here and below, see Christensen, in *Minnesota History*, 8:372, 376; U.S. Works Projects Administration, Minnesota, Historical Records Survey: Churches, 1936–41, Brown, Cottonwood, Dodge, Olmsted, Redwood, Steele counties, in MHS, hereafter cited as WPA, Church Records; Thomas P. Christensen, "De Danske i og omkring Geneva og Ellendale, Minn.," and "Danske i og omkring Sleepy Eye, Minn.," in *Danske i Amerika*, 287–303.

[16] Here and below, see Christensen, in *Minnesota History*, 8:372; G. Everett Arden, *Four Northern Lights*, 101 (Minneapolis, 1964); Knudsen and Mortensen, *Danish-American Immigrant*, 7, 13; Paul C. Nyholm, *The Americanization of the Danish Lutheran Churches in America*, 115 (University of Copenhagen, *Studies in Church History*, series 2, no. 16 — Minneapolis, 1963); Mortensen, *Danish Lutheran Church*, 84. See also Enok Mortensen, *Schools for Life: A Danish-American Experiment in Adult Education*, 10–20, 75–96 (Solvang, Calif., 1977).

[17] Here and below, see Mortensen, *Danish Lutheran Church*, xii–xiv, 15, 128, 250, 258; Knudsen and Mortensen, *Danish-American Immigrant*, 11, 14, 16, 19; Jensen, *United Church*, 49–54; Karl T. Jacobsen, comp., *Library of Congress Classification Schedules for the Lutheran Church*, 17 (Board of Christian Education Evangelical Lutheran Church, vol. 2, no. 3 — [St. Paul, 1953]);

U.S. Census Bureau, *Special Reports, Religious Bodies: 1936*, 2:904, 990; Michael Salomon, ed., *Salomon's Almanak for 1916*, 46 (Seattle, 1916).

[18] Here and below, see Christensen, in *Minnesota History*, 8:377; Enok Mortensen, *Seventy-Five Years at Danebod*, 7, 53 (Askov, 1961); Centennial History Committee, *Lincoln County, Minnesota, 1873–1973*, 48 (Lake Benton, [1974]); U.S. manuscript census schedules, 1880, and Minnesota manuscript census schedules, 1905, tabulations in MEHP Papers; taped interview of Grace Sonderlind Marti, Iver Andersen, Hans Krog, and Hanna Thompsen Krog by Arthur L. Finnell, March 10, 1973, in Southwest Minnesota Historical Center, Marshall. Danes in Ruthton and in Diamond Lake Township, Lincoln County, established their own Lutheran churches; MHS has a microfilm copy of their records. Danish Baptists sent a missionary to Tyler and owned a farm there. See Danish Baptist General Conference, *Minutes, 1937*, 8, 10 ([Cedar Falls, Ia., 1937?]).

[19] Kristian Østergaard, "The Danish Settlement at Tyler, Minnesota," in *Scandinavia*, April, 1924, p. 22. See also "De Danske Kolonier i Lincoln, Lyon, og Pipestone Countier, Minnesota," in *Danske i Amerika*, 473–507.

[20] Here and below, see Mortensen, *Seventy-Five Years*, 7, 12, 17, 60, 79–83, 93, and *Danish Lutheran Church*, 85, 272. For an example of the school's promotional literature, see *Danebod Folk School, Summer Session, 1936*, in MHS.

[21] Mortensen, *Seventy-Five Years*, 55, 72; Danebod Lutheran Church, Parish Records, 1888–1966, Book 2, p. 396, microfilm in MHS; *Tyler Tribune*, September 11, 1980, p. 1; interview of Elsie Hansen by author, December 12, 1980, notes in MEHP Papers.

[22] *Tyler Tribune*, June 15, p. 1, June 22, p. 1, 1977.

[23] *Tyler Tribune*, June 9, 1980, pp. 1, 9; Hansen interview, December 12, 1980.

[24] Mortensen, *Danish Lutheran Church*, 90, 149; Christensen, in *Minnesota History*, 8:381–383; Nyholm, *Americanization of the Danish Lutheran Churches*, 123; Centennial History Committee, *One Hundred Years in Pine County*, 79 (Askov, 1949). Stories of life in Askov are printed in Danish Ladies Aid, *From Partridge to Askov* (Askov, [1946]) and in *Scattered Seeds: A Gathering of Minnesota Memories*, vol. 1, no. 3 (1974).

[25] David Lloyd, "Askov: A Study of a Rural Colony of Danes in Minnesota," in Edmund D. Brunner, ed., *Immigrant Farmers and Their Children*, 161 (Garden City, N.Y., 1929); [A. Hermina Poatgieter], "In East-Central Minnesota: How the Land Is Used," in *Gopher Historian*, Spring, 1959, p. 7; Nyholm, *Americanization of the Danish Lutheran Churches*, 123.

[26] Centennial History Committee, *One Hundred Years in Pine County*, 83; [Ludwig Mosbaek], *A Brief Historical Outline of the Askov Community, Compiled for the 25th Anniversary of the Askov Creamery Association*, 7 ([Askov, 1936?]).

[27] Pine County Farm Bureau, *Pine County: Where Folks Are Home Owners*, 5 ([Askov, 1926]).

[28] Lloyd, in *Immigrant Farmers*, 165, 173, 176; Hugh J. Hughes, "'Now, Up at Askov–,'" in *Farmer's Wife*, 23:67, 86 (August, 1920).

[29] *Duluth News-Tribune*, January 9, 1977, p. 1B; *Askov American*, December 14, 1972, pp. 1, 7, 18.

[30] U.S. manuscript census schedules, 1880, Minnesota manuscript census schedules, 1905, tabulations.

[31] Christensen, in *Minnesota History*, 8:373; Franklyn Curtiss-Wedge, *History of McLeod County, Minnesota*, 378–381, 385, 387, 389, 395 (Chicago, 1917); McLeod County Historical Society, *McLeod County History Book, 1978*, 117 (Dallas, 1979); Anna Christensen Anderson, Andrew Anderson, and Mary Anderson, "History of Early Danish Settlers, Hutchinson, McLeod County,

Minnesota, from 1867 to 1883," 2, undated typescript, copy in MHS. MHS has copies of the Danish-Norwegian Seminary catalog from 1910 to 1928.

[32] State of Minnesota, *Census, 1895*, 192; Dwight E. Woodbridge and John S. Pardee, *History of Duluth and St. Louis County: Past and Present*, 1:333, 2:624 (Chicago, 1910); WPA, Church Records, St. Louis County.

[33] U.S., *Census*, 1880, *Population*, 1:539; 1890, 1:373, 671; 1920, 3:521, 522.

[34] Dan Armitage, "The Curling Waters: A West Bank History," in *Minnesota Daily*, Orientation Issue, August, 1973, pp. 9, 30, copy in MHS; Jerilee R. Niedenfuer, "Temporary Home: The Immigrant in Minneapolis 1895–1910: Milwaukee Avenue, A Case Study," 2, typescript, 1974, in MHS; WPA, Church Records, Hennepin County; *Minneapolis City Directory, 1912*, 55, 57, 58. The churches were Immanuel Lutheran (East 22nd St. and 28th Ave.), St. Peder's Lutheran (2003 South 9th St., moved to 32nd St. and 35th Ave. South in 1921), First Norwegian and Danish Baptist (13th Ave. and South 7th St.), and Norwegian-Danish Methodist Episcopal (13th Ave. and South 9th St.).

[35] St. Paul City Planning Board, "Foreign Born Population Studies: Saint Paul, Minnesota," [15], (1934); *St. Paul City Directory, 1909*, 57, 60–62; WPA, Church Records, Ramsey County. The churches were St. Stephen's Danish Evangelical (Orleans and Stevens sts.), Danish Lutheran (Exchange and 3rd sts.), First Norwegian-Danish Baptist (Woodbridge and Milford sts.), First Norwegian and Danish Methodist Episcopal (Broadway and 13th St.), and Dano-Norwegian Golgotha Presbyterian (196 Thomas).

[36] Salomon, ed., *Salomon's Almanak for 1916*, 47; Danish Brotherhood in America, *Souvenir Program: The Twenty-First National Convention*, 1, 93 ([Minneapolis, 1943]); Karl Jørgensen, *Dansk Amerika*, 86–89 (Holbaek, Den., 1930). St. Paul Sons of Denmark Papers, 1906–12, 1934–51, are in MHS.

[37] *Hans Christian Andersen Festival and Bazaar Program, April 27–29, 1892*, in pamphlet file, MHS.

[38] Here and below, see Armitage, in *Minnesota Daily*, August, 1973, pp. 9, 11, 29; *St. Paul Pioneer Press*, December 29, 1885; Jørgensen, *Dansk Amerika*, 86; Carl G. O. Hansen, *My Minneapolis*, 29 (Minneapolis, 1956). The Norwegians later also left Norden "because of the overwhelming Swedish majority," according to Hansen, 29.

[39] Mortensen, *Danish Lutheran Church*, 165; *Ungdomsforeningen af 1905*, 9, 24, 26, 45 ([Minneapolis, 1926?]); Jørgensen, *Dansk Amerika*, 90–97; Women's Co-operative Alliance, *A Study of Community Conditions, South District*, 52 (No. 68, series 3 — Minneapolis, 1926); *Minneapolis City Directory, 1917*, 570, *1933*, 291, *1934*, 291.

[40] Martin Nelson, "'Danebo' the Danish Old Peoples Home in Minneapolis," in Danish Brotherhood in America, *Souvenir Program, Twenty-First Convention*, 57; Olaf Juhl, *Danebo Home 50th Anniversary Festival*, [1–5] ([Minneapolis, 1974]), copy in MEHP Papers.

[41] Here and below, see "Introducing the Danish American Fellowship Institute and the Danish American Center," flier, [1971?]), "Danish American Center," undated flier, and interview of Annelise Sawkins, president of the Danish American Fellowship, by author, December 15, 1980 — copies and notes in MEHP Papers.

[42] Hansen, *My Minneapolis*, 113, 127; Arne H. Jensen, *Dansk Amerikanske Portrætter*, 97 (Copenhagen, 1928); Jørgensen, *Danske Amerika*, 90; Marion T. Marzolf, *The Danish-Language Press in America*, 83–90, 210 (New York, 1979). MHS has *Ugebladet* (1890–1931), *St. Paul Tidende* (1903–1927), *Det Danske Ugeblad* (1939–1945), and *Midwest Scandinavian* (1945–1959). See also *Minneapolis City Directory, 1917*, 570; *1969*, 340.

[43] *Minneapolis Star*, September 7, 1964, p. 10A, March 29, 1968, p. 1; taped interview of Hjalmar Petersen by Russell W. Fridley and Lucile M. Kane, May 28, 1963, typed transcript in MHS.

[44] WPA, Church Records, Freeborn, Hennepin, and McLeod counties; Centennial History Committee, *One Hundred Years in Pine County*, 80.

[45] Author's interviews of Rev. Daniel Pearson, St. Peder's Lutheran Church, December 15, 1980, and Annelise Sawkins, November 15, 1980, notes in MEHP Papers; *Minneapolis City Directory, 1960*, 664. A similar pattern in Norwegian-American Lutheran churches is suggested in Duane R. Lindberg, "Norwegian-American Pastors in Immigrant Fiction, 1870–1920," in *Norwegian-American Studies*, 28:306 (1979).

[46] Hansen interview, December 12, 1980.

CHAPTER 14

The Icelanders

Ann Regan

THE SEEMINGLY INFINITE rolling grassland of southwestern Minnesota near the town of Minneota in Lyon County bears little resemblance to the rocky seacoasts, rugged volcanoes, and steep waterfalls of Iceland. In order to get any feeling of height on the Minnesota prairie near Lyon County, one must drive to nearby Lincoln County, where a particularly large land swell known as the Coteau des Prairies presents a view of almost 20 miles — and an overwhelming sense of horizontal space. Yet it is on this high prairie that the Icelandic immigrants formed their second largest colony in the United States, exchanging fishing nets for plows and learning to raise grain. The Icelanders in Minnesota offer a fine example of the 19th century's ideal of immigration: they came, they saw, and they acculturated.

Figures for Icelandic immigration are difficult to determine. In the Minnesota state censuses for 1895 and 1905, they appear only as footnotes to the figures for "other" nationalities. As Danish subjects, Icelanders were counted with Danes in the federal censuses until 1930, 12 years after Iceland had become a self-governing country in a crown union with Denmark. Mother-tongue figures provide another clue to the group's size. The state's Icelandic stock probably peaked about 1925, when the Minneota colony in Lincoln, Lyon, and Yellow Medicine counties had an estimated 1,000 first- and second-generation Icelanders. By 1970 Minnesota listed only 56 Icelandic born and 474 born of Icelandic parents (see Table 14.1).[1]

Although the figures are small, Icelandic emigration was proportionally larger than that of many northern European

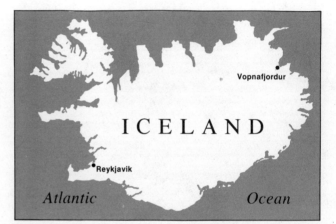

Map 14.1. Iceland

countries during the last quarter of the 19th century. Iceland's population in 1870 was only about 70,000. In the next 30 years it sustained an emigration of at least 12,000, almost half of which occurred in the 1880s. The outflow was heaviest from the northern and eastern parts of the island, the areas farthest from Reykjavik (see Map 14.1).[2]

Economic and political circumstances encouraged this migration. Iceland's economic development, like that of many European countries, did not match its population growth in the early decades of the 1800s. Because it did not industrialize, the little island had to rely on traditional means of livelihood. Fishing, which was to become the country's major industry in the 1970s, was very poorly developed at that time; individual fishermen working in open boats eked out a bare existence from the sea. Farmers in the valleys and lowlands near the coast raised what crops the short growing season would allow, but agriculture fell on hard times. The eruption in 1875 of Askja, Iceland's largest volcano, blanketed a large area with volcanic ash, making it temporarily unfit for cultivation. Sheep raising, then the country's principal industry, sustained repeated heavy blows in the mid-19th century. Flocks that had barely recovered from severe epidemics in the late 1850s were further ravaged by unusually bad weather, which reduced all livestock. The number of animals on farms declined to its lowest point during the 1880s, the decade of heaviest emigration.[3]

Table 14.1. Icelanders in Minnesota, 1895–1970

	foreign born	foreign stock
1895	522*	
1905	386**	
1910	304***	
1920	330***	
1930	266	
1940	189	
1960	141	608
1970	56	474

Source: Minnesota, *Census, 1895, 1905*; U.S., *Census*, 1930, 1940, 1960, 1970.
*Includes only Lincoln, Lyon, Yellow Medicine, Roseau, Stearns, and Kittson counties.
**Includes only Lincoln, Lyon, and Yellow Medicine counties.
***Includes only foreign-born Icelanders of Icelandic mother tongue.

290

Political dissatisfaction also helped produce a climate favorable to emigration. Denmark loosened its political and economic control of Iceland in 1874 by granting the country local self-government, but Icelandic desires for independence remained unsatisfied. A popular nationalist newspaper advocated emigration to Brazil and North America as a final means of escape from Danish domination.[4]

Favorable reports from earlier emigrants were an important factor in starting large-scale emigration. The first Icelanders to reach the Middle West (a few had immigrated earlier to the Mormon settlements of Utah in 1855) seem to have been four young men who migrated to Wisconsin in 1870, inspired by letters from a Dane to friends living in Iceland. Their enthusiastic reports, printed widely in newspapers, encouraged additional emigration. Many Icelanders also read a Norwegian pamphlet entitled *Breve fra Amerika* (Letters from America), published in Reykjavik in 1871, which reprinted letters from Norwegian emigrants that had originally appeared in a Norwegian newspaper. With the establishment in 1873 of the country's first emigration agency, the Allan Line, the numbers of Icelanders who left for North America grew rapidly.[5]

After peaking in the 1880s, emigration from Iceland fell off, especially after 1900 when economic conditions improved. Modernization of the fishing industry began to provide work for the excess population, and the development of dairy co-operatives brought new wealth to the countryside. Political grievances against Denmark lessened in 1918 with the Danish-Icelandic Act of Union, which gave the island home rule. In the first half of the 20th century net emigration from Iceland averaged about 200 persons a year. An unknown number of them must have reached the United States, for the country had as many foreign-born Icelanders in 1960 (2,780) as in 1930 (2,764). Certainly some were women who married American servicemen during World War II. Emigration increased in the late 1960s when high unemployment caused laborers to seek temporary work abroad, especially in other Scandinavian countries. In 1970 the census counted 2,895 first-generation and 6,875 second-generation Icelanders in the United States.[6]

Because they usually settled in colonies, tracing their principal destinations is relatively easy. Most of them went to "New Iceland," a colony founded on the shores of Lake Winnipeg in Manitoba in 1875. One offshoot of this settlement was a group in Pembina County, North Dakota, the largest concentration in the United States. Others who immigrated directly to the United States went first to Milwaukee, Wisconsin, which became a distribution point for Icelanders. Small groups settled in Wisconsin (on Washington Island in Lake Michigan and in Shawano County), in Nebraska, in major metropolitan areas such as Chicago, Boston, and New York City, and, later, on the West Coast. Many moved to the larger settlements in Minnesota, North Dakota, and Manitoba. Because few Icelanders spoke English, they often chose to settle with other Scandinavians.[7]

The Minneota Colony

Migration via Dane County, Wisconsin, provided Minneota's first Icelandic settlers, the Gunnlauger Petursson

family, who had emigrated in 1873. They were part of a group of 50 immigrants whom Pall Thorlaksson, an Icelandic Lutheran minister, had placed as hired hands among Norwegian Lutheran farmers in Wisconsin so that they might learn unfamiliar farming techniques before taking up claims of their own. When Petursson's Norwegian neighbors decided to move to Minnesota, he went with them.[8]

On July 4, 1875, Petursson claimed land on the Yellow Medicine River in Lyon County, seven miles northeast of what became Minneota in 1878. Local legend has it that he passed up richer lands to the south in order to take a plot that looked favorable for raising sheep. A few Icelandic families from Wisconsin joined him in 1876, and late in the summer of 1877, 50 settlers arrived directly from Iceland. Because land in Lyon County was rapidly claimed by other immigrants, the Icelanders began to spread into adjoining Yellow Medicine County in 1877 and into Lincoln County the following year. The largest single group to move to Minnesota was composed of 160 people who arrived in 1879, most of them from Vopnafjordur in northeastern Iceland.[9]

The colony came to consist of four land areas separated by settlers of other nationalities: (1) the western district, located in Limestone, Royal, and Lake Stay townships of Lincoln County; (2) Marshall, the seat of Lyon County, 12 miles southeast of Minneota; (3) the eastern district, which was made up of Westerheim and Nordland townships in Lyon County and Swede Prairie Township and the village of Canby in Yellow Medicine County; and (4) Minneota.[10]

The number of Icelanders, however, remained small. The eastern and western settlements never exceeded 28 and 55 homesteads, respectively. In 1880 Minnesota's Icelandic population (including natives of Iceland and their American-born children) totaled only 416, residing almost entirely in Lincoln, Lyon, and Yellow Medicine counties. Immigration to the colony dropped off after 1890. The number of foreign born fell from 452 in 1895 to 386 in 1905. By 1925 the first- and second-generation Icelandic population of the area was about 1,000.[11]

The immigrants were successful in both agriculture and business. On the rich farmlands they raised grains, vegetables, and livestock. In 1886 they formed a co-operative store, the *Verslunarfjelag Islendinga*, or Icelandic Mercantile Company, which operated in Minneota for 10 years. In Marshall and Minneota at the turn of the century Icelanders were working as day laborers and as skilled craftsmen, servants, merchants, and officials. They owned or operated many of the businesses in Minneota. The *Minneota Mascot*, an English-language newspaper which had been founded by Yankees, was taken over in 1900 by Gunnar Bjornson, an Icelander. For six years Bjornson also published *Vinland*, the only Icelandic-language newspaper ever printed in the United States. A monthly with a literary emphasis, *Vinland* appeared from 1902 to 1908. From 1897 to 1905 the *Mascot* shop also printed *Kennarinn* (The Teacher), a quarterly edited by Icelanders in North Dakota for use in Icelandic Lutheran Sunday schools.[12]

Minneota's best-known Icelandic business was the Big Store, founded in 1896 by two unrelated Icelanders, O. A. Anderson, who owned a clothing store, and S. A. Anderson,

THE BIG STORE, which shared a building with the Opera Hall, played a major role in the lives of Minneota's Icelanders from the 1890s until well into the 1950s. The lower picture shows the staff and some of the stock in the 1920s.

the grocer of the *Verslunarfjelag Islendinga*. In 1901 they erected a large brick building which became a trading and social center for the area. The Big Store "actually made Minneota, I think," asserted Dora A. Harvey, who was born in 1890 and was in 1978 the oldest living Icelander in Minneota. "People came from all around. . . . You were pretty sure of getting good things if you went to the Big Store." The business operated partially on a barter system, exchanging "trading checks," which could be applied toward purchases, for eggs, wool, and poultry.[13]

The second story of the building was the Opera Hall, which was rented out for meetings, dances, Chautauquas, and plays. A huge ballroom with a stage, it served as community center until the 1950s. By then the Big Store had competition from chain stores and supermarkets, as increased mobility changed shopping patterns. It closed in

1972 when age and ill health forced the retirement of the owner and several long-time employees.

Other community activities took place in the churches. Each of the four Minnesota settlement areas had an Icelandic Evangelical Lutheran congregation, all of which affiliated with the Icelandic Lutheran Synod 11 years after its formation in 1885. The four congregations shared a single minister and often sponsored joint functions. The record of their emergence and disappearance parallels that of the Icelanders in these settlements. (1) The Lincoln congregation, organized in 1879, built a church in Marble Township in 1899 that remained in operation until 1966. (2) The Marshall congregation constructed a church in 1890, but disbanded in 1911. (3) By 1891 settlers in the eastern district built Westerheim Lutheran Church in Westerheim Township. This congregation merged with the Minneota church in the early 1950s. (4) St. Paul's Lutheran Church, built in Minneota in 1895, affiliated with the Lutheran Church in America in 1963; it was the only one of the four surviving in the 1980s.[14]

Church organizations performed social and charitable, as well as religious, functions. Members of the Ladies Aid of the Lincoln church, the Westerheim congregation's *Ísafold* (Icefield), and St. Paul's *Kvenfjelag* (Women's Society), all women's groups, visited the sick and provided fellowship. The Lincoln church sponsored *skamtisamkomur*, or fun fests, for young people; Westerheim's Westerlites and St. Paul's Luther League provided activities for their young members. Brotherhood groups for men, organized by the Lincoln and Minneota churches in the 1950s, worked to promote the interests of the church.[15]

As the first and second generations aged and died, the use of Icelandic in the churches fell off. St. Paul's, which held its first English-language service in 1912, shifted to English in three out of four services in 1934. The minutes of its church meetings were kept in Icelandic until 1932; those of the Westerheim church were not recorded in English until 1942.[16]

On the whole, the Icelandic Lutherans experienced little friction with other religious and ethnic groups in the area. Although intermarriage was not common, they seem to have mingled with their Catholic neighbors to a greater extent than did the Norwegians. Catholics and Norwegian Lutherans each patronized businesses owned by members of their own groups, but the Icelanders, according to one of their descendants, shopped "wherever they damn' well pleased." The Icelanders, less pietistic than the Norwegian Lutherans and definitely not teetotalers, found drinking companions among the Belgians and Irish. According to the son of a Belgian farmer who grew up in Minneota in the 1950s, the Icelanders differed from the Belgians in their attitudes toward farm work. The Icelanders "always seemed to be two weeks behind the Belgians," he said. "They'd sit in town and argue over a cup of coffee while the Belgians got their crops in."[17]

This stereotypically Icelandic love of arguing and storytelling — a general preoccupation with language — reflected a strong literary tradition. Since literacy was required for church membership in Iceland, almost everyone could read. The sagas, the written legacy of Iceland's scalds (heroic poets), formed a rich national literature that promoted a love of poetry and stories among even the poorest parishioners. Those who immigrated to Minnesota carried their books and the eagerness for education with them. In 1878, even before a church had been organized, Icelanders in the Lincoln district formed the *Framfarafjelag* (Progressive Society) "to promote common enterprise, provide books and newspapers to readers, secure a cemetery in which to bury the dead, and bring about house services on holy days." Renamed and reorganized as the *Lestrarfjelag* (Reading Society) in 1884, the club built a meeting hall which was also used for church services. The society carried on at least until 1900.[18]

The Icelandic farmers had libraries of Icelandic and English books with which they educated themselves. "I grew up with the belief that every home had a library," recalled a second-generation Icelander born in Minneota in 1925. "I didn't draw a distinction between Icelanders and others — I thought that everybody had a big library." The books were not for show. The farmers, he remembered, not only read but also discussed them.[19]

As late as the 1950s, children of these farmers seemed to be far ahead of the other students when they started school. A third-generation Icelander recalled that "it was considered a disgrace if an Icelandic kid couldn't read before first grade." Second- and third-generation Icelanders often continued their educations through college. While some studied at such predominantly Scandinavian schools as Gustavus Adolphus College at St. Peter or St. Olaf College at Northfield, most attended the University of Minnesota. They became professionals, entering careers in law, medicine, engineering, and especially teaching. According to one writer, Minnesota's Icelanders supplied a disproportionately high number of teachers at all levels in the state's schools.[20]

As these second-generation Icelanders found jobs in the Twin Cities and in other states, Minneota's Icelandic population declined. A commemorative ceremony in 1945, marking the 70th anniversary of the founding of the colony, drew 400 persons of Icelandic descent, many from outside the community. By 1956 Minneota's Icelanders were estimated to number about 300, or a third of the area's peak in 1925. There are no figures for the centennial observation in 1975 of the colony's founding, but it seems to have been a smaller gathering. Although few Icelanders still farmed in the area, Minneota remained the gathering place for family reunions during the 1970s. By then the second generation, which was elderly and quickly disappearing, still spoke Icelandic; the third generation had lost the language.[21]

The Roseau County Icelanders

A much smaller settlement in the northwestern corner of the state attracted Icelanders from North Dakota's Pembina colony. They began to homestead in the early 1890s in Pohlitz and Dieter townships of Roseau County on the flat, wet lands near the Roseau River. By 1895 there were 65 first-generation Icelanders in the county. But many, finding that their hard work was not bringing enough return, soon discovered better opportunities in Canada. From 1897 to 1899, they left for Piney, Manitoba, a town about five miles north of Roseau County's border with Canada, and in 1902

many moved to new Icelandic settlements in Saskatchewan. The Canadian Northern Railway drew others north in 1907, building a line through Piney two years before the Great Northern Railway reached the town of Roseau.[22]

One of the remaining families moved in 1904 from its homestead in Pohlitz Township to the town of Dieter, where the nine children received a typically Icelandic dose of formal education. While many Norwegian youngsters in the area attended school for the legally required minimum of 40 days per year, and then proclaimed, "I got my days in, I'm gonna quit!" the Icelandic children "lived betw[e]en two schools in the same district, each of which had 4½ months of school, and we attended both" for the full nine months. All nine children went to high school in the town of Roseau, boarding with their aunt, and several attended college. Like other Icelandic families, they scattered widely, moving to Minneapolis, Washington, D.C., New York City, and Flint, Michigan. Only one stayed in Roseau County. By 1980 the settlement had virtually disappeared, with only a few second- and third-generation Icelanders left.

The Twin Cities

The third Icelandic settlement area in Minnesota, the Twin Cities, received immigrants both from these rural colonies and directly from Iceland. Minneapolis and St. Paul had served as stopping-off places for Icelanders on their way to Minneota. Some had stayed, most of them in Northeast Minneapolis. Early population figures are again elusive, but in 1920 Minneapolis had 41 foreign-born residents of Icelandic mother tongue and St. Paul had 12. By 1960, however, the Icelandic population had grown to 89 foreign born and 230 native born of foreign or mixed parentage in both cities. In 1970 only 18 first-generation and 98 second-generation Icelanders were counted in Minneapolis and St. Paul.[23]

Although the group was small, its women established their own organization in 1925 to help Icelanders in need and to promote Icelandic culture. The Twin Cities Hekla Club, which took its name from Iceland's most famous volcano, grew from 17 charter members to about 75 members, who lived throughout the metropolitan area in 1980. The club met monthly in homes and made donations to Icelandic causes such as a high school in Winnipeg and a home for aged Icelanders in Mountain, North Dakota. Several members, with other Icelandic women, formed an Icelandic Chorus in 1938. They also sponsored cultural exchanges, such as an exhibit in 1980 of contemporary Icelandic art. Since 1926 the Hekla Club has sponsored an annual *Samkoma* (literally, a gathering) with a banquet and speakers. Between 1926 and 1966, attendance averaged about 135 people; in the 1970s, from 150 to 250 participated. The club exhibited an interesting adaptation of the earlier Icelandic literary tradition in 1979 when the members volunteered their time in support of a public television fund-raising drive.[24]

As Minnesota's Icelanders worked to regain some of their ethnic identity in the 1970s, intriguing traces remained around the town of Minneota. Hundreds of Icelandic books gathered dust in attics and barns. William Holm, Minnesota poet and third-generation Icelander, carried on the traditions of the Icelandic scalds in his storytelling and poetry. The cemeteries of the Westerheim and Lincoln County churches, still in use, contained gravestones that recorded the Americanization of Icelandic names. Testimony to Icelanders' argumentative character remained in the Lincoln County church itself. The simple white frame building stood alone on a county road, surrounded by cornfields, exactly as it was when it closed in 1966: prayer books lay on the altar, and the pump organ still functioned. The women's group of St. Paul's Church in Minneota cleaned the building every year. Holm explained the situation straightforwardly. "They are Icelanders," he asserted. "They can't agree on what to do with it." [25]

Reference notes

[1] Jakob Benediktsson, "Icelandic Emigration to America," in *Le Nord*, 1:41 (1942); Thorstina Jackson, "Icelandic Communities in America: Cultural Backgrounds and Early Settlements," in *Journal of Social Forces*, 3:684 (May, 1925). The author wishes to acknowledge the helpful suggestions she received during her work on this chapter from William Holm of Minneota and Dr. Oliver Olafson of Minneapolis.

[2] Benediktsson, in *Le Nord*, 1:35, 37; Thorsteinn Thorsteinsson, ed., *Iceland: 1946*, 17 (Reykjavik, 1946). Maps printed in Harald Runblom and Hans Norman, eds., *From Sweden to America* (Minneapolis, 1976), after page 128, show Icelandic emigration rates by province for each five-year period from 1865 to 1914.

[3] Benediktsson, in *Le Nord*, 1:35; Amy E. Jensen, *Iceland: Old-New Republic*, 48 (New York, 1954); Knut Gjerset, *History of Iceland*, 458 (New York, 1924); W[ilhelm] Kristjanson, *The Icelandic People in Manitoba: A Manitoba Saga*, 9 (Winnipeg, 1965); Helgi S. Kjartansson, "The Onset of Emigration from Iceland," in *American Studies in Scandinavia*, 9:87 (1977).

[4] Gjerset, *History of Iceland*, 409, 425; Benediktsson, in *Le Nord*, 1:36. A group of Icelanders did leave for Brazil in 1863, but transportation difficulties turned emigration to North America; see Kristjanson, *Icelandic People*, 11.

[5] Thorstina Walters, *Modern Sagas: The Story of the Icelanders in North America*, 33, 34, 39 (Fargo, N. Dak., 1953); Halldor Hermannsson, *Islaenderne I Amerika*, 4 (Copenhagen, 1922); Kjartansson, in *American Studies in Scandinavia*, 9:88.

[6] Gjerset, *History of Iceland*, 449, 453; John C. Griffiths, *Modern Iceland*, 40, 47 (London, 1969); Johannes Nordal and Valdimar Kristinsson, eds., *Iceland 874–1974: Handbook Published by the Central Bank of Iceland on the Occasion of the Eleventh Centenary of the Settlement of Iceland*, 31, 204 (Reykjavik, 1975); Jensen, *Iceland*, 342; U.S., *Census*, 1940, *Population*, vol. 2, part 4, p. 31 (included 1930 figure); 1970, vol. 1, part 1, sec. 2, p. 598. The 1960 figure is from Valdimar Bjornson, "Icelanders in the United States," in *Scandinavian Review*, September, 1976, p. 41. Iceland became an independent republic in 1944.

[7] Benediktsson, in *Le Nord*, 1:39, 41, 43; Bjornson, in *Scandinavian Review*, September, 1976, p. 40.

[8] Valdimar Bjornson, "America in the Making," in *Icelandic Canadian*, Winter, 1949, p. 47; Walters, *Modern Sagas*, 40, 52.

[9] Torgny Anderson, *The Centennial History of Lyon County Minnesota*, 119 (Marshall, 1970); *St. Paul Dispatch*, September 4, 1877; Carl and Amy Narvestad, *A History of Yellow Medicine County Minnesota 1872–1972*, 789 (St. Paul, 1972); "Landnám Íslendiga í Minnesota," in Ólafur S. Thorgeirsson, ed., *Almanak 1900*, 58 (Winnipeg, 1899); Bjornson, in *Icelandic Canadian*, Winter, 1949, p. 49. U.S., *Census*, 1880, *Population*, 877, reported some sheep in the county, but not a disproportionate number.

[10] Thorgeirsson, ed., *Almanak 1900*, 54. See also tabulated figures on these townships compiled from U.S. manuscript census schedules, 1880, in MEHP Papers, MHS.

[11] *Minneota Mascot*, July 6, 1956, p. 7B; U.S. manuscript census schedules, 1880, in MEHP Papers; State of Minnesota, *Census, 1895*, 169, 170, 207; *1905*, 154, 155, 192; Arthur P. Rose, *An Illustrated History of Lyon County Minnesota*, 88 (Marshall, 1912); Jackson, in *Journal of Social Forces*, 3:684.

[12] Thorgeirsson, ed., *Almanak 1900*, 59, 60; interview of Valdimar Bjornson by Byron Nordstrom, August 8, 1974, notes in MEHP Papers; *Minneota Mascot*, December 26, 1974, p. 1B; Gjerset, *History of Iceland*, 463. MHS has a nearly complete set of *Vinland* issues, and its Southwest Minnesota Historical Center, Southwest State College, Marshall, has copies of *Kennarinn*. The principal newspapers and periodicals serving the Icelanders, including *Lögberg-Heimskringla*, were published in Winnipeg. On Gunnar Bjornson, see *St. Paul Pioneer Press*, September 16, 1957, p. 21; on the career of his son Valdimar, long-time Minnesota state treasurer (1951–54, 1956–74), see Bjorn Bjornson, "Valdimar Bjornson," in *Icelandic Canadian*, Summer, 1977, pp. 21–23.

[13] Here and below, see Thorgeirsson, ed., *Almanak 1900*, 60; *Minneapolis Tribune*, July 23, 1972, sec. P, pp. 10, 16; taped interviews of Anna Anderson, Sigrid Frost, and Theodore Anderson by Arthur Finnell and Warren Gardner, August 16, 17, 1973, and of Dora A. Harvey and Cora Monseth by Jan Louangie and Pat Fruin, June 9, 1977 — all in Southwest Minnesota Historical Center, which also has the Big Store records. Those interviewed were long-time employees of the Big Store.

[14] St. Paul's Evangelical Lutheran Church, *Eightieth Anniversary 1887–1967*, frames 13, 14, 17, 19, Icelandic Evangelical Lutheran Churches in Lyon and Lincoln counties, Minnesota, microfilm in MHS (hereafter cited as Icelandic Lutheran Church Records); Rose, *History of Lyon County*, 151. For more on the Icelandic Lutheran Synod, formed in Winnipeg, see K. K. Olafson, *The Icelandic Lutheran Synod: Survey and Interpretation* ([Winnipeg, 1935]), and P. E. Kretzmann, "The Icelandic Lutherans in America," in *Concordia Historical Institute Quarterly*, 2:1–7, 55–60, 82–86 (April, July, October, 1929). The synod disbanded in 1963 with the formation of the Lutheran Church in America. See Mrs. John Ousman, "Earlier Memories of St. Paul's Church," in Charles Vandersluis, ed., *Ninety Years at St. Paul's*, 37 (Marshall, 1977).

[15] Icelandic Evangelical Lutheran Church Records, frames 19, 21.

[16] Dates of change for the other churches were not available. Icelandic Lutheran Church Records, frames 319, 502; "Laconic Remarks by Frank A. Josephson," and Charles Vandersluis, "Survey of the Last Sixty Years of St. Pauls," in Vandersluis, ed., *Ninety Years at St. Paul's*, 26, 43.

[17] Interviews of Leonard L. Coequyt, July 20, 1978, and William Holm, August 8, 1978, by author, notes in MEHP Papers.

[18] Thorgeirsson, ed., *Almanak 1900*, 64; Jackson, in *Journal of Social Forces*, 3:682. On the Icelandic language, sagas, and literary tradition, see Gjerset, *History of Iceland*, 116–149; Jensen, *Iceland*, 90–137. The colony probably benefited from exchange programs sponsored by the Icelandic National Patriotic League, an organization founded in 1919 to preserve Icelandic language and culture in America and to foster contacts with Iceland. No evidence of a local chapter was found. Benediktsson, in *Le Nord*, 1:47.

[19] Taped interview of Stephen Guttormson by Arthur Finnell, July 2, 1978, in Southwest Minnesota Historical Center.

[20] Coequyt interview, July 20, 1978; Holm interview, August 8, 1978; Guttormson interview, July 2, 1978; Bjornson, in *Icelandic Canadian*, Winter, 1949, p. 51; Rose, *History of Lyon County*, 88.

[21] Bjornson interview, August 8, 1974; *Minneota Mascot*, August 17, 1945, p. 1, July 6, 1956, p. 7B, July 10, 1975, p. 1; Bill Holm,

"The Smallest Minority," in *Voices*, April, 1976, a publication of the Southwest Minnesota Arts and Humanities Council, copy in MEHP Papers.

[22] Here and below, see Minnesota, *Census, 1895*, 191; Eric Jonasson, *Tracing Your Icelandic Family Tree*, 11 (Winnipeg, 1975); Roseau County Historical Society and Warroad Bicentennial Committee, *Pioneers! Oh Pioneers!: A History of Early Settlers in Roseau County, 1885–1910*, 166, 191, 255 ([Warroad, 1976?]); Sigfus Olafson to the author, July 17, 1980, Oliver Olafson to the author, December 6, 1980, and interview of Oliver Olafson by author, August 19, 1980, letters and notes in MEHP Papers; T. D. Regehr, *The Canadian Northern Railway: Pioneer Road of the Northern Prairies, 1895–1918*, 206 (Toronto, 1976). On the Saskatchewan settlements, see Walter J. Lindal, *The Saskatchewan Icelanders: A Strand of the Canadian Fabric*, 131 (Winnipeg, 1955).

[23] Bjornson interview, August 8, 1974; Valdimar Bjornson to Conan Bryant Eaton, April 19, 1963, in MHS; U.S., *Census*, 1930, *Population*, 2:381; 1960, vol. 2, part 25, p. 342; 1970, vol. 2, part 25, p. 513. A few Icelanders also stayed in Duluth, which was on the route of those who immigrated by way of the St. Lawrence Seaway. In 1905 St. Louis County's Icelandic-born population was listed as 46; Minnesota, *Census, 1905*, 178.

[24] Helga Brogger, "The Early Years of the Hekla Club," and membership list, 1973, in Hekla Club Papers, MHS; Frances Gunlaugson, "History of the Twin City Hekla Club 1925–1975," and Vera J. Younger, "Twin Cities Hekla Club," both in *Icelandic Canadian*, Autumn, 1975, pp. 34–36, Summer, 1979, p. 35; interview of Frances Gunlaugson by author, July 8, 1980, notes in MEHP Papers.

[25] Holm interview, August 8, 1978.

CHAPTER 15

The Finns and Swede-Finns

Timo Riippa

Finns

FROM 1920 THROUGH 1940 Minnesota was the home of more Finns than any other state except Michigan, and they constituted its fourth largest group of foreign-born immigrants. The earliest Finnish arrivals had homesteaded on the mixed prairie and woodlands of south-central Minnesota in 1864; the second cluster formed in the west-central part of the state, notably near New York Mills in Otter Tail County, in the 1870s; and the third and largest influx moved from Finland and from Michigan to Duluth and northeastern Minnesota after the opening of the iron ranges there in the 1880s and 1890s. Among them was a distinctive subgroup that had lived in southern Finland since the 12th century. Known as Swede-Finns or Finland Swedes, their retention of Swedish as a mother tongue and their common heritage sets them apart.[1]

Taking into account the fact that Finns as a separate group do not appear in United States census figures before 1900, the total Finnish immigration to the country up to 1920 has been estimated at about 300,000. Illness, accidents, homesickness, the language barrier, poor adaptation to American conditions, intentionally temporary stays, and other reasons resulted in about 20% of the immigrants returning to Finland, a rate comparable to that of other Nordic countries, although it varied greatly in various parts of Finland. Of these returnees, 20% to 25% in turn eventually sailed for America once again. Minnesota's return rate was much lower — about 8% (see Table 15.1). The peak for foreign-born Finns in both the nation and the state occurred in 1920 with 149,824 and 29,108 people, respectively. After that the enactment of restrictive immigration laws by the United States in the 1920s, the Depression of the 1930s, and World War II in the 1940s reduced the flow to 11,093 arrivals for the entire period between 1924 and 1960. Between 1960 and 1978, 7,685 Finns immigrated to the United States.[2]

The homeland these people left is a country of lakes and forests resembling northern Minnesota in general appearance. Today it shares borders with the Union of Soviet Socialist Republics on the east and with Sweden and the tip of Arctic Norway on the west (see Map 15.1). However, Finnish is not linguistically related to the languages of Scandinavia. The ancestral home of the Finns is believed to have

Table 15.1. Finnish Migration to and from Minnesota

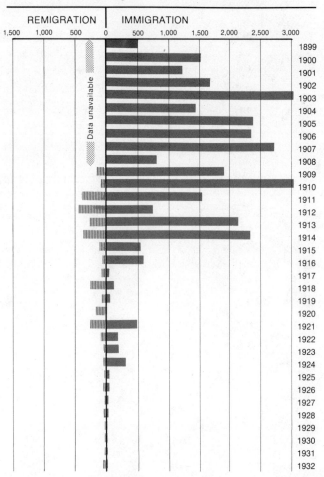

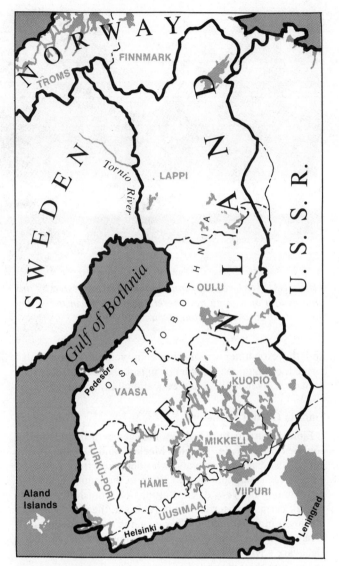

Map 15.1. Finland

agricultural production and infant industries were able to support. The crown retained large amounts of land, while the subdivision of individual farms among numerous heirs and tenants resulted in small holdings incapable of providing livelihoods for their owners. Of the farms in Finland, 70% were less than 22 acres in size in 1901 and over 30% were less than 5 acres. Between 1815 and 1875 tenants increased at twice the rate of landowners, while landless workers multiplied more than five times as fast. As a result, large numbers of crofters (tenant farmers) were forced to become migrant workers. Many of these landless people moved to Sweden, where they found employment in the forests, or to Helsinki, "the front porch of America," where some took ship for "the land of gold."[4]

Other factors also entered the picture. In the mid-1860s northern Finland endured a series of famines which drove Finns to migrate to the mining and fishing regions of Arctic Norway, where their countrymen had lived since the mid-16th century and more than 5,000 of them were to be found by 1865. At approximately the same time, tar distilling declined in Finland, following a drastic drop in prices on the world market. For decades this industry had provided limited employment, decimated the forests, and retarded the development of other wood products which became important in the Finnish economy in the 20th century.[5]

In 1863 the Finnish language gained official acceptance, 28 years after the first publication of *Kalevala*, the folk epic that gave great impetus to the nationalist movement. But the rise of Finnish political and cultural national aspirations in the late 19th century collided with the more stringent Russification and pan-Slavic policies of Czar Nicholas II. After 1898 these policies, which included military conscription and political repression, led to increased emigration. A striking example may be found in the exodus of Finns following the issuing of the czar's so-called February Manifesto, which nullified Finland's special autonomous status in 1899 and decreed the conscription of Finns into the Russian army. In the three years from 1896 through 1898, 10,568 Finns emigrated; in 1899 alone a total of 12,075 people did so, and in 1902 a record 23,152 Finns left the country. A few years later, both before and after the Finnish war of independence in 1917, numerous Socialists and political activists fled to the United States to escape imprisonment or execution.[6]

Before 1883 no official emigration records were kept in Finland, although personal data were collected on passport applications, by steamship companies, and in church parishes. In 1883 and 1884 the two northern provinces of Oulu and Vaasa, then the areas of heaviest emigration, began keeping records, but statistics for the entire country are officially available only from 1893. Estimates of emigration between 1865 and 1882 range from 7,000 to 15,000 people. Between 1883 and 1892 about 40,000 Finns emigrated, while some 250,000 to 265,000 largely unskilled laborers left from 1893 to 1914. The pre-1899 emigrants were drawn primarily from the rural, northern provinces, while the bulk of those in the later period left from the cities and farms of southern Finland. In 1873 farmers and the children of farmers constituted 53.6% of Finnish emigrants; in 1893 the figure was down to 34.3%, and by 1913 it was only 28.4%. Only 8.7% of

been an area extending from the middle Volga River to the Ural Mountains. Finnish belongs to the Finno-Ugric branch of the Uralic language family and is most closely allied to Estonian and Lappish and more remotely to Hungarian. Somewhat larger in area then Norway and like it possessing little good arable land, Finland was ruled for some 600 years by Sweden before Russia took over in 1809 as a result of the Napoleonic Wars. Thus in the early 19th century its educated classes spoke Swedish, and Finnish as a literary language was not widely used. For more than a century after 1809, during the principal period of Finnish emigration, Finland was a semi-independent Grand Duchy of Czarist Russia until it declared its independence in 1917.[3]

Why did the Finns emigrate? During the 19th century Finland experienced the same population explosion that was such a basic factor throughout the great European migration to America. Between 1811 and 1900 Finland's population rose from 1,053,000 to 2,700,000, outrunning the limits its those leaving in 1873 were city workers; by 1902 this figure had risen to 19.8%, and in 1913 to 24%. Between 1899 and 1909, 50.2% of the arriving Finns were common laborers.[7]

The immigrants who arrived from 1900 to 1914 were young. Over 53% of them were between the ages of 16 and 25, and those from rural Finland were slightly younger than the arrivals from urban areas. The sex ratio for the years from 1869 to 1914 was 64 men to 35 women, but appreciable numbers of single women (4,000 to 7,000 per year) began to leave only after 1900, taking jobs as domestics in large eastern American cities. From 1905 to 1909, for example, 34.1% of all Finnish immigrants were women. Many of these later moved on to the Midwest as a result of want-ad courtships, which were regular features of the Finnish newspapers. The percentage of women among the Finns was lower than that for other Scandinavian peoples but higher than among the South Slavs and Italians with whom the Finns frequently settled. Nevertheless the ratios varied with times and places. In newly founded Eveleth on the Mesabi Range, for example, in 1895 the male-female ratio was 87.3 to 12.7. Ten years later the Finnish ratio of the range as a whole had changed to 72.8 men to 27.2 women.[8]

The multifaceted roles of Finnish women in the immigrant community offer a rich field for further study. Although it was said among rural Finns that the only time a man took his wife to town was when he needed her signature on the mortgage, the fact remains that often "the wife . . . supplied more than an equal amount of the labor and intelligence that was necessary to maintain an existence on a marginal farming operation." Finnish-American women were in some ways more visible than those of virtually any other nationality. They contributed prominently to the rich organizational variety among Finnish Americans in which a strong anticlerical tradition vied with a countervailing belief in pietistic Lutheranism, and both shared a common dedication to education. They had received the right to vote in Finland as early as 1906, 14 years before woman suffrage came to the United States. They participated in the American suffrage movement and in the establishment and development of Finnish-American temperance societies, churches, workers' clubs, co-operatives, and other forms of associative life. Finnish women also established and conducted two newspapers of their own — *Lehti* (Journal), begun in 1896 in New York City and later moved to Calumet, Michigan; and *Toveritar* (Woman Comrade), a Socialist paper started in 1911 in Astoria, Oregon. Both journals championed education and self-development for their women readers.[9]

Although often linked in the popular mind with Norwegians, Danes, and Swedes, the Finnish immigrant response to America was notably different. For one thing, the Finns by and large reached the United States in a later period than did most Scandinavians and other northern Europeans, arriving in the milieu at the turn of the 20th century rather than in the mid-19th. Since the free farmlands of the earlier years were no longer a ready option in Minnesota, the Finns took jobs in the industries of a preunionized nation. Some were active in the struggle for better wages and working conditions in the iron mining and timberworking industries, the fight for women's rights, as well as the Socialist party,

THE UNUSUAL role of Finnish women is suggested by this photograph of women pallbearers at a funeral in the settlement of Angora in St. Louis County in 1916.

and the consumer co-operative movement. Others also farmed, often on marginal lands in isolated areas where they built their own cultural and educational organizations.

Finns in Central Minnesota

Finnish settlement in Minnesota began in the south-central counties of Renville, Wright, Meeker, and Douglas in the mid-1860s. The first arrivals, who debarked from a Mississippi River steamboat at Red Wing in the summer of 1864, were among the very earliest groups of Finnish immigrants to seek permanent settlement in America, the forerunners of the larger movement that followed in the next three decades. (They were preceded, of course, by Finns who had settled in Delaware's New Sweden colony in 1638.) Their trip to Minnesota was the second leg of a migration that had begun in the northern Finnish provinces, when poverty and famine in the 1860s drove thousands to seek work in the fishing and mining regions of Finnmark and Tromsø, Norway. At that time the Midwest was a principal destination of Norwegian immigrants. From them, from emigration agents, and from America letters, the Finns and Lapps in Arctic Norway learned that free and fertile lands were to be had in Minnesota.[10]

In 1864 the first group of three Finnish families and several single men left Tromsø. They arrived at Red Wing, then the state's main Mississippi River terminal for Scandinavians and Germans, after a transatlantic voyage of seven weeks and an inland trip via Chicago of five weeks by rail and steamboat. After working for a time as hired hands on Norwegian farms in Nicollet County, the men moved up the Minnesota River Valley to homestead in Birch Cooley Township, Renville County, where partially wooded land was still available.[11]

There the first permanent Finnish settlement in Minnesota was established the following year in the area that included later the village of Franklin. By 1883 it had some 40 families composed of over 200 Finns. In 1895, in spite of additions from Michigan's copper-mining country, only 157 foreign-born Finns were counted in Renville County; 10 years later the number had dropped to 117, and by 1930 there were 40. The 1970 census recorded six foreign-born Finns and 34 persons of Finnish stock (see Table 15.2).

A second settlement of Finns from Norway was begun in 1865 when four men walked from Minneapolis to stake 80-acre claims near Cokato Lake in Wright County. Returning in the spring of 1866, they built the first Finnish homes in this predominately Swedish region. As news of the Cokato settlement spread, more Finns arrived from Norway, from the Finnish villages on the Swedish side of the Tornio River in northern Sweden, from Värmland in southwestern Sweden, and from the copper mines of Michigan (see Map 12.1). By 1875 there were 50 families. Three years later the village of Cokato was incorporated. Not all of the Finns were able to purchase land immediately, and the men continued to work at times in the Minneapolis brickyards or on the railroads. Others rented two- or three-acre plots from older settlers until they were able to accumulate enough money to buy their own farms, a practice reminiscent of a tenant farming system prevalent in Finland in the 19th century.[12]

By 1880 the Cokato area was the largest Finnish rural settlement in the United States, a distinction it would yield to New York Mills during the next decade in spite of continuing growth. When Isak Barberg, one of the pioneers, took a census of Finns in 1879 he found 79 families totaling 450 persons, about 400 of whom lived on farms. The area he tallied measured approximately 35 by 50 miles and included Cokato and adjoining French Lake townships in Wright County along with Kingston and Dassel townships in nearby Meeker County. Barberg noted that very little unclaimed land remained. The 1920 federal census recorded 661 foreign-born Finns in Wright and Meeker counties. In 1970 census takers were still able to tabulate 77 foreign-born Finns and 567 persons of Finnish parentage there (see Table 15.2).[13]

The third of the early permanent settlements in central Minnesota was Holmes City, farther to the west in Douglas County, to which four Cokato Finns journeyed by oxcart during a week of rain and sleet in the fall of 1866. Like Cokato, the new area grew gradually throughout the 1870s as more settlers arrived from Michigan and Finland. When homestead lands ran out, others reasonably priced at about $5.00 an acre with 10 years to pay could still be found. By 1880, however, all the available land had been taken up. A

Table 15.2. Finns in Minnesota by County, 1880–1970

County	1895 foreign born	1905 fb	1905 foreign mixed	1920 fb	1930 fb	1930 fm	1970 fb	1970 fm
Aitkin	198	417	664	885	699	1,111	85	390
Anoka	3		2	32	45	25	14	429
Becker	326	357	862	526	426	1,128	11	332
Beltrami		47	47	96	47	70	14	86
Benton	9	4	14	13	10	18		20
Big Stone		4	12	3				6
Blue Earth				2		15		24
Brown				2	3	6		10
Carlton	466	1,730	2,785	2,140	1,828	3,100	440	1,772
Carver		1	1	1		1		25
Cass	12	103	144	94	67	134	53	77
Chippewa		1	1					6
Chisago		2	2	2	5	9	7	30
Clay	6	7	6	6	10	17		77
Clearwater		10	19	3	5	16		15
Cook		60	61	55	94	61		100
Cottonwood			9			1		9
Crow Wing	251	252	479	530	472	704	119	242
Dakota		4	32	30	40	28	21	165
Dodge				1		3		7
Douglas	103	119	323	116	99	229	6	139
Faribault					1	1		18
Fillmore		6	8		2	3		
Freeborn					1	6		7
Goodhue		7	13	4	3	15		27
Grant	1		1	2	1	7		8
Hennepin	45	882	1,290	1,169	1,218	2,576	398	3,352
Houston		4	13	1		7		
Hubbard	16	7	27	22	22	57		65
Isanti	3	4	11	5	5	17	5	25
Itasca	54	416	449	1,607	1,602	2,035	239	1,001
Jackson	5					3		11
Kanabec				3	3	8		32
Kandiyohi			1	22	53	16		27
Kittson	6	9	14	1	1	2		13
Koochiching				394	191	154	20	141
Lac qui Parle			2		1	1		
Lake	24	309	363	761	467	532	119	410
Lake of the Woods					10	27		14
Le Sueur				1		2		

Table 15.2. Finns in Minnesota by County, 1880–1970 (*continued*)

County	1895 foreign born	1905 fb	1905 foreign mixed	1920 fb	1930 fb	1930 fm	1970 fb	1970 fm
Lincoln	1					2		
Lyon	3	3	3	2	2	6		
McLeod				1	2	1		15
Mahnomen				3	5	4		
Marshall		18	31	74	56	158	7	17
Martin						2		7
Meeker	167	237	385	233	191	452	42	146
Mille Lacs	5	32	56	33	24	40	6	51
Morrison	143	42	57	41	16	17		13
Mower	1				2	18		19
Murray	11	14	18	3	1	4		
Nicollet		16	23	16	19	12		23
Nobles			2	1		3		
Norman		3	8	6		1		
Olmsted				14	24	22	15	39
Otter Tail	971	1,054	2,617	1,145	955	1,968	74	589
Pennington				14	16	28	6	12
Pine	181	366	563	270	241	408	8	112
Pipestone				1				
Polk	53	19	34	4		3		35
Pope		2	3	2		2		9
Ramsey	147	74	143	101	92	239	101	753
Red Lake		41	84	50	51	134	6	25
Redwood		2	11	2	1	5		6
Renville	157	117	227	55	40	65	6	34
Rice			6	7	7	67		38
Rock						3		
Roseau	65	3	7	2	1	4	18	36
St. Louis	3,225	12,076	18,135	17,342	14,309	18,276	2,579	10,288
Scott						1		45
Sherburne		2	14	11		17		
Sibley						1		7
Stearns		4	19	17	11	29	25	97
Steele					5	1	10	38
Stevens	9			1	1	2	6	6
Swift	11	9	17		1	3		
Todd	25	33	82	20	22	39		20
Traverse	2				1	5		
Wabasha				1	2	3		8
Wadena	428	609	1,320	625	491	1,179	143	540
Waseca		2	2			4		
Washington	5	6	18	44	22	16		82
Watonwan						2		5
Wilkin			2	2	1	10		7
Winona				3	3	3		14
Wright	479	300	1,195	428	317	837	35	421
Yellow Medicine		1	6		1			
Total	7,617	19,847	32,743	29,108	24,360	36,250	4,628	22,669
Published census figures	(7,652)	(19,847)	(32,730)	(29,108)	(24,360)	(36,250)	(4,628)	(22,669)

Source: See Appendix

count in 1883 found 133 adult Finns living in the area, all of whom were said to have emigrated originally from the province of Oulu. The state census of 1905 tallied 119 foreign-born Finns in Douglas County, and in 1970 there were 145 people of Finnish stock (see Map 15.2).[14]

A fourth major concentration of Finns in central Minnesota began to form around a sawmilling operation at New York Mills in Otter Tail County in the 1870s. The first two Finnish families arrived there in 1874 after learning of the availability of homestead land from Swedish coworkers in the lumber camps near Brainerd, where they had been drawn by the promotional activities of the Northern Pacific Railroad. Although Minnesota farmlands had attained a good reputation by this time, Finns in Michigan also began moving to the wheatlands of eastern Oregon after Elias Peltoperä of Cokato started a Finn settlement at Pendleton in

1876. Indian wars three years later again diverted the migrant stream to Minnesota and to New York Mills. Thirty families, primarily from Michigan, arrived in 1879.[15]

By the 1890s New York Mills, which was platted in 1883, had replaced Cokato as the focal point of Finnish rural settlement in central Minnesota. Finnish-language newspapers published there as early as 1884 proved to be effective in attracting new settlers until the "community of Finns in and around New York Mills" was said to number "nearly 4,000 souls" by 1889. Many of the men farmed in summer and cut railroad ties and cordwood in winter.[16]

After the homestead lands south of New York Mills were claimed in the 1880s, settlers moved into the village itself, to nearby Blowers and Paddock townships in Otter Tail County, as well as north to Becker County and east to Wadena County. In southeastern Becker County Finns arrived begin-

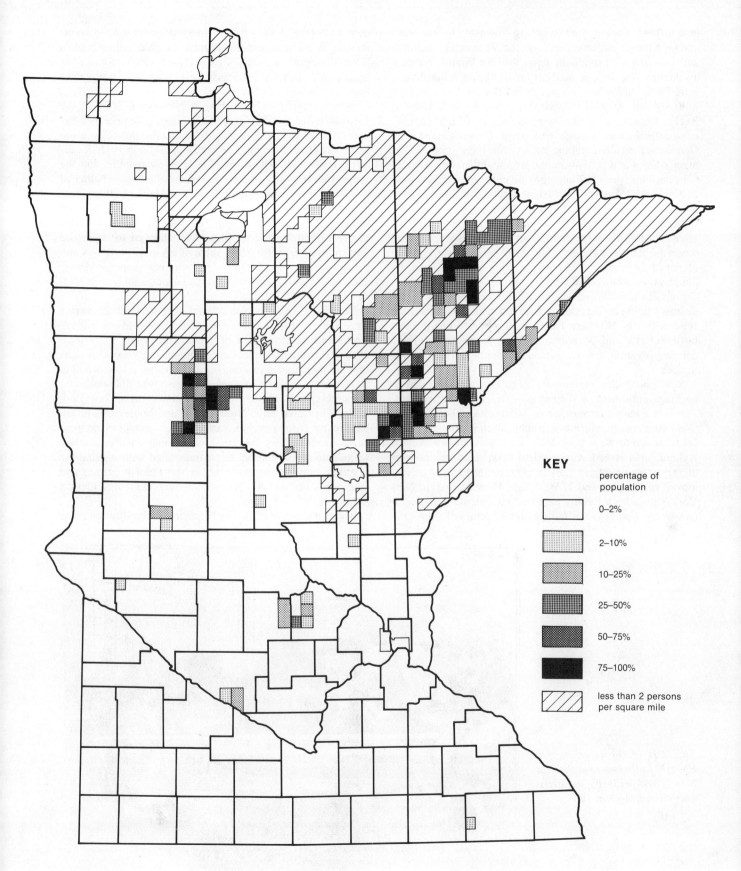

Map 15.2. Finns in Minnesota Rural Areas, 1905

KEY

percentage of population

0–2%

2–10%

10–25%

25–50%

50–75%

75–100%

less than 2 persons per square mile

ning in 1882. They named Runeberg Township for the well-known Finnish national poet and the villages of Snellman and Lönnrot for prominent figures in the Finnish national awakening. By 1906 a majority of Runeberg's inhabitants were Finns. Some had traveled from Michigan to New York Mills by rail, then proceeded by oxcart to Wolf Lake in Becker County, a trip that required six weeks and necessitated cutting a trail through thick woods for most of the way. One settler recalled trading rabbits for sugar, coffee, and other staples and cultivating the land with handmade hoes.

In the same decade Finns took up cutover pinelands near Sebeka and Menahga in western Wadena County, where they were joined in the 1890s by lumberjacks and miners from northern Minnesota's Vermilion Iron Range. Sebeka got its start as a storage depot from which logs were floated down the Red Eye River, while some of the early Finns at Menahga made their first home in a log hut abandoned by lumberjacks who had moved on after harvesting the pine. For all of these areas New York Mills continued to be the nearest trading center, post office, and railroad station until 1891, when the Northern Pacific built a branch line through both Sebeka and Menahga. After that the developing dairying region found it easier to market butter and milk in Sebeka.[17]

New York Mills also became an early center for Finnish-language publishing, a distinction it retained in the 1980s. The first Finnish newspaper in Minnesota, *Uusi Kotimaa* (New Homeland), which began publication in Minneapolis in 1881, moved to New York Mills in 1884. Its owner, August Nylund, also issued *Aamu Rusko* (Daybreak), a monthly literary magazine, from 1884 to 1889. In 1889 *Uusi Kotimaa* moved to Oregon, and J. W. Lähde filled the gap in New York Mills with a weekly paper called *Amerikan Suometar* (American Finn). When *Uusi Kotimaa* returned from Ore-

gon in 1890, the two papers merged under Lähde's editorship. In 1919 the resulting journal was sold to the People's Voice Cooperative Publishing Company, which continued to issue it in New York Mills until 1931, when it was moved to Superior, Wisconsin.[18]

Other newspapers published at New York Mills in the 1890s included the short-lived *Raittiuslehti* (Temperance Paper) and *Valoa Kansalle* (Light for the People). Two more were started in the depths of the Depression in 1932: *Keski-Länsi* (Midwest), which lasted only a few months, and the successful *Minnesotan Uutiset* (Minnesota News) launched by Carl A. Parta and Adolph Lundquist, both of whom were experienced newspapermen. By the 1950s *Uutiset* boasted the largest circulation of any Finnish-American newspaper in the United States. Its name was changed to *Amerikan Uutiset* in 1960. With 3,300 subscribers in 1978, it was still the largest biweekly Finnish-American newspaper in America, and the only surviving foreign-language journal in Minnesota at the end of that year.

New York Mills, which "brags that it is the country's largest agricultural community of Finnish Americans," wrote Ruth Hammond in 1979, was still visibly Finnish indeed. "Downtown stores have supplementary wooden signs that list their trades in Finnish. . . . The bakery sells 300 to 500 loaves of flatbread a week," Finnish was still spoken on the streets, and Saturday was still sauna night in New York Mills. The town had "well-kept frame homes, many enhanced by front porches with wooden spindles and neat yards decorated by flowers. . . . Young children, nearly white-haired and bearing last names filled with u's and k's say they don't know much about the Finnish culture and language," she added. "But people over 30 seem to know a little of both."[19]

Beginning in the 1870s the Northern Pacific Railroad was

SKETCH of the interior of a Finnish Lutheran church near New York Mills by an artist who visited there in 1888.

also responsible for making Brainerd a small hub of Finnish settlement in Crow Wing County' when numerous Finns passed through the village on their way west. As part of its land promotion program, the railroad provided free quarters for the settler and his family in its reception centers while they looked for land. To those who purchased, the company also offered free transportation to their new homes. In December, 1873, for example, eight Finnish families totaling 30 people were spending the winter at the Brainerd reception center.[20]

In the 1880s small numbers of Finns began to settle permanently in Crow Wing County, where they worked for the railroad, in the lumber camps, and later in the iron mines of the Cuyuna Range. Henry Pajari, a Finn on his way to homestead in Otter Tail County, stopped off in Crow Wing County in 1882. There he achieved a place in history by becoming the first man to make a real search for iron ore on what became the Cuyuna Range. After the range opened in 1911, Finnish miners were also to be found at Crosby. By 1900 the federal census counted 237 foreign-born Finns in Crow Wing County, and at their peak in 1920 the figure was 530.

Finns in Northeastern Minnesota

The last region closely identified with Finns — northeastern Minnesota — was also the one in which they became most numerous (see Map 15.2). The port of Duluth at the western end of Lake Superior and the six adjoining counties of Aitkin, Carlton, Cook, Itasca, Lake, and St. Louis contained 71.2% of the state's Finns and Finn stock in 1905 and 63.8% in 1970. The progress of the Northern Pacific Railroad westward from Duluth in the 1870s made the city an important dispersal point for Finnish immigrants who had traveled to Minnesota via the Great Lakes route.[21]

Exactly when the first Finns reached Duluth is uncertain. A few were present as early as 1868, and some Finnish fishermen were living on Minnesota Point in 1870. As immigrants arrived in greater numbers after 1880, some of them remained in the city to work on the docks and railroads, in the sawmills that ringed the bay, and in the nearby lumber camps. Others became fishermen. By 1895 clusters of Finns were to be found at the base of Minnesota Point, in the west end, and in the suburb of West Duluth — where three separate retail and residential concentrations existed. In them, as the population grew (see Table 15.3), the city's Finnish boardinghouses, churches, halls, restaurants, saunas, and businesses were built.[22]

As early as 1873 Finns began to clear small farms near the sawmilling village of Thomson and in Knife Falls Township of Carlton County. In the eastern part of the county sizable settlements grew up at Esko, where Finnish homesteaders arrived in 1877, as well as in Kalevala Township, at Moose Lake and Kettle River to the south in the 1880s, and among the Czechs, Scandinavians, and French Canadians around Cromwell and Wright to the west in the 1890s. Esko was named for Peter Esko, one of the early Finns, while Kalevala took its name from the Finnish folk epic. Carlton County, along with the farming sections of Beaver, Rice River, Workman, Tamarack, and Salo townships in adjoining Aitkin County, became one of the densest areas of Finnish population in the state. Between 1900 and 1910 the number of foreign-born Finns in Carlton County increased from 882 to 2,135; by 1920 they made up 37% of its foreign-born population.[23]

Many Carlton County Finns found work at Cloquet, where the town's first sawmill was built on the banks of the St. Louis River in the 1870s. By 1906 Cloquet was booming, with "five mills, supplied with logs from forty-odd camps," wrote Walter O'Meara, who grew up there. The mills were operated by the Cloquet Lumber, the Northern Lumber, and the Johnson-Wentworth companies, all of which were owned by the Weyerhaeusers. Cloquet's Finntown, recalled O'Meara, "was distinguished by a huge frame boardinghouse, a community sauna, and houses painted in vivid shades of pink, green, blue, and mauve — people called them Finlander colors."[24]

The family of one of O'Meara's boyhood friends "had a sauna in their back yard, next to the cowshed. It wasn't much like the streamlined saunas that even city apartment dwellers boast of nowadays." It "had a rough brick firebox stoked with birch logs, and above it was a bed of smooth, round stones. When the stones became practically white hot, you threw a pail of water on them to produce steam. Then you climbed up on a tier of plank seats (the higher you climbed, the hotter it got) and gasped for breath. Next, you splashed on a little water, soaped up, and beat one another with bundles of sweet-smelling cedar twigs. Finally, you escaped to the anteroom where a couple of barrels of ice-cold water stood, emptied a bucket over your head, and yelled bloody murder."

Cloquet and Moose Lake were completely destroyed by a disastrous forest fire that swept over 250,000 acres of northern Minnesota, killing at least 538 people on October 12, 1918. The toll among Finns was heavy; perhaps as many as 80% of those who died were Finns. One of the first organizations to rebuild was the Cloquet Cooperative Store, which had been organized by Finns in 1910. By 1937 it was said to be the "largest retail cooperative society in point of sales in North America," and it was still flourishing as a general store in the 1950s. By then Cloquet, a well-developed wood-products center, boasted one of Minnesota's few paper mills and counted many residents of Finnish descent. The 1920 census had recorded 2,140 foreign-born Finns in Carlton County; 50 years later there were 440 foreign-born and 1,772 Minnesotans of Finnish parentage in residence.[25]

But neither farming nor lumbering served as the principal magnet that attracted the largest migration of unskilled Finnish workers to northeastern Minnesota. Rather it was the

Table 15.3. Finns in Major Minnesota Metropolitan Areas

	1900	1910	1920	1930		1970	
	foreign born	fb	fb	fb	foreign mixed	fb	fm
Duluth	702	2,772	3,210	3,040	3,138	687	2,134
Minneapolis	348	875	1,120	1,154	2,460	283	1,989
St. Paul	51	73	97	87	231	88	437

Source: See Appendix

opening of the Vermilion and Mesabi iron ranges in northern St. Louis County in the 1880s and 1890s that drew migrants from the mines of Wisconsin and Upper Michigan as well as from Finland itself. By 1895 there were 3,225 Finns in St. Louis County. Ten years later the figure had risen to 12,076, or about 60% of the foreign-born Finns in Minnesota of whom 10.7% lived in Duluth. In 1920 St. Louis County's Finnish population peaked at 17,342.

By the 1880s Finnish immigrants were already experienced mine laborers, for their work in northern Michigan had already established a lasting, mine-oriented, occupational niche both for those who would later move to other regions as well as for Finns who were yet to arrive in America. Like the South Slavs and Italians, the Minnesota Finns' history after 1884 is closely tied to the development of iron mining. It provided them with employment, occasionally with company housing, and more often with company-contributed land for churches and temperance halls. It also offered low wages, long hours, dangerous work, and periodic unemployment — conditions that led to bitter strikes on the Minnesota ranges in 1907 and 1916.[26]

Soon after the first shipment of ore launched the Vermilion Range in 1884, Finns traveled from Michigan to settle in the new towns of Tower and Soudan. In 1886 ore was discovered near what became Ely. Again Finns were not far behind, arriving to work in the Chandler Mine and others opened in the Ely area from 1888 to 1899. The far larger Mesabi Range made its first shipments from the Mountain Iron Mine in 1892. After that town after town sprang up, and Finns appeared in communities all along the range as soon as jobs were available. They were said to have reached Biwabik and Eveleth in 1892 and Virginia and Hibbing at least by 1893. By 1905 Finns constituted the largest of the six major foreign-born immigrant groups on the Mesabi, and they made up some 40% or more of the foreign-born population in 12 of its towns and villages.[27]

The early comers were men who emigrated without their families. An old-timer, who went to Chisholm in 1900 when the Clark Mine opened, recalled that about half of its inhabitants were young Finnish men who had arrived not long before. Not until they were settled did they send for their families, a fact apparent in the sex ratios on the Mesabi. In 1895 the over-all ratio among 1,993 Finns there was about 4 males to 1 female. In some towns like Mountain Iron it ran as high as 6 to 1. Ten years later the ratio among 7,369 Finns had narrowed to 3 to 1.[28]

The decades near the turn of the century witnessed a movement to the land by Finnish immigrants in Minnesota as well as elsewhere in the country. Attracted by the inexpensive acreage offered in northern regions by promoters, lumber companies, and railroads, Finns as well as southern and eastern Europeans moved to homesteads, which were often located in cutover or submarginal farming areas. In Minnesota some Finns worked as seasonal laborers until they earned money to buy a few acres. They cleared the land where possible and planted around the stumps and boulders where plowing was impossible. A study of 15 homesteads in Salo Township, Aitkin County, from 1888 to 1907 revealed that the average holding totaled 120 acres, of which the set-

tler cleared an average of 1.3 acres per year in the first five to seven years. While clearing the land, these Finns usually spent about three months annually working at other occupations. When the time came to file the final papers on the claims, 80% of the Salo farmers were married.[29]

The strong pull of the land for some Finns was illustrated by a widely told and partly apocryphal story which related how four miners left Virginia on foot in 1902 after having worked the night shift. They supposedly walked 15 miles to Angora, staked their claims in a newly fallen snow, and then walked back to Virginia, arriving just in time to go to work the following night. During the next summer and fall, the men spent whatever time they could clearing the land. As a result, two of them were ready to move into their own cabins by Christmas, 1903.[30]

Land developers were quick to capitalize on the Finns' desire for farms. The Oldenburg-Jasberg Land Company acquired large holdings in the 1890s in central Pine County near present Finlayson. Through astute newspaper advertising, the firm sold them rapidly to land-hungry Finns. Writing in 1924, John Wargelin, president of Suomi College at Hancock, Michigan, observed that many Finn farmers were compelled "to work in the mines or the woods during the winter months in order to earn means of subsistence." Because of the Finns' affinity for stump farms, he added, "Mr. J. H. Jasberg . . . who has sold more land to the Finns than any other man in America, said that the only language the stumps understand . . . is the Finnish language." The Oldenburg-Jasberg firm maintained offices in Minneapolis and West Superior, Wisconsin, from which they also exchanged money and sold steamship tickets.[31]

In 1903 the Finnish Colonization Company of St. Paul was touting the low swampy lands of Aitkin County as the best farm sites ever offered to Finns. In 1910 Antero W. Havela, a businessman who had moved from Wyoming to Duluth, developed a Finnish settlement near Middle River in Marshall County. Two years later his firm, the Pellervo Land Company, acquired the right to sell some of the Itasca Lumber Company's cutover lands in the Suomi district near Little Bowstring Lake in Itasca County, another northern area that attracted numerous Finns who tried dairy farming augmented by mining, logging, and seasonal work in the wheat fields of the Dakotas.

Most of them, however, remained in St. Louis County. Finns moved in the 1890s to Floodwood Township in the southwestern tip of the county, to Embarrass Township and the Pike River Valley south of the Vermilion Range, and to the Brimson-Toimi area on the border of adjoining Lake County. By 1905 they had spread into the Palo-Markham region south of Biwabik and to Alango (meaning lowland in Finnish) and Field townships south of Cook (see Map 15.2).[32]

A reminder of this era in the state's agricultural history — the Eli Wirtanen Finnish farmstead at Markham, homesteaded in 1905 — has been preserved by the St. Louis County Historical Society. Like many other Finn farmsteads, it exhibits what Arnold R. Alanen called "a basic beauty and integrity of log building craftsmanship." Like others, too, it includes a sauna, an institution of considerable cultural significance in Finnish family and social life. According to legend, the sauna often served as a family's first home until a house could be built.[33]

Contrary to a commonly accepted notion, it was not the resemblance of the landscape to Finland which initially attracted the Finns to northern Minnesota and Michigan. Rather it was the occupational opportunities available in the mines and forests. Once there, in order to become farmers the Finns turned to what was available close at hand — the nearby stumplands with their stony, thin soils. They tended to settle in clusters, seeking homes near other Finns of the same religious or political persuasion.

A 40-acre piece of cutover, or better still, land with some standing timber, seemed large when compared to the two- or three-acre plots of Finland. Such small farms provided for many of their owners' needs — wood, game, fish, vegetables, a cow or two — which could be supplemented by staples purchased with paychecks from part-time work in the mines or logging camps. Those who had timber on their land sold it, often to the railroads. Frequently they turned to dairy farming to eke out a marginal living on soils too poor and too far north to grow good, cash, field crops.[34]

By 1920 there were 4,703 farms operated by the 60% of Minnesota's Finnish population that lived in rural areas. (For the 1905 rural distribution, see Map 15.2.) The hard times of the 1930s, however, forced large numbers to withdraw from full-time agriculture. World War II in the 1940s saw a further exodus as sons and daughters moved away for military service or to take jobs in industrial centers. In recent decades the movement away from farms has continued.[35]

To suggest more clearly the transformation that occurred over the years, let us look at the settlement of Finland in the cutover forests of Lake County. The community, which includes Isabella and Cramer, got its start in 1895, but the biggest influx of Finns arrived between 1902 and 1906, traveling by boat up the north shore of Lake Superior and then walking inland. By 1906 most homesteads had been taken up by Finns who moved there from the Vermilion Range mines at Ely and Tower. At first no roads existed, and the isolated settlement was served from 1907 to 1921 by a logging railroad. After that auto roads, graveled by 1934 and later paved, made their appearance.[36]

In 1934 the population of the area totaled about 160. Composed largely of Finnish dairy farmers, the people were interrelated and elderly. The average farm totaled about 100 acres, of which only 20 acres were cleared. Potatoes, hay, oats, and barley were raised, but the sale of milk was the leading source of cash income. Homes and farm buildings were frame or log; there was no electricity (the power line arrived in 1939) and few conveniences. Farming was supplemented whenever possible by work on roads, fire fighting in the nearby state and national forests, work in summer resorts on the north shore of Lake Superior, trapping, and jobs in the woods. A co-op store, started in 1913, had receipts of $30,000 in 1934. Many farms homesteaded before 1906 had been abandoned by 1934, and tax delinquency in the depths of the Great Depression was a problem. Most of the young people left in search of work opportunities elsewhere.

SAUNA on the Eli Wirtanen farm preserved by the St. Louis County Historical Society near Markham. Below, a sketch of the interior of a Finnish sauna at New York Mills in 1889.

By 1956 the population of Finland had nearly tripled. Although it was still heavily Finnish, its people were no longer farmers. Only one bona fide farm remained in the study area (it too was abandoned by 1960). Over half the community's residents were by then employed in nearby taconite installations and by a United States Air Force radar station established at Finland in 1950. Tax delinquency was no longer a problem, and many new dwellings had been built.

By 1976 few traces of the original agricultural community remained. Many of the clearings so laboriously created had been allowed to return to forests, and summer homes dotted the stony landscape. The flourishing co-operative store, established originally to serve the farming community, had its own building and a house for its manager. Patronized by people who came from miles around, its receipts in 1971 totaled $446,000.

The community still regarded itself as Finnish, and descendants of some original settlers were to be found there. For one of its bicentennial events in 1976 Finland chose to celebrate St. Urho's Day in honor of the mythical patron saint of Finnish vineyard workers who banished the grasshoppers from Finland and thus saved its grapes. Its historian described the event of March 16, also marked by other Finnish-American communities, as "not really a Finnish Celebration," but something "thought up by Finnish-Americans as a fun day to upstage the Irish" St. Patrick's Day on March 17. In a cold, blustery March, 1976, Finland with tongue in cheek staged a parade of 30 floats, a potluck dinner for about 300 people, a varied program of music and speeches, an exhibit on the community's history, and a dance to the music of Bobby Aro, "a Fabulous Finn from the Range." Buttons carrying the message, "The grasshoppers will get your grapes," were sold, and Finnish businesses were decorated in red, white, and blue.[37]

Organizations

The period after 1886 witnessed not only the growth of farms in northeastern Minnesota, but also the emergence of a rich variety of Finnish organizations — churches, temperance societies, workers' clubs, and co-operatives. For the earliest homesteaders in rural areas, there had been little opportunity for recreation beyond attendance at religious gatherings. For the stricter Finns, social activities like dancing were considered sinful. But at the turn of the century, as ever-greater numbers of immigrants began to arrive, the Finns responded to the need for additional group support.

Finnish immigrants organized small, independent, predominantly Lutheran congregations wherever they settled. It has been estimated, however, that only one in four Finnish Americans chose to belong to any church, although practically all of them had been nominal members of the Lutheran State Church in Finland. Once in the United States, they abandoned organized religion in large numbers.[38]

Various explanations for this shift have been offered. Among them were the powerful attractions of Socialism, the antipathy of religion to organized labor, and the unsympathetic attitude of the State Church in Finland toward emigration (for example, until 1923 it regarded weddings performed in the United States as illegal). Moreover the emigrants themselves changed over time. While the orientation of the earlier 19th-century arrivals was rural and religious, that of the 20th-century ones was frequently urban and secular. Scholars have suggested that the distinction can be explained in part by the fact that Finnish migrants before 1905 left directly from the rural provinces of Vaasa and Oulu, while later-comers worked for a time before emigrating from the cities, where they had been "alienated from the church" and "exposed to Marxist ideals."

Finnish immigrants to Minnesota in the first two decades after 1864 were largely Laestadians or Apostolic Lutherans, followers of Lars Levi Laestadius, a Lutheran minister who led a pietistic revival that swept the northern regions of the Scandinavian countries in the mid-19th century. While the structure of the Lutheran State Church in Finland was broad enough to encompass such movements emphasizing lay leadership and participation, churchgoing Finns in the United States fractured into three main groups — the Finnish

Apostolic Lutheran Church (the Laestadians), the Finnish Evangelical Lutheran Church of America (Suomi Synod) which most closely resembled the State Church, and the Finnish-American National Evangelical Lutheran Church.[39]

The first Finnish church in the state and the second in the United States was built in 1876 at Cokato by followers of Laestadius. The Apostolic Lutheran congregation at Holmes City got started in 1870. Its church, a small frame structure erected in 1877, retained its original appearance and furnishings in the 1980s. Prayer meetings in private homes in the Franklin area were led by Laestadian lay pastors until an Apostolic church was formally organized with assistance from fellow Laestadians at Cokato in 1875. Five years later a rigorous revival of Laestadian principles occurred at Franklin when Angelica Charlotta Jokela, the daughter of Lars Laestadius, moved into the community. The New York Mills church, built in 1877, was by 1950 the largest Finnish Lutheran congregation in the state.[40]

Finnish-American Laestadians have traditionally flourished in rural settlements, where adherents have practiced a spartan, family-centered life-style emphasizing faith and hard work. Of 42 congregations in the state in 1926, for example, 33 were rural; of 7,722 members, only 1,096 resided in urban areas. As a result of doctrinal differences among themselves and with other Lutherans, the Apostolics by the 1970s had formed into five groups independent of any ties to other Lutherans. Relatively isolated in rural areas, some have maintained their ethnic identity. In 1980 weekly services in both Finnish and English were still held in strongly Finnish areas like New York Mills and Cokato.[41]

The first steps toward the founding of the second major religious group — the Suomi Synod — got under way in Minneapolis in 1886, when several Finnish Lutheran leaders met informally to discuss the formation of a new church body. Not until 1890, however, did their efforts bear fruit in a gathering at Calumet, Michigan. The third organization — the Finnish-American National Evangelical Lutheran Church — came into being at Rock Springs, Wyoming, in 1898 as a rejection of the Suomi Synod. The founders inserted the word "national" into its name in order to emphasize its democratic character as opposed to what they regarded as the rigid authoritarianism and too close affinity of the Suomi ministers to the State Church in Finland.[42]

Both the Suomi Synod and the National Church were strongest in northern Minnesota, where they helped perpetuate the Finnish language and heritage. The synod was especially active in this regard. In 1906 it counted 20 congregations with 1,548 members in the state, while the National Church had 27 congregations with 2,589 members. By 1926 synod membership had jumped to 5,819 in 40 congregations, 28 of which were rural. Its rival was even more clearly rural, with 2,524 members in 30 congregations, only 4 of which were urban.[43]

In the Sunday and summer school programs of the Suomi Synod's Zion Lutheran Church in the Mesabi Range city of Virginia, for example, children learned Finnish history, language, and culture along with catechism and Bible study.

THE FINNISH Lutheran congregation in Mountain Iron gathered in front of the Temperance Hall in 1896.

The congregation's transition to English did not begin until 1932, when an English-language Sunday school session was inaugurated, but the minutes continued to be kept in Finnish until 1945.[44]

As the use of Finnish declined and the churches lost their strong ethnic orientation, the way was opened for merger with other American Lutheran groups. In 1963 the Suomi Synod joined the Lutheran Church in America; a year later the National Church merged with the Lutheran Church, Missouri Synod. By 1981 only the Apostolic Lutherans continued to maintain their separateness.[45]

Other Protestant denominations also found support among Minnesota's Finns. They included the Methodist, Congregational, Baptist, and Unitarian churches. The first Finnish Methodist congregation was established near Moose Lake in 1891, and a log chapel was erected the following year. By 1911 there were six churches in Minnesota with a total membership that ranged from 500 to 800. In the 1950s only the Methodist Church in Chisholm retained some Finnish activities.

In the early 1920s the Finnish-American Free Church Congregationalists (also known as the Evangelical Mission Society) sent missionaries from Ohio to minister to Free Church Finns in Duluth and on the Mesabi Range. By 1928 they had added new congregations in Duluth, Eveleth, Cloquet, Stony Brook, Hibbing, and Palo. During the 1960s Finnish activity came to an end as the congregations became English-speaking and second and third generations affiliated with American Congregational churches. In 1980 Cloquet was the only community that still had occasional Finnish "cottage services" held in private homes.[46]

The first Finnish Unitarian Church in the United States was organized at Virginia in 1911 by Risto and Milma Lappala, a Finnish couple who were both ordained ministers. By 1937 the membership had risen to 142. A second Unitarian congregation was founded at Alango in October, 1916, and a

church was built there three years later. Both were served by the Lappalas. In 1949 the Alango congregation had 92 members.[47]

On the Mesabi Range, however, Finnish congregations were not the first institutions to emerge. When mining began there, saloons with their "backroom gambling dens and upstairs quarters for the prostitutes" were the only centers of social life available. By 1910 out of a total of 356 saloons in 15 range towns, 59 were owned by Finns. "It used to be the custom of the single men in the boarding houses," wrote a sociologist, "to hurry off to the saloons Saturday evening and arrive home just in time to change clothes and report for work at the mines Monday morning." In this setting it is not surprising that temperance societies came into being before churches were organized. Indeed, many pioneer range congregations held their first services in temperance halls, which were often two-story frame structures with stages and large meeting rooms.[48]

The first such group to be organized in Minnesota was the *Pohjan Leimu* (Northern Light) society, established at Tower-Soudan on the Vermilion Range in 1886, only two years after the Soudan Mine opened there. Like many others, its hall was erected on land contributed by the mining company. Between 1886 and 1940 more than 50 such clubs were formed in northern Minnesota, 21 of them from 1890 to 1900, the period that saw the large Finnish immigration to the Mesabi. Strong organizations, these societies quickly became complete social, cultural, and fraternal institutions, offering activities and benefits that attracted large numbers of members. Almost a third of the Finnish adults (1,177) in Virginia, for example, were members of the *Valontuote* (Producer of Light) Temperance Society in 1903.[49]

In addition to weekly meetings, the local groups sponsored a wide variety of events. They held frequent evening socials, lectures, debates, plays, and bazaars. Each usually had a women's sewing circle, various athletic groups, a debating club, a drama society, a band and choir, and a library, where members could read newspapers and borrow popular and inspirational books. In Hibbing, for example, the Finnish band was "prominent in the village's musical life" at the beginning of the 20th century.

Nationally known Finnish and Finnish-American women lecturers like Alma Hinkkanen, Maggie Walz, and Linda Malmberg toured communities in the Midwest, carrying the temperance message to local societies. In May, 1908, for example, Hinkkanen spoke to audiences of 300 people in Ely and Hibbing and 600 in Virginia. A direct result of these tours was the establishment of local temperance schools for children. In 1906–07 the Hibbing, Virginia, Eveleth, Soudan, and Ely societies had temperance schools, although all were short-lived because of the lack of qualified teachers.[50]

At least two temperance newspapers in the Finnish language were published in Minnesota. One was *Päivälehti* (Daily News) of Duluth, which was started in 1901 and expanded to carry more general news. It claimed a circulation of nearly 15,000 in the early years of the century. Another was the short-lived *Raittiuslehti* (Temperance News) published in New York Mills.

The temperance halls soon became important gathering places, wrote Arthur E. Puotinen, for they "symbolized various aspirations for the immigrant Finns: A way of maintaining friendships, a means of preserving Finnish language and folkways, a place of entry for newcomers into mining town society, a center for organizing people's interests in reform, a forum for proclaiming or questioning Christian beliefs. In effect, the various modes of Finnish hall life constituted coping devices with which immigrants responded to their economic and social environment." Another scholar remarked that "For many participants the local hall and its activities represented a bridge between two worlds."[51]

With its libraries, plays, newspapers, and benefits to sick and deceased members, the Finnish temperance movement has rightly been called "an immigrant social, fraternal, and cultural, as well as a crusading, institution" against the evils of alcohol. The societies were generally tolerant toward those who broke their pledges against drinking. In 1895 the Hibbing group allowed members to backslide three times during a three-month period before placing the offender on probation for three months. Over a 25-year span the Ely society counted 862 violations among its 2,104 members.

The temperance movement was not limited to Finnish Americans, nor was it confined to Minnesota. At first many local societies like *Pohjan Leimu* at Tower-Soudan affiliated with the Scandinavian-American Good Templars, a branch of the national Independent Order of Good Templars. Then in 1888 the Finnish National Temperance Brotherhood was formed. Two years later a second rival group, the Finnish-American Friends of Temperance, was created.

Various developments caused the divisions among these groups. Although the early temperance societies were secular organizations, their ideals had attracted large numbers of clergy and church Finns. Meetings took on a religious orientation, opening and closing with prayers. Dancing, card playing, theater going, and even strike breaking were sometimes banned. Opposition to such policies and objections to clerical influences split the temperance movement in 1889. Further dissension in the 1890s opened the way for the transformation of some temperance locals into Socialist chapters. In 1897 when the Hibbing society divided, for instance, one faction became a workers' club; later entire societies in Eveleth and Nashwauk, for example, were transposed into Socialist clubs, which retained their temperance ideals and social activities and added Socialist lectures, card playing, and dancing. A further decline ensued after 1919 when the states ratified the 18th amendment to the Constitution, prohibiting the manufacture, sale, or transportation of intoxicating beverages. Many members left the movement, feeling that its mission had been accomplished. In 1941 only 16 "active" chapters comprising about 650 members could be found in Minnesota. By 1960 the Finnish Temperance Brotherhood existed in name only.[52]

The cause that stood to gain the most from the feuding within the temperance ranks was Socialism, which offered immigrant workers an alternative secular organization. Its forebears can be traced in part to Finland, where in the second half of the 19th century a broad, nationalistic, reform movement, known as the Finnish national awakening, established workers' clubs and night schools to promote education. Marxist class consciousness developed within these organizations about the turn of the century. But the "conception . . . that the immigrants brought their socialism with them as part of their European baggage is not borne out by the evidence. . . ," contended historian Hyman Berman. "Finnish Social Democracy did not really firm up until 1899 and its strong center was in industrial Southern Finland, whereas most of the Mesabi Finns came from the rural provinces of Oulu and Vaasa. Many of the Finnish socialist clubs on the Range were organized before there was an effective network of socialist clubs in Finland." Among the numerous immigrants from southern Finland in the decade after 1900, however, were lecturers and writers who provided ideological direction for the blossoming Finnish-American Socialist movement.[53]

The American industrial scene itself supplied a powerful spur to the movement's development. When the unskilled immigrant went to work in the mines, he was generally assigned to the hardest, dirtiest, and most dangerous jobs. In 1908 about 870 Finnish miners were employed by the Oliver Iron Mining Company, the largest firm on the Minnesota ranges, and most of them were on the lowest rungs of the economic ladder with little hope of improving their working conditions.[54]

In August, 1906, 40 delegates from Finnish workers' and Socialist clubs in 12 states met at Hibbing to establish the Finnish Socialist Federation, the first and soon the largest of the foreign-language associations within the Socialist party. In 1911 near the peak of its strength, the federation had 13,667 members, but only 1,693 of them were citizens (and thus voters) of the United States. At that time Minnesota listed more members than any other state — 2,824 (2,308

TYÖVÄEN OPISTO, the Work People's College in Duluth as it looked in 1914.

men and 576 women) in 47 chapters. By 1912–13 the 273 Finnish chapters throughout the country accounted for almost 12% of the party's total membership. The Reverend William J. Bell, a knowledgeable observer who conducted a survey on the Mesabi Range, estimated that a third of the Finns there in 1913 were Socialists. In that year the party ran losing candidates in many range towns, but in 1914 it was successful in Aurora, and two years later it "took the measure of the mining company candidates in Chisholm."[55]

Minnesota was also the home of the Work People's College of Duluth, an educational institution which trained many local Finnish Socialist leaders. Founded in 1903 by the National Evangelical Lutheran Church as the Peoples' College and Theological Seminary, it was modeled at first somewhat along the lines of the older Suomi College in Michigan. In 1907 the Peoples' College was taken over by Socialists, who in a complex maneuver had become majority stockholders. Renamed the Work Peoples' College, its curriculum was expanded along Marxist lines. The fundamentals of Socialism were taught along with courses in economics, Finnish language and literature, English, mathematics, typing, and accounting. When a split occurred in the Finnish Socialist Federation in 1914, control passed to the radical wing associated with the Industrial Workers of the World (IWW or Wobblies). The school became a center for that union's militant activities, continuing to operate until its last classes disbanded in 1940. In its 37-year life, the college instructed several thousand miners' children, who carried the Socialist message back to their local halls.[56]

Like the temperance societies and the churches, Socialist chapters served important social functions. Their halls at the simplest were small, one-room, rectangular buildings. The larger ones, like the imposing Opera House in Virginia, were elaborate multistoried structures complete with theater, auditorium, meeting rooms, library, and pool hall. Attesting to the popularity of the social and cultural activities was the frequent accusation that members were devoting more time to them than they were to the organization's political work. In fact, one former Finnish radical leader estimated that as many as 80% of the members joined for the social life. As a result, the Finns were sometimes derisively referred to as "hall Socialists," whose principal interests were more social than political.[57]

Be that as it may, Finnish Socialists were responsible for an important segment in the history of Minnesota labor. It began with their definitive role in the first major strike on the Mesabi in 1907 in which 75% of the strikers were estimated to be Finns. Not only did the walkout earn for the range Finns a reputation for radicalism, it aggravated already strained relations within the Finnish-American community in ways that endured in the 1980s. The church Finns accused the Socialists of jeopardizing the good reputation of all

POSTER for the Aurora Fire Department's ball in 1915, held in the Socialist Workers' Hall.

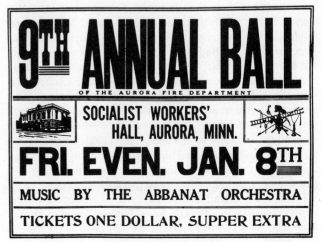

Finns, while the Socialists believed the church had sided with the mining companies and betrayed the workers. When the strike ended in failure after four months, it was claimed that effective blacklisting by the companies barred almost 1,200 Finns from employment in the mines.[58]

After the strike large numbers turned toward more militant industrial unionism. In 1914 a split in the Finnish Socialist Federation resulted in 3,000 members withdrawing or being expelled. Many were Minnesotans who then affiliated with the IWW. The Finnish Wobblies formed their own association, built their own halls, and founded their own newspaper in Duluth. Begun in 1914 as *Sosialisti* (The Socialist), the paper became the *Industrialisti* (The Industrial Worker) in 1917. Closely associated with the Work People's College, it was published in Finnish by the Workers' Socialist Publishing Company, which also issued books for IWW members. In 1919 it boasted 10,000 subscribers. When it ceased publication in 1975, *Industrialisti* was one of the very last foreign-language IWW journals in the United States.[59]

Although they were no longer the dominant leaders they had been in 1907, Finnish Wobblies helped organize a dock workers' strike in Duluth in 1913 to force the installation of safety devices, participated strongly in a second unsuccessful Mesabi strike in 1916, and helped initiate the large-scale walkout in 1917 of lumberjacks and sawmill hands from northern Minnesota mills and camps. The timberworkers strike was especially directed against the operations of the Virginia and Rainy Lake and the International Lumber companies in Beltrami, Itasca, Koochiching, and St. Louis counties. Like the earlier miners' strikes, the month-long walkout was broken by the concerted action of company and law enforcement officials. Nevertheless while it lasted over 3,000 jacks streamed out of the woods, and some mills were closed for short periods. Eveleth and Virginia banned Wobblies from their streets, ordering them to leave town or face arrest. Coupled with the jailing of strikers and their leaders, these and other tactics banished the IWW from the scene. The union "promised to return to the camps and the mines, but before it could launch another offensive the nation entered World War I."[60]

The strikes and Socialist activity drew attention to the Finns after the United States entered the war. In Minnesota the establishment of the ultra-patriotic, antilabor Commission of Public Safety initiated a witch hunt. "With a vigor reinforced by patriotism, local slacker-hunters raided the Socialist Halls on the Range and arrested all those who did not have draft cards," wrote Hyman Berman. "Many Finnish workers who were not citizens of the United States, in a mistaken belief that aliens did not have to register for the draft, had failed to do so. They were caught up in the dragnet, tried, jailed, and released only on their promise that they would loyally work in the mines for allied victory. . . . Under the prodding of the Public Safety Commission, public dissent was eradicated on the Range. The Finnish I.W.W. newspaper, *Industrialisti*, was temporarily silenced."[61]

Perhaps one example will convey the atmosphere of the period. In 1918 the *Duluth News-Tribune* reported that a Finn who intended to renounce his first citizenship papers was tarred and feathered by a group known as the Knights of Loyalty. Declaring that they had 2,000 members in the city and 75,000 in Minnesota, the local chapter of the Knights distributed circulars which, said the newspaper, reported that they intended to "bring the craven coward and the guilty exponent of sabotage alike, be he citizen or alien, to his just desserts and brand him publicly before every true and loyal American. . . . Let every coward and slacker take notice."

"On the iron range agitation continued among die-hard Finnish Wobblies, who conducted minor demonstrations during and immediately after World War I," wrote John E. Haynes. The wartime Public Safety Commission, however, "thoroughly infiltrated the organization and frustrated it at every turn." Its national leaders were prosecuted and jailed by the federal government. Not until the period of the New Deal were the Minnesota mines successfully organized. In the 1930s and 1940s Finns joined the Mine, Mill and Smelter Workers Union, which preceded the triumphant efforts of the Congress of Industrial Organizations (CIO) to organize the steel industry. They were also to be found on the political front in the Farmer-Labor, Socialist Workers, and Communist parties. From this radical, activist union tradition came such leftist luminaries as Gus Hall, long-time chairman of the Communist party of America, who was born of Finnish parents and raised on the Mesabi.[62]

Socialists in northern Minnesota were in the forefront of yet another kind of mutual support effort organized by Finnish-American immigrants — the co-operative. While individual co-ops sought to satisfy the immediate material needs of their members, the movement's ultimate theoretical objective was the creation of an alternative system without the faults of capitalism. Socialists found these principles compatible, holding that co-ops helped liberate the miner, worker, and farmer by offering a more democratic system to counter monopolistic business practices. Thus the "father of cooperation was Socialism — a strange parent," wrote John Kolehmainen, "reluctant to embrace the child wholeheartedly and blind to its unique possibilities in its own right."[63]

Although Finnish Socialists gave impetus to the movement, they were by no means responsible for all co-operatives, even among Finns. The first such group in the state, the *Sampo* of Menahga, for example, was established in 1903 with $170 raised by 13 Wadena County farm families who objected to the poor quality of merchandise and to being paid by local merchants for their butter, eggs, etc., in scrip instead of American currency. To market their products more effectively, the people of Sebeka also organized a co-operative creamery in 1908.[64]

During the 1907 strike year on the iron ranges, co-operative stores and boardinghouses came into being, for example, in Hibbing, Biwabik, and Nashwauk. The latter quickly expanded into a purchasing unit for foodstuffs and work supplies with its own building. The original members of the unit, which was named the Elanto Company (from a Finnish word meaning "livelihood") were Socialists. In 1909 long-lived co-operatives were born at Ely, Virginia, and Embarrass. At Cloquet what became a large and successful retail store developed in 1910 from a Finnish Socialist workers' society, whose hall the co-op later took over. A store society was begun at Floodwood in 1912, and others were formed at Gilbert, Orr, and 12 other Minnesota mining towns and rural areas after the disastrous strike of 1916.[65]

In 1917 representatives of 19 midwestern co-ops met in Superior, Wisconsin, and founded the Cooperative Central Exchange, a general wholesale and purchasing organization. Minnesota was represented by delegates, all of whom were Finns, from Cloquet, Fairbanks, Nashwauk, and Petrell. Despite adverse economic conditions in the country, the exchange grew and prospered. In its first year its sales were $25,574. By 1928 it had 71 member stores and its sales totaled more than $1,500,000. In 1960 they exceeded $34,767,000.[66]

With the dissension among Socialists and the formation of the Communist International in 1919, many within the Finnish co-operative movement supported the Communist program. But when the Communist party in 1929 sought to dominate the Central Exchange, an intense conflict developed between party followers and those who favored building the co-operative movement according to Rochdale principles on the broadest possible base. After a long and bitter debate that raged in local co-ops throughout Minnesota and the Midwest, the Communists were defeated at the 1930 annual convention. The Central Exchange then adopted a nonpolitical course, and in 1941 changed its name to Central Cooperative Wholesale.[67]

The co-operative movement offered a way of life for many members of the first generation, providing for their social, cultural, and material needs. Co-op halls throughout Minnesota were the sites of dances, concerts, evening socials, lectures, and plays. Unusual features begun in the 1920s were the women's guilds, composed at first entirely of Finnish women, which sprang up as auxiliaries to local co-op stores. In the 1930s they sponsored locally produced vaudeville-musicals that toured the Midwest promoting co-ops and their products. The guilds also sponsored summer camps held through the 1950s to teach Rochdale principles to young people.[68]

With changing times and conditions, the social and cultural functions of co-operatives decreased in importance. As the first generation died, control passed into the hands of the American born. The Central Cooperative Wholesale hired its first non-Finnish-speaking fieldman in 1930 and held its last bilingual session in 1948. During the 1940s and 1950s the ethnic composition of the co-ops shifted, so that by 1952 only an estimated 25% of the members were of Finnish descent. Nevertheless, out of 26 Minnesota co-operatives, two in 1952 still conducted general membership meetings completely in Finnish, and eight held them in both Finnish and English. With the growth of mass merchandising and discount stores after World War II, many — but not all — of the immigrant-established co-ops found it increasingly difficult to stay in business, especially in larger cities. After several years of discussions, Central Cooperative Wholesale merged with the Minneapolis-based Midland Cooperatives, Inc., in 1963.[69]

"With the Finnish-sponsored workers' halls and temperance groups having already faded into oblivion, it is the cooperative, as well as the church, which remain as viable

THE SUCCESSFUL *Elanto Co-operative Company's store in Nashwauk in the late 1930s.*

units within the American institutional system," wrote Arnold Alanen in 1975. "Interestingly enough, both the Finnish churches and cooperatives adapted to changing requirements of contemporary society by joining larger organizations. . . . It could indeed be argued that by becoming immersed in the greater mainstreams of American organizational endeavor, the perpetuation of at least some Finnish-sponsored institutions was ensured."

Acculturation

To the first-generation Finns, who had built and devoted their lives to various ethnic institutions, the preservation of a strong Finnish community was important. The problem, of course, was the second generation. "There are countless families that know only Finnish," one writer noted in 1915, "in which the children despise the culture of the home. Idealizing the culture they are taught at school, they would rather be Americans." Another, writing in 1924, saw "a serious breach . . . developing between the older and the younger members of the family," because older members lacked fluency in English and because of the "different interests and traditions" of the Finnish-born and American-born generations. Most Finnish-American leaders insisted that it was the responsibility of parents, especially the mother, to see that the language and culture were preserved. As one pastor put it, "The sheer love of one's race should encourage every parent to see to it that their children acquire a general knowledge of Finnish history."[70]

Americanization efforts reached a peak during the patriotic fervor of World War I, when many government and school officials pictured the Finns as "socialists of the worst sort" for whom the only remedy was education. In St. Louis County, however, the Americanization drive continued into the 1920s. Concerned with the prevalence of foreign languages, especially Finnish, among their pupils, St. Louis County school authorities adopted the then-popular idea that foreigners must be acquainted with English before they could appreciate American ideals. In 1924 they initiated a "Speak English" program. To this end, *Koti-Home* reported, they handed out to the children "We Speak English" buttons and certificates which read: "We, the undersigned, believe that in order to be true Americans we must speak the language of America. We, therefore, pledge ourselves to speak English at school at all times, and at home as far as possible, and to encourage and teach others to do the same."[71]

Some Finns objected to such methods, which they regarded as extreme. One recalled an overly zealous teacher in a Finnish community who asked her pupils to pledge "themselves never to speak Finnish anywhere," not even at home. "Some of the children," he wrote, "became very enthusiastic followers of her instructions. One girl, for example, whose father owned a store, refused to sell the customers anything until they asked for things in English. The children would not speak Finnish to their parents."

The question of language and cultural maintenance became particularly sensitive in the churches and the co-operatives as the gradual change to English took place from the 1920s to the 1940s. In many congregations controversy became bitter and heated. Much as other non-English-speaking immigrant groups in America, Finns tended to view the change to English as an attack on the Finnish heritage itself, and there was considerable resistance even to the introduction of English services for the English-speaking second generation. Nevertheless, as acculturation proceeded, English had with few exceptions become the primary language by 1960.[72]

Referring to the persistence of the Finnish language in the co-operative movement, one of its pioneers, writing in 1930, pointed to the exclusiveness of the co-op stores which were considered "a sort of Finnish club." In them, he said, Finns gathered, "hung on the counters, and stood in groups around the floor talking to each other in nothing but Finnish." If a non-Finn entered, a "clerk asked just enough in English to find out what groceries the customer wanted, made change and abruptly ignored his presence to engage in a lively conversation in Finnish." Thus, he concluded, there "is no inducement to the English-speaking people to join the co-operative," which they think of "as exclusively Finnish."[73]

A hybrid new dialect, often called Finglish or Fingelska, combining Finnish and English, developed to bridge the gap. In it, for example, corn flakes became *corn flakesiä*, potato *potaatti*, cake *keeki*, streetcar *striit kaara*, etc. A study conducted in northern Minnesota in 1940 recorded some 1,300 English loan words or adaptations of them in the speech of Finns on the Vermilion and Mesabi ranges. In the 1970s the hybrid attracted the attention of linguists in Finland, who visited Minneapolis and other American centers to record the language of American Finns.[74]

When Joshua Fishman published his monumental study of *Language Loyalty in the United States* in 1966, he did not consider the prospects very bright for the maintenance of Finnish. It was, he pointed out, one of the languages which had suffered sharp losses (more than 50%) in the number of its speakers from 1940 (230,420 in the United States) to 1960 (110,168). In the number of persons who claimed to speak

Finnish as a mother tongue, it ranked 20th in a list of 23 languages and 23rd out of 23 in the estimated prospects for its maintenance in the United States.[75]

The Finns were generally ahead of most recently arrived immigrant groups from southern and eastern Europe in becoming naturalized, although they were below the average for all foreign-born in the United States. In 1907, 34.9% of the Finnish workers employed by the Oliver Iron Mining Company on the Minnesota ranges were said to be naturalized, and 54.4% reportedly spoke English. In 1920, 47.8% of all foreign-born men 21 years of age or older and 39.2% of Finnish men were citizens. By that time relatively more women than men from Finland were naturalized. The political split in the Finnish community led many to seek citizenship. By becoming naturalized conservative Finns sought to demonstrate their loyalty to the new country, while Socialists sought to register their views by voting.[76]

In 1905 Eveleth businessman John Saari became the first Finn to be elected to the Minnesota House of Representatives. In 1920 Oscar J. Larson, a Duluth lawyer, became the first Finnish-American congressman from Minnesota and the only one elected up to 1980. Larson was actively involved in the World War I Americanization effort, founding the Lincoln Loyalty League, a patriotic, anti-Socialist organization among Finns at Duluth. Some scholars have voiced the opinion that Finnish Americans lacked interest in national politics. Socialists excepted, generally speaking they were fond of President William McKinley and tended to favor Republican candidates from about 1900 until the 1930s, when many shifted to the Democratic party of Franklin D. Roosevelt. As for local politics, a total of 15 Finns served in the Minnesota legislature through 1980.[77]

Language and cultural maintenance also played a part in events on the Finnish-American left. Although ideologically opposed to ethnic nationalism, the Socialists and later the Communists nonetheless carried on their activities in Finnish within the confines of an ethnic language federation. When the Communist party in 1925 abolished the language federations, a majority of Finnish-American Communists decided to retain their workers' clubs, halls, and ethnic activities. As a result, three-quarters of them refused to join a reorganized party structure.[78]

Ultimately a combination of social, economic, and cultural factors determined the outcome for the second generation. Speaking English and possessing access to education, its members were not locked into a few occupations as many of their parents had been. Their social needs were fulfilled by American institutions. Many moved away from the Finnish settlements to seek better employment opportunities in urban areas, where intermarriage with non-Finns further speeded the acculturation process.[79]

Minneapolis may be regarded as a case in point. Although small numbers of Finns were present there as early as 1865, it was not until the 1890s that a distinct Finnish neighborhood began to take shape along both sides of Glenwood Avenue between North Penn and Girard avenues. At that time organizational activity started when the Apostolic Lutherans began to hold religious services in homes. In 1895 the first secular Finnish organization in the city, a women's literary club, was established. The Vesa Society, a temperance organization established later in 1895, existed until about 1900. Local Lutherans incorporated the congregation that became the Morgan Avenue Lutheran Church and affiliated with the Suomi Synod. The temperance society was revived in 1901, and in 1903 a majority of its members joined a newly formed Finnish Socialist Workers' Association, turning over the temperance assets for the construction of a workers' hall.[80]

The next three decades saw steady growth in the ethnic community as Finnish shops, restaurants, halls, and churches were built (see Table 15.3). The Minneapolis Finns worked in brickyards, sawmills, and manufacturing firms. Women found employment as domestics and as garment workers in the Munsingwear Company's factories near Finntown. The boom years of World War I attracted Finns from elsewhere in Minnesota as well as from Wisconsin and South Dakota. By 1920 the city's Finnish foreign-born population had risen to 1,120.

With the Depression of the 1930s, World War II, and the subsequent spread into the suburbs, the ethnic enclave began to disappear. As one long-time resident of the area observed in 1972, "There has been a gradual splintering. Now the vast majority [of Finns] are spread all over town. . . . You couldn't really say the Finnish community exists here anymore." The 1970 census counted a total of 2,272 in Minneapolis, 283 of whom were foreign-born Finns, while the surrounding metropolitan suburban area recorded a total of 10,116, of whom 559 were foreign born, 4,227 second generation, and 5,530 third generation.[81]

The legacy of Finntown was still reflected in the 1980s in numerous churches which stemmed from the old Finnish community but which had also dispersed into the suburbs. Apostolic Lutheran congregations were located in Blaine, Brooklyn Center, Golden Valley, Hopkins, and Plymouth. The ethnic background of their membership remained solidly Finnish, but only a few still held monthly services in the language in 1981. The congregation at Plymouth, for example, was in that year composed of approximately 80% Finnish stock, but the church no longer held services in Finnish. The former National Lutheran Church in New Hope had become a Missouri Synod congregation, and about 30% of its members were of Finnish descent. Morgan Avenue Lutheran Church, the former Suomi Synod congregation, remained in old Finntown. An estimated two-thirds of its members were of Finnish stock, but services in the Finnish language were held only on such special occasions as Christmas morning.[82]

Despite the cultural assimilation of Finnish Americans, there has been a continued affinity to the ethnic heritage through aspects of folk culture such as observances of Finnish festivals. Since 1903 Finns have sponsored an annual *Juhannusjuhla* (midsummer festival) in Minnesota. Both New York Mills and Menahga have summer celebrations which derive from traditional observances of St. John's Day on June 24. The *Laskiainen* (sliding down hill) winter sporting festival at Palo-Makinen, an annual outdoor February event from the earliest days of settlement there, was revived

in 1937. Since that time it has been sponsored by the St. Louis County school system. A recent addition to Minneapolis area activities has been the Finnish Christmas Festival held annually at Beautiful Savior Lutheran Church in New Hope.[83]

In the forefront of the effort to preserve and promote Finnish culture and language were the Knights and Ladies of the Kaleva, secret benevolent orders fashioned somewhat on the Masons and the Eastern Star. The Knights were started by a Montana Finnish immigrant in 1898, and a parallel organization for women was begun there six years later. Gradually lodges sprang up nationally wherever sizable Finnish communities existed, including Duluth and the iron ranges. Their rituals, as well as the names of the lodges, were drawn from the *Kalevala*.[84]

Imbued with the spirit of romantic nationalism, the Knights and Ladies aimed to enlighten the Finnish community, preserve its traditions, and cultivate the Finnish national spirit. Since 1932 they have operated a youth camp in northern Minnesota, where in the 1980s young people learned Finnish folk dances, crafts, songs, folk tales, and language. Beginning in 1968 the orders provided scholarships to college-age Finnish-American and Finnish-Canadian young people.

Along with this growing interest in "Finnishness," two other organizations — The Finnish American Heritage (formerly the Finnish American Society) and the Minnesota Finnish-American Historical Society — have become increasingly active. The former was born in 1941 out of American sympathy for the Finns' defiance of the Soviet Union during the Winter War of 1939–40 and the Finnish War Relief effort headed by former President Herbert Hoover. Its aims have been to encourage an understanding of American institutions among the immigrants and to perpetuate Finnish cultural traditions. In 1979 the group had 500 members in the metropolitan Twin Cities area. In addition to commemorating traditional holidays, it has also been active in supporting the Finnish Language Village program conducted by Concordia College, Moorhead, and in popularizing the uniquely Finnish-American ethnic festival, St. Urho's Day.[85]

The Minnesota Finnish-American Historical Society came into being in 1943 when plans were undertaken to present the Minnesota Historical Society with a commemorative painting by the noted Finnish artist, Juho Rissanen. In 1949 the organization grew as it participated in the Minnesota Territorial Centennial celebration, and shortly thereafter it commissioned the writing of a history of Minnesota Finns which appeared in 1957 in both Finnish and English. The society also underwrote the annual *Siirtokansan Kalenteri* (Immigrant Calendar) from 1951 to 1978, when it ceased publication. Like the Finnish American Heritage, the historical society also sponsored yearly charter flights to Finland in the 1970s. In 1980 the society's eight chapters (seven of which were located in northern Minnesota) had a combined membership of approximately 640.

The Twin Cities chapter, with a 1980 membership of 250, has been a regular participant in organizing Finnish exhibits for the International Institute of Minnesota's Festival of Nations, and in the 1970s — along with its parent organization

— it supported such projects as the Finn Creek open air museum at New York Mills and the Finnish Language Village for young people. The Finn Creek project, begun in 1975, has been financed in part by successful benefit fund raisers stressing ethnic themes and by the sale of ethnic T-shirts and calendars. The local Finnish-American organizations also periodically sponsor programs highlighting various aspects of Finnish folk culture.[86]

Through the 1970s Minnesota's Finnish Americans became increasingly involved in the study and the promotion of their ethnic heritage through organizations, projects of various kinds, and the writing and publishing of books and journals. Much of the activity came from third- and fourth-generation Finnish Americans, many of whom were only vaguely aware of their own historical and cultural ties to Finland. There has also been some resurgence in language study at community schools and at the University of Minnesota. This renewed interest in "Finnishness" was not a nostalgic attempt to preserve the ethnic identity intact as the first generation had tried to do. Rather, it emerged as a sense of wonderment and curiosity about an ethnic heritage — one extending back beyond the immigrant generation to Finland itself. Thus the folk customs and traditions that were a living reality for the immigrants have now become a source of fascination and pride for their grandchildren and great-grandchildren.[87]

The Swede-Finns

THE SWEDE-FINNS or Finland Swedes, as they are sometimes called, are Swedish-speaking people who for centuries have inhabited the coastal areas of southern and western Finland, as well as the Aland Islands in the southwestern archipelago between Sweden and Finland (see Map 15.1). While they share a country with the Finns, a language with the Swedes, and a history with both, they have traditionally regarded themselves as a distinct group.

Caught up in the same social and economic conditions as the Finns, they too joined the migratory stream to America. In United States statistics these Swedish-speaking Russian subjects were classified as Finns. Nor were they listed separately in Finland's figures. Thus how many made the journey to the United States can only be estimated. Available counts from Swedish communities in Ostrobothnia indicated that the emigration was heavy. In 1900 when Swede-Finns constituted 13% of the total population of Finland, their mass departure was substantial enough to cause concern. An organization known as *Finlandssvenska Emigrantföreningen* (Finland-Swedish Emigrant Union) was formed to discourage Swede-Finns from emigrating, an activity the union regarded as "the most dangerous sickness of our time."[1]

A reasonable estimate is that 20% to 25% of all Finnish immigrants to Minnesota were Swede-Finns. Most were from Ostrobothnia and the Aland Islands and the majority were young, single people. Applying these percentages to the United States as a whole produces an estimated 60,000 to 70,000 Swede-Finn immigrants for the period from 1870 to 1924, perhaps a third of whom returned to Finland.[2]

The greatest number arrived in the years between 1885 and 1914, settling primarily in Massachusetts, Michigan, Minnesota, and Washington. A 1920 national occupational survey indicated that 18% worked in mines, 17% in the building industry, 14% in manufacturing, 14% in farming, and 11% in lumbering. Since many of the Swede-Finns had emigrated from southern Ostrobothnia, where they enjoyed a reputation for carpentry and shipbuilding, it is not surprising that they tended to gravitate to the building trades in Minnesota as well. In any case, they soon established a local reputation for carpentry. One Swede-Finn in Eveleth recalled being asked by an American how it was that all Swede-Finns were carpenters![3]

Although the first known Swede-Finn in Minnesota was said to have arrived in Minneapolis in 1869, most such immigrants did not reach the state until the 1880s or later. A majority chose the northern part of Minnesota, notably St. Louis County. The early arrivals' first impressions of Duluth were sometimes disappointing. One woman recalled that she cried when she reached there by train from Michigan. Expecting a large city, she found instead a primitive town with shacks, brush, stumps, and a few wooden sidewalks. The earliest Swede-Finns in Duluth lived on Grass Island in St. Louis Bay or in shanties near sawmills on the sand flats where Garfield Avenue was later located. Some of them became fishermen, but as the lumbering industry grew, many worked in the logging camps and sawmills. In the winter they headed for the forests as loggers and in the summer they returned to Duluth to work in sawmills and lumberyards. Others found employment on the railroads building into the city or on the ore docks and in the grain elevators that ringed the bay. Women found work in laundries, a match factory, and as domestics.[4]

The earliest business enterprises operated by Swede-Finns were a shoe and clothing store, a cabinet shop, and the service of a former saloon owner who drove a water wagon and sold water to residents for $.05 a bucket. Known as "Vesi Aakust" (August the Waterman) by the Finns, the man later found it more lucrative to go back to saloonkeeping. Gradually the Swede-Finns moved from the flats to West Duluth, where by 1903 there were an estimated 300 to 700 persons "depending upon the season." A number of new business establishments included a Swede-Finn meat market, a drugstore, several new saloons, and a grocery that grew into the West Duluth Mercantile Company. Several Swede-Finns drew upon their carpentry experience and became building contractors, erecting many of the houses in West Duluth. In 1928 an estimated 2,000 Swede-Finns and their descendants lived in the Duluth area.[5]

From the time they first arrived in the city, Swede-Finns began dispersing into the farming and mining regions of Aitkin and St. Louis counties. They moved to Ely on the Vermilion Range when mines were opened there in the 1880s, and by 1906 there were 20 families in the area. During the depression of 1893–94 about 20 who had worked in logging camps and sawmills moved from Duluth to the Palisade-Lawler farming region in Aitkin County. After 1900 a large number were also farming in the Cloquet vicinity. Between 1894 and 1898 Swede-Finns began moving to Eveleth and other Mesabi Range towns from Ely, Tower-Soudan, and Michigan. By 1903–04 they numbered from 300 to 400, and many of them worked in the building trades or the iron mines. One Eveleth Swede-Finn worked his way up from a mine laborer to St. Louis County mine inspector. Others who had been miners moved to Cook in 1907 to take up farming on cutover lands they cleared with an ax, pick, and dynamite.[6]

Along the north shore of Lake Superior Swede-Finns lived in Two Harbors, French River, and Larsmont, which was originally called Larsmo by a pioneer Swede-Finn woman in honor of a town in Finland. They worked at fishing, logging, and in sawmills. The first settlers in the village of Finland in Lake County were said to be a Swede-Finn and a Finn who walked 40 miles from Two Harbors to stake their claims.

Minnesota's Swede-Finns did not live exclusively in the northern part of the state. After the arrival of the first one in Minneapolis in 1869, the man's brother joined him in 1881 and his nephew followed in 1888. The earliest large group arrived between 1910 and 1915 and found employment with building contractors and in grain elevators and mills. In the 1890s Swede-Finn families arrived in Hopkins, where the men worked in the Moline Farm Machinery factory. By 1908, 15 families lived in Hopkins, while some who had resided there earlier had by then moved to Milaca to farm. Like the Czechs in Hopkins, Swede-Finns there developed berry-growing businesses. While the men worked in factories, their wives and families cultivated large berry patches which helped supplement the family income.

St. Paul's first known Swede-Finn was a sea captain named Niklas Gregg who arrived in the 1870s, went back to Finland in 1883, and returned to St. Paul in 1885. Swede-Finns from Pedersöre and Lövö began arriving in the 1890s, working as carpenters and painters for construction firms and the Northern Pacific Railroad. Until World War I about 10 Swede-Finn families and a number of single men lived near the Northern Pacific railyards in the vicinity of Churchill Avenue and Front Street. In 1941 a long-time St. Paul Swede-Finn observed that most of his countrymen in that neighborhood had died or moved away.

At the turn of the century, before the establishment of social organizations, the social life of Swede-Finns was often limited to weekend get-togethers held in private homes. Saloons also functioned as social centers, where men would pass the time playing cards. During the early phases of immigration, Swede-Finns occasionally participated with Finns in associational life, but their activities in organizations developed by Scandinavians or by other Finns seems to have been very limited. Swede-Finns joined the Finnish National

Temperance Brotherhood and several congregations of them joined the Suomi Synod. But the language barrier was too great an obstacle, and at the turn of the century they formed their own organizations.[7]

Swede-Finns "have been in a particularly difficult position in respect to their relationships with other Scandinavians," wrote a scholar in 1940. "Since they are derived from Finland, they have been charged as being Finns; but inasmuch as they do not speak Finnish, and are subject to the hostility which the Finns learned to show to the Swedish ruling minority in Finland, their association with the Finns has been impossible. As one informant said, 'We are people without a country. The Swedes high-hat us, and we can't talk to the Finns.' . . . The result has been that the amount of association between the various Scandinavian peoples has never been large."[8]

In 1900 Swede-Finns established their own fraternal benefit society, the *Svensk-Finska Sjukhjälpsförbundet av Amerika* (Swedish-Finnish Sick Benefit Society of America) at Bessemer, Michigan. Shortly thereafter similar groups were created in Duluth, Hibbing, and Chisholm. The first Swede-Finn temperance societies in Massachusetts and Michigan belonged to the Finnish National Temperance Brotherhood, but they soon withdrew to found a completely Swedish-speaking organization, the *Svensk-Finska Nykterhetsförbundet av Amerika* (Swedish-Finnish Temperance Society of America), which was born at Crystal Falls, Michigan, in 1902 with representation from only one Minnesota local society — that at Eveleth — whose delegate was elected the first president. The Eveleth chapter had gotten off to an early start in 1898, becoming the first Swede-Finn temperance society in Minnesota. By 1913 not only Eveleth, but also Chisholm, Crosby, Hibbing, Palisade, Two Harbors, and West Duluth had societies. Of all these, that at Eveleth was the largest at its peak with 103 members. It still had 82 members in 1954. Like the Finnish temperance societies those of the Swede-Finns fulfilled important social functions, operated halls and libraries, and boasted at least a choral group if not a brass band or an orchestra.[9]

In many communities these mutual benefit and temperance societies had duplicate memberships and sometimes even the same officers. After differing points of view on abstinence were resolved, a merger took place in 1920. The resulting organization was called *Runebergorden*, or the Order of Runeberg, in honor of Johan L. Runeberg, the famous poet. After the merger *Ledstjärnan* (Guiding Star), the temperance newspaper, became the official publication of the new group. In time the temperance function diminished (as a goal it disappeared from the bylaws in 1946). But the Order of Runeberg lived on as a fraternal and social society, often with its own halls. When its membership declined in the 1930s, it recruited from the second generation with some success. In Eveleth, for example, the order had 128 members in 1940; in 1968 the number was 42. In 1961 the society had been reorganized as the International Order of Runeberg with the aim of establishing closer relations with the Swedes in Finland. In recent years it has sponsored scholarships to Turku University in Finland for the children of Swede-Finns.[10]

Like the Finns in general, the majority of Swede-Finns were Lutherans. By 1930 they had established about 20 active congregations throughout the United States, most of them affiliated with the Swedish-American Augustana Lutheran Synod. It appears that the Swede-Finns in many areas saw no point in establishing their own congregations when there was a Swedish-Lutheran group in their community. One early historian estimated that about 12,000 Swede-Finns of two generations were members of Augustana, but that only about one-third of them belonged to "distinctly Finland-Swedish churches." But Duluth Swede-Finns in 1897 founded Bethel Lutheran Church, whose 1980 membership was still composed largely of their descendants.[11]

A small number of the immigrants had been members of Baptist congregations in Finland. In 1901 they formed the Finnish Baptist Mission Society (later known as the Mission Union), whose stated purpose was to carry on mission work among Finnish and Swede-Finn immigrants. At least two congregations resulted from the effort — the Finska Ebenezer Church organized in Duluth in 1904 and the Betfage Baptist Church founded in Chisholm in 1906. In addition, a short-lived Baptist congregation was organized in 1909 in East Little Fork. In 1918 the Duluth congregation took the unusual step of introducing services in the Finnish language, and for many years the Mission Society sponsored religious broadcasts in Finnish over three radio stations in northern Minnesota. In 1961 all the Swede-Finn congregations affiliated with the Baptist General Conference.[12]

The acculturation of second-generation Swede-Finns and Finns proceeded along generally similar lines. As the young moved out into American society, their principal language became English. As a result, during the 1920s and 1930s Swede-Finn organizations realized the importance of adapting in order to survive, although this did not always occur without resistance. But a change in language usage was inevitable. Anders M. Myhrman, the principal student of the Swede-Finns, noted that "In both churches and lodges of the Order of Runeberg it became necessary to shift to English in order to interest the native-born generation and secure them as members of the organization and as active participants in its activities."[13]

The switch to English occurred not only in organizations but also in family life. When the children entered school, English became their principal language, and many families switched from Swedish to English at home. Often parents spoke Swedish among themselves. Sometimes they spoke Swedish while the children responded in English. But in the end, English won out even in bilingual homes.[14]

Certainly this accounts in part for the Swedish-American dialect spoken by many Swede-Finns. As with all immigrants to America who found themselves in conditions for which they had no vocabulary, they developed a new hybrid to fill everyday needs. Words like *loggare* (logger), *oredocken* (ore dock), *boardinghus* (boardinghouse), *enjoya* (enjoy), and *unloada* (unload) were borrowed with only slight adaptation from English. Often familiar English expressions were taken over intact. Swede-Finns who went back to visit relatives in Finland were called "the yes-wellers" because that expression, acquired in the United States, was so prevalent in the Swedish they spoke.[15]

FINNS — *Reference notes*

[1] United States, *Census*, 1920, *Population*, 2:698; 1930, 2:235; 1940, vol. 2, part 1, pp. 43, 88, part 4, pp. 30, 31. The Finnish population of the Mesabi Range alone was even higher, totaling 39.8% of the foreign born in 1905; see Matti E. Kaups, "The Finns in the Copper and Iron Ore Mines of the Western Great Lakes Region, 1864–1905," in Michael G. Karni *et al.*, *The Finnish Experience in the Western Great Lakes Region: New Perspectives*, 75–85 (University of Turku Institute for Migration, *Migration Studies C3* — Vammala, Fin., 1975). Permanent Swedish colonies in what is now Finland were established as early as the 6th century; about 7% of Finland's population in the 1970s spoke Swedish compared to 13% in 1900; see *Statistical Yearbook of Finland: 1979*, 11 (Helsinki, 1980); *Finland in Figures, 1979*, 4 (Helsinki, 1979). The author wishes to acknowledge the many helpful suggestions he received during his work on this chapter from Carl Ross of Minneapolis and Matti Kaups of the University of Minnesota-Duluth.

[2] U.S., *Census*, 1950, *Population*, vol. 2, part 23, pp. 23–52; Reino Kero, *Migration from Finland to North America in the Years Between the United States Civil War and the First World War*, 26, 28, 36 (University of Turku, Institute for Migration, *Migration Studies C1* — Turku, Fin., 1974); Kero, "The Return of Emigrants from America to Finland," in University of Turku, Institute of General History, *Publications Studies*, 4:29 (Turku, Fin., 1972); Keijo Virtanen, *Settlement or Return: Finnish Emigrants (1860–1930) in the International Overseas Return Migration Movement*, 62–66, 69–74,

225 (Finnish Historical Society, *Studia Historica*, vol. 10 — Helsinki, 1979); Virtanen, "Problems of Research in Finnish Re-emigration," in Karni *et al.*, *Finnish Experience*, 205.

[3] For theories on the linguistic origins of Finnish, see Peter Hajdu, *Finno-Ugrian Languages and People*, 30–75 (London, 1975). See also John H. Wuorinen, *A History of Finland*, 7–20, 34–37, 47, 110–117, 138, 213–224 (New York, 1965); Eino Jutikkala and Kauko Pirinen, *A History of Finland*, 7–9, 187–192, 253 (Revised ed., New York, 1974).

[4] Wuorinen, *History of Finland*, 80–83, 180–193, 197, 259–263; Kero, *Migration from Finland*, 56–67; Stephan Thernstrom, ed., *Harvard Encyclopedia of American Ethnic Groups*, 364–366 (Cambridge, Mass., 1980); Timo Orta, "Finnish Emigration Prior to 1893," and A. William Hoglund, "No Land for Finns: Critics and Reformers View the Rural Exodus from Finland to America," both in Karni *et al.*, *Finnish Experience*, 21–35, 37–40, 43–48. Finnish America letters detailing reasons for emigrating have been collected but not extensively studied. Some 14,000 letters from the Etelä-Pohjanmaa, Satakunta, and Varsinais Suomi areas of Finland may be found on 57 reels of microfilm in IHRC. For samples, see Marsha Penti-Vidutis, "The America Letter: Immigrant Accounts of Life Overseas," in *Finnish Americana*, 1:22–40 (1978).

[5] John I. Kolehmainen, "Finnish Overseas Immigration from Arctic Norway and Russia," in *Agricultural History*, 19:225, 232 (October, 1945); Vilho Niitemaa, "The Finns in the Great Migratory

Movement from Europe to America 1865–1914,'' in Niitemaa, ed., *Old Friends — Strong Ties*, 70, 73 (Vaasa, Fin., 1976); Wuorinen, *History of Finland*, 192, 267, 270–272.

⁶ Wuorinen, *History of Finland*, 141–175, 202–213; Jutikkala and Pirinen, *History of Finland*, 200–206, 229–232; Kero, *Migration from Finland*, 65, 92; Carl Ross, *The Finn Factor in American Labor, Culture and Society*, 47–53, 141 (New York Mills, 1977).

⁷ For various figures, see Kero, *Migration from Finland*, 24, 26, 28, 36, 85, 94; Hans R. Wasastjerna, ed., *History of the Finns in Minnesota*, 55–59 (Duluth, 1957); U.S. Immigration Commission, *Immigrants in Industries*, 78:28 (61 Congress, 2 session, *Senate Documents*, no. 633 — serial 5677).

⁸ Kero, *Migration from Finland*, 91–96, 117; Kaups, in Karni *et al.*, *Finnish Experience*, 77, 79, 80; A. William Hoglund, *Finnish Immigrants in America 1880–1920*, 83–85 (Madison, Wis., 1960).

⁹ Arnold Alanen, ''In Search of the Pioneer Finnish Homesteader in America,'' 9, typed manuscript, to be published in *Finnish Americana*, vol. 4 (1981), copy in MEHP Papers; Ralph Andrist, ''A History of the Finns of Minnesota,'' 57, in Works Projects Administration, Writers' Project Papers, MHS, hereafter cited as WPA Papers; Carl Ross, ''The Feminist Dilemma in the Finnish Immigrant Community,'' in *Finnish Americana*, 1:74–83; Ross, *Finn Factor*, 22, 30–35, 139, 188; Hilja J. Karvonen, ''Three Proponents of Women's Rights in the Finnish-American Labor Movement from 1910–1930,'' in Tyomies Society, *For the Common Good: Finnish Immigrants and the Radical Response to Industrial America*, 195–216 (Superior, Wis., 1977). On the role of Finnish farm wives, see John I. Kolehmainen and George W. Hill, *Haven in the Woods: The Story of the Finns in Wisconsin*, 59 (Madison, Wis., 1951). For other sources on Finnish immigrant women, see ''Recapturing History: Immigrants and Their Daughters,''in IHRC, *Spectrum*, July, 1980, pp. 3–11; taped interviews with Minnesota Finnish foreign- and American-born women in Audio-Visual Library, MHS; and ''Notes and Interviews'' with Finns in WPA Papers.

¹⁰ Tauri Aaltio, ''A Survey of Emigration from Finland to the United States and Canada,'' in Ralph J. Jalkanen, *The Finns in North America: A Social Symposium*, 63–65 (Hancock, Mich., 1969); Kolehmainen, in *Agricultural History*, 19:227, 228, 230; Salomon Ilmonen, *Amerikan Suomalaisten Historia*, 2:19–24 (Jyväskylä, Fin., 1923); Niitemaa, in Niitemaa, ed., *Old Friends*, 73–75, 80, 148.

No published studies of American Lapps have been located. A copy of a four-page typed paper by Rudolph Johnson of Duluth entitled ''En Samisk Pioner,'' brought to my attention by Helen M. White, represented the sole scrap located. A copy is in MEHP Papers. On Lappish languages, see Hajdu, *Finno-Ugrian Languages and Peoples*, 203–213.

¹¹ On Renville County here and below, see Ilmonen, *Historia*, 2:25–28, 133, 143; Wasastjerna, *Finns in Minnesota*, 93–98; Franklyn Curtiss-Wedge, comp., *The History of Renville County*, 1:335, 336 (Chicago, 1916); Andrist, ''History,'' 24–43. Finns continued to arrive at Red Wing in the 1860s, and it is certain that at least 25 died in the cholera outbreak of 1866. See Ilmonen, *Historia*, 2:142. On Upper Michigan, especially Hancock, which served as a first stop after 1870 for many Minnesota Finns, see Armas K. E. Holmio, *Michiganin Suomalaisten Historia*, 124–138 (Hancock, Mich., 1967).

¹² On Wright County, see Wasastjerna, *Finns in Minnesota*, 98–102; Ilmonen, *Historia*, 2:27, 146–152, 156–175; Andrist, ''History,'' 32, 49, 52; Franklyn Curtiss-Wedge, *History of Wright County*, 2:703–707 (Chicago, 1915). Cokato's development was aided by its location on the Great Northern Railroad.

¹³ For Barberg's figures, see Ilmonen, *Historia*, 2:151. For difficulties between Finns and Irish there, see Andrist, ''History,'' 49–51, 56. On the geography of the area at the time of settlement and

the extent of Finnish holdings in 1897 and 1920, see W. R. Mead, ''A Finnish Settlement in Central Minnesota,'' in *Acta Geographica*, vol. 13, no. 3, pp. 3–16 (1954).

¹⁴ John I. Kolehmainen, ''The Finnish Pioneers of Minnesota,'' in *Minnesota History*, 25:320 (December, 1944); Ilmonen, *Historia*, 2:182–186; Douglas County Historical Society, *Douglas County Album of the Ages*, 248, 391–410 ([Alexandria, 1979?]). A partial translation of the reminiscences of Johan Piippo, one of the four, may be found in Wasastjerna, *Finns in Minnesota*, 115; they appeared originally in *Uusi Kotimaa* (Minneapolis), December 17, 1881. A 1939 interview with Johan's son, C. J., is in WPA Papers.

¹⁵ Reminiscences prepared by a descendant of Tuomas Autio, one of the early arrivals, may be found in *New York Mills: 75 Years of Progress, 1884–1959*, 20–22 (New York Mills, 1959). See also Ilmonen, *Historia*, 2:192–195; Finnish American Historical Society of the West, *The Pendleton Area Finns*, February, 1971, pp. 2, 6, 10; Wasastjerna, *Finns in Minnesota*, 144–163; John L. Harnsberger, ''Land Speculation, Promotion and Failure: The Northern Pacific Railroad, 1870–1873,'' in *Journal of the West*, 9:33–45 (January, 1970).

¹⁶ Here and two paragraphs below, see *New York Mills*, 9; Ilmonen, *Historia*, 2:195; Andrist, ''History,'' 70–77; Wasastjerna, *Finns in Minnesota*, 171–179, 192, 196, 197; Alvin H. Wilcox, *A Pioneer History of Becker County*, 671, 676 (St. Paul, 1907); Eugene V. Smalley, ''A Finnish Settlement in Minnesota,'' in *Northwest Magazine*, March, 1889, pp. 3–5. Johan L. Runeberg (1804–77), Johan V. Snellman (1806–81), and Elias Lönnrot (1802–84) were the enlightenment figures honored by these place names.

¹⁷ *History of the Sebeka Pioneers, 1882–1957*, [7, 18, 21] ([New York Mills?], 1957); Wasastjerna, *Finns in Minnesota*, 180, 187, 192; Andrist, ''History,'' 75. For memories of homesteading at New York Mills and Sebeka in the 1880s, see taped interview of Mrs. Emma Mattala by Robert Weber, 1956, in MHS. On the Sebeka Cooperative Creamery, see note 64, below.

¹⁸ Here and below, see Andrist, ''History,'' 74; Wasastjerna, *Finns in Minnesota*, 128, 149–152; A. William Hoglund, ''Finnish Immigrant Fiction and Its Evolution from Romanticism to Realism in the United States, 1885–1925,'' in University of Turku, Institute of General History, *Publications*, 9:16 (Vaasa, Fin., 1977); interview of Russell Parta by the author, December 28, 1978; MHS newspaper department records. On Adolph Lundquist, see Finnish-American Bicentennial Committee, *Finnish American Horizons*, 95–97 (New York Mills, 1976). For a listing of Finnish-American newspapers and periodicals, see John I. Kolehmainen, *The Finns in America: A Bibliographical Guide to Their History*, 75–97 (Hancock, Mich., 1947).

¹⁹ *Minneapolis Tribune*, August 4, 1979, pp. 1B, 4B.

²⁰ Here and below, see James B. Hedges, ''The Colonization Work of the Northern Pacific Railroad,'' in *Mississippi Valley Historical Review*, 13:320–322 (December, 1926); *St. Paul Daily Pioneer*, December 17, 1873; *Minneapolis Tribune*, January 13, 1874; Andrist, ''History,'' 68, 70; Wasastjerna, *Finns in Minnesota*, 136–143; David A. Walker, *Iron Frontier: The Discovery and Early Development of Minnesota's Three Ranges*, 248 (St. Paul, 1979); U.S., *Census, 1900, Population*, 1:762. On Crosby, see Paul Lekatz, ''Crosby Cooperatives,'' and ''Crosby Branches of the Socialist Party,'' 1938 — both in WPA Papers. For correspondence between Northern Pacific officials concerning Finnish immigrants, see Karl Möllersward to George B. Hibbard, June 2, 1873, and George Sheppard to Hibbard, July 5, 1873, roll 11, Northern Pacific Railway Company, Land Dept., Letters Received and Related Records, 1870–76, microfilm edition, MHS.

²¹ Kaups, in Karni *et al.*, *Finnish Experience*, 71.

²² Matti Kaups, ''Finns in Urban America: A View from Duluth,'' paper given at Finn Forum, 1979, Toronto, Ont., copy in MEHP

Papers; Matti Kaups, "Finnish Place Names As A Form of Ethnic Expression In the Middle West, 1880–1977," in *Finnish Americana*, 2:28 (1979); Andrist, "History," 84–90; J. C. Ryan, "The Duluth Lumber Industry," in Ryck Lydecker and Lawrence J. Sommer, eds., *Duluth Sketches of the Past: A Bicentennial Collection*, 167 (Duluth, 1976). The participation of Finns in the state's lumbering industry has not yet been studied. Certainly they were well represented, for example, in the St. Louis County Alien Registrations for the Virginia and Rainy Lake Lumber Company's large Cusson camp in 1918, present in the Minnesota Commission of Public Safety (PSC) Records in State Archives, MHS. It is also known that Finns continued to follow a farm-and-forest cycle, cutting timber on the farm plots they owned. See, for example, C. M. Oehler, *Time in the Timber*, 19, 24–27, 41, 53, 56 (St. Paul, 1948), for Finns in the Cusson camp in 1928; Bennett A. Beck, *Brief History of the Pioneers of the Cromwell, Minnesota, Area*, 29, 51, 91, 93, 117, 131, 142, 144 ([Cromwell?, 1962]), for farmer-lumberjacks; Benhart Rajala, *The Saga of Ivar Rajala* (Grand Rapids, 1972) on logging in the Bigfork River Valley. See also note 60, below.

[23] Andrist, "History," 84; Ilmonen, *Historia*, 3:185–190 (Hancock, Mich., 1926); Wasastjerna, *Finns in Minnesota*, 624, 630, 634, 644; Beck, *Pioneers of Cromwell*, 24, 29, 37, 39, 50–53, 56, 67, 71, 89–124, 131, 142, 144; Wuorinen, *History of Finland*, 267; U.S., *Census*, 1900, *Population*, 1:762; 1910, 2:998; 1920, 3:521.

[24] Here and below, see Walter O'Meara, *We Made It Through the Winter: A Memoir of Northern Minnesota Boyhood*, 14, 15 (St. Paul, 1974). On long-lasting boardinghouses in Chisholm and Duluth, see interview of Veda Ponikvar by Marjorie Hoover, February 10, 1981, notes in MEHP Papers; *Duluth Herald*, January 25–29, 1954, p. 1.

[25] Stewart H. Holbrook, *Burning an Empire: The Story of American Forest Fires*, 33–39 (New York, 1943); Wasastjerna, *Finns in Minnesota*, 635–653; Leonard C. Kercher, Vant W. Kebker, and Wilfred C. Leland, Jr., *Consumers' Cooperatives in the North Central States*, 219–238 (Minneapolis, 1941); Florence E. Parker, *The First 125 Years: A History of Distributive and Service Cooperation in the United States, 1829–1954*, 391 (Superior, Wis., 1956).

[26] Kaups, in Karni et al., *Finnish Experience*, 55–59; Neil Betten, "The Origins of Ethnic Radicalism in Northern Minnesota, 1900–1920," in *International Migration Review*, 4:44–55 (Spring, 1970); Ross, *Finn Factor*, 106–118. On the strikes, see note 58, below, and Neil Betten, "Riot, Revolution, Repression in the Iron Range Strike of 1916," in *Minnesota History*, 41:82–93 (Summer, 1968).

[27] Walker, *Iron Frontier*, 58, 70, 105; Ilmonen, *Historia*, 3:166–171, 182; Wasastjerna, *Finns in Minnesota*, 369, 415, 458, 481, 506; Kaups, in Karni et al., *Finnish Experience*, 73, 74. The largest numbers of Finns on the Mesabi in 1905 resided in Chisholm, Virginia, Hibbing, Eveleth, Sparta, Biwabik, Buhl, Nashwauk, and Mountain Iron; the six major Mesabi groups emigrated from Finland, the Austro-Hungarian Empire, Sweden, Canada, Italy, and Norway. See Kaups, in Karni et al., *Finnish Experience*, 75, 77.

[28] Oskar Pohjonen biography, in E. A. Aaltio, *Minnesotan Suomalaisia: Liikemiehiä-Lakimiehiä-Lääkäreitä*, 11–14 (Vammala, Fin., 1953); Kaups, in Karni et al., *Finnish Experience*, 72, 73, 77, 78.

[29] A. William Hoglund, "Flight from Industry: Finns and Farms in America," in *Finnish Americana*, 1:5–9 (1978); Kolehmainen and Hill, *Haven in the Woods*, 53; Alanen, "Pioneer Finnish Homesteader," 6, 12, 12A. The extent to which the strikes of 1907 and 1916 affected the growth of rural areas near the Minnesota ranges has yet to be examined in detail. Landis saw the 1907 strike as one of the factors in the rise of St. Louis County's rural population from 20,531 to 47,211 between 1900 and 1910. Karni considered it "a significant influence" in the increase of inhabitants in largely Finnish Alango Township from 32 in 1905 to 335 in 1910. See Paul H. Landis, *Three Iron Mining Towns: A Study in Cultural Change*, 50 (Ann Arbor, 1938); Michael G. Karni, "The Founding of the Finnish Socialist Federation and the Minnesota Strike of 1907," in *For the Common Good*, 82.

[30] Henry Antilla interview, October 12, 1938, transcript in WPA Papers; Wasastjerna, *Finns in Minnesota*, 556. According to the latter, the four men were Jack Latikka, Kusti Mäki, Henry Ronback, and one Pekkola.

[31] Here and below, see *Uusi Kotimaa*, April 27, 1893; Centennial History Committee, *One Hundred Years In Pine County*, 52–54, 61 ([Pine City?], 1949); John Wargelin, *The Americanization of the Finns*, 74 (Hancock, Mich., 1924); Wasastjerna, *Finns in Minnesota*, 200, 621, 628; Hoglund, in *Finnish Americana*, 1:2; Aaltio, *Minnesotan Suomalaisia*, 22–24. See also Suomi Historical Committee, *50 Years and More of Suomi*, [4], [12] (Suomi, [1967?]), which included numerous Finnish family histories. Other memories of growing up on subsistence homesteads were preserved in taped interviews of Clifford E. Ahlgren (Brimson) by Newell Searle, 1976; of Helmi J. Gawboy, Emily S. Maki, and Helmi S. Dyhn (all near Ely) by Lynn Laitala, 1975, 1976, 1977 — all in MHS. From 1900 to 1920 Finns also moved from the iron ranges to farms in Wisconsin; see Kolehmainen and Hill, *Haven in the Woods*, 49–53, 58, 65n, 81, 86.

[32] On Finn farming settlements in St. Louis County, see Ilmonen, *Historia*, 3:173, 175, 180; Eino M. Norha, *Embarrass Township in Historia* (Embarrass, 1960); Henry and Nancy Raihala, comps., *Floodwood Diamond Jubilee 1893–1968* (Floodwood, 1968). Eugene Van Cleef, "The Finnish Farmer of Northeastern Minnesota," in *Northland Farmer and Dairyman*, September, 1917, p. 5, offered an idealized view of Palo-Markham Finn farms, counterbalanced by Irja W. Laaksonen Beckman, "Echoes from the Past," typed manuscript, in MHS, a reminiscence of farming near Virginia. See also Finnish Activities file, Embarrass, 1936; "Brief Resume of the Early History of Brimson-Fairbanks Area," in *Erämaan Oras*, June, 1938, pp. 3–5; Vermilion Pioneer Assn., "History of Pioneer Days," pp. 1–5, and "History of Vermilion Lake Township," pp. 7–10, in *Reunion Programs*, 1938, 1939, respectively; "Pioneer of the Wilderness — Alango-Sturgeon-Field," 1938, pp. 2–5 — all in St. Louis County Historical Collection, Northeast Minnesota Historical Center, Duluth.

[33] Andrist, "History," 85; Michael Karni and Robert Levin, "Northwoods Vernacular Architecture: Finnish Log Building in Minnesota," and Karni, "Honey-heat and Healing Vapors," in *Northwest Architect*, 36:92–99, 37:69, 76–79, 92 (May–June, 1972, March–April, 1973); Cotton Mather and Matti Kaups, "The Finnish Sauna: A Cultural Index to Settlement," in Association of American Geographers, *Annals*, 53:494–504 (December, 1963); Alanen, "Pioneer Finnish Homesteaders," 13, 16. Of the Finn homesteads in Salo Township, 53% had saunas within five to seven years after the filing of the initial claim, according to Alanen, 12A.

[34] For an examination of the theory of geographical determinism, see Matti Kaups, "Patterns of Finnish Settlement in the Lake Superior Region," in *Michigan Academician*, 3:77–91 (Winter, 1971). See also Wasastjerna, *Finns in Minnesota*, 540–542; Hoglund, in *Finnish Americana*, 1:11; interview of Mrs. Carl Hultkrantz by William Liukkonen and Runar Gustafson, January 5, 1939, in WPA Papers; Kalevi Rikkinen, *Kalevala, Minnesota: Agricultural Geography in Transition*, 12–17 (Helsinki, 1979).

[35] Karni, in *For the Common Good*, 82; Hoglund, in *Finnish Americana*, 1:15–17.

[36] Here and three paragraphs below, see Ilmonen, *Historia*, 3:184; Darrell H. Davis, "The Finland Community, Minnesota," in *Geographical Review*, 25:382–394 (July, 1935); John R. Borchert, *A Quarter-Century of Change In The Finland Community of Northeastern Minnesota*, [9–15] (University of Minnesota Social Sciences Trust Fund, *Publication no. 2* — Duluth, 1960); Finland Schools

Reunion Committee, *Keeping Our Heritage: Finland Minnesota, 1895–1976,* 3, 7–28, 69, 99, 146–148 (Finland, 1976).

[37] On St. Urho's Day, see Finland Schools, *Keeping Our Heritage,* 99; *Midland Cooperator* (Superior, Wis.), March 9, 1970, p. 1, 12, March 5, 1973, p. 12; *St. Paul Pioneer Press,* March 13, 1978, p. 4; *Duluth News-Tribune,* March 19, 1978, p. 1B. For other folklore, see Marjorie Edgar, "Finnish Charms and Folk Songs in Minnesota," in *Minnesota History,* 17:406–410 (December, 1936).

[38] Here and below, see Andrist, "History," 3, 36, 57, 102; A. William Hoglund, "Breaking with Religious Tradition: Finnish Immigrant Workers and the Church, 1890–1915," in *For the Common Good,* 23, 45–59; Douglas J. Ollila, Jr., "The Suomi Synod: 1890–1920," in Ralph J. Jalkanen, ed., *The Faith of the Finns: Historical Perspectives on the Finnish Lutheran Church in America,* 167, 254 (East Lansing, Mich., 1972); Ollila, "The Finnish-American Church Organizations," in Niitemaa, ed., *Old Friends,* 146; Kero, *Migration from Finland,* 48–55, 61.

[39] Ollila, in Niitemaa, ed., *Old Friends,* 152, 162; Hoglund, *Finnish Immigrants,* 42.

[40] Wasastjerna, *Finns in Minnesota,* 96–98, 104, 116; Tom Hiltunen, ed., *Finnish Pioneer Day Memorial Program,* 21 (Duluth, 1949); Ilmonen, *Historia,* 2:138; Neil A. Markus, "Areal Patterns of Religious Denominationalism in Minnesota 1950," 99, master's thesis, University of Minnesota, 1961. Microfilm copies of the records of the New York Mills Apostolic Church are in IHRC.

[41] U.S. Census Bureau, *Special Reports, Religious Bodies: 1926,* 2:827; Douglas J. Ollila, "The Finnish American Experience," in Anthony V. Codianni, comp., *American Ethnic Profiles: Background Papers,* 4 (Minneapolis, 1978); interview of Rev. George Wilson, Apostolic Lutheran Church, New York Mills, by the author, December 27, 1978; Uuras Saarnivaara, *The History of the Laestadian or Apostolic-Lutheran Movement in America* (Ironwood, Mich., 1947). On the hymns and songs preserved and adapted by congregations at Cokato, Kettle River, and Crystal, see Kenneth A. Swanson, "Music of Two Finnish Apostolic Lutheran Groups in Minnesota," in Johannes Riedel, ed., *Student Musicologists at Minnesota,* 4:1–36 (1970–71).

[42] Ollila, in Niitemaa, ed., *Old Friends,* 153, 156–158; Ollila, in Jalkanen, ed., *Faith of the Finns,* 158–172; J. E. Nopola, *Our Threescore Years: A Brief History of the National Evangelical Lutheran Church,* 1–3 (Ironwood, Mich., 1958).

[43] U.S. Census Bureau, *Religious Bodies: 1926,* 2:806, 822.

[44] Zion Lutheran Church, *Faith of Our Fathers, 60th Anniversary, 1894–1954* (Virginia, 1954). The records of the Virginia church, as well as those of several other Minnesota Suomi Synod congregations collected by the University of Turku project, are in IHRC.

[45] Ollila, in Niitemaa, ed., *Old Friends,* 170.

[46] Charles N. Pace, ed., *Our Fathers Built: A Century of Minnesota Methodism,* 131–134 (Minneapolis, [1952?]); Wasastjerna, *Finns in Minnesota,* 496; Ollila, in Niitemaa, ed., *Old Friends,* 160; Arvid M. Steece, "A Century of Minnesota Congregationalism," 336–338, Ph.D. thesis, Harvard University, 1957; *Congregational Year-book, 1928,* 162–164 (New York, 1928); interview of Rev. Charles Saarion by the author, February 20, 1981. Rev. Saarion was a minister in the Finnish Evangelical Mission Society before its merger with the Congregational church in the late 1950s. "Palvelija," the congregational newsletter of the Evangelical Mission Society, still appeared monthly in 1980 in *Amerikan Uutiset.*

Pentecostal and Baptist groups have also found support particularly in Duluth, where the Baptists were active among Swede-Finns; Wasastjerna, 221. Very few Finns have become Roman Catholics except for those converted as a result of marriage. The records of Blessed Sacrament Church, Hibbing, show that out of a total membership of 5,454 in 1923, only four were second-generation Finns. According to interview of Father Peter Pritza of St. Michael's Orthodox Church, Hibbing, by the author, December 20, 1979, notes in MEHP Papers, a similar situation prevailed in 1979. See George A. Gallik, *Seventy-fifth Anniversary of Blessed Sacrament Parish, Hibbing, 1894–1969,* 24 ([Hibbing, 1969]); Wasastjerna, *Finns in Minnesota,* 383, 384.

[47] Ollila, in Niitemaa, ed., *Old Friends,* 160; Wasastjerna, *Finns in Minnesota,* 383, 426, 561. The success of the Unitarians may perhaps be attributed to the alienation of miners during the labor strife on the ranges when many felt the established churches had sided with the mining companies. One historian suggested that many of the Unitarians were former Finnish radicals and agnostics who found this church most to their liking; Walfrid J. Jokinen, "The Finns in Minnesota: A Sociological Interpretation," 92, master's thesis, Louisiana State University, 1955.

[48] Immigration Commission, *Immigrants in Industries,* 78:342; Timothy L. Smith, "Religious Denominations as Ethnic Communities: A Regional Case Study," in *Church History,* 25:210 (June, 1966); Landis, *Three Iron Mining Towns,* 62–68.

[49] Here and below, see John I. Kolehmainen, "Finnish Temperance Societies in Minnesota," in *Minnesota History,* 22:391, 397, 402 (December, 1941); Michael G. Karni, "The Finnish Temperance Movement in Minnesota," in *Range History,* December, 1977, pp. 1–3, March, 1978, p. 7; Arthur E. Puotinen, *Finnish Radicals and Religion in Midwestern Mining Towns 1865–1914,* 154 (New York, 1979); John Syrjamaki, "Mesabi Communities: A Study of Their Development," 300, Ph.D. thesis, Yale University, 1940; *History of the Sixty Years of Valontuote Temperance Society,* 14 (Virginia, 1953). See also the records of societies in Tower-Soudan (1886–1925), Ely (1894–1942), Sparta and Gilbert (1897–1921), and Virginia (1893–1968), as well as Edith Koivisto, "Lupaus: Hibbingin Suomalaisen Raittiusliikkeen Historia," a history of the Hibbing society from 1895 to 1957, unpublished typescript — all in IHRC. Some of these records are on microfilm.

[50] Here and below, see K. Marianne Wargelin-Brown, "A Closer Look at Finnish-American Immigrant Women's Issues: 1890–1910," 2–4, 6, a paper presented at Finn Forum, 1979; Karni, in *Range History,* 3:7; Holmio, *Michiganin Suomalaisten Historia,* 143; *Juhlajulkaisu: Suomalaisen Kansallis-Raittius-Veljeysseuran 25-vuotisen toiminnan muistoksi,* 164–166, 243 (Ishpeming, Mich., 1912).

[51] Here and two paragraphs below, see Puotinen, *Finnish Radicals,* 148, 153–156; Kolehmainen, in *Minnesota History,* 22:395, 397–403; John I. Kolehmainen, *The Finns in America: A Students' Guide to Localized History,* 20 (New York, 1968); *Juhlajulkaisu,* 19; Pohjan Leimu Temperance Society (Soudan), Minutes, May 30, 1886, in IHRC. For memories of temperance society activities in Ely, see taped interview of Ida P. Erickson by Lynn Laitala, 1976, in MHS.

[52] Taped interview in Finnish of Fred Torma by Auvo Kostiainen, March 24, 1974, in IHRC, partial translation by Timo Riippa in MEHP Papers; Hyman Berman, "Education for Work and Labor Solidarity: The Immigrant Miners and Radicalism on the Mesabi Range," 20–22, typed paper, 1963, copy in MHS; Hoglund, *Finnish Immigrants,* 95–98; Kolehmainen, in *Minnesota History,* 22:391; Reino Kero, "Finnish Immigrant Culture in America," in Niitemaa, ed., *Old Friends,* 118; Syrjamaki, "Mesabi Communities," 303; Kolehmainen, *Finns in America,* 21; Elis Sulkanen, *Amerikan Suomalaisen Työväenliikkeen Historia,* 455 (Fitchburg, Mass., 1951). In the Rocky Mountain states over 50 temperance societies became Socialist chapters; see Salomon Ilmonen, *Amerikan Suomalaisten Sivistyshistoria,* 1:132 (Hancock, Mich., 1930). On the Finnish-American temperance movement as a whole, see *Juhlajulkaisu,* 5–317.

[53] Reino Kero, "The Roots of Finnish-American Left-Wing Radi-

calism," in University of Turku, Institute of General History, *Publications*, 5:45–55 (Turku, Fin., 1973); Wuorinen, *History of Finland*, 198–201; Berman, "Education for Work," 19; Puotinen, *Finnish Radicals*, 167. For an alternative view, see Michael G. Karni, "Yhteishyvä — or, For the Common Good: Finnish Radicalism in the Western Great Lakes Region, 1900–1940," 92–108, Ph.D. thesis, University of Minnesota, 1975.

Among the Minnesota Socialist leaders was Dr. Antero F. Tanner, who founded the first Socialist local in the U.S. at Rockport, Mass., and served as the first editor of the newspaper *American Työmies* in 1900. He moved to Ely, where he built and operated a hospital and remained for the rest of his life. An early apostle of Socialism in both Finland and the U.S., he made numerous speaking tours among Finnish communities in the East and Midwest. A prestigious woman leader was Ida Pasanen, one of the founders of the Finnish Socialist Federation, who lived in Cloquet. Her daughter, Viena Johnson Hendrickson, continued in her mother's footsteps as an advocate of women's rights; taped interviews of Hendrickson by Gloria Thompson, 1972, in MHS, and by Timothy Madigan, 1973, in Northwest Minnesota Historical Center, Moorhead, transcript in MHS. On Tanner and Pasanen, see Auvo Kostiainen, "Finnish-American Workmen's Associations," in Niitemaa, ed., *Old Friends*, 208; Michael G. Karni, "The Founding of the Finnish Socialist Federation," and P. George Hummasti, "Finnish-American Working Class Newspapers, 1900–1921," both in *For the Common Good*, 68–70, 168; Ross, *Finn Factor*, 60; Ross, in *Finnish Americana*, 1:77–79.

[54] Berman, "Education for Work," 7–19; George O. Virtue, *The Minnesota Iron Ranges*, 346–353 (U.S. Bureau of Labor, *Bulletin*, no. 84 — Washington, D.C., 1909).

[55] *Minutes, Resolutions and Proceedings of the Hibbing Convention of the Finnish Socialist Federation* (Hancock, Mich., 1907); Berman, "Education for Work," 18, 25, 34; Kostiainen, in Niitemaa, ed., *Old Friends*, 212, 214; Ross, *Finn Factor*, 67–70; Wasastjerna, *Finns in Minnesota*, 226; Sulkanen, *Työväen Historia*, 91; *Suomalaisten sosialistiosastojen pöytäkirja 1912*, 41 (Fitchburg, Mass., [1913]). Finnish Socialist Federation, National Executive Committee, Minutes, 1915–25, as well as published minutes of national and district conventions, 1906–21, may be found in IHRC.

[56] Taped interview of Aune Helenius by Irene Paull, 1968, in MHS; Douglas J. Ollila, Jr., "The Work People's College," in *For the Common Good*, 90–113; Ollila, "From Socialism to Industrial Unionism (IWW)," in Karni *et al.*, *Finnish Experience*, 159–164, 167, 169, 184; Auvo Kostiainen, "Marx vs. Christ: Finnish Socialists Capture the People's College and Theological Seminary," 1–28, typed paper, 1973–74, in IHRC, which also holds the school's records for the entire period of its operation.

[57] Hoglund, *Finnish Immigrants*, 98; taped interview of Ero Koski by Irene Paull, 1968, MHS; Jokinen, "Finns in the United States," 150. The estimate appeared in John Wiita, "Cultural Life of Finnish American Labor Movement," 2, in John Wiita Papers, IHRC. The activities of various Socialist clubs in Hibbing (1902–61), Virginia (1931–51), and Nashwauk (1909–37) may be traced in their records in the Finnish language in MHS. See also taped interview of Lauri Lemberg by Helen M. White, 1969, in MHS.

[58] On the 1907 strike and its effects, see Betten, in *Minnesota History*, 40:343; Michael M. Passi, "Introduction," and Karni, in *For the Common Good*, 16, 78–84; Edward Marolt, "The Development of Labor Unionism in the Iron Mining Industry of the Virginia-Eveleth District," 49–51, 57, master's thesis, University of Minnesota, 1969. For examinations of Socialist and church Finn attitudes, see Arthur E. Puotinen, "Ameliorative Factors in the Suomi Synod Socialist Movement Conflict," and Jacob W. Heikkinen, "Theological Insights," both in Jalkanen, ed., *Faith of the Finns*, 227–233, 272. For the so-called Judas Resolution condemning the Socialists

by a church-led group in Eveleth, see Karni, in *For the Common Good*, 80. On blacklisting, see taped interview of John T. Bernard by Irene Paull, 1969, in MHS.

[59] Auvo Kostiainen, *The Forging of Finnish-American Communism, 1917–1924*, 37–43 (University of Turku, *Migration Studies C4* — Turku, Fin., 1978); Douglas Ollila, Jr., "A Time of Glory: Finnish American Radical Industrial Unionism, 1914–1917," in University of Turku, Institute of General History, *Publications*, 9:32; Hummasti, in *For the Common Good*, 182–184, 186, 189. MHS has a full file of *Industrialisti*. See also taped interviews of Ivor Vapaa, its editor, by Helen M. White, 1968, and of Samuel E. Swanson of Ely by Jack Spiese, 1967, original at Pennsylvania State University, typed copy in MHS; as well as the Workers Socialist Publishing Company Papers, 1910–57, MHS.

[60] Andrist, "History," 152; Industrial Workers of the World, *The I.W.W. Its First Seventy Years (1905–1975)*, 77, 101–105 (Chicago, 1976); John E. Haynes, "Revolt of the 'Timber Beasts': IWW Lumber Strike in Minnesota," in *Minnesota History*, 42:163–174 (Spring, 1971). Work in the camps and the activities of the IWW were touched on in taped interviews of Martin Kuusisto and Ilmar Koivunen by Irene Paull, 1968; of Nick Kuitunen by Lynn Laitala, 1975; of John Ollila, 1976, and William Kaukola, 1977, by Robert Wheeler; and of Swanson, 1967 — all in MHS.

[61] Berman, "Education for Work," 57–60. For the quotations below, see *Duluth News-Tribune*, September 20, 1918, p. 8.

[62] Haynes, in *Minnesota History*, 42:174; Ross, *Finn Factor*, 145–164; Donald G. Sofchalk, "Organized Labor and the Iron Ore Miners of Northern Minnesota, 1907–1936," in *Labor History*, 12:225–242 (Spring, 1971); Kostiainen, *Finnish-American Communism*, 120–127; Ollila, in Karni *et al.*, *Finnish Experience*, 156–171. On Farmer-Labor politics and Finns in St. Louis County, see Millard L. Gieske, *Minnesota Farmer-Laborism: The Third Party Alternative*, 215, 272, 286, 298, 299, 314, 321 (Minneapolis, 1979). Hall, general secretary of the Communist party U.S.A. since 1959, was born Arvo Kusta Halberg near Virginia in 1910, the son of a blacklisted Finnish miner. He legally changed his name to Hall in the 1930s and was repeatedly a candidate for president on the Communist ticket. Charles Moritz, ed., *Current Biography Yearbook 1973*, 165–168 (New York, 1973).

[63] Michael Karni, "Struggle on the Cooperative Front," in Karni *et al.*, *Finnish Experience*, 188–190; Kercher *et al.*, *Consumers' Cooperatives*, 15, 28, 31; Kolehmainen and Hill, *Haven in the Woods*, 137.

[64] *Sampo* was named for a "magic mill" in the *Kalevala*. See *Forty Years of Community Building with the Farmers' Co-operative Sampo, Menahga*, 1 (Superior, Wis., 1943); "History of Sebeka Cooperative Creamery Association," typed manuscript, 1938, in MHS. Records of the Sebeka creamery may be found in IHRC.

[65] Arnold Alanen, "The Development and Distribution of Finnish Consumers' Cooperatives in Michigan, Minnesota and Wisconsin, 1903–1973," in Karni *et al.*, *Finnish Experience*, 110–112n; Andrist, "History," 160–164; Howard H. Turner, *Case Studies of Consumers' Cooperatives: Successful Cooperatives Started by Finnish Groups in the United States*, 166–171, 314 (New York, 1941); Torma interview, March 24, 1974, and "Minnesota Memories Visits the Range," in *Scattered Seeds*, vol. 2, no. 1, pp. 34–36 (1974); Walter Kykyri, "Co-op Store," Gilbert, 1938, in WPA Papers; Kercher *et al.*, *Consumers' Cooperatives*, 219, 251, 281, 293; Wasastjerna, *Finns in Minnesota*, 482, 542; Virginia Co-operative Society, *The Story of Virginia Co-operative Society Through 30 Years of Progress*, 5–11 (Virginia, 1939); U.S., *Census*, 1930, *Retail Distribution*, 1:1333.

[66] Alanen, in *Finnish Experience*, 114–117; Walfrid J. Jokinen, "The Finnish Cooperative Movement," in Niitemaa, ed., University of Turku, Institute of General History, *Publications Nr 7*, 10–17

(Vammala, Fin., 1975). See also Central Cooperatives, Inc., *1961 Year Book*, 5 (Superior, Wis., 1961); Central's sales from 1917 through 1960 and other financial data are summarized on p. 48; its records (1917–62) are in IHRC.

[67] Karni, in Karni *et al.*, *Finnish Experience*, 191–201; Parker, *First 125 Years*, 117–124; taped interviews of Jacob (Jack) Anderson, Anton Antilla, Sr., and Walter Harju by Irene Paull, 1968, MHS. The three basic Rochdale principles were (1) open and voluntary membership; (2) democratic control; each member has only one vote no matter how many shares he owns; (3) limited interest rate on capital and return of surplus earnings to patrons in proportion to patronage. Wilfrid J. Jokinen, "Economic Activities of Finns in the United States," in Niitemaa, ed., *Old Friends*, 113. For a respected text, see V. S. Alanne, *Fundamentals of Consumer Cooperation* (8th Revised ed., Superior, Wis., 1946).

[68] Andrist, "History," 158; Torma interview, March 24, 1974; Parker, *First 125 Years*, 201–203; Turner, *Case Studies*, 195. On the guilds, see Maiju Nurmi, ed., *10th Anniversary Album: A History of the Northern States Women's Co-operative Guild*, [5–9] (Superior, Wis., 1939); Sylvia Torma Silvola, "Virginia: A City of Co-operatives," 7–9, typed manuscript, ca. 1958, in Silvola Family Papers, in IHRC, and the records of the Home Coop Club, Inc., Nashwauk, 1909–65, in MHS.

[69] Jokinen, in Niitemaa, ed., *Old Friends*, 107–110; Parker, *First 125 Years*, 202; Midland Cooperatives, Inc., *Fifty Years of Service*, 32 ([Minneapolis, 1976]); Alanen, in Karni *et al.*, *Finnish Experience*, 121–129. The quotation below appears in Alanen, 130. Andrist, "History," 170–185, outlined Finns' work in the development of federations as well as oil, fire insurance, and other co-op groups in Minnesota. The records of the Range Cooperative Federation, Virginia, 1929–32, may be consulted in MHS.

[70] Hoglund, *Finnish Immigrants*, 141–143; Jaakko Paavolainen, "First Generation Finnish-Americans Serve the United States," and John I. Kolehmainen, "Americanization and the Search for Identity," both in Niitemaa, ed., *Old Friends*, 250, 271; David T. Halkola, "Kielikysymys: The Language Problem in the Suomi-Synod," in Jalkanen, ed., *Faith of the Finns*, 278; Evert Määttälä, *Miksi Tahdon Olla Suomalainen?*, 4 (Hancock, Mich., 1915); Wargelin, *Americanization of the Finns*, 144–146; A. R–hti, "Lapset Kesäkouluun," *Kirkollinen Kalenteri, 1918*, 106 (Hancock, Mich., 1917).

[71] E. A. Freeman to H. W. Libby, April 8, 1918, in Speakers Bureau, PSC Records; "The Speak English Movement in the St. Louis Co. Rural Schools," in *Koti-Home*, September, 1922, p. 9. For the quotation below, see Wargelin, *Americanization of the Finns*, 146.

[72] Halkola, in Jalkanen, ed., *Faith of the Finns*, 279–290.

[73] Turner, *Case Studies*, 195. See also Jokinen, in Niitemaa, ed., *Old Friends*, 110.

[74] Leslie Leinonen, "The Influence of English on the Finnish Spoken in Rural Northern Minnesota," 51, master's thesis, University of Minnesota, 1940; Andrist, "History," 111–113; Reino Virtanen, "The Finnish Language in America," in *Scandinavian Studies*, 51:152–160 (1979). See also Kaups, and Marianne Blomqvist, "Finland-Swedish Immigrants: Lexical Innovation in Their Mother Tongue as a Result of Bilingualism," both in *Finnish Americana*, 2:28–65; Donald W. Larmouth, "Finnish Surname Change in Northern Minnesota," in *American Speech*, 40:31–37 (February, 1967).

[75] Joshua A. Fishman *et al.*, *Language Loyalty in the United States*, 42, 44, 46 (The Hague, 1966).

[76] Virtue, *Minnesota Iron Ranges*, 348; Hoglund, *Finnish Immigrants*, 113–120. As this chapter was being completed in 1981, naturalization records were beginning to come into the Minnesota State Archives; those for St. Louis County alone ran to hundreds of volumes — an as yet largely untapped resource for immigration

historians. An analysis of some Mesabi Range naturalization records for five-year periods from 1915–35 revealed that Finns were exceeded only by Austro-Hungarians in the numbers naturalized; see Syrjamaki, "Mesabi Communities," 407.

[77] Wasastjerna, *Finns in Minnesota*, 131, 181, 327; Paavolainen, in Niitemaa, ed., *Old Friends*, 248–255; O. J. Larson to John S. Pardee, July 15, 1917, in PSC Records; Wargelin, *Americanization of the Finns*, 171, 176; Kolehmainen, *Finns in America*, 34.

Finns in the Minnesota legislature after John Saari (1905–08) included in the 1930s and 1940s Senator Arvid Ruotsinoja and Representatives John Antila, J. William Huhtala, and George Sahlman; in the 1940s and overlapping the 1950s Senators J. William Huhtala and Henry W. Mattson, Representatives Richard Silvola, J. A. "Turp" Anderson, and R. R. Ryti; in the 1960s Representatives George W. Karvonen, Birger Nurminen, and Duane Rappana; in the 1970s Representatives William R. Ojala, Marvin Ketola, and Arlene I. Lehto. Mrs. Lehto remained in office in 1981.

[78] Kostiainen, "The Finns and the Crisis Over 'Bolshevization' in the Worker's Party, 1924–25," in Karni *et al.*, *Finnish Experience*, 171–185.

[79] Ross, *Finn Factor*, 168; Kolehmainen, in Niitemaa, ed., *Old Friends*, 271, 273, 275–278. On intermarriage in Duluth, see Kaups, "Finns in Urban America," 17.

[80] John E. Sala, "History of the Organizations and Cultural Activities of the Finnish People in Minneapolis," 3, in WPA Papers; Wasastjerna, *Finns in Minnesota*, 119–121, 125; interview of Rev. Chester R. Heikkinen by the author, March, 1973, notes in MEHP Papers; Sulkanen, *Työväen Historia*, 445. In August, 1881, *Uusi Kotimaa* estimated the Minneapolis Finnish population at about 200, but the following December it noted only 40 Finns living in the city, most of them single. At the turn of the century there were perhaps 1,000 in Minneapolis; Wasastjerna, 119.

[81] Ilmonen, *Historia*, 2:179; U.S., *Census*, 1970, *Population*, vol. 1, part 25, pp. 514, 515; *Minneapolis Star*, March 22, 1972, p. 1B. Over the years St. Paul's Finnish population has remained small; only about 97 foreign born at most were counted by census takers in the 20th century. See Wasastjerna, *Finns in Minnesota*, 129; Table 15.3.

[82] Information on the Finnish churches was provided to the author by Rev. Kenneth Hendrickson of Plymouth Apostolic Lutheran Church, February 26, 1981; Rev. Vernon P. Gundermann of New Hope Beautiful Savior Lutheran Church, February 27, 1981; Rev. Heikkinen, former pastor of Morgan Avenue Lutheran Church, November 28, 1980. The Plymouth congregation had 650 baptized members, Beautiful Savior 1,015, and Morgan Avenue Lutheran 170 in February, 1981.

[83] Wasastjerna, *Finns in Minnesota*, 470–473; St. Louis County Rural Schools Extension Department, *Laskiainen Year Book 1937*, 2–12 (n.p., 1937); *Midland Cooperator*, February 23, 1981, p. 4. For an example of midsummer festivals, which the Minnesota Finnish-American Historical Society sponsored and which rotated among various cities where Finns lived, see *Juhannusjuhla: 66th Mid-Summer Festival, Virginia, June 21, 22, 1969*, pamphlet in MEHP Papers. These society-sponsored festivals ended in the mid-1970s. By then many communities were holding their own celebrations. See also "Minnesota Memories Visits the Range," in *Scattered Seeds*, vol. 2, no. 1, pp. 24–36 (1974).

[84] Here and below, see Ross, *Finn Factor*, 83; Wasastjerna, *Finns in Minnesota*, 272–277, 467; Folke W. Sandstrom, ed., *Kalevainen 1898–1977*, 35 (New York Mills, 1977). For biographical sketches of members, see Aaltio, *Minnesotan Suomalaisia*.

[85] Here and below, see Wasastjerna, *Finns in Minnesota*, 278, 283, 286, 289–293; interviews by the author of Lillian Mikkola, February 12, 1979, Matti Mannoja, February 14, 1979, and Dr. Donald W. Nelson, March 2, 1981. In 1980 the Minnesota Finnish-

American Historical Society received a grant from the MHS to support the collection of written and taped histories of Minnesota families of Finnish-American descent; Minnesota Finnish-American Historical Society, *Seuranlehti*, Winter, 1980, p. 1.

[86] Interview of Darryl Nicholson of Finn Creek by the author, March 13, 1979. See also *Minneapolis Sunday Tribune*, June 11, 1978, pp. 13F, 20F; *Midland Cooperator*, July 3, 1978, p. 7.

[87] Ross, *Finn Factor*, 191–193. Some scholars feel that Finnish-American historiography of the 1970s was biased, since so much of it dealt with Finnish-American political radicalism. Since 1978 Camp Salolampi, a two-week summer camp for young people from 8 to 18, has been held in northern Minnesota under the auspices of the Language Village Program of Concordia College, Moorhead. Out of 52 campers in 1980, 34 were from Minnesota; *Salolampi Sanomat*, 2:4 (1981); *Viltis: A Magazine of Folklore and Folkdance*, May, 1978, p. 4.

SWEDE-FINNS — *Reference notes*

[1] Wuorinen, *History of Finland*, 7–11; Anders M. Myhrman, *Finlandssvenskar i Amerika*, 17 (Helsingfors, Fin., 1972); *Finland in Figures 1979*, 4; Anders Myhrman, "The Effects of Finland-Swedish Emigration upon the Homeland," in *Swedish Pioneer Historical Quarterly*, 31:197 (July, 1980); Tom Sandlund, "Patterns and Reasons in Emigration of Swedish Finns," paper given at Finn Forum, 1979.

[2] Kaups, in *Finnish Experience*, 76; Kero, *Migration from Finland*, 19, 91–93, 117–127, 206; Carl J. Silfversten, *Finlandssvenskarna i Amerika*, 76–83 (Duluth, 1931). See also Willcox, ed., *International Migrations*, 1:775–782.

[3] Myhrman, in Niitemaa, ed., *Old Friends*, 182–185; Johannes Näse, "Finlandssvenskarna i Amerika," in *Arkiv för Svenska Osterbotten*, 1:260 (Vaasa, Fin., 1922); Myhrman, *Finlandssvenskar*, 260.

[4] Anders M. Myhrman, "The Finland-Swedes in Duluth, Minnesota," in *Swedish Pioneer Historical Quarterly*, 14:20, 21 (January, 1963); Myhrman, *Finlandssvenskar*, 246, 254; taped interviews of Hjalmer Mattson and other Swede-Finn fishermen, in Northeast Minnesota Historical Center, Duluth.

[5] Myhrman, in *Swedish Pioneer Historical Quarterly*, 14:20–23; Myhrman, *Finlandssvenskar*, 245, 247. The waterman's name was August Signer.

[6] On the Minnesota settlements here and three paragraphs below, see Silfversten, *Finlandssvenskar i Amerika*, 113–120; Myhrman, *Finlandssvenskar*, 256–265, 267. See also Wasastjerna, *Finns in Minnesota*, 204. The mine inspector was Edward Smith; Myhrman, 261.

[7] Myhrman, in *Swedish Pioneer Historical Quarterly*, 14:22; Myhrman, in Niitemaa, ed., *Old Friends*, 186; Wasastjerna, *Finns in Minnesota*, 362, 461.

[8] Syrjamaki, "Mesabi Communities," 259.

[9] Myhrman, in Niitemaa, ed., *Old Friends*, 186–190; Wasastjerna, *Finns in Minnesota*, 186–190, 459, 461, 494, 517; Myhrman, *Finlandssvenskar*, 249, 265–267.

[10] Myhrman, in Niitemaa, ed., *Old Friends*, 190–194. On the order and its chapters in Eveleth, Hibbing, Chisholm, West Duluth, and Biwabik, see Anders M. Myhrman, ed., *Memorabilia of the International Order of Runeberg, 1898–1968*, 26, 32, 50–52, 66, 73, 76–80, 82 ([Seattle, 1968?]). On Crosby, see Wasastjerna, *Finns in Minnesota*, 142.

[11] Myhrman, *Finlandssvenskar*, 247, 255, 264; Anders M. Myhrman, "The Finland-Swedes and Their Cultural Organizations in America," in American Swedish Historical Foundation, *Yearbook 1957*, 24 (Philadelphia, 1957); Silfversten, *Finlandssvenskarna i Amerika*, 216, 268–271. The Bethel Church was served for many years by Rev. Carl J. Silfversten, an early historian of the Swede-Finns. He edited a monthly religious newsletter, the *Svensk-Finska Sändebudet* (Swede-Finn Messenger), which circulated among the group's congregations in the U.S. from 1909 to 1925; see *Old Friends*, 198.

[12] Myhrman, *Finlandssvenskar*, 263; Myhrman, in Niitemaa, ed., *Old Friends*, 198; Silfversten, *Finlandssvenskarna i Amerika*, 272–276.

[13] Myhrman, in American Swedish Historical Foundation, *Yearbook 1957*, 24.

[14] Blomqvist, in *Finnish Americana*, 2:55, 57.

[15] Ragna Ahlbäck *et al.*, *Amerika Trunken: Emigranter berättar om sig själva*, 196 (Borgå, Fin., 1976); Blomqvist, in *Finnish Americana*, 2:51, 58–65.

CENTRAL
AND
SOUTHERN
EUROPEANS

CHAPTER 16

The Baltic Peoples
ESTONIANS, LATVIANS, AND LITHUANIANS

Timo Riippa

THE STORY OF BALTIC PEOPLES in Minnesota can be described as twofold. The first part offers a familiar immigration scenario, unique in specifics, but essentially similar to the histories of many other groups that reached the United States at the turn of the century. The second part presents still another aspect of the human drama of uprootedness — survival and self-exile as refugees from the devastated Europe of World War II sought new homes in the state.

The Baltic countries of Estonia, Latvia, and Lithuania form a geographical unit on the vast east-European plain which extends from the eastern coast of the Baltic Sea to the Ural Mountains (see Map 16.1). On the eve of World War II in 1939, Latvia was the largest of the three countries with an area of 25,500 square miles and a population of 2,000,000, while Lithuania had the greatest population (2,500,000) and an area of 20,500 square miles. Estonia, the smallest of the three, had 1,100,000 people and encompassed 18,400 square miles. The region is believed to have been occupied by the ancient forebears of these peoples since about 2,000 B.C.[1]

The languages of Latvia and Lithuania belong to the Baltic subfamily of Indo-European. "Today the two [languages] are not mutually intelligible," an authority has observed, "but even a cursory comparison of their vocabulary is sufficient to show their common origin." Estonian, however, belongs to a different linguistic grouping, the Finno-Ugric language family, a non-Slavic, non-Germanic language whose closest relative is Finnish.[2]

The flat, marshy lands and the relatively mild climate of the east Baltic made the area well suited for agriculture, which with livestock breeding has dominated the economies of the region since ancient times. Christianity was introduced to the Latvians and Estonians in the 12th and 13th centuries through the missionary and colonizing zeal of the Danes, the Kievan Slavs, and the Teutonic Order, while the Lithuanians converted without conquest. In the era of the Reformation, Lithuania remained loyal to the Roman Catholic church, while Latvia and Estonia became early adherents of Lutheranism. Thus during the peak period of immigration about 1900, the prevailing faith of the Lithuanians was Roman Catholicism, while a majority of Latvians and Estonians were Lutheran.[3]

Although all three countries shared an ancient, colorful,

and complex development characterized by war, political union, annexation, and foreign domination, their history as a whole was largely a story of resistance to domination by more powerful neighbors, notably the Germans, Poles, Swedes, and Russians. Estonia and part of Latvia passed from Swedish to Russian hands in 1721 after Sweden's defeat in the Great Northern War. Lithuania and most of Lat-

Map 16.1. The Baltic Countries

KEY ——— Soviet Republics
- - - - Independent nations, 1920–39

via were absorbed by the Russians by 1795. The countries' social and cultural life was dominated by a Russo-Polish upper class in Lithuania and by Baltic-German nobles in Latvia and Estonia. With the collapse of Czarist Russia in the revolution of 1917, however, the three Baltic nations regained their independence.[4]

Long before that Estonians, Latvians, and Lithuanians are known to have made their way to Colonial America. Latvians were present in the settlement of Swedes and Finns on the Delaware River as well as in Pennsylvania, Massachusetts, and perhaps New Amsterdam. At least two Estonians lived in the colonies, a drummer in New Sweden on the Delaware and a saddle maker who settled in New York. Lithuanian soldiers served as mercenaries in the Dutch military in New Amsterdam in the 1650s and soon others were to be found there as well as elsewhere. Lithuanians (as well as Poles) claim as their own Brigadier General Thaddeus Kosciuszko of the Continental Army.[5]

A number of factors contributed to the emigration from the Baltic states in the 19th century. Agrarian reform allowed people to become more mobile, resulting in a movement to industrial areas from where mass emigration to the New World was already under way; a systematic policy of Russification by czarist authorities threatened to obliterate Estonian, Latvian, and Lithuanian national identities, and compulsory service in the Russian army provided an added impetus for many young men to emigrate. Finally there was the lure of adventure and the promise of greater opportunity in industrial America. During the California gold rush, for example, sailors from all three countries jumped ship upon reaching San Francisco to seek their fortunes.[6]

Between 1868 and 1914, about half a million Lithuanians emigrated to the United States. Some 5,000 Latvian revolutionaries and a number of Estonians arrived as a result of the 1905 revolution in Russia with its subsequent uprisings in the Baltic countries. The first waves of these Estonian and Latvian political exiles included nationalists, Socialists, and those who objected to Russian military conscription.[7]

The often complex issues of nationalism and Socialism factionalized the immigrant communities, which were then located predominantly on the East Coast, creating numerous competing political, social, cultural, and religious organizations. Within each of the three ethnic groups, the period was characterized by a heightened political consciousness fostered by events in Europe, which were then interpreted and debated by the Baltic exiles in America. Uprisings in czarist Russia in 1905 had considerable impact on the immigrants. As one Latvian put it: "After the revolution . . . then things started to go crazy! Then there were church upholders; there were baptists and social-democrats, and communists: and Latvians divided themselves into some twenty parties. Then people derided each other, cussed, and fought each other in the tavern." Between 1905 and 1907 all three groups established Socialist organizations which became foreign-language sections within the Socialist party of America. In 1918–19 these organizations underwent ideological splits that reflected the international division between Socialism and Communism.[8]

Several factors complicate census data for all three groups. The decision of United States officials to classify immigrants by country of origin does not permit precision in ethnic identification. For much of the pertinent period those from the Baltic countries carried Russian passports. Although Lithuanians were listed in immigration records after 1899, they were not included in the census until 1920 after the country became independent. Estonians and Latvians were not so recorded until 1930. Earlier the three groups were often misclassified as Russians, Germans, or Poles. Included with the Lithuanians were sizable, but undetermined, numbers of Jews, who in the 1890s made up 13% of the country's total population. They were heavily concentrated in Vilnius and Kaunas, where much of the emigration originated and where they comprised 45% and 36% of the cities' population, respectively.[9]

The Early Immigrants

In 1897 there were an estimated 1,000 Latvians in the United States. Most of them lived in such urban areas as Boston, which had the first major organized Latvian community in the nation, as well as in Baltimore, Philadelphia, and New York City. By 1900 the figure had risen to 4,309, reflecting the negative reaction of these Baltic people to the czar's intensified Russification policies.[10]

A unique Latvian settlement began in Lincoln County, Wisconsin, in 1897. An estimated 1,500, mostly single men from Chicago, Philadelphia, and Latvia itself, arrived between 1901 and 1908 to join a farm colony near Gleason — the only such Latvian rural settlement in the United States. The colony, which was promoted by the Reverend Hans Rebane and by lumber companies, advertised in and was endorsed by the *Amerikas Vestnēsis* (American Herald), a Latvian-language newspaper published in Boston. While many moved back to the cities, approximately 500 immigrants settled in the area on about 200 farms. As early as 1900 the immigrants organized the Latvian Evangelical Lutheran Church of Martin Luther. Six years later, with the help of a lumber company which provided the land and materials, the congregation dedicated the first Latvian-built church in the United States. While it is possible that some of these Wisconsin Latvians migrated to Minnesota, no proof that they did so has been found.[11]

Very little is known about Latvians in Minnesota before 1930. It is probable that, like their urban countrymen on the East Coast, most of them lived in Minneapolis and St. Paul, where they were employed as laborers and skilled workers such as carpenters and bricklayers. In 1911 *Strahdneeks* (or *Strādnieks*, The Worker), a Latvian Socialist newspaper, claimed that a Lettish labor group had existed in Minneapolis since 1908. Records of the Minnesota Commission of Public Safety in 1918 indicated that a Latvian Socialist chapter existed in Minneapolis and that Charles Dirba, secretary of the Socialist party in the state, was a Latvian. How many people belonged to this chapter, we do not know.[12]

In 1930 the census for the first time delineated Latvians as a separate group and provided a demographic sketch of them. Nationally there were 20,673 foreign born and 17,418 native born, 73% of whom lived in New York, Illinois, Massachusetts, Pennsylvania, New Jersey, and California. Of 523 Latvians in Minnesota, 255 were foreign born and 268 were native born. Of the latter, both parents of 200 were born abroad. Of the remaining 68, 53 had only foreign-born fathers, while 15 had only foreign-born mothers. Urban Minnesota Latvians numbered 417, while 56 were designated as rural-farm and 50 rural-nonfarm. Ten years later only 188 Latvian-born persons were counted in the state. Of these, 80 lived in Minneapolis, 43 lived in St. Paul, and 8 lived in Duluth. (See Table 16.1).[13]

Early Estonian urban communities in the United States existed in New York and San Francisco in the 1890s. While no record of any Estonians in Minnesota prior to 1905 has been located, Wisconsin and South Dakota were the sites of two of the earliest Estonian rural settlements in the country. In 1894 a group of seven families settled near Fort Pierre, South Dakota. There three years later they established the first Estonian Lutheran congregation in America. The Wisconsin settlement was in the Irma-Gleason area, near the Latvians.[14]

Yet another rural settlement, called Estonia, was established in 1906 in northwestern Wisconsin near Hayward. Like the nearby Latvian settlement, the community was encouraged by Rebane and by a lumber company interested in promoting an Estonian farm colony on its cutover lands. Also interested in the settlement was Konstantin Päts, an influential Estonian political activist and newspaperman later to become president of independent Estonia, who went to the United States to investigate the possibility of founding a large rural colony of Estonians. After seeing a model farm he initially endorsed the idea of such a colony, but when he was later advised of the actual condition of the cutover lands, he withdrew his endorsement.

While most Estonians left the community near Hayward, the settlers in the Irma-Gleason area grew in numbers. Except for a settlement in Liberty County, Montana, this was the largest Estonian rural community in the United States. These Estonians and the neighboring Latvians were at first served by the same pastor. The Estonians founded their own Lutheran congregation in 1902, however, and built a church near Gleason in 1914.[15]

If little is known about the early Latvians, even less is known about the Estonians, who were fewer in number. In 1930, the first year they were counted by the census, there were 5,317 Estonians in the nation and only 55 (foreign and native born) in Minnesota (see Table 16.1). Nine of the 30 who were of foreign birth lived in Minneapolis, 7 in Duluth, and 2 in St. Paul. The first to arrive in the state in 1905

reputedly emigrated to escape conscription into the Russian army.[16]

It was Lithuania that contributed the largest number of immigrants from any Baltic country. Before immigration officials identified them separately in 1899, perhaps 50,000 Lithuanians were counted as Russians. From 1899 to 1914, according to a Lithuanian estimate based on immigration reports and census figures, approximately 252,600 arrived. The sex ratio was 208.44 men to 100 women. During this period only 387 intended to settle in Minnesota (see Table 16.2); larger numbers were found in Pennsylvania, Illinois, New York, Massachusetts, Connecticut, and New Jersey, where they worked mainly as servants and as laborers in coal mines, factories, and steel mills. Even after the census began to list Lithuanians in 1920, some of them were still counted as Poles, Russians, or Germans. And all of the figures were complicated by the fact that approximately 20% of the early comers returned to Lithuania.[17]

The first Lithuanian immigrants to Minnesota were young men, whose arrival preceded that of their families. On the Mesabi Range they were one of the ethnic groups active in underground mining after 1900 and in open-pit operations after 1905. Among those on the iron ranges were a number of Lithuanian Jews, who went into business or the professions.[18]

Some of those in the Twin Cities joined family members who had arrived earlier. For example, Nathan and Bertha Eisenstadt, a Lithuanian Jewish couple who migrated to Minneapolis by 1887, were sponsored by Herman Borovsky, Bertha's brother. They were soon followed by Bertha's parents, who were accompanied by their younger children. Another example of relatives as a magnetic force in chain migration can be seen in the Mondykes of St. Paul. At the age of about 19, Anna traveled to the coal mining region of Pennsylvania, where her aunt ran a saloon. There in 1912, about 16 months after her arrival, Anna married Frank Mondyke, a miner who had also emigrated to join an aunt. After Frank became ill from working in the mines, the family moved to St. Paul, where in 1913 his brother, Anthony, was already in residence.[19]

Others arrived by way of large settlements in the East, sometimes finding new homes through a sense of adventure. Lithuanian Jusepas Jonas Jwanouskos, for example, was a construction engineering student in a German institution of higher learning when he and a friend decided to see the world by signing up for work on a cruise ship. In 1906 they embarked from Rotterdam for America, the "Golden Land," and entrained for Philadelphia after their arrival in

Table 16.1. Minnesota Baltic Peoples, 1930–70

| | 1930 | | 1940 | | 1960 | | 1970 | |
	foreign born	foreign stock*	fb	fs	fb	fs	fb	fs
Lithuania	1,283	2,887	1,290	3,330	785	3,105	418	2,445
Latvia	255	523	188		1,837	2,494	1,509	2,517
Estonia	30	55	25		321	430	242	381

Source: Country of origin statistics in U.S., *Census,* for the years listed.
*Foreign stock includes foreign born and native born of foreign or mixed parentage.

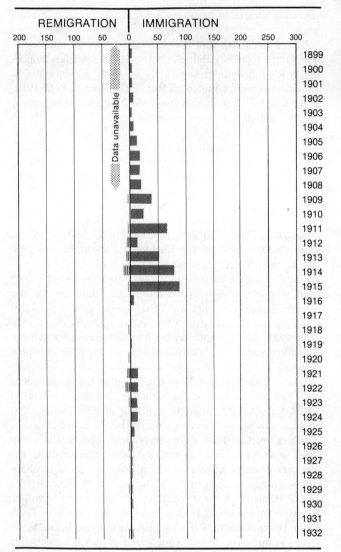

Table 16.2. Lithuanian Migration to and from Minnesota

New York City. While working at odd jobs in the city, Jwanouskos married a recently arrived Lithuanian woman. Three years later he heard of better opportunities out west. Leaving his family temporarily behind, he rode freights to St. Paul, where he found employment as a laborer on the Soo Line and, later, the Great Northern railroads. Jwanouskos became a leader in the Minneapolis-St. Paul Lithuanian-American community as well as a successful contractor who was one of the early builders of houses in the Como Park district.[20]

Like many immigrants, Lithuanians also emigrated to escape the drudgery of Old World rural life. George Bart (originally Bartkus) was born about 1880 into a large family on a farm near the east Prussian border. Most of his brothers and sisters died before reaching maturity. As a boy he herded sheep; from the age of 12 to 17 he operated a one-horse plow. His father then sent him to work for lumber contractors in the nearby forests; most of his earnings went to his parents. When he turned 21, the home farmstead was

willed to him, and he worked it for several years with his younger brother. During this time he married a girl from the village. At about the age of 26 Bart decided to leave for America, using money loaned to him by an uncle living in Minneapolis. He arrived in 1906, followed soon after by his wife and family. At first he found jobs in quarrying, lumbering, and construction before becoming a carpenter for the Soo Line Railroad.[21]

Like Lithuanians elsewhere, those in the Twin Cities secured employment primarily as manual laborers in factories and on the railroads. Like immigrants everywhere, they found themselves in competition or conflict with various other nationalities. Thomas A. Sieleini, a Lithuanian who worked as a second cook on the Chicago Great Western Railroad before moving to St. Paul, remembered that he "couldn't speak hardly any English and . . . was the butt of many jokes by my fellow workers, who chuckled loud and teasingly at my ignorance of American dishes." In 1911 he found work as a second roast cook at the Hotel St. Paul. "But the Italian cook put in another Italian," he recalled, "and I quit. I had asked the chef to give me the chance as the first roast cook, but he favored one from his own nationality."[22]

Like George Bart, many of the early Lithuanian immigrants left rural areas of their homeland, carrying with them the values of an agrarian society. To make the hard adjustment to American industrial society often involved a change in cultural priorities. As one woman, who immigrated to Minneapolis about 1906, put it: "In old country, in summer work, in winter, rest a little. Here work all the time. Watch clock. Didn't watch clock in old country. Too much rush. Easier, some ways. Washing machine, iron. Things. But too much rush." Others disagreed, pointing out that the higher living standard was worth the price. Another Lithuanian-American woman visited the Old Country in 1935 and returned with a negative impression. Reflecting perhaps her own Americanization acquired during a 30-year residence in Minneapolis, she commented on the lack of ambition she observed and on people's beliefs in the validity of "age-old notions" about what was or was not "desirable."[23]

According to the 1930 census, out of 2,887 Lithuanians in Minnesota 1,283 were foreign born and 1,604 native born (see Table 16.1). They lived primarily in cities: 2,620 were urban, 168 rural-farm, and 99 rural-nonfarm. Minneapolis was the major population center with 1,262 of the total. Residing in St. Paul were 447, while Duluth had 440. The 1940 census indicated that of 1,290 foreign born, 521 lived in Minneapolis, 235 in Duluth, and 194 in St. Paul.[24]

The Lithuanian Americans in the Twin Cities were dispersed rather than concentrated in well-defined ethnic communities. A 1934 Minneapolis housing survey, for example, showed Lithuanian families living in 11 of the city's 13 wards. In ten of them, the number of families ranged from one to six. Only in Ward 3, close to the industrial area along the Mississippi River, was there a marked concentration of 20 families.[25]

Twin Cities Lithuanians were brought together by the Twin Cities Lithuanian American Benevolent Society, a fraternal benefit organization. It had been founded at an informal gathering of Lithuanians at the home of Jusepas Jwanouskos in St. Paul on June 22, 1913. At its peak in the 1920s and 1930s, when the society had chapters in both Minneapolis and St. Paul, it sponsored picnics, socials, and dances, holding them alternately in each city in parks and rented facilities like the Deutsche Haus on Rice Street in St. Paul. As it became increasingly difficult to get young people involved, activity declined, and in the 1950s the organization disbanded. Social and cultural functions were continued by the Lithuanian American Women's Society, which organized the Lithuanian participation in the Festival of Nations. By 1979, however, attendance at the monthly meetings averaged less than 12 members.[26]

By the late 1930s the process of assimilation was at work, a fact disturbing to many of the elders who wanted to preserve Lithuanian culture and language. A number of crosscurrents impeded the attempt. Immigrants whose experience in the homeland had been largely negative deliberately chose not to preserve the culture they had left behind. While in many families children remained bilingual, parents in others made no attempt to speak the language.

In one large family, for example, both married daughters knew Lithuanian because they had grown up speaking it. Both married non-Lithuanians. Their parents read *Saulė* (Sun), a weekly, miner-oriented, Lithuanian-language newspaper published at Mahanoy, Pennsylvania, but neither participated in the local Lithuanian men's or women's organization. Since there were no Lithuanian parishes in the Twin Cities, the family attended the nearest Catholic parish. The lack of an ethnic church probably hastened the relatively rapid assimilation of the second generation.[27]

The Baltic Peoples as Displaced Persons

In June, 1940, the Soviet Union occupied the three Baltic states, reorganizing their governments into "People's Diets," whose members were selected by the Soviets. These diets then officially "requested" the incorporation of the Baltic states into the Soviet Union as Socialist republics, whose legality the United States has refused to recognize to the present day. In 1941 during World War II the Germans occupied all three countries. In 1944 the Soviets again reentered them, resulting in massive flights of refugees to the West to reach the Allied forces.[28]

When the war ended, the refugees were placed in Displaced Persons (DP) camps in Germany, Austria, and Italy, where many of them spent from three to five years waiting for sponsors in various host countries. Most eventually reached the United States, although large Baltic communities also exist in Canada, Australia, West Germany, Great Britain, and Sweden.[29]

The wait in the camps was a long and trying process for people who had lost their possessions, their relatives, and their homelands. In 1949 representatives of some Latvians in a camp in Germany wrote to then Minnesota Governor Luther W. Youngdahl. "We are waiting a long time for [a] solution of our problem," they said, "but without results." The same frustration was echoed in another letter from Estonians at Geislingen, Germany, who told the governor, "We

are able to work and we cannot understand why we should live on charity we are not accustomed to."

In the camps the refugees established an entire social, cultural, and educational milieu, which included institutions such as Baltic University at Pinneberg, Germany, completely staffed by refugee academicians; the Estonian Foresters Association, which appealed to the Northern Pine Manufacturers Association of Minneapolis from the Geislingen camp in 1947; and vocational organizations like the Association of Estonian Farmers at Geislingen, where a group of 326 farmers petitioned Youngdahl for admittance to Minnesota in 1948. Characteristic of the refugees was their high level of education and the fact that they included a large percentage of professional people.[30]

The refugee Latvians, Estonians, and Lithuanians transported to the United States intact their religious affiliations, voluntary associations, newspapers, and educational institutions. One authority stated, for example, that Latvian DPs "carried into exile their strong national loyalty and zeal to preserve the Latvian culture in exile — its institutions, traditions, symbols, values." "Actually," he continued, "the exile population constituted a microcosm of the Latvian state, complete with social, political, economic, educational and other cultural leaders to re-establish an organizational system that could be successfully transplanted from the DP camp life of Germany and Austria to centers throughout the world." As a result, in the 1970s about 85% of Latvian Americans belonged to one or more of the Latvian social, cultural, or professional societies. Ethnic organizations also proliferated among the Estonians, who, according to one estimate, had one society for every 65 first- and secondgeneration Estonian Americans. An inherent aspect of the "diaspora consciousness" that these organizations reflected was the determination that regardless of what might happen in the homeland, its culture would be preserved in exile.[31]

In 1948 Congress enacted the Displaced Persons Act, which allowed for the admission of 200,000 European refugees to the United States. Its provisions were extended in 1950, and by 1952 when the law expired about 395,000 refugees had been admitted. About three out of four were part of a family unit, while the rest were single adults. The overall sex ratio among the DPs was 119.3 males to 100 females. Initially a preference in the law, given to those from countries annexed by a foreign power, favored the Baltic states. Reflecting this "Baltic preference" was the large number of Latvians admitted. Constituting 10.4% of all DPs, they were exceeded only by Poles and Germans. In addition Lithuanians comprised 6.8% of the total and Estonians 2.9%.[32]

The act required that all Displaced Persons must have sponsors, who guaranteed that the refugees had adequate housing, a job which did not replace an American, and paid transportation from the port of entry to their destinations. Numerous public and private agencies administered the program. Among those active in aiding the resettlement of Baltic peoples in Minnesota were the National Lutheran Council, the National Catholic Welfare Council, the Church World Service, the National Association of Evangelicals, the Minnesota Commission for the Resettlement of Displaced Persons, and several local organizations.[33]

While the refugees waited to be sent to specific Minnesota communities, many of them stayed at the "Welcome Home," a resettlement house supported by the Lutheran Welfare Association and located at 398 Case Avenue in St. Paul. The home provided an opportunity for rest after the trip from Europe as well as a brief orientation to the more positive aspects of American life, especially for those refugees whose first impressions of the United States had been formed by newspaper reporters and photographers demanding pictures and stories about "the typical immigrant." A 1949 Latvian newspaper noted that between June and November, 1949, over 400 people stopped in the Welcome Home. Of them, 300 were Latvian, 60 Estonian, 30 Hungarian, and 10 Lithuanian. The average stay was several days in length, while the maximum allowed by the home was three months.[34]

At first, difficulties in the resettlement program occurred in trying to match the refugees' skills with available jobs. With few exceptions, professional people who had been part of the political, business, educational, artistic, and scientific strata of their respective countries had to take jobs initially in the unskilled labor force as janitors, construction workers, and farm laborers. Generally occupational adjustment varied with the profession. For example, physicians, engineers, and clergy tended to find positions more readily than teachers or lawyers who lacked expertise in the English language as well as in the American educational and legal systems. Some refugees eventually had to change professions or take graduate work in American universities. Nevertheless two factors tended to diminish the adverse impact of occupational adjustment: first, many of the unemployed professionals viewed any occupation as preferable to the dreary life in the DP camps; second, the higher standard of living in the United States and the rise in the individual's economic status tended to compensate for a decline in social or occupational status.[35]

A resettlement questionnaire circulated in Minnesota in 1952 identified problem areas as (1) the language barrier, (2) misunderstandings between sponsors and Displaced Persons, and (3) sponsors' "expecting too much before there was an understanding of American way of life." In addition the refugees' impatience, born of having undergone five years of war and an additional five years in the camps, led many to feel they had to make up for lost time.

Employers were generally eager to hire Displaced Persons because they found them to be reliable workers. On one occasion a Minneapolis union complained that an employer was hiring too many refugees and displacing union workers. The employer responded by saying that the union had either failed to provide people or those who had applied were unreliable, whereas the DPs he had hired were excellent workers. The issue was resolved by getting union cards for the Displaced Persons.[36]

Occasionally Minnesota farmers expressed dissatisfaction with the resettlement program because the refugees did not arrive in time for the harvest, lacked experience, and/or left after a year. One farmer, for example, claimed that he had been assigned a dairyman whose only experience had been washing floors in a bottling house. The Displaced Persons,

for their part, often felt that they were being exploited as cheap labor.[37]

Not all DPs worked as laborers. Among the professional people who found immediate employment was Dr. Edmund Smits, a former professor of systematic theology at the University of Riga in Latvia. After fleeing to Germany, he continued teaching at the refugee Baltic University in Hamburg during his stay at a DP camp. In 1950 he arrived with his family in St. Paul, where he taught pastoral psychology at Luther Theological Seminary. Another Latvian academic who also reached Minnesota by way of a camp was Karlis Kaufmanis, professor of astronomy, who accepted an invitation to teach at Gustavus Adolphus College at St. Peter in 1949. In 1962 he moved to the University of Minnesota, where for 16 years he has given his popular introduction to astronomy course to an estimated 26,000 students.[38]

Despite difficulties at the outset, refugees generally adapted to American life, although there were numerous cases where the Displaced Person's experience, isolation in the United States, and unsatisfactory adjustment to a strange culture caused psychological disruption and problems ranging from alcoholism and depression to divorce. Nevertheless within several years most had adapted in varying degrees to middle-class American life. The adaptation was not without reservations. Resisting assimilation, they regarded their sojourn in the United States as a stay that would last only until conditions were right for a return to the homeland.[39]

Between 1948 and the end of 1951, 37,505 Latvian refugees were admitted to the United States; by 1952 the number was estimated at 45,000. Of the total, about 1,300 Latvians were sent to Minnesota, more than arrived from any other Baltic country. Although they were widely scattered in the state, Minneapolis predominated as the point of first location with 163 refugees, followed by St. Peter with 122, St. Paul with 96, Northfield with 59, and Duluth with 42. After a while many seemed to drift toward the Twin Cities. For example, six families placed in the Red River Valley moved to Minneapolis after about a year when they discovered that "the Latvian people were congregating" there.[40]

Religious activity began as soon as the refugees reached Minneapolis. The Latvian Evangelical Lutheran Church was established at 3152 17th Avenue South in a building acquired from the Bethany Lutheran congregation. In a historic and symbolic event, the new group received in 1958 the bell from the abandoned Martin Luther Church in the Lincoln County, Wisconsin, settlement, which, as we have seen, was the first built by Latvians in the United States.[41]

Eleven years later a split occurred in the new group, which led to the formation of the Latvian Evangelical Lutheran Jesus congregation; however, the two groups reunited in 1978. As a result of differences of opinion concerning the use of English in religious instruction, still another split occurred in 1972, and a third congregation was formed in Minneapolis — the Latvian Evangelical Lutheran Christ Church. In 1980 the latter congregation, which met in St. Luke's Lutheran Church at 3751 17th Avenue South, had 315 members, while the earlier Latvian Evangelical group had 946 members. Both congregations were affiliated with the American Lutheran Church.[42]

Since its establishment in 1948, Latvian House at 2337 Central Avenue Northeast has been a cultural center for art fairs, special celebrations, and ethnic festivals. Among the active organizations in Minneapolis in 1980 were the Latvian Women's Society, the Latvian Youth Theatre, the Latvian Student Corporation (an umbrella organization for fraternities and sororities), the Latvian Association in Minnesota, and the Latvian Youth Organization.

A Latvian Saturday school offered an example of how the culture was passed on to young people. Each Saturday morning parents took their children to the Latvian Lutheran Church, where they were instructed in the language and the cultural heritage of songs, poems, folk tales, and customs. Using such musical instruments as the *kokle* (a wood and string instrument), *stabule* (recorder), and *trideksnis* (a percussion instrument), the children practiced and the Latvian dance group rehearsed. From such training grounds came performing groups featured at the Festival of Nations in St. Paul, in which Latvians have participated since 1952.[43]

The influx of refugees raised the number of foreign-born Latvians in Minnesota substantially over the 188 recorded in the 1940 census. In 1960, 1,837 foreign born and a total Latvian foreign stock of 2,494 were counted. In 1970 the foreign born declined to 1,509, while the native born rose from 657 in 1960 to 1,008. The Twin Cities were clearly a center for Latvians by 1970, with 828 residing in Minneapolis and 413 in St. Paul.[44]

The number of Estonian refugees fell far short of the Latvian surge. By the end of 1951, only 10,674 had arrived in the United States, and as few as 209 of them went to Minnesota. Like the Latvians, the Estonians scattered to many Minnesota communities. Minneapolis again was the favored location with 56 refugees, while St. Paul followed with 23.[45]

Although the Estonian population of the state was augmented by the DPs' arrival, it remained small. In 1940 it

YOUNG LATVIANS in Minnesota have continued traditions of group singing, accompanied by the ancient national stringed instrument, the kokle.

totaled 25 foreign born. By 1960 this figure had risen to 321, with a total foreign stock of 430. Ten years later, however, Estonian foreign stock had declined to 381, of which 242 were foreign born and 139 native born. The pattern of preference for the Twin Cities persisted. In 1970, 81 of the foreign stock lived in Minneapolis and 39 in St. Paul. Most other Estonians in Minnesota were to be found in or near the seven-county metropolitan area within reach of the Twin Cities center of their social and cultural activities.[46]

Like other Baltic peoples, the Estonians quickly established religious organizations, holding their first church service in Minneapolis in July, 1949, with 47 people attending. Two years later the Estonian Evangelical Lutheran Church was established, and from 1955 on it held weekly services in the Latvian Lutheran Church at 3152 17th Avenue South.[47]

Other activities were also begun in the early years of resettlement. The *Eesti Selts* (Estonian Society), a social and cultural organization, was founded in 1951. It issued a monthly newsletter, the *Minnesota Postimees*, to inform people about activities, general news, and births and deaths. By 1980 the newsletter was appearing on a quarterly basis. The *Naiskoondis* (Women's Club) was organized about the same time, but it was separate from the *Eesti Selts*.

Under the superstructure of the Estonian Society many subsidiary organizations came into being, among them a choir, a folk-dance group, a chess club, and a hunters' and fishermen's club. Beginning in 1955 Estonians participated in the International Institute's Festival of Nations in St. Paul. The same year the society bought a building on East Lake Street and established Estonian House as a center for social activity. The house also had a lending library of works in Estonian for its members.[48]

The early and mid-1970s witnessed declining social and cultural activity. It became increasingly difficult to get people to attend frequent social functions as the older generation aged, and young people married and moved from the area. The upkeep of Estonian House became burdensome, and in 1978 it was sold.

In 1980 two yearly gatherings still drew large numbers of young and old. One was the *Eesti Vabariigi Aastapäev* (Estonian Independence Day) celebration on February 24. The other was *Jaanipäev* (Midsummer Day) on June 24. Estonian church services were still held once a month in the Latvian Lutheran Church. In addition Estonian-language services were broadcast twice a month on Sundays from the St. Olaf College radio station in Northfield.

Although the 25,368 Lithuanian refugees admitted to the United States by the end of 1951 were far more numerous than the Estonians, they were the smallest of the three Baltic DP groups to find new homes in Minnesota. Only 143 reached the state between 1949 and 1952, scattering to such communities as Northfield, Mankato, St. Peter, St. Paul, Minneapolis, and Duluth.[49]

Despite the small number of refugees, however, Lithuanians constituted the largest segment of Baltic peoples in the state in 1960, totaling a foreign stock of 3,105. When the number of Latvians rose and that of the Lithuanians dropped to 2,445 in 1970, the Latvians emerged as the leading group.[50]

Predictably, the number of foreign-born Lithuanians declined from 785 in 1960 to 418 in 1970. Predictably, too, concentrations of the group remained in large urban areas, despite the scattering of the DPs. The metropolitan area of the Twin Cities counted 2,262 in 1960, and there were 746 in Duluth-Superior.

Although they shared the same religion and ethnic origin with earlier Lithuanian immigrants, the Lithuanian refugees of the 1940s and 1950s differed from them in a number of ways. Like other Displaced Persons, they tended to be well-educated, professional people who felt they had little in common with the other Lithuanian Americans. Their social, cultural, and political perspectives differed considerably from those of their American cousins, and as a result they did not participate to any great degree in the activities of the existing ethnic community. Many of them apparently sought better occupational opportunities in Chicago or other cities in the East with large Lithuanian settlements. "They were educated people," remembered a Lithuanian-American woman who helped in the placing of DPs. "They just couldn't find what they wanted here." [51]

Primary characteristics of refugees from all three nations were their staunch anti-Communism, well-defined ethnic self-consciousness, and high degree of political awareness. In American politics they supported conservative candidates, although the second and third generations tended to be more moderate. In addition the DPs were deeply committed to the ideals of preserving their cultures in exile and someday freeing their countries from Soviet domination. For example, the American Latvian Association, representing over 200 Latvian secular and religious organizations in the United States, was said to devote "all available efforts and resources to preserving the Latvian cultural heritage and securing self-determination for the Latvian people." In a similar vein, Estonian Americans not only celebrated their cultural heritage "but also reaffirm[ed] the dedication of Estonians in the West to the fight for freedom and independence for Estonia." [52]

In spite of the nurturing of these ideals of diaspora consciousness in the social, cultural, and political organizations of the Baltic peoples of the United States, the younger generation exhibited cultural assimilation. A Lithuanian authority has noted that "Second- and third-generation Lithuanians continue to associate informally with each other, to establish ethnic families, and to participate in various ethnic activities, but the number of those who are deeply committed to preserving their language and ethnic affiliations gradually continues to decline." A Latvian writer reinforced this point. "During the last 25 years," he observed in 1976, "the structure of the Latvian communities in America has changed. The first generation of post W[orld] W[ar] II immigrants is aging and passing away. Many socially active immigrants are being replaced by their children who, unlike their parents, have lost much of their patriotic zeal." [53]

These children had no memories of the war or the homeland, which constituted such vivid realities for their elders. Although they had grown up within a milieu that emphasized the preservation of culture in exile, the younger generation

COMMUNITY WOMEN made food as well as the needlework displayed here to sell at annual Christmas bazaars in Minneapolis' Estonian House.

also faced strong assimilative forces, especially from the school system and the mass media. Professional success brought with it the accouterments and values of middle-class American life to those who pursued careers in fields such as business, law, medicine, and education. Ironically these achievements of which the refugee generation was most proud have simultaneously undermined their homeland-directed goals.

Refugee organizations have actively sought to counter the threat. To foster intramarriage and prevent out-migration, social activities have been organized through major voluntary organizations which placed young people in settings, such as camp retreats and conventions, where the culture and heritage were emphasized and there was ample opportunity to form romantic attachments. In addition, since a high percentage of refugees' children attended college, Lithuanians and Latvians have responded by transplanting the national fraternities and sororities of the homeland to American universities. [54]

Heavy stress has been placed on education to maintain the respective languages, foster national loyalty, and promote ethnic solidarity. Saturday schools have been one aspect of this emphasis. The Estonians have also provided scholarships to send students from the United States to Finland for postgraduate work in Estonian language and culture. These measures and organizational activity have helped preserve and maintain the Baltic peoples' cultures in exile and their intense nationalism. Only the future will reveal how effectively and how long the socio-cultural-political structures erected by the refugees will preserve the diaspora languages and cultures.

Reference notes

[1] Kennth Katzner, *The Languages of the World*, 15 (New York, 1975); Peter Hajdu, *Finno-Ugrian Languages and Peoples*, 36 (London, 1975); August Rei, *The Drama of the Baltic Peoples*, 11 (Stockholm, Swed., 1970); Juris Veidemanis, "Social Change: Major Value-Systems of Latvians at Home, as Refugees, and as Immi-

grants," 38, Ph.D. thesis, University of Wisconsin, 1961. The author wishes to acknowledge the helpful suggestions he received during his work on this chapter from Andris Straumanis and Professors Edgar Anderson and Tönu Parming.

[2] Katzner, *Languages of the World*, 15, 86, 115, 116, 119.

[3] Marija Gimbutas, *The Balts*, 21, 33 (London, 1963); Georg von Rauch, *The Baltic States: The Years of Independence, Estonia, Latvia, Lithuania, 1917–1940*, 4 (London, 1970); Hajdu, *Finno-Ugrian Languages and Peoples*, 193; Veidemanis, "Social Change," 54–57; Stephan Thernstrom, ed., *Harvard Encyclopedia of American Ethnic Groups*, 665 (Cambridge, Mass., 1980).

[4] Von Rauch, *Baltic States*, 4, 16; Rei, *Drama of the Baltic Peoples*, 11–24; Thernstrom, ed., *Harvard Encyclopedia*, 340, 638, 665, 673.

[5] Maruta Kārklis, Līga Streips, and Laimonis Streips, *The Latvians in America 1640–1973*, 1 (Dobbs Ferry, N.Y., 1974); Jaan Pennar, Tönu Parming, and P. Peter Rebane, *The Estonians in America 1627–1975*, vii, 1 (Dobbs Ferry, N.Y., 1975); Algirdas M. Budreckis, *The Lithuanians in America 1651–1975*, 1 (Dobbs Ferry, N.Y., 1976).

[6] *Encyclopedia Lituanica*, 2:149 (Boston, 1972); Von Rauch, *Baltic States*, 16; Budreckis, *Lithuanians in America*, 4; Pennar et al., *Estonians in America*, 2; Kārklis et al., *Latvians in America*, 1.

[7] Here and below, see Budreckis, *Lithuanians in America*, v; Joseph S. Rouček, *American Lithuanians*, 5–8 (New York, 1940); Kārklis et al., *Latvians in America*, 6; Pennar et al., *Estonians in America*, 8.

[8] The quotation is from Juris Veidemanis, "A Twentieth Century Pioneer Settlement: Latvians in Lincoln County, Wisconsin," in *Midcontinent American Studies Journal*, 4:19 (Spring, 1963). See also Pennar et al., *Estonians in America*, 8, 14; Thernstrom, ed., *Harvard Encyclopedia*, 340, 640; Veidemanis, "Social Change," 383–386.

[9] *Encyclopedia Lituanica*, 2:523 (Boston, 1972). There are 1910 mother-tongue statistics for Lithuanians and Letts (Latvians) grouped together for both the state and for cities with populations of 100,000 or more, in United States, *Census*, 1910, *Population*, 1:1005, 1014. For Minnesota 636 were listed, for Minneapolis 157, and for St. Paul 49.

[10] Kārklis et al., *Latvians in America*, 2–5; Thernstrom, ed., *Harvard Encyclopedia*, 639; Veidemanis, in *Midcontinent American Studies Journal*, 4:14.

[11] Kārklis et al., *Latvians in America*, 4, 8; Veidemanis, in *Midcontinent American Studies Journal*, 4:13–23; Tönu Parming to Jean A. Brookins, March 24, 1981, in MEHP Papers.

[12] Announcement, "Celebration of the Anniversary of Russian Socialist Soviet Republic," December 14, [1918], and "Report Covering Friday, Nov. 15th, 1918," both in File 100, Minnesota Commission of Public Safety Records, Minnesota State Archives, MHS. See also Christopher J. Bittner, "The Socialist Heritage of the Latvian Immigrants in the United States," 138, master's thesis, State University of Iowa, 1924.

[13] Joseph S. Rouček, "Latvians in the United States," in *Baltic Countries*, 2:38 (May, 1936); U.S., *Census*, 1930, *Population*, 2:233, 295, 318, 325, 331; 1940, vol. 2, part 4, pp. 31, 168, 175, 182.

[14] Here and below, see Pennar et al., *Estonians in America*, 3, 6, 9; Joseph S. Rouček, "The American Estonians," in *Baltic Countries*, 2:193 (September, 1936); Parming information, March 24, 1981.

[15] Veidemanis, in *Midcontinent American Studies Journal*, 4:17, 26; Pennar et al., *Estonians in America*, 6; Parming information, March 24, 1981.

[16] U.S., *Census*, 1930, *Population*, 2:235, 268, 273; International Institute, *Festival of Nations, 1958*, 19 (St. Paul). According to the latter source, the reputed first immigrant was Martin Schonberg.

[17] Budreckis, *Lithuanians in America*, 151–154; J. P. Balys, "The American Lithuania Press," in *Lituanus*, 22:42 (Spring, 1976). The sex ratio was calculated from figures given in Budreckis, 151.

[18] John Sirjamaki, "The People of the Mesabi Range," in *Minnesota History*, 27:211–214 (September, 1946).

[19] Bess Eisenstadt Confeld, "Borovsky Family History," manuscript, 1967, in MHS; interview of Mrs. Frank Mondyke by Alfred M. Potekin, May 10, 1939, in Works Projects Administration (WPA), Minnesota, Writers Project Files, MHS; *Minneapolis City Directory, 1887–88*; *St. Paul City Directory, 1939*.

[20] Interview of Jwanouskos by Alfred M. Potekin, [1939?], in WPA, Writers Project Files; International Institute, *Festival of Nations, 1958*, 30. The name is variously given as Joe Jwanouskos and Jusepas Jonas Iwanouskas.

[21] Interview of George Bart by Ben Gallob, May, 1939, in WPA, Writers Project Files.

[22] Interview of Thomas A. Sieleni by Alfred M. Potekin, [1939?], in WPA, Writers Project Files.

[23] Interviews of Josephine (Mrs. John) Skriebes, May 23, 1939, and Mary (Mrs. John) Chase, May 25, 1939, both by Ben Gallob, in WPA, Writers Project Files.

[24] U.S., *Census*, 1930, *Population*, 2:295, 318, 325, 331; 1940, vol. 2, part 4, pp. 31, 72–74, 168, 175, 182.

[25] Herman E. Olson, *Minneapolis Property and Housing Survey* (Minneapolis, 1934).

[26] Jwanouskos interview, [1939?]; information provided to author by Mrs. Anne Lauth, August 12, 1980.

[27] Bart interview, May, 1939; Balys, in *Lituanus*, 22:45.

[28] Budreckis, *Lithuanians in America*, 34–37; Pennar et al., *Estonians in America*, 24–27; Kārklis et al., *Latvians in America*, 27–30.

[29] Here and below, see Memorandum, H. Voldemars Ritums and Viktors Kaminskis, representatives of "Dzintarzeme," to [Governor Luther Youngdahl], March 16, 1949; Agr. P. Köpp, Association of Estonian Farmers, to Youngdahl, [April, 1948] — both in National and International File, Minnesota Dept. of Public Welfare Records, Minnesota State Archives. See also Thernstrom, ed., *Harvard Encyclopedia*, 340, 674.

[30] Interview of Pastor Edvard Lind by author, June 22, 1980, notes in MEHP Papers; Osvalds Akmentins, *Latvians in Bicentennial America*, 5, 45 ([Waverly, Ia.?], 1976); Köpp to Youngdahl, [April, 1948]; H[ans] Kosenkranius and K[arl] Aasa, Estonian Foresters' Assn., to Northern Pine Manufacturers' Assn., October 29, 1947, in Northern Pine Manufacturers' Assn. Records, MHS. The records also include "Estonian Foresters' Association Bulletin," September 1, 1948, which reviewed the education, professional experience, and publications of 18 foresters. For an extensive discussion of Latvian culture in the camps, see Veidemanis, "Social Change," 222–296.

[31] The quotation is from Veidemanis, in *Midcontinent American Studies Journal*, 4:23. See also Budreckis, *Lithuanians in America*, 42–66; Pennar et al., *Estonians in America*, 27–29; Thernstrom, ed., *Harvard Encyclopedia*, 342, 640.

[32] United States Displaced Persons Commission, *The DP Story: The Final Report*, 23, 26, 37–41, 242–246, 366 (Washington, D.C., 1952).

[33] *Displaced Persons Resettled in Minnesota, 1949–52* (and tables compiled from these records, in MEHP Papers), and John W. Poor to H. Voldemars Ritums and Viktors Kaminskis, April 19, 1949, in National and International File, both in Minnesota Displaced Persons Commission Files, Minnesota Dept. of Public Welfare Records.

[34] Osa Kappers, "Our First Impression of U.S.A.," undated, in Student Speeches and Letters File, International Institute of Minnesota Papers, IHRC; *Laiks*, December 3, 1949, p. 2.

[35] Here and below, see Minnesota Displaced Persons Commission, Resettlement Questionnaire, Response of the Lutheran Resettlement Service of Minnesota, August 11, 1952, in Minnesota Displaced Persons Commission Files, Reports for 1952, Minnesota Dept. of Public Welfare Records; Lind interview, June 22, 1980; Leo J. Alilunas, ed., *Lithuanians in the United States: Selected Studies*, 166, 168, 171, 182 (San Francisco, 1978).

[36] Memorandum, John F. Bach to John W. Poor, July 7, 1950, in Minnesota Displaced Persons Commission Files, Complaints and Problem Cases, Minnesota Dept. of Public Welfare Records.

[37] Minnesota Farm Employment Advisory Council, Minutes, November 29, 1951, enclosed in Victor Christgau to John F. Bach, January 15, 1951; Paul W. Kunkel to John W. Poor, December 19, 1951 — both in Minnesota Displaced Persons Commission Files, Minnesota Dept. of Public Welfare Records. See also Lind interview, June 22, 1980.

[38] "Latvian DP Professor Teaches Here," in *Minnesota Welfare*, June, 1952, pp. 6–8; *Minnesota Daily* (Minneapolis), May 26, 1978, p. 4.

[39] Lind interview, June 22, 1980; information provided to author by Andris Straumanis, April 23, 1980.

[40] U.S. Displaced Persons Commission, *DP Story*, 376; Kārklis et al., *Latvians in America*, 32; Minnesota Farm Employment Advisory Council, Minutes, November 29, 1951 (quotation); Displaced Persons Resettlement Tables, in MEHP Papers. The total number of Latvians recorded was 1,310. However, seven of this number went to Wisconsin.

[41] Straumanis information, November 26, 1980; Veidemanis, in *Midcontinent American Studies Journal*, 4:23.

[42] Here and below, see Straumanis information, April 23, 1980; Supplement, in *Ceļa Biedrs*, 6:9 (July/August, 1980).

[43] *Minneapolis Star*, March 16, 1978, p. 1C; International Institute, *Festival of Nations, 1952*, 26 (St. Paul). See also Veidemanis, "Social Change," 394–396, for a discussion of Latvian schools.

[44] U.S., *Census*, 1960, *Population*, vol. 1, part 25, pp. 340–342; 1970, vol. 1, part 25, p. 512.

[45] U.S. Displaced Persons Commission, *DP Story*, 376; Displaced Persons Resettlement tables, in MEHP Papers.

[46] U.S., *Census*, 1940, *Population*, vol. 2, part 4, p. 31; 1960, vol. 1, part 25, pp. 340–342; 1970, vol. 1, part 25, p. 512.

[47] Here and below, see Lind interview, June 22, 1980, and interview of Mrs. Ingrid Lagus by author, June 23, 1979, notes in MEHP Papers. The Minnesota *Eesti Selts* Collection in IHRC includes many programs and other publications documenting the Estonians' social and cultural activities.

[48] Here and two paragraphs below, see Lind and Lagus interviews, June 22, 1980, and June 23, 1979, respectively. On the Festival of Nations, see International Institute, *Festival of Nations, 1955*, 22 (St. Paul).

[49] U.S. Displaced Persons Commission, *DP Story*, 376; Displaced Persons Resettlement tables, in MEHP Papers.

[50] Here and below, see U.S., *Census*, 1960, *Population*, vol. 1, part 25, pp. 194, 254, 340; 1970, vol. 1, part 25, p. 512.

[51] Anne Lauth information, August 12, 1980.

[52] *American Latvian Association*, undated leaflet, and *Estonia Estland Estonie Eesti*, a leaflet published by the Estonian American National Council, 1979, both in Vertical File, IHRC; Thernstrom, ed., *Harvard Encyclopedia*, 343, 640.

[53] Thernstrom, ed., *Harvard Encyclopedia*, 675; Akmentins, *Latvians in Bicentennial America*, 7.

[54] Here and below, see Grace DeSantis and Richard Benkin, "Ethnicity without Community," in *Ethnicity*, 7:140 (June, 1980); Thernstrom, ed., *Harvard Encyclopedia*, 342.

CHAPTER 17

The Czechs

C. Winston Chrislock

THE CZECHS are a Slavic-speaking people concentrated in the historic provinces of Bohemia and adjoining Moravia in the western two-thirds of contemporary Czechoslovakia. They began to join the emigrant stream in quantity after 1848, continuing to reach the United States in sizable numbers until World War I. By 1910 the census counted 539,392 foreign-born and second-generation Czechs in America; 33,247 of them lived in Minnesota, which ranked seventh among the states after Illinois, Nebraska, Ohio, New York, Wisconsin, and Texas. Primarily farmers, the Czechs settled in southern Minnesota as early as 1855, thus becoming the principal Slavic group to reach the state in the pioneer period.[1]

European Beginnings

Although Czechoslovakia did not come into being until the 20th century, the Czech heritage of political and cultural development reaches back more than a millennium. Since the 9th century, when they became Christians, the Czechs were successively an important component of the Great Moravian Empire, the kingdom of Bohemia, which was a part of the Holy Roman Empire, and the Austro-Hungarian Empire. They achieved political distinction in the 13th and 14th centuries under the rule of the Přemyslid family and Charles IV (1316–78) of Luxembourg. By the 15th century a religious reformation sparked by Jan Hus (1369–1415) converted many Czechs to an early form of Protestantism known as Hussitism. These people were much persecuted after 1526 when the Austrian Habsburgs were elected kings of Bohemia, and members of that dynasty began a century-long struggle to centralize their control with the help of a powerful bureaucracy, the army, and the Catholic church. The Czech nobility, which was largely Protestant, resisted but was finally crushed at the battle of White Mountain (*Bílá hora*) in 1620.[2]

In the aftermath of White Mountain, the independence of the Czechs as a nation was virtually extinguished. The Habsburgs confiscated the lands of the nobility, many of whom were among the 36,000 Protestant families who were forced to flee the country, causing the disappearance of the Czech aristocracy. Jesuit missionaries combed the countryside Catholicizing the peasants and destroying books in the Czech language, presumably because of their heretical content. Czech culture in the urban areas all but disappeared.

Charles University, which had been founded in Prague in 1348, took on an entirely Germanic character. Protestantism went underground. Some Czech Protestants made their way to the American colonies, including the Moravian followers of Hus who settled first in the provinces of Silesia and Saxony, where they became Germanized before moving on to Pennsylvania and North Carolina. Only among the peasantry did a sense of Czechness survive until enlightenment scholarship, industrialization, and romantic nationalism rekindled signs of Czech life in the 19th century. Nevertheless the people remained under the control of Austria-Hungary until after World War I.

While the Czechs never successfully wrested recognition of their historic Bohemian state from the Habsburgs, industrialization and urbanization intensified after 1850 to such an extent that by World War I portions of Bohemia were among the richest industrial centers of Europe. In 1846 three-fourths of the Czech people worked in farming; by 1910 only one-third were so engaged, although the population had increased from about 6,000,000 to 9,000,000. At the same time Bohemia began the transformation from labor-intensive to capital-intensive farming that characterized much of Europe during the mid-19th century. Transportation and communication networks (railroads and telegraph lines) opened the region to competition with American and Russian grain production. By the 1860s this led to changes in land use, particularly after improved methods of extracting sugar from beets were devised. Bohemia increasingly imported its wheat, and large tracts of land were given over to commercial sugar beet farming.[3]

None of these changes really benefited the southern portions of Bohemia and Moravia, where the Budějovice-Tábor area in the Lužnice River Valley and the Bohemian-Moravian Highlands were to be the principal sources of Czech immigration to Minnesota (see Map 17.1). In the former the soil was inferior and the only industries of note were brewing and the cultivation of carp, a Christmas delicacy in Czechoslovakia. In the latter the soil was stony and the terrain hilly. Large tracts of land belonged to the crown, the Austrian nobility, or the Catholic church. After the 1780s the peasants were permitted to own land. Some families owned as many as 70 acres, while others had no more than five, supplementing their incomes by hiring out their services and work animals. Still others, who had as little as two acres and no work animals, had to hire out for even longer periods of time. At the bottom of the complex class structure were the day laborers, who worked for others and had no land of their own. Forced labor ended in 1848, but not until 1867 could a peasant leave without the estate owner's permission.[4]

Life in the villages was unpretentious, revolving around the family, the church, the inn, and periodic festivals and carnivals. Potatoes and cabbages were the mainstays of the peasant diet. From the 1840s on the people went to school when they could, usually learning simple reading, spelling, and arithmetic in local elementary schools. (In 1900 literacy among Czechs was placed at 97%.) Politics and religion were heavy handed. There was virtually no self-rule, said one scholar, for "the Germanic imperial bureaucracy was the all-important factor in the government." Czech peasants were expected to be obedient to the Austrian Empire and to the Catholic church, but neither commanded deep-seated loyalty. While 96% of them were nominally Catholic, the facts that the church was led by German-speaking clergy imposed from above, and that it took a generous share of the peasants' earnings, made it unpopular with many. Unlike neighboring Poland, where Catholic influence was strong, the church had little ideological impact on the Czechs, except in portions of southern and eastern Bohemia. Indeed, many immigrants (some estimates run as high as 50% to 70%) simply discarded Catholicism after their arrival in the United States.[5]

The number of people departing from the Czech provinces in the 1850s was small, ranging from 287 in 1850 to 6,573 in 1854 "with an almost even ratio of males and females." Although some scholars believe these figures are much too low, various factors "militated against emigration on a larger scale" during that period. Passports were costly and difficult to obtain and borders were closely patrolled. Steamship companies were not allowed to maintain agents or to advertise within the Austrian Empire. After 1859 most of these restrictions were gradually removed. Transportation companies and American states then actively encouraged emigration from the ports of Hamburg, Havre, Antwerp, and Bremen. By the 1860s pamphlets in German extolling the virtues of Minnesota appeared in Bohemia. In the 1870s Northern Pacific Railway literature, also in German, called attention to the availability of Minnesota land; at the beginning of that decade the fare from Prague to St. Paul was $61.80.[6]

While it is easy to generalize about the over-all causes of Czech emigration in various periods, such generalizations obscure the thousands of extremely personal reasons that prompted people to leave their homelands. A series of Minnesota interviews in the 1930s revealed that Czech reasons for departing had ranged from a desire to escape a hopelessly drunken wife to mounting debts which the emigrant could see no way of repaying. Nevertheless it can be said that changes in inheritance laws in 1868, which permitted the

Map 17.1. Western Czechoslovakia, the Czechs' Homeland

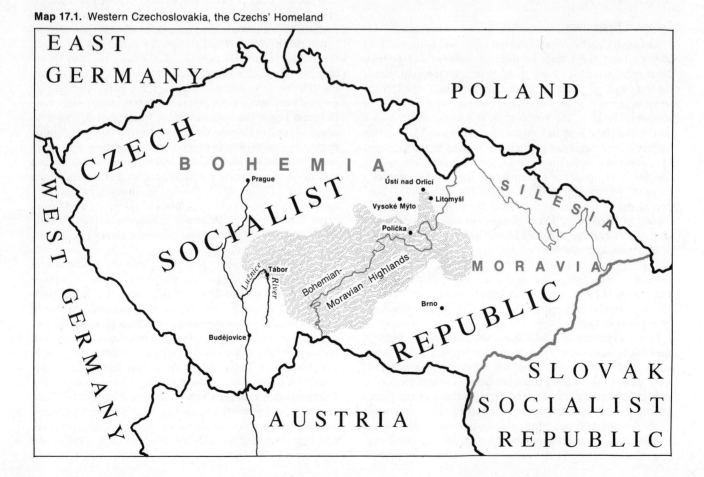

further subdivision of a peasant family's freeholdings, contributed to the breakup of the land into smaller and smaller parcels, making it impossible to earn a living from farming by the primitive methods then in use. A severe agricultural depression in 1873 and growing political repression in the mid-1880s prodded increasing numbers of Czechs to seek better opportunities in America. For others a desire to avoid three years of compulsory military service provided an incentive. Introduced in 1867, the conscription law, replacing the previously erratic impressment of men into the Austrian army, applied to all males 20 years of age. As was the case with many other Europeans, however, the Czechs' desire for better economic opportunities seemed to have been their most important reason for leaving the Austrian Empire during this period.[7]

Two closely related factors sustained emigration from Bohemia once it got under way. The first was emigration fever; everyone seemed to be leaving. The second was the letters written by Czechs who settled in Minnesota to relatives and friends back home, spreading news of the opportunities across the Atlantic. This information from America fed the emigration fever. In the mid-1850s, for example, many families left the Bohemian-Moravian Highland districts near Vysoké Mýto, Litomyšl, and Polička for Wisconsin, where the first Czech farming communities soon sprang into being.[8]

Patterns of Settlement

Czechs (then usually referred to as Bohemians), arriving in Minnesota in the 1850s, established communities that attracted their fellow nationals until World War I. By the mid-1850s such settlements had appeared in four distinct areas: the Lake Minnetonka-Hopkins region of western Hennepin County; Steele County south of Owatonna; Le Sueur, Scott, and Rice counties centering at what was to become New Prague; and Fillmore County in the vicinity of

Chatfield. By 1858 a fifth nucleus appeared in McLeod County with its focus at Silver Lake, Hutchinson, and Glencoe. That same year a few Czechs took land in Freeborn and Wright counties.[9]

By the early 1860s a few were also to be found in Winona, St. Paul, and Minneapolis. Subsequent settlement occurred in the Alexandria area of Douglas County (1868), Yellow Medicine County around Canby (1874), and in Wilkin (1874), Polk (1880), and Jackson (1882) counties. Then the flow swirled north and east for a time, backtracking into the cutover lands of Pine, Mahnomen, and St. Louis counties between 1890 and 1915. A final Czech community took shape near Meadowlands in St. Louis County in 1915 (see Table 17.1).

To these areas Czechs made their way directly from abroad or from such states as Iowa, Illinois, and Wisconsin. Settlers from Caledonia and Racine, Wisconsin, moved to McLeod County, Minnesota. The same staged migration process brought other family groups from southern Bohemia to Iowa and from there to Le Sueur County as the nucleus of the New Prague colony, from Ústí nad Orlicí in northeastern Bohemia via Wisconsin to Steele County, and from the Budějovice region to Le Sueur, Rice, and Scott counties.

Vojtěch Dolejš, for example, who ultimately settled at Montgomery in Le Sueur County, arrived in the 1850s from Bohemia because he heard "much talk about the good life." The Wondra family, living in the Budějovice district, learned of opportunities to be found in Minnesota in 1868. They sent their children in stages to Montgomery and at last followed themselves. Antonin H. Zeleny, father of future Yale and University of Minnesota scientists, left a comfortable life in Bohemia in 1869 for Wisconsin because he had a friend there; he moved west to Hutchinson in McLeod County in 1873. Jan Pavelka sold all his possessions in Bohemia and moved to Chatfield in Fillmore County in 1870 because his

Table 17.1. Bohemians and Czechoslovakians in Minnesota by County, 1860–1970

| County | Bohemians | | | | | | | | | | Czechoslovakians | | | |
| | 1860 | | 1880 | | 1895 | 1905 | | 1930 | | 1970 | |
	foreign born	foreign mixed	fb	fm	fb	fb	fm	fb	fm	fb	fm
Aitkin						13	27	36	62		7
Anoka			12	2	10	6	22	108	256	68	460
Becker					2	4	15	59	191	20	108
Beltrami						2	5	86	148	22	87
Benton			8	2	11	12	52	57	143	29	100
Big Stone			1	3		3	10	2	11		16
Blue Earth			29	23	16	10	47	15	53		57
Brown	67	6	575	357	617	7	11	241	606	6	48
Carlton					4	25	45	41	93		31
Carver	17	8	37	37	44	5	23	14	58		53
Cass			1		20	18	70	34	73	5	59
Chippewa					8	1	9	10	30		26
Chisago			4	4	4	5	11	7	17		36
Clay			4		2	9	18	17	59	10	144
Clearwater								40	56	17	68
Cook								3	9		
Cottonwood			12	4	10	11	33	13	53		
Crow Wing					14	18	44	32	80	36	82
Dakota			9	2	28	21	95	141	219	44	451
Dodge			23	23	51	17	49	27	67		14
Douglas			24	26	141	164	397	129	334	23	211
Faribault			14	15	10	5	20	8	43		15

Table 17.1. Bohemians and Czechoslovakians in Minnesota by County, 1860–1970 (*continued*)

County	Bohemians 1860 foreign born	1860 foreign mixed	1880 fb	1880 fm	1895 fb	1905 fb	1905 fm	Czechoslovakians 1930 fb	1930 fm	1970 fb	1970 fm
Fillmore			62	45	73	58	144	24	93		25
Freeborn	10	3	267	85	252	207	562	137	406	16	267
Goodhue			7	15	11	7	28	8	38		36
Grant			5	2	7	1	2	3	10		16
Hennepin	40	7	407	257	815	834	1,826	2,868	6,614	852	4,578
Minneapolis						388	946	2,308	5,302	599	2,440
Houston			17	5	13	11	31	6	22		38
Hubbard					1	3	2	35	44	14	66
Isanti								1	14		4
Itasca					2	14	21	112	236	21	133
Jackson			13	3	341	269	673	272	777	12	288
Kanabec					1		1	12	48		28
Kandiyohi			1		16	53	143	24	82	6	24
Kittson					3	5	11	2	7		
Koochiching								20	29		40
Lac qui Parle			1		1	2	3		4		12
Lake						2	8	13	25		25
Lake of the Woods								30	38		42
Le Sueur	131	13	1,220	968	1,226	1,019	3,016	524	1,647	21	585
Lincoln			13	16	27	40	106	20	77		15
Lyon						5	19	11	42		39
McLeod	26	6	869	407	974	534	1,414	470	1,238	12	443
Mahnomen								109	318	20	152
Marshall				4	21	29	74	41	116	20	73
Martin					10	10	16	4	32		13
Meeker						4	13	11	33		30
Mille Lacs					1	2	5	38	96	12	42
Morrison			61	28	76	35	54	140	293		101
Mower			60	23	134	115	411	185	460	19	341
Murray			6	1	2	13	17	23	55		7
Nicollet			244	154	85	7	26	26	48		32
Nobles					10	11	25	20	45		43
Norman					12	2	2	15	56	5	20
Olmsted			14	7	14	26	67	42	146	14	146
Otter Tail			24	7	16	15	35	32	81		92
Pennington								54	130	6	80
Pine			19	12	2	359	949	499	1,080	44	419
Pipestone				1	5	7	16	6	24		7
Polk			3	5	323	197	661	199	668	13	264
Pope			61	73	62	55	155	32	137	7	80
Ramsey	14	2	643	422	1,245	1,071	2,741	1,576	3,675	417	1,879
St. Paul						1,065	2,732	1,513	3,551	358	1,378
Red Lake						23	84	9	38		27
Redwood			17	11	78	106	302	87	288	7	72
Renville			66	98	463	348	973	206	633	11	191
Rice	2		648	503	847	617	2,004	301	1,310		290
Rock			1	6	2	5	16		5		
Roseau					33	127	283	104	235	16	105
St. Louis			2	7	25	30	155	511	986	111	603
Duluth						20	48	110	274	23	232
Scott	74	3	644	391	537	420	1,140	286	814	16	264
Sherburne					4	5	13	23	73		5
Sibley	19	2	19	21	14	4	5	9	33		9
Stearns	1		64	58	84	37	158	149	417	20	118
Steele	48	20	764	471	740	772	1,733	478	1,529	28	727
Stevens							15	8	27		11
Swift			5	5	2	3	11	12	38		26
Todd			21	18	104	113	258	133	451	6	145
Traverse			1		2	6	16	4	22		
Wabasha			26	31	4	4	8	14	43	8	29
Wadena			1		11	17	44	18	54		37
Waseca	17	2	52	39	24	39	107	19	64	6	17
Washington			9		4	5	39	24	68	9	171
Watonwan			8	4	2	8	6	4	14	5	19
Wilkin			51	32	71	98	253	74	224	20	90
Winona	3	2	362	135	300	57	170	73	237		92
Wright	28	4	89	110	138	124	301	75	249		129
Yellow Medicine			6	3	26	57	187	30	126		50
Total	497	78	7,626	4,981	10,288	8,403	22,561	11,415	29,623	2,080	15,825
Published census figures			(7,759)		(10,327)	(8,403)	(22,562)	(11,415)	(29,623)	(2,080)	(15,825)

Source: See Appendix

brother, who had lived there for 17 years, wanted him to witness his wealth. Jan Hrdlicka immigrated to Pope County in 1874 because his brother-in-law had settled there a year earlier. And so it went until Minnesota boasted some 12,500 persons of Czech stock in the 1870s.[10]

By then the state's largest Czech concentration was well established in the triangle of Le Sueur, Scott, and Rice counties. There, as elsewhere in rural Minnesota, Bohemians sought out land and started farming. New Prague, Montgomery, and Lonsdale became the commercial and social centers of this region, but other villages such as Budejovice, Trebon, Veseli, and Heidelberg — the last named by the Germans who got there first — were important from 1860 to the end of the century.

Budejovice, for example, attracted numerous Czechs in the late 1860s. One early arrival wrote that to get there from St. Paul, he and his colleagues had traveled by river and on foot for two and a half days to reach the New Prague area. Then they continued farther south because "the land there was taken up mostly by Luxembourgers." At first the settlers called their community Nemanice (the place where people have nothing); later they renamed it Budejovice for their homeland region. Once established, these farmers had to transport their grain by wagon 25 miles to Shakopee in order to market it. When the railroad came through in 1877, it ran about three miles east of Budejovice. As a result the community was soon outstripped by Montgomery.[11]

Later Lonsdale supplanted Veseli in a similar way. Writing in 1886, a settler described Veseli as "the only, purely Czech town in the United States." It was, he said, divided into eastern and western sections, which together had seven saloons, three blacksmith shops, a general store, a restaurant, a drugstore, a dance hall, and a Catholic church and school. After 1901 when the Milwaukee Road built a line through Lonsdale, Veseli faded in commercial, though not in cultural, significance. The railroad drew Czechs to the Lonsdale area. Many would work for it, save money, and gradually acquire farmland.[12]

Railroads were important to Czech settlements in other parts of the state. The Omaha and Western Railroad yards in St. Paul provided employment for the Bohemians clustered in the West 7th Street area. When the Chicago and Northwestern Railway built a line in 1899 through Lucan in Redwood County, Czechs settled in that town. Near the Czech community of Tabor in Polk County many people both farmed and worked for the Great Northern. A Moravian employed by the Duluth, Missabe and Iron Range Railroad, who was described as a "fast talker," lured scores of Czechs to Meadowlands in St. Louis County in the years from 1915 to 1919. There they found bogs and forests instead of the prime agricultural land he had promised.[13]

The period from 1860 to 1880 was the most active for Czech settlement across southern Minnesota. The rural areas with the heaviest Czech concentrations were in Rice, Scott, Le Sueur, and McLeod counties (see Table 17.1). Steele, Renville, Redwood, and Wright counties tapered off in the size of their immigrant populations after 1905. Of the southern counties, Jackson on the Iowa border showed the largest increase in "Czechoslovak" foreign born through the 1930 census. (Since Czechs and Slovaks were counted together after 1920, this increase may be attributable to the influx of Slovaks.)[14]

Immigration to the Twin Cities area peaked considerably later. The cities may have received the bulk of Czech arrivals counted after 1899 (see Table 17.2); their numbers dropped sharply during World War I. The high point for foreign-born Czechs in Ramsey and Hennepin counties occurred in 1930 (see Table 17.1). For Ramsey County, which included St. Paul, this figure represented mostly Czechs, but for Hennepin at least some of the people counted were Slovaks who settled near St. Cyril's Roman Catholic Church in Northeast Minneapolis, in the vicinity of 21st Avenue South and 2nd Street, and on the Bohemian Flats beneath the Washington Avenue Bridge in Southeast Minneapolis. By 1930 the two cities together had over 12,600 first- and second-generation "Czechoslovaks." Other towns (those with populations of more than 2,500) held another 5,600, and rural Minnesota counted nearly 23,000. Thus farming and the trades and services in the small towns associated with farming provided the livelihood for perhaps two-thirds of the Czechs who settled in Minnesota before 1930.[15]

One community in which urban and rural elements merged

NEW PRAGUE looking south about 1909. The large church of St. Wenceslaus can be seen in the left background.

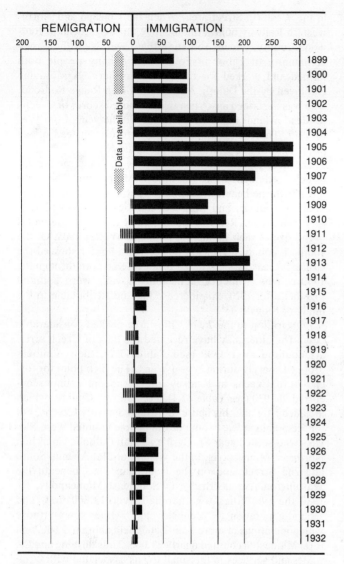

REMIGRATION | IMMIGRATION

200 150 100 50 0 50 100 150 200 250 300

Data unavailable

1899
1900
1901
1902
1903
1904
1905
1906
1907
1908
1909
1910
1911
1912
1913
1914
1915
1916
1917
1918
1919
1920
1921
1922
1923
1924
1925
1926
1927
1928
1929
1930
1931
1932

Table 17.2. Czech (Bohemian) Migration to and from Minnesota

McLeod County. One Czech recalled that the Indians put half of the town of Hutchinson to the torch and that the 14 Czech families living there clustered together on one farm, where they built a fortification. They brought their animals within the protected area and left it to work only the land within the range of their guns until an army contingent lifted the siege.[17]

The Development of Institutions

Minnesota Czechs were quick to form varied institutions around which they developed their religious, social, and cultural life. Among them were Roman Catholic and Protestant churches, fraternal lodges, free-thought reading societies, cemetery associations, and gymnastic groups. Perhaps as much as 70% of the state's Czech population was affiliated with the Catholic church, a figure below that of the Old Country but higher than in some other states. For example, in Wisconsin, an early center of Czech settlement, a very active free-thought movement won over as many as half the Czechs.[18]

Possibly learning from this experience, the Catholic church in Minnesota sought to draw them to the fold. In this it enjoyed a fair degree of success, but Czechs did not develop the fierce loyalty displayed by many Poles. They were, wrote historian Esther Jerabek, "prone to drop religious affiliations upon arriving in the United States, particularly if they settled in cities." Nevertheless the degree of Catholic efforts among them is suggested by a guide published in 1910 which listed no fewer than 13 Czech parishes in the state. Even more impressive is the fact that almost every Minnesota Czech Catholic family known to the author retained a copy of this book in 1980.[19]

Several parishes were organized early, including that of St. Wenceslaus Church in New Prague, which traces its history to 1858. Others sprouted later — Sacred Heart (originally a mixed parish) at Owatonna (1866), Holy Trinity at Veseli (1874), Holy Trinity at Litomysl (1878), Holy Redeemer at Montgomery (1881), Immaculate Conception at Trebon (1886), and St. Joseph at Silver Lake (1895).[20]

For a parish to be formed, the diocese required that a community turn over 40 acres of cleared land. This requirement was usually met by donations from several farmers in a given area, and the parish was then incorporated in the names of the bishop, the vicar general, the parish priest, and two laymen from the congregation. Occasionally this procedure led to misunderstandings, as it did at New Prague in 1875–76 when parish members refused to sign over the promised property, fearing that it might be lost to heirs of the bishop or those of the parish priest.[21]

According to the 1910 guide: "The parishioners did not understand what was meant by the term incorporation, therefore they stubbornly refused. . . . The bishop could not arrive at any other solution than to issue an interdict over the whole parish. Things looked very sad . . . ; no priest to serve mass, holy days were not kept, there were quiet funerals without a priest . . ." until at last "the parishioners recognized their unproductive actions" and "regretted their errors." After that "the interdict was lifted and the parish was again sent a priest."[22]

was Hopkins. In the 1850s and 1860s several Czech families moved from Caledonia, Wisconsin, where in 1854 they had heard about the "abundance of available land" in Minnesota, wrote one, "and that it would be suitable to settle there and begin farming." By the 1880s Hopkins had become noted for the cultivation of raspberry bushes, for the innovative Czech farmers had experimented and had solved the problem of wintering them. By the 1870s the railroad linked Hopkins with Minneapolis, and a farm implement factory provided work for more immigrants. Consequently Hopkins developed a community of Czechs employed on the railroad, in the implement plant, or as berry farmers and landowners.[16]

Accounts of the formative years of Czech life in rural Minnesota chronicled familiar themes. Land was acquired and opened to the plow — sometimes an acre at a time — capital was slowly built, and bad weather and pestilence were endured. On at least one occasion there were Indians to be fought. The Dakota War of 1862 slowed settlement in

When it was not possible to procure national churches, Czechs living in areas of mixed nationalities worshiped in territorial parishes with Poles, Germans, or Irish. In communities such as St. Paul, Silver Lake, and Owatonna, this created unhappiness. In St. Paul the early Czechs attended predominantly German Assumption Church downtown, but by 1872 St. Stanislaus of Kostka was built in the West 7th Street neighborhood to serve both Czechs and Poles. When a Czech priest was sent to St. Stanislaus in 1874, the Poles objected, and in 1880 they formed their own Church of St. Adalbert, located northwest of the state Capitol.[23]

The opposite transpired at Silver Lake. There a Czech Catholic cemetery, begun in 1867, preceded the organization of a chapel in 1873. Both were located at Bear Creek about four miles south of Silver Lake. This was too far for the Silver Lakers to travel, so until 1895, when they built their own St. Joseph's Church, the Czechs worshiped with the Silver Lake Poles at a church also named for St. Adalbert. On the other hand, Sacred Heart Church in Owatonna became Czech by a process of elimination. When it was incorporated in 1866, it served all the Catholics in town, but the Germans and the Irish formed their own parishes in 1891 and the Poles separated in 1901, leaving the Czechs and a few Bohemian Germans in full possession. As early as the 1890s, Czech Catholics decided to transfer from Northeast Minneapolis and establish a national parish, Our Lady of Perpetual Help Church, at 21st Avenue and 5th Street Southeast above the Bohemian Flats. Although its original membership had been Czech, by the 1920s and 1930s it was diluted as the Czechs moved out of the area and diverse other groups moved in.

By 1910 an extensive network of parishes and church-related institutions had been established for Czechs. It was led in part by priests born and educated in Bohemia joined after 1900 by some Minnesota-born, Czech-speaking clergy. Father Jan Rynda, who was assigned to St. Stanislaus from 1886 to 1924, was especially influential. Born in Moravia in 1859, Rynda immigrated to Minnesota in 1886, serving briefly at a church in Delano, Wright County. After he moved to St. Paul, he also held services in Czech areas throughout southern Minnesota, was active in various Czech societies, and was the leading personality in the League of Czech Priests, a group that sought to persuade Archbishop John Ireland to establish Czech national parishes to keep Czechs loyal to the church.[24]

Such parishes were particularly important because many of them supported grade schools where the Czech language was taught. As late as 1922 in southern Minnesota 10 parishes had over 1,000 children enrolled in such schools. New Prague also had a parochial high school, begun in 1903. This network of classrooms and churches helped preserve the language and other elements of ethnicity through World War I. Not until the late 1920s and 1930s did the use of Czech slowly fade from church services and parochial schools.[25]

A smaller number of Czechs were members of Protestant churches. For the most part, they had emigrated from the Bohemian-Moravian Highlands, where for several centuries Protestants had withstood the persecutions of the Counter Reformation and the forced re-Catholicization which followed the Thirty Years' War. During the latter part of the 19th century, American churches — especially the Presbyterian — sent missionaries to Bohemia, and Oberlin College in Ohio offered a two-year program to train Czech clergy, which was lengthened to three years in 1890. In addition to the seminary curriculum, the students were expected to take two years of instruction in the language. After 1900 the Presbyterians established Czech-language districts in the United States; the one that included Minnesota existed from 1910 to 1948. In 1926–28 it published *Naše prace* (Our Work), Minnesota's only Czech Protestant paper, which was edited at Silver Lake.[26]

Of Protestant denominations, Presbyterian and Congregational groups came into being in the Minnesota Czech settlements beginning about 1870. For example, immigrants from the Bohemian-Moravian Highlands began holding services in their homes at Hopkins about 1869. By 1888 they had started a cemetery and erected John Hus Presbyterian Church. Before 1900, when a full-time pastor was secured, traveling Czech clerics preached at first sporadically and then regularly.[27]

A similar pattern was apparent at Silver Lake, where Protestants worshiped in homes before completing a church in 1881. At first named the Czech Evangelical Reformed Church but later known as the Czech Brethren Presbyterian Church, it remained without a full-time pastor until 1891. When the congregation in that year had an opportunity to call a young Czech seminary student, who had on occasion preached in Silver Lake, the members voted not to do so. Dissatisfied, a minority then split off, called the student, and founded the Free Reformed Church, which in 1897–98 joined the Congregationalists. Both Silver Lake congregations established Saturday schools offering instruction in Czech literature, language, and history, and both held services in the mother tongue. On rare special occasions, the two congregations worshiped together. Still another group, started in St. Paul in 1886 by Czechs from the Bohemian-Moravian Highlands, became Cyril Congregational Church located near St. Stanislaus in the West 7th Street area. With 50 to 65 families as members, it, too, had a Saturday school and conducted weekly Sunday services in Czech until 1945.[28]

Other Protestant efforts to work among the Czechs were not particularly successful, although the Baptists built a church at New Prague and won some converts in St. Paul. A few Czechs affiliated with Lutheran and Baptist churches organized by Slovaks in Minneapolis in 1888 and 1917, respectively. But many were either indifferent or hostile to organized religion in any form. To some the Presbyterian and Congregational churches were too puritanical in their attitudes toward drinking alcoholic beverages and dancing, both of which were favorite Czech pastimes, while to others, who carried with them attitudes forged in the homeland, the Catholic church was the historic enemy.[29]

Writing in 1971 of five elements which, in his opinion, led to the "decatholicization" of Czechs in the United States, Karel D. Bicha listed: "(1) the history and culture of Old Bohemia, that is, its role as a religious battleground, the predilection of its people for religious controversy, its early and successful protestantization, and the forced and brazen nature of its recatholicization; (2) the marginal sincerity of Catholicism in the peasant villages of Bohemia; (3) the elimination, by emigration itself, of the most meaningful elements in the religious commitment of the peasants, that is, the elements associated with the folk tradition and the physical and cultural milieu of the village; (4) the fortuitous, yet strategic, arrival on the American scene of a group of able, articulate ex-clergymen and seminarians, many of them refugees from the Bohemian political and social upheavals of 1848 and the 1860's; and (5) the domination by these religious radicals of Czech-language communications, especially the press, in the formative years of the immigrant community.''[30]

Possibly as many as half of the Czech immigrants in the 19th century were affected by free thought, or religious liberalism, as it was sometimes called. It found expression in the Czech-American press and the founding of fraternal lodges, reading societies, and cemetery associations not associated with any church. Minnesota never boasted a strong and enduring Czech-language press, but nearby Chicago and neighboring Wisconsin did. From the 1860s and 1870s until after World War II, religious radicals published at Racine such long-lived and influential papers as *Slavie* (Glory) and *Pokrok* (Progress) and at Chicago, *Svornost* (Harmony). These publications had sizable readerships among Minnesota Czechs, some of whom had never seen a newspaper before they immigrated. Small wonder then that exposure to the ideas espoused in their pages made an impact.[31]

While the free-thought movement was not as popular in Minnesota as it was in some other states, there are scattered glimpses of its influence. *Minnesotské noviny* (Minnesota News), which appeared from 1904 to 1914 as a St. Paul supplement to *Osvěta americká* (American Enlightenment) of Omaha, reflected religiously liberal views in its columns. On March 5, 1910, for example, it attacked the Catholic church and called for the development of a positive free-thought philosophy.

The publishers of *Svornost* also produced *Amerikán: Národní Kalendář* (American: National Almanac) from 1878 to 1957, which called attention to Minnesota examples through the years. In 1898 a freethinker from Heidelberg, a hamlet in Le Sueur County near New Prague, reported that the priest in his community had so fanaticized people against him that they threatened to stab him with a pitchfork during threshing. A writer from Montgomery announced that his eyes had been opened and even the threat of going to hell would not bring him back to the church. A man in Pope County wrote that in the early years of the Czech colony there, many people had so resented the priest's interference that they separated from the church and agreed to purchase a parcel of land for a nonsectarian cemetery. He added that the priest got even by ordering the families of the dissenters who had relatives buried in the Catholic cemetery to remove flowers from the graves. When they did not comply, he went to the cemetery and tore them down.[32]

The establishment of such nonsectarian cemeteries, sometimes in advance of churches, was not uncommon, and an organization known as the Bohemian National Cemetery Association was created to fill the need. A national group

with headquarters in Chicago, its purpose was to provide burial plots for people without church affiliations. In order to acquire plots, the members were expected to donate labor and money toward the maintenance of the cemeteries, which were to be found in many Minnesota Czech communities during and after the 1870s.[33]

In addition to founding cemeteries, freethinking Minnesotans also formed benefit associations, reading societies, and gymnastic groups. *Česko-slovanský Podporující Spolek* (Czecho-Slovanic Benefit Society) known as CSPS for short, was the oldest Czech free-thought fraternal organization in the United States. Founded in St. Louis in 1854, it at first charged members $.50 a month, in return for which they were entitled to receive a $2.50 weekly sickness benefit and $20.00 in burial expenses; widows of deceased members were paid $4.00 a month. In time, the functions of CSPS were extended to encompass cultural and educational enterprises, theater and music groups, and the construction of halls which became community or neighborhood social and cultural centers for Czechs throughout the United States.[34]

The first CSPS lodge in Minnesota was started in St. Paul in 1876. New Prague, Owatonna, Minneapolis, and Montgomery soon had them as well, and by 1896 there were 11 in the state. In 1887 St. Paul erected a handsome three-story hall (renovated in 1917 and partially restored in 1980) in the heart of the Czech neighborhood near West 7th Street, and 10 years later the Owatonna Czechs built a similar structure. The halls hosted lodge meetings, dances, dramatic and musical performances, lectures, Czech-language schools, and yearly festivals. Antonín Dvořák appeared at the St. Paul hall in 1893.[35]

The cultural impact of St. Paul's CSPS Hall drew a grudging comment from a strait-laced Czech Protestant in 1900: ''Several of the free thinkers believe completely in their hall and the cultivation of their nationality by partaking in hops [*beer*],'' he remarked. ''Their children are instructed very quickly in that as well. Several, however, are inclined to our [*Congregational*] mission, they send their children to Sunday school, but they do not look after their own spiritual needs.'' In 1932 CSPS merged with several other Czech fraternal groups to form the Czechoslovak Society of America.[36]

A second fraternal organization that attracted freethinkers was the Western Bohemian Fraternal Union, better known as the ZCBJ (*Západní Česká Bratrská Jednota*). It came into being in 1897 when Slavic people in the western United States, believing that their injury and mortality rates were lower than those of the miners and industrial workers in the East, decided they should be entitled to lower rates and broke with CSPS. Like CSPS, ZCBJ established a network of lodges across Minnesota, built a number of halls — Canby and Meadowlands still had them in 1980 — and supported programs of Czech cultural activities. Still active in 1980 as the Western Fraternal Life Association, ZCBJ had 24 lodges with 5,152 members in Minnesota.[37]

Another important organization sympathetic to free thought was the Sokol (Falcon), which originated in Bohemia in 1862 to foster Czech nationalism and unity through educational activities and gymnastics. By 1865 Sokol had been transported to the United States. The first Minnesota lodge was organized in St. Paul in 1882. By 1927 nine others existed — in Hopkins (1906), Owatonna (1908), New Prague and Minneapolis (1912), Montgomery (1913), Foley and Denham (1919), Hutchinson (1923), and Meadowlands (1927). These groups sponsored gymnastic festivals, mass drills, folk dances, Czech plays, and old-time dances, and joined with other organizations in discussing topics of interest to Czechs.[38]

The St. Paul Sokol, like most of the others, rented the local CSPS Hall for its activities. But in 1978, it changed its name to Sokol Minnesota, purchased the building from the Czechoslovak Society of America, and became the most active surviving Czech group in the city.[39]

Through the years gymnastics were the core of its program. Members participated in district, regional, national, and international *slets* (gymnastic festivals) sponsored by the American Sokol Union, with which the local chapter was affiliated. In 1938, for example, five St. Paul Czechs took part in a *slet* held in Prague, Czechoslovakia. Commemorating 20 years of that nation's independence, the event was closely linked to the Czech heritage, for it was also held on July 6, the 523rd anniversary of the martyrdom of Jan Hus.[40]

The Czech free-thought reading and discussion societies, which often took the place of churches for their members, also abounded in Minnesota in the late 19th and early 20th centuries. One of those popular in the 1860s and 1870s was known as *Slovanská Lípa* (Slavic Linden Tree). Owatonna had such a circle as early as 1866 and St. Paul by 1870; eventually the CSPS absorbed both.

A similar organization was *Český Čtenářský a Vzdělanecký Spolek* (Czech Reading and Educational Society), which had as its objectives the preservation of the Czech language in the United States and the elevation of the moral, spiritual, and material welfare of the Czechs. It was most active in the Silver Lake area, where in 1883 it built Komensky Hall about midway between Silver Lake and Hutchinson. From there it conducted its activities until World War

WOMEN'S SOKOL unit performing at a Meadowlands slet in August, 1929.

II. They included sponsoring a Czech-language school, producing Czech plays, and carrying out such other functions as having members present at the funerals of deceased colleagues.[41]

To meet the threat posed by the free-thought movement, the Catholic church initiated and underwrote Catholic fraternal lodges. Among the most successful was *Katolický Dělník* (Catholic Workingman), which was organized in 1891 with headquarters at New Prague. It gained a substantial membership in Minnesota as well as in nearby states, and in 1929 it absorbed a similar group, the *Západní Česká Katolická Jednota* (Western Czech Catholic Union).[42]

Beginning in 1906 *Katolický Dělník* published a monthly and sometimes bimonthly Czech-language periodical of the same name, which was issued at New Prague and later in such cities as St. Louis, Chicago, and Omaha. The publication, one of a number backed by the Catholic church over the years in an attempt to counteract the influence of free-thought periodicals, was the second such effort to be published in Minnesota. The first was *Obzor* (Horizon), which appeared weekly in St. Paul from 1891 to 1894.[43]

Assimilation and Preservation

Assimilation has been defined as "the substitution of one nationality pattern for another." Generally Czechs had little difficulty adapting to American life, but the degree of assimilation or retention of Czech culture in Minnesota varied with conditions in particular settlements. Militating against preservation was the Czechs' tendency — somewhat greater than that of other Slavic peoples — to marry non-Czechs. (For example, 23.6% of second-generation Czechs in the United States in 1910 had mixed Czech and native or Czech and other foreign-born parents, against 6.1% for Slovaks.) Other factors included the breakup of Czech neighborhoods or towns, decline and loss of the language, and pressure from the host culture to shed features of Czech origin. Factors working for preservation included strong concentrations of Czechs in specific areas, effective organizations interested in perpetuating selected features of Czech culture, competent leadership, and uniting causes, such as the crusade for a Czechoslovak state during World Wars I and II or the interest aroused by the new ethnicity growing out of the pluralism of the late 1960s.[44]

In the state's largest Czech concentration — the New Prague-Montgomery area — retention was possible because the Czechs had the advantage of numbers. The 1930 census indicated over 4,000 first- and second-generation Czechs still residing in the Le Sueur-Rice-Scott triangle. At that time Catholic schools there retained some Czech-language classes in the curriculum. St. Wenceslaus Church in New Prague served as a focus of religious life, and the headquarters of *Katolický Dělník* (which continued to publish a bilingual newspaper) remained there. Such other institutions as the Bohemian National Cemetery and CSPS and ZCBJ lodges were active as well.[45]

The presence of Czechs drew more of their countrymen to the triangle area, and the expansion of industries made population growth economically feasible. Over the years New Prague became more than a marketing town, gradually assuming the trappings of an industrial center. A foundry was established in 1889, and the New Prague Flouring Mill, parent plant of what is now the International Multifoods Corporation, was born in 1896. As for Montgomery, Czechs were attracted there by the railroad and later by the canning industry and a Munsingwear plant built after World War II.[46]

While it still claimed the state's largest ZCBJ lodge (689 members) in 1980, only faint glimmerings of its Czech heritage could be discerned in Montgomery's most popular festival, Kolacky Days. Held annually since 1929 (except for the war years of the 1940s), the event was named for the *kolač* — a round Bohemian bun with a fruit or poppy-seed filling — on the theory that few people would know what it was, and they would want to find out. For the first festival a local bakery was asked to produce 20,000 *kolačky*, but it managed to turn out only 11,000, which were not enough to go around. The 1929 parade, too, was rated a "dud." It had only "5 floats 3 of which were . . . Minnesota Valley Canning Co. corn wagons piled up with empty pea and corn boxes."[47]

Nevertheless the idea caught on, and after a second try, Kolacky Days became a yearly event. At first it was held in October as a harvest festival, but in recent years it has usually been celebrated on the last Sunday in July. In 1980 over 20,000 people congregated to participate in what had by then become a typical Chamber of Commerce gathering with few ethnic overtones. Czech foods were still available, however, and the program of parades, tractor pulls, queen candidates, softball games, and *kolačky*-eating contests usually included some music and dances reminiscent of the area's ethnic heritage.

Czech music is the centerpiece, however, of a festival sponsored since 1968 by Holy Trinity Catholic Church at Veseli. Known as the Veseli Ho-Down, it attracted thousands of Czech-Americans, many of whom still spoke Czech, in August, 1980.[48]

St. Paul owes its vestiges of Czech life in part to the fact that many first- and second-generation Czechs continued to live in the West 7th Street area near St. Stanislaus and Cyril

Congregational churches and the CSPS Hall. Not until the late 1940s and 1950s did they depart in substantial numbers for such suburbs as Mendota, Roseville, and Woodbury. In the 1950s the membership of Cyril Church moved away, and in 1958 the congregation dissolved. Its building, still standing in 1980, had been converted to a dwelling. St. Stanislaus remained, continuing to serve elderly Czechs, Germans, and others who lived in the neighborhood in 1980. It might be added that St. Stanislaus and the CSPS Hall stand about 50 yards apart. While both have looked after Czech cultural life, each in its own way, there has been very little cooperation between them over a 90-year period, except during World Wars I and II.[49]

The Sokol and the CSPS Hall remained more active than the churches. Over the years the organization regularly used the old landmark for gymnastic classes and monthly business meetings, as well as for numerous cultural and social events important to the preservation of Czech life in the city. Twice a year through the 1920s and into the 1930s, the Sokol produced Czech-language plays, which were performed before large audiences in the hall's second-floor auditorium and then taken on tour to such communities as New Prague, Montgomery, and Silver Lake. Through World War II so many other organizations also used the hall that the rental income was sufficient to operate and maintain it.[50]

Even after the war, the hall's importance as an ethnic center continued. Among the many events still held there in 1980 was *Šibřinky*, sponsored by the Sokol. Although the word may imply a harvest festival, St. Paul's *Šibřinky* occurred in the spring just before the beginning of Lent. Held regularly since 1908, it attracted people in Czech costumes who enjoy dancing polkas and mazurkas and singing familiar Czech songs. Other Sokol-backed activities that continued were weekly sings, an annual picnic at the Sokol camp near Pine City, and Czech dinners with abundant quantities of *knedlíky* and *zelí* (dumplings and sauerkraut) accompanied by *jíternice* (a stuffed liver sausage) or roast pork.[51]

The persistence of both Sokol Minnesota and the CSPS Hall in the life of the city owed much to the leadership of

THE MAIN STREET of Montgomery as it looked during Kolacky Days in 1933.

THE CSPS Hall in St. Paul with Most's Grocery and Kriz Brothers Bakery on the ground floor in 1968.

Joseph Pavlicek. Born in the Bohemian-Moravian Highlands in 1890, he immigrated to McLeod County in 1908, studied accounting, and in 1921 accepted a post in the St. Paul Public Works Department, which he held until his retirement in 1961. During that period Pavlicek, as treasurer of the hall's board of trustees, organized and led hundreds of activities associated with Czech cultural, social, and political life. In the 1920s he edited a paper called *Sokolská Hlídka* (Sokol Outlook), which appeared first in Czech and later in English.[52]

One of his major concerns was the preservation of Czech culture. To this end he arranged for musical performances and programs to mark the anniversaries of Czechoslovak independence, lectures on the importance of maintaining an awareness of Czech origins, and the showing of Czech films. The latter were screened monthly for 200 to 300 people at the Garden Theater on West 7th Street from the late 1930s to the 1950s, when the supply was curtailed. Pavlicek arranged for the rental of such Czech classics as *Svět patří nám* (The World Belongs to Us), *Dvořák, Svatební cesta* (Wedding Journey), and many others. After each showing he carefully recorded the number of adults and children who attended, the total amount of money taken in, the profit, and his opinion of each film in brief comments that ranged from "Exceptional" through "Nothing extra" to "No good." After the films had been shown in St. Paul, Pavlicek arranged to send them on to other communities in Minnesota and Wisconsin.[53]

In Minneapolis, Czech cultural and social life was not as durable as it was in St. Paul, perhaps in part because the people were not concentrated in any one neighborhood. In spite of its name, the Bohemian Flats had more Slovak residents than Czechs, but all were essentially squatters along the Mississippi River in an area that teemed with life from about 1884 until the 1920s, when the city of Minneapolis threatened eviction. After a protracted court battle, the city forced the last resident to leave the area in 1931.[54]

Minneapolis had several ZCBJ lodges with at least one hall on the north side which was sold at the time of World War II, depriving the Czech organizations of a center. Writing in 1952 to the president of the St. Paul Sokol, Joseph Pavlicek pinpointed the problem: "We know from personal observations what has happened to Minneapolis Sokol Society since the Western Bohemian Lodge sold their hall, we also know that in Hopkins, with much larger Czech population than in St. Paul, Sokol activities are non-existent. I doubt very much that the membership of the St. Paul Sokol Society wishes to face the same difficulties encountered by their fellow members in Minneapolis and Hopkins," he went on, "and for that reason, they should recognize the fact that . . . the time has arrived for younger blood to take over."[55]

At the time Pavlicek wrote, the Czech groups in Hopkins were also suffering a decline. Until the 1950s Hopkins had boasted an effective leadership and strong ethnic organizations. John Hus Presbyterian Church had been served by Czech-speaking pastors from the 1920s, and not until 1950 did it hold services exclusively in English. The Hopkins Sokol and the ZCBJ lodge had active programs. In 1939 they had pooled their resources to sponsor harvest festivals, which were common among Czechs and Slovaks in both the Old Country and the United States. The event brought together Czechs in national costume, gymnastic displays, a harvest pageant, and Czech food, music, and dancing.[56]

Somewhat more successful were the Czechs in McLeod County in preserving elements of their heritage. Since the two most visible groups in Silver Lake were Poles and Czechs, there was less pressure to assimilate totally into American culture. Indeed, some competition may have existed between the two in the maintenance of their respective cultures. "[Sometimes] they fought at weddings," remembered one resident in 1974. "When the Polish had a wedding, it was their wedding; when the Bohemians had a wedding, it was their wedding. The older Bohemians and Polish used to always say they had their own butcher shops and they used to walk on separate sides of the street." Until the 1960s little intermarriage took place between them. In 1980 both maintained their own Catholic churches, and both operated their own parochial schools. Fittingly the community's summer festival, started in 1971, was called Pola-Czesky Days.[57]

Writing in 1934, Esther Jerabek, a Czech historian who grew up in Silver Lake, noted that the first generation of Czech settlers there "adhered to the language, habits, and customs of their native land, mingling but little with their neighbors of other nationalities. Their solidarity was such that men and women who came to the community fifty and sixty years ago have never been obliged to learn English in order to transact business or have social intercourse. . . . With the education of the second generation in the public schools, a bilingual group has developed. Although its members have discarded many of the picturesque customs of their forebears and have adopted those of Americans, they have preserved enough Czech traditions to serve as a . . . link between their parents and the third generation. . . .

"Until about 1914 the Bohemian language was in general use on the public school playground," and a "large number of children entered school without knowing English. . . . [But] one now [*1934*] rarely hears Czech spoken by the school children. It is used today chiefly by some of the older citizens and in part of the church services. Modes of dress are also changing. The kerchiefs formerly worn by women in place of hats and the large imported shawls once used instead of coats have almost disappeared. . . .

"As in other immigrant colonies, the ways of the Old World have given place to those of the New in nearly all the ordinary routine of living. Fifteen years ago [*1919*] a homesick young Czech . . . could still allude to Silver Lake . . . as 'little Prague.' But with the gradual disappearance of the pioneer settlers little remains to distinguish it from other small villages and farming districts of southeastern Minnesota."

Until the 1950s Silver Lake's Protestant churches had a succession of Czech-born or Czech-American pastors — the Congregational Church until 1954 and the Czech Brethren Presbyterian Church, as it was renamed in 1948, until 1958. In the former, services were conducted in Czech until 1928, when the congregation opted for English every second Sunday. In 1947 the church records were no longer kept in Czech, and services in that language were limited to one a month; seven years later they were eliminated entirely. In the Presbyterian Church Czech predominated in services, meetings, and records until the late 1930s. After that the use of English gradually increased until it completely replaced Czech in 1958. The church operated a lending library, and its records show that no Czech-language books have been borrowed since 1956.[58]

Other Czech organizations that continued to function in Silver Lake in 1980 included the Bohemian National Cemetery Association and an unusually active ZCBJ lodge. The latter acquired a fine, brick building formerly used as a school to which it transferred the books of the old Bohemian Reading and Educational Society's library (disbanded with the onset of World War II in 1941) as well as mementoes of the ZCBJ and other Czech organizations in the area.[59]

Two other rural communities that also successfully resisted complete assimilation until World War II were Tabor in Polk County and Meadowlands in St. Louis County. In Tabor institutional life revolved around Holy Trinity Church, which had Czech priests until 1941, and Tabor Presbyterian Church, which merged with that at Angus in 1951. The community has also sponsored an annual Czech Days festival, which usually takes place in June.[60]

In Meadowlands the ZCBJ Hall has served as a center of Czech activities since the 1920s. Here the residents gathered for lodge activities, Sokol gymnastics, Czech movies and plays, and other community activities. Two ZCBJ lodges were formed, one in 1918, which held its meetings in Czech, and a second in 1935, which used English. The two merged in 1975. A Sokol unit, active in the 1920s and 1930s, declined after World War II. In the 1930s an unemployed artist was commissioned to decorate the interior of the hall with paintings of castles and landmarks in Czechoslovakia. He also embellished the stage curtain with a pastoral scene and bilingual advertisements of local merchants. In 1980 the building remained in good repair, a symbol of the commitment of older Czechs in the area to their cultural legacy.[61]

In other parts of Minnesota visible signs of Czech culture had disappeared before World War I. In Chatfield, for example, Czech family names were Americanized. Joseph Underleak, a community leader and a state legislator in the 1890s, wrote in 1930 that his family name had originally been Anderlik, but that it had been changed after his older brother's teacher misspelled it. In Renville, Redwood, Todd, and Yellow Medicine counties, Czechs were virtually submerged by other ethnic groups. Although ZCBJ lodges still operated in Todd and Yellow Medicine counties in 1980, many officers of the latter were Scandinavians or Germans who had married Czechs.[62]

In Steele County, where a Czech National Cemetery is located in Owatonna, Czechs were a sufficiently important element of the population as late as 1931 to draw Governor Floyd B. Olson (whose wife Ada Krejci was of Czech extraction) as a speaker on the occasion of the 75th anniversary of Czech settlement there. Yet less than 12 years later, when Nazi oppression had kindled new interest in their homeland, Czech leaders in Owatonna had to scuttle 10 months of preparation for a Czech festival. One of the organizers of the canceled event noted in 1943, "It seems that everyone around here in a busy farming community has so much to do that it is impossible to work up the necessary interest to successfully promote a Czech Day as planned." By 1953 a prominent Czech leader commented that "National life here is completely dead." And it remained so dead that *kolačky* were referred to as "stuffed buns" at a Litomysl church festival attended by the author in 1979.[63]

Czech and American Causes and Ethnicity

National and international developments in the 20th century made a significant impact on Minnesota Czechs. Unlike German Americans, who found themselves in an awkward situation when the United States entered World War I in April, 1917, most Czech Americans were enthusiastic supporters of the war effort. They were especially interested in the wartime movement organized abroad by Tomáš G. Masaryk, Eduard Beneš, and Milan Štefaník in 1915 with the hope of creating an independent Czechoslovak state upon the defeat of Austria-Hungary. Vojta Beneš, Eduard's older brother who worked among Czech organizations in the United States to gain backing for an independent state, visited Minnesota in 1917. He reported that he found much support, particularly in Silver Lake.[64]

The Czech National Alliance, formed in 1914, and the Czechoslovak National Council, organized in 1918, worked for independence and for American recognition of a Czechoslovak state. Minnesota members of these groups were probably among those who welcomed Masaryk on May 3 and 4, 1918, when he briefly visited St. Paul while on his way from Siberia to Chicago. His stay was not publicized, but his presence was discovered. He agreed to make a brief appearance at his hotel before a crowd of Czech enthusiasts, who then accompanied him to Union Station, where he boarded the train. His entry into Chicago on May 5, 1918,

THIS well-preserved curtain, which advertised local businesses around scenes in Czechoslovakia, hung in the ZCBJ Hall at Meadowlands in 1980.

was his official welcome to Czech America. Tacit American recognition of Czechoslovakia's right to independence was achieved in April, 1918, and full recognition in September. In a rare co-operative effort, Catholic, free-thinking, and Protestant Czech and Slovak groups in the state staged a four-hour demonstration in the St. Paul Auditorium on September 29, 1918, to celebrate.[65]

In New Prague Minnesota Czechs were accused of over-enthusiasm in their backing of the war. Local members of the Nonpartisan League, who were largely of German extraction, complained in a petition to the city that league members had been molested, insulted, and accused of being pro-German. A response to the petition, signed by 91 persons with Czech names, suggested that some German Americans in the league had expressed disloyal sentiments, with which the Czech signers did not agree.[66]

While events leading to the creation of an independent Czechoslovakia were stimulating to Czech Americans, the decades of the 1920s and 1930s saw the decline of various ethnic institutions. Improvements in communications such as radio, telephone, and widespread use of the automobile invaded the isolation of rural Czech communities. Official American popular culture increasingly replaced ethnic traditions and language. Many rural Czechs moved to the cities, where they did not necessarily live in Czech neighborhoods or associate with other Czechs. Restrictions imposed by the National Origins Act of 1924 slowed movement from Europe at the same time the forces of Americanization were enjoying a heyday.

As early as November, 1919, a Minnesota Sokol leader expressed concern about the strength of these organizations in various communities. Those in St. Paul, Owatonna, and Minneapolis were found to be thriving, but membership was slackening in New Prague and Montgomery, and new leadership was called for in Silver Lake and Pine City. Hopkins,

too, was judged to be in some difficulty. During the Depression of the 1930s many Sokol units vanished; others retrenched and made plans to survive.[67]

In the late 1930s the threat posed by Nazi Germany renewed the initiative of Czech-American organizations. The Czech National Alliance was reactivated in May, 1938, and the Czechoslovak National Council again served as a federalizing agent for Czech and Slovak organizations committed to a liberated Czechoslovakia. The Czech American National Alliance, led by Joseph Pavlicek, performed the Czechoslovak National Alliance's educational and fund-raising tasks in Minnesota. Throughout the war, it sponsored exhibits at the state fair, depicting the beauties of Czechoslovakian scenery and the bravery of its patriots fighting the Nazis. Anniversaries of its independence and birthdays of famous Czechs were noted by musical performances, lectures, and celebrations, all of which raised money for relief.[68]

Although these efforts were financially successful, they pointed up the changing preoccupations of the group. One touring speaker remarked that while Czechs in St. Paul were active in the effort, only the older people in rural communities were doing any work for the Czech cause. She also noted that people over 60 were the ones who spoke Czech in southern Minnesota.[69]

The years after World War II saw a further decline in Czech ethnic life in Minnesota. Rural communities lost younger members to the cities, and even the bastion of St. Paul Czech strength on West 7th Street was weakened by suburban flight. Sokols outside the metropolitan area disbanded. Members of the ZCBJ, which renamed itself the Western Fraternal Life Association in 1971, were generally over 50 years old. The loss of Czech language noted above reflected reduced Czech immigration as well as Americanization. Of more than 337,000 immigrants admitted to the

United States under the Displaced Persons Act of 1948, only 2.4% (8,482) were Czechs and Slovaks. Of these, 151 were sent to sponsors in Minnesota.[70]

Communist control of Czechoslovakia also took its toll, for the cessation of emigration prevented continuing ethnic revival from that source. Throughout the 1950s the CSPS Hall hosted lectures by recent emigrés, politicians, and news commentators who delivered anti-Communist speeches. As late as 1964 Pavlicek organized the Vojta Beneš Branch of the Czechoslovak National Council. Established to carry on anti-Communist activities, it found little support, as did the national Czech organization's attempts to purge Communists in the 1960s. Dissatisfaction with these trends may have forced some Minnesota Czechs to drop their affiliations with the organized groups. The postwar immigrants, including those who fled the Soviet invasion of Czechoslovakia in 1968, also showed little interest in the surviving organizations.[71]

By 1980 Czechs had been in Minnesota for over 125 years. Manifestations of popular Czech-American culture combined a successful adaptation to the American setting and a reviving interest in their heritage among the immigrants' descendants. Old-time bands in southeastern Minnesota, like that of Eddie Shimota, performed songs in Czech. New Prague's singers and dancers and St. Paul's dance group added color and music to area festivals. Sokol Minnesota and some ZCBJ lodges continued to hold regular Czech song fests. Czech-language classes, offered in New Prague, Montgomery, Silver Lake, Hopkins, and St. Paul in the late 1970s, drew students who had Czech grandparents but only a sketchy knowledge of their backgrounds. The festivals actively promoted by the towns' businessmen inspired local interest.[72]

Sokol Minnesota offered good examples of adaptation and retention of Czech culture. Its membership also reflected several aspects of the group's history in the state. Most members were older people, children of the Czech immigrants of the 1890s, who had belonged all their lives. Some Displaced Persons also joined, often constituting the most politically active faction. Those who arrived after the Russian invasion of 1968 were much less interested and less active. The younger members came largely from assimilated families who were interested in finding out about the Czech heritage they had lost. Some of their spouses, of German, Irish, and Norwegian extraction, also participated.

St. Paul's CSPS Hall remained the center of Sokol activities. The threat of demolition in 1976 inspired the group to buy it from the Czechoslovak Society of America and have it placed on the National Register of Historic Places. The members felt that without a hall they would have no Sokol. While a few of them still lived in the West 7th Street neighborhood, the majority commuted, some as far as 30 miles, to gymnastic classes, song fests, and dinners in the hall in 1980. Co-operation with other ethnic groups helped pay the bills. An organization that promoted traditional Irish and British music and dance rented space on the ground floor.

Assessing the degree of assimilation of a group is a precar-

ious business. On any relative scale, however, it can be said that Minnesota's Czechs successfully blended into the new culture, while retaining a few traditions from the old. In keeping with their national heritage, a number of Minnesota Czech Americans have been active in the musical, theatrical, artistic, and political circles of their adopted state. While they never formed a permanent ethnic voting bloc in local politics, Czechs have frequently filled posts on county and school boards in areas where they resided. In the state legislature they appeared as early as 1878 with Frantisek Vrabek, and three legislators of Czech descent were serving in 1980. The trappings of Old Country culture visible in the festivals we have described may be neither authentic nor essential to the lives of present-day Czech Americans, but their popularity is indisputable. A 400-page cookbook published by the women of Sokol Minnesota in 1979 perhaps provided the best record of the present situation in the Minnesota Czech-American community. It included numerous recipes for certain popular ethnic foods as well as many others that were quintessentially products of the American Midwest, dishes which would be found on the tables of the peoples of varying ethnic backgrounds who chose to make Minnesota their home.[73]

Reference notes

[1] United States, Census, 1910, Population, 981. While the term "Czech" specifically describes the people of the historic province of Bohemia, and "Moravian" applies to those of the province of Moravia, both are usually regarded as Czechs, and the term will be so used in this chapter. From 1860 to 1910 they were listed in the U.S. Census as Bohemians, but that term lacks precision since it could also include German-speaking people from that province. After Czechoslovakia became independent in 1918, Czechs were listed as Czechoslovaks, a term also unacceptable, since Slovaks constitute a distinct, though linguistically related, ethnic group. In the 1970s Czechoslovakia had about 14,000,000 people: somewhat over 9,000,000 Czechs, about 4,000,000 Slovaks, and the remainder consisting of Magyar, German, Polish, Rusin, and Gypsy minorities.

[2] For the background here and below, see Thomas Čapek, The Čechs (Bohemians) in America: A Study of Their National, Cultural, Political, Social, Economic and Religious Life, 1–5, 9–19, 29–31, 123 (Boston and New York, 1920); Vera Laska, comp., The Czechs in America 1633–1977, 133, 134 (Dobbs Ferry, N.Y., 1978).

[3] Jozef Butvín and Jan Havránek, Dějiny Československa, 3:313 (Prague, 1968); Milan W. Jerabek, "Czechs in Minnesota," 31, master's thesis, University of Minnesota, 1939; Čapek, Čechs in America, 1–5, 9, 19.

[4] M. Jerabek, "Czechs in Minnesota," 34–41; A. J. P. Taylor, The Habsburg Monarchy 1815–1918, 72 (New York, 1965).

[5] Čapek, Čechs in America, 53, 54, 119; Butvín, Dějiny Československa, 3:326; M. Jerabek, "Czechs in Minnesota," 7, 20, 25. On freethinking and Protestant Czechs, see p. 341, below.

[6] Here and below, see M. Jerabek, "Czechs in Minnesota," 28, 44–56. On routes and costs, see Čapek, Čechs in America, 27–29, 30, 34–36.

[7] Interviews and other details may be found in M. Jerabek, "Czechs in Minnesota," 28–30, 40, 52, 144, 146–148, 150.

[8] For some Czech letters, see M. Jerabek, "Czechs in Minnesota," 41–44. See also K. H. Breuer, "Česká osada Veselí v Minnesotě," Josef Mikulecký, "Paměti Osadníků Českých v Americe," and Frant[išek] Kovář, "Dějiny Čechů v okresu Steele v Minne-

sotě," all in *Amerikán: Národní Kalendář*, 9:163 (Chicago, 1886), 15:198 (1892), 56:192 (1933).

9 Here and two paragraphs below, see M. Jerabek, "Czechs in Minnesota," 54, 58, 61, 64, 70–77; Joseph Underleak to Esther Jerabek, September 24, 1930, in Milan W. Jerabek Papers, MHS; Čapek, *Čechs in America*, 31; Liga Českých Kněží Arcidioecese St. Paulské, *Průvodce českých katolických osadách v arcidioecesi St. Paulské ve Spojených Státech Severoamerických*, 157, 169, 190 (St. Paul, 1910); Michael Karták, "První Počátky Čechů v Saint Paul, Minnesota," and Josef Raiman, "Paměti Českých Osadníků v Americe," both in *Amerikán: Národní Kalendář*, 9:177 (1886), 24:275 (1911). An English translation of the Karták article on Czech pioneers in St. Paul is in MHS.

10 M. Jerabek, "Czechs in Minnesota," 61; Jan Pavelka, "Ze života J. Pavelky v Chatfield Fillmore Co., Minn.," Vojtěch Dolejš, "Paměti Českých Osadníků v Americe," Antonín Zelený, "Paměti Českých Osadníků v Americe," Albína Wondrová-Kunzová, "Frank a Josefína Wondrovi v Montgomery, Minnesota," Kovář, and Frank Yonák, "Zkušenosti Frank Yonaka z Buffalo, Minn." — all in *Amerikán: Národní Kalendář*, 9:182 (1886), 21:201 (1898), 33:306–309 (1910), 59:183 (1936), 56:191 (1933), 73:175 (1950). See also "Early Sketches of Hutchinson: The Anthony H. Zeleny Family, 1910–47," typescript, in MHS, and Table 17.1.

11 "Čechové v Lensburgu, okres Le Sue[u]r, Minn.," and Dolejš, both in *Amerikán: Národní Kalendář*, 6:181 (1883), 21:201 (1898). See also Montgomery Bicentennial Committee, *Montgomery: From the "Big Woods" To The "Kolacky Capital": 1856–1976* (Montgomery, 1976).

12 Breuer, in *Amerikán: Národní Kalendář*, 9:157.

13 *Průvodce českých katolických osadách*, 204; interviews of Albert Vanek, retired farmer, Tabor, Minnesota, and Mary Marvel, secretary of the Meadowlands ZCBJ, by the author, July 31, August 1, 1979; M. Jerabek, "Czechs in Minnesota," 77.

14 The diaries (1869–77) and other papers of Zdenka Sojka Rypka, a second-generation Czech schoolteacher in southern Minnesota, are in IHRC.

15 U.S., *Census*, 1930, *Population*, vol. 3, part 1, p. 1194, 1221, 1223. On the Slovaks, see Chapter 18.

16 Jan M. Částek, "Paměti Českých osadníků v Americe," in *Amerikán: Národní Kalendář*, 28:270 (1905); Czechoslovak National Council of America, *Panorama: A Historical Review of Czechs and Slovaks in the United States of America*, 51 (Cicero, Ill., 1970).

17 Laska, *Czechs in America*, 85; Esther Jerabek, "The Transition of a New-World Bohemia," in *Minnesota History*, 15:28 (March, 1934).

18 Jan Habenicht, *Dějiny Čechův Amerických*, 435 (St. Louis, [1904]); M. Jerabek, "Czechs in Minnesota," 86. On the freethought movement in America, see Karel Bicha, "Settling Accounts with an Old Adversary: The Decatholicization of Czech Immigrants in America," in *Histoire Sociale-Social History*, 8:45–60 (November, 1971). The editors wish to acknowledge the helpful suggestions received during their work on this chapter from Professor Bicha of Marquette University.

19 E. Jerabek, in *Minnesota History*, 15:32n; informal conversations with Czech Catholics in Minnesota by the author. The handbook is *Průvodce českých katolických osadách*.

20 *Průvodce českých katolických osadách*, 46, 69, 113, 135, 153; Catholic Archdiocese of St. Paul and Minneapolis, Parish Questionnaires, 1948, originals in Catholic Historical Society, St. Paul Seminary, St. Paul, microfilm in MHS, hereafter cited as Parish Questionnaires; N. E. Sladek, "Litomysl," in *Sokol Slovo*, May, 1979, p. 11.

21 M. Jerabek, "Czechs in Minnesota," 90. For an example, see *Průvodce českých katolických osadách*, 113.

22 *Průvodce českých katolických osadách*, 50, author's translation. See also M. Jerabek, "Czechs in Minnesota," 90.

23 Here and below, see E. Jerabek, in *Minnesota History*, 15:30; *Průvodce českých katolických osadách*, 81, 175, 193; Parish Questionnaires; John N. Pivo, "The Catholic Parish of the Sacred Heart of Owatonna, Minn.," [1935], in Milan Jerabek Papers; Works Projects Administration, Minnesota, Historical Records Survey: Churches, 1936–41, MHS, hereafter cited as WPA, Church Records. St. Stanislaus built a parochial school in 1886. According to [Andrew F. Jensen], "Interview with Charles Srsen," [4] ([1935?]) in MHS library, Owatonna Czechs had a circulating library as early as the 1860s. At the time of the interview, probably in the 1930s, Srsen estimated that about 50% of them were Protestant.

24 *Průvodce českých katolických osadách*, 86, 101. Another priest who had a long career was František Tichy, who served New Prague from 1880 to 1906 and Silver Lake from 1906 to 1925. See E. Jerabek, in *Minnesota History*, 15:31.

25 *Naše zahraničí*, 2:198–201 (February, 1922); WPA, Church Records; Parish Questionnaires. The locations of schools and number of pupils were: Heidelberg 50, Jackson 110, Lonsdale 125, Montgomery 180, New Prague 350, Olivia 175, Owatonna 90, St. Paul 250, Tabor 142, Veseli 85, Winona 68.

26 Vilém Šiller, Václav Prucha, and R. M. DeCastello, *Památník českých evanjelických církví ve spojených státech*, 18, 194 (Chicago, 1900).

27 M. Jerabek, "Czechs in Minnesota," 60; John Hus Presbyterian Church, *A Historical Sketch*, [2] ([Hopkins, 1938]).

28 E. Jerabek, in *Minnesota History*, 15:34–36; Czech Brethren Presbyterian Church, [*History*] *1876–1976*, 3–5 ([Silver Lake, 1976]); First Congregational Church, *50th Anniversary*, 1–8 ([Silver Lake, 1941]), and *75th Anniversary*, [1] ([Silver Lake, 1966]); Šiller et al., *Památník českých evanjelických církví*, 53–55, 59, 60, 211–218; Church Register, 1956–58, pp. 227, 233–237, in Cyril Congregational Church Records, MHS. Trčka was Cyril's pastor from 1906 to 1940. A Presbyterian congregation at Tabor held its first services in a creamery before a church was built in 1891. Its first permanent pastor was Jaroslav Dobiaš. See Šiller et al., 57.

29 Šiller et al., *Památník českých evanjelických církví*, 56; Vaclav Vojta, *Czechoslovak Baptists*, 212–225 (Minneapolis, 1941); Holy Emmanuel Lutheran Church, *75 Years of Grace*, [5] (Minneapolis, 1963). For more on these churches, see Chapter 18.

30 Bicha, in *Histoire Sociale-Social History*, 8:48.

31 In addition to those mentioned in the text of this chapter, other periodicals known to have been issued or edited in Minnesota were: *Čecho-Amerikán*, a weekly supplement published by *Montgomery Star*, 1886–87; *Minnesoťan*, a weekly supplement, 1898–1902?, to *Svit* (Cedar Rapids, Ia., edited and published in St. Paul by F. B. Matlach); *Minnesotský pokrok* (Minneapolis, St. Paul, Omaha) 1908–20; *Orgán Česko-slovanské dělnické podporující jednoty ve Spoj. Státech* (St. Paul), monthly, 1912?–29; *Pokrok* (St. Paul), weekly, 1897–99; *Severo-západní herold* (Owatonna), weekly a few weeks in 1900 and *Svobodná Obec* very briefly after that; *Vytrvalost* (New Prague), supplement to *Pokrok západu* (Omaha), 1892; *Sokol Slovo* (St. Paul) irregular 1965–79, when it became *Sokol Minnesota Slovo*. See Esther Jerabek, *Czechs and Slovaks in North America: A Bibliography*, 316–348 (New York, 1976); M. Jerabek, "Czechs in Minnesota," 94–101. For the "Creed of the Freethinkers," see Laska, *Czechs in America*, 97.

32 Vojtěch Vrtiš, "Ze zkušeností starších osadníků českých v Americe," Tomáš Mareš and Jan Faktor, "Paměti českých osadníků v Americe," Jan Hrdlicka, "Paměti z mého života" — all in *Amerikán: Národní Kalendář*, 14:191 (1891), 21:199 (1898), 51:252 (1928).

33 Bessie Pessek, "Bohemian National Cemetery Association," undated typescript, copy in MEHP Papers.

[34] Laska, *Czechs in America*, 13; M. Jerabek, "Czechs in Minnesota," 109; Marlin Heise, "Founders Day," in *Sokol Minnesota Slovo*, May, 1980, p. 6.

[35] M. Jerabek, "Czechs in Minnesota," 116–118; Bozena Vanek, "Czechs in Minnesota 1854 to 1948," 21 ([1948]), typescript in MHS library; *Sokol Minnesota Slovo*, August–September, 1980, p. 1; Lionel B. Davis and Kenneth Carley, "When Minnehaha Falls Inspired Dvorak," in *Minnesota History*, 41:134 (Fall, 1968).

[36] Šiller *et al.*, *Památník českých evanjelických církví*, 211, author's translation; Laska, *Czechs in America*, 54.

[37] M. Jerabek, "Czechs in Minnesota," 115; Laska, *Czechs in America*, 38, 54; *Fraternal Herald*, July, 1972, p. 3; "Western Fraternal Life Association Members & Insurance Exhibit: Minnesota 5/1/79–5/1/80," copy in MEHP Papers. For an example of the rules of a local lodge, see *Domácí pravidla řádu Lumír, č. 34, ZČBJ, v Hutchinson, Minn.* (Omaha, 1917), in MHS.

[38] M. Jerabek, "Czechs in Minnesota," 122–124; Vanek, "Czechs in Minnesota," 25; and from the author's knowledge as a Sokol member. *Minnesotské Noviny* and *Minnesotský Pokrok* published news of Sokol activities between 1910 and 1920.

[39] Heise, in *Sokol Minnesota Slovo*, May, 1980, p. 6.

[40] *Tenth Sokol Congress: Prague, Czechoslovakia*, [1] ([Prague, 1938]), and Všesokolský Slet v Praze folder, both in Joseph Pavlicek Papers, IHRC; *St. Paul Dispatch*, March 9, 1938, p. 11. For an example of a *slet* program, see St. Paul Sokol Gymnastic Society, *Sokol Slet, Western District A.S.O., June 24 and 25, 1972*, copy in MHS. The Pavlicek Papers were uncataloged when this chapter was written. Citations used here are as complete as possible.

[41] M. Jerabek, "Czechs in Minnesota," 102; *Stanovy českého čtenářského spolku v Hutchinson, McLeod County, Minn.*, 1 (Omaha, 1897); Bessie Pessek, "The Bohemian Reading and Educational Society (Hutchinson Township)," 1–3 (n.d.), copy in MEHP Papers. The "Creed of the Freethinkers" is reprinted in Laska, *Czechs in America*, 97.

[42] Vanek, "Czechs in Minnesota," 22; M. Jerabek, "Czechs in Minnesota," 112.

[43] E. Jerabek, *Czechs and Slovaks in North America*, 325; M. Jerabek, "Czechs in Minnesota," 97.

[44] Henry P. Fairchild, ed., *Dictionary of Sociology*, 276 (New York, 1944), as quoted in Milton Gordon, *Assimilation in American Life*, 64 (New York, 1964); U.S., *Census*, 1910, *Population*, 1:963. The higher rate of Czech intermarriage may be due to their earlier arrival in the U.S.

[45] U.S., *Census*, 1930, *Population*, vol. 3, part 1, p. 1221. These figures include Slovaks, but there were no major Slovak settlements in the area.

[46] Win V. Working, "Czechs Settle Garden Spot in 'Big Woods,'" in *Southern Minnesotan*, 2:14 (January, 1932); *Minneapolis Tribune*, February 4, 1978, pp. 1B, 4B, December 8, 1979, p. 2B; *St. Paul Pioneer Press*, February 11, 1962, Pictorial magazine, p. 7.

[47] Here and below, see Joseph T. Rynda, "History of Kolacky Day," 1 (1935), in Rynda Papers, MHS; *Sokol Slovo*, June–July, 1979, p. 6; *Montgomery Messenger*, July 24, 31, 1980, p. 1.

[48] *Sokol Slovo*, June–July, 1979, p. 9; observations of the author, who participated in the event.

[49] Church Register, 1956–58, p. 227, Cyril Congregational Church Records; Sokol Minnesota membership list, 1979, copy in MEHP Papers. For memoirs of a third-generation Czech girlhood in St. Paul, see Patricia Hampl, *A Romantic Education* (Boston, 1981).

[50] Programs and reviews of plays from 1924 to 1931 are in Divadla-Pohostinská, Scrapbook, Pavlicek Papers; these papers also contain many records of activities in, benefits for, and groups affiliated with the hall. Backdrops of Old World scenes painted by Victor Hubl, Sr., remain on the hall's stage.

[51] See, for example, "Financial Report from the Sokol Camp Picnic, July 17, 1938," in Pavlicek Papers; *Sokol Slovo*, June, 1978, p. 8. The Pavlicek Papers contain records for the 1928, 1930–38, 1940, 1941, and 1944 *Šibřinky*.

[52] *Sokol Slovo*, November, 1979, p. 4. Copies of *Sokolská Hlídka*, 1927–28, and biographical information on Pavlicek in McLeod County are in Pavlicek Papers.

[53] The Pavlicek Papers contain many examples of cultural activities. See, for example, Dvořákův Program — St. Paul Auditorium 12 Října 1941 folder, Czechoslovak Independence Day folders, Česká Divadla — (Filmová) 1945–1946–1947 folder. The 1924 lecturer was Josef Havránek, organizer of the Union.

[54] E. Jerabek, in *Panorama*, 48; WPA, Writers' Program, *The Bohemian Flats*, 2, 23, 47 (Minneapolis, [1941]); *Minneapolis Journal*, April 29, 1931, p. 17.

[55] Joseph Pavlicek to Jerry Roch, May 21, 1952, CSPS Hall Benefit folder, Pavlicek Papers.

[56] John Hus Church, *Historical Sketch*, [2–5]; "Western Fraternal Life Association: Minnesota 5/1/79–5/1/80"; Obžinky-Hopkins, Minn., September 7, 1947, folder, Pavlicek Papers; *Hennepin County Review*, September 21, 1939, p. 1, September 11, 1947, p. 1, September 16, 1948, p. 7. For more on harvest festivals, see Svatava Pirkova-Jakobson, "Harvest Festivals among Czechs and Slovaks in America," in *Journal of American Folklore*, 69:266–280 (1956). Hopkins leaders included Joseph Kaminsky, Rev. Joseph Havlik, and Josef C. Vesely. In 1980 Hopkins had the second largest active ZCBJ lodge in the state with 548 members. Many non-Czechs who married into the community joined these lodges for the insurance benefits.

[57] Here and below, see E. Jerabek, in *Minnesota History*, 15:37, 38, 42; "The Silver Lake Story," in *Scattered Seeds: A Gathering of Minnesota Memories*, vol. 1, no. 4, p. 20 (1974); interview of Rev. Kayton Palmer by author, July, 1979; *Minneapolis Tribune*, May 6, 1978, p. 1B.

[58] First Congregational Church, *75th Anniversary*, [2]; Czech Brethren Church, *[History] 1876–1976*, 9–11; church records, First Congregational Church, and church and library records, Czech Brethren Presbyterian Church, Silver Lake.

[59] Pessek, "Bohemian Reading and Educational Society," 3.

[60] Here and below, see *Minneapolis Tribune*, June 18, 1978, p. 6F; interview of Jerry Vanek by author, August 1, 1980. From the 1920s until his death in 1966 Paul Sramek, who served as mayor of Meadowlands for over 20 years, provided leadership for the ZCBJ and the Sokol units.

[61] Marvel interview, August 1, 1979.

[62] Underleak to Esther Jerabek, September 24, 1930, in Milan Jerabek Papers.

[63] K[arel] E. Sršeň, "Sedmdesát pět let české osady v Minnesotě," in *Hospodář*, February 5, 1932, pp. 74–76; Walter Bruzek to Emily Welcl, [1943], and Karel Sršeň to Joseph Pavlicek, February 22, 1953, both in Czechoslovak National Council folders, Pavlicek Papers; [Jensen], "Interview with Charles Srsen," [5]; observation of author who was present at the event.

[64] Vojta Beneš, *První vojáci nejzápadnější fronty*, 149 (Prague, 1946); E. Jerabek, in *Minnesota History*, 15:41. For an example of support in Silver Lake, see Edmund Wrbitzky to Knute Nelson, February 5, 1918, in Knute Nelson Papers, MHS.

[65] Laska, *Czechs in America*, 46; *Minnesotský Pokrok*, May 9, p. 1, October 2, p. 1, 1918.

[66] Petition dated June 4, 1918, in Scott County file, Correspondence with Counties, Main Subject Files, Minnesota Commission of Public Safety Records, Minnesota State Archives, MHS.

[67] Based on author's impressions from folders of Sokol activities in Pavlicek Papers. For examples, see *Minnesotský Pokrok*, November 6, 1919, p. 1; Joseph T. Pleva to Joseph Pavlicek, [October,

1940], E.J.C. to Joseph Pavlicek, October 11, 1940, in Sokol Education folder, and *Sokolská Hlídka*, December, 1927, p. 1 — all in Pavlicek Papers.

⁶⁸ Laska, *Czechs in America*, 54; Czechoslovak National Council folders, 1943 and 1944 State Fair folders, Masaryk 90th and 100th Anniversary Celebration folders, Dvorak Concert folder, all in Pavlicek Papers. For examples of successful fund raising, see Financial Records, Czechoslovak Day, June 9, 1940, and American Relief for Czechoslovakia, Collections Record Book, January 15, 1946–August 16, 1947, in Pavlicek Papers.

⁶⁹ Emily Wecl folder, Pavlicek Papers.

⁷⁰ United States Displaced Persons Commission, *The DP Story: The Final Report*, 366 (Washington, D.C., 1952); Minnesota Displaced Persons Commission, Displaced Persons Resettled in Minnesota, 1949–52, in Minnesota Public Welfare Dept. Records, Minnesota State Archives; tables compiled from these records, and Sokol Minnesota membership list, 1979, both in MEHP Papers; *Fraternal Herald*, July, 1972, p. 12.

⁷¹ Czechoslovak National Council folder, Zájezd Dr. Hřebík folder, both in Pavlicek Papers; *Sokol Minnesota Slovo*, October, 1980, p. 7; Laska, *Czechs in America*, 61.

⁷² For Czech-American musicians and an actress, see Davis and Carley, in *Minnesota History*, 41:134; John K. Sherman, *Music and Maestros: The Story of the Minneapolis Symphony Orchestra*, 245–247 (Minneapolis, 1952); *St. Paul Dispatch*, June 4, 1979, p. 11; Esther Jerabek, "Antonin Jurka, A Pioneer Czech Schoolmaster in Minnesota," in *Minnesota History*, 13:271 (September, 1932); Antonin Jurka, "Vzpomínky Starého Čecha," in *Americán: Národní Kalendář*, 30:285 (1907); Blanche Yurka, *Bohemian Girl: Blanche Yurka's Theatrical Life*, (Athens, Ohio, 1970).

⁷³ Conversation with Rep. Robert Vanasek, August 17, 1980; *Favorite Recipes of Sokol Minnesota* (St. Paul, 1979).

CHAPTER 18

The Slovaks

M. Mark Stolarik

SLOVAK IMMIGRANTS began to arrive in Minnesota as early as 1875 to work in the mills and foundries of the booming city of Minneapolis. In the 1880s and 1890s larger numbers migrated to the mining towns of the iron ranges and to small farming communities in widely separated areas of the state. They settled most heavily, however, in the eastern and east central states, where jobs in coal mines and steel mills offered wages far higher than they could earn in their homeland. Minnesota's and the nation's Slovak-speaking population peaked in 1920, when four-fifths of them lived in the six states of New York, New Jersey, Connecticut, Pennsylvania, Ohio, and Illinois. That year Minnesota had 2,744 foreign-born and 3,734 second-generation Slovak speakers, or 1% of the nation's total (see Table 18.1). By 1970 the first, second, and third generations in the state who claimed Slovak as a mother tongue numbered 4,735; with the fourth generation and those who grew up speaking English, the total was perhaps as high as 20,000 in 1980.[1]

Table 18.1. Slovak Speakers in Minnesota, 1910–70

	foreign born	foreign stock*
1910	1,427	2,740
1920	2,744	6,478
1930	2,339	
1940	1,260	3,460
1960	929	
1970	599	4,735

Source: Mother-tongue data in U.S., *Census*, for years listed.
*Foreign stock includes foreign born and native born of foreign or mixed parentage.

The ancestors of these Slovaks were originally part of a group of Slavic peoples who settled in central Europe sometime before 500 A.D. But at the beginning of the 10th century their territory was conquered by the Magyars of Hungary and isolated from western Europe for almost a thousand years. When the Turks occupied southern Hungary in the 16th century, the Magyar rulers migrated north to what became Slovakia (see Map 18.1), until that area, which constituted only 27% of the Hungarian lands, supported 53% of its nobility. The Magyars, a non-Slavic people from western Asia, concentrated their political, social, and religious life in the land of the Slovaks, who paid most of the country's taxes. Cut off from their linguistic near relatives and fellow West Slavs, the Czechs, forced to give up the best lands to their Magyar overlords, and subjected to a determined campaign of Magyarization, the Slovak people experienced cultural and economic repression that gave them an identity distinct from that of the Czechs and Hungarians. Through alliances made by the Magyars in the 1520s, however, they like the Czechs were drawn into the Habsburg Empire and subsequently into the dual monarchy of Austria-Hungary, created in 1867.[2]

At about that time, the Slovaks began to leave their homeland in large numbers for three basic reasons: a population explosion, a lack of land, and a lack of industrial development. The population of Slovakia more than doubled between 1720 and 1840, growing from 1,100,000 to 2,400,000. In the four easternmost counties of Spiš, Šariš, Zemplín, and Abov, it multiplied six times, from 149,000 to 861,000; this region subsequently sent the majority of Slovak immigrants to America.[3]

This larger population had ever less arable land on which to live. The abolition of serfdom in the Habsburg Empire in 1848 was not followed by any redistribution of land among former serfs. Indeed the nobles of Hungary continued to enclose more land, building ever larger estates. As a result, a landless peasant class, wandering the countryside in search of work, grew throughout the 19th century.[4]

While some western European countries partially solved similar problems of overpopulation and unemployment by promoting industrialization, the Austro-Hungarian government in Vienna preferred to industrialize Austria and to keep Hungary as a source of agricultural products and raw materials for the dual monarchy. As a result the increasingly desperate landless agricultural workers sought employment outside the kingdom. In the 1870s they began to respond to advertisements from American rail and coal companies that were searching Europe for cheap labor.[5]

Although the exact number of Slovaks who immigrated to the United States cannot be precisely determined, educated estimates exist. Historians and demographers, who have wrestled with this problem in the last quarter century, agree that while only 5,000 entered the United States in the 1870s, about 200,000 did so between 1880 and 1899. There are no exact United States figures for these years because until 1899 the Slovaks were lost among all the polyglot peoples covered by the rubric "Austria-Hungary." After that the United States Bureau of Immigration and Naturalization began counting arrivals by "race or people" rather than by country of origin.

More than 460,000 Slovaks immigrated in the short period from 1900 to 1914. The influx peaked in 1905 when 52,367 made the journey. But many of these people also returned to their homeland; at least 39% of the number immigrating between 1908 and 1914 did so. From 1915 to 1919, during World War I, movement was severely restricted, but more Slovaks left the United States than arrived. Although the early 1920s saw a heavier influx, the numbers never returned to their prewar highs, perhaps due to legislation restricting immigration and the changes in Slovakia's status with the dismemberment of Austria-Hungary. Minnesota's immigration patterns closely followed the nation's in this period (see Table 18.2).[6]

The total Slovak population of the United States, however, is more difficult to ascertain. Not until 1910 did the United States census differentiate by native languages or mother tongues. Although the numbers are suspect, the 1910 census counted 166,474 foreign-born Slovak speakers and 117,970 born of foreign or mixed parentage. It was thought at the time that these figures were low, since it seemed likely, said one leader, that some Slovaks were counted as "Hungarians, Austrians, Slavs, Slavonians, or God knows what kind of absurd name." Indeed, the printed census listed 35,000 "Slavic, not specified," who were described as Slav, Slavic, Slavish, and Slavonian. Using annual immigration tables to figure back from the more accurate 1920 census, it would seem that the 1910 figures were indeed too low, and that the foreign born of this group then numbered over 195,000. The 1920 census recorded 274,948 first- and 344,918 second-generation Slovak speakers. Subsequent censuses counted

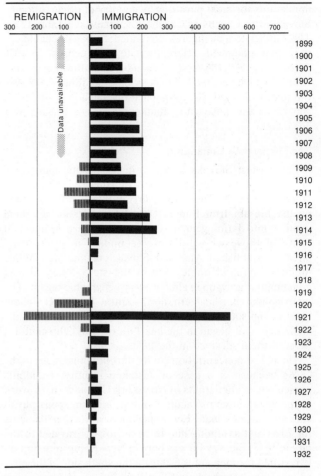

Table 18.2. Slovak Migration to and from Minnesota

Map 18.1. Eastern Czechoslovakia, the Slovaks' Homeland

immigrants for most purposes by country of origin, lumping Slovaks with Czechs as Czechoslovakians (see Table 17.1). The mother-tongue figures continued to be unreliable, as they were compiled differently with each census. In 1970 there were 510,366 first-, second-, and third-generation Americans who claimed Slovak as a mother tongue. By 1980 the total estimated Slovak population, including the fourth generation and those whose mother tongue was English, was 2,000,000.[7]

The Minneapolis Community

The earliest Slovaks to arrive in Minnesota immigrated directly from the Slovak districts of Hungary in search of work in the 1870s. They settled first in Minneapolis and then on the Mesabi Iron Range. Only later did some of them venture into farming in northern and western Minnesota; many of those who did were secondary migrants from already established American-Slovak communities. While individuals found homes across the state, small Slovak communities grew up in almost every geographic region. The metropolitan, northeastern, north-central, Red River Valley, central, and southwestern sections of Minnesota each had a settlement that began in the late 19th or early 20th century. Most of them survived in the 1980s.

The oldest concentration got its start in Minneapolis in the 1870s because of a case of mistaken identity. Handbills passed out to immigrants in New York City advertised work at the warehouses of Jacob S. Elliot, a Minneapolis physician and businessman. Five single men, mistaking his name for Eliáš and assuming him to be a Slovak, traveled to the city in 1875. Elliot, who was born in New Hampshire, initially boarded the men at his estate on the south side of the city, an area that later became Elliot Park.[8]

From this small beginning the community grew in the 1880s as others arrived from the eastern United States and Slovakia, primarily from the eastern county of Šariš and especially the village of Zborov. After the men found work in the saw and flour mills, they sent for their wives and children. These families settled in an area known as the Bohemian Flats along the Mississippi River under the Washington Avenue Bridge where the coal docks were located in 1980. Though named for their linguistic relatives, the Czechs, Bohemian Flats was the major Slovak concentration in the Twin Cities until the beginning of the 20th century.

Their neighbors were Danish, German, Czech, Irish, Swedish, Polish, and French, but the Slovaks were apparently the largest group and the one that held to its customs most tenaciously. They lived in many small homes, some no more than shacks, crowded together on three main streets, paying rents ranging from $6.00 to $25.00 per year. The men who worked as laborers earned $1.50 to $2.00 a day, and their families supplemented this meager income in many ways. Many married Slovak women cooked and washed for boarders. Unmarried women worked as domestics in homes and boardinghouses on the bluffs above the flats. Children contributed by gleaning wood from the river both for sale and for the family's own fuel. "It is a very novel spectacle," wrote an observer in 1887, "to see the way they manage to secure the valuable flotsam that the waters are always bringing to them at their door. . . . With crooked sticks or pronged instruments they grasp the . . . wood that comes in reach, and land it usually, with much dexterity."[9]

In the early years of the settlement peasant customs persisted among the residents. Women washed clothing in the Mississippi River and baked bread in outdoor community ovens. In the fall families gathered sacks of mushrooms along the river banks. In winter they skated on the ice and sledded down the bank. In spring they battled the floods that regularly sent those living on the lowest tier to higher land with their possessions. Holidays and weddings were celebrated in traditional fashion, including dress, food, music, and religious services identical to those they had known in the Old Country.[10]

By the turn of the century other Slovak communities were

CATCHING DRIFTWOOD from the Mississippi River on the Bohemian Flats in Minneapolis about 1905.

forming around churches in three parts of the city — Roman and Greek Catholic ones in the Northeast, and Lutheran and other denominations in South and Southeast Minneapolis. The groupings reflected two Slovak traits — deep religiousness and fracturing along denominational lines. The Reformation and Counter Reformation of the 16th and 17th centuries left Slovakia with four major faiths. By 1930 their relative sizes within Slovakia were: Roman Catholics 72%, Lutherans 12%, Greek Catholics 6% (most of whom were Rusins), and Calvinists 4%. In America further splintering occurred, with conversions to the Congregational and Baptist faiths.[11]

As Slovaks arrived in Minneapolis in the 1880s and 1890s, they began to organize along religious lines. Among the first to do so were the Roman and Greek Catholics. On November 12, 1888, 11 of them met at George Ihnat's boarding-house at 14 Lower Levee Street and established the *Slovenski Rimsko Katolicki Nemoci podporujuci Spolek Svateho Cirila a Methoda Svatich apostoloch* (Slovak Roman Catholic Sickness Support Society of Saints Cyril and Methodius, Holy Apostles). Although its members were primarily Roman Catholic men, Greek Catholic men were also eligible, but women were not. Besides providing sickness and death insurance, the society held balls and picnics on special occasions, and organized a band that later joined in festive parades. In 1890 the Minneapolis lodge joined others from Pittsburgh and Cleveland to form the First Catholic Slovak Union of the United States. The Minneapolis group had been founded earlier than the other two, but it was designated Branch no. 3 in the new union because "it was located the greatest distance from the East."[12]

Members of this branch aided in the founding of two congregations in Northeast Minneapolis — St. Mary's Greek Catholic Church and St. Cyril's Roman Catholic Church. Both broke away from the Roman Catholic Polish parish of Holy Cross, where they had initially worshiped. The Greek Catholics were the first to leave. In 1887 they joined with their more numerous coreligionists, the Rusins, who also immigrated from northern Hungary, to establish St. Mary's as a Greek Catholic parish. The story of the founding of this church, its difficulties with Archbishop John Ireland of St. Paul, and its subsequent union with Russian Orthodoxy, is told in Chapter 21.[13]

The second church came into being in 1891 when members of the Saints Cyril and Methodius Society asked Archbishop Ireland to allow them to leave the Polish congregation and form their own Roman Catholic Slovak national parish. He granted their request, but turned down a proposal to name the church after both patron saints, reasoning that one saint was enough. Thus the new Church of St. Cyril was built in 1893. With a membership of almost 300 families or 1,000 persons in 1918, it had become the largest single Slovak congregation in Minnesota.[14]

During its first decades St. Cyril's members faced many problems in their relations with their priests. Slovak immigrants, accustomed to a system by which the noble who erected a church controlled the appointment of its priest, assumed that since they paid for the church in the new country, they had the same right. The Irish hierarchy of the American Catholic church disagreed. Financial problems and disagreements over Americanization and language use ensued until the congregation in 1926 received a priest who had been raised in the community. Using his knowledge of St. Cyril's internal workings, he ended the system of lay trusteeism there, but the process was difficult. As a result, some people left the parish in 1932 to attend other Catholic churches, including St. Boniface, a German congregation in Northeast Minneapolis, Our Lady of Perpetual Help, a Czech parish near the Bohemian Flats, and Immaculate Conception, a mixed parish in the northeastern suburb of Columbia Heights.[15]

Lutheran Slovaks, a smaller group, also lost little time in getting together. In the early 1880s they held services in homes on the Bohemian Flats. In 1888 with the help of a pastor from the nearby Missouri Synod German Lutheran Church, they secured the services of a Czech-speaking minister, who persuaded them to form the Slovak Evangelical Church of Holy Emmanuel. Before the year ended they purchased a frame church from a Swedish congregation on the flats. Twenty years later, when the congregation outgrew this structure, it moved to a new location in Southeast Minneapolis. In 1970, as the expansion of the University of Minnesota crowded this site, its members built a new church in the southern suburb of Bloomington. First-generation members who still lived in Southeast Minneapolis in 1980 made the long trip to Bloomington for Sunday services. Many of the second generation, however, then lived in Bloomington and in the suburbs of Richfield and Burnsville.[16]

Like the Catholics, the Lutherans suffered from internal divisions. After 1910 several of them, who had immigrated from Važec in the Liptov district, responded to the missionary efforts of a Moravian Baptist woman who was soon joined by other lay preachers. The Baptist account of the conversions in these years spoke of an enthusiasm "so great" that it alarmed the Slovak community in Minneapolis. In 1917 the First Slovak Baptist Church was organized in South Minneapolis with 56 members, and three years later a new church was built on 15th Avenue South.[17]

A short while later a second, and larger, group of Lutherans broke away from Holy Emmanuel. They evidently disliked the conservatism of the Missouri Synod and wished to establish a closer relationship with the Slovak Evangelical Union, a national fraternal organization that was traditionally a thorn in the synod's side because it stressed the independence of the lay members from the clergy. In 1923 these dissidents, numbering 20 families, established Holy Trinity Church on 29th Avenue in South Minneapolis, which eventually affiliated with the Lutheran Church in America. The site may have been chosen simply because it was available. Most of its members, who lived near the parent church, had to walk to services. Explained one, "We didn't have cars, and we couldn't afford to take the streetcar. We all had too many children."[18]

By 1937 Holy Trinity had surpassed Holy Emmanuel in size with 406 members to 340. In 1956, as Slovaks moved to newer sections of the city, this congregation built a new church still farther south in Minneapolis which they named Prince of Glory Lutheran. Second- and third-generation Slo-

THE SLOVAK Evangelical Lutheran Church of Holy Emmanuel and a house on the Bohemian Flats about 1900.

vaks who had moved to St. Paul and the Minneapolis suburbs of Columbia Heights and Edina by 1980 remained loyal to the congregation, returning to worship with new members who joined the church because they lived nearby. By then about half the congregation was of Slovak descent.

The movement of the Lutheran churches and congregations left the city with clearly defined Slovak neighborhoods based on religious ties. In the 1980s Roman and Greek Catholics by and large lived among fellow Slavs, either in Northeast Minneapolis or nearby suburbs such as Columbia Heights. Slovak Lutherans followed their German and Scandinavian coreligionists to South Minneapolis, and, ultimately, to the southern suburbs.[19]

Not only did Minneapolis Slovaks help found these five churches between 1888 and 1923, but they also set up a wide variety of fraternal and church-related organizations. As we have seen, the earliest of these was the influential Saints Cyril and Methodius Society, which initially excluded women from its membership. In 1892 a group of women not only set up their own local benefit society, but also, like the men, went on to participate in the creation of the First Catholic Slovak Ladies Union, a national fraternal organization which was formed in Cleveland the same year. St. Mary's Lodge in Minneapolis became Branch no. 3 of the

national union. By 1970 the men's and women's federations each claimed about 100,000 members, making them the largest Catholic Slovak organizations in the world.[20]

Old Country rivalries in these Minneapolis lodges, however, prompted some members to secede and establish a new chapter whose membership was influenced by regional loyalties. The initial men's lodge no. 3 of the First Catholic Slovak Union was composed largely of men from Zemplín and Šariš counties in Slovakia. Seventeen dissidents, largely from Zborov, a village in Šariš, withdrew in 1895 and formed St. Joseph's Lodge, Branch no. 226. Similarly 12 years later 35 women withdrew from St. Mary's and organized St. Ann's Lodge, Branch no. 249 of the Ladies Union.[21]

Younger Slovaks set up their own clubs. In 1909 a group of 17 young Greek and Roman Catholic men organized St. George's Assembly no. 34 of the Slovak Catholic Sokol. Founded in Passaic, New Jersey, in 1905, this group emphasized athletics. By 1965 it had a national membership of over 50,000. Young Slovak women in Minneapolis organized a similar Sokol, known as the St. Veronica Wreath, in 1913. In 1980 the men's and women's groups in Minneapolis had 160 and 170 members, respectively, whose ages averaged about 35. Junior branches for boys and girls under 16 each had about 40 members. The group sold insurance, sponsored Christmas parties, picnics, and dinner dances, and sent a team to participate in the biennial track and field meets held by the national organization.[22]

Led by three Lutheran men, the St. John the Baptist Slavonic Society of Minneapolis came into being by 1896 as a nondenominational benefit lodge. This group, which also included both Roman and Greek Catholics, immediately affiliated as Assembly no. 46 with the National Slovak Society, organized in Pittsburgh in 1890. Nationalistic in outlook, it never developed the appeal of religious fraternals, and it folded by the early 1970s.[23]

In addition to these fraternal-benefit societies, Minneapolis Slovaks also supported a variety of other associations, most of which were church related. These included prayer groups, women's associations, choirs, and youth clubs. St. Cyril's had the St. Cecelia Dramatic Club, which staged plays in the church basement in the 1930s. Holy Emmanuel in 1960 sponsored a Slovak Lutheran Hour, which was broadcast over station WCAL on the St. Olaf College campus in Northfield. Holy Trinity's choir sang Slovak carols at members' houses on Christmas. Both Lutheran churches had softball teams that provided entertainment for many families, winning city-wide, church-league championships in the 1920s. At that time every woman in Holy Trinity's congregation belonged to the Ladies Aid, which sponsored many bake sales. When one was planned, remembered an older member in 1973, "there was no question of anyone being too busy to help out. Everyone would work two or three days to make the food — lushka [*halušky*], noodles, kolache [*koláče*] — and prepare for the sale. If there was anything left over after the sale ended, they bought it themselves."[24]

Along with their churches, the Slovaks of Minneapolis established schools. In 1921 the Lutherans at Holy Emmanuel set up a school for children in grades 6, 7, and 8 who wished to study for confirmation in the church; this effort lasted until 1945. After that they relied upon Sunday and summer school classes to prepare children for full acceptance into the adult congregation. Not until 1937 did Slovak Roman Catholics in Minneapolis build a parochial school to which they invited as teachers the Sisters of Notre Dame, headquartered in Mankato. Within two years, the church had set up a Mother's Club, three choral groups, and other associated organizations to support the school, which had expanded to include nine grades. It remained open in 1980.[25]

Churches, lodges, and schools worked together to give each Slovak religious group a community center. The churches used the familiar means of baptisms, confirmations, weddings, and funerals to establish the positions of members in the community. Catholic churches in particular also marked the passage of the religious year by staging colorful rituals and parades such as the blessing of Easter baskets, the procession around birch-tree altars on Corpus Christi Sunday, summer picnics, fall retreats, Christmas Eve festivities, and Mardi Gras balls. The lodges in Minneapolis also held regular dances with Slovak bands, occasionally performed plays, and celebrated the dates of their founding or the anniversaries of their patron saints. Both lodges and churches sponsored baseball, basketball, and other athletic teams.[26]

The same cultural factors that predisposed Slovaks in Minneapolis to live and worship with other Slavic groups also influenced their relations with those less like them. The Slovaks, as part of the growing immigration of southern and eastern Europeans at the turn of the century, became victims of American nativists, who found their numbers and differing cultures threatening.

Stereotypes of violence and radicalism were attached to Slavs in the East who struck for higher wages in the coal fields, but their small numbers in Minneapolis did not pose the same kind of threat. No studies have as yet been made of this group in the early 20th century, but the lack of information in general sources may suggest that Minnesota Slovaks accepted with good grace the efforts of Americanizing leaders during World War I.[27]

Other frictions were economic. Older immigrants feared that the eastern Europeans would displace them by working for lower wages. In general, however, the new immigrants provided a large unskilled labor pool for low-paying manual work, thus increasing the demand for English-speaking foremen and other skilled workers. Indeed, Minneapolis Slovaks complained that the Norwegians, Swedes, Danes, and Irish held the best jobs in the city's mills and lumberyards.[28]

Miners and Farmers

While a major portion of Minnesota's Slovaks settled in Minneapolis, small numbers also made their way to the Vermilion and Mesabi iron ranges in St. Louis County and to farming communities in various parts of the state. Some who had worked on the Michigan ranges sought similar employment in the mines near the newly established towns of Ely, Eveleth, Hibbing, McKinley, and Virginia soon after the Minnesota ranges opened in the mid-1880s and 1890s. The greatest numbers, however, arrived after 1905, settling also in the port cities of Duluth and Superior, Wisconsin, at the head of Lake Superior.[29]

These Slovaks were generally recent immigrants. An employee survey taken in 1907 by the Oliver Iron Mining Company revealed that 73% of the firm's 359 Slovak workers had lived in the United States for five years or less. Over half (55%) were married. Only 40% spoke English, a rate slightly lower than the average for all the company's 10,114 immigrant employees. About a third of those who had been in the country for five years or more had become citizens, a proportion which was about average for southern and eastern European employees.[30]

To provide some financial help in case of accident or death in the dangerous work of mining, these Slovaks organized branches of the national benefit societies. By 1908 Hibbing, Eveleth, and Virginia had branches of the First Catholic Slovak Union. Eveleth, McKinley, and Soudan, a town on the Vermilion Range to the north, each had an assembly of the National Slovak Society; Ely had three such groups.[31]

The number of Slovaks in northeastern Minnesota was so small, however, that they never established their own churches. Instead, Roman Catholic Slovaks worshiped with Slovenes and Croats at St. Elizabeth's in New Duluth; with Slovenes, Croats, Poles, and Germans at Holy Family in Eveleth; with Slovenes, Croats, and Ruthenians at St. Joseph's in Chisholm; and with Slovenes, Croats, Canadians, Irish, and Poles at Blessed Sacrament in Hibbing. With the end of World War I, as demand for labor declined, the Slovaks almost disappeared from the Mesabi Range.[32]

Small groups also tried their hands at farming, eventually establishing several rural communities in Minnesota. At the turn of the century they settled among the Swedes in the northern pine forests of Moose Park and Alvwood townships in Itasca County and in Hornet and Blackduck townships in Beltrami County. Some homesteaders like the Michael Zustiak family arrived directly from the Old Country, while others like Andrew Michaliček worked in the foundries of a Minneapolis machinery manufacturer for five years before buying a partially cleared farm of 120 acres for $700 in 1910. Eventually these people organized the Evangelical Free Church at Alvwood and the Evangelical Lutheran Church of Holy Trinity in Hornet Township in 1921. The isolation of the latter community may have helped them retain their Slovak character, for as late as 1937 some of the older people there spoke no English. Few of the second generation remained, however, preferring to move to urban areas. According to school records, attendance at Moose Park peaked at 43 pupils in 1929, declining to only 9 in 1944 when the school closed.[33]

Anna Zustiak, who arrived at Moose Park from Slovakia as a small girl in 1901, recalled that it was necessary to walk 18 miles to Blackduck to obtain such food supplies as salt pork, lard, sugar, salt, and coffee, which were then back-packed over a rough trail through the woods another 18 miles back to the homestead. At that time, she said, the pine had not yet been cut, and there were no roads through the deep forests. Porcupine served "with baking powder biscuits was a delicacy," she remembered, and boiled salt pork and

A SLOVAK FAMILY gathered for this photograph on the Minnesota iron range in the early 20th century.

sauerkraut were eaten with "sour dumplings which were substantial enough to be felt or heard when they hit the stomach." School lunch might consist of "a cold pancake smeared with lard or bacon fryings and sometimes a little sugar."

The northwestern Minnesota Czech community of Tabor, established in Polk County in the Red River Valley in 1880, attracted about 50 Slovak families by 1904. Catholics among them attended the local Czech church, but Lutherans established Holy Trinity Slovak Lutheran Church in 1889. Several of Holy Trinity's pastors were from Minneapolis. The settlement also had a branch of the National Slovak Society. Another Red River community, that of Elizabeth in Otter Tail County, had a few "Slavonians" who were probably Slovaks in the mixed congregation of its Roman Catholic church, St. Elizabeth.[34]

A stronger and more diversified Slovak community in central Minnesota developed around South Elmdale in Morrison County and neighboring Holdingford in Stearns County. A group of Slovaks who had immigrated in 1883 to Pittsburgh and Braddock, Pennsylvania, moved to South Elmdale several years later. By 1896, when about 30 families of various faiths had located there, a Slovak theology student from Oberlin College in Ohio arrived to spend the summer. Since the area had no church and the student had been converted to Congregationalism, he soon persuaded several families to join that denomination. In 1897, with the help of the Czech Congregational Missionary Association and ministers from the Czech settlement at Silver Lake in McLeod County, the Slovak Congregational Church of South Elmdale was established. It is one of the very few Slovak churches of this denomination in the United States, although Germans, Swedes, and Norwegians have also attended. The church maintained close ties with Silver Lake, exchanging ministers and guest speakers. Membership

totaled 106 in 1972. A more usual pattern developed at neighboring Holdingford where Roman Catholic Slovaks worshiped with Polish farmers at St. Hedwig's Church, which was founded in 1910.[35]

Other Slovaks from Pennsylvania also settled in central Minnesota near Browerville. Some of the men had worked as coal miners near McKeesport, Pennsylvania, for several years before moving with their families to Hartford Township in Todd County. At least 15 Greek Catholic families took up farms and built a small concrete-block church east of Browerville. Although they were unable to support a priest, they held meetings with several Ruthenian Greek Orthodox families who lived in the area. The church was abandoned in the 1940s. Most of the Slovaks intermarried with other groups and attended German or Polish Roman Catholic churches.[36]

Southern Minnesota also hosted two Slovak farming communities. The smaller appeared in Mound, just west of the Twin Cities, where the Slovaks joined German settlers in Our Lady of the Lake Roman Catholic Church, founded in 1909. Immigrants from one of the first Slovak settlements in the United States started a larger Slovak community in Jackson County. Two families left the bituminous coal fields near Streator, Illinois, which had attracted Slovak miners in the early 1870s, and moved to Lakefield in 1888. Others soon joined them. Sixteen Lutheran families organized a congregation in 1896 and built Holy Trinity Evangelical Lutheran Church in 1901. Roman Catholic Slovaks attended the Czech parish of St. Wenceslaus in the town of Jackson. In 1898 they formed a lodge of the First Catholic Slovak Union and in 1901, 40 families established their own church, St. John the Baptist, in Minneota Township.[37]

These Slovak settlements, not as large as those in the Twin Cities, participated on a smaller scale in many of the same activities. Churches organized Sunday schools and women's societies, and men's lodges offered needed financial support to members. Apparently they did not sponsor as many or as varied entertainments for Slovak families.[38]

Closely attuned to community activities in large cities and small towns was the Slovak press. Although there were not enough in Minneapolis or in the state to support their own daily or weekly newspapers, Minnesota Slovaks had access to the printed word in their own language. Catholic Slovaks subscribed to such weekly publications as *Jednota* (Union), issued in Middletown, Pennsylvania, as the official organ of the First Catholic Slovak Union, and *Katolícky Sokol* (Catholic Falcon), published in Passaic, New Jersey, by the society of the same name. These papers carried news about the activities of countrymen in Minnesota. Lutherans read the liberal *Slovenský Hlásnik* (Slovak Spokesman), the official organ of the Slovak Evangelical Union of Pittsburgh. Those who disagreed with its policies could subscribe to *Hlas sv. Emmanuela* (Voice of Holy Emmanuel), published by Holy Emmanuel Church in Minneapolis from 1920 to 1926, apparently the only Slovak periodical in the state. Also available was *Svedok* (Witness), issued in Pittsburgh by the Slovak Lutheran Synod. Two popular nondenominational weeklies with nationwide circulations were *Slovák v Amerike* (Slovak in America) and *Slovenská Obrana* (Slovak Defense), published in New York City and Scranton, Pennsylvania, respectively.[39]

Although some of these periodicals took strong stands in the debate on the future of Slovakia during both World Wars, the issue apparently drew little reaction from Minnesota Slovaks. In 1918 national debate split between Lutherans and secularists, who favored a close union with the Czechs, and the Catholics, who wanted an autonomous Slovakia in a federated state. Those in Minnesota evidently reflected this split pattern. Although neither religious group participated in a parade of St. Paul Czechs celebrating "Czecho-Slovak" independence in 1918, the pastor of Holy Emmanuel sent congratulations on behalf of "the Slovak peoples" of Minneapolis.[40]

As immigration declined and Slovaks in Minnesota followed the national patterns of urbanization and suburbanization, they lost their command of the Slovak language. Joshua A. Fishman, an expert on language retention, maintained that the two are connected: greater interaction with American culture in the cities, he said, tended to weaken the old cultures. His research showed Slovak language retention to be among the lowest of those he studied nationally, and here again Minnesota Slovaks were no exception. While a majority of the second generation had learned the language in childhood, very few members of the third generation spoke it at all. The second generation evidently saw little reason to teach their children such a minor Slavic language. Some feared that if their children spoke Slovak, they would be branded as "Hunkies," as the first and second generations had been. Small Slovak parochial schools, erected long after the group's arrival, did little to promote the language. Although Lutherans at Holy Emmanuel in Minneapolis supported their own school from 1920 to 1945, it included only grades six through eight, and its emphasis was on the perpetuation of Lutheranism, not Slovak ethnicity.[41]

The Slovak language did not, however, disappear entirely. In 1980 Holy Emmanuel still offered a weekly Slovak-language service, drawing a group of about 25 every Sunday. The Slovak Catholic Sokol initiated Slovak-language classes in September, 1980, teaching over 30 participants.[42]

Other indications of continued Slovak ethnicity suggested a shift in values and a changing perception of which ethnic attributes were important and which were not. While the Slovak language was discontinued in most church services, the Minneapolis churches themselves prospered, drawing members from St. Paul and from distant suburbs who remained loyal to their parents' congregations. Most assemblies of the National Slovak Society in Minnesota disappeared with a decline of Slovak nationalism, but the Saints Cyril and Methodius branch of the First Catholic Slovak Union remained active, perhaps because the union shifted its emphasis to Catholic fraternalism. The Slovak Catholic Sokol became a social organization, no longer renting halls for gymnastic practice but still working to attract younger people with an interest in sports.[43]

Slovak cooking declined in part because it was so time consuming. As one third-generation Slovak observed, "It was not the kind of meal the working parent whips up in the hour between getting home from work and taking off for the Little League game." Cooks received help from four second-generation women who gathered every week during the winter at Prince of Glory Church to make 32 pounds of noodles, filling orders from some 100 customers. In 1980 Holy Emmanuel sponsored an annual fall "Slovak Smorgasbord," so named as a concession to its Scandinavian neighbors in the state.[44]

Finally the nationwide interest of the 1970s in ethnic "roots" seemed to strike a chord among some Slovaks and to give a few of their lodges, churches, and national newspapers a new vitality. One demonstration of continued Slovak identification shows a certain symmetrical finality: the members of those Roman Catholic families who left St. Cyril's in Minneapolis in the 1930s were still returning 40 years later to be buried with their grandparents in the Slovak national parish.[45]

Reference notes

[1] Josef J. Barton, "Eastern and Southern Europeans," in John Higham, ed., *Ethnic Leadership in America*, 163 (Baltimore, 1978); Czechoslovak National Council of America, *Panorama: A Historical Review of Czechs and Slovaks in the United States of America*, 9 (Cicero, Ill., [1970]); United States, *Census*, 1920, *Population*, 2:984; 1970, vol. 1, part 25, p. 514. The 1980 figure for Minnesota Slovaks is an educated guess based on the author's analysis of average Slovak family size; Mark Stolarik to Ann Regan, October 13, 1980, in MEHP Papers.

[2] R[obert] W. Seton-Watson, *A History of the Czechs and the Slovaks*, 11, 251, 253, 255 (London, 1943); Stephen Janšák, "The Land Question in Slovakia," in *Slavonic Review*, 8:618, 620 (March, 1930); Arthur J. May, *The Hapsburg Monarchy 1867–1914*, 10, 12, 37, 236 (New York, 1951).

[3] Ján Hanzlík, "Vývoj obyvateľstva na Slovensku v období 1869–1961," in *Geografický časopis*, 19:7 (1967); Július Mésároš, "Roľnícka otázka na východnom Slovensku v 19, storočí," in *Príspevky k dejinám východného Slovenska*, 183 (Bravislava,

Czechoslovakia, 1964). Some of the emigrants from eastern Slovakia were Rusins and Magyars; see Chapters 21, 22.

[4] Karold Rebro, "Agrárne reformy v habsburskej monarchii od začiatku 18. storočia do r. 1848 s osobitným zreteľom na Slovensko," in *Historické štúdie*, 13:11–13 (1968); Július Mésároš, *Roľnícka a národnostná otázka na Slovensku, 1848–1900; k problematike feudálnych prežitkov*, 15–25 (Bratislava, Czechoslovakia, 1959).

[5] Endré Arató, "K hospodárskym dejinám Slovenska od r. 1849 do 1900," in *Historický časopis*, 1:432 (1953); Emily Greene Balch, *Our Slavic Fellow Citizens*, 239 (New York, 1910).

[6] Hanzlík, in *Geografický časopis*, 19:10; Ján Svetoň, "Slovenské vysťahovalectvo v období uhorského kapitalizmu," in *Ekonomický časopis*, 4:171–179 (1956); U.S. Slovak statistics, in MEHP Papers, MHS, compiled by Jon A. Gjerde from U.S. Dept. of Labor, Bureau of Immigration, *Annual Reports*, 1909–39, and U.S. Justice Dept., Immigration and Naturalization Service, *Annual Reports*, 1940–75, hereafter cited as Gjerde, Slovak statistics.

[7] U.S., *Census*, 1910, *Population*, 1:961, 976; 1920, 2:973; 1970, vol. 1, part 1, p. 599; *Národné Noviny* (Pittsburgh), April 7, pp. 3, 4, April 21, p. 4, 1910. The 1910 estimate was calculated by subtracting the net immigration for 1910–20 (figured from Gjerde, Slovak statistics) from the 1920 census total. For an explanation of the comparability of mother-tongue figures, see U.S., *Census*, 1960, *Population*, vol. 1, part 25, p. xxii. For an explanation of the 1980 estimate, see note 1.

[8] Here and below, see *Memoirs of the Golden Jubilee of the St. Cyril and Methodius Society, Branch 3, First Catholic Slovak Union, Minneapolis, Minn., 1888–1938*, 8–10, 42 ([Minneapolis, 1938]), hereafter cited as *Golden Jubilee Memoirs*; Warren Upham and Rose Dunlap, eds., *Minnesota Biographies, 1655–1912*, 205 (St. Paul, 1912); First Catholic Slovak Union, Membership Lists, Lodge No. 3, 1896–1907, in IHRC; St. Cyril's Parish, Birth Records, 1893–95, in the parish rectory, Minneapolis; Works Projects Administration (WPA), Writers' Program, *The Bohemian Flats*, 9, 16, 47 (Minneapolis, [1941]). The five first settlers were George and John Gogola, John Zelenák, Joseph Martonik, and Thomas Ovšak.

[9] WPA, *Bohemian Flats*, 9, 11, 15–17.

[10] WPA, *Bohemian Flats*, 19–24, 30–39.

[11] *Katolícke Slovensko . . . 833–1933*, 155 (Trnava, Czechoslovakia, 1933).

[12] Jednota, Sts. Cyril and Methodius, Lodge No. 3, Minutes, November 12, 1888, in IHRC; *Golden Jubilee Memoirs*, 11–14, 21. For examples of activities, see Sts. Cyril and Methodius, Lodge No. 3, Minutes, December 1, 1889, September 7, 1890, February 10, 1894, March 10, 1895, August 13, 1899, October 19, 1902; taped interview of Andrew Hudak by author, August 25, 1976, in IHRC.

[13] Sts. Cyril and Methodius, Lodge No. 3, Minutes, January 5, March 2, August 3, 1890; St. Mary's Russian Orthodox Church, *Fortieth Anniversary Memorial Book, 1889–1929*, 11–17 (Minneapolis, 1929), and *Diamond Jubilee Album, 1887–1962*, 17–23 (Minneapolis, 1962); Anna Potosnak Beeman, a former parishioner of St. Mary's, to the author, February 2, March 10, 1979, copies in MEHP Papers, originals in the author's possession. St. Mary's was built at 5th St. and 17th Ave. Northeast.

Slovak Greek Catholics who did not wish to become Russian Orthodox may either have worshiped at St. Cyril's or eventually joined St. John the Baptist Eastern Rite Catholic Church, which was organized in 1907 at 22nd Ave. Northeast and 3rd St. by Rusin immigrants. But Rev. Joseph Fedyszak, pastor of St. John's in 1980, denied that any Slovaks ever joined the church. St. John the Baptist Eastern Rite Catholic Church, *Golden Jubilee, 1907–1957*, 10 (Minneapolis, 1957); interview of Rev. Fedyszak by Ann Regan, June 5, 1980, notes in MEHP Papers.

[14] St. Cyril's Church, Articles of Incorporation, February 23, 1891, and Statistical Report, January 1, 1918, both in Archdiocese of St. Paul Archives, St. Paul Seminary; St. Cyril's Church, Parish Committee Minutes, May 11, 1909, in IHRC; St. Cyril's Church, *Historical Sketch 1891–1941*, 1–9 ([Minneapolis,] 1941), copy in IHRC. The church, built at 16th Ave. Northeast and Main St., was moved to 2nd St. and 13th Ave. Northeast in 1909.

[15] Interview of Rev. Joseph J. Balent by Ann Regan, June 20, 1980, notes in MEHP Papers; Hudak interview, August 25, 1976; Mark Stolarik, "Immigration and Urbanization: The Slovak Experience, 1870–1918," 85, 90–93, Ph.D. thesis, University of Minnesota, 1974. The chapter pertaining to Catholic Slovaks was included in Keith P. Dyrud, Michael Novak, and Rudolph J. Vecoli, eds., *The Other Catholics* (New York, 1978).

[16] Slovak Evangelical Church of St. Emmanuel, *História cirkve Sv. Emmanuela*, 3–20 (Pittsburgh, [1919]); Holy Emmanuel Lutheran Church, *75 Years of Grace, 1888–1963*, [5, 7, 11] ([Minneapolis, 1963]); *Minneapolis City Directory, 1950*, 572; *Minneapolis Suburban Directory, 1970*, 551; interview of Rev. Emil Velebir, pastor of Holy Emmanuel Church, by Ann Regan, August 18, 1980, notes in MEHP Papers. In the church's early publications, its name was mistranslated as St. Emmanuel. Its Southeast Minneapolis location was the corner of Essex and Ontario streets; the Bloomington address in 1980 was 201 East 104th St. The author wishes to acknowledge the helpful suggestions of Rev. Velebir in the preparation of this chapter.

[17] WPA, Minnesota, Historical Records Survey: Churches, 1936–41, in MHS, hereafter cited as WPA, Church Records; Václav Vojta, *Czechoslovak Baptists*, 217–219 (Minneapolis, 1941). The first church was at 2009 Washington Ave. South; the second was built at 215 15th Ave. South.

[18] Here and below, see George Dolak, *A History of the Slovak Evangelical Lutheran Church in the United States of America*, 130–135, 138 (St. Louis, 1955); WPA, Church Records; St. (*sic*) Emmanuel Slovak Lutheran Church, *Golden Jubilee, 1888–1938*, 15, 29 ([Minneapolis], 1938); Prince of Glory Lutheran Church, *Dedication Booklet*, 4–6 ([Minneapolis, 1957]), and *50 Years Together in Ministry*, 6 ([Minneapolis, 1973]); interview of Rev. John Ellison, pastor of Prince of Glory Church, by Ann Regan, June 23, 1980, notes in MEHP Papers. Holy Trinity was built at 2900 29th Ave. South and Prince of Glory at 4401 Minnehaha Ave.

[19] Stolarik, "Immigration and Urbanization," 36; Ellison interview, June 23, 1980; Velebir interview, August 18, 1980.

[20] St. Cyril's Church, *Historical Sketch*, 8; *Slovakia, 1970*, back cover (Middletown, Pa.).

[21] Sts. Cyril and Methodius, Lodge No. 3, Minutes, December 8, 1895, and Applications for Membership, Branch No. 3, Minneapolis, 1908–1912, Branch No. 226, Minneapolis, 1908–1912, First Catholic Slovak Union Records — all in IHRC; St. Cyril's Church, *Historical Sketch*, 8; Balent interview, June 20, 1980.

[22] *Slovák v Amerike* (New York), October 5, 1909, p. 2; *Jednota* (Middletown, Pa.), October 9, p. 1, November 6, p. 2, 1912; St. Cyril's Church, *Historical Sketch*, 9; Jozef G. Pruša, "Review of the Slovak Catholic Sokol History," in Slovak Catholic Sokol, *Pamätnica XXII. Hlavného Sletu Zavodov Slovenského Katolíckeho Sokola*, [33] (Passaic, N.J., 1965); interview of James J. Genosky by Ann Regan, August 11, 1980, notes in MEHP Papers. *Sokol* is the Slovak word for falcon.

[23] "Declaration for the Formation of a Fraternal Life and Casualty Insurance Society: St. John the Baptist Slavonic Society of Minneapolis," in National Slovak Society Papers, Assembly No. 46, St. John the Baptist, Minneapolis, IHRC; Slovak Evangelical Church of St. Emmanuel, *História cirkve Sv. Emmanuela*, 16.

[24] St. Cyril's Church, *Historical Sketch*, 5–7; Holy Emmanuel

Church, *75 Years of Grace*, [12, 15]; Prince of Glory Church, *50 Years Together*, 8–10; Rev. Emil Velebir to Ann Regan, November 11, 1980, in MEHP Papers.

[25] Holy Emmanuel Church, *75 Years of Grace*, [9]; St. Cyril's Church, *Historical Sketch*, 4–7.

[26] For examples of such activities, see St. Cyril's Church, *Historical Sketch*, 5–9; St. Cyril's Church, Parish Committee Minutes, December 31, 1905, March 3, 1907; and notes 12 and 24, above.

[27] John Higham, *Strangers in the Land: Patterns of American Nativism 1860–1925*, 88 (New York, 1963); *Minnesota in the War* (Minneapolis), February 15, 1919, p. 3.

[28] Higham, *Strangers in the Land*, 88; Peter Roberts, *The New Immigration: A Study of the Industrial and Social Life of the South-eastern Europeans in America*, 50 (New York, 1912); Isaac A. Hourwich, *Immigration and Labor: The Economic Aspects of European Immigration to the United States*, 7, 305 (New York, 1912); Brinley Thomas, *Migration and Economic Growth: A Study of Great Britain and the Atlantic Economy*, 154 (Cambridge, Eng., 1954); *Slovák v Amerike*, May 21, 1896, p. 7.

[29] John Syrjamaki, "Mesabi Communities: A Study of Their Development," 131, Ph.D. thesis, Yale University, 1940. For evidence of Slovaks in Superior, see Applications for Membership, 1909–11, Branch No. 358, Superior, Wis., First Catholic Slovak Union Records.

[30] George O. Virtue, *The Minnesota Iron Ranges*, 345, 348 (United States Bureau of Labor, *Bulletin*, no. 84 — Washington, D.C., 1909).

[31] Applications for Membership, 1908–11, Branch No. 106, Virginia, Branch No. 500, Hibbing, Branch no. 579, Eveleth, First Catholic Slovak Union Records. Assemblies 179, 328, 341 Ely, 213 Soudan, 348 Eveleth, and 380 McKinley are mentioned in the inventory of the National Slovak Society Papers, IHRC. Of these groups, only continuing records for the McKinley assembly have survived. In 1949 it had 27 male and female members receiving insurance; by 1972 there were only 4. Its founding is mentioned in Beeman to Stolarik, February 2, 1979.

The immigrants in at least one of these towns apparently migrated by village. Half of the 32 Slovaks who joined the Eveleth branch between 1908 and 1911 were born in Lomná, a village in Orava County of north-central Slovakia; 11 of the others were also from villages in Orava.

[32] Duluth Roman Catholic Diocese, "Annual Reports of Parishes," in Bishop's Office, Duluth Chancery, membership abstracts compiled by Marjorie Hoover, in MEHP Papers; Catholic Archdiocese of St. Paul and Minneapolis, Parish Questionnaires, 1948, originals in Catholic Historical Society, St. Paul Seminary, St. Paul, microfilm in MHS, hereafter cited as Parish Questionnaires; Blessed Sacrament Church, *75th Anniversary, 1894–1969*, 24 ([Hibbing, 1969]); *Catholic Outlook* (Duluth), January, 1926, pp. 56, 133; Syrjamaki, "Mesabi Communities," 123.

[33] Here and below, see Warren Upham, *Minnesota Geographic Names*, 253 (Reprint ed., St. Paul, 1969); Melvin C. Kruger, "The Slovaks of Moose Creek," in *Leatherleaf* (Grand Rapids), vol. 1,

no. 2, pp. 4–6, no. 3, p. 16 (1973), copies in MHS library; WPA, Church Records.

[34] Jan Habenicht, *Dějiny Čechův Amerických*, 431; *Jednota*, February 16, 1910, p. 5; Slovak Evangelical Lutheran Church of the Holy Trinity, *Poriadok Slávnostných Služeib Božích pri 50. Výročí Cirkvi*, 8–10 (Tabor, 1939); John W. Mason, *History of Otter Tail County, Minnesota*, 1:390–392 (Indianapolis, 1916). Assembly 536, Tabor, is listed in the inventory of National Slovak Society Papers, IHRC; none of the group's financial records is in the collection.

[35] South Elmdale Congregational Church, *Fiftieth Anniversary, 1897–1947*, [2–5, 8] ([Upsala, 1947]), and *75th Anniversary, 1897–1972*, [8] ([Holdingford, 1972]); WPA, Church Records; Parish Questionnaires. The Oberlin theology student was John Sabol.

[36] Irene Delsing to Deborah Stultz, [September, 1980], and interview of Samuel Roman by Ann Regan, September 11, 1980, letters and notes in MEHP Papers.

[37] Parish Questionnaires; *Jednota*, February 17, 1904, p. 3; Holy Trinity Evangelical Lutheran Church, *A Brief History Commemorating the Fiftieth Anniversary of Its Congregation, 1896–1946*, [5] ([Lakefield, 1946]); Membership List and Applications for Membership, 1908, Lodge No. 298, Lakefield, in First Catholic Slovak Union Records. Eight men founded the lodge; by 1908 there were at least 17 members. Information on St. John the Baptist is included with the Lakefield parish of St. Joseph's, of which it became a mission in 1912. On Streator, see Stolarik, "Immigration and Urbanization," 83.

[38] For examples of these activities, see Anna Beeman to author, February 2, 1979, copy in MEHP Papers; South Elmdale Congregational Church, *Fiftieth Anniversary*, [2, 5]; Holy Trinity Lutheran Church, *Fiftieth Anniversary*, [9, 19, 21].

[39] Konštantín Čulen, *Slovenské časopisy v Amerike*, 51–54, 58, 120–126, 129, 151 (Cleveland, 1970); WPA, Church Records; Esther Jerabek, "Czechs and Slovaks in Minnesota," in Czechoslovak National Council of America, *Panorama*, 50; Holy Emmanuel Church, *75 Years of Grace*, [13]; Hudak interview, August 25, 1976.

[40] Mark Stolarik, "The Role of American Slovaks in the Creation of Czecho-Slovakia," master's thesis, University of Ottawa, 1967; *St. Paul Pioneer Press*, September 30, 1918, p. 10.

[41] Joshua Fishman et al., *Language Loyalty in the United States*, 42, 44, 47, 135 (The Hague, 1966); Hudak interview, August 25, 1976. See also note 24, above.

[42] Velebir interview, August 18, 1980; Genosky interview, August 11, 1980.

[43] Ellison interview, June 23, 1980; Velebir interview, August 18, 1980; taped interview of Peter Kavchar, president of Sts. Cyril and Methodius Society of Minneapolis, by author, January, 1968, in IHRC; Genosky interview, August 11, 1980.

[44] Interview of Mary Van Devere by Ann Regan, August 12, 1980, notes in MEHP Papers; *Minneapolis Star*, July 2, 1980, p. 3T.

[45] Balent interview, June 20, 1980; author's observations of and research in Slovak communities across the U.S. between 1966 and 1980.

CHAPTER 19

The Poles

Frank Renkiewicz

THE SETTLEMENT of Poles in Minnesota, beginning on the eve of the Civil War, loosely resembled that of Poles elsewhere in the United States. The Minnesota community, so far as it differed notably from the norm in Polish America, was based more heavily in the Prussian partition of the old republic and had a more rural flavor; it resembled the largely Germanic and agricultural ethnic and economic pattern of the state. Peasant villages in Upper Silesia, Kaszubia, and Poznan — all within Prussia as a result of events in 1740–1815 — were the homes of the first Polish migrants to Minnesota as they were of most American Poles until the 1880s (see Map 19.1).[1]

It is nearly impossible to estimate the number of Poles in Minnesota until early in the 20th century when death had carried off many of the first settlers and the censuses of 1880 and 1890 had lost many others as "Prussians." The state census of 1905 recorded about 27,000 first- and second-generation Poles, a figure believed to be far short of their true numbers. Other estimates ranged as high as 84,000. Assuming a minimum of 7,000 families in the state, and a modest average of six to eight members, one could put the number of Poles in a range from 42,000 to 56,000. While these figures may be too high, the Poles were a typically young and fertile immigrant population (see Table 19.1).[2]

Emigration was associated with a variety of factors mostly related to the agricultural revolution in East Elbian Prussia after the mid-19th century. The emancipation of peasants from serfdom, completed by 1848, was followed by the integration of the region's agriculture into an expanding capitalist and industrial German economy. Based on more efficient technology, the consolidation of small holdings, the appropriation of commons land, a mobile labor force, a few commercial crops, and eventually upon tariff protection, large commercial estates and peasant farms gradually replaced the traditional manorial economy.[3]

Agricultural modernization, however, forced tens of thousands of peasants to leave the countryside. Traditional woodcrafts, shepherding, and fishing, which had long supplemented or substituted for farming in many districts, were subjected to the same pressures and proved unable to absorb a growing population. As the network of print communications and railroads reached into east-central Europe, the attention of many young peasants was focused upon the United States and upon such Latin American countries as Brazil. Their emigration abroad reached a peak in the 1880s, after which the newly profitable agriculture and the lure of industrial employment in the nearer Rhineland made America less attractive.[4]

A number of political and cultural factors were also at work. The threat of conscription into the Prussian army in the 1860s influenced at least a few young men to leave rather than risk or postpone the establishment of families. Kaszubs, a West Slavic people with strong ties to Polish culture living west and south of Danzig, were early objects of Germanization. In the 1850s the Maritime Navigation Company of Hamburg induced many Kaszubs to sell their land in exchange for passage to the United States. The company in turn sold the land to ethnic Germans. German landlords in Upper Silesia also encouraged their Polish tenants to emigrate, hoping to replace them with German colonists whom they considered more efficient and energetic. There is little evidence, however, that the more systematic Germanization policies later in the century gave much encouragement to emigration, except to spur the departure of some members of the intelligentsia.

Patterns of Settlement

In 1855, foreshadowing the pattern of Polish immigration to the state, parts of two families from the Wiele village region in southern Kaszubia arrived in Winona just as that new town was beginning its rise to eminence as a grain shipment and lumber center. They encouraged others, chiefly friends and family, to invest the $60.00 or so needed for the three-month voyage by sea from Bremen, by rail from New York to the Mississippi, and finally by river boat to Winona.[5]

The first large party of about 25 reached the city in 1857. Working as farm laborers or as railroad track hands, in lumberyards, and (in the case of women) in heavy domestic service, they began in the 1860s to purchase farms in Trempealeau County across the Mississippi River in adjacent Wisconsin or to settle permanently in the city. By 1864 there were about 50 Polish families in Winona. Their number grew rapidly through 1888 to about 700 families concentrated in the east end of the city and in a small pocket on the west side. Living within easy walking distance of the sawmills, foundries, and railroad yards which employed them, they began to build homes on narrow half-lots with cheap or free wood from the immense stocks of local lumber companies.

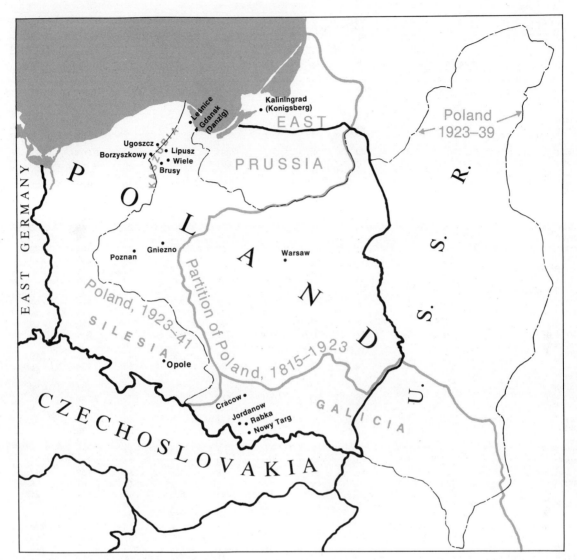

Map 19.1. Poland in Three Eras

Table 19.1. Poles in Minnesota by County, 1860–1970

County	1860 foreign born	1860 foreign mixed	1880 fb	1880 fm	1890 fb	1905 fb	1905 fm	1930 fb	1930 fm	1970 fb	1970 fm
Aitkin			1			3	8	12	27	14	41
Anoka	4	1			2			175	391	94	1,045
Becker						7	7	47	111		38
Beltrami						8	11	39	70	9	62
Benton			101	60	213	144	415	300	1,118	25	458
Big Stone			2		6	6	29	8	19		
Blue Earth			4	3	18	3	12	41	93	46	71
Brown	1		3			1	2	22	42	6	33
Carlton					32	201	415	172	451	54	372
Carver	1	2	10	7	3	3	12	26	45		63
Cass					6	3	8	23	45	13	42
Chippewa			1	1				2	14		17
Chisago			1	4	11	7	9	10	22	9	18
Clay					1	4	9	16	48	17	59
Clearwater								6	9		
Cook						3	6	9	3		
Cottonwood			7	2	1	2	14	30	82		19
Crow Wing			9	4	3	1	22	65	133	11	169
Dakota			68	40	89	55	106	245	524	136	742
Dodge			6		3	2	11	13	48	7	50

Table 19.1. Poles in Minnesota by County, 1860–1970 (*continued*)

County	1860 foreign born	1860 foreign mixed	1880 fb	1880 fm	1890 fb	1905 fb	1905 fm	1930 fb	1930 fm	1970 fb	1970 fm
Douglas			18	6	3	3	11	21	55		32
Faribault			65	31	111	20	51	118	294	58	147
Fillmore	4		2	1	1		4	8	15		25
Freeborn			3	6	19	17	32	30	110	13	79
Goodhue			3	3	2	8	34	18	39	9	48
Grant					1	1		6	20		
Hennepin	12	2	39		392	897	1,431	4,692	8,603	1,579	7,289
Minneapolis					381	891	1,415	4,555	8,325	1,080	4,600
Houston			7	9	4			2	4		40
Hubbard						3	3	20	38	5	5
Isanti						2	14	12	44	12	34
Itasca						17	30	68	143		126
Jackson							6	9	27		28
Kanabec								23	43	6	15
Kandiyohi			1		4	1	1	20	19		7
Kittson			1	11	5	20	49	50	164	8	37
Koochiching								139	244	8	121
Lac qui Parle						3	6	8	21		8
Lake					3	42	41	9	23		31
Lake of the Woods								13	20		
Le Sueur	17	1	7	1	147	74	204	68	226	12	213
Lincoln			1		209	333	890	166	619	15	165
Lyon			1		21	30	67	49	133	29	105
McLeod	1		317	157	440	219	700	108	370	10	127
Mahnomen								6	34		
Marshall					117	183	532	147	536	19	227
Martin			2	5	104	24	76	65	234	5	154
Meeker					1			6	10		7
Mille Lacs					3	5	16	44	101	58	46
Morrison			356	283	769	412	1,297	570	2,142	47	880
Mower			2		1		1	16	17	8	48
Murray					5	1	1	9	20	7	7
Nicollet	2	3	3		6			27	36		33
Nobles					1				2		17
Norman						1	13	7	17		
Olmsted	8	1	4	10	15	8	17	74	111	35	163
Otter Tail			154	97	163	138	360	250	552	12	122
Pennington								18	61	6	26
Pine					92	225	503	246	498	21	190
Pipestone						1	2	6	14		13
Polk					3	8	17	28	71		121
Pope						1	2	12	20		
Ramsey	4	5	254	132	1,099	1,345	3,162	2,701	5,224	868	3,797
St. Paul					1,015	1,225	2,703	2,610	4,917	770	2,934
Red Lake						21	27	4	12		
Redwood					2	4	8	5	14		19
Renville	2	3	3	1	3			14	38		12
Rice			7	2	5	2	5	17	95	6	74
Rock				2				2	2		
Roseau						95	262	68	183		112
St. Louis			164	94	930	1,342	2,786	2,051	4,062	395	2,394
Duluth						1,046	2,207	1,280	2,492	243	1,381
Scott			3	9	2			10	15		67
Sherburne					11	11	26	11	50		48
Sibley	1		1	1	17			14	50	14	46
Stearns	1	2	113	61	245	79	257	317	1,085	86	568
Steele			257	40	145	102	297	162	349	16	105
Stevens			2		4		2	6	28	7	10
Swift			21	5	2	28	101	21	95		24
Todd	1		17	9	72	246	810	268	762	20	192
Traverse			1	2	5	6	35	11	27		
Wabasha	1		1	1	3	4	5	17	43		15
Wadena					1			2	11		36
Waseca			16	5	2	4	6	21	48	8	63
Washington	1		13	1	6	2	4	56	101	26	310
Watonwan							4	20	39		14
Wilkin			8		11	6	12	21	52		27
Winona			58	36	1,840	1,401	3,900	675	2,267	38	849
Wright	8	1	129	47	54	22	91	46	101	26	126
Yellow Medicine					14	11	30	26	98		55
Totals	69	21	2,267	1,189	7,503	7,881	19,337	15,015	33,896	3,933	22,998
Published census figures	(127)		(2,218)		(7,503)	(7,881)	(19,343)	(15,015)	(33,896)	(3,933)	(22,998)

Source: See Appendix

POLES applying for passports in Warsaw in 1924.

At the end of the century the Polish population of the city stood at about 5,000. Four-fifths were Kaszubs drawn largely from the area near the villages of Ugoszcz, Borzyszkowy, Brusy, Leśnice, Lipusz, and Wiele (see Map 19.1). Winona held a large minority of the 90,000 Kaszubs in the United States, ranking fourth after the Stevens Point, Wisconsin, area with 10,000, and Buffalo, New York, and Detroit, Michigan, with 5,000 each. The remainder of the state's 4,000 Kaszubs (over 600 families) lived mainly in rural Sturgeon Lake, New Brighton, and St. Paul.[6]

Other non-Kaszub Poles, who are sometimes referred to as "pure" Poles, emigrated primarily from Poznania, the heart of ancient and early historic Poland, and from Upper Silesia. About 1,000 lived in Winona. The large community at Silver Lake in McLeod County was begun in 1860 by a Poznanian whose path had taken him north from Texas' Polish colonies. Gnesen, a smallish colony north of Duluth, was established by 1878 by people from Poznan, who named it for Gniezno, the first historic center of Polish culture.[7]

Emigration fever, which gripped Upper Silesia in the 1850s, uprooted whole villages and provided the second largest provincial base for Polish settlement in Minnesota. Opole in Stearns County, founded in 1860, was a classic case, carrying the very name of the village-parish from which most of its members hailed. During the next 25 years homogeneous and substantial Silesian Polish settlements appeared in such widely scattered parts of the state as Browerville in Todd County, Delano in Wright, Wells in Faribault, North Prairie in Morrison, and elsewhere (see Table 19.1).[8]

Probably the key to the location and development of these rural settlements was held by the railroads then laying a network of tracks in Minnesota. Construction, advertising, land sales, and emigration agents focused the interests, sometimes by chance, of potential Polish farmers. Frequently an entrepreneur, a cleric, or a colonization company served as an intermediary in the settlement process. Gilman in Benton County grew out of the purchase of 25,000 acres of timberland from the St. Paul and Pacific Railroad by a Chicago group in which a Polish publisher took a leading part in 1877–78. Probably many of the farmers established themselves by cutting timber for or working in the sawmill at Gilman.[9]

A few years later the Michigan agent of the St. Paul, Minneapolis, and Manitoba Railway's emigration bureau made something of a career of establishing Polish farm colonies. Following a success in Illinois, he helped found the community at Stephen in the Red River Valley in 1881–82. Wilno in Lincoln County in the extreme southwest was the planned product in 1881–83 of collaboration among the Chicago and Northwestern Railroad, two Minnesota Catholic clerics, and a Polish promoter in Chicago.

If Wilno was a rare example of a planned Polish colony in Minnesota, it was not for lack of interest. The colonization of urban Poles was a major item on the agenda of the Polish National Alliance's 1887 convention in St. Paul and an object of its continuing interest through the early 20th century. Railroads, too, often encouraged such schemes by donating land for churches or cemeteries. In any case the reaction to both lay and clerical Polish promoters in the Red River Valley by the late 1890s revealed disenchantment with ambitious colonization schemes. The practice of the Minnesota Colonization Company, which retained Polish agents with good contacts in the community, may have seemed a more reliable if less dramatic device to both company-owner and prospective land purchaser.[10]

Early in the 20th century interest in farm life declined among Polish Americans. Perhaps the reports of difficulties on poorer land discouraged buyers. More likely the capital investment required for success was beyond the means of immigrants from Russian and Austrian Poland. The price of land varied considerably. Near Owatonna in 1886 it had sold for as little as $.65 an acre. The price at Sturgeon Lake in 1896 might be $5.00 an acre with five to 10 years to pay and in the northwestern corner of the state $5.00 to $7.00. Near Wilno in 1900 land was $20.00 an acre, a factor which may have limited the colony's growth, even though Poles were known as hard workers, savers, and good credit risks.[11]

Rural settlement formation continued until the early 1920s. At least 10 Polish colonies appeared in each decade from 1866 to 1915, with the greatest growth in 1876–90, 1896–1900, and 1911–15. By 1925, when the founding of new settlements through migration into the state had tapered off, there were between 90 and 100 clusters of Poles in rural Minnesota. The 30 largest of these — ethnically homogeneous and moored solidly in institutions — appeared throughout the half-century but especially in 1881–85 and 1896–1900.[12]

If one assumes that the Poles in Winona, Ramsey, Hennepin, and St. Louis counties were all urban and those in all other counties were rural (a moderate exaggeration in both directions), then Minnesota's Polish population was divided about 3 to 2 urban to rural in 1905 and 1930 (see Map 19.2). One careful estimate of the entire Polish-American population in 1920 put the ratio at about 6 to 1 which, even if there were wide error, differs significantly from Minnesota's.[13]

The first Poles reached the state's cities and large towns at

LETTERHEAD used by an immigration society promoting three Polish settlements in northwestern Minnesota in 1896.

about the same time and from the same sources as those in the rural communities. St. Paul, Minneapolis, and Duluth had at least a few Poles by 1870, and they arrived in St. Cloud, Little Falls, and Owatonna by the mid-1880s. As in Winona, work dictated their locations. Those in St. Cloud lived near the granite quarries on the northwest side of town. In Minneapolis they lodged at first in boardinghouses on the "Bohemian Flats" close to the mills and factories along the Mississippi River. Like the men, the women found work cleaning downtown offices through the agency of community brokers (usually saloonkeepers and boardinghouse owners) who provided the early immigrants with a wide range of services. Many of the men worked out of town in the lumber industry, emerging from the woods at Eastertime for a physical and spiritual spring cleaning. By the mid-1880s, as single males gave way to families, stable working-class neighborhoods grew up north and east of the flats with houses at first reminiscent of those left behind in Poland — earthen floors spread with sweet flag, flower gardens in front, vegetable gardens and orchards in the rear.[14]

The growth of urban Polish communities after 1885, particularly in Minneapolis and St. Paul (see Table 19.1), was facilitated by the availability of unskilled and semiskilled jobs. It depended also on conditions in the Austrian and Russian partitions. Emancipation from serfdom in 1864 had been more favorable to peasants in Russian Poland than in either of the other partitions. There the pressure to emigrate was exerted not so much by efforts to rationalize agriculture and consolidate holdings into commercial estates as it was by the difficulty of supporting a growing population with existing technology. Regions near the German border were the first to be affected as seasonal migrations to work on Prussian farms became a way of life for many families. The

conscription of young males and increasing Russification influenced a few to emigrate. Though Russian Poles were not numerous in Minnesota, Sturgeon Lake on the rail line between St. Paul and Duluth was a good example of a rural settlement which grew through their presence.[15]

Galicia, Austria's share of the old Poland, was the poorest, least industrialized, and least literate of the partitions. Twenty years after its Polish peasants were emancipated on relatively favorable terms in 1848 as punishment for a landlord uprising, the Habsburg monarchy reversed field by granting Galicia political autonomy under the domination of gentry and high nobility. The province was also the freest of the partitions culturally. Nevertheless Galicia became increasingly a land of inefficiently cultivated small holdings growing progressively smaller. Despite heavy seasonal and permanent migration after 1880, its population virtually doubled from 4,500,000 in 1850 to 8,000,000 in 1910.[16]

Factors such as these drove people increasingly from the poor pasture and woodlands near the villages of Rabka and Jordanow and the town of Nowy Targ in Podhale in the foothills of the Carpathians (see Table 19.2). For $45.00 to $60.00 they might travel as far as Minnesota. Northeast Minneapolis was their principal destination, particularly at the turn of the century, but they also scattered throughout the state and occasionally into rural communities like Gilman.

None of the partitions was ethnically homogeneous. The Poles themselves were divided by regional cultures, dialects, and the varied economic and cultural policies of their rulers. These differences persisted well into the 20th century, although the trend at the time of the Great Migration was toward the imposition of a national Polish culture. Germans, Lithuanians, White Russians, Ukrainians, Rusins, and Slo-

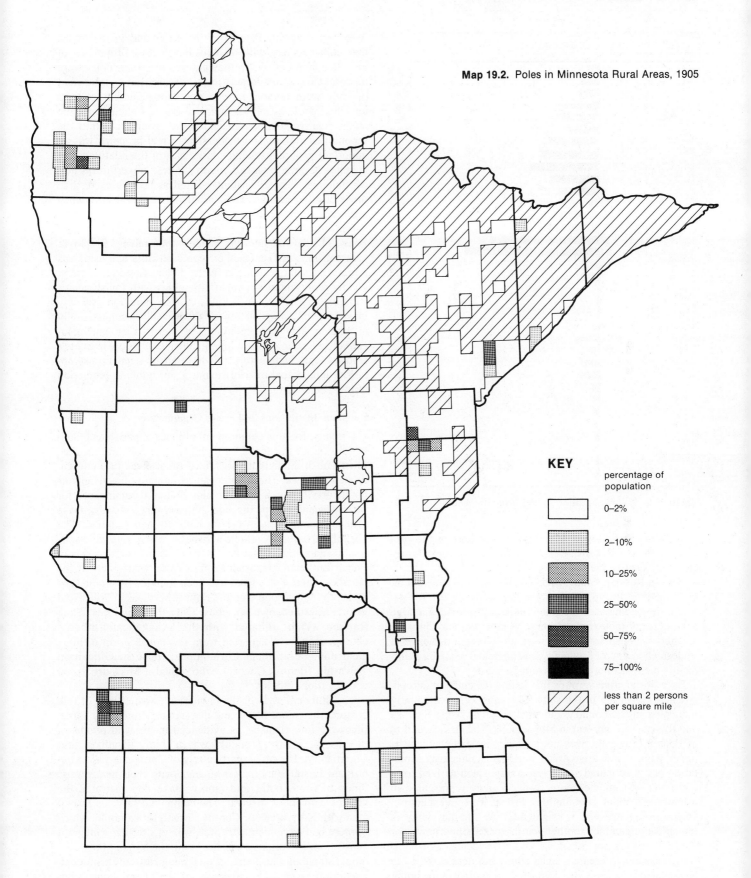

Map 19.2. Poles in Minnesota Rural Areas, 1905

KEY

percentage of
population

0–2%

2–10%

10–25%

25–50%

50–75%

75–100%

less than 2 persons
per square mile

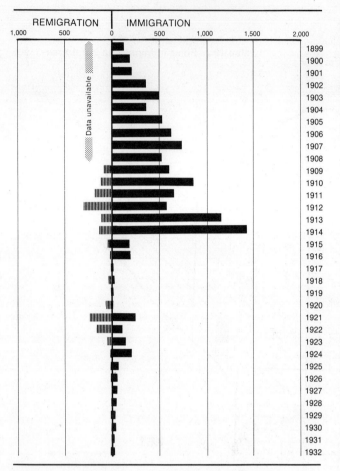

Table 19.2. Polish Migration to and from Minnesota

By any measure Polonia in the cities and towns was a blue-collar society with an unusually heavy proportion of unskilled laborers. When they entered the state, Poles were much like other immigrants in this regard, but as time went on they were notable for the continuing number of their unskilled workers and for failing to improve their economic status relative to other major ethnic groups late into the second generation. The ownership of real property was an important goal, consuming a large part of the relatively low incomes of both town and country Poles. Nevertheless Polish holdings were consistently listed as less valuable than those of other groups. Their progress was great only when measured against prospects in Poland.[19]

It is difficult to explain the persistent low economic rank of Poles, but several answers suggest themselves. Employer paternalism, which defused or repressed labor activism, was a factor at least in Winona in the 1880s. Cultural barriers, vividly represented by Anglo difficulties with Polish names and customs, and various kinds of discrimination probably played a part. A popular genetic theory, still circulated orally in Winona, held that generations of intermarriage among local Poles accounted for a high incidence of "slow learners" among them. Such factors may have encouraged a presumption of intellectual inferiority and a self-fulfilling prediction of low social status.[20]

Religious Institutions and Other Organizations

Possibly, too, the commitment of Poles to parish and family outweighed the desire for mobility and economic success. Most Polish immigrants organized themselves into church-related parishes. These units can be thought of as neighborhoods or villages, a fact of major if altered significance for their descendants in the late 20th century. Usually these primary communities were formally Roman Catholic. The six Polish National Catholic parishes in Minnesota were spiritually and socially their kin. Nor did the two settlements of Polish Lutheran Mazurian farmers differ that much. If the parishes where Poles lived had been founded by ethnic Germans, the Poles soon won the right to services in Polish and to organize their own societies. Only the group near Sauk Rapids, which affiliated with the Evangelical Lutheran church, may have departed from the Polish norm of liturgical and hierarchical Christianity; those in Gilmanton Township (Benton County), who joined a Missouri Synod congregation, did not.[21]

The liturgical style of the immigrants was a blend of folk custom, the cult of Mary, and messianic nationalism. Sometimes the folk element, as evidenced in the wild pranks of *dyngus*, or Easter Monday, was a thinly disguised pre-Christianity. The ritual, particularly of Christmas Eve (*wigilia*) and Easter Blessing (*swięcone*), with their near-mystic union of food, faith, and family, have demonstrated the greatest powers of survival. The communal services associated with Holy Week or Corpus Christi, for example, which bordered on monumental theater, waned after the immigrant generation. Devotions associated with the Virgin Mary were long a staple of church life, which mingled freely with commemorations of the anniversary of the liberal Polish constitution of 1791, an important, nominally secular holiday on

vaks were mixed together in varying numbers in the predominantly Polish territories as well as dominating the regions adjacent to them.[17]

Jews in Russian Poland and Galicia were the largest non-Polish ethnic group. They were important in the towns, where they dominated the small trades and provided a large percentage of industrial workers. As poor as their Christian neighbors, Polish Jews, who were often tavern owners and tradesmen in country villages, engendered economic resentment which was perceived as anti-Semitism.

Each of the ethnic groups that joined the emigrant stream affected Polish life in the state. Germans were particularly influential in the country and smaller cities, while Slovaks and Rusins were present in Minneapolis. The class structure of Poland, however, was not well duplicated. Neither the upper gentry and aristocracy nor the intelligentsia, composed of the educated social leadership which derived from the lower and middle gentry, was strongly represented in Minnesota's ethnic communities. Priests were an exception. One consequence was a heightened role for the clergy in Polish-American life; another was increased opportunity for the few artisans, intelligentsia, and lower gentry as well as some peasants to create a small ethnic business class. Both clerical and business elites competed for control of the immigrant community's wealth.[18]

May 3. Outdoor shrines honoring the Virgin were common in Wells at least, and notable paintings of the madonnas of Czestochowa and Mount Carmel were transported from Poland to grace the churches at Delano and Opole.[22]

The messianism of Polish Catholicism appeared in the very naming of churches. Many bore the names of such heroic medieval saints as Stanislaus, Adalbert, Hedwig, and Casimir, who were associated with the militant defense and expansion of Catholicism. Others were reminiscent of the suffering nation of modern times. Bishop John Ireland of St. Paul chose "Holy Cross" for the mother church in Minneapolis to symbolize both the faith and the fate of Poles. Services like Forty Hours, the Bitter Lamentations of Holy Week, and others focusing on the Virgin of Czestochowa sustained that symbolism throughout the church year.[23]

Both men and women participated actively in the liturgical life of the parish, albeit in different ways and in separate organizations. One Polish traveler recalled the nearly magical effect upon him of a service in Winona in 1874. Though most members of the congregation had adopted the prosaic broadcloth and silk Sunday-best of American workers, "more than one old country coat and cap of transatlantic cut . . . testified to the fact that the older generation clings to the clothing they brought with them from Europe as to a reliquary." As in Poland, the sexes were segregated by seating, with men on the right and women on the left.[24]

"The music," he went on, "remembered from childhood, and the Latin liturgy, transported me into a kind of hypnosis. So also did the garb of the priest, with his head gray as a dove, the heads of the worshippers, bowing in humility, and the sermon, delivered in a tongue almost never heard. Politics and half-American customs and religious views that had become a part of me, — all these fled at once from my mind. In the company of these children I too became a child. I humbled myself and drank in the words of the liturgy and the teachings of the sermon. The elderly priest instructed his flock in a manner not too involved nor above their understanding, and it was not for me to criticize, as the entire community listened attentively to his message."

Some parishes, such as the one at Opole, were also literally institutional successors to the Polish village and its increasingly vigorous associational life in the 19th century.[25] Minnesota parishes, however, were significantly different. They were, for example, more nationally Polish ones since frequently members in the cities and sometimes those in the country came from diverse regions in Poland or the United States. Though regional memories lived long, the parish tended to subsume them in a larger Polish identity.

Minnesota parishes also offered more and greater variety in social services through voluntary associations. Some societies of women, men, or children dedicated formally to a particular liturgical function were attached directly to the church and provided important material and moral support for its work. Many other organizations, although nominally independent, drew their members from and acted within the parish framework. Some were broad based, like the Association of Polish Farmers in Sturgeon Lake. Usually, however, the lay societies served specialized cultural, gymnastic, paramilitary, educational, or temperance functions.[26]

No matter what the purpose, parochial and lay groups normally adopted a mutual benefit feature to protect members from temporary unemployment due to sickness or, in an age when death was a major community event, to help families meet the costs of funerals and burials. In 1893, for example, the paramilitary Polish Legion of Winona required a $5.00 initiation fee and $.25 monthly dues in exchange for a death benefit of $100 and a sick benefit of $3.50 per week.[27]

Most voluntary associations had obvious economic value to their members and still more to their organizers and officers. But that factor would not have been enough to sustain them. They were also, broadly speaking, educational and ethnic in purpose, part of the effort to adapt peasant culture to conditions of modern life, which was an essential ingredient in the minds of nationalists in creating and sustaining Polishness. The movement, known as "organic work" in Poland, called for a nonviolent, nonpolitical nationalism in the wake of the failure of armed uprisings earlier in the century.[28]

The ethnic lodges, societies, and associations were dedicated not only to economic improvement but also to the education of the community to Polishness. To achieve their goal of creating a Polish nationality (as opposed to loyalty to a region or village) through cultural work and history, they institutionalized meetings, demonstrations, and exhortation. By 1900 they focused on the anniversary of the Polish constitution of 1791, the uprisings of 1830 and 1863, and the life of Thaddeus Kosciuszko, whose career was conveniently and patriotically both Polish and American. Community theater in the immigrant generation was also, as one Chicago writer put it, "the great school of national virtues and the higher emotions." The lodges of the Polish National Alliance in Duluth, Minneapolis, and St. Paul and several Roman Catholic churches maintained substantial libraries for the education of their adult members.[29]

The founders of *Wiarus* (The Veteran), a Winona newspaper, put themselves squarely in this tradition. "Our slogan," they proclaimed in the first issue, "is God save 'Polonia,' under this slogan we wish to unify our forces so as to be firm against our adversities, to preserve our holy faith in its purest form, to save our ethnic traditions, to educate our youth and to secure for ourselves a respectable position in the United States in political and economic fields." They soon recruited editor Hieronim (Jerome) Derdowski to carry out their purposes.[30]

The Minnesota parish also differed from its Polish ancestor in being subject to more control by its members. Given the scarcity of the gentry in the immigration and the total absence of the state, the two forces that had controlled church appointments and finances in Poland, parish democracy resulted. Other factors, some of them accidents of immigration, emphasized the tendency toward practical congregationalism.[31]

A lay committee usually took the initiative in establishing a parish, sometimes in conjunction with a roving mission priest. For example, Reverend Francis Szulak, a Jesuit working out of Chicago throughout the Middle West, assisted in organizing the first St. Casimir Society in Winona in 1871 and in giving that city's Polish community its first institutional focus. At other times the church committee was aided by advice from a nearby resident priest or by the chance appearance of a clergyman interested in a permanent position. Frequently committees petitioned bishops who recruited Polish clergy for their dioceses. Some of the state's most important clerics were brought from Europe as a result. The availability of a clergyman trusted by both bishop and people was in the long run the best guarantee of communal stability, be it in the narrow parochial or in the larger neighborhood sense.

Parish formation was associated, nevertheless, at times with communal instability. The governing committees often represented the nascent Polish-American middle class, whose members competed among themselves for economic advantage. Pastors, however chosen, easily became rivals for influence and for control of the community. Representing the community-congregation and elected at well-attended annual meetings, the committees were factors in parish governance long after they were legally superseded by boards of trustees composed of pastor, bishop, and appointees. Their power was grounded firmly in the ability to raise money, enforce moral behavior, and freely encourage Polishness.[32]

Bishops, of course, appointed pastors, but the independence (some called it unreliability) of parish committees and mission priests frequently rendered episcopal power more nominal than real. The early financing of parishes through pew rents, special pledges, and social events arranged by the societies, rather than through anonymous collections or unrewarded gifts, brought in considerable sums of money, but it also encouraged a spirit of independence among the member-contributors.

In the short run, there was little the bishops could do about practically autonomous nationality parishes, but they followed policies which brought the parishes more effectively under their authority by the end of the immigrant generation. Since American-born Poles were not available at first as priests, the bishops tried to recruit from abroad men who would complete their training for the priesthood in the United States. Bishop Joseph B. Cotter of Winona finally insisted that he would not appoint any pastor who had not been ordained in his diocese.[33]

In any case, Poles developed an American-born, American-trained clergy early in the 20th century, earlier, for example, than the Germans among the large Catholic ethnic groups. Its strongly blue-collar background and loyalty to the community may have enabled it to identify more closely with the ethnic parish than some Polish-born priests, who had gentry backgrounds or sophisticated training in European seminaries. Bishops also took care to reinforce the authority of reliable pastors by cloaking them in the prestige of monsignorships or by seeking their advice as diocesan consultors.[34]

Looking well ahead, Archbishop John Ireland, who more than any church leader tried to influence the future of Catholicism in the Upper Midwest, followed the path of realistic compromise. He favored teaching religion in the mother tongue in order to win the support of parents for Catholic instruction and to maintain the integrity of the family through the use of a common liturgical language.

The youth, he believed, should be encouraged gradually to adopt English in order to articulate and defend the Catholic faith in the American future.

Parish schools logically became the most important social service institutions in Polish communities. Only the smallest parishes did not open them. The elementary literacy they promised, which was a matter of no small importance for Galicians, who were only two-thirds literate, was indispensable to that "respectable position . . . in political and economic fields" which all Polish-American leaders wanted.[35]

Beyond the acquisition of useful knowledge for blue-collar or business-clerical occupations, the parish schools' purposes were, not surprisingly, the transmission of community values. Effectively, they taught at first a national (that is, Polish) and later an ethnic (that is, Polish-American) identity, a Polish religious style, and a respect for discipline and authority similar to that expected within the family. These purposes were not strictly compatible beyond the immigrant generation, but the distinguishing mark of Polish-American education was its effort to include all of them in a single system.[36]

Laymen, often the church organist or choirmaster, conducted the first parish schools. They might be gifted and well qualified by language and background to uphold the community's ethnicity. Increasingly, however, in the 1880s the parishes turned to sisters of various orders who were perhaps better able to teach in English and to uphold local religious and family values. Preparation for first communion, an event which occurred fairly late in childhood, was the most important of the school's religious-cultural functions. Soon afterward, by about the fifth or sixth year, boys began to enter the work world. Girls might remain in school longer, possibly strengthening their ethnic identity and accounting for some cultural conservatism in later years. In cities and towns, neighborhood public schools offered the further possibility of completing an elementary education and meeting compulsory school attendance requirements.[37]

Sisters came to dominate parochial education for other reasons. For one, they were inexpensive labor, an important fact in a working-class community. For another, the sisterhood offered women a socially acceptable and convenient route to an education and improved social position. Recruitment took place in ever-increasing numbers through the parochial schools maintained by American congregations but especially by the American branches of older German and Polish congregations and by new Polish-American foundations. In 1907 one-quarter of the Franciscan sisters of Rochester (founded by German and Luxembourger women) were teaching in four of Minnesota's largest Polish schools. Half of all the order's students (about 3,000 children) attended these four schools. When the Polish members of the Franciscan community formed an independent province with headquarters in Ohio in 1916, responsibility for most of these students was transferred to them. Other schools in Minnesota were staffed by sisters of Notre Dame from Milwaukee (later Mankato) and by Minnesota Benedictines — both orders of German origin — and by Polish Felicians, an order established in Warsaw in 1855.[38]

Sometimes the sisters were blamed for failing to live up to

ST. STANISLAUS Catholic Church in Winona, an important Polish religious and educational institution, in 1973.

the purposes of the schools. On one notable occasion in 1894 the inability of several Notre Dame nuns to speak Polish was a factor in the disruption of St. Stanislaus parish in Winona. However, the ethnic issue was seldom so clear-cut. When the "Irish" principal was forced out of St. Stanislaus, the editor of *Wiarus* sharply criticized both the Notre Dame and Franciscan orders for failing to prepare their sisters to teach in Polish schools.[39]

Yet at the Holy Cross parish school in Minneapolis, which the Rochester Franciscans took over in 1894, a "German" principal was said to speak Polish "tolerably well," while another sister teaching in the lower grades was safely Polish. Together they taught the 3R's in English, as well as reading, religion, and Polish history in Polish, and in a moment of cross-cultural enthusiasm staged a drama entitled "The Polish Uncle Sam." They labored, like many other sisters, under the burden of a high student-teacher ratio — 65 to 1 when Holy Cross opened.[40]

Nevertheless in later years the sisters and the schools they staffed were criticized (unjustly perhaps, when one remembers that they were not asked by their constituents to prepare an upwardly mobile generation for professional careers) for a curriculum, teaching methods, and emphasis on the Polish language which limited the ambitions, social skills, and economic opportunities of their pupils.[41] It is hard to resist the conclusion that overall they prepared their charges as the parents would have wanted.

A mixture of social service, instruction, liturgy in Polish, self-conscious ethnicity, parochial autonomy, and loyalty to a distant Rome defined most Polish parishes. Their emergence was accompanied not only by discord within the communities but also with some other Catholic ethnic groups whose patterns of settlement placed them in close relationships with Poles. There is some evidence of economic competition and incompatibility within churches between Poles and Germans, but in Winona long-standing tensions, which normally went no further than street fights, came close to communal riot between Poles and Irish during the church crisis of 1894 over various issues, including the location of a new church. In Duluth, where Poles and Irish once shared the same church, the Poles fell out with the Irish bishop over the location of their cemetery. For years they buried their dead in unconsecrated ground rather than accept what they believed to be an onerous trip to a cemetery symbolic of Irish control. And, though Bishops Ireland and Cotter sincerely tried to meet the needs of Poles, their views on education, temperance, and the ultimate fate of ethnic identity in America were not widely popular in immigrant Polonia.[42]

By contrast Poles and Czechs, who resembled each other in important ways, sometimes worked well together, sharing church facilities or pastors in Silver Lake, Browerville, Minnesota Lake, Sturgeon Lake, St. Paul, Minneapolis, and Winona. Necessity occasionally put other Slavic groups in secondary positions in Polish parishes with only moderate difficulty as the result. Thus Polish parishes had Bohemians and Rusins in Minneapolis, Slovaks and Croatians in South St. Paul, Lithuanians in Sturgeon Lake, and Slovenians in Browerville.[43]

Usually the intramural conflicts within Polish parishes were brought on by struggles for power and economic advantage among competing lay groups and clerics. The earliest of these to be recorded in Minnesota occurred in Winona in 1874. It involved a pastor who publicly called his parishioners "empty heads," and then sued them for failing to pay pew rents. Disputes over the location of new church buildings, clearly related to personal gain and convenience, badly divided the Poles in Browerville, Alberta, Morrill-Ramey, and Winona. The desire for a more pliable Polish priest, fueled by the appointment of an attractive, new assistant, was a factor in Winona in 1893. The pastor of Holy Cross in Minneapolis was accused of sexual irregularity, unwillingness to perform priestly duties for which parishioners believed they had paid, and misappropriation of parish moneys in 1907–15. The result was a major schism and the formation of a national parish. In Duluth the pastor himself led the organization of an independent parish.[44]

Understandably church administrators might lose patience with the mysterious inner workings of Polish parishes. During the turmoil in Winona, Archbishop Ireland was alleged to have told the parish committee in effect "that the Polish were so very quarrelsome everywhere that a bill might be passed in Congress to expel them from the country." Probably he or Cotter was closer to the truth when, in a calmer and more charitable moment, one of them told the recently besieged sisters at St. Stanislaus in Winona that "these fusses and little quarrels of the Poles do not harm much; so long as they fight about their religion they are not in danger of losing it."[45]

It did not take much for parochial "fusses" to assume an ideological character and raise questions of ethnic definition. What especially were the nature and relative importance of Polish traditions, Catholic values, loyalty to Rome, and social class in defining Polish America? The earliest and most pervasive of these debates was between clerics who saw the Polish community in sectarian (Roman Catholic) terms and nationalists whose pluralist approach embraced a variety of values while recognizing the preponderance of Catholics within Polonia.[46]

Their views were institutionalized in the Polish Roman Catholic Union of America (PRCUA), founded in 1873, and in the Polish National Alliance (PNA), organized by lay businessmen in 1880. The rivalry between them remained academic until the mid-1880s when the PNA consolidated its offices in Chicago and both fraternals expanded their operations with ambitious insurance programs, new or stronger publications, mortgage loans, and other services to members. The PRCUA, meanwhile, had come under the influence of the Chicago province of the Congregation of the Resurrection, a powerful community of Polish clergy whose headquarters were in Rome.

The debate about the meaning of Polonia assumed special meaning for Minnesota when Julian Szajnert, a businessman who was one of the founders of the PNA, moved to Minneapolis where he helped in 1884 to start the Harmony Society, one of the alliance's oldest lodges. Along with two other businessmen, Frank (Grygla) Gryglaszewski of Minneapolis and Theodore Helinski of Duluth, Szajnert promoted the alliance vigorously in the state and assumed leadership positions in the national organization in the 1880s and 1890s.[47]

These men succeeded in large part by establishing good working relations with local Catholic pastors. PNA lodges met in church halls and schools, easily combined national and Catholic insignia in their costly and treasured collections of banners, and contributed conspicuously to church support. The national convention of 1887 held in St. Paul, which refused membership to Socialists, anarchists, and members of forbidden societies, was applauded by Polish clergy in Minnesota and by Archbishop Ireland. However, when the next convention refused to ban "Jews and notorious infidels" and it was discovered that Gryglaszewski was a Mason, the moderate clerical party withdrew.[48]

Led by Father Dominic Majer, a St. Paul priest and patriarch of Minnesota Polonia, the moderates established the Polish Union of America in 1889–90 to steer a course between the comprehensive nationalism of the PNA and the sectarianism of the Resurrectionists. It was this approach that Hieronim Derdowski, the widely read, maverick journalist of Winona, came closest to supporting in *Wiarus* during the turbulent 1890s.[49]

During that decade the Polish Union enjoyed some success in Minnesota with a financial program comparable to other federations. Monthly dues were determined by age: $.50 for those 18 to 30 years old; $.60 for those 30 to 45; and $.75 for those 45 to 50. Women were not insured directly. A benefit of $750 was paid on the death of a member; $250 when a member's wife died. Five lodges were soon organized in the Twin Cities and one each in Owatonna and Duluth, but the locus of membership, power, and the official organ *Słońce* (Sun) shifted eastward by 1900. A series of reorganizations in the next decade led to the formation of the Polish Union of the United States with headquarters in Wilkes-Barre, Pennsylvania, and the Polish Union of America in Buffalo, New York.

The other insurance fraternals which took root in Minnesota also had lay or moderately clerical orientations: the purely local Polish Roman Catholic Union of Winona, organized and guided by Father James Pacholski from 1898; the Polish Women's Alliance and the Polish Falcons, resembling the Polish National Alliance in outlook, each with one lodge; the Polish White Eagles Association, founded in Minneapolis in 1906; and the Federation Life Insurance of Milwaukee, which built a lodge out of the rebellion in Holy Cross Church in Minneapolis, probably in 1914.[50]

None of the fraternals could match the position of the Polish National Alliance with its more sophisticated approach to insurance, broader initial membership base, active women's department, and practical nationalism. In 1905 the PNA had 14 lodges and over 1,100 members in Minnesota. Its principal rival, the Polish Roman Catholic Union of America, lost members in the 1890s, notably in Winona, because of high assessments, doubts about its financial stability, and suspicion of Resurrectionist influence. The union's growth in Minnesota resumed during World War I, but the organization was never the major element in the state's Polish fraternal structure that it was elsewhere. Just prior to World War I, the alliance spearheaded the formation of the first partially successful central organization of Polish groups in Minnesota, the forerunner of the wartime National Department in the Twin Cities.[51]

At nearly the same time in 1916, *Nowiny Minnesockie* (Minnesota News), began publication in St. Paul-Minneapolis. When *Wiarus*, managed by Derdowski's daughter Helene after his death in 1902, ceased publication in 1919, *Nowiny* absorbed its subscription list. Under the direction of John Kolesky, it became the most successful Polish-language newspaper in the state's history. It adopted a generalized national-ethnic outlook but otherwise served as a nonideological medium of communication of almost all Polish organizations in the region until 1978. In its last years it claimed a circulation of 14,000.[52]

Preservation of the parish as the Polish institution par excellence promoted sensitivity to its ethnic character and to perceived threats among all factions. Loyalist Catholic priests, though divided among themselves, constituted the large majority of Polish clergy and represented most immigrants. They were put on their guard to maintain Polishness in the parish through the school and the liturgy, by opening the church to nationalist organizations, by lobbying for more Polish clergy and for Polish representation in the hierarchy, and by assisting in the care of Polish immigrants at American ports of entry. Father Majer was the founder and first president of a regional Society of Polish Priests in 1886 to pursue those goals, and he included a Union of Polish Priests as a special lodge in the Polish National Union in 1894.[53]

The agitation of the clerics was one element in the decision of Rome to send the Polish Archbishop Francis Symon to investigate conditions among American Poles in 1905. Symon visited Duluth, the Twin Cities, and Winona amid much pomp and high hopes for recognition in the American church. Three years later Polish hopes were partially fulfilled with the appointment of Paul Rhode as an auxiliary bishop of Chicago, effectively a bishop for American Poles.[54]

Symon's tour was made more urgent by the growth of religious independency based on formal control by parishioners of church property, financial affairs, and pastoral appointments. Cases of schism, scattered in the 1880s, became alarmingly frequent in the 1890s. Disputes in Winona and Little Falls raised issues and involved at least one priest figuring in later independency. Separatism in the form of the Polish National Catholic Church formally established itself in Minnesota after 1907 at several locations. However, only congregations in Duluth and Minneapolis survived. All, especially the rural ones, were plagued by small numbers, factionalism, a shortage of priests, and a succession of unreliable pastors. Above all, the co-operation of Roman Catholic clerics and nationalists in the state undermined the principal cultural argument for separatism.[55]

Twentieth-Century Transitions

On the eve of World War I, the broad geographical, social, institutional, and ideological outlines of Minnesota Polonia were visible in forms which were still recognizable in 1980. The war subtly but surely altered the development of the community. Most obviously it crystalized Polish nationalism. Efforts to educate Polish immigrants in a national tradition and prepare them for the resurrection of a Polish state began in Minnesota at least as early as 1864. They became consistently and overtly political between 1885 and 1895 as a new, activist generation emerged for whom the insurrection of 1863–64 was a fairly remote and less discouraging memory. The Polish Legion, a paramilitary fraternal association, was founded in Winona in 1886, and two years later Polish leaders in the city held the first of a long series of annual commemorations of the 1863–64 uprising. The message of Polish aspirations was carried to even the remotest immigrant community during the next 20 years.[56]

The prospect of a general war in Europe, which might affect the future of Poland, stirred American Poles of all opinions to organize. During the years before American entry into the war, they confined themselves to relief for Poland, discreet propaganda on behalf of Poland's historic rights and culture, and demonstrations of loyalty to the United States. These activities were carried out at first by the Minnesota segment of a Committee for National Defense organized in 1913 and later by the state branch of an umbrella organization known as the Polish Central Relief Committee of America. The National Department in the Twin Cities was the strongest voice in the state committee, especially in setting political policy. After American entry in April, 1917, Polish Americans freely sided with the political goals of pro-Allies Polish nationalists like Ignace Paderewski, Joseph Haller, and Roman Dmowski. Several hundred Minnesota men volunteered for the Polish American Army and fought in France, while the women of the community contributed heavily in supporting services. The Americanization campaign in the state was a real but apparently nonthreatening movement to Polish Minnesotans.[57]

President Woodrow Wilson's sympathetic attitude toward Poland helped to reverse 15 years of declining Polish support for the national Democratic party. Poles had normally voted Democratic at all levels until 1900, probably because Democrats identified with the cultural values of Catholic immigrants in such matters as temperance, private education, and legislated morality. That pattern continued in local elections. Poles normally produced Democratic state legislators, county commissioners, and township officers. Less frequently Polish Republicans appeared in places like Rochester which lacked Polish voting blocs or in areas like Winona where Republicans nominated Poles in the hope of making incursions into the Democratic majority. Nationally the Republican and Progressive parties of Theodore Roosevelt and William Taft won a majority of Polish votes in 1904–12, a tendency which reasserted itself somewhat after Wilson's retirement. Support for national Democratic candidates picked up strongly again by 1928, continuing to 1980 with some downturns in the early 1950s and early 1970s.[58]

Chronologically arbitrary as they seem, World War I and the restoration of Poland also formed a watershed in the evolution of ethnic Polish identity. Immigration restrictions in the early 1920s ended new infusions of native Poles for more than a generation, allowing the children and grandchildren of immigrants to shape their communities and encouraging them to look inwardly.[59]

The new Poland confronted Polish Minnesotans with important choices. Few returned to the homeland, confirming the status of even the Polish born as permanent residents of the United States. They confined their relationship to letters, remittances, and occasional visits. The politics of the Old Country, and probably national Polish-American projects as well, inspired apathy if not outright cynicism at the grass roots. Commemorations of the uprisings of 1830 and 1863 declined, while the constitution of May 3 and the heroics of Casimir Pulaski, events more compatible with an ethnic Polish identity, grew in importance.

Between World Wars I and II the roots of ethnic cultural transmission in the family also showed significant changes along geographic lines. Urban settlements, particularly that in Northeast Minneapolis, recorded fewer marriages and baptisms along with a trend to marriage outside the ethnic group. Marriage dates, now chosen throughout the year (with the exception of Lent and Advent), reflected American custom instead of the Polish village practice of marrying in the postharvest season. The immediate result was a demographically stabler community, though the prospects for change in the future were considerable.[60]

Rural settlements, exemplified by that in Wright County, showed strong tendencies to endogomous marriage, residential stability, and social isolation as late as the 1940s. A probably similar social pattern in McLeod County was supported by an economy of intensive farming and the division of land among all heirs, behavior reminiscent of Poland and in sharp contrast to that of their non-Slavic Minnesota neighbors.[61]

More difficult to measure were the less tangible values and patterns of personal development. Families were still nuclear and relatively large, though the spacing of births suggested some effort at family planning. They valued privacy and autonomy, qualities apparent in their reluctance to display material wealth or to accept public welfare and private charity. Child rearing still stressed discipline and loyalty to communal standards over affectionate understanding or "helping out" when children deviated from social norms. Discipline was reinforced in school through physical punishment, but perhaps more effectively through sports. To some outsiders Polish Americans' enthusiastic participation in sports, particularly by males of all ages, looked like rowdyism, but it promoted community pride, cohesion, and discipline.[62]

Residential patterns stabilized as immigration slowed in the 1920s, but they were in 1980 still oriented to work and especially to the church. Neighborhood institutions like the fraternal societies or the St. Paul Home Company facilitated the purchase of homes locally, while important investments in parish plants in the 1920s reinforced the old focus of community life. Roman Catholic pastors practically ended the power of parish committees and checked the growth of the Polish national church. The education of the clergy became more conventionally American, and the education of children in parish schools lost much of its specifically ethnic character as teaching in the Polish language declined. Before World War I in the Holy Cross school, Polish and English had been used equally in classes; by 1930 it was employed only in teaching religion, although 31% of all the families in Northeast Minneapolis still spoke the Polish language in the mid-1930s. Attendance in high schools and the integration of neighborhood public schools reinforced the trend to English. Despite some complaints about the quality and decline of Polish, the strong tendency in 1915–30 was toward the adoption of English as a second language in church services and as the sole language in second-generation organizations.[63]

A LOCAL CHAPTER of the Polish National Alliance sponsored a Winona baseball team, shown in East End Park in 1939.

By the third or fourth generations English became the normal mother tongue. Facility in speaking and writing it was ostensibly a prized advantage, but the performance of Polish children on standardized tests was low in parish schools in comparison to non-Polish youths. Nor did parish school children register high occupational ambitions. In the high schools Poles had begun to attend, the trades and business were their favored programs, consistent with a philosophy of education which did not encourage social or geographic mobility. The consequences were apparent in adult life. Poles in Minneapolis during the interwar period and Winona in the 1970s still comprised a more predominantly blue-collar community than their neighbors. Furthermore they continued to occupy a low social and economic status compared to other major ethnic groups.[64]

That basic fact was obscured by the success of such individual members of the generation of 1920–60 as bankers Val Yokiel in Wells and Sylvester J. Kryzsko in Winona, civic leader Valentine Kasparek in North Prairie, Mayors Harry (Miszewski) Maze and William Galewski in Winona, priests like Monsignor John Grupa, scholar-teachers like Reverends Ladislas Sledź and John Rolbiecki, businessmen like the Bambenek brothers (founders of the Peerless Chain Company) of Winona and the Krawczyks and Kozlaks of Minneapolis, writers like Victoria Janda and Monica Krawczyk in Minneapolis, and lawyer-judges Edward Libera in Winona and Francis (Frank) Nahurski of St. Paul.[65] Their successors among the upwardly mobile in the next generation point to the persistence of the paradox of individual achievement and communal blue-collar stability — Mayor Alex P. Smetka in Rochester, political activist and feminist Koryne Horbal, United States Senator David Durenberger (whose ancestry is German and Polish), and others.

New institutions and modifications in old ones reflected the changes in Polonia between the wars. Members of the Polish American Army organized local branches of the Association of Polish American War Veterans, while accidents of geography turned some American Legion posts into ethnic organizations. The Minneapolis Commercial Club, composed largely of young businessmen of Polish descent, conducted its business solely in English and published a journal with no apparent ethnic content. The Polish National Alliance embarked on a vigorous youth insurance sales campaign which it complemented with a variety of programs for families and children — scouting, Polish Supplementary Schools, sports teams, and scholarships.[66]

And there were other developments. The PNA Women's Lodge abandoned its patriotic and intellectual Polish focus in favor of a more purely social program. For a few years in 1927–32 it also conducted its business in English. The National Department of the war years transformed itself into a central organization of Polish societies by 1932 and dedicated itself entirely to local concerns. The Polish American Civic Club and Pulaski Hall in St. Paul, the PNA Home in Minneapolis, and the Athletic Club in Winona offered alternatives to church halls and clerical guidance for meetings and institutional development.[67]

Another schism apparent in Polonia in the interwar years reflected the evolution of the community. It was in many ways reminiscent of the old division between folk and national cultures during the age of immigration. Native-born working and business-clerical people provided a participant audience for a new ethnic or Polish-American pattern of life. "Polka culture," as it was called later, was built on sports like wrestling, baseball, and bowling; on tavern-restaurants which served as community social centers; on the transformation of a workingman's diet, *kielbasa* or Polish sausage, for example, into *the* ethnic cuisine; on the celebration of folk heroes like an Americanized Casimir Pulaski; and, of course, on popular dances like the polka.[68]

The new, college-educated middle class preferred to express itself instead through a conscious and conscientious revival of the old folk and newer national cultures of Poland. Its members were often employed as public schoolteachers or as social workers with the International Institute of St. Paul, institutions traditionally alien to the ethnic community which were used to promote and legitimize Polish culture. The institute and its Festival of Nations were particularly helpful in preserving, re-creating, and sometimes adapting the old peasant culture to American tastes. "The International Institute has given the Polish people in St. Paul back their culture," said one community leader. "Very few of our parents had any opportunity for education in the Polish villages under Russian, German, or Austrian rule from which they migrated. They had very little knowledge about their own country or its culture to pass on to their children. Even in America they were expected to forget Poland. But the Festival of Nations has awakened the interest of the second generation in their own background."[69]

The Polanie Club, founded in 1926, served as another bridge between the ethnic neighborhood and the larger world. Its membership of middle-class women sponsored cultural programs and small university scholarships. In the late 1930s the first American-born students traveled to Poland to drink at the sources of their heritage. World War II, the Cold War of the 1950s, and new pressures to Americanize interrupted normal contacts with Poland, but the Polanie Club initiated a successful series of publications based on Polish folk culture and Polish-American life.[70]

The ethnic revival and the growth of travel to Poland in the late 1960s and the 1970s encouraged newer forms of ethnic identification. The Wasie Foundation, founded by a successful Minneapolis trucker, undertook to help young Polish Americans meet the costs of higher education. The Minnesota Polish American Congress, fitfully active in the Twin Cities, and other groups sponsored commemorations of major events in Polish history and programs to educate people generally to the nature of Polish-American life. Professional historical studies were encouraged by the Immigration History Research Center at the University of Minnesota. Popular folk festivals sprang up in Ivanhoe, Sobieski, Minneapolis, St. Paul, and Winona, and newly organized heritage associations and dance groups, sometimes joined by old community organizations, provided some institutional continuity.[71]

World War II, in which the Polish question was if anything more central than it had been in World War I, was a clear test of Polish Americanization. An outpouring of communal sympathy and humanitarian aid in the fall of 1939, similar to the movement of 1914–17, was channeled through a new Polish American Council. Led by Maria Sokolowska and such PNA activists as Thomas Gratzek and Boleslaw Olinski, the council acted as the community's major instrument for Polish relief, collecting money and clothing, collaborating with the War Chest and the state's establishment to mobilize money and moral support, and representing the cause of Poland in a general way to the larger public. The League for Religious Assistance to Poland, founded in 1943, took advantage of the Roman Catholic parochial structure to direct additional aid to the war-torn country. Though some young Poles may have enlisted in the Canadian military forces prior to Pearl Harbor, there was no effort this time to build a separate Polish-American army. The military patriotism of Polish Americans was concentrated in "American" units.[72]

As the war drew to a close, Poles in Minnesota focused upon the threat or possibility of Soviet influence in liberated Poland. So far as they displayed any political concern, they favored the aims of the Polish American Congress (founded in Buffalo in 1944) to promote an enlarged Poland as a bulwark against Soviet power in eastern Europe. The congress was never a vital force in Minnesota, but it expressed the attitudes of many Polish Americans as well as such state institutions as the Polish National Alliance.

Though Polonia could do nothing to reverse the tide of events in eastern Europe in 1944–48, it continued its relief work after the war and dealt generously with some of the consequences of war by assisting in the placement of refugee Poles in 1948–53. The influx was great after Congress passed the Displaced Persons Act in 1948. By 1952 the Poles constituted 37% of the DPs who sought a haven in the United States, the most numerous of all the refugee groups. Of these new Polish immigrants, 2,780 went to Minnesota. The infusion of new Polish blood tempered somewhat the Polish Americanization of the community, at least in the Twin Cities where about half the newcomers settled.[73]

World War II and its aftermath pointed up both the origins and evolution of Minnesota's Poles. A coolness soon crept into the relationships between Polish Americans and the new immigrants, who were on the average better educated and drawn from higher social classes than the old Polish settlers. Whenever the newcomers expressed their ethnicity they fitted into Polonia's older institutions, but they seldom assumed leadership positions and were not as committed to the geographic neighborhood and its way of life. The war veterans of the two immigrations, for example, were not compatible, and the newcomers were compelled to organize separately in a unit of the Association of Polish Combatants. Added to the mixture was a still newer immigration, a trickle of Poles motivated almost entirely by economic opportunities who continued to enter Minnesota, mainly through Northeast Minneapolis, in the 1960s and 1970s.[74]

Old neighborhoods and villages, though not expanding as they had in the first half of the century, still served many of their traditional purposes as centers for new immigrants, community services (often for an aging population), cheap housing, and easy access to work. By mid-century, they were coexisting somewhat uneasily with newer communities. Sometimes the new was a physical extension of the old. Sometimes the new was more scattered and mobile — populated by the middle-class descendants of the old and new immigrants using modern means of communications (telephone, automobile, radio, and television) instead of territorial proximity to sustain ethnic identity.

Finally Polish Americans had demonstrated anew the diverse as well as the tenacious and adaptable character of ethnic identity in Minnesota. Presumptions of a common sense of ethnicity gave way again before attempts to define Polishness. Poles in Minnesota had never been able to come to any agreement on what it was to be Polish, much less to translate ethnic identity into any state-wide institution. It was not merely that a state's boundaries describe a somewhat artificial unit; American Poles generally defied efforts to classify or organize them outside of such vague categories as Roman Catholic, and even then there were major problems of definition. In the Upper Midwest the dominant German-Scandinavian cultural atmosphere and agricultural economic base further distinguished the region's Poles from those in the urban, industrial settlements of the Great Lakes Basin and northeastern states. Separate and isolated development, especially in rural colonies, left them relatively unaware of distant others of their kind. Frequently they felt closer to Poles in adjacent southwestern Wisconsin or the eastern Dakotas than to Poles elsewhere in their own state. At best, small communities followed parallel paths of development, but the parish-neighborhood-village, where the ideal of ethnic cohesion had its best chance to be realized, was itself frequently riven by ideological, provincial Polish economic and generational struggles. Those struggles and the social history they represent may provide more fruitful lines of analysis than holistic models of ethnic community structure, consciousness, and evolution.[75]

Reference notes

[1] On Polish immigration to the U.S., see Frank Renkiewicz, comp. and ed., *The Poles in America, 1608–1972* (Dobbs Ferry, N.Y., 1973); Victor Greene, "Poles," in Stephan Thernstrom, ed., *Harvard Eycyclopedia of American Ethnic Groups*, 787–803 (Cambridge, Mass., 1980).

[2] William L. Crozier, "A Social History of Winona, Minnesota, 1880–1905," pp. 56–59, 62, 65, 70, 86, 89–101, 136–41, 168, Ph.D. thesis, University of Nebraska, 1975; *Wiarus* (Winona), May 11, 25, 1899; Wacław X. Kruszka, *Historya Polska w Ameryce*, 11:5 (Milwaukee, 1907); William J. Galush, "Forming Polonia: A Study of Four Polish-American Communities, 1890–1940," p. 110, Ph.D. thesis, University of Minnesota, 1975. The *Duluth Herald*, October 12, 1937, p. 18, estimated the number of Poles in the state at 150,000.

[3] Mack Walker, *Germany and the Emigration 1816–1885*, 161–174, 184–194 (Cambridge, Mass., 1964); Adam Galos and Kazimierz Wajda, "Migrations in the Polish Western Territories Annexed by Prussia (1815–1914)," in Celina Bobińska and Andrzej Pilch, eds., *Employment-Seeking Emigrations of the Poles World-Wide XIX and XX C.*, 53–75 (Kraków, 1975); Władysław Rusiński, "The Role of the Peasantry of Poznan (Wielkopolska) in the Formation of the Non-agricultural Labor Market," in *East Euro-*

pean Quarterly, 3:509–524 (January, 1970); Stefan Kieniewicz, *The Emancipation of the Polish Peasantry* (Chicago, 1969); *Polish Encyclopedia*, 2:30, 123–140, 435–451; 3:45–224 (Geneva, 1921–22); William I. Thomas and Florian Znaniecki, *The Polish Peasant in Europe and America*, 1:87–302 (Reprint ed., New York, 1958).

[4] Here and below, see Helen L. Ulbrech, *The Losinski Family History*, 9–11 ([Trempealeau, Wis.?], 1978); Lawrence D. Orton, *Polish Detroit and the Kolasinski Affair*, 12, 197 (Detroit, 1981); T. Lindsay Baker, *The First Polish Americans: Silesian Settlements in Texas*, 19 (College Station, Tex., 1979); Andrzej Bukowski, *Działalność Literackai Społeczna Hieronima Derdowskiego w Ameryce (1885–1902)*, 1–13, 82 (Gdańsk, 1961); Kruszka, *Historya*, 11:18; Sister M. Teresa, "Polish Settlements in Minnesota, 1860–1900," in *Polish American Studies*, 5:66 (July–December, 1948); St. Stanislaus Kostka Church, *Jubilee Memoirs, 1873–1948*, n.p. (n.p., n.d.), in Catholic Archdiocese of St. Paul and Minneapolis, Parish Questionnaires, 1948, originals in the Catholic Historical Society, St. Paul Seminary, St. Paul, microfilm in MHS, hereafter cited as Parish Questionnaires.

[5] Here and below, see *St. Paul Daily Press*, May 12, 1868; *Winona Daily Republican*, May 23, 1894; Paul Libera, "Polish Settlers in Winona, Minnesota," in *Polish American Studies*, 15:21–25 (January–June, 1958); Ulbrech, *Losinski Family*, 10, 13–15; Baker, *First Polish Americans*, 32–36; Crozier, "A Social History of Winona," 17, 54, 168; Jerzy W. Borejsza, *Emigracja Polska po Powstaniu Styczniowym*, 32 (Warsaw, 1966); *Wiarus*, February 11, 1886. See also T. Kuklinski to M. Anton Kochanek, January 30, 1864; Anton Durayewski to *Echo z Polski*, February 26, 1864; J. Walenty von Radomskj to *Echo z Polski*, March 26, 1864; these letters, located in the Rapperswyl (Switzerland) Papers, Polish Museum of America, Chicago, are transcripts of originals destroyed during the invasion of Warsaw, September, 1939.

[6] *Wiarus*, February 11, 1886, May 11, 25, 1899; Kruszka, *Historya*, 11:17; Crozier, "A Social History of Winona," 96.

[7] *Wiarus*, February 22, 1894, May 11, 25, 1899; "The Silver Lake Story," in *Scattered Seeds: A Gathering of Minnesota Memories*, vol. 1, no. 4, pp. 20–32 (1974); P[atrick] J. Lydon, comp., *History of the Diocese of Duluth*, 61 (Duluth, 1914); *Duluth Herald*, September 22, 1939, p. 17; Kruszka, *Historya*, 11:40.

[8] St. Casimir's Church, Wells, Faribault County, in Works Projects Administration, Minnesota, Historical Records Survey: Churches, 1936–41, MHS, hereafter cited as WPA, Church Records; Kruszka, *Historya*, 11:26, 27; Sister Teresa, in *Polish American Studies*, 5:68. See also the following in Parish Questionnaires: St. Joseph's Church, Browerville, Todd County; St. Joseph's and St. Mary's churches, Delano, Wright County; Holy Cross Church, North Prairie, Morrison County; Our Lady of Mount Carmel, Opole, Stearns County.

[9] Here and below, see *St. Paul Dispatch*, December 31, 1877; *Minneapolis Tribune*, November 27, 1877, January 5, September 26, 1878, July 16, August 17, 24, 1881; Sts. Peter and Paul Church, Alberta Township, Benton County, in WPA, Church Records; Kruszka, *Historya*, 11:44; Sister Teresa, in *Polish American Studies*, 5:69–72; Edward A. Chmielewski, "Polish Settlement in East Minneapolis, Minn.," in *Polish American Studies*, 17:16, 27 (January–June, 1960); *Red River Rezerwacya: Red River Dolina w Minnesocie* (Chicago, 1896), a pamphlet in Land Dept. Circulars, Great Northern Railway Company Records, MHS; St. John Cantius Roman Catholic Church, Wilno, Lincoln County, in Parish Questionnaires. Additional details are in the records (1883–1976) of this church on microfilm in IHRC. Sources cited above give information on later colonization efforts by the railroads and Polish agents as well as activities in the 1870s and 1880s. The two clerics were Bishop John Ireland and Father Romuald Byzewski of Winona.

[10] Edward A. Chmielewski, "Minneapolis' Polish Fraternals

1962); *Sprawozdania na Sejm XIX–ty Z.N.P. w St. Louis, Mo., 1886–1914*," in *Polish American Studies*, 19:93, 95 (July–December, 18–20, 100 (Chicago, 1911); *Wiarus*, November 29, 1894, April 4, May 23, 1895, July 22, 1897, October 25, 1900, February 17, 1910; Charles H. Babcock to Samuel Hill, May 21, 1898, in Samuel Hill File No. 782, Eastern Railway Company of Minnesota, Great Northern Railway Company Records; C. W. Mott to P. W. Corbett, May 3, 1898, Northern Pacific Presidents' Subject File No. 207, Northern Pacific Railway Company Records, MHS. See also Stanley A. Libold, "Brief History of St. Isidore's Church at Sturgeon Lake [Pine County], Minn.," 1, typed manuscript, 1949, and St. John Cantius Church, Wilno, Lincoln County — both in Parish Questionnaires.

[11] *Wiarus*, October 1, 1896, March 2, 1899, August 9, 1900; Sister Teresa, in *Polish American Studies*, 5:67; *Red River Rezerwacya*, 4, 7.

[12] Conclusions based on the author's analysis of settlement dates found in Parish Questionnaires; WPA, Church Records; Kruszka, *Historya*; other sources cited in this chapter.

[13] The 1905 and 1930 ratios were calculated from State of Minnesota, *Census, 1905*, 193–195; United States, *Census, 1930, Population*, 3:1220. On the 1920 estimate, see Mieczysław Szawleski, *Wychodźtwo Polskie w Stanach Zjednoczonych Ameryki*, 24 (Lwów-Warsaw-Kraków, 1924).

[14] *St. Paul Pioneer*, May 30, 1869; *Nowiny Minnesockie* (Minneapolis-St. Paul), October 4, November 22, 1917; Kruszka, *Historya*, 11:6, 25; *Duluth Tribune*, May 12, 1873; Stanisław A. Iciek, *Samochodem przez Stany Zjednoczone*, 1:115 (Piastów, Pol., 1934); Ss. Peter and Paul Catholic Church, *Ss. Peter and Paul's: A Faith Community 75 Years Growing, 1901–1976*, 3 ([Duluth, 1976]); Sister Teresa, in *Polish American Studies*, 5:67; *St. Paul Dispatch*, May 16, 1874; John J. Dominik, comp., *Three Towns into One City, St. Cloud, Minnesota*, 97 (St. Cloud, [1977?]); Edward A. Chmielewski, "Minneapolis' Polish-American Community, 1886–1914," in *Polish American Studies*, 18:88, 91 (July–December, 1961); Chmielewski, in *Polish American Studies*, 17:20; Galush, "Forming Polonia," 89; Richard Wolniewicz, *Ethnic Persistence in Northeast Minneapolis: Maps and Commentary*, 5 ([Minneapolis?], 1973); Wolniewicz, "An Outlook at the Study and Understanding of Polish American History," 4, undated manuscript in the possession of author; St. Adalbert's Church, St. Paul, Ramsey County, in WPA, Church Records. See also the following in Parish Questionnaires: St. Adalbert's Church, St. Paul; *Commemorating the Dedication of the New Holy Cross School, Minneapolis, Minnesota, April 30, 1950* ([Minneapolis, 1950]); Holy Cross Church, Minneapolis, Hennepin County; and Richard Wolniewicz, "Northeast Minneapolis: Location and Movement in an Ethnic Community," 217–229, Ph.D. thesis, University of Minnesota, 1979.

[15] Zbigniew Stankiewicz, "The Economic Emigration from the Kingdom of Poland Portrayed on the European Background," in Bobińska and Pilch, eds., *Employment-Seeking Emigrations*, 27–52; R. F. Leslie, *Reform and Insurrection in Russian Poland 1856–1865*, 44–88 (London, 1963); Joseph Obrebski, *The Changing Peasantry of Eastern Europe*, 21–77 (Cambridge, Mass., 1976); *Polish Encyclopedia*, 3:385–416, 531–552; Galush, "Forming Polonia," 89, 91; Sister Teresa, in *Polish American Studies*, 5:66, 69; Libold, "Brief History," in St. Isidore's Church, Sturgeon Lake, Pine County, in Parish Questionnaires. For two letters from a Browerville Pole in 1891 to relatives, probably in Russian Poland, see Witold Kula, Nina Assorodobraj-Kula, and Marcin Kula, *Listy Emigrantów z Brazylii i Stanów Zjednoczonych, 1890–1891*, 300 (Warsaw, 1973).

[16] Here and below, see Andrzej Pilch, "Migrations of the Galician Populace at the Turn of the Nineteenth and Twentieth Centuries," in Bobińska and Pilch, eds., *Employment-Seeking Emigrations*, 77–101; *Polish Encyclopedia*, 3:237–259, 343–348; Galush,

"Forming Polonia," 7–12, 27–35; Chmielewski, in *Polish American Studies*, 18:88; *Wiarus*, February 15, 1894.

[17] Here and below, see Galush, "Forming Polonia," 12, 38–40; Wolniewicz, *Ethnic Persistence*, 4.

[18] Wolniewicz, *Ethnic Persistence*, 4; Galush, "Forming Polonia," 7–10; John J. Bukowczyk, "Steeples and Smokestacks: Class, Religion, and Ideology in the Polish Immigrant Settlements in Greenpoint and Williamsburg, Brooklyn, 1880–1929," p. 168–180, Ph.D. thesis, Harvard University, 1980.

[19] Crozier, "A Social History of Winona," 69–75, 110–118, 141–161; Galush, "Forming Polonia," 280, 296.

[20] Chmielewski, in *Polish American Studies*, 17:21–23; Crozier, "A Social History of Winona," 123, 127–134, 169; *Stillwater Gazette*, February 19, 1879, transcript in Works Projects Administration, Minnesota, Writers Project, MHS; *Winona Daily Republican*, April 7, 1894. The comment on the genetic theory is based on the author's conversations with various Winonans since 1962.

[21] *Wiarus*, September 10, 1896; Trinity Evangelical Lutheran Church, Sauk Rapids, *Fiftieth Anniversary, 1887–1937*, 8 ([Sauk Rapids, 1937?]); Trinity Evangelical Lutheran Church, Sauk Rapids, and St. John's Lutheran Church, Mayhew Lake Township — both Benton County, in WPA, Church Records. The evolution of St. John's from the First Polish Lutheran Church of Unaltered Confession of Augsburg and the First Polish-German Evangelical Lutheran Congregation, with divisions and the locations involved, is explained in St. John's Lutheran Church Parish Registers, 1908–78, microfilm edition, in MHS.

[22] *Wiarus*, April 18, 1889, March 22, 1894; St. Mary's Church, Delano, Wright County, in Parish Questionnaires; "Our Lady of Mount Carmel, Opole, Minnesota," undated typed manuscript in Central Minnesota Historical Center, St. Cloud; interview of Margaret Driscoll by author, August 2, 1975, notes in author's possession; Helen S. Zand, "Polish American Holiday Customs," in *Polish American Studies*, 15:81–90 (July–December, 1958). Zand's series of articles in *Polish American Studies*, 1949–50 and 1955–61, is an excellent introduction to Polish folk culture in the U.S.

[23] Holy Cross Church, Minneapolis, *Commemorating the Dedication*, in Parish Questionnaires; *Wiarus*, May 6 and 20, 1897.

[24] Here and below, see Marian Moore Coleman, trans., Sygurd Wiśniowski, *Ameryka 100 Years Old: A Globetrotter's View*, 49 (Chesire, Conn., 1972).

[25] Our Lady of Mount Carmel, Opole, Stearns County, in Parish Questionnaires; Galush, "Forming Polonia," 42.

[26] *Wiarus*, January 12, February 16, March 22, 1888, May 15, 1891, April 18, 1895, March 5, 1896, January 13, 20, April 21, 28, 1898, May 18, 1899; *Daily Minnesota Tribune*, March 6, 1884; *Winona Daily Republican*, September 11, 1893, p. 3; *Duluth Herald*, September 1, 1951, p. 3, November 22, 1958, p. 3; *Minneapolis Tribune*, June 5, 1886; Edward A. Chmielewski, "Minneapolis' Polish Priests 1886–1914," in *Polish American Studies*, 19:34 (January–June, 1962); Chmielewski, "Holy Cross Parish, Minneapolis, Minn., 1886–1906," in *Polish American Studies*, 18:11 (January–June, 1961); Stanisław Osada, *Historia Związku Narodowego Polskiego, 1880–1905*, 643, 684 (Chicago, 1957).

[27] *Wiarus*, July 27, 1893, March 1, 1894, August 26, 1897; Osada, *Historia*, 642–644, 663, 664, 677, 684, 696, 722, 726; Galush, "Forming Polonia," 90, 91.

[28] Stanislaus A. Blejwas, "The Origins and Practice of 'Organic Work' in Poland: 1795–1863," in *Polish Review*, Autumn, 1970, pp. 23–52; Adam Bromke, *Poland's Politics: Idealism vs. Realism*, 13 (Cambridge, Mass., 1967); Galush, "Forming Polonia," 146, 189.

[29] *Wiarus*, January 26, 1888, December 20, 1894, May 23, 1895; Chmielewski, in *Polish American Studies*, 18:90–93; Galush, "Forming Polonia," 145, 189–192; Thomas and Znaniecki, *Polish Peasant*, 2:1564 (quotation); Osada, *Historia*, 643, 644, 677; St.

Hedwig's and St. Philip's churches, Minneapolis, Hennepin County, in WPA, Church Records.

[30] Bukowski, *Działalność*, 21; Kruszka, *Historya*, 11:20. The quotation is cited in Crozier, "A Social History of Winona," 169. Derdowski was a Kaszub journalist and writer.

[31] Here and below, see *St. Paul Daily Globe*, October 25, 1881; *Winona Daily Republican*, May 23, 1894; *Wiarus*, April 18, 1895, February 13, 1896, January 20, 1898, June 22, 1899; "Our Lady of Mount Carmel"; Galush, "Forming Polonia," 92; St. Adalbert's and St. Casimir's churches, St. Paul, Ramsey County, in WPA, Church Records; Holy Cross Church, Minneapolis, *Commemorating the Dedication*, in Parish Questionnaires; *Nowiny Minnesockie*, November 22, 1917, March 7, 1924, January 21, March 31, 1944; Kruszka, *Historya*, 11:7; Sister Teresa, in *Polish American Studies*, 5:68; Francis X. Szulak, Journal (ca. 1869–1903), pp. 36, 37, microfilm in IHRC. Among the clerics brought from Europe were J. Barszcz, Dominic Majer, and Roman Guzowski of St. Paul, James Pacholski of Minneapolis and Winona, Alexander Zalewski of Wilno and Silver Lake, John Hanak (a Czech) of Minnesota Lake and Wells, and Stanislaus Iciek of Duluth.

[32] Here and below, see *Winona Daily Republican*, September 17, 1892, March 26, 1894; Sacred Heart of Jesus Polish National Catholic Church, Alberta Township, Benton County, in WPA, Church Records; Chmielewski, in *Polish American Studies*, 18:13, 84; Galush, "Forming Polonia," 156–158, 222.

[33] Kruszka, *Historya*, 11:8; *Catholic Outlook*, January, 1926, p. 141; St. Adalbert's Church, St. Paul, in WPA, Church Records; Holy Cross Church, *Commemorating the Dedication*, in Parish Questionnaires; Galush, "Forming Polonia," 161; Daniel P. O'Neill, "St. Paul Priests, 1851–1930: Recruitment, Formation and Mobility," 29, Ph.D. thesis, University of Minnesota, 1979; *Wiarus*, May 24, 1900.

[34] Here and below, see Daniel O'Neill, "The Development of an American Priesthood: St. Paul's Native Sons 1863–1930," manuscript in the possession of O'Neill, Winona; O'Neill, "St. Paul Priests," 121, 127–130; Chmielewski, in *Polish American Studies*, 18:15; 19:28, 30; Galush, "Forming Polonia," 92.

[35] Galush, "Forming Polonia," 38n. The quotation is cited in Crozier, "A Social History of Winona," 169.

[36] Galush, "Forming Polonia," 164, 182–184.

[37] Holy Cross Church, *Commemorating the Dedication*, in Parish Questionnaires; Chmielewski, in *Polish American Studies*, 18:10, 11; Galush, "Forming Polonia," 94, 172–174, 181–183; Minnesota Dept. of Labor and Industries, Report on the Polish Catholic Church School, Sacred Heart of Jesus, Minneapolis, [1918?], in Women in Industries File, Council of National Defense, Women's Committee, Minneapolis Division, War Records Commission (WRC) Records, Minnesota State Archives, MHS; *Winona Daily Republican*, September 29, 1893, February 3, 1894.

[38] Thaddeus C. Radzialowski, "Reflections on the History of the Felicians in America," in *Polish American Studies*, Spring, 1975, pp. 19–28; Sisters of Notre Dame, St. Stanislaus Kostka Parish, Winona, Convent Journal, [1887], p. 1, original in the possession of the convent, photocopy in the possession of William Crozier, Winona, hereafter cited as Convent Journal; Sister M. Caedmon Homan, "Years of Vision: A History of the Sisters of the Third Order Regular of Saint Francis of the Congregation of Our Lady of Lourdes, Rochester, Minnesota," 20–30, master's thesis, Catholic University of America, 1956; Kruszka, *Historya*, 11:25, 27, 33, 35, 38, 39; *Catholic Outlook*, January, 1926, p. 56; "Saint Stanislaus Church, Sobieski, Minnesota," 2, undated typed manuscript in Parish Files, St. Cloud Diocesan Office, St. Cloud; St. Casimir's Church, St. Paul, in WPA, Church Records; *Ss. Peter and Paul's*, 6.

[39] *Winona Daily Republican*, July 16, 19, 28, September 4, 1894; Convent Journal, 1893–94, p. 4–7; *Wiarus*, July 1, 1897; Homan,

"Years of Vision," 40. Homan pointed out that Polish was being taught in the Franciscan mother house in Rochester in 1909.

[40] Holy Cross Church, Minneapolis, *Commemorating the Dedication*, in Parish Questionnaires (quotation); Galush, "Forming Polonia," 94, 178; Chmielewski, in *Polish American Studies*, 18:87.

[41] Galush, "Forming Polonia," 169, 184–189; Anthony Kuzniewski, "Boot Straps and Book Learning: Reflections on the Education of Polish Americans," in *Polish American Studies*, Autumn, 1975, pp. 5–26.

[42] Crozier, "A Social History of Winona," 170–172; *Wiarus*, March 1, 1888, January 23, 1890, June 12, 19, 1891, May 19, 1892, January 25, February 1, 1894, October 22, 1896, March 3, 1898, October 19, 1899; St. Joseph's Church, Browerville, Todd County, in Parish Questionnaires; *Winona Daily Republican*, August 17, 18, 1894; Iciek, *Samochodem przez Stany Zjednoczone*, 115; Kruszka, *Historya*, 11:10, 27, 39. Kruszka included comments on difficulties between the Poles and Irish in Virginia.

[43] *Winona Daily Republican*, August 4, 1894; Kruszka, *Historya*, 11:6, 10, 13, 23, 27; *Catholic Outlook*, January, 1926, p. 133; "The Silver Lake Story," in *Scattered Seeds*, vol. 1, no. 4, p. 21; Chmielewski, in *Polish American Studies*, 18:5n, 7–9. See also the following in Parish Questionnaires: St. Joseph's Church, Browerville, Todd County, including a clipping from the *Long Prairie Leader*, September 1, 1932; Holy Cross Church, Minneapolis, including *Commemorating the Dedication*; St. Adalbert's Church, St. Paul; Holy Trinity Church, South St. Paul, Dakota County; St. Isidore's Church, Sturgeon Lake, Pine County.

[44] *St. Paul Dispatch*, May 28, 1874 (quotation); Wiśniowski, *Ameryka*, 50; *Wiarus*, March 9–May 25, 1893, February 15, 1894; *Winona Daily Republican*, June 20, July 1, 3, 10, 1893, June 4, July 14, 1894; Iciek, *Samochodem przez Stany Zjednoczone*, 106–108; Chmielewski, in *Polish American Studies*, 19:31, 35; Galush, "Forming Polonia," 221–226; Lydon, *History of the Diocese of Duluth*, 46, 52. See also the following in WPA, Church Records: Holy Mother Rosary Polish National Catholic Church, Pierz; St. Joseph's Church, Morrill; St. Hedwig's Church, Morrill Township, all in Morrison County.

[45] The first quotation is from the *Winona Daily Republican*, August 10, 1893; the second is from Convent Journal, 1895, p. 8.

[46] Here and below, see Victor R. Greene, *For God and Country: The Rise of Polish and Lithuanian Ethnic Consciousness in America, 1860–1910*, 85–91, 117, 119, 138 (Madison, Wis., 1975); Frank Renkiewicz, "The Profits of Non-Profit Capitalism: Polish Fraternalism and Beneficial Insurance in America," in Scott Cummings, ed., *Self-Help in Urban America: Patterns of Minority Business Enterprise*, 117–121 (Port Washington, N.Y., 1980); Chmielewski, in *Polish American Studies*, 19:94.

[47] Galush, "Forming Polonia," 90, 140, 150; *Wiarus*, February 18, 1886; Kruszka, *Historya*, 11:37; Sister Teresa, in *Polish American Studies*, 5:69; Chmielewski, in *Polish American Studies*, 19:92, 96, 97.

[48] Osada, *Historia*, 268–273, 624, 643, 644, 653, 664, 677, 684, 726; Chmielewski, in *Polish American Studies*, 19:29, 95, 96 (quotation cited); Galush, "Forming Polonia," 51, 138, 224; St. John the Baptist Church, Virginia, St. Louis County, in WPA, Church Records.

[49] Here and below, see Galush, "Forming Polonia," 51, 91; *Historja Unji Polskiej w Stanach Zjednoczonych Północnej Ameryki*, 48 (Wilkes Barre, Pa., 1940); *Wiarus*, September 13, 1894, January 14, February 4, 11, 18, 1897, November 2, 1899; Bukowski, *Działalność*, 83; Helene Derdowska Zimniewicz and Norah O'Leary Sorem, "Polish Troublemaker: Pioneer Trouble Shooter," in *Gopher Historian*, November, 1949, pp. 2–4, 13; Chmielewski, in *Polish American Studies*, 19:27. Father Majer, who died in 1911, and Father Pacholski, who succeeded him as senior Polish cleric in the state, served as chaplains to the Union.

[50] *Wiarus*, May 16, 23, 1895, January 6, 1898, January 11, May 17, 1900, January 17, 24, 1901, January 13, 1910; Galush, "Forming Polonia," 91, 223, 251.

[51] Osada, *Historia*, 642–644, 653, 664, 677, 684, 696, 722, 726; Chmielewski, in *Polish American Studies*, 19:99; Galush, "Forming Polonia," 73, 139, 203; *Wiarus*, June 11, 1896, January 14, 1897; Mieczysław Haiman, *Zjednoczenie Polskie Rzymsko-Katolickie w Ameryce, 1873–1948*, 539, 544, 545 (Chicago, 1948). Local PNA policy probably delayed or contained the growth of independent, national churches. See Galush, "Forming Polonia," 224.

[52] *Nowiny Minnesockie*, October 11, 1917, October 13, 1944; *Directory of Canadian Polish and Polish American Periodical Publications*, 15 (Orchard Lake, Mich., 1976); interview of John Kolesky by author, April 2, 1971, notes in author's possession.

[53] *Wiarus*, November 25, 1886, November 19, 26, 1891, April 12, 1894; *Nowiny Minnesockie*, September 20, 1917; Chmielewski, in *Polish American Studies*, 19:29; Galush, "Forming Polonia," 53.

[54] Convent Journal, July 31, 1905, p. 23; "Reception Royal," clipping in Duluth Churches, Roman Catholic File, Duluth Public Library; Greene, *For God and Country*, 141, 162–170.

[55] *Winona Daily Republican*, July 21, August 18, 1894; *Wiarus*, January 20, 1898, November 9, 1899, May 10, August 30, 1900; *Duluth Herald*, May 16, 1941, p. 5; St. Josephat's Parish, *Forty Years of Christian Service: St. Josephat's Parish Polish National Catholic Church, Duluth, Minnesota, 1908–1948*, 13 ([Duluth, 1948]); Galush, "Forming Polonia," 225–237, 263–265. See also the following in WPA, Church Records: St. Joseph's Church, Morrill; Holy Mother Rosary Polish National Catholic Church, Pierz; Polish National Catholic Church, Little Falls — all in Morrison County; Sacred Heart of Jesus Church, Alberta Township, Benton County. Several collections in IHRC are useful for understanding the history of the Polish National Catholic Church in Minnesota, particularly the parishes in Duluth and Minneapolis. See especially Polish National Catholic Church, Western Diocese, Sacred Heart Church, Parish Records, 1914–65, microfilm copy, and Józef Lebiedzik Zawistowski Papers, ca. 1914–67.

[56] T. Kuklinski to M. Anton Kochanek, January 30, 1864; Anton Durayewski to *Echo z Polski*, February 26, 1864; J. Walenty von Radomskj to *Echo z Polski*, March 26, 1864 — all in the Rapperswyl Papers; *Wiarus*, January 26, 1888, May 15, 1891, December 20, 1894, May 23, 1895; St. Adalbert's Church, *Seventy-fifth Diamond Jubilee History, 1881–1956*, 17 ([St. Paul, 1956]), in Parish Questionnaires; Chmielewski, in *Polish American Studies*, 18:90–93; Galush, "Forming Polonia," 145.

[57] Galush, "Forming Polonia," 203, 205–210, 214, 249, 255; Convent Journal, January 22, 1916, p. 47, May 2, 1917, p. 53; *Nowiny Minnesockie*, June 21, August 23, September 20, November 15, 22, December 2 — all in 1917; *Minneapolis Journal*, May 5, 1918, p. 11; Iciek, *Samochodem przez Stany Zjednoczone*, 116; Holy Cross Church, North Prairie, Morrison County, St. Casimir's Church, *Golden Jubilee, 1892–1942*, 66, 70 ([St. Paul, 1942]) — both in Parish Questionnaires. On Americanization efforts, see, for example, J[an K.] Komarniski to Hester M. Pollock, January 16, 1919, and [Pollock] to Komarniski, February 25, 1919, in Americanization Committee, County Files, Minnesota Commission of Public Safety Records, Minnesota State Archives.

[58] Richard J. Jensen, *The Winning of the Midwest: Social and Political Conflict, 1888–1896*, 300 (Chicago, 1971); Crozier, "A Social History of Winona," 181–185, 187, 193–195, 198, 213, 256–260; Wiśniowski, *Ameryka*, 34, 48; *Winona Daily Republican*, November 10, 1894; Kruszka, *Historya*, 11:8; *Nowiny Minnesockie*, January 28, 1944; *Minneapolis Tribune*, February 8, 1979, p. 2B; Sister Teresa, in *Polish American Studies*, 5:72; Donald E. Pienkos, "The Polish American Congress — An Appraisal," in *Polish American Studies*, Autumn, 1979, p. 43.

[59] Here and below, see Stanisław A. Iciek, *Samochodem przez Stany Południowe*, 387 (Ware, Mass., 1937).

[60] Galush, "Forming Polonia," 110, 256, 303–305; St. Philip's Church, Minneapolis, in Parish Questionnaires.

[61] Lowry Nelson, "Intermarriage among Nationality Groups in a Rural Area of Minnesota," in *American Journal of Sociology*, 48:585–592 (March, 1943); Wolniewicz, "An Outlook," 12; Galush, "Forming Polonia," 107.

[62] Convent Journal, May 2, 1917, p. 53, May, 1937, p. 120; Driscoll interview, August 2, 1975; Galush, "Forming Polonia," 110; Wolniewicz, "An Outlook," 12; Iciek, *Samochodem przez Stany Południowe*, 388; Chmielewski, in *Polish American Studies*, 18:86; St. Hedwig's Church, Minneapolis, Hennepin County, in WPA, Church Records.

[63] Galush, "Forming Polonia," 107, 257, 258, 260, 261, 285; *Nowiny Minnesockie*, December 18, 1917, January 4, 1924; *Sts. Peter and Paul's*, 9; Convent Journal, January 17, August 9, 1917, pp. 52–54, October 12, December 21, 1935, p. 115, April 25–26, 1936, p. 116, June 8, 13, 1937, p. 121, December 14, 1937, p. 125. Iciek, *Samochodem przez Stany Południowe*, 387; "Saint Stanislaus Church, Sobieski, Minnesota," 3, in Parish Files, St. Cloud Diocesan Office, St. Cloud; Alex Simirenko, *Pilgrims, Colonists, and Frontiersmen: An Ethnic Community in Transition*, 67 (New York, 1964). See also the following in WPA, Church Records: St. Hedwig's, Holy Cross, and St. Philip's churches — all in Minneapolis, Hennepin County; St. Lawrence Church, St. George Township, Sts. Peter and Paul Church, Alberta Township, Trinity Evangelical Lutheran Church, Sauk Rapids — all in Benton County; St. Isidore's Church, Moran Township, Todd County; St. Mary's Church, Czestochowa, Franklin Township, Wright County; St. John the Baptist Church, Minnesota Lake, Faribault County; St. Scholastica's Church, Heidelberg, Le Sueur County.

[64] Galush, "Forming Polonia," 115–121, 280, 291–294, 296; Minnesota Dept. of Labor and Industries, Report on Polish Catholic Church School, Sacred Heart of Jesus, Minneapolis, [1918?], in Women in Industries file, WRC Records; Stanley Pollock, "Window on Winona Data Archive," 1976, cited in William L. Crozier, "The Polish People of Winona, Minnesota, 1880–1905," manuscript in Crozier's possession; Crozier, "A People Apart: The Polish Community of Winona, Minnesota, 1880–1905," p. 23, manuscript, 1980, in Crozier's possession; interview of Della Jancoski (Mrs. Joseph) Ulbrich by Helen Davis, Sue Maher, Teresa Seliga, and Nancy Pilgrim, June 9, 1976, tape in MHS. For two memoirs of Minnesota working-class life between the wars see Institute of Social economy, *Pamiętniki Emigrantów: Stany Zjednoczone*, 484–499 (Warsaw, 1977).

[65] Iciek, *Samochoden przez Stany Południowe*, 388; Driscoll interview, August 2, 1975; "Synopsis of Life History and Civic Activities of Mr. Valentine E. Kasparek, June 22, 1950," typed manuscript, in MHS. See also Sylvester J. Kryszko Papers (1950–75) in Southeast Minnesota Historical Center, Winona, and Victoria Janda Papers (ca. 1934–61) in IHRC.

[66] Galush, "Forming Polonia," 253, 287, 307–310; *Nowiny Minnesockie*, January 18, 1924; Gertrude Anderson, "Polish Folk Customs," mimeographed manuscript, April 30, 1936, in Polish Societies Vertical File, Northeast Minnesota Historical Center, copy in MEHP Papers; *Duluth News-Tribune*, October 1, 1939, p. 14.

[67] Galush, "Forming Polonia," 205, 251, 255; *Nowiny Minnesockie*, September 13, 1917.

[68] Jim Klobuchar, "She Dazzled the Polka Crowd," in *Minneapolis Star Saturday Magazine*, February 10, 1979, p. 4; Anderson, "Polish Folk Customs."

[69] *Nowiny Minnesockie*, January 15, 29, 1932; Alice L. Sickels, *Around the World in St. Paul*, 12, 76, 82, 95, 195, 224 (Minneapolis, 1945); International Institute, *Festival of Nations, 1939*, 53, *1958*, 34 (St. Paul).

[70] Galush, "Forming Polonia," 253; interview of Edmund Lukaszewski by the author, February 13, 1976, notes in author's possession. See Josepha K. Contoski, ed., *Treasured Polish Songs with English Translations*, 4 (Minneapolis, 2nd ed., 1968) for the list of Polanie Club publications, 1942–64.

[71] *St. Paul Area Downtowner*, May 3, 1978, p. 6, August 9, 1979, p. 9; Edward V. Kolyszko, "Preserving the Polish Heritage in America: The Polish Microfilm Project," in *Polish American Studies*, Spring, 1975, pp. 59–63; Frank Renkiewicz, comp., *The Polish American Collection* (University of Minnesota, Immigration History Research Center Ethnic Collections Series, no. 6 — 2nd ed., Minneapolis, 1977); *Insight* (Minneapolis), May 17, 1978, p. 10; IHRC, "Dances of the Immigrants," mimeographed program, October 14, 1979; *Minnesota Pol Am Newsletter* (Minneapolis), [September, 1979]. See also Poles in Minnesota, Vertical File, IHRC, for a number of newspaper clippings describing Polish social and cultural events.

[72] Here and below, see *Duluth News-Tribune*, February 11, p. 4; 22, p. 1; March 16, pp. 1, 3 — all 1940; *Duluth Herald*, February 10, p. 3, 16, p. 15 — both 1940; September 21, 1942, p. 5; *Minneapolis Tribune*, November 6, 1942, p. 4; *Nowiny Minnesockie*, January 21, February 25, March 10, May 19, June 9, August 18, September 22, October 6, 27, December 8 — all 1944; Sickels, *Around the World*, 156, 159, 163, 169; Holy Cross Church, *Diamond Jubilee Memory, 1886–1961*, 17 ([Minneapolis, 1961]), in Parish Questionnaires.

[73] Just under half the total number of Displaced Persons destined for Minnesota between 1948 and 1952 were Poles. United States Displaced Persons Commission, *The DP Story: The Final Report*, 26, 37–41, 366 (Washington, D.C., 1952); Displaced Persons Resettled in Minnesota, 1949–52, and John W. Poor to Stanley Bandur, July 12, 1951, in Local File B4B — both in Minnesota Displaced Persons Commission Files, Minnesota Dept. of Public Welfare Records, State Archives. See also tables on resettled DPs compiled from the 1949–52 records, in MEHP Papers.

[74] Here and below, see Wolniewicz, *Ethnic Persistence*, 6–8; Wolniewicz, "An Outlook," 3–11; *Congressman Bruce Vento's Washington Report*, September, 1979, p. [4]; *Frogtown Forum* (St. Paul), October, 1979, p. 7; *Minneapolis Tribune*, July 5, 1981, p. 4B; *St. Paul Sunday Pioneer Press*, July 5, 1981, p. 10F.

[75] The question of cohesion in Polonia has been discussed at length or is implicit in the work of Theresita Polzin, *The Polish Americans: Whence and Whither* (Pulaski, Wis., 1973); Greene, *For God and Country*; Helena Znaniecki Lopata, *Polish Americans: Status Competition in an Ethnic Community* (Englewood Cliffs, N.J., 1976); Bukowczyk, "Steeples and Smokestacks." The author also acknowledges his indebtedness to Professor William J. Galush, Loyola University, Chicago, for his comments on this chapter and for his insight into and interpretations of Polish-American history. See particularly his "Faith and Fatherland: Dimensions of Polish-American Ethnoreligion," in Randall M. Miller and Thomas D. Marzik, eds., *Immigrants and Religion in Urban America*, 84–102 (Philadelphia, 1977), and "Being Polish and Catholic: Immigrant Clergy in the American Church," an unpublished manuscript in author's possession.

CHAPTER 20

The South Slavs

BULGARIANS, CROATIANS, MONTENEGRINS, SERBS, AND SLOVENES

June D. Holmquist, Joseph Stipanovich, and Kenneth B. Moss

COLLECTIVELY the South Slavs are composed of the peoples known as Bulgarians, Croatians, Macedonians, Montenegrins, Serbs, and Slovenes, whose homelands in the Balkan Peninsula are now largely encompassed by Yugoslavia and Bulgaria (see Map 20.1).[1] In Minnesota they exhibited a staggered pattern of settlement in two separated periods in three principal areas. In the 1860s small numbers of Slovene farmers made their way to Stearns County. From the mid-1880s to the early 1920s larger numbers of South Slav workers clustered in northeastern Minnesota's iron-mining region and in South St. Paul, a meat-packing center.

How many South Slavs emigrated to the United States and to Minnesota cannot be ascertained with accuracy. Most scholars feel that these groups were badly underrecorded. Nationally at least 887,600 South Slavs reached the United States between 1899 and 1976. Perhaps 60% were Croatians. Most emigrated before World War I, peaking in 1907 with 82,393 arrivals. In 1910 the United States census reported 332,065 speakers of South Slav languages in the country and 19,829 in Minnesota (see Table 20.1). The latter constituted almost 6% of those in the nation, placing Minnesota fourth behind Pennsylvania, Illinois, and Ohio. By 1930, however, Minnesota's South Slav foreign stock had dropped to eighth place, where it remained in 1960.[2]

Several characteristics of the South Slav migration were important. In the late 19th and early 20th centuries the movement was overwhelmingly composed of men, who entered the unskilled work force. Nationally, from 1899 to 1910, 95.7% of the Bulgars, Serbs, and Montenegrins arriving in the United States were male, 84.9% of the Croats and Slovenes, and 92.3% of those from the provinces of Bosnia, Hercegovina, and Dalmatia. Thus it is not surprising that the return rates for South Slavs were relatively high. For the years 1899 through 1923, 49% of the Bulgars, Serbs, and Montenegrins, and 44.2% of the Croats and Slovenes returned to their homelands. After the creation of Yugoslavia as an independent nation in 1918, the rate until 1937 was even greater (110.5%), particularly among Serbs. Remigrants were especially numerous from 1918 through 1922, when 37,723 returned either permanently or to visit their families after World War I. Available Minnesota figures reflected similar trends, with more South Slavs returning than arriving in 1918–20 and 1922 (see Table 20.2). Although returnees have not yet been studied, existing records make it clear that some men made the Atlantic crossing many times.[3]

The aftermath of World War II, which left many Yugoslav citizens homeless, produced a more recent wave of South Slav immigration to the state — 530 Displaced Persons who arrived in Minnesota between January, 1949, and April, 1952. Unlike the earlier immigrants, most of these were family units, which included 165 children under the age of 18.

Table 20.1. South Slav Language Groups in Minnesota, 1910–70

	Serbo-Croatian		Slovenian		Bulgarian	
	foreign born	foreign stock*	foreign born	foreign stock*	foreign born	foreign stock*
1910	6,888	7,901	6,701	10,661	1,223	1,267
1920	5,587	9,003	5,690	13,803	556	621
1930*	3,385		5,516		280	
1940*	2,140	5,140	4,640	13,920		
1960	1,622		2,040			
1970	1,008	5,196	753	5,072		

Source: Mother-tongue statistics in U.S., *Census,* for the years listed.
*Foreign stock includes foreign born and native born of foreign or mixed parentage. The 1930 foreign born included 2,267 Croatian speakers, 1,118 Serbian speakers. 1940 included 780 Serbian speakers, 1,360 Croatian speakers. 1940 foreign stock included 1,840 Serbian speakers and 3,300 Croatian speakers.

Map 20.1. Yugoslavia and its Historic Components

Moreover the adult sex ratio of 131 men to 100 women was much more even than in earlier periods. St. Louis County (including the iron range communities and Duluth) received 41.5% of the new arrivals, while the Twin Cities (including South St. Paul and other suburbs) gave 22.2% a home. Since 86% of the women listed their occupational category as "service" and 44% of the men as "agricultural," many were doubtless forced to find new occupations or to move from the places they were originally sent. Augmented by this trickle of new residents, South Slavs in Minnesota totaled about 2,200 foreign born and 10,000 persons of Yugoslav and Bulgar foreign or mixed parentage in 1970 (see Table 20.3) out of a total of about 467,800 recorded in the United States in that year.[4]

European Background

Culturally and politically the multiethnic South Slavs have posed challenges to linguists and historians as well as European diplomats at least since the Middle Ages. Unified only since 1918 largely within Yugoslavia (the name itself, adopted in 1929, means country of the South Slavs) and Bulgaria, South Slav concentrations may also be found in modern Austria, Italy, Hungary, Greece, and Romania. Linguistically these people are all part of the large Slavic family, with Slovenes, Serbs and Croatians, Macedonians, and Bulgars having independently developed languages. There is considerable dispute among Serbs and Croats over whether they speak distinct languages or merely dialects of the same tongue. Certainly much of Serbo-Croatian or Croato-Serbian, as it is called by linguists, is mutually intelligible despite variations in words, grammar, and spelling.

Serbs, Bulgarians, and Macedonians use the Cyrillic alphabet, while the other languages employ the Latin alphabet.[5]

South Slavs were early divided into followers of the Roman Catholic, Eastern Orthodox, and Moslem religions. When the Christian world split between Rome and Byzantium (Constantinople) in the 11th century, the schism also left its mark in the Balkans. Slovenes and Croats were drawn toward Rome, while Serbs, Montenegrins, Macedonians, and Bulgarians followed the Eastern Orthodoxy of Byzantium. Matters were further complicated by the fall of Constantinople to the Moslem Turks in 1453; Islam then swept into the Balkans with the conquering armies of the Turkish Ottoman Empire (see Map 20.1). Several hundred thousand Serbs and Croats in the area of Bosnia-Hercegovina (within present Yugoslavia) became Mohammedans. Although Islam has been a significant factor in the history of South Slav peoples, those who emigrated were followers of the Roman Catholic church and to a lesser extent of the Eastern Orthodox faith.[6]

The geography of South Slav national origins is perhaps even more confused than their linguistic and religious backgrounds. When substantial emigration began about 1880, most South Slavs were under the nominal control of the Austro-Hungarian Empire ruled by the Habsburgs in the western Balkans or the Ottoman Empire ruled by the Turks in the eastern Balkans. These tottering institutions proved unable to accommodate the forces of ethnicity and nationalism which surfaced throughout Europe in the mid-19th century. At immense political and human cost, independent Serb, Montenegrin, and Bulgar states slowly emerged from the two empires. Bulgaria as well as Montenegro and Serbia (now two of the six republics within Yugoslavia) became for varying lengths of time separate kingdoms (see Map 20.1). Slovenia, Croatia, and Bosnia-Hercegovina (three of the other four republics of present Yugoslavia) remained parts of Austria-Hungary until after World War I, while the fourth, Macedonia, was partitioned in 1913 among Greece, Serbia (now Yugoslavia), and Bulgaria.[7]

Only a small proportion of the Serbian migration to the United States and to Minnesota originated from the independent regions; most of the Serbs as well as the Slovenes and Croats immigrated from portions of the two empires — largely from Austria-Hungary. Bulgars, Montenegrins, and Macedonians in Minnesota appear to have been much less numerous than other South Slav groups, as indeed they were in their homelands.

Wherever they lived, similar economic and social factors pushed South Slavs toward emigration. As a result of mass political upheavals in 1848, serfdom was abolished throughout the Austro-Hungarian Empire, and land ownership became possible for peasants. Different laws governed different areas, but all hastened the breaking up of land that had been held communally. A small proprietary peasant class of independent farmers developed, along with greater differentiation among peasants as a group, since some obtained more and better lands and many could not afford any at all. Later the fragmentation of peasant holdings among offspring increased the breakup and created farms too small to support individual families. It was from the land-owning peasant class that most South Slav emigrants were drawn. Additional push factors were lack of industrialization to absorb the surplus labor and the poor soils of the mountainous and limestone desert regions from which large numbers emigrated.[8]

Increasing population, the need for funds to buy land, rising aspirations, growing literacy in Austria-Hungary after 1867, and the development of railroad transportation and inexpensive books and newspapers as means of communication encouraged migrations of labor. Initially many peasants moved from depressed farming areas within the empire to jobs in the expanding industrial cities of Germany, Austria, and the Low Countries. Much of this movement was temporary, however, for most migrants hoped to earn enough money to return to their native regions. Nevertheless these

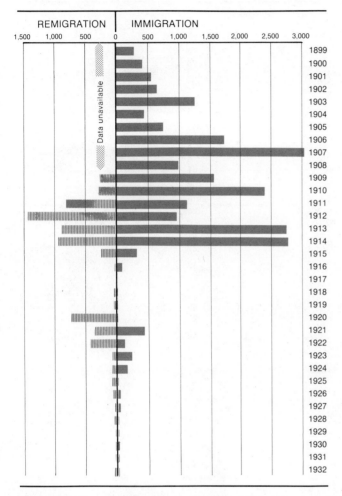

Table 20.2. Yugoslav Migration to and from Minnesota

Table 20.3. Yugoslavs in Minnesota by County, 1920–70

County	1920 foreign born	1930 fb	1930 foreign mixed	1960 fb*	1960 foreign stock	1970 fb	1970 fm
Aitkin	4	2	9		22		5
Anoka	26	3	1	12	112	11	137
Becker	1	4	14				27
Beltrami	5	29	35		29	14	20
Benton	20	5	12		43	5	26
Big Stone	5						
Blue Earth	8	5	8		12		12
Brown	6	4	6		7	7	7
Carlton	11	10	21	4	129	12	70
Carver	3	1			8	8	26
Cass	1	3	7		17	21	19
Chisago	1	1			7		12
Clay	3	1	2		4		14
Cook	1	10	2				
Cottonwood	1				8		
Crow Wing	332	321	556	78	361	51	128
Dakota	132	350	380	133	475	90	292

Table 20.3. Yugoslavs in Minnesota by County, 1920–70 (*continued*)

County	1920 foreign born	1930 fb	1930 foreign mixed	1960 fb*	1960 foreign stock	1970 fb	1970 fm
Dodge	1	1			4		
Douglas	3				5		18
Faribault	10		1		3		
Fillmore	3						
Freeborn	3	3	12		4		
Goodhue	5	11	15		20		22
Hennepin	170	134	144	211	1,233	239	1,034
Minneapolis	163	123	131		767	119	452
Houston		2	5		7		6
Hubbard	2				14		11
Isanti		1	4		12		
Itasca	588	802	1,176	311	1,043	204	675
Jackson	3	9	28		16		
Kanabec					8		
Kandiyohi	1	10	10		4	6	
Koochiching	79	86	180	7	51	6	61
Lac qui Parle	2						5
Lake	54	15	17		59		29
Lake of the Woods			1		5		5
Le Sueur		6	8		4		
Lyon	5	1	10		4		11
McLeod	3				20		26
Mahnomen	1	6	12		4		
Marshall	1		1				
Martin	6	2	10		13		
Meeker	1						
Mille Lacs			1				
Morrison	17	14	11		34	8	23
Mower	1	10	18		55		7
Nicollet	6	2			27		21
Nobles	2				17	7	
Olmsted	7	4	2	8	59	8	62
Otter Tail	5	30	5		49		12
Pennington			1		8		6
Pine	2	3	11		19		
Pipestone	2						
Polk	6	5	14		8	5	7
Pope	4						
Ramsey	340	205	200	61	712	164	546
St. Paul	334	200	189		558	117	288
Red Lake	2	4	8		7		
Redwood	24	1	1				
Renville	9	5	6		4	12	19
Rice	8	2	15		33		17
Rock	3	1					12
Roseau	3	6	15		13		17
St. Louis	8,563	6,635	12,721	2,748	11,001	1,242	6,288
Duluth	791	782	1,064		1,339	183	722
Scott	9	2	1		8		6
Sherburne	3	2	4		8		8
Sibley					4		
Stearns	102	86	263	8	115	3	129
Steele	8						7
Stevens	2				8	8	42
Swift		1	1		8		
Todd	8	3	12		20	9	33
Traverse	1	3	4		4		
Wabasha	5	3	2				
Wadena					4		
Waseca	1				4		7
Washington	40	10			33	32	69
Watonwan	1	2	8				
Wilkin	6	4	11				
Winona	1	4	4		19	7	51
Wright	4	3			16		
Yellow Medicine	1				8		
Totals	10,697	8,888	16,026	3,581	16,074 **	2,179	10,087
Published census figures	(10,697)	(8,888)	(16,026)		(16,074)	(2,179)	(10,087)

Source: See Appendix
*Figures are based on mother tongue
**Includes 4,328 foreign born and 11,746 native born of foreign or mixed parentage

migration patterns — especially for Croats and Serbs — created an assembling stage for potential overseas movement from the larger towns and cities.[9]

After 1890 the American labor market pulled increasing numbers of unskilled South Slav peasants directly to such growing segments of industry as mining, steelmaking, and meat packing. While a surplus of unskilled labor in most European industrial centers kept wages low, a shortage of workers in the United States kept wages high enough to compensate for the cost of travel. Information about jobs was not difficult to find, particularly for Slavs living in the urban staging areas, where American business and transportation companies as well as government agencies published appeals in native languages. Once South Slavs reached the United States, letters, firsthand accounts of returning workers, remittances, and the more formal efforts of immigrant associations sparked additional migration based upon kinship, village, and regional ties. In 1908–09, for example, 88.3% of the emigrating Bulgars, Serbs, and Montenegrins and 96.3% of the Croats and Slovenes left to join friends and relatives.[10]

South Slavs have been characterized as "ambitious" and "self-uprooted." Although a few emigrated to escape military service, their reasons for leaving were at base almost wholly economic. In the view of some scholars, conditions in Croatia were exacerbated by the oppressive rule of Austria-Hungary. But whether one regards the primary motivation for departure in this case as economic or political, most South Slavs emigrated to make money. They remained emotionally attached to their native lands, where they fully intended to return. It is interesting to note that similar factors were involved in the post-World War II exodus of large numbers of Yugoslav workers to other European countries.[11]

Slovene Beginnings

Two of the three South Slav concentrations in Minnesota — those in the northeast and in South St. Paul — were associated with specific industries. The Stearns County

Slovene settlements, the first rural ones, exhibited quite different patterns. They were founded in the 1860s, 20 years before the first iron mine opened, by a group of Slovenes interested in farming.

Like many of their German-speaking neighbors, these Slovenes found their way to Stearns County through the efforts of Father Francis Xavier Pierz, a pioneer Slovene priest, who published glowing descriptions of Minnesota in newspapers that reached both Slovenes and Germans. There is some evidence that a tiny vanguard arrived by 1856. Among them may have been the priest's nephew, Bartholomew Pierz (or Pirz), who served three terms in the Minnesota legislature in the 1870s — undoubtedly the first South Slav in the state to do so.[12]

In 1864 Father Pierz, who was then 79 years old, visited Slovenia. While there he successfully persuaded a band of some 50 to 60 "Krainers," as the Germans called residents of the Slovene province of Carniola, to make the journey to Minnesota for the purpose of establishing a New Slovenia. The following year some members of the group homesteaded west of St. Cloud, in what they organized in 1872 as Krain Township, where they developed the community of St. Anthony. Others took land north of St. Cloud, where they formed a settlement at first named Brockway and later St. Stephen. In 1869 and 1870 Father Pierz's Slovenian assistant, Father Joseph F. Buh, visited both groups and aided them in erecting log churches. That at St. Stephen — the first in the United States built by Slovenes — was completed in 1871. The St. Anthony church and school were in use by 1874. Both parishes flourished. An analysis of plat maps of Brockway and Krain townships in 1896, 1925, and 1973 revealed that Slovene holdings remained remarkably stable.[13]

A revealing glimpse of the communities in transition was provided by Father Alexius Hoffmann of St. John's Abbey at nearby Collegeville. The settlers, he wrote, "for a long time retained their European garb, as they did their language, customs and religion." The "men folk still had their tight fitting trousers, multibuttoned vests and short coats

CEMETERY of St. Stephen Catholic Church, Stearns County, where many Slovenian pioneers are buried.

and wide brimmed hats, the women — of all ages — from childhood to old age — wore ample but short dresses. . . . Over their heads, instead of hats,'' the children ''wore white . . . or cream colored handsomely embroidered scarfs . . . old women usually wore a black scarf that was knotted below the chin. . . . In the [18]70's the young ladies began to Americanize and wore hats over elegant coiffures, and their gowns were longer. . . .[14]

''Do not believe that they were illiterate; they all had to go to school in Europe, [but as] a consequence of their adherence to their national language, their homes were bare of 'literature.['] The old folks did not care to read German, because they had been compelled to study German in the schools. . . . the German settlers looked down upon the Krainers, whom they contemptuously called 'Schlawaken,' a name which the latter resented, for they were not Slovaks but Slovenians. . . . In general, they (the Krainers) were deemed inferior because they did not speak good German. . . . The Slovenians, many of them, readily learned German, but I never heard of a German learning the Slovenian language.'' In the 1970s that language had largely disappeared from the Stearns County communities, but the people continued to preserve some Slovene traditions, foods, and customs in their churches and festivals.[15]

Father Buh served as a link between these early rural communities and those in St. Louis County to which he moved in the 1880s. Mining began in northeastern Minnesota at Tower-Soudan on the Vermilion Range in 1884. Although South Slavs were not among the very first arrivals, a half dozen or so were there when the state census was taken in 1885. Some historians claimed that they immigrated directly from Slovenia, having heard of jobs from Father Buh. Others maintained that they migrated from Michigan, where they learned of the new work opportunities from another Slovenian priest, Father Bernard Locnikar.[16]

In any case, by 1888, when Buh became the first resident priest at Tower, he estimated that one-fourth (300 families) of the people there were Slovenians. By 1909 they were said to constitute 40% of Tower's population of about 2,000. At nearby Ely operations began with the opening of the Chandler Mine in 1888. By 1895 at least 114 Slovenes, many of whom had moved from Tower, were counted in Ely's population of 2,260, and by 1909 they constituted about one-third of its residents.[17]

Slovene miners were blamed in part for the first recorded strike in the Minnesota iron mining industry at Tower-Soudan in June, 1892. It was said to have been precipitated by Slovene and Italian workers who preferred to go to church rather than to work on Corpus Christi Day. (Perhaps a more plausible reason was the miners' belief that it was unlucky to work on that day, a superstition reportedly still current among Slovenes in 1952.) When the company retaliated by laying off 315 men for two weeks, ''trouble broke out,'' as the local newspaper put it. The mining firm quickly obtained sheriff's deputies and several companies of state militia, setting a precedent that was to be repeated in the 20th century. Not a great deal happened, however, and in six days the difficulties seemed to be over.[18]

Slovene Institutions

Churches and other organizations ministering to the needs of the Slovenes quickly appeared in the Vermilion Range settlements. Buh enlarged St. Martin's Catholic Church at Tower, built in 1885, and founded the predominantly Slovenian parish of St. Anthony at Ely in 1888. Indirectly at first and then directly he was also responsible for the establishment of *Amerikanski Slovenec* (American Slovene), the first national newspaper for Slovenes in the United States and one of only three South Slav papers known to have been published in Minnesota. Started in 1891 in Chicago, it had ceased publication after 10 weekly issues. Unwilling to see the effort die, Buh bought the paper, and the eleventh issue appeared at Tower on March 4, 1892, with the priest as editor and publisher. Aided by Slovenian seminarians from St. Paul, notably Mathias Šavs, Buh managed the journal until 1899, when it was transferred to Joliet, Illinois. The priest was also responsible for the publication at Tower of the first Slovenian book in the United States in 1895, three volumes of a yearly Slovene almanac, a catechism, and other works.[19]

Through *Amerikanski Slovenec*, Buh and Šavs were instrumental in helping to found in 1894 the Grand Carniolian-Slovenian Catholic Union (*Kranjsko-Slovenska Katoliška Jednota*), a national benefit society usually known as KSKJ. Restricted to Catholics, it offered an insurance plan that paid $800 upon the death of the worker-member and $200 upon the death of his wife. By 1898 KSKJ, with headquarters in Illinois, had 2,142 members in 46 lodges throughout the United States. In 1963 the organization's name was

THE FLOURISHING GARDEN of the John Kalsich family of Ely in 1922.

changed to the American Slovenian Catholic Union. It had 14 lodges in Minnesota in 1980.[20]

Dissatisfaction with KSKJ's high rates for iron miners led to the formation of the South Slavonic Catholic Union (*Jugoslovenska Katoliška Jednota* or JSKJ) at Ely in 1898. In 1913 it added a department to insure children, and by 1924 it was publishing its own newspaper, *Nova Doba* (New Era), printed in New York. In 1941 the organization's name was changed to the American Fraternal Union and all ethnic and religious requirements were dropped. In 1980 the union was still headquartered at Ely.[21]

Meanwhile a second split in 1904 created the Slovene National Benefit Society (*Slovenska Narodna Podporna Jednota* or SNPJ). Formed by freethinking, Socialist-minded Slovenes who objected to the older Catholic lodges' insistence on attendance at Mass and confession, SNPJ also attracted many Croats and Serbs. The first SNPJ lodge in Minnesota was formed at Ely in 1905. The national society had a juvenile department and was unusual in extending equal benefits to women almost from its beginnings, a fact that soon made it the leading Slovene group. The first women's lodge in the state was organized in 1909. In 1980 the organization had 15 lodges in Minnesota and about 2,300 members.[22]

The Slovenes also began to emerge on the political scene. Their first political club in Ely had been formed in 1908, but eight years passed before they succeeded in electing George L. Brozich as Ely's first Slovenian mayor. About the same time a Slovene became president of the Aurora school board, and others held various offices in Kitzville. Since then hundreds of South Slavs have appeared among elected officials at all levels. Up to 1968, for example, at least 10 mayors of Ely had been Slovenes. South Slavs have served steadily in the state legislature since the 1930s, and northeastern Minnesota has been represented in Congress continuously since 1941 by the descendants of Slovene immigrants. In 1976–78 Rudolph G. Perpich of Hibbing, the son of Croatian immigrants to Minnesota in 1920, became the first South Slav to serve as governor.[23]

South Slavs on the Mesabi

As important as the Vermilion communities were, the largest Minnesota concentration of South Slavs developed on a second St. Louis County iron range — the giant Mesabi, some 70 miles northwest of Duluth. When commercial mining operations began in the early 1890s, the Mesabi was a wilderness of forests and swamps. By 1910, 13 communities contained 50,000 residents, including 3,600 Slovenes, 3,410 Croats, 2,650 Montenegrins, 515 Serbs, and some 30 other national, regional, or ethnic groups.[24]

That South Slavs were present on the Mesabi from the beginning was indicated by the activities of Father Buh. The second mine to open there was the Biwabik, which began shipping in June, 1893, on the eve of a severe depression. In August, Buh visited Biwabik and found five "Austrian" families who had lived on flour and water for two weeks because they could not speak English and did not know where to ask for help. That other South Slavs may well have

been in residence is indicated by the fact that Buh organized St. John's Catholic congregation in Biwabik during his 1893 visit and conducted the first services in Slovene and three other languages.

An exact date for the beginnings of Serb and Croat migration is difficult to pinpoint, but it is certain that they reached the Mesabi in numbers before 1900. One source estimated about 2,000 Croats in Minnesota by 1901, and the *Virginia Enterprise* reported that "Austrians" then composed about half the workers in the mines there. The stripping and open-pit mining techniques widely utilized on the Mesabi after 1905, as opposed to the underground methods on the Vermilion, created an increased need for unskilled workers. Some arrived from the older ranges, while Slovenes from the Stearns County rural settlements were reported to have moved to Buhl and Nashwauk in 1901.[25]

As demand continued to exceed supply, labor agents were employed to recruit workers from the older Slav centers in Pittsburgh, Cleveland, and Chicago, as well as directly from Europe. In May, 1907, the work force of the Oliver Iron Mining Company, the largest firm then operating on the range, totaled 12,018 men; 84.4% were foreign born, and almost half had been in the United States for a maximum of two years. South Slavs made up over 30% of the firm's foreign-born workers, and their percentages were even higher in succeeding years.[26]

Like the Slovenes before them, very few of the Croatians, Serbs, Bulgars, and others arriving directly from southeastern Europe had any previous experience in mining. Nearly 80% of them had been peasant farmers or farm laborers who often worked in such unskilled, low-paying surface jobs as dump men, trammers, and tracklayers. For example, of the Croats surveyed on the Minnesota ranges in 1909, 49.4% earned from $12.50 to $15.00 a week, 13.6% from $15.00 to $17.50, and 1.1% earned $17.50 or more. Moreover the seasonal nature of open-pit mining made regular employment uncertain. Less than half (49.2%) were employed for a full 12 months; nearly 17% worked less than six months a year. By contrast 69% of the Slovenes worked year-round in underground mines and 51.5% made from $15.00 to $17.50.[27]

It has been claimed that inexperience in mining, illiteracy, and inability to speak English condemned South Slavs to low-paying jobs. The sparse statistics available cast some doubt upon inability to speak English as a satisfactory explanation. In May, 1907, 79% of the Slovenes employed by Oliver Mining, 30.8% of the Croats, 27.5% of the Montenegrins, and 14.7% of the Serbs reportedly could do so. Two years later the United States Immigration Commission listed a similar figure for the Slovenes but much higher ones for Croats and Serbs — 70.8% and 47.8%, respectively.[28]

Like that of most mining regions, the South Slav population was young and the sex ratio was very unbalanced at first. The over-all ratio in northeastern Minnesota communities in 1885 was 249.5 men to 100 women; 10 years later it was 233 to 100. For Serbs during the Mesabi's opening years it was not uncommon to find proportions as high as 25 men to one woman. One of the earliest Serbs to settle at Hibbing in 1900 recalled that he had been there for three years before he saw a woman of his own nationality. For Croats and Slovenes the ratios stood above 5 to 1 until 1909; a survey of Hibbing in 1903 reported a Slovene population of 30 families and 500 single men.

The high number of spouses left behind in the homeland, coupled with the low rates of naturalization, suggest that many men hoped their stay would be temporary. A 1909 survey showed that more than two-thirds (66.7%) of the married Croatian workers in Minnesota had left their wives abroad, as had 43.6% of the Slovenes. In eight northeastern Minnesota communities in 1918, the figure for Croatians was 72% and for Serbs 46.2% (see Table 20.4).

The outbreak of World War I in 1914 and the quota laws of the 1920s giving preference to northern Europeans interrupted the family immigration chain. Thus many of the men who chose to remain in Minnesota continued to seek wives in older Slav communities elsewhere as they had earlier or to marry outside of their national or ethnic group.[29]

Forming Communities and Institutions

The ways in which communities are formed and maintained over time continue to occupy social scientists. For many emigrant groups the patterns were strikingly similar. The migrants were often from the same regions or from certain villages within those homeland regions, although all of the present provinces of Yugoslavia were represented in the state. Numerous Minnesota Slovenes emigrated from Carniola and Styria; many Croats and Serbs arrived from Lika-Krbava in western Croatia; Niksic and other parts of western Montenegro ruled by Turkey until 1878 were home for many Serbs, and Bansko for many Bulgars. In the usual pattern of immigrant groups, as soon as a few people arrived from a given area, they reported back on travel routes and sent remittances or information on wages, living conditions,

and availability of jobs. But the process of family and community formation was marked by a great deal of mobility. If the mines closed or better employment seemed available elsewhere, South Slavs often moved on.[30]

In northeastern Minnesota arriving relatives and fellow villagers clustered together in mining locations or logging camps, establishing crude communal living facilities independently or with the assistance of the companies. For example, when a Serb from Lika obtained employment in a logging camp near Hibbing in 1906, he found there about 150 men from his native region. South Slavs concentrated on the south side of Chisholm, at the Kitzville and Carson Lake locations near Hibbing, and at the Spruce and Adams locations at Eveleth. Chisholm and Eveleth especially became known as South Slav cities. In some places South Slavs represented the largest single group; in others they were second only to the Finns in number. Later, after the opening of the Cuyuna Range in 1911, numerous Serbs settled at Crosby and Ironton.[31]

In a report based upon a house-to-house canvass in 1913, the Reverend William J. Bell wrote that he regarded the Kitzville Location near Hibbing as "typical." It was composed, he said, of 25 Slovene households, 8 Croat, 1 Serb, 1 Bulgar, 10 Italian, 2 Finnish, and 2 American for a total of 49. In the nearby Harold Location, Bell counted "eleven different" ethnic groups represented. "One boarding house extended its hospitality to 35 Croatians, a second to 27, a third to 13," he wrote, "while a fourth furnished a home for 14 Finns."[32]

In addition to the kinship and regional loyalties evident among South Slavs, such ancient symbolic ties as godfatherhood (*kumstvo* in Serbo-Croatian) were helpful in preserving group identity. *Kumstvo* involved persons unrelated by blood, who were obligated to assist and co-operate with each

SOME EVELETH HOMES of South Slavs.

THE KITZVILLE LOCATION about 1915.

other for life. In some South Slav communities in Europe and the United States, a few persons might become *kum* or *kuma* (godfather or godmother, known as *boter* and *botra* among the Slovenes) to all other families. A *kum* might also be a marriage witness or a confirmation sponsor. Such relationships, when intertwined with the transitional institutions developed by South Slavs, fostered ethnic ties and promoted a sense of community.[33]

Among the important transitional institutions utilized by Slovenes, Croats, and Serbs must be placed the ethnic boardinghouse, saloon, and store — all of which gave rise to an entrepreneurial leadership class within the immigrant community. Boardinghouses, particularly among the Croats and Serbs, developed in response to the male workers' need for lodging and their desire to save money for their return to the Old Country. One study reported that nearly half of the population of Tower-Soudan on the Vermilion Range in 1885 was composed of boarders or lodgers, 58% of whom shared a household with others of their national group, although frequently they were not blood relatives. Another 16% lived in boardinghouses or hotels run by nonkin. Of 40 Minnesota Croatian families studied in 1909, almost three-fourths had boarders, compared to only one-third of the Slovenes.[34]

By using the 1918 Minnesota Public Safety Commission alien registration forms in the Minnesota State Archives, the situation on the iron ranges can be compared with prewar years. In general, South Slav demographic characteristics remained similar (see Table 20.4). Men still heavily outnumbered women, and while about half were married, many of their wives remained in Europe. Of equal importance, however, was the variation among South Slav groups. The Bulgarians were almost entirely male. Although more Bulgars were married than members of the other two groups, only a small fraction of their wives immigrated to Minnesota. On the other side of the spectrum were the Serbs, who had the most even sex ratio and the highest percentage of wives present. These differences point to dissimilar strategies within the groups. They suggest that Serbs were more committed to remaining in America than were Bulgars, who probably intended to return to their families in the Old Country.

Communal living establishments were run co-operatively by the men under the direction of a boardinghouse boss or by couples in which either the man or woman might be in charge. Whether the female or male head of the household served as supervisor varied from family to family. Among both Croats and Serbs the male boardinghouse boss, or *burtinbasova*, was common. At their best, these ethnic board-

inghouses resembled the more highly structured *zadruga*, or communal patriarchal households of the Croatian homeland. At their worst, reported the Immigration Commission, they were merely tarpaper shacks where "refuse of all kinds is generally thrown on the ground immediately adjoining the buildings without regard for cleanliness." Company-owned boardinghouses, which included various nationalities and were often the scenes of fights among them, were much less favored by South Slavs.[35]

The son of a Croatian miner from Lika who went to Nashwauk about 1906 recalled that when his father arrived the town was a "mud hole," consisting only of "twenty-four saloons, company stores, and boardinghouses." His mother followed his father to the United States in 1910, and the couple secured "a big frame house" and took in boarders until 1928. "Mother cooked for the men, some of whom worked underground [in the Hawkins Mine] on different shifts, so she worked practically night and day," the son wrote. "There were twenty-four boarders to care for. . . . To cook twenty or thirty pounds of meat was an everyday task for Mother, who also had five boys in those years. She often tells how the boarders would watch us while she did her work."[36]

A Serb who immigrated directly to Chisholm in 1912 described his boardinghouse, which was a *društvo* or co-operative household run by a boarding boss. The houses, he wrote, "were built of wooden planks and were of poor quality, without toilet facilities or running water. They were rather uniform in style of architecture and consisted predominantly of three rooms on the first floor and one bedroom on the second floor where the boarders slept, whether there were ten, twelve or twenty of them. For the grounds upon which the house was built a rental fee of five or six dollars a year was assessed by the owner, usually the mining company.[37]

"Everyone had a garden where potatoes and other vegetables were raised. Furthermore, to supplement their meager income, each family kept a milk cow, hogs and chickens. For heating purposes, wood, which was plentiful and near at hand, was cut and hauled in[to] the yards. . . .

"The local mines worked in two shifts (*sifte*). The men who worked nights arrived home about six A.M., ate breakfast and then retired, two in each bed. They arose about 5 P.M., ate supper with the miners who had just arrived after completing the day shift and then returned to the mines for their evening work. Supper usually consisted of a one-dish meal, cabbage and meat, beans and bacon, or goulash of beef

Table 20.4. Characteristics of South Slavs on the Iron Ranges, 1918*

	Age		Arrival		Males	Men Married	Wife in U.S.
	20–29	36–39	1904–11	1912–14			
Bulgars (N=124)	40.3	41.1	18.5	73.4	98.4	55.7	4.4
Croatians (N=92)	40.2	44.6	53.3	38.0	87	53.7	27.9
Serbians (N=37)	45.9	35.1	35.1	51.3	81.1	43.3	53.8

Source: Based on a sample of alien registration forms in Minnesota Commission of Public Safety Records, 1918, for Biwabik, Stuntz (Hibbing), Virginia, Buhl, Ely, Cusson, Midway, and Franklin.

*All figures as percentage of sample.

A MINERS' BOARDINGHOUSE at Nashwauk on the Mesabi Range in 1910.

and vegetables. At work the men carried tin dinner pails which were divided into two sections, the lower half for liquids and the upper part for solids, such as pork chops, bread, cake and fruit. The boarders alternated in the use of the beds, the night shift taking over after the day shift arose around 5 A.M. . . . .

"The boarders paid a fee of $3 a month to the boarding boss for the cooking, washing and, sometimes, patching services. The food was ordered from the grocer. . . . At the end of the month the whole charged monthly grocery bill was divided equally among all the boarders. The total cost for the cooking, washing and groceries usually approximated from $12 to $15 a month per person."

For married couples, a boardinghouse was a valuable source of additional income. In 1909, for example, the prevalence of boarders in Minnesota range communities pushed the average annual family income among Croats to $1,370, over $300 above that of the native born, although the latter commanded higher wages. The Slovenes, with fewer boardinghouses, had average yearly incomes of $869. For both the operators and the boarders, such living arrangements offered a chance to accumulate enough capital to return

home, to bring other family members to the United States, or to buy property. Of 49 Croat families living in Minnesota range towns in 1909, 46.9% owned their own homes. Of 28 Slovenes, 71.4% did so. (No comparable figures were given for Serbs.)[38]

Because boarders in a house were often related or from the same homeland region, they served as an extended family for married men separated from their own families for years at a time. As those immigrants who intended to return to Europe or to bring their families to Minnesota did so, more households were established. Although not all South Slavs were quickly formed into small family units, ethnic boardinghouses declined in the late 1920s. They did not entirely disappear, however, and some could still be found in northern Minnesota in the 1960s.[39]

The development of the saloon as a social institution important to industrial immigrants is a recurring theme in immigration history. In 1909 the Immigration Commission counted 356 saloons in 15 towns on the Mesabi and Vermilion ranges. Of these, 91 were run by South Slavs — 48 by Slovenes, 34 by Croats, 8 by Montenegrins, and 1 by a Serb. Organized along ethnic lines, such saloons were much more than drinking establishments. They provided newcomers with a convenient social club, where crucial information concerning wages and opportunities for work and lodging could be readily exchanged, where letters could be received, translated, written, or read, where documents and unfamiliar customs could be explained, and where money orders could be sent home. The saloon was usually the new arrival's most accessible, and sometimes his only, source of such information. Indeed the saloonkeeper frequently served as labor agent, banker, and general adviser. Many also rented rooms and operated pool halls, card rooms, and dance halls in connection with their establishments. After the immigrants became citizens, the saloon owner often assumed the role of political boss, usually as an advocate of the Democratic party.[40]

Mesabi Range newspapers frequently chronicled crimes associated with South Slav saloons, and the activities of the saloon owners themselves were also considered newsworthy. The tone of many such accounts left little doubt that these men were regarded as prosperous main street businessmen. The transformation of one such saloonkeeper into a multifaceted entrepreneur can be traced in the pages of the Chisholm Herald. During 1905 the paper noted that the man was visited by relatives from Ohio, remodeled the upper floor of his saloon into a hall, returned to the Old Country for a visit, was thinking of starting a clothing store, and was fined $100 for keeping a disorderly house. During 1906 the saloonkeeper presented a chalice to the Catholic church and made another trip to Europe. In 1907 he announced that he was giving up the saloon business and was planning to operate a livery stable. By mid-1908 he had rented a building for a drug store, and late in the year he was moving into a new business building and purchasing an adjacent lot.[41]

Even after free immigration ended in the 1920s and Prohibition was repealed in 1933, the saloon retained its importance as a social center, although it was no longer the only one available to the South Slav community. Political meetings could be conducted in the omnipresent rooms above it, weddings or receptions could be held there, and parties and concerts could be given. More than a dozen South Slav taverns were listed in five towns on the Mesabi and Vermilion ranges in 1937. Although they lost their informal ethnic exclusiveness over the years, bars and lounges have retained their importance as social centers for South Slavs. In them traditional ethnic music could still be heard in Minnesota in the late 1970s.[42]

The ethnic store, be it all-purpose grocery, meat market, or specialty shop, was another useful transitional institution which grew out of the immigrants' language difficulties and their desire for items they had known in the homeland. Inability to communicate effectively in English or to secure credit on reasonable terms made the ethnic store attractive during the early decades. That it was a highly volatile enterprise was indicated by the frequent openings, closings, and moves from one iron range town to another reported in the local newspapers. As patrons acquired skill in English and familiarity with the new society's patterns, few retail stores catering solely to a single ethnic group survived. Nevertheless as late as 1937 more than 30 groceries and meat markets

were operated by South Slavs in seven towns on the three ranges. Other exceptions which persisted into the 1970s included bars, funeral homes, auto parts and repair operations, insurance agents, and franchise outlets for various national products. To survive, these later South Slav operators enlarged their clienteles to include members of other ethnic groups.[43]

Basic kinship and Old Country ties visible in the boarding-house, saloon, and store helped ease the process of accommodation, a service churches performed for certain other immigrant groups. Among Croats and Serbs, however, the ethnic church did not figure prominently as a transitional institution. The two groups, traditionally unfriendly in their homelands, were divided sharply by religion. Many Minnesota Serbs migrated from Croatia, where their ancestors had settled as refugees from the Turks between 1520 and 1700. The mainstay of their efforts to maintain cohesiveness as a minority people during their centuries of migration and struggle against the Turks was the Serbian Orthodox religion, which was closely identified with Serbian ethnicity. Yet the church was not a factor in the daily lives of the early Serbian immigrants in Minnesota; its role was rather that of a historical force in forming national identity. For example, not until 1910 and 1923 were Serbian Orthodox churches organized in Chisholm and Duluth due to a lack of priests.[44]

As for the Croats, a long-standing anticlerical tradition existed among them. Some participated, however, in Roman Catholic parishes organized by Slovenes in Minnesota communities, and some Croats and Serbs responded to the mission efforts of the Reverend William J. Bell, whose non-denominational Iron Range Parish served isolated communities there from 1913 to the early 1930s. Nevertheless it is significant that no Croatian national churches were established in the state. One scholar estimated that perhaps 50% did not attend any church.[45]

Like the Slovenes, Croats and Serbs founded benefit societies soon after they arrived. There were, however, two important differences in these organizations: (1) unlike the Slovenes the local Croatian and Serbian groups were chapters of societies founded elsewhere, and (2) initially these fraternal organizations were not church-related. The Bulgars and Macedonians, on the other hand, do not appear to have established major organizations in the state, but rather to have participated in those of the Croats and Slovenes.

The leading Croatian fraternal group was the Croatian Union of the United States (Hrvatska Zajednica u Sjedinjenim Državama), which was started in Pittsburgh in 1894. After several name changes, it became the Croatian Fraternal Union of America (Hrvatska Bratska Zajednica u Americi or HBZ) in 1925. As the largest Croatian society in the United States, it provided insurance, operated an orphanage, and offered social and political activities in local lodges, of which there were at least 40 in Minnesota in 1937.[46]

For a time this and other Slav organizations were accused of being under Communist party influence and fell prey to the repressive tactics of Senator Joseph McCarthy of Wisconsin in the early 1950s. Under new leadership in the 1960s, the union attracted members among second- and third-generation Croats, offered scholarships, encouraged Croatian language courses, and perpetuated Croatian music and folklore. In 1979 it had 15 lodges in Minnesota with 1,406 members.

The Serbs also established lodges and associations based elsewhere. In 1896 they had four federations of 269 lodges with 20,000 members nationally. A merger of three older groups created the Serb National Federation (*Srpski Narodni Savez* or SNF) in Pittsburgh in 1929. In 1937 Minnesota had at least 19 chapters, and 10 remained active in 1981.[47]

The important aspect of these fraternal organizations was not simply that they existed, but rather how they functioned and what roles the members of the immigrant community played in their operation and development. In "the fragile economic security" offered by mining, they fulfilled a "need for a more formal basis for community," observed one historian. Their structures were based upon lodge systems which enabled individuals to develop a local body with its own idiosyncrasies. Great latitude existed within the Croatian Fraternal Union which soon developed English-speaking lodges; the Serbs, however, were not so tolerant of diversity, perhaps because of their smaller numbers. Religious-minded Croats could create locals to their liking, while more secular-minded immigrants could develop anticlerical or Socialist chapters — all within the framework of the union.

In fact, following World War I secularization and social democratic leftist politics were so pronounced within the Croatian Fraternal Union that the Catholic clergy in 1921 felt compelled to establish the Croatian Catholic Union (*Hrvatska Katolička Zajednica* or HKZ) as an alternative organization. Although HKZ became the second largest Croatian society in the nation by the 1960s, only two lodges in Hibbing and Keewatin were listed in the state in 1973.[48]

The local lodges of these various South Slav organizations were beehives of activity for many decades because they provided forums for the discussion of pertinent issues, mechanisms for community service, avenues for the development of status and prestige, and focal points for the collection of funds to be used in the local and national ethnic community. Originally preoccupied with providing life and accident insurance for industrial workers, they later moved into such diverse fields as home mortgages, care of the aged, preparation for citizenship, and aid in legal matters stemming from immigration. Sizable sums of money were invested and utilized in their efforts, and in the process scattered immigrant groups were welded together, creating a capital base for their populations as a whole. By 1930 the economic organizations of the Serbs, Croats, and Slovenes (with Bulgars, Macedonians, and others as individual members) had amassed a national working capital exceeding $18,000,000. By 1944 this figure had risen to about $40,000,000, money which was at the disposal of members of the immigrant communities and their descendants.[49]

Over the years, however, the needs of the people changed in response to general processes at work in the American economy. For example, the collapse of private welfare systems during the Depression of the 1930s and the subsequent involvement of government in such programs lessened the need for some benefits the ethnic societies had provided. As a result, they have declined in varying degrees, and the activities they carried out have come to be shared by a host of other organizations in which South Slavs became active in the larger society, including labor unions and the Socialist party.

Effective labor organizations in the iron ore industry were slow in developing. Intimidation by mining company agents effectively discouraged participation. In addition, immigrants who intended to return to Europe were reluctant to chance interrupting their wages. Troublesome, too, for organizers was the number of languages spoken among the miners and the antagonisms among various immigrant groups. A long-time union organizer in Minnesota recalled, for example, "there was one thing the Austrians insisted that you know: they were not Austrian; they hated Austrians. They were either Bosnians, Herzegovinians, Montenegrins, Rumanians, Bulgarians, Croatians, Slovenians, Serbians, or some other group. . . . And some of them didn't mind being called Bohunks, but others didn't like it, either." The first serious efforts to improve working conditions grew out of the Socialist movement, which emerged in northern Minnesota between 1900 and 1906. Relations between South Slavs and Socialist Finns, who took the lead in attempting to organize the workers, were mixed. Contemporary accounts from 1892 to 1900 record numerous fights in Mesabi saloons with names like Matt Baudek's Slovenski Dom or Crooked Neck Pete's Scandinavian Saloon. South Slav Socialists were never as numerous or as powerful as the Finnish groups. They built no halls on the range and formed only three clubs in Chisholm, Aurora, and Ely which affiliated with the South Slavic Socialist Federation by 1910.[50]

Nevertheless both Finn and South Slav Socialists and non-Socialists supported the disastrous and unsuccessful iron range strikes of 1907 and 1916. Although they did not achieve immediate improvements in the harsh working conditions, these serious labor disputes induced unexpected demographic changes. The 1907 strike temporarily increased the Montenegrin population, many of whom were brought in as strikebreakers. Reportedly 1,124 Montenegrins were sent to the Mesabi in August, 1907, alone, but many of these men left or were fired within a year.[51]

The strikes also led to some loss of Finn and Slovene families. During the 1907 walkout, for example, Eveleth lost 20% of its population. Several hundred people a day were leaving, the *Eveleth News* reported on July 24, their possessions packed in satchels, suitcases, or trunks, bound for the Old Country, for their woodland claims, or for visits to friends.[52]

South Slavs and others with a desire to farm formed a number of rural communities. Some in the cutover region of north-central Minnesota were being boomed for settlement in the early 20th century. Slovenes from Ely and Nashwauk homesteaded at Rauch in Koochiching County in 1906 as well as at Greaney and at Gheen in western St. Louis County. The nucleus of Nebish in Beltrami County is said to have been formed in 1914 by four South Slavs, who were followed by others from Illinois in 1922. Croatian and Serbian families moved to Goodland in Itasca County before 1913, where they mingled with Finns and Swedes as well as a group of German-American Lutherans who migrated from Iowa. By 1937 South Slavs were found in no fewer than 48 Minnesota settlements.[53]

In 1907 and 1916 they helped write a chapter in Minnesota's labor history that was to have long-lasting effects, a chapter that left a bitter legacy inherited by succeeding generations of immigrant miners' children. The failure of the 1916 strike, coupled with the companies' adamant opposition and espionage activities, deterred attempts to unionize the miners until the Congress of Industrial Organizations (CIO) seriously set out to do so in 1936–37. Even then it was not until 1943, under the aegis of Franklin D. Roosevelt's New Deal, that the CIO Steel Workers Organizing Committee successfully signed contracts with the Minnesota iron mining industry. These events may help to explain the area's enduring "radical" tradition, its consistent support of the labor movement, and its loyalty to the Democratic and Democratic-Farmer-Labor parties.[54]

Even before the union was recognized by the Oliver Mining Company, South Slavs had been active. As early as 1937, 10 South Slavs out of a total of 26 members were elected to the CIO Iron Range Industrial Union Council. At the beginning of 1940, 9 of 22 delegates to the council were South Slavs, including a trustee, the treasurer, and the sergeant-at-arms.[55]

World War I and Americanization

The violent strike of 1916 was part of the militant atmosphere of the World War I era, a period characterized in Minnesota by antilabor, antiforeign, and anti-Catholic hysteria. United States entry into the war in 1917 triggered a massive assault on immigrant groups launched by a special state agency known as the Minnesota Commission of Public Safety (PSC). South Slavs were among those who came under its scrutiny. Not only were they suspect because they were "different," but they were regarded as Austrians, a country then among the enemy.[56]

A Serbian immigrant in Chisholm recalled, "There was a conspicuous difference between the native born Americans and us immigrants, not only in the way we lived but also in our outward appearance. Most of us had large handle bar mustaches which neither the scissors nor the razor had marred. We shaved on the average of once a week. On the streets we strolled lazily in groups, talking loudly in our Serbian tongue and gesticulating wildly and expressively. Under these circumstances we were closely scrutinized and observed with suspicion by the Americans."[57]

Native-born Americans and northern European immigrants quickly formed stereotypes of South Slavs. Mine superintendents were said to regard Serbs, Montenegrins, and Croats as unsuitable for any but the most menial work. They were characterized as "dark, shagged, stoop-shouldered, and forbidding," as well as unreliable because they sometimes walked off the job in large numbers. In 1916 readers of the national magazine *Survey* were informed that South Slavs on the Mesabi lived "very much like cattle" and "spend much of their money for liquor. . . . Of such matters as sanitation or the proper respect for women, and other

factors of American progress which we deem vital, they know nothing." Moreover, said the magazine, because their presence acted "as a dead weight pulling down the wage-scale" for American workers, further South Slav immigration should be prevented.[58]

Minnesota South Slavs were loyal to the Allies during World War I. Some 250 of them returned to Europe to fight in the Serbian, Montenegrin, or French armies. Colonies of Bulgars near Hibbing and Chisholm, once numbering as many as 300, "dwindled down to nearly nothing," and Montenegrins disappeared. Others enlisted in the United States armed forces, and the draft brought more into the ranks. At home, South Slavs bought Liberty Bonds and contributed to the South Slav Committee in London, which was working for Allied recognition of South Slav independence. The creation of the Jugoslav Republican Alliance, which pressed President Woodrow Wilson to support the establishment of a South Slav republic, also gained adherents in Minnesota. Nevertheless, in view of the recent 1916 strike, the iron range communities were among the Public Safety Commission's principal targets (another was the German city of New Ulm), for the agency clearly regarded the strikers and their leaders in the Industrial Workers of the World (IWW or Wobblies) as dangerous.[59]

Along with other organizations, the wartime agency's women's committees endeavored to Americanize the immigrants, especially those from southeastern Europe, but in this effort the PSC was a short-lived johnny-come-lately. As early as the 1890s Slovenian churches in Ely and Tower had begun on their own initiative to offer English courses, and in 1908 Slovenian Socialists had promoted naturalization and political education among their members. But the first large-scale efforts were undertaken in the early 1900s by the local public school systems of the range towns, which offered adult classes.[60]

Attended by miners and their wives, often at night, the classes enrolled large numbers of South Slavs. "Cooking, sewing, and commercial work were offered," one principal recalled, but the "interest was in English" classes. After women received the right to vote in presidential elections in Minnesota in 1917, federal judges took the position that a woman could no longer receive naturalization through her husband, nor could the husband become a citizen until his wife also passed the test. Women were less versed in English, according to a sample of PSC alien registration forms for St. Louis County in 1918. While 71.1% of the men said they could speak or read at least a little English, only 23.8% of the women said they could do so.[61]

After 1917 the attendance of women in the night schools as well as in home classes often exceeded that of men. Home classes were started in 1917 to teach English and homemaking (including American cooking) to immigrant women in small groups in neighborhood homes. In 1923–24 those in Hibbing, for example, had a total enrollment of 262, of whom 29% were South Slavs, primarily Croatians and Slovenes. In January, 1924, 11 range towns and Duluth had a total adult school enrollment of 6,806, of whom 3,638 were men and 3,170 were women. Of these 3,130 were in English classes. In that year 1,051 people were naturalized in St. Louis

County; 834 were graduates of the classes and 224 were women.

Also active in the Americanization movement were the old ethnic organizations of the South Slavs as well as a few new ones. About 1,500 delegates (largely Slovenes and Croatians) founded the American Jugoslav Association of Minnesota (AJAM) in 1925. Croats established in 1926 the American United Yugoslav Association of the State of Minnesota (AUYA), which had 12 chapters by 1940. These groups tried to help individuals deal with Americanization by assisting their education and their quest for citizenship. Thus, instead of fighting the pressures to Americanize, they pushed their members toward greater participation in American society.[62]

In the accommodation, however, they also helped to protect individual and cultural identity. Since 1935 AJAM has sponsored an All-Slav Day annual picnic to emphasize "the preservation and perpetuation of Yugoslav folklore, culture, traditions, and heritages." Both AJAM and AUYA promoted educational attainment, and AJAM emerged as a political voice for South Slavs that survived in the 1980s. Since 1964 it has also carried on a successful scholarship program. Nor did all the organizations represent only a single language group. In 1932, in the hope of overcoming national rivalries, South Slavs created the American Yugoslav Club. Within a few years, it had chapters throughout the state.

South Slavs in Duluth

There is some evidence that migration from the iron ranges led to the growth of a South Slav community in Duluth during the opening years of the 20th century. Clinging to the shores of Lake Superior, Duluth and neighboring Superior, Wisconsin, developed into the major metropolitan area in northern Minnesota after the discovery of iron ore. As lake ports and railroad hubs, they provided jobs and funneled thousands of immigrants to the mines of the Vermilion and the Mesabi and to the wheat fields of the Dakotas. The first Slovene workers probably passed through Duluth in the 1880s on their way to the newly opened Soudan Mine on the Vermilion. Just when the city's South Slav colony got its start is not certain; perhaps it was about 1893 when the Duluth, Missabe and Northern Railroad tracks and piers were built there. The first 30 or so Serbian men are said to have settled in Duluth between 1902 and 1906, working on the Thomson Dam completed by the Great Northern Power Company in 1907.[63]

It seems probable that the colony was well under way before April 13, 1911, when the first issue of *Narodni Vestnik* (National Herald) made its appearance in the city. The second and last Slovene newspaper to be published in Minnesota, it began as a weekly and ended in 1917 as a biweekly, which had operated under at least six different editors. Initiated by the Slovenian Printing and Publishing Company, the paper and the firm were apparently the brainchild of George L. Brozich, an Ely banker, who was listed as the firm's president in 1911. Near the end of its life on May 18, 1917, the paper's masthead proclaimed it the organ of the Slovenian-Croatian Union of Calumet, Michigan, the Western Slavonic Association of Denver, Colorado, and the Independent Benevolent Society of La Salle, Illinois. Its best-known editor was Ivan Zapan, popularly called Mike Cegare, a pseudonym under which his humorous writings became familiar to Slavs throughout the Northwest.[64]

Existing copies have a page of Minnesota news, reporting on Slovene activities in Duluth and in the range towns. In its first issue, for example, the paper listed by name Slovenian businessmen in Eveleth (11), Gilbert (10), Chisholm (10), Ely (10), Aurora (5), Virginia (4), Duluth (4), New Duluth (1), Hibbing (3), Buhl (2), and Pineville (1), suggesting that the Duluth Slovene community was not as yet so well established as others on the ranges. By 1917, however, some Duluth businesses, including the Slavenski Saloon on West Michigan Street, were regular advertisers. A second journal, *Radnička Obrana* (Workers' Sentinel) was also being published by Croatian Socialists in Duluth in 1916, although nothing more is known of the periodical and little is known about the Socialist movement among the Slavs there.

During this period, too, Josip Jurkovic and Matija Sojat founded a short-lived Croatian bookstore in the city, and a Serb who arrived in 1913 reported that three groceries were owned and operated by countrymen from Hercegovina. Others from Montenegro, Lika, Bosnia, Banija, and Kordun are mentioned among the residents in 1913 (see Map 20.1). "Occasionally Russian Orthodox Missionaries spent brief periods among us," wrote one, holding services in private homes, "but, in those days, the Serbian colony in Duluth was an integral part of the Chisholm church. This arrangement continued until the arrival" in 1916 or 1917 of Father Danilo Kozomora, "who, on Sundays, first blessed a pool room and then served the holy liturgy."[65]

From these beginnings St. George Serbian Orthodox

THE INTERIOR of St. George Serbian Orthodox Church, Duluth, 1939.

Church in the Duluth suburb of Gary came into being in 1923. By 1957 the city was reported to have about 150 Serbian Orthodox families as well as two lodges of the Serb National Federation (SNF) and an active Circle of Serbian Sisters. In 1970 a second church, Mala Gospojina (Little Holy Lady) Free Serbian Orthodox Church, was consecrated in Gary. This congregation was formed by Displaced Persons who objected to control of the Serbian church by the hierarchy in Yugoslavia. The result was a schism within the church in the United States. St. George remained loyal and continued to grow. In 1971 it constructed a new fellowship hall. By 1980 it had about 250 members, including some from Crosby and Ironton.[66]

Evidence indicates that the number of South Slavs in Duluth increased after work began on the United States Steel Corporation's plant in Gary in 1910. Serbs, who were hired to clear land for the building, quickly sent word to others. After that Slovenes, Croats, and Serbs worked for the steel company and in the adjacent Universal Atlas Cement Company's plant for over 50 years, living nearby in New Duluth, Gary, or West Duluth. There they organized units of JSKJ, KSKJ, SNPJ, SNF, and other lodges. One disgruntled member of SNPJ, which had about 50 members in 1914, said, "We got a church and a priest. Soon it had its circle. But whoever would not dance to the priest's music was blacklisted at the plant. Many Slovenes were discharged because of this, and some of the more progressive were compelled to move away."[67]

Whatever the truth of this charge, other sources suggest that at that time there was "a strong group of Slovenian settlers and St. Elizabeth was their parish." In 1910 no Catholic church existed in Gary or New Duluth, so the people attended St. James in West Duluth or held services in their homes and halls. In 1913 St. Elizabeth was built in New Duluth, and in 1928 the congregation completed the construction of a parish hall in which the KSKJ, JSKJ, Altar Society, Boy Scouts, Degree of Honor, and the Croatian Cultural Club met regularly.[68]

From its founding until at least the 1950s St. Elizabeth conducted services in Croatian and Slovene, although Poles and Italians also attended. Its South Slav membership peaked in 1929 with 135 Slovenes and 200 Croats. By 1938 these figures had dropped to 98 Slovenes and 142 Croats in a total membership of 1,514, for the Depression was severe in northern Minnesota and many people left in search of work. On its 24th anniversary in 1938 festivities at St. Elizabeth featured music by both Slovene and Croatian choirs, and not until 1942 did the church switch to English-language services.

By the mid-1920s the South Slav community of Gary-New Duluth had its own merchants, clubs, and activities. Along Commonwealth Avenue, the main street running through both towns, South Slav businesses included six Slovene and Serb groceries, three Serb and Croat barbers, a Slovene tailor, and a Serb cafe, as well as confectioneries, soft drink dealers, hardware and clothing stores, a Serb coal, feed, and hay emporium, a Romanian auto company, a billiard parlor, a Slovene saloon, and at least five boarding and lodging houses from 96th to 99th avenues West. Residents recalled

attending lodge functions, the Sunday baseball games of the Gary Athletic Club, which celebrated its 50th anniversary in 1980, and many activities sponsored by the Raleigh Street Center of the International Institute of Duluth, which opened under YMCA auspices in 1919 and became a separate agency there in 1930.[69]

The South Slavs kept big gardens, and most had cows, pigs, geese, and chickens. They usually had a smokehouse for pork, and they made lots of sauerkraut and wine. For the latter, they purchased grapes from their Italian neighbors, who ordered them by the railroad carload. During the Depression many survived on the fish they caught in the nearby St. Louis River and the produce they raised. When they could afford to buy meat from the butcher, he called at the door in the mornings and delivered the orders in the afternoons, dispensing news and gossip as he made his rounds.[70]

Wakes were held in the homes, and most babies were born there, sometimes with a midwife and sometimes with the help of neighbors or family members, "and no one stayed in bed long afterwards," recalled one woman, "because there was too much to do." She said that one of her own children "was born on the back step" as she was going to get help from her neighbor. She "picked it up, brought it inside, cleaned it up and never bothered my neighbor." Serbian interviewees said they kept many Old Country traditions, especially those for Christmas. One remembered that she always cut a small birch tree and decorated it with fruits, nuts, and candy as a substitute for the young cherry or plum tree she would have had in Yugoslavia.[71]

By the 1930s South Slavs were the largest of 26 groups reported in Gary, numbering an estimated 3,000 to 5,000, largely employed in the steel and cement works. In the 1970s both plants closed, and in 1980 the effects were still visible in Gary-New Duluth. There were many vacant lots and empty buildings. In spite of the addition of refugee families after World War II, the area seemed in decline. Many younger people had moved away. Only St. George Serbian Church seemed to be flourishing. And of all the South Slav groups in Duluth, the Serbs, anchored by their church, appeared to have most tenaciously preserved their traditions.[72]

The South St. Paul Community

The third South Slav geographical concentration in Minnesota took shape in the Twin Cities metropolitan area community of South St. Paul.[73] Although it evolved during the same period as the St. Louis County settlements, South St. Paul had a different economic base, for it developed as a major livestock exchange and meat-packing center. The St. Paul Union Stockyards Company opened there in 1887; Swift and Company started a meat-packing plant in 1897; and Armour and Company joined them in 1919. By 1925 the South St. Paul market ranked second in the United States in calf and hog receipts and fourth in cattle. Superficially dissimilar from the mining and steelmaking in which South Slavs were employed in northern Minnesota, the livestock and meat-packing industry shared a common need for a large number of unskilled workers.[74]

It is said that a Croat arrived to work in the Swift and Company plant soon after its opening in 1897, and that sever-

Table 20.5. Characteristics of South Slavs in South St. Paul, 1918*

| | Age | | Arrival | | | | |
	20–29	30–39	1904–11	1912–14	Males	Men Married	Wife in U.S.
Bulgars (N=34)	41.2	44.1	35.3	58.8	100	44.1	6.7
Croatians (N=31)	32.3	45.2	45.2	48.4	74.2	43.5	30.0
Serbians (N=32)	53.1	40.6	50.0	46.9	59.4	63.2	91.7

Source: Based on a sample of alien registration forms in Minnesota Commission of Public Safety Records, 1918.
*All figures as percentage of sample.

al Serbs journeyed to the growing new town before 1908. There are various versions of where these early arrivals came from. One asserts that they migrated from the iron ranges; another maintains that a group of Serbs from the Pennsylvania coal fields were bound for the iron ranges when they learned of the jobs available in South St. Paul from Polish immigrants in the St. Paul railroad station. The Serbs crossed the bridge over the Mississippi River, so the story goes, and walked to South St. Paul, where they obtained work. It is certain that more joined them there, migrating from other South Slav centers and from Europe. By 1910 the Serbian colony in South St. Paul numbered perhaps 60 persons, including 11 women and 3 children. Before the outbreak of World War I, about 600 Croats and Serbs were estimated to have settled there. Although the war and the years that followed drew some back to Europe, South Slavs built a community that persisted in the 1980s.[75]

Its early years were reminiscent of those in northern Minnesota. The unskilled men obtained low-paying jobs in the stockyards and packing plants, where, with hundreds of other urban workers, they labored 12 to 16 hours a day. According to one researcher, "The livestock exchange yards in South St. Paul were almost exclusively reserved for Serbs and some other immigrants and they took care of the cleaning and feeding of the animals." In later years (1930s and after) women as well as men worked in the plants until Swift closed in 1967 and Armour in 1978. But in the beginning men far outnumbered women in the community. Couples shared rented houses, taking in boarders whom they charged about $10.00 a week in the 1920s. These boardinghouses apparently did not persist as long as they did on the iron ranges; by 1930 they were no longer numerous in South St. Paul. Indeed as early as 1914 about 10 Serbian families were able to buy their own homes, thanks to the fact that work in the stockyards and packing plants was steadier than that in the mines.[76]

In the early 1900s, wrote one of the few scholars to study this ethnic community, "South St. Paul was a dispersed town surrounded by farms. The livestock exchange area was below a relatively steep hill in a wide flat area along the Mississippi River. The [stock]yards were located next to a railroad line, and next to it was a gravel road. . . . Along the road and railroad there were several hotels, stores, and shops. Farther along the steep hill and on the hill were located the houses. The people who worked in the yards walked downhill to their jobs and uphill to go back home."[77]

Samples of the foreign-born Serb, Croat, and Bulgar populations of South St. Paul registered in 1918 revealed

differences similar to those noted earlier on the iron ranges. While Bulgars were at one end of the spectrum and Serbs at the other, the South St. Paul community as a whole had a more even sex ratio and more wives present than did the northern component (see Tables 20.4, 20.5).

A majority of the men in all three ethnic groups were employed as unskilled laborers — 75.5% of the Bulgars, 58% of the Croats, and 50% of the Serbs. There were also bakers, barbers, carpenters, a candymaker, an iceman, a cook, and a farmer. Of the women, none worked outside the home, but 15.3% operated boardinghouses. It was apparent from the names and addresses that many Bulgar men lived together in boardinghouses on North Concord or 2nd Avenue South and that some of these men were related. The boarders ranged in age from 19 through 37 with one 60-year-old; 64.7% had lived in South St. Paul one year or less; the others from 16 months to 5½ years.[78]

Early arrivals among the Croats had entered the United States via the port of Baltimore; those in the 1912–14 period overwhelmingly went through New York City. A total of 96.8% of the Serbs also arrived there. The Bulgars were the only one of the three groups to travel via Canada in any appreciable numbers; 23.5% did so. None of the Bulgars had taken out first papers declaring their intention to become American citizens, 3.2% of the Croats had done so, and 28.1% of the Serbs. On the other hand, 67.6% of the Bulgars reported that they intended to return to Bulgaria after World War I, and apparently many of them did so.

By that time various South Slav organizations had been

THE SERBIAN HALL in South St. Paul as it looked in 1980.

created in South St. Paul. Among the first was the St. Sava chapter of the Serb National Federation established in 1909 with about 28 members. By 1941 it had 107 members, a junior lodge, and a ladies' auxiliary which had come into being in 1930. Lacking a congregation of their own faith in the Twin Cities, the Serbs joined with Russian immigrants to form the Russian-Serbian Holy Trinity Orthodox Church in St. Paul in 1916.

Eight years later the colony built a Serbian Hall on 3rd Avenue. In it was an office for the SNF benefit society and a small library. A singing group was active, and the hall became a South St. Paul social center, "where Serbian foods were served, and people had a chance to hear . . . ethnic songs or play the *tamburica* [*a stringed instrument*] or *gajde* [*bagpipes*]. Sometimes the whole audience was involved in songs and music, as well as in dancing the *kolo*," a circle dance. The hall also provided a setting for children's Serbian-language classes and for the celebration of family pa-

tron saints' days, which pass down from generation to generation. On that day Serbs "invite their relatives and friends to break bread with them and invite the Priest to bless their *Kolac*," a special yeast bread. It served also as a chapel for St. Sava's Eastern Orthodox congregation, which held services there from 1950 to 1953, when its church was completed.[79]

Like those in northern Minnesota, the Croatians in South St. Paul did not form their own congregations but worshiped with other groups in nearby St. Augustine, St. Adalbert, or Holy Trinity Roman Catholic churches. In 1918, however, they established an active chapter of the Croatian Fraternal Union with a membership of between 60 and 70 families and at once erected a Croatian Hall on 2nd Avenue. Locally owned by shareholders rather than by the national union, it was in 1980 the only Croatian hall in the state. A second English-speaking lodge came into being in South St. Paul in the early 1930s. The Croatian Hall quickly became and re-

A SOUTH ST. PAUL Croatian tamburitza *orchestra in 1938. Front left to right, Joseph Krizanic, Tony Spraitz, Albert Palla; back, John Kendall and Frank Jankovich. The men earned a total of $10 to $12 a performance.*

PARADE marking the opening of the Croatian Hall in South St. Paul in 1920. The houses in the background on 1st Street South were still occupied in 1980.

mained a lively community center. Language lessons were taught within its walls, *tamburitza* orchestras and *kolo* dancers practiced for appearances at the Festival of Nations sponsored by the International Institute of Minnesota, and social gatherings of all sorts were held, including dinners following the funerals of members in which the lodges marched carrying black and Croatian flags.[80]

As the Great Depression gathered over the United States in the early 1930s, one informant recalled that some South Slavs moved from northern Minnesota to South St. Paul to take advantage of the more stable employment in meat packing. When hard times hit with full force, said another, "the life of the Serbian Hall became less exciting, the amount of food was not as large as before; so we could dance and sing much less because bread and onions were not good fuel." A Croatian woman remembered the "kettles and kettles" of soup that were prepared and distributed in some South Slav communities. A man recalled that he and other Croatians in South St. Paul did not apply for welfare but shared and borrowed from one another to make do. "I didn't like onions for a long time after that," he said.[81]

Nevertheless as the Depression waned, it was apparent that South Slavs were becoming established in many Minnesota communities. A directory published in 1937 listed independent businessmen, artisans, and contractors offering varied products and services from food to pool halls, as well as a sprinkling of such professionals as doctors, dentists, lawyers, and numerous public officials in the range areas. The operation of small butcher shops (many of them on 3rd Avenue) was especially popular among South St. Paul Croats.

After autos became more common in the late 1930s there was considerable social interchange between South St. Paul and northern Minnesota Slavs. Lodge-arranged Croatian festivals have been held annually since 1960 in various locations. To attend them northerners traveled to South St. Paul and vice versa. The 19th annual Croatian Day, for example, was held in 1979 at the hall in South St. Paul, the 20th in 1980 near Duluth. At that time the lodge's membership included second- and third-generation Croatians as well as many non-Croats. One man of German ancestry who married into the South St. Paul Croat community was named an honorary Croatian and participated in the Croat national bowling tournament. A number of Bohemians were accepted from the earliest days of the settlement. Serbs, on the other hand, have their own festivities, centering in recent years more frequently in their churches than in the Serbian Hall. The first annual Minnesota Serbian Day, for example, was proclaimed by the state's governor in 1947, and the Serbian church in Chisholm seemed to have been the focus of the day's annual commemorative program for at least 10 years.[82]

Assimilation and Retention

In a broad sense, ethnicity concerns the cultural baggage people carry through time, including their decisions on what to discard or retain. By whatever definition one adopts, ethnic survivals among South Slavs in Minnesota are difficult to measure with precision. In 1980 religion, food, and music were the most obvious examples of cultural persistence.

Among foods, durable survivals still served in Minnesota homes included *potica* (Slovene), known as *povitica* in Croat and *pavititsa* in Serb (a kind of rolled cake with a filling of nuts or raisins), buckwheat crumbles, various kinds of dumplings and noodles, *sarma* (cabbage rolls), kidney beans and sauerkraut, apple and cheese strudel, tomato soup, *bakalar* (a cod dish), and *polenta* (cornmeal mush). Almost equally durable were the polka bands and accordion music of the Slovenes and the *tamburitza* orchestras of the Croats and Serbs accompanied by *kolo* dances and singing groups. While none was known to be performing in the state by the 1970s, poet-singers, or *guslar*, were also to be found in Minnesota until well after World War II. (A *gusle* is a one-stringed instrument played with a bow.)[83]

The cultural persistence of customs carried by the immigrants from their Slavic homelands was not, however, limited to food and music. Serbs and Croats continued to observe their patron saint days, to act as *kum* and *kuma*, and to carry on certain Christmas and Easter traditions. Serbs, who use the Julian calendar in their churches, observe Christmas on January 7 and bake *chesnitsa*, a Christmas bread containing a silver coin for good luck. But such customs as scattering grain or straw on the floor or carrying a kettle containing a lighted coal through the house on Christmas Eve were dying by 1950, and any celebration of St. Nicholas Day rather than Christmas was "completely" gone among Slovenes by 1976. Only two decades before, however, Sister Mary Daniel O'Neill had been able to collect hundreds of Slovene folk tales, sayings, songs, and superstitions in Virginia, Eveleth, New Duluth, Soudan, and Mountain Iron.[84]

As for languages, a 20.3% gain in Serbian and Croatian speakers was recorded with the influx of refugees into the United States from 1940 to 1960, the third largest gain among the languages studied. The use of Slovene, however, declined during the same period by 62.4%. The only serious language survey thus far carried out among Minnesota South Slavs confirmed the latter decline. In 1976 Joseph Paternost, himself an iron ranger, studied the use of Slovene there. He found that religious services were conducted in English and that the use of Slovene was restricted to special occasions. "Generally speaking," wrote Paternost, "there is no stable bilingualism among the Slovenes here. . . . I was unable to find one person of the third generation who could speak Slovenian," although a number could understand it. In the fourth generation (the great-grandchildren of the immigrants), Paternost found that "the Slovenian language has not 'touched' them at all."[85]

While first- and second-generation South Slavs kept their languages alive and preserved certain traditions, these age groups were rapidly disappearing in the 1970s. In addition the boom-and-bust economy of the iron ranges, the closing of various plants in South St. Paul and Duluth, and rising education and aspiration levels have led many younger people to migrate elsewhere in search of better opportunities. Although few attempts have been made to measure this out-migration, it has obviously occurred. And the perceptive suggestion has been made that those who have remained in northern Minnesota are coming to regard themselves more as "iron rangers" than as members of any particular ethnic group — that a regional consciousness is beginning to replace the old ethnic loyalties.[86]

Other notable changes are apparent in the role of the church in South Slav communities. Ethnic parishes and priests have disappeared among Slovenes, but Serbian Orthodox congregations have probably been strengthened by the arrival of more Serbian priests in recent years and by the organization of new churches.

Thus it seems safe to say that South Slav communities, like all viable social organisms, have changed and are continuing to do so, preserving some old values and adopting new ones in relation to the host society and their ethnic pasts. Two small examples might be pointed out in conclusion. In the extremely diverse ethnic atmosphere on the iron ranges, some traits of one ethnic group have been adopted by another. Bocce ball, originally an Italian bowling game played on a dirt court, early became popular among South Slavs there. During the governorship of Rudy Perpich in 1976–78, the entire state became acquainted with the game, thanks to the fact that Perpich popularized it. In the second example, another form of adaptation was in evidence. In May, 1973, Father Frank F. Perkovich, a Croatian, held the first polka Mass in Minnesota and the second in the United States in Resurrection Catholic Church at Eveleth. Set to the music of older South Slav secular melodies, the Mass was well accepted by second- and third-generation Slavs, but was criticized in the South Slav religious press and by members of the older generation who could recall the words of a Croatian love song, for example, which provided the melody for the offertory hymn. Subsequently recorded and repeated many times, polka Masses have since become widely popular.[87]

Reference notes

[1] Like many other groups, the South Slavs exhibit problems of definition and statistical confusion. Since the United States census counted immigrants only by country of origin until 1910, South Slavs were undistinguishable among Turks, Austrians, and Hungarians. See Chapter 8, note 8, above. Montenegrins by religion and language are regarded by most scholars as Serbs, while residents of Bosnia, Hercegovina, and Dalmatia may be either Croats or Serbs. Numerous studies of Macedonians have failed to achieve agreement on the problems they present, while the Bulgars have been virtually ignored; see Nikolay G. Altankov, *The Bulgar-Americans*, xiv, 20, 21 (Palo Alto, Calif., 1979).

[2] South Slav statistics in MEHP Papers, MHS, compiled by Jon A. Gjerde from U.S. Bureau of Immigration, *Annual Reports*, 1909–75, and other sources, hereafter cited as Gjerde, South Slav statistics. See also Appendix, below; United States, *Census*, 1910, *Population*, 1:981; George J. Prpic, *The Croatian Immigrants in America*, 135, 442 (New York, 1971); Branko M. Colakovic, *Yugoslav Migrations to America*, 44–51, 90, 115 (San Francisco, 1973). The authors wish to acknowledge the helpful suggestions they received during the preparation of this chapter from Professor George J. Prpic of John Carroll University as well as the aid given by Bernard M. Luketich, former president of the Croatian Fraternal Union.

[3] U.S. Immigration Commission, *Emigration Conditions in Europe*, 12:376 (61 Congress, 3 session, *Senate Documents*, no. 748

— serial 5870); Colakovic, *Yugoslav Migrations*, 52–58, 65–67, 95; Gjerde, South Slav statistics; Yugoslavia Direktsija drazharne statistike, *Statistički Godišnjak, 1929*, 154, 160, 161 (Belgrade, 1932, 1939). Some figures were calculated from Walter F. Willcox, ed., *International Migrations*, 1:432–443, 476, 479, 494, 498, 887 (Reprint ed., New York, 1969).

[4] In addition 20 DPs went to Stearns County and 74 Dalmatians arrived, 40 of whom were sponsored by Immaculate Conception Roman Catholic Church, Eveleth. See Minnesota Displaced Persons Commission files, 1949–52, in Minnesota Public Welfare Dept., Minnesota State Archives, MHS, tabulations by Sarah Rubinstein in MEHP Papers; *Range Facts* (Virginia), October 1, 1949, family sec., 1; U.S., *Census*, 1970, *Population*, vol. 1, part 1, sec. 2, p. 1–598; vol. 1, part 25, p. 25–512. On DPs in the Duluth suburb of Gary, see interview of George and Marion Orescanin (Mrs. Orescanin was director of the Duluth International Institute in the 1950s) by Marjorie Hoover, April 25, 1980, notes in MEHP Papers; *Duluth News-Tribune*, February 19, 1950, Brotherhood Week sec., p. 2.

[5] Vladimir Dedijer et al., *History of Yugoslavia*, 103, 505–507 (New York, 1974); Emily Greene Balch, *Our Slavic Fellow Citizens*, 13–22 (New York, 1910); George J. Prpic, *South Slavic Immigration in America*, 21, 24, 27–40, 247 (Boston, 1978). On the historic and linguistic development of the South Slav peoples, see Dmitri Obolensky, *The Byzantine Commonwealth: A History of Eastern Europe, 500–1453* (London, 1971).

[6] Dedijer et al., *History of Yugoslavia*, 80, 180; Obolensky, *Byzantine Commonwealth*, 134–163; Prpic, *South Slavic Immigration*, 24, 27–40, 103. Many Moslems were and are concentrated in Bosnia; some Protestant groups were present, particularly among Bulgars.

[7] Here and below, see Stephan Thernstrom, ed., *Harvard Encyclopedia of American Ethnic Groups*, 187, 247–256, 918, 934–942 (Cambridge, Mass., 1980); Dedijer et al., *History of Yugoslavia*, 275, 290–292, 425; Johann Chmelar, "The Austrian Emigration 1900–1914," in *Perspectives in American History*, 7:308–315, 333–335 (1973); Ivan Čizmić, "O iseljavanju iz Hrvatske u razdoblju 1880–1914," in *Historijski zbornik*, 27:27–47 (1974). For statistics on South Slavs admitted to the U.S., 1899–1924, from Hungary, Austria, and Turkey, broken down by various groupings, see Willcox, ed., *International Migrations*, 1:483, 484, 489. On Serbs, Croats, and Slovenes in the Austro-Hungarian Empire during the late 19th century, see essays in *Austrian History Yearbook*, vol. 3, part 2 (Houston, 1967).

[8] Ivan T. Berend and Gyorgi Ranki, *Economic Development in East-Central Europe in the 19th and 20th Centuries*, 37–58 (New York, 1974); Balch, *Our Slavic Fellow Citizens*, 37–49; Jozo Tomasevich, *Peasants, Politics, and Economic Change in Yugoslavia*, 210–216 (Stanford, Calif., 1955); Colakovic, *Yugoslav Migrations*, 20–27.

[9] Literacy rates and communication and transportation development varied among South Slav areas, with the Slovenian progressing about twice as fast as the Croatian and Serbian regions. See Daniel T. Rodgers, *The Work Ethic in Industrial America, 1850–1920*, 171 (Chicago, 1978); Balch, *Our Slavic Fellow Citizens*, 50–56; Ruth Trouton, *Peasant Renaissance in Yugoslavia 1900–1950: A Study of Yugoslav Peasant Society Development as Affected by Education*, 83–117 (London, 1952); Colakovic, *Yugoslav Migrations*, 13, 31–34, 46, 69; Joseph Stipanovich, "In Unity Is Strength: Immigrant Workers and Immigrant Intellectuals in Progressive America: A History of the South Slav Social Democratic Movement, 1900–1918," pp. 36–63, Ph.D. thesis, University of Minnesota, 1978; J. Puskás, "Emigration from Hungary to the United States Before 1914," in *Etudes Historiques 1975*, 2:9–17 (Budapest, 1975).

[10] Immigration Commission, *Emigration Conditions*, 12:59, 363, 377; Colakovic, *Yugoslav Migrations*, 27–31, 61–64; Balch, *Our Sla-*

vic Fellow Citizens, 452; Frank P. Blatnik, "Culture Conflict: A Study of the Slovenes in Chisholm," 121–123, incomplete master's thesis, University of Minnesota, 1942, partial copy in MEHP Papers, used with the author's permission. On remittances, see Frances Kraljic, *Croatian Migration To and From the United States, 1900–1914*, 46, 71–74, 95, 98 (Palo Alto, Calif., 1978), which concluded that economic factors motivated both Croatian immigration and repatriation.

[11] Immigration Commission, *Emigration Conditions*, 12:361; Dinko A. Tomašić, "Americans from Croatia," 7A, 58, 63, typed manuscript, [1930s], in IHRC; John Syrjamaki, "Mesabi Communities: A Study of Their Development," 139–143, Ph.D. thesis, Yale University, 1940, offered Minnesota examples. On post-World War II movements, see Ivo Baucic, "Some Economic Consequences of Yugoslav External Migrations" and other essays in Leszek A. Kosinski, ed., *Demographic Developments in Eastern Europe*, 266–283 (New York, 1974).

[12] William P. Furlan, *In Charity Unfeigned: The Life of Francis Xavier Pierz*, 3, 16, 196, 236 (St. Cloud, 1952); Sister Grace McDonald, "Father Francis Pierz, Missionary," in *Minnesota History*, 10:117–125 (June, 1929). On Bartholomew Pierz, see Joseph Gregorich, "History of Jugoslav People in Minnesota," in Minnesota American Jugoslav Assn., *25th Annual State Convention*, [19] (Gilbert, 1949); Edward D. Neill, *History of the Upper Mississippi Valley*, 412 (Minneapolis, 1881); William B. Mitchell, *History of Stearns County*, 2:1266 (Chicago, 1915).

[13] On the Stearns County settlements, here and below, see *St. Cloud Visitor*, July 1, 1971, p. 4; *Memorable Events in the History of St. Stephen's Parish* ([1971]) and *Historical Highlights of Saint Anthony's Parish, 1870–1970*, 7–11, 18, 43–45 ([1970]) — leaflets in Stearns County Historical Society, St. Cloud; "Church of Saint Stephen," 3, 5, 6, a typed manuscript, 1964, in the files of the *St. Cloud Visitor*, St. Cloud; John L. Zaplotnik, "Life of Abbot Bernard Locnikar, O.S.B.," 71–91, a typed translation containing firsthand data on St. Anthony, where Locnikar served in the 1870s, in St. John's Abbey Archives, Collegeville, copy in MHS. The material was published as a series in *Novi Svet* (Chicago) in 1944–46. See also Sisters Bernard Coleman and Vernona LaBud, *Masinaigans: The Little Book: A Biography of Monsignor Joseph F. Buh*, 69–71, 83, 98, 202 (St. Paul, 1972). The latter contains a list of 58 Slovene priests, many of whom served in Minnesota; see pp. 281–304. Stearns County plat books for the years cited are in the MHS library.

[14] Here and below, see Alexius Hoffmann, O.S.B., "Natural History of Collegeville," 70–72, 123, manuscript, 1926–34, original in St. John's Abbey Archives, Collegeville, copy in MEHP Papers. On kerchiefs, see also Ellen Jugovich, "Jugoslavian Immigration," 31, typed reminiscence, 1941, in MHS.

[15] Bea Wolak, *Recipes and Customs from the First Rural Slovenia Settlement in the United States*, 6–13 ([St. Stephen], 1971). German and Slovenian languages were gradually dropped from St. Stephen services in the 1920s, but 10% of the confessions were still made in those languages in 1964, according to "Church of Saint Stephen," 6. In the early 20th century, a third Slovene settlement developed at Sartell in Stearns County, where work opportunities in a paper mill attracted South Slav immigrants in 1906; see Lawrence De Zurik, "Sartell, Minnesota U.S.A.," 21 (June, 1975); "St. Francis Xavier Church, Sartell," 5 (June, 1973) — typed manuscripts in Stearns County Historical Society, St. Cloud.

[16] David A. Walker, *Iron Frontier: The Discovery and Early Development of Minnesota's Three Ranges*, 55–57 (St. Paul, 1979); Minnesota manuscript census schedules, Breitung Township, Tower, and Ely, St. Louis County, 1885, roll 41, microfilm in MHS; Timothy L. Smith, "Factors Affecting the Social Development of Iron Range Communities," 10, typed paper, 1963, copy in MHS;

Minnesota American Jugoslav Assn., *25th Annual State Convention*, [21].

[17] Coleman and LaBud, *Masinaigans*, 167, 168; U.S. Immigration Commission, *Immigrants in Industries*, 78:298 (61 Congress, 2 session, *Senate Documents*, no. 633 — serial 5677); Minnesota manuscript census schedules, Ely, 1895, roll 94.

Two other groups of statistics shed a little further light upon the life of 20th-century Slovenians in Ely. An analysis of municipal court records from 1903 to 1914 showed a total of 1,194 arrests, of which a possible 384 involved South Slav males and 16 South Slav females. A similar analysis of marriages performed by Ely municipal judges from 1914 to 1956 revealed 46 in which both partners were South Slavs, 11 in which the man was, and 13 in which South Slav women married non-South Slavs. Ely court and marriage records, Minnesota State Archives, MHS.

[18] Walker, *Iron Frontier*, 72; Sister Mary Daniel O'Neill, "A Survey and Interpretation of Slovenian Folk Culture on the Minnesota Iron Range," 126, master's thesis, University of Minnesota, 1952.

[19] Coleman and LaBud, *Masinaigans*, 167, 174–187; Anthony C. Schulzetenberge, "Life on the Vermilion Range Before 1900," 24, typed manuscript, 1963, copy in MHS; *Dedication of the New St. Anthony's Catholic Church*, 6, 7 (Ely, 1958).

On the newspaper, see J. M. Trunk, *Amerika in Amerikanci*, 446 (n.p., 1912). A partial file of *Amerikanski Slovenec*, which continued until 1946, is in IHRC. On Šavs, see St. Paul Seminary Register, 1896, p. [6], in St. Paul Seminary Archives, St. Paul; *St. Paul Pioneer Press*, May 19, 1944, p. 14; Julius A. Coller II, *The Shakopee Story*, 670–678 (Shakopee, 1960).

[20] Coleman and LaBud, *Masinaigans*, 190; Božidar Purić, *Naši iseljenici* (Belgrade, 1929); Jože Zavertnik, *Ameriški Slovenci*, 371–382, 555 (Chicago, 1925), translations from this source by Ann Regan are filed in MEHP Papers; Thomašić, "Americans from Croatia," 80; Robert L. Kosmerl, secretary, to June D. Holmquist, February 20, 1980, in MEHP Papers. KSKJ Board of Directors, Minutes, 1894–95, are in IHRC: Josef Stukel of Tower was its first president.

[21] Jugoslav National Home, *Program, July 14, 1935* (Ely, 1935), in IHRC; Zavertnik, *Ameriški Slovenci*, 375; Josephine I. Shepel, "The Jugoslavs in Minnesota," 9, term paper, 1941, University of Minnesota, copy in MHS; Douglas L. Aldrich, secretary, to June D. Holmquist, February 27, 1980, in MEHP Papers.

[22] Interview of Sophie Malkovich by Marjorie Hoover, February 28, 1980; Edward R. Hribar, secretary, to June D. Holmquist, March 21, 1980, notes and letter in MEHP Papers; Stipanovich, "In Unity Is Strength," 5–11, 76–79; Zavertnik, *Ameriški Slovenci*, 371, 375, 376; Minnesota American Jugoslav Assn., *25th Annual State Convention*, [36]; Frank Zaitz, "O Naših Ljudeh v Severni Minnesota," in *Ameriški Družinski Koledar*, 21:125–165 (Chicago, 1935), translation by Regan in MEHP Papers; Blatnik, "Culture Conflict," 143, 147–150. There were about 300 Minnesota subscribers in 1940 to SNPJ's newspaper *Prosveta* (New Era) published in Chicago; see SNPJ Papers, 1904–66, including membership records, in IHRC.

[23] Zavertnik, *Ameriški Slovenci*, 379; Marie Prisland, *From Slovenia To America*, 118 (Chicago, 1968); Walter Van Brunt, *Duluth and St. Louis County, Minnesota: Their Story and People*, 1:385 (Chicago and New York, 1921); Trunk, *Amerika*, 494, 499; Kitzville Village Council, Minutes, 1914–24, in Northeast Minnesota Historical Center, Duluth. For Slovene political units in Chisholm, see Blatnik, "Culture Conflict," 153–156.

South Slav descendants in the Minnesota legislature included Croatians Thomas D. Vukelich, 1939–65, Peter S. Popovich, 1941–46, A. J., George F., and Rudolph G. Perpich, 1960s–80s; and Slovenes John A. Blatnik, Jr., 1941–46, and Peter X. Fugina,

1955–61, 1963–65, 1971. In Congress Blatnik represented northeastern Minnesota, 1947–74; he was succeeded in 1975 by James L. Oberstar, whose father emigrated from Slovenia. See Bruce M. White et al., *Minnesota Votes: Election Returns by County for Presidents, Senators, Congressmen, and Governors, 1857–1977*, 220, 224 (St. Paul, 1977); Blatnik speech to Yugoslav Convention, Virginia, Minn., October 14, 1956, in Blatnik Papers, MHS; taped interviews of Perpich, 1978, in MHS, and of his parents, Anton and Mary Perpich, 1977, tapes 154–156, in IRRC. On Nick Begich, Alaska Congressman, and his brother Joe, mayor of Eveleth, see *Zajedničar* (Pittsburgh), October 25, 1972, p. 2.

[24] Here and below, see Immigration Commission, *Immigrants in Industries*, 78:301; Norman J. Setnicker, "The Development of the Biwabik Mine from 1892–1920," 38, 58–61A, master's thesis, University of Minnesota, 1968; Coleman and LaBud, *Masinaigans*, 177.

[25] Here and below, see Josip Marohnić, *Popis Hrvata u Americi*, ix, 59 (Allegheny, Pa., 1902); Setnicker, "Biwabik Mine," 97, quoting *Virginia Enterprise*, August 23, 1901; John Sirjamaki, "The People of the Mesabi Range," in *Minnesota History*, 27:207, 209, 210, 211, 213 (September, 1946); Edward Marolt, "The Development of Labor Unionism in the Iron Mining Industry of the Virginia-Eveleth District," 26, master's thesis, University of Minnesota, 1969; Minnesota American Jugoslav Assn., *25th Annual State Convention*, [19]; Mike Povich interview, tape 53, in IRRC.

[26] George O. Virtue, *Minnesota Iron Ranges*, 345–347 (U.S. Bureau of Labor, *Bulletin*, no. 84 — Washington, D.C., 1909).

[27] Immigration Commission, *Immigrants in Industries*, 78:308, 311, 314, 315, 320, 331; Smith, "Factors," 10. Neil Betten, "The Origins of Ethnic Radicalism in Northern Minnesota," in *International Migration Review*, Spring, 1970, p. 50, maintained that wages were overreported by the companies.

[28] Here and below, see Immigration Commission, *Immigrants in Industries*, 78:378, 381; Virtue, *Minnesota Iron Ranges*, 348; Smith, "Factors," 13–15. For the 1885 and 1895 figures plus extensive tables on age, sex, nativity, and households, see Joseph Stipanovich et al., "Report of the Iron Range Historical-Cultural Survey, Oct. 1, 1978–Sept. 30, 1979," 74, 122–126, 144–199, 203, 206, typed manuscript, 1979, copy in MHS.

[29] Immigration Commission, *Immigrants in Industries*, 78:368. On the 1920s laws, see Introduction. Few Croatians in South St. Paul married within their group, according to interview of Joseph W. Yager by Deborah Stultz, August 2, 1979, notes in MEHP Papers. Iron range sources also indicated that intermarriage was commonplace; for the Slovenes many mixed marriages occurred in the second generation and were the rule in the third, often occurring with non-Catholics although rarely with Finns. See Timothy L. Smith, "New Approaches to the History of Immigration in Twentieth-Century America," in *American Historical Review*, 71:1278 (July, 1966).

[30] The sample used in Tables 20.4, 20.5, showed that Minnesota registrants had owned property or registered for the draft in 13 other states. They also moved around within Minnesota. John Muhar interview, tape 48, in IRRC, recalled that he was the only one of 10 children in his family to remain in Itasca County. For the odyssey of a Minnesota Croatian miner and logger who worked in the Cusson camp and dozens of other places, see Andrew Devich Autobiography, 1976, in IHRC. See also Stipanovich et al., "Survey," 109; Immigration Commission, *Emigration Conditions in Europe*, 12:387; Syrjamaki, "Mesabi Communities," 130. Croatian remittances to the homeland, 1892–1902, were estimated at $13,000,000; Prpic, *Croatian Immigrants*, 153, 213, 402.

[31] Peter Cviyanovich, in St. Vasilije Serbian Orthodox Church, *Golden Jubilee Souvenir Book*, [i] (Chisholm, 1960); Walker, *Iron Frontier*, 246–258; Syrjamaki, "Mesabi Communities," 126, 242, 243; Duluth Roman Catholic Diocese, "Annual Reports of

Parishes," in Duluth Chancery, membership abstracts by Marjorie Hoover in MEHP Papers. For Carson Lake, see also Mrs. Barbara Raich interview, tape 43, and an undated map showing South Slav households by street and by family name, both in IRRC.

On Cusson, a Virginia and Rainy Lake Lumber Company logging camp, see Alien Registration forms, in Minnesota Commission of Public Safety (PSC) Records, St. Louis County, Cusson, Minnesota State Archives, MHS; C. M. Oehler, *Time in the Timber*, 15, 16, 19, 48 (St. Paul, 1948).

[32] Bell, "The Mesabe and Vermillion Ore Ranges," 4, in William J. Bell Papers, MHS.

[33] *Kumstvo* survived in Minnesota in the 1980s. See Helen Vujovich, "The Serbians," 2, typed paper, 1979, in MEHP Papers; joint interview of Lillian and John Kendall, Matt Kovacic, Helen Badalich, and Mildred Palla of South St. Paul by Deborah Stultz, August 2, 1979, notes in MEHP Papers, hereafter referred to as Croatian Hall interview.

[34] Blatnik, "Culture Conflict," 58–62, 103–109, 124, 134; Immigration Commission, *Immigrants in Industries*, 78:321, 323; Stipanovich, "Survey," 144, 157–160. Smith, in *American Historical Review*, 71:1270, 1274, and Tomašić, "Americans from Croatia," 194–215, 236, called attention to the "mediating" role of ethnic businessmen. See also Josef J. Barton, "Eastern and Southern Europeans," in John Higham, ed., *Ethnic Leadership in America*, 150–161, 166–168, 170 (Baltimore, 1978).

[35] Immigration Commission, *Immigrants in Industries*, 78:348–350; LeRoy Hodges, "Immigrant Life in the Ore Region of Northern Minnesota," in *Survey*, 28:708 (September 7, 1912); Setnicker, "Biwabik Mine," 86; Prpic, *Croatian Immigrants*, 153–156; Virtue, *Minnesota Iron Ranges*, 357–359.

On *zadruga* see, for example, Dinko A. Tomašić, *Personality and Culture in Eastern European Politics*, 149–205 (New York, 1948). On the persistence nationally of patriarchal households and other practices, see John Bodnar, "Immigration and Modernization: The Case of Slavic Peasants in Industrial America," in *Journal of Social History*, 10:46 (Fall, 1976); Gerald Rosenblum, *Immigrant Workers*, 123–128 (New York, 1973); and oral history data on coal and copper miners available for comparison in South Slav Archive, Marriott Library, University of Utah, Salt Lake City.

[36] Thomas A. Dasovich, "My Yugoslav Background," in *Minnesota History*, 28:250–252 (September, 1947).

[37] Here and three paragraphs below, see Theodore Vuicich, in St. Vasilije Church, *Golden Jubilee Souvenir Book*, 32. Additional reminiscences on South Slav boardinghouses may be found in Devich autobiography and Anthony Grebenc, "Tales of the Old Country and Activities of the Immigrants," chapters 2, 4 — both in IHRC; taped interviews of Rade Popovich, Helen Drazenovich Berklich, and Mary Furlong, tapes 19, 34, 113, in IRRC; interview of Angela Blatnik by Marjorie Hoover, April 30, 1980, notes in MEHP Papers.

[38] Immigration Commission, *Immigrants in Industries*, 78:252, 277, 321; Govorchin, *Americans from Yugoslavia*, 182–184.

[39] For a broader look at the role of the boardinghouse in the U.S., see John Modell and Tamara K. Hareven, "Urbanization and the Malleable Household: An Examination of Boarding and Lodging in American Families," in *Journal of Marriage and the Family*, 35:467–479 (August, 1973). See also "Passing of an Era," in Pickands Mather Company, *PM Iron News*, August–September, 1959, p. 12; *Chisholm Free Press*, August 8, 1963, p. [11]; Stipanovich, "Survey," 159; Croatian Hall interview, August 2, 1979; interview of Mildred Palla by Deborah Stultz, June 25, 1979, notes in MEHP Papers.

[40] Immigration Commission, *Immigrants in Industries*, 78:341, 342; Chambers, "Social Welfare Policies," 4; Smith, "Factors," 16; Govorchin, *Americans from Yugoslavia*, 191–193; Louis Adamic, *Laughing in the Jungle: The Autobiography of an Immigrant in*

America, 107 (New York, 1932); Stipanovich, "In Unity Is Strength," 80, 98–109.

[41] Murders and shootings were reported, for example, in *Eveleth News*, May 22, 1907, p. 1, September 25, 1907, p. 1; *Hibbing Tribune*, February 14, 1907, p. 3, September 18, 25, 1907, p. 1, August 14, 1908, p. 1. Balch, *Our Slavic Fellow Citizens*, opposite p. 307, pictured a Croatian saloon in Hibbing. On the saloonkeeper described in the text, whose name was Steve Zgonc, see *Chisholm Herald*, February 3, March 3, July 21, August 11, October 6, 1905; April 20, May 11, 1906; January 11, March 15, 1907; July 17, November 20, December 11, 1908. All these stories appeared on page 1.

[42] Prpic, *Croatian Immigrants*, 158; Mladineo, ed., *Narodni Adresar*, 350, 361, 362, 366, 370. On ethnic music, see note 83, below.

[43] For opening, moving, and closing of local stores, see, for example, *Chisholm Herald*, May 4, 1906, January 11, 1907, October 2, 1908 — all p. 1. Grocery and meat markets in 1937 were listed in Chisholm, Crosby, Ely, Eveleth, Gilbert, and Keewatin; on these and other Minnesota South Slav businesses, see note 69, below; Mladineo, ed., *Narodni Adresar*, 345–370; ads in American Yugoslav Assn. of Minnesota, *Golden Anniversary Booklet*, 3, 4, 6, 8, 14, 26, 28, 31, 32 ([Chisholm?], 1974), copy in Iron Range Historical Society, Gilbert; South St. Paul Commercial Club, *South St. Paul and Inver Grove Directory, 1915*, 44 (South St. Paul, [1915]).

[44] Here and below, see Stipanovich, "In Unity Is Strength," 55, 76–79; Sava Vuković, ed., *The Serbian Orthodox Church Through 750 Years* (Cleveland, 1969); Bozidar Dragicevich, "American Serb," 81–85, 90–95, 100–112, master's thesis, University of Minnesota, 1973; Prpic, *South Slavic Immigration*, 193–195. Three additional Minnesota Serbian churches existed in 1981: St. Sava (South St. Paul) built in 1950, St. Michael's Orthodox Church (Hibbing) chartered in 1959, and Mala Gospojina Free Serbian Orthodox Church in the Duluth suburb of Gary dedicated in 1970. See Dragicevich, "American Serb," 108–114, 118–125.

[45] Prpic, *Croatian Immigrants*, 193; Gunther Rothenberg, *The Military Border in Croatia, 1740–1881*, 12 (Chicago, 1966); Chambers, "Social Welfare Policies," 65–76, 81.

Croatians were among the members of at least 13 Roman Catholic churches in range communities, where the shift to English services began as early as 1903 in Virginia and, except for special occasions, was carried out in the 1930s by those at Aurora, Buhl, Chisholm, Eveleth, Gilbert, Mountain Iron, Nashwauk, and Tower; Catholic Archdiocese of St. Paul and Minneapolis, Parish Questionnaires, 1948, originals in Catholic Historical Society, St. Paul Seminary, St. Paul, microfilm in MHS, hereafter cited as Parish Questionnaires; Works Projects Administration (WPA), Minnesota Historical Records Survey: Churches, 1936–41, in MHS; Duluth Diocese, "Annual Reports of Parishes."

[46] Here and below, see Prpic, *Croatian Immigrants*, 125–127, 264, 416–420; Govorchin, *Americans from Yugoslavia*, 117, 133; Vladimir Markotic, comp. and ed., *Biographical Directory of Americans and Canadians of Croatian Descent With Institutions, Organizations, Their Officers and Periodicals*, 4:151–154 (Research Centre for Canadian Ethnic Studies, *Occasional Monograph No. 1* — Calgary, 1973); Bernard M. Luketich, president, to June D. Holmquist, September 11, 1979, in MEHP Papers.

[47] Govorchin, *Americans from Yugoslavia*, 118; Notes on Serbian Organizations, in Writers' Project, Yugoslavs in Minnesota file, WPA Papers; Dragicevich, "American Serb," 74–79; Mladineo, ed., *Narodni Adresar*, 338–382; Robert R. Stone, president, to June D. Holmquist, January 26, 1981, in MEHP Papers.

[48] Bodnar, in *Journal of Social History*, 10:51; Prpic, *Croatian Immigrants*, 262–265, 420; Zaitz, in *Ameriški Družinski Koledar*, 21:124–165; Markotic, *Croatian Directory*, 120. For a comparison of

the bylaws of various South Slav lodges, see Tomašić, "Americans from Croatia," 97–114, 278, 281, 286, 289, 301.

[49] Tomašić, "Americans from Croatia," 186; Govorchin, *Americans from Yugoslavia*, 327; Joseph Stipanovich, "Collective Economic Activity Among Serb, Croat, and Slovene Immigrants," in Scott Cummings, ed., *Self-Help in Urban America: Patterns of Minority Business Enterprise*, 160–176 (Port Washington, N.Y., 1980). On the decline of fraternals, see Robert H. Leibman, "Yugoslavs on the Range," 10, typed report, 1978, of a survey made in connection with the Iron Range Historical Society and the Minnesota Folklife Center, used with the author's permission, copy in MEHP Papers.

[50] Interview of Samuel E. Swanson by Jack Spiese, October 27, 1967, p. 36, original at Pennsylvania State University, University Park, Pa., typed copy in MHS; Syrjamaki, "Mesabi Communities," 206; Hyman Berman, "Education for Work and Labor Solidarity: The Immigrant Miners and Radicalism on the Mesabi Range," 22, 24, typed paper, 1963, copy in MHS; Marolt, "Development of Labor Unionism," 162–167; Setnicker, "Biwabik Mine," 98. The Jugoslav Socialist Federation Papers, 1906–52, are in IHRC.

On the Socialist movement among South Slavs, see Berman, "Education for Work," 32, 34; Stipanovich, "In Unity Is Strength," 93–139, 155, 159–164; Charles Leinenweber, "The American Socialist Party and 'New' Immigrants," in *Science & Sanity*, 32:17–25 (Winter, 1968). On the Finns, see Chapter 15, above.

[51] Berman, "Education for Work," 38–42; Marolt, "Development of Labor Unionism," 33, 44–50; *Hibbing Tribune*, September 5, 1907, p. 1.

On the strikes, see Neil Betten, "Strike on the Mesabi — 1907," and "Riot, Revolution, Repression in the Iron Range Strike of 1916," in *Minnesota History*, 40:340–347, 41:82–93 (Fall, 1967, Summer, 1968); Setnicker, "Biwabik Mine," 128–135; Marolt, "Development of Labor Unionism," 61–95; Chapters 15, 24.

[52] *Eveleth News*, p. 1, quoted in Marolt, "Development of Labor Unionism," 25; Berman, "Education for Work," 43.

[53] On Rauch, Gheen, Greaney, and Silverdale, see Trunk, *Amerika*, 498; John Skraba interview, tape 5, in IRRC; Charlotte Von Alman *et al.*, comps., *Silverdale Rauch Bramble*, 24, 30, 37, 38, 42, 45, 48, 55, 56, 89, 126 (Marceline, Mo., 1979). On Nebish, see Catholic Diocese of Crookston, *Our Northland Diocese*, September, 1960, p. 4.

On Goodland and Greaney, see interview of Sister Mary Margaret Radaich by Deborah Stultz, June 1, 1979, notes in MEHP Papers; Duluth Diocese, "Annual Reports of Parishes"; Lydon, in *Acta et Dicta*, 5:273; "Greaney, Minn.," in *Ave Maria Koledar, 1930*, 219 (Chicago, [1930?]); Alien Registration forms, in PSC Records; Zaitz, in *Ameriški Družinski Koledar*, 21:163 (1935). The number of settlements in 1937 is in Mladineo, ed., *Narodni Adresar*, 911.

[54] Donald G. Sofchalk, "Organized Labor and the Iron Ore Miners of Northern Minnesota," in *Labor History*, 12:217, 239–242 (Spring, 1971); Betten, in *International Migration Review*, Spring, 1970, pp. 44–55. For brief histories of existing Steel Workers locals in Calumet, Duluth, Ely, Eveleth, Hibbing, Nashwauk, and Virginia, see Minnesota CIO, *Directory and Fourth Annual Convention Brochure, 1941*, 39–41 ([Hibbing?], 1941). For a useful review of ethnicity theories and voting choice, see James E. Wright, "The Ethnocultural Model of Voting: A Behavioral and Historical Critique," in *American Behavioral Scientist*, 16:653–674 (May–June, 1973). See also Millard L. Gieske, *Minnesota Farmer-Laborism: The Third-Party Alternative*, 325–328 (Minneapolis, 1979).

[55] CIO Iron Range Industrial Union Council, Minutes, October 10, 1937, March 10, 1940, in MHS. A South Slav biographical card file compiled by Joseph Stipanovich in MEHP Papers shows interesting interrelationships during this period.

⁵⁶ For background on the PSC, see Introduction, above. On South Slavs in PSC Records, see, for example, Ely Slavonic Catholic Union telegram to President Wilson, December 7, 1917; Anthony Pleva to John Lind, August 26, 29, 1917, April 29, 1918, and to the commission, November 14, 1917; E. A. Bergeron to W. I. Prince, October 15, 1917; George L. Brozich to H. W. Libby, March 11, 1918; B. Vosnjak to the commission, March 21, 1918; Slovenian Republican Alliance loyalty resolutions, Ely, Aurora, and Eveleth branches, April 14, 16, May 8, 1918; Aimee Fisher to Mrs. M. M. Booth, January 2, 1919, enclosing the Americanization report of the Minnesota Woman's Committee, Council of National Defense and Commission of Public Safety.

For overlapping records, see Anthony Pleva to John Lind, July 14, 1917, attached to Lind to Burnquist, July 20, 1917, Burnquist Papers, Governor's files, Minnesota State Archives; M. I. Pupin, Serbian consul, to T. G. Winter, July 13, 1917; reports of investigators D.J.G., June 3–July 25, 1917, and no. 45 of the Pinkerton Detective Agency, August 5–16, 1917, in Report files, Correspondence and Miscellaneous Records, Woman's Committee (Minneapolis), Council of National Defense, War Records Commission Records, State Archives.

⁵⁷ Vuicich, in St. Vasilije Church, *Golden Jubilee Souvenir Book*, 32.

⁵⁸ Immigration Commission, *Immigrants in Industries*, 78:340; *Biwabik Times*, July 7, 1907, quoted in Setnicker, "Biwabik Mine," 124; C. Whit Pfeiffer, "From 'Bohunks' to Finns: The Scale of Life among the Ore Strippings of the Northwest," in *Survey*, 36:13 (April 1, 1916); J. S. Roucek, "The Image of the Slav in U.S. History and in Immigration Policy," in *American Journal of Economics and Sociology*, 28:29–48 (January, 1969).

⁵⁹ For reports on South Slav volunteers in the earlier Balkan wars and their loyalty activities in the U.S. in World War I, see *Commercial West*, November 23, 1912, p. 10; *Duluth News Tribune*, October 19, 1912, p. 3; *Duluth Herald*, October 10, 1918, p. 12; *Chisholm Tribune-Herald*, April 13, 1917, p. 1; *Eveleth Mining News*, July 12, 1917, p. [1]; *Ely Miner*, March 22, 1918, p. [1]; KSKJ, *Jubilejna Spomisnka Knjiga*, 57 (Cleveland, [1924]). On the disappearance of Bulgars and Montenegrins, see Syrjamaki, "Mesabi Communities," 123, 124. See also Joseph P. O'Grady, ed., *The Immigrants' Influence on Wilson's Peace Policies*, 173–203 (Lexington, Ky., 1967); Kraljic, *Croatian Migration*, 102. Jugoslav Republican Alliance Papers may be found in IHRC.

⁶⁰ Smith, "Educational Beginnings," 11, 14; Herbert Blair to J. W. Richardson, April 8, 1924, copy in Grace Lee Nute Papers, University of Minnesota-Duluth Library, used with permission.

⁶¹ Here and below, see calculations for St. Louis County sample, in MEHP Papers; C. C. Alexander, "Survey of Hibbing Night Schools from 1909 to 1922," 1, 2, 4; Florence Lang, "Americanizing Our Foreign Born," 1, 8; anonymous, "Americanizing the Immigrant Woman Through the Home Teacher," 1–5, 8 [1924?]; R. K. Doe, ["History of the Americanization Movement in Northern Minnesota, 1906–1924"], 1–9 — all in Nute Papers.

⁶² Here and below, see Minnesota American Jugoslav Assn., *25th Annual State Convention*, [42], and *Golden Anniversary Booklet*, 15; membership data in John Tomavich notes, August 20, 1940, Nute Papers; United American Slavs of Minnesota, *By-Laws* (Minneapolis and St. Paul, 1939), copy in MHS; *Centennial Roaring Stoney Days, Ely, 1888–1958*, 93. On AJAM, see *Eveleth Clarion*, October 29, 1925, p. 1; *Duluth News-Tribune*, July 24, 1980, region sec., 8A; Blatnik, "Culture Conflict," 144, 150; Rudy Perpich to Frances Kosnik, secretary, April 6, 1971, in Perpich Papers.

⁶³ Walker, *Iron Frontier*, 62, 116; Dragicevich, "American Serb," 13; interviews of Dan Bastie, May 19, 1980, and Eli and Dorothy Kovich, George Knezevich, Father Varnava Minich, Katie Bruich, Millie Belich, Joseph R. Balach, all by Marjorie Hoover, February

14, 1980, hereafter cited as St. George Fellowship Hall interview, notes in MEHP Papers; Minnesota Power and Light Company, *Contact Magazine*, June–July, 1976, p. 5.

⁶⁴ Zavertnik, *Ameriški Slovenci*, 273; Trunk, *Amerika*, 446; Zaitz, in *Ameriški Družinski Koledar*, 21:151. Here and below, see *Narodni Vestnik*, April 13, 1911, pp. 2, 3; August 10, 1911, p. 2; May 18, 1917, p. 2, microfilm in IHRC. No complete file has been located. On the Croatian journal, below, see Govorchin, *Americans from Yugoslavia*, 157.

⁶⁵ Prpic, *Croatian Immigration*, 207, 327; St. Vasilije Church, *Golden Jubilee Souvenir Book*, 28.

⁶⁶ St. George Serbian Church, *40th Anniversary Souvenir Booklet*, 1 (Duluth, 1963), and *Golden Anniversary*, n.p. (Duluth, 1973); Mala Gospojina Free Serbian Orthodox Church, *Consecration Ceremonies* (Duluth, 1970) — all in Northeast Minnesota Historical Center, copies in MEHP Papers. The names of those who served as *kum* for various structures are given in these booklets. See also *Duluth News-Tribune*, January 6, 1957, p. 40, November 28, 1971, p. 14; St. George Fellowship Hall interview, February 14, 1980; interviews of Mr. and Mrs. Rade Bruich, February 21, 1980, and Steve Balach, March 20, 1980 — all by Marjorie Hoover, notes in MEHP Papers. Additional data may be found in Dragicevich, "American Serb," whose author served as pastor of St. George from 1961 to 1979. On DPs in Duluth, see note 4, above.

⁶⁷ *Duluth Budgeteer*, July 27, 1977, pp. 4, 21; Zavertnik, *Ameriški Slovenci*, 273. Other employers of South Slavs were also primarily metal-working firms, such as Zenith Furnace Co., Atlas Iron and Brass Works, and during World War I, McDougall-Barnes Shipbuilders; see Industries file, Duluth Public Library. See also S. Balach and Bastie interviews, March 20, May 19, 1980.

⁶⁸ Here and below, see Tone Zrnec, C.M., *Po Baragovi deželi*, 106 (Toronto, 1969), Regan translation; St. Elizabeth Church, *25th Silver Jubilee*, n.p. (Duluth, 1938); interviews of Bastie, May 19, 1980, and Father Willard Spehn of St. Elizabeth, May 26, 1980, by Hoover, notes in MEHP Papers; Zavertnik, *Ameriški Slovenci*, 273; "New Duluth," in *Ave Maria Koledar, 1930*, 227–229; Duluth Diocese, "Annual Reports of Parishes"; Parish Questionnaires, 1948; *Duluth News-Tribune*, December 8, 1938, p. 11. In the 1920s and 1930s, according to the above-cited Parish Reports, Slovenes and Croats also attended Good Shepherd Roman Catholic Church and to a lesser extent St. John the Evangelist and St. Margaret Mary. St. Elizabeth erected a new building in 1958.

⁶⁹ *Duluth City Directory, 1920, 1924, 1926*, extracted by Hoover, in MEHP Papers; interviews of S. Balach, March 20, 1980, Mr. and Mrs. Alex Smolnikar, February 26, 1980, and Nick Borovac, March 19, 1980, by Hoover, notes in MEHP Papers; "The Gary Athletic Club Story, 1930–1980," in Northeast Minnesota Historical Center. For a brief history of the International Institute of Duluth, see *Duluth News-Tribune*, October 9, 1955, feature sec., p. 27.

⁷⁰ Interviews of Smolnikars, February 26, 1980, St. George Fellowship Hall, February 14, 1980, Orescanins, April 25, 1980, S. Balach, March 20, 1980. See also Ida B. Davis, "A Social Study of Gary-New Duluth," 8, typed report, 1929, International Institute of Duluth Papers, Northeast Minnesota Historical Center.

⁷¹ Orescanins interview, April 25, 1980; interview of Sophie Malkovich, Minnie Boben, and Sophie Churchya, by Hoover, February 28, 1980, notes in MEHP Papers.

⁷² *Duluth Budgeteer*, July 27, 1977, pp. 4, 21; Duluth Planning and Development Dept., *Gary-New Duluth Neighborhood Plan*, 4–6 (Duluth, 1978); International Institute, "Report of Joint Study Committee . . . Meeting with Miss Ethel Bird, September 7, 1939," p. 1, International Institute of Duluth Papers.

⁷³ No recognizable South Slav communities in the Twin Cities were revealed by the MEHP. South Slavs are said to have migrated there from South St. Paul, obtaining work at first as unskilled labor-

ers or factory hands. Minneapolis had a scattered 30 families in 1903, over 1,100 persons in 1910, 398 in 1920, and only 290 in 1930. St. Paul had 207 and 90 in 1920 and 1930, respectively, a fair number of whom lived in Wards 8 and 10 north of Marshall Ave. between the Capitol and Lexington Ave. A chapter of the Serb National Federation is said to have operated in Minneapolis from 1909 to 1932 when it merged with one in South St. Paul. A housing survey in Minneapolis in 1934 identified only 28 families of Bulgars and Serbs scattered through the city's 13 wards. Slovenians and Croatians were not listed, and it is assumed they were among the 441 families designated merely as "Slav." By the 1930s Slovenes were reputedly living on small farms near the Twin Cities, where they were active in beekeeping, an enterprise fostered by Francis Jager, a Catholic priest who farmed at St. Bonifacius west of Minneapolis and taught beekeeping at the University of Minnesota farm school in St. Paul from 1913 to 1928.

See U.S., *Census*, 1910, *Population*, 1:1013; 1920, 3:524; 1930, 2:381, 384; Herman E. Olson, *Minneapolis Property and Housing Survey* (Minneapolis, 1934); Trunk, *Amerika*, 499; Zaitz, in *Ameriški Družinski Koledar*, 21:163; Tomavich notes, August 15, 1940, in Nute Papers; Zivka Scheglowski, "Serbs in South St. Paul and Minneapolis," 15, course paper, 1972, University of Minnesota, copy in MEHP Papers. For a brief history of Russian-Serbian Holy Trinity Orthodox Church, founded in 1916 in St. Paul, see *25th Year Jubilee*, 5–8 ([St. Paul], 1941), in International Institute of Minnesota Papers, IHRC.

[74] H. Bruce Price, ed., *The Marketing of Farm Products: Studies in the Organization of the Twin Cities Market*, 108 (Minneapolis, 1927); Charles E. Bottemiller, "Meat and Men in Minnesota — The St. Paul Union Stockyards to 1907," 47–51, 70–72, master's thesis, University of Minnesota, 1963.

[75] On the "first" Croats and Serbs, see Frank Rech notes, [1940], and Tomavich notes, 1940, Nute Papers; Scheglowski, "Serbs in South St. Paul," 13, 14.

[76] Croatian Hall interview, August 2, 1979; Palla interview, June 25, 1979; Scheglowski, "Serbs in South St. Paul," 14, 15.

[77] Scheglowski, "Serbs in South St. Paul," 14.

[78] The samples here and below were drawn from Alien Registration forms, Dakota County, South St. Paul, PSC Records. See also Palla interview, June 25, 1979; Croatian Hall interview, August 2, 1979. In 1920 an estimated 80 Serb families lived in the hilltop settlement along with perhaps 250 Croats; Scheglowski, "Serbs in South St. Paul," 17.

[79] Russian-Serbian Holy Trinity Orthodox Church, *Short History 1916–1941*, 5, 9, in International Institute of Minnesota Papers; Tomavich notes, August 15, 1940, Nute Papers; Vujovich, "The Serbians," 2; Scheglowski, "Serbs in South St. Paul," 17. On St. Sava Church, see *South St. Paul Reporter*, August 7, 1963, p. B11.

In 1980 *kolac*, as baked by a Duluth woman, was a round loaf on top of which she made a cross in the dough. In each quarter of the cross she placed the letter "C." The four "C's" stood, she said, for a Serbian saying meaning "Only unity saved the Serbs." K. Bruich interview, February 21, 1980.

[80] Here and below, Croatian Hall interview, August 2, 1979; Festival of Nations programs in International Institute of Minnesota Papers; interviews of Ellen Wold, June 27, 1979, Pallas, June 25,

1979, Anna Dragich, June 19, 1979, Mary Spraitz, June 20, 1979, and J. Kendall, October 18, 1979, by Stultz, notes in MEHP Papers. See also Grace Lee Nute, "Trip to South St. Paul to Rehearsal of the Tambouritza Orchestra at Croatian Hall with Dr. Frank Gouze," December 4, 1946, and Rech notes — both in Nute Papers.

[81] Here and below, see Scheglowski, "Serbs in South St. Paul," 18; interview of Dave Petek by Stultz, June 19, 1979, notes in MEHP Papers; J. Kendall interview, October 18, 1979; interview of Mrs. Blanche Casanova, July 27, 1977, typed transcript, in West Central Minnesota Historical Center, Morris; South St. Paul Commercial Club, *South St. Paul and Inver Grove Directory, 1915*, 28, 44; Mladineo, ed., *Narodni Adresar*, 337–382, 900–908.

[82] Petek interview, June 19, 1979; Wold interview, June 27, 1979; Croatian Hall interview, August 2, 1979; *South St. Paul Sun*, August 20, 1980, p. 1A; Mladen D. Trbuhovich, ed., *10th Jubilee Minnesota Serbian Day, 1957*, 10 (Chisholm, 1957).

[83] On food, see Joseph Paternost, "Slovenian Language on Minnesota's Iron Range: Some Sociolinguistic Aspects of Language Maintenance and Language Shift," in *General Linguistics*, 16:135 (Summer, Fall, 1976); Dragicevich, "American Serb," 168; interview of L. Kendall by Stultz, February 7, 1980, notes in MEHP Papers; Mary Hart column in *Minneapolis Tribune*, January 24, 1980, p. 6C. On music and dance groups, see Paternost, 16:136; James R. Baldrica, "Tamburitza Music, History and Origin on the Iron Range of Minnesota," Plan B paper, University of Minnesota, 1978, copy in MHS; Leibman, "Yugoslavs on the Iron Range," 48–68; Shepel, "Jugoslavs in Minnesota," 12–16; Thomas F. Magner, "Minnesota Guslar," in *Minnesota History*, 34:296 (Autumn, 1955), on Risto Grk, perhaps the last of the state's *guslar*, who was still performing in South St. Paul in the 1950s. Several writers mentioned especially the popularity of "Moja Decla" as "practically an Iron Range theme song" to which many people knew the Slovene words but few understood their meaning; see, for example, O'Neill, "Slovenian Folk Culture on the Iron Range," 117.

[84] Vujovich, "The Serbians," 2; Croatian Hall interview, August 2, 1979; *Duluth News-Tribune*, January 6, 1957, p. 40; Dragicevich, "American Serb," 85–88; Paternost, in *General Linguistics*, 16:141; O'Neill, "Slovenian Folk Culture on the Iron Range," 47–89, 93, 98–108, 124, 133–150.

[85] Joshua A. Fishman *et al.*, *Language Loyalty in the United States*, 42, 46 (The Hague, 1966); Paternost, in *General Linguistics*, 16:103, 107, 109, 113, 145.

[86] For some information on South Slav internal migrations, see Colakovic, *Yugoslav Migrations*, 128–136. The comment on the development of an "iron ranger" concept was made by Mrs. Veda Polnikvar, editor of the *Chisholm Free Press*, in an interview by Carlton Qualey, October, 1973, notes in MEHP Papers. The concept is also apparent in a poem entitled "Why Is a Ranger?" in H. E. Lager, *Happy Depression On The Iron Range*, 102 (Virginia, 1979). For a comparison, see David E. Whisnant, "Ethnicity and the Recovery of Regional Identity in Appalachia," in Sallie TeSelle, *The Rediscovery of Ethnicity*, 124–138 (New York, 1973).

[87] *Midland Cooperative Builder* (Superior, Wis.), March 6, 1975, p. 1; Paternost, in *General Linguistics*, 16:137–141; Grebenc, "Tales of the Old Country," 4; *Zajedničar*, August 28, 1974, p. 5.

CHAPTER 21

East Slavs
RUSINS, UKRAINIANS, RUSSIANS, AND BELORUSSIANS

Keith P. Dyrud

IN THE CENTURY from the 1870s to the 1970s an estimated 500,000 to 600,000 East Slavic people who referred to themselves as Ruthenians, Rusins, Ukrainians, or Russians immigrated to the United States from eastern Europe. By 1980 some 1,800,000 East Slavic immigrants and their descendants lived in the United States. Although Pennsylvania, New York, and New Jersey were the major early centers of East Slavic settlement, some 5,000 to 10,000 found their way to Minnesota (see Table 21.1), where they made their homes primarily in the Twin Cities but also in smaller communities in the northern and central parts of the state.[1]

The first such immigrants, who seem to have migrated as individuals, reached North America long before the 19th century, but the mass migration of East Slavs did not get under way until the 1870s; it continued until the outbreak of World War 1. A number of political refugees emigrated after World War I following the 1917 revolutions in Russia; a larger number of political emigrants known as Displaced Persons arrived after World War II. Minnesota received few of the first group, but several thousand East Slavic Displaced Persons reached the state in the late 1940s and early 1950s.[2]

The main difficulty in discussing East Slavic peoples occurs in distinguishing the various groups among them. Complexity is the outstanding feature in the history of eastern Europe, not least in the areas where East Slavs lived.

Geography, language, and religion are three criteria which may separate one culture from another. The geographic criterion of the origins of the East Slavs in the borderlands of present Romania, Poland, Czechoslovakia, and the Union of Soviet Socialist Republics is not particularly helpful in this effort (see Map 21.1). For example, Ruthenian settlement centered in and near the Carpathian Mountains, which formed part of the boundary between Poland and Hungary. Though they were a geographic and political border area, the Carpathians functioned only in a limited way as a cultural demarcation: East Slavs lived on both sides of the mountains.[3]

As for the second criterion — language — many East Slav immigrants and their descendants are either uncertain of the language of their ancestors or believe that Russian, Ukrainian, Belorussian, and Carpatho-Rusyn are simply dialects of one language, which they often refer to as Russian, or Slavish, or simply *po-nashomu* (which means, literally, in our own way). Many others, especially those who identify themselves as Ukrainians, make clear distinctions between Russian, Belorussian, and Ukrainian, each of which they consider a distinct language.[4]

In certain time periods, the third criterion — religious affiliation — can be helpful in determining which East Slavic group was which. In the 19th century, for example, some were members of the Byzantine Rite Catholic church, called at the time the Greek Catholic or Uniate church, which combined Eastern Orthodox ritual and practice with recognition of the pope in Rome as its head. Others belonged to the Russian (or Eastern) Orthodox church, which had successfully Russified the Ukrainian Orthodox church after the Great Russian political takeover of Ukraine in 1654. But, as we shall see, even the religious lines between certain groups became blurred in the United States.[5]

The pieces of this puzzle germane to Minnesota include Rusins (Ruthenians), Ukrainians, Belorussians, and Great Russians. Ruthenians, or Rusins, who were for the most part members of the Byzantine Rite (or Greek) Catholic church, emigrated from three regions of eastern Europe

Table 21.1. Ukrainians, Ruthenians, and Russians in Minnesota, 1910–70

	Ukrainians & Ruthenians		Russians	
	foreign born	foreign stock	foreign born	foreign stock
1910	66	80	823	1,517
1920	585	715	4,232	8,562
1930	647		3,443	
1940	520	1,020	4,180	7,380
1960	1,947		2,447	
1970		1,120		3,392

Source: Mother-tongue data in U.S., *Census*, for years listed; 1940 *Special Report: Nativity and Parentage of the White Population, Mother Tongue.*

Note: In 1930, 206 of the foreign born were Ruthenians. Foreign stock includes foreign born and native born of foreign or mixed parentage.

Map 21.1. East Slavs' Homelands

which were part of Austria-Hungary until after World War I: (1) eastern Galicia, now in the western portion of the Ukrainian Soviet Socialist Republic; (2) Subcarpathia, now divided between northeastern Czechoslovakia and the Transcarpathian region of the Ukrainian Soviet Socialist Republic; and (3) Bukovina, now partly in northern Romania and partly in Soviet Ukraine.

Ruthenian was a generic term used to describe all Byzantine Rite (Greek) Catholics who immigrated to the United States before 1914 from eastern Galicia, northern Bukovina, and Subcarpathia. Because of new patterns of religious and national associations that evolved in the United States, those Ruthenians from eastern Galicia and northern Bukovina came to identify themselves as Ukrainians or as Carpatho-Russians (or sometimes simply as Russians), while those

from Subcarpathia continued to identify themselves as Ruthenians or more often as Rusins or Carpatho-Rusins. In this essay, "Rusin" will refer to immigrants and their descendants from Subcarpathia; "Ukrainian" or "Galician" will refer to immigrants and their descendants from eastern Galicia and northern Bukovina.[6]

The term "Russian" is often used in Minnesota sources to identify members of Russian Orthodox churches regardless of their geographical place of origin in eastern Europe. Some who called themselves Russians, at least in the early period of Minnesota immigration, were Greek Catholics from Subcarpathia and Galicia who converted to Russian Orthodoxy after their arrival. Others were Russian Orthodox immigrants who left eastern Ukraine or Bukovina before Ukrainian nationalism became widespread among the peasants there. A few Belorussians (also known as "White Russians") and "Great Russians" from Russia proper immigrated to Minnesota, but most of the people who arrived from the Russian Empire and who often described themselves as Russians were actually Jews (see Tables 21.2, 21.3).[7]

The geographic, linguistic, and religious criteria applicable to the East Slavs, though relatively objective, are complicated enough. But another more desirable way of defining an ethnic group — in terms of its people's own changing perceptions of who they are — is nearly impossible to trace for the East Slavs in an essay of this scope. Until recently scholars have achieved little agreement in attempts to define the shifting identities of East Slav groups.

Such an effort does not grow easier as one progresses in time from the 19th to the 20th centuries. For example, though the Ukrainians had defined themselves as such by the period between World Wars I and II, many of those who arrived in Minnesota in the 1950s joined a Russian Orthodox church newly founded by refugees who considered themselves Russians and hoped eventually to return to Russia. Apparently these Russian and Ukrainian immigrants felt they had more in common with each other than with members of earlier-established Russian and Ukrainian churches.[8]

The Rusins, if they continued to identify themselves as such in the second generation, sometimes found that their relatives in the Old Country did not consider themselves a part of any national group. One Minnesota-born man whose parents had emigrated from the village of Stebník in the Sáros district in Hungary (now Šariš County in Czechoslovakia) visited his first cousins there in 1966. One of them "stated emphatically that they are not Russians, not Ukrainians, not Slovaks, not Czechs, not Hungarians, but merely Sarizane." The American did not at first understand, but he later realized that his cousin "was merely saying that he was a resident of Šariš, which is equivalent to my saying I am a Minnesotan."[9]

On the other hand, people who may at one time have considered themselves Rusins — or maybe just Šarišane — by converting to Russian Orthodoxy in Minnesota came to regard themselves as Russians rather than Rusins. It does them no favor, therefore, to insist on calling them Rusins if they refer to themselves as Russians — once we understand that their origins in eastern Europe were not within the 19th-century Russian Empire. But some of the descendants of converts apparently felt ambivalent about the matter. One observed in 1973 that in his opinion those in Minneapolis were "inclined too slavishly to emphasize purely Great-

Table 21.2. Ruthenian Migration to and from Minnesota

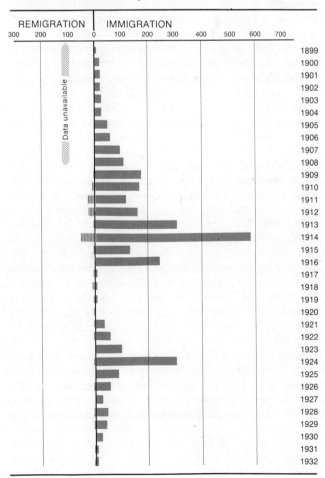

Table 21.3. Russian Migration to and from Minnesota

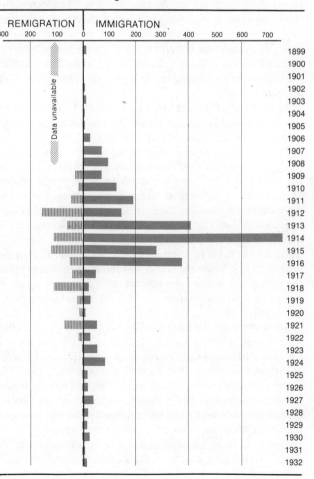

Russian customs, dances, music and to ignore our real Rusyn ethnic heritage."[10]

The Twin Cities

The earliest East Slavs to arrive in the state in any numbers were Rusins, who began to migrate to Minnesota in 1878 from one of the poorest parts of eastern Europe or from Pennsylvania, where some of them had settled earlier. After the elimination of serfdom in Austria-Hungary in 1848, population increases, excessive subdivision of peasant holdings, loss of land to creditors, and laws passed to help the former landlords regain economic control over the former serfs forced many landholding peasants to leave rather than face starvation or the social ignominy of being reduced to the status of propertyless day laborers. Many emigrated from the mountain villages of Becherov, Komlós, and Stebník, north of Prešov in Šariš County. They settled in Northeast Minneapolis and sent word of employment opportunities to friends and relatives. Almost all the men worked as unskilled laborers in the railroad yards or in saw or flour mills. More Ruthenians joined them, including some from Galicia.[11]

Many families bought land "bordering the city on 7th Avenue Northeast near the Mississippi River, built homes and gardens and went to German and Polish parish priests" until 1887, when there were enough of them to begin organizing their own Byzantine Catholic congregation. The existence of this congregation and the small frame church its members built in Northeast Minneapolis touched off a controversial series of events which were to affect East Slavs in both the United States and Europe, events which ultimately involved the highest policy-making levels in Austria-Hungary, Russia, and the Vatican.

At the heart of the controversy was the effort to establish the Byzantine Rite in the United States. Like many other immigrant groups, the Minneapolis Ruthenians wished to continue to practice their faith in the new country. Thus in 1888 they completed St. Mary's Greek Catholic Church on the corner of 17th Avenue and 5th Street in the Northeast Minneapolis neighborhood where many of them lived. The congregation's founders then wrote to the bishop of Prešov in what was then Hungary, requesting that a priest be sent to them. After some delay, the bishop sent Father Alexis G. Toth, who held his first services at St. Mary's on Thanksgiving Day, 1889. Since the parish was too poor to support him, the new priest opened the community's first grocery store, operating it in addition to carrying on his religious duties until 1891.[12]

Some three weeks after holding his first services, Father Toth visited Archbishop John Ireland of St. Paul to present his credentials and receive diocesan authorization to serve as St. Mary's priest. But Ireland was not receptive. The meeting was acrimonious and, according to Toth, both men lost their tempers. As a result, Ireland rejected Toth's credentials because he had been married (although he was at the time a widower), refused to permit the Byzantine Rite to be practiced in his diocese, and ordered the members of St. Mary's to attend a nearby Polish Roman Catholic church.[13]

When Toth reported Ireland's decisions to the congregation, the members rejected them and began to investigate alternatives. Toth continued to serve St. Mary's for about a year without Ireland's blessing while the parish considered various options. In the end the people decided to forego Catholicism and turn to the Russian Orthodox church. Through the Russian consul in San Francisco, the congregation was placed in touch with Bishop Vladimir Sokolovsky, who traveled from San Francisco to Minneapolis to visit St. Mary's. On March 25, 1891, he welcomed both the congregation and its priest to Orthodoxy. By October, 1892, the church was an official member of the Russian Orthodox Diocese of Alaska and the Aleutian Islands. In 1980 the official name of the Minneapolis congregation, St. Mary's Russian Orthodox Greek Catholic Church, reflected both its origin and its conversion.

That the Russian Orthodox hierarchy did not consider this congregation to be composed of Great Russians was clearly stated in 1892 by Paul Petrovich Zaichenko, who was sent from San Francisco as St. Mary's first parish teacher and choir director. "There was not a single man from Russia in the city of Minneapolis," he wrote. Nevertheless the Russian government desired that those who converted to Orthodoxy under the jurisdiction of its state church would become Russified in the process, and an effort to persuade the members of St. Mary's to consider themselves Russians began.

St. Mary's conversion could have meant the end of an unpleasant incident, but alas, it was only the beginning. In succeeding years over 100 Greek Catholic congregations in the United States followed St. Mary's into the Russian church. The controversy escalated from the ecclesiastical to the international diplomatic level, and Minneapolis became the center of a propaganda war between Hungary and Austria on one side and Russia on the other.[14]

Although the Ruthenians in Europe were then subjects of the Austro-Hungarian Empire, they were also open to influence from Russia, to which many of them looked for cultural leadership. In the period just before World War I, the Russian government wished to annex the Ruthenian lands; therefore winning the loyalty of these people became a Russian objective. The institution most suited to making Russians out of Ruthenians was the Orthodox church.

That the effort extended to Minneapolis was apparent in a 1910 report on the cultural activities centered in St. Mary's "Reading Room." It was prepared by Leonid J. Turkevich, an early pastor from the Russian Empire who later became Metropolitan of North America. He wrote that 66 meetings had been held in the room that year, of which two were semiannual business meetings and no less than 35 were classes in Russian. Turkevich reported that at least six newspapers were available in the room, five of which were either published in Russia or were pro-Russian in outlook.[15]

St. Mary's Church clearly occupied a favored, and indeed unique, place among American institutions of the Orthodox faith, for it alone received a subsidy directly from the Russian government rather than through church channels. For the maintenance of the parish in 1892 St. Mary's was the recipient of $1,100 from the imperial treasury, an annual stipend continued each year until 1917. St. Mary's in turn sponsored a mission chapel of the same name for Rusin

A BRASS BAND enlivened an ice cream social near St. Mary's Russian Orthodox Greek Catholic Church in Minneapolis about 1905.

farmers who had settled in Morrison County, near the central Minnesota community of Holdingford. The first chapel there was built in 1897. Three years later a permanent church, still occasionally used in the 1980s, was erected in Two Rivers Township.[16]

The Minneapolis church also became the base for a school to prepare promising young Russian Orthodox students from all over the United States for leadership in American churches. Some of its graduates were chosen to study in Orthodox seminaries in Russia. Begun in 1897 by Bishop Nicholas Zerov, the school was located across the street from St. Mary's Church on the site of the present parish center. In 1905, under Archbishop Tikhon Belavin, the school became the first Orthodox seminary in the United States, making it no longer necessary for young Americans to travel to Russia for study. And, perhaps partially as a result, Minneapolis was the place where a Russian Orthodox worship service was first conducted in English about 1906, after a translation of the Orthodox liturgy had been officially authorized. The congregation also established a parochial elementary school, whose stated goal was "to help protect the children of the parish from the secularizing influence of the public schools." It operated from 1905 to 1917, after which funds from the Russian government were cut off by the revolutions.[17]

The successful mission activity of the Russian church in the United States eventually reached back to the areas from which the Minneapolis Rusins had emigrated, a state of affairs the Hungarian government found objectionable. A number of Minneapolis Rusins had returned to Becherov, their homeland village, where they had successfully converted many others. Hungarian leaders of both state and church, wishing to stop the conversion of Greek Catholic immigrants to Russian Orthodoxy in order to quash "anti-Hungarian propaganda" at its source, proposed to do so by establishing the Byzantine Rite in the United States.

In 1902 they secured the appointment of Andor Hodobay as papal representative to investigate the need for a Byzantine Rite bishop in the United States. He spent the next five years in America trying to bring administrative order out of ecclesiastical chaos on behalf of the Greek Catholic church and the Hungarian government. In 1906, along with the prime minister of Hungary, various leading Hungarian churchmen, and others, Hodobay recommended that Pope Pius X approve the establishment of the Byzantine Rite in the United States. Pius did so, and the following year he appointed Father Sotor Ortinsky to the post of bishop for Byzantine Rite Catholics in America.[18]

Meanwhile Hodobay visited the Rusin community in Minneapolis in 1906 and determined that a number of families from Subcarpathia would willingly join a Byzantine Rite church if one were established. He then wrote two letters concerning that possibility. He sent one to the Hungarian prime minister, proposing that the government provide temporary financial support for the proposed church. He addressed the other to Archbishop Ireland, suggesting that a Greek Catholic church in Minneapolis would significantly slow or even halt the conversion of Rusin Catholic families to Orthodoxy. By 1906 Minnesota's three Russian Orthodox churches — St. Mary's in Minneapolis and in Morrison County and St. Nicholas in Kittson County, discussed below — counted 964 members among them. Men outnumbered women by 548 to 416, and the Minneapolis church accounted for 866 of the total.[19]

Ireland's answer revealed that his attitude had changed considerably in the 16 years since he had expelled Father Toth from his office. He wrote: "I shall be very glad to see a good priest of the Greek Rite established in Minneapolis. I will cooperate with him to the best of my ability to make his mission a success.

"Of course you easily understand that the priest coming to Minneapolis must be celibate. The presence of any other would be the occasion of great scandal . . . and I should feel obliged to protest against it."[20]

As a result, St. John the Baptist Eastern Rite Catholic Church was organized early in 1907. An existing Polish church building was purchased for $350 and moved to five lots on the corner of 22nd Avenue and 3rd Street Northeast, only a few blocks from St. Mary's. On Thanksgiving Day, 1907, fully 18 years after Father Toth held his pioneering Greek Catholic services in Northeast Minneapolis, the first Greek Catholic Mass sanctioned by the Roman Catholic hierarchy was celebrated in the city by Father J. A. Zaklynsky in the new church. The next year the recently appointed American Greek Catholic bishop visited and blessed St. John's Church.[21]

By 1910 most of the East Slavs who attended St. Mary's and St. John's made their homes with other Slavs in Ward 1 of Northeast Minneapolis. A local newspaper article on the community published in 1916 noted that the "little Russian colony" of 350 families lived for the most part on 5th Street Northeast between 10th and 18th avenues and that most of the men still worked as laborers in railroad shops, though a few were skilled tradesmen or merchants. The reporter described the costumes and customs at weddings and wakes, including such festive foods as *loshish* (borscht), a cold soup "made of beef and beetroot cooked in sour cream," and *konlibia*, a huge pie of salmon, pancakes, and spinach. Group activities, which were connected with the churches, played an important role in the lives of these immigrants. Although men used the saloons of Northeast Minneapolis as social centers and women visited in each others' homes, all gathered in their chosen churches. So vital was this interaction to their well-being that Minneapolis Rusins who moved to North Dakota to farm "almost invariably returned to the community," unhappy and dissatisfied without a group life.[22]

The East Slav immigrants discussed thus far were peasants, many of whom had little schooling. What national consciousness they developed was generally acquired in the United States. Another much smaller group, who reached Minneapolis from about 1910 to 1917, was composed of intellectuals active in the movement for Ukrainian independence. They promoted Ukrainian ethnicity and assumed leadership roles that gave them a significance out of proportion to their numbers. These activists provided cultural stimulation for the wave of East Slavic immigrants who arrived in the Twin Cities in the first decades of the 20th century.

The earlier settlers in Northeast Minneapolis had emigrated principally from Subcarpathia and considered themselves Rusins or Russians. The intellectuals, as well as other later arrivals, were largely from Galicia, and they increasingly identified themselves as Ukrainians. Since they did not feel at home in either of the older Minneapolis churches, they organized a congregation of fewer than 50 families in 1912, and a year later completed still another Catholic church in Northeast Minneapolis — St. Constantine Byzantine Rite.[23]

A congregation also came into being in St. Paul just before the United States entered World War I. But this one was different because it had both Belorussian (East Slav) and Serbian (South Slav) members. The Belorussians, who migrated to Minnesota for the most part between 1910 and the Russian revolutions of 1917, worked mainly in the meat-packing plants of South St. Paul. In 1916 the two groups, with the help of the Russian Orthodox Mission of North America, organized the Russian-Serbian Holy Trinity Orthodox Church.[24]

Northern Minnesota

In the closing decades of the 19th century and the opening ones of the 20th, when some East Slavs were settling in Minneapolis, others were entering northern Minnesota. Some emigrated directly from Galicia and Subcarpathia about 1900 to work in the iron mines of the Mesabi Range, especially in the Chisholm area. A Russian machinist quit the roving life of a railroad construction worker when he arrived there, "because I found a lot of my own people here." Five years later there were a sufficient number of them on the Mesabi to form a fraternal benefit society. Starting in 1906 Ukrainians and Russians arrived on the iron ranges in increasing numbers. "In some cases they [and some South Slavs] replaced or pushed upward off the lowest rungs of the economic and social ladder the Finns and other Slavic laborers." A researcher on the Mesabi in the 1930s found that people he called Carpatho-Russians made up the largest group of East Slavs there, but that there were also Ukrainians from eastern Ukraine and a scattering of Great Russians. What had lured them there from eastern Europe or from industrial Pennsylvania was jobs. A Russian miner told the researcher he went to the United States to earn money, intending to return to Galicia. "'If you had told me I would still be in this country after thirty years when I left, I would have said you were crazy.'" Once they settled there, however, two questions arose which were being asked by many East Slavic communities in the United States. The first concerned church affiliation and the second, national identity.[25]

Most of the East Slavs in Chisholm had been Byzantine Rite Catholics. By 1915 the United States had a Catholic bishop of the Byzantine Rite, so they did not face the difficulties that had earlier confronted St. Mary's in Minneapolis. But by that date the question of nationality had become a major issue for East Slavs in America. Although those in Chisholm were probably numerous enough to form a church by 1905, they could not agree on either national identity or religious affiliation. Among Byzantine Rite adherents, immigrants from Galicia generally considered themselves Ukrainians, while those from Subcarpathia usually identified themselves as Rusins. As in Minneapolis and Morrison County, the Orthodox faithful aligned themselves with Russia. In the end two churches resulted.[26]

In 1912 some of the East Slavs on the Mesabi organized St. Nicholas Russian Orthodox Greek Catholic Church, which at first met in the Serbian Hall in Chisholm. The members tried several sources of financial aid, including the Russian government, before they were able to erect a building in 1916. Legend has it that the czar agreed to help them, but the Russian revolutions intervened and St. Nicholas never got any money. On the other hand, since 54% (29) of the families in the church worked for the Oliver Mining Company in

1922, the congregation may well have received a contribution from that firm, which made a practice of donating to churches attended by its employees.

In the same year Catholic followers of the Byzantine Rite built Saints Peter and Paul Catholic Church in Chisholm. Its membership, which included both Galicians and Subcarpathians, totaled some 25 families. Such mixed congregations were assigned to the administrative unit within the church — either Subcarpathian Rusin or Galician Ukrainian — chosen by a majority of the members. Saints Peter and Paul Church apparently chose the Ukrainian jurisdiction, since it was so identified in the 1970s.[27]

Despite the presence of both Russian Orthodox and Byzantine Catholic churches in Chisholm, St. Joseph's Roman Catholic Church there counted Greek Catholics with their parish totals for some years. Between 1918 and 1928 the number varied from 350 down to 200 and back up to 300 "Ruthenians and Greek Catholics."

Other East Slavs who settled in the northern tier of counties had originally crossed the Atlantic as part of a massive migration bound for Canada. From there they moved southward to Minnesota. Many of these people emigrated from eastern Ukraine, then a part of the Russian Empire, which had tried with mixed success for over 300 years to Russify the Orthodox church there. Others were from Bukovina, then a part of Austria-Hungary.[28]

Some of the Bukovinians became Minnesotans by accident. At the turn of the century, a handful of families migrated southwest from the Winnipeg, Manitoba, area seeking good farms. Finding acceptable land, they settled in what is now Caribou Township of Kittson County in the extreme northwestern corner of Minnesota, where in 1905 they built St. Nicholas Orthodox Church. Four years later a joint American-Canadian commission arrived to mark the boundary between the two countries, and the residents of Caribou discovered that they lived on the Minnesota side of the line. Nevertheless they continued to participate in the larger community on the Canadian side of the border.[29]

That other Ukrainians took land elsewhere in Kittson County is clear from the story of a woman who moved from North Dakota to Hill Township just after World War I. Her life offers an example of how some fairly isolated rural dwellers among Minnesota's Ukrainians were able to retain and transmit elements of their culture. Helen Sajkiwich emigrated from a small Ukrainian village in 1907 at the age of 13, working in a tailor shop operated by a countryman in Chicago for six years before marrying. With her first husband she moved in 1916 to a farm located among other Ukrainians near Pembina, North Dakota, but he died in an influenza epidemic only a year later.[30]

In 1918 she married Anton Kiriluk, a Ukrainian immigrant to Manitoba in 1909 who had subsequently moved to the Northcote area of Kittson County. The couple bought a 580-acre farm in Hill Township in 1919, and Mrs. Kiriluk spent the next years "raising children, turkeys, bees, sheep, vegetables and milking cows, baking, canning, sewing and helping her husband clear and develop a farm." The nearest Ukrainian church was at Pembina, too far away for the Kiriluks to attend. So for a 10-year period they made do with an occasional Mass or baptism performed in their home by a visiting priest from Tolstoy, Manitoba. Mrs. Kiriluk became an American citizen in 1933. Her older children (she had six) spoke only Ukrainian when they started school, and in 1976 they still conversed with their mother in Ukrainian, which was "frustrating" for their spouses. By that year, when an account of her life was written, Mrs. Kiriluk was again widowed. She continued to take pride in doing fine Ukrainian embroidery and in making Ukrainian Easter eggs every year.

Other northern Minnesota concentrations of East Slavs may be found in Koochiching County on the Minnesota-Ontario border. Following a migration route through Canada, some of these immigrants, who were largely Ukrainians, reached the area about 1915, drawn by the work available in the paper mills of International Falls. Before World War I another group of some 30 or 40 families settled at Bramble in the southwest corner of the county. Though the village no longer appeared on maps in 1980, a number of the people and their descendants still lived there. In 1918 they began to build Saints Peter and Paul Russian Orthodox Church, which remained in use until 1932. In 1968 on the 50th anniversary of its founding, the structure was reopened for what became an annual summer festival, which in the 1970s attracted celebrants from as far away as Chicago.[31]

The Bramble settlers further illustrate some of the knotty problems in ethnic labeling so characteristic of East Slavs. Although at least some of them emigrated from Ukraine near Kiev, the church they built was Russian Orthodox, which suggests that they looked upon themselves as Russians rather than Ukrainians. For example, Onufry Diachok, who reached Bramble in 1919, knew only that he had emigrated from the Russian Empire and that his grandfather had been a priest of the Russian Orthodox church. As a young man he earned money for his passage to Canada by smuggling emigrants across the Russian border. He charged the emigrant $1.00, kept $.50, and paid the border guards $.50 to look the other way. He landed in Canada with $50.00 and worked his way across the country giving haircuts to lumberjacks. At one point he spent $20.00 to pay someone to teach him English. Despite Bramble's Russian Orthodox Church, however, the community was labeled Ukrainian by the son of two early settlers. Stephen Hricko's parents homesteaded there in 1919, and his daughter and grandson continued to practice some Ukrainian dances and the traditional painting of Easter eggs.[32]

Nor did all the pioneers follow Diachok's route to the area via Canada. A more usual pattern may have been emigration from Galicia to Pennsylvania to work in the coal mines about the turn of the century, a later move to Minnesota's iron ranges to find employment as a miner, and finally the pursuit of a free homestead in Koochiching County after World War I. Several families went to the area from Chisholm. The men combined seasonal employment on the Mesabi Range for two or three months of the year with clearing and farming the rest of the time. A map of Summerville Township in 1976 showed Saints Peter and Paul Church in the northwest corner of section 33, with much of the surrounding land owned by its East Slavic parishioners. The congregation started with a membership of approximately 20 families and reached a peak of 30 families, a few of whom remained in 1979. Since the church was always too small to support a regular pastor, monthly Masses were performed by priests from Mesabi Range towns, most often from Chisholm. Another area where East Slavs farmed was Meadowlands, south of the Mesabi in the southern part of St. Louis County not far from Duluth. Fifteen families reportedly still lived there in 1980, attending occasional church services in Chisholm.[33]

There have been small numbers of East Slavs in the Duluth area throughout the 20th century, but no churches were built there and no organizations survived in 1980. A Duluth-born daughter of Russian immigrants recounted that her father immigrated to the United States in 1912, worked as a logger in the Bemidji area, then went to the Duluth suburb of Gary to work in the steel plant in 1916. Her mother was not able to join him until 1927. Three or four other Russian families lived in the area when she was growing up, but most of the single Russian men who had lived in boardinghouses there in 1910–12 had either returned to the Old Country during World War I or moved to Detroit.[34]

A Ukrainian who arrived in Duluth via Canada in 1916 from a town near Lviv planned to return after the war. Since his home then came under Polish jurisdiction, he decided to stay, working on the Duluth, Missabe and Iron Range Railroad for several decades. Some of his friends from the same part of eastern Europe worked at the steel plant. A 1930s account of Duluth ethnic groups and their occupations noted that Ukrainians were listed in the 1930 census as Russians. It added: "More of the Russians work at the steel plant than in any other industry; some work at the cement plant in Gary."

Some Russians and Ukrainians arrived in Duluth as Displaced Persons immediately after World War II, sponsored by clubs, churches, or individuals. At least one Russian family remained there in the 1980s. When their children were young they traveled to Russian events in the Twin Cities; in later years they entertained Russian visitors to the port, helped with the city's annual Folk Festival, and worked in the public schools' ethnic program.

The small numbers of compatriots and the absence of an ethnic community meant that intermarriage and attendance at churches other than Russian Orthodox and Greek Catholic characterized quite a few of the East Slavs in Duluth throughout the century.

World War I and the East Slav Community

The outbreak of World War I had a decided impact on East Slavs in the United States. At the war's outset in 1914 the United States remained neutral, but East Slav loyalties were divided between Germany and Austria-Hungary on one side and Russia, which was allied with France and Great Britain, on the other. The Subcarpathian Rusins who wished their homeland to be free of the Hungarian yoke openly supported Russia. Most Russian Orthodox Rusins from both Subcarpathia and Galicia also supported Russia and its allies. The leaders of the Ukrainian movement, however, were ambivalent. In general they leaned toward Austria-Hungary, since the Russian attitude clearly indicated that a victorious Russia would annex at least Galicia and would not tolerate an independent Ukraine.[35]

For the most part, the average East Slav in Minnesota tried to keep a low profile both before and after America entered the war. The late entry of the United States in 1917 placed Russia among its allies and Austria-Hungary among its opponents. But the political climate in the state demanded 100% patriotism, especially on the part of immigrants from countries with whom the United States was at war. These people found keeping a low profile difficult, since local officials insistently pressured them to buy Liberty Bonds.

One of many examples of the extreme measures taken to force purchases was the case of four Bukovinian Ukrainians, a case investigated by the Swedish embassy which handled the affairs of the Austria-Hungary government in the United States during the war. The Bukovinians were among those rounded up by International Falls police in September, 1918, because they had failed to subscribe to any of the three previous bond drives. The four men were unwilling to buy bonds, they said, because they were loyal subjects of Austria-Hungary, not citizens of the United States. They had families in the homeland and planned to return there. If they bought bonds, they feared they would be threatened.[36]

When the Ukrainians refused, they were thrown into jail. A few hours later they were released to a masked mob that bound them and marched them to Rainy Lake, where one man's head was held under water until he — not surprisingly — indicated a willingness to purchase. Intimidated, the other three also agreed. At least one person who was on the bond committee knew how much each man had in savings. As a result each was required to put all of his money into bonds. One of the four, who did not trust banks, was accompanied to his boardinghouse by the police to make sure he, too, bought bonds.

When investigators from the Swedish embassy pointed out the clear violations of law in this incident, Governor Joseph A. A. Burnquist refused to investigate on the grounds that it was a federal matter because, he said, the regional director of the bond drive worked for the United States Treasury Department. Burnquist headed the militant Minnesota Commission of Public Safety, which was concerned with "the preservation of order and public safety . . . the relations between labor and capital . . . discouragement of disloyalty and promotion of patriotism, cooperation with the military authorities [and] the government's loan drives," among other tasks.

International Falls officials claimed they had acted upon Public Safety Commission orders, but they seemed unable to describe the details of the incident for the Swedish investigators. A policeman remembered accompanying a man to his boardinghouse but could not recall whether the man had been tied up; the police chief could not be positive about any of the evening's events; the mayor, who according to the police had ordered the arrests, was unsure whether he had been at the bond headquarters on the night in question, but said that if he had ordered the arrests, he had done so "pursuant to the Safety Commission's order for further investigation." Told by an investigator that the bonds had been sold under duress, the chairman of the Koochiching County bond campaign replied "that was what the bond committee was there for[,] to sell bonds; that these men were buckers and should have been put in jail and kept there for a long time."

In July, 1919, United States Secretary of State Robert Lansing informed Burnquist: "It would appear that these aliens have not received the protection in their persons and property to which even alien enemies residing in the United States are entitled."[37] Thus was a deprivation of liberty carried out in the name of a Liberty Bond campaign.

Other immigrant groups, especially Germans but including Russians, South Slavs, and Finns, were the targets of surveillance not only by various government agencies but by their neighbors as well. Preserved files contain numerous reports in which Public Safety Commission informants observed supposedly radical activities. Typically one wrote on August 25, 1918, that he had attended a "Russian-Slavic Picnic on Hendon Avenue, between Minneapolis and St. Paul on the Como-Harriet Car line." He said that "the speaking lasted for over an hour and was very radical, I understand, but as it was in Russian, I only got what was interpreted to me by Russians who I was acquainted with."[38]

Such activities were part of a panicky chapter in Minnesota and American history often called "the Red Scare." The events of that brief period were not, however, simply a one-sided response to the Russian revolutions of 1917. Rather they were a complex reaction to happenings in the United States, including the end of the war, rapid industrialization, the rise of labor unions, Socialist activity, a troubled economy, and many other social changes that threatened the status quo. Not the least of these was the increase in immigrants from southern and eastern Europe who were perceived as more alien than northern Europeans, partly because they were not Protestants.[39]

Members of the state's power structure also associated Russian immigrants with Socialist or Communist political activity, but neither official records nor newspaper accounts indicated that the charges of radicalism were generalized to apply to the whole immigrant group. Russians who did not participate in radical movements were not necessarily considered guilty by association or solely because of their nationality.[40]

Nevertheless the Russian revolutions posed an indirect threat to the good name of Russian immigrants. A speech given by Marion D. Shutter in March, 1919, undoubtedly reflected the opinion of an influential segment of Minnesota society. Addressing the Citizens Alliance, a group of businessmen whose objective was to keep organized labor out of the Twin Cities, the Reverend Shutter, who was minister of the Universalist Church of the Redeemer in Minneapolis as well as chairman of that city's charter commission, outlined the threats he felt Communism and Socialism posed to the American way of life. Then he addressed a related problem, noting that "rumors have reached us that three millions of Russians intend to come to the United States after the War! No! If necessary slow down the indus-

tries till we have gotten our bearings. Then let us take on the foreigner only so fast as he can be subjected to the melting-pot. Have we not had enough 'Little Italys,' 'Little Russias,' 'Little Germanys,' and 'Little Swedens?' Let us cease being an aggregation and become an organism."

Other American organizations, individuals, and the federal government responded with sympathy and compassion to the tremendous suffering and starvation that followed the civil war in Russia. In 1922 the Minneapolis Trades and Labor Assembly contributed $400 to the Trade Union National Committee for Russian Relief. Minnesota businessmen raised thousands of dollars to send wheat and seed. They formed a Minnesota Russian relief committee which, among other activities, organized a "say it with flour" campaign in 1922 that produced nearly $2,000. While these amounts were not large compared to the magnitude of the Russian famine, they were all part of a national effort for which Congress appropriated $20,000,000.[41]

By January, 1924, the *Minneapolis Star* was beginning to sort out its editorial response to the Soviet revolution. Boris Berkman, a Russian journalist then in Minneapolis, contributed an editorial which decried the Communists' success in 1917, but advocated that the United States recognize and trade with the new Soviet government. This, Berkman believed, would reassure the peasants and entrepreneurs that they had not been deserted by the outside world and would inspire them to use their power to limit Communism and turn Russia into a vigorous, prosperous, non-Communist state.[42]

The "three millions" of Russian immigrants that Shutter had feared did not materialize, but about 100,000 political refugees left Russia after the revolutions. Few made their way to Minnesota; those who did entered as individuals. Often well educated, they found professional employment. An example of such a political immigrant was Pitirim A. Sorokin, an internationally recognized sociologist who taught at the University of Minnesota from 1924 to 1930 before founding and heading the sociology department at Harvard University.[43]

The Interwar Period

The 1920s and 1930s were times of change for the state's East Slavic communities, as indeed they were for all Americans. Economic hardship and the effects of the war slowed cultural activities beyond the Twin Cities almost to a standstill. The churches at Caribou and Bramble closed and those in Chisholm struggled to remain active. For occasional years in the 1920s, 1930s, and 1940s Saints Peter and Paul was served once a month by Minneapolis priests. In 1934 the parish women organized the Sisterhood of the Blessed Virgin Mary. Its purposes were to promote "good home life" and respect for "their Byzantine Rite, language, customs, and . . . Catholicism and the frequenting of the sacraments." The church counted 45 families as members in 1936. St. Nicholas Russian Orthodox Church received similar help from St. Mary's in Minneapolis and from St. Vasilije Serbian Orthodox Church in Chisholm. An effort to organize a Ukrainian club in Duluth just before World War II failed for lack of interest.[44]

In the Twin Cities, by contrast, both religious and secular activities increased. At Minneapolis' St. Constantine Ukrainian Catholic Church in 1934, for example, the organizations included *Sitch*, a branch of a national group, the Society of St. Mary, a Ukrainian chorus, and a ballet class with 47 members. Six years later the following groups were "actively utilizing the . . . parlors" of St. Michael's Ukrainian Orthodox Church in Minneapolis: the Ukrainian National Home, branches of several national organizations including one for "the Restitution of the Ukrainian National Independent State," a drama club, and the Ukrainian Folk Ballet and Chorus of the Twin Cities.[45]

In the Russian community, too, many activities remained within the church. A Russian-American Club was founded in 1922 at St. Mary's which, among other objectives, supported a "united front in the political life of our country." (Indeed St. Mary's has supplied Minneapolis and Hennepin County with more than its share of judges and other elected officials.)[46] The St. Mary's Mothers Club, started in 1928, participated in such national American activities as Red Cross work during World War II, while helping to preserve the ethnic background of its people by publishing a cookbook of traditional Russian foods. Also associated with the church was St. Mary's R Club, a young people's organization designed to encourage them to remember their Russian heritage; begun in 1936, it was still active in 1980.

But active communities frequently spark disagreements over policies and sometimes over personalities, and several East Slav churches in the Twin Cities experienced major disputes in the 1920s and 1930s. Thirty families from St. Mary's split off in 1926 to form a separate congregation in the Minneapolis suburb of Columbia Heights, where its members built Saints Peter and Paul Russian Orthodox Church six years later. For some years the parish shared a priest with the Morrison County-Holdingford congregation. When a permanent pastor arrived later in the Depression years of the 1930s, the Columbia Heights congregation was unable to support him. The Reverend Theodore Turchenko-Vesely then undertook to support himself until economic conditions improved "by part-time farming, selling insurance, and religious services in the community." But membership dwindled, and the building was sold in 1956.[47]

The mixed congregation of the Russian-Serbian Holy Trinity Orthodox Church in St. Paul became involved in a dispute so serious it ultimately had to be resolved by the courts. The disagreement developed over what constituted the highest authority governing the organization: the congregation or the rules of the church as interpreted by the bishop. The Russian members divided into two factions on the issue, and the Serbs supported the one that favored subordination to the Russian Orthodox Church in America rather than an independent church. The Minnesota Supreme Court ruled in 1938 in support of the principle that hierarchical church denominations are governed by hierarchical rules and congregational denominations are governed by congregational rules. In this case, the Russian church, not the congregation, would and did take precedence.[48]

Controversy also reared its head among the Rusins, leading a group of families that preferred to follow the Julian, or

Old Style, calendar, to leave St. John's and form St. Nicholas Greek Catholic Carpathian Orthodox Church in Northeast Minneapolis in 1942. It supported a pastor until 1969.[49]

Nor was the Ukrainian community exempt from both religious and political divisions. After the Russian revolutions of 1917, Ukrainians in Kiev established in November the Ukrainian National Republic, which maintained a federative relationship with Russia until January, 1918, when it chose to fight for complete independence. With the end of World War I in November, 1918, Galician Ukrainians established a Western Ukrainian National Republic in eastern Galicia. It was immediately invaded by Polish forces. In an effort to halt the Polish advance, the Western Ukrainian Republic united with the Ukrainian National Republic in January, 1919.[50]

Transcarpathia, however, did not join Galicia and Bukovina in becoming part of the new Ukrainian republic. Instead, for various reasons including the strong influence of 200,000 American Rusins, the people of Subcarpathia in May, 1919, chose to attach themselves to the new republic of Czechoslovakia. Their choice was ratified by the 1919 Versailles peace conference which ended World War I, although the Rusins fought for the next 20 years to achieve the autonomy within the Czechoslovak republic guaranteed them by the treaty.

Meanwhile the Ukrainian National Republic did not last long. Poland got Galicia, Romania obtained Bukovina, and the Russians eventually made their 1919 declaration of the existence of the Ukrainian Soviet Socialist Republic prevail in what remained of eastern Ukraine. Pieces of an independent Ukraine existed for a few years before all were submerged once again in the shifting intricacies of eastern European political geography.

The Orthodox church in its turn became embroiled in a division which endured for a few years longer than did independent Ukraine. For centuries the church in eastern Ukraine had been subordinated to the Russian Orthodox patriarch in Moscow. During the early 1920s Ukrainian nationalists felt this arrangement was incompatible with Ukrainian independence. Therefore a number of Ukrainian priests set about establishing the Ukrainian Autocephalous church and electing one of their own priests to head it. These moves angered Russian Orthodox leaders in both Russia and the United States, but the independent Ukrainian church continued to grow among immigrants and their descendants in North America. In Ukraine it lasted only until 1930, when the so-called period of Ukrainization ended.[51]

The fostering of Ukrainian nationalism and the rejuvenation of the Ukrainian church were factors in the creation of a new congregation in Northeast Minneapolis in 1925. Led by Alexander Granovsky, a group of ardent nationalists left St. Constantine Byzantine Catholic Church to organize St. Michael's Ukrainian Orthodox Church. The St. Constantine historian explained that "led on by a false notion of nationalism a number of the parishioners abandoned their Catholic faith and their rich Catholic heritage and attached themselves to a newly founded sect of Ukrainian Orthodoxy." But St. Michael's chronicler offered three reasons for its founding: its members felt that Byzantine Rite Catholic churches like St. Constantine were being Latinized; they wished to foster a Ukrainian national identity; and they were stimulated to do so "by the power of rebirth of the ancient Ukrainian National Orthodox Church in 1921 from the domination of the Russian Orthodox Church." [52]

Nevertheless the members of St. Constantine continued to think of themselves as Ukrainians. In 1925 they incorporated the Ukrainian Educational Home, which until the mid-1940s was the social and cultural center of the parish.

The 1930s saw the Ukrainians announce to the Twin Cities that they existed and that they had a cultural heritage to share which could enrich the entire community. Events leading to that development may perhaps be explained by taking as an example the activities of community leader Marie Sokol Procai, who settled in Minneapolis in 1914 and became a nationally recognized authority on Ukrainian folk culture, especially on the art of decorating Easter eggs. Her story contains elements common to the history of many Minnesota Ukrainians of this period.

Marie Sokol arrived in the United States from western Ukraine in 1912 and spent two years with her brother in Pennsylvania before moving to Minneapolis. Soon after her arrival she joined the newly founded St. Constantine Ukrainian Catholic Church and its young people's drama society, which performed plays in the Ukrainian language. The company toured Ukrainian communities in the Upper Midwest, playing primarily in the Twin Cities, Duluth, and Superior, Wisconsin. Between 1915 and 1930, Sokol (who married Anthony Procai during those years) starred in 87 plays. Thereafter she helped lead Ukrainian efforts to reach out to the larger community, often by means of newspaper articles on folk art and culture with the decorated egg gradually coming to symbolize that art in the minds of many non-Ukrainian Minnesotans. [53]

This outreach effort resulted from Ukrainian determination to make their native land known in their new home despite its incorporation into other eastern European countries for most of the previous 300 years. Other nationalities did not feel so great a need to acquaint others with their culture, Mrs. Procai believed, because they had countries of their own they could point to and look to; Ukrainians did not.

World War II and Postwar Developments

Marie Procai continued her involvement in the Ukrainian community after World War II, when Ukraine was united for the first time in centuries, although under Soviet rule. Thousands of Ukrainians who had been displaced by the war chose not to return to their homes under those circumstances. Many of them emigrated to the United States, where their countrymen in the Twin Cities and elsewhere worked hard to find them homes and jobs. The Procai family sponsored more than 80 families. Mrs. Procai opened a Ukrainian art shop in her living room in 1949. She thereby became an employer, and all those who contributed handicrafts and art to her shop became her employees, enabling her to sign the papers which would satisfy their immigration requirements. The shop still existed in the 1980s in a home of its own on Central Avenue in Northeast Minneapolis,

where Procai and her daughters carried on the Ukrainian traditions she helped make more visible in Minnesota.

The Ukrainian Folk Ballet and Chorus, founded in March, 1934, became the best-known Ukrainian cultural organization in the state. Still going strong in 1980, the group had given hundreds of performances throughout the Twin Cities, including appearances at every Festival of Nations sponsored by the International Institute of Minnesota in all the years since 1934. In 1959 the ballet and chorus performed in Mazeppa, a small town in Wabasha County in southeastern Minnesota named for Ivan Mazeppa, a Ukrainian Cossack leader killed in 1709 in the battle of Poltava and immortalized in Byron's poem, "Mazeppa." The town was not settled by Ukrainians and, as far as anyone could determine on the 250th anniversary of the battle in 1959, no one of Ukrainian descent lived there. Nevertheless the ballet and chorus appeared at the Mazeppa Festival, acquainting many in the audience for the first time with the culture which had provided the town's name. [54]

While they were engaged in creating a viable Ukrainian-American culture, the immigrants and their descendants in Minnesota were again drawn into European concerns with the beginning of World War II. The group's leaders in the United States and Canada realized there could be no hope of re-establishing an independent Ukraine while its lands were occupied by Poland and Russia. Because Nazi Germany opposed both countries, some leaders in Berlin favored the Ukrainian movement because it could be used to weaken Hitler's enemies. As a result Ukrainian nationalists in the United States were often regarded as pro-Nazi Germany. Even before the German invasion of Poland in September, 1939, Ukrainian spokesmen took great pains to refute the charge and to present their true position. The Ukrainian nationalists said they were willing to make the extreme sacrifice of allowing their homeland to become a battlefield in a war between the Soviet Union and Nazi Germany in the hope that a postwar settlement would make Ukraine an independent and united nation. It was clear from the beginning that in such a confrontation Ukrainians had the most to lose. From 1941 to 1945 they paid a greater price than they could have dreamed possible, but they did not win the prize of independence. [55]

The Ukrainian point of view was generally understood in Minnesota and newspapers there took some care to explain it. No anti-Ukrainian hysteria was reported in the state during World War II like that which had existed toward Austrian and German subjects during World War I. Following the defeat of Hitler in 1945, more than a million people, mostly from eastern Europe, who had been displaced as forced laborers for German factories, refused to return to their Soviet-occupied homelands. These people became the estranged Displaced Persons of World War II. Although exact figures are not known, it is probable that several thousand arrived in Minnesota in the decade and a half following the war, the largest single influx of East Slav immigrants in the state's history. [56]

One example of the trauma of these people must stand for many. The following brief saga was written by a high school student in Northeast Minneapolis in 1961. "When the Ger-

ELABORATELY PAINTED Easter eggs were sold in 1948 at the Ukrainian Art Shoppe in Minneapolis, with proceeds going to the Ukrainian Refugee Fund.

mans came into Russia they took all of the people they could back to Germany to work in the mills and factories," he began. "They were sent by thousands at a time, almost all on foot or riding in wagons. They were always hungry and most of the time bare. The Russians bombed them trying to make them turn back. They worked eleven months for the Germans. Then the Americans came and liberated them in 1945. They lived in what they called a *Taburr*. It was like a camp. The displaced persons lived there, and the Americans took very good care of them. Then I was born." The boy and his family had to wait five years in the camp before they could go to the United States; others waited even longer.[57]

When the family got to the United States, the boy wrote, his father "found a job right away." That a job was available at once was the result of careful planning. Minnesota Russian and Ukrainian Americans alike worked with state and federal agencies to find homes and employment for thousands of their countrymen. It was a massive task, especially in a postwar economy where unemployment was generally high and sponsors were supposed to find jobs for immigrants which did not displace American citizens. Aided by the United Ukrainian American Relief Committee (UUARC), displaced East Slavs entered Minnesota from eastern European countries including Poland, Romania, Russia, and Ukraine. Many arrived in family groups. The occupations they listed ranged from farmers and farmhands through housewives and domestics to the occasional bookkeeper or teacher, and included laborers and skilled workers as well.[58]

Minnesota did an exemplary job of providing for its new residents. The state's Displaced Persons Commission, headed by John W. Poor, was the agency charged with settling them. It received few serious complaints and was quick to respond. Rather most of the queries sent to it concerned citizens' fears that the displaced people were not being treated well enough.

Only a handful of the postwar East Slavic immigrants found their way to the Mesabi Range, where Chisholm's St. Nicholas Russian Orthodox Greek Catholic Church increased its congregation by about 15 families and its Byzantine Rite Catholic Church added a few new members. By 1976, when Saints Peter and Paul closed, the membership of 45 families was approximately the same as it had been 40 years earlier. Members subsequently attended St. Joseph's Roman Catholic Church in Chisholm.[59]

The impact of the displaced people, which was felt largely in Minneapolis and St. Paul, resulted in the organization of a number of new churches and other institutions to accommodate the divergent interests of this new migration. At first many of the newcomers who identified themselves as Russians joined St. Mary's, but this association was not entirely satisfactory to some of them for various reasons. For one thing, St. Mary's was several generations old, and English was rapidly becoming its dominant language. For another, it continued to recognize the authority of the Moscow Patriarchate, a factor the displaced Russians found difficult to accept.[60]

In the years following the Bolshevik Revolution of November, 1917, the Soviet government had actively intervened in church affairs, imprisoning Patriarch Tikhon, who, before returning home as archbishop, had founded the seminary in Minneapolis in 1905. Many Russian Orthodox bishops left the Soviet Union and organized a Synod of Bishops in exile, declaring themselves the supreme ecclesiastical authority of what came to be known as the Russian Orthodox Church Outside of Russia. Meanwhile the earlier Russian Orthodox Church, which had existed in the United States since before World War I, continued to recognize the authority of the patriarch in Moscow, although in practice it functioned as an autonomous organization known as the Metropolia. Therefore a majority of its congregations, including St. Mary's in Minneapolis and Holy Trinity in St. Paul, saw no need for a formal break with Moscow. Many parishes in other states, as well as St. Panteleimon Russian Orthodox Church in Minneapolis, established largely by Russian and Ukrainian exiles who had left their homelands after the revolutions or World War II, accepted the authority of the Synod of Bishops in the Russian Orthodox Church Outside of Russia.[61]

Not all the displaced immigrants started new churches, however. St. Constantine grew from a small, struggling congregation to a strong, prosperous one whose renewed vigor was symbolized by a new Byzantine-style church built in the 1970s on the site of the old one. St. Michael's doubled its membership but did not sustain this phenomenal growth when many of the new immigrants left in 1950 to form St. George's Ukrainian Orthodox Church in Southeast Minneapolis. The East Slavs who settled in St. Paul also wished to have their own congregations, so two more Ukrainian churches appeared there: St. Stephan's Ukrainian Catholic Church on the East Side, a mission of St. Constantine, and Sts. Volodymyr and Olga Ukrainian Orthodox Church in the Summit Avenue area.[62]

Since not all the Ukrainian immigrants were Catholic or Orthodox, a group of Protestants among them established the First Ukrainian Evangelical Baptist Church in South Minneapolis about 1945. The congregation began with 11 members, primarily Displaced Persons who immigrated to Minnesota from Germany after World War II. Starting in the late 1960s, Ukrainians who had lived since the war in the South American countries of Brazil, Argentina, Paraguay, and Uruguay began leaving there in order to improve their economic lot. Some of them were acquainted with the pastor of the Ukrainian Baptist Church in Minneapolis, so Minnesota became their destination. At about the same time the church moved in 1969 to Northeast Minneapolis, where in 1980 it had 62 members despite a split in which some of the South American Ukrainians left to form the second Ukrainian Baptist Church. The latter's 36 members lived primarily in South Minneapolis and Apple Valley in 1980, and the congregation met in Edgewater Baptist Church in South Minneapolis. In 1980 services in both churches were primarily conducted in Ukrainian, although the church in Northeast Minneapolis had English services twice a month. In addition to a young people's group, a choir, and an orchestra, it sponsored a Ukrainian-language radio broadcast in the Twin Cities on Sunday afternoons.[63]

Only two of the East Slav churches in the Twin Cities were virtually unaffected by the post-World War II migration — Holy Trinity in St. Paul and St. John's in Minneapolis. While there probably were in this period some immigrants from Subcarpathia who still identified themselves as Rusins, apparently few arrived in the Twin Cities. As for the persistence of the Russian community, a 1960 study found 15 second-generation families living in the border area between Minneapolis and Columbia Heights. These American-born members of St. Mary's maintained close contact with those living in Northeast Minneapolis and, among themselves, called their neighborhood "Little Moscow."[64]

East Slavic Displaced Persons in Minnesota also worked to create links with the larger Twin Cities community. In addition to continuing such earlier Ukrainian methods of communicating their culture as festivals and art exhibits, the new immigrants and many of the older ones as well identified

themselves with anti-Communism. In January, 1952, for example, they sponsored a "mass protest meeting against Russian and Communist Imperialism" in the Minneapolis Auditorium.[65]

Despite the varying perspectives of Ukrainian immigrants to Minnesota and their descendants and despite the variety of organizations the community spawned, in 1980 the Ukrainian Congress Committee of Minnesota, a member of the national organization of the same name, acted as the umbrella group for Ukrainian organizations in the state. Made up of representatives from 29 local bodies, it included churches and their allied organizations, independent youth groups such as the Association of Ukrainian Youth, a veterans' association, political organizations like the Ukrainian Republican Club and the Ukrainian Democratic Club, and benevolent associations. Among the latter was the Gold Cross, which raised funds and collected materials for needy people all over the world. In addition there were also single-purpose organizations dedicated to freeing Ukraine or monitoring the Helsinki agreement which pledged member nations, including the Soviet Union, to uphold human rights.[66]

Though the Ukrainian Congress Committee represented diverse elements, it managed to serve as the united voice of the community, handling such tasks as organizing Ukrainian participation in the Festival of Nations and electing the Ukrainian representatives to the advisory committee of the Immigration History Research Center, both in St. Paul.

Members of Holy Trinity and especially St. Mary's Orthodox churches also at various times have taken part in Russian programs at the Festivals of Nations. In 1949 the St. Mary's participants described the qualities which they believed set them off from the larger Minnesota community and perhaps from their fellow East Slavs as well. "The parishioners who, for three generations, *have patterned their private and social lives after the manner of their adopted country*," they wrote, "still retain in their devotion to the church of their fathers a highly personal type of service. Like the pioneers who built it with their own hands, craftsmen of the parish voluntarily do the repair work, the women scrub the floors of the sanctuary and the parish hall, the young girls collect contributions for decoration of the church at Easter, the women's societies bake and serve for benefits to raise money for the widows and sick among them." The implication was strong that Russian ethnicity among these people rested primarily in their religion. Minnesota Ukrainians, on the other hand, appeared to have retained their Old Country language, foodways, artistic and other secular cultural influences, as well as religious loyalties and a strong political interest in their homeland.[67]

Despite these differences, organized religion has played a vital role in the maintenance of East Slavic ethnicity in Minnesota, as it has for other groups. It may be, however, that the Byzantine Rite shared by both Catholic and Orthodox East Slavs is different enough from mainstream American churches to encourage further distinctiveness. Moreover the Ukrainian community in particular has had what might be called a political reason for maintaining its cultural identity and making the larger Minnesota society aware of it. As

ST. PAUL UKRAINIANS adopted a Minnesota Scandinavian word to describe the buffet of foods offered at Sts. Volodymyr and Olga Ukrainian Orthodox Church in 1981.

Marie Procai suggested in 1980, the lack of a recognized, independent homeland served as a stimulus to keep alive among those in the diaspora the idea of Ukraine and the hope of its liberation from what many of them considered Soviet tyranny.

Reference notes

[1] The figures in this paragraph are from the articles on Belorussians (181–184), Carpatho-Rusyns (200–210), Cossacks (245), Russians (885–894), and Ukrainians (997–1009) by Paul R. Magocsi in Stephan Thernstrom, ed., *Harvard Encyclopedia of American Ethnic Groups* (Cambridge, Mass., 1980). The problem of determining how many East Slavs arrived in the U.S. and in Minnesota is difficult using American statistics, for federal and state censuses and immigration service figures offer only spotty information. Michael J. Kozak, chairman of the Minnesota Ukrainian Bicentennial Committee, estimated that there were in 1976 about 10,000 Minnesotans of Ukrainian descent alone; Minnesota Ukrainian Bicentennial Committee, *Minnesota Ukrainians Celebrate the Bicentennial of the U.S.A.*, English section, 4 [Minneapolis, 1976?], copy in MHS.

Another way of treating the numbers problem for the U.S. as a whole is to say that if there were 1,500,000 Ukrainians in the country in 1979, as many writers estimated, about half were Carpatho-Rusins; Paul R. Magocsi, "Problems in the History of the Ukrainian Immigration to the United States," in Magocsi, ed., *The Ukrainian*

Experience in the United States: A Symposium, 4 (Cambridge, Mass., 1979). For Carpatho-Ruthenian centers, see Frank Renkiewicz, comp., *The Carpatho-Ruthenian Microfilm Project: A Guide to Newspapers and Periodicals*, [1] (St. Paul, 1979). For a useful summary of what might be called the "Ukrainian problem" in Europe and the U.S., see Joshua A. Fishman *et al.*, *Language Loyalty in the United States*, 318–357 (The Hague, 1966).

[2] Myron B. Kuropas, *The Ukrainians in America*, 37, 39 (Minneapolis, 1972); St. Michael's Ukrainian Orthodox Church, *Golden Jubilee*, 43 ([Minneapolis, 1975]), copy in IHRC. The so-called Russian Revolution of 1917 had two major parts: the overthrow of the imperial government and its replacement by the Provisional Government and the Petrograd Soviet in February, 1917, and the coup in which the Bolshevik-dominated Petrograd and Moscow soviets took over from the Provisional Government in October, 1917; see William H. Chamberlin, *The Russian Revolution*, 2 vols. (Reprint ed., New York, 1965).

[3] Probably the most helpful recent scholarship defining East Slavic groups in this context has been that of Paul R. Magocsi of the Harvard Ukrainian Research Institute, whose comments on this chapter were much appreciated. His essay cited in note 1 and his *The Shaping of a National Identity: Subcarpathian Rus', 1848–1948* (Cambridge, Mass., 1978) were particularly useful.

[4] Paul R. Magocsi to Deborah M. Stultz, November 10, 1980, in MEHP Papers; Magocsi, *National Identity*, 132; Peter V. Masica to the editor, in *The Orthodox Church*, October, 1973, p. 4, monthly publication of the Orthodox Church in America, formerly the Russian Orthodox Greek Catholic Church of America, copy in IHRC.

[5] For explanations of the differences among the various Catholic rites and practices, see Athanasius Pekar, O.S.B.M., *Our Past and Present: Historical Outlines of the Byzantine Ruthenian Metropolitan Province*, 36–39 (Pittsburgh, 1974); Michael Lacko, S.J., *The Union of Uzhorod*, 42–46, 187–190 (Cleveland, 1976); Charles Zoltak, "Ukrainian Independence and the Russian Church-State Configuration," in *Ukrainian Quarterly*, 35:124, 131–133 (Summer, 1979). In the U.S. many of these differences have gradually eroded, with the Eastern Rite changing to conform to Roman Catholic Latin Rite practices. See Walter C. Warzeski, *Byzantine Rite Rusins in Carpatho-Ruthenia and America* (Pittsburgh, 1971); Stephen C. Gulovich, *Windows Westward: Rome, Russia, Reunion* (New York, 1947).

[6] A Rusin scholar noted that the term "Ruthenian" originated in a Vatican effort to distinguish Greek Catholic from Orthodox East Slavs. He contended that of the total Ruthenian immigration to the U.S., some 60% was Rusin. "They spoke several dialects which were akin to the Ukrainian and Russian language and referred to themselves by a variety of national designations, such as Carpatho-Ruthenians, Ruthenians, Ugro-Russians, Rusins, Rusnaks, and Russkis." A Ukrainian scholar, writing in the same volume, pointed out that the ancestors of the Rusins and Ukrainians "were anthropologically and linguistically related" but that "cultural and political differences have developed between their descendants because of the dissimilar socioeconomic fortunes of the Rusins under Hungarian control and of the Ukrainians under Austrian rule." Here and below, see Walter C. Warzeski, "The Rusin Community in Pennsylvania," and Bohdan P. Procko, "Pennsylvania: Focal Point of Ukrainian Immigration," both in John E. Bodnar, ed., *The Ethnic Experience in Pennsylvania*, 175, 218 (Lewisburg, Pa., 1973); Magocsi, *National Identity*, 277–281; Magocsi to Stultz, November 10, 1980.

[7] Here and below, see Alex Simirenko, *Pilgrims, Colonists, and Frontiersmen: An Ethnic Community in Transition*, 40–42 (London, 1964); interview of Onufry Diachok by author, spring, 1971, notes in author's possession. For definitions of the identities of each East Slavic group in the U.S., see the articles by Paul R. Magocsi in

Harvard Encyclopedia cited in note 1. For Russian Jews, see Chapter 26, below.

⁸ A. A. Sollogub, ed., *Russkaja Pravoslavna ja Tserkov Zagranitsei*, 1:753 (New York, 1968); author's interviews of Professor and Mrs. Wassili Alexeev, Minneapolis, officers of St. Panteleimon Russian Orthodox Church, August 6, 1979, notes in author's possession. For a discussion of the organization of that church, see p. 416.

⁹ Masica, in *Orthodox Church*, 4. Not content to allow the identity of the Rusins to remain an internal battle within the East Slavic language family, some Slovaks, speakers of what is usually defined as a West Slavic tongue, claim that Ruthenians or Rusins from northeastern Czechoslovakia are Slovaks. The Rusins in Europe, led by their clergy, attempted during the 1960s and 1970s to develop a Carpatho-Rusin identity partly to protect against a Ukrainian takeover of their Catholic church and partly to deflect "the attempts of some Slovak nationalists who are intent on identifying the entire Carpatho-Ruthenian community with the Slovak nation." For secular attempts to develop "ethnonational consciousness," see *Carpatho-Rusyn American*, the quarterly newsletter of the Carpatho-Rusyn Research Center in Fairview, N.J.; for religious efforts, see Vasyl Markus, "The Ancestral Faith Transplanted: A Century of Ukrainian Religious Experience in the United States," in Magocsi, ed., *Ukrainian Experience*, 105–128. A helpful source on national developments in Europe during the 1960s and 1970s is Pavel Mačů, "National Assimilation: The Case of the Rusyn-Ukrainians of Czechoslovakia," in *East Central Europe*, 2:101–135 (1975).

¹⁰ Masica, in *Orthodox Church*, 4; Simirenko, *Pilgrims, Colonists, and Frontiersmen*, 37–44. In his sociological study of St. Mary's Russian Orthodox Greek Catholic Church in Minneapolis, Simirenko referred to the members of the congregation only as "Russians." He noted in his preface (p. x) merely that they "came from Slavic peasant villages in the Austro-Hungarian Empire when the national loyalties of the people in that region were still in the process of crystallization." Later (p. 171), however, he added that Minneapolis Russians "Politically and religiously, have identified themselves with the Russians, while linguistically and ethnically they have nothing in common with the true Russian background." It has been estimated that of all the immigrants from greater Ukraine to the U.S. between 1876 and 1914, 40% remained Rusin "in ethnocultural orientation," 20% became Russian, and 40% became Ukrainian. "Ukraine" is here defined as Galicia, Bukovina, eastern Ukraine, and Carpatho-Ukraine or Subcarpathia. Myron B. Kuropas, "The Centenary of the Ukrainian Emigration to the United States," in Magocsi, ed., *Ukrainian Experience*, 39, 41.

¹¹ Here and below, see St. Mary's Russian Orthodox Greek Catholic Church, *Diamond Jubilee Album, 1887–1962*, 17, 18 ([Minneapolis, 1962]), copy in MHS; Emily Greene Balch, *Our Slavic Fellow Citizens*, 49–52, 138 (Reprint ed., New York, 1969); C. A. Macartney, *Hungary*, 234 (London, 1934); Simirenko, *Pilgrims, Colonists, and Frontiersmen*, 40. For a detailed listing of immigrants from the Carpathians to Minneapolis and the villages from which each came, see Mitro Jurchisin, comp., *Carpathian Village People: A Listing of Immigrants to Minneapolis, Minnesota, from the 1880's to 1947* ([Minneapolis, 1981]), copy in MHS.

¹² St. Mary's Church, *Diamond Jubilee*, 18–20; Keith S. Russin, "Father Alexis G. Toth and the Wilkes-Barre Litigations," in *St. Vladimir's Theological Quarterly*, 16:128–149 (1972), copy in IHRC. Simirenko, in *Pilgrims, Colonists, and Frontiersmen*, 42, noted that Toth persuaded John Mlinar to take over the store beginning in 1891. Minneapolis city directories from 1892 through 1933 show a number of Mlinars running grocery stores on 5th St. Northeast. John H. Mlinar was a partner in Mlenar (*sic*) and Jaroscak at 1525 5th St. Northeast in 1892; three years later Mlinar and Masby were grocers at 1531. By 1900 John Mlinar operated the store by himself before moving to Wisconsin in 1901 or 1902. Directories from 1903–33 list a

grocery at the latter address run by William Mlinar, who had partners in the early years. William died about 1933 and his widow, Pearl, ran the store during 1934. By 1935 no Mlinar-owned store was listed, but in 1980 there was still a small grocery to be found at 5th St. and 15th Ave. Northeast.

¹³ Here and two paragraphs below, see St. Mary's Church, *Diamond Jubilee*, 21; Russin, in *St. Vladimir's Theological Quarterly*, 16:132, 135; Simirenko, *Pilgrims, Colonists, and Frontiersmen*, 44; Keith P. Dyrud, "The Rusin Question in Eastern Europe and in America, 1890–World War I," 1, Ph.D. thesis, University of Minnesota, 1976. The St. Mary's booklet gave the impression that it was the congregation's idea to convert to Russian Orthodoxy; Russin, 134, using Toth's papers, claimed that the priest decided to convert to Orthodoxy and prayed for help to convince his "unenlightened parishioners."

¹⁴ Here and below, see Dyrud, "Rusin Question," 1, 4, 63, 65, 285, 295.

¹⁵ *Svit* (Wilkes-Barre, Pa.), February 2, 1911, p. 8, a Russian-language weekly newspaper, whose name translates as "The Light," published by the Russian Orthodox Catholic Mutual Aid Society of the U.S., a pro-Russian group. The IHRC has copies. A metropolitan in the Russian church hierarchy is equivalent to a Roman Catholic archbishop.

¹⁶ The transaction is described in the annual report of the Holy Synod, the governing body of the Russian Orthodox Church, *Otchet Ober-Prokurora Svjateshago Synoda*, 1892–93, p. 43 (St. Petersburg, Russia, 1895). The microfilm copy used by the author is in the private collection of James Cunningham, St. Paul; the Library of Congress and the Holy Trinity Monastery in Jordanville, N.Y., also have copies. Before the fall of the czar in 1917, the Holy Synod spent more than $77,000 annually to support the Russian Orthodox Mission in America; Procko, in Bodnar, ed., *Ethnic Experience in Pennsylvania*, 226. See also St. Mary's Church, *Diamond Jubilee*, 81; Works Projects Administration, Minnesota, Historical Records Survey: Churches, 1936–41, MHS, hereafter cited as WPA, Church Records; bronze plaque in churchyard of St. Mary's in Morrison County examined by author, August, 1979. The Holdingford group in turn seems to have spawned an even smaller agricultural settlement in nearby Todd County, apparently the only other place in central Minnesota with a Ruthenian community. Four or five families left the Holdingford area for Hartford Township there. Some later returned to Holdingford; those who remained kept up family ties with the earlier settlement and went back there for church services and festivities. They did not build a church of their own. One family continued to operate their original farm in the 1980s. A Minneapolis Rusin-American priest recalled that settlement in 1980. Byzantine Catholic priests had traveled there to hold Easter services in the 1940s. Interview of Father Joseph Fedyszak by Deborah Stultz, August 11, 1980, notes in MEHP Papers. Also in Hartford Township was a somewhat larger group of Greek Catholic Slovak settlers who are discussed in Chapter 18. Irene Delsing to Deborah Stultz, [September, 1980], in MEHP Papers.

¹⁷ St. Mary's Church, *Diamond Jubilee*, 26, 30–33, 62. In 1912 the seminary was moved to New Jersey to be nearer the area from which it drew most of its students. Its Minneapolis building was demolished in 1956 to build a parish center and school; see Simirenko, *Pilgrims, Colonists, and Frontiersmen*, 51; *Minneapolis Star*, December 13, 1956, p. 6C, October 21, 1957, p. 11A.

¹⁸ Here and two paragraphs below, see Dyrud, "Rusin Question," 206, 230–235, 256–259, 266. The primary sources for this incident are the Hungarian Prime Minister's Archives, parts of which are available on microfilm in the IHRC. The originals are in Budapest.

¹⁹ U.S. Census Bureau, *Special Reports, Religious Bodies: 1906*, 1:216, 388. By 1916 the three Minnesota Russian Orthodox churches

had a combined membership of 3,279; 10 years later the number of churches had increased to five, four urban and one rural, but the number of members had decreased to 2,515 urban and 219 rural. By 1936 another rural church had been added, with the membership dwindling to 1,987 urban and 140 rural. U.S. Census Bureau, *Special Reports, Religious Bodies: 1916*, 2:262; *1926*, 2:508, 509; *1936*, 2:583.

[20] Ireland to Hodobay, December 31, 1906, Hungarian Prime Minister's Archives, reel 13, IHRC.

[21] Catholic Church of St. John the Baptist, Eastern Rite, *Golden Jubilee*, 10 (Minneapolis, 1957). Simirenko, in *Pilgrims, Colonists, and Frontiersmen*, 53, wrote that because Father Turkevich organized the Society of the Defenders of Orthodox Religious Life at St. Mary's, only a few of that church's members returned to the Uniate fold.

[22] Simirenko, *Pilgrims, Colonists, and Frontiersmen*, 45; *Minneapolis Tribune*, August 6, 1916, sec. 11, pp. [1], 9.

[23] On St. Constantine Church, also called St. Constantine Ukrainian Catholic Church, at University and 6th Ave. Northeast, see its booklet, *Golden Jubilee*, n.p. (Minneapolis, 1963).

[24] On the Russian-Serbian Holy Trinity Orthodox Church, at 956 Forest St., St. Paul, see its *Russian-Serbian Day 25th Year Jubilee*, 5–7 ([St. Paul, 1941]), copy in International Institute of Minnesota Papers, IHRC; interview of Father Gregory Krutchek by author, May 29, 1980, notes in MEHP Papers. On Serbian involvement in the church, see Chapter 20. A few people described as "Byelo-Russians from Bessarabia" attended the ethnically mixed St. Thomas Church in the Wilkin County village of Kent on the North Dakota border. Catholic Archdiocese of St. Paul and Minneapolis, Parish Questionnaires, 1948, originals in Catholic Historical Society, St. Paul Seminary, St. Paul, microfilm in MHS, hereafter cited as Parish Questionnaires.

[25] Michael J. Kozak, *Ukrainians on the Minnesota Iron Range*, 5 (Minneapolis, 1978); Sts. Peter and Paul Catholic Church, *Golden Jubilee Bulletin*, 38 (Chisholm, [1966]); interview of Very Rev. Father Dragoslav Kaseric, priest of both St. Nicholas Church and St. Vasilije of Ostrog Serbian Orthodox Church, Chisholm, by Deborah Stultz, June 23, 1980, notes in MEHP Papers; Dyrud, "Rusin Question," 131; Timothy L. Smith, "Factors Affecting the Social Development of Iron Range Communities," 11, typescript, 1963, in MHS. For more on East Slavs on the Mesabi, see John Syrjamaki, "Mesabi Communities: A Study of Their Development," Ph.D. thesis, Yale University, 1940, especially pp. 110, 130, 131, 139, 167, 243, 262, 288, 358.

[26] Here and below, see WPA, Church Records; interview of Mrs. Eva Kosiak, Chisholm, by Deborah Stultz, June 16, 1980, notes in MEHP Papers; Kaseric interview, June 23, 1980; John H. McLean to M. H. Godfrey, September 18, 1922; Godfrey to McLean, September 21, 1922, both in Oliver Iron Mining Company Papers, MHS. For a Ukrainian viewpoint tending to identify all iron range East Slavs as Ukrainians, see Kozak, *Ukrainians on the Range*, 5, where the author asserted that those who joined St. Nicholas "lost their Ukrainian identity, and assumed the Russian heritage."

[27] Here and below, see Sts. Peter and Paul Catholic Church, *Golden Jubilee*, 38, 40; Kozak, *Ukrainians on the Range*, 5; Isidore Sochocky, "The Ukrainian Catholic Church of the Byzantine-Slavonic Rite in the U.S.A.," in *Ukrainian Catholic Metropolitan See Byzantine Rite U.S.A.*, 273 (Philadelphia, 1959). Father Joseph Fedyszak, pastor of St. John's Byzantine Rite Church in Minneapolis, said in 1980 that most of the first members of Sts. Peter and Paul had been Rusin, but since only Ukrainian priests could be found to serve there, it came to be regarded as a Ukrainian Greek Catholic church; Fedyszak interview, August 11, 1980. See also Duluth Roman Catholic Diocese, "Annual Reports of Parishes," in Bishop's Office, Duluth Chancery, membership abstracts compiled by Mar-

jorie Hoover, in MEHP Papers, hereafter cited as Duluth parish membership abstracts.

There were also East Slavs in the St. Louis County towns of Cusson (1918) and Greaney, where the Slovenes at St. Bridget's were joined by some Byzantine Rite Ukrainians. A parish census of Blessed Sacrament Roman Catholic Church in Hibbing in 1923 counted three Russian born and four of Russian parentage as well as four Ukrainian born and 11 of Ukrainian parentage. An undated issue of the *Evening School Review* (Chisholm) included essays by students in its English classes. Pete Ivanca's "My Home in Galicia" recounted, "In Galicia we lived along side the Carpathian Mountains. The people make their living by farming." Mrs. L. S. Frisch wrote about "Marriage Customs in Russia." See Alien Registration forms, St. Louis County, Cusson, in Minnesota Commission of Public Safety (PSC) Records, Minnesota State Archives, MHS; Parish Questionnaires; Blessed Sacrament Parish, *75th Anniversary, 1894–1969*, 24 ([Hibbing, 1969?]); copies of the *Evening School Review* may be found in the Grace Lee Nute Papers, University of Minnesota, Duluth, Library; used with permission.

[28] Volodymyr Kubijovyč, ed., *Ukraine: A Concise Encyclopaedia*, 1:74, 2:155–167 (Toronto, 1963, 1971), a detailed history of Ukraine and its people in Europe and America.

[29] *The Carillon* (Steinbach, Man.), September 3, 1975, sec. 3, p. 10, incorrectly identified the church as St. Michael's, as did Kittson County Historical Society, *Our Northwest Corner: Histories of Kittson County, Minnesota*, 495 (Dallas, 1976); WPA, Church Records, called it St. Nicholas in 1936. An interview of George Kowaliuk, Caribou, by author, August 23, 1979, revealed that the correct name has always been St. Nicholas. A picture of the church and cemetery appeared on the cover of *Gopher Gazette*, April, 1979, published in Duluth.

[30] Here and below, see Kittson County Historical Society, *Our Northwest Corner*, 229.

[31] *Gopher Gazette*, April, 1979, p. 3; Paul L. Berg, "The Incredible Story of the Forgotten Church," in *Orthodox Church*, June–July, 1968, pp. 6, 7.

[32] Berg, in *Orthodox Church*, June–July, 1968, pp. 6, 7; Diachok interview, spring, 1971; necrologue, in Sts. Peter and Paul Orthodox Church, *4th Annual Tikvin Festival Schedule* [1971], copy in MEHP Papers; Charlotte Von Alman *et al.*, comps., *Silverdale Rauch Bramble*, 37 (Marceline, Mo., 1979).

[33] Von Alman, *et al.*, comps., *Silverdale Rauch Bramble*, 25, 41, 42, 54, 126, 131, 170; interview of Wasyl Halich by Marjorie Hoover, July, 1980, notes in MEHP Papers.

[34] Here and three paragraphs below, see interviews by Marjorie Hoover of Martha Laine, February 26, 1980, Lucas Policka, July, 1980, Mrs. Alex Taly, July, 1980 — notes in MEHP Papers; "Nationalities, and Their Occupations in Duluth," undated typescript in "Nationalities" vertical file; "Duluth Refugees" vertical file, both in Northeast Minnesota Historical Center, Duluth.

[35] For an analysis of national newspaper and pamphlet accounts of this struggle, see Dyrud, "Rusin Question," 275–312. See also Peter Kohanik, *The Austro-German Hypocrisy and the Russian Orthodox Greek Catholic Church* (New York, 1915); Paul R. Magocsi, "The Political Activity of Rusyn-American Immigrants in 1918," in *East European Quarterly*, 10:351 (Fall, 1976); Gustaf F. Steffen, *Russia, Poland and the Ukraine* (Jersey City, N.J., 1915), a pamphlet in Ukrainian Collection, IHRC.

[36] Here and three paragraphs below, see the report on this incident by Frank O. Pelto, June 7, 1919, in the Joseph A. A. Burnquist Papers, MHS; Franklin F. Holbrook and Livia Appel, *Minnesota in the War with Germany*, 2:7 (St. Paul, 1932), quoting *Minnesota in the War*, official bulletin of the Minnesota Commission of Public Safety.

[37] Lansing to Burnquist, July 25, 1919, Burnquist Papers.

[38] "Report Covering Aug. 25, 1918," in file no. 100, PSC Records; for another example, see Burton J. Randolph to O. R. Hatfield, July 29, 1917, in B. J. Randolph Report files, Correspondence and Miscellaneous Records, Woman's Committee (Minneapolis), Council on National Defense, War Records Commission Records, both in State Archives.

[39] Robert K. Murray, *The Red Scare: A Study in National Hysteria, 1919–1920*, 263, 265 (Minneapolis, 1955). The more shocking manifestations of hysteria included bombings, government raids, mass deportations, and mob violence.

[40] Mesabi Range East Slavs experienced some political problems after the Russian revolutions, however, but many of them stayed. Syrjamaki, "Mesabi Communities," 262, noted that "The Russians on the Range, while they have been anti-Soviet among themselves, have had to endure the charges raised by other groups against Soviet Russia, and to be accused of Bolshevism."

Here and below, see *Policy and Principles of the Citizens Alliance of Minneapolis*, undated pamphlet in correspondence and miscellaneous papers, 1903–23, and Marion D. Shutter, *From Constitution to Chaos in Russia and America*, n.p. (Minneapolis, 1919), in St. Paul, General file, both in Citizens Alliance of Minneapolis Papers, MHS; Warren Upham and Rose B. Dunlap, eds., *Minnesota Biographies*, 702 (St. Paul, 1912). For a labor viewpoint, see, for example, resolution, January 10, 1919, in "Russia" folder; letter to L. C. K. A. Martens from the secretary of the Trades and Labor Assembly of Minneapolis and Hennepin County, June 26, 1920, both in Central Labor Union of Minneapolis and Hennepin County Papers, MHS.

[41] Joseph Manley and Frank Morrison to Dan W. Stevens, February 2, 1922, both in Central Labor Union Papers; *St. Paul Pioneer Press*, February 26, 1922, sec. 4, p. 5.

[42] *Minneapolis Star*, January 3, p. 6; 4, p. 14; 5, p. 4 — all 1924.

[43] Philip A. M. Taylor, *The Distant Magnet: European Emigration to the U.S.A.*, 254 (London, 1971); Stanley J. Kunitz, *Twentieth Century Authors*, 1st supplement, 936–938 (New York, 1955).

[44] On the Bramble church, see *Duluth Sunday News-Tribune*, May 26, 1968, Cosmopolitan sec., 3. The Caribou church was used only for "special services or funerals" beginning in the 1940s; see Kittson County Historical Society, *Our Northwest Corner*, 495. For the Chisholm churches, see Sts. Peter and Paul Catholic Church, *Golden Jubilee*, 42; WPA, Church Records; Kaseric interview, June 23, 1980; Duluth parish membership abstracts; Policka interview, July, 1980.

[45] Here and below, see St. Constantine Church, *Memorial Book of Golden Jubilee of Ukrainian-Greek Catholic Church in U.S.A. and Twentieth Anniversary of St. Constantine Church*, n.p. ([Minneapolis, 1934]); St. Michael's Ukrainian Orthodox Church, *Fifteenth Anniversary*, n.p. ([Minneapolis], 1940); St. Mary's Church, *Diamond Jubilee*, 90, 91, 96–98; St. Mary's Mother's Club, *A Cook Book of Traditional and Favorite Recipes* (Minneapolis, 1970), copy in MHS; interview of Dorothy Borgstrom, parish secretary, by Deborah Stultz, March 28, 1980. Some Minneapolis East Slavs participated in the Americanization effort of the 1920s: in 1919–21, 50 Russian men and 12 women, 7 Ukrainian men and 2 women attended Americanization classes in that city, while 14 Russian men, 24 Russian women, 2 Ukrainian men, and 3 Ukrainian women took part in home classes. U.S. Dept. of Labor, Immigration and Naturalization Service, "Government Report for Americanization Classes," October 20, 1919–March 19, 1920; January 7, 1920–July 1, [1921], in National Archives Record Group 85, copies in MEHP Papers.

[46] Among the politically active members of St. Mary's were district Judge Paul J. Jaroscak, state Senator Harold Kalina, and lawyer William G. Kohlan; see *Minneapolis Star*, May 28, 1951, p. 1, December 1, 1956, p. 9A, January 18, 1954, p. 26, in clipping file, Alex Simirenko Collection, IHRC.

[47] Simirenko, *Pilgrims, Colonists, and Frontiersmen*, 63, 70. The Columbia Heights church was located at Central Ave. and 44th St. One problem was related to a dispute over the ownership of church property at St. Mary's; for a discussion of that type of problem here and below, see Myles C. Stenshoel, *Religious Neutrality under the Constitution: An Analysis of Alternative Rationales of the First Amendment Religion Clauses*, 190 (Minneapolis, 1966), copy in Augsburg College Library, Minneapolis.

[48] Holy Trinity Orthodox Church, *25th Year Jubilee*, 5.

[49] Fedyszak interview, August 11, 1980; the building still stood at 1929 5th St. Northeast in 1980.

[50] Here and two paragraphs below, see Kubijovyč, ed., *Ukraine: A Concise Encyclopaedia*, 1:737, 754, 759, 788, 2:70, 73, 74. See also Taras Hunczak, ed., *The Ukraine, 1917–1921: A Study in Revolution* (Cambridge, Mass., 1977).

[51] Kubijovyč, ed., *Ukraine: A Concise Encyclopaedia*, 2:167–177, 204–208; "Ukrainians Accepted by Constantinople?" and "The Ukrainian Issue," both in *Orthodox Church*, March, August, 1973, pp. 1, 4, respectively; Zoltak, in *Ukrainian Quarterly*, 35:132, 135.

[52] Here and below, see St. Michael's Church, *Golden Jubilee*, 37, 38; St. Constantine Church, *Golden Jubilee*. On Alexander A. Granovsky, the chronicler of St. Michael's, see note 58, below. The Ukrainian Home at Jackson and Summer sts. was sold after usage declined in the 1940s.

[53] Here and two paragraphs below, see interview of Mrs. Procai by author, April 17, 1980, notes in MEHP Papers. Procai and Alexander A. Granovsky appear in *Ukrainians of North America: A Biographical Dictionary of Noteworthy Men and Women of Ukrainian Origin in the United States and Canada*, 84, 262 (Champaign, Ill., 1975).

[54] *The Ukrainian Folk Ballet and Chorus*, 1934, and *Mazeppa Festival*, 1959, programs in MHS; International Institute, *International Folk Festival 1934*, 13 (St. Paul), and subsequent programs of the triennial St. Paul Festival of Nations, in IHRC; *Minneapolis Star*, October 5, 1959, p. 15A.

[55] Here and two paragraphs below, see explanation and defense of the Ukrainian position in G. W. Simpson, *Ukraine*, a published speech from the "Frankly Speaking" radio series of CFCQ, Saskatoon, Sask., broadcast on January 3, 1939, copy in Halich Collection, IHRC; *Duluth Herald*, April 17, 1939, p. 6.

[56] The statistics are still debated, but H. Stuart Hughes, *Contemporary Europe: A History*, 364 (Englewood Cliffs, N.J., 1961) referred to "more than a million — mostly anti-Communists from Eastern Europe — who refused to go home." St. Michael's Church, *Golden Jubilee*, 43, cited the figure 5,000 coming to Minnesota; the author believes this estimate is too high.

[57] Here and below, see Nicholas Jarmulowicy, "The Tragedies of War," May 26, 1961, and "Father Since I've Known Him," June 5, 1961, in Birdella M. Ross manuscript family histories, MHS.

[58] Documentation for activities described here and below may be found in Displaced Persons Resettled in Minnesota, 1949–52, and John F. Bach to John W. Poor, October 11, 1949, in Minnesota Displaced Persons Commission files, Minnesota Public Welfare Dept. Records, State Archives; tables compiled from these records in MEHP Papers. On Displaced Persons in general, see U.S. Displaced Persons Commission, *Memo to America: The Displaced Persons Story* (Washington, D.C., 1952). For information in English on the United Ukrainian American Relief Committee (UUARC), see Mykola Kulycky, *Resettlement of Displaced Persons in the United States* (Philadelphia, 1950). Alexander A. Granovsky, who led the Minnesota UUARC, was one of a number of educated Ukrainians who played major roles in the development of the state's Ukrainian community. He arrived in Minnesota in 1913 as an adult and became a prominent entomologist at the University of Minnesota. In addition to acting as a moving force behind the organization of St.

Michael's Ukrainian Orthodox Church in Minneapolis, he promoted post-World War II immigration to Minnesota. See Irene T. Granovsky, *Who We Are: A Genealogy of Our Family*, 103–150 (St. Paul, 1974), copy in MHS. The papers of the UUARC are in the IHRC.

[59] The Sts. Peter and Paul cookbook committee continued to market its *Favorite Recipe Cookbook*, however, which by 1980 had sold some 20,000 copies since it was first printed in the 1950s to sell at the church's booth at the state fair; MHS has a copy. Sts. Peter and Paul Church, *Golden Jubilee*, 42; interview of Julia Soroko, Chisholm, by Deborah Stultz, August 19, 1980, notes in MEHP Papers; Kaseric interview, June 23, 1980. Father Kaseric in 1980 had been serving St. Nicholas Church twice a month for 19 years in addition to his duties at St. Vasilije Serbian Orthodox Church. Late in the 1950s some Hibbing members of St. Nicholas began attending St. Michael's, a newly organized multiethnic Orthodox church there; see telephone interview of Father Peter Pritza, Hibbing, by Deborah Stultz, December 20, 1979, notes in MEHP Papers.

[60] Here and below, see Simirenko, *Pilgrims, Colonists, and Frontiersmen*, 71; Dmitry Grigorieff, "The Orthodox Church in America from the Alaska Mission to Autocephaly," in *St. Vladimir's Theological Quarterly*, 14:208–211 (1970).

[61] Alexeev interviews, August 6, 1979; St. Mary's Church, *Diamond Jubilee*, 32; Sollogub, *Russkaja Pravoslavna*, 1:753. In March, 1956, St. Panteleimon, composed about 60% of Ukrainians, moved to its present location on East Franklin Ave., Minneapolis.

[62] St. Constantine Church, *Golden Jubilee*; St. Michael's Church, *Golden Jubilee*, 44; interviews of Father Andrew Kist, former priest of St. Michael's, retired priest of St. George's, June 18, 1980, and Msgr. Stephen Knapp, priest at St. Constantine and St. Stephan's, June 13, 1980, both by Deborah Stultz, notes in MEHP Papers.

[63] Interview of Michael Kozak by author, August 8, 1979, notes in author's possession; interviews of Urii Maruschak, secretary of the second church, June 23, 1980, and Rev. Paul Basiecznik, assistant pastor of the first church, June 30, 1980, both by Deborah Stultz, notes in MEHP Papers.

[64] Simirenko, *Pilgrims, Colonists, and Frontiersmen*, 126. The 1960 census listed 2,022 foreign-born Russian speakers in the Twin Cities metropolitan area and 1,707 foreign-born speakers of Ukrainian. For more on speakers of East Slavic languages in Minnesota, see Table 21.1. Many of the Russian speakers were Jews.

[65] Examples of activities included a Ukrainian Day Festival, with speeches, an exhibit, food, and dancing, held in the fall of 1950; 30 years later the Ukrainian Chorus "Dnipro" and the Ukrainian Dance Company performed in costume on Nicollet Island in Minneapolis in connection with the eleventh annual Mississippi River Ramble. In the spring of 1951 the Minnesota Group of Ukrainian Artists exhibited 65 paintings and sculptures created by 13 recent immigrants to the state; as late as 1976 the Bicentennial Ukrainian Heritage exhibit at the Minnesota Museum of Art in St. Paul revealed a strong attachment among Ukrainian-American artists to prerevolutionary Ukrainian motifs. See John W. Poor to Alexander A. Granovsky, September 21, 1950; Poor to Lillian L. Mates, May 1, 1951; "Mass Protest Meeting Against Russian and Communist Imperialism," typescript — all in Minnesota Displaced Persons Commission files, in Minnesota Public Welfare Dept. Records. See also the monthly neighborhood newspaper *Southeast* (Minneapolis), October, 1979, p. 7; *Ukrainian Heritage* (catalog of the exhibition), n.p. (St.Paul, 1976), copy in MHS. On Ukrainian concern with the homeland, see Peter Vaughan, "They dream of free, independent Ukraine," in *Minneapolis Star*, March 21, 1972, p. 1C.

[66] Here and below, see interview of Luba Mensheha, president of the Ukrainian Congress Committee of Minnesota, by author, April 16, 1980, notes in MEHP Papers. The Ukrainian Chorus "Dnipro" of the Twin Cities published *Herald*, a Ukrainian-language music and art quarterly, for several years beginning in 1960. "Dnipro" was following a pattern among Ukrainian arts groups in Minneapolis and St. Paul: the Ukrainian Folk Ballet had issued a monthly Ukrainian-English newsletter called *The Ukadet* from 1941 to 1965 from St. Michael's Church; it was reinstated in 1971 by the Ukrainian Orthodox Junior League at St. Michael's. Copies of *The Ukadet* and *Herald* from some of those years are in MHS.

[67] Italics added; International Institute, *Festival of Nations, 1949*, 37 (St. Paul).

CHAPTER 22

The Hungarians

Paul Kirchner and Anne R. Kaplan

WHEN ÁRPÁD THE CONQUEROR and his Magyar horsemen crossed the Carpathian Mountains to the valley of the middle Danube in 896 A.D., they are said to have beheld "a great plain, rich in game and green pastures, between two great rivers rich in fish, surrounded by mountains." In later times, invaders, conquerors, and settlers — Tartars, Turks, Germans, Romanians, Serbs, Croats, Slovenes, Slovaks, Rusins, and Jews — inundated the Magyars, shaping the cultures and political destinies of the central European area known as Hungary (see Map 22.1). By the mid-19th century Hungary, ruled by the Habsburg dynasty, contained a conglomerate of peoples (half of whom were Magyars) locked together in a pre-industrial socioeconomic system characterized by class distinctions and archaic patterns of land use resembling feudalism. A complex interplay of geographical, political, economical, and sociological factors would lead Hungarians of all ranks to emigrate during the ensuing one hundred years.[1]

Although Minnesota's fields, forests, and mines were ready for development as successive waves of Hungarians reached America, relatively few of the immigrants were lured to the North Star State. As late as 1907 (the peak year of their emigration), Hungary was still 78% rural, and 67% of those who arrived in the United States declared themselves to be farmers or farm laborers. But when "the Hungarian immigrant left home," wrote a historian in 1948, "he underwent a remarkable sea change," turning "his back on the soil" and his face "toward the mine and the blast furnace." The majority of the immigrants went no farther inland than was necessary to obtain work, settling primarily in New York, New Jersey, Pennsylvania, Ohio, and West Virginia, as well as in the midwestern states of Indiana and Illinois.[2]

Like other states, Minnesota has received six distinct series of Hungarian immigrants since the 1850s, each propelled by a political or economic upheaval in the homeland and characterized by emigrants of similar socioeconomic and educational backgrounds and skills. Magyar nobles were followed by landless peasants, who were in turn succeeded by four groups of increasingly urban, technically trained, and politically alienated refugees. From a slow start in the mid-19th century, Minnesota's Magyar population rose to 2,823 in 1920, a decade after the peak in immigration. Over the years, as the characteristics of the immigrants changed, so did the composition of the Minnesota population. In the

mid-20th century scientists, scholars, engineers, technicians, and artists joined the state's earlier arrivals.

The First Series, 1850–69

While some scholars infer from slender evidence that a native speaker of Magyar sailed with Leif Ericson in 1000 A.D., it was not until the failure of the Hungarian Revolution of 1848–49 that significant numbers of Hungarians left for America. In the 1850s and 1860s an estimated 4,000 of those who had supported the unsuccessful revolutionary government of Lajos Kossuth against the Habsburg dynasty fled to the United States. Numbered among them were army officers, doctors, ministers, engineers, musicians, scholars, and students of the humanities. These "cultured people of middle or upper class origin," wrote a Hungarian-American scholar, were often forced to find employment as laborers and farm hands. Beginning in the 1860s, they were joined by merchants, craftsmen, and adventurers.[3]

Although groups of Hungarians settled in Wisconsin and Iowa in this period, only one family is known to have resided in Minnesota during these years. According to a travelogue published in 1858 by Samuel Ludvigh, himself a Hungarian exile, Joachim and Theresa Kállay and their three children farmed under spartan conditions on a homestead in Nicollet

Map 22.1. Hungary during the Austro-Hungarian Empire and in Modern Times.

County. While traveling from St. Peter to New Ulm in September, 1857, Ludvigh stopped at Nicollet, a hamlet of five houses and one store. From there he made a detour in order to visit Dr. Kállay, with whom he had studied law in Sárospatak, Hungary. At the Kállay cabin he learned from his hosts of the scarcity of food staples, the troublesome winters, and their fear of Indian attack. The fate of the family is unknown, but since Kállay was the legally protected name of a famous Hungarian noble family, and since according to the 1860 census the youngest child was born in Minnesota in 1852, political refugees of the Revolution of 1848–49 appear to have been among Minnesota's first Hungarian settlers.[4]

The Second Series, 1870–1918

The second period of Hungarian immigration, which lasted from the 1870s to the end of World War I, was economically motivated. Although by the late 19th century Budapest, the capital city, had been industrialized, Hungary was still predominantly agrarian and firmly tied to its archaic system of large estates and entailed landholdings. Poverty, starvation, and exploitation by many Hungarian magnates and squires drove some of the peasants off the land and out of the country. In general, however, it was not the downtrodden or the penniless who left Hungary during this period. Studies of northeastern Hungary — the home of 40% of the Hungarian settlers in America between 1899 and 1913 — showed that people were most likely to emigrate to the New World if they resided in a population center with a history of geographic mobility, if they had access to reliable information about their destination, and if they were able to finance the journey. In any case, most Hungarians left with the intention of returning once they earned enough money to purchase land of their own.[5]

The flood tide of emigration from 1890 to 1910 coincided not only with the beginnings of industrial and agrarian reform in Hungary but also with the opening of what has been called "the golden age of iron and steel" in the United States. Apparently the attraction of employment at wages at least five to six times higher than those in Hungary more than offset the gradual improvement in economic conditions there. At first it was the young "emigrants . . . at the peak of their work capacity" who ventured overseas. In 1905–07, for example, 59.9% of them were under 30 years of age and 84.8% under 39. At the turn of the century 66% were men, but by the beginning of World War I women were leaving in equal numbers. By 1910, 315,283 Magyar speakers were counted in the United States, 2,374 of them in Minnesota.[6]

Admittedly such decennial census totals obscure the dynamics of international migrations. For example, in 1907 alone 60,071 Magyars left their homes, while in the two years from 1908 to 1910, 50,333 elected to return to Hungary, where they probably served as walking advertisements of the prosperity to be found in America. After 1910 the tide slowed somewhat. Nevertheless by 1914 the United States had gained another 62,154 Magyars — 118,743 immigrants minus 56,589 returnees. In fact, it is estimated that more than a quarter of all the Hungarians who emigrated between 1899 and 1913 attained their economic dream and were repatriated.

In accordance with the national trend, Minnesota's Hungarian population increased greatly during this era. The census recorded 209 Hungarian-born residents in 1870 and peaks of 5,582 in 1910 and 4,277 in 1920. While immigration in the decade from 1910 to 1920 declined, total Hungarian stock increased. Of the state's 5,582 foreign-born Hungarians in 1910, however, only 28.6% claimed Magyar as their mother tongue. By 1920 the number of native speakers had increased only slightly (see Table 22.1). The steady growth of Minnesota's Hungarian population from 1900 to 1920 may be attributed to direct immigration and internal migration, which combined to offset the losses from remigration to the homeland. For example, 161 Magyars expressed an intention to settle in Minnesota in 1909 while 58 others left, the net gain being 103. In 1910 an influx of 86 was tempered by the return to Hungary of 61, leaving an increase of only 25, and so forth (see Table 22.2).[7]

Despite the overwhelmingly agricultural image of Minnesota, most of its Magyar immigrants — like their compatriots in other states — lived in the cities. So much has been made of the "complete reversal in living habits of former rural Hungarians," however, that an important continuity in their behavior is often overlooked. "The trip to the United States did not bring a conceptual change in the lifestyles of most of them," pointed out a Hungarian scholar, "as migrant work had had a long tradition in Hungary. Landless peasants or those with small plots often contracted for migrant labor, such as harvesting, earth-moving, or construction work, both in the country and in cities, even if the opportunities were far away from their homes. America was even further away, but that was practically the only difference."[8]

True to form, 60% of Minnesota's Magyars (and 54% of all foreign-born Hungarians) lived in the Twin Cities by 1910. From 1880 St. Paul led all cities with respect to Hungarian-born residents, and by 1910 it had 1,032 first- and second-generation Magyar speakers compared to Minneapolis' 404. In 1920 when the Twin Cities' Magyars accounted for only 48.9% of the state's total, the St. Paul population had risen to 1,079. Minneapolis had dropped to 329, and Duluth, tallied for the first time, had 71. Mother-tongue totals were not

Table 22.1. Hungarians in Minnesota, 1870–1970

	by country of origin		by mother tongue	
	foreign born	foreign stock*	foreign born	foreign stock*
1870	209			
1880	356			
1890	1,256			
1900	2,182	6,405		
1910	5,582	8,001	1,597	2,374
1920	4,277		1,338	2,823
1930	1,681	5,940	919	
1940	1,697		980	1,740
1950	1,508	4,808		
1960	1,297	4,640	841	
1970	791	3,741	615	1,928

Source: Country of origin and mother-tongue statistics in U.S., *Census*, for the years listed.

*Includes foreign born and native born of foreign or mixed parentage.

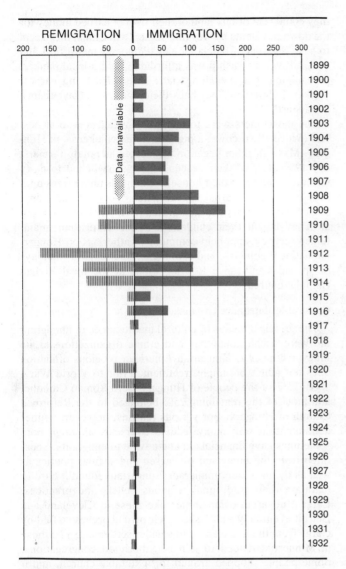

Table 22.2. Hungarian Migration to and from Minnesota

recorded in 1920 for other Minnesota cities, but in 1910 there were 103 Hungarian nationals in Virginia, 13 in St. Cloud, 5 in Stillwater, 4 in Winona, and 1 in Mankato.[9]

Once settled, however, Minnesota's urban Hungarians did not form tight, geographically concentrated ethnic communities. Drawn to the Twin Cities by employment opportunities, they were as scattered or as centralized as the firms that needed laborers. For some, the lure of old acquaintances and the opportunity to work exerted a combined pull. People from the Hungarian village of Csekefalva in Transylvania (a part of Hungary annexed by Romania in 1918) chose to settle in St. Paul because friends were employed at Armour or Swift, meat-packing firms in South St. Paul that regularly hired immigrants.[10]

Although it lacked a "Little Hungary," St. Paul had several identifiable Magyar neighborhoods, where homeowners commonly took in as boarders Hungarian men who were single or who had immigrated without their families. The

oldest area, located south and west of Lake Como, included Ward 12 and parts of Wards 10 and 8. Settled in the early 1900s, the Como area in 1980 still had a cluster of Hungarian families. Within it were four of the principal turn-of-the-century employers of Hungarian immigrants — the Northern Pacific and Great Northern railways, St. Paul Foundry, and Koppers Twin City Coke. (American Hoist and Derrick, located in Ward 6, was another common Magyar workplace.) By 1920 Hungarians had also established themselves near Rice Street north of University Avenue and near the meat-packing plants in South St. Paul. These areas were not isolated units. One Hungarian American who lived in the Como district remembered packing the whole family into their first car for Sunday visits to friends in South St. Paul; another recalled late-night trips by streetcar to attend wakes or other events in that part of the city.

Ward statistics sharpen the boundaries of settlement but blur those of ethnic communities in two ways. First, the wards were political subdivisions resulting from a grid superimposed on existing settlement. They did not necessarily match the residents' perceptions of their own neighborhoods, which might span several wards or merely occupy a corner of one. Second, while settlers might easily identify Magyar, Austrian, German, or Romanian communities within one area, the statistics lumped together all immigrants from pre-World War I Hungary as Hungarians, thus compounding the difficulty of pinpointing ethnic settlements. Nevertheless the figures are useful as general guidelines. In 1910 Hungarians lived in all 12 of St. Paul's wards and all 13 in Minneapolis, but in each city they were concentrated in four contiguous wards. St. Paul had 270 foreign-born Hungarians in Ward 12, 882 in Ward 8, 290 in Ward 9, and 349 in Ward 5 — the area from Lexington Parkway east to Mississippi Street, and south and west from downtown. None of the other wards had more than 73, and some had as few as 7.[11]

In Minneapolis Hungarians lived in the section bordering the Mississippi River west and north of City Hall, where there were 140 foreign-born Hungarians in Ward 1, 198 in Ward 3, 104 in Ward 4, and 565 in Ward 6. Numbers elsewhere ran from a high of 51 in Ward 9 to a low of 6 in Ward 12. The Pillsbury Company, the city's major employer of Hungarians, was all but surrounded by the first four wards.

The Hungarian influence on milling in Minnesota reached beyond Pillsbury's immigrant laborers. As early as 1878 both Charles A. Pillsbury and Cadwallader C. Washburn, Minneapolis milling magnates, were toying with the "Hungarian process," a technique that used rollers as well as traditional millstones to crack wheat. Washburn imported a Hungarian miller to run his experimental B Mill in 1878. In the same year, Pillsbury reportedly sneaked some steel rollers out of Budapest. By 1881, when interest in the Hungarian milling process was diminishing in Minnesota at the same time Hungarian immigration was rising, both companies were employing the new method in some form in their world-famous establishments. During the next quarter century Budapest was gradually displaced as the flour-milling center of the world by Minneapolis.[12]

It is virtually impossible to distinguish Hungarian nationals from native speakers of Magyar outside the Twin Cities, since mother-tongue figures were consistently printed only for the state, Minneapolis, and St. Paul. By 1890 Hungarians had been officially counted in most of Minnesota's counties, but it is safe to assume that not all of them were Magyars (see Table 22.3). Of the 938 Magyars (40% of the 1910 total) said to be living outside the Twin Cities, only 210 can be located precisely.[13]

They were to be found working in the iron mines of St. Louis County. Like meat-packing, mining employed the unskilled of many nationalities, and some Magyars had been miners in northern Hungary. In 1907 the Oliver Iron Mining Company, the largest Mesabi Range employer, had on its payroll 210 foreign-born Magyar workers, of whom 72 (34.3%) could speak English. One hundred of them (54.9%) were married, but the nationality of their spouses is unknown. The company's figures, however, provide some clues to the rate of Magyar migration to the Minnesota iron ranges. In 1907, 19 of the total 210 had lived in the United States for less than 1 year, 34 for only 1 year, 46 for 2, 21 for 3, 36 for 4, 24 for 5, 10 for 6, 1 for 7, 4 each for 8 and 9 years, 2 for 10, and 9 for more than 10 years. Seven of the 54 who were eligible for naturalization had become citizens.[14]

An assessment of the capabilities of the various nationalities in the Oliver work force lumped together all those from the mixed ethnic population composing Austria-Hungary. They were "regarded by the mining companies as the most desirable workers next to the Scandinavians and Finns. The promise given by their large frames and muscular build of being efficient workers is not, however, wholly borne out. . . . While very docile, they lack the initiative of the Scandinavians and the Finns, and thus require a great deal of supervision. Even in physical endurance they have not in the mining region proved the equal of those races. This is often explained by their different standard of living. They live in large numbers in camps near their work, and their fare consists largely of rye bread and the cheapest cuts of beef boiled with vegetables."

Where most of the other 728 Magyars then living outside the Twin Cities were to be found remains a mystery. In 1910 foreign-born Hungarian household heads made up only .29% of those in Minnesota's foreign-born farm population. Since the Magyars made up only 30% of the Hungarian-born population at the time, they presumably constituted but a fraction of that farming total.[15]

Nevertheless the Hungarian farmers of Elk River, Sherburne County, presented a contrast to the stereotype of the urban immigrant laborer. These people came to North America expressly to buy land and settle, following a trail to Elk River broken about 1890 by the Fazekas family — three brothers, a sister, and their mother who homesteaded there and in 1896 won title to the land. A few relatives and countrymen joined them; they wrote to friends and advertised in a Hungarian newspaper in order to gather Magyars around them. Some relocated from as far away as British Columbia and as near as East Chicago, Indiana, to form the nucleus of a community which in 1980 included about 30 family names. While some of the settlers cut brush for a local farmer until

they could rent or buy land of their own or earned money for the down payments by working in the Twin Cities, they seem to have regarded urban labor as a temporary measure. Land in Elk River Township was affordable, and a local banker, recognizing that the Hungarians "were hard and earnest workers [who] would pay back their loans . . . gave them a good start."[16]

The newcomers were former small villagers who at best had owned "two cows, a pig, and some chickens" in Hungary. Many of them began in Minnesota as potato farmers. (By 1980 most of their descendants had switched to dairy farming.) They tied their household animals under trees until they could build barns, saved choice spots for gardening, and created a settlement that prided itself on being traditional. They taught their children to speak Hungarian, maintained their cuisine, held community gatherings on Hungarian national holidays, and commemorated religious holidays of special significance to Hungarians at the local Roman Catholic church.

Cultural Maintenance Organizations

The principal means of cultural maintenance in immigrant life were usually churches and ethnic organizations. Like Magyar ethnicity, Hungarian-American religious affiliation does not admit of simple treatment. Prior to World War I about 75% of the people of Hungary were Roman Catholic, and most of the remaining 25% belonged to the Reformed Church of Hungary. For various reasons, however, neither denomination sent many leaders overseas, although both sometimes gave financial aid and advice to emigrants. Separated from the homeland by sacred and secular politics as well as by an ocean, immigrant Hungarians found it hard to maintain their traditional religious beliefs and practices. Large Hungarian communities like those in Cleveland and Detroit eventually established their own churches staffed by clergy from the homeland, but smaller settlements like those in Minnesota tended to join neighborhood congregations. Some people shopped around for a suitable church, and it was not uncommon for a family to change its congregational membership or even its denominational affiliation according to its conviction or convenience.[17]

Catholics, Presbyterians, and Baptists were to be found among St. Paul's Hungarians. This diversity was conditioned by previous denominational affiliation but modified by neighborhood settlement patterns, linguistic affinity, and personal belief. Among Catholics, the interplay of these factors sent Hungarians to three congregations — the Churches of St. Agnes, St. Bernard, and St. Andrew, established in 1887, 1890, and 1895, respectively. Organized as German-language parishes on St. Paul's North Side, St. Agnes and St. Bernard each attracted a contingent of German-speaking Hungarians from the Rice Street neighborhood. Magyars from the Como district also regularly attended St. Andrew and St. Agnes — especially from 1912 to 1921, while Hungarian-born Father Ernö Rückert served the latter as assistant pastor — but some were drawn back to St. Andrew when a parochial school was opened there in 1920. St. Andrew, established as a territorial parish to serve all Catholics in the Como district, was popularly regarded as Hungarian because

ST. PAUL'S Hungarian community, lacking a national parish, gathered to attend a Mass offered by a visiting Hungarian priest in 1922.

of its numerous Magyar members. Services were conducted in Latin and English, but the Magyar presence was nonetheless noticeable. Until the 1930s both the American and the Hungarian flags were displayed at the altar on traditional European holidays such as Holy Trinity Sunday, and as late as 1980 the parish retained an intangible but pervasive ethnic influence.[18]

The Baptist faith enjoyed brief popularity among Hungarians in the Como neighborhood, where a lay preacher, Andrew Kandler, an Austrian patternmaker, carpenter, and former Catholic, lived and in 1912 founded the Church of God Baptist Mission. The congregation, meeting in a tiny edifice, was subsequently renamed a German, then a Hungarian, and finally a Hungarian and German Baptist Mission. Its members varied in number, nationality, and religious background, although most of them were disaffected Catholics. In order to reach as many neighbors as possible, Kandler preached in both German and Hungarian, learning the latter language solely for that purpose. In its heyday during the early 1920s, the mission claimed 25 members and 20 adherents, and Kandler issued *Vallásos Lap* (Religious Gazette), a weekly publication in the Hungarian language. But the congregation was "never very big or very regular." Older members died, younger ones strayed, and the mission was finally closed in 1937.[19]

Other Protestant Hungarians attended Warrendale Presbyterian Church, which was also located in the Como neighborhood. Organized in 1889 as a mission of the House of Hope Church, it was not originally intended to serve the Hungarians, who soon became its active, pioneering members. Hungarian men donated their labor to improve the physical facilities of the church, and families hosted goulash dinners and bazaars to raise funds for congregational purposes. As early as 1898 a traveling Hungarian minister married couples in traditional ceremonies using Warrendale's Hungarian song and prayer books.[20]

In fact, it was through association with "the Protestant Hungarians of St. Paul" that the church acquired its first resident pastor. In 1921 the group arranged to pay $360 annually to finance a Hungarian service on Sunday after-

noons. Thus the church, self-supporting for the first time in its history, issued a call to the Reverend George de Földessey Fisher, a graduate of the Hungarian Seminary in Dubuque, Iowa.

Fisher's work during the ensuing six years illustrated the gradual process of cultural adjustment. "The Hungarian children attend the English Sunday School," he wrote, "and when ready are received as members in the American Church. . . . There are twenty Hungarian families associated with our American Church. On the average, we receive three young people a year into the fellowship of the church. The youngsters attend only English services. The Hungarian service is maintained for the benefit of those who do not understand English." When Fisher accepted a pulpit in East Grand Forks in 1927, the Warrendale congregation tried but failed to find a similarly bilingual pastor as his successor.

But even before Minnesota's Hungarians had religious services in their native language, they had established at least one all-Hungarian society. The tendency to form associations was shared by Hungarians in America regardless of their social background, religion, or political preference. These various fraternal, cultural, and benefit societies served the diverse needs of people removed from home and family. From 1890 to 1914, "the formative period of Hungarian-American organizational life," 2,092 societies were established in the United States: 1,046 benefit, 317 religious, 638 social, and 91 political groups. Yet their combined memberships totaled a mere 67,000. The benefit and funeral societies were the most durable, since they provided monetary aid for which immigrants today can apply to public or private welfare agencies. Many other Hungarian-American organizations were short-lived because of dissension, which has been called "the Magyar curse."[21]

Typical of these ventures was the Gábor Baross Social and Sick Benefit Society of St. Paul, which provided health and funeral insurance to Minnesota Hungarians from 1892 until its official dissolution in 1973. At the time of the founding, Gábor Baross had only 25 members. Their number reached 100 in 1912 and 113 (the maximum) in 1917; it was still 91 in 1957. According to its bylaws, the society was nondenominational, welcoming any "law-abiding native sons and daughters of Hungary," as well as their descendants. The majority of members, however, were Protestants. In the year following its founding, Gábor Baross established a Hungarian-language school, which until 1910 received grammars, readers, and atlases from the Association of Hungarian Museums and Libraries in the homeland. The Hungarian government also supplied 20 books — mostly novels — specially bound and imprinted with the society's name. The extant records of the society do not mention the school after 1910, and its size, duration, and accomplishments are unknown.[22]

During 1904 the Holy Trinity Roman Catholic Benevolent Society was founded at the Church of St. Agnes in St. Paul. While little precise information has survived about this organization, we know that its affairs were conducted in the Hungarian language, that it provided social occasions as well as insurance, and that, like the Baross society, it began to falter with the decline of the Hungarian immigrant generation in the 1950s.[23]

Such societies and the churches were the major agents of cultural preservation for Minnesota Hungarians. Sacred or secular, they united the immigrants in traditional ceremonies or social activities. Hungarian wakes were commonly held in homes, and in Elk River, for example, the community gathered to celebrate traditional religious holidays such as the feast day of St. John. While Hungarian ways sometimes influenced religious services, the churches themselves were most important for their role in language maintenance.[24]

It remained for the Gábor Baross Society, joined after 1918 by the Holy Trinity Society, to uphold some of the ethnic traditions. Singly or jointly, they marked national holidays such as the feast day of St. Stephen (August 20), honoring the ruler who had established the Hungarian Christian kingdom in 1000 A.D., and March 15, the first day of the Hungarian Revolution of 1848–49. These celebrations were often held in rented halls on Sunday afternoons — regardless of the precise calendar date — so that community members of all religions and occupations could attend. The Elk River contingent regularly turned out, making the all-day trip to St. Paul three or four times annually to mingle with their countrymen and friends. Through the 1920s, at least, some people attended these events wearing their national costumes, and diligent children recited patriotic poetry in the mother tongue.

The two societies also sponsored purely social events at which everyone was welcome. Each held an annual Grape Dance, a traditional Hungarian harvest celebration for which the ceiling of a rented hall was draped with the fruit, and St. Paul and Elk River Magyars of all ages danced to live music. Hungarians in the Como district also held an annual picnic, where "strictly traditional" activities were mixed with informal socializing and softball. These social events, like the religious and nationalistic celebrations, served the additional purpose of helping to maintain some traditional cooking, dancing, singing, and instrumental music.

While Hungarian dishes continued to appear at community gatherings and on family tables, they were also introduced to a larger public by St. Paul entrepreneurs. By 1915

several Hungarians had opened bars or small lunch counters catering to people in the Rice Street area. John Stoyka and Joseph Konnad, however, operated downtown restaurants that attracted Hungarians as well as a wider clientele "whose names," reported the *St. Paul Pioneer Press*, "meant power and social position."[25]

Stoyka, the most successful Hungarian restaurateur in Minnesota, arrived in St. Paul in 1902 at the age of 32. In 1915 he opened his own saloon. Four years later he owned John Stoyka's Restaurant, which featured "Hungarian Dishes (genuine)." In addition, he canned and marketed Home Cooked Stoyka's Goulash to groceries, delicatessens, and meat markets. The goulash venture lasted for only a few years, but Stoyka continued to own and manage restaurants at various downtown St. Paul locations in the 1930s. His death in 1935 was front-page news, and his obituary referred to him as the owner of "one of St. Paul's most popular cafes."

Stoyka's name must have carried some weight as early as 1920 when Konnad, a former photographer turned bartender, opened a cafe complete with "Hungarian Kitchen" and advertised his former association with John Stoyka. His menu of goulash, paprika chicken, stuffed green peppers and cabbage, paprika schnitzel, and wiener schnitzel survived two moves in the ensuing years, but by 1928 Konnad had abandoned the food trade and resumed photography.

World War I, which ultimately found Hungary and the United States on opposing sides, abruptly ended the second period of Hungarian immigration and crystallized the divided loyalties of Hungarians and other European settlers. Faced with the escalating antiforeign feelings of more established Americans, Hungarians were suddenly forced to create an acceptable image from the complicated ingredients of ethnic loyalty, sentimental nationalism, and economic pragmatism. The Hungarian-American press, an excellent barometer of its readers' opinions, took both sides during the course of the conflict, as well as several positions in between, before concluding in 1918 "that in this great war America is also fighting Hungary's war for independence."[26]

Perhaps it was the rural Hungarian *ideal* — the fertile land, the home village, the extended family, the Magyar tongue, and the traditional customs — to which the typical immigrant remained loyal. Certainly the dream of rejoining his family as a landowner strengthened his nationalism. In any case, at the outset of the war the Hungarian government outlawed emigration and called for the return of its nationals. "At first great numbers were repatriated, but the . . . collapse of the country caused this movement to die down rapidly." Those who returned found "lawlessness, unemployment, poverty, and political unrest." The initial surge quickly subsided as many immigrants elected to remain in America.[27]

The response of Minnesota Hungarians to the war was quiet and cautious. As immigration and remigration slowed and then stopped (see Table 22.2), settlers by choice or by circumstance attempted to preserve elements of their heritage without appearing un-American. United in their societies, they evolved a pattern of action that long outlasted the volatile war era. While the solution — selective loyalty to both their native land and adoptive country — appeared contradictory, it was in fact the first tangible sign that the temporary immigrants had become Hungarian Americans. In April, 1918, for example, the members of the Baross society resolved to join the Hungarian American League of Loyalty, a national organization that sought to anticipate and dispel the anti-Hungarian suspicions or accusations likely to arise during the war. (This resolution appears to have been the extent of their involvement with the league.) At the same meeting the society also agreed to buy a $100 United States Liberty Bond. In general, however, Minnesota's Magyars eschewed public politics unless outside events forced them to take a stand.[28]

They were far more inclined to support activities aimed at maintaining the status quo or easing their adjustment to American society. There was, for example, the effort to establish a community center similar to those erected in the early 1900s by Hungarians elsewhere in the country. The members of the Gábor Baross Society first discussed the possibility of building such a Magyar House in 1918 and allocated $800 toward the cost of construction. The proposed center was envisioned as a cultural stronghold, a place where all Hungarians of different backgrounds could meet, socialize, and maintain their traditional customs. In 1922 representatives of the Holy Trinity Society offered to participate in this project, but despite the efforts of both groups it languished until 1928, when it was abandoned for lack of funds occasioned by "hard times."[29]

The Third Series, 1921–48

In 1919, when ocean travel to Europe resumed, Minnesota Magyars who wished to do so were free to return to Hungary. The exodus from the state was short-lived. Only in 1920 and 1921 did returnees significantly outnumber new arrivals (see Table 22.2). A large group is said to have left from St. Paul, perhaps hoping to buy land reportedly freed by the dissolution of large estates, to rejoin their families, or to emigrate again in the company of relatives made destitute by the war.[30]

International politics ruined many such plans. As early as 1919 political unrest erupted in Hungary, and returnees who had never served in the Hungarian army were conscripted despite their American citizenship. Then in 1920 the Treaty of Trianon gave 72% of Hungary's land and 62% of its population to Czechoslovakia, Romania, and Yugoslavia, ending dreams of prosperous repatriation and inaugurating decades of irredentist plans (see Map 22.1). Finally, passage by the United States Congress of the Emergency Quota Act of 1921 and the Immigration Act of 1924 greatly reduced the number of Hungarians allowed to enter the United States.

Subsequent Hungarian settlement in America was no longer a question of the pull of the New World or the push of the Old Country; rather, the third period of Hungarian immigration (roughly from 1921 to 1948) may be best characterized as a squeeze. America was still the land of opportunity for certain Hungarians: those who wanted to join relatives, laborers, skilled professionals, and political exiles. From 1921 to 1924 approximately 25,000 Hungarians were admitted to the United States, many of them women and children who were joining family members already in the country.[31]

After that the Immigration Act reduced the annual total of Hungarian immigrants to 869 and favored technicians and professionals. The Great Depression of the 1930s put a further crimp in admissions, just as increased numbers of Jews and other political refugees sought to escape from Hungary's growing anti-Semitism and Nazism. Then World War II virtually halted immigration. Figures vary, but it is estimated that no more than 2,500 Hungarians entered the United States from 1940 to 1945. The third period of immigration as a whole was marked by a shift in the ratio of female to male immigrants as well as a change in their socioeconomic and educational backgrounds.

Hungarian ethnic communities already established in the United States would be minimally affected by the changed patterns of third-series immigration. Often the educated newcomers did not mingle with the earlier settlers, whom they considered either as hopelessly Americanized or as socially, educationally, and culturally inferior. These differences prevented the revitalization of the ethnic communities and encouraged the quick assimilation of newly arrived professionals into the American mainstream. One result of this factionalism was the accelerated bloom and rapid decline (hastened by the Depression and World War II) of a hybrid Hungarian immigrant culture which exposed a bilingual second generation to local versions of Hungarian music, dance, literature, newspapers, and religious institutions. Like their parents, the members of this maturing generation were stigmatized as an ethnic minority. Labeled "American" by the new immigrants and "foreign" by the Americans, they, too, saw the attractions of joining the mainstream. If the 1920s was the "golden age of Hungarian language maintenance efforts," the 1930s and 1940s were periods of cultural erosion.[32]

The only issue to unite Hungarian Americans in the interwar years was the desire for a revised Treaty of Trianon which would restore Hungary to its prewar dimensions — a desire, said one historian, that assumed "the proportions of an elemental force." In February, 1929, the Gábor Baross Society resolved to support Hungarian irredentism. The following year the organization formally expressed its sympathy with the Revisionist League, an international arm of the Hungarian governments of the 1920s and 1930s, which sought to publicize Hungary's right to the recovery of its lost territories. There is no evidence, however, that the Gábor Baross Society did anything beyond passing these resolutions. Its members devoted neither time nor money to publicizing or promoting the cause of revisionism.[33]

Minnesota Hungarians, although too few in number to play dominant roles in these efforts, followed the general population trends visible in the country as a whole. Yearly totals of new immigrants steadily decreased from a high of 56 in 1924 to a low of 3 in 1932, the last year for which figures are available (see Table 22.2). The number of those identified as foreign-born Magyar speakers in the state also declined from 1920 to 1930, rising only slightly in 1940 (see Table 22.1).[34]

These new settlers bolstered the Hungarians' predominantly urban profile in Minnesota. In 1930, 730 of them were living in cities (420 in St. Paul, 191 in Minneapolis, 12 in Duluth, and the others in unspecified places); 189 were identified as rural residents, of whom 140 lived on farms. For the first time the Hungarian population of Minneapolis gained in proportion to that of St. Paul. In 1910 Minneapolis had 34% fewer Hungarian foreign born than St. Paul; in 1920 this figure fell to 30%, but by 1930 it had risen to 45%. It appears probable that Hungarian technicians, scientists, and scholars settled in Minneapolis in comparatively larger numbers because of its greater opportunities for employment.

In the decade following World War I, Hungarians in the Twin Cities pursued the courses they had set earlier in the century. Families continued to attend the same churches, which were, in most cases, still located in their immediate neighborhoods, but by 1927 services in the Hungarian language had ceased. The Gábor Baross and Holy Trinity societies remained strong and essentially nonpolitical. Maintaining the stances adopted during the war, they were sparing both in their expressions of American patriotism and in their support of organized opposition to Hungarian political regimes. In 1928, for instance, the Gábor Baross Society chose to ignore an invitation to join the Anti-Horthy League of New York, a group opposed to the increasingly right-wing, anti-Semitic policies of consecutive parliamentary governments under the regency of Nicholas Horthy.[35]

During the 1930s and 1940s the more traditional elements of Hungarian immigrant culture in Minnesota began to erode; those that survived underwent a curious transition. Culture took to the stage as family and community customs became material for public festivals and parades. Among the complex reasons for this evolution were the Great Depression and the subsequent international crises leading to World War II. Both catastrophes hastened the dissolution of the Hungarian-American home as a unit of language and culture retention.[36]

Minneapolis and St. Paul Hungarians interviewed during the research for this book cited this general period as the beginning of the end of Hungarian community life. Fewer Grape Dances were held; holy days were no longer celebrated by the display of Hungarian symbols in the churches, and the older Hungarian restaurants closed. Elderly immigrants died; others moved away; the second generation spoke less and less Hungarian and, losing interest in the old ways, "didn't keep things up."[37]

In Elk River, possibly because it was a tighter, more isolated Hungarian community with fewer nontraditional distractions, the picture was somewhat different. The public celebration of events like St. John's Feast or St. Stephen's Day lapsed, but the traditional home environment was maintained. Thus Hungarian speech, cooking, and many social customs remained the accepted patterns of behavior without special efforts to preserve them.

At least one successful Hungarian business was launched in Minneapolis during this era. Herman Sirmai (or Szirmai), its owner, typified the immigrant success story while remaining homesick for pre-World War I Hungary. Arriving in Minneapolis about 1910, he worked as a mailer for the *Min-neapolis Tribune* before returning to Hungary to marry. In 1911 he brought his wife to Minneapolis and resumed work. By the 1920s he was an auctioneer; in 1929 he opened a grocery store. By 1934 Sirmai had expanded, and he was then selling "beverages" (beer). Two years later he opened the Budapest Gardens, a bar and grill. Until 1961, when the business passed briefly to his son, Sirmai "had what some connoisseurs called the best-stocked bar in town" with a clientele ranging from union laborers to captains of industry. By 1964 business had fallen off, Herman Sirmai had died, his son was training to be a stockbroker, and the Budapest Gardens was sold.[38]

The story of this Hungarian-Jewish Minnesotan born in Transylvania should warn against rigid ethnic classifications. Nostalgic for his homeland, Sirmai clearly regarded himself as Hungarian. Esther Sirmai, his wife, and her Jewish compatriots named their organization the American Hungarian Ladies Benevolent Society. (The group did charity work from the pre-World War I era to the early 1960s, aiding among other places a hospital in Minnesota and a kibbutz in Israel.) Depending upon the circumstances, immigration and census authorities might have labeled the Sirmais as Hungarian, Magyar, Romanian, or Jewish. Similarly, they and doubtless many others sometimes regarded themselves as Hungarians, sometimes as Jews, and sometimes simply as naturalized Americans. Their case is not unique. National, religious, racial, and linguistic threads interweave to yield tapestries that change with the viewer's perspective.[39]

Paradoxically, the most successful local, public efforts to preserve and publicize the traditional cultures were initiated not by immigrants and their descendants but by other Americans. In response to the escalating antiforeign feelings aroused by the Depression and the impending World War II, the staff of the International Institute of St. Paul saw a need to extol the virtues of cultural diversity. In 1932 the institute sponsored the first Festival of Nations, an elaborate event which featured the foods, dances, music, and crafts of 15 of St. Paul's ethnic groups. Hungarians participated, although it was noted that "there were no youthful dancers in the community" and "their costumes were somewhat makeshift." Moreover one of the dancers' children reportedly said, "I don't like that old-country stuff."[40]

The presence of the same child as an elaborately costumed dancer in the next festival four years later underlined the irony of such cultural preservation efforts, which came from without, were often a revival of discontinued or dying practices, and almost always presented a frozen sample or a mechanical approximation of living European customs. Americanization — the adjustment of immigrant traditions to current living conditions — was regarded not as change but as loss. The Hungarians had emerged from the melting pot with vital parts of their culture intact, but by the mid-20th century their lives included much more than the customs and traditions of an increasingly remote homeland. Nevertheless the festival was accepted as a vehicle of cultural preservation by community members. In the 1980s it remained a colorful showcase for the famous Hungarian embroidery, wood painting, "gypsy" violin music, cuisine, and dances.

WOMEN in traditional dress with a display of Hungarian folk crafts at the 1964 Festival of Nations in St. Paul.

Displaced Persons and Freedom Fighters, 1948–56

Hungarian Americans had declared their loyalty to the United States well before the end of 1941 when the two countries officially became enemies in World War II. Nevertheless some touchy issues remained. Many Hungarian Americans, especially irredentists, maintained that Hungary, by pursuing the legitimate recovery of its lost territories, had become a pawn of Mussolini and Hitler. They pledged allegiance to the United States while agitating for the creation of an independent Hungary with its "ancient boundaries" intact. The events of the war dispelled such idle pipe dreams. The Hungarian war effort, the German and then Russian occupation of Hungary, and the provisions of the 1947 peace treaties affecting the country led in the end to both territorial and population losses. In the postwar era the fourth and fifth series of Hungarian immigrants — the Displaced Persons (DPs) and the Freedom Fighters — joined the already stratified Hungarian Americans. From 1948 to 1952, under the terms of the Displaced Persons Act, the United States received 16,000 Hungarians who had refused repatriation. In 1956–57, following the Hungarian revolt against Soviet Russian dominance, 30,000 Freedom Fighters arrived. These two waves of immigrants differed substantially from each other and from previous Hungarian settlers in the United States.[41]

In general, the DPs were members of the educated, urban, middle and upper classes. Many arrived as families. Like the immigrants following World War I, they tended to form their own social stratum, viewing most of the old Hungarian Americans as "farmers." But there the similarity between the two groups ended. Many of the DPs represented the right-wing, nationalistic points of view that had caused their immediate predecessors to leave Hungary. Consequently the immigrants of the third and fourth periods rarely mingled.[42]

·The procedure for admitting foreigners to the United States under the Displaced Persons Act was intricate and time-consuming, and the federal regulations created new — and in many cases short-lived — settlements. Not until 1949 did any Hungarian DPs arrive in Minnesota. When they did, the official requirement of sponsors and assurances of employment frequently placed them in areas with no previous Hungarian residents. Records of the Minnesota Department of Public Welfare showed that between 1949 and 1952, 162 Hungarian men, women, and children arrived in the state. Half of the recorded three-year total were sent to the state's three largest cities: 33 to Duluth, 26 to Minneapolis, and 23 to St. Paul. The other 80 were scattered singly or in families from International Falls in the north to Caledonia in the south.[43]

Some appear to have been placed according to their skills or preferences. A farming family of six members and a single farmer were sent to Balaton, a village in rural Lyon County named after Lake Balaton in western Hungary. A nurse went to Roseau's Budd Hospital; a housemother to the Hammer School in Wayzata; students to Macalester College (St. Paul), the College of Saint Teresa (Winona), and St. John's University (Collegeville); and two children to the St. Cloud Orphan Home. Twenty-three of the women found employment as domestics. While ministers, chemists, physicians, engineers, machinists, lithographers, and a chocolate-maker were represented among the 162 refugees, farmers, farm hands, and their families accounted for 40% (64) of the total number. This relatively high percentage may help explain the rural placements, although one wonders what a farm hand and his family of seven did in Duluth. Few of those who went to rural Minnesota remained there; most of them stayed in their assigned places for only six months before moving to an area with a greater Hungarian population. Some migrated to Minneapolis, but many left for Hungarian havens such as Cleveland and other cities on the East Coast.

While the resettlement of DPs dominated the immediate postwar era, other notable Hungarians also settled in Minnesota during those years. Both Loránd Andaházy, a choreographer and former dancer with the Ballet Russe de Monte Carlo, and Antal Dorati, who had conducted operatic, symphonic, and ballet music on four continents, had left Hungary many years before they reached the Twin Cities. Each had an established professional reputation and each lent his energy and prestige to various Twin Cities Hungarian refugee relief organizations in the ensuing years. Dorati, who arrived in the United States in 1941, directed the Minneapolis (now Minnesota) Symphony Orchestra from 1949 to 1960, often placing the works of his countrymen and former teachers on the programs he conducted. Andaházy, who served as an officer in the United States Army and led the first American tanks across the Rhine, settled in St. Paul after World War II. In 1952 he and his wife Anna Adrianova founded the Andaházy Ballet Borealis Company and the Andaházy Choreographic Schools, which were still operating in the 1980s.[44]

Until 1956 the Hungarians were just one among the many groups of Displaced Persons uprooted by events in central and eastern Europe as well as the Balkan peninsula. In 1956, however, the abortive Hungarian Revolution of late October and early November swiftly created an estimated 200,000 refugees. Thirty thousand reached the United States by April, 1957; approximately 300 of them were settled in the Twin Cities area by the following November. In general they shared the nationalistic, anti-Communist feelings of their immediate predecessors, the DPs. They were, however, considerably younger. Many were single adolescent males or university students. They included many more technically or professionally trained persons than the previous series of Hungarian immigrants.[45]

The resettlement of the Freedom Fighters in the United States coincided with the last two effective months of the Refugee Relief Act of 1953, the sequel to the Displaced Persons Act which had expired in 1952. Consequently the national network established to process earlier postwar refugees was simply maintained for the newest influx. The Joyce Kilmer Reception Center in New Jersey, where they stayed until they could be matched with sponsors, homes, and jobs, received the Hungarians through May, 1957. Each state formed a Governor's Committee for Refugee Relief to co-ordinate the work of all public and private agencies engaged in refugee resettlement. The state programs reported to the President's Committee for Refugee Relief (after 1956 known as the President's Committee for Hungarian Refugee Relief), which disseminated information and determined national policy.[46]

In Minnesota the committee appointed by Governor Orville L. Freeman included representatives of the major religious faiths, state commissioners of public welfare, business development, agriculture, and employment, members of the media, and private citizens. And it had a full schedule, for the Hungarian crisis caught the popular imagination. Minnesotans initiated and participated in a wide variety of relief efforts which progressed in four phases: sending aid to survivors in Hungary, arranging to bring refugees to the United States, finding them homes and jobs in Minnesota, and then helping them to learn English and adjust to life there.

Predictably, local Hungarians were active in all stages of the state's relief programs. Old organizations were mobilized, new ones were formed, and special events were launched with the twofold purpose of raising money and the national consciousness. In order to centralize and thereby maximize local resources, the Gábor Baross and Holy Trinity societies temporarily merged. By November 2, 1956, the president of the combined societies suggested that they coordinate the collection of clothing and funds, which the Red Cross would then forward overseas.[47]

The American Red Cross later initiated a campaign to raise $5,000,000 for the relief of Hungarian refugees in Austria. Cities were assigned quotas, ranging, for example, from $40,000 in Minneapolis and $22,000 in St. Paul to $345 in Pipestone. Also early in November, the Council for the Liberation of Captive Peoples from Soviet Domination was founded in the Twin Cities. Its members included Hungarians, Latvians, Ukrainians, and Estonians. The council issued a resolution calling on the United Nations to "deny recognition to the present Hungarian puppet government," apply social and economic sanctions against the Soviet Union, and call up an international police force which would operate under the United Nations charter. On November 24, 1956, the council sponsored a parade through Minneapolis and St. Paul culminating in a rally by several hundred local residents on the steps of the state Capitol, where Dorati and Andaházy were among the speakers who protested against "atrocities in Hungary."

The month of December, 1956, was even busier. The Minneapolis Symphony Orchestra — conducted alternately by Dorati and Zoltán Rozsnyai, a recent refugee from Hungary — played a concert for the benefit of Hungarian refugees in Austria. The program, featuring works of Bartók, Kodály, and Liszt, was intended to commemorate "the heroism and artistic genius of the Hungarian people." This benefit performance netted about $2,300.

The Governor's Committee for Refugee Relief expected Minnesota to accommodate 500 to 600 Hungarian refugees, and the various firms, clubs, and religious as well as private organizations worked hard to make the resettlement a smooth one. They were joined by the Minnesota Hungarian Emergency Committee, created during the previous month by Senator Edward J. Thye. Composed of prominent citizens throughout the state, the group was empowered to raise funds, to collect clothing, and to seek sponsors for the incoming refugees. It worked closely with the Governor's Committee, which did not have fund-raising duties. Newspaper and radio announcements helped the relief agencies secure sponsors. Reportedly, one radio broadcast alone netted 200 letters promising homes and jobs "for dentists, domestic and farm help, factory workers and specialists."[48]

While clothing was being gathered and rented homes furnished in anticipation of the Freedom Fighters' arrival, other imaginative proposals were put into action. Macalester College students worked to raise full tuition scholarships for five Hungarian refugees during the 1956–57 winter semester. Students at St. Mary's College in Winona formed the American Council of the World Action for Hungarian Freedom "to keep Hungary's plight in the forefront of Americans' thought." To this end, they designed and printed stamps picturing the Hungarian flag with the Communist hammer and sickle torn out. They mailed these stamps to students at other colleges and universities, asking only for contributions to cover their expenses.[49]

Another project engaged the attention of University of Minnesota students. They collected $1,200 and 5,000 pounds of clothing for the faculty and students of Sopron College of Forestry and Mining, who had recently escaped from Hungary to Austria. The Minnesota Hungarian Emergency Committee then suggested to the President's Committee

HUNGARIAN Freedom Fighters arriving in 1956.

that the college could be relocated in the former Pipestone Indian School in southwestern Minnesota. It further proposed that the United States government might operate the college for a year, after which it would depend upon private financing. Although the State Department was reportedly "immensely interested," the project was never developed.[50]

Equally inventive, as well as representative of the response of Minnesota's citizens, was the suggestion of a Duluth businessman that refugees be resettled on cutover timberlands about 50 miles from Duluth. In a letter to President Dwight D. Eisenhower, Jeno Paulucci, the president of Chun King Sales and Wilderness Valley Farms, Inc., explained that his firm had successfully grown vegetables on the land, 10 acres of which would easily support a family. Although Paulucci offered his company's facilities and heavy equipment for the venture, the proposal was not accepted, presumably because few Hungarians chose to settle in Minnesota. In any case, not many farmers turned up among the Freedom Fighters, most of whom had been urban residents.[51]

The first refugee to arrive in the state was a mechanical engineer who joined his great-aunt in St. Paul in late November, 1956. The first groups did not arrive until late December. Then, of the 75 expected in the Twin Cities, only 42 appeared. The others preferred to spend Christmas with their compatriots at Camp Kilmer before being dispersed throughout Ramsey and Hennepin counties, including the Twin Cities and 25 rural communities. Similarly, of the 11 who were sent to Duluth, only six arrived before the holiday.[52]

Although the number of arrivals fell short of expectations, Minnesotans supported the resettlement of Hungarians throughout 1957. Donations continued to appear from unusual sources. In January the Minnesota Motion Pictures Exhibitors, operators of theaters owned by the Minnesota Amusement Company, contributed $10,551 to the Minnesota Hungarian Emergency Committee, but by then energies had shifted from collecting money to "meeting the actual needs

of the bewildered families as they arrive." Thus Mrs. Klára Dorati, a member of the Emergency Committee, established a center where volunteers answered questions, compiled helpful information, and found interpreters to aid the newcomers. Arranging work for the adults and schooling for the children proved the most difficult tasks.[53]

At the same time, the Governor's Committee was trying to persuade Minnesota colleges and universities to provide tuition scholarships for student refugees, most of whom were said, with considerable exaggeration, to be interested in engineering. While efforts were under way to create and fund 20 such grants at the University of Minnesota, the committee received a check for $8,000 from the Roman Catholic Bishop Peter W. Bartholome of St. Cloud for scholarships at St. John's University, St. Mary's College, and the College of St. Thomas (St. Paul).

Still, as late as March 15, 1957, Minnesota had received only 130 Hungarians. On May 1, 1957, Camp Kilmer closed, signaling the end of the federal government's special involvement. Thereafter, Hungarians were processed at various ports of entry by the Immigration and Naturalization Service, and it became the responsibility of state and local committees "to make a complete and lasting job of resettlement."[54]

In their long-term reception of the DPs and Freedom Fighters, Hungarians in Minnesota once again proved a microcosm of the nation. After the initial crises had subsided, both the older residents and the newcomers tacitly acknowledged that they had little more than language in common. All told, there were only 841 foreign-born Hungarian speakers in the state by 1960, roughly half of whom had arrived since 1948. But nationality alone could not bridge the social, economic, educational, and political gulf, not to mention the generation gap. As in other states, "The expectation of the old American Hungarian organizations that these newcomers should revitalize their aging lodges was just partially fulfilled." Although some of the new immigrants joined the Gábor Baross and the Holy Trinity societies, the late 1950s marked the beginning of the end for both groups. Some members of the older generations died, and the newer arrivals found their needs for insurance and companionship satisfied elsewhere.[55]

Hungarian organizational life, however, did not end in the 1950s. Immigrants from Hungary still felt an urge to associate for the sake of religious and cultural continuity, rather than the economic and social security sought by their predecessors around the turn of the century. Consequently in 1959 Father Ferenc (Francis) Túrmezei, professor of comparative education at the College of St. Thomas, himself a DP, founded the St. Paul chapter of the Hungarian Catholic League of America. Its aims were fourfold: to support the spiritual, educational, cultural, and social welfare of all Hungarians, but especially Catholics — including those "behind the Iron Curtain." Túrmezei directed the chapter for 18 years. Its membership grew to 45 in 1960, decreasing gradually thereafter.[56]

In structure and in some functions the organization resembled the earlier benefit societies. There were fairly regular monthly meetings, minimal membership dues, and the customary commemorations of St. Stephen's Day and the anniversaries (March 15 and October 23) of the first days of the revolutions of 1848–49 and of 1956. Notable social events included an annual Shrove Tuesday Ball and a Christmas Festival complete with a special Mass. The chapter also operated a short-lived Hungarian language school which met at Holy Name Church in South Minneapolis on weekends in 1965–66. In addition, the chapter sponsored dinner dances and brought Hungarian entertainers to town. One of the major attractions for the older members was the showing of Hungarian films from the 1930s and 1940s, particularly comedies of manners. They commemorated a period of Hungarian culture — a way of life characterized by morals, manners, and a brand of humor — that had vanished after 1945.

But the local Hungarian Catholic League also developed a split in its ranks. By the early 1960s those who preferred to rally around ethnicity rather than the Roman Catholic religion formed a new organization known as the Minnesota Hungarians. This small, informal group held its meetings, dinners, dances, cultural events, and celebrations at the International Institute in St. Paul. For almost 20 years the two organizations coexisted, although by the late 1960s the league's activities were on the wane. During this time they occasionally cosponsored commemorations and performances. In 1965 the Minnesota Hungarians, the Hungarian Catholic League, and the remnants of the Gábor Baross Society joined in celebrating the anniversary of the 1956 revolution — the one tie binding the disparate Magyar factions together. Again the next year the united Hungarian groups actively sponsored or encouraged a month-long series of public events commemorating the 10th anniversary of the unsuccessful uprising.[57]

By 1972 the Minnesota Hungarians organization had 122 members (including some non-Hungarian-American spouses and friends) living in the Minneapolis-St. Paul metropolitan area, Stillwater, Chaska, and the college towns of Winona, Rochester, Northfield, Collegeville, and St. Peter. By 1973 they were operating according to a set of "loose bylaws."

Amended in 1977, the bylaws stated that the purpose of the group was "to provide a social, recreational, cultural, and charitable program for interested Minnesotans and other upper midwesterners of Hungarian origin and their families . . . as well as to serve as the Hungarian section of the International Institute of Minnesota." And so it happened that the small Minnesota population of Hungarian DPs and Freedom Fighters supported two groups similar in function, if not in philosophy, until the Catholic League disbanded in 1977 at Father Túrmezei's death.

The Sixth Series, 1960–?

Since the settlement of the Freedom Fighters by the end of the 1950s, only a trickle of Hungarians has reached the United States and Minnesota despite the relaxation of the quota system. In 1970 the state listed only 1,928 Magyar speakers, of whom 1,029 were first-generation Americans, 284 second-generation, and 615 foreign born. The vast majority lived in the most populous areas: 1,412 in metropolitan Minneapolis-St. Paul and 72 in Duluth-Superior. The remaining 344 were sprinkled in groups of 10 and 20 throughout the state except the southwest counties (see Table 22.3). There has been little solidarity in the ranks of the newcomers. Dissidents as well as apolitical emigrants have settled in the United States, the latter either because they were engaged or related to American Hungarians, or because they were seeking better professional or economic opportunities. In the early 1970s a small Hungarian neighborhood formed in South St. Paul in a manner reminiscent of the earliest settlements. The first family to arrive (sponsored by a local church) soon informed friends and relatives in the United States and abroad. By the end of the year there were 12 families, most of whom stayed in the immediate area.[58]

Few in number and mixed in age and outlook, the latest immigrants were nevertheless heirs to the patterns of the past. Although some joined the Minnesota Hungarians — then the state's only active Hungarian organization — they were not comfortable with their predecessors. In 1979 the group revised its bylaws, began using English rather than Hungarian at meetings, and changed its name to the Hungar-

Table 22.3. Hungarians in Minnesota by County, 1890–1970

County	1890 foreign born	1910 fb	1910 foreign mixed	1940 fb	1970 fb	1970 fm
Aitkin		5	2	3		13
Anoka	5	36	31	27	7	155
Becker		1		3		41
Beltrami		6	2	2	8	20
Benton		8	13	3	7	27
Big Stone				1		
Blue Earth		4	4	5	11	35
Brown	1	7	2	4		
Carlton	4	2		6		8
Carver	3	4	3	2	6	21
Cass		14	13	5		24
Chippewa			1	1		
Chisago		1		3		22
Clay		3		2	11	10
Clearwater				2		
Cook				1		
Cottonwood	1			1		7

Table 22.3. Hungarians in Minnesota by County, 1890–1970 (*continued*)

County	1890 foreign born	1910 fb	1910 foreign mixed	1940 fb	1970 fb	1970 fm
Crow Wing		7	1	9		9
Dakota	29	326	89	66	98	207
Dodge	3			5		
Douglas		3		1		
Faribault	3		1			7
Fillmore					7	4
Freeborn		5		2		5
Goodhue		8	4	1		6
Hennepin	271	1,197	510	424	371	949
Minneapolis	269	1,176	506	401	194	428
Hubbard		3		4		
Isanti				1		
Itasca		106	24	13		13
Jackson	1	43	73	1		
Kandiyohi				3		
Kittson		2		1		
Koochiching		4		8		5
Lac qui Parle	1	1		2		
Lake		2				13
Lake of the Woods						11
Le Sueur	26	51	51	3		7
Lincoln		1				
Lyon		1	2			
McLeod	92	50	82	1		19
Mahnomen				1		9
Marshall	3	3	5	3		22
Martin				1		
Meeker		20	12	10		18
Mille Lacs		1		6		14
Morrison	9	83	117	6	8	12
Mower	1	1		3		24
Murray	2			3		
Nicollet	6	5	3	9		6
Nobles		3	2	1		6
Olmsted	3	14	2	9		38
Otter Tail		4		6		9
Pennington				2		8
Pine		17	31	3		19
Pipestone				1		
Polk	3	9	18	1	6	
Ramsey	442	2,020	798	781	187	721
St. Paul	410	1,989	785	753	159	549
Red Lake				2		6
Redwood			1	3		6
Renville		3	1	1		20
Rice	7	3	2	1		14
Rock				1		
Roseau				5		19
St. Louis	31	1,124	201	80	3	98
Duluth	10	76	22	25		42
Scott	1	2		10	6	
Sherburne	3	16	13	38	22	48
Sibley	25	13	6	4	6	23
Stearns	205	188	217	24		57
Steele	8					
Stevens	1	6	3	2		
Swift	2	1		2		
Todd	4	10	16	6		7
Traverse	4	1				
Wabasha		69	4	4		
Wadena		3		5		
Washington	12	16	9	22	22	53
Watonwan	10	5	2			5
Wilkin		2		2		11
Winona	16	9	1	13		32
Wright	18	27	42	9	5	7
Yellow Medicine		3	4	2		
Total	1,256	5,582	2,419	1,697	791	2,950
Published census figures	(1,256)	(5,582)	(2,419)	(1,697)	(791)	(2,950)

Source: See Appendix

ian Organization, Incorporated. Soon thereafter internal disagreements caused some of the older members to leave.

The history of the Hungarians in Minnesota is a study in ethnic complexity. In little more than one century, six distinctive series of immigrants have called the state home. Their far-reaching and abiding differences at any given moment have caused some to question the existence of an ethnic community. As the Reverend Túrmezei put it, "There are too few of us, and in any case we are scattered, and each of us tends to be an island entire unto himself." Yet small groups did form, tempering life in Minnesota with varying allegiances to the national integrity, the language, the arts, crafts, and customs of Hungary. In the end, none would deny that all were or had been Hungarians. Their history of conflict, consensus, and change offers an example of the dynamics of intragroup diversity.[59]

Reference notes

[1] International Institute, *Festival of Nations, 1958,* 22 (St. Paul); Emil Lengyel, *Americans from Hungary,* 14, 17 (Philadelphia, 1948). On the multiethnic, multinational composition of Hungary, see Julianna Puskás, *Emigration From Hungary to the United States Before 1914,* 30 (Budapest, 1975). The authors wish to thank Paul Rupprecht, George Grossman, Katherine Tezla, and Kriszta Mandics for their help.

[2] Here and below, see Lengyel, *Americans from Hungary,* 126–128; United States, *Census, 1920, Population,* 1:995. For a higher but unverified population estimate, including distribution of settlement, see D. A. Souders, *The Magyars in America,* 51, 55 (New York, 1922). On the characteristics of Hungarian emigration, see Gustav Thirring, "Hungarian Migration of Modern Times," in Walter F. Willcox, ed., *International Migrations,* 2:411–438 (Reprint ed., New York, 1969); J. Kosa, "A Century of Hungarian Emigration, 1850–1950," in *American Slavic and East European Review,* 16:501–514 (December, 1957); Puskás, *Emigration From Hungary,* 1–36.

A note on the terms "Hungarian" and "Magyar" should be added. The latter is more precise, as it specifically names the ethnic group, differentiating it from the many others which reached the United States from Hungary. The former includes all residents of Hungary regardless of background or affiliation. In the literature and popular usage, however, the two terms are often interchanged. American immigration and census reports, for example, labeled immigrants by country of origin. Thus although figures exist for Hungarians in Minnesota as early as 1870, the number of Magyars is not known. Consequently mother-tongue tallies, which offer a surer but by no means infallible index of ethnicity, have been used in this chapter wherever possible, and the terms have been employed as specifically as source material permits. For the additional complications created by the Treaty of Trianon partitioning Hungary in 1920, see p. 429. On the problems of counting Magyars, see Leslie Konnyu, *Hungarians in the United States: An Immigration Study,* 5 (St. Louis, 1967); Lengyel, *Americans from Hungary,* 120–124; Erdmann C. Beynon, "The Hungarians of Michigan," in *Michigan History,* 21:92 (Winter, 1937). For criticism of mother-tongue statistics, see Joshua A. Fishman, *Hungarian Language Maintenance in the United States,* 5, 50 (Bloomington, Ind., 1966).

[3] Konnyu, *Hungarians in the United States,* 5, 11, 14; Joseph Széplaki, comp., *The Hungarians in America 1583–1974,* 5 (Dobbs Ferry, N.Y., 1975). For information on early Hungarian explorers, see Rezsoe and Margaret Gracza, *The Hungarians in America,* 8–16

(Minneapolis, 1971); Lengyel, *Americans from Hungary*, 19–36. On the Hungarian Revolution and the period preceding the formation of the Austro-Hungarian Empire, see C. A. Macartney, *Hungary: A Short History*, 155–170 (Edinburgh, Scot., 1962); Denis Sinor, *History of Hungary*, 264–273 (New York, 1959).

[4] Samuel Ludvigh, "Nach dem Westen," in *Die Fackel* (The Torch), 11:218, 219 (Baltimore, 1858). As late as the 20th century, family names ending in "y" — equivalent to the German "von," French "de," or English "of" — signified the possessor of a hereditary title. Hungarian law forbade commoners to assume such names. The family's name is spelled "Kallia," a plausible English representation of the Hungarian sounds, in U.S. manuscript census schedules, 1860, Nicollet County, roll 572, microfilm in MHS. On Balaton, platted in 1879 and purportedly named by political emigrés, see note 43, below. On the Wisconsin and Iowa settlements, see Konnyu, *Hungarians in the United States*, 11; Széplaki, *Hungarians in America*, 4, 6; Lengyel, *Americans from Hungary*, 33–35, 50–52; Gracza, *Hungarians in America*, 15.

[5] W. B. Bovill, *Hungary and the Hungarians*, 301–312 (New York, 1908); "Hungary," in *Encyclopaedia Britannica Micropaedia*, 5:210 (Chicago, 1975); Gracza, *Hungarians in America*, 35; Konnyu, *Hungarians in the United States*, 20; Kosa, in *American Slavic and East European Review*, 16:502; Lengyel, *Americans from Hungary*, 101, 104, 111; Arminius Vámbéry, *The Story of Hungary*, 7 (New York, 1891); Puskás, *Emigration From Hungary*, 17; József Gellén, "Emigration in a Systems Framework: The Case of Hungary, 1899–1913," paper presented at IHRC, October 17, 1979, copy in MEHP Papers. For more detail on 19th-century Hungary, especially the lot of the peasants, see Lengyel, 94–134; Konnyu, 15–21; Vámbéry, 7–10; Bovill, 299–314.

[6] Here and below, see Konnyu, *Hungarians in the United States*, 15, 20; Lengyel, *Americans from Hungary*, 98, 125, 129; Julianna Puskás to Paul Rupprecht (in Hungarian), summer, 1979, pp. 1, 6, copy in MEHP Papers; Puskás, *Emigration From Hungary*, 5–8, 14–16; Willcox, ed., *International Migrations*, 1:436, 438, 494, 495; U.S., *Census*, 1910, *Population*, 1:1005; 1920, 2:973. For more detail on remigration, see Széplaki, *Hungarians in America*, 27; Julianna Puskás, "Some Recent Results of Historic Researches on International Migration," in *Acta Historica Academiae Scientarum Hungaricae*, 23:164 (Budapest, 1977).

[7] U.S., *Census*, 1870, *Population*, 340; 1880, 494; 1910, 1:836, 1005; 1920, 2:995. For net immigration, see Minnesota Hungarian Statistics, in MEHP Papers, compiled by Jon A. Gjerde from U.S. Dept. of Labor, Bureau of Immigration, *Annual Reports*, 1909–39. These figures, however, are only approximations. They were taken from declarations of *intended* residence and do not include interstate migration. Unlike the Balkan peoples (see Chapter 20), relatively few Hungarians left just before or during World War I. Many had completed their military service prior to immigrating, others may have hesitated to join the Central Powers; Konnyu, *Hungarians in the United States*, 20.

[8] Andrew Vázsonyi, "The Cicisbeo and the Magnificent Cuckold, Boardinghouse Life and Lore in Immigrant Communities," in *Journal of American Folklore*, 91:641 (April–June, 1978).

[9] Konnyu, *Hungarians in the United States*, 21; U.S., *Census*, 1880, *Population*, 540; 1890, 676; 1900, 796; 1910, 1:836, 856, 1005, 2:1014, 1015; 1930, 2:377, 1020, 1026.

[10] Here and below, see interviews of John Préda, Károly and Julia Kovács by Kriszta Mandics, summer, 1979; Ann Heinz, July 23, 1980, Steven Gunda and Irene Rotz, August 1, 1980, Helen Zupfer, August 5, 1980, by Anne Kaplan — all notes in MEHP Papers.

[11] Here and below, see U.S., *Census*, 1910, *Population*, 2:1018. Information on Hungarian life in Minneapolis is sparse, but those interviewed showed some signs of ethnic confusion. One contended that the South St. Paul settlement was predominantly Romanian,

others asserted that it was Magyar, and still another felt that ethnic distinctions made no difference, since immigrants of different nationalities left from the same central European area, knew each others' languages, and were on good terms. In any case, Hungarian neighborhoods in the Twin Cities were never as large or cohesive as those in New York City, Buffalo, New Brunswick (N.J.), Pittsburgh, Cleveland, Detroit, and Chicago. See Konnyu, *Hungarians in the United States*, 27–30, 33, 35, 39, 40–42, 47; see also Chapter 23.

[12] John Storck and Walter D. Teague, *Flour for Man's Bread*, 246, 251, 253 (Minneapolis, 1952); Pillsbury Mills, "Historical Sketch," 1, November 9, 1953, copy in MEHP Papers, original in Technical Library, Dept. of Scientific Research and Technical Development, Pillsbury Mills, Inc.; "Pillsbury A Mill," in *Earth Journal*, vol. 5, no. 1, 1975, p. 61; *St. Paul Pioneer Press*, July 4, 1977, p. B18. For a detailed discussion of the invention and adaptation of milling technology, see also Robert M. Frame III, "The Progressive Millers: A Cultural and Intellectual Portrait of the Flour Milling Industry 1870–1930," Ph.D. thesis, University of Minnesota, 1980.

The slow but steady trickle of Hungarian millers to Minneapolis, begun at the end of the 19th century, continued at least into the 1950s. By the mid-20th century the immigrants who found jobs in the city's milling industry were mostly mechanical engineers introduced to the mills by their Hungarian-American predecessors; interview of Paul Rupprecht by Anne Kaplan, December 18, 1980, notes in MEHP Papers.

[13] Calculated from U.S., *Census*, 1910, *Population*, 1:1005.

[14] Here and below, see Puskás, *Emigration From Hungary*, 7; George O. Virtue, *The Minnesota Iron Ranges*, 345, 348, 349, 355 (U.S. Bureau of Labor, *Bulletin*, no. 84 — Washington, D.C., 1909).

[15] Calculated from U.S., *Census*, 1910, *Population*, 1:1005; 1910, *Agriculture*, 5:180. There were eight Magyar families in Bovey in 1912, according to William J. Bell, "The Mesabe and Vermillion Ore Ranges," [1914], in Bell Papers, MHS. For an account of the few Hungarians in Duluth, see interview of Mrs. L. Chepel by Marjorie Hoover, summer, 1980, notes in MEHP Papers.

[16] Here and below, see interview of Steve Nemeth, a native of Elk River, by Anne Kaplan, October 10, 1980, notes in MEHP Papers; Rotz interview, August 1, 1980; Title Atlas Company, *Atlas of Sherburne County, Minnesota*, n.p. (Minneapolis, 1962). Most attended the Church of St. Andrew, Elk River.

In 1910 there were 16 foreign-born and 13 native-born Hungarians in Sherburne County; by 1920 their number had jumped to 45 foreign born (native-born Hungarians were not counted that year). U.S., *Census*, 1910, *Population*, 2:1010; 1920, 3:521.

[17] Dezsö Ábrahám, *Hungarian Reformed Churches in America*, 3, 15 (n.p., 1960); Lengyel, *Americans from Hungary*, 161, 180–183; Stephen Torok, "Hungarian Catholics and Their Churches in America," in Keith P. Dyrud, Michael Novak, and Rudolph J. Vecoli, eds., *The Other Catholics*, 2 (New York, 1978); John Dikovics, *Our Magyar Presbyterians* (New York, 1945); interview of Adele Gross by Anne Kaplan, August 8, 1980, notes in MEHP Papers.

[18] Church of St. Agnes, *50th Anniversary*, 32 (St. Paul, 1937); Church of St. Bernard, *Golden Jubilee*, 73 (St. Paul, 1940), and *Pictorial Directory* (St. Paul, 1969); Kenneth J. Pierre, "The Church of St. Andrew St. Paul, Minnesota, 1895–1945," 33, master's thesis, St. Paul Seminary, 1966; interviews of Father Ted Koziol (St. Andrew), July 22, 1980, Michael Ettel, July 23, 1980, Gisele Gubasta, July 25, 1980, by Anne Kaplan — all notes in MEHP Papers; interviews of Heinz, July 23, and Gross, August 8, 1980.

Rückert information from Father Urban Wagner, Chancery Office, Archdiocese of St. Paul, July 30, 1980; Lucille Kampa, St. Agnes Church secretary, August 18, 1980, notes in MEHP Papers. Rückert (also called Ernest Rickert) served as assistant pastor at St. Bernard's from August through November, 1912, and was then transferred to St. Agnes. In 1921 he was sent to the Cleveland diocese, where he died in 1947. While in St. Paul he was a member of the Hungarian Library Committee, a six-person group formed to increase the number of Hungarian-language publications in that institution. Acclaimed as the first scholar of American-Hungarian literature, Father Rückert compiled the earliest anthology of poems by American Hungarians. Entitled *Amerikai Magyar Költők*, it was published in Budapest in 1920; Széplaki, *Hungarians in America*, 26; Gábor Baross Social and Sick Benefit Society, Minutes, May 5, 1918 (in Hungarian), in IHRC.

[19] Souders, *Magyars in America*, 87, 142; *St. Paul City Directory, 1912–38*; Gross interview, August 8, 1980; interview of Ann Jurgenson, Kandler's daughter, by Anne Kaplan, August 12, 1980, notes in MEHP Papers.

[20] Here and two paragraphs below, see Warrendale Presbyterian Church, *75th Anniversary* (St. Paul, 1964); George de Földessey Fisher to William P. Shriver, Home Missions Board, n.d., in Dikovics, *Our Magyar Presbyterians*, 37, 38; interview of Helen Zupfer by Anne Kaplan, July 21, 1980, notes in MEHP Papers.

The traveling minister was Rev. Alex Harsanyi, who also published at Pittsburgh a weekly paper, *Amerikai-Magyar-Reformatusok Lapja*, for Presbyterian and Reformed churches in America; Souders, *Magyars in America*, 141; Zupfer interview, July 21, 1980. Of all the American Protestant denominations at the turn of the century, Presbyterians were noted for their efforts to include Magyars in the church. Warrendale itself continued to emphasize foreign and national missions through the 1970s. See Ábrahám, *Hungarian Reformed Churches*, 15; Ann G. Kaloides, ed., *Histories of Presbyterian Churches in the Twin Cities Area* ([Minneapolis-St. Paul?], 1976), copy in MEHP Papers.

[21] Fishman, *Hungarian Language Maintenance*, 6; Lengyel, *Americans from Hungary*, 167. For more on societies and churches as cultural trusts, see Ábrahám, *Hungarian Reformed Churches*, 13–16; Gracza, *Hungarians in America*, 36.

[22] Gábor Baross Society, books and undated inventory, bylaws and annual membership records, in IHRC. Gábor Baross was the Hungarian minister of transportation (1886–89), who helped develop steamboat navigation on the Danube, nationalize the railways, and lower the fares. Within the framework of a government program to curtail emigration, he also officially encouraged and assisted one group of Transylvania Hungarians to resettle in central Hungary and to work for the Hungarian National Railways; Bálint Hóman and Gyula Szekfű, *Magyar Történelem*, 5:497 (Budapest, 1936); István Rácz, *A paraszti migráció és politikai megitélése Magyarországon 1849–1914*, 168 (Budapest, 1980).

[23] Gábor Baross Society, Minutes, June 1, 1919; interview of John Préda by Anne Kaplan, July 23, 1980, notes in MEHP Papers.

[24] Here and two paragraphs below, see interviews of Heinz, July 23, Rotz, August 1, Gunda, August 1, Zupfer, August 5, and Nemeth, October 10, 1980; Gábor Baross Society, Minutes, June 7, 1918, March 2, 1919.

[25] Here and two paragraphs below, see *St. Paul City Directory, 1915–36*; Shubert Theatre playbills (St. Paul), September 24, 1919, January 11, 1920, copies in MHS; *Capitol Theatre Magazine* (St. Paul), February 2, 1924, p. 9; *St. Paul Pioneer Press*, December 13, 1935, p. 1; Rotz interview, August 1, 1980.

[26] Lengyel, *Americans from Hungary*, 200.

[27] Gracza, *Hungarians in America*, 40; Konnyu, *Hungarians in the United States*, 20; Lengyel, *Americans from Hungary*, 129; Thirring, in Willcox, ed., *International Migrations*, 2:433.

[28] Gábor Baross Society, Minutes, April 7, 1918. The exact number of Hungarians in Minnesota during the war is not known, but other sources offer much higher estimates than the 1,431 foreign born in the census: 2,000 in St. Paul alone, according to Alice Sick-

els, *Around the World in St. Paul*, 11 (Minneapolis, 1945); 5,000 in the state, according to Souders, *Magyars in America*, 51.

There is no evidence that Hungarians during this period were the targets of American chauvinists or public safety commissions. While many remembered English classes, naturalization proceedings, and buying war stamps in grade school, none recalled any undue pressure. Nor is there any record that the Baross Society went beyond voicing mere support of the League of Loyalty. See interviews of Heinz, July 23, Gubasta, July 25, Gunda, August 1, and Rotz, August 1, 1980. The Minnesota Public Safety Commission's publication, *Minnesota in the War* (St. Paul), February 15, 1919, p. 3, noted that "work is being done among the . . . Magyars"; copy in Minnesota Commission of Public Safety Records, Minnesota State Archives, MHS.

[29] Gábor Baross Society, Minutes, May 5, 1918, February 2, March 4, 1922, April 1, 1928; Fishman, *Hungarian Language Maintenance*, 29; Konnyu, *Hungarians in the United States*, 42; Préda interview, July 23, 1980.

[30] Here and below, see Gracza, *Hungarians in America*, 41; Konnyu, *Hungarians in the United States*, 54; Kovacs interview, summer, 1979; Theodore Saloutos, "Exodus U.S.A.," in O. F. Ander, ed., *In the Trek of Immigrants*, 208 (Rock Island, Ill., 1964); Souders, *Magyars in America*, 102. The Dual Monarchy collapsed in 1918. From 1920 to 1944, the parliamentary governments under the regency of Nicholas Horthy discouraged emigration; Kosa, in *American Slavic and East European Review*, 16:508; Gracza, *Hungarians in America*, 41. On U.S. legislation, see Introduction, above. Irredentists were those who sought the restoration of Hungary's lost territories.

[31] Here and below, see Gracza, *Hungarians in America*, 43–45; Kosa, in *American Slavic and East European Review*, 16:509–511; Puskás to Rupprecht, summer, 1979, pp. 2, 3. On politics in Hungary, see Macartney, *Hungary*, 209–235; on the immigration of Hungarian scholars, scientists, and artists, see Laura Fermi, *Illustrious Immigrants: The Intellectual Migration from Europe, 1930–41*, 25–27, 53–59 (Chicago, 1968).

One such immigrant was Eugene Ormandy, who became a famous conductor. Ormandy arrived in the U.S. in 1921; from 1931 to 1936 he was the music director and conductor of the Minneapolis Symphony Orchestra. Under his aegis the orchestra enhanced its reputation and won a major recording contract. See John K. Sherman, *Music and Maestros*, 195–226 (Minneapolis, 1952).

[32] Fishman, *Hungarian Language Maintenance*, 7–9.

[33] Lengyel, *Americans from Hungary*, 173; Gábor Baross Society, Minutes, February 3, 1929, July 6, 1930.

[34] U.S., *Census*, 1920, *Population*, 2:995, 1020, 1026; 1930, 2:372, 377, 381, 384; 1960, vol. 1, part 25, p. 195. It should be noted that as the century progressed tallies of the mother tongue of the foreign born became less accurate estimates of population size, for they failed to account for the generations born in America and used restrictive criteria to define mother tongue.

[35] Gábor Baross Society, Minutes, July 1, 1928. In Hungary the Dual Monarchy had been followed by a Socialist republic, a Communist regime ("the red terror"), and then a lawless period of anti-Communist reprisals and anti-Semitic pogroms ("the white terror") which ended in 1920 with the re-establishment of the monarchy and a parliamentary form of government under the regency of Nicholas Horthy. The Anti-Horthy League was founded by Hungarian Americans who either sympathized with the regimes of 1918 and 1919 or believed that the subsequent Hungarian governments failed to prosecute the instigators of the white terror with sufficient vigor or were drifting into a right-wing and anti-Semitic orbit; Gracza, *Hungarians in America*, 41.

[36] Fishman, *Hungarian Language Maintenance*, 11–13.

[37] Here and below, see interviews of Heinz, July 23, Rotz, August

1, Gunda, August 1, and Nemeth, October 10, 1980. Sickels, *Around the World in St. Paul*, 11, claimed that "In 1920 there were nearly two thousand foreign-born Hungarians in St. Paul, but in the next 10 years half of them moved away." Community members thought that those who left were seeking better employment; Gubasta interview, July 25, 1980.

[38] *Minneapolis City Directory, 1912–65*; *Minneapolis Tribune*, May 10, 1980, p. 10A; interview of Esther Sirmai by Anne Kaplan, August 28, 1980, notes in MEHP Papers.

[39] Sirmai interview, August 28, 1980. Another example was the Hungarian Grill, featuring "American and Hungarian Cooking Kosher style," which opened in 1931 in St. Paul but had closed by 1932; *St. Paul City Directory, 1931, 1932*; Shubert Theatre playbill, March 1, 1931. In the homeland, many Jews considered themselves first and foremost patriotic Hungarians; Lengyel, *Americans from Hungary*, 223. On Jewish and Catholic Hungarians' changes of affiliation in America, see Fishman, *Hungarian Language Maintenance*, 11.

[40] Here and below, see Sickels, *Around the World in St. Paul*, 71, 73, 79; Heinz, Préda interviews, both July 23, 1980. Once the ice was broken, public displays of culture-for-a-cause became common. Folk songs, dances, and costumes were all part of the show. In 1966 Fishman noted that annual events — picnics, festivals, dances — might become the only contact the younger generations have with their traditional culture; see *Hungarian Language Maintenance*, 33.

For more on the conception of the Festival of Nations, see Sickels, *Around the World in St. Paul*; on attempts to create tolerance through cultural display, see Anne Kaplan, "The Folk Arts Foundation Of America: A History," in *Journal of the Folklore Institute*, 17:56–75 (January–April, 1980); on the Hungarians' retention and commercialization of customs, see Beynon, in *Michigan History*, 21:100–102.

[41] Lengyel, *Americans from Hungary*, 174–176. For a sketch of Hungary's part in World War II, see Gracza, *Hungarians in America*, 45–47. A final estimate placed the number of Freedom Fighters in the U.S. at 38,045 "by the late 1950s"; Puskás to Rupprecht, summer, 1979, p. 4.

[42] Fishman, *Hungarian Language Maintenance*, 13; Konnyu, *Hungarians in the United States*, 57; Kosa, in *American Slavic and East European Review*, 16:511–513.

[43] Here and below, see Minnesota Displaced Persons Commission, Displaced Persons Resettled in Minnesota, Minnesota Public Welfare Dept. Records, January, 1949–April, 1952, in State Archives; interview of Olga Zoltai by Anne Kaplan, October 1, 1980, notes in MEHP Papers; interviews of Gubasta, July 25, and Nemeth, October 10, 1980. None of the refugees was sent to Elk River although friends and relatives of community members did settle in the state. On Balaton, see Fishman, *Hungarian Language Maintenance*, 49; Warren Upham, *Minnesota Geographic Names*, 312 (Reprint ed., St. Paul, 1969); interview of Mr. and Mrs. Texas Swanjord of Balaton by Anne Kaplan, July 19, 1980, notes in MEHP Papers.

[44] International Institute, *Festival of Nations, 1958*, 22; Gracza, *Hungarians in America*, 59, 60; Sherman, *Music and Maestros*, 289–298.

[45] The President's Committee for Hungarian Refugee Relief, Memorandum, February 14, 1957, Dept. and General Files, Orville L. Freeman Papers, in Minnesota State Archives (hereafter cited as Freeman Papers); "Displaced Persons," in *Encyclopedia Americana*, 9:166–168 (New York, 1960); Konnyu, *Hungarians in the United States*, 57; unidentified St. Paul newspaper clipping, November 10, 1957, p. 1, in "The Hungarian Revolution and Refugees in the Minnesota Press 1956–1957," scrapbook in International Institute of Minnesota, Special File on Hungarians, 1938–58, in IHRC (hereafter

cited as International Institute, Hungarians). On the Hungarian Revolt, see Macartney, *Hungary*, 236–243.

[46] On the relief efforts here and below, see Kenneth Bjork, "Report of the Conference on Hungarian Refugee Resettlement for Chairmen of the Governor's Committees, April 1–2, 1957" (hereafter cited as Bjork, "Report"), and Governor's Committee for the Refugee Relief Program, roster, n.d., both in Freeman Papers; National Council of the Churches of Christ in the United States of America, "Information Memorandum no. 25," February 15, 1957, in International Institute, Hungarians.

[47] Here and below, see *St. Paul Pioneer Press*, November 2, p. 1; December 1, p. 1; 20, p. 10 — all 1956; *St. Paul Dispatch*, November 24, 1956, p. 4; *Pipestone County Star*, December 27, 1956, p. 2; Council for the Liberation of Captive Peoples from Soviet Domination, "Resolution, November 24, 1956," in International Institute, Hungarians.

[48] Governor's Refugee Relief Committee, Minutes, December 10, 1956, p. 2, Freeman Papers; *St. Paul Dispatch*, December 4, p. 17; 12, p. 75; 20, p. 5; 22, p. 1 — all 1956; *St. Paul Pioneer Press*, December 4, 1956, p. 1. The accredited relief agencies in Minnesota were the International Institutes of Duluth and St. Paul, Minneapolis Council of Americanization, Catholic Charities, Church World Service, United Hebrew Immigration Aide Service, Inc., and Lutheran Welfare Society. All of the Minnesota refugees arrived under the auspices of the Catholic Charities or the Lutheran Welfare Society; Else Miller to Lorena Scherer, May 21, 1957, in International Institute, Hungarians.

[49] *St. Paul Pioneer Press*, December 9, 1956, 5th sec., 1; *St. Paul Dispatch*, December 13, 1956, p. 13.

[50] *Pipestone County Star*, December 10, 1956, p. 1. Students who had received help from Minnesota reportedly enrolled at the University of Vancouver, British Columbia; *St. Paul Pioneer Press*, January 8, 1957, p. 1.

[51] *St. Paul Dispatch*, December 27, 1956, p. 17.

[52] *St. Paul Dispatch*, November 23, p. 13; December 22, p. 1, 1956; *Duluth News Tribune*, December 21, p. 1; 22, p. 2, 1956.

[53] Here and below, see *St. Paul Dispatch*, January 8, 1957, p. 7; unidentified newspaper clippings, January 11, June 27, 1957, in "Hungarian Revolution," scrapbook, in International Institute, Hungarians; Peter W. Bartholome to Kenneth Bjork, May 27, 1957, Freeman Papers. On the tuition scholarships, see also *Minneapolis Star*, June 6, 1957, p. 10A.

[54] Bjork, "Report," Freeman Papers.

[55] Interviews of Gubasta, July 25, Gunda, August 1, Rotz, August 1, and Zoltai, October 1, 1980; Konnyu, *Hungarians in the United States*, 57; American Immigration Conference, National Council on Naturalization and Citizenship, "Hungarian Refugee Resettlement in the United States," 12 (New York, 1958), copy in International Institute, Hungarians; U.S., *Census, 1960, Population*, vol. 1, part 25, p. 145. Of the Minnesota Hungarians, 740 were urbanites, 44 were farmers, and 57 were classified as rural nonfarming residents. The 1960 census, however, did not count native-born speakers of the mother tongue and used only a 25% sample. Thus its findings do not give a total picture.

[56] Here and below, see Hungarian Catholic League of America, St. Paul chapter, financial records, 1959–77, and "Aims of the Hungarian Catholic League of America," n.d., both in Ferenc Túrmezei Papers, in IHRC. Twenty-five students of kindergarten and primary school age attended the Hungarian school. While the benefit societies had also sponsored social events, these occasions were not their primary function.

[57] Here and below, see Zoltai interview, October 1, 1980; conversation of Anne Kaplan with Paul Rupprecht, October 8, 1980, notes in MEHP Papers; membership roster, 1972, Amended Bylaws

of the Minnesota Hungarians, March 5, 1977, and Invitations, 1965, 1966 — all in Papers of the Minnesota Hungarians, in IHRC. Members in the metropolitan area lived in South St. Paul, West St. Paul, Minnetonka, Coon Rapids, Cottage Grove, Wayzata, and Circle Pines.

[58] Here and below, see Puskás to Rupprecht, summer, 1979, p. 4; U.S., *Census*, 1970, *Population*, vol. 1, part 25, p. 514. For the county distribution of Hungarians, see Minnesota Analysis and Planning System, *Minnesota Socio-Economic Characteristics From the 4th Count Summary Tape of the 1970 Census*, vol. 3, n.p. (St. Paul, 1972); Zoltai interview, October 1, 1980. The counties without Magyar speakers were Big Stone, Swift, Lac qui Parle, Yellow Medicine, Chippewa, Lincoln, Lyon, Redwood, Pipestone, Murray, Cottonwood, Rock, Nobles, and Jackson. In 1970 Minnesota also had 2,950 native-born citizens of Hungarian stock, some of whom, no doubt, considered themselves ethnic Hungarians although they did not speak the language.

[59] Túrmezei to Mindszenti House (a Hungarian Catholic school in Austria), 1968, in Túrmezei Papers.

CHAPTER 23

The Romanians

Louis M. deGryse and Anne R. Kaplan

THE ROMANIANS of Minnesota belong to the immigration of the late 19th and early 20th centuries. None was recorded in the state until 1900, when the federal census counted 483 from the kingdom of Romania, almost all concentrated in Hennepin (419) and Ramsey (52) counties. Their numbers increased until 1930, when they totaled 5,754, the vast majority of whom settled in the metropolitan area of Hennepin, Ramsey, and Dakota counties (see Table 23.1). Thereafter growth was stunted by the combined effects of United States' immigration quotas, World War II, and Soviet restrictions on emigration. By 1970 Minnesota's foreign-stock Romanian population had diminished to 2,357.[1]

From the start the Romanians settled in a few particular neighborhoods: near the stockyards in South St. Paul, in the North End and Frogtown areas of St. Paul, and in North Minneapolis. Although some were also to be found in Austin, Duluth, and elsewhere in St. Louis County, the story of Minnesota's Romanians is largely a part of the history of the Twin Cities area, the site of their only churches and fraternal organization in 1980.[2]

The ethnic Romanians are the largest branch of a widely scattered people who call themselves Rumans. Prior to the World War I peace settlement of 1919, the kingdom of Romania (see Map 23.1) embraced only Wallachia, Moldavia, and Dobruja, leaving a great many Romanians in Austria-Hungary (Transylvania, Bukovina, and the Banat), Serbia, and Russia (Bessarabia). Others were scattered in various areas of present-day Bulgaria, Yugoslavia (the Istrian peninsula, near Trieste, the city of Dubrovnik, the mountains of Macedonia), and in the Pindus Mountains and Acarnania (western Sterea Hellas) in Greece (see Maps 20.1, 25.1). Language and religion have been the mainstays of their identity. All of the Romanians speak closely similar Latin-derived dialects. They are predominantly Eastern Orthodox in religion, with a leaven of Uniates in northeastern Transylvania, Bukovina, and the Banat.[3]

Given the complexity of ethnicity in southeastern Europe and the very frequent changes of political frontiers in the period since 1890, nationality as recorded by immigration officials often bore little relation to an immigrant's ethnic identity. From 1901 to 1910, for example, only 3.5% of the Romanian emigrants came from the kingdom of Romania; 93% derived from the Hungarian provinces of the Banat and Transylvania and Austrian-ruled Bukovina, while the re-

maining 3.4% left Russian Bessarabia, Serbia, Greece, Bulgaria, and Turkey. Conversely, of the 61,073 emigrants whose last residence was Romania admitted to the United States from 1899 to 1910, 89.8% were Jews, 3.9% were Germans, Greeks, Bulgarians, Serbians, and Montenegrins, and only 5.8% were of pure Romanian stock.[4]

The causes of this emigration were complex and varied somewhat from region to region. In general, poverty and oppression were the lot of the peasant in all areas of Romanian habitation between 1890 and 1919 where the small industrial base could not absorb the growing rural population. In the kingdom land was largely in the hands of the *boiars* (nobles), and even the secularization and redistribution of extensive church holdings did not palliate the peasants' land hunger. Divisibility of inheritances led to fragmentation of the already small plots and an inevitable dependence on low-paid labor on the large estates. Taxes were high, incomes low, and the peasant was all but disfranchised by the electoral laws and literacy tests.[5]

In Austria-Hungary, too, the agrarian economy was severely depressed and the peasant was at the mercy of the landlord. But there the situation was further complicated by cultural distances and a more systematic oppression. The Hungarian policy of Magyarization had very definite economic results: the average Romanian paid four times as much tax as his Magyar neighbors, was effectively disfranchised, and was heavily fined or jailed for the least infractions. He was daily exposed to the sight of neighbors living a better life at his expense, a goad at once to ambition and to discontent. Magyarization went to the heart of Romanian life, denying children schooling in their own language, forcing teachers and the intelligentsia to speak in the Hungarian tongue, and generally creating an atmosphere of intense ethnic antipathy. In Bessarabia similar Russification policies produced parallel results. Bukovina was under Austrian administration and therefore free from the burdens of Magyarization but it, too, produced a crop of Romanian emigrants.[6]

Regardless of their country of origin, the Romanian emigrants were overwhelmingly unskilled male agricultural workers. Over 30% were illiterate. Many had some vague notions of possible destinations such as Philadelphia, Detroit, or Chicago, places extolled in America letters or praised by returned friends or by railroad and steamship

Table 23.1. Romanians in Minnesota by County, 1900–70

County	1900 foreign born	1930 fb	1930 foreign mixed	1970 fb	1970 fm
Aitkin		2	6		
Anoka		5	14	7	12
Becker		4	10		
Beltrami		2			
Big Stone		2	3		
Blue Earth		3	2	13	
Brown		1	2		13
Carlton		2	24		29
Carver		1	7		16
Cass		12	11		
Chippewa				6	
Chisago	2			4	
Clay	1	4	12		5
Crow Wing	2	1	4		5
Dakota		296	227	54	75
Dodge		1	1		16
Douglas	1	1		9	
Fillmore		1	1		
Freeborn		2	2		
Goodhue	1		2		11
Grant			1		
Hennepin	419	1,610	1,771	332	934
Minneapolis	417	1,599	1,757	94	322
Houston				9	
Isanti	1		1		
Itasca		3	6		
Kanabec		2	1		8
Kandiyohi		3	1		
Kittson		16	60		
Koochiching		67	33	6	13
Lake of the Woods		20	29		6
Le Sueur		1			
Lyon		3	1		
McLeod		1	3		
Mahnomen		5			
Marshall	1				4
Martin		1	3		
Mille Lacs		1	4	6	
Morrison		2	1		
Mower		2			15
Nicollet		1	1		
Norman		2	4	7	
Olmsted		10	10		42
Otter Tail	1	7	3	5	5
Pine		5	11		12
Pipestone		4	5	6	
Polk		5	10	6	
Pope		1	3		
Ramsey	52	596	510	142	374
St. Paul	52	589	507	125	310
Red Lake		1	3		
Redwood		1			
Rice		3	6	12	8
St. Louis	1	82	92		27
Duluth	1	61	59		27
Scott		4	3		
Sherburne		1	3		
Sibley		1	1		7
Stearns		9	6		
Steele				7	7
Stevens			3		8
Todd		1	9		6
Traverse	1				
Wabasha		1	3		
Wadena				7	
Washington		5	1		24
Wilkin					13
Winona		2	2	9	8
Wright			2		7
Yellow Medicine			1		
Total	483	2,819	2,935	647	1,710
Published census figures	(483)	(2,819)	(2,935)	(647)	(1,710)

Source: See Appendix

agents. In a number of instances whole villages picked up stakes and moved, and some resettled *en bloc* in America. Even so, men usually left first, sending for wives and sweethearts later. In other cases when immigrants from the same villages or districts arrived in the United States, they were hired by agents as unskilled labor and were promptly shipped to various factories, mines, railroad yards, or meat-packing plants. Despite their agrarian backgrounds, over 90% of all Romanian immigrants entered industrial occupations in the United States. From the outset they were concentrated in New York, Ohio, Pennsylvania, Illinois, and Michigan, with states such as Minnesota standing fairly low on the scale.[7]

But just as characteristic as the tendency to settle in industrial centers was the very heavy incidence of Romanian returnees. Like immigrants of many nationalities during this era, most planned to make their fortunes, return to their homes, buy land, and live out their lives in comfort. This goal was expressed in the popular phrase "a thousand dollars and home again." Between 1899 and 1924, 148,251 Romanians were admitted to the United States, and, during the same time, 97,861 (66%) departed.

Establishing Settlements: 1900–1930

This picture of immigration was faithfully reflected in Minnesota (see Table 23.2). While it is probable that the 483 Romanians reported in 1900 were chiefly Jews, the 639 who arrived between 1899 and 1910 represented the immigration commission's attempts to record "by race or people as well as by country of birth or origin." Although almost all of the Romanian regions sent immigrants to Minnesota, the majority about whom we know — those in St. Paul and South St. Paul — were from the Banat. Some settlers arrived from Austro-Hungarian lands: Transylvanians were well represented in the Duluth community and formed the second largest contingent in South St. Paul, and Bukovinians made up a small share of the populations of both cities. In addition, a few immigrated from Moldavia and Wallachia, and there is a record of one family from Macedonia.[8]

As of about 1904 some dozen men from the Banatean village of Toracul Mare had found their way to South St. Paul, attracted by work in the Swift and Armour meat-packing plants. In 1905 four more arrived. They were joined in 1906 by a particularly interesting group of eight who had first gone to Toledo, Ohio, to work in railroad construction. Finding themselves ill-treated by a foreman, they decided to walk to St. Paul since they lacked money to travel otherwise. This epic expedition took six weeks. The adventurers in turn invited five friends to join them, who encouraged the sixth, a married man, to bring his wife and open a boardinghouse.[9]

A common feature of immigrant life in the United States, boardinghouses were focal institutions in the early communities. As one Romanian put it, "The few men who brought their wives with them soon discovered that keeping a boardinghouse for fellow nationals brought more money into the family till than by working — often irregularly — in factories." The house was usually a two-story frame building with seven or eight rooms, and the average number of Romanian boarders ranged from 25 to 30, although some places

Map 23.1. Romania

housed as many as 60. Boarders rarely slept alone, and there were often two shifts a day for each bed. The men frequently gathered after supper to sing plaintive songs about their homeland or to listen to someone in the group play the shepherd's flute, a traditional Romanian instrument. "At the end of each month the housekeeper bought a four gallon keg of beer and 'treated' his boarders. . . . If some owner appeared to be stingy about it, he soon lost some boarders." [10]

There is good reason to believe that this pattern was enacted in South St. Paul. Between 1907 and 1909 some 200 to 400 Romanians, mostly single men or those who had left their families overseas, settled there. Many were employed by Swift and Company, but community entrepreneurs also emerged fairly early. The first "restaurant and saloon" appeared in 1907, followed by eight others. At the same time there were three barbers, three bakers, four grocers, and one Romanian hotelkeeper. By 1911 the area was served by nine boardinghouses, all but one of them located on North Concord Street. In these early years, wrote a community historian, "The little social life for which they had time, after 12 or 14 hours of work daily centered in the respective board-

inghouses' large dining rooms and later in the [Romanian] saloon . . . at 217 North Concord Street." [11]

Until 1907 Romanians in the United States had no churches of their own. Hymns and cantiques were often sung in the saloons on Sundays, until gradually the men were able to sing the whole service. For deaths, marriages, and christenings, the Eastern Orthodox often resorted to the services of Serbian, Greek, or Russian priests. Where possible Uniates attended Roman Catholic Hungarian churches, as they could understand some of the Magyar language. In St. Paul the Church of St. Bernard attracted many from the burgeoning Romanian colony in the North End. The South St. Paul community relied on the services of the nearest clergy, usually Catholic or Lutheran. [12]

Early reports of the St. Paul neighborhood are less detailed, but it seems to have developed along similar lines. In 1910 the federal census found 392 Romanian speakers in the city proper, although, as ever, their ethnic affiliation is open to question. We do know, however, that many arrived after 1910, drawn to the area by the prospect of employment in the Northern Pacific Railway's Como shops or in the grain elevators. [13]

By 1918 between 180 and 200 ethnic Romanian families lived in St. Paul's North End and Frogtown neighborhoods, a combined area bounded by Western Avenue and Jackson Street on the west and east, by Larpenteur Avenue on the north, and the Burlington Railroad tracks near the state Capitol on the south. They settled thickly around the intersection of Woodbridge and Atwater streets, which soon became central to the community. Almost all were former residents of the villages of Toracul Mare and Beba Veche in the Banat, which had been home to many of the South St. Paulites as well. In the decade from 1920 to 1930 there was some movement within the general neighborhood, as Romanians were among those who replaced the Swedes in Wards 1 and 8, immediately west and east of the North End colony.

After 1902 Romanians in various cities began to form sick- and death-benefit associations. In addition to providing for members, these societies soon gained an informal educative value, as meetings became places to discuss problems of adjustment to life in America. Cultural societies also appeared, and as early as 1906 a first attempt was made to

Table 23.2. Romanian Migration to and from Minnesota

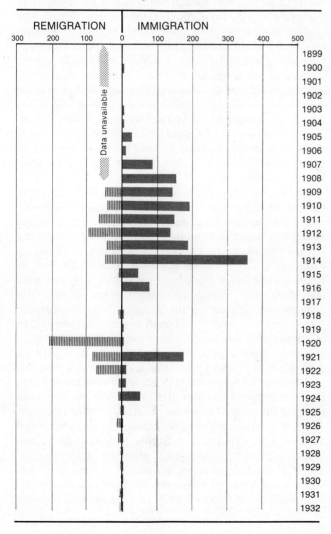

form a national organization known as the Union of Romanian Beneficial and Cultural Societies. A rival organization called the League and Help soon sprang up, and active competition for membership ensued. By 1928 the advantages of merger became apparent, and the Union and League of the Romanian Societies of America, Inc., resulted.[14]

Beneficial and cultural societies both preceded and facilitated the formation of Romanian Orthodox churches. Until a basis in practical organization existed, provision for churches could not be made, as the home church lacked both funds and personnel to promote missionary activity. When Romania finally sent priests to serve in the United States, competition for control of the communities soon arose between the already established lay leaders and the newly arrived clergy. In 1918 a Convention of Laymen and Priests acknowledged the problem and agreed to recognize the archbishop of Bucharest as their spiritual head. Thereafter the Americans promoted a movement to create a new diocese known as The Romanian Orthodox Episcopate of America. Organized in the United States in April, 1929, it was not endorsed by the powers in Bucharest until 1935 when they assigned Bishop Policarp Moruşca to the new diocese, which had its offices in Cleveland and its cathedral in Detroit. This proved to be the beginning of decades of feuding which finally culminated in a rift in the American Episcopate and a break with Bucharest. The Minnesota communities were, from the first, in the thick of these developments.

The North End settlement in St. Paul was the site of Minnesota's first two Romanian institutions. In 1910 the combined St. Paul and South St. Paul communities founded Augustina, a fraternal society named for the month in which it was established. As was the case with many such organizations, Augustina did more than pay out sick and death benefits. Members were friends who socialized and grieved together. As early as 1911 at the first Romanian burial in St. Paul, "Members of Augustina . . . led by a funeral band, followed the casket to the cemetery."[15]

But the group was probably best remembered for its efforts in organizing the state's first Romanian Orthodox parish, The Falling Asleep of the Ever-Virgin Mary, in May, 1913. Land was purchased at the corner of Atwater and Woodbridge streets, and by 1914 the parish had completed St. Mary's Romanian Orthodox Church, allegedly a replica of one in San Nicolaul Mare, Romania. It soon became the focal point of an active social as well as sacred life. Adults presented Romanian-language plays, and younger members formed *calusheri*, traditional dancing groups.[16]

Although sustaining a parish was said to be more difficult than founding one, the congregation proved its mettle. As one of about 16 Romanian Orthodox churches in the United States in 1917, St. Mary's survived both the break in overseas communications caused by World War I and the political-religious vicissitudes of the home church. Not until after the war did it receive a priest. Shortly thereafter a language school was begun for the benefit of the youngsters. The church was not officially consecrated, however, until 1935 when Bishop Policarp arrived in America, five years after members had voted to join to the Episcopate. By 1938 St. Mary's served 80 families. It had a women's auxiliary, a

Sunday school, a Young People's Club, and a social and cultural hall.

Nowhere else in the state is the record as clear as for the above two groups. It is especially vague for the Romanian settlement in Minneapolis. Although the federal census of 1910 found 878 speakers of Romanian there, mother tongue, as we have seen, was no guarantee of ethnicity. The statement of a Romanian from South St. Paul that "Minneapolis . . . attracted some Romanians" hardly accounted for a mother-tongue tally more than twice the size of St. Paul's. Lacking any positive proof that these people were Romanians — they had no churches or organizations despite their large numbers — it seems safe to conclude that most of them may have been Jewish.

Almost all of the pre-1895 Romanian immigrants in the United States were Jews from Moldavia, Bessarabia, and Bukovina. In Minneapolis, according to one historian, "On the South Side . . . there were an estimated 3,500 [Jews] . . . most of them Rumanians." As early as 1888 a sufficient number in Minneapolis consciously identified with their homeland to start an Orthodox synagogue, the Rumanian Hebrew Congregation, in Ward 6 — the heart of the densest concentration of the "Romanians" listed in the 1910 census. Furthermore a survey of the 1905 state census schedules revealed that many of those who reported Romania as their country of origin had names such as Cohen, Goldenberg, Rosenzweig, Schwartz, Segal, Finkmeyer, and the like; not ethnic Romanian names in any case.[17]

Not until about 1930 did a distinct ethnic Romanian settlement form in North Minneapolis. According to a long-time neighborhood resident, it extended from a block south of Broadway on Dupont Avenue near Ascension Catholic Church eastward to the Mississippi River and southward to the vicinity of Plymouth Avenue. Ascension Church itself functioned as a religious center for some of these people, a situation which poses several questions: Why, in the era of parish building and the creation of the American Episcopate, did the Minneapolis Romanians attend a Catholic church? Were they too few to organize their own? Before the creation of St. Mary's, Romanians depended upon the nearest clergy, Catholic and Lutheran alike, for baptism and funeral services. But why in the 1930s did "only two or three families" attend the church in St. Paul? Were they, perhaps, Uniates?[18]

The Romanians of the Duluth area, although few in number, organized at an early date. In 1900 the one Romanian in all of St. Louis County lived in that city. By 1910 the population had grown to 79, and in 1920 there were 66 Romanian speakers, 47 of them foreign born, out of 84 residents of Romanian stock. They congregated in New Duluth, the city's western industrial sector. There, in 1916, 17 Romanians, most of them Transylvanians, established *Campul Libertatii* (Field of Liberty), a cultural and benefit society destined to reach beyond its local beginnings. Apparently less successful was the attempt of 10 New Duluth families to establish St. Nicholas Church sometime in the mid-1920s. No further mention of the venture has been found, and the congregation was not included in any of the religious censuses of the period. Instead, by 1938 St. Mary's in St. Paul listed "sons" from both New Duluth and Minneapolis among its congregants.[19]

Romanian workers put in a relatively brief appearance on the Mesabi Iron Range. They were, according to one study, among the "recent immigrants" who, arriving on the Mesabi after 1905, were put to work in the pits and dumps of the surface operations. In 1907 five of the Oliver Iron Mining Company's 12,478 employees were Romanians, two of whom spoke English. None had been in the country for more than three years. Shortly thereafter the tide turned; "Romanians were present on the Range in large numbers for some years after 1907." Although never numerous enough to support their own lodges, they were credited with "maintain[ing] a separate ethnic existence," while joining the organizations of "those whose religious affiliation was similar to their own." There were both Eastern Orthodox and Uniate churches in Chisholm after 1911, but the Romanian presence there must have been short lived. After 1912 they, along with Montenegrins, Bulgarians, Serbs, and Macedonians, were called back to Europe to fight in the Balkan Wars. At about the same time, economic depression followed by mechanization of the mining process decreased the need for unskilled labor. By World War I, the range's Romanians were reported to have "disappeared virtually to the last man."[20]

ST. MARY'S Romanian Orthodox Church in St. Paul, noted for its distinctive onion dome, as it looked in 1964.

ROMANIAN WOMEN demonstrated traditional embroidery styles and spinning techniques at Duluth's International Institute festival in 1941.

World War I and the Growth of Immigrant Institutions

The war had a far-reaching impact on Romanian-American life, intensifying some aspects and altering others. Initially neutral, Romania joined the Triple Entente in 1916, hoping for territorial gains in the peace settlement. When the United States entered the conflict in 1917, at least one Romanian who was forced to register as an alien in Minnesota used the registration form to define his status beyond all doubt. For place of birth, he listed Austria-Hungary; for the country to which he claimed allegiance, he chose the United States. In the space for miscellaneous remarks, he laid other pertinent questions to rest, declaring: "I am Roumanian of Nationality born in Transylvania (Hungary). God bless Roumania and Uncle Sam." [21]

Although defeated and forced into a separate peace by the Germans, Romania remained sympathetic to the Allies, and at the war's end became one of the chief beneficiaries of the peace, acquiring Transylvania, a large part of the Banat, Bukovina, and Bessarabia. Many migrants from those regions returned to Europe after the war. Not only were their homelands now legally joined with Romania proper, but the land reforms enacted there in 1921 promised to permit realization of the emigrants' original dreams. The exodus from Minnesota began in 1918 and peaked two years later;

nevertheless, in the decade from 1920 to 1930 Minnesota lost 298 Romanians and gained only 163 (see Table 23.2). [22]

Romanian ethnic awareness reached a fever pitch among those who chose to remain in the United States during this time. It was expressed locally in the formation of new organizations. The Romanian population of South St. Paul, at least, had been steadily, if slowly, growing despite losses from re-emigration and interstate migration. It was time for the residents, as one put it, to "avoid the long streetcar rides they had to make every Sunday to go to church and lodge in St. Paul." The first move toward self-sufficiency came on January 1, 1918, when 47 men, mostly Transylvanians, founded the fraternal and cultural society, *Alexandru Cel Bun* (Alexander the Good). Like other such associations, this one paid thousands of dollars in sick benefits during the course of its existence. [23]

Other organizations soon took shape. In 1922 *Clubul National Roman* (Romanian National Club) was incorporated as a cultural and mutual aid society. This group, the first to include women among its charter members, was composed chiefly of former Banateans. It was thus the third of the four Romanian fraternal societies in the state which formed according to Old Country residence. Apparently the ethnic awareness of the era did not develop into pan-Romanianism. On the contrary, according to one descendant, the settlers "were most comfortable dealing with people of their own villages." Settlements at home were remote and the immigrants carried their rivalries and loyalties with them to Minnesota. Only as the generations passed did a sense of being St. Paul, South St. Paul, or Minnesota Romanians replace original Old Country regional identities. [24]

As had happened earlier in St. Paul, the formation of one organization quickly led to another. By 1922 when South St. Paul had an estimated 500 Romanians, the area undertook to support a church of its own. Under the leadership of *Clubul National Roman*, the Orthodox parish of St. Stefan was organized in 1923, and a church was built the following year. In 1927, according to a parishioner, the club "united" with the parish, donating all of its resources and artifacts to the church. The following year St. Stefan's gained a women's aid society, and by the 1930s it had a church choir and Sunday school as well.

Three more events marked this era of growth. In January, 1929, a group of 22 men and women in South St. Paul formed *Ardealul si Banatul*, still another mutual aid society. Six months after being established, it merged with *Campul Libertatii*, the predominantly Transylvanian society in Duluth. The result, *Campul Libertatii si Ardealul si Banatul* affiliated with the recently merged national organization, the Union and League of Romanian Societies of America. In St. Paul, the Augustina society also joined the Union and League, leaving only *Alexandru Cel Bun* in South St. Paul as an independent benefit society. [25]

The third and last organization to be formed during this era was the Romanian Youth Club, founded in 1934 in South St. Paul. Its purpose, according to a community historian, was "holding together American youth of Romanian descent in South St. Paul," suggesting that the Romanian community was feeling the pinch of Americanization. [26]

To combat the drift away from their heritage, members of the Romanian Youth Club organized some very traditional activities. Much like the church group in St. Paul, it offered plays and songs, presumably in the Romanian language. The club was closely linked to St. Stefan's Church, which provided the site for its activities and received the proceeds of its performances. Meetings were suspended during World War II, when many of the members either went off to fight or devoted their time to other duties. After the war, it was reconstituted as a chapter of the American Romanian Orthodox Youth (AROY), newly founded by the Episcopate in hopes of retaining its younger members.

War and Schisms, 1940–45

World War II and subsequent politics in the homeland directly affected the churches and communities in the United States. In 1940 Romania aligned with Germany, entering the conflict the following year. By 1944 a change of regimes effected a change of sides, and the country finished the war with the Allies. Later developments saw the establishment of a Communist-controlled coalition government, succeeded in 1947 by the People's Republic of Romania.[27]

While Romanians in Minnesota and elsewhere in the United States explicitly supported their adopted country, they were unwilling to deny their heritage. In 1940 the Cultural Association for Americans of Romanian Descent was established in Cleveland. Coincidentally or not, its purposes were perfectly suited to deflecting any wartime anti-Romanian propaganda. The association vowed to "disseminate information regarding the contributions made by Romanian Americans to the United States, to help Americans of Romanian descent to better understand their ethnic background, and their place in the American society." From 1942 to 1948 it published the *New Pioneer*, the only all-English Romanian journal in existence in the United States at that time. As early as 1942 the magazine listed among the association's members one from St. Paul, one from South St. Paul, and the entire *Campul Libertatii si Ardealul si Banatul*.[28]

The *New Pioneer* scrupulously reported the patriotic activities of its constituents. Its Minnesota entries showed churches and benefit societies busily organizing community war efforts. The Romanians of St. Paul, led by Father Petru Moga of St. Mary's Church, contributed both cash and the clothing made by the Ladies' Auxiliary to the American Red Cross. Moga estimated in 1942 that 100 Romanian families in the city had purchased about $28,000 worth of war bonds and contributed $1,800 to other service agencies. In South St. Paul, *Campul Libertatii* and *Alexandru Cel Bun*, respectively, invested 50% and 75% of their funds in war bonds. Each also made small donations to the Red Cross, as did the women of South St. Paul who organized a benefit tea for the organization.[29]

During this period, the ecclesiastical politics that eventually split the Romanian church in America came to a head. In 1939 Bishop Policarp of the American Episcopate took certain grievances to the patriarchate in Romania and while there was placed under house arrest. In the United States a power struggle evolved between those loyal to the absent bishop and those who, hoping to take his place, intrigued to prevent his return. The Minnesota parishes remained loyal to Policarp, with Father Moga as a prominent agitator for his cause.[30]

Relations among the Americans and between them and Bucharest became more and more strained, especially after the establishment of the Communist regime in Romania. The rift came in 1950 when the Holy Synod of Romania officially retired Policarp and appointed one of his most ardent opponents in his place. Representatives of dissenting parishes, including those in Minnesota, convened in Chicago in 1951, broke with the synod, elected their own bishop, and proclaimed themselves the Romanian Orthodox Episcopate of America. For them these acts marked the end of religious affiliation with the homeland, for in 1960 the diocese, which had been without canonical ties since the split, entered the jurisdiction of the Russian Orthodox Metropolia in the United States.

The years of infighting and the final schism had surprisingly little effect on daily life in the parishes. No doubt the members of St. Mary's noticed when Father Moga banned copies of the diocesan publications from his church, but the local reaction to his activities is not known. The Episcopate, however, was not pleased to learn in 1944 that he was "reading a goodly portion of the Holy Liturgy in English," and "publishing a review called *Orthodoxy*, attacking the Catholics." We can only conjecture that Moga was trying to keep his parishioners within the faith, hold onto the bilingual or English-speaking second generation, and perhaps attract outsiders to St. Mary's. But, according to a church historian, the lay faithful "seldom worried about largely theoretical spiritual problems . . . the Church meant having a priest for Sunday, for baptizing and funerals." Father Moga left St. Paul in 1945. He was neither the first nor the last of a series of controversial priests who served the parish.[31]

Evolution of Ethnic Communities after 1945

The story of the Romanians in Minnesota is in some ways one of ethnic decline. Although particular neighborhoods seemed to grow in the 1900s, the census showed a steady population decrease after 1930 (see Table 23.3). Following World War II the Displaced Persons did little to swell the ranks. In 1949 only three of the 558 Displaced Persons reported in Minnesota were Romanian. By February, 1950, there were 26, and as of May, 1952, Minnesota Public Welfare Department records showed only 64 "destined for Minnesota." A detailed tally in that year listed 74 who were resettled in the state, but judging by last names and places of birth, well over half of them may have been Poles, Austrians, Germans, Hungarians, and Jews.[32]

Ethnic organizations began to falter after the war. As a result, all of the state's Romanian benefit societies consolidated into one, *Romanii din Minnesota* (Romanians in Minnesota) about 1964. In 1980 the group maintained a list of approximately 120 policy holders but had, at most, 80 active members.[33]

Other elements of immigrant life, purely Romanian in origin, have fared no better in the state. Folk music and dancing, once so prominent a part of the culture, declined with

Table 23.3. Romanians in Minnesota, 1900–1970

	by country of origin		by mother tongue	
	foreign born	foreign stock*	foreign born	foreign stock*
1900	483			
1910	2,008		1,588	1,900
1920	2,385		1,504	2,253
1930	2,819	5,754	1,156	
1940	1,995		700	1,160
1950	1,249	3,339		
1960	902	2,896	567	
1970	647	2,357	297	767

Source: Country of origin and mother-tongue statistics in U.S., *Census*, for the years listed.

*Includes foreign born and native born of foreign or mixed parentage.

the increasing difficulty of recruiting musicians competent to play native instruments. In 1978 a Romanian-American journal, critical of federal census counts, compiled figures "based not only on church and lodge memberships but also on information gathered over a period of many years." It found only 500 ethnic Romanians in "St. Paul, South St. Paul, Duluth, etc." In 1980 evidence of Minnesota's Romanian culture could regularly be found in few settings: in traditional church activities, in homes where customs such as ethnic cookery were still practiced, in such events as the Festival of Nations organized by the International Institute in St. Paul.[34]

Churches and neighborhoods, the traditional strongholds of ethnic life, were seriously weakened by this general decline. Through much of their history, the St. Paul and South St. Paul settlements and institutions had seemed remarkably free of the divisions and factions that afflicted the larger Romanian-American community. But with a diminishing population, differences were accentuated. During the diocesan schism Minnesota churches, in addition to their competition for parishioners, became further alienated by a controversy over ecclesiastical discipline and canon law, which led to the exclusion of St. Stefan from the American diocese in 1954. Such divisions, for whatever reasons they arise, do not make for ethnic solidarity.[35]

Some of St. Mary's parishioners, furthermore, were deeply pessimistic about the future of their church. The first generation had been devoted to Romanian traditions and raised their children accordingly. As a result, the North End community remained strong until the 1960s. The second generation, however, tended to be exogamous and upwardly mobile, so that the third was territorially dispersed and did not speak Romanian. Many children of mixed marriages were lost to the church. As of 1980 most of the faithful parishioners were scattered through St. Paul's suburban areas. While St. Mary's still drew a preponderantly Romanian flock, services were offered in English on Saturday afternoons, 80% in Romanian at Sunday matins, and approximately 98% English at Sunday Mass.[36]

Whether the experience of St. Mary's represented the condition of all second- and third-generation Romanians in Minnesota is uncertain. In South St. Paul the community seemed to grow and prosper until World War II, but thereafter the same forces of acculturation and mobility appeared to take their toll. In 1980 the neighborhood, unlike the North

End, was still known as a Romanian area, where the mother tongue was commonly spoken and the priest adhered to a purely Romanian liturgy. It was the site of the Twin Cities' only Romanian restaurant. South St. Paul also initially attracted the state's few post-1952 immigrants from the People's Republic of Romania. These younger and more professionally trained newcomers, however, tended to learn English and move away, finding that they shared little more than language with older community members. As a result, the South St. Paul community, although extant in 1980, did not appear to be growing.[37]

Minnesota's Romanian communities, few in number and small in size, have nonetheless participated actively in the evolution of Romanian-American life. Like many other ethnic groups, Romanian or not, their history contains a full complement of neighborhoods, clubs, churches, and societies. In this sense, theirs has been a common experience. In another light, however, the state's Romanians provide an outstanding example of small-group ethnicity. In 1980, despite diminishing population, social and geographic mobility, and changing values, they maintained two churches, two separate communities, and one distinctive neighborhood. The pessimism of some was balanced by the cautious optimism of those who foresaw an era of ethnic revival. The future of the state's Romanian-American communities, however, was unclear.

Reference notes

[1] United States, *Census*, 1900, *Population*, 1:763; 1930, vol. 3, part 1, p. 1194; 1970, vol. 1, part 25, p. 512. These figures were based on country of origin. For a comparison with mother tongue figures, see Table 23.3. Rozeta M. Metes, *The Iuliu Maniu American-Romanian Relief Foundation: A Quarter Century of Activity 1951–1976*, 2 (Reprint ed., Cleveland, 1977); Valentin Hurgoi, "The New Romanian Immigrants," in *American Romanian Review*, 2:18 (May–June, 1978); Christine A. Galitzi, *A Study of Assimilation Among the Roumanians in the United States*, 28 (New York, 1929).

Although both groups are commonly called Romanians, the distinction between ethnic Romanians and all the other emigrants from the kingdom and, later, the nation is an important one. This chapter concentrates on the former but provides statistics for both groups.

[2] John Stefan, "The Romanians in South St. Paul, Minnesota," in *New Pioneer*, January, 1945, pp. 42, 43; Herman E. Olson, *The Minneapolis Property and Housing Survey* (Minneapolis, 1934); Peggy Korsmo-Kennon and Robert Drake, *Discover St. Paul*, 41 (St. Paul, 1979).

[3] Galitzi, *Assimilation*, 11, 41; Leon Dominian, *Frontiers of Language and Nationality in Europe*, 159 (New York, 1917). Uniates were members of the Byzantine Rite Catholic church, which combined Eastern Orthodox ritual and recognition of the pope in Rome as its head.

[4] Galitzi, *Assimilation*, 25; figures for 1899–1910 computed from U.S. Immigration Commission, *Statistical Review of Immigration, 1820–1910*, 20:61 (61 Congress, 3 session, *Senate Documents*, no. 756 — serial 5878); Dominian, *Frontiers*, 154–173.

[5] The exception to this rule was Oltenia, which yielded the greatest number, proportionately, of emigrants in the kingdom. Nowhere in Romania were peasant conditions better (granting that they were none too good), and commerce was also more active in Oltenia than in any other region. This suggests that a downtrodden, poverty-ridden, traditionalist peasantry may be less ripe for emigration than

more prosperous and mobile rural populations. See Galitzi, *Assimilation*, 48.

[6] Galitzi, *Assimilation*, 50; "Alexander III," in *Encyclopædia Britannica Macropaedia*, 1:478 (Chicago, 1975).

[7] Here and below, see Galitzi, *Assimilation*, 27–29, 33, 38, 40, 62; Gerald J. Bobango, *The Romanian Orthodox Episcopate of America: The First Half Century, 1929–1979*, 4, 7 (Jackson, Mich., 1979); Stephan Thernstrom, ed., *Harvard Encyclopedia of American Ethnic Groups*, 1036 (Cambridge, Mass., 1980).

[8] Stefan, in *New Pioneer*, January, 1945, pp. 42, 49; Immigration Commission, *Statistical Review of Immigration 1820–1910*, 20:4, 318. This report found two Romanians headed for Minnesota in 1900, 12 in 1903, 6 in 1904, 29 in 1905, 14 in 1906, 87 in 1907, 161 in 1908, 136 in 1909, and 192 in 1910.

[9] Stefan, in *New Pioneer*, January, 1945, p. 43.

[10] "The Boarding House," in *New Pioneer*, January, 1945, p. 6.

[11] Stefan, in *New Pioneer*, January, 1945, pp. 43, 50.

[12] Galitzi, *Assimilation*, 89, 94; Stefan, in *New Pioneer*, January, 1945, p. 44; interview of Philip Toconiţa, Jr., by Anne Kaplan, November 14, 1980, notes in MEHP Papers.

[13] Here and below, see Korsmo-Kennon and Drake, *Discover St. Paul*, 39, 41, 43; U.S., *Census, 1920, Population*, 2:1026; Katherine Spear, *Foreign Born Population Studies, St. Paul, Minnesota*, 7 (St. Paul, 1934); interview of Father Romey Rosco, St. Mary's Romanian Orthodox Church, by Louis deGryse, September, 1979.

[14] Here and below, see Galitzi, *Assimilation*, 90–97; Vladimir Wertsman, comp., *The Romanians in America 1748–1974*, 5, 9 (Dobbs Ferry, N.Y., 1975); Bobango, *Romanian Orthodox Episcopate*, 93.

[15] Here and below, see Stefan, in *New Pioneer*, January, 1945, pp. 43, 44. The funeral service was led by the pastor of St. Paulus Lutheran Church.

[16] Here and below, see St. Mary's Romanian Orthodox Church, *65th Anniversary*, 2 (St. Paul, 1978); H. F. Koeper, *Historic St. Paul Buildings*, 110 (St. Paul, 1964); Romanian Orthodox Episcopate of America, *Calendarul Solia*, 105 (Detroit, 1938); Bobango, *Romanian Orthodox Episcopate*, 19, 27; Mary Leuca, "The Romanian School in America," in *American Romanian Review*, 3:8–10 (January–February, 1979); Toconiţa interview, November 14, 1980.

[17] U.S., *Census, 1920, Population*, 2:1020, 1026; Stefan, in *New Pioneer*, January, 1945, p. 43; Bobango, *Romanian Orthodox Episcopate*, 2; Rhoda Lewin, "Stereotype and Reality in the Jewish Immigrant Experience in Minneapolis," in *Minnesota History*, 47:263 (Fall, 1979); W. Gunther Plaut, *The Jews in Minnesota*, 119 (New York, 1959); Minnesota manuscript census schedules, 1905, Hennepin County, pp. 95–496, roll 122, microfilm in MHS. See also Chapter 26.

[18] Interview of Harry Davis by Louis deGryse, October, 1979, notes in MEHP Papers; Toconiţa interview, November 14, 1980. In 1919–20, the Minneapolis Board of Education enrolled only 12 Romanians (7 men and 5 women) in its naturalization and citizenship classes; see Government Report for Americanization Classes, enclosed in Katherine M. Kohler to Raymond F. Crist, July 17, 1920, in U.S. Department of Labor, Immigration and Naturalization Services, General Education Correspondence Files, Minnesota State Convention, Minneapolis, May, 1920, National Archives Record Group 85, copy in MEHP Papers.

[19] Stefan, in *New Pioneer*, January, 1945, p. 48; Bobango, *Romanian Orthodox Episcopate*, 49; U.S. Census Bureau, *Special Reports, Religious Bodies: 1926*, 2:503; *1936*, vol. 2, part 1, p. 578; U.S., *Census, 1900, Population*, 1:799; 1910, 2:1014; 1920, 2:1032;

1930, 2:377; Romanian Orthodox Episcopate of America, *Calendarul Solia*, 105.

The society was named for the Transylvanian field where Romanians met to demand freedom and equality with Hungarians during the Revolution of 1848. For later developments, see p. 445, below.

[20] John Syrjamaki, "Mesabi Communities: A Study of Their Development," 115, 121, 134, 288, 315, Ph.D. thesis, Yale University, 1940; George O. Virtue, *The Minnesota Iron Ranges*, 347–349 (U.S. Bureau of Labor, *Bulletin*, no. 84 — Washington, D.C., 1909).

[21] Alien Registration form of Octavian Bulgaria, Dakota County, South St. Paul, in Minnesota Commission of Public Safety Records, in Minnesota State Archives, MHS.

[22] Gerald J. Bobango, "Romanians," in Thernstrom, ed., *Harvard Encyclopedia*, 880; Minnesota Romanian statistics, in MEHP Papers, compiled by Jon A. Gjerde from U.S. Dept. of Labor, Bureau of Immigration, *Annual Reports*, 1909–39. In 1930 the number of foreign-born Romanians emigrating to the United States reached its maximum; see E. P. Hutchinson, *Immigrants and Their Children*, 4 (New York, 1956).

[23] Stefan, in *New Pioneer*, January, 1945, p. 44.

[24] Here and below, see Stefan, in *New Pioneer*, January, 1945, p. 45; Toconiţa interview, November 14, 1980.

[25] "National Organizations," in *New Pioneer*, July, 1945, p. 42; Stefan, in *New Pioneer*, January, 1945, pp. 45, 48. Since "Ardealul" is a Romanian term for Transylvania, the name of this new group implied some sort of union between the two previously separate regional enclaves.

[26] Here and below, see Stefan, in *New Pioneer*, January, 1945, p. 49; Chapter 22, above. The Youth Club in St. Paul also joined AROY after World War II, but neither chapter survived long. There were too few youths in the small communities to sustain the groups; Toconiţa interview, November 14, 1980. For more on AROY, see Bobango, *Romanian Orthodox Episcopate*, 324–342.

[27] Here and below, see Wertsman, *Romanians in America*, 12, 13, 15, 17.

[28] Membership roster, in *New Pioneer*, November, 1942, p. 30.

[29] Events and News, in *New Pioneer*, November, 1942, p. 17; July–September, 1943, p. 50; July, 1944, p. 36.

[30] Here and below, see Bobango, *Romanian Orthodox Episcopate*, 125–222; Wertsman, *Romanians in America*, 21.

[31] Bobango, *Romanian Orthodox Episcopate*, 48, 151, 253; Toconiţa interview, November 14, 1980.

[32] Minnesota Displaced Persons Commission, Displaced Persons Resettled in Minnesota, 1949–52, in Minnesota Public Welfare Dept. Records, in Minnesota State Archives.

[33] Rosco interview, September, 1979; Toconiţa interview, November 14, 1980.

[34] Unsigned note, in *American Romanian Review*, 2:16; U.S., *Census, 1970, Population*, vol. 1, part 25, pp. 512–515; interview of Mrs. Philip Toconiţa, Jr., by Louis deGryse, October 18, 1979, notes in MEHP Papers; International Institute, *Festival of Nations Program*, 1934–80, copies in IHRC. The Romanians have been a part of the St. Paul Festivals of Nations since the early 1930s.

[35] Rosco interview, September, 1979; Bobango, in Thernstrom, ed., *Harvard Encyclopedia*, 883; Bobango, *Romanian Orthodox Episcopate*, 245. In 1980 St. Stefan's was one of the five independent Orthodox churches in the United States.

[36] Rosco interview, September, 1979.

[37] Here and below, see Toconiţa interview, November 14, 1980.

CHAPTER 24

The Italians

Rudolph J. Vecoli

FOR MORE THAN A CENTURY, Italy has been among the foremost countries of emigration in the world. Over 25,000,000 Italians left their native land between 1876 and 1980. Initially those from its northern regions went to northern Europe and South America. By 1900, however, the tide of migration had shifted, carrying its human cargoes predominantly from the central and southern regions to the United States. From 1820 to 1980 some 6,000,000 Italians have entered the country. Over half arrived during the first 15 years of the 20th century.[1]

Only a small portion chose Minnesota. Of the more than 2,000,000 Italian immigrants between 1899 and 1910, fewer than 10,000 designated the state as their destination (see Table 24.1). Its Italian-born population peaked in 1910 at 9,668 and then fell while other midwestern states were still registering increases. This pattern continued even after passage of the liberalized Immigration Act of 1965. For example, only 29 of the 25,000 who arrived in 1970 listed Minnesota as their intended residence. In that year of the over 4,000,000 first- and second-generation Italian Americans in the United States, 12,910 were counted in Minnesota.[2]

Like other migrating peoples, Italians left for a variety of motives: spirit of adventure, quest for economic opportunity, flight from persecution. For some, however, migration was a tradition. For centuries wandering craftsmen, such as sculptors, musicians, stonecutters, plaster workers, and barbers, had vended their skills throughout Europe. These well-established migrant types were the trail blazers of emigration to the United States and to Minnesota.[3]

The diaspora of the late 19th and early 20th centuries, however, was propelled by powerful demographic and economic forces. Between 1861 and 1936 Italy's population doubled, although its economy remained largely agricultural and traditional. Growing families caused the fragmentation of landholdings until they were reduced to *fazzoletti* (handkerchiefs). The new Italian kingdom espoused policies which favored capitalist enterprise in the north at the expense of the south. Thus oppressive taxes were added to the adversities of poor soil, recurring drought, malaria, and exploitive landlords.

Although most Italian immigrants were tillers of the soil, they were not a rural people in the American sense. Their typical abode was the *paese*, an agro-town of thousands of inhabitants with complex social relationships, intense communal life, and entrenched folk traditions. Within the peasant culture the family was the primary institution. While most were Roman Catholics, history had taught them to be skeptical of the church and the clergy. A deeply felt folk religion prevailed among them, drawing upon pagan as well as Christian sources. Their sense of community extended only within earshot of the church bell, a parochialism termed *campanilismo*. Beyond that, regional identities were significant, for the various areas of Italy embodied great cultural and linguistic differences. Intense antipathies between northern and southern Italians were major obstacles to unity both at home and abroad.[4]

The great majority of the peasant immigrants hoped to work in America until they had saved enough money to return and purchase land in their villages. Perhaps as many as half did in fact repatriate, while others made several crossings. Predominantly male and youthful, these "birds of passage" constituted a floating labor force responding to the shifting demands of the American economy. For the most part, they were unskilled laborers employed in the hardest, dirtiest, and lowest-paying jobs. But the $1.25 or more that they could earn each day compared well with the $.20 in the *paese*.[5]

News of such grand wages caused an epidemic-like reaction, *la febbre d'America* (America fever). Where it struck, entire villages were depopulated of their able-bodied men. A process of chain migration ensued; the first migrants often sent back prepaid steamship tickets for relatives and friends, who in time sent for their relatives and friends. Once families were reunited (or formed) on American soil, the sojourner had taken a major step toward becoming a permanent immigrant. In this fashion, people from certain villages were recruited and channeled to particular destinations, where kinship and hometown ties were reconstituted.

Settlement Patterns

It is an irony of Italian immigration that these tillers of the land were destined to become urban, industrial workers. This occurred primarily because they intended to earn as much money as quickly as possible, and the cities offered more economic opportunities. In 1890 over 80% of the state's Italians were clustered in St. Paul, Minneapolis, and Duluth — cities that, with the iron ranges, remained major concentrations (see Table 24.2). After 1900 St. Paul was the

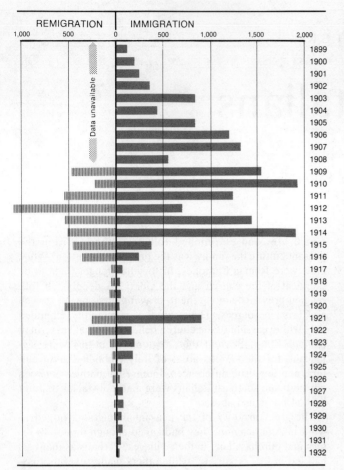

REMIGRATION	IMMIGRATION

Table 24.1. Italian Migration to and from Minnesota

single largest center, averaging about 20% of the total; Minneapolis and Duluth each accounted for about 10%, and iron range cities and villages together recorded another 40%. Reflecting the persistence of initial settlement patterns, in 1970 over 80% of all Minnesota Italian Americans resided in Hennepin, Ramsey, St. Louis, and Itasca counties.

Unlike Wisconsin, which had two successful agricultural

colonies, Minnesota developed no large Italian farming settlements. Italians were not among the favored nationalities recruited by the State Board of Immigration or by the railroads. A few took up isolated homesteads in northern Minnesota, and some engaged in market gardening on the outskirts of the Twin Cities or Duluth. From the 1890s on, for example, Sicilian families in Little Canada grew fruits and vegetables for roadside stands and the downtown market in nearby St. Paul.[6]

Because of his avoidance of farming in a state which was largely rural and agricultural, the Italian remained an exotic in most of Minnesota. In 1930 only 173 foreign-born Italians were reported in the "rural-farm" category; out of 87 counties 35 recorded none, and 37 reported fewer than 10 Italians (see Table 24.3).[7]

From the 1850s on, a vanguard of artisans and merchants reached Minnesota from the regions of Liguria, Lombardy, and Tuscany (see Map 24.1). Quickly making a place for themselves in the commercial life of the Twin Cities and Duluth, they peddled fruits, vegetables, confectionery, ice cream, and cigars, at first from carts and then from stands and stores. By 1888, joined by "thrifty and industrious" Sicilians from Termini Imerese, they were operating some 20 fruit stores scattered about St. Paul's business district from which in time developed wholesale houses such as those of Ciresi and DeLisi. In 1892 at least 13 Italians were engaged in confectionery and cigar businesses in Duluth. A manufacturing concern, the Italian Macaroni and Vermicelli Company, was established in St. Paul in 1889.[8]

Among the early arrivals were practitioners of the arts and crafts which Italy had been exporting for centuries. The *Minnesota Pioneer* of June 19, 1851, noted the presence of an Italian engaged in the manufacture of "beautiful statuettes and busts." He was one of the *figurinai* (image makers) from the hill towns of Lucca who for centuries had been making and peddling statues. In the 1890s the Giuliani brothers established a St. Paul company which became a major producer of ecclesiastical art in the Midwest. As they prospered, they recruited numerous artisans from Barga and nearby towns, employing some 40 workmen by 1910. Italian craftsmen from Lombardy, Veneto, and Friuli monopolized

Table 24.2. Italian Concentrations in Minnesota, 1890–1970

	1890*	1900	1910*	1920	1930	1940	1950	1960	1970
Minneapolis									
foreign born	140	222	653	766	785	702	565		242
foreign stock**	177	425	932	1,577	2,200			2,032	1,395
St. Paul									
foreign born	317	529	1,994	1,685	1,722	1,503	1,209		490
foreign stock**	393	892	3,044	3,515	4,683			3,294	2,663
Duluth									
foreign born	212	292	648	836	787	657	506		239
foreign stock**	252	528	1,051	1,904	2,225			1,617	1,255
St. Louis County									
foreign born	250	859	4,184	3,909	3,043	2,559	1,925		744
foreign stock**			5,466		7,928			5,015	3,726
Itasca County									
foreign born		3	530	481	320	323	273		119
foreign stock**			649		908			696	434

Source: Country of origin statistics in U.S., *Census*, for years listed.
*Foreign stock figures in 1890 and 1910 include foreign born plus only those native born with *both* parents born in Italy.
** Foreign stock figures, except those for 1890 and 1910, include foreign born and native born of foreign and mixed parentage.

Table 24.3. Italians in Minnesota by County, 1920–70

County	1920 foreign born	1930 fb	1930 foreign mixed	1970 fb	1970 fm
Aitkin	17	9	24		7
Anoka	12	20	30	21	224
Becker					14
Beltrami	1	1	5	7	29
Benton	3	4	14		12
Big Stone	2		1		
Blue Earth	3	3	1		39
Brown	2	1	8		8
Carlton	28	12	19		90
Carver		3	3		14
Cass	4	1	5	4	24
Chippewa	2				
Chisago		2	1		21
Clay	75	57	88	13	86
Clearwater		1			6
Cook		1	3		
Cottonwood	3				8
Crow Wing	73	50	92		52
Dakota	33	28	54	51	285
Dodge	1		6		14
Douglas			1		
Faribault	4	2	10		
Fillmore	6	1			
Freeborn	3				32
Goodhue	9	2	25		52
Grant	3			7	
Hennepin	793	824	1,452	412	2,413
Houston			2		12
Hubbard	1	2	4		7
Isanti			2		29
Itasca	481	320	588	119	315
Jackson			1		6
Kanabec	3	1	3		
Kandiyohi	3	8	2		
Kittson	2		1		9
Koochiching	40	52	50	20	31
Lac qui Parle			1		
Lake	11	7	8	8	32
Lake of the Woods			2		6
Le Sueur	1	2	4		12
Lincoln		1	2		
Lyon	3		3		
Marshall	2	3	8		6
Martin					7
Meeker					10
Mille Lacs	3	2	3		5
Morrison	4	4	18	20	52
Mower	6	5	7		14
Murray			1		7
Nicollet	11	16	3		28
Nobles	8	8	6	6	24
Olmsted	4	21	17	46	123
Otter Tail	26	16	30		13
Pennington					8
Pine	7	7	17		58
Pipestone	2				9
Polk	2	4	5		
Pope	2	2	4		
Ramsey	1,707	1,756	3,036	617	3,002
Red Lake	1				6
Redwood	1		2		7
Rice	2	7	20		13
Rock	1				
Roseau			2		1
St. Louis	3,909	3,043	4,885	744	2,982
Scott	1		3		19
Sherburne	9	5	12		26
Stearns	18	11	23		34
Steele			1		13
Stevens	3				
Swift		1	4		7
Todd	2	7	8		14
Wabasha		2	7		

Table 24.3. Italians in Minnesota by County, 1920–70 (*continued*)

County	1920 foreign born	1930 fb	1930 foreign mixed	1970 fb	1970 fm
Wadena					6
Waseca	5	2	2		6
Washington	66	59	128	45	269
Wilkin	3		3		14
Winona	2	1	1		66
Wright	1	1	5	5	22
Yellow Medicine	2				6
Total	7,432	6,401	10,774	2,145	10,765
Published census figures	(7,432)	(6,401)	(10,774)	(2,145)	(10,765)

Source: See Appendix

mosaic, tile, and terrazzo work in the Twin Cities. In time several established their own firms. There was hardly a religious, public, or commercial building in the Twin Cities which did not profit from a "fine Italian hand."[9]

Musicians were also among the first settlers. By the 1870s the presence of street musicians playing harps and fiddles was remarked upon in the Twin Cities and Duluth. St. Paul boasted an organ-grinder in the early 1900s. Every town in southern Italy had a brass band, and uniformed, marching bands were quickly formed in Minnesota to play for saints' day processions, Columbus Day parades, and funerals. Among the conductors and musicians from Italy who helped establish various organizations were Errico Sansone (St. Paul Symphony Orchestra and College of Music), Francesco Amendola (St. Paul Institute of Musical Arts), Luigi and Ada Lombardi (Iron Range Symphony Orchestra and the Lombardi Conservatory of Music in Hibbing). These Italian teachers and performers had a significant influence on the state's musical culture.[10]

"In Minnesota there are Italian professors of language, painters, sculptors, musicians, printers, farmers, successful businessmen, and so on," asserted Father Nicola Carlo Odone, an early chronicler of the Italians, in about 1905. "I could give you here a catalogue of at least forty trades and occupations at which we find the Italians working." This versatility was more characteristic of the early immigration than of the mass of peasant sojourners who followed. The merchants, shopkeepers, artists, and artisans who intended to stay formed the stable nucleus of the Italian community. Differences of social status and often region of origin kept these immigrants and the sojourners apart, a dichotomy that had important consequences for the social and institutional development of Minnesota's Italian communities.[11]

By 1900 when the *contadini* of the southern regions were forming the Little Italies on St. Paul's Upper Levee beneath the High Bridge and in Swede Hollow along Phalen Creek, older settlers had already established their own distinctive residential areas. In St. Paul the Genoese were concentrated between West Central Avenue and Summit Place (north of the present Cathedral of St. Paul), the Tuscans lived near East 7th and Rosabel streets, and the Termini Imeresani were to be found on the hill north of the city market around

Map 24.1. Principal Regions of Italian Emigration to Minnesota

Robert Street and East Summit Avenue (now Columbus Avenue). In Minneapolis a smaller cluster of Sicilian families was located along the eastern end of Western Avenue (now Glenwood Avenue) not far from that city's market. The other northern Italians (Lombards, Venetians, and Friulani) tended to live near the Genoese and Tuscans. By the early 1900s "scattered families" living in mixed residential areas in "beautiful and ornate houses" were said to be "the most progressive of all [the Italians] . . . they come nearer being 'Americanized' than those who herd together and cling to the manners, customs, and language of their native land."[12]

The established Italian community was inundated after 1900 by a wave of newcomers from the *mezzogiorno*, or southern Italy. Unskilled laborers of peasant origin, these sojourners responded to the demand for workers to build and maintain the railroads running west to the Pacific. In the 1880s Italians had begun to replace the Irish and Scandinavians on the Great Northern and the Northern Pacific crews. Tens of thousands were recruited and shipped from Chicago

to the "railroad frontier" each year. A 1905 survey reported that the approximately 60,000 track laborers in Illinois, Wisconsin, Minnesota, and Iowa were mainly Italians and Slavs. A cryptic message from the Great Northern Railroad in 1897 reflected the invidious distinctions made by railroad management between "dagoes" (Italians) and "white men" (Americans and northern Europeans): "White men coming to Duluth will not work. Dagoes only men who will work," it read. "Send more dagoes and shut off white men."[13]

The life of the railroad laborer was hard. He was at the mercy of the *padrone* (boss), who recruited and managed the labor gangs. Usually the *padrone* charged the worker a fee for the job and overcharged him for inadequate, often spoiled food, clothing, and tools, as well as rent for a crowded and filthy boxcar in which to sleep. On occasion the workers were duped by an employment agent. A gang of laborers shipped from Chicago to Minneapolis, for example, found there was no work for them on arrival.[14]

Working conditions were brutal. The men labored 10 or

more hours a day in all kinds of weather under the eye of a tyrannical boss for a daily wage of about $1.50. When the abuses became intolerable, they would quit in a body or strike spontaneously, often precipitating violent battles with strikebreakers and deputies. Injury and death from explosions, cave-ins, exposure, and train collisions were common. Yet the sojourners were eager for such jobs, which enabled them to earn money to hasten the day of their return to Italy.

Because railroad work was seasonal, running from April through November, the men either went back to Italy or wintered over in an American city. Chicago was favored, but Minneapolis, Duluth, and especially St. Paul also served as winter quarters and recruiting centers. In 1910 it was estimated that St. Paul's Italian-born population of about 2,000 more than doubled during the winter months. The housing, feeding, and care of several thousand migrant workers provided opportunities for business-minded Italians.[15]

Italian *padrones*, speaking English and being somewhat "Americanized," became intermediaries for employment agencies, organizing labor gangs and providing transportation, food, and lodging. The *padrone* usually operated a saloon and grocery, *Banca Italiana*, steamship agency, and boardinghouse. Even the honest ones could make handsome profits, but some took advantage of the workers' helplessness and ignorance. Because of the sentiment of *campanilismo*, the laborers tended to trust only someone from their own *paese* or region. From the ranks of the *padrones* emerged a number of wealthy and influential leaders of St. Paul's Italian colony.

Some of the wintering laborers, deciding to stay in Minnesota, sent for wives or sweethearts from their villages. Given the high ratio of men to women, a wife was an asset, for by taking in five to ten boarders at $3.00 a month, she could almost equal her husband's earnings. For $.10 a day the men had a place to sleep and, while they bought their own foods, *la bossa* (the woman boss) would prepare their meals and wash their clothes. Although relatives and fellow townsmen were favored as boarders, the presence of single men often threatened the integrity of the families and caused domestic tragedies. Amy Bernardy, an Italian social worker who visited St. Paul in 1910, termed the boarding system the "most dangerous and shameful plague of the Italian colonies." A survey in 1917 revealed that over 30% of St. Paul's Italian families kept lodgers. For many, doing so was an economic necessity.[16]

Distinct Italian neighborhoods were formed in two St. Paul locations — on the flats of the Upper Levee and in Swede Hollow. These settlements grew by a process of chain migration, well described by an Italian priest in St. Paul: "first the father comes; then the father calls the son; then the rest of the family follows; and then part of the village or perhaps the entire village follows."[17]

In the 1880s a few Italians joined the Germans and Poles as squatters on the Upper Levee, building shacks from scraps of lumber, tin, and tarpaper and setting them on piles to keep above the spring floods. Gradually, as the land was built up with refuse from the city, the Italians purchased title to the lots, built more substantial houses, and planted vegetable gardens and grape arbors. By 1910 some 60 families were living on the flats.[18]

Isolated from the rest of the city by bluffs and railroad tracks, the Upper Levee was an Italian enclave where immigrant culture survived for a half century. In 1904 it was described as "a village of southern Italy transported as if by magic from the wild mountains of Abruzzo and Molise and placed on the banks of the Father of Waters." Bernardy observed that the neighborhood had a rural flavor, populated by ducks, chickens, goats, and even a cow or two. With the exception of a few families, the people of the Upper Levee emigrated from the province of Campobasso in the region of Molise, particularly from the villages of Ripabottoni and Casacalenda.[19]

When Alice Sickels of the International Institute of St. Paul studied the area in the 1930s, she found it little changed. Nearly 100 families, most of whom owned their own homes, totaled 410 persons; 80% were Italian. A high rate of endogamy and residential stability had maintained the neighborhood's ethnic character. The men worked in railroad section gangs (some throughout their lives), as laborers on city or county public works, or in the nearby J. T. McMillan meat-packing plant. While a few residents established saloons and a grocery, the community remained solidly blue collar through the second generation.

A second area settled by Italian railroad laborers was known as Phalen Creek or Swede Hollow on St. Paul's East Side. A steep ravine surrounded by high bluffs through which ran a polluted stream, it had served as a port of entry for Irish and Swedes before the Italians arrived in the 1880s. By 1910 there were some 60 Italian families numbering several hundred persons living in shacks which clung precariously to the hillside. The settlers paid land rent of $24.00 a year but owned the houses, which many had built themselves. The area lacked city water and city sewers. A 1917 survey of housing conditions in St. Paul concluded that Swede Hollow and the Upper Levee constituted the "lowest types of residential districts" in the city.[20]

Still Swede Hollow was fondly remembered by its former residents. "It was just like a town in Italy," one recalled. Its inhabitants were drawn from several regions: the Abruzzi (especially the mountain villages), Puglia (especially the province of Foggia), Campania, and Calabria. Despite regional diversity, peace and harmony generally prevailed. As on the Upper Levee, isolation enabled the Hollow's immigrant families to maintain their old ways. In 1910 an American observed of it: "You might not imagine yourself in the United States, so completely are the people isolated, and so completely foreign is the atmosphere." Despite nostalgic memories, these families seemed eager to move out of the Hollow and "up on the street" as quickly as possible. For some families this took longer than for others, but in time all made it out, to be succeeded in turn by Mexicans.[21]

The larger Italian neighborhood on St. Paul's East Side was known as Railroad Island or Lower Payne Avenue for the main thoroughfare on which were located Italian saloons, groceries, and restaurants. As on the Upper Levee, many of the men here were employed in the section gangs or roundhouses of the nearby railroads. In time some took jobs

THE UPPER LEVEE community nestled under St. Paul's High Bridge about 1889. The settlement's isolation protected its rural atmosphere.

in Hamm's brewery and elsewhere, while others worked for the city. As recently as 1960, Italian Americans still constituted a majority of the population in the Lower Payne neighborhood.[22]

In Northeast Minneapolis Italian railroad workers settled in the district known as Maple Hill or Dogtown. In 1905 the neighborhood was still composed largely of Swedes, Germans, and Poles, with only 18 Italians. Over the next two decades, the latter increased to a peak of about 150 families. By 1920 about 40% of the 766 Italians in Minneapolis were concentrated in this small area bounded by Hennepin on the south, Fillmore on the west, Johnson on the east, and Broadway on the north.[23]

As they did in St. Paul, Italians lived in small detached houses, which they usually owned. The neighborhood was noted for its flourishing gardens and its variety of barnyard animals — important sources of food. With the exception of those few who established grocery stores or saloons, the Italians for the most part worked in the section gangs or shops of the Soo Line Railroad. In time a considerable number secured sought-after jobs in Pillsbury flour mills. As in Swede Hollow, the Italians of Maple Hill comprised a mix of regional groups from the *mezzogiorno*. Certain towns of Calabria and the Abruzzi were strongly represented. Maple Hill (which in 1948 was renamed Beltrami) remained a coherent Italian community until well after World War II.

Two other distinctive railroad settlements appeared with significant connections to the Little Italies of the Twin Cities. In Cumberland, Wisconsin, some 200 families had formed an agricultural settlement by 1900. While the land was being cleared, the men continued to work on the railroads, shipping out from St. Paul. The original settlers from Abruzzi-Molise were joined by a goodly number from Calabria and a few from Sicily. Cumberland became a feeder for the Swede Hollow and Maple Hill colonies. When the Northern Pacific opened its shops in Dilworth, four miles east of Moorhead in the Red River Valley, laborers for its section gangs and roundhouses were recruited from Cumberland and St. Paul. Dilworth's Little Italy, on the south side of the tracks, at one time numbered some 45 families. Many were from Molise, and others were from Campania, Calabria, and Sicily.[24]

In the 1880s Duluth's pioneer settlers began to arrive from Lombardy as well as from southern Italy. They were joined by others moving westward from the coal mines of Pennsylvania or the copper and iron mines of Michigan. Early arrivals operated fruit and confectionery stores and worked as stonecutters, masons, or in other skilled trades. The city also served as winter quarters for railroad workers and mine laborers from the Mesabi Range. In 1884 the *Duluth Tribune* of August 8 commented upon a tenement filled with Italian laborers as "a nuisance to everybody in the neighborhood."[25]

Duluth's Italians were predominantly from the *mezzogiorno*, with the major contingent from Abruzzi-Molise. In the early 1880s some dozen families constituted the city's foreign-born Italian population. By 1900 it had increased to 292, and it peaked in 1920 at 836. Despite their small numbers, the Italians formed several distinct settlements according to place of origin and occupation. These settlements persisted over time; in 1940 more than two-thirds of Duluth's Italian Americans resided in these same neighborhoods. Within the city proper, Lombards were concentrated on the edge of the business district, especially from 5th to 6th avenues West. Southerners comprised the largest Little Italy, which was located at 11th Avenue West and Superior Street in a hilly area known as "Point of Rocks," within easy walking distance of the railroad yards and coal docks where many of them worked. A small number lived in Hunter's Park near a prosperous Scottish neighborhood where the men worked as gardeners, while the women cleaned and washed clothes for the well-to-do families.[26]

In the city's industrial West End, Italians were to be found in West Duluth, Gary, and New Duluth. By 1914 over 50 southern Italian families had settled in West Duluth, where they worked at the Clyde Iron Works and the Zenith Furnace Company. The Italians shared the neighborhood between 54th and 60th avenues near Raleigh Street with a predominantly South Slav population.[27]

The western industrial zone of Gary-New Duluth attracted still another group of Italians, especially after the opening of the Morgan Park steel plant in 1915. Most of these came from the *paesi* of Cordenons and Pordenone in Friuli with a smaller number from the Veneto and Austrian Istria. Many had migrated from the Michigan copper country after the 1913 strike. Located between 96th and 105th avenues West, these people lived in shacks and boardinghouses, grew vegetables, and raised chickens, pigs, and cows.[28]

Duluth's Italians pursued a variety of occupations and realized vastly different degrees of economic success. The craftsmen of Lombardy and Friuli were much in demand, at good wages, for constructing retaining walls and buildings along the city's steep hillsides. Many more were employed in the West End steel plants. Unlike those in the Twin Cities, others entered Duluth's garment industry, where women worked as machine operators and men as cutters, pressers, and tailors. In 1924, however, the largest single category was still laborers — "gandy dancers" in section gangs, car cleaners for the Northern Pacific Railroad or the Duluth Street Railway, navvies on the coal and ore docks, ditchdiggers, and street cleaners.[29]

Professionals were few and far between in the Duluth community, but a considerable number of Italians succeeded in commercial ventures. Beginning often as peddlers, some became quite prosperous operating grocery, fruit, confectionery, and cigar stores, saloons, and wholesale and import firms. Less usual was the Duluth Macaroni Company (later the Puglisi Spaghetti Factory), which was established in 1909. Attilio Castigliano was the dominant figure in the

THE GLEN (also known as Skunk Hollow), pictured in 1887, was part of Duluth's Little Italy. The dwellings remaining in the 1970s were razed; two apartment buildings and a park now occupy the site.

Duluth colony in the first two decades of the 20th century. The Italian consular agent, he was also a kind of *padrone*, serving as interpreter, legal adviser, and employment agent. Castigliano invested in a cheese factory in Wisconsin which became the basis of the Stella Cheese Company, the largest producer of Italian cheeses in the United States.

The third, and largest, concentration of Italians in Minnesota developed in the iron range towns and mining locations of St. Louis and Itasca counties, where over 4,000 foreign-born Italians were counted in 1910 (see Tables 24.2 and 24.3). Despite its general decline in the mid-20th century, that area still accounted for about one-fourth of the state's Italian Americans in 1970.

Along with Cornishmen, Swedes, and Finns, northern Italians, who had been employed in the Michigan mines since the 1860s, were drawn to the newly discovered Vermilion Range, where by 1890 Tower and Ely each listed about 100. Many more, however, settled on the vast Mesabi Range, with its rich surface deposits and open-pit operations. There the earliest Italians to arrive reached Mountain Iron in 1892, the year the first Mesabi ore was shipped. By 1909 they constituted 10% of the labor force of the Oliver Iron Mining Company, the largest firm on the ranges. Of these, 837 worked on the Mesabi and 30 on the Vermilion.[30]

A process of ethnic succession took place due to the rapid expansion of the Mesabi and the urgent demand for unskilled labor for stripping as well as for constructing railroads and other facilities. Castigliano observed that those from northern and central Italy tended to be employed underground, while those from southern Italy worked in the open pits. Many of the northerners (Tyrolese, Venetians, Lombards, Piedmontese, and Marchegians) had previous experience in the mines of France, Luxembourg, and Alsace-Lorraine, but fewer of the southerners (Calabrians, Sicilians, and Neopolitans) who arrived after 1900 possessed any acquaintance with mining.[31]

Officials on the Minnesota ranges described the southern

Italians as "inefficient and worthless . . . fit for but the lowest grades of work in the open-pit mines." In 1911 the United States Immigration Commission reported a "consensus of opinion of all representative persons in the region . . . that the northern European races are the most desirable, while the South Italians, Montenegrins, Serbians, and Croatians are the least desirable." Such prophecies were self-fulfilling; southern Italians were hired only for the most menial jobs, and an invidious distinction came to be made on the ranges between "white men," meaning northern Europeans, and the "black races," meaning people from southern Europe. Opportunities for advancement for Italians were slight; the "white men" had a monopoly on supervisory and skilled jobs.[32]

Life in northern Minnesota during the early years was hard and dangerous. Living conditions were primitive. A frontierlike atmosphere prevailed; saloons, brothels, and violence provided miners with a release from a relentless cycle of exhausting work. Drunkenness was common among all nationalities. Of the 317 saloons on the Mesabi in 1910, 32, described as "nearly all low-class places," were operated by Italians.[33]

The absolute power of the mining companies was personified by the captains and foremen, who appeared to take particular satisfaction from driving the new immigrants "toward whom they felt extreme racial antagonism and superiority." Men were hired and fired at will; wages were raised and lowered according to the labor supply. Accidents were daily occurrences. Between 1906 and 1909 one of every 200 workers was killed each year. Of the 292 fatalities during this period, 38 were Italians. But the high death rate attracted little attention because most of the victims were foreigners.[34]

Wages in 1908 ranged from $2.45 and $2.17 per day for underground miners and laborers to $1.98 for surface workers. Since the open pits closed for the winter, the work season for most employees was only six or seven months. In 1910 the average yearly earnings of southern Italian heads of households were $623, below the average for all ethnic groups. And the cost of living was quite high.

No wonder the rate of labor turnover was high. Teofilo Petriella, a labor organizer, observed in 1906 that two-thirds of the men remained only one or two years. Many Italians returned home, often bitterly disillusioned by their American experiences (see Table 24.1).[35]

Scattered along the 80-mile length of the Mesabi Range from northeast to southwest were dozens of towns, villages, and mining locations. Since the eastern end of the range was developed first, men from northern and central Italy tended to be more heavily represented there, while southern Italians were concentrated on the western portion, which was opened later. The most important center was Hibbing, which, said Castigliano, had more than 2,000 of his countrymen in 1913. The cities of Eveleth, Chisholm, and Virginia also contained significant numbers.[36]

Many recent immigrants, however, lived in "locations" adjacent to mines. A few of these had company housing, but most inhabited squatters' camps hastily constructed of boards covered with tarpaper. Overcrowding was common, with several families sharing a house; many families also took in boarders.

As the population stabilized, permanent Italian communities emerged. In certain small and isolated "locations" all the people might have emigrated from a particular region of Italy. But in towns like Hibbing and Eveleth there was a mix of regional groups, often with residential clustering. Boardinghouses were segregated by regions; marriages were arranged within regional groups; and businesses operated by fellow townsmen were patronized.[37]

The leaders among the Italians on the range were often saloonkeepers or merchants who were in effect *padrones*. These men, usually former miners themselves, served as middlemen between the more recent arrivals and the Americans. They contracted with the mining companies for labor gangs, recruited workers, provided them with lodging, food, and drink, banked their money or sent it to Italy, and sold them steamship tickets. Labor leader Petriella regarded this as a "form of slavery" in which the miners were kept by "their merchant and politician countrymen."[38]

The growing Italian population also required a variety of goods and services which provided opportunities for immigrant businessmen. Italian groceries, bakeries, barbershops, coaldealers, and shoemaking shops multiplied in the various towns. By the 1920s one could also find in the larger communities Italian doctors, lawyers, pharmacists, teachers, and nurses, often American born or at least American educated. One study concluded, however, that Italians were somewhat slower than other ethnic groups entering into businesses and professions on the ranges.[39]

Certain enterprising Italians capitalized on their countrymen's penchant for wine making, which, on the Mesabi alone, required ten or more carloads of California grapes each autumn. In Buhl the Satori brothers from the Veneto began as peddlers with a horse and wagon, established a general merchandise store, and then became wholesale grape and liquor merchants. John Fena established a winery in Hibbing and founded the Fena Wholesale Fruit Company. Cesare Mondavi was dispatched to California by the Italian mutual benefit society *Roma* of Virginia each year to select grapes for the members. After several trips he bought a vineyard in the Napa Valley. The Mondavi family subsequently purchased the Charles Krug Winery, and one of the sons eventually established his own winery.[40]

By the end of World War I, the iron ranges had ceased to attract new immigrants. In fact, the Italian population decreased between 1910 and 1920. Increased mechanization and the exhaustion of ore deposits at the eastern end of the Mesabi reduced the demand for unskilled labor. Unemployment caused many men to leave for other parts of the country.[41]

The exodus continued during the Great Depression of the 1930s, when the level of employment declined to an all-time low of 3,000 (it had been over 20,000 in 1910). Some communities became ghost towns, and certain ethnic groups largely disappeared from the region.

Many second-generation Italians left for Duluth, the Twin Cities, and elsewhere, for the range had little to offer in the way of economic opportunity during the interwar years. But the Italians did not disappear. For the old-timers who had acquired property after long struggles this was home; they were loathe to leave.

At least until World War II, deep hostility based on ethnic differences existed between northern and southern Europeans. Hibbing and Virginia were referred to as "white men's towns," while Chisholm and Eveleth were stigmatized as being controlled by "blacks." While strict residential segregation did not exist, a high degree of social segregation did. Southern Europeans were excluded from Anglo-Scandinavian middle-class social and professional circles. Although ethnic conflict rarely erupted into violent confrontation, it became more bitter in times of economic depression or labor strife.[42]

The tendency of Italians to remain within their own group was due in part to choice and in part to ostracism by the dominant Anglo-Scandinavian element. As a consequence, Italians gradually came to realize that their common national identity was more important than their regional differences and that only through unity could they muster the clout to challenge the entrenched "whites."

Italians played a significant, if at times equivocal, role in efforts to organize the Minnesota mining industry. For a half century the Oliver Iron Mining Company and other firms refused adamantly to bargain collectively with their employees and used every means, including blacklisting and espionage, to frustrate organizing attempts.[43]

Nevertheless sporadic walkouts occurred as well as two major revolts in 1907 and 1916. A spontaneous work stoppage in July, 1907, shut down the mines throughout the range. Teofilo Petriella, a Socialist and former schoolteacher from Campania, was appointed special organizer for the Mesabi Range by the Western Federation of Miners. But using special deputies and strikebreakers, the companies outlasted the workers. By October the strike was over. Petriella, who had been attacked as that "alien Dago anarchist," left under a shadow, suspected of having appropriated strike funds. Unlike many Finns, the Italians were not blacklisted by the mining companies, suggesting that their support of the struggle was lukewarm. After that, a decade of uneasy peace was broken by occasional protests — such as the riot of Italians in Eveleth against unemployment in 1914 — but little organized labor activity.

In 1916 Joe Greeni, an Italian miner and agitator, touched off a second serious revolt. Working at the St. James Mine at Aurora, Greeni one payday threw down his pick and walked off the job, taking the entire shift with him. Within a few days, all mining operations on the Mesabi were closed down.[44]

Responding to the strikers' appeal, the Industrial Workers of the World (IWW or Wobblies) sent its leading organizers to the area. Among them was Carlo Tresca, a Socialist agitator in his native Abruzzi who became a labor leader among the Italian immigrants. With characteristic passion, he exhorted the miners to join the IWW and remain steadfast in the struggle.[45]

A majority of the strikers were Italians and South Slavs

who were characterized as "the lowest paid, the worst housed, and the most abused by the mine bosses."[46] (The English-speaking workers who received favored treatment were largely opposed to the walkout.) The demands called for the abolition of the contract wage system, a flat wage-rate of $3.50 a day, and an eight-hour day. The companies responded by hiring private police and attacking the IWW as un-American. One incident in Biwabik resulted in the killing of two men. Although they were not present at the shooting fray, the IWW leaders were arrested and indicted for murder on the charge that they had told the strikers to defend themselves.

Tresca's arrest evoked a storm of outcry in both the United States and Italy. Protest meetings were held throughout Italy and money was sent for his defense by Italian comrades. His case was discussed in the Italian Chamber of Deputies, but the government failed to lodge a formal protest. Charges against Tresca and the other IWW leaders were dropped when three miners pleaded guilty to manslaughter. Meanwhile, after four months of resistance, the strike ended in total defeat.[47]

Many Italians had joined the IWW during the strike. Pietro Pieri, a miner who served as secretary of the strike committee, later became an organizer for the union. Detailed accounts of the strike by Efrem Bartoletti were published in *Il Proletario*, the Italian syndicalist organ in New York City. A native of Umbria, Bartoletti had worked in the mines of Luxembourg before going to Hibbing in 1909. A Socialist and a poet, he described in verse the life of the immigrant and the miner.[48]

Disappointment over the failure of the strike and the impact of World War I caused many Italians to break with the IWW. By June, 1917, an agent of the antiunion Minnesota Commission of Public Safety could report: "The Italians and Austrians have practically all withdrawn from the I.W.W. as they have come to realize the fact that the Finnish members of that organization are too active and radical and always stir up trouble of some kind or other." It was the Finns' opposition to the wartime Allies (particularly Russia) that especially antagonized the Italians. Pietro Nigro, an IWW organizer, thought that most of them withdrew from the IWW for this reason. But the political climate had also made it unhealthy to be associated with the Wobblies, for foreign radicals were the favored target of the Public Safety Commission.[49]

For two decades no significant movement to organize Minnesota's mine workers occurred. The strikes of 1907 and 1916 had taught them that the power of the mining companies could not be directly challenged. While many nourished deep resentments against Oliver, they found politics a more effective weapon than labor organization. Only when the rules of the game were changed by the New Deal administration in the 1930s was a new and successful effort made to unionize the iron ranges.[50]

Italians and South Slavs were most active in the organizing work initiated by the Steel Workers' Organizing Committee of the Committee for Industrial Organization in 1937. When locals were formed, Italians were conspicuous among their elected officers, and the director of the Steel Workers

Organizing Committee on the range was John T. Bernard, who had been born in Corsica of Italian parents. Taken to Eveleth as a boy in 1907, Bernard had worked as a miner but was blacklisted for political activities. A man of strong progressive views, he was elected to Congress on the Farmer-Labor ticket in 1936.[51]

The Steel Workers' campaign finally achieved victory in 1943 when the Oliver Iron Mining Company signed a contract. Eventually the United Steel Workers of America came to embrace every mine. In 1953 the union had 14,000 members in northern Minnesota, a large percentage of whom were Italian Americans. Some filled important leadership roles. Henry Pappone, for example, was president of Virginia Local No. 1938, president of the Iron Range Assembly, and a vice-president of the Minnesota AFL-CIO.[52]

Religious Organizations

Although they were with few exceptions Roman Catholics, immigrants from Italy posed for the American church what was referred to as the "Italian Problem." Regular attendance at Mass, generous financial support, and respect for the clergy were not common traits, especially among the men. In addition, the Italian kingdom had achieved its goal of unification only over the obdurate opposition of the papacy. Italian nationalists tended to be strongly anticlerical. In Minnesota, where the dominant Catholic figure for many years was Archbishop John Ireland, the immigrants encountered a church strongly Hibernian in flavor.[53]

Because there were few Italian priests in America, the immigrants were left to shift for themselves as far as religious services in their language were concerned. In St. Paul, noting their neglect, Father John Shanley began to say Mass for the Italians in 1874. For some years, an Italian mission was ministered to by Irish-American priests, who like Shanley had studied in Rome and were familiar with the Italian language. From 1888 to 1896 Father Alessandro Cestelli, a professor at St. Thomas Seminary, cared for the Italians both in Minneapolis and St. Paul.[54]

In 1899 Father Nicola Carlo Odone, a Genoese, arrived at the invitation of Archbishop Ireland to take charge of the Italian mission, which was designated Holy Redeemer parish in 1906. Odone also from time to time ministered to the Italians of Minneapolis, Stillwater, Little Canada, Duluth, the iron ranges, and Cumberland, Wisconsin. A talented artist and writer, perhaps less skillful as an administrator, he struggled valiantly for a decade to create a unified congregation and to build a church. He encountered numerous obstacles: rampant factionalism among the Italians; fierce anticlericalism on the part of some; and a general niggardliness with respect to giving.[55]

During this period attendance at Holy Redeemer fluctuated from 500 on Easter to 50 or fewer on an ordinary Sunday. Odone encouraged the celebration of the feast days of the patron saints and madonnas of the various groups of *paesani*; 19 such days were celebrated in 1907. Odone was criticized by American priests for catering to traditional customs and thus hindering the Americanization of Italians.

Despite Odone's efforts to secure an independent church, Italians continued to meet in the *basamento* of the cathedral.

Although adorned with statues and pictures (some by Odone) before which banks of candles burned, the crypt was still dark and humid. Odone expressed to the congregation his sense of humiliation at "having to meet under the feet of a different people which looks at us from above with contempt." Other nationalities, he reminded them, had their own churches, except "we children of Catholic Italy."[56]

All of his appeals fell on deaf ears. Archbishop Ireland, intent on building his new cathedral, prohibited Odone from seeking contributions from wealthy American Catholics and insisted that the Italians provide their own church. For their part, many Italians made it a condition of their support that the church and land must be owned by the Italian colony and not by the archbishop. Nor could those on the East Side and those on the West Side agree on a building site. In 1910, Odone, discouraged and embittered, resigned. Finally under one of his successors, Father Giacinto D. Ciebattone, a site on West College Avenue was chosen and Holy Redeemer Church was built in 1915 at a cost of $42,000. Still attendance was low, fluctuating around 150, with most of the parishioners from the Upper Levee and the Sicilian enclave.[57]

In the early 1900s few of those in the Phalen Creek-Swede Hollow area attended the cathedral's basement chapel. When Odone attempted to hold services in a private home there in 1908, he encountered such indifference and outright hostility that after some weeks he abandoned the effort. The area was then neglected until the Presbyterian Committee on Home Missions established Hope Chapel on Bradley Street in 1911. Soon Italian families were attending the chapel in goodly numbers and sending their children to its Sunday school.[58]

Suddenly Archbishop Ireland decided that St. Paul should have two Italian parishes. With a gift of $5,000 from Clara Hill, a daughter of railroad builder James J. Hill, a small brick church on Bradley Street was purchased and named for St. Ambrose in 1911. This parish had a checkered career. It was closed, reopened in 1917, attached to Holy Redeemer as a mission in 1925, and at last established as an independent church in 1954. With a new building erected in the late 1950s, St. Ambrose survived in 1980 as the only Italian national parish in Minnesota.[59]

The appointment of Father Luigi Pioletti in 1925 as pastor of both Holy Redeemer and St. Ambrose churches revitalized the Italian parishes. From the province of Turin, a former seminary professor and soldier, Pioletti became a father figure for the St. Paul Italians, warm and loving, but also a stern disciplinarian. Under his tutelage, Holy Redeemer and St. Ambrose became centers of community life for their respective neighborhoods. Each developed an array of organizations — ladies' sodalities, Rosary and Holy Name societies, Young Men's and Young Ladies' clubs, choirs, and Boy Scout troops. The church halls became the scenes of events sponsored by Italian organizations; festivals and bazaars, which by the 1930s assumed a more American flavor, including popcorn and pop music to appeal to the young people; and observances of feast days which until World War II continued to be the most colorful events of the year.[60]

The Phalen Creek Italians were also the beneficiaries of

MEMBERS of the St. Ambrose congregation in St. Paul carried a statue of the Virgin Mary on the Feast of the Assumption in 1927.

Christ Child Center, a Catholic social settlement, established in 1911 under the auspices of the Guild of Catholic Women with the purpose of caring for the Italian children of Swede Hollow and the Upper Levee. Under the guidance of Eleanor G. Dowling, its forceful director for many years, the center gained acceptance among Italians, and its auditorium, library, gymnasium, clubrooms, and medical and dental clinics were widely utilized. To the Italians, the center was known as *la Scuola* because of the citizenship classes held there. In the 1940s the facility was moved north to Edgerton Street and renamed Merrick Center.[61]

Minneapolis Italians, fewer in number and more dispersed, had to wait even longer than those in St. Paul for their own church. For many years they were visited occasionally by an Italian priest. After one was regularly assigned to them in 1907, Mass was said in the school annex of the Immaculate Conception Church in a "small, bare, poorly lighted, unheated room." In 1910 an old church was purchased at Main Street and 7th Avenue Northeast, and dedicated to Our Lady of Mount Carmel. Not easily accessible to the majority of the city's Italians, it failed to become self-supporting, and it was sold to a Syrian congregation in 1919.[62]

Services were then held in the Margaret Barry House, a Catholic settlement in the Maple Hill neighborhood, until 1938, when a second Church of Our Lady of Mount Carmel was rededicated as the Italian parish. Located at Summer and Fillmore Streets Northeast, it was now in the heart of Minneapolis' Little Italy. Like the St. Paul churches, it became the focus of social as well as religious life in the community.[63]

Margaret Barry Settlement House had been established on the corner of Pierce Street and Broadway Northeast, in November, 1915, as a result of the efforts of Margaret Barry, aided by the Minneapolis League of Catholic Women, to establish a kindergarten for Italian children. In time the house offered the full range of social services, providing clinics, gymnasium, library, and activities for the entire family until it closed its doors in 1973.[64]

In Duluth a separate "Italian Congregation," numbering 224 men, women, and children, was in existence by 1901. Four years later its members purchased a former French church at 11th Avenue West and Superior Street and founded St. Peter's Italian Church. From 1907 to 1920 and again from 1939 to his death in 1965, St. Peter's was the domain of Father Giovanni Zarrilli. An important figure in the Catholic history of Duluth and the iron ranges, he was instrumental in founding churches in West Duluth, Hibbing, Eveleth, Virginia, and elsewhere.[65]

Born in the province of Avellino, Zarrilli had an eventful and stormy career in the diocese of Duluth. Unrelenting in reminding parishioners of their obligations, he went so far as to deny the services of the church to those who did not pay their dues. By these means he managed to keep St. Peter's solvent, but he also generated a great deal of animosity.

In 1920 Zarrilli accepted a transfer to the Church of the Immaculate Conception in Hibbing. But there he quickly became embroiled in a bitter and complex controversy with Bishop John T. McNicholas. As a result, Zarrilli was exiled in 1923 to Two Harbors, where he remained for 16 years.[66]

Meanwhile, under the leadership of Father Bartolomeo Zucchi, St. Peter's in Duluth erected a handsome edifice. Italian craftsmen contributed their labor or agreed to work for half wages. When the new church was dedicated on December 18, 1927, the program proudly boasted that it had been "constructed entirely by the parishioners."[67]

During his second tenure at St. Peter's, the now elderly Zarrilli continued to maintain, as he had earlier, that Italians would be better off in territorial rather than national parishes, that by mixing with Catholics of other nationalities they would become "loyal and practical Catholics." St. Peter's as a national parish, he declared in 1939, was "finished," for "more than two thirds, probably [,] of the people who came from Italy have died and the rest are dying pretty fast, the young Italians intermarry, move to different parts of the city, and are importuned to join the parish into whose territory they move."[68]

St. Peter's did not become a territorial parish in Zarilli's lifetime. Upon his death the priest bequeathed $35,000 to St. Peter's on the condition that it be declared a territorial parish within two years or forfeit the money. His wishes were carried out in 1967, but his posthumous vindication was short-lived. St. Peter's was soon administered by a priest from Sacred Heart parish, making it in effect a mission. The church itself, built of native stone quarried a few blocks away, still stood in 1980, a Romanesque Gothic monument to the skill and devotion of Italian craftsmen.[69]

On the iron ranges, Italians for the most part were either unchurched or they belonged to mixed parishes which served the polyglot populations of the mining towns. In Chisholm and Nashwauk, for example, they shared churches with Slovenes, Croats, Poles, French Canadians, and other nationalities. Because such mixed parishes were often troubled by ethnic conflicts, the bishop established national parishes. Among these was Zarrilli's Church of the Immaculate Conception started in Hibbing in 1906. Only three years

later, however, it was reported that Hibbing Italians seldom attended, often were not married in church, and did not baptize their children. Having emigrated predominantly from north-central Italy, many of them apparently held strong anticlerical views.[70]

Elsewhere on the ranges, Italians were largely neglected by the Catholic church until Presbyterian missionary William J. Bell, a recent graduate of Princeton Seminary, was sent to begin work among the immigrants in 1913. Aided by Gaetano A. Lizzi, a Waldensian preacher, he visited isolated mining locations armed with portable organ, stereopticon, and tracts in Italian. Meetings in the Presbyterian Church at Eveleth were soon attracting as many as 150 Italians, precipitating what Zarrilli later described as "the terrible struggle in 1914–1920 to combat the large scale propaganda of the Protestants among the Italians."[71]

Both the Catholic and Presbyterian churches brought in forceful Italian preachers to persuade the immigrants of the truth of their respective faiths. A *Savonarola Circolo Educativo*, an anticlerical organization of which Lizzi was the leader, was formed. This religious conflict kept the Italian communities in a state of turmoil for several years. The level of rhetoric escalated to personal attacks, both verbal and physical, culminating in a federal court case involving Lizzi and Vincenzo Cimino, publisher of *Il Corriere Italo-Americano* (Italian American Courier) of Duluth. Cimino was charged with threatening to defame certain persons, while Lizzi was accused of sending an obscene letter to Zarrilli. The simultaneous prosecution of Cimino and Lizzi by the American authorities smacks of a concerted effort to silence these critics of the Italian representatives of church and state.[72]

When Bell closed down his range mission in the 1930s, he had difficulty answering the question put by the Presbytery of Duluth: how many converts had he made during his ministry? Among the Italians, the number appeared to be few. The primary effect of Bell's Italian mission seemed to have been, as Zarrilli observed, that its challenge stimulated Catholic attention to the neglected Italian immigrants.

The establishment of the Church of the Immaculate Conception in Eveleth, for example, was one immediate response to the Protestant threat. The Eveleth parish had a rocky history with a succession of priests until 1941, when it was entrusted to the Pious Society of St. Charles, an Italian religious order. The Immaculate Conception Church survived until the late 1970s when it was declared that there was no longer a need for an Italian ministry. But the closing of the church caused a good deal of resentment on the part of Eveleth Italians.[73]

The Hibbing church also had a turnover of pastors every few years until the arrival of Father Dominic Strobietto, who served from 1923 until his death in 1954. Like Pioletti, he was from near Turin and had served in the Italian army during World War I, and he too became a loved and revered father to his congregation. In 1950, with some 3,500 souls, the Church of the Immaculate Conception of Hibbing was probably the largest Italian parish in the state. Strange to say, Strobietto was the last of the church's Italian pastors.

Italians living in various scattered settlements elsewhere

in the state usually had no choice but to attend the local parish church. Such was the case with a small group of Lombards who settled in Stillwater in the 1870s to work in the sawmills; they joined St. Joseph's Church, which had originally been French Canadian. In International Falls an even smaller Italian colony that emigrated from the Veneto about World War I to work in the paper mill belonged to St. Thomas Church.[74]

Dilworth's Italians never had a church of their own. St. Elizabeth's was located on the north side of town, while the Italians, who made up the majority of the parishioners, lived on the south side. For many years the pastor was a German who did not know Italian.[75]

Since many Dilworth Italians were from Montefalcone di Valfortore in the province of Benevento, where the cult of Our Lady of Mount Carmel was zealously observed, they formed a society in her honor and from 1912 on celebrated her feast day. In time it became a three-day community celebration with Mass, procession, music, sports competitions, food, and a fireworks finale. The Italians built a sacristy on the south side where the *festa* was held. But this cult transplanted from southern Italy to the Great Plains came to an end during World War II, when the Italians were advised that since the United States and Italy were at war, they should not hold the festival in 1942. The Lady of Monte Carmelo Society was disbanded at the same time. In 1980 only the statue of Our Lady of Mount Carmel remained, ensconced in the back yard of Christine Verdi, one of the last of the Italian immigrant generation in Dilworth.

Organizations

Like the churches, Italian organizations in Minnesota reflected the regional prejudices, parochialism, and political differences which made for disunity and conflict. It was not always this way. In 1888 a journalist declared "union and concord reign among the Italians of the two cities." The *Società Italiana Dante Alighieri*, formed in 1883, embodied this spirit of harmony. It included practically all the Italians of St. Paul and Minneapolis from whatever region of Italy. Membership was open to "persons of good character who can speak the Italian language."[76]

The *Dante* was the first of many Italian mutual aid societies as well as a social organization, sponsoring balls, banquets, and picnics. For their monthly dues, members were entitled to sick and death benefits as well as a proper funeral with their lodge brothers marching in unison behind the casket, flags waving, while a band played appropriate dirges. Nationalist and anticlerical in character, the *Dante* initiated the celebration of September 20 to commemorate the military triumph of the kingdom of Italy over the papal states. This observance was particularly obnoxious to the Catholic church, and Archbishop Ireland sought to have it suppressed. After he condemned the commemoration in 1905, the society, accompanied by a band playing the "Italian Royal March" and "Garibaldi's Hymn," marched under the windows of the cathedral residence.[77]

The formation in 1904 of *Sant'Antonio di Padova*, a Catholic mutual aid society, was in part a reaction to the *Dante*'s anticlericalism. The *Sant'Antonio*'s membership, which was restricted to Catholics, was composed largely of southern Italians. In addition to its insurance functions, it sponsored fund-raising events for Holy Redeemer Church, took part in parades of Catholic societies, and planned elaborate celebrations of the feast day of St. Anthony, its patron saint.[78]

As an increasing number of southerners joined the *Dante*, some of the northerners withdrew and formed the *Società Monte Bianco* in 1911. This mutual aid society, which was militantly anticlerical, appealed particularly to the statuary workers from Tuscany. Those from south of Rome were excluded from membership. At its inaugural banquet, Giovanni Pieri, the organization's secretary and a Socialist, made a speech attacking the pope, and a band played "Garibaldi's Hymn."[79]

The years following World War I were marked by a flurry of organizational activity. The Italian-American Legion, made up of veterans of either the American or Italian armies, was formed by sculptor Carlo Brioschi, who was a captain in the Minnesota militia. In 1921 the creation of the *Società Armando Diaz*, a mutual aid organization, sparked further friction among St. Paul Italians. Its founder, Santo Speranza, was expelled from the *Sant'Antonio* on the grounds that he was causing division within the colony. Also formed at this time were the Romolian Club and its auxiliary, the Marconi Social Club, the *Società Femminile Maria ss. dell'Assunta* (the first women's mutual aid society), and the *Società Mutuo Succorso* (or *M.S.*) *Santa Caterina*, a mutual aid society of *paesani* from the town of Santa Caterina Villarmosa in Sicily.[80]

This proliferation of small organizations, most with fewer than 100 members, often sponsored competing activities. A growing appreciation of the negative effects of such splintering produced efforts to achieve greater unity. In 1930, led by a new generation of younger Italian Americans, four mutual aid societies merged to form the *Società Italia di Mutuo Soccorso*, which through its enlarged resources was able to construct a new building to provide clubrooms for itself and facilities for the Christ Child Center in St. Paul.[81]

Since the mutual aid societies barred organizational participation in politics, the Italian-American Club of St. Paul came into being in 1921 to enhance the political standing of Italians, help them become naturalized, and defend them from unjust slander by the American press. The club urged Italians to unify and put aside hatreds stemming from regionalism, provincialism, or *campanilismo*.[82]

In Minneapolis only two city-wide organizations were formed over the years by Italians. After belonging to the *Dante* for some years, they created the *Società Cristoforo Colombo* in 1896. In addition to offering mutual benefit provisions, it sponsored, often in conjunction with the *Dante*, patriotic observances. In 1912 it organized a joint Columbus Day parade for Italian societies of the Twin Cities.[83]

The second city-wide organization was the Progressive Club founded by a group of younger Italian Americans in 1933. It assumed responsibility for the annual Columbus Day banquets and initiated a movement to erect memorials to Giacomo C. Beltrami, an Italian who searched for the source of the Mississippi River in Minnesota in 1823. Through the

THE Società Italia di Mutuo Soccorso, *also known as the Italia Club, celebrated the opening of its new building in St. Paul in 1930. The facility, which also housed the Christ Child Center, was near Swede Hollow.*

efforts of the Beltrami Memorial Association, its offshoot, bronze tablets celebrating the explorer's exploits were placed in 1948 at Fort Snelling and in Beltrami Park (formerly Maple Hill Park) in Minneapolis.

Italians in Duluth, on the other hand, spawned a wide range of organizations. The *Società Cristoforo Colombo*, organized in 1893 by Lombard merchants, was the city's first mutual aid society. Lacking the anticlerical scruples of the *Dante*, it participated in Catholic affairs. For many years beginning in 1901 it sponsored an annual picnic in Enger Park as a benefit for St. Peter's.[84]

Reflecting their several locations, organizations emerged from the various neighborhoods. About 1910 Venetian businessmen in Gary-New Duluth formed the *Società M.S. Figli d'Italia Independente*. Some years later working-class southerners established the *Loggia Principe Ereditario Umberto II*, affiliated with the Sons of Italy in America, and in 1919 the *Società M.S. Bersaglieri* was organized in West Duluth. All of these organizations sponsored a variety of social activities and community projects, including fund raisers for the churches and war relief.

In 1922 the Italian-American Progressive Club of Duluth was created as a chapter of the Minnesota State Federation of Italian American Clubs to assist immigrants in securing citizenship and to aid them with legal problems. The club's Americanization Committee helped teach the English language and American civics to Italians during the 1920s. With its auxiliary, the Italian-American Daughters Lodge, the organization was still active in World War II, raising funds for the Red Cross and purchasing war bonds. Yet both this club and the local Sons of Italy affiliate succumbed to the anti-Italian climate fostered by the war.[85]

Two of the mutual aid societies continued to exist through the 1960s, but *Cristoforo Colombo*, reduced to a handful of old-timers, disbanded in 1975. In that same year, however, a

new Italian American Club and its Women's Auxiliary, both composed of second-generation persons, were formed. Their activities, which have been entirely social and cultural, included revival of the Italian picnic at Enger Park, dinner dances, scholarships, and participation in the Duluth Summer Folk Festival.[86]

On the iron ranges, numerous mutual aid societies were created in the various towns and villages, initially on the basis of regional and *paese* origins. To a greater extent than those in the Twin Cities or Duluth, Italians there developed a common identity. Thus it was they who took the initiative to achieve greater unity, first in the region and then among all Italians in the state. In Eveleth three mutual aid societies and a women's auxiliary founded from 1902 to 1917 merged to become the *Società M.S. Italo-Americana* in 1922. In Chisholm in 1918 the *Società Cristoforo Colombo* and the *Società Fratellanza* joined to form a single mutual aid group. Virginia, perhaps reflecting the preponderance of central Italians in its population, had one major organization, *Società Italiana M.S. Roma*, which had its own hall, as did the Italian societies in Eveleth and Hibbing.[87]

In Hibbing, the Tyrolese and Piedmontese were the first to organize and the last to abandon their exclusive regional character. In 1924 the *Società M.S. Gugielmo Marconi* (1905) and a lodge of the Sons of Italy merged as the Marconi Lodge of the Sons of Italy with a membership of 210 and a handsome bank balance. Its building, completed in 1931 at a cost of $40,000, became a center of Italian community activities in Hibbing. Over the years the lodge lobbied for the teaching of Italian in the local high school, protested against restrictive immigration laws, supported a weekly Italian radio program, contributed to the building of Immaculate Conception Church, and purchased bonds during World War II to demonstrate that it was "100% American."

A significant development in the 1920s was the creation of

the Minnesota State Federation of Italian American Clubs, which began as a network of Italian Americanizaton Clubs on the ranges. The avowed purpose was to promote naturalization and to defend the Italian reputation. The larger objective was to mobilize politically in order to advance the interests of Italians vis-a-vis other ethnic groups. Delegates from the various clubs gathered annually at a meeting of the state federation to discuss problems and plan strategy. With the affiliation of the Duluth club and links with Twin Cities organizations, the Italians for the first time had forged a vehicle for state-wide unity of action.[88]

Columbus Day, October 12, became the most important ethnic observance for Minnesota Italians because it provided an opportunity to celebrate and reconcile their dual identities as Italians and Americans. Until they began to sponsor observances the day had generally been ignored in the state.

In 1904 a Columbus Day entertainment was held in St. Paul for the benefit of Holy Redeemer Church. It became an annual event held under the auspices of the *Società Sant'Antonio* until 1913. After that the United Italian Societies provided a sumptuous banquet at which churchmen and state, city, and county officials paid for their supper with rotund oratory.[89]

Meanwhile the State Federation of Italian American Clubs was sponsoring Columbus Day celebrations on a range-wide basis. In 1927, when Congressman Fiorello LaGuardia of New York was the guest speaker in Hibbing, the Progressive Club of Duluth proposed that a monument to Columbus be erected in the state. Meeting in Eveleth the following year, the state federation enthusiastically endorsed the project and launched the Columbus Memorial Association of Minnesota.[90]

Plans for the monument went forward. In all, 14 chapters of the memorial association were formed. Ten were on the iron ranges; the others were in Duluth, International Falls, and the Twin Cities. After several years of unprecedented state-wide effort, a bronze statue of Columbus by St. Paul sculptor Carlo Brioschi was placed on a granite base on the grounds of the state Capitol across from the Minnesota Historical Society. It was dedicated on October 12, 1931, with a parade, a banquet for 2,000 people, and elaborate ceremonies broadcast over national radio and attended by more than 25,000 Italians from all over the Northwest.

The unity of purpose which Minnesota's Italians achieved during the campaign for the Columbus monument proved to be ephemeral. On the ranges Columbus Day celebrations continued to be held jointly, but in Minneapolis and St. Paul Italians went their separate ways. The Columbus Memorial Association of St. Paul has continued its observances with a ceremony at the monument and a banquet at which scholarships are presented to high school graduates of Italian descent. From 1933 on, first the Progressive Club and then the Italian American Club of Minneapolis have also sponsored a Columbus Day dinner and scholarship program.[91]

For several decades Italians agitated for the establishment of Columbus Day as a legal holiday in Minnesota. The atmosphere engendered by World War II, when Italy was an enemy, seemed an unlikely time for such a measure, yet it was during the 1945 legislative session that the bill was finally passed. Vigorous lobbying by Italian-American groups from the Twin Cities and northern Minnesota, with the Columbus Memorial Association taking a leading role, had done the trick.[92]

During the interwar years, the Minnesota Italian-American community underwent marked changes in its social and institutional character. With the restrictive immigration legislation of the 1920s, the Italian population achieved demographic stability. Gone were the days of the seasonal migration of railroad workers. The Italian neighborhoods were now composed of settled families who often owned their own homes; more men had secured steady city jobs or factory work. After severe growing pains, Italian institutions had developed qualities of permanence and maturity.

But most important, a new generation born in America was coming of age. By 1940 the second generation outnumbered the first by a ratio of two to one.[93] The native-born young people (or those who had immigrated as small children), while raised in immigrant families, were also the products of American schools and American popular culture.

From this generation a new Italian-American leadership began to emerge during the 1930s and 1940s. With the more assimilated leaders of the immigrant generation, they aspired to a larger role in American society both for themselves and for the Italian ethnic group. They perceived that only through unity could Italian Americans attain acceptance, respect, and political power.

Fred A. Ossanna and William C. Davini exemplified this new leadership. Born in Norway, Michigan, the son of a miner, Ossanna quickly developed a successful law practice in Minneapolis following his graduation from the University of Minnesota. But he was also deeply involved in politics and civic affairs, and became a national as well as a state leader in Italian-American organizations. He served as president of the Italian-American Civic League from 1933 to 1938. Through the league, Ossanna pushed for the teaching of Italian in the public schools and for scholarships for Italian-American students. Davini was a St. Paul native and an educator. He too was active in many civic and fraternal organizations. In 1942 he was the first president of the newly formed Twin Cities National Unico Club, a service organization. When the Italian-American Civic League and the National Unico Clubs merged in 1946, Davini was elected national president of the UNICO National. Through these organizations, Ossanna and Davini established important links between Minnesota Italians and the larger Italian-American ethnic group.[94]

World War II marked a dramatic turning point in the history of all Italian Americans, including those in Minnesota. In the conflict between country of origin and country of adoption, their loyalty was clearly with the United States. Earlier sympathies with Fascist Italy proved to be superficial. Although the Italian Americans experienced little overt hostility during the war, they were anxious to dispel the cloud of suspicion by demonstrating their total patriotism. The *Società Italia* became the *Società America*. Other Italian organizations disbanded and community functions were suspended. Fearful of the public's response to their participation in the 1942 Festival of Nations, St. Paul Italians decided to forego the event, although a few did take part. Columbus Day, 1942, however, was a day of rejoicing for Italian Americans, because United States Attorney General Francis Biddle took the occasion to announce that the Italian-American community had been found to be completely loyal and that unnaturalized immigrants would no longer be treated as enemy aliens. Meanwhile the young men went off to war, over 50 from St. Paul's Upper Levee alone, and some did not return.[95]

The war unleashed disruptive forces in the old neighborhoods. Wives and daughters left home for industrial jobs. Full employment and high wages brought a new affluence to the Little Italies. Military service, work opportunities, the G.I. bill, and marriage to non-Italians — all served to draw young people increasingly out of the ethnic enclaves. Those left behind tended to be members of the aging immigrant generation; unreplenished by newcomers, they became fewer with each passing decade.[96]

Natural and political forces also appeared to conspire against the old neighborhoods. Spring floods, which inundated the Upper Levee in 1951 and 1952, inspired the city of St. Paul to rezone the area for industrial use. Despite their protests, the last residents were evicted in 1959, and the Upper Levee became the site of the Kaplan Scrap Iron Company. Meanwhile, in Minneapolis, over stubborn opposition from the community, one-third of the homes in the Beltrami area were destroyed to make way for Interstate 35W. The Lower Payne Avenue neighborhood in St. Paul also suffered from "urban renewal," as did the near-downtown Italian district in Duluth. These forced removals were especially traumatic for the old-timers. For some the loss of homes, gardens, and neighbors was too much; they simply died.[97]

The Italian communities appeared unable to mobilize politically to resist these encroachments, but the threat to Holy Redeemer Church posed by the construction of Interstate 94 aroused determined resistance. Led by the aged and ill Monsignor Luigi Pioletti, the parishioners fought a protracted struggle extending over a decade to save the church. Yet despite vigorous lobbying, fund raising, and publicity efforts, the movement failed. Holy Redeemer was demolished in 1967, and a petition to build a new and smaller church on the same site was denied by Archbishop Leo Binz. Although the diocese re-established Holy Redeemer parish with an Italian-American priest in the St. Paul suburb of Maplewood, the old parishioners would have none of it. More than a decade later, empty land and a parking ramp marked the old site, and bitterness lingered among St. Paul's Italian Americans over the loss of their mother church.[98]

The breakup of the old neighborhoods was also an expression of the increased occupational mobility of the second generation. By and large, Italian Americans remained solidly blue collar, but by 1980 relatively few were unskilled laborers. Rather, they had become skilled craftsmen and service and semiskilled workers. More of them were going on to higher education and entering business and the professions. Names ending in vowels became common in lists of attorneys, physicians, professors, and corporate personnel.[99]

But food and liquor still provided a distinctive field for Italian-American enterprise. Spaghetti houses, pizza parlors, and cocktail lounges proliferated, catering to a broad American clientele. For some these proved to be the highway to success. Jim and Rose Totino, for example, established a restaurant in Northeast Minneapolis, branched out into frozen pizza, and eventually sold out to the Pillsbury Company for $22,000,000. In the process of this occupational differentiation, the Italian-American population became highly stratified, from the very rich to the very poor.

Many made their way into the ranks of white-collar workers, particularly in government agencies. Since the 1930s Italian Americans had voted rather solidly for Minnesota's Farmer-Labor and then Democratic-Farmer-Labor parties. Following World War II they were elected to public office with greater frequency. The iron ranges and St. Paul sent several to the state legislature. Fred A. Cina, son of a miner, for example, served in the Minnesota House of Representatives for over two decades and as majority leader for several terms. In 1976 Bruce F. Vento, an Italian American from St. Paul's East Side, was elected to Congress.

The exodus from the old neighborhoods, however, did not result in a random dispersion of the Italian-American population throughout the Twin Cities metropolitan area. Rather they tended to concentrate in certain sections of the cities and suburbs. Thus community ties were not necessarily ruptured by the migration, but became more elastic with the aid of the telephone and automobile. Families traveled considerable distances to attend their former national parishes. The second and third generations kept alive some of the organizations which their immigrant forebears had established. In 1979 the *Società Sant'Antonio*, for example, celebrated its 75th anniversary with a dinner and dance attended by over 500 persons.[100]

The Italian presence has contributed flavor and color to the composite culture of Minnesota. Certainly Italian food has become an important part of the state's culinary heritage. On the iron ranges, where Italian influence was stronger, certain folkways such as the game of *bocce* have been incorporated into the regional culture.[101]

Nevertheless the folk cultures nurtured by the immigrants have been largely abandoned. The religious *feste*, once so important, have not been celebrated in the Old Country manner for several decades. In 1980 Giovanna D'Agostino (Mama D), a Minneapolis restaurant owner, continued the observance of St. Joseph's Day by offering a free meal to all comers, but the family ritual of St. Joseph's table appeared extinct. Winemaking, canning, gardening, raising barnyard animals — skills which were so important in feeding the immigrant family — were practiced by few. Of the oral traditions, folk tales, and humor, only a minority of an aging second generation have recollections. Although almost 13,000 persons in Minnesota claimed Italian as their mother tongue in 1970, the majority had at best an elementary knowledge of the language.

Still there was a consciousness of being Italian American

among them. Often this was expressed through the cultivation of things Italian — music, fashions, and foods — within the company of family and friends. Ties of kinship and sentiment also attracted them to contemporary Italy. For many, family connections have survived a half century and more of separation, renewed from time to time by the occasional letter or gift. In recent years a growing number of the American born have returned in search of their roots, seeking out the *paesi* from which their ancestors departed.

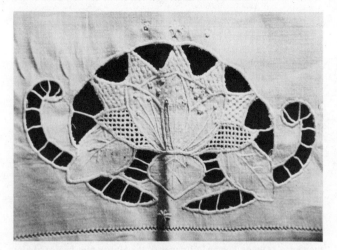

MADEIRA open-work embroidery by Mary Crescenzo, a resident of Duluth who was born near Naples. Second-generation Italian women, like their mothers before them, decorated their household linens with fine needlework.

It was such attachments that inspired the response of Italian Americans to the disasters which have afflicted their land of origin. From the eruption of Mount Vesuvius in 1906 to the earthquake of 1980, Minnesotans have contributed generously to the relief of victims of these recurring calamities. They have also succored their compatriots during time of war. St. Paul Italians contributed an ambulance to the Italian Red Cross in World War I and sent clothing and other relief to Italy during World War II.[102]

The ethnic identity of Minnesota's Italian Americans has also been influenced by their experience of prejudice and discrimination. A conspicuous minority in the midst of the state's Nordic population, they were long regarded with antipathy. But the most persistent and insidious stereotype has been that of the Italian as criminal. From the turn of the century, Italians have been depicted in newspapers and other later mass media as bloodthirsty members of the Mafia. Despite their protests, this biased characterization has resurfaced again and again. In recent years films such as *The Godfather* have given new life to the *mafioso* image. The Twin Cities press has made flagrant use of such labels. But Italian Americans have been passive and quiescent in the face of such pejorative treatment. In fact, certain Italian-American restaurateurs have adopted a Mafia theme in advertising their places of business.[103]

In 1980 the lack of organized response to group defama-

tion was indicative of the current state of Italian Americans in Minnesota. No umbrella organization existed through which they could speak with a united voice. Their factionalism, itself an ethnic trait, persisted unto the third generation.

Just as they had no antidefamation league, they had few institutions for maintaining Italian language and culture in the state. The national parishes, with one exception, were defunct. The surviving organizations served primarily social functions.

In 1976 the *Stella del Nord* Chapter of the American Italian Historical Association was formed to gather, preserve, and interpret the history of the Italians in the Upper Midwest. An Italian Nationality Group was also established in the 1970s to co-ordinate participation in the International Institute of Minnesota's Festival of Nations. On the iron ranges and in Duluth, the Minnesota Federation of Italian American Clubs sponsored an annual *bocce* tournament and Columbus Day observance. Columbus Day was still celebrated with dinners and scholarship-award programs in the Twin Cities. But that was about the sum total of Italian-American cultural activity in Minnesota in 1980. The language was rarely taught in the high schools or colleges of the state, and Italian Americans had taken little initiative in maintaining their mother tongue.

After a century the future of Italian Americans in Minnesota appeared problematical. Few of the immigrant generation were left, and the second generation in 1980 was middle-aged or older. A third generation was coming of age which possessed little knowledge of the traditional culture of their immigrant grandparents. There were few Italian-American institutions to provide them with the solid substance of language, culture, and history to fill out the ethnic identity many of them felt.

Curiously, Italian Americans in Minnesota had not yet made the transition from the primordial ethnicity of the *paese* to the conscious, institutionalized ethnicity of modern America. As the 1980s began, their history was at a fork in the road, one leading through conscious effort to a revitalization of ethnic consciousness, the other to extinction as a community.

Reference notes

[1] The best general work on the subject remains Robert F. Foerster, *The Italian Emigration of Our Times* (Cambridge, Mass., 1919). More recent histories of Italian immigration include Alexander De Conde, *Half Bitter, Half Sweet: An Excursion in Italian-American History* (New York, 1971), and Luciano J. Iorizzo and Salvatore Mondello, *The Italian-Americans* (New York, 1971). For a more interpretive treatment, see Richard Gambino, *Blood of My Blood: The Dilemma of the Italian-Americans* (New York, 1974).

[2] Iorizzo and Mondello, *Italian-Americans*, 219; U.S. Immigration Commission, *Statistical Review of Immigration, 1820–1910*, 290 (61 Congress, 3 session, *Senate Documents*, vol. 20 — serial 5878); U.S. Dept. of Justice, Immigration and Naturalization Service, *Annual Report 1970*, 58 (Washington, D.C., 1971).

[3] Here and below, see Gianfausto Rosoli, ed., *Un secolo di emigrazione Italiana 1876–1976* (Rome, 1978); Emilio Sereni, *Il capitalismo nelle campagne (1860–1900)* (Turin, 1947); John S. Mac-

Donald, "Agricultural Organization, Migration, and Labour Militancy in Rural Italy," in *Economic History Review*, 16:61–75 (August, 1963); Francesco Barbagallo, *Lavoro ed esodo nel sud 1861–1971* (Naples, 1973); Francesco Paolo Cerase, *Sotto il domino dei borghesi* (Rome, 1975).

[4] For more on Italian peasants and their adjustment to the U.S., see Rudolph J. Vecoli, "*Contadini* in Chicago: A Critique of *The Uprooted*," in *Journal of American History*, 51:407–417 (December, 1964), and "Cult and Occult in Italian-American Culture: The Persistence of a Religious Heritage," in Randall M. Miller and Thomas D. Marzik, eds., *Immigrants and Religion in Urban America*, 25–47 (Philadelphia, 1977); Franco Molfese, *Storia del brigantaggio dopo l'Unitá* (Milan, 1974); Renzo Del Carria, *Proletari senza rivoluzione* (Milan, 1970); Luigi Villari, *Italian Life in Town and Country* (New York, 1902), and *Gli Stati Uniti d'America e l'emigrazione italiana* (Milan, 1912); Amy A. Bernardy, *Italia randagia attraverso gli Stati Uniti* (Turin, 1913).

[5] Here and below, see Robert F. Harney, "The Padrone and the Immigrant," in *Canadian Review of American Studies*, 5:101–118 (Fall, 1974), and "Ambiente and Social Class in North American Little Italies," in *Canadian Review of Studies in Nationalism*, 2:208–224 (Spring, 1975); John S. and Leatrice D. MacDonald, "Chain Migration, Ethnic Neighborhood Formation and Social Networks," in *Milbank Memorial Fund Quarterly*, 42:82–97 (January, 1964).

[6] On the Wisconsin settlements, see U.S. Immigration Commission, *Abstracts*, 1:559–565 (Washington, D.C., 1911); Alexander E. Cance, "Piedmontese on the Mississippi," in *Survey*, 26:779–785 (1911). Italian-American newspapers frequently carried advertisements for railroad lands in Texas, Mississippi, and New Mexico, but only one for Minnesota has been found. See *L'Italia* (Chicago), June 16, 1888; Nancy C. Anderson, "James J. Hill and the Promotion of the Northwest," 23–26, typed paper, 1980, copy in IHRC; G. F. Di Palma-Castiglione, "Vari Centri Italiani negli Stati di Indiana, Ohio, Michigan, Minnesota e Wisconsin," in *Bollettino dell'Emigrazione*, 14:591 (Rome, 1915). Di Palma-Castiglione observed that the Immigration Office of the State of Minnesota had not issued any land circulars in Italian. For examples of truck gardeners, see Vadnais Heights Bicentennial Commission, *Vadnais Heights: A History, 1845–1976*, 29 ([Vadnais Heights], 1976); Martha Campanaro obituary, September 28, 1969, in Clippings, John Vannelli Papers, IHRC; Paul Mohrbacher, "The Vitales," in *Metropolitan*, August–September, 1978, pp. 23–25. The Vannelli Papers contain thousands of newspaper clippings, both loose in folders and pasted into unpaginated, unnumbered scrapbooks. Most are not fully identified by name of paper, date, and page. Citations in these footnotes contain as much information as was available.

[7] U.S., *Census*, 1930, *Population*, vol. 3, part 1, pp. 1194, 1220.

[8] Book of Peace and Information, 5:26, 61–65, 125 (1920–24), and "Italians in Minnesota," [2], in Manuscripts, Italians in Minnesota, n.d., — both in Nicola Carlo Odone Papers, IHRC; John A. Vannelli, "Italian Presence in St. Paul," Vannelli Papers; *L'Italia*, April 14, 1888; *St. Paul Pioneer Press*, January 2, 1910, sec. 4, p. 7; *Catholic Directory of Duluth and Almanac for 1892*, 11, 23, 31, 45, 46, 50, 51, 55 (Duluth, 1892); Columbus Memorial Association of Minnesota (Attilio Castigliano and Fred A. Ossanna, eds.), *Columbus: A Collection of Historical Facts*, 62, 66 (St. Paul, 1931); *Northwest Magazine* (St. Paul), August, 1897, p. 29. About the pioneers of the 1850s and 1860s little is known but their names and occupations: Adriano d'Orsolino, sculptor, Fernando Monti, merchant, and C. H. Del Vecchio, barber, to name a few.

The Odone Papers contain diaries (1904–47), correspondence, newspaper clippings, announcement books and church censuses of

Holy Redeemer Church in St. Paul (hereafter cited as HR Announcement Books and HR Censuses, respectively), printed materials, and Odone's own writings on the Italians in St. Paul and Minnesota. Except for newspaper clippings, unless otherwise indicated, all material cited from this collection was written by Odone. The diaries, the church censuses and announcement books, and Odone's Books of Peace and Information (5 vols.) have both dated and undated entries, and not all are paginated. In citing these volumes, dates of entries were used when possible; if there were no dates, volume numbers and pages were used, and the inclusive dates of the volume were supplied in the first citation. For more on Odone, see below, p. 458.

[9] Diary, 2:57 (1907–08), and "Memorie raccolte per servire a scriver la Storia della Missione e Parrocchia Italiana in Saint Paul, Minnesota," in Diary, 8:33 (1912), both in Odone Papers; *St. Paul Dispatch*, March 25, 1948, p. 13, April 13, 1968, p. 11, June 16, 1977, p. 27C; *St. Paul Pioneer Press*, August 3, 1975, Metropolitan sec., 1; *Minneapolis Tribune*, August 24, 1979, p. 1B; "List of Italians in St. Paul taken from 1906 City Directory," in Notebook, Vannelli Papers; Columbus Memorial Assn., *Columbus*, 81. Among the local firms were the Arrigoni Brothers, the Grazzini Brothers, and the Venice Art Marble Co. Giuseppe Capecchi, Giovanni B. Garatti, and Carlo Brioschi were outstanding sculptors.

[10] Two other St. Paul organizations were the Chiarini Band and the Verdi Band, the latter directed by Guido Arrigoni. Arthur E. Wascher and Thomas C. Ingham, *Who's Who in Music and Dramatic Art in the Twin Cities*, 10, 157 (Minneapolis, 1925); Oliver Towne, "Passing of the 'Maestro of Summit Avenue,'" April, 1976, in Clippings, and three items in Scrapbooks — "Minnesota's Italian Pioneers," Oliver Towne, "Echoes of the Hurdy-Gurdy," Arrigoni obituary, September 12, 1958 — all in Vannelli Papers; "Luigi Lombardi," Vertical File, Northeast Minnesota Historical Center, University of Minnesota-Duluth; Luigi Lombardi, *Pages of My Life* (Fond du Lac, Wis., 1943); Diary, February 24, 1909, Odone Papers; Matti Kaups, "Europeans in Duluth," in Ryck Lydecker and Lawrence J. Sommer, eds., *Duluth: Sketches of the Past*, 73 (Duluth, 1976); Gentille Yarusso, "Musical Memories," undated typescript in IHRC; *St. Paul Pioneer Press*, February 15, 1976, p. 12. The *Minneapolis Tribune* of July 6, 1876, reported that Italian street musicians "disgusted the citizens with their everlasting squeaky fiddles."

[11] Rev. S. N. [N.C.] Odone, "A Sketch of the Italian Colony in Minnesota," in newspaper clippings, [1908?], Odone Papers. See also Di Palma-Castiglione, in *Bollettino dell'Emigrazione*, 14:595–598.

[12] "Memorie raccolte," in Diary, 8:34, "La Colonia Italiana di St. Paul, Minnesota," 1–7 (1904), in Manuscripts, Italians in Minnesota — both in Odone Papers; *St. Paul Pioneer Press*, January 2, 1910, sec. 4, p. 7.

[13] Frank J. Sheridan, *Italian, Slavic and Hungarian Unskilled Immigrant Laborers in the United States*, 434, 445–468 (U.S. Bureau of Labor, *Bulletin*, no. 72 — Washington, D.C., 1907); Ja[me]s N. Hill to F. I. Whitney, August 18, 1897, in James N. Hill to Louis W. Hill Subject Files, Eastern Railway of Minnesota, Great Northern Railway Papers, MHS. The author is indebted to Nancy C. Anderson for this citation and related material. See also Foerster, *Italian Emigration*, 361. On Chicago as a center of Italian railroad labor, see Rudolph J. Vecoli, "Chicago's Italians: A Study of the Adjustment of a Peasant Group to an Urban Environment," Ph.D. thesis, University of Wisconsin, 1963. On the building of Minnesota's railroads, see Henry A. Castle, *History of St. Paul and Vicinity*, 1:218–228 (Chicago, 1912).

[14] Dominic T. Ciolli, "The 'Wop' in the Track Gang," in *Immigrants in America Review*, 2:61–64 (July, 1916); *L'Italia*, Novem-

ber 19, 1887, June 2, 1888, July 4, 1891; G. T. Slade to Ja[me]s N. Hill, July 14, 1899, in James N. Hill to Louis W. Hill Subject Files, Eastern Railway of Minnesota, Great Northern Railway Records; Industrial Commission of Wisconsin, *Labor Camps in Wisconsin*, 3–13 (Madison, Wis., [1913?]).

[15] Here and below, see John Koren, *The Padrone System and the Padrone Banks*, 113–129 (U.S. Bureau of Labor, *Bulletin*, no. 9 — Washington, D.C., 1897). *St. Paul Pioneer Press*, September 13, 1908, sec. 4, p. 8, describes the labor agencies along East 3rd St. Father Odone recorded the coming and going of the railroad laborers in his diary; he also noted the operations of the *padrones*, commenting that one was reputed to have been "the wolf of the Italian colony of St. Paul who sucked the blood of the Italian workers." Diary, April 20, 1921.

Various St. Paul *padrones* catered to men from their home regions: Paolo Carbone to the *Calabresi*, Santo Speranza to the Sicilians, Angelo Goduto to the *Pugliesi*, Frank James (Francesco Di Joia) to the *Abruzzesi* and *Molisani*. Among the earliest and most successful *padrones* were Andrea Di Gloria and Pasquale Di Re. See Diaries, 1:10 (1904–07) and March 13, 1910, HR Census, 1899–1903, p. [3], and March 10, 1910, HR Announcement Books, December 20, 1908, and April 18, 1909 — all in Odone Papers; Oliver Towne column, 1964, in Scrapbooks, Vannelli Papers. See also Amy A. Bernardy, "Sulle condizioni delle donne e dei fanciulli Italiani negli Stati del Centro e dell'Ovest della Confederazione del Nord-America," in *Bollettino dell'Emigrazione*, 1:26 (1911).

[16] Bernardy, in *Bollettino dell'Emigrazione*, 1:161–163; Carol Aronovici, *Housing Conditions in the City of Saint Paul*, 52 (St. Paul, 1917); Kathryn Boardman, "Payne's True Story; No Mafia Myth," in *St. Paul Dispatch*, 1969, clipping in Vannelli Papers.

[17] *Guida Pratica della Parrocchia del SS. Redentore in St. Paul, Minnesota* ([Savona, Italy]), April, 1909, p. 11, Odone Papers. Odone published four numbers of this guide to provide information and instruction to his parishioners.

[18] HR Census, 1899–1903, p. [3], "Memorie raccolte," in Diary, 8:34, both in Odone Papers; Bernardy, in *Bollettino dell'Emigrazione*, 1:70; *St. Paul Pioneer Press*, October 15, 1908, p. 4, January 2, 1910, sec. 4, p. 7, April 19, 1959, p. 7.

[19] Here and below, see "Memorie raccolte," in Diary, 8:34, Odone Papers; Bernardy, in *Bollettino dell'Emigrazione*, 1:70; Alice L. Sickels, "The Upper Levee Neighborhood," 6, 18, 20, 27, 34, 35, 58, master's thesis, University of Minnesota, 1938; *St. Paul Dispatch*, April 25, 1978, p. 19. See also Cindy Kunz, "The Upper Levee: Reviewed, Remembered, in Perspective," typescript, 1977, in IHRC.

[20] Aronovici, *Housing Conditions*, 11; Bernardy, in *Bollettino dell'Emigrazione*, 1:72; Book of Peace and Information, 5:116, Odone Papers; *St. Paul Pioneer Press*, January 2, 1910, sec. 4, p. 7; *St. Paul Dispatch*, November 15, 1910, p. 1; Di Palma-Castiglione, in *Bollettino dell'Emigrazione*, 14:593.

[21] Boardman, "Payne's True Story," clipping, and Gareth D. Hiebert, "Italian Way of Life Lingers in St. Paul," July 9, 1950, in Scrapbook, both in Vannelli Papers; Polly Nyberg and Jerome Bette, "Swede Hollow," in *Common Ground*, Fall, 1974, pp. 4–11; *St. Paul Pioneer Press*, January 2, 1910, sec. 4, p. 7; Gentille Yarusso, "An Italian Symphony of Aromas," undated typescript, IHRC. A file of Yarusso's unpublished writings, containing many affectionate and charming accounts of life in the hollow, is in IHRC.

[22] Boardman, "Payne's True Story," clipping, Vannelli Papers; Joel S. Torstenson and David A. Nordlie, *Phalen Park: An Urban Community in a Midwest Metropolis*, 29–31 (Minneapolis, 1965); Gentille Yarusso, "Little Red Caboose," undated, and "The Backyard Classics of Swede Hollow," January 5, 1977, in IHRC.

[23] Here and below, see Lisa Knazen, "The Maple Hill Commu-

nity 1915–1940," 21, 23, 70, typescript, 1973, in IHRC; Barry Morrow, "The Beltrami Neighborhood Remembered," in *Common Ground*, Spring, 1974, pp. 4–10; Women's Co-Operative Alliance, *A Study of Community Conditions: East District*, 8, 13 (Publication 68, series 2 — Minneapolis, [1925]); Richard Wolniewicz, *Ethnic Persistence in Northeast Minneapolis: Maps and Commentary*, 6 (Minnesota Project on Ethnic America, *Research Study No. 1* — Minneapolis, 1973); *Minneapolis Tribune*, September 17, 1977, p. 2B, April 8, 1978, p. 1B. By 1917 at least 150 Italians were employed in the flour mills, according to "D.J.G. Reports," St. Paul, July 13, 1917, in Correspondence and Records, Woman's Committee (Minneapolis), Council of National Defense, War Records Commission (WRC) Records, in Minnesota State Archives, MHS.

[24] Newton S. Gordon, ed., *History of Barron County, Wisconsin*, 1098 (Minneapolis, 1922); Immigration Commission, *Abstracts*, 1:559–565; Book of Peace and Information, 5:103, Odone Papers; *The Forum* (Fargo-Moorhead), June 27, centennial sec., 3, July 1, 1979, p. F9; author's interviews of Thomas St. Angelo and Albert H. Miller, August 7, 1966, Frank and Margaret Oliver, July 29, 1980, Tony Altobelli, August 20, 1980, notes in author's possession.

[25] Among Duluth's pioneer settlers were Biaggio and Angelina Somma, who arrived by way of Winnipeg in 1880 from the town of Brebbia, Lombardy. Others were from Boiano and Chivita in Molise and Guardia Lombardi in Campania. Jaqueline R. Moran, "The Italian-Americans of Duluth," 10, 32–38, master's thesis, University of Minnesota-Duluth, 1979. A breakdown of Duluth's Italian families in 1916 listed 107 from Abruzzi-Molise, 47 Calabria and Sicily, 36 Lombardy, 25 Campania, 16 Basilicata, 10 Veneto and Tyrol, and 7 Marche-Lazio-Tuscany. See Chiesa Italiana di S. Pietro, *Resoconto Finanziario Annuale, 1915–1916* (Duluth, 1916), in Giovanni Zarrilli Papers, Diocese of Duluth Archives, College of St. Scholastica, Duluth. The author is indebted to Rev. John Whitney Evans for his generous assistance in the use of this collection.

[26] Moran, "Italian-Americans," 7, 13, 27, 200.

[27] Moran, "Italian-Americans," 21. West Duluth, observed a social worker, exhibited "a 'right' and 'wrong' side of the tracks situation, with middle-class Protestant Scandinavians on one side and Catholic Italians and Yugoslav peasants, turned industrial, on the other." See Ethel Bird to Vera V. Karabut, May 14, 1942, International Institute of Duluth Papers, in Northeast Minnesota Historical Center.

[28] Moran, "Italian-Americans," 25.

[29] Here and below, see Moran, "Italian-Americans," 31–61, 98–105; Columbus Memorial Assn., *Columbus*, 68; Attilio Castigliano, "Origine, sviluppo, importanza ed avvenire delle colonie italiane del Nord Michigan e del Nord Minnesota," and Di Palma-Castiglione, both in *Bollettino dell'Emigrazione*, 7:739–742 (1913) and 14:575, respectively.

[30] Castigliano, in *Bollettino dell'Emigrazione*, 7:723–739; *L'Italia*, January 1, 1887, April 7, 1894, July 19, 1902, p. 1; John Sirjamaki, "The People of the Mesabi Range," in *Minnesota History*, 27:206–208 (September, 1946); George O. Virtue, *The Minnesota Iron Ranges*, 347 (U.S. Bureau of Labor, *Bulletin*, no. 84 — Washington, D.C., 1909); U.S. Immigration Commission, *Immigrants in Industries*, 78:291–305 (61 Congress, 2 session, *Senate Documents*, no. 633 — serial 5677).

[31] Castigliano, in *Bollettino dell'Emigrazione*, 7:733–739; Immigration Commission, *Immigrants in Industries*, 78:307–314, 330; Virtue, *Minnesota Iron Ranges*, 356.

[32] Immigration Commission, *Immigrants in Industries*, 78:340.

[33] Immigration Commission, *Immigrants in Industries*, 78:341; John Syrjamaki, "Mesabi Communities: A Study of Their Development," 187, Ph.D. thesis, Yale University, 1940; Hyman Berman,

"Education for Work and Labor Solidarity: The Immigrant Miners and Radicalism on the Mesabi Range," [1963?], photocopy in IHRC. Although Berman does not deal specifically with Italians, his study provides a thorough analysis of living and working conditions among the miners.

[34] Here and below, see Syrjamaki, "Mesabi Communities," 188; Virtue, *Minnesota Iron Ranges*, 367–376, 389–394; Immigration Commission, *Immigrants in Industries*, 78:318–323, 339.

[35] *The Miners Magazine* (Denver), August 22, 1907, p. 8; Syrjamaki, "Mesabi Communities," 142.

[36] Here and below, see Syrjamaki, "Mesabi Communities," 120; Castigliano, in *Bollettino dell'Emigrazione*, 7:737; Columbus Memorial Assn., *Columbus*, 70–78; Immigration Commission, *Immigrants in Industries*, 78:318–323, 348–350; Virtue, *Minnesota Iron Ranges*, 356–359.

[37] Syrjamaki, "Mesabi Communities," 126, 249; Columbus Memorial Assn., *Columbus*, 70–78.

[38] Syrjamaki, "Mesabi Communities," 253; Sirjamaki, in *Minnesota History*, 27:211; "Report of Teofilo Petriella," in Western Federation of Miners, *Proceedings of the Fifteenth Annual Convention, 1907*, 190 (Denver, 1907), in Western Federation of Miners/Mine, Mill Archives, Western Historical Collections, University of Colorado, Boulder.

[39] Columbus Memorial Assn., *Columbus*, 70–78; Syrjamaki, "Mesabi Communities," 129. The business activities of the Italians are also described in such community histories as Anniversary Book Committee, *Nashwauk "From Timber to Taconite": The Story of Nashwauk Minnesota* (Nashwauk, 1978).

[40] Walter Van Brunt, *Duluth and St. Louis County, Minnesota*, 3:1040 (Chicago, 1921); *Minneapolis Star*, June 20, 1979, p. 17T; Moran, "Italian-Americans," 181.

[41] Here and below, see Paul H. Landis, *Three Iron Mining Towns: A Study in Cultural Change*, 19 (Ann Arbor, Mich., 1938); Syrjamaki, "Mesabi Communities," 371–381; Adolfo Vinci, "Le miniere di ferro nel Minnesota," in *Bollettino dell'Emigrazione*, 20:16–20 (1923).

[42] Here and below, see Landis, *Three Iron Mining Towns*, 23; Syrjamaki, "Mesabi Communities," 245–247, 257, 378, 435.

[43] Here and below, see *Vermilion Iron Journal* (Tower), June 23, 1892; Anthony C. Schulzetenberge, "Life on the Vermilion Range before 1900," 40, typescript, 1963, copy in MHS. The 1907 strike has been thoroughly studied in Berman, "Education for Work and Labor Solidarity," 38–45; Neil Betten, "Strike on the Mesabi — 1907," in *Minnesota History*, 40:340–347 (Fall, 1967); Edward J. Marolt, "The Development of Labor Unionism in the Iron Mining Industry of the Virginia-Eveleth District," master's thesis, University of Minnesota, 1969.

Unlike the Italian miners in Illinois, Colorado, and elsewhere who organized branches of the *Federazione Socialista Italiana* and printed Socialist publications, those on the iron ranges appear not to have engaged in organized activities. The only Italian radical newspaper published in Minnesota was *La Campana* (Minneapolis), an anarchist sheet edited by Calogero Speziale, and only one issue of that (October, 1917) seems to have appeared. A microfilm copy is in author's possession. On Petriella, see "Petriella, Teofilo," *Casselario Politico Centrale, Ministero dell'Interno, Direzione Centrale di Pubblica Sicurezza, Archivio Centrale dello Stato* (Rome), and "Report of Teofilia Petriella," in Western Federation of Miners, *Fifteenth Annual Convention*, 185–190.

[44] On the 1916 strike, here and below, see Berman, "Education for Work and Labor Solidarity," 46–55; Neil Betten, "Riot, Revolution, Repression in the Iron Range Strike of 1916," in *Minnesota History*, 41:82–93 (Summer, 1968); Donald G. Sofchalk, "Organized Labor and the Iron Ore Miners of Northern Minnesota, 1907–1936," in *Labor History*, 12:214–242 (Spring, 1971).

[45] On Tresca, see *Dictionary of American Biography, Supplement Three, 1941–1945*, 776–778 (New York, 1973).

[46] Sofchalk, "Organized Labor," 229.

[47] On the Italian government's reaction, see Macchi di Cellere to Ministry of Foreign Affairs, September 12, 1916, in "Tresca, Carlo," *Casselario Politico Centrale, Ministero dell'Interno, Direzione Centrale di Pubblica Sicurezza, Archivio Centrale dello Stato*, which also contains reports of the protests throughout Italy on Tresca's behalf. See also Arturo Caroti, *Per Carlo Tresca* (Milan, 1916). The Italian ambassador explained his inaction by saying that the strike was financed by Germany and Austria, the strikers were almost all Austro-Hungarians, and any action by Italy in Tresca's behalf would "predispose the mine owners against our workers who have already suffered much for the unwise strikes which occurred in years past."

[48] *New York Call*, May 11, 1919, p. 1. Bartoletti's collected poems were published by the IWW in *Nostalgie Proletarie* (Brooklyn, n.d.). *Il Proletario*, July 15, 1916, and subsequent issues, carried Bartoletti's articles; his 1916 strike poem was entitled "I Ribelli del Minnesota."

[49] John Michaela, an Italian assistant chief of police for Oliver Mining, reported that his "secret informants" told him "95% of the Italians and Serbs have dropped out of that organization [*IWW*] solely on account of the firm stand taken by the Finnish members against the war and conscription." "D.J.G. Reports," June 29, July 1, 3, 1917; "#45 Reports," August 18, 1917, in Correspondence and Records, Woman's Committee (Minneapolis), Council of National Defense, WRC Records.

[50] Here and below, see Syrjamaki, "Mesabi Communities," 204, 226; Landis, *Three Iron Mining Towns*, 111; Marolt, "Development of Labor Unionism," 140–160; Rudolph Pinola, "Labor and Politics on the Iron Range of Northern Minnesota," 75–83, Ph.D. thesis, University of Wisconsin, 1957; Anniversary Book Committee, *Nashwauk "From Timber to Taconite,"* 75. See also the correspondence of range locals in United Steelworkers of America District 33, sub-district Hibbing, Papers, MHS.

[51] On Bernard, see Barbara Stuhler, "The One Man Who Voted 'Nay': The Story of John T. Bernard's Quarrel with American Foreign Policy, 1937–1939," in *Minnesota History*, 43:84, 90–92 (Fall, 1972); interview of John T. Bernard by author, September 11, 1978, notes in author's possession.

[52] Pinola, "Labor and Politics," 91–93. For examples of Italians in union leadership, see clippings, Vannelli Papers.

[53] Rudolph J. Vecoli, "Prelates and Peasants: Italian Immigrants and the Catholic Church," in *Journal of Social History*, 2:217–268 (Spring, 1968). Informative sketches of the Italian national parishes in Minnesota are in Giovanni Schiavo, *Italian-American History*, 2:683–694 (1949).

[54] Francis J. Schaefer, "Parish of the Most Holy Redeemer, St. Paul, Minn., for the Catholics of Italian Descent," in *Acta et Dicta*, 2:243 (July, 1910); U.S. Works Projects Administration, Minnesota, Historical Records Survey: Churches, 1936–41, in MHS, hereafter cited as WPA, Church Records. Among the very earliest Italians in Minnesota Territory were two priests, Francis de Vivaldi, a missionary to the Winnebago Indians in 1851, and Demetrius de Marogna, one of the founders of St. John's Abbey in 1857.

[55] During his years as pastor of Holy Redeemer, Odone made detailed notations on his experiences and observations. His diaries and parish records provide abundant documentation on the early history of Holy Redeemer. See especially HR Announcement Books, 1899–1909, Odone Papers. On citation style for this collection, see note 8. In his struggle to raise funds for the church, he warned his parishioners that in the U.S. stinginess to the church was a mortal sin; HR Announcement Book, June 10, 1906. On attend-

ance and *feste,* below, see HR Announcement Book, April 11, 1909, Diary, 3:11 (1908–09), Odone Papers.

[56] HR Announcement Book, 1906–08, p. [9], Odone Papers.

[57] Diaries, May 22, 1913, April 2, 1915, Odone Papers; "Weekly Bulletin of Holy Redeemer Church, December 22, 1940," Luigi Pioletti Papers, IHRC; *Catholic Bulletin* (St. Paul), November 29, 1913, January 15, 1916, clippings in Vannelli Papers. Odone wrote the history of his efforts to establish an independent Italian church in "Ragguaglio del movimento per la chiesa italiana in St. Paul, Minn.," in Diary, 7:1–66 (1911–12). He described an appeal for funds to James J. Hill which Hill ended abruptly by saying, "I have no money"; Diary, 3:70.

[58] Diaries, August 7, 1908, 2:185, April 4, 1911, HR Announcement Book, July 11, 1909, "Memorie raccolte," in Diary, 8:73–75 — all in Odone Papers; *St. Paul Dispatch,* April 12, 1910, p. 2; *St. Paul Pioneer Press,* April 13, 1910, p. 16.

[59] Diaries, April 7, August 31, September 7, 9, 13, October 11, 1911, January 26, 1912, "Ragguaglio," in Diary, 7:59–66 — all in Odone Papers; James Reardon to Pioletti, July 7, 1960, in Pioletti Papers; Church of Saint Ambrose, *Souvenir Issue Commemorating the Dedication,* 15 ([St. Paul, 1957]). Odone reported that Archbishop Ireland wanted the Italian church around East 7th to counteract the Protestant mission among the Italians in the hollow.

[60] WPA, Church Records; clippings, July 20, 1931, August 17, 1933, in Vannelli Papers. On Pioletti, see *Italian American Who's Who,* 2:304 (New York, 1937); Herm Sittard, "Shepherd to Italians: Msgr. Pioletti Lives, Disciplines," in *Catholic Bulletin,* January 7, 1966, and Joseph L. Baglio, "Priest Traveled Lifelong Pilgrimage," in *Catholic Bulletin,* 1971, both clippings in Vannelli Papers.

[61] Diary, April 7, 1911, HR Announcement Book, April 7, 1911, both in Odone Papers; Kathleen B. Spear, *Recreation Survey of St. Paul Minnesota,* 81 (St. Paul, 1934); Torstenson and Nordlie, *Phalen Park,* 50; Gentille Yarusso, "I'll Meet Ya, at the Center," undated typescript, in IHRC.

[62] Diaries, 1:38, 121, November 3, 1907, August 19, 1919, C. A. Moore to Odone, January 9, 1910, in General U.S. Correspondence, Odone Papers; "The New Church of Our Lady of Mount Carmel, Minneapolis," in *Acta et Dicta,* 3:172 (July, 1911).

[63] Margaret Barry to Odone, March 5, 1928, in General U.S. Correspondence, Odone Papers; Odone to B. Zucchi, October 21, 1931, in Miscellaneous, Zarrilli Papers; "Italian Parish in City Revived," August 4, 1938, and *Catholic Bulletin,* March 4, 1977, in Scrapbooks, Vannelli Papers; Knazen, "Maple Hill," 74–77. Margaret Barry House Announcements Book, 1927–33, and Documents, 1927–33, are in the Odone Papers.

[64] Margaret Barry obituary, in Scrapbooks, Vannelli Papers; *Irish Standard* (St. Paul), anniversary issue, [September], 1915, p. 11; Knazen, "Maple Hill," 79; Women's Co-Operative Alliance, *A Study of Community Conditions, East District,* 25; Alice O'Brien Lahiff, *Young at Sixty-Five: Minneapolis League of Catholic Women, Inc.,* [8–24, 48, 58] ([Minneapolis, 1976]).

[65] Here and below, see Sacred Heart Cathedral, *Directory,* 79–83 (Duluth, 1901); St. Peter's Italian Church, *Dedication 1927,* 12 ([Duluth, 1927]); Good Shepherd Church, *Dedication Book,* 26 ([Duluth, 1960]); Zarrilli to Joseph Ciarrocchi, May 23, 1951, Private Personal-Vescovi d'Italia, Zarrilli to Thomas Welch, July 28, 1941, Zarrilli Papers; McNicholas to Peter Fumasoni-Biondi, August 17, 1923, McNicholas-Zarrilli Papers, 1920–28, in Records of the Administration of John T. McNicholas, Bishop of Duluth, Diocese of Duluth Archives, College of St. Scholastica.

For a concise history of St. Peter's parish see Moran, "Italian-Americans," 62–84. For more on Zarrilli's management of the church, see Scrapbook, 1915–16, and financial records of the church, both in Zarrilli Papers.

[66] See Zarrilli to McNicholas, April 12, 1923, March 12, May 10, 1924; McNicholas to Fumasoni-Biondi, August 27, September 7, 1923; McNicholas to "My Dear Monsignor," July 22, 1924 — all in McNicholas-Zarrilli Papers; *Duluth News Tribune,* August 28, 1923, *Hibbing Daily Tribune,* August 31, 1923, *Il Progresso Italo-Americano* (New York), September 17, 1923 — all in Scrapbooks, Zarrilli Papers.

[67] St. Peter's Church, *Dedication,* 14–16.

[68] Zarrilli to Bishop Thomas A. Welch, February 20, August 18, 1939, June 9, 1941, October 1, 1949, in Zarrilli Papers. He had earlier argued the issue with Bishop McNicholas (Zarrilli to McNicholas, August 26, 1923) and in his writings. See John Zarrilli, *A Prayerful Appeal to the American Hierarchy in Behalf of the Italian Catholic Cause in the United States* (Two Harbors, 1924).

[69] Fortieth, Forty-fifth, and Fiftieth Annual Parish Financial Reports, St. Peter's Church, 1944, 1949, 1954, in Zarrilli Papers; Moran, "Italian-Americans," 77. Zarrilli succeeded in establishing a parochial school in 1948; a new school, built despite misgivings by St. Peter's in 1959, was closed in the 1960s.

[70] Syrjamaki, "Mesabi Communities," 312; Office of the Bishop, Diocese of Duluth, to U.S. Steel Corp., undated memorandum, in 1918–25 Correspondence, McNicholas Papers; Moran, "Italian-Americans," 71; P. G. Lyden, *History of the Diocese of Duluth,* 66 (Duluth, 1914); Diary, 3:148, Odone Papers; Zarrilli to McNicholas, October 15, 1923, McNicholas-Zarrilli Papers. On the ethnic mix in particular parishes, see WPA, Church Records; Catholic Archdiocese of St. Paul and Minneapolis, Parish Questionnaires, 1948, originals in the Catholic Historical Society, St. Paul Seminary, St. Paul, microfilm in MHS, hereafter cited as Parish Questionnaires.

[71] "The Mesabe and Vermilion Ore Ranges of Minnesota: A Report to the Administrative Missions Committee, Presbytery of Duluth, [1914]," Bell to William P. Shriver, November 24, December 2, 1913 — all in William J. Bell Papers, MHS; Zarrilli to Cristoforo Carullo — July 4, 1951, in Zarrilli Papers. Shortly after his arrival on the iron ranges, Bell noted that the Italians and South Slavs were "isolated from Catholicism and socialism was spreading among them." On Bell's "Iron Range Parish," see Clarke A. Chambers, "Social Welfare Policies and Programs on the Minnesota Iron Range — 1880–1930," 65–76, typescript, 1963, copy in MHS.

[72] Church of the Immaculate Conception, *Silver Jubilee Souvenir,* 7 ([Eveleth?, 1940]), copy in Parish Questionnaires; Chambers, "Social Welfare Policies," 65–76; Zarrilli to Carullo, July 4, 1951, and Scrapbook, 1915–16, both in Zarrilli Papers; Book of Peace and Information, vol. 3, December 20, 1918, Odone Papers; Moran, "Italian-Americans," 101–103. The court file (United States of America *v.* Vincenzo Cimino, Criminal cases file 242, in the office of the clerk of U.S. District Court, Duluth) was made available to the author by Ms. Moran.

[73] Here and below, see Church of the Immaculate Conception, *Silver Jubilee Souvenir,* 6–16; Book of Peace and Information, vol. 3, February 24, 1919, Odone Papers; Parish Questionnaires; *Eveleth News-Clarion,* July 31, 1947, historical sec. 1, p. 2; Lorenzo Sabatini, Superiore Provinciale, to Giovanni Simonetto, Superiore Generale, June 5, 1978, in Archives of the Missionaries of St. Charles, Centro Studi Emigrazione, Rome; clipping, October 12, 1952, and Strobietto obituary, July 11, 1954, both in Vannelli Papers; Schiavo, *Italian-American History,* 2:692–694.

[74] Diaries, 1:11, September 9, 1919, Book of Peace and Information, 5:32, 35, both in Odone Papers; *Stillwater Evening Gazette,* December 1, 1954, p. 1; Parish Questionnaires; interview of Charles H. Salmore by author, August 20, 1980, notes in author's possession. On International Falls, see Columbus Memorial Assn., *Columbus,* 79; clipping, June 24, 1951, in Scrapbooks, Vannelli Papers. Although Stillwater had an Italian merchant in the 1840s, more sustained settlement began after 1879. In 1904 Father Odone noted some 35 families there. Many departed after World War I for the

logging operations of Montana or for St. Louis, Mo., where there was a substantial colony of their fellow townsmen from Coggiono and Inveruno. A few resettled in the Twin Cities and only a handful remained in Stillwater.

⁷⁵ Here and below, see *The Forum*, June 27, 1978, centennial sec., 3, July 1, 1979, p. F9; Parish Questionnaires; Lady of Monte Carmelo Society, *Ninth Annual Festival Programme* (Fargo, N. Dak., 1937); author's interviews of Frank and Margaret Oliver, July 29, 1980, Tony Altobelli, August 20, 1980, notes in author's possession.

⁷⁶ *L'Italia*, April 21, 1888; *The Republican* (Red Wing), March 1, 1884; Diary, 3:141, HR Census, 1904–07, [98], both in Odone Papers; Columbus Memorial Assn., *Columbus*, 60.

⁷⁷ HR Announcement Books, 3rd Sunday after Pentecost, 1901, and May 31, 1908, Diary, 1:13–17 — all in Odone Papers.

⁷⁸ See, for example, Diary, 1:8, HR Announcement Books, June 18, 1905, June 13, 1906, and May 31, 1908, "Ragguaglio," in Diary, 7:58–60, "Memorie raccolte," in Diary, 8:13, 29, and two clippings — *St. Paul Daily News*, December 19, 1909, and *Minneapolis Journal*, December 19, 1909 — all in Odone Papers. Materials relating to *Sant'Antonio* are in Holy Redeemer Congregation Mutual Benefit Society, 1904–05, Odone Papers. In 1903 an Italian women's court of Mount Carmel of the Order of Catholic Foresters was also established, but it had few members and seems to have disappeared after a few years.

⁷⁹ Diaries, February 27, March 15, 1911, November 18, 1912, December 13, 1914, Giovanni Pieri to "Conscocio e Fratello," n.d., in U.S. Correspondence, Form Letters 1896–1942, and clipping, November 17, 1912 — all in Odone Papers.

⁸⁰ F. Jarusso to "Signore," March 7, 1921, in Holy Redeemer Congregation Mutual Benefit Society, and Diary, June 18, 1921, both in Odone Papers; Columbus Memorial Assn., *Columbus*, 61; clipping, 1932, in Scrapbook, Vannelli Papers.

⁸¹ Società Italia di Mutuo Soccorso, *Grand Opening August 12, 1933, Program,* in Rose Ciresi Papers, IHRC; *St. Paul Pioneer Press*, August 13, 1933, sec. 1, p. 8. References to these societies can be found in Scrapbooks, Vannelli Papers.

⁸² Italian American Club di St. Paul, *Appello a Tutti gli Italiani di St. Paul e Dintorni*, January 22, 1921, in Manuscripts, Italians in Minnesota, Odone Papers.

⁸³ Here and below, see Gonnella obituary, in newspaper clippings, 1909, and Diary, September 21, 1912, both in Odone Papers; Progressive Club of Minneapolis, *Thirteenth Annual Columbus Day Banquet* (Minneapolis, 1946) in Fred A. Ossanna Papers, IHRC; Frank Puccio to Richard Sackett, February 14, 1948, *Beltrami Memorial Dedication*, 5, 8 ([Minneapolis], 1948), both in Beltrami Memorial, 1947–49, Minnesota Territorial Centennial, St. Paul, Papers, MHS.

⁸⁴ Here and below, see Duluth Churches-Roman Catholic, clippings in Duluth Public Library; Moran, "Italian-Americans," 86–90; Columbus Memorial Assn., *Columbus*, 68; Christopher Columbus Mutual Benefit Society of Duluth, *42nd Annual Italian-American Picnic* ([Duluth], 1942), in Zarrilli Papers.

⁸⁵ Moran, "Italian-Americans," 86–95.

⁸⁶ Moran, "Italian-Americans," 92–95.

⁸⁷ Here and below, see *Eveleth News-Clarion*, July 31, 1947, historical sec. 3, p. 7; Columbus Memorial Assn., *Columbus*, 70–76. The records of the Guglielmo Marconi Lodge, Order of Sons of Italy in America, Hibbing, including minutes (1922–55), an account book (1905–23), and correspondence, are in MHS.

⁸⁸ *Duluth Herald*, February 6, 1928, *Tribune Herald* (n.p.) August 11, September 1, 1932, *Duluth News-Tribune*, January 10, December 6, 1939, March 7, December 13, 1941 — all clippings in Vertical File, Northeast Minnesota Historical Center; *Eveleth News-Clarion*, July 31, 1947, historical sec. 1, p. 7.

⁸⁹ *St. Paul Pioneer Press*, October 13, 1904, p. 10, October 12,

1913, sec. 2, p. 5; Diary, 1:8, Odone Papers. The 1925 banquet, for example, was reported under the headline, "Value of Christopher Columbus' Discovery to the History of World Stressed at Yearly Fete; Part Played by Countrymen of Explorer in Building United States Pointed Out"; see clipping in Pioletti Papers. The event was also reported in *The American Citizen-Il Cittadino Americano*, October 25, 1925, an Italian-language newspaper published by Alfred C. Pini that was launched in St. Paul in the early 1920s. At least five issues appeared; several are in Pioletti Papers.

⁹⁰ Here and below, see *St. Paul Pioneer Press*, October 13, 1928, and undated clippings, Columbus Memorial Assn. materials, both in Pioletti Papers; *Duluth Herald*, February 6, 1928, p. 9, October 14, 1931, p. 3; Columbus Memorial Assn., *Columbus*, 8–16, 72; *Il Progresso Italo-Americano*, October 17, 1931, clipping, Columbus Memorial Assn. of Minnesota, *Official Dedication Dinner Program* (n.d., n.p.), both in Ciresi Papers; "The Columbus Celebration," in *Minnesota History*, 13:83–85 (March, 1932). A portrait of Giacomo C. Beltrami was donated at this time to the Minnesota Historical Society by the painter, G. A. Micheli. An article in the *Duluth Herald*, October 14, 1931, clipping in Vannelli Papers, was headlined, "Impressed by Great Size of Italian Vote; Columbus Day Celebration in St. Paul Opened Politicians' Eyes." The general chairman of the association was John B. Michela, then superintendent of police for the Oliver Iron Mining Co.

⁹¹ Jim Klobuchar, "When 400 Italians Convene," clipping, Vannelli Papers; Richard Ritchie to Donald Scalzo, September 12, 1963, Scalzo to Ritchie, September 18, 1963, both in Columbus Memorial Assn. of St. Paul Papers, IHRC.

⁹² Minutes of Meeting, July, 1945, J. V. Weber to Mrs. A. Goduto, October 6, 1945, both in Columbus Memorial Assn. Papers. Information on attempts to obtain the holiday is in clippings, Ciresi Papers.

⁹³ U.S., *Census*, 1940, *Population*, vol. 2, part 4, p. 31; 1960, vol. 1, part 25, p. 194 (contains 1940 second-generation figure).

⁹⁴ National Italian-American Civic League, *Sixth Annual Convention Program* ([Milwaukee], 1937), *Italian-American Progressive* (Omaha), March 1, 1932, and *Omaha Bee-News*, February 20, 1932, all clippings, and Theodore Mazza, "UNICO National — its birth, growth; its objective," in UNICO National, *Golden Anniversary Issue, 1972*, 3–11 — all in Ossanna Papers; "Ralph J. Davini, St. Paul, Minnesota," unidentified reprint in author's possession. On Ossanna, see *Italian American Who's Who*, 2:274 (New York, 1937).

⁹⁵ "Interview with Mrs. Alice Sickels of the International Institute on October 13, 1943," in St. Paul and Ramsey County War History Committee Papers, MHS; Alice Sickels, *Around the World in St. Paul*, 161–166 (Minneapolis, 1945). The text of Biddle's address is in the Columbus Memorial Assn. Papers, IHRC. Mike Colallilo of Duluth was awarded the Congressional Medal of Honor. See *Raleigh Street Reunion*, [14], (Duluth, 1975). For more examples of Italians in the armed services, see Scrapbooks, Vannelli Papers. Seven servicemen from St. Peter's Church in Duluth were killed in the war. Zarrilli to My Dear Boy, November 15, 1945, Zarrilli Papers.

⁹⁶ Yarusso, "I'll Meet Ya, at the Center," 9; Sickels, *Around the World*, 10; Moran, "Italian-Americans," 183–189.

⁹⁷ Kunz, "The Upper Levee," 11–13, 35; Knazen, "Maple Hill Community," 101; Morrow, "Beltrami Neighborhood," 9; *St. Paul Pioneer Press*, April 19, 1959, News and Feature sec., 7; *Minneapolis Tribune*, September 7, 1977, p. 2B.

⁹⁸ Kunz, "Upper Levee," 35; *Catholic Bulletin*, September 20, 1968, *St. Paul Dispatch*, October 30, 1968, both in clippings, Vannelli Papers; Binz to Pioletti, June 22, 1967, in Pioletti Papers. The correspondence and a scrapbook of the Steering Committee to Save the Church of the Holy Redeemer are in Ciresi Papers. On Pioletti,

see *Italian American Who's Who*, 2:304; *Catholic Bulletin*, January 7, 1966, Joseph L. Baglio, "Priest Traveled Lifelong Pilgrimage," in *Catholic Bulletin*, 1971, both in clippings, Vannelli Papers.

[99] For examples, here and two paragraphs below, see *St. Paul Dispatch*, July 29, 1976, p. 29; *Minneapolis Tribune*, June 14, 1980, p. 2B; "Fred Cina," in Vertical File, Northeast Minnesota Historical Center; *Aurora Diamond Jubilee 1903–1978*, 54 (n.p., [1978]); clippings, Vannelli Papers; Sickels, "Upper Levee," 87–97, and *Around the World*, 10; Moran, "Italian-Americans," 59; Torstenson and Nordlie, *Phalen Park*, 32–38.

[100] U.S., *Census, 1970, Census of Population and Housing, Census Tracts, Minneapolis-St. Paul SMSA*, PHC (1)–132, *Duluth-Superior SMSA*, PHC (1)–60; Behm, Sullivan and Associates, Inc., *Comprehensive Feasibility Report for the Physical Development of the Parish Building Program, Parish of Holy Redeemer*, in Pioletti Papers, includes a map of parishioners' residences in 1966. The annual Columbus Day banquet programs, sponsored by the Columbus Memorial Assn. of St. Paul and the Progressive Club of Minneapolis, listed the same societies decade after decade. For examples of activity in the 1970s, see clippings, Vannelli Papers.

[101] Here and below, see Elizabeth Mathias, "Summary of Findings of Italian American Culture on the Iron Range," [2], typed manuscript, 1978, copy in Iron Range Historical Society, Gilbert;

"Mama D. Day in Minneapolis, November 16, 1978," packet in author's possession; U.S., *Census, 1970, Subject Reports: National Origin and Language*, 236–241, 368–370.

[102] HR Announcement Books, 15th Sunday after Pentecost, 1906, and December 31, 1908, Frank Lorenzi to Odone, April 24, 1918, in General U.S. Correspondence, and two clippings, *St. Paul Dispatch*, April 13, 1906, and *St. Paul Pioneer Press*, April 14, 1906 — all in Odone Papers. See also American Committee for Italian War Relief of St. Paul, Papers, 1943–48, and Italian Flood Relief Committee of St. Paul, 1952, Papers, both in MHS. In 1980 over $80,000 was raised by the Minnesota Italian community for relief of the earthquake victims.

[103] Odone, "A Sketch of the Italian Colony in Minnesota," clipping, [1908?], clipping, October 11, 1915, *St. Paul Pioneer Press*, March 29, 1906 — all in Odone Papers; *Minneapolis Tribune*, August 22, 1979, p. 17A, December 16, 1979, p. 1, December 30, 1979, p. 1, April 6, 1980, p. 1B, February 22, 1981, p. 11; *St. Paul Pioneer Press*, October 30, 1974, p. 25, October 29, 1977, p. 5; *St. Paul Dispatch*, August 31, 1972, p. 33, May 17, 1974, p. 1, November 18, 1975, p. 15, February 22, 1977, p. 19, January 23, 1981, p. 1. *Duluth News Tribune*, June 4, 1893, headlined an article, "Dark Deed of a Dago"; the *Minneapolis Tribune* of March 27, 1977, p. 1B, headlined a story, "Mafia grabs a pizza da rural cheese action."

CHAPTER 25

The Greeks

Theodore Saloutos

ONE would have expected Greeks, accustomed to a warm Mediterranean climate, to seek out a state with weather more hospitable than Minnesota's; yet late in the 19th century a small number arrived, followed by considerably more in the 20th century. Although the Greeks were primarily a rural people and agriculture then dominated Minnesota's economy, the early settlers chose the city as a source of livelihood, reasoning that city life offered better prospects for ready advancement than did rural existence. The pace in Greek-American communities was set early by a Greek-born, middle-class, small-business-oriented group responsive to the pressures of the host society. They remained in control of community affairs through the World War II years, when the leadership gradually passed into the hands of the second generation, many of whom were born and educated in Minnesota.

Information on the early immigrants is fragmentary. While we know who some of these people were, we cannot name the first Greek to arrive in Minnesota, the time he arrived, or the place he settled. Not a single Greek was counted in the state by the census compilers in 1880, but 14 were found in 1890 and 75 in 1900. Minnesota, according to the census, had 10 Turks among its residents in 1880 and 45 in 1890. Since Turkish emigration in this period was not sizable, it is likely that most of those recorded as Turks in 1890 were actually Greeks, Serbians, Montenegrins, Bulgarians, Armenians, and others from the European portion of the Turkish Ottoman Empire (see Map 20.1). Members of the large, restless Greek population of Macedonia, now divided between Greece and Yugoslavia, did emigrate during the period of Ottoman rule. American law, however, determined nationality by country of birth rather than by ethnic affiliation. Thus, an immigrant born of Greek parents in Macedonia, who spoke Greek, observed Greek customs and traditions, and considered himself a Greek was nevertheless listed as a Turk if he entered the United States from the Ottoman Empire.[1]

Most Greeks who emigrated between 1890 and 1920 were from the Peloponnesos, especially from Sparta and neighboring villages. Gradually others arrived from all parts of the Peloponnesos, as well as from central Greece (Sterea Hellas), the Greek Islands, Crete, Epirus, the Dodecanese Islands, and the Asian portion of Turkey (see Map 25.1). Economic reasons caused most to leave, although political and religious discrimination also figured in the Greek exodus from Turkey.[2]

Population patterns in Minnesota were comparable to those in neighboring states and in the nation. The sharpest increase in numbers occurred in the first decade of the 20th century (see Table 25.1), when the Greek population rose from 75 in 1900 to 1,840 in 1910. Some 1,660 of the latter were born in Greece, leaving only 180 born in the United States of Greek or mixed parentage.[3]

Foreign-born Greek Americans continued to outnumber those of Greek or mixed parentage through the 1930 census. American-born Greeks exceeded the immigrants by 1940, when the peak in Minnesota's Greek foreign-stock population — a total of 3,861 — was reached. Arrivals from Greece after World War II were few compared with those before and after World War I, despite the relaxation of American immigration laws. By 1970, however, slightly more than two of every three Greeks counted by the census takers in Minnesota were born in the United States.[4]

Of the 182,558 immigrants who gave Minnesota as their intended destination at a port of entry between 1899 and 1910, only 606 were Greeks (Table 25.2). Ninety-five of them arrived between 1899 and 1905, and 511 between 1906 and 1910. The general upsurge in Greek emigration to the United States and better knowledge of the opportunities in Minnesota probably accounted for the increase.[5]

In fact, more than 100 listed Minnesota as their intended destination each year from 1911 through 1917, when the United States's entry into World War I brought emigration almost to a standstill. The largest number in any single year (444) arrived in 1914; the second largest (210) in 1913. Some of them were new to the state, but a sizable number must have been volunteers who had left Minnesota in 1912 to return to Greece in order to serve in the Balkan Wars (see Table 25.2).[6]

By 1910 clusters of Greeks had begun to appear throughout the state. Hennepin, St. Louis, and Ramsey counties consistently attracted the largest numbers; few of the others maintained stable Greek populations. Elsewhere totals were too small to carry much weight, especially given the imprecision with which census takers recorded ethnicity. Nevertheless, it appeared that by 1920 noticeable population shifts — both gains and losses — had occurred throughout the state

Map 25.1. Greece

(see Table 25.1). Kittson apparently lost its entire Greek settlement, and Carlton, Cass, Douglas, Itasca, Otter Tail, Polk, Stearns, and Wilkin counties were not far behind. Blue Earth, Chippewa, Crow Wing, and Koochiching, on the other hand, more than tripled their Greek populations during those same years, and Ramsey and St. Louis counties showed similar growth.[7]

From the beginning Greeks demonstrated a preference for city life. More than a third of Minnesota's Greeks in 1910 lived in the three largest cities: 463 in Minneapolis, 129 in St. Paul, and 57 in Duluth. Smaller cities with total populations from 10,000 to 25,000 also attracted Greeks: St. Cloud had 87, Virginia 17, Mankato 6, Winona 4, and Stillwater 2.[8]

Concentration in the cities became even more pronounced by 1920 when employment on the railroads declined, families began to increase in number, and a more settled life developed. Slightly more than three-fifths of the 2,391 Greeks in Minnesota lived in the same three major cities: Minneapolis had 873, St. Paul 354, and Duluth 230 (see Table 25.1). Hibbing was close behind with 203, Virginia had 55, Austin 44, Mankato 24, Rochester 15, Faribault 13, St. Cloud 11, and Winona 9.[9]

Foreign-born Greeks resided in all 13 Minneapolis wards in 1920, but the largest number lived in Wards 4 and 5 (from

the central business district west to the city limits, bounded by 6th Avenue to the north and Franklin Avenue to the south), which had 243 and 222 Greeks, respectively, and accounted for over half of the 873 Greeks in that city. The smallest number (8) lived in Ward 10 (bounded by the city's north and west limits). Almost half of the 354 Greeks in St. Paul in 1920 lived in Ward 4 (the downtown area); elsewhere their numbers ranged from 53 in Ward 9 (north of Ward 4 to the city limits) to 3 in Ward 12 (the Lake Como area).

Table 25.1. Greeks in Minnesota by County, 1910–70

County	1910 foreign born	1920 fb	1940 fb	fb	1970 foreign mixed
Aitkin		2	4		
Anoka	7	8	16	7	42
Becker		5	3		
Beltrami	9	6	4		
Benton	7	10	2	4	
Big Stone		2			
Blue Earth	6	25	13	8	
Brown	1	3			
Carlton	60	14	13	6	28
Carver	1				16
Cass	37	2	3		7
Chippewa		19	4		
Chisago					9

Table 25.1. Greeks in Minnesota by County, 1910–70 (*continued*)

County	1910 foreign born	1920 fb	1940 fb	1970 fb	1970 foreign mixed
Clay	19	18	19	8	27
Clearwater			1		
Cottonwood	1	4	2		15
Crow Wing	1	39	32	5	50
Dakota	53	35	21	18	81
Dodge	20				
Douglas	22	3	5		
Faribault		6	3		
Fillmore		2			
Freeborn	4	15	9		5
Goodhue	9	15	8	13	6
Grant	6	1			
Hennepin	531	877	807	466	871
Minneapolis	463	873	765	262	356
Hubbard	6	2	5		
Isanti	5	1			
Itasca	104	31	15	6	8
Jackson	3	8			
Kanabec		2			10
Kandiyohi	7	12	10	14	
Kittson	30				
Koochiching		14	12	8	
Lac qui Parle		3			
Lake	2	4	6		
Le Sueur	1				
Lyon	8		3		
Mahnomen	2				
Marshall		2			
Martin	3	8	6		
Mille Lacs		1	7		10
Morrison		2	2		
Mower	42	48	27		50
Nicollet	1	6	9		17
Nobles	1	9	1		
Olmsted	6	15	67	13	49
Otter Tail	33	7	4		
Pennington		3	4		
Pine	5	17	7		
Pipestone	7	4			
Polk	24	5	7		
Pope	9		3		
Ramsey	136	355	264	129	317
St. Paul	129	354	260	117	221
Red Lake	12	1			
Redwood			1		
Renville			1		
Rice	5	15	24		
Rock	13	8	1		
Roseau	1				
St. Louis	223	601	263	158	245
Duluth	57	230	140	122	160
Scott		6		5	18
Sherburne		6			
Sibley					6
Stearns	89	14	7	7	14
Steele	1	8	3		
Stevens		2	2		
Swift	1	1	1		
Todd	6	14	7		
Traverse	2		1		
Wabasha	8	2			
Wadena		3	3		
Waseca		4	2		
Washington	2	8	10	12	30
Watonwan		1			
Wilkin	53	15	1		
Winona	4	9	4		8
Wright	6	3			7
Yellow Medicine	5		2		
Total	1,660	2,391	1,761	887	1,946
Published census figures	(1,660)	(2,391)	(1,761)	(887)	(1,946)

Source: See Appendix

Most Greeks arrived with little money; they needed earnings to sustain them and to send home to anxious parents as proof of their success in America. The city offered quicker ways of accomplishing these goals, providing employment with regular wages at the end of the day or week. It also allowed newcomers to live closer to relatives, friends, and compatriots who spoke the same language, observed the same customs and traditions, faced the same problems, and were easier to reach in times of need.[10]

Perhaps nothing influenced the upwardly mobile Greek more than the belief that his future lay in the city and the business opportunities it offered. The Greek aversion to farming may be traced to several factors. Among them were bitter memories of hard times, poor soil, short crops, and few returns in the homeland; the isolation of farm life in the United States, unlike Greece, where farmers worked their plots during the day and returned to the village when finished; and the presence of few compatriots, outnumbered by farmers of many nationalities speaking many different languages. Moreover, farming in the United States required techniques, equipment, and substantial amounts of capital

Table 25.2. Greek Migration to and from Minnesota

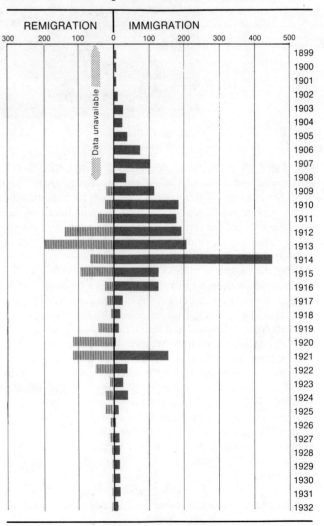

that the Greeks did not possess. Of the 846 Greek farmers in the United States in 1920, only 12 lived in Minnesota. Eleven were farm owners and one was a tenant. Together they owned a total of 1,130 acres of land, of which 624 were improved.[11]

Once settled in a city, Greeks were quick to establish their own churches and import pastors from Greece. Traditionally a central thread in the fabric of community life, the Greek Orthodox church, when transplanted to America, took on new dimensions. In Greece where Orthodoxy was the state religion, the problems of religion and politics were intertwined. Most Greek priests, whether well educated or not, were steeped in their national traditions, which they fully expected to perpetuate in the United States. In a predominantly Protestant country, however, where church and state were formally separated and the pull of Americanization was strong, the Greek Orthodox church faced social and cultural challenges different from the political vicissitudes in the homeland. In America, the church became the stronghold of ethnic identity — the repository of language and custom, the center of social life, and a forum for political debate. Tied to the fortunes of their communities, churches split, reunited, enlarged, diminished, directed acculturation, and were, in turn, shaped by Americanizing members. In a retrospective letter to the youth of his community, a Minneapolis Greek summarized the various functions ultimately linked to the church: "We have gathered from various parts of Greece, and as genuine Greeks, our duties are to build our church, to keep our Orthodox religion, and also to organize a Greek school, so that we may teach our children our immortal language, make them true legitimate Greeks, and upstanding American citizens."[12]

Establishing Communities, 1890s–1920s

At least three distinct periods stand out in the story of the Minnesota Greeks. The first, from the 1890s into the early 1920s, was characterized by an immigrant population composed largely of Greek-born bachelors. Ties to the homeland were close and loyalty was intense. While becoming businessmen was the goal of the more ambitious, a substantial percentage belonged to the state's floating labor supply. Social life revolved around the Greek Orthodox church. The second phase, which opened after World War I, saw Greek involvement with the homeland diminish. Organizations designed to meet the needs of those who chose to remain permanently in the United States began to form, and determined efforts were made to win the approval and good will of the larger American community. During the third phase, which started after World War II, the immigrant generation gradually relinquished its hold on the administration of parishes, church-related organizations, and other groups to members of an American-born and American-educated generation. In this period a small number of newcomers from Greece trickled into the communities, promoting a new wave of ethnicity in the late 1960s and 1970s with their efforts to rehellenize what appeared to them the almost completely assimilated American Greeks.

Among the first to settle permanently in Minneapolis, and perhaps in Minnesota, was Peter Boosalis, who became prominent in Greek circles of both the city and the state. A native of Niata, Boosalis was among the first Peloponnesians in the United States, arriving in 1887 as a young man of 24. The following year he found his way to Minneapolis, where he wheeled a pushcart through the streets selling fruit until he discharged his family obligations and accumulated enough money to open a small fruit and vegetable market on Washington and 1st Avenue South (now Marquette). By 1912 he was the proprietor of the billiard rooms in the impressive West Hotel and president of the Minnesota Pan-Hellenic Union.[13]

New arrivals tended to cluster according to the village or district of Greece from which they emigrated. Within two or three years relatives and other Spartans followed Boosalis until two groups assumed leadership roles in the emerging

THE LAVISH INTERIOR of the Boosalis Brothers' Olympia Fruit and Confectionery in Minneapolis, around 1905.

Greek community of Minneapolis: those from the village of Niata and those from Sparta, both in the province of Laconia. They were joined by emigrants from Arcadia, traditionally rivals of the Laconians in Greece. Referred to as the Tripolis group, the Arcadians seemed to gain an early hold on shoeshining in the city.[14]

Business-minded Greeks, who lacked capital and a sufficient working knowledge of the English language but were determined to become their own bosses, followed a pattern of upward mobility similar to that of Boosalis. Some became railroad construction workers or performed other menial jobs until they could launch out on their own or establish a partnership with a compatriot. The first Greeks in St. Paul, for instance, were construction and maintenance men for the Great Northern or Northern Pacific railroads. During the March to October season they lived on the trains; winters were spent in the city on temporary jobs.[15]

In 1900 St. Paul had only 25 Greeks and 4 Greek-owned stores, but "Little by little, the winter jobs became the permanent ones and the monies saved for [repatriation in] Greece became the nucleus of privately-owned businesses." In Minneapolis with its older and more settled Greek community, it was customary for newcomers to work for established countrymen. This arrangement provided an attractive alternative to factory or railroad jobs, gave the new workers immediate business experience, and at the same time increased community solidarity and stability. This work, however, was not an end in itself — an immigrant who did not eventually start out on his own earned the label "one who always worked for others."

The minimal amount needed to start a business seemed to be $300. A business directory in the Greek language reported that of the 300 Greeks in the state's three largest cities in 1907, about 25 in Minneapolis, 6 or 7 in St. Paul, and 7 or 8 in Duluth owned confectionery stores, shoeshine parlors, and florist shops. As in Minneapolis, some of these small entrepreneurs had probably worked for relatives and friends in these cities or in other parts of the United States before branching out for themselves.[16]

Greek-owned small-business establishments increased so noticeably with the growth of the Greek population that one business directory reported an American quip: "When Greek meets Greek, they open a restaurant." A casual tally in downtown Minneapolis and St. Paul gave the impression that Hennepin and Washington avenues and Wabasha and St. Peter streets were little more than a succession of Greek cafes and confectioneries. Of the 107 Greek merchants in Minneapolis in 1915 for whom information was available, 25 owned confectionery stores, 21 restaurants, 18 shoeshine parlors, 11 fruit stores or stands, 7 billiard parlors, 4 bowling alleys, 4 florist shops, 3 hat-cleaning shops, 3 grocery stores, 2 coffee clubs (a more sophisticated name for coffee houses which had gained notoriety as gambling dens), 2 barber shops, 2 hotels, 2 bakeries, 1 shoe shop, 1 laundry, and 1 tavern. Of these merchants it was known that 3 had been in the country for only 2 years and another 3 for 28, 15 had been in the United States for 20 or more years, 11 from 15 to 19 years, and 16 between 2 and 5 years. The youngest was 20 years of age and the oldest 56, 34 were between the ages of

TWIN CITY CAFE in downtown Minneapolis in 1922, when Greek-owned restaurants served American-style food.

20 and 29, 30 between 30 and 39, 11 between 40 and 49, and 4 between 50 and 56 years of age. Forty had become citizens of the United States by 1915, and another 17 had declared their intentions to do so.[17]

Some Greek merchants displayed a willingness to accept non-Greek women as wives, as three of the first four Greeks to settle in Minneapolis demonstrated. One cannot underestimate the influence that mixed marriages, naturalization — in Minneapolis at a rate above the national average for Greeks — and early acceptance into the life of the larger community had on Greek social progress. By 1915 one Minneapolis Greek had reputedly enrolled 60 compatriots in the Catholic lodge known as the Knights of Pythias, an event which also indicated acceptability.[18]

Between 1900 and 1925 increasing numbers of Greeks settled and opened businesses in St. Paul. By 1910 there were 100 residents, including 30 permanent families and 20 stores; by 1923 the city had 88 permanent families and 78 Greek-owned shops. While the St. Paul community never rivaled Minneapolis' in size, it took a similar shape. Of the 26 Greek merchants in St. Paul in 1915 for whom information was available, 12 owned restaurants, 6 confectionery stores, 3 billiard parlors, 2 shoeshine parlors, 1 saloon, 1 barber shop, and 1 grocery store. Of the 15 for whom age information existed, the oldest was 40 and the youngest 18; 5 were in their 30s and 8 in their 20s. Of these same 15, 1 had lived in the United States for 27 years, 2 between 17 and 18 years, 6 between 11 and 15 years, 3 between 7 and 8 years, and 3 between 3 and 5 years. Seven of the 26 merchants had become citizens and 4 intended to do so. No information on mixed marriages among St. Paul's Greek merchants has been found, but one would expect a higher rate there, owing to the large number of bachelors and the presence of even fewer Greek women than in Minneapolis.[19]

By 1900 Twin Cities Greeks had organized weekly church services and secured a pastor from Greece. They first worshiped at the Ancient Order of United Workmen (AOUW)

Hall in downtown Minneapolis; in 1906 they established St. Mary's Greek Orthodox Church on land later claimed by the University of Minnesota. In 1909 the group bought land on East Lake Street, a location chosen for its proximity to both communities, and built the second St. Mary's, which for the next three decades ministered to the cities' Greek population. It was there that the Greek school (a program of afternoon language classes) began in 1917, that the Sunday school was established in the early 1920s, and that the short-lived parochial school was started in 1923. In later years the church also housed various lodges, clubs, and auxiliaries.[20]

Outside of the metropolitan area, Greek entrepreneurs often located in the smaller population centers, while laborers congregated wherever they found suitable employment. Any generalizations about settlement and occupation during this era, however, are speculative; conclusions must be drawn from fragmentary evidence such as census figures, state accident reports, newspaper articles, letters, and interviews. We know that many Greeks settled temporarily in the Twin Cities, trained in a friend's or relative's business, learned some English, and then set out for "places like Faribault or Fergus Falls" to open their own cafes, confectioneries, and food supply firms. A very general picture of Greek occupations outside of the food trades can be gleaned from state industrial accident reports. Of the 59 Greeks injured in 1901–12, for example, 21 were in lumbering and woodworking, 9 were in iron mining, 5 in meat packing, 2 in railroad shops, and 1 in metal working. The figures, however, give no breakdown by county; aside from the miners, there is no clue to the locations of these workers.[21]

The record is considerably more precise for St. Louis County. In Duluth most of the Greeks worked in restaurants, shoeshine parlors, groceries, and other small stores until they earned enough money and learned enough English to establish businesses of their own. Elsewhere they were employed on the Mesabi Range, especially after open-pit and strip-mining activities increased. The Oliver Iron Mining Company, the only firm to furnish information for a 1907 study, employed three Greeks at the time. Two of them were reported to be capable of speaking English, and one had become a naturalized citizen of the United States. Many Greeks, however, left the mines as soon as possible. Some were able to open their own shops, such as confectioneries; others turned to peddling fruits and vegetables or working in food-related stores.[22]

Greeks from the mainland and the Greek Islands "appeared in large numbers" in the iron range country especially after 1910, "on the section crews of the Duluth, Missabe and Northern and the Duluth, Winnipeg and Pacific railroads, having been hired chiefly through labor exchange offices in the near large cities." Others worked for the Great Northern.

Services were available to Greeks and other Balkan peoples of the Eastern Orthodox faith on the Mesabi Range in the St. Vasilije of Ostrog Serbian Eastern Orthodox Church, organized at Chisholm in 1910. Since the church remained Serbian in character, however, other groups, including the Greeks, usually sought the priest's services only for funerals and weddings. In 1915 Russians in Chisholm established St.

Nicholas Russian Orthodox Greek Catholic Church, which drew Greeks and Bulgarians away from St. Vasilije. In the early 1920s Greeks from Hibbing, Virginia, and Eveleth occasionally traveled to Duluth to attend the newly organized Twelve Holy Apostles Greek Orthodox Church.[23]

The Greek population of Duluth during this period was composed primarily of immigrants from Macedonia. Many eventually opened small businesses but most began as workers on the railroads, in the mills and mines, or in the city's restaurants and grocery stores. The steel plant at Gary (a Duluth suburb) employed large numbers of them, who formed the nucleus of the second of about five Hellenic neighborhoods in the city.

In 1918 when Twelve Holy Apostles, the second Greek Orthodox church in the state, was organized, the foreign-born Greek population of St. Louis County was increasing from 223 in 1910 to 601 in 1920. Its members felt a pressing need for a priest who spoke their language and observed their customs and traditions. After raising $4,000 in Gary and $7,000 in Duluth-Superior, they purchased a building from a Jewish Reform congregation. Services were first held there in 1921.[24]

THE ARCADE, a Greek-owned grocery in Duluth, in the early 1920s.

While Twelve Holy Apostles attracted some single men, mostly unskilled laborers as well as Greeks and Bulgarians from the Mesabi, families and small businessmen gave the community and the parish the continuity and stability it needed to survive. Services were conducted solely in the Greek language, and as late as 1931 the priest was capable of conversing only in Greek. Church records were kept in English and Greek, however, for the benefit of members adept in only one of these languages. Except for several years after World War II, the Duluth parish consistently had a Greek or foreign-born priest. The decline in employment during the Great Depression and the drift of population from Duluth and the iron ranges to other parts of the state or nation took its toll: church membership decreased from 245 in 1918 to 160 in 1939.

Duluth's first Greeks also established a number of secular institutions that endured for many years. Alexander the Great, a social-philanthropic group, was their major organization. The dinners and celebrations it sponsored on traditional feast days raised funds for local philanthropic projects. Other monies were allocated to relief efforts in Macedonia: to support a rug factory, aid the poor, contribute to girls' dowries, and send Christmas and Easter gifts to the homeland. The group also helped sponsor Greeks in America.[25]

Another organization, smaller in scale, was the Bachelors' Club, also called the Diogenes Club. Members gathered frequently at local coffeehouses for refreshment, card playing, and meetings. This group, too, raised money for worthy causes. While Alexander the Great was headquartered in Duluth with relatively few members in towns like Deer River and Virginia, the Bachelors' Club was a gathering place for Greeks from Superior and many of the range cities as well as Duluth. In addition to clubs, the community members rented space in the early 1920s and organized a Greek school, where their children were taught the language, history, and culture of the homeland. In 1980 the school continued to function, meeting weekly at Twelve Holy Apostles Greek Orthodox Church.

It is probable that Rochester owes much of its Greek population to the Mayo Clinic. Entrepreneurs recognized that the facility would attract large numbers of temporary residents who would need, perhaps, more goods and services than a settled population. According to a second-generation resident, whose father left Duluth to open a restaurant in Rochester, most of the Greeks arrived in the 1920s, although some settled there as early as 1909. They came for medical reasons, to take advantage of business opportunities, or to join relatives. "Most of them were in business, mainly in . . . restaurant[s], but some operated shoe repair shops. Some were cooks, and there was an occasional doctor."[26]

The ephemeral Greek populations of Kittson, Wilkin, and Cass counties are not so well documented. Census takers found no Greeks in any of these areas in 1905, considerable numbers in 1910, and a dramatic decline by 1920 (see Table 25.1). Given the Greek penchant for city life, tempered by a willingness to begin work as a menial laborer, it is possible that these residents were seasonal workers who either earned enough to open businesses elsewhere or moved away in search of better jobs. In Stearns County, a similar pattern of growth and decline emerges among the nonrural Greeks. In 1910, 87 of the total population of 89 lived in St. Cloud as did 11 of the 14 remaining in 1920.[27]

Greeks outside of the state's two Orthodox parishes often relied on the services of the closest pastor. The Reverend Averkios Demakopulos, who accepted the call to the Minneapolis church in 1911, also served communities within a 500-mile radius of his home base. Even the settlement of Greeks in southeastern Minnesota suffered a "spiritual void," as did the "vast numbers of other Orthodox Christians who journeyed from all over the world to the Mayo Clinic" until the Rochester community organized Saints Anargyroi Greek Orthodox Church in 1947 and acquired a pastor in 1949.[28]

Mobility among the Greeks in the Minnesota labor force was influenced by a series of events over which they had no control. The first decade of the 20th century saw tensions mount between Greece and Turkey, its traditional enemy. Many Greeks returned to their homeland to fight in the Balkan Wars that broke out in 1912. World War I began in 1914, touching off economic dislocation on the iron ranges. After the initial shock of the conflict lessened, the mines became more mechanized, driving some Greeks out of the Mesabi country. And when the United States declared war in 1917, many Greeks enlisted in the American armed forces. During the years 1916 to 1918, others began to quit the railroads, taking employment in the tracklaying and dump gangs of the iron range open pits. They also "transferred from mining and railroad work to the management of restaurants, in which they have been successful."[29]

In Minneapolis the degree of Greek response to Balkan tensions was apparent when the volunteer unit organized and sponsored by the Pan-Hellenic Union paraded down Hennepin Avenue on Greek Independence Day in 1911. Although emigration had been draining Greece of young men when war with Turkey loomed, the loss was tolerated because the country received economic assistance from its nationals abroad and could count on their return when the call to arms was sounded. Although details are lacking, it was in this spirit that the Minneapolis unit was formed.[30]

In the absence of a Greek consul in the city, Peter Boosalis, as president of the Minnesota Pan-Hellenic Union, took charge of arrangements for the departure of volunteers in the fall of 1912. The Reverend Demakopulos "stirred the patriotic blood of his countrymen" as preparations were being made to send the first contingent from Minnesota. Seventy-five were reported ready to leave on October 10 and another 50 later in the week. Much of the $2,000 raised for the expenses of the departing volunteers represented the partial savings from the contributors' years of toil in this country. A trench digger for the city of Minneapolis donated $1,000 or one-third of his savings, but a less fortunate Greek, who was robbed of his travel funds ($177 in cash and a draft for $300) en route, said he would be unable to leave.[31]

News stories of departing Greeks appeared frequently during the month of October. "Every train from the Northwest passing through the Twin City today and last night," reported the *St. Paul Dispatch* on October 11, 1912, "carried groups of Greek reserves on their way to the fatherland." Fifty Greeks employed by the Great Northern Railroad in Fergus Falls quit their jobs and were reportedly returning to Greece by way of Superior, Wisconsin. Another firm announced that 68 of the 85 employees attached to one of its units had left. Although early reports suggested that as many as 3,000 Greeks in and around the Minneapolis-St. Paul area were prepared to depart by October 21, only 300 volunteers had done so and another 350 were being held in readiness. Most Greeks, however, were expected to work the remainder of the fall season and sail during the winter months.

Meanwhile, Thomas Louis, president of the Greek Red Cross Society of the Twin City, solicited assistance for the wounded soldiers of Greece and "fatherless families" in Minneapolis and St. Paul. The Minnesota Pan-Hellenic Union and the Greek Red Cross Society also appealed to St.

Paul Mayor Herbert P. Keller, who made a contribution and asked the citizens of St. Paul to do so.[32]

Like most ethnic groups in America during World War I, Minnesota's Greeks were subject to suspicion despite their participation in the war effort. Greece became an ally of the United States in 1917, allaying some fears that Greek Queen Sophia's ties to her brother, Kaiser Wilhelm, might bring the country into the war on the side of the Central Powers, thereby exposing Greeks in America to the indignities encountered by enemy aliens in times of war. Nevertheless the Greeks were among those that the Americanization Committee of St. Paul was determined to reach.[33]

Greeks demonstrated their loyalty to the United States in a number of ways. One impassioned confectioner from Worthington wrote Governor Joseph A. A. Burnquist, "I would like to fight Germany, Austria, Turkey, and Bulgaria. . . . You will find that lots of the Greek born boys are willing to do their duty." How many waived their exemptions from military service is unknown, because the War Department did not compile statistics on volunteer enlistments by ethnic origin. It is believed, however, that a sizable number, although subjects of a foreign nation, nevertheless volunteered from Minnesota. In Hibbing, for instance, the newspaper reported that 200 members of the Doris Society, a local Greek benefit organization and fraternal lodge, were serving in the army.[34]

Greek women also engaged in war work. In St. Paul the Women's Auxiliary of the Minnesota Commission of Public Safety discovered that they had done "a good deal for Red Cross, and that they are interested in war work but are shy and clannish and feel they have not had recognition for the things they have done." On the strength of this assessment, the auxiliary and the Ramsey County Women's War Organization, the same groups that sponsored Americanization activities, made special efforts to enlist their aid. In Minneapolis, Helen and Peter Boosalis sponsored a volunteer sewing project staffed by Greek-American women. While Peter bought 31 sewing machines, allocated a shop in one of his rental properties, and collected fabric for the effort, Helen organized the women to sew Red Cross supplies and nightshirts for wounded veterans at Fort Snelling. Several of the volunteers cooked and served meals so the sewers could work without interruption.[35]

The 1920s to 1940s

Although Minnesota Greeks anxiously awaited news of Greece's fortunes in the postwar years, their overriding concerns were in the United States. The collapse of Greek ambitions in Asia Minor in 1922 was a blow to their pride, but the rising tide of antiforeign, antiradical, and pro-American sentiments was an even greater immediate problem. The realization that open allegiance to their homeland or customs might threaten their image as loyal Americans presented a conflict to many Greek Americans.[36]

Members of the various Minnesota Greek communities demonstrated a range of responses to this problem which were evident in their business activities, their organizations, and the general tone of their community affairs. For some, resolution meant visible and self-directed acculturation; for

others, it meant a return to Greece. Between these two extremes lay the varying degrees of assimilation, acculturation, and cultural maintenance — part and parcel of any group's transition from the status of national minority to ethnic community. Various social, business, and public relations organizations arose to promote a smooth transition, while inter- and intracommunity dissension sometimes testified to the difficulty of this process.

The small businessmen who came in daily contact with the general public, for example, contributed to the slowly developing acculturative trend. In Minneapolis businesses named the New Nicollet Flower Shop, the Palace Cafe, American Beauty, Rainbow Restaurant, Princess Candy Shop, and University Sweet Shop outnumbered the occasional Akropolis Candy Store or Sparta Candy. Much the same process was under way in St. Paul, where Greek-owned businesses included the Savoy Restaurant, Boston Cafe, Majestic Cafe, Colonial Lunch, Twin City Linen Supply, and Cosmopolitan Pool Room, although one Greek preferred to name his restaurant the Marathon Cafe. In Duluth Greeks owned or managed hotels bearing names such as the Hotel Alvarado, the State, the Park, and the Victor, while Greek-owned restaurants and confectionery stores carried names comparable to those in Minneapolis and St. Paul.[37]

Another step in the acculturative process was taken in 1919 with the formation of the Hellenic Post of the American Legion in Minneapolis, comprised of Greeks who had served with the armed forces of the United States. Such an organization might have been accepted as a matter of course by members of a larger, better-represented, and better-known ethnic group, but it had a special significance to the Greeks. For the first time in their history they had served with the United States Army in sizable numbers, and they wanted their non-Greek friends and neighbors to know that they, too, had fought to defend their adopted country in 1917–18. Hellenic Post No. 129, the first American Legion post in the United States composed of veterans of Greek descent, was also the first service organization established in the Minneapolis Greek community.[38]

Restaurant owners also sought to improve their public images. While the exact date of the formation of the Greek Restaurant Men's Association in Minneapolis is unknown, it is known that the Greeks as a group worked long hours, were highly competitive in business, and were sometimes the targets of abuse from competitors. The association helped refute unfair stereotypes: that Greek restaurants were unsanitary, or that they ignored their patriotic duty on meatless and wheatless days. A statement in 1925 read: "The Greek Restaurant Men's Association of Minneapolis is already proving the value of the idea of unity, not only to the restaurant owners themselves, but also to the public they are there to serve."[39]

The formation of chapters of the American Hellenic Educational Progressive Association (AHEPA) in Minneapolis in 1925, in Rochester in 1929, and in Duluth and St. Paul in 1930 was perhaps the most visible element of the acculturative trend. Destined to become the longest-lived and most influential Greek-American organization of laymen in Minnesota and in the nation, AHEPA had several objectives: to counteract the antiforeign sentiment encountered by Greek businessmen, to encourage naturalization and greater use of English, to foster participation in the affairs of the larger American community, and to support the public school system. It reported members' meritorious community service and provided leadership for those who had made the United States their permanent homes. Membership was open only to men; women joined the auxiliary, Daughters of Penelope. Although AHEPA members as a rule were born in Greece or neighboring countries and belonged to the Greek Orthodox church, the organization officially chose to be nonsectarian, a stand which angered traditionalists who believed that Greek alone should be spoken and that Greek Orthodoxy should be the official religion of the order. Significantly, a chapter of the Greek American Progressive Association, a rival organization formed in Pittsburgh in 1923 which espoused these principles, never gained a footing in Minnesota.[40]

Acculturation of the Greeks as a community was accelerated by the departure of 407 Greeks from Minnesota in the years from 1919 to 1926, presumably to return to Greece. If what is known of those who left other parts of the United States at about the same time applies to the Minnesota contingent, their reasons ranged from fulfilling their original objective of repatriating themselves after amassing some money in America to a preference for the more leisurely, less demanding, and more satisfying life of Greece. Family heads who had strong ethnic loyalties often expressed a desire to rear their children in Greece, where they would be better able to maintain their Hellenic heritage.[41]

Despite their decision to Americanize, Minnesota's Greeks could not totally divorce themselves from politics overseas. After World War I, they kept an eye on developments at the Paris Peace Conference in 1919. As expected, a request for the support of Greek claims in Paris reached the Minneapolis community early. Nicholas I. Cassavettes, director of the Pan-Epirotic Union and father of Hollywood director-actor John Cassavettes, sent a form letter dated March 21, 1919, to the president of St. Mary's parish. The letter suggested that the civilized world owed much to the "Greek race," and that this was an appropriate time to pay part of the debt by granting freedom to the descendants of those who gave the concept of political liberty and the "blessings of democracy" to the civilized world. On February 13, 1921, the Greeks of Minneapolis and neighboring communities appealed to Prime Minister David Lloyd George of England to use his "good offices and influence to prevent a revision of the Treaty of Sevres" to safeguard "our race." They also denounced the recall of King Constantine to the Greek throne and expressed their "confidence and faith in the foreign policy of Mr. [Eleutherios] Venizelos," who had been named prime minister.[42]

During the 1920s and 1930s the Minneapolis Greek community became embroiled in the struggle between King Constantine, who had favored neutrality for Greece during the war, and the liberal Venizelos, who had steered Greece toward the Triple Entente, asserting that its future lay with the nations of the West. The state church, subject to the changing political fortunes of the country, inevitably became involved in this debate. When Venizelos was named prime minister in 1917, he had replaced the Metropolitan of Athens, who presided over the Holy Synod of the Church of Greece, with one more favorable to his own policies. Since the synod also had jurisdiction over Greek churches in the United States, this change had serious repercussions in America. Wherever possible, priests favorable to the king were replaced with those sympathetic to the policies of the new metropolitan and Venizelos. Apparently the resulting dissension in the Minneapolis parish was not enough to cause disaffected members to secede and form a new church.[43]

That was not true, however, after King Constantine returned to the throne in late 1920 and reinstated the former metropolitan. Differences in Minneapolis reached the breaking point in 1921–22 when supporters of the king seceded from St. Mary's to form a second parish in Minneapolis, St. George's. Thus the city's Greeks, who were having difficulties supporting one church, found themselves saddled with two.[44]

In 1931 the archbishop of the Greek Orthodox Church of North and South America visited parish after parish, including Minneapolis, urging the divided community to unite. The reconciliation, which was effected in the early 1930s, has been attributed, however, to more local powers of persuasion. Members of St. Mary's board of trustees argued against the expense of maintaining two congregations; AHEPA chapters, which had remained neutral despite their members' affiliations with both churches, urged that the community bury past grievances; and the war clouds again hanging over Europe convinced Greek Americans of the need for unity at home. Parish sources, however, credit the women of both churches with the reunification. They formed the Elpitha (Hope) Society, a group that concealed its real motive of reconciliation beneath the stated purpose of helping the poor.[45]

While the unified church once again bore the name St. Mary's, the community also used the former St. George's church building for special occasions. More spacious than St. Mary's, it was the site of Holy Week and Easter services and of large weddings as well. Not until the early 1950s was it sold to a Ukrainian Orthodox congregation when the Minneapolis Greeks were planning to consolidate in one structure at a new location.[46]

In the wake of the split, few changes had been wrought. Lack of support forced the parochial school, founded in 1923, to become a night school. It folded soon thereafter, but other social, educational, religious, and service clubs proliferated. The reunited St. Mary's hosted dances, attended by Greeks of both Minneapolis and St. Paul, which provided occasions for well-chaperoned courting as well as for informal socializing. AHEPA and the Daughters of Penelope continued to meet at the church. In 1938 the young people of the congregation formed Sigma Tau Nu, a group which served religious, secular, and recreational interests.[47]

By 1941 church-related organizations included a board of trustees, Greek school, ladies' auxiliary (Philoptochos), an auditing committee, the Hellenic Post of the American Legion, and a bachelors' club. World War II fatally weakened

Sigma Tau Nu, as most of its young men enlisted. The remaining members published a newsletter, *Sigma Tau News*, which was sent to those overseas, not only keeping them in touch with their community, but also mediating between parents unable to write English and children unable to read Greek. After the war, a chapter of the national Greek Orthodox Youth of America supplanted Sigma Tau Nu among the young adults; in 1952 graduates of the original group formed the Mr. and Mrs. Club, which became quite influential in church and community affairs.

The Greeks in St. Paul, long overshadowed by their more numerous and assertive compatriots across the river, began to press for an identity of their own during World War I. Their early efforts to develop a community life had been hampered by the presence of a transient bachelor population offset by only a few Greek families. A local church might have focused community spirit, but there was no real need for one, since St. Mary's on East Lake Street in Minneapolis was convenient to both cities. In fact, by mutual agreement the two communities enjoyed equal membership privileges there. Although St. Paulites chose sides during the schism in the 1920s, "Most of the new-born children of St. Paul were baptized at St. Mary's and most of the wedding ceremonies also took place there." Thus it was a social organization known as the Greek Community of St. Paul, founded on October 2, 1916, and incorporated on May 23, 1918, that guided community development. Members met several times each year at social events, and on August 13, 1922, the group held its first annual picnic.[48]

Local pride and the fear that some day a new church would be built in a less accessible section of Minneapolis were powerful prods to action. Soon after it was formed, the community organization began a collection to buy property, as the first step in establishing a St. Paul church. While the Minneapolis congregation bickered, the St. Paul contingent proceeded to buy land about a half mile west of the state Capitol. The purchase later proved its worth, although no church ever occupied the site.

By 1930 St. Paul was strong enough to support its own chapter of AHEPA; a local Daughters of Penelope unit followed five years later. While some members of the Minneapolis groups transferred to their hometown organizations, relations and rivalries between the two were amicable. The fact that the St. Paul chapter was five years younger than its Minneapolis counterpart did not prevent its leaders from winning the right to host the national convention in 1936. This victory, which was financial as well as symbolic, proved pivotal in establishing the St. Paul community's identity.[49]

The church fund grew along with the community, and by 1939 both were ready for action. A mansion at Summit and Lexington avenues was purchased for $10,000, partly financed by the sale of the lots near the Capitol. The St. Paul chapter of AHEPA donated $4,000 — its total earnings from the national convention — and the community made up the rest. The honor of naming the church was reserved for the largest individual contributor, and so, in the face of a community preference for the name "St. Paul," St. George

Greek Orthodox Church came into being. The Reverend Constantine Capoyannis, formerly pastor of Twelve Holy Apostles in Duluth, became St. George's first priest. It was he who convinced the Athena, the church's ladies aid society, to affiliate with Philoptochos, the national organization. With the subsequent addition of a Sunday school, a Greek language school, a church choir, and a youth group, the St. Paul church and community attained a full complement of social and religious activities.[50]

The Greeks of the Twin Cities might have swelled with pride when Dimitri Mitropoulos arrived in 1938 to head the Minneapolis Symphony Orchestra, but they were soon disappointed when the maestro maintained a stiff aloofness from the Greek community. "Local dignitaries of the Greek church have long been deeply offended," reported the *Minneapolis Star-Journal*, "because on the few occasions when he attends services, he shows a preference for Minneapolis' biggest Presbyterian congregation." Mitropoulos, according to a native of Minneapolis born of Greek parents, had an aversion to foreign-born Greeks, whom he viewed as "corrupt," and a preference for those born in the United States. Such self-imposed estrangement of the foreign-born artist or intellectual from the ethnic community was to prove common among Greeks, as similar experiences with academicians and graduate students from Greece in the post-World War II years would demonstrate.[51]

The Greek community in Rochester, a small but vigorous group estimated at more than 50 in the early 1920s, was dominated by businessmen. Like their compatriots in St. Paul, they organized an AHEPA chapter before they could establish a church. The chapter gave the Greek community an identity during the first decades of its existence. Early in 1933 it boasted a membership of 53 in good standing and a treasury capable of withstanding the expense of sending a large delegation to a district convention in Cedar Rapids, Iowa. Members rented space in downtown Rochester where, in an "atmosphere like an English or Irish pub," the men gathered to play cards and exchange news. Twenty-five cents per card game was set aside for the rent, a practice lucrative enough to secure the space until 1955, when the group began meeting in the new Saints Anargyroi Church, to which it had donated $14,000.[52]

Ahepans used the "Know Rochester" column of the local newspaper to inform the general public of their part in city affairs. On occasion they met in such nearby towns as Faribault (60 miles away) to enable members throughout the area to attend. The Rochester chapter also reached Greeks in La Crosse, Wisconsin, where new members on one occasion chartered a bus to take them and their wives to the initiation ceremonies. Special efforts were also made to entertain non-Greek friends, neighbors, and their families as a means of cultivating better understanding. In 1936 the secretary of the Rochester chapter reported that the order was helping members become loyal citizens, improve their "American speech," co-operate with each other, and learn to "say good things only."[53]

By December, 1941, when the United States formally entered World War II, the interests of Greeks were largely identical with those of other Minnesotans. Many if not most had become naturalized citizens. Their American-born children had attended or were attending the public and private schools of the state. Many had graduated from high school and a growing number from college. The sons of many immigrants had reached or were approaching military age. As in 1917, Greece's alignment with the Allies — this time after being invaded by Mussolini's forces on October 28, 1940 — relieved Greek Americans of the fear that their homeland might side with the Axis nations. Greeks in Minnesota, as elsewhere, were closing ranks, raising money and collecting clothes for the Greek War Relief Association, thus helping the Allies before the United States formally declared war.[54]

Once the United States entered World War II, AHEPA headquarters in Washington, D.C., informed members that the interests of the United States came first; it ordered the chapters to direct the sale of United States government bonds in their communities. Every conceivable device was employed by Minnesota Greeks to encourage bond sales, and for a time it seemed as though Greeks were outdoing each other in displaying their loyalty. In Minneapolis "Chris Legeros, proprietor of the famed Rainbow Cafe out on Hennepin and Lake, is up to his neck in war bond selling," reported the *Minneapolis Star-Journal* of December 7, 1942. "He offered one of his steak sandwiches with all the trimmings with every $1,000 bond purchased in the cafe. First patron to buy after the deal went in and bought a $25,000 bond which made Chris owe him 25 steak sandwiches. The next customer popped for a $10,000 bond. Chris came through again. He's also offering a second cup of coffee with every baby bond purchased." The Minneapolis AHEPA chapter sold more than $1,000,000 in bonds and the Duluth group over $200,000. Figures for St. Paul and Rochester chapters are unavailable, but indications also point to brisk sales.[55]

1945 to the 1980s

After World War II American interest in Greece focused on the guerrilla warfare waged there from 1946 to 1949, the Truman Doctrine which in 1947 selected Greece and its historic enemy Turkey for United States assistance, the various aid programs sponsored by public and private agencies, and the gradual resumption of international trade and travel. In Minnesota the arrival of Greek students, immigrants, or students turned immigrants, the growing popularity of Greek foods and folk dances, and the various degrees of encouragement given to modern Greek study programs bolstered interest in Hellenic culture and history. But these developments did not divert Minnesota Greeks from their pursuit of Americanization.

Given Orthodoxy's traditional opposition to acculturation, events at St. Mary's provided a striking example of Americanization. In 1948 sermons were preached in English for the first time, demonstrating the consensus of the Greek-born priest and older congregants that young members should receive instruction in their native language. In 1955 the church moved to a new building overlooking Lake Calhoun. The move, engineered largely by the Mr. and Mrs. Club, was partly financed by an annual Greek Smorgasbord instituted by the group in 1955. The influence of this club, which folded after members became integrated into the community power structure, marked the beginning of the transition of leadership to the second generation.[56]

The St. Paul community and church, too, continued to grow and change. "Today is the time to plan for the needs of tomorrow," asserted the three women who in 1960 asked church permission to start a building-fund committee. When fire destroyed the interior of the old church in 1967, the committee was able to replace the structure a year later with a larger one. Social and cultural innovations continued into the 1970s as Americanization and ethnicity were no longer seen as mutually exclusive loyalties. A Mr. and Mrs. Club was formed to promote fellowship among congregants, and the Karyatides, a Greek music and folk dance group, was organized "to preserve the Greek culture . . . and to raise funds for our Church and [non-Greek] charities." Congregants felt free to proclaim, "We don't mind that our Greek

CLAD in native costumes, "Loyal Americans of Greek Descent" marched in a Minneapolis Civilian Defense Parade in May, 1942.

pride shows; in fact, we want our Greek heritage to go on forever." Twice a year in the 1980s, at the Spring Smorgasbord and the Bazaar-Food Fair in the fall, St. George continued to open its doors to its non-Greek neighbors.[57]

The Greek community in Duluth, while no longer the center of Hellenism in northern Minnesota, has nevertheless maintained its institutions, its organizations, and contact with neighboring countrymen. In 1980 local chapters of Philoptochos, AHEPA, Daughters of Penelope, and Greek Orthodox Youth of America continued to function. Twelve Holy Apostles had an active membership of about 80 families and counted another 80 at special events; in addition, they were sometimes joined by compatriots from the Orthodox churches on the iron range. Since the late 1970s the congregation has also exchanged visits with the community at Thunder Bay, Ontario, each attending the other's cultural events. The mother tongue was still spoken in Duluth by the elderly parishioners as well as by the 15 to 20 students aged 6 to 17 who attended the weekly Greek School.[58]

In Rochester sacred and secular developments took a slightly different turn, as local chapters of AHEPA, Daughters of Penelope, Greek Orthodox Youth of America, and Philoptochos predated the church, some by as much as two decades. Saints Anargyroi Greek Orthodox Church was not chartered until 1947. Services began in 1949 when its members hired a pastor and organized a Sunday school and choir. At first congregants worshiped in the hall rented by AHEPA; in 1949 they acquired an old house in downtown Rochester. Plans to build a church and rectory on the site, however, proved untenable, and the property served only as a temporary parsonage. It was sold, a new location was secured, and in 1953 construction began. Donations from community members and all four of the Greek organizations in town, local businesses and citizens — many of them non-Hellenic — and Greek groups and residents of other Minnesota cities as well as some in Iowa, Michigan, Illinois, New York, Wisconsin, and Pennsylvania helped finance the youngest Greek Orthodox church in the state. In selecting a name for their church, completed in 1954, Rochester's Greeks considered both their heritage and their American hometown, which they proudly called "the biggest medical center." They chose to name the new church for two sainted brothers who "spent their whole life serving and curing the sick . . . rich and poor without expecting to be paid."[59]

As in other Greek communities, the church was a center for social and cultural events. Each year it held a Greek Independence Day dinner at which children donned Greek costumes, sang songs, and recited poetry. An annual parish picnic was instituted in the 1950s. Non-Greek friends were invited to attend, and their enthusiasm encouraged parishioners to host a yearly Greek Festival. Since the first festival in 1964, Rochester's Greeks and Grecophiles, joined by compatriots from other towns, have gathered every August to sample an ethnic meal and to dance to a Greek band from Minneapolis. In fact, so popular was Greek food in Rochester that in 1977 the community began selling *souvlakia* at the yearly Olmsted County Fair.

Despite these activities, the relatively small size and decentralization of Rochester's Greek community has caused difficulty in maintaining ethnic organizations. Through the 1950s at least, the area supported strong and active chapters of Greek Orthodox Youth, Daughters of Penelope, Philoptochos, and AHEPA. By 1980 the local AHEPA and Philoptochos were still thriving, but the Daughters of Penelope and the youth group had become inactive. There were no longer any song or dance groups, and over the years the Greek language school passed into and out of existence. But some of the Displaced Persons who settled in Rochester in the 1950s have helped keep the mother tongue alive, and six family-style restaurants continue to sell Greek food. In addition to the traditional businessmen, the Rochester Greek community in 1980 included "a sizable number" of physicians, lawyers, engineers, and Mayo Clinic employees. The doctors especially represented both American-born and Greek-born residents. Some of the latter planned to return to Greece; others settled in Rochester permanently.

In fact, a dramatic reduction in the number of Greek-owned restaurants throughout the state has been attributed to the second generation's decision to enter the professions rather than business or the trades. The 1930s were transition years for many. Businesses were sold or went bankrupt as "the boys followed different fields — became lawyers, doctors, real estate owners." While the elaborately decorated confectioneries and many of the small cafes and restaurants are gone, Minnesota's Greeks have not abandoned the food trade. In the 1960s a new phenomenon — the Greek restaurant often featuring belly dancers, music, travel scenes, or other flourishes evocative of the Old World and serving nothing but Greek food — began to appear. In addition, in 1980 Greek-owned family-style restaurants around the state still offered a sampling of ethnic cuisine along with steak sandwiches, prime rib, pizza, or coney islands.[60]

Change also characterized the aims and purposes of the AHEPA organizations in the post-World War II years. Since the need for naturalization was no longer great and anti-Greek feeling was not the problem it had been, the organization shifted its focus more and more to philanthropy. Largely through the efforts of AHEPA, Minnesota's Greeks established committees to assist returning veterans. They also sent aid to Greece and supported the state refugee program which, under the amended Refugee Act of 1953, made more visas available to Greek as well as to Italian and Chinese refugees.[61]

The census of 1950 reported a slight increase in the Greek-born population of the state, but in 1960 and 1970 the trend again turned downward. Whatever determination the newly arrived Greeks might have exhibited to steer the community into a more Hellenic orbit was overshadowed by the American-born, American-educated, and American-oriented element which controlled the community's affairs and was determined to pursue an American course.[62]

Mixed marriages had a long history in the Greek communities of Minneapolis and St. Paul, despite the official opposition of the Greek Orthodox church. Beginning with World War II the church gradually relented, but only because it had no alternative. The rate of mixed marriages in the Minneapolis church remained above 50% in the late 1970s, despite the arrival of later immigrants from Greece. In St. Paul it was reportedly even higher and still climbing. In St. George parish there the Reverend Parry A. Paraschou estimated in 1979 that one parent in at least a third of the 180 families was a non-Greek. More converts were females than males, and most were confirmed. The continued high percentage of mixed marriages seemingly indicated that social and economic status counted more than ethnic background in choosing a mate.[63]

Further evidence of Minnesota's acceptance of its Greek-American citizens may be seen in their successful bids for public office. Candidates elected on the local level fall into two distinct categories: those whose interests revolved almost exclusively around the domestic scene, and those who showed special concern with American foreign policy in the eastern Mediterranean. Most representatives of the former were the members of the American-born generation; of the latter, some were Greek born, and some American born.

Notable among those whose primary concern was state and local politics were Thomas N. Christie, a Democrat and the first Greek-born member of the Minnesota House of Representatives (1946–59); George J. Vavoulis, Independent Republican and the first and only American-born Greek elected mayor of a large Minnesota city (1960–66) up to that time; and Democratic-Farmer-Labor member Sam G. Solon, the first Minnesota-born Greek elected to the Minnesota Senate (1972–   ). Despite differences in era and party affiliation, their lives showed striking similarities. All three worked hard, participated in various civic and fraternal organizations, belonged to the Greek Orthodox church, and married non-Greek women. If their attachments seem more philhellenic than Hellenic, their experiences nevertheless proved that in the post-World War II years, unlike the era following World War I, Greek backgrounds and memberships in obviously Greek organizations were not obstacles to success.[64]

The arrival of newcomers from Greece, however, injected a new and in some ways disquieting element into the otherwise placid Minnesota Greek community life. Immigrants during the late 1950s, 1960s, and 1970s had life experiences, values, and priorities different from American-born Greeks. Many viewed the local communities, which generally consisted of a parish church and its satellite organizations, with discontent, displeased with the inroads that Americanization had made and with the few remnants of Hellenic life left intact. Traditionalists found the use of English in church disturbing. They feared not only for the complete dehellenization of the institution but also for the loss of their national identity. The fact that three of the four priests serving the "dehellenized" congregations in Minnesota in 1979 were Greek born added an ironic sidelight to this situation. Although the shortage of American-educated priests probably explained why the hierarchy looked to Greece for its clergy, the desire to rekindle a stronger Hellenic spirit in the parishes might have been another reason.[65]

Students from Greece enrolled at the University of Minnesota, few of whom attended church, represented yet another disparate aspect of Greek life in America. Student and intellectual attitudes toward the church in the United States were generally based upon opinions formed in Greece. Among other things, the state church in Greece was resented for its extensive, tax-exempt property holdings; insensitive, if not calloused, attitude toward the problems of the poor; collaboration with "the forces of reaction" or with the junta that had seized control of the Greek government in 1967; and the scandalous behavior of some churchmen. One of their biggest grievances stemmed from the belief that Greek Americans, including the archbishop of the Greek Orthodox Church of North and South America, either acquiesced in or failed to protest the military rule of Greece from 1967 to 1974. The students and their sympathizers first denounced those recent immigrants who openly supported junta rule and then concentrated their displeasure on Greek Americans for their presumed projunta sympathies.[66]

These activists were either unaware or unaccepting of the fact that many Greek Minnesotans opposed having the priest, the parish, or both take any stand on a political issue. Other Greek Minnesotans were simply disinterested in events in Greece. The activists concluded that those who did not oppose the Greek junta supported it. They would accept no other explanation.[67]

The Turkish invasion of Cyprus in 1974 elicited a greater response from the Greek communities in the Twin Cities than had the threat of invasion in 1964 or the junta takeover in 1967. In 1975 a group known as the Minnesota Friends of Cyprus began to advocate grass-roots action to oppose Turkish persecution of Greek Cypriots. The organization, one of many Cyprus groups formed in the United States at that time, was unique in its explicit pursuit of non-Greek members and in its policy of making direct, personal contact with legislators and other officials. By 1977 Minnesota Friends of Cyprus had a regular quarterly newsletter and a program that featured a series of events for the benefit of Greek Cypriots. A dinner honoring Ambassador Nicos Dimitriou of Cyprus, a concert at the College of St. Thomas, and a bake sale at St. Mary's church netted $10,000 for the fund. Signed petitions were forwarded to Congress and the State Department urging that military aid to Turkey be withheld until that nation complied with American law governing the use of military supplies provided for the defense of North Atlantic Treaty Organization (NATO) allies and demanding that Turkish troops be withdrawn from Cyprus. In 1976 the University of Minnesota housed a "Cyprus Forum"; exhibits of Cypriot art and handicrafts were also displayed at the university and other colleges. Local stations aired television and radio programs exploring the issue. AHEPA chapters raised money and placed advertisements in the Minneapolis and St. Paul newspapers. Letters were sent to churches of all denominations in the state and to clergymen in the greater metropolitan area of the Twin Cities alerting them to the Turks' destruction of Greek Orthodox churches in northern Cyprus. As of 1980, although Minnesota Friends of Cyprus had discontinued its fundraisers and social events, members continued to gather and disseminate information and to lobby legislators and other concerned citizens.[68]

By the 1970s a growing interest in modern Greek studies became evident in the Twin Cities. The newest immigrants from Greece, with their missionary zeal to rehellenize the local communities, had promoted that concern, and the earlier presence of a Greek art historian at the University of Minnesota had indirectly contributed to the trend. Courses in modern Greek studies were added to the university curriculum in the late 1960s. This program was enhanced in 1978 when Mrs. Basil Laourdas presented to the university her late husband's 4,000-volume library. Literary critic, scholar, and director of the Institute for Balkan Studies in Thessaloniki, Greece, Basil Laourdas was considered the foremost exponent of modern Greek studies. In conjunction with this gift, the university instituted the Basil Laourdas Fellowship for Modern Greek Studies and Greek-Slavic Relations, and, through the special collections division of its library system, established an Annual Celebration of Greek Letters. In May, 1978, the First Annual Celebration marked the installation of Laourdas' library as a special collection of the O. Meredith Wilson Library. Thereafter, the event has co-ordinated the Basil Laourdas Lecture, devoted to the work of a modern Greek scholar, with an exhibit of the author's manuscripts, first editions, and inscribed texts. The result of these activities has been the creation in Minnesota of an internationally acknowledged center for the study of modern Greek culture.[69]

Preliminary data compiled by the census bureau in 1970 yielded more quantitative information on Greek-American education in the Twin Cities. Census figures showed that American-born Greeks living in the Minneapolis-St. Paul metropolitan area compared favorably with other Twin Cities ethnic groups. The average median school years completed by males or females, 25 years or older, who were born in the United States of foreign or mixed parentage, was 12.1; the Twin Cities averages were 12.9 and 12.7 for Greek-American men and women, respectively. Minneapolis-St. Paul residents born in Greece did not score as well. The average median school years completed by all foreign-born males, 25 years or over, residing in the metropolitan area, was 10.4 years for males and 9.8 years for females. Local Greeks in this range completed only 8.3 and 7.4 years, respectively.[70]

The census also gave some indications of the financial standing and language loyalty of Greek Minnesotans. The median income of all families of foreign or mixed parentage in the Minneapolis-St. Paul area in 1969 was $11,915; for Greek- or mixed-parentage families it was $12,960. As for language, census findings indicated that Greek had been retained at least by the older generations. In 1970, 1,341 American-born Twin Citians of Greek or mixed parentage were asked to specify "what language, other than English, was spoken in [your] home when [you were] a child?" Over half (838) reported that Greek was spoken, 409 grew up hearing only English, while the remaining 94 were raised in households speaking Norwegian, German, Polish, Czech, or Yiddish.

By the mid-1970s most Greek Minnesotans were comfortably acculturated. Functionally American, they were nevertheless sufficiently proud of their Hellenic heritage to boast about it, eat Greek foods, dance Greek folk dances, celebrate Greek Independence Day (March 25), take periodic

trips to Greece, and identify with Greek causes. The growth of the second generation, the long history of mixed marriages, the Americanization of the Greek Orthodox church, the community and civic spirit that they adopted for self-preservation, the acceptance of Greek Minnesotans by the general public had helped ease their transition to an American life-style. So did the ability of many to maintain a low profile while they scaled the social and economic ladder. As Americans' interest in their heritages mounted, public displays of ethnicity were not only tolerated, they were welcomed. St. Mary's and St. George's smorgasbords serve thousands of non-Greeks annually, and Minnesotans of all ages can be found sampling the food, listening to the music, or learning the dances at local Greek restaurants or at events like the Festival of Nations in St. Paul. The adoption of more substantive modern Greek studies programs and success in arousing American interest in Greek causes may, if continued, promote and perpetuate this philhellenic trend.

Reference notes

[1] United States, *Census*, 1880, *Population*, 495; 1890, p. 609; 1900, 1:733; John Sirjamaki, "The People of the Mesabi Range," in *Minnesota History*, 27:214 (September, 1946); Theodore Saloutos, *They Remember America: The Story of the Repatriated Greek Americans*, 8 (Berkeley, Calif., 1956). The author and the editor wish to acknowledge the help received during the preparation of this chapter from the Reverend Anthony Coniaris of St. Mary's Greek Orthodox Church, Minneapolis, Professor Theofanis Stavrou of the University of Minnesota, and Sam Solon of Duluth.

[2] Theodore Saloutos, "Causes and Patterns of Greek Emigration to the United States," in *Perspectives in American History*, 7:391–393, 397 (1973); "The Greeks of Minneapolis," "Commercial Section," and "St. Paul, Minnesota," in *Greek-American Merchant*, 2:17, 25–35, 41–44 (May, 1915).

[3] Here and below, see U.S., *Census*, 1910, *Population*, 2:991; 1960, vol. 1, part 25, pp. 194, 195; 1970, vol. 1, part 25, p. 231.

[4] Marion T. Bennett, *American Immigration Policies: A History*, 89, 338 (Washington, D.C., 1963).

[5] U.S. Immigration Commission, *Statistical Review of Immigration 1820–1910*, 20:288, 318 (61 Congress, 3 session, *Senate Documents*, no. 756 — serial 5878).

[6] U.S. Bureau of Immigration, *Annual Report*, 1911, p. 33; 1912, p. 87; 1913, p. 59; 1914, p. 57; 1915, p. 77; 1916, p. 33; 1917, p. 33; 1918, p. 86; 1919, p. 114.

[7] Before 1920 clusters of Greek lumbermen from Macedonia worked in the forests and sawmills near Deer River, Itasca County, and the sawmills and railroads in Cloquet, Carlton County. Many later followed the pine west to Washington, although some switched occupations and moved to Duluth or iron range cities. See interviews of John Kardon, Evelyn Gerogeorge, Steve Kontonikas by Marjorie Hoover, Duluth, fall, 1980, notes in MEHP Papers.

[8] U.S., *Census*, 1910, *Population*, 2:1014, 1015.

[9] Here and below, see U.S., *Census*, 1920, *Population*, 3:521, 523. The development of the Greek community in St. Paul (below) is a perfect example of the movement from railroad employment to city living. See also George Leber, *The History Of the Order Of AHEPA*, ix (Washington, D.C., 1972).

[10] Peter Robert, *The New Immigration*, 171 (New York, 1920); Thomas Burgess, *Greeks in America*, 169 (Boston, 1913); *Greek-American Merchant*, 2:17.

[11] Theodore Saloutos, *The Greeks in the United States*, 59 (Cambridge, Mass., 1964); U.S., *Census*, 1920, *Agriculture*, 5:318–333.

[12] Chris Legeros, "A Message To Our Youths," in Greek Eastern Orthodox Church, *Annual Picnic Souvenir Program* (Minneapolis, 1937).

[13] *Minneapolis Times-Tribune*, November 4, 1940, pp. 15, 21; *Minneapolis Argus*, October 3, 1963, p. 1B; *Greek-American Merchant*, 2:17.

[14] *Greek-American Merchant*, 2:17. The Niatans were a particularly cohesive group. They not only formed the Niata Club, which maintained close ties with their home village, but they also tended to consider other Twin Cities Greeks as "foreigners." According to a retired Rochester restaurateur, the Niatans, who were prominent among Twin Cities confectioners, were friendly to other Greeks but would teach their trade secrets only to other Niatans; telephone interview of George Margellos by Anne Kaplan, May 19, 1980, notes in MEHP Papers.

On Greek intracommunity organizations, see Karen Bruce, "The Social Organization of the Greek Community in Minneapolis," 9–12, term paper, University of Minnesota, 1961, copies in MHS and St. Mary's Greek Orthodox Church library.

[15] Here and below, see St. George Greek Orthodox Church, *Consecration Album*, 11 (St. Paul, 1975); April Holter, "The Greeks in Minneapolis," 1, term paper, University of Minnesota, [1972], copy in IHRC.

[16] Interview of James D. Dimopoulos, St. Paul, by the author, April 23, 1979; Seraphim C. Canoutas, *Greek-American Guide*, 194 (New York, 1907).

[17] C. D. Chapralis, *The Greek-Americans and the Greek-Canadians*, 135 (Chicago, 1948); *Greek-American Merchant*, 2:25–35.

[18] *Minneapolis Times-Tribune*, November 4, 1940, pp. 15, 21; *Greek-American Merchant*, 2:20–22, 24.

[19] *Greek-American Merchant*, 2:41–43; St. George Church, *Consecration Album*, 11.

[20] St. Mary's Greek Orthodox Church, *Consecration Album* (Minneapolis, 1961); *Tower Talks* (Minneapolis neighborhood newspaper), October, 1980, p. 10.

[21] Minnesota manuscript census schedules, 1905, Kittson, Wilkin, Otter Tail counties, rolls 131, 140, 157, 162, microfilm in MHS; interview of Elsie Boosalis by Deborah Stultz, December 7, 1979, notes in MEHP Papers; Greek Eastern Orthodox Church, *Annual Souvenir Book* (Minneapolis, 1931, 1937, 1941); John Syrjamaki, "Mesabi Communities: A Study of Their Development," 134, Ph.D. thesis, Yale University, 1940; Minnesota Bureau of Labor, *Biennial Report*, 1911–12, pp. 91, 108, 123, 137, 177, 228.

[22] Here and below, see George O. Virtue, *The Minnesota Iron Ranges*, 348 (U.S. Bureau of Labor, *Bulletin*, no. 84 — Washington, D.C., 1909); Syrjamaki, "Mesabi Communities," 115, 121, 134; interviews of Henry Tempelis, John Pappelis, Frank Lagios, John Kardon by Marjorie Hoover, Duluth, fall, 1980, notes in MEHP Papers.

[23] Syrjamaki, "Mesabi Communities," 135; Sts. Peter and Paul Catholic Church, Byzantine Rite, *Golden Jubilee*, 38 ([Chisholm, 1966]).

[24] Here and below, see Kontonikas interview, fall, 1980; Twelve Holy Apostles Greek Orthodox Church, *Consecration Album*, 9 (Duluth, 1966); U.S., *Census*, 1910, *Population*, 2:996–1013; 1920, 3:521. On language loyalty, see U.S. Works Projects Administration, Minnesota, Historical Records Survey: Churches, Greek Orthodox Community of Duluth, in MHS. Information on the decline in membership was drawn from author's interview of Senator Sam Solon, St. Paul, April 26, 1979.

Despite this decline, St. Michael's Orthodox Church in Hibbing was established in 1958 to serve Greeks, Russians, and Serbs who found Duluth or Chisholm too far to commute. According to Rev. Paul Pritza (see interview by Deborah Stultz, December 20, 1979,

notes in MEHP Papers), more than a quarter of the church membership of about 100 families was Greek. Some held dual memberships, attending St. Michael's and belonging simultaneously to Twelve Holy Apostles. In the absence of a local Greek Orthodox church or priest, range Greeks maintained their community identity through traditional name-day celebrations. Greek attendance at this interethnic church is an interesting development in light of the earlier desertion of St. Vasilije. Perhaps holding dual memberships satisfied the urge to identify as Greek Orthodox while worshiping closer to home.

[25] Many of Duluth's Macedonians came from the village of Katafigion, near Mount Olympus. After World War I they were gradually outnumbered by immigrants from the Lidoriki area of central Greece and from the Peloponnesos, including Spartans and Niatans. When Alexander the Great disbanded in 1973, the $7,000 in its treasury was sent "to the girls in Katafigion." Here and below, see interviews of Tom Pratchio, John Kardon, Evelyn Gerogeorge, Steve Kontonikas, Coula Perros by Marjorie Hoover, fall, 1980, notes in MEHP Papers; Solon interview, April 26, 1979.

[26] George Margellos to Anne Kaplan, May 22, 1980. MEHP Papers.

[27] U.S., *Census*, 1910, *Population*, 2:996–1012; 1920, 3:521, 522.

[28] *Greek-American Merchant*, 2:18; Margellos interview, May 19, 1980; Sts. Anargyroi Greek Orthodox Church, *25th Anniversary* (Rochester, 1979). The church, which hired its first pastor in 1949, served Greeks in the surrounding communities of Austin, Faribault, Owatonna, Winona, and Albert Lea, as well as in La Crosse and Sparta, Wis.

[29] Saloutos, *Greeks in the United States*, 108, 117; Syrjamaki, "Mesabi Communities," 77, 121, 122, 134; Ch. Kanelos, *Greek-American Guide of the North-West*, 22, 25 (Milwaukee, 1923); Seraphim G. Canoutas, *Hellenism in America*, 301–303 (New York, 1918).

[30] *Greek-American Merchant*, 2:18; Saloutos, *Greeks in the United States*, 77, 114. Similar units began to appear in major United States cities as early as 1907.

[31] Here and below, see *St. Paul Dispatch*, October 3, p. 1; 9, p. 3; 10, pp. 2, 11; 11, p. 3; 12, p. 1; 14, p. 1; 21, p. 9 — all 1912.

[32] *St. Paul Dispatch*, October 25, p. 24; November 11, p. 2, 1912.

[33] For conflicting views on Greece's choice of sides, see Paxton Hibben, *Constantine I and The Greek People* (New York, 1920); George M. Melas, *Ex-King Constantine And The War* (London, 1920); V. I. Chebithes, *AHEPA And The Progress Of Hellenism In America*, 21 (New York, 1935). For a Greek version addressed to Greeks of the U.S., see Adamantios Th. Polyzoides, *Greek Neutrality and King Constantine* (New York, 1917). Polyzoides was the editor of *Atlantis*, the royalist daily published in New York City. On Americanization, see Carol Aronovici to Mrs. J. T. Hale, April 11, 1918, in Correspondence and Reports, Woman's Committee, Council of National Defense, War Records Commission (WRC) Records, in Minnesota State Archives, MHS.

[34] M. G. Pappas to the Governor of Minnesota, August 16, 1917, in File no. 169, Minnesota Commission of Public Safety Records, in Minnesota State Archives; Canoutas, *Hellenism in America*, 310.

[35] Aimee Fisher to Mrs. J. T. Hale, March 21, 1918, in Mrs. T. G. Winter Correspondence, Correspondence and Reports, Woman's Committee, Council of National Defense, WRC Records, in Minnesota State Archives; Boosalis interview, December 7, 1979; *Minneapolis Times-Tribune*, November 4, 1940, p. 21.

[36] See Chebithes, *AHEPA*, 22–25, for a brief expression of this feeling.

[37] *California* (a Greek weekly published in San Francisco), August 23, 30, September 6, 1924; Kanelos, *Greek-American Guide*, 14–36, 37–57, 61–78.

[38] *California*, December 1, 1923, March 29, 1924; Kanelos, *Greek-*

American Guide, 23; St. Mary's Church, *Consecration Album*. Nicholas B. Phillips or Philosopoulos was elected president about 1921. The formation of the Minneapolis post is especially interesting in light of the fact that elsewhere "the American Legion led a virulent campaign against all aliens, especially the Greeks," according to Helen Papinokolas, "The Exiled Greeks," in *The Peoples of Utah*, 427 (Salt Lake City, 1976).

[39] Saloutos, *Greeks in the United States*, 163; *The AHEPA*, Pre-Convocation Number, September, 1925, p. 123. A bi-monthly publication of the Order of AHEPA (see below), this magazine has appeared since 1927 under the title *The Ahepa* and, after 1940, *The Ahepan*. Two annual issues in 1925 and 1926, labeled "Pre-Convocation Number," predated this regular format. The MHS and IHRC have partial files.

[40] Order of AHEPA, *Annual Report*, 1976, p. 205; *The AHEPA*, Pre-Convocation Number, August, 1926, pp. 3–8, 211–214; Greek American Progressive Assn., *Fifth Annual Convention*, 30 (1930). The founding dates of the four AHEPA chapters in Minnesota were Minneapolis, April 21, 1925; Rochester, June 14, 1929; Duluth, July 27, 1930; St. Paul, October 17, 1930. Organization of the chapter in St. Paul was delayed because the Minneapolis group had difficulty enrolling the required number of members without help from Greeks in St. Paul.

In addition to their formal objectives, AHEPA conventions may perhaps have been an important institutionalized way of finding a mate; Bruce, "Social Organization," 19. No Minnesota chapters of the Greek American Progressive Assn. existed in 1930.

[41] U.S. Bureau of Immigration, *Annual Report*, 1919, p. 117; 1920, p. 123; 1921, p. 61; 1922, p. 58; 1923, p. 75; 1924, p. 69; 1925, p. 78; 1926, p. 72; Saloutos, *They Remember America*, 29–50.

[42] Nicholas I. Cassavettes to Worthy Mr. President, March 21, 1919, form letter in Greek and English; Peter Boosalis to Premier Lloyd George, February 15, 1921, both in the possession of Elsie Boosalis, Minneapolis.

[43] J. P. Xenides, *The Greeks in America*, 120–122 (New York, 1922); Saloutos, *Greeks in the United States*, 140, 281.

[44] Kanelos, *Greek-American Guide*, 12; *California*, August 23, 1924. When Prince Paul of Greece, who became king in 1947, visited the Twin Cities in 1926, he attended services only at the royalist St. George's; *California*, February 23, 1926.

[45] George Papaioannou, *From Mars Hill to Manhattan*, 70–81 (Minneapolis, 1976); Bruce, "Social Organization," 16, 24; St. Mary's Church, *Consecration Album*. In 1922 the Archdiocese of North and South America had been established to solidify the decentralized, politically polarized Greek Orthodox churches in America. It is therefore especially significant that St. Mary's, despite its reunification, did not vote to join the Archdiocese until 1959. For details on the founding of the Archdiocese, see Theodore Saloutos, "The Greek Orthodox Church in the United States and Assimilation," in *International Migration Review*, 7:397 (Winter, 1973).

[46] Interview of Rev. Anthony Coniaris by Anne Kaplan, April 11, 1980, notes in MEHP Papers.

[47] Here and below, see Bruce, "Social Organization," 21, 25, 40; Greek Eastern Orthodox Church, *Annual Picnic Souvenir Program* (Minneapolis, 1941).

[48] Kanelos, *Greek-American Guide*, 37–39; St. George Church, *Consecration Album*, 11. Here and below, see also interview of Athanasia Daltas by Anne Kaplan, April 24, 1980, notes in MEHP Papers. In 1980 the picnic was still an annual event.

[49] *The Ahepa*, 10:2–7, 15 (September–October, 1936); *The AHEPA*, Pre-Convocation Number, August, 1926, p. 213; St. George Church, *Consecration Album*, 25, 26.

[50] Author's interviews of Dimopoulos and James P. Paulos, April 23, 1979; Daltas interview, April 24, 1980; St. George Church, *Consecration Album*, 11.

[51] *Minneapolis Star-Journal*, February 14, 1946, p. 23; conversation of the author with Deano Geannakopoulos, New Haven, Conn., August 20, 1970.

[52] Margellos interview, May 19, 1980; Sts. Anargyroi Hellenic Orthodox Church, *Consecration Album* (Rochester, 1955).

[53] *The Ahepa*, 9:29 (July–August, 1935), 10:24 (May–June, 1936); *The Ahepan*, 14:24 (January–February, 1940).

[54] Saloutos, *Greeks in the United States*, 344–350.

[55] *The Ahepan*, 21:74, 128 (July–August, 1947); *Duluth Herald*, February 21, 1941, p. 12; *Minneapolis Star-Journal*, December 7, 1942, p. 17.

[56] Bruce, "Social Organization," 24, 27, 41; St. Mary's Church, *Consecration Album*.

[57] St. George Church, *Consecration Album*, 11, 26, 28, 29.

[58] Interview of Rev. Ted Trifon, Twelve Holy Apostles, by Marjorie Hoover, fall, 1980, notes in MEHP Papers.

[59] Here and two paragraphs below, see Margellos interview, May 19, 1980; Margellos to Kaplan, May 22, 1980; Sts. Anargyroi Church, *Consecration Album*. "Anargyroi" means "with no money."

The festival, which absorbed the parish picnic in 1968, drew an estimated 1,200 guests in 1979. In 1980 the church decided to hold its first parish-only picnic in 12 years. Margellos estimated that the Rochester church probably served about 160 people in town and 220 in outlying areas. At one time Rochester had 14 Greek-owned restaurants; the remaining six have from 10% to 60% Greek items on their menus. Like their compatriots in Rochester, church-affiliated Greeks in Duluth and St. Paul in 1980 regularly sold ethnic foods at public events such as the Festival of Nations in St. Paul and the Duluth Folk Festival.

[60] Conversations of Anne Kaplan with Anna Legeros (Rainbow Cafe), May 27, 1980, and Frances Arvanitis (The Original Coney Island, established in St. Paul in 1923), April 24, 1980; interviews of Margaret Apostole and Coula Perros by Marjorie Hoover, Duluth, fall, 1980 — all notes in MEHP Papers; Margellos to Kaplan, May 22, 1980; *St. Paul Dispatch*, June 9, 1980, p. 11A; *Twin Cities Reader*, September 10, 1980, p. 17; *Southeast* (Minneapolis neighborhood newspaper), July, 1980, p. 13, copy in MEHP Papers. Many of the new ethnic restaurants were established by Greeks who immigrated in the 1950s.

[61] Bruce, "Social Organization," 51; St. Mary's Church, *Consecration Album; The Ahepan*, 20:11 (January–February, 1946), 28:11 (October, 1964), 29:4 (March, 1965); "Refugee Relief Program in Minnesota," and "Groups Eligible for Admission to U.S. under Refugee Relief Act of 1953 — Public Law 203," undated typescripts, both in Governor's Committee for the Refugee Relief Program, Governor's files, in Minnesota State Archives; Order of AHEPA, *1964 Yearbook*, A3, 24, D29, 30.

[62] U.S., *Census*, 1960, *Population*, vol. 1, part 25, p. 195; 1970, vol. 1, part 25, p. 231.

[63] Saloutos, in *International Migration Review*, 7:399; *An Eastern Orthodox Looks at Mixed Marriage*, a folder distributed by Eastern Orthodox Pamphlets, apparently associated with St. Mary's Greek Orthodox Church, Minneapolis; author's interviews of Rev. Parry A. Paraschou, St. Paul, April 7, 1979, and Rev. Anthony Coniaris, Minneapolis, April 24, 1979.

[64] For Christie, who died while serving his sixth term, and Solon, see Minnesota, *Legislative Manual*, 1959–60, p. 75, 1977–78, p. 78. For Vavoulis, who served three terms as mayor of St. Paul, see Orin Nolting and David Arnold, eds., *Municipal Year Book, 1961*, 544 (Chicago, 1961). Another native of Minneapolis to achieve prominence in local politics was Helen Geanakoplos Boosalis, who served as a councilwoman in Lincoln, Neb., before being elected mayor of that city. See *Hellenic Chronicle* (Boston), May 15, 1975, p. 1.

[65] Ann Eggebroten, "Americanizing Greek Orthodoxy," in

Christianity Today, 14:998 (July 31, 1970); author's interview of Evangelos Kalambokidis, Minneapolis, April 21, 1979. Rev. Coniaris of St. Mary's, a native of Massachusetts, was the only American-born priest of the Greek Orthodox church officiating in Minnesota in 1981.

[66] *New York Times*, April 5, 1962, p. 5; November 22, 1965, p. 11; November 23, 1965, p. 12; July 19, 1973, p. 9; January 13, 1974, p. 3; Kalambokidis interview, April 21, 1979.

[67] Theodore Saloutos, "Ethnic Politics: The American Hellenic Model," unpublished manuscript.

[68] Interview of Theofanis Stavrou by Anne Kaplan, March 11, 1980, notes in MEHP Papers; *Minnesota Friends of Cyprus Newsletter*, January, 1977, p. 2, copy in MEHP Papers.

In August, 1964, delegates from all four AHEPA chapters in the state attended the national convention in Toronto, where they sup-

ported the claims of Cyprus, petitioned the president to "suspend all economic and military aid to Turkey in strict harmony with existing law," and endorsed the proposal of the Johnson administration to liberalize the immigration laws of the United States. Support was expected from Vice-President Hubert H. Humphrey, who had joined AHEPA in 1945 when he was mayor of Minneapolis.

[69] "Stavrou Brings Greek Literary Renaissance to Minnesota," in University of Minnesota, *Report*, 2, 7 (September, 1978); program from an exhibit, "Homage to Pandelis Prevelakis," University of Minnesota, Minneapolis, May 18, 1979, copy in MEHP Papers; Stavrou interview, March 11, 1980. The art historian was Dimitri T. Tselos, whose papers are in the IHRC and whose collection of works on modern Greek art is in the Laourdas Collection.

[70] Here and below, see U.S., *Census*, 1970, PC (2) IA, 236–240, 368–370.

CHAPTER 26

The Jews

Hyman Berman

JEWS were among the settlers of Minnesota Territory soon after its creation in 1849. Always small in proportion to the total population, they concentrated in the Twin Cities and Duluth. Jews have also resided in many of the state's market towns, performing vital services in their economies. A critical mass, consisting at a minimum of a few families, was needed, however, to activate group life — to form religious congregations, burial societies, and fraternal and cultural institutions. This requirement limited community life in the state to a small handful of towns. Minneapolis, St. Paul, Duluth, Mankato, Virginia, Hibbing, Eveleth, Chisholm, and sometimes Rochester have been the settings for Minnesota's Jewish communities.[1]

The earliest Jewish settlers arrived in Minnesota from the eastern and southern United States, from central Europe (mostly the Germanic lands), and in small numbers from the western sections of eastern Europe. From the 1880s until the close of mass migration to the United States in the 1920s, Jews reached Minnesota largely from the Russian Empire's Pale of Settlement (Poland, Ukraine, White Russia, and the Baltic provinces), from the Galician sections of the Austro-Hungarian Empire, and from Romania (see Map 26.1, Table 26.1). They emigrated as individuals and as families, driven from their homes by religious, cultural, political, economic, and social disabilities or attracted by opportunities in the New World.[2]

They arrived speaking German, Yiddish, Polish, Romanian, Russian, Hungarian, and a multiplicity of other languages. Most had left self-contained Yiddish-speaking urban village communities which were breaking down under the pressures of modernization and industrialization. Many, particularly those from eastern Europe, retained the cultural characteristics of Orthodox piety, including Old World styles of dress.[3]

The Jewish population of Minnesota reached an estimated peak of 43,700 in 1937. By 1977 approximately 34,270 Jews were counted in the state (see Table 26.2). Some 22,000 lived in Minneapolis and its suburbs, 9,500 in St. Paul and its suburbs, and about 1,000 in the Duluth area. Elsewhere only Virginia and Hibbing on the Mesabi Range and Austin and Rochester in southern Minnesota recorded more than 100 Jews. Thus, although they constituted only 1% of the total population of the state, they accounted for better than 2% of the population of the Twin Cities metropolitan area.[4]

Controversy still abounds as to the definition of a Jew. Does religious affiliation determine identity? If so, what of those Jews who refused to participate in sacred institutions? How does one classify a person born of Jewish parents who converted to a Christian denomination? Questions of this kind occur and recur to plague scholars who attempt to analyze the Jewish group experience.

Jews are a people with common historical and cultural traits as well as a shared core of religious identity. Some commentators identify Jews as a nation and others have erroneously called them a race. We have chosen to regard them as an ethnic group. Given the diversity of national origins, the heterogeneity of religious affiliations, the Babel of languages, and the complexities of diverse historical experiences, the only safe definition must be an eclectic one which depends upon self-perception. A person or group of people who identify themselves as Jews, participate in institutions or activities — religious, cultural, philanthropic, political, or social — that seek to perpetuate Jewish group identity will here be regarded as Jews.[5]

The Pioneer Era

Individual Jewish settlers trickled into Minnesota Territory in the 1850s, attracted by mercantile and commercial opportunities opening up in the region, especially in St. Paul. Some arrived with savings or access to investment capital which enabled them to launch commercial careers. Clothing and dry-goods merchants predominated among them, but others were involved in general merchandising, junk collecting, and itinerant selling in the hinterland. Through the process of chain migration, early settlers were followed by family members, friends, and acquaintances from their European homes.[6]

The first phase of Jewish group life in Minnesota was characterized by the middle-class status of members who lived within the context of the German cultural milieu. These newcomers grew in numbers and by 1856 were able to establish the Mount Zion Hebrew congregation of St. Paul. This action signaled the beginnings of organized Jewish group life in Minnesota. Not all Jews in the territory joined Mount Zion, although for a time there were too few unaffiliated persons to organize other Jewish institutions. But in spite of the factionalism that plagued the congregation in its early years, everyone utilized the Mount Zion Cemetery, for burial in hallowed ground was a universal custom followed by even nonaffiliated Jews.[7]

Individuals from the early Jewish group participated without hindrance in Minnesota politics. During the territorial years from 1849 through 1857, Jacob Jackson Noah, son of a prominent New York Jacksonian Democrat, played a leading role. Arriving in St. Paul in 1849, he became an attorney and worked closely with such early political leaders as Henry H. Sibley and Alexander Ramsey. He was appointed clerk of the Dakota County District Court, and elected as the first clerk of the state Supreme Court in 1857. That same year Noah also served as secretary of the Democratic half of the Constitutional Convention. He was identified by his col-

leagues as a Jew, and he lectured on the history of the Jews to diverse audiences. Although Noah left the state after the Civil War, his activities inaugurated Jewish participation in the Minnesota political arena.[8]

After the Civil War, Jewish migration gathered momentum. Immigrants from Russia, Lithuania, and Poland (then part of Russia) were quickly absorbed into the framework of Jewish life in the state. Successful as peddlers, storekeepers, light manufacturers, and in licensed professions such as medicine, they nevertheless felt different from their German fellow Jews. By 1872 there were enough eastern Europeans in St. Paul to organize a separate religious congregation known as the Sons of Jacob. Neither distance nor

Map 26.1. Pale of Jewish Settlement in the Russian Empire about 1890 Superimposed on a Map Showing Modern and Historic Boundaries in Eastern Europe

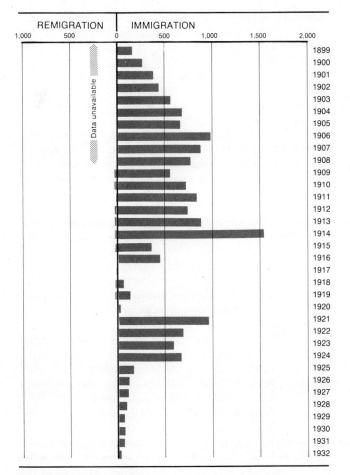

Table 26.1. Jewish Migration to and from Minnesota

Organized Jewish life was focused in the pioneer synagogues, and Mount Zion and Shaarai Tov remained the central institutions of the German settlers until the 1880s. Although small in size (as late as 1882 the membership of Mount Zion did not exceed 50 families), the synagogues spawned social and cultural subgroups which provided the communities with burial and charitable services. Embryonic educational activities for children were also begun.[11]

The existence of such separate institutions did not indicate that the German Jews were totally excluded from the state's general communal or political activities. This was particularly true in St. Paul, where they participated in such German cultural institutions as the *Turnverein*, a social and athletic club, and the *Sängverein*, a singing society. Residential patterns, however, reinforced a tendency to cultivate their own institutions.[12]

As residents became more settled and successful in their economic life, rounds of entertainment, balls, and parties were held in their homes. Leisure-time pursuits moved away from the synagogues. Social clubs, discussion groups, and fraternal organizations began to play increasingly prominent roles for middle-class Jewish families in St. Paul and Minneapolis. Lodges of *B'nai Brith* (Sons of the Covenant), a national, primarily German-Jewish fraternal organization founded in 1843, were established in St. Paul in 1871 and in Minneapolis in 1877. In addition, in 1875 St. Paul Jewish merchants organized the Standard Club as a place to make social and business contacts away from home and synagogue. Similarly Minneapolis, beginning in the early 1880s, had a series of short-lived social organizations, including the Apollo and two different Phoenix clubs.

Economic success did not always result in social acceptance, as the spread of discrimination against German Jews in the eastern states showed. In Minnesota, however, few such manifestations were recorded in the early years. On the contrary, a substantial number of affluent Jews seem to have married outside of the group or voluntarily disassociated from it, often by converting to other religious faiths.[13]

Such assimilationist conversions caused concern in the Minnesota community, but they were soon overshadowed by a more serious challenge — the unexpected arrival of large numbers of eastern European Jews, different in culture, appearance, and language, suffering from want, and challenging the western style of Judaism built up since the territorial years.

On Friday morning, July 14, 1882, just hours before the onset of the Jewish Sabbath, the community was shocked by the unannounced arrival at the St. Paul railroad depot of some 200 hungry, tired, dirty, and impoverished refugees

belief separated German from eastern European Jew during this era; they lived near each other and subscribed to the same religious tenets. Rather it was language, social practices, and attitudes that divided the two groups.[9]

By 1875 the Jews of Minneapolis, which had become a thriving industrial town, were chastised by the *American Israelite*, a national newspaper, for their failure to found Jewish institutions and start a synagogue. A few months later the Montefiore Burial Society and *Baszion* (Daughter of Zion), a women's benevolent association, came into being. Practical necessity dictated the establishment of the burial society, for it was physically difficult to transport the dead to the St. Paul cemetery during the harsh winter months. Two years later in 1878 the Shaarai Tov congregation (now known as Temple Israel) was incorporated.[10]

Table 26.2. Jews in Minnesota and Its Three Major Cities, 1900–77

	1900	1910	1920	1930	1937*	1955*	1960	1971*	1977*
Minnesota	6,000	13,000	31,462	43,197	43,700	38,000	34,900	34,475	34,270
Minneapolis			15,000	22,000	20,700	23,000	20,000	21,640	22,090
St. Paul			10,000	13,500	14,000	10,400	10,200	10,000	9,500
Duluth			2,300	4,000	3,700	3,100	3,000	1,300	1,000

* **Source:** *American Jewish Year Book*, 1899–1900, 1910–11, 1920–21, 1930–31, 1938–39, 1956, 1961, 1972, 1978.
* Figures for 1940, 1950, 1970, 1980 unavailable.

from Russia. Men, women, and children, they taxed the philanthropic resources of the entire city.[14]

Emergency aid was quickly granted by Governor Lucius F. Hubbard, Mayor Edmund Rice, the city council, and the chamber of commerce. The refugees were fed, temporarily housed — first in the St. Paul, Minneapolis and Manitoba Railroad's immigrant house and then in a vacant school building — and welcomed amid the confusion. Within a few days they were settled in a temporary tent city on St. Paul's West Side, across the Mississippi River from the downtown district, in an area that was to become the main residence for subsequent eastern European Jewish settlers in St. Paul. Although not the first Russian-Jewish refugees to reach the state, this unannounced group awakened Minnesotans to the problems of absorbing refugees rather than immigrants.

A number of factors propelled these people from eastern Europe. Added to the rapidly disintegrating social and economic bases of Jewish life resulting from the early stages of modernization in Russia were the political and religious discriminations dictated by the czar and the Russian Orthodox church. The Jews, designated as scapegoats to pacify increasing popular resentment against Czar Alexander II, were singled out for further persecution after revolutionaries assassinated him in March, 1881. A series of laws promulgated in May of that year restricted Jewish residency rights, limited the geographical extent of the Pale of Settlement, and dispossessed large numbers of Jews from rural districts, compelling them to concentrate in already overcrowded villages in the western provinces of the Russian Empire (see Map 26.1). Economic and residential dislocation was followed rapidly by governmentally stimulated attacks. These pogroms hastened the decisions of many to flee. By the spring and summer of 1882 a mass exodus to western Europe was under way.

Fear that this influx would upset the delicate balance of Jewish intergroup relations on the continent and in England prompted efforts to divert the refugees across the Atlantic. In England the Mansion House Committee of London was formed to offer aid and to assure that the refugees would not inundate the island. The work of the committee, in uneasy alliance with the Hebrew Emigrant Aid Society of New York, led in part to the shipment of the unannounced group that reached Minnesota.[15]

The hysterical exodus of the summer of 1882 subsided, but the patterns of Jewish settlement in the nation and the state were drastically altered. Chain migration caused a sustained flow of people to the New World. Continued repressive actions, pogroms, and social or economic dislocations periodically heightened the incoming levels. Only economic depression or war disrupted or slowed the movement.[16]

Before 1882 the entire Jewish population of the United States did not exceed 250,000. From that year until 1924, 3,000,000 to 4,000,000 arrived from eastern Europe. This pattern in microcosm can be traced in Minnesota. It is estimated that there were fewer than 1,000 Jews in the state prior to the 1880s. By the 1920s, when immigration quotas slowed the flow, some 30,000 to 40,000 Jews resided there. [17]

The year 1882 saw some 600 Jewish refugees settle in Minnesota, a number almost equal to the old-time, well-established Germanic element. The result was the evolution of a second distinct Jewish group composed of laborers and charity clients who were Yiddish speaking and more traditional in custom and outlook. The two communities lived in symbiotic relationship, sometimes exhibiting co-operative characteristics, but more often remaining at arm's length and displaying quiet hostility.[18]

Relatively quickly, however, bridging institutions sought to promote communal integration. Early in the 20th century *B'nai Brith* opened its lodges to active and successful eastern European men, while their wives joined such organizations as the National Council of Jewish Women (NCJW). The latter, founded in Chicago in 1893, attempted to provide activities which would address the concerns of American Jewish women. In 1894 NCJW sections were organized in Minneapolis and St. Paul. Superseding earlier Jewish women's associations, these chapters energetically tackled educational and philanthropic needs. At the beginning of the 20th century they also became involved in the international peace movement and in the campaign for women's rights, including the right to vote.[19]

At first the activists in the NCJW were upper-class women from Mount Zion and Temple Israel, but before long the council's program also attracted young women from eastern European families. Fanny Fligelman Brin, who emigrated from Romania as a child in 1884 and who was a 1907 Phi Beta Kappa graduate of the University of Minnesota, joined the Minneapolis chapter, where she carried out her commitments to women's rights, world peace, and her Jewish heritage. From 1932 to 1938 Fanny Brin served as the ninth president of the national NCJW, signaling by her election the integration of eastern European Jews into the country's as well as the state's Jewish life.[20]

Despite such examples, many of the eastern Europeans remained poverty-stricken and dependent. Without family or social-support networks to fall back upon, they were perceived as a burden and as a potential threat by settled Jews. The St. Paul group fulfilled its charitable obligations without stint, while continuing to regard the newcomers as uneducated and thus backward dependents who must be elevated to a higher plane. Fearful that such large numbers of refugees would swamp the local community, St. Paul Jews, like those in England, New York City, and Cincinnati, attempted to restrict the flow or divert it into other channels.[21]

One proposed alternative was to stimulate the settlement of Jewish migrants on the land. In Europe agriculture was increasingly viewed as the way to regularize and modernize the Jewish occupational pyramid. It was held that the absence of Jewish agrarians created a void which was a major source of social dislocation and anti-Jewish prejudice. The legal prohibition against Jewish farming in Russia was seen as a major cause for dispersion. Hence it was reasoned that the Russian exodus could be transformed into an opportunity to right a major occupational and social wrong. This thinking motivated the actions of several western European Jewish organizations and stimulated philanthropist Baron

Maurice de Hirsch of Germany to create an international fund to assist in the establishment of a class of Jewish farmers in Palestine, Argentina, and the United States.[22]

The dream of Jewish farming communities also captivated young idealists who believed that their individual actions would liberate the whole Jewish people from medieval backwardness. A group of these intellectuals organized a colonization society called *Am Olam* (Eternal People), which, borrowing from Russian populist thought, sought to create agricultural communes in the United States. A few of these young men found their way to St. Paul in the spring of 1882, some months before the appearance of the refugees. They quickly succeeded in gaining the support of Rabbi Judah Wechsler of Mount Zion Temple. Wechsler agreed to sponsor the establishment of a Jewish agricultural settlement in Burleigh County, Dakota Territory (now North Dakota), near Painted Woods on the Missouri River.[23]

A few months before the rabbi decided to assist in founding such a colony, the New York-based Hebrew Emigrant Aid Society commissioned one of its members to study the possibilities of colonizing Russian refugees in the "West." During April and May, 1882, Julius Goldman visited Minnesota and Dakota Territory, consulted with Roman Catholic Bishop John Ireland, personally inspected a number of possible agricultural sites, and wrote a report on his findings. He concluded that colonization on homestead or railroad lands was feasible, that it should be organized on an individual rather than a communal basis, and that the endeavor should be based upon business rather than charitable considerations.[24]

Two agricultural settlements in present North Dakota were started along these lines in 1882, one at Painted Woods and the other at Devils Lake. Three years of crop failures followed by a year of drought ended the Painted Woods experiment of 54 families, in spite of generous financial support from the St. Paul community. A number of the failed farmers from that ill-fated colony found their way to Devils Lake after 1886, but by the winter of 1888–89 recurring problems of poor crops and bad weather forced the Jewish communities of the Twin Cities to come to the rescue. This time the initiative in raising funds and relief supplies was taken by Temple Israel in Minneapolis. Later technical and financial assistance was also received from the national Jewish Agricultural Society formed in 1891. Devils Lake weathered the crisis, and Jewish farming persisted there well into the 20th century.[25]

The belief that agriculture was the economic road to social salvation for the Jewish people led to a third short-lived settlement — this one in Minnesota. Early in 1891 Jacob H. Schiff, a New York investment banker active in Jewish affairs, attempted to establish an agricultural settlement at Milaca in Mille Lacs County. A long correspondence with James J. Hill resulted in the leasing of Great Northern Railroad lands for this endeavor. Apparently both men believed that a community situated on a railroad line and close to the Twin Cities would succeed. Schiff, with the permission of the Baron de Hirsch Fund, guaranteed that each family sent to Minnesota would have $500 to $600 in cash. Hill in turn completed arrangements to build 40 or 50 houses, each on 40 acres. Before the severe depression of 1893 made such ventures especially risky, a number of Jewish families were placed in the area. By 1898, however, only 13 families had been settled, and their fate is not known.[26]

During the first decade and a half of the 20th century, more attempts at rural settlement were made. The Industrial Removal Office of New York City succeeded in placing 1,371 Jews in 40 Minnesota rural towns and villages. Although a majority of these families engaged in mercantile pursuits, a number successfully undertook dairy and truck farming — if by successful we mean that they farmed for a decade or more.[27]

They were among the infinitesimal minority of Jews attracted to farming. By 1910 the Jewish Agricultural and Industrial Aid Society counted only 13 agricultural families in the state. The dilemma of Jewish farming in Minnesota was that communal agriculture failed, yet the cultural, religious, and social needs of Jewish life required a population core unattainable under conditions of individualized, dispersed agriculture.[28]

City Life

By the beginning of the 20th century most Jewish immigrants lived in urban centers to which they had been attracted by job opportunities and by the well-established networks of religious, cultural, fraternal, and philanthropic institutions. By 1900 St. Paul alone had developed three major Jewish residential areas with a total population of 4,450–5,000. The older, more prestigious, and largely German families lived in the downtown area and on the bluffs overlooking the state Capitol; some had begun to make inroads in the Summit Avenue neighborhood. Eastern Europeans — mainly small merchants, peddlers, and factory workers in the developing garment trades of the city — resided on the West Side. With increasing economic success they began moving across the Mississippi River and up the bluffs to the Selby-Dale neighborhood (see Map 26.2).[29]

Paralleling the rapid population growth of Minneapolis, Jewish areas there began to exceed the size of those in St. Paul. By 1900 approximately 5,000 Jews lived in Minneapolis, an increase of 4,500 since 1880. Although the economic and cultural gap between the German and the eastern European Jews was not as wide as that in St. Paul, distinct residential districts nevertheless developed (see Map 26.3).[30]

The earliest arrivals centered in the downtown area close to their businesses and to their synagogue, Temple Israel, which from 1888 until 1928 was located at 10th Street and 5th Avenue South. Newer arrivals from Romania and the Russian Empire concentrated in two separate neighborhoods, the Romanians on the South Side near the intersection of Franklin Avenue and 15th Street South, and the Russians, Poles, and Lithuanians on the North Side near Washington Avenue and 5th Street North.[31]

The South Side remained relatively stable until the 1940s as a self-contained family neighborhood. Residents lived near their jobs or businesses and were not pressured by other ethnic groups competing for housing. In contrast, fluid-

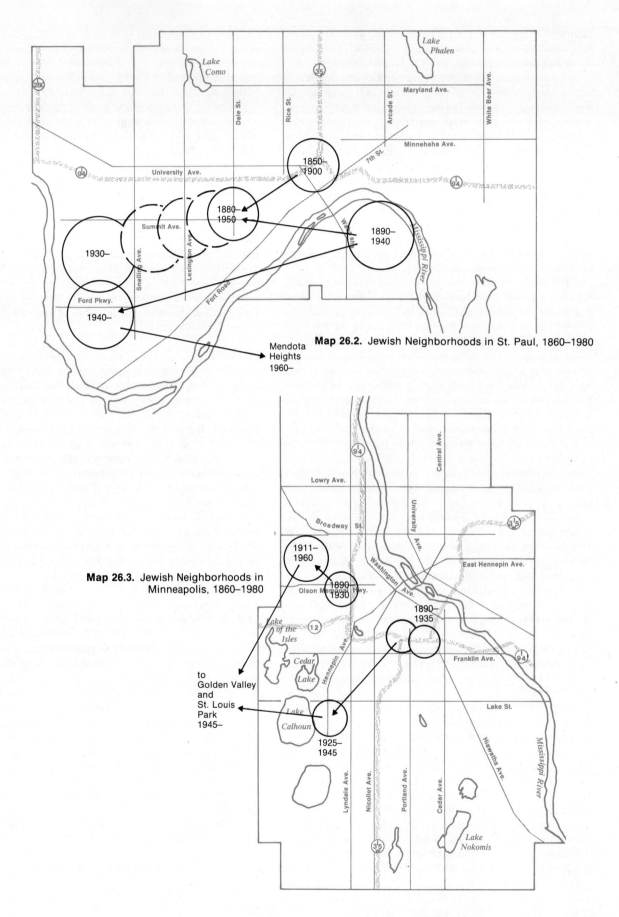

Map 26.2. Jewish Neighborhoods in St. Paul, 1860–1980

Map 26.3. Jewish Neighborhoods in Minneapolis, 1860–1980

THE JEWISH NEIGHBORHOOD in North Minneapolis about 1909. At left children stand before a kosher grocery store at 6th Avenue North and Lyndale. Nearby, Jews lived in tenementlike houses located at 6th Avenue North and 3rd Street.

ity rather than stability was the rule on the North Side. By 1915 residents were beginning to leave that district as a consequence of both economic improvement and pressures from the growing Black population there. Most of the Jews located farther north and west in the Homewood district based at North Plymouth and Penn avenues. Through World War II this area had the heaviest concentration of Jews in Minneapolis.[32]

In Duluth, where individual Jews had appeared as early as the 1870s, a range of organizations did not emerge until the city itself became a viable business center after the opening of the Mesabi Iron Range in the 1890s. The earliest arrivals, fairly Americanized Jews from the eastern United States, established businesses and bought houses in the affluent area east of Lake Avenue. Decades later the eastern European laborers settled in the city's West End, many of them renting low-cost housing between 12th and 24th avenues. Never numerous, Duluth Jews totaled at their height in the 1930s about 4,000 people (see Table 26.2). Although they exhibited the same demographic split — an older German and a newer eastern European component — the arrival of one within a decade of the other precluded the wide divisions that characterized the St. Paul and, to a lesser extent, the Minneapolis experience. By 1900 Duluth had four synagogues. Organized Jewish communities with religious, educational, philanthropic, and cultural institutions were also to be found in the range cities of Hibbing, Eveleth, Virginia, and Chisholm. Although populations on the Mesabi fluctuated with the rise and decline of the iron ore industry, Jews continued to live in these northern Minnesota cities in the 1980s.[33]

The neighborhoods reflected the economic circumstances of the residents. Eastern Europeans who continued to settle in the state in large numbers during the first 15 years of the 20th century at first lacked the capital resources to follow the patterns of the well-established earlier arrivals. Carpenters, tailors, shoe repairmen, and other craftsmen frequently set up workshops in their homes; butchers, bakers, and grocers opened small shops nearby. Butchers in particular were in demand because of the Kosher dietary laws almost universally followed by their neighbors. Some immigrants without craft skills acquired them to become "Columbus' Tailors" in the New World.[34]

Many Jews with some knowledge of trading practices learned in their eastern European villages attempted to eke out a livelihood peddling. Although neither Minneapolis nor St. Paul reproduced the pushcart jungles of New York, many hawkers of fruits, vegetables, dry goods, pins, needles, and other cheap commodities were to be found. Some who were able to purchase or hire a horse and buggy expanded their routes beyond the Jewish neighborhoods.[35]

Peddling became widespread throughout the state, and many a hawker settled down as a retail merchant in one of the smaller market towns. Morris Kaplan of Bemidji, for example, began his career that way. He opened a general store in Bemidji in 1908, built the Kaplan Glass Block in 1910, participated in the city's political and economic life, and became active in the state's Socialist party, running for Minnesota's United States Senate seat in 1934.[36]

Few if any Jewish Minnesotans were to be found in such major economic endeavors as iron mining or flour milling, but a handful became grain merchants. Others followed the paths of their New York and Boston counterparts, pioneering as proprietors and entrepreneurs in the manufacture of specialty apparel such as furs and other types of winter clothing. Banking in the state was closed to Jews, as was the lumber industry. Employment in garment and cigar factories did not become widespread until a core of Jewish employers was established in the early 1900s, thus allowing

AGUDATH ACHIM Synagogue in Hibbing in 1972.

Orthodox employees to follow their religious practices by closing on Saturdays and on Jewish holidays.[37]

Organizations

The proliferation of organizations has been a characteristic of Jewish communities throughout the United States, and those in Minnesota were no exception. Jews in the state enthusiastically embraced the principle of voluntary association, founding a bewildering array of fraternal, charitable, cultural, political, and religious groups. Philanthropy became a key ingredient of the voluntary organizations spun off from the pioneer temples, and self-help dominated their philosophies. The Hebrew Ladies Benevolent Society, organized by prominent members of Mount Zion in 1871, raised money to help indigent Jews by holding bake sales, strawberry festivals, and charity balls. The *Baszion* Society in Minneapolis served a similar function. In 1880 it formally incorporated, changing its name to the Hebrew Ladies Benevolent Society, as well.[38]

Fraternal benefit societies, some affiliated with national organizations and many purely local, developed as a preferred means of self-help for Minnesota Jews. These groups collected small monthly payments, insured members against death, and in some cases provided a primitive form of prepaid health benefits. Emergency collections taken up at lodge meetings frequently supplemented these payments to sick or destitute fellow members. The most prominent of the self-help fraternal orders was *Brith Abraham* (Covenant of Abraham), which at its peak prior to World War I enrolled a few thousand members in its lodges in Minneapolis, St. Paul, Duluth, and the iron range towns.[39]

The ever-increasing demands of local, national, and international fund raisers and their apparent duplications and inefficiencies led to an effort to consolidate such endeavors in the Twin Cities. In 1910, with *B'nai Brith* taking the initiative, the major groups in each city combined to form the Associated Jewish Charities of Minneapolis and the United Jewish Charities of St. Paul. Professionalization of social welfare services followed after 1915. By 1918 the Minneapo-

lis organization had been so well accepted that the local War Chest, and its successor the Community Fund, invited the Associated Charities to participate in the city's consolidated fund drive.[40]

As larger numbers of Jews found themselves working downtown, social clubs sprang up to meet their needs. In St. Paul the 19th-century Standard Club in time accepted eastern European Jews. Not until the 1920s when the St. Paul Athletic Club opened its doors to Jewish members, did the Standard go out of existence. In Minneapolis the need for a downtown club was felt when it became apparent that existing city organizations were reluctant to enroll Jews. In addition, those moving from the older neighborhoods wished to remain in touch with their friends. In 1908 a group of University of Minnesota graduates founded the *Gymal Doled* Club, named for the third and fourth letters of the Hebrew alphabet. Primarily a social and athletic organization, it also served lunch and sponsored cultural events.[41]

Other downtown clubs, such as the Atlas, Pro-North, and Ampliora, were by 1919 absorbed by *Gymal Doled*. With increasing acculturation, the members decided in 1945 to change its name to the Standard Club. In 1980 this institution still existed largely as a businessman's group, although in the previous decade such exclusive bastions as the Minneapolis Club and the Minneapolis Athletic Club began to welcome some prominent Jews into their ranks.[42]

Another cluster of organizations came into being to serve the large numbers of Jewish students who attended the University of Minnesota in Minneapolis. As early as 1904 a Jewish Literary Society began meeting regularly there. In 1911 it joined the national *Menorah* (Enlightenment) Society, formed to help students cope with the coldness of campus life. By the 1920s Minnesotans had assumed positions of leadership in this national movement.[43]

By the dismal Depression years of the 1930s the absence of a Jewish center on the campus was especially felt, in part because of the rising tide of anti-Semitism at home and abroad. With support from the national *B'nai Brith* and the Jewish communities of Minneapolis and St. Paul, Hillel House was built and formally opened in 1940. It was still in use in 1981.[44]

Despite regional, cultural, and class differences, for most Jews the synagogue remained the central institution of their communal life. It was not only a place to worship and study the *Torah* (the Five Books of Moses) and the *Talmud* (scholarly commentaries), but also a major social institution and a home away from home, especially for the eastern Europeans. These immigrants attempted to reproduce as closely as possible the Old World practices they had known. Twice daily worship services, strict adherence to dietary laws, sharp physical separation of the sexes in the synagogue, complete abstinence from labor on the Sabbath, rigid adherence to all religious laws, firm following of the family practices during holidays, religious instruction in Hebrew for male children, ritual baths for women, daily study of the *Talmud* — all this was conducted under the watchful eye of a learned rabbi who was both teacher and interpreter of the laws. The rigid requirements of Jewish law, followed meticulously by Orthodox Jews, the desire to worship with people from the same European country or locality, as well as regional variations in practices and customs produced a proliferation of synagogues located within the various Jewish residential areas of the Twin Cities. St. Paul alone had six congregations, founded between 1872 and 1900; in Minneapolis 11 Orthodox synagogues were formed from 1884 to 1905. These "lands man" congregations were to be found primarily in the early phases of the immigrant experience. By the first decade of the 20th century, Old World geography was no longer a viable organizing principle for local synagogues.[45]

As a minority group subject to the pressures of the surrounding society, many Jews gradually modified their traditional practices, but institutional forms were much slower to change. As long as Jews remained in the compact geographical areas where they were a dominant majority, they continued to attend Orthodox synagogues while moving away from the strict requirements as individuals. This was especially true of children who encountered a wider world and a competing culture in the public schools. The lure of the streets and the acculturative attractions of the secular world of the public schools constituted major threats to cultural and religious survival. Thus Jewish communities in the Twin Cities founded several new institutions to deal with these problems. One was the parochial school; the other was the settlement house.[46]

As in most immigrant communities, Jewish education in the Twin Cities was chaotic. Largely the work of old-fashioned itinerant teachers whose use of rote-learning methods was resented by children, such tutelage failed to meet the heightened need for cultural survival. As a result, the Minneapolis Talmud Torah was founded to perpetuate Jewish learning in modern, secular, urban America. It opened in 1894 as the Hebrew Free School in a vacant butcher shop. Its evolution into a modern afternoon school, with a full curriculum of Jewish subjects from elementary through secondary levels, awaited the creative volunteer efforts of Dr. George J. Gordon, an immigrant from Lithuania who bridged the gap between traditionalism and modernism, medical science and the Jewish heritage. He introduced modern pedagogy, graded classes, and a rigorous curriculum into the new Talmud Torah, which opened on Minneapolis' North Side in 1911.[47]

Within a few years the school had become the Jewish community's dominant educational institution. It refused to associate with any religious congregation. By 1928 its educational reputation was world wide, and Gordon gave up his medical practice to assume full-time direction. Even after a second and third generation replaced the immigrant children, its enrollment remained high. Talmud Torah expanded, set up branch schools on the South Side, and in the mid-20th century followed the Jewish population to the suburbs. Not until the period from 1965 to 1972 did the institution report a 35% decline in enrollment.

A Minneapolis parochial school, Torah Academy, was established in 1944 by a minority of Orthodox Jews who were dissatisfied with the Hebrew cultural emphasis of Talmud Torah and wanted to provide a total Jewish religious education for their children. No comparable schools were

A CLASS in the Jewish Educational Center in St. Paul in the fall of 1931.

created in either St. Paul or Duluth. An attempt in St. Paul failed, because the school was considered too closely tied to the synagogues. Thus it never evolved into a community institution. In Duluth, Jews were simply not numerous enough to follow the Minneapolis example, although religious education was provided there by week-end or Sabbath schools, as it was by other major synagogues throughout the state.[48]

In St. Paul fears for the values and economic well-being of Jewish youths prompted the founding of a settlement house on the river flats of the West Side in 1895. Neighborhood House, initially called the Industrial School, begun as an effort of the Hebrew Ladies Benevolent Society of Mount Zion, was intended to provide industrial training for Jewish immigrant children following the economic crisis of 1893. Rapidly expanding its services to meet additional needs, Neighborhood House was by 1897 a true social settlement, offering recreational as well as formal and informal educational opportunities.[49]

Even though it remained closely associated with the welfare initiatives of Mount Zion, the house was reorganized on a nonsectarian basis in 1903. After 1905 it employed professional workers to organize the clubs, day-care centers, and physical educational efforts, which succeeded in luring immigrant youngsters off the streets. For two generations Neighborhood House helped reinforce Jewish values, despite the clash of cultures and the pressures of assimilation accompanying the Americanization drives during and following World War I. By World War II the ethnic composition of the West Side flats had changed, and Neighborhood House was serving primarily a Mexican clientele.

In the 1920s Minneapolis followed St. Paul's example by establishing South Side Neighborhood House and Emanuel Cohen Center on the North Side. The South Side institution was modeled on that in St. Paul, but Emanuel Cohen Center emerged from the expanded activities of Talmud Torah. A social service department organized within the school in 1914 outgrew its quarters seven years later, and in 1924 a new center opened for the North Side community with modern clubrooms, a gymnasium, auditorium, and swimming pool. Named for the attorney who was its major benefactor, it also provided inexpensive health and dental care facilities. The center's primary role, however, was to offer an alternative to the street, a function it continued to play until the North Side Jewish community dispersed after the 1950s.[50]

As the rigid traditionalism of Orthodox Judaism was increasingly challenged by American secular life, a national network of Reform (or Liberal) congregations had been established in 1875, with a rabbinical school in Cincinnati. An ideology of intellectual and theological justification had been worked out for Reform Judaism, culminating in a formally adopted outlook which rejected the concepts of Jewish nationhood and ethnic and cultural distinctiveness for Jews in America. Following the western European, German, and British examples, it postulated the Jew as an American of the Hebrew faith. This new philosophy conformed perfectly to the life-styles of the older German Jews, particularly in St. Paul and to a lesser extent in Minneapolis.[51]

Mount Zion Temple embraced the Reform ideology enthusiastically. Ritual and theological changes further dramatized the separation of the German and eastern European Jewish groups, and physical removal from the immigrant neighborhoods completed the separation process. Between 1900 and 1910 most members of the older immigrant community had moved from downtown to the Hill District, and in 1903 Mount Zion followed, constructing a new building at Avon and Holly avenues near prestigious St. Paul churches. A new rabbi emphasized nontraditional elements of religious practice and even moved to Sunday services in conformity with Christian neighbors.[52]

Temple Israel, Minneapolis' Reform congregation, avoided the theological and ritual extremes experienced in St. Paul. Although it exhibited tendencies to Liberal practices as early as 1880 and adopted the Reform prayer book in 1894, there was no sharp conflict with the Orthodox community for several reasons. The temple and its members were not physically separated from the newer immigrants, and they had accepted Reform practices and ideas before the mass arrival of the eastern Europeans. Moreover Minneapolis lacked St. Paul's long tradition of German-Jewish integration into the wider community, a fact that was to have considerable bearing on the city's attitudes toward Jews in general.[53]

In addition Samuel N. Deinard, the rabbi apppointed to serve Temple Israel in 1901, was a moderate reformer, a nationalist who did not reject cultural Jewishness. Throughout his 20-year career there, he sought to bridge the gap between his congregants and the Yiddish-speaking Jews of the community. To this end in June, 1912, Deinard began to publish in English a newspaper called the *Jewish Weekly* (known after 1915 as the *American Jewish World*). As editor, he successfully involved other Jewish leaders in the work of the paper, consciously seeking to balance his editorial opinions with various viewpoints. The newspaper kept readers informed of local, national, and international events of Jewish concern, pointed out needed changes and reforms, and galvanized the community in times of crisis. In the 1980s the

American Jewish World was still widely read by Jewish families in Minnesota.[54]

Less successful was an attempt to publish a Yiddish-language weekly launched in 1921. Although over 13,000 foreign-born Minnesotans named Yiddish as their mother tongue in 1920, the *Shabbosdige Post* (Saturday Post), which first appeared on September 23, 1921, lasted only three years. During its final year of publication, its pages were evenly divided between Yiddish and English material. Several factors may have contributed to its failure: competing national Yiddish dailies were being published in New York, and Americanizing pressures dictated a move away from Yiddish. Thus the success of Deinard's English-language weekly and the failure of the Yiddish one might be interpreted as manifestations of the increased acculturation of Minnesota Jews.[55]

The Reform ideology of Judaism did not, however, attract all those who sought an accommodation between Jewish practices and modern needs. For some, a third alternative was to be found in Conservative Judaism, a movement which emerged nationally in the first decade of the 20th century with the founding of the Jewish Theological Seminary in New York City. Its efforts were directed toward conserving traditional Judaism while modifying it to meet modern conditions.[56]

In Minneapolis Adath Jeshurun, a South Side Orthodox congregation, moved into the Conservative camp as early as 1907, and Beth El was started on the North Side in 1921 by a group of young people who had grown up there. In St. Paul the Temple of Aaron emerged from a congregation organized in 1910. When a new building, erected at Ashland and Grotto in the Hill District, was opened in 1916, a graduate of the Jewish Theological Seminary was chosen as spiritual leader.

Despite the inroads of Reform and Conservative ideologies, Orthodox synagogues continued to proliferate. In Minneapolis, two on the North Side merged to form Kenesseth Israel in 1891. The maturity and stability of the local community was demonstrated by the dedication of a new synagogue building during the depths of the depression of 1893. Kenesseth Israel became the most influential Orthodox congregation in the city and was still thriving in the 1980s. After 1900 four additional Orthodox synagogues on the North Side and three on the South Side continued to serve the growing eastern European population of Minneapolis. Similarly in St. Paul at least four new congregations were established after 1900.[57]

The steady erosion of membership in Orthodox synagogues, however, compelled a modest modernization effort both nationally and locally. Kenesseth Israel in Minneapolis and Sons of Jacob in St. Paul increased the use of English in services, utilized rabbis trained in America, and encouraged the involvement of their leaders in the nonreligious aspects of Jewish and American communal life. Nonetheless both insisted upon holding to all the laws and practices of Orthodoxy, making it more and more difficult to retain adherents. For example, as Jews dispersed to the western suburbs of Minneapolis and the southern ones of St. Paul, distances were too great to walk to the synagogues, yet auto travel was precluded by the Orthodox admonition not to ride on the

Sabbath or holy days. Although reduced in numbers, Orthodox congregations remained viable in Minnesota in the 1980s.

Dramatic changes also took place in Reform congregations between 1940 and 1980. Attracted by the greater freedom of Reform practices and the overt commitment to the wider community and to broad social justice, large numbers of the children and grandchildren of eastern European immigrants joined Temple Israel and Mount Zion. In the process, more traditional elements found their way into the congregations, softening the sharp edge of Reform with increased use of Hebrew, a greater appreciation of Yiddish, a general acceptance of the concept of the Jews as a nation rather than merely a religious group, the reinstitution of *Bar Mitzvah* ceremonies, and the inclusion of Jewish cultural content in temple programs.[58]

The absence of large numbers of Jews outside the Twin Cities precluded similar institutional religious developments elsewhere. In the smaller communities the divisions were not as wide and compromise usually moved the congregation into the Conservative mode. Only Duluth had enough Jewish families to enable differentiation. In 1945 Tifereth Israel changed from Orthodox to Conservative; in 1970 it merged with the Reform Temple Emanuel to create a new congregation, Temple Israel. By 1973 only one Orthodox synagogue, Adas Israel, remained.[59]

Although always a distinct minority, nonreligious Jews were present in the Minnesota population from territorial times. In the early 20th century their numbers included a group that identified with Socialism, saw the salvation of the Jewish people in the attainment of a classless society, favored the use of Yiddish for cultural and artistic expression, and attempted to create institutions to serve its needs. Among the members were veterans of the revolutionary struggles in the Russian Empire who had belonged to the Jewish Socialist Workers Association of Russia, Poland, and Lithuania (the *Bund*). This group had broken with Lenin and the Bolsheviks after 1903 over the question of cultural autonomy, for it wished to maintain the use of Yiddish within the revolutionary movement. The failed Russian Revolution of 1905 compelled many members to seek asylum in the United States, where some found their way to Duluth, the North Side of Minneapolis, and the West Side of St. Paul.[60]

During the life of the first immigrant communities in these cities, Yiddish Socialists constituted a creative, but often disruptive, minority. They established a vibrant network of cultural, political, fraternal, and educational institutions and successfully attracted a number of second-generation followers. Clubs were formed which affiliated with the Jewish Socialist Federation of the Socialist party. Actively involved in the labor and political struggles of the Twin Cities, this group was helpful in 1916 in electing Thomas Van Lear, the only Socialist mayor Minneapolis ever had.[61]

Self-help with a Socialist and Yiddish twist was the objective in forming the 1910 Minneapolis and St. Paul branches of the Workmen's Circle, a fraternal organization which provided medical and insurance benefits to members. The circles also organized Yiddish libraries, performed Yiddish plays, established Yiddish-language schools, and sponsored prominent Yiddish lecturers. A similar group in Duluth, founded in 1911, remained viable through the 1930s.[62]

Although the Bolshevik Revolution of 1917 in Russia caused a split within this movement, with one group eventually affiliating with the Communist party and the other remaining in the Socialist camp, both wings remained dedicated to the perpetuation of Yiddish secularism with a radical, anticapitalist orientation. In 1915, at the height of their influence, Yiddishist radicals built the Labor Lyceum as a nonreligious, social center on the Minneapolis North Side. But the movement gradually waned, a victim of acculturation. By the end of the 1940s, with the gradual disappearance of a Jewish proletariat, only a small remnant could still be found in the city.[63]

During the period when the Socialists were most active, the focus of Jewish charitable activities shifted from integrating the immigrant into the community to dealing with the indigent and problem families. Reflecting the new emphasis, the Associated Jewish Charity's name was changed to the Jewish Family Welfare Association in 1924 and in 1946 to the Jewish Family Service Association (later called the Jewish Family and Children's Service). Whatever its name, however, this organization served as the primary social welfare agency of the Minneapolis Jewish community. Similar groups were active in St. Paul and Duluth. By the time the Great Depression descended on the nation in the 1930s, these agencies were engaged in multifaceted case work rather than merely direct relief.[64]

Despite the efforts of the Jewish Family Welfare Association, educational, social, political, and international relief concerns produced duplication and proliferation. By 1936 some 94 separate organizations were to be found in Minneapolis alone, with St. Paul and Duluth not far behind in the variety and diversity of organized groups. The idea of combining fund raising for all groups into one effort had long been advocated by professional workers, but it was not until 1930 that the Minneapolis Federation of Jewish Service was incorporated. Successfully directed by an executive board and co-ordinated by a small professional staff, the federation endured in 1981 as the principal organization integrating the numerous Jewish agencies in Minneapolis. In St. Paul the United Jewish Fund and Council performed a similar function.[65]

Politics: Actions and Reactions

Over the years events affecting the well-being of Jews in Europe frequently concerned those in Minnesota. When political anti-Semitism emerged in western Europe at the end of the 19th century, the St. Paul Jewish community responded with protests and political actions. After the Dreyfus Affair in France in the 1890s, its protests were echoed by many non-Jewish Minnesota religious leaders. The massacres of Jews in Kishinev, Russia, in 1903 and the government-sponsored pogroms following the failure of the 1905 revolution stimulated a rare unanimity among local Jews, who joined in relief activities abroad and political agitation at home in an attempt to persuade the United States to repudiate its trade agreement with Russia.[66]

After the outbreak of World War I in 1914, when Jews living in the battle zones between the Russian and German armies seemed to be in jeopardy, all factions of Minnesota Jewry again responded. Workers donated a day's wages to relieve the starving Russian Jewish masses, the left-wing People's Relief Committee raised funds among its Jewish adherents, and others participated in national campaigns directed by the American Jewish Committee and the Joint Distribution Committee.

Relief efforts during and immediately after World War I and following the Russian Revolution gave Minnesota's eastern European Jews opportunities to assume leadership positions. When alleged "undemocratic" control of international efforts by affluent Jews on the American Jewish Committee was challenged, and a more representative body known as the American Jewish Congress resulted, it was supported by large numbers of Minnesota Jews. The congress sought postwar guarantees of Jewish rights in the newly created European states. In this effort, however, it was to be disappointed.

The rise of Fascism and Nazism in the 1930s, with their threats to the very survival of European Jewry, drew mass protests from Minnesota Jews. When Hitler's government proclaimed the racist Nuremberg Laws in 1935, depriving German Jews of various rights and forbidding them to marry non-Jews, a small number of the state's Jewish leaders advised quiet diplomacy. A majority, however, opted for mass demonstrations, a boycott of German goods, and agitation for immigration of Jewish refugees from Germany to the United States.[67]

Not until 1948 were Displaced Persons permitted to enter the country. By 1952, 269 families, consisting of about 800 people, had settled in Minneapolis, 168 families (365 people) in St. Paul, 28 families in Duluth, and a smaller number were sent to other parts of the state. Since that time the Jewish population of Minnesota has remained relatively stable for three decades (see Table 26.2).[68]

The revelation that between 5,000,000 and 6,000,000 European Jews were exterminated by the Nazis during the 1940s exerted a profound and traumatic impact on American Jews. Shocked and guilt ridden that they had not done enough to rescue their brothers and sisters, those in Minnesota resolved to react with greater vigilance to every threat to the further survival of the Jewish people. A communal pledge that the Holocaust would never be repeated supplied a uniting force for the diverse elements of the state's Jewish communities.[69]

As a result, Zionism gained support in Minnesota. The rise of the Zionist movement, which emphasized creating a Jewish homeland, uniting the Jewish people, and bringing about a Hebrew cultural renaissance, had attracted limited attention in the state during the decade preceding World War I. Embraced by numbers of eastern European Jews, Zionism was at first opposed by many Reform religious leaders, by Socialists, and by well-integrated German Jews, especially those in St. Paul. The leadership provided by Louis C. Brandeis, who served as a United States Supreme Court Justice from 1916 to 1939, reassured German Jews that Zionism was

not the divisive expression of disloyalty to the United States that they had at first thought.[70]

After the British proclamation of the Balfour Declaration in 1917 supporting Zionist objectives and the establishment of the Palestine Mandate by the League of Nations in 1922, Minnesota Zionists worked tirelessly to assist in the building of a Jewish national presence in Palestine. Women organized Hadassah groups to provide support for the development of educational, medical, and philanthropic institutions, and the Jewish National Fund was created to raise money to purchase land. In the 1930s Labor Zionists established a training farm north of Minneapolis in Champlin to prepare potential communal farmers for life on the kibbutz, but only a small number of Minnesota Jews emigrated to Palestine. Zionism remained a minority movement in Minnesota with fewer than 2,500 members in its various organizations in 1920. It did not achieve majority status until after 1945.

Although most Minnesotans continued to be supporters from afar, the establishment of the state of Israel in 1948 brought forth a spontaneous celebratory demonstration as well as a massive fund drive. Arab military attacks on Israel in 1948, 1967, and 1973 resulted in extraordinary financial, political, and emotional efforts by Minnesota Jewish groups. And regularly the annual fund drives conducted by the Jewish federations in the Twin Cities raised money to support institutions in Israel. Minnesota Jews bought bonds, contributed to the Jewish National Fund, to Hadassah Hospital, to Hebrew University, and to social service agencies working to integrate Jews from Europe and from the Arab countries into the new state. Thus events accomplished a redefinition of Zionism. For most Minnesota Jews, it came to mean support for Israel's survival and identification with its aspirations through institutional ties with the Jewish homeland.[71]

In the fall of 1946 Minnesotans were disturbed to find Minneapolis described by the noted journalist Carey McWilliams as "the capital of anti-Semitism in the United States." Jews were not surprised, for they had long lived with job discrimination, housing restriction, stereotyped views, hostility, and other manifestations of anti-Jewish sentiment. Late in the 19th century anti-Semitism had found expression in *Caeser's Column*, a novel by Minnesota Populist leader Ignatius Donnelly, which characterized Jewish middlemen as social enemies. Expressions of anti-Semitism in the 20th century were heard from the pulpits of such popular Minneapolis evangelists as William Bell Riley and Luke Rader. Social discrimination was manifested by the inability of Jews to gain membership in many local groups. Jewish country clubs, like Oak Ridge in Minneapolis and Hillcrest in St. Paul, had been started in the 1920s because existing clubs were closed to them. As late as 1948 Jews were excluded from membership in the Minneapolis Automobile Association, the Minneapolis Athletic Club, the Kiwanis, Rotary, Lions, and similar organizations.[72]

They could not buy homes in certain sections of Minneapolis, and Jewish realtors were excluded from the local realty board. Jewish physicians had difficulty acquiring hospital residencies, compelling the Minneapolis community to build Mount Sinai, a Jewish hospital which opened in 1948. Nationally teaching was becoming an upward-mobility route for educated second-generation Jews, but few were employed in Minneapolis. And Jews were conspicuous by their absence as employees of major Minneapolis retail, banking, and manufacturing establishments. Similar patterns of discrimination were discernible to a lesser degree in other parts of the state.

But it was the successful use of anti-Semitism as a political weapon during the 1930s that caused Minnesota Jews to organize countermeasures. Coinciding with the rise of Nazism, countless Fascist political groups acquired recruits in the state. Particularly successful were the Silver Shirts and Father Charles Coughlin's Social Justice movement. By calling attention to the fact that some Jews were prominent supporters of Governors Floyd B. Olson and Elmer A. Benson of the Farmer-Labor party and that a number were employed by state agencies and the governor's office, these groups attempted to equate Jewishness with radicalism and Communism.[73]

Although such propaganda was not overwhelmingly successful, some elements among Minnesota's old economic and political elites employed the same tactics to discredit and defeat the Farmer-Labor administration. Anti-Semitic whispering campaigns, posters, and pamphlets were used by Ray P. Chase and one segment of the Republican party to defeat Elmer Benson's re-election efforts in the 1938 race for governor. The participation of Jewish trade unionists Sander D. Genis, Rubin Latz, and Michael L. Finkelstein in the industrial union organizing drives of the 1930s gave anti-Semites further reasons to raise funds from leading Minnesota banks and companies to end Farmer-Labor domination of the state's executive branch. Their efforts were successful. After Benson was defeated, Republicans occupied the Minnesota governorship until 1955.

In response the Minnesota Jewish Council came into being as an investigative, lobbying, and educational agency. Under the energetic leadership of Samuel L. Scheiner, its executive director during 1939–44, 1946–51, and 1953–74, the council worked openly and secretly to combat anti-Semitism. Little progress was achieved, however, until after national attention had spotlighted the Minneapolis situation. Coming so soon after the nation was repelled by the revelations of Jewish genocide in Europe, the 1946 pronouncement forced Minneapolitans to recognize that only a narrow line separated racial prejudice from genocide.[74]

Elected in 1945, Mayor Hubert H. Humphrey headed a new city administration which undertook to eliminate this blot on Minneapolis' reputation. Humphrey appointed a blue-ribbon Mayor's Council on Human Relations, which surveyed the local situation and, in the course of the years from 1946 to 1949, proposed ordinances to assure civil rights and discourage housing and job discrimination. On the state level Republican Governors Edward J. Thye and Luther W. Youngdahl sponsored measures to outlaw discrimination and participated in educational efforts to eliminate anti-Semitism. Prominent ministers joined rabbis and community leaders to prevent rabid anti-Semites like Gerald L. K.

Smith, leader of the America First party, from using city-owned halls to preach his message of hate. Public educational endeavors were intensified by the Catholic archdiocese, the American Lutheran church, and other Christian bodies. Pulpit exchanges between rabbis and priests were instituted. Candidates for public office were closely questioned about their attitudes toward civil rights. The onslaught of these activities, coupled with the economic boom that followed World War II, abated many overt manifestations of anti-Semitism and discrimination.

Nevertheless Jews remained vigilant. The Minnesota Jewish Council, which evolved into the Minnesota Jewish Community Relations Council and then merged with the Anti-Defamation League of B'nai Brith in 1975, continued to function as an educational and lobbying body on human rights and human relations. One legacy of the earlier troubles was a continuing commitment to civil rights and the fostering of a society of opportunity for all free from discrimination. As early supporters of the Urban League and the National Association for the Advancement of Colored People, Jewish leaders regarded civil rights for all as a guarantee of human rights for Jews.[75]

These attitudes help to explain the consistently liberal voting record of Minnesota Jews since the 1930s. Before that time their allegiance had been almost evenly divided between Republican and opposition candidates, but after the advent of the New Deal, they voted overwhelmingly for Farmer-Labor and Democratic candidates. In the 1970s, however, as some successful Jews began voting their economic and social self-interest, the balance again shifted toward a more even Democratic Farmer-Labor and Independent Republican split.[76]

As they became more secure after the 1950s, Jews also ran for public office with greater frequency instead of occupying less visible staff and support positions as they had in the past. Their success at the polls, not only in legislative and local offices but also in the state-wide arena, was one measure of declining prejudice. Arthur E. Naftalin served as mayor of Minneapolis from 1961 to 1969; Lawrence D. Cohen filled that post in St. Paul from 1972 to 1976; and Rudolph E. Boschwitz became a United States senator from Minnesota in 1978.[77]

Jewish Communities in the Postwar Era

By the 1950s the early social and ethnic divisions between German and eastern European Jews in Minnesota had weakened. Communal integration had at last been achieved in part because the eastern Europeans and their descendants had attained geographic and occupational mobility, and in part because of their numerical predominance in the Twin Cities. The bastions of German-Jewish exclusiveness slowly gave way, until by the 1950s even in such old, elite institutions as Mount Zion Temple distinctions between the two groups could no longer be discerned.[78]

The change had come gradually. Until the end of World War II, poverty among eastern European Jews was endemic. Most petty traders remained at that level for their entire lives, living a hand-to-mouth existence. Fewer than 1 in 10 were able to make the trek from peddling to small retail shops to the wholesale trade to real estate development that marked the successful. As late as 1936, some 126 Jewish families were displaced in the slum clearance that preceded the construction of the low-income Sumner Field Housing Project on the North Side of Minneapolis. Moreover Jews were eligible to occupy almost one-fourth of the living units in the completed project.[79]

For those Jews stuck at the lowest rung of the occupational and income ladder, hope centered on their children. A strong faith in formal education as the path to success led many parents to live on the edge of subsistence in order to assure that one or more of their children would benefit from secondary school or college. Yet the full flowering of this upward effort was not apparent until after the 1940s. In 1947 a study by the Minneapolis Mayor's Council on Human Relations showed that 44% of the Jews were employed in clerical and sales jobs, while only 1.5% were professional or semiprofessional workers. Even more noteworthy was the finding that about 42% of Minneapolis Jews were craftsmen, factory employees, and laborers, but only a little over 6% occupied proprietary or managerial posts.

At that time about 60% of Minneapolis Jews still lived on the North Side, although the migration westward had already begun. After 1945 Jewish families in both the North and formerly stable South sides moved west to such suburbs as St. Louis Park, Golden Valley, and Minnetonka. Within the city itself, the areas of Kenwood, Lake of the Isles, and Lakes Harriet and Calhoun saw an expansion of Jewish settlement patterns. Not until the late 1960s, when the local consequences of the Black revolution made themselves felt on the North Side, did the final remnants of Jewish population and institutions leave that part of the city (see Map 26.3).[80]

Dramatic changes occurred in the occupational distribution of Minneapolis Jewish men and women during the 25 years from 1945 to 1970. The influence of the school, the settlement house, and the cultural trait of close family ties had assured that a significant number of the immigrants' children would be able to rise occupationally and economically. Although a small percentage had opted for sports, petty crime, and bootlegging after the onset of Prohibition in 1919, success was achieved largely through professional and mercantile pursuits. By 1971 less than 10% of all Jews in Minneapolis were craftsmen, factory operatives, laborers, and service workers; 90% were in professional, clerical, managerial, and proprietary occupations. Professional and technical employment accounted for 28.2% of the total; 41.4% of the men, 12.2% of the women, and 32.3% of all gainfully employed Minneapolis Jews were managers, proprietors, or administrators. Clerical and sales occupations engaged 21% of the males, 53% of the females, and almost 31% of all Minneapolis employed Jewish adults. In contrast was the sharp decline in blue-collar occupations from 48.4% in 1947 to only 8.8% in 1971.[81]

The same study showed that the median household income for Minneapolis Jews was $1,805 higher than that reported for all Hennepin County households, and that the educational level was substantially higher than their non-Jewish neighbors. Only 10% reported less than a high school education, and 63.4% cited college attendance, graduation, or postgraduate degrees. Nevertheless 17.8% of Minneapolis Jewish households in 1971 had annual incomes of less than $8,000.

Although no comparable statistics have been compiled for other Minnesota cities, it is probable that the findings would be similar for St. Paul. In Duluth, however, educational achievement and upward mobility have resulted in Jewish out-migration. Informed opinion suggests that professional and educational achievement resulted in geographical migration to major metropolitan centers from the smaller market towns. The Jews remaining behind were mainly engaged in mercantile activities.[82]

Congregational or religious affiliation remained the single most significant mode of Jewish self-identification in Minnesota. Although comparable figures are not available for the rest of the state, a 1971–72 report on Minneapolis indicated that over 88% of all Jewish adults identified themselves with one of the three major branches of Judaism — 52.9% with Conservatism, 27.5% with Reform, and 7.9% with Orthodoxy. (Of the remaining 12%, 2.9% were secular, 2.2% fell into the "other" category, and 6.7% did not reply.) Yet only 77% of the heads of households claimed congregational membership, and the records of synagogues affirmed that 65.7% were indeed members. Most knowledgeable observers believed that similar proportions existed in St. Paul and perhaps Duluth.[83]

In the same survey a sample of approximately 10% of the community showed that nearly 90% of Minneapolis Jews over the age of six had completed at least one year of formal Jewish education. But its attractions were declining. In 1971–72 only 43% of the children aged 5 to 17 were enrolled in Jewish educational programs. In 1957 the same age group had a 55% attendance rate. Although most parents reported that they were highly satisfied with their children's learning experiences, the children themselves were not so enthusiastic.

In 1980 Jewish communities in Minnesota supported synagogues, centers, social service organizations, and educational efforts. The belief that continuity depended upon the transmission of religious and cultural values and information to the young explained the formidable investment of community funds allocated to educational purposes — from synagogue schools to Talmud Torah, from summer camps to support for the Jewish Studies Program established at the University of Minnesota in the 1970s. Nor were the elderly ignored. Homes for them with educational and social programs were also communally supported.[84]

Minnesota Jews were primarily an English-speaking people in 1980. Ten years earlier 9,209 had declared Yiddish as their mother tongue, but fewer and fewer were able to function in that language with each passing year. The cultural revival associated with the establishment of Israel had brought about increased efforts to teach the Hebrew language to the young, but few Minnesotans had more than a bare acquaintance with it. They might have been able to read Hebrew prayers, but most could not read, write, or speak the language.[85]

A HEBREW SERVICE in the Jewish Home for the Aged in St. Paul about 1925. In 1981 the expanded residence was known as the Sholom Home.

Secure and stable in 1980, Minnesota Jews still had apprehensions. They were concerned that their numbers were not growing. Intermarriage increasingly seemed to be making inroads among their young. They were worried and vigilant lest a revival of racism and intolerance jeopardize their standing in the state and nation. They were committed to religious and cultural survival in American terms, which they saw as a function of their own efforts and the continued adherence of American society to the principles of pluralism. The Holocaust had a profound and indelible impact on their consciousness; thereafter, Minnesota Jews saw an inexorable nexus between the survival of Israel and their own well-being. They were determined that the democratic, caring values integral to both their Jewishness and their Americanness persist and prevail for the benefit of all.

Reference notes

[1] W. Gunther Plaut, *The Jews in Minnesota: The First Seventy-five Years*, 8–15, 123–125 (New York, 1959); John Syrjamaki, "Mesabi Communities: A Study of Their Development," 128, 131, Ph.D. thesis, Yale University, 1940.

[2] On the origins of Jewish mass migration to the U.S., see Zoza Szajkowski, "How the Mass Migration to America Began," in *Jewish Social Studies*, 4:291–310 (October, 1942); Ezekiel Lifschutz, "The First Russo-Jewish Mass Immigration and the American Jews," (Yiddish), in *Yivo Bleter*, 4:312 (November–December, 1932).

[3] On the religious-cultural traits of the eastern European immigrants, see Hutchins Hapgood, *Spirit of the Ghetto: Studies of the Jewish Quarter of New York* (New York, 1976); Irving Howe, *World of Our Fathers* (New York, 1976); Moses Rischin, *The Promised City: New York's Jews, 1870–1914* (Cambridge, Mass., 1977).

[4] H. S. Lenfield, "The Jews of the United States, Numbers and Distribution," in *American Jewish Year Book, 5700*, 41:185 (Philadelphia, 1939), hereafter cited as *AJYB*; Alvin Chenkin, "Jewish

Population in the United States, 1977," in *AJYB, 1978*, 78:251, 256 (1977).

A survey of the Minneapolis Jewish population in 1936 produced a count of 16,260, whereas the *AJYB, 5703*, 44:426 (1942), estimate for 1937 was 20,700. The survey method, however, may well have resulted in an undercount; see Sophia M. Robison, "The Jewish Population of Minneapolis, 1936," in Sophia M. Robison, ed., *Jewish Population Studies*, 152–159 (New York, 1943).

[5] For a succinct summary of the vast literature on Jewish identity, see Salo W. Baron, *The Jewish Community*, 3–10 (Reprint ed., Westport, Conn., 1972); for a recent discussion focusing on St. Paul, see Arnold Dashefsky and Howard Shapiro, *Ethnic Identification Among American Jews*, 1–31 (Lexington, Mass., 1974).

[6] Albert I. Gordon, *Jews in Transition*, 12–14 (Minneapolis, 1949); Plaut, *Jews in Minnesota*, 39. On German-Jewish migration to the U.S., see Eric Hirschler, ed., *Jews from Germany in the United States* (New York, 1955), especially the chapter by Bernard D. Weinryb, "The German Jewish Immigration to America: A Critical Evaluation," 116–119. On chain migration, see Mark Wischnitzer, *To Dwell in Safety: The Story of Jewish Migration Since 1800*, 98 (Philadelphia, 1948).

[7] W. Gunther Plaut, *Mount Zion 1856–1956: The First Hundred Years*, 11–14 (St. Paul, [1956]) and *Jews in Minnesota*, 30–35.

[8] Plaut, *Jews in Minnesota*, 16–21.

[9] Plaut, *Jews in Minnesota*, 54–57, 312; Hiram D. Frankel, "The Jews of St. Paul," in *Reform Advocate* (Chicago), November 16, 1907, p. 45; Sons of Jacob, *75th Anniversary Book* (St. Paul, 1953).

[10] *American Israelite* (Cincinnati), December 24, 1875; Ruby Danenbaum, "A History of the Jews of Minneapolis," in *Reform Advocate*, November 16, 1907, pp. 7, 13, 20, 29; Albert G. Minda, *The Story of Temple Israel, Minneapolis, Minnesota. A Personal Account*, 4 (Minneapolis, 1971).

[11] Plaut, *Jews in Minnesota*, 57, 95; Minda, *Story of Temple Israel*, 4–7.

[12] Here and below, see Plaut, *Jews in Minnesota*, 51, 58–60; Danenbaum and Frankel, in *Reform Advocate*, November 16, 1907, pp. 8, 30, 47; Edward E. Grusd, *B'nai Brith: The Story of a Cove-*

nant, 12 (New York, 1966). For more on the *B'nai Brith* lodges in Minnesota, see Hiram D. Frankel Papers and Independent Order of B'nai Brith, Chicago, Papers (Grand Lodge District Number 6), both in MHS.

[13] Gordon, *Jews in Transition,* 206; Plaut, *Mt. Zion,* 23.

[14] Here and two paragraphs below, see *St. Paul Pioneer Press,* July 16, 17, 18, 20, 23, 26, 1882; Plaut, *Jews in Minnesota,* 90–95. For more on conditions leading to the mass emigration, see Simon Dubnow, *History of the Jews in Russia and Poland,* 2:269–330 (Reprint ed., Philadelphia, 1946).

[15] Wischnitzer, *To Dwell in Safety,* 39, 44–49. The *St. Paul Pioneer Press,* July 17, 1882, attributed the shipment of the 200 refugee Jews to the Mansion House Committee, which it erroneously located in Liverpool, England.

[16] The announced policy of the Russian government was to induce mass migration, conversion, or use extermination to eliminate Jews from the Empire. This policy, formulated by Constantine Pobiedonostsev, the Procurator of the Holy Synod, was effected by expelling Jews from Moscow (1891), inciting pogroms by the Black Hundreds, and stimulating peasant attacks on Jewish communities in addition to passing legal prohibitions against Jews in designated occupations. Mass Jewish emigration also resulted from the internal revolutionary upheaval and defeat by Japan in 1905. See Dubnow, *Jews in Russia,* 2:336–373, 399–413; Wischnitzer, *To Dwell in Safety,* 67–70, 105.

[17] Wischnitzer, *To Dwell in Safety,* 66; Minnesota population estimated from *AJYB, 5688,* 29:242 (1927), and U.S. Census Bureau, *Special Reports, Religious Bodies: 1926,* 2:648.

[18] Plaut, *Jews in Minnesota,* 95, 110–114. For fictional recreations based on life in Minneapolis and St. Paul, see Myron Brinig, *Singermann* (New York, 1929); Jennie Rosenholtz, *Upon Thy Doorposts* (New York, 1936); Harry Bloom, *Sorrow Laughs* (New York, 1959); and a series by William Hoffman: *Those Were the Days* (Minneapolis, 1957), *Tales of Hoffman* (Minneapolis, 1961), *Mendel* (South Brunswick, N.J., 1969).

[19] Plaut, *Jews in Minnesota,* 149–151, 230–236. *American Jewish World,* September 22, 1922, p. 23, claimed that the Minneapolis chapter was founded in 1893, but *AJYB, 5661,* 2:84 (1900) confirmed the date.

[20] Nina Morais Cohen, daughter of one of the founders of the Jewish Theological Seminary and wife of Emanuel Cohen, a prominent local layman (see p. 497, below), was the founder and a longtime prominent force in the Minneapolis chapter of the NCJW; Plaut, *Jews in Minnesota,* 147–151. For Brin and Cohen, see Barbara Stuhler, "Fanny Brin, Woman of Peace," in Barbara Stuhler and Gretchen Kreuter, eds., *Women of Minnesota: Selected Biographical Essays,* 284–300 (St. Paul, 1977); Ruth F. Brin, "She Heard Another Drummer: The Life of Fanny Brin and Its Implications for the Sociology of Religion," master's thesis, University of Minnesota, 1972. The Fanny Fligelman Brin Papers, in MHS, contain comprehensive documentation of both the Twin Cities chapters and the national activities of the NCJW.

[21] Plaut, *Jews in Minnesota,* 101. For a theory on the continual hostility between the German and eastern European Jews, despite or perhaps because of the former's charitable contributions to the latter, see Jessie Bernard, "Biculturality: A Study in Social Schizophrenia," in Isaque Graeber and Stuart H. Britt, eds., *Jews in a Gentile World,* 272 (New York, 1942). Bernard's "Milltown" is believed to be Minneapolis.

[22] Wischnitzer, *To Dwell in Safety,* 78–82. For more on the philanthropist, see Samuel Joseph, *History of the Baron de Hirsch Fund* (New York, 1935).

[23] Plaut, *Mt. Zion,* 56–58, and *Jews in Minnesota,* 96; Abraham Menes, "Di Am-Olem Bavegung," in Elias Tcherikower, ed.,

Geshichte fun der Yiddisher Arbeter Bevegung in di Vereinigte Shtaten, 2:203–238 (New York, 1945); Leo Shpall, "Jewish Agricultural Colonies in the United States," in *Agricultural History,* 24:125–128, 137, 145 (July, 1950).

[24] Julius Goldman, *Report on the Colonization of the Russian Refugees in the West,* 1–3, 6, 15–24 (New York, 1882). For more on the man and his work, see Julius Goldman Papers in the Jewish division of the New York Public Library.

[25] Leonard G. Robinson, "Agricultural Activities of the Jews in America," in *AJYB, 5673,* 14:61, 93 (1912); Plaut, *Jews in Minnesota,* 96–109; Shpall, in *Agricultural History,* 24:144.

[26] Cyrus Adler, *Jacob H. Schiff: His Life and Letters,* 2:87 (Garden City, N.Y., 1929); Plaut, *Jews in Minnesota,* 108. The Schiff-Hill correspondence is also in President's File, Great Northern Railroad Papers, in MHS.

[27] Plaut, *Jews in Minnesota,* 109.

[28] Robinson, in *AJYB, 5673,* 14:77, 78 (1912).

[29] Frankel, in *Reform Advocate,* November 16, 1907, pp. 45–47; *American Jewish World,* September 22, 1922, p. 55; Plaut, *Jews in Minnesota,* 157–159, 189. Population figures, here and below, are rough estimates, generally composites of synagogue and society memberships. On the difficulties of gauging populations, see *AJYB, 5661,* 2:624 (1900).

[30] Plaut, *Jews in Minnesota,* 110, 117.

[31] Gordon, *Jews in Transition,* 14, 19; Minda, *Story of Temple Israel,* 6; Herbert S. Rutman, "Defense and Development: A History of Minneapolis Jewry, 1930–1950," 8–10, Ph.D. thesis, University of Minnesota, 1970.

[32] Gordon, *Jews in Transition,* 6; Calvin F. Schmid, *Social Saga of Two Cities: An Ecological and Statistical Study,* 77–79, 151, 152 (Minneapolis, 1937).

[33] Duluth's Orthodox synagogues were Tifereth Israel (1892 or 1893), founded by Russian Jews; Adas Israel (late 1890s), founded by Lithuanian Jews; and B'nai Israel (late 1890s). Temple Emanuel, founded in 1891, was a Reform congregation. Plaut, *Jews in Minnesota,* 123–125, 132–139; Thelma C. Covner, "The New Wilderness: Building the Jewish Community in Duluth, Minnesota, 1870–1975," 3–10, typescript, [1975?], copy in MHS; Jewish Welfare Federation of Duluth, *Social, Recreational, and Educational Survey of the Jewish Community of Duluth, 1944,* 5–20 ([Duluth, 1944]); Agudath Achim Synagogue, *31 Years of Jewish Life on Iron Range of Northern Minnesota,* 8–31 (Hibbing, 1938).

[34] Nathan Goldberg, *Occupational Patterns of American Jewry,* 15–19 (New York, 1947); Judith R. Kramer and Seymour Leventman, *Children of the Gilded Ghetto,* 51 (New Haven, Conn., 1961).

[35] Plaut, *Jews in Minnesota,* 112, 129, 156; Gordon, *Jews in Transition,* 18; Hoffman, *Those Were the Days,* 135–139.

[36] Morris Kaplan and Mildred Kaplan Light, "Reminiscences," unpublished manuscript in Morris Kaplan and Family Papers, in MHS.

[37] Council of Jewish Federations and Welfare Funds, *Minneapolis Jewish Communal Survey,* 3:1–3 ([Minneapolis, 1936]); Frankel, in *Reform Advocate,* November 16, 1907, p. 41. On Jewish business families, see, for example, the Papers of Hiram D. Frankel, of Joseph H. Schanfeld, and of Fanny F. Brin, all in MHS. Even for those who achieved modest success, economic gains were, at times, precarious. The depression of 1893 drove many Jewish merchants to the brink of failure, and cries for reductions in their synagogue obligations reached a peak in 1894–95. Most survived these difficulties, but their economic success should not be exaggerated; Minda, *Story of Temple Israel,* 6.

[38] Mt. Zion's HLBS subsequently divided into a ladies' auxiliary and the Jewish Relief Society of St. Paul; see Plaut, *Jews in Minnesota,* 57, 141–143, 153; Danenbaum, in *Reform Advocate,* Novem-

ber 16, 1907, p. 20; *American Israelite*, October 15, 1903, p. 3. Minute books and annual reports of the HLBS (St. Paul) are in MHS.

[39] Danenbaum, in *Reform Advocate*, November 16, 1907, p. 30; Gordon, *Jews in Transition*, 173–175; Plaut, *Jews in Minnesota*, 120, 138; Rutman, "Defense and Development," 44–46.

[40] Gordon, *Jews in Transition*, 39; Plaut, *Jews in Minnesota*, 221–223; Rutman, "Defense and Development," 85–88. See also Annual Reports, 1930, 1931, and minutes of the Jewish Family Welfare Association, Jewish Family and Children's Service Papers, in MHS.

[41] Plaut, *Jews in Minnesota*, 292–294; Gordon, *Jews in Transition*, 24.

[42] Standard Club, *50th Anniversary Souvenir Book*, 21–24 ([Minneapolis, 1958]). Gordon cites 1921 as the date of the merger, but the anniversary book is more authoritative. On the name change, see Gordon, *Jews in Transition*, 62–64; *American Jewish World*, August 10, 1945, p. 8, September 7, 1945, p. 46, October 19, 1945, p. 7.

[43] Menorah Society of the University of Minnesota, *Annual, 1926*, 1–4, *1927*, 11 ([Minneapolis], 1926, 1927), hereafter cited as *Menorah Annual*. Gordon, *Jews in Transition*, 25, and Plaut, *Jews in Minnesota*, 168, erroneously dated the origins of the Jewish Literary Society as 1905 and 1903, respectively.

[44] *American Jewish World*, July 13, 1945, p. 1; *Menorah Annual, 1927*, 13–15, discussed the need for a Hillel House on campus; Gordon, *Jews in Transition*, 187.

[45] Plaut, *Jews in Minnesota*, 56, 115–121, 202; Gordon, *Jews in Transition*, 19–21, 71–73, 152–163; Danenbaum, in *Reform Advocate*, November 16, 1907, pp. 34, 38. St. Paul's Orthodox congregations were: Sons of Jacob (1872), known as the Polish synagogue; Sons of Zion (1883), formed by immigrants from Russia; Beth Hamedrash Hagodol (1888); Russian Brotherhood (1888); Sherey Hesed va-Emet (ca. 1900); and Sons of Abraham (1900). Sons of Moses and Adath Yeshurun were organized in the early 1900s and joined Sons of Jacob and Sons of Abraham in the Hill district, while the other synagogues served the vast immigrant population on the West Side flats.

Minneapolis' South Side synagogues were: Adath Jeshurun (1884); Rumanian Hebrew (1888), the forerunner of B'nai Abraham (1896); Nachlus Israel (1896); and Agudas Achim (1902). On the North Side were: Ohel Jacob (1888); Beth Medrash Hagodol (1888); Anshei Russia (1890), which changed its name to Mikro Kodesh in 1895; Tiferes B'nai Israel (1890), which became Tiferes B'nai Jacob in 1920; Anshei Tavrig (1902), which merged with Gemilas Chesed in 1915; Beth Aaron (1905), later called Sharai Zedeck.

[46] Henry L. Feingold, *Zion In America: The Jewish Experience from Colonial Times to the Present*, 135 (New York, 1974); Rutman, "Defense and Development," 15–17, 34–36.

[47] Here and below, see Plaut, *Jews in Minnesota*, 170–173; Judith B. Erickson and Mitchel J. Lazarus, *The Jewish Community of Greater Minneapolis: A Population Study*, ch. XIII, 10 (Minneapolis, 1972); *American Jewish World*, September 22, 1922, pp. 18–20, 75, October 26, 1951, p. 3.

[48] Gordon, *Jews in Transition*, 183; Nancy J. Schmidt, "An Orthodox Jewish Community in the United States: A Minority Within A Minority," in *Jewish Journal of Sociology*, 7:179–183 (December, 1965); Plaut, *Jews in Minnesota*, 174–176; Covner, *"New Wilderness,"* 11.

[49] Here and below, see Plaut, *Jews in Minnesota*, 152–155; Hoffman, *Those Were the Days*, 163–169; Lorraine Esterly Pierce, "St. Paul's Lower West Side," 36–40, 65, 87, 89, 121, master's thesis, University of Minnesota, 1971; Neighborhood House Association Papers, in MHS.

[50] Angelo Cohn, "A Long Way From Ninth Street," in *Identity* (Minneapolis), April, 1971, p. 11; Plaut, *Jews in Minnesota*, 229; Gordon, *Jews in Transition*, 40, 182; *American Jewish World*, February 7, 1919, p. 376, March 7, 1919, p. 439.

Legacies of the St. Paul and Minneapolis settlement houses are two Jewish Community Centers, one in each city, which in 1980 continued to provide cultural and recreational opportunities to middle-class Jews. Each is in a predominantly Jewish neighborhood: St. Louis Park in Minneapolis, and Highland Park in St. Paul. See, for example, Erickson and Lazarus, *Jewish Community*, ch. XIII, 1.

[51] Feingold, *Zion in America*, 96–112; David Philipson, *The Reform Movement in Judaism*, 334–339 (Rev. ed., New York, 1931). For more on the 19th-century organizer of Reform Judaism in the U.S., see Isaac Meyer Wise, *Reminiscences* (New York, 1901); J. G. Heller, *Isaac M. Wise, His Life Work and Thought* (New York, 1965).

[52] Plaut, *Mt. Zion*, 74–76, and *Jews in Minnesota*, 183–190.

[53] Rutman, "Defense and Development," 58–62; Plaut, *Jews in Minnesota*, 190.

[54] Michael G. Rapp, "Samuel N. Deinard and the Unification of Jews in Minneapolis," in *Minnesota History*, 43:213–221 (Summer, 1973).

[55] United States, *Census*, 1930, *Population*, 2:360; Plaut, *Jews in Minnesota*, 298; Gordon, *Jews in Transition*, 175–178. Gordon claimed that the *Shabbosdige Post* began publishing in 1917 and lasted for three years, but Plaut's evidence for the 1921 beginning date is more conclusive.

[56] Here and below, see Feingold, *Zion in America*, 179–193. On the development of Conservative Judaism in the U.S., see Moshe Davis, *The Emergence of Conservative Judaism: The Historical School in 19th Century America* (Philadelphia, 1965); for the practices and beliefs, see Marshall Sklare, *Conservative Judaism: An American Religious Movement* (New York, 1972).

[57] Here and below, see Plaut, *Jews in Minnesota*, 119, 195–207, 314; Gordon, *Jews in Transition*, 153, 157–159, 162. Ohel Jacob and Beth Medrash Hagodol merged to form Kenesseth Israel. On the other synagogues, see note 45, above.

A small group of Twin Cities Jews joined the Lubavitcher Chasidim after 1960. This sect, tracing its origins to an 18th-century eastern European pietistic revival, attempts to persuade all Jews to perform all ritual functions and family obligations in a context of joy. The Minnesota group is part of a world-wide movement, looking to the Lubavitcher Rebbe (holy man) for guidance. See Feingold, *Zion in America*, 309; Gerald S. Strober, *American Jews: Community in Crisis*, 260–264 (Garden City, N.Y., 1974).

[58] Author's observations of membership and programs at Mount Zion and Temple Israel since 1962; discussion with Rabbi Max Shapiro, Temple Israel, December, 1980. The *Bar Mitzvah* is a ritual in which males, considered to be men upon turning 13, are accepted as adult members of the faith.

[59] Covner, "New Wilderness," 10, 21.

[60] Dubnow, *Jews in Russia*, 3:55–58. For a comprehensive study of the *Bund*, see Ezra Mendelsohn, *Class Struggle in the Pale: The Formative Years of the Jewish Workers Movement in Czarist Russia* (Cambridge, Mass., 1970).

[61] Herz Burgin, "Kurtze Geshichte fun der Idisher Arbeter Bavegung in di Vereinigte Shtaten," in *Almanac: 10th Jubilee of the International Workers Order* (Yiddish), 222–266 (New York, 1940); Erickson and Lazarus, *Jewish Community*, ch. XII, 2; David P. Nord, "Minneapolis and the Pragmatic Socialism of Thomas Van Lear," in *Minnesota History*, 45:3 (Spring, 1976).

[62] Plaut, *Jews in Minnesota*, 224n; Gordon, *Jews in Transition*, 175–177. For a sample of meetings of Yiddish Socialists and the Workmen's Circle in Duluth, see *Labor Leader* (Duluth), September 21, 1917, p. 10; *Truth* (Duluth) November 16, 1917, p. 1, February

22, 1918, p. 3, March 8, 1918, p. 2. The *American Jewish World* throughout the 1920s, 1930s, and 1940s reported similar meetings in Minneapolis and St. Paul. For a general history, see Judah J. Shapiro, *The Friendly Society: A History of the Workmen's Circle* (New York, 1970).

The International Workers' Order (IWO), founded in 1930, was the left-wing counterpart to the Workmen's Circle. Branches in St. Paul, Minneapolis, and Duluth constituted the core of IWO organization in Minnesota which lasted until destroyed by government action during the Cold War; see *Almanac: 10th Jubilee,* 576, 579; *New York Times,* June 26, 1951, p. 12.

[63] The 30th anniversary of the Labor Lyceum was celebrated in December, 1945, with Mayor Hubert H. Humphrey as the main speaker; *American Jewish World,* December 7, 1945, p. 15; Burgin, in *Almanac: 10th Jubilee,* 245–248.

[64] Plaut, *Jews in Minnesota,* 218–224; Gordon, *Jews in Transition,* 40; *American Jewish World,* January 31, 1930, p. 4, November 16, 1945, p. 11. For more on family welfare, relief, and care for the aged, see Council of Jewish Federations and Welfare Funds, *Minneapolis Jewish Communal Survey,* 1:1–9 ([Minneapolis, 1936]).

[65] Gordon, *Jews in Transition,* 10; Council of Jewish Federations, *Minneapolis Jewish Communal Survey,* 3:2; Rutman, "Defense and Development," 89–97; [Rhoda G. Lewin], *Minneapolis Federation for Jewish Service: Moving Into the 80's,* 3–6 ([Minneapolis, 1980]); *American Jewish World,* February 7, 1930, p. 3. Duluth followed a similar pattern of consolidation, first of social service agencies and then of all Jewish communal organizations. See Ida B. Davis Papers, in MHS.

[66] Here and two paragraphs below, see Plaut, *Jews in Minnesota,* 87–89, 248–253; Feingold, *Zion in America,* 244–249. For accounts of Minnesota Jews' efforts on behalf of coreligionists in the war zones, see, for example, *American Jewish World,* May 26, 1916, pp. 657, 659, July 21, 1916, pp. 787, 794, June 13, 1919, p. 689, May 30, 1919, p. 656. On the activities of Minnesota Jews in the American Jewish Congress, see *American Jewish World,* January 3, 1919, p. 303, January 10, 1919, p. 307.

[67] Feingold, *Zion in America,* 283. For local reactions to Nazi Germany's treatment of its Jews, see *American Jewish World,* March 22, 1935, pp. 1, 4, and throughout the 1930s.

[68] Figures compiled from Displaced Persons Resettled in Minnesota, January, 1949–April, 1952, and Minnesota Displaced Persons Commission Files, both in Minnesota Public Welfare Department Records, State Archives, MHS; Minneapolis figures from *Newsletter of Jewish Family and Children's Service,* January, 1952, n.p., in Minneapolis Section, National Council of Jewish Women Papers, in MHS. For more on Jewish DPs, see Wischnitzer, *To Dwell in Safety,* 260–273.

During the 1970s a small number of Soviet Jewish families settled in Minnesota (about 230 in Minneapolis, 140 in St. Paul, and six in St. Cloud), and a continuing flow of Jewish professionals and academics took up employment in the state. This immigration was balanced, however, by a steady loss of Jewish Minnesotans to professional opportunities elsewhere and a larger flow of retired persons to the sun belt states; Erickson and Lazarus, *Jewish Community,* ch. VI, 1, 5. Information on Soviet Jews from Sidney Hurwitz, St. Paul Jewish Family Service, Irving Mendel, Minneapolis Jewish Family and Children's Service, February 19, 1981; *Minneapolis Star,* March 9, 1981, p. 1A.

For more on Soviet Jews in the Twin Cities, see two articles by Stephen C. Feinstein, "Soviet-Jewish Immigrants in Minneapolis and St. Paul: Attitudes and Reactions to Life in America," in Dan N. Jacobs and Ellen Frankel Paul, eds., *Studies of the Third Wave: Recent Migration of Soviet Jews to the United States,* 57–75 (Boulder, Col., 1981), and "Aspects of Integrating Soviet Jewish Immigrants in America: Attitudes of American Jewry

Toward the Recent Immigration," presented at the Baltimore Hebrew College symposium on Soviet Jewish resettlement, Baltimore, Md., 1981, copy in MEHP Papers.

[69] There is a vast literature on the Holocaust and its impact on American Jews; see, for example, Arthur D. Morse, *While Six Million Died: A Chronicle of American Apathy* (New York, 1968); Henry L. Feingold, *The Politics of Rescue: The Roosevelt Administration and the Holocaust 1938–1945* (New Brunswick, N.J., 1970). *American Jewish World,* 1945–46, gave a dramatic account of Minnesota Jews' reactions.

[70] Here and below, see Melvin I. Urofsky, *Louis D. Brandeis and the Progressive Tradition,* 87–103 (Boston, 1981); W. Gunther Plaut, "How Zionism Came to Minnesota," and Seymour Leventman, "Zionism in Minneapolis," both in Raphael Patai, ed., *Herzl Year Book,* 5:221–235, 237–246 (New York, 1963); Gordon, *Jews in Transition,* 26, 34, 37, 197, 306–308; Rhoda G. Lewin, "Some New Perspectives on the Jewish Immigrant Experience in Minneapolis: An Experiment in Oral History," 141–143, Ph.D. thesis, University of Minnesota, 1978. For more on Zionism, see Feingold, *Zion in America,* 194–207; Naomi W. Cohen, "The Reaction of Reform Judaism in America to Political Zionism (1897–1922)," in *Publications of the American Jewish Historical Society,* 40:361–394 (June, 1951).

[71] *American Jewish World,* March 30, 1945, p. 18, October 19, 1945, p. 1, January 4, 1946, p. 4, June 21, 1946, p. 1, May 14, 1948, pp. 1, 3, 5, May 21, 1948, p. 7, June 9, 1967, pp. 1, 4, June 23, 1967, p. 1. On American Jewish support of Israel, see Strober, *American Jews,* 9–25.

[72] Here and below, see Carey McWilliams, "Minneapolis: The Curious Twin," in *Common Ground,* Autumn, 1946, pp. 61–65; Norman Pollack, "Ignatius Donnelly on Human Rights: A Study of Two Novels," in *Mid-America,* 47:99–112 (April, 1965); Gordon, *Jews in Transition,* 44–48, 64; Plaut, *Jews in Minnesota,* 273–277, 280; *American Jewish World,* September 22, 1922, p. 54, March 9, 1945, p. 1, March 1, 1946, p. 5, October 5, 1948, p. 7. Riley was minister of the First Baptist Church, and Rader was minister of the River Lake Tabernacle. For an evaluation of McWilliams' research and conclusions, see Plaut, *Jews in Minnesota,* 282–284.

[73] Here and below, see Hyman Berman, "Political Antisemitism in Minnesota during the Great Depression," in *Jewish Social Studies,* 38:247–264 (Summer–Fall, 1976).

Genis was the manager of the Twin Cities Amalgamated Clothing Workers Union, vice-president of the national union, and, in the later 1930s, president of the Minnesota Industrial Union Congress. Finkelstein was the local leader of the Ladies' Garment Workers Union; on both men, see John R. Steelman, *Who's Who in Labor,* 111, 128 (New York, 1946). Latz was a leader of the Laundry Workers Union and the organizer of the United Labor Committee for Human Rights; see *Minneapolis Tribune,* December 26, 1948, p. 12, *Minneapolis Labor Review,* December 30, 1948, p. 1. All three were active in Farmer-Labor politics.

[74] Here and below, see Charles I. Cooper, "The Minnesota Jewish Council in Historical Perspective — 1939–1953," 1–7, typescript, November, 1953, copy in MHS pamphlet collection; papers, reports, self-survey, conclusions, and recommendations of the Minneapolis Mayor's Council on Human Relations, in the Papers of Hubert H. Humphrey, Douglas Hall, and the Jewish Community Relations Council, all in MHS; *American Jewish World,* April 6, p. 11; 13, p. 4; May 4, p. 4; October 12, p. 4 — all 1945; August 9, p. 7; 30, pp. 4, 11; February 8, p. 1 — all 1946; September 12, 1947, p. 7; November 5, 1948, p. 1; Gordon, *Jews in Transition,* 55–58.

[75] Jewish Community Relations Council, Anti-Defamation League of Minnesota and the Dakotas, Annual Reports, 1975–80, in the agency's office, Minneapolis; Gordon, *Jews in Transition,* 54.

[76] Plaut, *Jews in Minnesota,* 112, 259. For the national voting trends of Jews after 1930, see Stephan D. Isaacs, *Jews In American*

Politics, 140–142, 150–156 (New York, 1974); for Minnesota patterns, see election-day editorials and news in *American Jewish World.*

[77] Information on Cohen and Naftalin from St. Paul and Minneapolis mayor's offices, February 19, 1981; *Minnesota Legislative Manual 1979–1980,* 438 (St. Paul, [1979]).

[78] Plaut, *Mt. Zion,* 93; Kramer and Leventman, *Children of the Gilded Ghetto,* 46, 48.

[79] Here and below, see Gordon, *Jews in Transition,* 6, 9, 292, 294; Erickson and Lazarus, *Jewish Community,* ch. V, 8. The Jewish poor have been a singularly invisible part of the community, except during times like the Great Depression, when charitable organizations were overwhelmed; Rutman, "Defense and Development," 98–102.

[80] Erickson and Lazarus, *Jewish Community,* ch. IV, 3–7; *American Jewish World,* September 9, 1966, p. 28, December 30, 1966, p. 3.

[81] Here and below, see Kramer and Leventman, *Children of the Gilded Ghetto,* 129–150; Erickson and Lazarus, *Jewish Community,* ch. V, 9–11, 18, 20, 30, 32.

[82] Covner, "New Wilderness," 22.

[83] Here and below, see Erickson and Lazarus, *Jewish Community,* ch. VII, 3, 4; ch. XIII, 2, 6, 13–15.

[84] Kramer and Leventman, *Children of the Gilded Ghetto,* 153; Covner, "New Wilderness," 22; Erickson and Lazarus, *Jewish Community,* ch. VIII, 2, ch. XI, 12–27, ch. XII, 12–19.

[85] U.S., *Census, 1970, Population,* vol. 1, part 25, p. 514; Gordon, *Jews in Transition,* 106, 168.

MIDDLE EASTERN
AND
ASIAN PEOPLES

CHAPTER 27

Middle Easterners

SYRIANS, LEBANESE, ARMENIANS, EGYPTIANS, IRANIANS, PALESTINIANS, TURKS, AFGHANS

Deborah L. Miller

PEOPLE FROM THE MIDDLE EAST, traditional crossroads of Europe, Asia, and Africa (see Map 27.1), have long migratory traditions which include emigration to the western hemisphere. Among those who chose Minnesota late in the 19th century and early in the 20th were both Arabs and non-Arabs, Muslims and Christians. They included Syrian (or Lebanese) and Armenian Christians and Turkish Muslims who settled in St. Paul, Minneapolis, Duluth, the Red River Valley, and elsewhere in southern and northeastern Minnesota. After World War II they were joined by smaller numbers of Egyptians, Iranians, Turks, Palestinians, and Afghans. Most of the later immigrants were part of the three great postwar movements of people to the United States: the influx of students to American universities, the so-called brain drain of professionals from less-developed countries, and the flight from political or religious oppression in their homelands.

By the late 1970s there were an estimated 1,500,000 Arab

Americans[1] in the United States, but the number of Middle Eastern migrants to Minnesota was small (see Tables 27.1, 27.2). The largest group in the state was composed of Syrians and Lebanese. The 1970 census counted only 1,037 first- and second-generation Lebanese in the state, but some estimates placed the total number of Middle Easterners at about 10,000. Perhaps as few as 1,000 of them were Muslims. Minnesota had a smaller percentage — by two-thirds — of Arab Americans of all generations than the country as a whole (see Table 27.3).[2]

SYRIANS AND LEBANESE

Of the people who left the Middle East for Minnesota, the earliest and most numerous were the Syrians or Lebanese, who began arriving in the late 1880s. They scattered throughout the state as farmers and settled on the iron ranges and in the cities of St. Paul, Minneapolis, Duluth, Mankato, Crook-

Map 27.1. The Middle East in 1981 and the Ottoman Empire of 1900

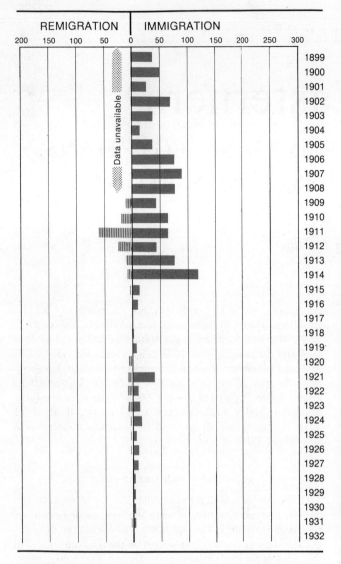

Table 27.1. Turkish, Armenian, and Syrian Migration to and from Minnesota

Table 27.3. Arabic Speakers in Minnesota, 1910–70*

	foreign born	foreign stock*
1910	440	694
1920	859	1,649
1930	707	
1940	600	1,160
1960	257	
1970	464	1,572

Source: Mother-tongue statistics in U.S., *Census*, for the years listed. The 1910 and 1920 figures given here appeared under the heading "Syrian-Arabic."

*From 1910 through 1940 the state's Arabic speakers were primarily Syrian or Lebanese; thereafter Egyptians and some other groups discussed in the chapter were included as well. Foreign stock includes foreign born as well as native born of foreign or mixed parentage.

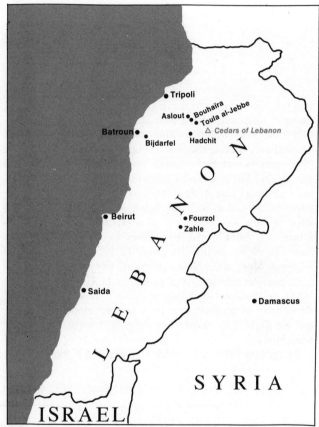

Map 27.2. Lebanon

Table 27.2. Middle Easterners in Minnesota, 1890–1970.

	1890	1900	1910		1920		1930		1940	1950	1970	
	foreign born	fb	fb	foreign stock*	fb	fs	fb	fs	fb	fb	fb	fs
Turkey	45	125	1,226	1,528	130	818	90	188	112	80	177	371
Syria							670	1,764	597	385	60	403
Lebanon										130	241	1,037
Palestine					25		35	63		5		
U.A.R. (Egypt)											205	351
Other North Africa											110	200
Armenia					174		60	107				

Source: Country of origin statistics in U.S., *Census*, for years listed.

Note: People listed as born in Turkey before 1920 could be Syrians, Lebanese, Armenians, Turks, or even Greeks. In 1940 Syrian figures included Palestine. In 1950 the Palestine figure is for "Arab Palestine." Neither Iran nor Afghanistan appears in the statistics for Minnesota.

*Foreign stock includes foreign born as well as native born of foreign or mixed parentage.

ston, and Moorhead as laborers and businessmen. Some were from what is now Syria, an area then occupied by the Ottoman Empire of the Turks. Most, however, emigrated from small villages in the partly autonomous district known as Mount Lebanon, the coastal mountain region between the Syrian port cities of Beirut and Tripoli (see Map 27.2). After that area gained its independence in 1946 as the country of Lebanon, the growth of national consciousness spurred many migrants to think of themselves as Lebanese, although earlier they may have used the term "Syrian" (these terms will be used interchangeably hereafter). By 1909 approximately 95% of those immigrating to the United States were joining friends and relatives who had arrived earlier. It is probable that Minnesota's Lebanese were part of that national pattern.[3]

Among them were a few Muslims, but most were members of two Christian groups, Maronite Catholics and Syrian Orthodox. The more numerous in Minnesota were the Maronites, sometimes called "the Irish of the East" because of their tendency to equate their ethnicity with their religion. Although affiliated with Rome, they practiced the Antiochian rite rather than the Roman or Byzantine rites more familiar to European Catholics. By 1980 a majority of the world's Maronites lived in the western hemisphere; the United States counted 49 Maronite parishes, two of which were in St. Paul and Minneapolis. The Syrian or Antiochian Orthodox, as they are more properly called, organized their own diocese in the United States in 1936. By 1980 St. Paul had two small Antiochian Orthodox congregations, the only ones in the state. Other Syrians joined various local churches, often Roman Catholic ones.[4]

Syrian and Lebanese Settlements

St. Paul's Syrians and Lebanese emigrated from a different cluster of villages from those left by their countrymen in Minneapolis, Mankato, and Crookston. Most St. Paul Lebanese Maronites moved from Toula al-Jebbe, Aslout, Bouhaïra, and Hadchit in the *coza* (county) of Jebbe southeast of Tripoli. A number of them arrived in St. Paul via Mexico. Almost 95% of the members of the city's only Maronite church in 1968 could trace their origins to a small district "not too far from the Cedars, a great pride of Lebanon." Minneapolis Lebanese left from Bijdarfel, Batroun, Jdabra, and other villages in the *coza* of Batroun, south of Tripoli, while nearly all of those who settled for a time in Crookston emigrated from the Jebbe village of Bouhaïra.[5]

Many Mankato Lebanese families who had roots in Fourzol or the nearby larger town of Zahle, which many Duluth Lebanese also called home, had known each other in the Old Country, as had people from the village clusters named above. Farmers there usually had a few acres of land on which they grew wheat and grapes and herded sheep and goats. Those who left did so for economic reasons: the Turks took too much of what they produced. Some of the first immigrants in Mankato arrived directly from Lebanon, but most had lived for a time in such cities as New York, Chicago, Cedar Rapids, Iowa, and Aberdeen, South Dakota.[6]

Nonchurch-related Lebanese organizations were often based on a common village of origin. The Knights of Ferzoul and the Aslout Relief Society, for example, each had small chapters in St. Paul and Minneapolis which met only irregularly by the 1970s.[7]

Syrians and Lebanese in Minnesota were largely urban dwellers, living in towns of varying size all over the state. St. Paul had the largest contingent, followed in approximate order by Minneapolis, Duluth, Mankato, Crookston, and Moorhead. Several iron range cities also counted Middle Easterners in the first quarter of the 20th century, though many probably did not stay long.

In 1895 St. Paul recorded 116 Syrians, a number which grew to 186 within 10 years. Minneapolis counted only 30 in 1895, but 136 in 1905. Few of the Syrians living in the Twin Cities in 1895 remained there 10 years later; most had moved on and been replaced by others. A study of American Syrians in 1911 found from 200 to 250 individuals in the Twin Cities, with some 75 families in Minneapolis. By 1920 a total of 818 were listed in the state, 263 in St. Paul and 240 in Minneapolis. Ten years later the number of foreign-born Syrians had declined to 670; there were 1,094 people of Syrian descent.[8]

Most of St. Paul's Syrians in 1895 lived in the 400 block of East 7th Street. Within 10 years the community had moved across the Mississippi River to the West Side, where its residents lived in or near buildings housing Syrian stores. Some occupied homes on the river flats, an area which was often flooded in the spring and which in 1981 was the site of an industrial park. Others lived on the West Side's hills, reported an observer in 1911, "where picturesque rocks towering above are, no doubt, a grateful reminder of the home land," and where they could cultivate gardens. Many single people and those whose families were in Syria stayed in rooming houses or boarded with families on the West Side in 1918.[9]

In Minneapolis "all the Syrians lived in Ward one on Main and Marshall Streets. In 1895, all 30 immigrants lived at 123 Main Street, the address of Mike Henne's store, and in 1905, 51 people lived at the address of his new store, 521 Marshall Avenue," according to one study. In 1918 patterns of Syrian residence in Minneapolis were similar to those found in St. Paul. Of the Syrian households counted, 104 were in the Northeast part of the city, two were in North Minneapolis, and two were in the central business district. A number of households continued to call Henne's building home.[10]

In 1910 the combined estimated total of Syrians in all Mesabi Range towns was 110. Those in Eveleth, like their South Slav and Italian fellows, lived under boarding-boss systems, paying $2.00 to $4.00 a month for lodging, laundry, and cooking and $10.00 to $15.00 for food. Some of this group, who may have been Muslims, apparently left during World War I. Virginia counted perhaps the most Middle Easterners (largely Syrians) in 1918, but Hibbing also had a few, as did Tower on the Vermilion Range and Floodwood in southeastern St. Louis County.[11]

Duluth's Middle Eastern community, composed of Syrians and a few Turks, numbered over 50 people in 1911. Seven years later the Rice Point-Garfield Avenue area was a center of their settlement, though a number lived on West Michigan, Superior, 1st, and 2nd streets as well.[12]

Mankato, a southern Minnesota town at the great bend of the Minnesota River in Blue Earth County, began attracting Syrians about 1890. By 1955 there were some 180 of them spanning three generations in the city of 30,000. In the 1950s two of the three early centers of Syrian settlement persisted, "one toward the southern periphery of the city along James Avenue and the other in the northern part . . . on 4th and 5th Avenues, near the area spoken of as 'the prairie.'" The remnants of a third center were still noticeable in North Mankato on Belgrade and Nicollet avenues. Mankato author Maud Hart Lovelace, who incorporated many aspects of the town's life into her books for children, called the southern settlement "Little Syria," describing it as a "strange wide beautiful valley" with "one big brick house and a row of tiny houses in the center." It was also called Tinkcomville for the American who lived in the big house and sold lots to the Syrians.[13]

During the second decade of the 20th century Crookston's Lebanese lived and had their stores either in the small section of town between the Red Lake River and the Great Northern Railroad tracks or on North Main and North Broadway. Between 1915 and 1979 their numbers decreased as many migrated to St. Paul, often becoming members of the Maronite church there. Before making that move permanently, a Crookston railroad worker "used his railroad pass often to come to St. Paul just to hear a Maronite Mass." At least one member of the St. Paul community went in 1924 to Crookston — rather than to Lebanon — to find a wife.[14]

Syrian and Lebanese Occupations

Like their countrymen all over the United States, many Minnesota Syrians became peddlers. The New York publishers of the 1938–39 *Syrian Business Directory* introduced their useful volume with a paean to the entrepreneurial spirit of the group. Alluding to those great maritime traders, the Phoenicians, from whom Syrians claim descent, the directory noted that American Syrians shared "their commercial inclination and instinct."[15]

Peddling was not a common Lebanese occupation in the Old Country, where it was more often practiced by Greeks, Armenians, and Jews. Nevertheless before 1914 some 90% of Syrian immigrants, including women and children, took up the work in the United States, at least for a short time. It was an ideal trade for immigrants; the profits were good and little training or command of English was needed. Communities formed around a supplier like Mike Henne in Minneapolis or George Toby in St. Paul, who provisioned varying numbers of salespeople. The peddlers, however, were independent; they could find other suppliers or become suppliers themselves in another town.[16]

"Initially a trade in rosaries, jewelry, and notions that would fit into a small case," peddling gradually expanded. Its practitioners had a high success rate, and a network of routes developed all over the United States. Some traveled over large areas, but most women and children, as well as older people, remained within range of their homes to which they returned in the evening. Peddling made a degree of acculturation both necessary and relatively easy. Learning English and accumulating capital were frequent results, as

was permanent settlement in the United States. Most former peddlers opened family businesses, often grocery or dry-goods stores in cities or small towns.

Although peddlers could be found at times in all the Minnesota towns noted above, St. Paul, Minneapolis, and Mankato apparently were the major centers of that activity. From St. Paul, they took their goods to Wisconsin as well as to Minnesota towns and farms. Mankato became home base for traveling salespeople who covered southern Minnesota, the Dakotas, and northern Iowa.[17]

A Mankato peddlers' supply store, opened by Charles Ramy in 1916 in Little Syria, carried Lebanese foods as well as supplies. At its peak it provisioned as many as 100 traveling salesfolk, who sold underwear and overalls among other things. At first they went by train with packs on their backs; later they used horses and buggies.

The first Syrians in St. Paul were peddlers who had worked for a time in Chicago before heading north in search of an area with less competition. Carrying rosaries to prove they were Christians and selling goods along the way, they eventually reached St. Paul, where business proved good. In 1889 George Toby opened a wholesale supply shop which carried linens, laces, and brasses in addition to more usual dry goods. From it each peddler, "fitted with a wooden box slung across his back by means of a leather belt and filled with trinkets and household necessities," was "sent out into the rural areas." Many Minneapolis peddlers got their supplies, as well as bed and board when they were in town, at Mike Henne's stores in Northeast Minneapolis.[18]

Women also became peddlers. While one St. Paul woman's husband worked for the Great Western Railroad, she took the train to Wisconsin and peddled from farm to farm. Her work, she recalled, allowed her to enjoy the countryside and learn about American life as she earned money to send to the children she had left in Lebanon. Defending the preference of Syrian women for peddling, Louise Houghton pointed out in 1911 that it was more appealing than factory work. "Why should she give up the open air, the broad sky, the song of the birds . . . to immerse herself within four noisy walls and be subject to the strict regime of the clock?" asked Houghton. "Why should she who has been . . . her own person, become a mere 'hand'?" In Mankato Hasna Jabbra and her husband crocheted lace collars which she peddled in the Dakotas during the years before she had children. For several weeks at a time Mrs. Jabbra traveled alone on the train, stopping in towns along her route.[19]

Smaller communities also had Syrian peddlers. In 1918 a 57-year-old woman marked her 14th year of peddling from a home base at Tower. Moorhead and Crookston too had a few peddlers in that year. A woman in northwestern Minnesota's Kittson County recalled that "A Syrian peddler . . . came once a year with his horse-drawn tall skinny green wagon with enclosed cab." A Muslim who peddled in Lincoln County in southwestern Minnesota, was described as "short, fat, round-faced and jolly." He "did not own a tape measure. A yard to him was the distance from the tip of his outstretched right arm to the . . . end of his nose, turned generously to the left. He kept no written records and his customers' accounts were kept in his head."[20]

MUSLIM PEDDLER Moham-med Ali Shami posed in his horse-drawn wagon at a south-western Minnesota farm on his regular route about 1900.

Although many Minnesota Lebanese got their start by peddling, it was not considered a permanent job for either men or women. An excellent example of the changes in Syrian occupational patterns may be seen in St. Paul between 1895 and 1905. In the earlier year three dry-goods stores, two confectioners, and two peddlers' suppliers provided the commercial base for the 49 peddlers, two laborers, and one shoemaker who comprised the employed Syrian population. Ten years later the total number of stores had decreased to four, there were 34 peddlers, and the community included some 200 laborers, an organ grinder, two farmers, a dress-maker, a seamstress, and a cook.[21]

One man whose experience provided a capsule summary of Syrian work patterns was a former Lebanese sponge diver who peddled out of Mankato and St. Paul before opening a confectionery in the latter city. In 1900 he and his family bought a farm near Annandale, but after five years they returned to St. Paul to open another confectionery. After it failed he found a job in the Swift & Company packing plant, and his wife became midwife to the Syrian community. Eventually they opened a successful grocery store, which they operated until his death.[22]

Even before 1920 Syrians in the larger communities became railroad workers, laborers in factories such as the American Hoist and Derrick Company and the Villaume Box Company in St. Paul, the B. F. Nelson Company in Minneapolis, and the Clyde Iron Works and Duluth Boiler Shop in Duluth. Several towns boasted such skilled workers as barbers, butchers, members of building trades, and cigar-makers, to list a few. Other Syrians worked as clerks or opened billiard parlors or small shops to sell groceries, dry goods, or confectionery. At Mankato some worked in local quarries; on the Mesabi Range they were miners as well as timberworkers.[23]

Employment for women also varied in the second decade of the 20th century. A young widow in West St. Paul listed "going out washing" as her occupation, while an unmarried woman operated "a large embroidery establishment" employing "American workers" from at least 1911 to 1914. But Crookston in 1918 offered the most vivid picture of the working lives of Syrian women. One, aged 18, lived with her parents and had a job as an ironer in a local laundry, where she earned $6.50 a week for 52 hours of work. A second teenager received $5.00 a week for 98 hours of washing dishes in a local hotel restaurant. Another woman supported her family by ironing 54 hours a week for $7.00, while a night cook put in 84 hours for about $9.00.[24]

Many Syrians who retired from peddling either bought a farm or opened a small shop with the money they had saved. A number of businesses started in this way remained in the family for two generations or more. In 1938 Northeast Minneapolis had four Syrian dry-goods establishments and five grocery stores. In addition pioneer Mike Henne still operated his establishment on Marshall Avenue. In Mankato Charles Ramy opened a downtown dry-goods store in 1920. His daughters ran it after he retired, and his son started the Ramy Seed Company, which he in turn planned to pass on to his sons.[25]

In Duluth the business headed in 1917 by Joseph Bourestom, a linen importer, was still conducted by the Bourestom family in the 1970s. The city in 1917 also had several Syrian-owned grocery stores and a billiard parlor. By the 1930s two Lebanese were operating fruit and confectionery stores, two were grocers, and one sold Oriental goods. In Virginia there were two Syrian-run dry-goods establishments at that time.[26]

In the Red River Valley Syrians ran at least two dry-goods shops and two grocery stores in Crookston in 1915, and the co-owners of one dry-goods store were Muslims who apparently did not stay in the area. Syrian merchants at Moorhead in 1918 included a clothing store operator and two pool hall owners. In the Norman County town of Shelly lived a Syrian-born man who married a Scandinavian-surnamed woman and ran a dry-goods store for some years. Later he owned and operated the Damascus Hotel and Restaurant until it burned in 1945. Some of his children remained in the area in the 1970s.[27]

Similarly Ahmed Abdallah Melouhay, a Muslim, arrived in Minnesota about 1900. After spending some time in Mankato, he moved to Minneapolis, where he married a Swedish-American woman and changed his name to Albert Abdallah. The couple parlayed a store at Lake Street and Hennepin Avenue — an emporium of ice cream, candy, fresh flowers, fruits, and cigars — into the Abdallah Candy Company, which was in 1980 in its third generation of family ownership.[28]

By 1913, however, a national Arabic-language publication claimed that most of the state's 2,000 Syrians were successful farmers, having moved from devoting all their time to peddling to dividing their energies between peddling and agriculture, and finally giving up peddling to farm full time. Local sources, however, have offered scant support for the publication's claim that Minnesota was "the distributing point of the Syrian farmers in the West." Only scattered examples of Syrian farmers have been found.[29]

Among them were couples who farmed in southeastern Minnesota near Mazeppa in Wabasha County and Carimona and Preston in Fillmore County. In western Minnesota perhaps some of the Syrian families who were members of Most Holy Redeemer Roman Catholic Church in Marshall, Lyon County, in 1949 were farmers. Floodwood in St. Louis County attracted at least one Syrian family in 1907 who farmed there for 11 years or more, and Syrians also farmed in the vicinities of Mankato, Minneapolis, and St. Paul — locations which allowed them more contact with countrymen in the cities. As late as the 1960s a Maronite family lived near Mound, where they raised pigs, chickens, and cattle, and ran two stores in town. They attended holiday services twice a year at St. Maron's Church in Minneapolis.[30]

Religion

Religion was among the factors which both united and divided the Syrian-Lebanese community, which organized Maronite Catholic and Syrian Orthodox churches only in the Twin Cities. Lebanese in Mankato and Marshall joined local Roman Catholic parishes, and some farmers who settled in heavily Scandinavian areas became Lutherans. Such differing religious affiliations, while divisive, by no means accounted for all of the church-related disputes that occurred, especially in the Twin Cities communities.[31]

St. Maron's Church, organized in 1906, met first in a Northeast Minneapolis home. The number of members rose from 100 in 1906 to 450 in 1948, which may have been a peak period. Of the parish's eight clubs in existence in 1949, one remained in the mid-1960s, when only 125 of the estimated 560 Maronites in Minneapolis attended services. The church that was in use in 1980 was built in the 1940s at 602 University Avenue Northeast.[32]

Between 1900 and 1915 St. Paul's Maronites joined Irish

MIDDLE EASTERN congregations in the Twin Cities in 1980 included St. Maron's in Minneapolis at bottom center and Holy Family in St. Paul at left, both Maronite Catholic. St. Mary's at right and St. George at top center, in St. Paul and West St. Paul, respectively, are both Antiochian Orthodox.

Roman Catholics at St. Michael's Church on the West Side instead of making the long trip to St. Maron's in Northeast Minneapolis. After 1913 the pastor of St. Michael's invited the priest of St. Maron's to conduct Mass each Saturday night until enough money was collected to buy a church building at Ada and East Robie.[33]

About 1915 the 300 parishioners in St. Paul organized the Church of the Holy Family, which followed the Maronite rite in the Arabic and Syriac languages. In 1936 the Mass was still said in Syriac, but the language of the spoken service was changed from Arabic to English "for the benefit of the younger people." By then the membership totaled 700. In the 1950s only some 65 families belonged to the church. Early divisions in the community had so thoroughly alienated some pioneers from Holy Family that their descendants never rejoined it. Difficulties there and in Minneapolis arose from two types of problems: village loyalties differed and the traditional policies of Old Country priests sometimes clashed with an Americanized congregation. One scholar blamed the priests for creating problems in Lebanese communities. "Often overzealous and poorly educated, the immigrant clergy helped transplant sectarian and religious factionalism to the New World," she wrote.

St. George Syrian Orthodox Church was organized in 1913 on St. Paul's West Side and moved in 1973 to West St. Paul when the upkeep of its old building became a problem and many of its members had left the neighborhood. Between 1913 and 1917 the congregation met in a hall on the second floor of a store owned by charter member George Toby at 26–28 East Chicago. In the latter year the 75 members bought an Episcopal church at Clinton and Isabel streets near their homes. Although the members spoke Arabic, the languages used in the service were Syriac and Greek.[34]

By the mid-1930s their number had grown to 170 and their cultural and social needs were met by events like the one reported in 1932. Lamese Hamati, daughter of the pastor, had organized an entertainment and dance for the benefit of the church. A one-act play, "The Rich Economist," was performed in Arabic along with musical selections in English and Arabic; the dance followed. By 1969 the congregation had decided to drop Arabic because many members were lost after an earlier refusal to do so. In 1980 St. George had some 45 families and several affiliated organizations, including an Arabic dance group.

In 1952 conflicts at St. George caused the priest to depart for newly organized St. Mary Antiochian Orthodox Church, also on the West Side. St. Mary's congregation purchased a church building and furnished it with art work and religious artifacts from Athens, Damascus, and Jerusalem. Most of the parishioners in 1980 were American-born Syrians, Lebanese, Palestinians, and Egyptians whose spouses represented many ethnic backgrounds, including Swedes and Germans.[35]

The lack of connections, not to say hostility, between Maronites and Orthodox was pointed up in the 1950s when the International Institute's attempt to combine them for participation in the Festival of Nations was a resounding failure. The president of the St. George women's organization explained that the Maronite "group use[d] to do things at the Institute[,] then the Orthodox group got involved. At the last Festival[,] since the two groups had the one booth and they were not able to work together[,] they split the days so one group had two days and the other group took two days."[36] Orthodox and Maronite women clearly saw the groups as separate entities as late as 1980.

Acculturation

While making some adjustments to life in Minnesota, Syrians and Lebanese retained for differing lengths of time a variety of customs and traditions, the Arabic language, and concern for the Old Country and friends and relatives there. The processes by which change occurs in an ethnic community are not always apparent to those who can only observe the results and read or hear about the way it used to be, but the host culture, for reasons of its own, sometimes sets up institutions to promote certain kinds of change, like Americanization. Many Syrians and Lebanese, for instance, changed their names as soon as they arrived in the United States, often under pressure from immigration officials. Thus early members of Holy Family "Hawash Youssef Saad became Howard Joseph; Shedid el Khatiar changed his name to John Thomas; Youssef George Abou Antionious became known as Joseph George; Eissa Daoud was translated to Isaac David; George Bishara Tannous became George Thomas."[37]

St. Paul's West Side Neighborhood House was one local institution concerned with Americanizing Syrians and others between about 1904 and 1936. In the latter year, some 70 Syrian families composed of 380 people made up 6% to 7% of the area's population, both on the flats and on the hills. Syrian men and boys joined night classes in English and citizenship held at the center in 1904. During World War I West Side Syrians apparently rallied patriotically; in 1917 more than 100 men and women attended a loyalty meeting with a Syrian speaker.[38]

Minneapolitans, who also busied themselves propounding the Americanization gospel, noted in 1920 that Syrians had the highest percentage of their group (along with Italians) in school and home Americanization classes. In 1931 it was Syrian women who most often showed up in English classes for foreign women at the North East Neighborhood House.

SYRIAN WOMEN baked and served cakes and coffee at an early St. Paul Festival of Nations in 1934.

Later in the 1930s the Syrian Dramatic Club was active there.[39]

In some ways Mankato's Lebanese acquiesced in their Americanization promptly and willingly. They attended Roman Catholic churches and some sent their children to parochial schools. Many learned English in night school classes organized by local townswomen. One second-generation man reported that "most of the Lebanese then became citizens as soon as they could learn enough to become citizens."[40]

Change, of which Americanization was only a part, occurred within the Syrian and Lebanese communities as it did within all of Minnesota's ethnic groups. In Minneapolis a number of educated Lebanese taught their countrymen English and the second generation Arabic, and tried to publicize important issues in the homeland. Solomon David, who immigrated to the city in 1909, organized the American Syrian Moral Revolutionary Association through which Minneapolis and St. Paul Lebanese were to fight Turkish rule of the Middle East. In connection with that organization, David published the semiweekly Arabic-language *Al-Omma* (Nation) for a few years in Minneapolis beginning in 1915. He taught English at the International Bible College near the University of Minnesota and later became a doctor. In 1923 David's fellow publisher, E. George Joseph, started an Arabic school with an enrollment of 75 children. Three years later, with the number of pupils reduced to seven, the school closed.[41] Probably the small size of the community, as well as the internecine strife that plagued the parishes, doomed both the paper and the school.

Responses to questions asked of Twin Cities Lebanese in the 1970s revealed how far change had proceeded, as well as what traits had been retained, and gave some idea of Lebanese-American ethnicity at that time. Naming the ethnic group to which one belonged was, in the case of these people, a revealing procedure. More than two-thirds of the respondents in all three generations considered themselves Lebanese Americans, while few of any generation identified themselves as Arabs or Arab Americans.[42]

Nearly 60% of the first generation had returned to the Old Country to visit relatives. Just over 30% and just under 12% of the second and third generations, respectively, had also visited the homeland. The first generation suffered from the divided-heart syndrome common to most immigrants. America was to them "the best country in the world," but Lebanon was in their hearts "like yeast." Their grandchildren had made the usual shift to being primarily Americans while retaining pride in their heritage.

Changes in women's roles were also apparent. A preference for large families dwindled from over 80% in the first generation to just over 21% in the third. Several second-generation women felt strongly "the crunch of divergent cultural attitudes" about dating, in which they were less free than their non-Lebanese friends because their parents would not permit them to go out without a chaperone. The subordination of wife to husband in a marriage was considered appropriate by half of the first-generation respondents, 30% of the second, and less than 10% of the third. Nevertheless almost two-thirds of the second generation "approved of the traditional division of roles giving the father supreme authority concerning important family matters and decisions."

Many of the immigrants were illiterate in Arabic and never learned to read or write English, but a sample of St. Paul members of the first generation in the 1970s showed that three-fourths had become fluent in speaking English. More than two-thirds of the second generation surveyed could speak Arabic at least fairly well, but the third generation knew very little of the language.

Food was another important aspect of ethnic culture and one which continued to play a vital role in the Twin Cities communities in the 1980s. Nearly three-fourths of the Lebanese of all three generations queried in the 1970s preferred Lebanese food, but its consumption was reserved for Sundays and special occasions because of the time required to prepare it. Many families ate Lebanese bread with every meal, however; first-generation women baked their own and others bought it at Lebanese grocery stores. At the annual dinners sponsored by each of the churches, Lebanese food was always served, with *kibbee* ("ground meat mixed with cracked wheat and spices, kneaded thoroughly, then baked or fried") a star item on the menu.

Interest in Arabic music and dancing remained strong in the 1970s, at least in the Twin Cities, though it was for the most part first-generation members who preferred Arabic music over other types. Social functions attended by large numbers of Lebanese rarely ended without a *dabke* (circle dance) performance.

First-generation Lebanese continued in the 1970s their Old Country patterns of leisure activities, including visiting friends and relatives and, among the women, baking, knitting, crocheting, and sewing. A researcher noted that "Some of them excelled at needlework and were proud to display their masterpieces fashioned according to typical old country designs; those craft skills are extinct among the younger generations." Friendships were extensive outside the ethnic community for all three generations, but most first-generation people reserved more close friendships for members of their ethnic church than did the second and third generations.

About the Mankato community Lovelace wrote that in the early 20th century the families of Little Syria raised goats and vegetables and that their children, who "still dressed in the old country way, girls in long skirts, earrings, with scarfed heads," attended the Catholic school on the other side of town. Describing the interior of one of the small houses, she noted the grandfather smoking a *narghile* or hubble-bubble pipe and the grandmother pounding lamb for *kibbee*. In other homes there were "women baking flat round loaves of bread" and "a boy playing a long reed flute [called] a munjaira."[43]

As Lovelace's books suggest, Mankato, a town made up largely of people of northern and western European extraction, apparently viewed its Lebanese community as exotic in the early years, in part because of their fights. One second-generation man remembered that "They sort of fought each other in loud voices because that was their old country style." Some fights were reported in the newspaper in 1901 under such lurid headlines as "Abdul Invades the Land of

Buschana'' and "Bunch of Assyrians Have a High Old Time Last Evening.'' The stories hinted at division and rivalry within the community and noted that arrests sometimes occurred when fighters crossed the line from verbal to physical violence.[44]

Accounts of those who grew up in the community indicated that many Lebanese customs were retained as late as the 1960s. Weddings lasted from three to five days, and at funerals friends and relatives "shared the deaths,'' taking the body home and crying over it for four days before the burial. Easter customs of colored eggs and visiting were also followed by many families. In some households both coffee and liquor were special treats for Christmas and Easter.[45]

For such small communities, the low number of marriages outside the group by first-generation Lebanese in the Twin Cities and Mankato was remarkable. The acceptance of arranged marriages probably accounted for the phenomenon. A man who had left the West Coast for St. Paul in 1919 to marry a woman his parents had selected from a family who had been their neighbors in the Old Country noted that "in those days it was a shame to marry somebody from another nationality.'' Minneapolis peddler Sadie Jacobs had to refuse a German woman on her peddling route who wanted Sadie to marry her son; Sadie's marriage had already been arranged "by her mother and sister with an immigrant from her own village of Bijdarfel.''[46]

Like most of those in the Twin Cities, first-generation Mankato Lebanese queried in the late 1950s had married other Lebanese Americans. By the second generation, however, only a third of those who had married chose spouses from within the group. Some of the city's estimated 30 Lebanese families in 1978 also maintained contact with fellow Lebanese Americans, most notably at an annual get-together in Sioux City, Iowa. Called a *mahrajan* (picnic), the party was a way "to keep them close together,'' explained one, "in case they want to see each other, that they might want to marry one of them, you know what I mean, otherwise there would be no contact.'' A three- or four-day event, it often featured entertainment by Danny Thomas or some other prominent Lebanese American.[47]

Lebanese traditions were strengthened by the arrival of new immigrants. Though some Mankato Lebanese departed to settle elsewhere, new immigrants from Lebanon continued to arrive. One second-generation man helped 18 or 19 people to settle in Mankato during the years between the 1920s and 1978. Some did not like it and returned home, but others stayed. In the late 1970s many Mankato Lebanese had Old Country relatives whom they visited and who comprised a pool of potential immigrants, especially in view of the troubles in Lebanon at that time.[48]

As was true in Mankato, a few new immigrants continued to arrive in St. Paul, joining relatives and friends, for instance, during the post-World War II period. A 1955 arrival lived with his cousins temporarily and eventually married a St. Paul woman. A man who immigrated in 1961 at the request of his St. Paul grandmother followed a similar pattern. By 1968 six postwar immigrants had joined the Church of the Holy Family.[49]

In 1980 a journalist who grew up in St. Paul's Lebanese

JOSEPH'S MARKET on St. Paul's West Side was one of several Lebanese-run grocery stores which catered to both Lebanese and Mexicans in the 1980s. The Lebanese flag, with its symbolic cedar tree, decorates the top of the building, and the American flag is painted on the side.

community tied together the Lebanese and the Americanizing experiences of life there: "In a way, the West Side has been like a little Lebanon for my parents. There are many Lebanese . . . and most of them attend the same church. . . . We hold ethnic dances, complete with a three-piece Lebanese band; church dinners, with everything from Lebanese bread to cabbage rolls; social clubs for youth and adults, and summertime picnics.'' On the other hand, the reporter believed that West Siders of whatever ethnic group — Lebanese, Mexican, Irish, Italian, or German — also shared a common neighborhood culture, one derived from "experiencing floods, urban renewal, stickball and backyard barbecues'' together.[50]

The Minneapolis Lebanese community's development closely paralleled that of St. Paul, though by the 1970s, at least, there seemed to be little organized contact between them. Members of the two groups attended the annual dinners sponsored by each of the churches, and they raised funds jointly for the noncontroversial and humanitarian St. Jude's Hospital, founded by Danny Thomas, but there seemed to be little other direct interaction.[51]

Political activity beyond a high voter turnout has been most apparent in Minnesota's Lebanese communities in recent years, when Northeast Minneapolis, for example, elected a Lebanese-American alderman in the 1960s and St. Paul and Mankato both had mayors of Lebanese extraction in 1980. All were members of the Democratic-Farmer-Labor party, reflecting the tendency of the first two generations of the state's Lebanese to vote Democratic. More of the third generation called themselves independents. Lebanese Americans Gerald D. Isaacs and George Latimer were both active in the city's DFL party in the 1970s. A political rally organized by Isaacs and held at Latimer's home in 1975 was followed by "a typical Lebanese meal with 'mezze' (elaborate Lebanese hors d'oeuvres), ice cream served in camel and cedar shaped molds and entertainment by an Arabic dance group from the Orthodox community."[52]

In 1976 the two ran against each other in the party's primary for mayor of St. Paul. Latimer, an attorney and University of Minnesota regent before his election, later characterized himself as "kind of an entrepreneur at heart, kind of a Lebanese tradesman really." His parents had owned a "4-by-4 grocery store" in Schenectady, New York, where he had waited on customers from the time he was eight years old.[53]

Along with participation in local government, political issues in the Old Country became important to Minnesota Lebanese in the 1960s and 1970s. Former Minneapolis alderman Donald P. Risk organized fund-raisers where Lebanese-American Senator James G. Abourezk, a South Dakota Democrat, was invited to speak about Middle East issues in hopes of conveying more accurate information than regular media sources provided and arousing the interest and concern of Twin Cities people of Middle Eastern descent. By 1978 the civil war in Lebanon provoked action from some St. Paul Lebanese in co-operation with local Jewish organizations. Two St. Paul Lebanese Americans spoke at the Jewish Community Center there, claiming that the first Lebanese rally in the United States had been held in the city on August 16 of that year. The reaction to the Syrian attack on Lebanon in July, 1978, had been one of anger in the Lebanese-American community, and participants in the march and rally urged the replacement of Syrian troops in Lebanon with United Nations forces. Members of both Maronite parishes joined some Protestant Lebanese in supporting these activities. Mankato Lebanese also had strong opinions about the situation in Lebanon. As early as 1976 Lebanese-American mayor Herbert Mocol announced that the community was making efforts "to help the victims of Lebanon's 15-month-old civil war."[54]

The American Lebanese Action Committee of Minnesota, also initiated in St. Paul, supported a blood drive for Lebanon and raised funds for medicine and long-range aid to war victims there. During this effort Minnesota Lebanese, including social organizations in Mankato and Crookston which traditionally supported scholarships, worked for the first time with two national groups, the Lebanese Research and Information Center and the American Lebanese League. That interest and concern continued could be seen in the annual St. Paul sales of Lebanese foods to raise money for the American Lebanese Association of Minnesota on behalf of Lebanese refugees in Lebanon. These began in 1979 and continued through 1981.

ARMENIANS

Armenians, another people with ancient roots in the Middle East (see Map 27.1), settled in Minnesota in far smaller numbers than the Lebanese. Also subjects of the Ottoman Empire, the Christian Armenians' centuries-old accommodation with the Muslim Turks disintegrated as the empire crumbled and Armenian nationalism grew. Their problems reached tragic proportions between 1894 and World War I

when the Turks killed more than a million Armenians in a series of massacres.[55]

By the late 1880s some 1,500 Armenians had emigrated to the United States, often encouraged by American missionaries. Between 1899 and 1910 only 51,950 Armenians, mostly young, single men, immigrated. Post-World War I migration, which began in 1919, saw 730,000 survivors of the massacres (52% women, 21% children) reach the United States before the quota system provided for in the Immigration Act of 1924 cut off the flow of survivors.

Between World War II and 1965 approximately 13,000 Armenians entered the United States, 4,500 of them as Displaced Persons from 1948 to 1952. Following passage of the Immigration and Nationality Act, which lifted quotas in 1965, more arrived, having escaped not only from Turkey but also from several other countries to which they had fled after the Turkish massacres. In the mid-1970s the Armenian-American community numbered between 350,000 and 450,000, with 45% living in East Coast states and 25% in California. Of the 15% residing in the Midwest, only a few had settled in Minnesota. As late as 1980 some 2,000 Armenians, mostly young and well educated, entered the United States yearly from various countries.

Many early immigrants were skilled as well as literate, but they had no money. Thus they began life in the New World as numerous other immigrants did — by taking jobs in mills and factories. There were few women among the early arrivals, but they, too, often worked in the garment industries. The Armenians achieved economic mobility most often by opening small shops as soon as they had saved the necessary capital. Selling Oriental rugs worked well for some because their Old Country knowledge kept pace with the widespread interest in such carpets in Victorian America.

Although men greatly outnumbered women, intermarriage with members of other groups was rare in the immigrant generation. Social assimilation, especially by the third generation, led to changes in marriage patterns as well as in other Old Country codes. Nevertheless Old Country politics and, more importantly, the church contributed to the retention of Armenian-American ethnicity. Vital parts of cultural and group maintenance included language, literature (especially fiction), music, dance, food, and, more recently, visits to Soviet Armenia.

Statistics on Armenians in Minnesota are spotty at best (see Table 27.4). So few Armenians immigrated to the state that it is difficult to discern a meaningful pattern in their settlement. They began arriving in St. Paul during the 1890s and often took up entrepreneurial occupations, most notably the carpet business, both there and in Minneapolis. Between

Table 27.4. Armenian Speakers in Minnesota, 1910–60

	foreign born	foreign stock*
1910	235	268
1920	177	213
1930	92	
1940	20	60
1960	56	

Source: Mother-tongue statistics in U.S., *Census,* for the years listed.
*Foreign stock includes foreign born and native born of foreign or mixed parentage.

1899 and 1917 only 67 Armenians planned to go to Minnesota when they landed in the United States. The only place in the state with more than 100 Armenians in 1919 was St. Paul. The next year Minneapolis counted some 50 Armenian born. By 1944 a national survey found only 100 Minnesota Armenians living primarily in the Twin Cities and Duluth; five years later an estimate of 200 in the Twin Cities alone was bandied about, but by 1958 the total had dwindled to 200 for the entire state. In 1981 there were an estimated 200 Minnesota households in which one or more adults were of Armenian birth or descent.[56]

Awareness of the early arrivals by the larger society increased with publicity about the massacres of Armenians in Turkey, which stimulated the formation of a number of relief organizations. In fact, the only formal Minnesota organizations for Armenian relief in the post-World War I period were groups apparently set up and run by non-Armenians. St. Paul and Minneapolis had Armenian and Syrian relief committees in 1917 and 1918, respectively. Thereafter the committees may have merged, for in 1919 the organization's name was changed to Near East Relief. The lack of formal organizations did not mean, however, that the community was inactive. A Minnesota-born Armenian recalled that in 1917 and 1918 some 40 to 45 Armenians met in a downtown St. Paul hall to raise money for survivors of the massacres. A social worker later noted that "During World War I the relief needs of Armenian orphans united [the St. Paul Armenians] in effort with the . . . colony in Minneapolis."[57]

Most Armenian men in the Twin Cities belonged to one of two political factions concerned with the fate of the homeland after the short-lived Armenian republic formed in 1918 became part of the Union of Soviet Socialist Republics two years later. The Tashnags were radicals who wanted to fight for an independent Armenia; the Ramgavars, whom the Tashnags accused of being pro-Communist, accepted the status quo on the theory that it could be worse and probably never would be better. A local Tashnag women's auxiliary later became an Armenian Red Cross group which held raffles and dances to raise money for Armenian causes.[58]

Armenian occupational patterns were diverse. A 1918 sample of some St. Paul wards reported seven Armenians, among them two families and two sets of brothers. One set included a repairer of Oriental rugs. Two brothers farmed 10 acres at Como and East Phalen avenues, and another man owned and operated the Capital Lunch on Wabasha Street.[59]

A Minneapolis sample during the same year counted 18 men, all single or with families in the Middle East, and a single woman who was a dressmaker in Dayton's department store. Again, only one of the men worked with carpets; the others were laborers, with a sprinkling of salesmen (two of whom sold popcorn), two billiard hall owners, a French instructor, and the house manager at Eitel Hospital. Eight of them lived at 250 Hennepin Avenue. Beginning in the 1920s three Minneapolis Armenians ran a combined Oriental Carpet Company and Armenian Rug Laundry on Hennepin Avenue; by 1940 neither remained in business. St. Paul counted both the Persian Rug Cleaning Company, Arsene Nakashian, proprietor, on Selby Avenue, and Krikor A. Keljik's Oriental Carpet Cleaning Company on Grand Avenue in 1917.

A daughter of an immigrant who started out in the rug business in St. Paul observed that Armenians in the Twin Cities tried to keep a low profile, exhorting their children to be "good people" so that Americans would like and accept them. They were frequently mistaken for Jews, Yugoslavs, or Greeks. The second generation, few of whom learned

MUSIC AND WINE contributed to the conviviality at this Armenian picnic about 1916 in St. Paul. Several of the men shown later fought in the Armenian Revolutionary Forces in the Russian Army during World War I to free Armenia from the Turks.

their parents' language, were often self-consciously aware that the foods they ate were different from those of the larger community. Okra, eggplant, yogurt, and bulgur were regular fare, along with pistachio nuts at Christmas and shish kebob grilled by the men over slow charcoal fires at community picnics. (Roasting meat was the only cooking chore performed by men.) Another second-generation St. Paul Armenian recalled seeing older Armenian women picking grape leaves on the east side of the High Bridge. They stuffed the leaves with meat, spices, and rice to make *dolma*.[60]

By necessity Minnesota Armenians associated with non-Armenians much of the time, but social events within the community pointed up the "we versus them" feelings of the immigrant group: a second-generation informant remembered that being with other Armenians was like being in a large family. St. Paul Armenians got together at picnics and other informal gatherings. They had no church, no coffee-house, no common neighborhood, although three or four families lived near their Selby Avenue businesses for a time. Representing varying religious persuasions, they attended infrequent Armenian Apostolic Masses performed by visiting priests. They often waited for those occasions to have their children baptized. Despite their small numbers, however, Armenians often sang, danced, and exhibited rugs and mementoes of their homeland in the triennial Festivals of Nations sponsored by St. Paul's International Institute, including a very early one in 1934.

Beginning in the mid-1950s, growing Arab nationalism in the Middle East drove Armenians from Egypt, Lebanon, Syria, Iraq, and Iran. Those who settled in Minnesota were for the most part professionals, including trained medical workers and scientists. The half-dozen Armenian families who arrived in the state from Iran in the late 1970s were only the latest example in the postwar pattern of flight from Islamification in various Middle Eastern countries. Some who tried life in Minnesota remained in the state, while others moved on to California.[61]

Some American-born Armenians regarded the newcomers with interest because they had retained their culture while living in the Middle East but outside the remnants of historic Armenia. The American Armenians, in contrast, felt that they had assimilated quickly and rather thoroughly, retaining for the most part only an interest in their heritage rather than a determination to continue it.

Clubs and societies in later years were few. Until 1979 an Armenian Student Organization existed intermittently at the University of Minnesota. In February, 1980, members of the Twin Cities community formed the Armenian Cultural Organization of Minnesota to foster interest in their heritage by sponsoring classes in cooking, dancing, history, and language, lectures on Armenian subjects, and concerts by Armenian-American musicians.

MUSLIM ARABS AND OTHERS

Other organized groups of Middle Eastern peoples in Minnesota included the predominantly Muslim Arabs, Turks, Afghans, and Iranians, the last also counting some followers of the Bahai religion. Most Egyptians in the state were

Arabs, but some were members of a tightly knit community of Coptic Christians. The number of Muslims was not large, either nationally or in Minnesota. Most of those in the state arrived after 1970; by 1980 a majority probably lived in the Twin Cities. Nationally Muslims totaled from 200,000 to 300,000, or about 1% of the population, in 1980. Like Christians, these followers of the prophet Mohammed are divided into a number of sects, the largest of which are the Sunni and the Shiite.[62]

The state's only Islamic place of worship in 1980 was the Islamic Center of Minnesota in the Minneapolis suburb of Columbia Heights. Members of all the Middle Eastern groups discussed in this chapter (except the Armenians and the other Christians) and scattered others joined Indians and Pakistanis as members. Some 80% were Sunnis, with most of the rest Shiites. Started in 1967 near the University of Minnesota in Minneapolis, where most of its early members were Middle Eastern or South Asian graduate students, the center counted 350 families in 1979. To make attendance easier the day of prayer was changed from the traditional Friday to Sunday. In addition to providing a place to worship, the center offered Sunday school and Arabic-language classes. Though few of its members were Iranian, the organization in 1979–81 suffered from American anger at Iran, where Muslim militants held American embassy personnel captive for 14 months. Vandals damaged the Columbia Heights center by throwing eggs and rocks.[63]

One Minneapolis Palestinian Muslim expressed concern about being a member of such a small religious community in the American environment in 1979. "It's very hard for our kids, living in the suburbs where everyone is blond and blue-eyed and Protestant," she said. "It's hard to be different. Their names are different, their religion, their background at home, their food."

Other organizations of Muslims in existence in the 1970s were the Islamic Cultural Society and the Women's Islamic Society, which met at the International Institute in St. Paul. Their purposes were "to promote and publicize Islamic culture and thus gain recognition for Islam in the American society . . . to promote Islamic educational and cultural activities among Muslim group members and the Twin City community." The Muslim Student Association at the University of Minnesota sponsored Friday prayers at noon in Coffman Union. One of the smaller Islamic sects was separately organized as the Shia Imami Ismalia Association in Minneapolis.

Associations among the state's Middle Easterners appeared to follow primarily religious lines. Egyptian Muslims joined with other Muslims; Egyptian Coptic Christians organized separately. Iranians of the Bahai faith associated with American Bahais rather than with other Iranians. An immigrating Maronite Catholic or Orthodox believer might join one of the Twin Cities churches of those denominations, but other connections between old and new immigrants from the Middle East seemed to be restricted to third-generation Lebanese Americans who participated in such groups as the Association of Arab-American University Graduates (AAUG), discussed below.

The word "Arab" was often used in 1980 to denote a

variety of people in and from the Middle East and North Africa, though it usually excluded Armenians, Coptic Christians, Afghans, Iranians, and Turks. It had a limited usefulness when applied to Middle Easterners and their descendants in the Twin Cities. In the past the term implied adherence to Islam as well as identification with nonreligious aspects of culture such as language, so Lebanese Christians, for example, did not use it to describe themselves. After World War II, however, Christians in the Middle East came to regard themselves as Arabs and helped to stimulate a growing Arab nationalism there.[64]

One result was ambiguous usage of the term in the United States, where not only Arabic-speaking student groups were referred to as Arab organizations, but also some third-generation descendants of Christian Syrian and Lebanese immigrants began to identify themselves as Arab Americans, while most of the rest of that community resisted such a label. Armed with the idea that they were Arabs, young American-born Lebanese founded the AAUG in 1967, primarily for professional people of Arabic-speaking descent. Explicitly nonsectarian and nonpolitical, the organization's declared purpose was to promote "knowledge and understanding of cultural, scientific, and educational matters" between Canada and the United States on the one hand and Arabic-speaking countries on the other.[65]

Its desire to "enhance the appreciation of the values of the Arabic-speaking countries in the United States and vice versa" led it, however, to deal with issues many regarded as political, such as the question of a homeland for Palestinian refugees in the Middle East. In 1972 the 1,000-member national organization praised Middle Eastern guerrillas, "accused Arab governments of hypocrisy," and passed a resolution calling for the creation of a democratic secular state of Palestine to be occupied by Arabs and Jews.

The Twin City chapter of the AAUG, later called the Minnesota chapter, was organized about 1970. Its members wrote letters to politicians and editors expressing their views on Middle East issues and sponsored talks on Middle Eastern subjects. They also established Arabic-language classes for their children, participated as a group in the Festival of Nations, sponsored an auction of Arab jewelry and crafts to raise money for the United Holy Land Fund, and met in each other's homes for occasional potluck dinners of Arab foods.

They had little success, however, in attracting members of the Twin Cities Lebanese communities who refused to think of themselves as Arabs. In 1970 only 12 to 15 people were in attendance at some meetings, and two years later an officer acknowledged that the AAUG had "found it to be almost impossible to recruit more members in the Twin Cities due to their conservatism. Many even feel that the AAUG is too radical or too political."

Arab student organizations included an Arab-American Club at the University of Minnesota, begun in 1956. In 1980 the group had some 150 members, 50 to 60 of whom were active. Although the club worked to include all Arabs in the community, most of the members were students. In 1975–76 political differences led to the formation of a splinter group known as the Organization of Arab Students. In 1980 it had 10 members and few activities. The Arab-American Club,

which included a dance group, tried to promote better understanding between Americans and Arabs, attempting to counteract what it regarded as negative images disseminated by the media. Members worked with community organizations and spoke in public schools about their ethnic and professional backgrounds. All three of these Arab organizations opposed the 1979 Israeli-Egyptian peace treaty.[66]

Like the Arabs, members of many of the other Middle Eastern groups present in the state in 1980 had arrived after World War II, frequently as students. Most of the 300,000 or so foreign students in the United States in the late 1970s, 75% of whom were men, planned to return to their home countries in a modern-day variant of the single men and women who arrived early in the 20th century intending to stay only long enough to accumulate whatever would improve their lives at home — money, education, eventually status. And like the earlier temporary migrants, some decided to remain permanently.[67]

Nearly 5,000 foreign students, many of whom were Iranians or Arabs, attended Minnesota colleges and universities in 1980. A large proportion of the latter were from Saudi Arabia, but few of them had settled permanently in the state by that year. More than half the Middle Eastern students were studying on the various campuses of the University of Minnesota, but the state universities of Mankato, St. Cloud, Bemidji, Moorhead, and Winona each had 100 or more, as did Macalester College in St. Paul and the Minnesota Mayo Medical School in Rochester.

While a large number of Middle Easterners in Minnesota in 1980 were students, there were also permanent residents, some of whom had married Americans. Several of those who chose to settle and take up careers in the state acquired citizenship as soon as they were able to do so, contributing to the so-called brain drain from their countries.

EGYPTIANS

A number of Egyptians, some Christian, some Muslim, arrived in Minnesota after World War II. In 1980 an estimated 1,200 to 1,400 (not including students) resided in the state. At least 379 had arrived after 1970. Small numbers lived in St. Cloud and Mankato, but most had settled in the Twin Cities. Even there, however, no identifiable neighborhood existed. The first to arrive were students, who did not become permanent residents. They were followed in the 1950s by others who remained. Most of those present in 1980, however, had immigrated as the result of an agreement between Egypt and the United States in 1965 which allowed educated Egyptians to leave the homeland. Some chose Minnesota as a destination because they had relatives or friends there, but the Egyptian embassy assigned others to the state because of their backgrounds in agriculture or other fields deemed appropriate for life in the Upper Midwest. Most of the immigrants had college educations. Many of those with agriculture degrees, however, found it difficult to break into the state's agribusinesses. Some took temporary jobs; others gave up and returned home. Eventually those who remained found better positions.[68]

Although some settled-out students and immigrant professionals joined University of Minnesota students in the Arab-American Club, a degree of social separation, if not friction, existed between the two groups of permanent residents. The majority of both groups settled in the Twin Cities, and they tended to live near the campuses of the University of Minnesota whether or not they were associated with the institution.

Some Egyptian immigrants were Coptic Christians, non-Arabs who consider themselves descendants of the people who lived in Egypt at the time of the pharaohs. The Copts began arriving in the state in the 1960s. By 1981 they totaled 37 families and 139 individuals, including children, most of whom immigrated in the early 1970s. All of them lived in the Twin Cities except for two associated with the Mayo Clinic in Rochester. A mixed group occupationally, there were in 1981 four with doctoral degrees, two physicians, an owner of a franchised doughnut shop in the suburb of Eagan, and an operator of a recently opened branch of a well-known Greek-owned steakhouse chain in downtown Minneapolis; the rest were laborers.[69]

Those who were sufficiently fluent in English attended services at St. Mary's Greek Orthodox Church in Minneapolis, but all of them belonged to a Coptic church in Cleveland, Ohio, which sent a priest to hold monthly services at St. Mary's in 1981. The Coptic congregation hoped to buy a church and find a resident priest by 1982.

Most of the state's Egyptians were Muslims, about half of whom participated in the activities of the Islamic Center of Minnesota. Efforts to form an Egyptian-American club, though hampered by other allegiances — mostly religious — or by the division between students and permanent residents, continued in the 1980s.[70]

By 1980, when few new immigrants were arriving from the homeland, the Egyptians in Minnesota formed a stable group whose members had good professional and technical jobs they were unlikely to leave. Among them were accountants, business people, and bankers who, according to one of their number, had more success than some other Middle Easterners partly because they expected to be treated in a normal American fashion and for the most part they were. Largely accepted as individuals, they encountered little prejudice in their work places, perhaps because most were at the upper levels of the economic scale.

Some Muslim members of the group may have distanced themselves from their fellow Arabs on April 8, 1979, when they joined Twin Cities Jews in celebrating the peace treaty signed by Israel and Egypt. More than 1,300 people attended a ceremony at the College of St. Thomas in St. Paul, during which for the first time in the Twin Cities "Egyptians and Jews read their prayers for peace together, jointly sang the national anthems of America, Egypt, and Israel and danced with one another following the program." Muslims as well as Coptic Christians participated in the celebration, which led to the formation of the Midwest Mideast Investment and Trade Committee, made up of Jewish and Egyptian community leaders and American businessmen.[71]

IRANIANS

Like many other Middle Easterners, most of Minnesota's Iranians apparently reached the state after World War II as students. Only a third of the 70,000 to 80,000 in the United States in 1970 were permanent residents, and how many of those were in Minnesota is not known. A very approximate estimate of the number in the state in the 1970s was 182, not including students. Predominantly Muslim, they nevertheless reflected Iran's religious diversity, for Bahais, Jews, and Christians were also represented.[72]

Job prospects and a lower inflation rate induced some to immigrate, and religious, political, and kinship considerations played important roles in their decisions. Those who stayed tended to associate according to their religious affiliations, but Muslims were seemingly less religiously cohesive than Bahais.

Although Iranians participated in St. Paul's Festival of Nations as early as 1958, the only group surviving in 1980 from that period was the Iranian Student Organization (ISA). Its national convention, held in Minneapolis in 1958, welcomed Shah Mohammed Reza Pahlavi to the celebration of the centennial of Minnesota statehood. In 1980 the local chapter had a membership of about 50 out of a total of 180 registered Iranian students at the University of Minnesota. Its members' views toward the shah had changed, however, reflecting the shifting political situation in Iran. During the hostage crisis of 1979–81, the 500 Iranian students in the state were frequent targets of American resentment.[73]

THREE ADDITIONAL SMALL MUSLIM GROUPS

A few people from Palestine, which like Syria was for many years part of the Ottoman Empire, were first recorded in Minnesota in 1918. Mostly men, they were laborers or salesmen; one was a waiter. Two had families in Jerusalem and two had wives in Minneapolis. The women did not work outside the home. Two of the unattached men lived with one of the families at 1315 Nicollet Avenue, across the street from two more single men who lived at 1408.[74]

As individuals and then as families, Palestinian immigrants appeared again in the 1970s in the Twin Cities, where they opened restaurants and operated small grocery stores. Approximately 62 permanent residents arrived from "Palestine" during that decade. Mostly Muslim, some were active in the Islamic Association of Minnesota. A few Christian Palestinians joined St. Mary Antiochian Orthodox Church on St. Paul's West Side.

Despite their small numbers the food businesses they operated made the larger community more aware of them than it otherwise might have been. Palestinians, many of them related to each other, ran four of nine newer Middle Eastern restaurants counted in Minneapolis and St. Paul in 1980. They continued to attract additional relatives to the area by reporting that life was good and by urging others to join them. They too suffered, inappropriately, during the

Iranian hostage crisis of 1979–81, from the inability of some Minnesotans to distinguish one black-haired, olive-complexioned person from another, thus pointing up the need for the educating and mediating mission of their eateries. A 1980 article describing one Minneapolis establishment made clear the possibilities: a construction worker entering the store in search of a bologna sandwich got instead "a falafil sandwich, its filling made of chickpea patties dipped in sesame seeds and fried. The man ate it and left, then returned with the whole construction crew. They all ate falafil, the 'hamburger of the Mideast.' " The proprietor "felt as if he'd accomplished something, broadened the Midwestern palate, so to speak." [75]

The primarily Muslim Turkish immigration to the United States before World War II was made up for the most part of working-class people, many of whom returned to Turkey. After the war the brain drain pattern, which characterized much immigration to the United States in that period, applied to Turkish newcomers as well. Among immigrant professionals, return migration was minimal. [76]

In Minnesota a few Turks took up residence before World War II (see Table 27.5). A history of a South Minneapolis Roman Catholic church noted that among its organizers in 1913 was a Turkish man who had married a Catholic and who had a furniture store on East Lake Street at that time. Five years later a few people in Minneapolis described themselves as being from Turkey. One had been at his 1918 address for five years, but most had lived at their residences for less than a year. Their occupations varied from laboring and railroad section work to food-related jobs; among them were cooks, a butcher, and a baker who owned a half interest in the Constantinople Bakery, with its two horses and wagons, at 802 Lyndale Avenue North. Some of these people were single; others had families in Minneapolis or in Turkey. Two bachelor men lived at the bakery, along with the baker and his family. [77]

St. Paul in 1918 showed a similar pattern, though most of the Turkish born there had resided at their 1918 addresses for five years or more — one for 15 years. Most lived among other Middle Easterners on the West Side. The majority were laborers, but one was a bookkeeper and another owned a confectionery store. Several had their families with them.

Turkish students in the Twin Cities first became permanent residents and established organizations about 1960. Some of them formed the Minnesota Turkish American Association, whose members maintained contacts with both

new Turkish students at the University of Minnesota and elsewhere and with the International Institute in St. Paul, where they participated in the Festival of Nations. In 1980 one of its officers estimated the organization had no more than 150 members, including children, all of whom lived in the Twin Cities. (Some 73 permanent residents had arrived in the state from Turkey during the 1970s.) The association's purposes were to enable the scattered Turkish people in the area to socialize with each other and to educate their fellow Minnesotans about Turkey by such means as sponsoring Turkish films at the University of Minnesota and giving public dinners at the International Institute. [78]

Members of the organization in 1980 neither knew nor knew of any Minnesota descendants of the few Turks who had settled in the state in earlier years, indicating that the latter eventually left the state or that their children disappeared into the larger community.

Afghans, among the later arrivals of Middle Easterners in Minnesota, left their homeland when "The institution of a Marxist regime in Afghanistan in 1978 and subsequent turmoil . . . caused [an] influx of immigrants to the United States." The number of Afghans in the United States in 1980 totaled some 2,500. Most were well-educated members of the elite in Afghanistan, a country which has been a recognizable social-political unit only since the mid-18th century. Before that time it was a grouping of tribes, and even in 1980 extended-family and tribal loyalties there tended to take precedence over nationhood. Located in a region long a crossroad of central Asia, modern Afghanistan has some 12,000,000 to 15,000,000 people, 99% of them Muslim. Well into the 1970s emigration to the United States was on an individual or extended-family basis. Afghans lived in nearly every state, with major concentrations in Los Angeles, Washington, D.C., and New York City. [79]

A few individuals had settled in the Twin Cities in the 1970s after studying at the University of Minnesota. Still small early in 1980, the group, which by then included 60 adult refugees, formed the Afghan Community of Minnesota, in part to support International Red Cross efforts to aid Afghan refugees in Pakistan. Members' occupations ranged from doctors and engineers to laborers; two ran restaurants. Abdul Kayoum, married to an American, opened his popular restaurant, Caravan Serai, in St. Paul in 1972. In 1980 a recently arrived family leased a Lake Street restaurant known as Shirley's Cafe where family members worked while they looked for jobs. The menu was the same as that of most small Lake Street eateries with a few Afghan dishes added. [80]

Almost all of the approximately 115 Afghans in the state were Muslims; the majority of the 85 immigrants in Minneapolis and St. Paul in 1981 were active in the Islamic Center of Minnesota, which had an Afghan president that year. Those not in the Twin Cities lived for the most part in Moorhead and Mankato.

The questions and comments of some Minnesota Afghans in 1980 revealed their special status as refugees rather than

Table 27.5. Turkish Speakers in Minnesota, 1910–60

	foreign born	foreign stock*
1910	106	121
1920	41	50
1930	24	
1960	103	

Source: Mother-tongue statistics in U.S., *Census,* for the years listed.
*Foreign stock includes foreign born and native born of foreign or mixed parentage.

ordinary immigrants. "Our country is going to be wiped off the world map — that's what scares us," said one. "Everything — country, traditions, language, culture — could all go soon. . . . How do you live when what you were and what made you isn't there anymore? Who *are* you after that happens?" Among Minnesota immigrants, perhaps Ukrainians and Indochinese could best identify with such questions, which the Dakota and Ojibway Indian people of the state have had to deal with for many decades.

Traditions: Continuity and Change

Although the number of emigrants from the Middle East to Minnesota was small, they were by no means swallowed up by the larger community in 1980. One reason for their visibility was the extraordinary number of restaurants they operated in comparison to their number and in contrast to, say, the few eateries specializing in Scandinavian food. One explanation may lie in the traditional role of food as a mediating and socializing part of culture. If food is one of the traditional customs likely to be retained the longest precisely because it is not a threat to the larger society, then opening restaurants may be a relatively "safe" way of mediating between one culture and another. In the Twin Cities, a society made up for the most part of people of northern European descent and carrying an image that reflects and even exaggerates that predominance, there is little need for restaurants to mediate between Scandinavians and the society as a whole. For a relatively exotic group like the Middle Easterners, on the other hand, food introduces members of the larger society to a different culture in a nonthreatening way.[81]

Since many Middle Easterners were entrepreneurs and small-business people, opening food establishments was a phenomenon in which both old and new immigrants took part, though the popularity of their food in the Twin Cities in 1980 was a trend of uncertain duration. The earlier restaurants were located in the Lebanese communities on St. Paul's West Side and in Northeast Minneapolis. The newer eating places, run by Egyptians, Palestinians, Syrians, an Afghan, and even a Pakistani couple, were located near colleges and universities, in downtown Minneapolis, South Minneapolis, the Highland area of St. Paul, and the Minneapolis suburbs. The food served was not what one would find in a Beirut restaurant; even the newer immigrants changed their recipes "so that they will be fit for the American taste."[82]

Aside from food, 1981 was too early to draw conclusions about the role of postwar Middle Eastern immigrants to Minnesota. By then only the Lebanese had been in the state long enough and in sufficient numbers to analyze their interaction with the larger society. Some of the conclusions drawn in the following paragraphs, however, may be applicable to the later groups as well.

After commenting on Arab family structure and American values and economic opportunities, one scholar noted that "Syrians readily became success-oriented free-enterprisers. No two more dissimilar molds could have produced more similar products."[83] Such an analysis, it seems to me, right-

ly calls into question the amount of Americanization necessary for Syrian-Lebanese success in the United States. Coming from a radically dissimilar culture, they managed, without relinquishing their distinctiveness, to parlay the little they brought with them into a relatively speedy American success story. The continuation of funeral customs, for instance, and the persistence of intragroup marriage despite the numerical odds against it, even in a town like Mankato which had no Lebanese church, indicate how little of the old was abandoned by the first and even the second generations in order to achieve success in the new society.

Nor did retention of "Arab" cultural traits prevent these immigrants and their descendants from considering themselves Americans. This self-perception helps explain why, for example, it took many of the local pre-World War II immigrants and their offspring until the 1970s to see any relevance in the Arab political and social issues which were of great concern to post-1948 immigrants from the Middle East. And "Even when they did, it was primarily as Americans and only secondarily as Arabs," one researcher noted.[84]

The lack of long-lasting organizations in the Lebanese community was not a sign of rapid Americanization, although most Twin Cities Lebanese immigrants became American citizens, but a result of the Syrian personality. One scholar of the Twin Cities communities quoted a study of Syrians in Pittsburgh, which ascribed the lack of organizational life to the "intense individualism" of the Syrians, which doomed the organizations from the start. "Each [immigrant] considers himself the sole and final judge of right and wrong, of justice, of community action."

Scholars have noted that Syrians and Lebanese were slow at social assimilation (for example, intermarriage) but quick to assimilate economically. What was retained, as the Minnesota communities demonstrate, were "food habits, crafts, music and dancing, the rites of hospitality, authoritarian family patterns, the closeness and warmth of family ties, and a religious ritual with many common features, whether the church was Maronite . . . or Eastern Orthodox."

The Mankato community, at least, would seem to call into question the conclusion of a Twin Cities scholar that "the Lebanese churches and their religious associations are the only vehicle . . . of a Lebanese or Arabic culture." It is clear from interviews and studies of the Mankato community that group life as well as Old Country customs continued, bolstered not by a church but by the periodic arrival of newcomers from Lebanon and by communication with other Lebanese Americans.

The transmission of traditional culture through generations of Minnesota Lebanese was visible at a performance of Middle Eastern dancers at a South Minneapolis neighborhood festival in May, 1980. Essny Abdo, grandmother of one of the dancers, was there to watch from her wheelchair. One of her daughters explained that her Lebanese-born mother "wouldn't miss this for anything. . . . She did these dances and she taught Margeaux's mother and me to dance. And now Margeaux's up there performing."[85]

Reference notes

[1] The author wishes to thank Professor Raouf J. Halaby, Ouachita Baptist University, Arkadelphia, Ark., for his helpful suggestions on this chapter. Some scholars of Middle Eastern immigration refer to all Arabic-speaking immigrants and their descendants as Arab Americans, a term unacceptable to many Minnesota Lebanese Christians, to whom the word "Arab" implies adherence to Islam. See, for example, Elaine C. Hagopian and Ann Paden, eds., *The Arab-Americans: Studies in Assimilation* (Wilmette, Ill., 1969) and other sources listed below; see also Viviane Doche, *Cedars by the Mississippi: The Lebanese-Americans in the Twin-Cities*, 84 (San Francisco, 1978). Therefore we have used "Arab American" only when referring to the entire United States. In speaking of Minnesota, "Arab" will refer primarily to Egyptian and Palestinian Muslims and to the sprinkling of their coreligionists from other Arabic-speaking countries. Not included are Armenians, Iranians, Afghans, and Turks, who are not Arabic speakers.

[2] Estimates of the total number of Arab Americans in the late 1970s ranged from "Slightly more than 1 million" to one and one-half million; see Alixa Naff, "Arabs," in Stephan Thernstrom, ed., *Harvard Encyclopedia of American Ethnic Groups*, 128 (Cambridge, Mass., 1980) and Beverlee T. Mehdi, comp. and ed., *The Arabs in America, 1492–1977*, viii (Dobbs Ferry, N.Y., 1978). For the Minnesota figures, see United States, *Census*, 1970, *Population*, vol. 1, part 25, pp. 512, 513; the 10,000 figure is a ball-park estimate by the author, to whom the figure 26,000 in the Mehdi volume (p. 137) seemed much exaggerated. A 1969 source also estimated that there were 10,000 Syrian-Lebanese of all generations in the state, which seemed more plausible; Abdo A. Elkholy, "The Arab-Americans: Nationalism and Traditional Preservations," 6, in Hagopian and Paden, eds., *The Arab-Americans*. For the number of Muslims in the state in the mid-1960s, see Abdo A. Elkholy, *The Arab Moslems in the United States*, 24 (New Haven, Conn., 1966).

The comparison at the end of this paragraph is not strictly accurate since the percentage of all Middle Easterners in Minnesota is set against the number of Arab Americans in the United States, but the great majority of the state's Middle Easterners are Arabic speakers or their descendants.

[3] Doche, *Cedars by the Mississippi*, 20, 37; Naff, in Thernstrom, ed., *Harvard Encyclopedia*, 128; Carol J. Landis, "Lebanese Immigration to the United States and the Twin Cities, 1890–1924," 53, master's thesis, University of Minnesota, 1967.

[4] Philip M. Kayal and Joseph M. Kayal, *The Syrian-Lebanese in America: A Study in Religion and Assimilation*, 78, 113–116, 120, 131, 132, 164 (Boston, 1975), compared the Maronites to the Irish and noted that "Ethnicity passing as religion seems to have more survival potential than pure social ethnicity, which simply attempts to keep a sociocultural community together for historical-emotional reasons." See also Paul R. Magocsi, "Eastern Catholics," and Thomas E. Bird, "Eastern Orthodox," both in Thernstrom, ed., *Harvard Encyclopedia*, 301, 302. For Minnesota particulars, see below.

[5] Doche, *Cedars by the Mississippi*, 40; Church of the Holy Family, *50th Jubilee, 1918–1968*, n.p. ([St. Paul], 1968); Landis, "Lebanese Immigration," 53, 54.

[6] Interviews by Karin Thiem of Roy Ramy, November 29, 1978, pp. 5, 6, and Effie and Mike Jabbra, October 30, 1978, pp. 9, 17, 18 (both taped, with transcripts), and T. R. Schaffler, "Community Integration of the Lebanese in Mankato, Minnesota," 3, typescript, 1958 — all in Southern Minnesota Historical Center, Mankato; Mehdi, *Arabs in America*, 5.

[7] Doche, *Cedars by the Mississippi*, 98. "Ferzoul" is probably another transliteration of the name of the village earlier referred to as "Fourzol."

[8] Landis, "Lebanese Immigration," 47; Louise S. Houghton, "Syrians in the United States," in *Survey*, 26:491, 494 (April–September, 1911); U.S., *Census*, 1920, *Population*, 2:699, 731; 1930, 2:236, 274.

[9] Landis, "Lebanese Immigration," 50; Houghton, in *Survey*, 26:494; Alien Registration forms, Ramsey County, in Minnesota Commission of Public Safety (PSC) Records, Minnesota State Archives, MHS.

[10] Neither of Henne's store buildings remained in 1981. Landis, "Lebanese Immigration," 50; Alien Registration forms, Hennepin County, in PSC Records.

[11] U.S. Immigration Commission, *Immigrants in Industries*, 78:350 (61 Congress, 2 session, *Senate Documents*, no. 633 — serial 5677); John Syrjamaki, "Mesabi Communities: A Study of Their Development," 134, Ph.D. thesis, Yale University, 1940; Alien Registration forms, St. Louis County, in PSC Records; Blessed Sacrament Parish, *75th Anniversary, 1894–1969*, 24 ([Hibbing, 1969]).

[12] Houghton, in *Survey*, 26:491; Alien Registration forms, St. Louis County, in PSC Records.

[13] Schaffler, "Community Integration," 3, 11, 16; Maud Hart Lovelace, *Over the Big Hill*, 7, 8 (New York, 1942); Michael Cabaya, "Maud Hart Lovelace," 13, unpublished paper, 1966, copy in Minnesota Valley Regional Library, Mankato.

[14] *Crookston City Directory, 1915–16, 1956*; Crookston telephone book, 1979; Brock & Company, *Standard Atlas of Polk County, Minnesota* (Chicago, 1930); Holy Family Church, *50th Jubilee*.

[15] S. A. Mokarzel and H. F. Otash, *The Syrian Business Directory, 1938–1939*, [introduction, 1] (New York, [1938?]).

[16] Here and below, see Naff, in Thernstrom, ed., *Harvard Encyclopedia*, 131.

[17] Here and below, see Ramy interview, 8, 9; Jabbra interview, 3.

[18] Alice L. Sickels, *Around the World in St. Paul*, 16 (Minneapolis, 1945); International Institute, *Festival of Nations, 1949*, 43 (St. Paul).

[19] Doche, *Cedars by the Mississippi*, 42; Houghton, in *Survey*, 26:661, 662; Jabbra interview, 3, 33.

[20] Alien Registration forms, St. Louis and Clay counties, in PSC Records; *Crookston City Directory, 1915–16*; Kittson County Historical Society, *Our Northwest Corner: Histories of Kittson County, Minnesota*, 6 (Dallas, 1976); Lincoln County Centennial History Committee, *Lincoln County, Minnesota, 1873–1973*, 184 (Lake Benton, [1973?]). Not all the peddlers were well received, however. Merchants in the Mesabi Range town of Keewatin in 1907 protested because the village had no ordinance requiring a license from peddlers, with the result that "many Arabians and Syrians are plying their vocation unrestricted," reported the February 14 *Hibbing Tribune*. Reflecting the stereotyped prejudices held by some, the article continued, "With shoddy stock they constantly beset the householders and with oily words and much persistence and cheap prices they are selling so much" that the business of the so-called legitimate merchants was suffering.

[21] Naff, in Thernstrom, ed., *Harvard Encyclopedia*, 131; Landis, "Lebanese Immigration," 48.

[22] Landis, "Lebanese Immigration," 50–52.

[23] Alien Registration forms, Ramsey, Hennepin, and St. Louis counties, in PSC Records; Ramy interview, 26; Jabbra interview, 2, 8, 11; Syrjamaki, "Mesabi Communities," 134.

[24] In 1912 Mrs. Mary Zien had a lace shop in St. Paul at 44 West 4th; for the next two years her "embroidery" or "art goods" establishment was at 9 East 6th St., but after 1914 she was no longer listed in city directories. See Alien Registration forms, Dakota County, in

PSC Records; Houghton, in *Survey*, 26:659; *St. Paul City Directory, 1913–15*; Women in Industry in Minnesota in 1918, Polk County, Crookston, in War Records Commission Records, Minnesota State Archives.

[25] Naff, in Thernstrom, ed., *Harvard Encyclopedia*, 131; Mokarzel and Otash, *Syrian Business Directory*, [143]; Ramy interview, 10, 13–17.

[26] *Duluth City Directory, 1917*; Duluth telephone book, 1976; Mokarzel and Otash, *Syrian Business Directory*, [143], 144.

[27] *Crookston City Directory, 1915–16*; Alien Registration forms, Clay County, in PSC Records; Norman County Heritage Commission, *In the Heart of the Red River Valley: A History of the People of Norman County, Minnesota*, 343 (Dallas, 1976).

[28] *Minneapolis City Directory, 1910–76*; interviews of Marie Oletzke and Vicki Hegedus, daughter and granddaughter of Albert Abdallah, by author, both in November, 1980, notes in MEHP Papers.

[29] James M. Ansara, "The Immigration and Settlement of the Syrians," 86, honors thesis, Harvard University, 1931, copy in IHRC, quoting B. M. Kherbawi, *Tarikh Alwalayat Almutihidat*, vol. 2 (Brooklyn, 1913). The latter is a history of the U.S. written in Arabic.

[30] Holy Family Church, *50th Jubilee*; Catholic Archdiocese of St. Paul and Minneapolis, Parish Questionnaires, 1948, originals in the Catholic Historical Society, St. Paul Seminary, St. Paul, microfilm in MHS, hereafter cited as Parish Questionnaires; Alien Registration forms, St. Louis County, in PSC Records; Wlademer Akekee, *Parishioners of St. Maron Church*, 58 ([Minneapolis, 1969?]); Landis, "Lebanese Immigration," 51. An early farm family which remained in rural Fillmore County was that of Amen Soffa, who began as a peddler in the 1890s between La Crosse, Wis., and Greenleafton. After he married Nazera Kimmel in 1901, they bought a 10-acre farm at Hazel Prairie, near Carimona, where they lived for 17 years and raised their family. In 1918 they moved to another farm, which they worked until their retirement in 1937, when they moved to Preston. Two of their children farmed in the same area. Barry M. Dahl, "Soffa Family History," 2–9, typescript, 1979, in IHRC.

[31] Doche, *Cedars by the Mississippi*, 43–45; Landis, "Lebanese Immigration," 60–65; Jabbra interview, 12; St. Paul Seminary, Most Holy Redeemer Church, Marshall, Lyon County, in Parish Questionnaires; Dahl, "Soffa Family History," 2.

[32] The history of St. Maron's provided an example of years of intraparish controversy, leading one student of the situation to conclude that "strife between pastor and parishioners or, perhaps, between parish factions, has been a constant factor in St. Maron's history." Landis, "Lebanese Immigration," 61–63. See also Parish Questionnaires; *Minneapolis Tribune*, November 23, 1959, p. 15. Among the church organizations in 1949 were an altar society, a young men's and a young women's group, a choir, and the Maro-Knight Veterans' Assn.

[33] Here and below, see Parish Questionnaires; Holy Family Church, *50th Jubilee*; Work Projects Administration, Minnesota, Historical Records Survey: Churches, in MHS, hereafter cited as WPA, Church Records; Landis, "Lebanese Immigration," 65; Doche, *Cedars by the Mississippi*, 44; Naff, in Thernstrom, ed., *Harvard Encyclopedia*, 132.

[34] Here and below, see an article on St. George Church in *A Tribute to the Old Church in the New World: Commemorating the 31st Antiochian Archdiocese Convention*, n.p. (San Francisco, [1976?]), copy in St. George Church office; WPA, Church Records; *Syrian World* (New York), May, 1932, p. 53, microfilm in IHRC; interview of Very Rev. John G. Khoury by author, November 14, 1980, notes in MEHP Papers.

[35] Doche, *Cedars by the Mississippi*, 45; interview of Very Rev.

Essa Kanavati by author, November 14, 1980, notes in MEHP Papers.

[36] Notes on conversations of unidentified International Institute worker with Mrs. Victor Zien, October 6, 1954, and Mrs. Nick Antoniades, October 12, 1954, in Syrian Group, Nationality Groups folders, International Institute of Minnesota Papers, IHRC.

[37] Doche, *Cedars by the Mississippi*, 68.

[38] "1936 Neighborhood Survey"; "Report on a study of the Neighborhood House" (1932?); 1917 Annual Report; Monthly Report, January 10, 1904 — all in Neighborhood House Association Papers, MHS.

[39] Government Report for Americanization Classes, enclosed in Katharine M. Kohler to Raymond F. Crist, July 17, 1920, in Dept. of Labor, Immigration and Naturalization Services, General Education Correspondence files, Minnesota State Convention, Minneapolis, May, 1920, National Archives Record Group 85, copy in MEHP Papers; Report from December, 1931, and Adult Education file, 1936–39, both in North East Neighborhood House Papers, MHS.

[40] Schaffler, "Community Integration," 6–8; Ramy interview, 4, 29, 30.

[41] Landis, "Lebanese Immigration," 56–60. Few remembered *Al-Omma* in 1980; no copies could be located. Most Twin Cities Lebanese who subscribed to an Arabic-language newspaper took *Al-Hoda*, published in New York City.

[42] Here and six paragraphs below, see Doche, *Cedars by the Mississippi*, 66, 70–72, 75, 84.

[43] Lovelace, *Over the Big Hill*, 49, 56, 119, 122.

[44] Ramy interview, 28; *Mankato Review*, July 30, 1901, pp. 5, 7.

[45] Ramy interview, 4, 19, 23; Jabbra interview, 31, 32.

[46] Doche, *Cedars by the Mississippi*, 39; Landis, "Lebanese Immigration," 56.

[47] Schaffler, "Community Integration," 5; Ramy interview, 18, 19.

[48] Ramy interview, 7; Jabbra interview, 13.

[49] Holy Family Church, *50th Jubilee*.

[50] Theresa Monsour, in *St. Paul Sunday Pioneer Press*, May 11, 1980, Focus sec., 1, 9.

[51] Doche, *Cedars by the Mississippi*, 98.

[52] Doche, *Cedars by the Mississippi*, 72, 76; information from Minneapolis City Clerk's Office, March 20, 1981, notes in MEHP Papers; *Mankato Free Press*, July 31, 1976, p. 1.

[53] *Minnesota Daily*, February 2, 1976, p. 5; Peg Meier, "St. Paul's Bearded Wonder," in *Mpls./St. Paul*, October, 1978, pp. 59, 60.

[54] Here and below, see Doche, *Cedars by the Mississippi*, 76; author's notes on speeches by Charlene Gubash and Tony Saber at the Jewish Community Center, St. Paul, October 8, 1978, in MEHP Papers; *Mankato Free Press*, July 31, 1976, p. 1; *St. Paul Area Downtowner*, April 5, 1979, p. 4; *Highland Villager* (St. Paul), January 28, 1981, p. 15. The good relationship between Jews and Lebanese recalled the days when they had lived together on St. Paul's West Side. One Lebanese American remembered fondly the neighboring Jewish families who owned businesses and helped the Lebanese. Doche, *Cedars by the Mississippi*, 39.

[55] Here and four paragraphs below, see Robert Mirak, "Armenians," in Thernstrom, ed., *Harvard Encyclopedia*, 136–149.

[56] M. Vartan Malcom, *The Armenians in America*, 71, 72n (Boston, 1919); Niles Carpenter, *Immigrants and Their Children, 1920*, 375 (Census Monograph no. 7 — Washington, D.C., 1927); James H. Tashjian, *The Armenians of the United States and Canada: A Brief Study*, 23 (Reprint ed., San Francisco, 1970); International Institute, *Festival of Nations, 1958*, 14 (St. Paul); interview of Var Kardashian, president, Armenian Cultural Organization of Minnesota, by author, March 13, 1981, notes in MEHP Papers.

[57] St. Paul and Minneapolis *City Directories, 1917–19*; interview

of Pat Nakashian Heilman by author, February 10, 1981, notes in MEHP Papers; Sickels, *Around the World in St. Paul*, 16.

[58] Author's interviews of Woodrow Keljik, February 11, 1981, and of Pat Nakashian Heilman, February 27, 1981, notes for both in MEHP Papers. For more on the Ramgavars and the Tashnags, see Mirak, in Thernstrom, ed., *Harvard Encyclopedia*, 145–147.

[59] Here and below, see Alien Registration forms, Ramsey and Hennepin counties, in PSC Records; Minneapolis and St. Paul *City Directories, 1910–40*. For a short time, probably in the 1910s, Arsene Nakashian and his mother Mariam marketed yogurt made in the family basement in porcelain kettles, under the brand name "Zozon." Doctors at St. Paul hospitals had requested that they make it for patients. Garo Rupenian delivered it to the hospitals daily, priced at $.02 a quart. Arsene's sister Prapeon had a small boutique near his rug shop at that time where she sold "Zozon," chocolates, and Armenian lace and handwork. Doctors patronized her store for its yogurt, but the food did not catch the fancy of the public then. Heilman interview, February 27, 1981; Heilman to author, March, 1981, in MEHP Papers.

[60] Here and below, see author's interviews of Pat Nakashian Heilman, January 22, 1981, and of Woodrow Keljik, February 12, 1981, notes for both in MEHP Papers; International Institute, *International Folk Festival, 1934*, and *Festival of Nations* programs for 1949, 1955, 1958, 1964, 1967 (St. Paul).

[61] Here and two paragraphs below, see interview of Var Kardashian by author, February 14, 1981, notes in MEHP Papers; Heilman interview, January 22, 1981; *Minnesota Daily*, October 18, 1978, p. 17; information from University of Minnesota International Center, December 10, 1980, notes in MEHP Papers.

[62] All Muslims "recognize the oneness of God (Allah) and the role of the 7th-century Prophet Muhammed as his last prophet," and are to pray five times daily, pay a tax to aid the poor, fast during the month of *Ramadan*, and make at least one pilgrimage to Mecca. The Koran is their holy book. Like Christianity, Islam transcends national and linguistic boundaries, counting adherents not only in North Africa and the Middle East, but in Pakistan, Indonesia, the Balkans, and elsewhere. Thomas Philipp, "Muslims," in Thernstrom, ed., *Harvard Encyclopedia*, 732.

[63] Here and two paragraphs below, see "Moslems in Minnesota," in *New Harbinger: A Journal of Amalgamation* (Minneapolis), Winter, 1976, p. 8; *St. Paul Sunday Pioneer Press*, April 1, 1979, Trends sec., 1, 10, 11; Islamic Center of Minnesota, *Newsletter*, December 1, 1973, copy in IHRC; *Minneapolis Tribune*, December 7, 1979, p. 7B; list of University of Minnesota international organizations, February, 1977, copy in MEHP Papers. Not many of the few Muslim Lebanese who immigrated to St. Paul or to the Dakotas to farm retained that faith. One Twin Cities woman who did tried to make a list of local Muslims only to find that "A generation or two ago [her relatives] had married Christians and their ties with Islam were gone." *Pioneer Press*, April 1, 1979. In 1981 efforts were underway to raise funds to build a mosque; see *Islamic Center of Minnesota Newsletter*, April–May, 1981, p. 8, copy in MHS.

[64] Naff, in Thernstrom, ed., *Harvard Encyclopedia*, 128; see also note 1, above.

[65] Here and three paragraphs below, see Doche, *Cedars by the Mississippi*, 84; Naff, in Thernstrom, ed., *Harvard Encyclopedia*, 128; AAUG Bylaws, 1972; *New York Times* clipping, November 13, 1972; "Twin-City Chapter Association of Arab-American University Graduates," typescript, [1970]; Edmond J. Yunis to Abdun Jabara, September 29, 1972; assorted minutes of local AAUG meetings; other miscellaneous items — all in Association of Arab-American University Graduates, Twin Cities Chapter, Papers, in IHRC; *St. Paul Pioneer Press*, November 26, 1971, Family Life sec., 26.

[66] Interview of Dale Sokkary by author, December 16, 1980, notes in MEHP Papers; *Minneapolis Tribune*, March 28, 1979, p. 5C.

[67] Here and two paragraphs below, see a series of articles by Joe Rigert in *Minneapolis Tribune*, March 23, 24, 25, 26, 29, 30, 1980, all on p. 1A; see also *Minnesota Daily*, May 30, 1980, pp. 1, 8.

[68] Here and below, see interview of Ghaleb Abdel-Rahman by author, December 15, 1980, notes in MEHP Papers; United States Middle Eastern statistics, in MEHP Papers, compiled by Jon A. Gjerde from U.S. Justice Dept., Immigration and Naturalization Service, unpublished tabulations in Statistics Dept., 1970–77, hereafter cited as Gjerde, Middle Eastern statistics.

[69] Here and below, see interview of Guirguis Ibrahim by author, February 12, 1981, notes in MEHP Papers.

[70] Here and below, see Abdel-Rahman interview, December 15, 1980.

[71] Lorraine Schweitzer to the editor, in *Minneapolis Tribune*, April 19, 1979, p. 7A; interview of Ghaleb Abdel-Rahman by author, January 22, 1981, notes in MEHP Papers.

[72] Here and below, see "Iranians," in Thernstrom, ed., *Harvard Encyclopedia*, 521–524; Gjerde, Middle Eastern statistics; *Minnesota Daily*, February 15, 1979, p. 1. The Bahai movement originated in Iran as a split from Shiite Islam in the mid-19th century. Having absorbed a number of non-Islamic features, the Bahais, with their "emphasis on the spiritual unity of mankind," have had "notable missionary success in the United States." Philipp, in Thernstrom, ed., *Harvard Encyclopedia*, 733. Minnesota counted some 70 Iranian adult Bahais in 1980, 40 of them in the Twin Cities area, 17 in Moorhead, 9 in Mankato, and scattered others. Author's interviews of Samira Samimi-Moore, December, 1980, and Jerry Wetterling, January, 1981, notes for both in MEHP Papers.

[73] International Institute, *Festival of Nations, 1958*, 43; Abdol Ali Khodadad to Orville L. Freeman, July 15, 1958, in Governors' files, Minnesota State Archives; *Minnesota Daily*, February 15, 1979, p. 1, January 19, 1981, p. 1.

[74] Naff, in Thernstrom, ed., *Harvard Encyclopedia*, 128; Alien Registration forms, Hennepin County, in PSC Records. People from Palestine were also recorded in the state in 1920, 1930, and 1950; see Table 27.2.

[75] Don Del Fiacco columns, in *St. Paul Dispatch*, December 18, 1979, p. 1, January 15, 1980, p. 21; *Minneapolis Tribune*, March 29, 1980, p. 2B; "Moslems in Minnesota," in *New Harbinger*, Winter, 1976, p. 8; Kanavati interview, November 14, 1980; Gjerde, Middle Eastern statistics.

[76] Talat Sait Halman, "Turks," in Thernstrom, ed., *Harvard Encyclopedia*, 992–996.

[77] Here and below, see Charles S. Neerland, "Monsignor Owen J. Rowan and the Church of St. Helena, 1913 to 1966," typescript, [1966], in MHS. There are also references to Turks on the Mesabi Range in the early 1900s, including a violinist and his wife in Virginia in 1918, but then the picture fades. Alien Registration forms, Hennepin, Ramsey, and St. Louis counties, in PSC Records.

[78] Here and below, see interview of Aynur Konar by author, December 10, 1980, notes in MEHP Papers.

[79] David C. Champagne, "Afghans," in Thernstrom, ed., *Harvard Encyclopedia*, 3–5.

[80] Here and two paragraphs below, see interview of Abdul K. Kayoum by author, January 20, 1981, notes in MEHP Papers; Larry Batson column, January 27, 1980, p. 7A, and Dennis Cassano, "Afghan Refugees Start Over in Minnesota," February 4, 1980, p. 1A, both in *Minneapolis Tribune*. Two middle-aged Afghan men sold hot tamales in Virginia, on the Mesabi Range, in 1918. Alien Registration forms, St. Louis County, in PSC Records.

[81] For more on ethnic foodways, see Henry Glassie, *Pattern in the Material Folk Culture of the Eastern United States*, 206 (Phil-

adelphia, 1968); Mary Douglas, "Deciphering a Meal," in Clifford Geertz, ed., *Myth, Symbol, and Culture*, 61 (New York, 1971).

[82] West Side restaurants serving Lebanese food in 1981 included Awada's and Whebbe's, the latter having opened in 1981; among those in the Northeast Minneapolis area were Emily's Lebanese Delicatessen and the 101 Bar. Of the eateries reflecting the newer immigration from the Middle East, Ali Baba was near Macalester College in St. Paul; Mother's Deli and the Baghdad Cafe set up shop in the vicinity of the University of Minnesota's Minneapolis campus; the original Java and Amir Afandy were located in downtown Minneapolis; the new Java and Abdul's Afandy opened in south Minneapolis, along with Food Paradise; and Caravan Serai

found a home in St. Paul's Highland area. See *Insight* (Minneapolis), March 17, 1980, p. 6, and assorted newspaper clippings and advertisements in MEHP Papers.

[83] Naff, in Thernstrom, ed., *Harvard Encyclopedia*, 130.

[84] Here and three paragraphs below, see Naff, in Thernstrom, *Harvard Encyclopedia*, 133; Landis, "Lebanese Immigration," 46, 63, quoting Morris Zelditch, "The Syrians in Pittsburgh," 45, master's thesis, University of Pittsburgh, 1936; Doche, *Cedars by the Mississippi*, 96, quoting Mary B. Treudley, "The Ethnic Group as a Collectivity," in *Social Forces*, 31:262 (March, 1953).

[85] *Minneapolis Tribune*, June 14, 1980, p. 2B.

CHAPTER 28

The Chinese

Sarah R. Mason

OVER THE COURSE OF THE CENTURY since the first Chinese arrived in Minnesota, much of the history of the Chinese community has been shaped by the unique environment of the Upper Midwest. Comparatively small and isolated from other Chinese settlements, the Minnesota community's pattern of development differed from that of most others in the United States, especially those in the Pacific states, the region of the earliest and most concentrated Chinese immigration. Many of the early settlers in Minnesota — largely men who were single or whose families remained in China — fled the West Coast to escape the racial violence and labor conflict of the anti-Chinese movement in the 1870s and 1880s. While the majority of Chinese in the West during the late 19th century were unskilled laborers, most of those who migrated to Minnesota became entrepreneurs who established small businesses such as laundries, restaurants, hotels, and import shops. In Minnesota they found an open social climate which contributed to a relatively high degree of interaction between the Chinese community and the larger society.[1]

The first Chinese arrived in the mid-1870s, and by 1885 approximately 100 had entered the state. At the end of the decade St. Paul, Minneapolis, and Duluth attracted the largest numbers, with others scattered throughout the state in smaller cities, towns, and villages, including Winona, Lake City, Faribault, Stillwater, Willmar, and Cloquet. By 1910 the Chinese population had grown to nearly 400, including over 100 on the Mesabi and Vermilion iron ranges, where they operated small businesses in Bovey, Eveleth, Virginia, Hibbing, Chisholm, Grand Rapids, Brainerd, Ely, and Tower.[2]

Nationally the Chinese population declined following enactment of the Chinese Exclusion Act in 1882, dropping from a high of 107,488 in 1890 to a low of 61,639 in 1920, then rising slowly as family life began to develop. In Minnesota, however, the Chinese population increased after 1882 because of internal migration, peaking in the late 1920s at an estimated 800 to 1,000. Immigration from China came to a virtual standstill during the Depression years of the 1930s in Minnesota and elsewhere, and some Chinese closed their shops and returned to their homeland. Following World War II, a large influx of Chinese wives of servicemen, families of earlier immigrants, students, and political refugees brought about another increase in the state's Chinese population, which totaled 1,270 in 1960 (see Table 28.1). After the liberalization of United States immigration law in 1965, Minnesota's Chinese population more than doubled, reaching approximately 4,000 by 1980.[3]

19th-Century Immigrants

The first significant Chinese immigration to the United States took place during the rush that followed the discovery of gold in California in 1848. Throughout the second half of the 19th century, hundreds of thousands of Chinese peasants, impoverished by famine and rebellion under the corrupt Manchu Dynasty — a regime under aggressive political and economic pressure from the West — fled the southeastern provinces and settled in Hong Kong, Macao, Southeast Asia, and North and South America. From 1850 to 1882 more than 300,000 crossed the Pacific to seek economic betterment in the *Gam Saan* (Gold Mountain), as the Chinese called San Francisco and California. Their labor constituted a major contribution to the opening of the West during the 1850s and 1860s. When the panic of 1873 brought economic

Table 28.1. Chinese in Minnesota, 1895–1970

	1895	1900		1905	1910		1920		1930		1940		1950	1960		1970	
	foreign stock*	foreign born	fs	fb	fb	fs	fb	fs	fb	fs	fb	fs	fs	fb	fs	fb	fs
Minnesota	116	153	166	171	237	275	355	508	314	524	293	551	720	621	1,270	974	2,422
Twin Cities	51	52		82	146			292	212	343	215	380	497	572	583		1,128
Duluth	27	22		9	38			85	30	51	19	40	47	119**	44**		90

Source: Minnesota, *Census, 1895, 1905*; U.S., *Census*, for other years cited.

*Chinese were badly undercounted. Census takers attempted to record what was termed the "Chinese race," a category which "did not reflect clear-cut definitions" but which sometimes included country of origin. We have listed these figures under "foreign stock," which from 1930 on included foreign born and native born of foreign or mixed parentage.

**Also included Superior, Wis.

depression and unemployment to the western states, however, the Chinese became scapegoats for American workingmen who feared their competition on the labor market. Mobs attacked Chinese settlements, lynched the immigrant laborers, and burned their houses. In the decades that followed, the anti-Chinese movement spread from the West Coast over the entire nation. Thousands of Chinese left the Pacific states, where the hostility was most severe, some returning to Hawaii or China and others migrating to the Midwest and the East Coast. By 1890 Chinese lived in every state and territory of the United States.[4]

The largest number of immigrants to the United States and Hawaii during the pre-World War II period were from Guangdong and Fujian provinces in southeastern China (see Map 28.1). Over 80% were from a small region in Guangdong province consisting of eight districts or political divisions comparable to American counties (see Map 28.2). Those immigrating to the continental United States were predominantly from an area known as *Sze Yup* (Four Districts), which included Enping, Kaiping, Xinhui, and Xinning later called Taishan (Toishan). By far the greater number — perhaps as many as 60% of the Chinese immigrants in the United States — emigrated from Taishan, a rocky, hilly area of small farms which produced only enough food for about a third of its population even in relatively stable times.[5]

Because of the great importance attached to preserving family and ancestral bonds in Chinese traditional culture, families in *Sze Yup* usually chose one male member to emigrate, while the others remained in the village to maintain the ancestral home and care for the family graves. The chosen person was expected to send regular remittances for the support of those left behind. Ideally he married before emigrating and left behind a pregnant wife who would bear his child, care for his aging parents, perform the proper ancestral rites, and ensure the young emigrant's eventual return to family and village. Virtually all the emigrants believed they would go back to China after a few years of work abroad, but gradual adaptation to the new environment, wars, and hard times often made this difficult, if not impossible.[6]

Early Settlement in Minnesota: 1876–1910

Three or four Chinese immigrants arrived in Minnesota in the spring of 1876 and established the Chinese Laundry in St. Paul and the Lung Wing Laundry in Minneapolis. Public reaction to their arrival combined a measure of curiosity with a certain respect for their apparent frugality and hard work. On May 31, 1876, the Minneapolis correspondent of the *St. Paul Pioneer Press* announced that "Two more California Chinamen have leased the basement under the City Hall drug store, and will run opposition to Wing Lung or any other man. . . . One excellent trait is discovered in John Chinaman: He is both cleanly and civil, and in this respect his example should be imitated by some who are now somewhat disposed to turn up their noses at him." The *Pioneer Press* editorialized on the same day, "The people of St. Paul can't see why the Californians should fret so much about the Chinese. In this city they conduct themselves in the most unexceptionable manner, pursuing their avocation in a way that wins general respect. Give the Orientals a chance —

who knows what good they may yet do on election days in offsetting some other nationality?"[7]

Eight months later the citizens' image of the Chinese people was greatly enhanced by the public addresses of a distinguished Chinese scholar, Wong Chin Foo. He spoke to overflow crowds at both the Academy of Music in Minneapolis and the Opera Hall in St. Paul in a series of lectures on such topics as "The Heathen Chinese" and "Domestic Life in China." On January 3, 1877, the *St. Paul Pioneer Press* noted that Wong was "a gifted speaker, as well as a curiosity." Wong apparently returned to the area in October, 1877, when he included Stillwater on his speaking circuit.[8]

The Chinese population in Minnesota grew steadily from 1876 to 1910, largely through migration from the western states. A few immigrants also arrived from China before 1882, and certified merchants and their families — exempt from the 1882 Exclusion Act — continued to arrive in small numbers throughout the period. St. Paul's Chinese settlement, the largest in the state until 1900, claimed some 35 residents in 1883. By 1885 there were 25 Chinese laundries in the capital city, 14 in Minneapolis, five in Duluth, and two in Stillwater, then a thriving lumber town. After the turn of the century Chinese businesses diversified to include import shops, hotels, grocery stores, and restaurants. In 1910 there were 10 Chinese restaurants in Minneapolis, which by 1880 was the state's largest city, and six each in St. Paul and Duluth. Chinese-owned hotels, restaurants, and laundries also appeared in iron range towns during this period, when rapid development of the mining industry caused an unprecedented population boom. The presence of many single, male miners in the area created a demand for the services Chinese businesses provided.[9]

Chinese immigrants had originated laundries as well as restaurants and other ethnic institutions on the West Coast in order to survive in an alien environment. These small business enterprises, which were the principal means of livelihood for Chinese in Minnesota, required little capital investment, did not compete with white labor, and provided employment for newcomers. Often based on partnerships of brothers or individuals from the same village in China, these businesses depended for their economic survival on unpaid family help and the low-paid work of new arrivals. Profits were virtually nonexistent during the early years of operation. Both the owners and the help lived extremely spartan lives, working long hours with little rest, separated from home and village, and isolated from the larger society by barriers of language and culture.[10]

During the 1876–1910 period Chinese businesses, which usually included living quarters, were generally located in downtown areas of Minnesota's larger cities and towns. While they did not constitute separate Chinatowns, they were close enough to each other to allow the formation of networks of mutual assistance and to provide for the social and material needs of the immigrants. Chinese businesses in St. Paul clustered in the area extending from St. Peter Street to Sibley Street between 3rd and 7th streets. In Minneapolis Chinese laundries and other enterprises were generally located in the Gateway district, from 1st Avenue North to

Map 28.1. China

Map 28.2. China's Guangdong Province

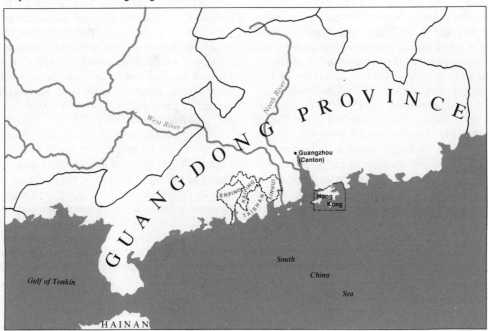

AH WING'S First Class Chinese Laundry operated in Winona about 1882. Seventy-nine years later the Poy Moy Hand Laundry in St. Paul was one of the last of its kind in the state.

8th Avenue South between 1st and 3rd streets, and also around Glenwood (then Western) Avenue and North 1st Street. In Duluth there were two areas of Chinese businesses. The largest was in the main commercial district on East Superior Street from 1st Avenue East to 5th Avenue West and extending southward along Lake Avenue South. The second area was in West Duluth on West Superior and West Michigan streets. In Stillwater four laundries were opened at various times during the early period on Chestnut and 2nd streets, close to the main business district.[11]

While the majority of the Chinese immigrants in this period came from the peasant class in China, in Minnesota a new merchant class emerged and developed a social hierarchy based on wealth and property acquired in the United States. Until about 1915 Minnesota had none of the Chinese immigrant organizations — family name associations, benevolent societies, and secret societies or tongs — that provided the power structure in Chinatowns on the West Coast and elsewhere. In their absence, early leaders were able to achieve a sense of solidarity and continuity through programs organized within the framework of established churches and social agencies in the larger society. Even after national immigrant associations were introduced, these leaders remained aloof and continued to assert their leadership in programs oriented toward greater interaction between the Chinese community and the larger society.[12]

One of the most respected of the early leaders in Minneapolis was Woo Yee Sing, who arrived about 1880 at the age

of 18. He soon established a laundry on Nicollet Avenue which became well known in the Lowry Hill neighborhood for its colorful horse-drawn delivery wagon. A few years later he opened an import shop, called Yee Sing and Company, on Glenwood Avenue. In 1882 Woo sent for his younger brother, Woo Du Sing, and in 1883 they opened the Canton Cafe, the first Chinese restaurant in Minnesota, on 1st Avenue South. Later the restaurant was moved to 28 South 6th Street, and the name was changed to Yuen Faung Low — "exotic fragrance from afar." Known as John's Place, it became one of the most popular restaurants in the Twin Cities, famous for its food and its decor, including mother-of-pearl inlaid teakwood tables and camphorwood carvings from China.[13]

Soon after his arrival in Minneapolis, Woo was converted to Christianity by an elder of the Westminster Presbyterian Church. Through Woo's influence many other immigrants began to attend a weekly Sunday afternoon service at the church conducted in the Chinese language. This program became a focus for Chinese community activities and a point of contact with the larger society.[14]

As the most prosperous of the Chinese businessmen in Minneapolis, Woo was widely recognized as the leader of the immigrant community. In this role he took a strong moral stand, reflecting both the traditional Confucian concept of leadership and his new Christian beliefs. Woo strongly opposed the gambling and other illegal activities later introduced by Chinese immigrant organizations to the Minneapolis community, and he would never allow them in any of his business establishments. He often served as intermediary in conflicts between the new organizations, and with other Chinese leaders he assumed responsibility for the collective welfare of the community. Woo also made an effort to establish good relations with the dominant society; each year he hosted a Chinese banquet to which he invited such local officials as the mayor and aldermen, as well as business associates from the broader community.

Another important leader during the early period was Chin D. Ong, a Duluth businessman. Born in San Francisco, Chin was taken to China as a small child to be educated. At 15 he returned to the United States, rejoining his merchant father in Boston, where he was enrolled in grammar school. After graduation he established a business in Chicago. In 1906 he moved to Duluth and opened the Quong Chong Hai import shop on 5th Avenue West and later the Mandarin Cafe on West Superior Street. Because of his education in both Chinese and English, he was appointed an official interpreter for the United States government in Minnesota, North Dakota, and Iowa. Chin was highly respected by the Chinese Duluthians for his business success, an important criteria for prestige among the immigrants, and for his education, the basis of social status and authority in traditional China. Because of his knowledge of immigration law, he was especially revered by many individuals who sought his help with immigration papers or problems in bringing relatives from China.[15]

Family life developed slowly in Minnesota's early Chinese community and elsewhere in the United States, due to the restrictions of immigration law, Chinese tradition, and the high cost of trans-Pacific travel. Nevertheless at least six

ELABORATE DECOR and imported furniture complemented the fine Cantonese cuisine at John's Place, a well-known Minneapolis restaurant, pictured in about 1915.

families were established in Minnesota before 1910. Since virtually all the early immigrants were men, these families were formed by marriages with Chinese women from the West Coast or China and by intermarriage with non-Chinese women.[16]

Woo Yee Sing's family exemplifies the first of these family forms. While on his way to *Sze Yup* to select a wife, Woo met a young Chinese woman, Liang May Seen, at a mission in San Francisco and decided to marry her instead of proceeding to China as planned. He returned with his wife to Minneapolis in 1893, after a honeymoon at the Columbian Exposition in Chicago. Woo's brother, Du Sing, on the other hand, traveled to *Sze Yup* about 1900 to marry, but in keeping with Chinese tradition, he left his wife and son in his parents' home there when he returned to Minnesota. It was not until 1911 that he could visit his family in China. He stayed in his home village for over two years, during which a daughter was born, and in 1914 he, his wife, and two children traveled to Minnesota, where another son was born later.[17]

The family of Hum Su, another early settler, illustrated a variation of the family formed by marriage between an immigrant and a woman in China. Hum first established a laundry with his brother in Duluth in the early 1880s. After a few years they moved to St. Paul and opened another laundry. In 1908 Hum went to *Sze Yup* to marry and stayed in his home village for two years. He took his wife Chee She to Minnesota on merchant papers in 1910. Hum and his brother operated a business in St. Paul for eight or nine years after his return, then moved to Minneapolis, where they owned shares in three restaurants — the Royal Garden, the New Peking, and the Golden Pheasant. Hum, his wife, and eight children lived during the 1920s and 1930s in another small concentration of Chinese residences and businesses which developed in downtown Minneapolis on 3rd Avenue South between 7th and 8th streets.[18]

An example of a third type, established by intermarriage with a non-Chinese member of the larger society, is the family of Hum Bing, who settled in Minnesota in the mid-1890s after working on the railroad in Montana. About 1895 he married a Canadian woman of Irish extraction whom he met in Montana. She was the widow of his friend, a fellow Chinese railroad worker killed in an accident. Hum took his wife to Willmar, where he opened a laundry and later purchased the Glarum Hotel. All but one of the couple's 12 children were born in Willmar before the family moved to Minneapolis about 1908. Despite the taboo on intermarriage in the Chinese tradition of *Sze Yup*, in Minnesota the Hum family and others formed by mixed marriages were an integral part of the immigrant community.[19]

The Pre-World War II Community: 1910–39

Old-timers claimed that Minnesota's Chinese community experienced considerable population growth during the 1910s and particularly the 1920s and declined somewhat in the hard times of the 1930s. Their claim is supported by the rise and fall in the number of known Chinese businesses from 1910 to 1935. In Minneapolis, the largest Chinese settlement in the state, laundries increased from 23 in 1910 to 73 in 1928, then dropped to 55 in 1935. Restaurants climbed from

10 in 1910 to 23 in 1928, then fell to 13 in 1935. In St. Paul, laundries numbered eight in 1910, rose to 19 in 1928, and declined to 15 in 1935. Restaurants increased from six in 1910 to 12 in 1928, decreasing to five in 1935. In Duluth the trend was similar.[20]

Several factors accounted for the marked flux in the Chinese population in Minnesota and elsewhere during the 1920s. While the 1924 Immigration Act defined merchants as international traders with a specified volume of import-export business, thereby making it more difficult for immigrants to enter under the merchants' exemption, earlier court decisions had affirmed the rights of merchants and American citizens to bring wives and children to the United States. By 1927 the courts had also affirmed the right of foreign-born children and grandchildren of American-born Chinese to derivative citizenship. These rulings were a significant factor in the growth of the community in this period. After decades of restrictive legislation, the rulings on derivative citizenship gave rise to the immigration slot racket, whereby Chinese merchants and Chinese-American citizens in the United States falsely registered the births of children in China in order to create slots for future immigrants. The slots could later be sold to others who wanted to bring sons to the United States but did not have merchant or citizen status. An undetermined number of "paper" sons and daughters joined their fathers in immigrant communities through this system. Migration from the western states and entry from Canada and Mexico were also important factors in population growth, as was the establishment of new families through marriages of the second generation.[21]

During the 1910s and 1920s new leadership developed in Minnesota's Chinese community with the introduction of tongs or secret societies (discussed in more detail below) by agents of the larger organizations in Chinatowns on the East and West coasts. In contrast to earlier leaders, tong leaders often avoided interaction with the larger society, both because of the secret nature of their associations and because, in addition to providing mutual aid and protection, they engaged in illegal activities.[22]

Wong Wen exemplified the tong leaders in Minnesota during the 1920s and 1930s. Born in Taishan, he emigrated as a young man to the West Coast, where he worked for a number of years before moving to Minnesota in 1908. He went to Taishan to marry in 1910, and after a son was born the following year, he returned to Minnesota, leaving his wife and child in his parents' home. About 1921 Wong took his family from China to the United States on merchant papers. He worked as a cook for a period, then with a partner opened the Eagle Cafe and later established the highly successful Kin Chu Restaurant, both in Minneapolis. As president of the On Leung, one of two tongs organized in Minnesota, Wong was an important leader in the Chinese community, acting with force to protect the businesses of the association's members. He also played an important role in the feuds between tongs that stemmed from business competition, rival claims to women (who were scarce in the early bachelor society), and quarrels between individuals that occasionally escalated into tong wars.[23]

In addition to the new tong leadership, younger men who remained independent of the organizations were also rising to important positions in the community during this period. One of these was Henry Yep, who, like Woo Yee Sing, was known as a "neutral," for his intermediary role in tong conflicts, and who favored interaction between the Chinese community and the dominant society. Born in Seattle in 1888, he was sent to China as a young boy for his education and marriage. He returned without his wife and son in 1918 to help in his father's laundry, located first in Wisconsin and later in Minnesota. In Minneapolis he became a leader of Westminster Presbyterian Church's Sunday afternoon Chinese-language services. Like many of the independent leaders, Yep spoke both English and Chinese and frequently served as interpreter for new immigrants. Under his leadership Chinese members of Westminster Church, assisted by a Chinese student at Hamline University, published a Chinese-language newspaper entitled *Sing Kee Po* (The Chinese Weekly). Each 24-page issue included foreign news — particularly items concerning China — domestic news, and advertisements of Chinese businesses.[24]

Kim Wah, popularly known as Walter C. James, was another neutral, independent leader who, like Woo and Yep, spoke both English and Chinese. Born in Yakima, Washington, James migrated to the Midwest as a young man in the early 1900s. After first establishing a successful restaurant in Chicago, he moved to Minneapolis in 1909. There three years later he opened the Canton Grill in the basement of the Dyckman Hotel. In 1919 he established the Nankin Cafe on South 7th Street, still a favorite among Twin Cities residents in 1981. James was strongly committed to establishing close ties between the Chinese and the larger Twin Cities society; he was also concerned about the welfare of new immigrants. In order to serve better as liaison between the Chinese and other Minnesotans, he became an active member of the Rotary, the YMCA, and the Salvation Army.[25]

Tongs were not established in the smaller Chinese community in Duluth, but a benevolent association was organized about 1911. Chin D. Ong remained a leader in Duluth until he

THE NEWSROOM of the Chinese Weekly *about 1925.*

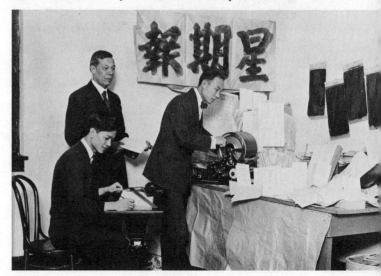

moved to Chicago in the mid-1930s. Thereafter no single leader emerged, although several businessmen assumed responsibility for maintaining harmony within the community and good relations with the larger Duluth society. One of these was Joe Huie, whose residence in Duluth had begun in 1909. While he was one of several leaders in the 1930s and 1940s, he emerged as the most prominent member of the immigrant community in the 1950s and 1960s.[26]

Born in Guangdong province in 1892, Huie worked in Duluth restaurants for six years before returning to his wife and son in China. He stayed for over a year, then went back to Duluth until 1933, when he again sailed for Guangzhou (Canton) in order to "help the people" and to remarry after his first wife's death. Huie returned alone to Duluth in 1937, staying for nine years before traveling again to Guangzhou, where he opened a pharmaceutical outlet in 1946. He fled the city after the Communists established control and returned to Duluth with his two oldest sons in 1951. In 1954 the rest of his family followed. Over the years Huie worked as dishwasher, cook, or manager in several Duluth restaurants before opening Joe Huie's Cafe in 1951. He gained prestige in the Chinese community through his business success, and as a Chinese leader gave generously to civic causes, including scholarships for students at the University of Minnesota in Duluth. He also provided employment in his restaurant and developed a reputation as a practitioner of folk medicine.

In smaller cities and towns where immigrant associations were not organized locally, leadership was generally based on business success and property ownership, as well as education and age. For example, in the southern part of the state Chinese in Austin and Albert Lea formed a close-knit community through frequent movement between the towns. Sammy Wong and Wong Hong were leaders in that area, and both promoted good relations with local businessmen and police. Some individual Chinese in the outstate communities belonged to tongs in the Twin Cities, but their participation consisted mainly of donating money when they visited Minneapolis.[27]

When Woo Yee Sing died in Minneapolis in 1925, his funeral was an intercultural event that reflected the esteem in which he was held by Chinese and non-Chinese alike. Combining both Christian rites and Chinese traditions, the funeral service began at Westminster Church and was followed by a procession that included a Chinese band which wound its way past Woo's home and businesses to collect his soul in the Chinese fashion. Woo's friends and relatives then attended a Chinese dinner, where they paid their respects in the customary way. Before departing, each guest received a coin wrapped with a block of sugar "to take away the bitterness." Woo was buried in Lakewood Cemetery in Minneapolis; he did not want his bones returned to China in the traditional way, because he considered Minneapolis his home.[28]

Although family life began to develop more fully in the Chinese community during the 1910–39 period, the population still consisted largely of men who were single or whose families lived in China. In the Twin Cities the number of families grew from about seven to 30. Some reached Minne-

sota on merchant papers, but the majority were formed by marriages of the second generation. Of 24 sons and daughters of immigrants who settled in the state before 1910, many married Chinese from the West Coast, while others married local non-Chinese. A few of the immigrants' daughters wed Chinese students attending the University of Minnesota, and a number of early settlers' sons married wives from China. In addition, a few children born to merchants who arrived after 1910 reached maturity and married before 1939. Most of the early immigrants' children remained in Minnesota after marriage, contributing to the development of Chinese family life there.[29]

For the more affluent Chinese merchants who could send for their wives and children, acculturation to Minnesota life became easier in normal family units. Many of the Chinese women, however, were secluded in their homes. Since they seldom learned English well enough to communicate easily, they had few social contacts outside their immediate families. A daughter of an early restaurant owner in Minneapolis recalled that her mother rarely went downtown — never more than once in two months — and only if there were an urgent need for some necessary item that she would select for herself. Usually her father took the children to buy clothing, or they went shopping with their uncle and aunt, who were considered westernized. Another woman remembered that her mother strongly opposed the Americanization of her children. The mother, like most Chinese, placed a high value on education, but she would not permit her daughters to participate in after-school activities for fear they would make friends with boys and girls outside the family.[30]

After 1914 students from China who enrolled at the University of Minnesota added another element to the Twin Cities community. Despite class, regional, and language differences — most students spoke northern dialects, while immigrants spoke Cantonese or the dialects of *Sze Yup* — they regularly visited settlers' homes and socialized with their children. During this period a number of the immigrants' sons and daughters also began to enter the University of Minnesota, where they often found common interests with the students from China.[31]

The first Chinese student to enroll was Pan Wen Ping, who arrived from Shanghai in 1914. An outstanding student — he held a Boxer Indemnity scholarship — he was also a fine athlete, having won a gold medal at the Olympics in the Philippines in 1913. Pan persuaded his brother and two Chinese students at other American colleges to transfer to the university. The four graduate students rented the upper floor of a house on 4th Street Southeast near the campus. In addition to their academic work, Pan and his brother played on the university basketball team. As students from a Christian family, they were also active in the campus YMCA, speaking often at other YMCAs and churches in the area.

During their first year at the university, they were invited to speak at the Whosoever Will Mission in Minneapolis. To put the students more at ease, the mission's pastor invited Hum Bing and his family to attend. The Pan brothers became close friends of the Hum family, who frequently entertained them and other Chinese students in their home. The older

Hum children, who were then in high school, taught the students American social dancing and invited them to a traditional American turkey dinner on Thanksgiving. The Hum home became a popular meeting place for Chinese students; in 1914 the Chinese Student Club was organized in this immigrant household.

Pan received a degree in mining engineering in 1919 and took a position with the Oliver Mining Company in Hibbing. He planned to return to China after a few years' experience on the iron range. But in 1923 he married May Hum, daughter of Hum Bing, and because of unstable conditions in China they postponed the voyage. As the years passed they established a family in Hibbing and decided to remain.

During the late 1920s and early 1930s, an average of five Chinese students arrived at the University of Minnesota each year. In 1934 this figure jumped to 15 and continued at over 20 until the Japanese invaded China in 1937. After that, the number of new students dropped to a dozen or fewer each year up to World War II. Of the 63 students who entered the university during the 1936–40 period, 43 were enrolled in the College of Agriculture, for the most part in the departments of entomology and plant pathology. While a few remained in the United States after graduation, the majority returned to China. Many of these professionals led the postwar agricultural reconstruction programs in both the People's Republic of China and Taiwan.[32]

World War II and the Postwar Era: 1939–81

The participation of Chinese in both military and civilian efforts during World War II represented the first time the community took part in a major activity of the larger society. While the young men served in the military forces, Twin Cities merchants turned their attention to the sons of Chinese immigrants, who were training at the War Department's Military Intelligence Service Language School (MISLS) at Camp Savage and later at Fort Snelling, near the Twin Cities. They organized recreational programs, holiday celebrations, and special Chinese meals at their restaurants to make the servicemen feel at home in Minnesota. Chinese businessmen also provided aid to students from China who were stranded in Minnesota by the war and cut off from supporting funds.[33]

The largest effort, however, went into the organization of the Twin Cities Chinese Emergency Relief Society to raise money for civilian relief funds and military supplies to be sent to China, an ally of the United States in the Pacific War. In 1941 alone the group raised $45,000 for relief and $20,000 for military aid in the small Twin Cities Chinese community of about 400 people. According to the *Minneapolis Star Journal*, three Chinese businessmen headed a relief committee that required every employed Chinese to contribute money each month. "Backsliders are almost unknown, and none escapes contributing his share in the end," the newspaper reported; an enforcement committee "makes certain that the individual does not fail in his duty to the group. Fines are imposed on delinquents." In Duluth, too, Chinese residents responded to the wartime needs of their countrymen by contributing to the local committee of the American Bureau for Medical Aid to China.[34]

While the war effort opened the door to greater participation in the larger society, rapid population growth and change at the war's end brought problems and tensions which consumed much of the energy of Chinese leaders. The first influx of new immigrants from China during the late 1940s and early 1950s included wives and children of earlier settlers, students, professionals, political refugees, and wives of servicemen — largely men from the Chinese-American community. Although no figures were available for Minnesota, Immigration and Naturalization Service records showed that Chinese entering the United States in the immediate postwar period reached an annual high of 7,203 in 1948. Following the establishment of Communist rule in 1949 new arrivals from China dwindled, but immigration from Taiwan and Hong Kong continued. Between the early 1940s and 1960 Minnesota's Chinese population more than doubled to approximately 1,270.[35]

The first wave of immigrants in the late 1940s was precipitated by changes made during World War II in United States immigration laws. After discriminatory legislation against Chinese became an embarrassment to the United States during its wartime alliance with China, President Franklin D. Roosevelt in October, 1943, called for an end to the exclusion of Chinese. In December Congress repealed Chinese exclusion, established a minimal quota of 105 immigrants per year, and gave naturalization rights to Chinese already in the United States legally. A number of bills were also passed to facilitate family reunification during the postwar years. The first, the act of August 9, 1946, exempted Chinese wives of American citizens from quota restrictions, while the wives of resident aliens were given preferential treatment within the quota. Second, the act of July 22, 1947, lifted the racial restrictions from the War Brides Act of 1945 and allowed approximately 8,000 Chinese women to enter the United States before it expired on December 30, 1949. Under the Refugee Relief Act of 1953, 2,000 Chinese were permitted entry and several thousand living in the United States on temporary visas became eligible for permanent resident status.[36]

Following liberalization of immigration law in 1965 greater numbers of Chinese entered the United States annually, peaking at 25,096 in 1967. The high level of immigration from China, Taiwan, and Hong Kong continued through the 1970s. In Minnesota 133 arrived in 1967 and 217 in 1977. A sizable portion of the state's Vietnamese population of 4,500 in 1980 was also ethnic Chinese.[37]

In the Twin Cities Chinese community leaders endeavored to help the numerous new immigrants adjust to the Minnesota environment. Many of the newcomers were drawn to tongs and the more recently introduced family name associations, but the needs of the women and children in particular could not be met by those groups. In the fall of 1948 over a dozen young wives of Chinese-American servicemen approached L. Jane Wilson, the superintendent of the Chinese Sunday school at Westminster Presbyterian Church, about the possibility of starting English-language classes. In response Wilson organized weekday English classes as well as Sunday afternoon religious programs geared to the special needs of the new arrivals. The classes, besides teaching English, served as a support group for some 20 women during a period of difficult adjustment; later their children formed friendships with other Chinese-American children at Sunday school which were crucial to their identity development.[38]

Walter James and Stanley Chong, a younger independent leader, responded to the influx of new immigrants by converting the third floor of the Nankin Cafe into clubrooms for the burgeoning Chinese community. English classes, Red Cross instruction for new mothers, day care, and entertaining Chinese movies were provided. James also frequently invited the new arrivals on outings to his farm at Howard Lake. The participants in these programs met informally as the Chinese American Club.[39]

The Westminster classes and the Chinese American Club were open to all new immigrants, but their programs were designed primarily for those from southern China who identified with the Twin Cities Chinese business community. Some northern intellectuals and political refugees — and a few southern professionals — joined a student Bible study group formed in 1949 and named the Chinese Christian Fellowship in 1958. While the primary purpose of the fellowship was religious, it also served as an ethnic support group. When there were more families, it provided a Chinese-language school and other programs for religious and cultural instruction of the children as well.[40]

The number of Chinese families in Minnesota grew steadily in the post-World War II era, but normal family life was not firmly established in the community until the 1970s. With the postwar influx of immigration, the ratio of women to men began to rise steadily (see Table 28.2). During the 1950s the ratio of 203.8 men to 100 women decreased to 155.5 to 100 in 1960. It was not until the 1965 Immigration Act had been in effect for two years, however, that a balance between the sexes in the community was approximated. In 1970 the ratio was 127 men to 100 women.[41]

Chinese students attending the University of Minnesota and other colleges in the state also increased markedly in number after World War II. Records are incomplete, but 1980 alumni lists showed that approximately 45 who attended the university during the late 1940s and early 1950s were from the People's Republic of China, while 228 were from Taiwan. Others were from Hong Kong and various parts of the United States. This indicated that at least 300 to 400 Chinese students attended the university during the immediate postwar period. Following the break in United States-China relations in 1950, the number declined considerably. During the McCarthy era, surveillance by the Federal Bureau of Investigation of Chinese organizations at the university caused Chinese student activities to break down as members tried to keep a low profile. Many moved to the East and West coasts to join the larger Chinese populations there; others returned to China.[42]

Chinese students from Taiwan and Hong Kong continued to enroll at Minnesota colleges during the 1960s and 1970s. Students from the People's Republic of China did not arrive until the late 1970s, when the end of the Cultural Revolution in China and the normalization of United States-China relations made study in the United States feasible. An exchange of faculty and students between the University of Minnesota and several institutions in the People's Republic sent 30 visiting scholars to the university during the 1979–80 academic year and 110 during 1980–81. In addition, 186 students from Taiwan, 183 from Hong Kong, and one from Macao attended the university in the latter year.

Beginning in the 1960s a sizable number of second-generation Chinese, largely children of the postwar immigrant group, also entered the University of Minnesota and other colleges. In an era of active protest against the Vietnam War and increased ethnic consciousness, this group became highly politicized. Those at the university, along with a number of second-generation Japanese, were instrumental in establishing the Asian American Alliance. The first local pan-Asian student organization, the alliance provided a base for the developing ethnic consciousness of the second generation in the immigrant community. A number of this group were also active in antiwar protests. After leaving the university, former members of the Asian American Alliance were instrumental in organizing in 1977 the Minnesota Asian American Project (MAAP), the first pan-Asian community organization in the state. MAAP was formed to promote affirmative action, civil rights, and legal services for the Asian community and to monitor legislative activity.[43]

Chinese Community Organizations

The On Leung and Hip Sing tongs, introduced into Minnesota between 1912 and 1915, were modeled on clandestine organizations prevalent in South China during the 19th century. Tongs in Chinese immigrant communities initially served to protect members from encroachment by rival Chinese businessmen and provided fraternal support in factional quarrels. Membership was drawn from businessmen who were largely immigrants from South China. During the 1920s and 1930s, Twin Cities tongs, like those in other parts of the country, were involved in violent conflicts as well as in illicit traffic in opium and gambling. But by the late 1930s local leaders had put a stop to these practices. One spokesman believed the tongs reformed in order to unify the community in efforts to send aid to China during the war against Japan. In 1940 about 150 On Leung members from throughout the United States held a convention in Minneapolis. Since the 1940s the Minnesota tongs — now referred to as merchant associations — have functioned largely as social clubs. Each holds an annual banquet to which members of the other group are invited. While both the Hip Sing and On

Table 28.2. Sex Ratios of Minnesota Chinese Population, 1900–70

Year	Sex Ratio*	Total population
1900	3,220.0	166
1910	2,955.6	275
1920	746.7	508
1930	413.7	524
1940	323.8	551
1950	203.8	720
1960	155.5	1,270
1970	127.0	2,422

Source: U.S., *Census*, 1970.
*Males per 100 females.

Leung are based in the Twin Cities, outstate Chinese contribute money and maintain social ties with them.[44]

Twin Cities businessmen from South China also established family associations modeled on clan organizations in southeast China. Like the tongs, family associations were formed by early immigrants on the East and West coasts and in Chinese communities all over the world. In China clan membership was determined by carefully kept lineage records, but overseas a common surname was the only requirement for eligibility. Thus the immigrants' family associations assumed many of the duties of the clan in China, including the provision of mutual aid, care of widows, sickness and death benefits, and hostels for traveling members. In addition association leaders exerted some social influence on the members, reminding them of their obligations to family and village in China and enforcing the traditional taboo on marriage to a person with the same surname.[45]

The larger of the two family associations in Minnesota in 1980 was the Wong Wun Son, comprised of community members with the surname Wong. Organized in the state in the 1940s, it hosted the 13th national convention of the Wong Wun Son in Minneapolis in June, 1979. The Moy Family Association, formed in Minneapolis somewhat later, in 1980 represented a considerably smaller family group.[46]

As the Twin Cities Chinese population became larger and more diversified in the 1950s and 1960s, a sharp division occurred between southern Chinese businessmen and northern Chinese intellectuals. The southerners formed a close-knit social structure of family name associations, tongs, church programs, and educational clubs. The northerners — with the exception of those who belonged to the Chinese Christian Fellowship — were more loosely organized in small, intimate groups of friends that evolved out of the Chinese Student Association at the University of Minnesota. When concern grew over the deepening cleavage, Chinese leaders agreed to establish an umbrella association in which northerners, southerners, students, professionals, and businessmen could be brought together. About 1968 the Chinese American Club was renamed the Chinese American Association of Minnesota (CAAM), with unification of the community as its primary goal.[47]

In 1970 CAAM organized all the Chinese groups to participate in the annual Aquatennial celebration in Minneapolis, the theme of which was "Seas of the Orient." An arch designed by architect Fred Hsiao, a member of the Chinese community, was erected on Nicollet Avenue, and Chinese arts and crafts were displayed in department store windows. The program included a parade with floats and performances of the lion and sword dances and the martial arts. Walter James provided funds to pay travel expenses for the well-known St. Mary's High School girls' drum corps in San Francisco's Chinatown to take part in the festivities.[48]

Despite this show of unity, the goals of the business community and those of the professionals were basically divergent, and tensions soon arose within the new organization. While the businessmen wanted to promote commercial success, the intellectuals were more interested in sponsoring scholarships, dinners, and other social events. The conflict reached a climax during discussions of whether the Minnesota Chinese community should participate in the national Miss Chinatown contest in 1970. Businessmen saw potential economic gains in such an event, while the professionals looked upon it with distaste. The latter eventually agreed to go along with the contest, with the understanding that those parents who did not favor beauty pageants would not permit their children to participate. The Miss Chinatown competition was held in Westminster Church with five candidates backed by various interest groups in the business community. The winner, Linda Shen, was feted in gala Minneapolis celebrations; she then went on to win the Miss Chinatown U.S.A. title the following year in San Francisco. After the local contest the businessmen broke away from CAAM and formed the Chinese Chamber of Commerce.[49]

Since the split, the Chinese Chamber of Commerce has sponsored an annual 4th of July picnic and a lunar New Year's dinner at Howard Wong's Restaurant. It has also supported the Chinese-language school at Westminster Presbyterian Church. CAAM's activities have included the awarding of two scholarships annually to students in the local community, publication of a newsletter, an annual banquet, and participation in the Festival of Nations and Aquatennial celebrations in the Twin Cities.[50]

The Chinese Sunday school program organized in 1882 at Westminster Church continued intermittently until the pre-World War II period when it became important as a meeting place for early Chinese settlers. In the postwar years under the leadership of L. Jane Wilson, who became a vital link between the Chinese community and the larger society, the church again served as a social and religious center for recent Chinese immigrants and their families. In 1969 the Walter James Foundation and Westminster Church cosponsored a new program for the Chinese community under the guidance of the Reverend Stephen Tsui. With Tsui's co-operation a Cantonese-language school was organized in 1972 by the Chinese Chamber of Commerce. In 1980 the classes enrolled 50 students.[51]

The Chinese Christian Fellowship, after outgrowing two houses it had purchased near the Minneapolis campus of the University of Minnesota, in 1975 bought an elementary school building in the St. Paul suburb of Lauderdale. The Reverend Joseph C. Wong, who was called as part-time pastor in 1967, became the full-time minister in 1970. While the original Bible study group was organized by northern Chinese students, it later included southerners as well. In 1980 the congregation was made up of professionals from the north and south, the majority of whom had been students in Minnesota during the 1960s. Wong preached in Mandarin, the language of the north, but those attending could use earphones to hear immediate translations into Cantonese and English. Youth groups and adult classes, as well as family fellowships, were divided by language groups into Mandarin, Cantonese, and English (for the second generation). The fellowship's Chinese-language school was conducted in Mandarin.[52]

The Minnesota Chapter of the National Association of Chinese Americans was organized in 1978. It provided an opportunity for Chinese Americans interested in the People's Republic of China to organize cultural events focused on the "New China." Its activities have included films, lectures, and social events.[53]

The Taiwanese Association of Minnesota, founded in 1966 as the Formosan Club, had become by 1981 the largest of three Taiwanese organizations in the Twin Cities. Its objectives were to promote the interests of its members and to bring together Taiwanese in the area for social and cultural activities. The association has organized seminars, sports fairs, picnics, and parties for the lunar New Year, the Harvest Festival, and Christmas, as well as an annual Taiwan Day. Average attendance at the events has been about 200.[54]

The Educational Fund for the Needy in Taiwan, established in the Twin Cities in 1974 as a nonprofit, educational charity, has assisted over 400 students. A third Taiwanese organization active in 1981 was the Formosan Christian Fellowship, a nondenominational congregation that met each Sunday for services, Bible study, and social activities. In addition to retreats, seminars, and a biweekly bulletin, it sponsored classes in the Taiwanese language for its membership of some 45 adults and 30 children.

Four organizations at the University of Minnesota in the Twin Cities in 1981 reflected the political differences among students from China, Taiwan, and Hong Kong. The largest and most active group was the Chinese Student Association, which was founded in 1914 as the Chinese Student Club. It has been oriented toward the northern Chinese who moved to Taiwan after the establishment of Communist rule in China in 1949. It has co-operated with CAAM in a number of community activities, including the compilation of a Chinese community directory. The Hong Kong Student Association, founded in the 1960s, in the past supported the People's Republic of China, although the membership in 1980 comprised students with various political views. The Chinese Student Service Center, more recently organized, has served students from the People's Republic and attempted to provide information on Chinese culture and history to the broader Twin Cities community. In 1980 the Taiwanese Student Association was comprised largely of native Taiwanese and worked closely with the Taiwanese Association of Minnesota in the Twin Cities. While it was not primarily a political organization, its members favored independence for Taiwan.[55]

Acculturation and Interaction

While acculturation varied among individuals in Minnesota's Chinese community, a few observations may be made concerning language retention, marriage customs, and burial rites. In general, Cantonese families in the business community have retained their language to a greater degree than have Mandarin speakers in the professional group. American-born Chinese men who married women from China after World War II have also succeeded in retaining Chinese as the language spoken in their homes. In many cases the oldest child in the immigrant family — who carries the greatest burden in fulfilling the parents' wishes — has married a Chinese and maintained the native language in the family. Twin Cities resident Margaret Woo Chinn, daughter of early settler Woo Du Sing, pointed out that children of pioneer immigrants who grew up in Minnesota in the 1910s and 1920s

had to speak Chinese at home because their parents and grandparents could not speak English. Nevertheless many like herself now find it easier to speak English because their children do not speak Chinese. The language she has retained is largely household Chinese. On the other hand, Albert Hum, the son of another early settler, Hum Su, noted that he and his brothers and sister all speak Chinese at home, and their children understand but do not speak the language.[56]

Most children of Cantonese businessmen who were born in the 1940s and 1950s speak only limited Chinese, and children of Mandarin-speaking professionals speak almost no Chinese. Several have pointed out that since both parents usually spoke English well, there was no need for the children to learn Chinese. University of Minnesota entomology professor Chiang Huai-chang, who arrived in the state as a student in 1945, observed that he and his wife had rarely spoken Chinese at home, but after visits to the People's Republic of China, they have found themselves using a number of Chinese slang phrases that "seem to express it just right."[57]

Modified forms of arranged marriage, particularly between immigrants' sons and women in *Sze Yup*, were maintained in Minnesota's Chinese community through the 1930s. Since then intermarriage has become increasingly frequent, despite the anxiety this has caused the immigrant population. Most Chinese parents in recent years have continued to emphasize the importance of marrying Chinese, some pointing out that marrying into another Asian group would be better than wedding a Caucasian. Professionals have also made it clear to their children that they should marry a Chinese of their own class rather than offspring of families in business. While there is a general recognition that intermarriage is inevitable in Minnesota, where the Chinese population is relatively small, a number of the second generation have observed that they have been disturbed when their children married Caucasians.[58]

The Chinese immigrants' practice of returning the bones of the deceased to his home village to be buried near his ancestors' graves — a practice limited to affluent merchants — was discontinued in the 1930s because of the Japanese invasion of China. Later, community organizations formed committees to maintain the immigrants' graves. While the caretaker groups no longer exist, most Chinese remember the deceased on Memorial Day, which has replaced the Chinese dragon festival as a day for honoring ancestors. For the most part traditional burial rites have not been retained in the post-World War II period, but incense sticks may still be seen in the Chinese section of Lakewood Cemetery in Minneapolis.[59]

Although Chinese Americans feel they have been generally well accepted in Minnesota, they have experienced overt discrimination since the early days. One instance occurred in 1925 during a nationwide wave of tong wars that flared briefly in the Twin Cities. During the summer of 1925 two local tong members were murdered in Minneapolis by out-of-town representatives of rival tongs. Although neither crime was committed by a member of the Twin Cities community, local police and federal agents responded to the

THE GRAVESTONE of Kia-Yick Yep in Duluth's Park Hill Cemetery. The inscriptions at lower right and left are place names; the characters under the English letters identify the deceased as a native of Taishan (Toishan) District. Yep died in 1934.

second murder with the mass arrest of 113 Chinese men as part of an effort to "determine the exact status of every Chinese living here and impress on the tongs that the Twin Cities are not a battle ground where murder can be committed with impunity." Eighty-eight of those arrested were able to prove at once that they had legally entered the United States; they were soon released, while the remaining men were subjected to an investigation that included the threat of deportation. The rights of those who were legal immigrants had clearly been violated.[60]

A more recent example of discrimination occurred in Lauderdale and involved the Chinese Christian Fellowship. For more than three years after the fellowship moved into the former school building, local residents repeatedly vandalized the structure, disrupted services by throwing rocks through windows, and damaged members' automobiles parked nearby. Discrimination in the Twin Cities housing market has long been evident. As recently as the 1960s Chinese were not able to buy houses in affluent suburbs. Name-calling in elementary school and dating problems in high school and college have been experienced by the second and third generations.[61]

Until the 1970s Chinese Americans were more concerned with the conflicts between the People's Republic of China and Taiwan and with United States' China policy than with American domestic politics. Deeply divided between the pro-Taiwan faction and those who favored the People's Republic, many in the community were ambivalent about President Richard M. Nixon's initiative in opening relations between the United States and China in the early 1970s, while others welcomed the opportunity to visit their homeland.[62]

During the 1960s some second-generation Chinese participated in the minority rights and antiwar movements, and a few subsequently became active in the Democratic-Farmer-Labor party. The Chinese community as a whole became more involved in local and national politics in the 1970s. Chinese contributed generously to Hubert H. Humphrey's senatorial campaigns and supported Donald M. Fraser's Minneapolis mayoral campaign in 1979. The Chinese Chamber of Commerce also made a significant contribution to the Hubert H. Humphrey Institute of Public Affairs at the University of Minnesota, established in honor of the late senator in 1978. Humphrey had long been considered a friend of the Minnesota Chinese because of his frequent assistance with immigration problems. Many also supported his pro-Taiwan position.[63]

Minnesota's Chinese-American community in 1981 comprised a complex variety of subgroups, including young couples and teenagers recently arrived from China, well-established businessmen, students, professionals, and second- and third-generation members. Their life-styles ranged from that of intellectuals in outstate college towns, who were well integrated into local social life, to recent immigrants in the Twin Cities who sought the support and intimacy of traditional Chinese organizations.[64] The rapid growth and fragmentation of the Chinese settlement in Minnesota after World War II brought many changes in the older organizations and a proliferation of new ones to meet the needs of the subgroups within the community. There is little doubt that the Chinese-American community in Minnesota will continue to change as more newcomers arrive.

Reference notes

Much of the information in this chapter is from the author's interviews of members of the Chinese-American community in Minnesota and selected others. Those interviews that were recorded on tape are so identified; the tapes are in the Audio-Visual Library, MHS. The author's notes for both taped and untaped interviews are in MEHP Papers, MHS.

[1] The approximate arrival date of the first Chinese immigrants is based on information from *Stillwater Gazette*, May 24, 1876; *St. Paul Pioneer Press and Tribune*, May 31, 1876; *Minneapolis Tribune*, July 3, 7, 1876; *St. Paul City Directory, 1876*; *Minneapolis City Directory, 1876*; United States, *Census*, 1880, *Population*, 396. On the Chinese in the West and the anti-Chinese movement, see Stanford M. Lyman, *Chinese Americans*, 54–85 (New York, 1974). A search in the records of the Great Northern and Northern Pacific railroads in MHS revealed no evidence that Chinese laborers were employed in Minnesota railroad construction, nor was any evidence found that they worked in farming, lumbering, or mining in the state.

[2] Minnesota manuscript census schedules, 1885, for counties cited, rolls 21, 27–30, 33, 36–39, 41, 45, 46, microfilm in MHS; *Duluth City Directory, 1887*; *St. Paul Daily Globe*, October 11, 1879, September 18, 1885; *Stillwater Gazette*, May 24, 1876, January 3, 1883; *Winona Herald*, September 22, 1876; *Rush City Post*, August

26, 1881; interview of May Hum Pan, August 15, 1979; Walter O'Meara, *We Made It Through the Winter: A Memoir of Northern Minnesota Boyhood*, 16 (St. Paul, 1974).

For information on Chinese on the iron ranges, see U.S. Immigration Commission, *Immigrants in Industries*, 78:301 (61 Congress, 2 session, *Senate Documents*, no. 633 — serial 5677); Donald L. Boese, *John C. Greenway and the Opening of the Western Mesabi*, 28, 30 (Grand Rapids, 1975); Anthony C. Schulzetenberg, "Life on the Vermilion Range Before 1900," 14, typed manuscript, 1963, copy in MHS; *Eveleth News-Clarion*, July 31, 1947, sec. 2, p. 1; *Iron Ranges of Minnesota: Historical Souvenir of the Virginia Enterprise* (Virginia, 1909); Carl Zapffe, *"75" Brainerd, Minnesota, 1871–1946*, 54 (Minneapolis, 1946); *Range Towns Directory of the Vermilion and Mesaba Iron Ranges in Northern Minnesota, 1907–1908*, 785, 786, 820, 821; *Duluth News Tribune*, January 22, 1911, p. 14.

It should be noted that Asians have been consistently undercounted in the U.S. censuses and that discrepancies occur between the national and state counts. The latter is probably more accurate. See Table 28.1. Another discrepancy is apparent between the 1910 U.S. census enumeration of 275 Chinese in Minnesota, and the U.S. Immigration Commission report published the same year (cited above) which counted 110 Chinese living on the iron ranges alone. U.S., *Census*, 1890, *Population*, part 1, p. 438; 1910, 2:991; see also Appendix.

³ H. M. Lai, "Chinese," in Stephan Thernstrom, ed., *Harvard Encyclopedia of American Ethnic Groups*, 223 (Cambridge, Mass., 1980); interview of Edward L. Thom, June 7, 1979; Minnesota Governor's Interracial Commission, *The Oriental in Minnesota*, 7 ([St. Paul], 1949). Estimates of Minnesota's Chinese population in 1980 do not include ethnic Chinese immigrants from Vietnam. The Chinese population in the U.S. in 1980 was estimated at between 800,000 and 900,000. Hum Mark Lai, Joe Huang, and Don Wong, *The Chinese of America, 1785–1980*, 93 (San Francisco, 1980). For more on U.S. immigration laws, see Introduction.

⁴ Lyman, *Chinese Americans*, 5, 58–62; Lai, in Thernstrom, ed., *Harvard Encyclopedia*, 218, 220. That the fear of cheap Chinese labor existed in Minnesota is indicated by published notices which (1) scotched rumors that Chinese would be hired by a new barrel factory in Minneapolis in 1878, and (2) reported that "200 Chinamen are to be introduced in Minneapolis to fill the demand for labor" in 1881; *Minneapolis Tribune*, May 29, 1878, October 5, 1881.

⁵ Betty L. Sung, *The Story of the Chinese in America*, 11–14 (New York, 1967); Lai, in Thernstrom, ed., *Harvard Encyclopedia*, 218.

⁶ Interviews of David Yep, June 12, 26, 1979; Sung, *Chinese in America*, 154–156.

⁷ *Minneapolis City Directory, 1876*; *St. Paul City Directory, 1876*.

⁸ *St. Paul Pioneer Press*, January 3, 16, 1877; *St. Paul Dispatch*, January 15, 1877; *Stillwater Gazette*, October 17, 1877. The Chinese name order — surname first — is used here and for names of all Chinese immigrants, except in cases where the immigrants or their children have adopted American given names.

⁹ Data compiled by Dennis Tachiki from Minneapolis, St. Paul, and Duluth *City Directories, 1876–1910*, in MEHP Papers; Plymouth [Congregational] Church (St. Paul), *The Records and Reports for 1883*, 7 (Red Wing, 1884); *Stillwater City Directory, 1885*; Paul H. Landis, *Three Iron Mining Towns: A Study in Cultural Change*, 19 (Ann Arbor, Mich., 1938). On the population growth of the cities, 1860–85, see William W. Folwell, *A History of Minnesota*, 3:480n (Reprint ed., St. Paul, 1969). An 1888 agreement allowed Chinese to re-enter the U.S. upon showing a certificate, issued prior to departure, that proved their rights as teachers, officials, students, merchants, and travelers. See Marion T. Bennett, *American Immigration Policies: A History*, 19 (Washington, D.C., 1963).

¹⁰ Sung, *Chinese in America*, 189–193.

¹¹ Tachiki data, 1876–1910.

¹² Interview of Margaret Woo Chinn, daughter of Woo Du Sing, July 3, 1979; Yep interviews, June 26, July 16, 1979. The author wishes to acknowledge helpful suggestions received during the preparation of this chapter from Margaret Woo Chinn. For more on Chinese immigrant organizations, see Stanford Lyman, "Strangers in the City: The Chinese in the Urban Frontier," in Amy Tachiki *et al.*, eds., *Roots: An Asian American Reader*, 166–169 (Los Angeles, 1971). "Several" Chinese men in Duluth in 1892 belonged to the Superior, Wis., lodge of Chinese Free Masons, organized about 1890. In 1894 the "Chinese and Japanese Grand Lodge of Masons of Northern Wisconsin and Michigan" was organized in Superior with some members from Duluth. See *Superior Evening Telegram*, March 5, 1892, September 24, 1894.

¹³ Interview of Howard Woo, November 22, 1980; M. Chinn interview, July 3, 1979.

¹⁴ Here and below, see John E. Bushnell, *The History of Westminster Presbyterian Church*, 76, 77 (Minneapolis, 1938); interview of Walter Girod, August 30, 1979.

¹⁵ *Duluth News Tribune*, January 22, 1911, p. 14; interview of Sing Chinn, nephew of Chin D. Ong, July 12, 1979.

¹⁶ Sung, *Chinese in America*, 154; interviews of Albert Hum, November 18, 1980, Marvel Hum Chong, June 8, 1979 (taped).

¹⁷ M. Chinn interviews, July 3, 1979, November 8, December 9, 1980, February 19, 1981.

¹⁸ Hum interviews, July 20, 1979, November 18, 21, 1980. The U.S. Supreme Court ruled in 1900 that wives and minor children of Chinese merchants in the U.S. were admissible with proper "merchant papers." S. W. Kung, *Chinese in American Life: Some Aspects of Their History, Status, Problems, and Contributions*, 96–98 (Seattle, 1962).

¹⁹ Pan interviews, August 15, 1979, November 18, 1980; M. Chong interviews, September 6, November 17, 1980. Both interviewees are daughters of Hum Bing. A number of early marriages involved Chinese men and Polish women who worked in the kitchens of Chinese restaurants; Chong interview, August 31, 1979.

²⁰ Thom interview, June 7, 1979; Governor's Interracial Commission, *Oriental in Minnesota*, 11; Minneapolis, St. Paul, and Duluth *City Directories, 1910, 1928, 1935*. On the inadequacies of U.S. census figures for this period, see Appendix.

²¹ Lai, in Thernstrom, ed., *Harvard Encyclopedia*, 223; Lyman, *Chinese Americans*, 105–112.

²² *St. Paul Dispatch*, November 11, 1912, p. 4; Yep interview, July 16, 1979.

²³ Interview of Betty Wong, August 22, 1979; Yep interview, July 16, 1979.

²⁴ Yep interviews, June 12, 26, July 16, 1979; *Hamline Oracle*, March 12, 1926, p. 1. No copies of *Sing Kee Po* were found; it is not known how long the paper was published.

²⁵ "Walter James and '35 Golden Years,'" in *Greater Minneapolis*, November, 1954, p. 9; taped interviews of Viola H. Hymes and Florence G. Greene by Rhoda G. Lewin, May 10 and August 13, 1976, respectively; taped interviews of Stanley Chong, June 28, 1979, and Marvel Chong, June 8, 1979. James also managed the Nankin Cafe in St. Paul at 7th and Wabasha in the 1920s; as a community leader he purchased a plot in Lakewood Cemetery, Minneapolis, for burial of single Chinese men without families. *Capitol Theatre Magazine*, May 26, 1923; M. Chong interview, July 3, 1979.

²⁶ Here and below, see M. Chinn interview, July 12, 1979; *Duluth City Directory, 1935*. See also Wing Young Huie, "Port Cities People: Joe Huie," in *Lake Superior Port Cities*, vol. 1, no. 2, pp. 9–12 (1979), copy in MEHP Papers; interview of Joe Huie, January 21, 1979.

²⁷ Interview of Michael Wong, August 29, 1979. For a fictionalized account of a Chinese family in Albert Lea in the 1950s, see

Eleanor Wong Telemaque, *It's Crazy to Stay Chinese in Minnesota* (Nashville, Tenn., 1978).

[28] *Minneapolis Tribune,* August 14, 1925, p. 8; Mary Lynn, "'And Unto the Following Generation' . . . ,'' in *M.A.C. Gopher,* May, 1939, pp. 9, 23–27; M. Chinn interview, July 3, 1979. The coin and sugar symbolized more sweetness in the future for the recipients. For a description of a similar, much earlier funeral in Minnesota, see *Winona Herald,* September 22, 1876.

[29] Hum interview, November 18, 1980; M. Chong interview, November 25, 1980.

[30] M. Chinn interviews, July 3, August 29, 1979; B. Wong interview, August 22, 1979.

[31] Here and three paragraphs below, see M. Chong interview, August 31, 1979, Pan interviews, August 15, 27, 1979. The three other students were Pan Wen Hua, Ling Pao Ching, and Harding Kwong. After the antiwestern Boxer uprising in China in 1900, the U.S. and other western powers exacted an indemnity for damages to property. Later the U.S. returned its share to China in the form of scholarships to outstanding Chinese students selected to study in the U.S. Sung, *Chinese in America,* 61.

[32] Data compiled by author from materials in "Chinese Foreign Students at University of Minnesota, 1920–40," a folder of information collected by Dennis Tachiki from holdings (primarily President's Files) in the University of Minnesota Archives, in MEHP Papers; see also interview of Joyce Yu, July 24, 1979.

[33] Interviews of Howard Chinn, former MISLS student, November 28, 1980, and Ginn Young, November 29, 1980. On the language school students, see *Memoirs, Fort Snelling, 1945,* a yearbook published by the Chinese servicemen, in possession of Ginn Young, Minneapolis. The Chinese were a small and largely unpublicized contingent within the MISLS, which became more widely known for its enrollment of Japanese Americans. See Chapter 30.

[34] *Minneapolis Star Journal, Sunday Magazine,* March 23, 1941, p. 5; *Duluth News Tribune,* June 15, 1940, p. 6, March 11, 1941, p. 6, March 19, 1941, p. 6.

[35] United States Asian Statistics, in MEHP Papers, compiled by Jon A. Gjerde from U.S. Dept. of Labor, Bureau of Immigration, *Annual Reports,* 1909–39, and U.S. Justice Dept., Immigration and Naturalization Service, *Annual Reports,* 1940–78, hereafter cited as Gjerde, Asian statistics; U.S., *Census,* 1960, *Population,* vol. 1, part 25, p. 43.

[36] Sung, *Chinese in America,* 78–80, 82, 156; Kung, *Chinese in American Life,* 103, 105, 106, 108, 112; Bennett, *American Immigration Policies,* 74.

[37] Gjerde, Asian statistics; interview of Jane Kretzmann, Minnesota Dept. of Public Welfare, March 11, 1980. On the Vietnamese, see Chapter 32.

[38] Interviews of L. Jane Wilson, former superintendent of Westminster's Chinese Sunday school, June 1, 1979, Judy Wong Hohmann, May 9, 1980; Francys E. Shull, *How Firm A Foundation: A History of the Westminster Service Guild, Westminster Church, Minneapolis . . . 50th Anniversary,* 26 (Minneapolis, 1968).

[39] S. Chong interviews, January 11, June 28, 1979.

[40] S. Chong interview, June 28, 1979; interviews of Rev. Joseph C. Wong, August 7, 1979, Tina Wu, October 8, 1979.

[41] U.S., *Census,* 1970, *Population,* vol. 1, part 25, p. 66. The sex ratio among Chinese Americans was equalized by the number of children born in the U.S. as well as by the influx of Chinese women after World War II.

[42] Here and below, see data on Chinese alumni of the University of Minnesota, compiled by Forrest Moore, former director, International Student Adviser's Office, in his possession; interview of Forrest Moore, November 7, 1979; University of Minnesota, *International Programs Newsletter,* June, 1975, p. 1; information from

John Albrecht, International Student Adviser's Office, University of Minnesota, July 27, 1981, in MEHP Papers.

[43] Yu interview (taped), June 4, 1979; M. Wong interview, July 3, 1979; Hohmann interview, May 20, 1980; *MAAP Newsletter,* June, 1977, pp. 1–5, copy in MHS.

[44] Yep interview, July 16, 1979; interview of James Wong, September 6, 1979; Girod interview, August 30, 1979; M. Wong interview, August 29, 1979; *St. Paul Dispatch,* October 16, 1924, p. 1; Sung, *Chinese in America,* 137. See also note 60, below. That tongs periodically brought Chinese prostitutes to the Twin Cities during the 1920s and 1930s was reported by one interviewee but not verified by other sources.

[45] Lai, in Thernstrom, ed., *Harvard Encyclopedia,* 222; Lyman, *Chinese Americans,* 30.

[46] J. Wong interview, September 6, 1979; interview of Helen Fong, November 30, 1980.

[47] Yu interview, June 4, 1979; S. Chong interviews, June 28, 1979, December 5, 1980.

[48] S. Chong interview, June 28, 1979; M. Chong interviews, June 8, 1979, February 20, 1981; *International Institute Newsletter,* March, 1972, p. 4. The Chinese arch was later moved to a site on the Minnesota State Fairgrounds.

[49] Yu interview, June 4, 1979; M. Chong interview, June 8, 1979; Fong interview, November 30, 1980.

[50] Hohmann interview, December 3, 1980; interview of Jacqueline Yue, May 13, 1980. Yue was president of CAAM.

[51] Hohmann interview, December 3, 1980; Fong interview, December 2, 1980 (Fong was principal of the Chinese-language school); Stephen Tsui, "A Report on the Chinese Community in the Twin Cities," 1–3, unpublished paper, 1975, copy in MEHP Papers.

Information on three other early schools for Chinese is sketchy. One was organized in 1883 in St. Paul as the Chinese Education Society; it held classes, apparently in English, for a total of 36 Chinese men during its first year. *Minneapolis Tribune,* November 18, 1884. The second was begun about 1885 by the First Presbyterian Church of Duluth. *Minneapolis Tribune,* April 29, 1885; First Presbyterian Church, *Centennial, 1869–1969,* 12, 25 (Duluth, 1969). The third was a class for a "half dozen" Chinese men held at the East Presbyterian Church in St. Paul in 1895. *St. Paul Pioneer Press,* August 26, 1895.

[52] Rev. Wong interview, August 7, 1979; (St. Anthony) *Park Bugle* (St. Paul), February, 1978, p. 7; Chinese Christian Fellowship, *A Brief Introduction,* an undated, printed chronology of the fellowship's history, copy in MEHP Papers.

[53] *NACA, Newsletter of the Minnesota Chapter of the National Association of Chinese Americans,* [January?], 1978, copy in MEHP Papers. NACA was founded in September, 1977.

[54] Here and below, see *Taiwanese in Minnesota,* a pamphlet published in 1977; a copy, updated by Edward Yu in 1980, is in MEHP Papers. The name of the Formosan Club was changed in 1979.

[55] Interviews of Carole Hasagawa, Asian-Pacific American Learning Resource Center, University of Minnesota, October 5, 1979, Cheong Kit Lan, Chinese Student Service Center, October 15, 1979, Edward Yu, January 20, 1981, Steve Wang, Chinese Student Association, October 10, 1979.

[56] M. Wong interview, February 22, 1981; M. Chinn interview, February 22, 1981; Hum interview, February 24, 1981.

[57] Yu interview, June 4, 1979; interview of Chiang Huai-chang, February 23, 1981.

[58] Yu interview, June 4, 1979; B. Wong interview, August 22, 1979; Yep interviews, June 12, September 18, 1979.

[59] M. Chinn interview, February 19, 1981.

[60] For local press coverage of the Twin Cities tong wars of 1924–25, see *St. Paul Dispatch,* October 16, 1924, p. 1; August 14, p.

6; 25, pp. 1, 7; 26, p. 11; September 7, p. 2; October 3, p. 1 — all 1925; *St. Paul Pioneer Press*, October 17, 1924, p. 1; March 8, p. 9; 12, p. 1; August 26, p. 5; 28, p. 15; September 11, p. 3; 16, p. 4; October 3, p. 1; 4, p. 1 — all 1925; *Minneapolis Tribune*, October 17, p. 12; 18, p. 16 — both 1924; August 14, p. 8; 26, p. 2; 27, p. 1; 28, p. 2; 29, p. 1 — all 1925.

[61] *Minneapolis Tribune*, June 12 (p. 1B), September 21, (p. 1B), 1978; (St. Anthony) *Park Bugle*, June, 1978, p. 1; Yu interview, September 26, 1978; interview of Frank Tsai, October 5, 1979.

[62] Yu interview, June 4, 1979.

[63] M. Wong interview, August 29, 1979; Yu interview, June 4, 1979; Tsai interview, October 5, 1979.

[64] On outstate Chinese Americans, see interviews of Amy and Lai Ling Chin, Duluth, July 12, 1979; Sen and Helen Fan, Morris, December 1, 1979 (taped); Sinmin and Betty Wu, Morris, December 2, 1979 (taped).

CHAPTER 29

The Filipinos

Sarah R. Mason

IN THE 70 OR MORE YEARS since immigrants from the Philippines first arrived in Minnesota, the Filipino[1] community has grown from a small settlement of about 200 students and workers in the late 1920s to an increasingly diversified population of 3,000 to 4,000 in 1980, a large proportion of whom are professionals and their families who arrived after 1965. While the Minnesota community is relatively small compared to larger settlements in New York, Chicago, Los Angeles, and Honolulu, Filipinos constitute one of the most rapidly growing immigrant groups in the state.[2]

Minnesota's Filipino community had its beginnings in a small group of 25 to 30 Filipino students — predominantly males — who enrolled at the University of Minnesota and other colleges during the late 1910s and early 1920s. A few workers arrived even before the students, but it was not until the late 1920s that systematic recruitment brought 150 to 200 Filipino laborers each spring and summer to Minnesota's sugar beet fields, truck farms, and canneries. Some seasonal workers stayed on each year to seek employment in the Twin Cities, and many of the students also remained as permanent residents. Although immigration from the Philippines virtually stopped during the Depression and World War II, Filipino farm workers continued to migrate to Minnesota from other states throughout the 1930s and early 1940s. Following Philippine independence in 1946, immigration to the state gradually increased, and by 1965 the community had grown from an estimated 500 in 1949 to over 1,000. Soon after the 1965 liberalization of United States immigration law, new arrivals from the Philippines began to increase dramatically, reflecting the large influx of Asian immigrants throughout the country. From 1965 to 1978, approximately 2,000 Filipinos settled in Minnesota, more than tripling the 1965 Filipino population (see Table 29.1).[3]

Filipino immigration to the United States began soon after American colonization of the islands in 1898, following the United States victory in the Spanish-American War. The first to arrive were the *pensionados*, or students on government stipends, who were sent to the United States under a program initiated by William Howard Taft, first civil governor in the colony. While only 209 *pensionados* took part in the program, which lasted from 1903 to 1910, many other students followed, totaling more than 14,000 by World War II. During the period from 1907 to 1934 workers recruited or enlisted by agents of the Hawaiian Sugar Planters' Associa-

tion constituted a much larger immigrating group than the students. While figures are not available for the entire period, at least 113,000 Filipino workers arrived in Hawaii between 1909 and 1931. As many as 18,600 of these later migrated to the West Coast, and during the mid-1920s immigration of workers from the Philippines to the continental United States also increased rapidly. While most Filipinos lived and worked in the Pacific Coast states, a sizable number of those who arrived in the 1920s migrated to the Midwest and East. After 1965 a far greater influx occurred, and from 1968 to 1978 Filipinos represented the second largest immigrating group in the United States following the Mexicans. During this period 329,785 Filipinos — two-thirds of whom were professionals and skilled workers — entered the country, and by 1980 the total Filipino population reached 400,000 to 500,000.[4]

The history of Filipino immigration to the United States and Minnesota has been shaped to a large extent by restrictive immigration laws passed by Congress during the 1920s and 1930s, a period of intensified nativism and racial exclusion (see Introduction). From the annexation of the Philippines by the United States in 1898 to the enactment by Congress of the Philippine Independence Act of 1934 — which granted the Philippines deferred independence — Filipinos were classified as United States "nationals." Unlike other Asians, Filipinos were exempt from immigration restrictions during this period because of their status as colonial subjects. Nevertheless the movement to ban all Asian immigrants from the United States had a marked effect on the course of Filipino immigration and the reception given Filipinos in this country even before 1934.[5]

Table 29.1. Filipino Immigration to Minnesota, 1961–78

1961	10	1970	144
1962	20	1971	194
1963	20	1972	192
1964	15	1973	211
1965	6	1974	160
1966	29	1975	176
1967	89	1976	247
1968	97	1977	209
1969	99	1978	169

Source: U.S. Dept. of Justice, Immigration and Naturalization Service, *Annual Reports,* for the years cited. The figures, covering fiscal years ending June 30, represent those expressing an *intention* to settle in Minnesota.

The exemption of Filipinos from the Asian exclusion provision of the Immigration Act of 1924, also known as the National Origins Act, resulted in accelerated recruitment of laborers from Hawaii and the Philippines for agricultural work in the western states. This recruitment began in 1923, while the immigration bill was still being debated in Congress, and continued through 1929. Reflecting these efforts, the average annual number of Filipinos entering the country increased from 7,019 in the 1920–23 period to 13,547 in the 1923–29 period. In Minnesota the Filipino population rose from 20 in 1920 to 236 in 1930.[6]

Despite the fact that the influx of Filipinos into the United States was still considerably less than the earlier Japanese and Chinese immigration, by the late 1920s a new movement was under way in Congress to add Filipinos to the list of excluded Asians. In 1928 Representative Richard J. Welch of California introduced a bill to remove the Filipino exemption from the 1924 immigration act. During public hearings on the bill, exclusionists — supported by labor leaders and nativists — used the same arguments previously employed against the Chinese and Japanese, claiming that cheap labor endangered the American standard of living and that Filipinos could never be assimilated into American society.[7]

Filipino leaders appearing at the hearings included Manuel Roxas, later president of the Philippines, who pointed out that no nation, no matter how imperialistic, had ever denied its colonial subjects the right to immigrate to the mother country. Camilio Osias, Philippines commissioner in the United States Congress, argued that if Filipinos were to be treated as aliens, they should first be given their independence. The moral arguments of the Filipino leaders were apparently effective, and the Filipino exclusion provision was not reported.

Following the hearings, however, the notion of independence as the only justifiable means of achieving Filipino exclusion gained wide acceptance, even among spokesmen for the growing independence movement in the Philippines. A compromise was eventually reached between American exclusionists and Filipino independence leaders which resulted in the Philippine Independence Act of 1934. By this act, the United States Congress granted deferred independence — to take place 10 years after a constitutional form of government was established — in return for acceptance by Filipino leaders of immediate restriction of immigration to a quota of 50 per year, the lowest permitted by law. Filipino leaders stipulated, nevertheless, that the quota must be based on national origin rather than race, and the Philippines became the first Asian nation to have a quota.

The Philippine Independence Act of 1934 was opposed by many Filipinos in Minnesota, because of the immigration restriction clause. Its most profound effect in the Minnesota community was to perpetuate the numerical predominance of Filipino men. Very few Filipinas had arrived in the state when the restriction became effective; consequently most Filipinos taking up permanent residence during the 1920s and 1930s married Americans. Such mixed marriages prevailed in the state until after World War II.[8]

During final negotiations on independence for the Philippines in 1946, the immigration quota for Filipinos was raised to 100 per year. Congress had also agreed that Filipino residents in the United States could — for the first time — apply for citizenship. In 1924 the Supreme Court had ruled that because Filipinos were United States nationals, and not aliens, they were ineligible for naturalization, since by statute only aliens could become naturalized citizens. As a result of this ruling, many Filipinos had resided in Minnesota for as long as 25 years without citizenship rights.[9]

The quota system, which continued to govern the immigration and settlement of Filipinos in the United States for two decades after World War II, was abolished by the 1965 immigration act. Effective July 1, 1968, this act opened a new period in the Minnesota Filipino community. Within 10 years New Immigrants, who began arriving in family groups in the late 1960s, equaled Old Timers, whose Minnesota history extended from World War I and the nativism of the 1920s.[10]

The Early Immigrant Community

The first Filipino residents in Minnesota appear to have arrived in 1910 or earlier and probably left before the first wave of immigration began. The only known evidence of their presence consists of the United States Census of 1910, which listed two Filipinos in the state, and a news item in the September 10, 1912, issue of the *St. Paul Dispatch*, which reported that two Filipinos living in St. Paul had tried to register to vote in the national elections. According to the *Dispatch*, the Filipinos were turned down by the assistant corporation attorney, who said that "unless the Filipinos were naturalized, they had no right to vote in the United States." There is no record of the two Filipinos after this date, however, nor is there any knowledge of them among the Old Timers of the present Filipino community.[11]

Of the students who arrived in Minnesota in the late 1910s the first was Juan C. Orendain, who left the Visayan Islands in the central Philippines in 1917 (see Map 29.1). He had attended a missionary high school in Iloilo province, where teachers from the Swedish Baptist General Conference in Minnesota encouraged him to continue his studies at Bethel Academy in St. Paul. Orendain attended the academy during the 1917–18 school year, and the next fall he entered the University of Minnesota in Minneapolis. He remained in the state for eight years, attending classes at the university, St. Paul College of Law, and the College of St. Thomas, while supporting himself by alternating periods of work and study.[12]

Like many students who followed in later years, Orendain discovered that practically the only jobs open to Filipinos in the Twin Cities were service positions. He worked as dishwasher, hospital orderly, and gardener, then served as a butler in the homes of wealthy businessmen, including John S. Pillsbury, John Washburn, and George C. Beckwith. Later, as a law student, he passed a civil service examination and obtained a position in Duluth during the summer of 1924 as navigation inspector for Lake Superior; after that he sold magazine subscriptions and brushes door to door.

As more Filipino students arrived in Minnesota, Orendain joined Filipino student groups and community organizations and took a lively interest in American politics as well as

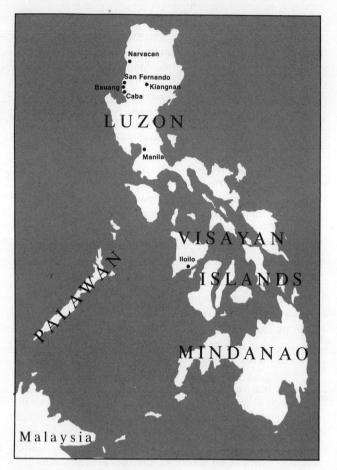

Map 29.1. The Philippine Islands

social and religious affairs. His marriage to a Scandinavian American set a pattern which was to become a prevalent feature in the state's Filipino community. After moving to Florida in 1925 for health reasons, he worked for the city of Miami Beach and completed his law studies at Stetson University. He returned to the Philippines in 1930 and embarked upon a distinguished career as a lawyer, writer, and adviser to Filipino and American officials.

In 1918 four Filipino students immigrated to Minnesota from Caba, a city in the province of La Union in northern Luzon. Their arrival marked the beginning of a chain migration from Caba to the Twin Cities, as the students wrote to relatives and friends and encouraged them to follow. The initial group included two cousins, Sixto F. Runez and Caledonio Maglaya, and two brothers, Dedimo M. and Eugenio M. Fonbuena. All four had attended La Union High School in San Fernando, La Union, where about half the teachers were Americans recruited by the United States government. Several were from Minnesota, including one whose sister owned a farm near Champlin in Hennepin County. This teacher and her sister, who visited San Fernando, urged the students to go to Minnesota to study.[13]

After the four students arrived, however, the teacher's sister took them to her Champlin farm and put them to work, which delayed the beginning of their studies for some time. All were children of government officials in La Union who hoped that an American education would enable their sons to enter professional careers. Thus their parents were surprised and dismayed when the students sent home photographs of themselves as farm workers in Minnesota.

In spite of this exploitation of the young Filipinos, the students from Caba subsequently completed their studies successfully. Two earned doctoral degrees, and three returned to the Philippines to pursue professional occupations. The fourth, a lawyer, married an American and settled in Washington, D.C. According to the Old Timers in Minnesota, marriage to an American usually led to the decision to remain in the United States. Although most Filipino students planned to return home after completing their education, their American wives frequently did not want to live in the Philippines.[14]

Several students from Caba arrived in the Twin Cities each year after 1918, encouraged by the Minnesota students, by American teachers, and by textbooks that fostered the "American Dream" of the United States as the land of democracy and economic opportunity. They were also motivated by the high value Filipinos placed on education and by the widespread belief that students in America could support themselves while they pursued their courses of study. The students chose Minnesota because of family and regional ties with earlier immigrants from Caba, a factor of major importance to early settlers in the 1920s and 1930s, as well as immigrants in the late 1960s and 1970s.[15]

The influence of family and regional ties is illustrated by the pattern of immigration among members of the Runez family who followed Sixto Runez and his cousin Caledonio Maglaya to Minnesota. In 1919 Sixto's cousin Abelardo B. Runez, who had grown up in Caba, arrived. He eventually married an American and remained as a permanent resident of the state. In 1922 Sixto's younger brother Rudolfo (later Americanized to Rudolph) also decided to go to Minnesota,

EDDIE MAGLAYA was among the Filipino students who worked as domestic servants in the 1920s.

where he married a Norwegian immigrant's daughter and became a resident. Later in the decade another younger brother, Antonio, and two cousins, Patricio A. Runtal and Henry B. Runez, immigrated to Minnesota. Both married Scandinavians and settled in the Twin Cities. Sixto's sister Josefina, a trained nurse, arrived in the state during the 1920s. She married Casimiro B. Lara, a Filipino doctor who was studying at the Mayo Clinic in Rochester on a fellowship from the Philippines government. They returned to the Philippines, but in 1956 their daughter and son-in-law arrived in the Twin Cities for a period of study, thus initiating the second generation of family ties between the two areas.[16]

While the earliest arrivals from Caba were sons of officials and teachers, other Filipino students in Minnesota during the early period were sons of farmers, ranging from wealthy landowners to subsistence farmers. The strong belief that education could bring social status and economic gain to the family motivated even those parents with meager resources to make sacrifices in order to send their children to America for professional training. Although the sons of poor farmers often arrived with scant funds, and therefore had less chance of achieving their educational goals than their compatriots from wealthier families, practically all the Filipino students in Minnesota, regardless of their background, had a difficult time supporting themselves.[17]

Since those who had to work in the Twin Cities could get only service positions, they found themselves in a difficult situation during the late 1920s and early 1930s, when even that type of employment became scarce. Many Filipino students dropped out of school entirely during this period, while new arrivals were not able to begin their studies. Because of the low rate of pay, those who had wives and families to support attempted to hold two or three menial jobs at once in order to survive. Single students who could not find work in the cities often joined Filipino seasonal laborers in the sugar beet fields and on truck farms in southern Minnesota.[18]

The experience of Paul C. Borge, an early immigrant, is an example of many Filipino students' struggles during the late 1920s and 1930s. Borge was born in 1904 in Narvacan, Ilocos Sur, another province of northern Luzon where many of Minnesota's early Filipino immigrants originated. His father was a farmer who grew rice, corn, and vegetables and also fished for the family's consumption. Members of Borge's family were very religious. During his earliest years they were Roman Catholic, but later they joined the Methodist Church, preferring the congregational singing, Bible reading, and warmth and liveliness of its atmosphere. Two of Borge's older cousins studied for the Methodist ministry at Northwestern University in Evanston, Illinois, and for years the youth pleaded that he be allowed to follow them to America. His father finally agreed, on the condition that he also study for the ministry, and sold a cow, a horse, and a piece of land to pay for the trip.[19]

Borge arrived in Seattle in 1926 on a ship with several hundred other Filipinos. Immediately he and his compatriots were besieged by recruiters from ranches and canneries who tried to pressure them into going to Alaska or to various towns in Washington. With no destination and little money, Borge paid a fee and joined a busload of recruits headed for Cosmopolis, Washington, where the recruiter had promised jobs and lodging. Upon their arrival they found that they had been tricked, for while there were a box factory and a hotel in the town, there were no jobs or housing awaiting them. Borge obtained a job in the factory but soon lost it after being injured by falling lumber.

During the following two years, Borge held several service jobs and also did farm work. In the summer he picked apples, hops, and potatoes near Seattle and worked on a lettuce farm near Monroe, Washington. In the winter he and other Filipinos stayed in a Japanese hotel in Seattle — the only one that would take them in — and survived by frequenting a Chinese gambling house that served free meals paid for by the winners.

In the spring of 1928 Borge signed on as a laborer for the Northern Pacific Railroad, working along the tracks in Montana with Japanese, Chinese, and Mexicans, as well as many other Filipinos. After six months he learned that his cousins had completed their theological studies and had moved to Minneapolis. He decided to ask for a railroad pass at the end of the summer in order to join his relatives in Minnesota.

When Borge arrived in Minneapolis in the fall of 1928, he first worked in a laundry and then as a bus boy in the Dyckman Hotel. After a short period of employment at Swift's meat-packing plant in South St. Paul, he took a job as bus boy in the Minneapolis Athletic Club, where Filipinos were often employed in the early years. During the 1930s Borge served as a butler for the family of Charles B. Sweatt, an executive of the Minneapolis Honeywell Company, and also in the home of Minneapolis businessman Cavour S. Langdon. In 1942 he heard that the Great Northern Railroad was hiring Filipinos to replace Japanese in service jobs on the trains. He applied and was employed as a personal attendant in a railway car reserved for the president of the Great Northern. Borge served the president his food, pressed his clothes, and kept the car clean. On some occasions the executive's family or other guests also rode in the car, with Borge attending to their needs as well.

Not long after his arrival in Minneapolis Borge enrolled at the Northwestern Bible College, where he hoped to begin studying for the ministry. As the Depression deepened, however, it became increasingly evident that he could never earn enough money to make this possible, and he abandoned the idea. In 1934 he married a Scandinavian American and remained in Minnesota as a permanent resident.

During his first years in the Twin Cities, Borge lived in the downtown area of Minneapolis, first on Harmon Place, where a number of other Filipinos lived at that time, and later on Clinton Avenue and 14th Street South. Throughout most of the 1930s he and his family resided in housing provided by the wealthy businessmen in whose homes he was employed. In the early 1940s a number of Filipinos migrated to Northeast Minneapolis, and Borge moved his family there when he began to work for the Great Northern Railroad. In the post-World War II years most of the Old Timers moved to the suburbs, as did Borge and his wife, who lived in Columbia Heights in 1980. Borge has participated in Filipino organizations throughout his years in Minnesota, and since his retirement in 1969 from the Great Northern Railroad, he has been active in a number of suburban church and civic groups, including the Community Methodist Church and the Kiwanis Club, of which he served as president in 1975. In 1980 he was elected to the National Commission on Race and Religion of the United Methodist Church.

From Narvacan to Seattle to suburban Minneapolis, and through a half century of active involvement in the Twin Cities' Filipino community, Paul Borge's experiences reflect those of many Old Timers. His life illustrates the linking of student and worker careers in the struggle for economic survival among the state's original Filipino immigrants.

In addition to the students, other Filipinos in the early immigrant community of the late 1920s and 1930s labored on farms and in canneries in southern Minnesota. They immigrated to the state from Hawaii or other parts of the United States or were recruited by representatives of canneries or sugar companies. During this period, for example, the American Crystal Sugar Company in Chaska sent a recruiter each year to the West Coast to find seasonal workers for Minnesota Valley farms, where the tasks of thinning, cultivating, and harvesting sugar beets were done by hand until 1950. While the Filipinos were employed by the farmers themselves, the sugar company handled the recruitment and advanced money to the farmers for workers' wages during the summer months. The Filipinos were housed on the farms and usually cooked their own food in a common kitchen. Each group was hired to complete only one task before moving on to seek work elsewhere in the Midwest. Some of them remained to look for employment in the Twin Cities, eventually becoming permanent residents of the state.[20]

The Minnesota Valley Canning Company also recruited seasonal workers among the Filipinos arriving on the West Coast. In 1929 a recruiter who was having difficulty persuading the Filipinos to go to the Midwest offered to pay an extra sum of money to one of the individuals, Filemon C. Balbuena, if he would talk others into going to Minnesota and act as their manager at a canning factory. Balbuena agreed to accompany 100 of his compatriots to Montgomery, in Le Sueur County, and to serve as supervisor of the group. Although he received the bonus, his pay as manager was never more than $.43 per hour, compared to $.25 per hour paid the others.[21]

Filipinos also arrived independently from other parts of the Midwest to look for farm work in Minnesota. Old Timers recalled that during the Depression they often traveled in groups by freight cars or old automobiles. One of those seeking employment during the 1930s was Stanley A. Sabado, who became a permanent resident and in 1980 lived in Glenville. Freeborn County. Sabado was the son of a subsistence farm family in the Philippines who emigrated to Hawaii in 1927 as a young man. His brothers had preceded him and found work in Chicago. They sent him money to join them and after he arrived in Chicago, Sabado got a job in the United States Post Office, where many other Filipinos were employed. After losing this position during the Depression, however, he decided to go to Minnesota to look for farm work.[22]

Sabado joined a group of Filipino sharecroppers near Albert Lea in Freeborn County. They leased land from local farmers for half the crop, which was shared among 20 to 25 people in the group. The Filipinos lived together in houses rented in such nearby towns as Hayward, Hollandale, and Glenville and raised onions, carrots, cabbage, and other vegetables, which they marketed through local wholesalers. Old Timers recalled that Filipinos on the truck farms often took bags of onions to their compatriots in the Twin Cities during the hard times of the 1930s.

Very few early Filipino settlers in Minnesota initiated business enterprises, but one who did was Pedro T. Velasco, who operated the Velasco Toy Company in Minneapolis from 1930 to 1949. Velasco arrived in 1920, planning to study medicine at the University of Minnesota. Like many other Filipino students, he found the long course of study very expensive and jobs difficult to obtain. After a short period he changed his course to chemistry, married an American, and took a position as chief chemist at the American Crystal Sugar Company in Chaska. In 1930 he opened the toy factory, which employed some 200 persons, including a number of Filipinos. Velasco's firm produced a variety of wooden toys which were marketed throughout the United States as well as in Canada and several South American countries.[23]

Another Filipino business established by Old Timers was the Balbuena Grocery Store operated by Filemon and Clara A. Balbuena from 1949 to 1975. A small shop in the Selby-Dale area of St. Paul, it carried American, Filipino, and other Asian foods.[24]

Aside from a few female students in Minnesota for short periods, there were only three women in the Filipino community during the 1920s and 1930s, which reflected a sex imbalance that existed until the 1960s. Each of the three played an important role in fostering cultural and social activities for Twin Cities Filipinos.

The first to arrive was Basilisa Garcia Epperly, whose husband, Samuel J. Epperly, had been a soldier in the Missouri Volunteers serving in the Philippines during the Spanish-American War. After the war Epperly taught in a Manila high school where Basilisa Garcia was a student. They were married in 1903 and continued to live in Manila until 1914, when Samuel Epperly became ill with tuberculosis and returned to the United States with their eldest son. Four years later Basilisa and the younger children followed. The Epperlys settled first in Onamia, in Mille Lacs County, and then moved to Minneapolis. From 1922 to 1930 they lived in a large house on 4th Street Southeast which became a center for Filipinos in the Twin Cities during the period. Several Filipino students roomed at the Epperlys' home, and on weekends there were dinners and parties for Filipino friends who played their musical instruments and sang songs from the homeland. Later the family moved to Mayer, in Carver County, and then to Mound, in western Hennepin County, but continued to be active in the Twin Cities Filipino community.[25]

The second Filipina to settle in Minnesota was Clara Balbuena, who traveled from the Philippines with her husband Filemon to Montgomery in 1929. During the summer she helped her husband manage a company restaurant serving food cooked in the Filipino style. Just 21 years old when she arrived in the United States, Clara Balbuena believed that she and her husband would visit friends for a few months before returning to the Philippines. As the months turned into years and the Depression worsened, it became difficult to save enough money for the return passage.[26]

Clara Balbuena never ceased longing to return to her homeland; in the meantime she became a leader in the Minnesota Filipino community and an articulate interpreter of its culture to the other residents of the Twin Cities. In addition to opening her St. Paul home to new immigrants and taking part in Filipino social activities, she attended classes at Hamline University and joined the Women's Institute of St. Paul. She also played an important role in organizing Filipino dance programs and exhibits for the Festival of Nations, a series of folk festivals sponsored by the International Institute of Minnesota.

The third Filipina in Minnesota was Petra P. Rigucera, who journeyed to the Twin Cities in 1930 to marry her fiancé, Miguel F. Custodio. Like Clara Balbuena, she was a young woman who believed that her stay in the United States would be temporary. During the first winter after their marriage, the Custodios shared a house with the Balbuenas. Petra Custodio contributed her talents and energy to the Festival of Nations as well as the Filipino American Club. Later the Custodios lived with their three young sons at several locations in downtown Minneapolis. Among them were the Euclid Hotel at 310 South 7th Street and an apartment building on Harmon Place in one of the few districts Filipinos found housing open to them. Many single, young Filipinos worked at the Minneapolis Athletic Club and several nearby hotels. Petra Custodio regularly invited them to her home for music, food, and companionship.[27]

Because Filipino culture has always been open to mixed marriages, the American wives of Filipinos were warmly welcomed into the Minnesota Filipino community, as were their children. Some of these women suffered harsh criticism and rejection by their own families after their marriages to Filipinos. Old Timers and their American wives recalled the sneers and taunts directed toward them when they appeared together in public during the early years.[28]

The early Filipinos established neither language schools nor ethnic churches because of the linguistic and religious diversity within the immigrant community. The Old Timers spoke a variety of Filipino languages and dialects, but English was the common language among the members of the small Minnesota settlement. The majority married American women and therefore spoke English at home, as did their children. Moreover in the Philippines English had been established in the schools by American colonial administrators and was considered prestigious as the language of the educated. Old Timers and their wives expected their children to use English at Filipino community functions as well as in the larger society, thus there was no demand for language schools.[29]

The ethnic church was equally irrelevant in the early Filipino community. Most of the Old Timers did not attend church regularly after their arrival, and the small group was divided between a majority of Roman Catholics and fewer Protestants. American wives of the early immigrants were often Protestant and the Filipinos usually went to their wives' churches. Whereas the ethnic church in many immigrant communities was extremely important in preserving the common language and religion, it could serve no such purpose for the early Filipinos in Minnesota.

The social and cultural life of these Filipinos centered in such organizations as Philippinesotans, started by students at the University of Minnesota in 1925; the Cabeñan Club, a regionally based organization comprised of immigrants from Caba, the Filipino Club of Minnesota in Minneapolis, and the Filipino American Club in St. Paul — all organized during the 1920s; the Filipino Club of St. Paul, founded in 1936;

FILIPINO members of the Cosmopolitan Club, an international student's organization at the University of Minnesota, rehearsed a play in about 1923.

THE Filipino American Club met at the Radisson Hotel in Minneapolis in 1931.

and the Helping Hand Club, organized in the late 1940s by Filipino employees of the Curtis Hotel in Minneapolis. During the early years the clubs' primary purpose was to provide celebrations of births, weddings, and baptisms, as well as the commemoration of revolutionary hero José Rizal. Later the organizations also emphasized mutual aid, cultural education of the youth, and service projects to help their compatriots in the Philippines.[30]

For a short period in the late 1920s, a Filipino newspaper, the *Philippines Echo*, reflected the immigrants' desire to maintain their culture and sense of community. The *Echo* was published in Minneapolis by Andrew P. Driz with the help of Felix Delsorio, a journalism student at the University of Minnesota. Written in both English and Spanish, the newspaper informed the Filipino community of events in the Philippines and provided information on the treatment of Filipinos in Minnesota to their friends and relatives in the home provinces. Driz hoped to develop a broad circulation both in the United States and in the Philippines, but with the onset of the Depression, the *Echo* failed after its first year.[31]

The New Immigrants

In contrast to the early Filipino settlers, the New Immigrants since 1965 have included both men and women professionally trained in the Philippines. Whereas the early arrivals sought education and economic gain in the United States to take back to the Philippines, those who have arrived since the enactment of the 1965 immigration act have been motivated by the desire for greater professional opportunities. The ongoing "brain drain" from the Philippines and other Asian countries has resulted from changes in the preference system of the 1965 act designed to meet the United States' needs for professional personnel in certain fields.[32]

The preference given to medical professionals under the current law — and the resulting influx of Filipino doctors and

nurses into Minnesota during the early 1970s — followed the precedent set by the active recruitment of Asian medical professionals by both the United States government and several private hospitals following World War II. For example, St. Mary's Hospital in Rochester, which provides bed care for patients at the Mayo Clinic, recruited 75 to 100 nurses per year from the Philippines and other Asian countries between 1957 and 1974. These nurses, the largest number of whom were Filipino, arrived in Rochester under the St. Mary's Exchange Program. The terms of the program required them to return to Asia when their two-year contracts expired, but provided a waiver of state licensing requirements during their stay in Minnesota. The program was terminated in 1974 for political reasons; the government of the Philippines objected to the drain on its supply of nurses, and the United States government claimed it could no longer absorb foreign nurses in large numbers.[33]

In addition to their desire for economic gain, the New Immigrants, like the Old Timers, were motivated by the "American Dream," which still prevails in the Philippines. Recent arrivals have reported that for some professionals it is almost a tradition to go to the United States after graduation. "In the Philippines, anything American is valued," according to Augusto A. Sumangil, who arrived in Minnesota in 1969. The teachers and history books say "everyone in America is rich. . . . [Filipinos] see it on television, they see it in the movies . . . the newspapers, and magazines." Pointing to the widespread notion that everything American is superior, an idea implanted in Filipino school children at an early age, Sumangil observed that colleges "use American textbooks . . . though there are Filipino authors who are equally as competent . . . and we have local books . . . and yet [there is] the Filipino colonial mentality of looking up to the Americans as the big brother, the best in everything." Although Sumangil grew up in the Philippines after it acquired independence, the educational program established during 40 years of American rule remained largely unchanged during his childhood. "We were trained to be American," he said.[34]

The New Immigrants are principally the sons and daughters of affluent businessmen, teachers, or officials who have themselves achieved a high level of education. They represent a variety of professions and businesses, but an unusually large number are medical professionals, including an estimated 60 to 70 practicing doctors and approximately 500 nurses. Many graduating nurses in the Philippines seek employment through advertisements in American nursing journals, which are readily available at their schools.[35]

Buenaventura D. de Leon, a doctor in Stillwater, pointed out that Minnesota is known throughout Asia as an important medical center and a good place to acquire specialized training. He decided to go to Minnesota in 1958, after completing medical school in the Philippines, to specialize in pediatrics and surgery. Later he returned with his American wife to practice at Kiangnan, Ifugao, a remote mountain area of northern Luzon where he had grown up. His wife found adjustment to life in that primitive area difficult, however, and after one and a half years they returned to Minnesota.[36]

Filipino social organizations continued to be the focus of cultural life in the decade after the New Immigrants began to arrive. Initially most professionals joined the Fil-Minnesotan Association, organized in 1954 to promote and interpret Filipino culture, to educate Filipino youth in their heritage, and to provide social activities within the community. The association established a dance group in 1972 and a youth group in 1978. Both have been featured in the annual performances of the association's cultural series known as the "Filipiniana," which began in 1976. Following a conflict within the Fil-Minnesotan Association in 1971 part of the membership left to form the Cultural Society of the Filipino Americans (CSFA). Its purpose is similar to that of its earlier counterpart, and both have sponsored community activities such as banquets, dances, and picnics. Like the Fil-Minnesotan, the CSFA organized a dance group which performed at various cultural presentations, and both continue to publish newsletters including articles on Filipino history and culture as well as local community news. In 1980 the membership of the two organizations differed, however; most of the medical professionals remained in the Fil-Minnesotan Association, while a large number of nonmedical professionals joined the CSFA. The latter organization also included a majority of the mixed couples among the recent immigrants.[37]

Old Timers have continued to organize their social activities within the Filipino American Club, which dates from the 1920s, although a few have also attended the banquets and special celebrations of the Fil-Minnesotan and the CSFA. In an effort to strengthen relations between the Old Timers and the New Immigrants, some of the latter have participated in the Filipino American Club's activities, and several have served as its officers in order to relieve the older members of administrative tasks.

Two professional organizations have been formed by Filipinos in the state. In the early 1970s doctors established the Philippine Medical Association of Minnesota, which affiliated with the Association of Philippine Practicing Physicians

of America in 1978. The Minnesota chapter has arranged annual clinical seminars for its members and provided assistance to young doctors arriving in the state from the Philippines. In 1978 Filipino nurses founded the Philippine Nurses Association, which provides members legal aid, assistance in preparing for state certification examinations, and opportunities to share cultural activities.[38]

The Second Generation

Second-generation Filipinos in Minnesota may be divided into three groups which reflect the changing character of the community from the 1920s to 1980. The first consists of the children of mixed marriages of the Old Timers, most of whom were mature adults with offspring of their own by 1980. The second comprises the children of both the Filipino couples who immigrated between 1945 and 1965 and the Old Timers who married Filipina wives after World War II. The majority of these were born in Minnesota and ranged from high-school age to young adults in 1980. The third group — which ultimately will be the largest — is the children of the New Immigrants who arrived after 1965. This includes both children born in the Philippines, who are now high school or college age, and younger ones born in Minnesota or elsewhere in the United States.

Without attempting a systematic analysis of the second generation, a few general observations may be made from information available in 1980. With the exception of the children of mixed marriages, the retention of Filipino values and cultural identity has been remarkably prevalent among the second generation. This was particularly evident in the children of families who participated actively in Filipino organizations or had relatives either living in the household or nearby. While the success orientation of many recent immigrant parents has led them to discourage the use of their Filipino language at home, they have nevertheless transmitted to their children the Filipino values of education and close family ties, as well as a strong sense of identity with the Filipino community. The older children of the New Immigrants are the only ones retaining fluency in their Filipino language, although their younger siblings born in Minnesota often understand but do not speak it.

The children of the two families of Benigno U. Andrada, who was married initially to an American in the pre-World War II era and to a Filipina in the postwar years, illustrate the first two groups of second-generation Filipinos. Virgil T. Andrada was born in 1933 in Minneapolis, where his father had immigrated in 1928 from Buaung in La Union province. His mother, Thina Brothern Andrada, was the daughter of Norwegian immigrants who settled at Clearbrook in Clearwater County. Prior to her marriage in 1930, Thina Brothern and her sister had moved to Minneapolis to seek employment and had rented an apartment on Harmon Place. As often happened, both married Filipino men. The sister married Henry Runez, one of Sixto Runez' cousins from Caba. Both the Andrada and Runez families continued to live on Harmon Place for several years.[39]

Virgil Andrada recalled the closeness of the two families during the early years on Harmon Place. He also remembered that even after his family moved from the central city to Wayzata, to be closer to his father's work, Filipino friends often visited on Sunday afternoons, fishing with his parents and enjoying a game of poker afterwards. There were also special Filipino celebrations and parties at the Andrada home. For extended periods, however, Virgil saw little of his father. During the Depression Benigno Andrada worked long hours as a butler and chauffeur for a well-to-do famliy; he even accompanied his employers to Florida during the winter months, leaving his own family in Minnesota.

During their father's absences, Virgil and his brothers spent a great deal of time with their mother's relatives, who still spoke Norwegian within the family and firmly maintained Norwegian traditions. Christmas, for example, was always celebrated with lutefisk and lefse prepared by Andrada's grandmother on her wood-burning stove. The Andrada children also often spent summers in the Clearbrook area. As Andrada grew up, the Norwegian influence of his mother's family was reinforced by the prevailing Scandinavian culture of the Twin Cities and later by his marriage to a woman of Swedish extraction.

As an adult Andrada has not participated in the activities of the Filipino cultural organizations in the Twin Cities, nor has he identified with the Filipino community, although he has recognized that they represent an important part of his roots. He continued to look upon his own cultural identity as essentially American and recalled few incidents of discrimination during his childhood which were related to his Filipino background.

Andrada's half-sisters, Marietta and Cristeta Paz Andrada, represent the second group — children of Filipino couples who established families in Minnesota from the late 1940s to the late 1960s. In 1957, two years after the death of his first wife, Benigno Andrada married Belen Martinez Santos, a Filipina graduate student at the University of Chicago. Marietta was born in Minneapolis in 1958, and Cristeta was born in suburban Richfield in 1964. Their father, a leader of the Filipino community before they were born, was a respected Old Timer until his death in 1980. Their mother has played a key role in bridging the gap which developed between the Old Timers and the New Immigrants during the late 1960s and 1970s. She has also strongly encouraged the involvement of the second generation in Filipino organizations, and served as a liaison between the Filipino community and the larger Twin Cities society.[40]

As a result of their parents' common heritage and active involvement in Filipino organization both Marietta and Cristeta have closely identified themselves with the community and participated in its social and cultural activities. Both have adopted Filipino cultural values, especially the importance of religion and close family ties. They learned these values not only from their parents, but also from many relatives in the United States and the Philippines with whom they have maintained strong bonds through visits and correspondence. Both have participated in programs for teenagers and young adults sponsored by Filipino organizations. Marietta has taken an active role in the Fil-Minnesotan Youth Group, and has also helped with a survey of the needs of elderly Filipinos in the Twin Cities.

Unlike their half-brother, Virgil, the sisters experienced taunting remarks and name-calling by fellow students during their elementary school years. As one of the first minority children to attend public school in Richfield, Marietta bore the brunt of the racial abuse directed toward Filipino children. It was not until she entered junior high school that she learned to cope with the daily incidents. On one occasion she walked out of her ninth-grade social studies class because the teacher made a biased remark about Filipinos. To her surprise, two of the most popular students in the class rose in her defense and challenged the teacher, who later apologized.

Other second-generation Filipino Americans have been considerably less interested in identifying with the Filipino community. In most cases they have reflected a similar attitude on the part of their parents. For example, the Andradas' first cousins, Benjamin S. and Melissa S. Arriola, have taken only a minimal interest in the activities of the Filipino organizations. Their parents, Benjamin G. and Ofelia S. Arriola, immigrated to Minnesota in 1960, living first with the Andrada family then buying a house nearby. Instead of participating in the cultural programs of the Filipino community, the senior Arriolas have focused their social life on the leisure activities of Benjamin G.'s fellow employees of an insurance company in Minneapolis, and they have encouraged their children to center their activities on school functions and social occasions in the homes of their student friends.[41]

The children of both families attended the same elementary and high schools, but Benjamin and Melissa Arriola — as well as Cristeta Andrada — had an easier time gaining acceptance than Marietta Andrada did. In addition to the fact that Marietta paved the way for them, by the mid-1960s when the Arriola children and Cristeta Andrada entered school, other minority groups were moving to Richfield and the schools were becoming integrated.

Because the elder Arriolas, like many others, have been primarily concerned with their children's success in American society, they have felt some ambivalence about preserving their Filipino culture and identity. Arriola has maintained that the family is important but has not been sure it will be as important for his children. On the other hand, he has always been convinced that a good education and a professional career is the ideal goal, — one he has emphasized in raising his children.

While the Arriola children have been less concerned than their cousins with maintaining their Filipino culture and identity, they have recognized the fact that they cannot simply put these aside. Benjamin, a high school senior, spoke for both: "Since we grew up here in the United States . . . we try to consider ourselves Americans, but we will always know that we have that Filipino heritage, and I don't think we'll totally break away."

The third group of second-generation Filipinos — the offspring of New Immigrants — includes both young American-born children and older children born in the Philippines. It was apparent in 1980 that many of the young professionals in Minnesota had spoken only English to their children from infancy. This practice was also current in the Philippines, where upwardly mobile families believed it would give their children an advantage in school. There were, however, a number of large Minnesota families in which the older children born in the Philippines have continued to use their Filipino language, and while they have adapted well to American life outside the home, the traditional family structure has been preserved to a large extent. A strong Filipino identity has been evident in the second generation of these New Immigrant families.[42]

The Alfredo de los Reyes family provides a good example of the large, close-knit families which include children born both in the Philippines and the United States. Arriving in Washington in 1968 with their six children, who ranged in age from 3 to 11 years, Alfredo L. and Nellie D. de los Reyes remained for a year with relatives in Seattle, where a seventh child was born. After their move to Minnesota in 1969, the oldest son married and established his own home, while the remaining members of the family settled first in South St. Paul and later in suburban Cottage Grove. The de los Reyes family has been active in the Fil-Minnesotan Association, of which Alfredo, Sr., served as president from 1972 to 1974. The family also has had close relatives nearby.

Of the six children at home in 1980, the four oldest have retained their fluency in Tagalog, the language of the Manila area where they were born. While the two youngest have not been as comfortable in speaking the language, their comprehension allows them to translate for friends visiting their home. All the children have identified themselves as Filipinos, although Marie-Rose, 14, and her brother Nelson, 15, have described themselves as "half and half," Filipino and American. Their brother Gene, 17, commented, "I don't feel like I'm American," and added that "maybe" he would go back to the Philippines to live; Carl, 20, said that although he was a United States citizen and grew up in America, he did not feel "really American." Marie-Rose observed that she and John-Mark, the two youngest in the family, felt more American than her older brothers did.

Traditional Filipino mores have been retained by the de los Reyes family to a greater extent than by many Filipino families in Minnesota. While most have dropped the traditional *mano po,* a gesture in which the back of the hand is placed on the forehead as a sign of respect for one's elders and parents, it has continued to be practiced by the de los Reyes children, who have indicated they would teach it to their own children. Most of the de los Reyes children also said it was important for them to participate with their parents in activities of the Roman Catholic church and the Fil-Minnesotan Association.

While retaining Filipino traditions as a family, the de los Reyes children have adapted well to American life outside their home. They have excelled in school work, sports, and music. As Alfredo, Jr., a high school senior, explained, "I'm Filipino here at home. . . . I know I'm Filipino, but when I'm at school I don't even think about it, I just blend in with the kids." Nelson, a junior high school student, said it took a couple of years to make friends after he arrived in Minnesota. As the only Filipinos in the South St. Paul parochial elementary school they attended, he and his brothers were subjected to unpleasant taunts by their classmates, but in junior high school he had two Filipino friends, and that made a big difference for him. While he felt accepted by his classmates, he liked having a Filipino friend "so we can talk about common things, and sometimes we can talk in Tagalog and just goof around."

All the de los Reyes children have experienced discrimination at school, largely in the form of name-calling and bullying. Such harassment has occurred most frequently in the parochial elementary school and in more subtle forms in the public high school as well. For the younger two in elementary and junior high school, it was a continuing problem through the 1970s.

The Filipino Community in 1980

During the rapid growth of the community in the 1970s tensions arose between the New Immigrants and the Old Timers. Overwhelmed by the large number of professionals taking over the leadership of new organizations, Old Timers often felt displaced and resentful of the newcomers. Nevertheless by 1980 conflicts between the two groups began to lessen, and the community again became a generally cohesive group conscious of its history. Since 1965 the Filipino population has been concentrated in the Twin Cities and suburbs, with a relatively small number living outside the metropolitan area. Some Old Timers and their families have continued to live in Northeast Minneapolis, but many have moved into the northern suburbs of Columbia Heights, Fridley, Brooklyn Center, and Brooklyn Park. New Immigrants have scattered more widely, with the largest numbers settling in Bloomington, Richfield, Cottage Grove, Golden Valley, and Minnetonka. Most of the Filipinos in recent years have been economically comfortable, and with the influx of new professionals, the average income has continued to rise each year.[43]

Filipino businesses have not been numerous in Minnesota, but several small grocery stores, gift shops, a restaurant, and a fast-food establishment have been opened by New Immigrants. Following a trend evident across the country, Filipinos in Minnesota have used savings from professional work to finance small businesses, indicating a probable future increase in Filipino enterprises in the state.[44]

Throughout the years, the Filipinos' views of American politics have reflected their interest in the issues of independence for their homeland, the alliance between the Philippines and the United States during World War II, United States relations with the martial-law regime of Ferdinand E. Marcos, and immigrant status for Filipinos. One of the first Filipinos in Minnesota, Juan Orendain, recalled that he learned from his father a great admiration for William Jennings Bryan, who favored independence for the Philippines after the Spanish-American War. Both Old Timers and New Immigrants have praised President Franklin D. Roosevelt as the great hero of the liberation of the Philippines during World War II, and also as an advocate of independence.[45]

While many Filipinos in Minnesota have been opposed to the Marcos regime, they have been reluctant to criticize it or American support of Marcos. Most have avoided active involvement in such political organizations as the Movement for a Free Philippines or Friends of the Filipino People — both of which have grown rapidly in California and New

York — because they fear it would endanger relatives in the Philippines or jeopardize their own chances for return visits to their homeland. Filipino college students in the Twin Cities, who formed the nucleus of a local chapter of the Movement for a Free Philippines during the mid-1970s, have become inactive since receiving warnings from their government to refrain from anti-Marcos activities while studying abroad.[46]

On the domestic scene, most of the Old Timers have been sympathetic to the Democratic party as the champion of the struggling Filipino immigrant, although their American wives — particularly those from Scandinavian immigrant families — were characteristically Republican. On the other hand, New Immigrant Benjamin Arriola observed that many recent arrivals have associated themselves with the Republican party as the party of the affluent class; they may, however, feel sympathetic toward the Democratic party because of the assistance Filipino immigrants received from Senator Hubert H. Humphrey. Vice-president Walter F. Mondale and former Representative Donald M. Fraser also gained in popularity among Filipinos in Minnesota after visits to the Philippines.[47]

The Arriola family is one of many Asian immigrant families that received the help and support of Senator Humphrey during the three decades prior to reform of the United States' immigration law in 1965. In 1959 the Arriolas decided to try to join their relatives in Minnesota, but they had difficulty obtaining visas. They wrote to Ofelia Arriola's brother-in-law, Benigno Andrada, who in turn sought the help of Senator Humphrey. Through Humphrey's intervention the Arriolas received visas and arrived in Minnesota in 1960. A few years later the Arriolas visited Washington, D.C., and stopped in Humphrey's office to thank him. To their surprise, the senator recognized their names and warmly welcomed them to the United States and Minnesota. Still later, the Arriolas met Humphrey by chance on a street in Minneapolis, and again the senator recognized and greeted them.[48]

Most Filipinos agree that Minnesota has been a relatively hospitable environment for immigrants from the Philippines, despite severe discrimination in the early years and incidents that still occur from time to time. New Immigrant Augusto Sumangil said he considered Minnesotans "very warm and friendly" because the state is "more of the provincial type" and its people "can always relate yet to being Swedish, or Norwegian, or Finnish, or Polish and . . . have an intangible kinship with a new immigrant. . . . They are more approachable; they accept us more as a person, because they could see in us the things that happened to their grandparents and father and mother."[49]

Reference notes

Much of the information in this chapter is from the author's interviews of Filipino Americans and other persons in Minnesota. Those interviews that were recorded on tape are so identified; the tapes are in the Audio-Visual Library, MHS. The author's notes for both taped and untaped interviews are in MEHP Papers, MHS.

[1] The term "Filipino" rather than "Pilipino" is generally used by the Minnesota community. "Pilipino," however, is the correct term in Tagalog, the official language of the Philippines, and appears with increasing frequency in recent publications.

[2] United States, Census, 1930, Population, 2:58; United States Asian Statistics, in MEHP Papers, MHS, compiled by Jon A. Gjerde from U.S. Dept. of Labor, Bureau of Immigration, Annual Reports, 1909–39, and U.S. Justice Dept., Immigration and Naturalization Service, Annual Reports, 1940–78, hereafter cited as Gjerde, Asian statistics; H. Brett Melendy, "Filipinos," in Stephan Thernstrom, ed., Harvard Encyclopedia of American Ethnic Groups, 362 (Cambridge, Mass., 1980). It should be noted that Asians have been consistently undercounted in the U.S. censuses and that discrepancies occur between national and state counts. Filipinos have been included in the federal census intermittently and under varying classifications. The Asian statistics used here are based on statements of intent to migrate to Minnesota; population estimates by local community leaders, however, tend to corroborate these figures. See also Appendix.

[3] For figures on Filipino students and Minnesota's Filipino population in 1949, see Governor's Interracial Commission, The Oriental in Minnesota, 32 (St. Paul, 1949); on farm workers, see interviews of Benigno U. Andrada, November 1 (taped), 9, December 9, 1978; Filemon C. Balbuena, November 27, 1978; Stanley A. Sabado, December 5, 1978; Joseph Axelson, November 9, 1978, June 15, 1979; Gjerde, Asian statistics.

The author is indebted to Benigno and Belen Andrada for information used throughout this chapter. Especially helpful was Belen S. Andrada, The Filipino Experience in Minnesota, 1918–1953 (Minneapolis, 1977).

[4] Melendy, in Thernstrom, ed., Harvard Encyclopedia, 354, 356, 357, 359, 362; Hyung-chan Kim and Cynthia C. Mejia, comps. and eds., The Filipino in America 1898–1974, (Dobbs Ferry, N.Y., 1976); Gjerde, Asian statistics.

[5] Robert A. Divine, American Immigration Policy, 1924–1952, 68 (New Haven, 1957); Paul L. Murphy, The Constitution in Crisis Times: 1918–1969, 90 (New York, 1972). For a report on problems concerning Filipino immigrants up to 1931, see Bruno Lasker, Filipino Immigration to Continental United States and to Hawaii (Chicago, 1931).

[6] U.S., Census, 1930, Population, 2:58; "Restriction of Immigration," in 71 Congress, 3 session, House Reports, no. 2405, part 4, p. 9 (serial 9326).

[7] Here and two paragraphs below, see Divine, American Immigration Policy, 68–73, 75; H. Brett Melendy, Asians in America: Filipinos, Koreans, and East Indians, 26 (Boston, 1977).

[8] Interview of Benigno U. Andrada, October 20, 1978. "Americans" is the term generally used by Filipinos in Minnesota to describe non-Filipinos in the U.S. Unlike California, Minnesota had no miscegenation law forbidding Filipinos to marry white women. Melendy, Asians in America, 52.

[9] Murphy, Constitution, 91; Divine, American Immigration Policy, 154; Toyota v. United States, 268 United States Supreme Court Reports 402 (1924).

[10] Gjerde, Asian statistics. The terms "Old Timers" and "New Immigrants" are used by Minnesota Filipinos to differentiate between early and recent groups of settlers in the community.

[11] U.S., Census, 1930, Population, vol. 3, part 1, p. 1187. On naturalization rights prior to the 1920s, see Murphy, Constitution, 90.

[12] Here and two paragraphs below, see interview of Rudolph F. Runez, November 28, 1978; interview of Juan C. Orendain by Helen M. White, March 20, 1959, transcript, and Juan C. Orendain, "Juan in Minnesota, 1917–1925," unpublished manuscript, copies of both in MHS. Runez and his wife, Ruby K., were close friends of Orendain and his first wife, Florence L.; the women were cousins.

[13] Here and below, see Rudolph Runez interviews, December 7,

1978, January 17, 1979 (taped); Andrada, *Filipino Experience,* 21.

[14] Rudolph Runez interviews, November 28, December 7, 1978, January 17, 1979.

[15] Rudolph Runez interviews, November 7, 18, December 7, 1978, January 17, 1979; Melendy, *Asians in America,* 71; interview of Belen Andrada, December 12, 1980. On the influence of family and friends on immigrants' choice of Minnesota, see Andrada, *Filipino Experience,* 8.

[16] Rudolph Runez interview, December 7, 1978.

[17] Rudolph Runez interview, January 17, 1979; Benigno Andrada interview, October 9, 1978 (taped); interviews of Paul C. Borge, October 27 (taped), November 30, 1978. Borge recalled that some Filipinos were hired for public works projects. They were eligible for employment on Works Progress Administration projects because they were nationals. See Melendy, *Asians in America,* 49.

[18] Benigno Andrada interview, October 9, 1978; Borge interview, October 27, 1978.

[19] Here and the following six paragraphs, see Borge interviews, October 27, November 30, 1978, December 18, 1980.

[20] Axelson interviews, November 9, 1978, June 15, 1979. Axelson, who retired as manager of the Field Labor Dept. of the American Crystal Sugar Company in 1975 and served as consultant until 1977, was a company interpreter for migrant laborers in 1945. His supervisor told him that during the 1920s and 1930s he went to Seattle every year to recruit Filipino field workers, who were taken to Chaska by the trainload. See also Andrada, *Filipino Experience,* 8.

[21] Balbuena interview, November 27, 1978. Balbuena and his wife (see below) settled in St. Paul, where they lived in 1980.

[22] Here and below, see Sabado interview, December 5, 1978; Benigno Andrada interview, November 9, 1978.

[23] Interview of Dorothy P. (Mrs. Pedro) Velasco, January 15, 1979; Andrada, *Filipino Experience,* 22.

[24] Interview of Clara A. Balbuena, November 27, 1978; Andrada, *Filipino Experience,* 25.

[25] Interview of Edward S. T. Epperly, son of Basilisa and Samuel Epperly, January 30, 1979.

[26] Here and below, see Filemon and Clara Balbuena interviews, November 27, 1978; Andrada, *Filipino Experience,* 26.

[27] Interview of Petra R. Custodio, January 31, 1979.

[28] Taped interview of Ruby K. and Rudolph F. Runez, January 17, 1979.

[29] Here and below, see Belen Andrada interview, January 29, 1981; Melendy, in Thernstrom, ed., *Harvard Encyclopedia,* 355.

[30] Rudolph Runez interview, January 8, 1979; interview of Angel Relopez, December 22, 1980; Borge interview, December 22, 1980. Only the Filipino American Club remained active in 1980. The Cabeñan Club was short-lived because it was considered too exclusive by many in the community. The Helping Hand Club, which expanded its membership to 20, was active for about a decade.

[31] Interview of Andrew P. Driz, November 24, 1978. No issues of this newspaper have been found.

[32] Taped interview of Augusto A. Sumangil, December 8, 1978; Charles B. Keely, "Effects of the Immigration Act of 1965 on Selected Population Characteristics of Immigrants to the United States," in *Demography,* 8:167 (May, 1971).

[33] Interviews of Buenaventure D. de Leon, Stillwater physician, December 7, 1978; Margaret A. Hermann, personnel assistant, St.

Mary's Hospital, Rochester, January 24, 1979. Within four years after the program ended, Minnesota as a whole was experiencing a severe shortage of nurses; St. Mary's Hospital, for example, offered employees a bonus of $100.00 for each new nurse recruited. See *St. Paul Pioneer Press,* December 12, 1978, Trends sec., 6.

[34] Taped interview of Rebecca N. and Augusto Sumangil, December 8, 1978.

[35] Interviews of Eugenio E. Siruno, February 15, 1979, and Alice Rosales Olson, February 15, 1979; Rebecca Sumangil interview, December 9, 1978. Siruno was president of the Philippines Medical Assn. of Minnesota in 1979; Olson was president of the Philippine Nurses Assn. Sumangil, a registered nurse in Minneapolis, received three job offers after responding to advertisements in American nursing journals. Along with the practicing physicians, the New Immigrants include many trained doctors who are not licensed to practice in Minnesota.

[36] De Leon interview, December 7, 1978.

[37] Here and below, see interviews of Augusto Sumangil, February 8, 1979 (taped); Glen Roderiguez King, February 9, 1979; Constancio F. and Luz A. Argueza, December 8, 1979. Sumangil was president of the Fil-Minnesotan Assn. in 1980; King was vice-president of the CFSA in 1979; the Arguezas, both certified public accountants who immigrated with two young children in 1972, have been officers of the Filipino American Club and active in other organizations.

[38] Siruno and Olson interviews, February 15, 1979.

[39] Here and three paragraphs below, see taped interview of Virgil T. Andrada, February 1, 1979.

[40] Here and two paragraphs below, see taped interviews of Benigno Andrada, October 9, Belen Andrada, October 20, Cristeta Paz Andrada, October 20, and Marietta Andrada, November 1 — all 1978; Benigno and Belen Andrada interviews, December 10, 1978.

[41] Here and three paragraphs below, see taped interview of Benjamin G., Benjamin S., and Melissa S. Arriola, January 13, 1979.

[42] Here and five paragraphs below, see taped interviews of Carl D., Alfredo D., Jr., Gene D., Nelson D., Marie-Rose D., and John-Mark D. de los Reyes, March 16, 1979.

[43] Belen S. Andrada *et al.,* comps., *Directory of the Filipino Community of the Twin Cities, 1978* ([Minneapolis, 1978]); Borge interview, January 29, 1979; Rudolph Runez interview, January 17, 1979. Other metropolitan area cities that had from 8 to 18 Filipino families in residence in 1978 were Anoka, Burnsville, Coon Rapids, West St. Paul, and South St. Paul.

[44] Interviews of Ely T. Arcilla and Marlou De Mira Hough, both June 1, 1979. Among the establishments of New Immigrants were the Phil-Oriental grocery and gift shop in St. Paul owned by Ely T. and Yvonne S. Arcilla; the Aliza gift shop in Edina owned by Nelson G. and Esther R. Paguyo; the Garuda Restaurant in St. Paul owned by Suzette P. De Mira, Marlou De Mira Hough and husband Mervyn H. Hough, and other members of the De Mira family.

[45] Orendain interview, March 20, 1959; King interview, February 9, 1979; interview of Barbara Posadas, February 9, 1979.

[46] King interview, February 9, 1979.

[47] Borge interview, January 29, 1979; King interview, February 9, 1979; Benjamin G. Arriola interview, January 13, 1979; Posadas interview, February 9, 1979.

[48] Benjamin G. Arriola interview, January 13, 1979.

[49] Borge interview, October 27, 1978; Sumangil interview, December 8, 1978.

CHAPTER 30

The Japanese

Michael Albert

JAPANESE AMERICANS were the largest Asian-American group in Minnesota until recently. In 1970 they numbered 2,693, which ranked Minnesota 18th nationally among states with populations of Japanese descent. Even so, they were a small group, representing less than 1% of Minnesota's inhabitants. A majority of them lived in the Twin Cities metropolitan area. Most had arrived during and after World War II (see Table 30.1), although there were a dwindling number of prewar settlers known as Issei. (Their American-born children are referred to as Nisei and their grandchildren as Sansei.) The 1970 census reported that Minnesota also had a small number of Japanese women who had married Americans stationed in Japan after 1945, some Japanese nationals who were students or recent immigrants, and a few postwar migrants of Japanese descent who had been born in Hawaii.[1] The present study focuses on the Issei immigrants and their descendants. (See Map 30.1 for areas of Japan represented by migrants who settled in Minnesota.)

A trickle of Japanese arrived in the United States during the 1860s, but immigration of any substance really began in 1884 when Japan legalized the emigration of laborers. At first they went to Hawaii under contract to work on sugar plantations; mainland United States did not attract large numbers until 1900, and even in that peak year fewer than 13,000 legal immigrants landed. Migrants from Hawaii and illegal entrants via Mexico and Canada increased the yearly totals somewhat, but for every 100 Japanese who entered the United States in 1910, 60 returned to Japan. The so-called Gentlemen's Agreement of 1907 between Japan and the United States curtailed the export of Japanese labor; under its terms the Japanese government stopped issuing passports to laborers, but it granted them to family members of workers already in the United States. While anti-Japanese movements to prevent aliens from owning land and to enact segregation legislation proliferated — chiefly on the Pacific Coast — it was not until 1922 that Japanese were denied the right of naturalization. Two years later Congress passed the

Immigration Act of 1924, which effectively prevented Japanese from entering the United States for the next 28 years. Remigration figures rose to 80% during the decade of the 1920s and continued to surpass arrivals until the 1940s.[2]

More than 88.5% of the nation's Japanese resided in the three Pacific Coast states in 1940 — chiefly in California. Notwithstanding their relatively small numbers, they were a visible minority because they were concentrated in particular areas and certain occupations — especially small-scale intensive agriculture, but also small businesses and service industries.[3]

Before World War II Minnesota, remote from West Coast ports of entry and offering few work opportunities not found in the West, attracted very limited numbers of Japanese in the early years of their immigration. The 1890 census counted only two Japanese in the state (see Table 30.1). During the rest of the decade a few may have drifted in to work here and there, but records of their identity and whereabouts are scanty.[4]

Contract labor on the railroads led to the arrival of the first significant Japanese population in Minnesota. As early as 1893, a West Coast Japanese firm approached the Great Northern Railway Company with an offer to supply Japanese section laborers, but the railroad apparently did not enter into such contracts until 1898. By 1900 the Great Northern secured at least 2,500 Japanese workers from the Oriental Trading Company of Seattle. Virtually all of them went to the Pacific and Mountain states, but a small crew of 56 was employed at $1.10 a day on the Eastern Railway Company of Minnesota (a Great Northern subsidiary) laying tracks between Swan River and Hibbing. This crew perhaps explains the increase to 51 Japanese reported by the 1900 census and the otherwise puzzling presence of 42 of them in St. Louis County. The Eastern Railway Company expressed dissatisfaction with the high cost of their Japanese laborers, and apparently they were not used in Minnesota after 1900.[5]

The fate of the section laborers employed in northern Min-

Table 30.1. Japanese in Minnesota, 1880–1970

	1880	1890	1900	1910	1920	1930	1940	1950	1960	1970
Minnesota	1	2	51	67	85	69	51	1,049	1,726	2,603
Twin Cities		2	5	58	65	48	37	905	1,320	1,965

Source: Harry H. L. Kitano, *Japanese Americans*, 162; U.S., *Census*, 1900, 1930, 1940, 1950, 1960, 1970.

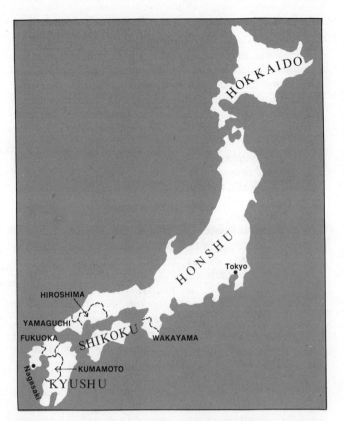

Map 30.1. Prefectures and Cities in Japan from which Emigrants Reached Minnesota

nesota in 1900 has not been discovered, but it is clear that after 1910 the bulk of the state's Japanese lived in the Twin Cities (see Table 30.1). Most of those who arrived from the West Coast in this period were single males. Unfortunately, little is known about these sojourners, for few married and stayed in the state. When this chapter was written in 1980, only one prewar Japanese couple was located in St. Paul. Like many prewar St. Paul Japanese, the man, who settled in Minnesota in 1928, worked for the Great Northern in various capacities until his retirement in 1968. Others were employed by the Soo Line, and their friendship ties were within these railroad groups.[6]

The Japanese population of Minneapolis in 1918 consisted of 36 adult males. Of these 28 worked in some phase of the restaurant business, largely as waiters in local restaurants or homes, and occasionally on Great Northern and Northern Pacific trains. Two were employed as chauffeurs, three as store clerks or owners, one as a butler, and two were university students. Several operated concessions at Como Park in St. Paul and at the Excelsior and White Bear Lake amusement parks.[7]

All were from 24 to 36 years old and 31 were single. Three had wives in Japan; two, who had wives in Minneapolis, had married Northern European women. According to Harry K. Habata, whose father moved to Minnesota and married a Finnish woman about 1913, most Japanese who married Caucasian spouses did so because there were no single Japanese women among the early settlers in the state.

The stable family-oriented portion of the population was small, and even the rare married couple did not always put down roots. Two such pioneer Twin Cities settlers migrated from Portland in 1905 to work at the Nicollet Hotel in Minneapolis. They stayed just a few years before fleeing from Minnesota winters, only to return as relocatees from an Idaho detention camp during World War II.

Because the prewar Minneapolis group was largely composed of single men (only six families were counted as late as 1934), Habata recalled, no sense of community existed. There were no formal ethnic organizations; friends assisted friends, and by and large, he said, "everybody took care of themselves, and accepted their lot as individuals, not as a people." Prejudice, he felt, did not seriously affect his life, although certain opportunities were closed — for example, membership in a number of organizations such as the Minneapolis Athletic Club and the Automobile Club of Minneapolis. Later, he recalled, conditions worsened briefly at the outbreak of World War II when the hostility other Americans felt for Japan spilled over to local Japanese residents.

The situation for Japanese Americans living on the West Coast in 1941 was, however, much more uncomfortable. Despised and distrusted already, they were after Pearl Harbor identified in the eyes of many with the enemy. The United States government, succumbing to racist agitation and fears concerning their loyalty, effected removal of Japanese Americans from California and most of Oregon, Washington, and Arizona. By mid-1942 more than 110,000, nearly two-thirds of whom were American citizens, had been relocated in 10 barbed-wire-encircled detention camps in southeastern Arkansas or in the nation's desolate western interior. Touring these centers in 1943, the Reverend Daisuke Kitagawa, who later became well known among Twin Cities Japanese Americans, commented: "As we visited one center after another, we became more and more impressed with the ingenuity of the government in finding such uniformly Godforsaken places." The army carried out the evacuation, but the camps were operated by the War Relocation Authority (WRA), a civilian agency. Recognizing the harmful environment of the camps, the WRA adopted a policy of relocating internees to other areas of the country. This policy was responsible for the arrival of the first large-scale Japanese-American migration to Minnesota.[8]

Settlement during World War II

Despite its harsh climate and relatively few jobs in war industries, Minnesota attracted a surprising number of Japanese resettlers. From 1940, when the state counted 51 persons of Japanese descent (more than half of whom were American born), the number rose to 1,049 a decade later. Three factors account for the increase: the establishment of the Military Intelligence Service Language School near the Twin Cities; the presence of numerous educational institutions which welcomed Nisei students; and the prompt mobilization of Minnesota agencies to aid resettlers moving into the area.[9]

Even before the Japanese attack on Pearl Harbor, the American military had foreseen a need for trained Japanese linguists to perform intelligence duties. Because only a handful of Caucasians were skilled in the Japanese language, the army decided to use Nisei, many of whom, it was hoped, would be able to serve with little or no training. A survey of 3,700 Nisei already in uniform in 1941 produced the surprising findings that only 3% were fluent in Japanese, another 4% were proficient, and a further 3% could be useful after prolonged training. Since the Americanization of the Nisei was clearly more complete than had been assumed, a special training unit, the Military Intelligence Service Language School, was designed to increase Nisei effectiveness as Japanese linguists. The school began operation with 60 students at San Francisco's Presidio in November, 1941, but was forced to seek a new location when the evacuation of Japanese from the West Coast began. Colonel Kai E. Rasmussen, a Danish-born naturalized citizen and an accomplished linguist, was the school's commandant. After making a nationwide survey, he chose to move the school to a former state-operated home for indigent, elderly men at Savage, Minnesota. According to one evaluation, the new site was selected in part because the army "pinpointed Minnesota as the geographic area with the best record of racial amity."

Growing from a class of 200 in June, 1942, to 1,100 by the beginning of 1944, the school was pressed for greater space. Thus it moved from Savage to Fort Snelling in the summer of 1944 and returned to the West Coast two years later. In the fall of 1945 enrollment surpassed 1,800. By June, 1946, when it left Minnesota, its graduates numbered 6,000 men, the overwhelming majority of whom were Japanese Americans. While the heroic deeds of the all-Japanese 442nd Regimental Combat Team in Europe have received much attention, the contributions of these Minnesota-trained Nisei linguists in the Pacific have not been widely acclaimed. Nevertheless they translated captured documents at the front, monitored Japanese radio broadcasts, interrogated captured enemy soldiers, and surely saved many fellow Americans' lives.

The Japanese-American population of the Twin Cities in 1980 was largely a legacy of the language school. Relatives, wives, sweethearts, and friends of many of its students left the detention camps to reside in the Twin Cities during the six- or nine-month course. A 1968 survey of metropolitan Nisei revealed that fully 50% had been stationed at Camp Savage or Fort Snelling or had a family member there. As mayor of Minneapolis in 1946, Hubert H. Humphrey recognized the school's contribution when he said: "During the war we came to know the Nisei well in connection with the fine patriotic service they performed at Fort Snelling and Camp Savage. It is a pleasure to note that many of them have chosen to make Minneapolis their permanent home, and that they are becoming a part of our social community." [10]

The evacuation was also responsible for the arrival in Minnesota of a second group of several hundred Nisei students, who had been enrolled in West Coast colleges. Assisted by the Japanese American Student Relocation Council, many of them transferred to schools in other parts of the country. The willingness of Minnesota institutions to accept them attracted more than 300 Japanese Americans to the state, again primarily to the Twin Cities. At Macalester College the student body voted nine to one in favor of accepting them. Hamline, St. Catherine's, St. Thomas, St. Cloud, and Carle-

ton also enrolled Nisei students in the 1942–43 school year. Conspicuously absent from the early list was the University of Minnesota. In the fall of 1942 its board of regents received a report on "the problem of admission to Japanese-Americans" but not until November of the following year did it approve such admissions. Even then registrations were not effective until each student had completed a "personal security questionnaire" and received clearance from the office of the provost marshal general. But other institutions, including hospitals, schools of nursing, and vocational training centers, accommodated many more, so that by the 1945–46 academic year only Chicago had more Nisei students than the Twin Cities area. [11]

The quick action of civic groups in organizing aid for the new arrivals also encouraged relocation in Minnesota. When it became clear early in 1942 that Japanese would be leaving the West Coast to escape forced evacuation, the St. Paul police chief at first attempted to bar any more from entering St. Paul. Failing that, he then tried to initiate a system whereby no Japanese could enter the city without a permit issued by him. A group of citizens protested these actions, and out of their protest the St. Paul Resettlement Committee was organized in the fall of 1942 under the auspices of the International Institute of St. Paul. In the summer of that year, a visit by representatives of the War Relocation Authority and the National Committee for the Resettlement of Japanese Americans stimulated the formation of a Minneapolis resettlement committee. The two committees, which were among the first to be organized in the United States, began operations before the WRA opened its own office in Minneapolis in February, 1943. Soon a WRA directory listed more than 80 Minnesota groups and individuals who offered services to resettlers. Some provided numerous recreation opportunities for resettlers and language-school students. The USO Center and YWCA Nisei Girls Club in Minneapolis and St. Paul's International Institute, for example, were among those that sponsored special programs. Over the next few years volunteers contributed countless hours to the resettlement effort. [12]

At first the Twin Cities committees undertook to find employment and housing for the new residents. Beginning in the fall of 1942 letters inquiring about job opportunities had been received from detention camp internees by organizations such as the Young Women's Christian Association and the International Institute. Late in that year Genevieve F. Steefel volunteered as a placement worker to help Japanese Americans at the Minneapolis office of the United States Employment Service. In April, 1944, a similar function was begun in St. Paul, where Ruth Gage Colby performed with the same devotion and efficiency as Mrs. Steefel. Between them, the two women helped more than 1,000 Japanese Americans secure work; Mrs. Colby alone found jobs for nearly 450 persons between April, 1944, and August, 1945. [13]

The employment policy of the WRA was to place the Nisei in a job as "closely matching his skills and qualifications" as possible. Because a sizable minority of the Nisei adults were college educated, this was not easy, for the Twin Cities at that time had a surplus rather than a shortage of labor. Nonetheless a number of job offers for Japanese Americans were received by the WRA and the resettlement committee volunteers; at first most of them were for domestics and gardeners, the stereotyped employments of Orientals.[14]

Temporary housing for Japanese while they searched for work became a pressing need. The YWCA, YMCA, and a few churches provided some lodgings in both cities, but they could not entirely meet the demand, especially in Minneapolis. The Board of American Missions of the United Lutheran Churches of America responded by opening a hostel at 127 Clifton Avenue in Minneapolis late in December, 1943. During its two years of operation, the hostel accommodated more than 1,000 Japanese Americans in friendly, comfortable surroundings. At first the smaller number of resettlers in St. Paul created a less critical need there, but as arrivals increased and the deadline for closing all the detention camps approached, the St. Paul Resettlement Committee leased an old hotel at 191 West Kellogg Boulevard, renovated it, and opened it to resettlers late in October, 1945. It remained in operation until 1948.[15]

Another complication existed in the fact that Japanese Americans were not equally distributed between the two cities, for Minneapolis received by far the greater share (see Table 30.2). Camp Savage and Fort Snelling, the greatest magnets for wives, relatives, and friends of those stationed there, were more accessible from Minneapolis than from St. Paul. All the gates through which Japanese Americans at first entered the Twin Cities were in Minneapolis: the WRA office with its various services; the Lutheran hostel; and the volunteer job-placement worker at the United States Employment Service. Once lodged in temporary housing in Minneapolis, resettlers were reluctant to go to St. Paul because of the distance and the double fare on streetcars. In the hope of encouraging a more even distribution between the two cities, the Minneapolis job-placement desk was closed in May, 1944, a month after the one in St. Paul began operations. This step, however, was only partially successful.

Religious leaders took an active role in the organization and operation of the resettlement committees from their in-ception. In the summer of 1944, the Minneapolis Church Federation sponsored the formation of the United Christian Ministry to Japanese Americans. Its purpose was to advise local people, "be they pastors, school teachers, or employers, as well as . . . the resettling Japanese Americans, with regard to the affairs which require special knowledge of Japanese American background, especially of things of spiritual and moral nature, so that Japanese Americans . . . in the Twin Cities area may soon become fully assimilated." The United Christian Ministry regarded their integration as a necessity, claiming that "no Japanese-American can be truly happy unless and until he becomes a part of the community in which he settles."[16]

The executive secretary of the United Christian Ministry was Daisuke Kitagawa, an Issei Episcopal minister who had moved to the Twin Cities in 1944 at the request of Colonel Rasmussen to work with the Minneapolis Church Federation as an unofficial civilian chaplain to the language school. He organized a Minneapolis congregation of Issei resettlers, whose limited ability in English dictated the need for a Japanese-language church. In St. Paul the Reverend Paul M. Nagano, another United Christian Ministry staff member, led the Japanese American Fellowship sponsored by the First Baptist Church. This group held Sunday afternoon services followed by Japanese-style suppers at the church. The Episcopal Cathedral Church of St. Mark in Minneapolis, the University YMCA, and Trinity Episcopal Church in St. Paul alternated to provide facilities for the Issei congregation, who needed easily accessible meeting places during the days before a community center was established.[17]

Although the WRA office tried promoting resettlement throughout Minnesota, relatively few Japanese Americans chose outstate destinations. Compared to the several thousand Japanese Americans in the Twin Cities, the largest outstate groups numbered only a few dozen persons. In Rochester a sizable segment consisted of nurses in training or assigned to hospital facilities. More arrived after it became known that Rochester hospitals would accept Nisei nurses. The Issei parents of some student nurses joined them

DIRECTOR Martha B. Akard showed Sergeant and Mrs. Shiro Omata through the Minneapolis Lutheran hostel for Japanese Americans at 127 Clifton Avenue in the mid-1940s.

Table 30.2. Minnesota Communities with 20 or More Japanese Americans, 1950–70

1950		1960		1970			
Minneapolis	670	Minneapolis	558	Minneapolis	686	White Bear Lake	32
St. Paul	184	St. Paul	193	St. Paul	241	Brooklyn Center	31
		St. Louis Park	119	Bloomington	122	Hopkins	29
		Bloomington	69	St. Louis Park	92	Maplewood	27
		Richfield	51	Rochester	85	Burnsville	26
		Duluth	43	Richfield	64	Columbia Heights	25
		Mankato	30	Roseville	63	New Hope	25
		Hopkins	29	Duluth	53	Coon Rapids	23
		Rochester	26	Fridley	44	St. Cloud	23
		Roseville	25	Golden Valley	42	Mankato	22
		Golden Valley	23	Edina	35	Crystal	22
				Minnetonka	34	Brooklyn Park	20

Source: U.S., *Census*, for the years cited.

in Rochester, where they received warm welcomes from three prewar Issei who worked in a local restaurant. In addition, the all-Hawaiian Japanese 100th Infantry Battalion, stationed for a time at Camp McCoy near Sparta, Wisconsin, sent numerous Nisei doctors and dentists to the Mayo Clinic for short courses before they went overseas. Perhaps as many as 60 Japanese Americans lived in Rochester at the end of World War II. Housing was a serious problem; except for nursing, employment opportunities were limited, and by 1945 the WRA considered confining resettlement in Rochester to single males and couples in domestic work.[18]

In Duluth there were about 35 Japanese Americans in 1946. The city's attitude was receptive; a resettlement committee was formed, but resettlers were few because of the scarcity of jobs. One firm, the Chun King Company headed by Jeno F. Paulucci, employed some Japanese to grow Oriental vegetables. Most of these people were from California, including Ben Furuta who was instrumental in establishing the profitable Bean Sprout Growers Association at 214 West 1st Street. This group produced the vegetable for national wholesale distribution. Within two years it employed eight men and harvested nearly two tons of sprouts per day. After a few years, Furuta returned to California, however, citing the bitter winters as his main reason.

WRA representatives traveled to many smaller cities and towns to explain the resettlement program. Usually the response was warm. Faribault and Red Wing, for example, formed resettlement committees to assist the anticipated newcomers, only to find that virtually none wished to move there. In the early days of the resettlement program, the WRA opened an office in Fargo to serve North Dakota and northern Minnesota. In seven months of operation in 1943, the unit placed fewer than 40 people, primarily in agricultural and low-paying domestic situations, before consolidating with the Minneapolis office. The relocatees were not interested in Red River Valley agriculture, which differed greatly from farm operations on the West Coast. Moreover the Nisei were turning away from the backbreaking intensive farming familiar to their parents.[19]

One problem faced by all the resettlers was their unfamiliarity with the area and their anxiety over the reactions of Minnesotans, who had had virtually no previous contact with Japanese Americans. Earl K. and Ruth Tanbara, the first Nisei to relocate in the Twin Cities, arrived in St. Paul in 1942. Mrs. Tanbara recalled that she was afraid to ride on the streetcar because of the stares of the passengers who "looked at us and didn't know if we were Chinese, Indians, or what." The Tanbaras, who received co-operation from some prewar Japanese residents of St. Paul, had moved there under WRA auspices to volunteer with the St. Paul Resettlement Committee, YWCA, and WRA public education efforts. Earl Tanbara became the local representative of the Japanese American Citizens League, which worked in conjunction with the other organizations to aid resettlers.[20]

While the efforts of civic agencies must not be discounted, it was also the generosity of the few long-time Japanese residents and early resettlers that made relocation less traumatic and helped it to succeed. Those still in the detention camps felt less apprehension about relocating or allowing children to do so if other Japanese Americans they knew had preceded them to smooth the way. "Please kindly guide . . . my still green boy," wrote one mother to the Tanbaras as her son prepared to leave an Idaho camp for St. Paul.

Minnesota was by no means free of discrimination, and nearly all residents can recount unpleasant incidents. During the war the Tanbaras and others often took resettlers into their homes. They also prepared numerous home-cooked meals for Nisei soldiers stationed at Fort Snelling. A neighbor, suspicious of these uniformed Japanese visitors, called the Federal Bureau of Investigation which sent an agent to investigate. Some businesses, such as barbershops, refused to serve Japanese customers. And one Nisei soldier, visiting a bar on Nicollet Avenue in Minneapolis, was turned away by the bartender who said, "We don't serve liquor to the Indians."[21]

Other incidents were more serious. The International Chick Sexing Association moved to Mankato from California early in 1942. The technique of quickly identifying the sex of chicks had been perfected in Japan and brought to California in 1933; most of the workers were Nisei. Since many resettlers had moved to Minneapolis, the association decided to conduct a training class there in 1944. Soon after the small class began in a North Side house, neighbors petitioned against it. They persuaded their alderman to attempt to remove the school by passing an ordinance requiring a license for it, arguing that it was a slaughterhouse and would attract rats. Although the residents claimed racism did not motivate their actions, a child playing outside the home where the petitioners met queried a reporter: "Mister, are we going to get rid of them Japs?" Various individuals and organizations rallied to support the school, and the problem was amicably resolved. Some neighborhood people joined with members of the Minneapolis Resettlement Committee to give the students a graduation party.

Discrimination was also evident in the housing market. Most resettlers had little money and did not own cars. All housing was in short supply during and immediately after the war, and frequently long hours were consumed by streetcar travel to check on scarce rental units. Then "you would find that you were last on the list anyway. . . . Even the real estate companies didn't want to bother with people who had little money," recalled one Japanese American. Most common was the "for rent" sign in the window of an apartment which had mysteriously been rented just before the resettler rang the doorbell. In one case two young Nisei girls were turned away from 36 apartments in St. Paul before finding one for rent to Japanese Americans. Mrs. Steefel wrote to Congressman Walter H. Judd: "The girls for whom we have found office jobs have a bitter experience when they go looking for apartments. Sometimes they are cruelly rebuffed, more often they are politely put off. When they do find space it is in poorer neighborhoods at better than current rentals."[22]

Those attempting to buy houses sometimes fared no better. In some cases an owner would agree to sell, only to change his mind when neighbors applied pressure. Petitions, obscene phone calls, and threatening letters were used against Japanese Americans who pioneered in some Twin Cities neighborhoods. Recalling his experiences, one Nisei veteran said: "Every house . . . apartment . . . we go to they look at me and say, 'Oh no, we don't want you.' Here I had spent two years overseas, and here I come back and get a kick in the butt." Twin Cities Japanese Americans remember fewer incidents of job discrimination, although outright refusal to hire on the basis of race, hostility of coworkers, and lower salaries for the same work performed by Caucasians were reported by some.[23]

For each hostile person and unpleasant incident, most Minnesota Japanese Americans can describe many more good experiences. The state branch of the American Legion, for example, roundly condemned an anti-Japanese article in the official Legion magazine and passed a resolution protesting this "violation of the constitution." The generally warm reception given the newcomers was echoed in the major newspapers, which early adopted a fair and friendly attitude toward them and published sympathetic stories during and after the war years. William P. Steven, city editor of the *Minneapolis Morning Tribune,* told a WRA relocation officer in 1946, "We realize that any new minority group is going to have hard sledding, and we felt it our duty to ease the situation for them as much as possible while still being consistent with good reporting and good newspaper operation."

Public education programs contributed to the largely favorable impression of the area most resettlers received. The Minneapolis and St. Paul relocation committees and WRA office provided speakers who made literally hundreds of presentations throughout Minnesota to acquaint people with the relocation program. The Tanbaras alone gave over 20 talks to civic groups between December, 1942, and February, 1943. The St. Paul Council of Human Relations exhibited at the Minnesota State Fair in 1944, showing a film explaining the Japanese American situation to over 15,000 people.[24]

Comments by Minneapolis Nisei reflected their views of the Twin Cities in 1944. A student in the language school praised church groups. "On Sundays most of the men leave Camp Savage to come into the city to go to church," he said. "They feel most welcome at any church they want to attend. They feel that every effort is being made to make us feel a part of the group. The men at the camp have often said that this is one of the most inspiring experiences they have had." Another affirmed that "There has been something in the air in Minneapolis. People are so kind and friendly. We have been permitted equal entry into the schools, the shops, the places of amusement. It has not been that way before, nor is it that way in other places. Like many other Japanese we will live here forever." One of the first students to reach Camp Savage in 1942 expressed amazement: "I couldn't believe how well they treated us up here. This place was like heaven." It was not heaven, but the instances of cruelty were apparently understood to be the acts of individuals, rather than the products of a pervasive climate of racism like that the Japanese Americans had experienced on the West Coast.[25]

Postwar Changes and Organizations

Prodded by the United States Supreme Court, the government at the end of 1944 revoked the evacuation orders and allowed some Japanese to return to the West. During the immediate postwar years, numerous other sojourners in Minnesota elected to go back to California, Washington, and Oregon. Despite their bitter experiences, many had left behind businesses, farms, friends, and memories. Over 50% of the 1940 Japanese-American population of California, for example, had returned by 1946. To the first-generation Issei, especially, these states were home.[26]

Nevertheless some Japanese Americans chose to put down roots in Minnesota. The war and subsequent relocation brought significant changes in the structure of Japanese-American communities. Many Issei who had lost their businesses and property were unable to recover economically and spent the rest of their working lives in menial service positions. Life in the relocation centers had weakened the traditional authority of the Issei father in his family. For the first time, Issei women were liberated from the kitchen to work in factories or other jobs, often at higher wages than their husbands. Thus the traditional husband-wife relationship changed. Nisei experiences in college, the army, and in establishing themselves on their own made them independent. Better able than their parents to deal with the postwar world, they assumed leadership in the new Japanese-American communities of the Middle West.[27]

The close-knit group of Issei in the Twin Cities shared this period of adjustment with one another. They took jobs in laundries, hospitals, hotels and restaurants, and greenhouses — frequently helped by their Nisei children during interviews. In 1946 the Reverend Kitagawa estimated that there were between 1,500 and 2,000 Japanese Americans in the Twin Cities and that "a good number of families are now settling down in this area." But by 1950 the Minnesota population had fallen to 1,049 (905 or 86% in the Twin Cities). Fewer than 10 remained in each of the two secondary resettlement areas of Rochester and Duluth. Those who stayed set about establishing families and careers as permanent Minnesotans.

No identifiable residential concentrations of Japanese Americans appeared in the Twin Cities. In early postwar years, many lived close to downtown Minneapolis in inner-city neighborhoods, where cheap housing and accessibility to mass transit were available. By the 1950s they had begun to move to the near south and west Minneapolis suburbs, where a cluster of Japanese Americans was welcomed by the newly established Jewish community of St. Louis Park, for example. Rapid development of this and other suburbs coincided with improved incomes, acquisition of automobiles, and the space requirements of growing Nisei families.[28]

Despite the fact that the resettlement committees, so vital in the earlier stage of in-migration, gradually phased out their programs, the small Twin Cities Japanese-American population spawned a number of activities and organizations in the 1940s and 1950s. Among them were four Minneapolis churches. Most Nisei joined congregations in their neighborhoods, but in 1946 the Twin Cities Buddhist Association, organized with the help of the Midwest Buddhist Temple in Chicago, began to meet first at the university and later in a Minneapolis Universalist church. Kitagawa, in addition to his many services to the United Christian Ministry, maintained the predominantly Japanese-speaking Issei congregation, which was formally organized in 1947 as the Japanese Christian Union Church. A group split from this congregation in 1951, taking a number of Issei and adding some Nisei members to form the Twin Cities Independent Church. Meeting first at the YMCA near the University of Minnesota, the independents in 1957 purchased a former Methodist Church in Northeast Minneapolis. Since 1977 the interdenominational Japanese Fellowship Church in Edina has held services in the Japanese language. A Saturday language school, begun in 1978 and sponsored by the government of Japan for aliens and their children, still met in the church building in 1980.[29]

Kitagawa was also instrumental in helping to establish a group for young married couples, primarily Japanese American, which in 1947 officially organized as the Rainbow Club with membership open to all. Its purpose was "to meet and get to know people as people, regardless of race, creed, or color." The club had a vigorous social program, but by 1980 many of the original Japanese-American members, once in the majority, had become inactive, and the group met less frequently.[30]

A Twin Cities chapter of the Japanese American Citizens League (JACL), the principal Nisei voice during and after World War II, was formed in 1946. At the national level it functioned effectively as a civil rights organization, advocating an assimilationist position for much of its history. The local branch maintained a low profile. The minutes of an early meeting urged "that social activities of the JACL be kept at a minimum to avoid undue attention being called to Japanese Americans as a group. Rather, work should be carried on to further acceptance as individual American citizens, which comes mainly through personal actions." Some recommended that the local chapter omit the term "Japanese Americans" from its name. As a result, the Twin Cities United Citizens League (UCL) became the only chapter of the JACL that did not use the parent organization's title.[31]

The league took steps to combat local instances of discrimination, while actively pushing for government compensation of property losses suffered in the evacuation, a goal partially achieved in 1948. It also mobilized local support for the successful national campaign to grant naturalization rights to the Issei which culminated in the passage of the McCarran-Walter Act in 1952.

Attempts to publish a Japanese-American newsletter in the Twin Cities began in January, 1947, with the *Northwest Nisei*, which appeared sporadically. The sheet, issued by several groups of volunteers, underwent three title changes before becoming the monthly *JA Journal*, published at the Japanese American Community Center in Minneapolis from 1952 to 1965.

The establishment of that center in 1949 was a pivotal event. As Charles Tatsuda, the chairman of its board of directors, explained when the center officially opened: "Ever since we first relocated to the Twin Cities we have felt a strong desire for a Japanese American Center. . . . Such a center might be used primarily as a focal point from which we could concentrate our effort in serving the community. . . . Second, it might be used as a common meeting place for Issei and Nisei organizations. Third, it might be used to promote and practice Japanese American culture."[32]

The National Council of the Episcopal Church and the Episcopal Diocese of Minnesota contributed $18,000 to purchase an old mansion at 2200 Blaisdell Avenue in Minneapolis. The agreement between the center's board and the diocese granted Japanese Americans full use of the property as long as they met its operating expenses. It also provided for the transfer of ownership to the local Japanese Americans if they could repay the diocese its original purchase price. The center served as a meeting place for two congregations (the Japanese Christian Union Church and the Twin Cities Buddhist Association), and for such clubs as the Rainbow, War Brides, Young Adults (mainly single Nisei), and Issei women. In addition it was used by the UCL, United Citizens League Credit Union, and the *JA Journal* staff. Various dance, flower arrangement, and cooking classes gathered there, and several thousand people attended public fundraising events that included a bazaar and one or more sukiyaki dinners.

During the late 1950s the activities of Japanese-American organizations intensified, with the peak occurring perhaps in 1961. That year the UCL, in addition to its regular meetings and social events, sponsored a benefit dinner and a live theater performance at an area theater, and hosted the four-day biennial convention of all the eastern and midwestern chapters of the JACL. The Japanese American Community Cen-

THE WOMEN participating in this Japanese exhibit at the 1949 St. Paul Festival of Nations included community leader Ruth Tanbara (center).

ter put on its usual bazaar, held two large fund-raising dinners, participated in the International Institute's Festival of Nations — a triennial celebration of Minnesota's ethnic cultures held in St. Paul — and constructed a float for the Minneapolis Aquatennial parade which won the top award in its category there and at the Hopkins Raspberry Festival. During a return visit in 1961, Kitagawa, who had moved from the Twin Cities in 1954, expressed amazement at the group's participation in so many community projects. For its size, he believed it to be one of the most active Nisei communities in the nation.[33]

Kitagawa also commented in 1959 that it was "really strictly and exclusively a middle class professional community." The high educational level among Nisei was reflected in their occupations and in their economic well-being. Not all were professionals, but virtually all had achieved at least lower-middle incomes by this time. Most of the Issei, then retired or in the late years of their working lives, could watch proudly as their children attained the economic and social acceptance denied them. Between 1952, when the right of naturalization was granted, and 1956 more than 90% of the 150 Issei in the Twin Cities had become citizens.[34]

The 1960 census reported 1,726 persons of Japanese descent in Minnesota, a 65% increase over 1950. The components of this growth were varied. Many children (the third generation Sansei) were born to Nisei resettlers in Minnesota during the 1950s. Secondly, Japanese women who married American servicemen arrived in increasing numbers, so that foreign-born Japanese reached 533 by 1960. At the same time there was also a steady trickle of out-migration from the state, as families moved back to California, where the Japanese population increased by 85% in the same period.

The sex ratio in Minnesota, which decreased from 112 males per 100 females in 1950 to 84 by 1960, reflected the arrival of the misnamed "war brides." Ten years later the state population showed an even more lopsided sex composition, with a ratio of 78 males to 100 females. Between 1947 and 1961 an estimated 46,000 American military or civilian personnel in Japan married Japanese women. Duluth's community, for example, grew from 7 Japanese in 1950 to 43 in 1960, of whom 34 were women. Thus, the distribution of original resettlers in the state was partially masked by the infusion of this newer, culturally somewhat different popula-

tion. The war brides usually did not become an integral part of the local Japanese-American communities. An attempt to maintain a social group for them in St. Paul failed during 1955. A similar effort the same year in Minneapolis was more successful; a war brides' club continued to meet at the Japanese American Center through the late 1950s.[35]

The vibrant Twin Cities Japanese-American community of the late 1950s and early 1960s was sustained by the energetic young adult Nisei and by a smaller group of mostly retired but still vigorous Issei. The pace and variety of their activities soon slackened markedly, however. Most Nisei had married during the 1940s and 1950s, and the demands of rearing a family restricted their participation in ethnic affairs. Developing careers also required hard work and sometimes long hours. Acceptance by their neighbors frequently meant absorption into churches and civic organizations, which, in turn, lessened their need for formalized ethnic group activities. As the average age of the Issei climbed, they became less mobile, more confined to their homes, and more dependent on the Nisei for transportation. All these factors combined to produce a shrinking core of Nisei who were able to donate their free time to Japanese-American organizations. One Nisei, referring to the upkeep of the deteriorating old building that housed the Japanese American Center, recalled that "It got to be expensive. . . . people got sick and tired of doing all the tasks. Most of us were married and had families growing and we didn't have time to spend away from home."[36]

The frenetic pace of activity in 1961 soon told on the Twin Cities group. In 1962 the Nisei bowling league folded, it was said, because of the members' increasing family responsibilities. The *JA Journal* appeared with less regularity despite the outgoing editor's impassioned plea to readers "not to lose it simply because of apathy." The future of the center, first discussed in the late 1950s, assumed more urgency because of the need for major renovations. One member remarked that "It would be utter folly to spend $6,200 on repairs." A move to end the wasteful duplication of efforts by merging the boards of the center and the UCL (which changed its name from UCL to Twin Cities chapter of the Japanese American Citizens League early in 1962) failed, despite approval by 81% of the Japanese Americans polled.

Declining membership and diminishing participation by

1963 produced operating losses for the center, which survived briefly on surpluses built up in preceding years. By mid-1964, however, the situation was so critical that a decision had to be made quickly. At year's end it was decided to sell the building. The center closed in July, 1965.[37]

The Issei probably suffered most in losing their gathering place, but the Sansei also lost a setting in which to meet with other young Japanese Americans. While many Nisei regretted the center's loss, they were unwilling or unable to retain the building or to acquire another. One Nisei, active in its affairs, said: "We spent most of our weekends repairing the place. . . . So many things happened there in the days when we had more hours than money. . . . The place was so broken down we thought we would be buying trouble to keep it. . . . We were closely knit then, but we lost contact. I wish we still had a Center. We made a mistake losing that place. Our Sansei could have used it too."[38] The 1960s, then, saw the decline of some of the institutions which had served the Japanese Americans during their years of adjustment. The Sansei generation began to reach adulthood during the later 1960s and 1970s, as the Issei passed from the scene.

Like the children of other immigrant groups, the Nisei reflected the culture of their parents and that of the United States into which the older generation had tried so hard to assimilate. For at least a few years during childhood most Nisei attended Japanese-language schools, where they also received traditional moral training emphasizing filial piety, respect for teachers and elders, and belief in the value of education and hard work. No doubt many Nisei heard the stories their parents had learned in Japan about the scholar who poured ice-cold water over his body in winter to stay awake in order to complete his schoolwork, or about the man who used a cageful of fireflies to provide light so that he could study at night. Issei, who had once hoped to make their fortunes quickly and return to Japan, became resigned to an arduous life in America; they endured so that their children could be educated and avoid similar ordeals. "If you don't study hard and be educated, you will end up doing hard work like your father," one Issei warned his son. These Japanese values, which were compatible in many ways with those of the American middle class, aided the Nisei in their efforts to become a part of Minnesota life. Local Nisei, like their counterparts elsewhere, gave remarkably uniform responses to questions about values they learned from their parents, although the language teaching was not notably successful among them.[39]

The impressive levels of education and economic progress recorded by Nisei and their Sansei offspring from 1950 to 1980 followed remarkably soon after the total disruption of their lives. This rapid development prompted one observer to speak of the Japanese Americans as America's "prize subnation," pointing out that "there is no parallel to this success story" in American history. By implication, other groups would do well to emulate this so-called model minority, a conclusion denounced by some Asian Americans. The attitude, shared by some Nisei, that "We made it, why can't they?" currently has as its chief exponent Senator S. I.

Hayakawa, who is unpopular with many liberal Sansei and Nisei.[40]

How real is the apparent success of Japanese Americans? The 1970 census confirmed their high level of education (12.5 school years completed versus 12.1 for the general population) and their heavy representation in white-collar occupations (see Table 30.3). Nevertheless discrimination has evidently persisted. Japanese earned only $43 for every $51 earned by whites in California in 1960, and this income lag continued. In 1970 regional disparities existed as well. A comparison of median family incomes of Japanese Americans and whites in Illinois (the only available Midwest census data) and California revealed that white incomes were virtually the same in the two states ($11,096 in Illinois, $11,093 in California), but in Illinois Japanese-American family incomes were significantly higher ($13,135) than those in California ($12,393). Although Japanese incomes exceeded the median for the total population in all regions except the South, they were probably achieved because most Japanese households had more than one wage earner. In over half of Japanese families both husbands and wives worked, whereas in 1970 only 39% of all families in the United States had employed husbands and wives.[41]

But what of Minnesota? Although data on incomes were lacking, a sample of local Japanese Americans revealed an occupational structure radically different from the national and the Illinois situations. The Twin Cities Japanese-American population is overwhelmingly white-collar and professional (see Table 30.3). This is not to say that they do not exhibit the high family employment typical elsewhere or that employment discrimination has not been a factor in the state. What the sample data suggest is that the Minnesota group may be significantly different in occupation structure and income from other Japanese Americans.

By 1970 Japanese Americans, while still concentrated in the Twin Cities metropolitan area, had dispersed into suburban communities (see Table 30.2). The residential preference for Minneapolis persisted, with the western and southern suburbs showing the greatest increase. The presence of persons of Japanese descent in high-income suburbs testified to both the comfortable economic position of many Japanese Americans and to the virtual disappearance of housing discrimination against affluent Japanese Americans.[42]

This study views Minnesota Japanese Americans as an ethnic community — that is, as a group of people bound together by ties based on a sense of common origin and interacting with one another. In the past, the term also connoted a geographical location in which numerous members of the group made their homes. Three areas — the community of residence, ethnic institutions, and informal social interaction — deserve further comment.[43]

Community need not be based on locality. However, the "affinity of a group for its own people and culture can produce a geographical community as the spatial manifestation of ethnicity." In Minnesota, Japanese Americans outside the Twin Cities have little contact with one another. For example, Charles Hazama, a Hawaiian-born Sansei who was

Table 30.3. Japanese-American Occupational Structure, 1970s (in percent)

	U.S. Population 1970	Japanese Americans			
		U.S.	Illinois	Twin Cities Nisei	Twin Cities Sansei
Professional and technical	14.3	26.4	30.3	46.2	85.7
Managers, officials, and proprietors	11.2	11.3	14.4	23.1	14.3
Subtotal	25.5	37.7	44.7	69.3	100.0
Craftsmen and foremen	21.2	12.8	21.3	25.6	0.0
Laborers	6.6	12.3	1.6	0.0	0.0
Other	47.7	37.2	32.4	5.1	0.0

Source: U.S., *Census,* 1970; Twin Cities data based on author's interviews, 1977–80.

elected mayor of Rochester in 1979, indicated that he knew of only one other Japanese-American family in his city. Even in the Twin Cities, little sign of an ethnic residential community can be found. Less than half (47%) of the metropolitan area's Japanese Americans remained in the central cities in 1970, with the rest scattered over dozens of suburbs. In a random sample of 75 Japanese-American households, 71% reported no others living within a two-block radius.[44]

Social interaction among Japanese Americans could function in lieu of geographical proximity as a means of bonding the group. In the absence of geographical concentration, ethnic institutions and the degree of interaction they promote may be important. Institutions can furnish the settings in which ethnic group members form friendships and carry on traditions.

In 1980 a limited number of ethnic institutions existed among Minnesota Japanese Americans. The Twin Cities chapter of the JACL continued to function as a civil rights organization, which occasionally expressed opinions on national issues. The chapter awarded scholarships to outstanding Japanese-American high school students. About 20 Sansei were eligible in 1980 and nine of them shared nearly $2,500 in awards, most of which were distributed at the annual community picnic in June. But the league's main function is social. Its community-wide activities include an annual picnic, a sukiyaki fund-raising dinner, and a banquet featuring a national Japanese-American leader as speaker. A significant proportion of the metropolitan Japanese-American population belonged to JACL, with membership fluctuating between 200 and 300 over the past 20 years; in 1980 it declined to about 150. Only about 22 were active members, however, and Sansei participation was low.[45]

The Twin Cities branch of the Japan America Society and the St. Paul-Nagasaki Sister City organization also had active Japanese-American participants, but they made up a minority in the memberships of both groups. The Rainbow Club continued its social functions with a small membership.

The older Protestant ethnic churches in the Twin Cities had all but faded away, and the Japanese Fellowship Church, although serving a youthful congregation, had less than two dozen members. The Japanese Christian Union Church dwindled to about a dozen members, the youngest of whom was 77. In 1978 membership in the Twin Cities Independent Church consisted of 11 widows and 2 elderly men, and the congregation was forced to sell its building. The Twin Cities Buddhist Association continued to hold services in a Universalist church. Eight times a year a priest from Chicago visited the group, whose membership consisted of about 35 persons — a number of Issei in their 80s and 90s and 10 Sansei, only a few of whom were active. The congregation has not sought to enroll Caucasians or members of other Asian backgrounds. Fewer than 50 Issei could be counted in the Twin Cities in 1980.[46]

From 1974 until 1979 the Minnihon Arts Center operated at 924 2nd Avenue South in Minneapolis. It was dedicated to the dissemination of Japanese culture to a wider public than just Japanese Americans and offered a variety of classes in dance, calligraphy, athletics, language, and other fine arts. Its supporting membership was always small (less than 125) and included many non-Japanese. Because of inadequate revenues, the center faced a continuous struggle for existence. It closed in January, 1979.[47]

In an attempt to meet mutual problems and advance cultural projects, members of various Asian-American ethnic groups formed the Minnesota Asian American Project (MAAP) in 1977. Japanese-American membership consisted mainly, but not entirely, of a relatively small group of younger adult Sansei who reacted more positively to the idea of Asian solidarity than did their elders. The project collected oral histories from elderly first-generation Asians in the Twin Cities, provided a legal defense and education service for Asians, and at this writing is at work on ambitious plans for a Minnesota Asian Center to house a library, cultural center, and office and retail space.[48]

Few Sansei are involved in the Japanese ethnic institutions that survive in the Twin Cities, though there is a small and relatively active group of JAYS (Japanese American Youth) affiliated with the league. Its aims are to bring Sansei together in a social atmosphere, to serve the Issei and the community at large, and to develop leadership ability and a sense of identity. There were 28 members in 1979, of whom 16 were fairly active.

The intensity of informal social interaction is one indicator identifying an ethnic community. In response to the question "Of your five closest friends, how many are Japanese Americans?" nearly half (49%) of the Twin Cities Nisei sample reported that a majority (three or more) of their closest friends were Japanese American. More than a quarter (27%) reported no close Japanese-American friends. Many Nisei have deep friendships that grew out of common experiences and adversity. The years of discrimination in the West, life in the detention camps, and the struggle to attain economic security and social acceptance in the Middle West forged strong bonds that have survived moves to the suburbs, the broadening of social networks beyond the ethnic group, and the decline of ethnic organizations. The Sansei have no such shared experiences beyond that of common ancestry. For them, in-group friendships depend much more on proximity or joint participation in activities. Among Twin Cities Sansei, three-fourths (76%) reported that none of their closest friends was Japanese American; none reported that a majority of their closest friends were.[49]

The nearly total intermarriage of the Minnesota Sansei with other groups is an inevitable outcome of the small Japanese-American population. It is also the greatest question mark on the future of the community. Of 46 Sansei marriages reported (half or more of the Sansei had yet to marry when the survey was made in 1978) 38 were to Caucasians, one to a Chinese American, two to Japanese nationals, and five to Japanese Americans, according to Andrew Otani. Among the Nisei, intermarriages were rare — less than 10% among the Twin Cities group sampled.

Sansei reared in Minnesota, especially those outside the Twin Cities, have grown up in an almost totally Caucasian society, probably with few Sansei classmates or acquaintances. Some reported that their parents emphasized traditional values such as respect for elders, the need to work harder than others to succeed, and the necessity of upholding the family image, but most did not recall the emphasis on moral training that the Nisei experienced. Nearly all Nisei described the Sansei as thoroughly Americanized, pointing out that traditions fell by the wayside because of the environment in which the third generation grew up. Some Nisei saw the Sansei as being more outspoken than they, although a few felt that because of their upbringing in easy circumstances their children had known no suffering and did not persevere in tasks. Most Nisei have accepted the loss of tradition, finding good features in the Sansei character. One declared that they "are much like young people all over — a lot more open and understanding of racial problems — more than we were. We're grateful that they don't have a chip on their shoulders."[50]

Differences between the second and third generations — whether in their participation in ethnic organizations, language retention, patterns of friendship, or intermarriage rates — are pronounced. This does not necessarily indicate a total loss of ethnic identity and culture, which, after all, are not completely tied up with place community and social community. Sansei are proud of their Japanese ancestry. As compared with the Nisei, however, a continued decline is apparent in the tangible aspects of a Japanese-American community.

Recent Japanese immigrants have not rejuvenated the ethnic community by fresh infusions of Japanese culture. As a rule, close relationships between these immigrants and local Japanese Americans do not exist. A Japanese-born engineer living in a Minneapolis suburb commented that most of his friends there were Japanese, not American Japanese, adding that he did not feel at home with the latter because "They are just like Americans." Another skilled young Japanese immigrant indicated that most of her relationships were with Caucasians and that the Japanese Americans she knew had "old-fashioned ideas and feelings" about family and culture. The elements of Japanese culture transmitted to the Nisei and Sansei are, after all, from turn-of-the-century Japan and must seem archaic to those raised in contemporary Japan.[51]

Ties between Minnesota Japanese Americans and relatives in Japan were not strong in 1980. Issei continued to communicate with their families in Japan, but as they died away such ties were further weakened. Not many Nisei and

JAPANESE-AMERICAN VETERANS of the Military Intelligence Service Language School donated this bentendo, or shrine, to the Japanese Garden at Normandale Community College, Bloomington, in appreciation for the reception they received in Minnesota during World War II. The garden was constructed during the 1970s.

very few Sansei were able to write Japanese well enough to keep in contact. There has been no flow of Japanese immigrants into Minnesota to join families that have been in the United States for generations, although some local Japanese Americans who have visited Japan spent time with relatives there.

Unless the form of Sansei ethnic identification undergoes change, the future of a close-knit Japanese-American community beyond the Nisei generation in Minnesota is doubtful. After the return migration to the West Coast following World War II, the Twin Cities community fell below the critical mass needed to support institutions such as churches, social and service organizations, and businesses that strengthen ethnicity. Along with this — or perhaps because of it — the population has dispersed throughout the area. With no places and few opportunities where ethnicity could be reinforced by contact with one another, some of the Sansei have ceased to be part of an ethnic community as defined in this study. There are and will be exceptions to this trend, but in a small Japanese-American settlement such as that in Minnesota, the ethnic community will become more a psychological than a geographical entity.

Reference notes

[1] United States, *Census, 1970, Japanese, Chinese, and Filipinos in the United States*, Subject Report PC(2)-1G, 1, table 1; interview of Rev. Andrew N. Otani, June 14, 1977, notes in author's possession. All interviews cited hereafter were conducted by the author unless otherwise noted. The author wishes to acknowledge helpful suggestions received from Rev. Otani during the preparation of this chapter.

[2] The standard work on early Japanese immigration is Yamato Ichihashi, *Japanese in the United States* (Stanford, Cal., 1932); see especially pp. 47–64, 65, 247. The most recent addition to the literature is Robert A. Wilson and Bill Hosokawa, *East to America: A History of the Japanese in the United States* (New York, 1980). See also U.S. Immigration Commission, *Abstract of Reports*, 1:113, 660, 661 (61 Congress, 3 session, *Senate Documents*, no. 747 — serial 5865); Dorothy Swaine Thomas, *The Salvage*, 573 (Berkeley, Cal., 1952); Takao Ozawa *v.* United States, 260 *United States Supreme Court Reports* 189 (1922). For a fuller discussion of the events through 1924, see Roger Daniels, *The Politics of Prejudice*, 65–78, 98 (New York, 1969). A legal history is Frank F. Chuman, *The Bamboo People: The Law and Japanese-Americans* (Del Mar, Cal., 1976). On the Immigration Act of 1924, see Introduction.

[3] U.S., *Census, 1940, Population*, vol. 2, part 1, p. 19, table 4.

[4] U.S., *Census, 1890, Population*, part 1, p. 442, table 17. A reference to Japanese laundrymen is in Mrs. Gerald Olson and Mrs. Joel W. Johnson, eds., *In the Heart of the Red River Valley: A History of the People of Norman County Minnesota*, 542 (Dallas, 1976). The *Herman* (Grant County) *Enterprise*, July 21, 1892, reported on a lecture by "a real live Japanese minister in native dress," who drew a large crowd.

[5] W. T. Matsuoka to James J. Hill, August 17, 1893; Oriental Trading Company to Russell Harding, August 30, 1898; P. T. Downs to Oriental Trading Company, January 10, 1900; G. T. Slade to D. M. Philbin, May 3, 1900 — all in Great Northern Railway Company Records, MHS; U.S., *Census, 1900, Population,* 1:571, table 21. Ichihashi, *Japanese in the United States,* 142, indicated that the Japanese laborers received more pay than the Mexicans, but less than European labor. See also Yuji Ichioka, "Japanese Immigrant Labor Contractors and the Northern Pacific and the Great Northern Railroad Companies, 1898–1907," in *Labor History,* 21:325–350 (Summer, 1980). Two Japanese worked for the Oliver Mining Co. in 1907; George O. Virtue, *The Minnesota Iron Ranges,* 345, 349 (U.S. Bureau of Labor, *Bulletin,* no. 84 — Washington, D.C., 1909).

[6] Interview of Johnny C. and Mary Ogura, early St. Paul residents, June 26, 1979, notes in author's possession. Among Japanese who were not associated with the railroads were the W. J. Akamatsu family members, who operated a gift shop in St. Paul for many years; Dr. Kano Ikeda, a pathologist at Miller Hospital; Tometaro Kitagawa, a Minneapolis gift shop owner; and Takashi Terami, who taught physics at St. Thomas College.

[7] Here and three paragraphs below, see Alien Registration forms, Hennepin County, Minneapolis, Ward 4, precinct 4, in Minnesota Commission of Public Safety Records, Minnesota State Archives, MHS; Herman E. Olson, *The Minneapolis Property and Housing Survey* (Minneapolis, 1934); interviews of Harry K. Habata, November 19, 1979, Ruth N. Tanbara, June 4, 1979, notes in author's possession. Ruth Tanbara's parents, Frank J. and Kiyo Nomura, had worked in Minneapolis in 1905.

[8] On events leading to the mass evacuation, see Roger Daniels, *Concentration Camps USA: Japanese Americans and World War II,* 1–41 (Hinsdale, Ill., 1971); Michi Weglyn, *Years of Infamy: The Untold Story of America's Concentration Camps* (New York, 1976); Daisuke Kitagawa, *Issei and Nisei, the Internment Years,* 154 (New York, 1967). See also *St. Paul Sunday Pioneer Press,* July 19, 1981, Metro sec., 3.

[9] Here and two paragraphs below, see U.S., *Census, 1940, Population,* 2:14, 1950, 2:44; Masaharu Ano, "Loyal Linguists: Nisei of World War II Learned Japanese in Minnesota," in *Minnesota History,* 45:273–287 (Fall, 1977); Military Intelligence Service Language School, *MISLS Album,* 8, 10, 15 (Minneapolis, 1946); *442nd Combat Team,* 2 (n.p., [1945?]). For more detailed information on Nisei linguists, see Joseph Harrington, *Yankee Samurai: The Secret Role of Nisei in America's Pacific Victory* (Detroit, 1979); see

especially pp. 36, 44, 113, 129–131. An outstanding accomplishment of the language-school graduates was the translation of the entire plan (captured from the Japanese) for the naval battle of the Philippine Islands; the information resulted in the greatest sea defeat suffered by Japan in World War II.

[10] Risa Palm, "Japanese American in Minnesota: A Historical Geography," 24, Plan B paper, 1969, University of Minnesota; U.S. Dept. of Interior, War Agency Liquidation Unit, *People in Motion: The Postwar Readjustment of the Evacuated Japanese Americans,* 21 (Washington, D.C., 1947).

[11] "Report," December 12, 1945, p. 2, in St. Paul Resettlement Committee Papers, 1942–53, MHS; Genevieve F. Steefel to Morris Robinson, February 11, 1944, in Minneapolis Committee on Resettlement of Japanese Americans Papers, 1942–44, MHS; Robert W. O'Brien, *The College Nisei,* 123, 138, 145 (Palo Alto, Cal., 1949); University of Minnesota Board of Regents, *Minutes,* September 26, 1942, p. 405, November 20, 1943, p. 159. According to Palm, "Japanese Americans in Minnesota," 24, of Twin Cities Nisei 20% had attended a Minnesota college; 46% indicated that they or a relative had done so.

[12] "Report," 1, in St. Paul Resettlement Committee Papers; Dillon S. Myer, *Uprooted Americans: The Japanese Americans and the War Relocation Authority during World War II,* 136 (Tucson, 1971). The Minneapolis committee was formed by the Minneapolis Federation of Churches, the Council of Church Women, the YMCA, the YWCA, and the Council of Social Agencies; War Relocation Authority, *A Directory of Agencies, groups, and individuals . . . in the North Central Area,* 13–18 (Chicago, n.d.), copy in MEHP Papers, MHS; Minutes, June 17, 1943, in St. Paul Resettlement Committee Papers, MHS; James H. Hiner, "Narrative History, War Relocation Authority, 1942–1946," 10, typewritten manuscript, in National Archives Record Group (NARG) 210, copy in Hiner Papers, MHS; *JA Journal* (Minneapolis), July, 1959, p. 8. The *Journal* was a monthly, mimeographed newsletter published by the Japanese American Community Center from 1952 to 1965; a partial file is in MHS.

[13] See, for example, Mioko Takagi to YWCA, November 12, 1942, and Violet Tagawa to YWCA, December 18, 1942, both in Minneapolis Committee on Resettlement Papers; "Report," 4, [8], in St. Paul Resettlement Committee Papers. Genevieve F. Steefel to Walter H. Judd, February 12, 1943, in Minneapolis Committee on Resettlement Papers, described the procedures she followed.

[14] "Report," 4, in St. Paul Resettlement Committee Papers; Harold Mann, staff memorandum, March 9, 1944, in NARG 210, copy in MHS. On job offers, see, for example, Arthur N. Phillips to Manzanar Relocation Authority, January 5, 1943, in Minneapolis Committee on Resettlement Papers.

[15] Here and below, see Hiner, "Narrative History," 8, 10–12; Minutes, October 31, 1945, March 17, 1948, in St. Paul Resettlement Committee Papers; Steefel to Daisuke Kitagawa, March 26, 1944, Genevieve F. Steefel Papers, MHS; "Annual Report, 1944," p. 1, in Minneapolis Committee on Resettlement Papers.

[16] Dan G. Long to Genevieve F. Steefel, September 22, 1944, in Steefel Papers.

[17] Kitagawa, *Issei and Nisei,* 164; Hiner, "Narrative History," 9; Norma Sommerdorf, *A Church in Lowertown: The First Baptist Church of Saint Paul,* 154, 156 (St. Paul, 1975); Long to Steefel, September 22, 1944, Steefel Papers; "Directory of Protestant Missionaries Engaged in Work among Japanese in the United States," mimeographed list, December 1, 1944, in International Institute of Minnesota Papers, IHRC; interview of Kimi and Sam Hara, November 12, 1979, notes in author's possession.

[18] Here and below, see interviews of Kimi and Sam Hara, December 7, 1977, November 12, 1979, notes in author's possession; Hiner, "Narrative History," 39, 40, 40b, 40c, 40d; Allen Aldrich to

George Sergeant, December 9, 1944, and Evelyn M. Carroll to Ben Furuta, March 27, 1945, both in NARG 210, copies in MHS; Tanbara interview, June 4, 1979. A list of 17 adults and 14 children in Duluth is appended to Elmer B. Isaksen to Roy E. Burt, February 21, 1945, in NARG 210, copy in MHS.

[19] Elmer B. Isaksen to Prudence Ross, September 6, 1944, March 27, 1945, in NARG 210, copies in MHS; Hiner, "Narrative History," 38.

[20] Tanbara interview, June 4, 1979; Alice L. Sickels to Annie Clo Watson, February 3, 1943, in International Institute of Minnesota Papers; Kinichi Suzuki to Earl and Ruth Tanbara, March 31, 1943, letter in possession of Ruth Tanbara, copy in MEHP Papers. An account of Earl Tanbara's helpfulness is given in Bill Hosokawa, *Thirty-Five Years in the Frying Pan*, 249–251 (New York, 1978).

[21] Here and below, see interviews of Tanbara, June 4, 1979; Harry T. Umeda, March 1, 1978; Sam Hara, November 12, 1979, notes in author's possession; interview of Sue Saiki, February 25, 1975, in Oral History Program, Blue Earth County Historical Society, Mankato; *Minneapolis Star Journal*, November 14, pp. 8, 11, November 15, p. 13, 1944; Hiner, "Narrative History," 9d. Difficulties between Nisei soldiers and Twin Citians are described in Tamotsu Shibutani, *The Derelicts of Company K: A Sociological Study of Demoralization*, 274 (Berkeley, Cal., 1978).

[22] Hara interview, November 12, 1979; Alice L. Sickels, *Around the World in St. Paul*, 205–208 (Minneapolis, 1945); Steefel to Judd, April 25, 1943, in Walter H. Judd Papers, MHS.

[23] Here and below, see Harry Umeda, quoted in Duane R. Shellum, *America's Human Secret Weapon*, 30 (Minneapolis, 1977); Hiner, "Narrative History," 23c; "Text of American Legion Protest on Racial Discrimination," [n.p., August 21, 1943], copy in MEHP Papers; author's interviews of Twin Cities Japanese Americans.

[24] Isaksen to Ross, September 6, 1944, NARG 210; list of speeches given by Earl and Ruth Tanbara, MEHP Papers.

[25] Audrey Johnson and Barbara Tosdal, "A Study of the Relocated Japanese Americans in Minneapolis," [1944?], NARG 210, copy in MHS; Toshio Abe, quoted in Shellum, *Secret Weapon*, 9. Some Nisei had unpleasant church experiences, however; see [Pastor Paul L. Grove] to "Dear Brother Ed," March 26, 1945, in possession of Ruth Tanbara, and Dr. Kano Ikeda to C. L. White, May 6, 1943, in NARG 210, copies in MEHP Papers.

[26] U.S. Dept. of the Interior, *WRA: A Story of Human Conservation*, 206 (Washington, D.C., 1946).

[27] Here and below, see Daisuke Kitagawa, "Twin Cities: 'Settling Down' Noted," in *Resettlement Bulletin*, April, 1946, p. 7, the final issue of a newsletter published by the Home Missions Council, New York, copy in MEHP Papers. See also U.S., *Census, 1950, Population*, vol. 2:4, 122; James K. Morishima, "The Evacuation: Impact on the Family," in Stanley Sue and Nathaniel N. Wagner, *Asian Americans: Psychological Perspectives*, 13–19 (Palo Alto, Cal., 1973); Ryoichi Fujii, *Shikago Nikkeijinshi*, 113–115 (Tokyo, 1968); Hara interview, December 7, 1977.

[28] Hara interview, November 12, 1979; Otani interview, June 14, 1977.

[29] The St. Paul committee considered continuing its work with service to urban American Indians but finally voted to dissolve late in 1952; St. Paul Resettlement Committee, Minutes, November 28, 1952, in St. Paul Resettlement Committee Papers. See also *JA Journal*, December, 1957, p. 9, July, 1959, p. 10; Kiyoshi T. Shiraishi, ed., *A Pictorial History of the Japanese Christian Mission in America*, 205 (Los Angeles, 1964); information from Takashi Matsuda, July 10, 1980.

[30] *St. Paul Pioneer Press*, May 4, 1975, Family Life sec., 3; *JA Journal*, December, 1957, p. 10; Hara interview, November 12, 1979.

[31] Here and two paragraphs below, see United Citizens League, Minutes, September 20, 1946, in private collection, notes in author's possession; U.S., *Statutes*, 66:163. For an account of JACL efforts to secure naturalization rights, see Bill Hosokawa, *Nisei: The Quiet Americans*, 435–453 (New York, 1969). A chronology of the *JA Journal* appears in the issue of July, 1959, pp. 1, 12.

[32] The *JA Journal* reported on community and church events and provided a calendar of future activities. Here and below, see the newsletters for October, 1956, June, 1957, February and June–July, 1964, April–May, 1965, all on p. 1, and July, 1959, p. 2.

[33] *JA Journal*, September, 1954, February, March, April, August, September, 1961, all on p. 1; March, 1963, p. 8. Sickels, *Around the World*, 73–98, describes the origin of the Festival of Nations.

[34] Here and below, see *JA Journal*, December, 1956, p. 6, September, 1959, p. 3; Hara interview, November 12, 1979; U.S. *Census, 1960, Population*, vol. 1, part 25, pp. 43, 340. Out-migration is reflected throughout the social news in the *JA Journal*; see, for example, issues of April, 1952, p. 5, June, 1953, p. 4, April, 1954, p. 3, February, 1955, p. 4, May, 1956, p. 3.

[35] U.S., *Census, 1950, Population*, 2:44; 1960, vol. 1, part 25, pp. 43, 195, part 24, p. 28; 1970, *Japanese . . . in the United States*, 1, table 1. On war brides, see John W. Connor, *A Study of the Marital Stability of Japanese War Brides*, 1, 65 (San Francisco, 1976); Andrew N. Otani, *Hope Shines in the White Cloud: An Issei's Story*, 170 (Minneapolis, [1974?]); *JA Journal*, July, 1959, p. 3; Nationality Clubs folder, in International Institute of Minnesota Papers.

[36] Here and below, see interview of anonymous Japanese American, notes in author's possession; *JA Journal*, March, 1959, p. 1, and March, p. 5, April, p. 3, May, p. 6, June, pp. 4, 8, August, pp. 1, 5 — all in 1962, March, 1963, p. 7.

[37] *JA Journal*, January, 1964, p. 4, April–May, 1965, p. 1.

[38] Interview of Dr. George T. Nishida, May 11, 1978, notes in author's possession.

[39] Isao Horiuchi, *Education Values and Preadaptation in the Acculturation of Japanese Americans*, 6, 31, 38 (Sacramento, 1967); interviews with Twin Cities Japanese Americans, notes in author's possession.

[40] William Petersen, *Japanese Americans, Oppression and Success*, 5 (New York, 1971); Petersen, "Chinese Americans and Japanese Americans," in Thomas Sowell, ed., *Essays and Data on American Ethnic Groups*, 65 ([Washington, D.C.], 1978); Yuji Ichioka, "Review of Petersen," in *Amerasia Journal*, 2:171–173 (1973); Daniel I. Okimoto, *American in Disguise*, 150–515 (New York, 1971); "Interview with S. I. Hayakawa," in Amy Tachiki *et al.*, eds., *Roots: An Asian American Reader*, 19–23 (Los Angeles, 1971). On the "model minority" see Harry Kitano, *Japanese Americans: The Evolution of a Subculture*, 146 (Englewood Cliffs, N.J., 1969).

[41] U.S., *Census, 1970, Japanese . . . in the United States*, 9, 42, tables 3, 9; *Census, 1970, Educational Attainment*, 2, table 1; Daniels, *Concentration Camps*, 182; U.S. Dept. of Health, Education, and Welfare, *A Study of Selected Socio-Economic Characteristics of Ethnic Minorities Based on the 1970 Census*, vol. 2, *Asian Americans*, 104, 108 (Washington, D.C., 1974).

[42] The evolution of the Japanese-American residential pattern is illustrated by maps drawn for 10-year intervals beginning in 1947 and based on Japanese surnames in Twin Cities telephone directory listings; Michael Albert, "Japanese American Communities in Chicago and the Twin Cities," 196, 198, 202, 204, Ph.D. thesis, University of Minnesota, 1980.

[43] Discussion of the concepts of assimilation and cultural pluralism continues among Japanese-American scholars. See Joe Feagin and Nancy Fujitaki, "On the Assimilation of Japanese Americans," Paul Takagi, "The Myth of Assimilation in American Life," and George Kagiwada, "Confessions of a Misguided Sociologist" — all

in *Amerasia Journal*, February, 1972, pp. 13–30, Fall, 1973, pp. 149–158, 159–164.

⁴⁴ Cathy L. Tanimoto, "Changing Japanese Ethnicity: A Case Study of Gardena, California," 28, master's thesis, Louisiana State University, 1975; U.S., *Census*, 1970, *Population*, vol. 1, part 25, pp. 80, 99. Mayor Hazama apparently excepts the doctors, nurses, and students at the Mayo Clinic who are recent migrants from Japan or other locations within the U.S.; *Pacific Citizen*, June 15, 1979, p. 1 (a weekly newspaper published by the JACL in Los Angeles). The sample is from a group of Japanese Americans selected at random from telephone listings and interviewed by the author between January and May, 1978.

⁴⁵ Here and below, see Hara interviews, November 12, 1979, December 2, 1980.

⁴⁶ Interviews of Otani, June 14, 1977, Matsuda, July 10, 1980, William Y. Hirabayashi, February 8, 1978, and George Ono, April 6, 1978, notes in author's possession.

⁴⁷ Interviews of Reiko Shellum, October 13, 1976, Frank Yanari, March 30, 1978, Tanbara, June 4, 1979, notes in author's possession. The center was founded by Duane and Reiko Shellum.

⁴⁸ Here and below, see *MAAP Newsletter* (Minneapolis), October–November, 1978, p. 1, 3; interview of Matthew Abe, July 31, 1979, notes in author's possession. Abe was president of the JAYS. Participants in MAAP include Chinese, Korean, Filipino, Vietnamese, and other southeast Asians.

⁴⁹ Here and below, see sample data compiled by author and described in note 44, above; Otani to the editor, April 10, 1980, in MEHP Papers. One Nisei whose four children all married non-Japanese said she "didn't expect anything different." Interview of Grace Ohama by Mary Cannon, July 30, 1980.

⁵⁰ Interview with Takeshi and Alice H. Osada, May 26, 1978, notes in author's possession.

⁵¹ Here and below, information is from interviews of Japanese nationals in Minneapolis during 1978; sample data compiled by the author.

CHAPTER 31

The Koreans

Sarah R. Mason

THE FIRST KOREANS to settle in Minnesota in significant numbers arrived during and after the Korean War (1950–53) and included students, wives of American servicemen, and war orphans adopted by American families. The population remained small until the 1965 liberalization of American immigration law which resulted in a dramatic increase in Korean immigration to the United States. Within a decade Koreans became the third largest immigrating group in the United States, while in Minnesota they were the second largest as early as 1969 — surpassed only by the Canadians — and largest by 1971. A peak was reached in 1976 (see Table 31.1), when approximately 933 Koreans entered the state, representing 34% of the total immigration to Minnesota in that year. By 1978, the last year for which figures were available, Koreans in Minnesota numbered more than 5,000 (not including students) out of a national total of approximately 350,000.[1]

Minnesota's Korean community has differed considerably from earlier ones in Hawaii and on the West Coast and has also diverged from the pattern of development of later settlements in such metropolitan centers as New York City, Washington, D.C., and Los Angeles. While Koreans in the West in the 1900s and 1910s were predominantly farm workers, the core community in Minnesota was composed of students and intellectuals at the University of Minnesota and other colleges. Arriving in the period following World War II, they found a relatively open social climate — both in the Twin Cities and outstate areas — and experienced little of the racial hostility encountered by Koreans in the West. With rapid growth in the late 1960s, Minnesota's Korean population became increasingly diversified, and by the mid-1970s blue-collar workers outnumbered professionals. In contrast to the Korean experience on the East and West Coasts, where sizable Koreatowns formed within or adja-

cent to Chinatowns and Japantowns, no separate residential and business community has emerged in Minnesota. While Korean businesses, churches, and cultural organizations have multiplied rapidly during the past decade and have been concentrated largely in the Twin Cities and suburbs, they have never been geographically isolated from the larger society.[2]

The first Korean immigrants arrived in American territory shortly after the Treaty of Amity and Commerce was signed with the United States in 1882. Like the 1868 Burlingame Treaty with China, the 1882 agreement opened Korea to American traders and missionaries and provided for free migration between the two countries. Students, political exiles, and merchants reached America in the 1880s, but it was not until 1903 that the first large-scale immigration occurred. Several circumstances led to the recruiting of Korean emigrants to work in Hawaii. One was a labor shortage on the islands that resulted from United States exclusion of Chinese immigrants in 1882 and from increased strikes and work stoppages by Japanese workers. In 1901 drought, famine, and a cholera epidemic struck Korea's northwestern provinces of Pyongan and Hwanghae. The following year, at the behest of the Hawaiian Sugar Planters' Association, the American minister to Korea, Horace N. Allen, and an American businessman, David W. Deshler, worked together to supply Korean laborers to the island plantations. Allen convinced the king of Korea that emigration to Hawaii was the solution to his nation's social and economic crises. He also persuaded American missionaries in Korea to encourage their parishioners to emigrate in order to better their lives. Between 1903 and 1905, 7,226 Koreans, 85% of them men, were recruited to work on the pineapple and sugar plantations in Hawaii.[3]

Early immigrants to Hawaii included laborers, former soldiers, policemen, and woodcutters from the cities of the northwestern provinces, a few farmers from the rural areas, and a small number of students who hoped to save enough from their plantation wages to continue their studies in the United States (see Map 31.1). A large number were Christians who were often the most educated of the early immigrants. Consequently they took the lead in organizing the immigrant communities in Hawaii around the church, which became the focal point of Korean cultural and religious ac-

Table 31.1. Korean Immigration to Minnesota, 1969–78

1969	157	1974	503
1970	189	1975	664
1971	316	1976	933
1972	502	1977	843
1973	564	1978	729

Source: U.S. Dept. of Justice, Immigration and Naturalization Service, *Annual Reports,* for the years cited. The figures, covering fiscal years ending June 30, represent those expressing an *intention* to settle in Minnesota.

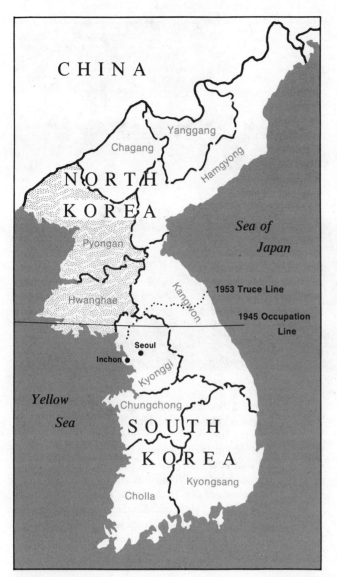

Map 31.1. Korea

tivities and later provided a base for the Korean independence movement in the United States. While traditional organizations such as the clan and sworn brotherhood were also transplanted by Korean immigrants to Hawaii, these did not play the central role of similar organizations in Chinese and Japanese communities in America.[4]

As early as 1904 Korean plantation workers began moving to the mainland in search of better wages. Many were recruited by railroad companies, including the expanding Great Northern, operating between St. Paul and Seattle. Others found work in mines and on farms throughout the western states. By 1907 approximately 2,000 had arrived at San Francisco, the first concentrated Korean settlement on the mainland. After 1910 the Korean population center shifted southward to Los Angeles.[5]

Emigration from Korea was suspended in 1905 under pressure from Japan, which had established a *de facto* protectorate in the country. The only exception to the ban were "picture brides" — women who contracted to marry Koreans in the United States after an exchange of photographs. Alarmed over growing agitation for Korean independence among immigrants in the United States, the Japanese allowed about 1,100 women to leave between 1910 and 1924 in the hope that marriage would dampen the political ardor of the single men.[6]

Between 1910 and 1919, when the independence movement was at its peak, a total of 541 anti-Japanese activists left Korea without passports and were accepted by the United States as "working students." They settled in the Midwest and East as well as on the West Coast, establishing Korean communities in such cities as Chicago, Washington, D.C., New York, and smaller college towns. Korean student associations were organized throughout the nation, providing bases of support for the independence movement. As Korean communities grew to include families and nonstudents, churches became the focal points of political, social, and religious activities, following the pattern established in earlier settlements in Hawaii and on the West Coast. After the Japanese ruthlessly suppressed a student-led demonstration in Seoul in March, 1919, however, political activity among the immigrants in America declined.[7]

With the enactment of restrictive immigration legislation in the United States in 1924 and increased limitations by Japanese authorities on student departures from Korea, the Korean population in the United States remained at a virtual standstill until after World War II. Although 1924 restrictions remained until the McCarran-Walter Immigration Act of 1952 provided a token quota of 100 entries per year, several nonquota groups began to arrive in the early postwar period. An estimated 6,000 students flocked to the United States after 1945 to resume their studies after long years of war and Japanese occupation. Following major involvement of American forces in the Korean War, Korean wives of American servicemen began to arrive in the early 1950s, reaching annual totals of 292 in 1956, 1,255 in 1966, and 2,155 in 1975. By 1978, 40,366 of these women lived in the United States. Another group which began to arrive in the early 1950s was the racially mixed and Korean orphans adopted by American families. Between 1950 and 1962, 4,162 children were admitted to the United States. Their number increased sharply during the 1970s, reaching a total of 29,608 by 1978.[8]

Minnesota's Korean Community: The Early Arrivals

Although few if any Koreans settled in Minnesota before World War II, a small number worked or studied in the state in earlier decades. Perhaps the first was a Korean mineworker employed by the Oliver Mining Company on the Mesabi Iron Range in the early 1900s. Little is known about this early sojourner. A company census in 1907 indicated that he was over 21 years of age, that he spoke English, and that he had been a resident of the United States for at least five years but was not a naturalized citizen.[9]

In the mid-1920s two Korean students were enrolled at Hamline University in St. Paul, but it was not until the early 1950s that a significant number arrived to attend college. Most of the early students enrolled at Macalester College in

AN INTENT AUDIENCE attended the 1958 Korean Independence Day celebration at Como Park in St. Paul.

St. Paul, which by the late 1950s accepted eight or nine Koreans each year.[10]

Korean students at Macalester initiated a small-scale chain immigration system by writing home to relatives, friends, and classmates, urging them to emigrate to Minnesota. For example, Young Pai, one of the earliest Koreans enrolled at the college, was instrumental in bringing in many students. Pai's father, the Reverend Min Soo Pai, had been stranded in the United States during World War II while a graduate student at Princeton University. He frequently visited the Macalester campus at the invitation of the Reverend Edwin Kagan, college chaplain and chairman of the religion department, who had met Pai while serving in Korea as a missionary. After returning to Korea at the end of the war, Pai sent his son to Macalester at the suggestion of Kagan. Young Pai arrived in 1948, and shortly thereafter wrote to two friends, Rok Shin and Philip Ahn, asking them to join him in Minnesota. Shin, a young doctor, arrived in 1950 to take an internship at St. John's Hospital in St. Paul. He brought his brother and sister, Roy and Kay Shin, to Macalester, as well as a friend, Edward Chang. Ahn, who had attended church and sung in the choir with Pai in Korea, arrived at Macalester in 1953. He brought his brother, Sam Ahn, to the college in 1955.[11]

Macalester College in the 1950s was a cosmopolitan campus that became the center of activities for Korean students in the Twin Cities. Encouraged by administrators, teachers, and the student body, the Koreans at Macalester participated in a variety of international events as well as sports and religious and musical activities. They were also invited to speak about their homeland to community groups both in the Twin Cities and outstate.

In 1953 three Koreans were enrolled at the University of

Minnesota, and a few others attended the Colleges of St. Thomas and St. Catherine and Hamline University in St. Paul. Because the supportive atmosphere of Macalester College did not exist on their campus, the university students took the lead that year in organizing the Korean Association of Minnesota to promote friendship and mutual assistance among the state's Koreans. In the 1950s the association met at Macalester College, with occasional visits to a Chinese restaurant near the university's Minneapolis campus, where members could enjoy food similar to that of their homeland.[12]

Virtually all of the Korean students in Minnesota in the 1940s and 1950s had planned to return to Korea upon completing their studies (largely in the sciences). A majority of them, however, remained in the United States — many of them settling in Minnesota — primarily because of the extremely unstable political and economic conditions at home during and after the Korean War. In Minnesota the expansion of opportunities in scientific fields during the 1950s and 1960s encouraged them to remain as professionals. As they established families it became increasingly difficult to return to Korea.

Between 1954 and 1962 Minnesota's small Korean community grew dramatically with the arrival in the Twin Cities of 229 Korean faculty members from Seoul National University. The newcomers were participants in a co-operative project arranged between their school and the University of Minnesota by former Governor Harold E. Stassen, then employed by the State Department. Seoul National University's campus had suffered large-scale destruction at the hands of both North Korean and American military forces during the Korean War. Under a contract with the State Department, the University of Minnesota provided technical assistance to the Seoul institution in reconstructing buildings and restoring its academic programs. Korean faculty members were sent to the university for periods of three months to two years of intensive study — initially in engineering, medicine, and agriculture, with nursing, veterinary science, public health, and public administration added later.[13]

The project and its participants brought considerable publicity to the University of Minnesota in Korea. It was undoubtedly a major factor in the increase in Korean enrollment at the university during the 1960s when 30 to 40 Korean graduate students attended each year and the focus of Korean student life shifted from Macalester to the university campus. Many of these decided to remain in Minnesota where professional opportunities were available. Along with some young professionals from other states, they formed the nucleus of Minnesota's growing Korean community, which by then included a few families as well.[14]

During the same period Korean wives of American servicemen also began to arrive in Minnesota. Because of class and educational differences, as well as their scattered locations, these women had difficulty participating in the activities of the Korean community. In numerous instances they were abused or abandoned by their husbands. Without formal organizations of their own, they banded together in small friendship groups for emotional support and protection against family violence. Two attorneys in the Twin Cities — one of them married to a Korean — provided legal assistance to some of the women, but many others had no such recourse. By 1980 estimates of the number of Korean wives in the state varied from several hundred to 1,000, but no official information was available.[15]

A KOREAN ORPHAN en route to Minnesota in 1959.

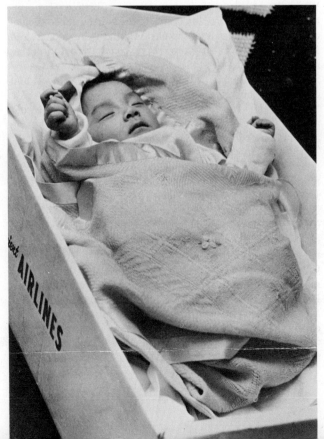

In the unfamiliar Minnesota environment, these women found a source of security in helping relatives from Korea enter the United States. As wives of American citizens they were entitled to citizenship in three years as opposed to five for most immigrants. This status gave them some advantage in arranging the immigration of parents and siblings with their nuclear families, for only immediate family members of alien residents are allowed to enter the country.[16]

Another group which began to arrive in the 1950s was the adopted children. While at first they were largely racially mixed offspring of American troops in Korea, in later years most were full Koreans. Early adoptions in Minnesota were arranged by the Minnesota Department of Public Welfare, but in the 1970s they were handled by private agencies including Lutheran Social Service, Catholic Charities, and the Children's Home Society. Adoptions in the 1950s were limited but rose steadily to a peak of 607 in 1975. The number then declined, partly as a result of the Korean government's attempt to limit and gradually end American adoptions. In 1979 only 279 children were adopted in Minnesota. It was estimated that in 1980, 4,000 adopted Koreans resided in the state, or 10% of the total in the United States.[17]

The children formed a group on the periphery of the Korean community, although they have comprised a large proportion of students attending classes at the Korean Institute in Minneapolis. Adoptive parents formed the Organization for a United Response (OURS) in 1968 and also participated actively in the institute's functions.[18]

Cultural and Religious Organizations

The Korean Association of Minnesota, organized by University of Minnesota students in 1953, originally served as a focal point of social and cultural activities for Korean students throughout the Twin Cities metropolitan area. Participation of the faculty members from Seoul National University, however, introduced a certain tension into the association due to the traditional formality in faculty-student relations — a reflection of the high value placed on respect for teachers in Korean culture. As a result of this situation, the students in 1955 formed the Korean Student Association, in which they organized their own activities while still taking part in those of the Korean Association.[19]

In 1959 Korean students in the Twin Cities also organized a Bible study group, the forerunner of the Korean Christian Fellowship, which became the center of Korean community activities during the late 1960s and early 1970s. The group started with about 10 to 25 Christian and non-Christian students who met each Sunday afternoon at the United Christian Campus Fellowship on the St. Paul campus of the University of Minnesota. Members took turns leading the discussion and worship, but the attendance of non-Christians indicated that, beyond its strictly religious function, the group served the broader need for an organized effort to establish a sense of fellowship and intimacy in the alien environment. Although most of the students during this period were men, a few women students as well as wives of graduate students and young professionals also participated in the meetings.[20]

During the 1960s, a period of moderate growth in the Korean community, Joo Ho Sung, a young professor in the medical school at the University of Minnesota, emerged as an adviser to Korean students and a leader in the immigrant community as well. Sung and his wife, Inchoong Kim, also a physician, arrived in Minnesota with their first child in 1962. They soon became involved with the Korean Student Association and also joined the Bible study group, although they were not Christians. Students often visited their home on holidays, when dormitories at the university were closed, to enjoy Korean foods prepared for special occasions such as Christmas or New Year's. Close friends among the students dropped in casually throughout the year and often stayed for a Korean meal.[21]

Sung also took a leading part in community activities in the 1960s, during which a co-operative mood prevailed. He served as president of the Korean Association from 1964 to 1966, after the Seoul faculty had returned to Korea. The number of settlers was still relatively small, but the students had grown to about 130, and most community activities were organized by the students in the Korean Association's subgroup, the Korean Student Association.[22]

After 1969, however, the settlement experienced rapid population growth resulting in a period of conflict. Sung again headed the Korean Association in 1970–71, when differences between students and settlers were becoming more evident. In 1970, amidst growing community concern over the friction between the two groups, Sung made an important speech in which he attempted to unite the two factions by emphasizing that the time had come for the Korean community to view itself in the context of the larger Minnesota society, rather than as a colony of sojourners. Although some Koreans would be leaving the community, he pointed out, it was more constructive to look upon themselves as a part of Minnesota society during their years of residence rather than to think only of departure. After the speech a Korean journalism student, Jung Woo Suh, wrote an editorial in the Korean Association newsletter supporting Sung's position. A brief period of unity followed in the summer of 1970 when all the factions joined to take part in the Minneapolis Aquatennial, an annual summer festival, the theme of which was "Seas of the Orient." Koreans participated with floats, craft exhibits, dance performances, foods, and a karate demonstration. The large-scale co-operation required for this effort drew the community together and also represented the first time it had participated in a social event organized by the larger Minnesota society.

A few years earlier the student Bible study group, after prolonged discussion, decided to become a community church rather than a student-oriented association. In 1966 the Reverend Daniel Kim, the first Korean pastor in Minnesota, had accepted a teaching position at Central Baptist Theological Seminary in Minneapolis. He brought with him five Korean seminary graduates who planned to further their studies at the seminary, and they became involved in the Bible study group. As the membership grew the seminarians urged the organization to become a church, but there was considerable opposition because in other Korean immigrant communities it had led to congregational splits over the pastor's salary, denominational affiliation, and various theolog-

ical and social issues. A committee established in 1967 studied the problem, and after much debate the group decided to form a church. Three goals were established by the members: first, the church should be based on the teachings of the Bible; second, there should be only one church in the community unless the membership became too large for one meeting place; and third, the church should be interdenominational to preserve the unity of the group.[23]

At this point a dispute arose over the inclusion of non-Christians. The Reverend Kim, a theological conservative, contended that if they were included the reorganized group could not be called a church. He suggested instead calling it the Korean Christian Fellowship, as a transition between the Bible study group and a church. His suggestion was accepted and the first session, held in July, 1968, was attended by 90 of the 120 Koreans invited, virtually all of the Twin Cities core community. From 1968 to 1972 the Korean Christian Fellowship was a major center of Korean cultural and religious activity, as well as the focal point of the group's ethnic identity. In addition to Sunday worship services, held first at the United Campus Christian Fellowship on the St. Paul campus of the University of Minnesota and later in the Weyerhaeuser Chapel on the Macalester campus, the fellowship also sponsored the first language school for the settlers' children. Organized by Joo Ho Sung and two graduate students, the classes held each Sunday morning after Sunday school also taught both Christian and traditional Korean values.[24]

A few years later the Reverend Kim again raised the question of a formal church despite opposition from many members. Early settlers continued to express their concern for the unity of the Korean community, pointing out that a formal church could not include Catholics as well as Protestants, believers and nonbelievers, as did the fellowship. While the problem of denominational affiliation also continued to be a source of conflict, one of the most crucial questions was the role of the pastor in the Korean church in Minnesota. Pastors in Korea were generally authoritarian and patriarchal, but settlers who had lived in the United States for a number of years preferred a more liberal and democratic church in which the minister might be seen as a "messenger," rather than an authoritarian figure. Recent arrivals, on the other hand, expected and supported a strong leader such as those they had known in Korea.

In 1972, after more than a year of discussion, the Reverend Kim and one faction of the membership left the Korean Christian Fellowship and formed the nondenominational Korean Church of the Twin Cities. That same year the Catholics, under the leadership of the Reverend Francis Choe, a Korean priest who had been studying at the College of St. Thomas and the University of Minnesota, left the fellowship and formed the Catholic Church for the Korean Community. The Korean Christian Fellowship then became inactive for several months but was finally reorganized by Hyun Sang Cha, a seminarian and social worker trained at Scarritt College in Tennessee, and Yun Ho Lee, one of the early organizers of the fellowship and a graduate of Jamestown College, in North Dakota. Members of the reorganized fellowship then called the Reverend Suh Young Baik, a Korean Methodist in Colorado, to serve as full-time pastor, and he arrived in the Twin Cities in 1973.[25]

In 1976, three years after the organization of the Korean Church in the Twin Cities, a group of families broke away to form the Korean United Methodist Church. In 1978 Kim's congregation was again split to form the Korean Presbyterian Church and the Korean Baptist Church. The Korean Church of the Twin Cities was then disbanded.[26]

Meanwhile Pastor Baik also urged the Korean Christian Fellowship to become a church, and in 1975 it was renamed the Korean Community Church. In 1979, however, the Reverend Baik and some of the more recently arrived members formed a new congregation, the Korean Evangelical United Methodist Church. The earlier settlers, including largely university professors and doctors, remained in the Community Church, calling a new pastor from Germany, the Reverend Yung Jae Kim. In late 1979 still another Korean Church was formed when a group of families who had been affiliated with the Seventh-Day Adventist Church in Korea banded together. This brought the number of churches to a total of seven in the relatively small Minnesota Korean community.[27]

Broadly speaking, the many church schisms in the Korean community during the 1970s may be seen as a reflection of the rapid population growth and change during that decade and of the increasing cultural differences between early settlers and recent arrivals. While most in the community valued the church as an instrument to preserve Korean culture, pastors and conservative members, often newcomers, feared the religious purpose of the church was losing ground to the social activities so important to the immigrant community. Despite these conflicts, however, Korean churches in the 1970s played a vital role in the community, one which has continued into the 1980s. For many immigrants the congregations took the place of the extended family in Korea as the center of social activities and mutual assistance. Korean pastors were untiring in their efforts to help new arrivals find housing, employment, and even emergency food supplies when necessary. For women the congregations provided close association with other Korean women, a supportive group in times of childbirth, illness, and death, when they particularly missed their own families in Korea. For all the settlers the churches were focal points of cultural identity and centers for the training of children in both Christian and Korean values.[28]

Secular organizations in the Korean community also grew during the 1970s, and while they did not provide the close fellowship of a church, they helped promote the welfare of the group and served as a liaison between the Korean community and the larger society. The Korean Association of Minnesota began to take on new responsibilities during this period. Under the leadership of Yung Lyun Ko, it established the Korean Institute in 1974 to take over the language training and cultural education of the children in the community after church splits had caused a serious division of resources. The association also organized Korean performing arts for the annual Festival of Nations in St. Paul and the Aquatennial in Minneapolis. Through its initiative Korea

Day — which included sports events, Korean foods, and entertainment — was proclaimed by Governor Rudolph G. Perpich in 1975 for the first Saturday of October. This annual occasion continued into the 1980s, bringing together all the Korean groups in preparations for the affair.[29]

New Korean organizations formed in the 1970s included the Minnesota Korean Medical Club and a number of generational clubs for young, middle-aged, and elderly members of the community. While the latter group had an active role in the extended family in Korea, in the immigrant community they were totally dependent upon their children, most of whom, including the women, were working full time. Some of the elderly cared for their grandchildren during the day, but others had little to occupy their time, and the senior citizens' club helped alleviate their isolation.[30]

The Korean Community in 1981

The Korean population in 1981 included servicemen's wives, adopted children, students, professionals, and blue-collar workers. The latter consisted of two subgroups. In the first were those who had completed college or professional training in Korea but had not attained certification in Minnesota and therefore worked in factories, at least temporarily. In some fields such as education, this might be permanent because their skills and training were not transferable to American society. In the second group were blue-collar workers from Korea who found comparable employment in Minnesota. Most of these were relatives of servicemen's wives.[31]

With the exception of the adopted children and servicemen's wives, the majority of the Korean population lived in the St. Paul-Minneapolis metropolitan area. An undetermined number of Korean professionals — largely doctors and college professors — have also settled in small towns in outstate areas. For example, two families and a single Korean lived in Morris, where they were associated with the University of Minnesota campus. (A third Korean family associated with that university had moved to the Twin Cities — even though the family head had to commute each week to Morris.) Those who remained were well integrated into the social life of the university and the town. Their children were quite Americanized and for the most part well accepted by their peers. Although they experienced some name-calling in elementary school, they also enjoyed the reputation of being excellent students.[32]

Korean-language newspapers were not published in Minnesota in 1980, but approximately 50% of the Korean population subscribed to two newspapers from Chicago, *Han Kook Il Bo* (Korea Times) and *Chung Ang Il Bo* (Central News). These carried Korean and American news and sometimes covered Minnesota affairs as well. Local and community news was also circulated through the *Minnesota Korean Newsletter*, published by the Korean Association of Minnesota.[33]

Korean businesses in 1981 were growing rapidly — particularly in the Twin Cities — and included restaurants, grocery stores, gift shops, and *tae kwon do* (Korean karate) centers. While some were operated by immigrants with business experience in Korea, others were owned by doctors, teachers, and other professionals who had not attained certification, as an alternative to factory work. One of the earliest Korean businesses in Minnesota, the First Oriental Food Store on Como Avenue in Southeast Minneapolis, expanded in 1981, moving to a new building on East Hennepin Avenue and consolidating its tofu plant and retail store. Begun in 1971 by a group of former university students, by 1981 the business had established a Chicago branch including a wholesale business and tofu factory. The Minneapolis store attracted not only Koreans but Chinese, Japanese, and Indochinese customers as well. In addition to groceries, it carried Korean monthly magazines and novels, chinaware, and cooking utensils such as woks and electric rice makers. It also provided customers with information on subscriptions to Korean newspapers and charter flights to Korea at reduced rates.[34]

The Minnesota community in 1981 differed from larger urban Korean settlements on the East and West Coasts in a number of ways. In the latter many in Koreatowns were isolated from the dominant society, rarely interacting with it in their day-to-day routines. Conflicts within the communities had increased rapidly as competition for housing and employment became exacerbated in the ghettolike settings. Racial discrimination — especially that directed against Asians — continued to be a far more serious problem on the West Coast than in the Upper Midwest.[35]

The Minnesota community, on the other hand, despite its own inner tensions, had a reputation among Koreans in the United States as a co-operative settlement that worked hard to retain its cultural identity. Some believed the University of Minnesota was an important factor in the community's development. Students and professionals at the university during the 1960s encountered no discrimination on campus — and relatively little in the larger society — and established a close-knit group with unusually capable leadership which set the tone for later years. Although professionals were outnumbered by blue-collar workers in the early 1970s, much of the leadership remained in the hands of the first group, and the goals and ideals of the early period remained largely intact.[36]

Reference notes

Much of the information in this chapter is from the author's interviews with members of the Korean community. Interviews that were recorded on tape are so identified and have been placed in the Audio-Visual Library, MHS. The author's notes for both the taped and untaped interviews are in the MEHP Papers, MHS.

A note on name order should be added. While Korean usage calls for giving the family name first, most Koreans in Minnesota have adopted the American form, which is used in the present chapter.

[1] Taped interviews of Philip Ahn, December 7, 1979, April 14, 1980; interviews of Evelyn Iverson, Lutheran Social Service, January 25, 1980, and Young-shil Song, March 29, 1981; Eui-young Yu, "Koreans in America: An Emerging Ethnic Minority," in *Amerasia Journal*, 4:117, 123 (1977); United States Asian Statistics, in MEHP Papers, compiled by Jon A. Gjerde from U.S. Dept. of Labor, Bureau of Immigration, *Annual Reports*, 1909–39, and U.S. Justice Dept., Immigration and Naturalization Service, *Annual Reports*, 1940–78. Figures from the latter include adopted children and serv-

icemen's wives but not students. In computing the national Korean population total for 1978, the author added 1977 and 1978 immigration figures to Yu's estimate of 290,000 for 1976.

[2] Linda Shin, "Koreans in America, 1903–1945," in Amy Tachiki *et al.*, eds., *Roots: An Asian American Reader*, 200–203 (Los Angeles, 1970); taped interview of Joo Ho Sung, February 7, 1980. The author wishes to acknowledge the helpful suggestions received from Joo Ho Sung throughout the preparation of this chapter.

Wives of servicemen and adopted children were not generally part of the core community and are discussed separately.

[3] Lee Houchins and Chang-su Houchins, "The Korean Experience in America, 1903–1924," in Norris Hundley, Jr., ed., *The Asian American: The Historical Experience*, 130–136 (Santa Barbara, 1976); Hyung-chan Kim and Wayne Patterson, comps. and eds., *The Koreans in America, 1882–1974*, 1 (Dobbs Ferry, N.Y., 1974); Shin, in Tachiki *et al.*, eds., *Roots*, 200; Fred H. Harrington, *God, Mammon, and the Japanese: Dr. Horace N. Allen and Korean-American Relations, 1884–1905*, 186 (Madison, Wis., 1944); Hyung-chan Kim, "The History and Role of the Church in the Korean American Community," in Hyung-chan Kim, ed., *The Korean Diaspora*, 48 (Santa Barbara, 1977). Deshler's business connections in Korea included a partnership in the American Trading Co. and interests in a steamship company later used to transport Korean laborers to Hawaii.

[4] Houchins and Houchins, in Hundley, ed., *Asian American*, 129; Warren Y. Kim, *Koreans in America*, 28–31 (Seoul, 1971); Kingsley K. Lyu, "Korean Nationalist Activities in Hawaii and the Continental United States, 1900–1919," in *Amerasia Journal*, 4:31–33 (1977); Shin, in Tachiki *et al.*, eds., *Roots*, 201; H. Kim, in Kim, ed., *Korean Diaspora*, 47.

[5] Shin, in Tachiki *et al.*, eds., *Roots*, 201; Houchins and Houchins, in Hundley, ed., *Asian American*, 136.

[6] Houchins and Houchins, in Hundley, ed., *Asian American*, 134, 140; W. Kim, *Koreans in America*, 22; E. Yu, in *Amerasia Journal*, 4:119.

[7] W. Kim, *Koreans in America*, 23–26, 91–98; Houchins and Houchins, in Hundley, ed., *Asian American*, 139, 156; Shin, in Tachiki, *et al.*, eds., *Roots*, 203; H. Brett Melendy, *Asians in America: Filipinos, Koreans, and East Indians*, 129 (Boston, 1977). On the Korean independence movement in the U.S., 1905–30, see Bong-young Choy, *Koreans in America*, 141–166 (Chicago, 1979).

[8] W. Kim, *Koreans in America*, 36, 53; Melendy, *Asians in America*, 130, 137; Bok-lim C. Kim, "Asian Wives of U.S. Servicemen: Women in Shadows," in *Amerasia Journal*, 4:98; interviews of Hyung-suk Han, January 23, 1980, and Ruth C. Weidell, Minnesota Dept. of Public Welfare, June 25, 1980; information on servicemen's wives and adopted children from Immigration and Naturalization Service, Washington, D.C., August 26, 27, 28, 1980, notes in MEHP Papers.

[9] George O. Virtue, *The Minnesota Iron Ranges*, 345, 349 (U.S. Bureau of Labor, *Bulletin*, no. 84 — Washington, D.C., 1909). Asians were not eligible for naturalization until World War II or after.

[10] Hyong Kyu (Fritz) Pyen graduated from Hamline in 1928 and later became a Methodist bishop in Korea. Chang Suk Yun, a nationalist leader, enrolled at Hamline in 1925 but returned to Korea before completing his studies because of hardships suffered by his family under Japanese rule. See *The Liner of Hamline University*, 1924, p. 115, 1925, pp. 136, 141, 148; *The Hamline Oracle*, October 6, 1925, p. 1; *St. Paul Pioneer Press*, February 1, 1925, p. 8; interview of Rev. Suh Young Baik, August 10, 1980. On the early Macalester students (including at least two women), see *The Mac Weekly*, April 5, 1957, p. 8; interview of P. Ahn, June 16, 1980.

[11] Rok Shin practiced medicine at Howard Lake, Minnesota, after

completing his studies, and Philip Ahn joined the staff of the University of Minnesota. Here and below, see interviews of P. Ahn, December 7, 1979 (taped), February 29, April 14, June 11, 1980.

[12] Here and below, see interviews of P. Ahn, February 29, June 11, 1980; Yun Ho Lee, December 14, 1979, April 18, September 29, 1980. Lee was an important leader first in the student community and later in the immigrant settlement. He was president of the Korean Association during three periods: 1954–64, 1967–68, 1971–72. In 1980 he owned and operated Lee's Apron Manufacturing Co.

[13] *St. Paul Pioneer Press,* June 27, 1962, p. 11; *Minnesota Daily* (Minneapolis), October 21, 1955, p. 8, July 31, 1956, p. 1; unsigned article, in *International Programs Newsletter* (University of Minnesota), December, 1969, p. 3; interviews of Y. Lee, April 18, 1980, Neal L. Gault, Jr., Dean of University of Minnesota Medical School, October 11, 1978.

[14] Interviews of Gault, October 11, 1978; J. Sung, April 22, 1980; P. Ahn, February 29, 1980.

[15] Interviews of Rev. Francis Choe, November 16, 1979; Y. Song (former serviceman's wife), June 10, 1980. Attorneys were Theodore G. Elmquist and Joseph Kominsky.

[16] Interviews of Y. Song, June 10, 1980; Hyun Sook Han, January 3, 1978 (taped); S. Baik, May 20, 1980.

[17] Interviews of Hyun Sook Han, June 24, October 10, 1980; Iverson, January 23, 1980; Weidell, June 25, 1980.

[18] Interview of Chan Soon Olson, September 29, 1978.

[19] Interviews of Y. Lee, April 18, 1980; P. Ahn, April 14, 1980; J. Sung, June 11, 1980.

[20] Interviews of J. Sung, February 7, March 10, 13, 1980 (taped); Inchoong Kim Sung, April 23, 1980; Y. Lee, April 18, 1980. The Bible study group was initiated by Sam B. Kim, a graduate student at the university, but leadership was assumed about a year later by Yoon Berm Kim, a graduate student who later became a professor at the University of Minnesota Medical School.

[21] Interviews of J. Sung, February 7, 1980; I. Sung, June 5, 1980.

[22] Here and below, see interviews of J. Sung, April 22, 1980; I. Sung, April 23, 1980.

[23] Interviews of J. Sung, March 13, 1980; John Kim, son of Rev. Daniel Kim, November 14, 1979.

[24] Here and below, see interviews of J. Sung, February 7, March 13, 1980. Language school organizers and teachers included Un Chul Shin, C. H. Chung, Jung Ja Suh, Chung Soo Han, Inchoong Kim Sung, and others. Most are still Minnesota residents.

[25] Interviews of J. Sung, March 13, 1980; Y. Lee, December 14, 1979; S. Baik, pastor of Korean Christian Fellowship, 1973–75, and Korean Community Church, 1975–79, October 3, 1979.

[26] Interviews of Henry Han, November 3, 9, 1979.

[27] Interviews of Henry Han, November 3, 1979; S. Baik, October 3, 1979, January 21, 1980; J. Sung, March 13, 1980.

[28] Interviews of J. Sung, February 7, 1980; S. Baik, October 3, 1979; Sung Boon Baik, November 9, 1979.

[29] Interviews of Yung Lyun Ko, president of the Korean Association, 1979–81, and Shuk Ko, December 17, 1979.

[30] Interviews of Han Kyung Imm, November 8, 1979; I. Sung, April 23, 25, 1980; J. Sung, February 7, 1980. The Minnesota Korean Medical Club was organized in 1971 by J. Sung and Yoon Berm Kim. In 1980 it had 35 members.

[31] Interview of S. Baik, November 20, 1980.

[32] Interviews of Pat and Sun M. Kahng, December 1, 1979; Chang Hee Chae, Wha Soon Chae, and Ching Ming Yeh, all December 2, 1979. S. Kahng, C. Chae, and C. Yeh were faculty members at the University of Minnesota, Morris.

[33] Interview of Y. Ko, December 17, 1979.

[34] Interviews of Y. Ko, December 17, 1979; Ki Yong Kim, owner of Kim's Oriental Grocery Store, St. Paul, February 27, 1979; Moon Kim, operator of Minnesota Tai Kwon Do Center, St. Paul, November 29, 1979; Chang Kee Sun, employee of First Oriental Food Store, Minneapolis, April 2, 1981.

[35] Interview of Sung Won Son, chief economist for Northwestern National Bank of Minneapolis, December 19, 1979.

[36] Interview of J. Sung, February 7, 1980.

CHAPTER 32

The Indochinese

VIETNAMESE, ETHNIC CHINESE, HMONG, LAO, CAMBODIANS

Sarah R. Mason

FROM 1975 TO 1981 Indochinese refugees constituted the most rapidly immigrating group in Minnesota. Of the 1,500,000 or more who fled their homes in Vietnam, Laos, and Cambodia during those years, approximately 445,000 settled in the United States and 21,500 in Minnesota. The state's Indochinese population in 1981 included Vietnamese, Lao, Cambodians, ethnic Chinese, Hmong, and a scattering of Yao, Tai Dam, Tinh, Guy, and other tribal groups from northern Laos. The first three represented the majority of peoples of the Laotian, Cambodian, and Vietnamese lowlands, where the ethnic Chinese were a predominantly urban minority. The latter groups were highlanders from northern Laos and Vietnam (see Map 32.1).[1]

In the late spring and summer of 1975 when an estimated 135,000 Indochinese — largely Vietnamese — arrived in the United States, approximately 4,500 settled in Minnesota. In the two years that followed, many of them moved to larger refugee settlements in California, Texas, and Washington, D.C., either to join friends and relatives or to seek a warmer climate and better employment opportunities. By October, 1977, Minnesota's Indochinese population had dropped to about 3,400. Beginning in 1976, however, Hmong, Lao, and Cambodians reached the state in increasing numbers, including numerous secondary migrants from other parts of the United States. Despite Minnesota's harsh climate, St. Paul became a clustering area for Hmong refugees, who increased in number from 350 to 1,000 in the last six months of 1978. At about the same time an influx of "boat people" — Vietnamese and ethnic Chinese who fled Vietnam in small fishing boats — further swelled the refugee community, which by December, 1979, totaled nearly 8,000. In 1980 the refugee population more than doubled, largely due to the rapid growth of the Hmong settlement. By November 30, Minnesota had 18,000 Indochinese, the sixth largest such population in the United States. In early 1981 refugees continued to arrive in the state, and the total reached nearly 21,500 in late February (see Table 32.1).[2]

The primary cause for the flight of the first group of Indochinese — most of whom were associated with American

military or civilian agencies in their homelands — was fear of reprisal by the Communist regimes which came to power in 1975. The Hmong were particularly targeted for their role in the Clandestine Army formed by the United States Central Intelligence Agency (CIA). The many Lao, Vietnamese, and Cambodians who were employed by American embassies or military bases were also endangered, as were those who worked for the various American-supported governments in Indochina.[3]

When the collapse of these governments became imminent in the spring of 1975, Indochinese working for the United States were assured of evacuation with American personnel, and a large number were flown to Guam or to the Philippines, while others were picked up from barges by the United States 7th Fleet. Because Communist forces took control sooner than expected, however, the official evacuation by air and sea became chaotic, and many were left behind to fend for themselves.[4]

Indochinese who departed on foot or in small boats in the ensuing months and years also feared the repression of the new regimes. In addition they suffered from the acutely depressed economic conditions which followed American withdrawal. At the start of the Indochina War most of the population was engaged in agriculture. Thirty years of intensive bombing and the use of defoliants during the period of most active American involvement from 1965 to 1975 had forced much of the rural population into the already crowded cities, causing severe food shortages and large-scale unemployment. Only massive aid from the United States and em-

Table 32.1. Estimated Minnesota Indochinese, 1981

Group	Population
Vietnamese (including ethnic Chinese)	7,500
Hmong	9,200
Lao	2,800
Cambodians	2,000
Total	21,500

Source: Minnesota Dept. of Public Welfare, Refugee Program Office, March 31, 1981.

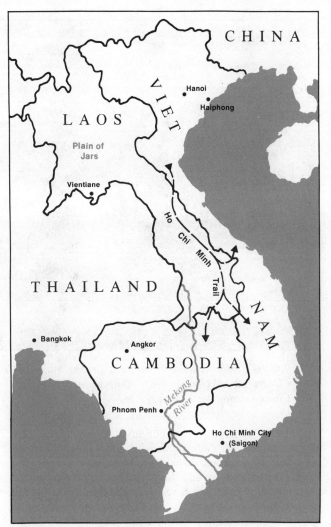

Map 32.1. Indochina

ployment of thousands in American military and civilian bureaucracies had prevented the economic collapse of the South Vietnamese, Laotian, and Cambodian regimes. With the abrupt departure of the Americans in 1975, the bubble burst and thousands left their homelands for economic as well as political reasons.

American involvement in Indochina began during World War II, when intelligence agents of the United States Office of Strategic Services (OSS), predecessor of the CIA, worked closely in North Vietnam with the Viet Minh, a coalition of Vietnamese anti-Japanese resistance groups led by Ho Chi Minh. After the Japanese defeat in 1945, Ho proclaimed Vietnamese independence from the French colonial rule that had been established in the late 19th century. When fierce fighting broke out between the French and Vietnamese in 1946, the United States was preoccupied with the Cold War in Europe and paid little attention. Not until the Communist victory in China in 1949 and the North Korean Communist invasion of South Korea in 1950 did President Harry S Truman turn his attention to building an anti-Communist bastion in Southeast Asia. In 1950 the United States began to send

military and economic aid to French forces fighting the Viet Minh, who were by then predominantly Communist.[5]

With the French defeat and withdrawal from Indochina in 1954, American military advisers began to enter Vietnam. In Laos the CIA trained Hmong and other highland tribesmen to attack North Vietnamese guerrilla forces along the Ho Chi Minh Trail, rescue downed American pilots, man weather stations, and carry out military missions against Pathet Lao Communist forces, which were made up largely of Lao along with some Hmong. In Cambodia the United States supported South Vietnamese army conducted incursions during the 1950s and 1960s, and in 1970 launched an American-South Vietnamese invasion, which included dropping nearly 400,000 tons of bombs on rural areas of Cambodia.

The 1970 invasion of Cambodia marked a turning point in the mounting opposition of the American public to the Indochina War. Hundreds of thousands took to the streets in protest, students organized their first national strike, and the United States Senate voted to repeal the Gulf of Tonkin resolution under which President Richard M. Nixon had taken action in Cambodia. In October, 1970, a public-opinion poll found that 61% of the American people favored withdrawal from Indochina, while a similar poll seven years earlier had reported that 66% favored sending in troops. While peace talks in Paris floundered after the 1970 invasion, President Nixon ordered the 1972 "Christmas Bombing" of Hanoi and the mining of Haiphong harbor, provoking further angry protests. A peace agreement, signed in Paris in 1973, established a schedule for American withdrawal. Communist forces continued to fight, however, until the United States-backed South Vietnamese, Laotian, and Cambodian governments collapsed in the spring of 1975.[6]

Shortly before withdrawal the United States government took steps to facilitate the evacuation and resettlement of Indochinese associated with the Americans. Receiving stations were established in the Philippines and Guam, from which refugees would be flown to four centers in the United States: Camp Pendleton, California; Eglin Air Force Base, Florida; Fort Indiantown Gap, Pennsylvania, and Fort Chaffee, Arkansas. On April 18, 1975, President Gerald R. Ford established the Interagency Task Force (IATF), comprised of representatives from 12 federal agencies, to co-ordinate planning for the refugee resettlement program. On May 24, 1975, Congress enacted the Indochinese Migration and Refugee Assistance Act, which provided funding for resettlement and placed primary responsibility in the Departments of State and Health, Education, and Welfare.[7]

The refugee centers were in operation from April to December, 1975. During that time 10 voluntary agencies under contract to IATF were given the task of finding sponsors for the 135,000 refugees in the first group to be resettled. The federal government provided each agency a cash grant, which varied over time from $300 to $500 per refugee, to help pay for interim transportation, lodging, food, clothing, and medical care, costs which usually far exceeded this amount. More than half the sponsors were American families, despite the significant expense involved in providing for the refugees until they became independent. Later arrivals, who had less education and familiarity with Western culture, required help for longer periods. Because sponsors increasingly found that they could not absorb such long-term costs, a shift of responsibility from sponsor to federal government was necessary. The Comprehensive Refugee Act passed by Congress in 1979 provided 100% federal reimbursement to states for up to four years of assistance.

Refugees who departed after the 1975 evacuation were fed and processed in camps in East and Southeast Asia under the supervision of the United Nations High Commissioner for Refugees while awaiting resettlement. This group suffered enormous casualties in escaping their homelands. In 1978 and 1979, when as many as 65,000 were leaving Vietnam each month, neighboring Malaysia, Indonesia, and Thailand refused to give them asylum and in some cases towed their boats back out to sea. In this emergency the United States agreed to double its monthly admissions from 7,000 to 14,000, and six other countries also increased their quotas.[8]

As refugees began to arrive in Minnesota in 1975, Governor Wendell R. Anderson established an Indochinese Task Force. Two years later responsibility for them was moved from the governor's office to the Minnesota Department of Public Welfare, which acted as co-ordinator for state and private service agencies. The department contracted with such voluntary organizations as Lutheran Social Service, Catholic Charities, Church World Service, and the International Institute of Minnesota to conduct English classes, provide information, and counsel refugees. It also co-ordinated educational programs offered under the auspices of the Minnesota Departments of Economic Security and Education in 34 vocational schools. In July, 1979, the state agencies and voluntary organizations formed the Minnesota Consortium to facilitate a more effective use of available resources. In September six Area Co-ordinating Centers were established to provide easier accessibility to services for refugees living outside the Twin Cities. Each center was assigned to one of the voluntary organizations operating in Austin, Rochester, Willmar, Moorhead, St. Cloud, and Duluth.[9]

THE VIETNAMESE

An estimated 4,500 Vietnamese refugees arrived in Minnesota in the summer and fall of 1975. Many left for California or Texas in the next two years, and by late 1977 fewer than 3,500 remained. With the influx of the boat people in late 1978 and 1979, however, the population began to expand. While it increased steadily thereafter, it was not until late 1980 that a substantial gain occurred. By the end of February, 1981, the Vietnamese population had reached an estimated 7,500 (including ethnic Chinese).[10]

Prior to the arrival of the refugees a small community of Vietnamese — largely students and wives of American servicemen — had developed in Minnesota. The first Vietnamese enrolled at the University of Minnesota in the 1950s. During the 1960s they were joined by South Vietnamese military and government personnel who attended Minnesota universities and colleges under State Department grants. In the early 1970s about 15 Vietnamese were enrolled at the University of Minnesota's Minneapolis, St. Paul, and Morris campuses, while others attended Mankato State University,

KIM LONG'S Vietnamese restaurant prospered on St. Paul's University Avenue in 1981, along with several other Twin Cities Vietnamese eateries.

Macalester College, and other institutions in the state. Approximately 60 Vietnamese wives of American servicemen had also settled throughout Minnesota by the early 1970s. Both the wives and the students who became permanent residents encouraged relatives and friends in Vietnam to join them in Minnesota, resulting in the community's growth through the process of chain migration. By 1975 it had between 200 and 300 members.[11]

In June, 1959, four University of Minnesota students led by Johannes Huyen formed the Vietnamese American Association in Minnesota. Its purpose was to bring together the area's Vietnamese for social and cultural activities such as summer picnics and the celebration of Tet, the lunar New Year. The organization had 90 members in 1973. Two years later its events were attended by 200 or more people, including families from Wisconsin and North Dakota. But in 1975 class differences between students and servicemen's wives resulted in a split, with the students withdrawing to form the Vietnamese Community Center. This, in turn, was dissolved in 1977.

When the first group of refugees arrived in 1975, earlier settlers made an attempt to welcome them and to provide assistance. In 1976, for example, the Vietnamese American Association sponsored a Tet celebration to which all were invited. With the rapid expansion of the Vietnamese population after 1975, however, tensions developed between the two groups, and refugees in the Twin Cities began to form their own religious, cultural, and mutual assistance organizations.

The refugees who arrived in 1975 were a heterogeneous group of military personnel, civil servants, government officials, embassy staff, writers, fishermen, and workers. Late in the year some of them met to discuss ways of bringing the community together and decided that only a religious organization could achieve this goal. Early in 1976, between 50 and 100 families in the Twin Cities formed a Buddhist group which later became the Vietnamese Buddhist Association of Minnesota, with playwright Vu Khac Khoan as chairman. After a period of meeting in homes, churches, and YMCAs, the association bought a small house on Dale Street in St. Paul to be used as a permanent place of worship — a pagoda. Although they did not have a regular monk, services were held on two Sundays per month, and special celebrations marked Buddha's birthday and enlightenment. In addition to its religious functions, the association also served as a mutual assistance organization, helping newcomers locate housing and employment. It also sponsored refugees from camps in Southeast Asia. In 1981 the association had 200 members, and religious celebrations were attended by 300 to 400 people.[12]

Another religious group was the Vietnamese Catholic Community, organized in 1978 for refugees in the Archdiocese of St. Paul and Minneapolis. A Vietnamese priest, the Reverend Peter Thanh, arrived in late December, 1977, to establish a congregation at St. Vincent's Church in St. Paul, where the refugees shared facilities with an American parish. In Vietnam before 1975 Catholics had comprised about 10% of the population; in Minnesota they represented approximately 40% of the Vietnamese community. Although about 70% of the Vietnamese in the state were professionals, most of the 700 congregation members were of the working class. Many were northerners who had fled to South Vietnam in 1954 after the country was partitioned.[13]

At St. Vincent's, Mass, confession, and Sunday school were held in Vietnamese for the refugees. English classes were also provided in the evening for adults. In addition the Reverend Thanh helped new arrivals find housing, jobs, and transportation and counseled those who were homesick or depressed. While he believed his parishioners should learn the functions of American parishes, Thanh also hoped that the church would play a vital role in helping Vietnamese retain important elements of their culture, such as strong family ties and respect for the elderly. Although primarily serving the Archdiocese of St. Paul and Minneapolis, he also made periodic trips to such cities as Duluth, Rochester, and Mankato, where he held Mass and heard confession in Vietnamese for outstate members of Catholic mutual assistance groups who also indirectly belonged to the Vietnamese Catholic Community. During most of the year these people attended American churches.

The Vietnamese Evangelical Church represented a smaller religious group in the community. Formed in 1975 under the direction of Pastor Tan Minh Phan, this congregation, affiliated with the Christian and Missionary Alliance Church, met initially on the old St. Paul Bible College campus. Like many Vietnamese who arrived in 1975, a considerable number of the original 150 members later left the state, and in 1978 the pastor himself departed for California. Leadership was then assumed by the Reverend John Van Tranberg (formerly Van Oan Tran), and in 1980 the congregation moved to the Grand Avenue Alliance Church, where it shared facilities with several other groups. Like many immigrant institutions, the Vietnamese Evangelical Church functioned both as a religious fellowship and as a mutual assistance group, with members providing aid and support to each other and to newcomers, some of whom were sponsored by the church itself. In 1981 the congregation numbered about 65.[14]

Among the secular organizations that emerged after 1975, the Vietnamese Cultural Association of Minnesota (VICAM) was the only one devoted primarily to promoting literature and fine arts. Formed by Vietnamese artists, writers, and musicians in the Twin Cities in the summer of 1977, the group by December had sponsored a week-long conference, "To Save and Maintain Our Culture," at the International Institute of Minnesota. Speakers included local Vietnamese and members of Vietnamese communities in other states. The highlight was the production of a modern Vietnamese play, *The Misunderstanding*, by Vu Khac Khoan, first president of VICAM and a Minnesota resident since 1975. In April, 1979, VICAM members participated in a lecture series, "The Immigrant Experience," organized by the Minnesota Historical Society. Two of their talks were repeated in Lindstrom at the request of a church group sponsoring refugees from Vietnam. In December the association presented an evening of Vietnamese culture at the St. Paul Civic Center which included entertainment by well-known artists who had recently escaped from Vietnam. Singer and composer Cung Thuc Tien, a resident of Minnesota since 1977, also performed, as did a number of Vietnamese students from the University of Minnesota. In 1981 VICAM had about 35 members.[15]

Two mutual assistance associations — also known as self-help groups — were formed soon after the refugees arrived. The Vietnamese Alliance was organized in 1975 and the Vietnamese League in 1976. Both provided services to the community and sponsored new refugees from Southeast Asia. Neither had formal memberships. In 1981 the two organizations merged to form the Vietnamese Community in Minnesota.[16]

A third mutual assistance group, the Fellowship of the Republic of Vietnam Armed Forces in Minnesota, was organized in 1978 by former military personnel. Its purpose was to promote friendship and solidarity among members and help them adjust to the new environment. The fellowship formed a food co-operative to buy in bulk from California and Chicago such Vietnamese staples as rice, rice paper, soy and fish sauces, and sticky rice. The organization sponsored a considerable number of refugees from Southeast Asia, including 35 families in 1980. Membership was limited to men and numbered between 150 and 200 in 1981. Most resided in the seven Twin Cities metropolitan counties, but some lived as far away as Mankato and New Ulm.[17]

A self-help group that emphasized cultural exchange and friendship between Vietnamese and Americans was founded in 1979 by a group of students and instructors at St. Paul Technical Vocational Institute. The Vietnamese American Friendship Association — modeled on an organization of the same name in pre-1975 Vietnam — included over 200 Vietnamese and American families in 1981, some of whom be-

LIKE MANY earlier immigrants, a Vietnamese child joined in pledging allegiance to the flag in Duluth in 1979.

longed to the Cleveland Avenue Methodist Church, where meeting space and office equipment were made available. The group published a newsletter entitled *Gop Y* (Mutual Support).[18]

One of the most active organizations was the Vietnamese Student Association at the University of Minnesota in Minneapolis. Formed in 1975 with 10 members, by 1981 it had grown to 420 — virtually all the Vietnamese enrolled there. The association published a monthly magazine, *Noi San Lien Lac* (Internal Magazine), with information concerning students, news of Vietnamese in Minnesota and elsewhere in the United States, short stories, poems, and an opinion column. Activities also included a tutoring program for Vietnamese students and music and dance groups which took part in cultural events at the university and in the community. On February 6, 1981, the group co-operated with Chinese student organizations in sponsoring a *Tet* celebration on the university campus in Minneapolis.[19]

Since 1977 most Vietnamese associations have annually joined together in early February to organize events for *Tet*, traditionally the most important holiday of the year. In 1981 Twin Cities Vietnamese gathered at the Bel-Rae ballroom in the northeastern Minneapolis suburb of Mounds View on February 7. Festivities began in the morning with remembrance of the ancestors and continued with traditional music, dance, an *Ao Dai* (traditional Vietnamese dress) contest, and the election of community representatives.[20]

Although most of the state's Vietnamese were concentrated in the Twin Cities, 100 or more settled at least temporarily in Duluth, St. Cloud, Rochester, and Willmar in 1975, while an unknown number went to scattered smaller towns. Many of them moved very quickly to the Twin Cities or to the West Coast, but core groups remained, attracting new arrivals and eventually developing into relatively stable communities. While in 1981 formal organizations had not yet evolved in the smaller settlements, Vietnamese gathered in their homes for companionship and mutual support.[21]

For example, approximately 450 Vietnamese were settled in northern Minnesota in 1975, 150 of them in Duluth. Some moved to Mesabi Range towns such as Chisholm and Hibbing — where the employment situation was better until 1979 — and others went to the Twin Cities, Texas, or California. Newcomers continued to arrive, however, and by 1981 Duluth's Vietnamese population had reached 140. Each year since 1976 this group has organized a *Tet* celebration that has drawn refugees from as far as Alexandria and generally attracted as many Americans as Vietnamese. In 1981 about 700 people took part in festivities which included skits, special foods, music, and dancing. In St. Cloud over 400 people from 16 counties attended the fifth *Tet* celebration in 1981, although the town's Vietnamese population totaled only about 250. In southern Minnesota about 1,000 persons — half of them refugees, the other half Americans — participated in *Tet* events jointly organized by Vietnamese in Rochester, Mankato, and Worthington.[22]

Since the Minnesota Vietnamese community had no weekly or biweekly newspaper, many residents subscribed to periodicals from the West Coast or Washington, D.C. These included *Van Nghe Tien Phong* (Literary Vanguard), formerly published in Saigon, and *Dat Moi* (New Land), which originated in the immigrant community in Seattle. Two members of the Vietnamese Cultural Association in Minnesota, Vu Khac Khoan and Cung Thuc Tien (whose pseudonym is Thach Chuong), frequently contributed to the latter.[23]

The Vietnamese impact on Minnesota varied considerably from small town to metropolitan area. Fewer in number outside the Twin Cities, the immigrants have participated more fully in the institutions of the host society. Since small-town life afforded personal relationships between sponsors and refugees, *Tet* celebrations have frequently become community affairs in which Americans were readily included.[24]

Hibbing may be taken as a case in point. The 70 to 80

refugees who settled there were well incorporated into the life of the town. Most obtained good jobs and some joined labor unions. They worked in foundries, in a radiator factory, and in iron mining. Lutheran Social Service had arranged for their resettlement in Hibbing, and Holy Trinity Lutheran Church, a Finnish congregation, played a key role in sponsoring and providing for them. Once settled, however, the refugees attended various churches where they had American friends and often took active parts in church functions. That the Vietnamese in turn have made their mark on Hibbing may be illustrated by the annual bazaar at Holy Trinity where the favorite item purchased by local townsfolk has changed from Finnish bread to Vietnamese egg rolls.

While the reception of Vietnamese in Minnesota has been relatively good, a number of incidents point to racial hostility. On July 4, 1979, about 50 white youths in St. Cloud, where the largest number of outstate Vietnamese were concentrated, attacked five Vietnamese teenagers in a city park. One of the victims was thrown into the river and was only semiconscious when pulled out by the police, while onlookers yelled racial epithets and obscenities.[25]

In November of the same year rumors that Indochinese were eating cats and dogs circulated widely in St. Paul. Vietnamese became particularly alarmed that the charges were directed at them, as they were the only group named in articles in both the *Minneapolis Tribune* and the *St. Paul Dispatch*. Leaders of the Vietnamese community organized several informal meetings in their homes, and the Department of Public Welfare's Refugee Resettlement Office sponsored a public forum to help resolve tensions. No evidence was ever produced to show that refugees did in fact eat dogs or cats, and the rumors evidently stemmed from misleading press reports.[26]

By 1981 acculturation was taking place as adaptations were made to the new environment. For example, services at the Buddhist pagoda were held on the first and third Sundays of the month rather than on the traditional days of the full and half moon. At Catholic gatherings men and women sat together as couples and shook hands with the priest, whereas in Vietnam they were seated separately and greeted the priest by bowing.[27]

Tet celebrations were also adapted. Instead of lasting for three days as was customary in Vietnam, most activities have been limited to New Year's Eve and New Year's Day in Minnesota, and in 1981 the main celebration took place on the Saturday after New Year's Day. Traditionally *Tet* was the time when Vietnamese forgot their troubles and visited their relatives, friends, and teachers. It was also a time to pay one's debts. Both of these practices have been modified. Many families have become separated, and paying one's debts was no longer possible, as Vietnamese were taking out loans to buy houses and cars in the American way.[28]

Politically the Vietnamese in Minnesota have been largely preoccupied with the crises of the Indochina War and the postwar developments which have affected virtually every family. Many were part of the Vietnamese resistance against the French in the North until 1949 when Communists gained control of the Viet Minh coalition. When the country was partitioned in 1954 a large number fled to the South where they found employment in the government or the American embassy. Others joined the Third Force which opposed both the Communists and the American-backed South Vietnamese government and sought alternative ways to end the war and reunify the country. Thus while most Minnesota refugees were firmly anti-Communist, they represented a diversity of political views.[29]

In their first political action in the state, students and members of every Vietnamese refugee organization staged a demonstration on the Capitol steps in St. Paul on June 22, 1979, to protest the forceful ouster of Vietnamese refugees seeking asylum in Malaysia. The deputy prime minister of Malaysia had announced that 76,000 boat people would be towed out to sea and that new arrivals would be shot on sight. When condemnation of this announcement poured in from around the world, the statement was retracted, but not until several thousand Vietnamese had been abandoned in unseaworthy boats on the high seas.[30]

Although it is premature to speculate on the ultimate roles of Vietnamese people in the political life of the state, the appointment of Johannes Huyen, a member of the pre-1975 group, as director of the St. Paul Department of Human Rights marked an important step in initiating their participation in American affairs. While Huyen's appointment by Mayor George Latimer in October, 1980, aroused opposition in the city's Black community, it was welcomed by the Indochinese. The office has been particularly heavily used by the Hmong.

ETHNIC CHINESE

Although ethnic Chinese refugees arrived in Minnesota after 1975 from all three Indochinese countries, a majority were from Vietnam. Their forebears had emigrated from South China to Southeast Asia in the 19th and early 20th centuries, encouraged by French colonial authorities who hoped to utilize their commercial skills in developing trade with the West. In South Vietnam the Chinese thrived as merchants, moneylenders, and traders, eventually monopolizing the rice and spice trades by acting as middlemen between European firms and Indochinese producers. In North Vietnam they competed with an emerging Vietnamese urban middle class, and the clash which resulted created considerable hostility toward them. During the Indochina War, ethnic Chinese in the North were suspected of being a fifth column, and the government imposed repressive measures barring them from higher education, the civil service, and the military.[31]

With the withdrawal of American aid to South Vietnam and the halting of Chinese aid to North Vietnam, the country's leaders turned for assistance to the Soviet Union. Tensions between China and Vietnam increased, and in 1978 Vietnamese leaders expelled 180,000 ethnic Chinese, whom they described as unproductive city dwellers who constituted a threat to security. With the onset of the border war between China and Vietnam in 1979, the latter began a systematic expulsion of ethnic Chinese from both the north and south, charging 10 taels of gold (more than $3,000) for each departure. The alternative to leaving was a move to a new economic area to labor on the land. While some Chinese accepted the government's offer to work in the countryside, others decided to leave, fearing that more repressive measures were in store.[32]

Late in 1978 as many as 17,000 refugees a month — about 80% of whom were ethnic Chinese — left Vietnam. By May, 1979, the exodus reached 65,000 a month. Departures continued at this high level until the convening of the Geneva Conference in July, during which the Hanoi government agreed to control the outflow because of problems in the receiving countries of Southeast Asia.

In Minnesota ethnic Chinese were not counted separately by state officials, but estimators believe that about 50 were among the first arrivals in 1975. Only 10 of these remained in the state in 1981. A far larger number were believed to have been among the boat people in 1978–79, but again no figures have been compiled.[33]

The state's ethnic Chinese were composed of two subgroups, one from North Vietnam and the other from South Vietnam. In southern Minnesota Chinese from the North predominated in such towns as Rochester, Austin, Albert Lea, and Hayfield, while Chinese from the South were more numerous in the Twin Cities. Because anti-Chinese feeling was strong in North Vietnam and because the North and South fought on opposing sides in the Indochina War, tensions between the two subgroups have persisted. Ethnic Chinese from North Vietnam did not attend the Vietnamese *Tet* celebration in Rochester in 1981, while virtually all those from South Vietnam took part. In the Twin Cities only the latter attended the Vietnamese festivities.

Ethnic Chinese have established two businesses in the Twin Cities, both operated under the same group ownership in 1981. One was the Vietnam Hong Kong International, a store in North Minneapolis marketing foods and gifts as well as Chinese and Vietnamese books and newspapers. Its clientele included all the refugee groups as well as Thai, Indonesians, and Filipinos. The store also supplied Chinese and Vietnamese restaurants in the state. The second business was the Ritz Theater, located near the store, where Chinese films from Hong Kong were shown to overflow crowds on weekends.

Two ethnic Chinese residents of the Twin Cities illustrate the varying experiences of this group. Trieu Tran was born in Guangdong province in South China in 1916. He immigrated with his parents to South Vietnam as a young boy, attended Chinese school there, and spoke Chinese at home. He became a fisherman and later a rice merchant in Kien Giang, a small town near Saigon. His wife, Lau Vong, was also of ethnic Chinese background, and they continued to speak Chinese at home, although their children attended a Vietnamese school.[34]

In March, 1978, before the large-scale expulsion of ethnic Chinese began, Tran decided to leave Vietnam. Communist authorities had nationalized his business and confiscated his property so that he could neither fish nor engage in trade. Tran and his family escaped in a fishing boat with 58 other ethnic Chinese and Vietnamese. After four months in a refugee camp in Malaysia, the family was sponsored by a Minnesota Vietnamese whom they had never met. Eleven

months after arriving in the Twin Cities the Trans knew only four other ethnic Chinese families. When asked if they identified themselves as Chinese or Vietnamese, the parents responded that they considered themselves Chinese, while the children (all born in Vietnam) said they felt more Vietnamese than Chinese. The Tran family was Buddhist, but they did not attend the Vietnamese pagoda in St. Paul.

Van Tong Sam, on the other hand, is the grandson of Chinese who were also from Guangdong province. They immigrated to North Vietnam, settling in Haiphong. Sam's father was a soldier in the French army. After the French defeat in 1954, he fled to Saigon, where Sam was born in 1959. His father later joined the South Vietnamese army and in 1969 got a job as a clerk in the American embassy. Sam's mother was also a second-generation ethnic Chinese, and his parents spoke Chinese at home, although Sam was sent to Vietnamese school.[35]

In October, 1978, when ethnic Chinese were being expelled from Vietnam, Sam's family decided that it would be best to send the two eldest children out of the country. His father thought that he was too old to go himself, but he wanted his children to be able to start a new life. Sam and his sister paid $5,000 each to the Vietnamese government for permission to leave the country. After six days at sea in a small boat with little food, they were picked up by the Malaysian navy and landed in Malaysia in October, 1978. The two spent 10 months in a refugee camp, then were accepted for resettlement in the United States and went to San Francisco. Following his sister's marriage, Sam decided to go to Minnesota to be with a friend he had met in the camp. Enrolled at the University of Minnesota in 1981, Van Tong Sam identified himself as Vietnamese although both his parents were ethnic Chinese.

THE HMONG

The first Hmong families arrived in Minnesota in 1976. During the two years that followed, the population grew moderately, reaching 350 by June, 1978. Shortly thereafter St. Paul became a clustering area for the Hmong, whose numbers surged to 1,000 by December, and more than doubled in 1979. But the most dramatic increase took place in 1980 when the Hmong population quadrupled. By the year's end the Twin Cities, with a settlement of almost 10,000, became the largest urban concentration of Hmong in the country.[36]

The majority in the Twin Cities settled initially in the Summit-University area of St. Paul and, by 1979, in South Minneapolis. Some went to smaller Minnesota towns, but few remained, as most preferred to live near their compatriots in the metropolitan area. The exception was a stable group of about 50 that emerged in Duluth in 1980–81.

Although the origins of the Hmong are obscure, their legends and early Chinese sources suggest that they migrated southward into China from Siberia or Mongolia between 2000 and 5000 B.C. Warring constantly with the Chinese as they advanced, the Hmong in 424 A.D. established a kingdom in the Hubei-Hunan-Guangxi region of southwestern China, an area with many ethnic minorities. From this stronghold they later moved into the neighboring provinces of Guizhou, Sichuan, and Yunnan. In the late 18th and early 19th centuries they migrated into North Vietnam, and during the second half of the century they entered Laos (see Map 32.1).[37]

The Hmong usually lived in mountainous areas, building their villages at or above 3,000 feet. Their economy was based on slash-and-burn agriculture, a system of burning a forest and using the ashes as fertilizer. The Hmong cultivated dry rice, buckwheat, millet, barley, corn, and various vegetables but had to move their villages frequently as the land became infertile rapidly. They also raised livestock, hunted, fished, and gathered herbs and fibers. The Hmong language belongs to the Miao-Yao family. As far as can be discerned it had no written form until the 1950s and 1960s when several systems were developed by Western missionaries.

During World War II Japan occupied Laos, and the Hmong, who offered their help to French and Laotian resistance forces, won a reputation as superior guerrilla fighters. After the war Touby Lyfoung, the Hmong field commander, gained power in a faction which later became the Royal Laotian government supported by the United States. Another Hmong leader attained prominence in the rival faction that became the Pathet Lao, and as a result the Hmong were split between opposing sides throughout the Indochina War. Those who settled in Minnesota were followers of Touby and Vang Pao, commander of the Hmong guerrilla army trained by the CIA.[38]

In the early 1960s, when the Pathet Lao gained control of Xieng Khouang, capital of the province where most of the Hmong lived, thousands were displaced from villages in surrounding areas. They fled to mountain guerrilla bases from which General Vang Pao's forces attacked the enemy on the Plain of Jars. Families living at these bases for a decade or more suffered severe hardships and the disruption of the traditional extended family system around which Hmong society was normally organized. Virtually all the men were recruited by the guerrilla army. Women and small children, attempting to farm the land near the bases, were often forced to move on before they could harvest the crops. While the guerrillas fought valiantly, they were eventually decimated by the much larger North Vietnamese and Pathet Lao forces. The Hmong suffered over 30,000 casualties, losses that affected every family.

When Communists took over the government of Laos in May, 1975, the CIA flew Vang Pao to the United States and settled him on a ranch in Montana. Despite the American promise to "take care of" the Hmong regardless of who won the war, only about 1,000 were airlifted to camps in Thailand. The remainder were left to the mercy of the Pathet Lao, who vowed to "exterminate" those who served the Americans. Over 10% of the estimated 70,000 who did not escape to Thailand were reportedly killed by the end of 1977. Meanwhile those who had escaped began long waits of up to five years in Thai camps before they were accepted for resettlement in the United States or elsewhere.

When the early families arrived in Minnesota, they were still suffering the effects of the war and its dislocations. In order to draw the community together and to overcome the difficulties of adaptation, the Hmong resorted to their traditional reliance on mutual assistance through kinship groups. Hmong social organization is based on the patrilineal clan, whose members are descended from a common mythological ancestor. Within the clan, descendants of a common known ancestor form lineages which are comprised of a number of households consisting of parents, their unmarried children, and their married sons with families. Members must marry outside the clan.[39]

A group of Hmong households whose male heads are closely related as brothers, uncles, or first cousins may also form lineage associations for mutual assistance. While it is the duty of all members of a lineage to help each other, those joined in an association — often known as "the group" and identified by the leader's name — have a much greater collective obligation. These associations, while based on lineage ties, were flexible enough to include a few outside individuals if they were loyal to the leader. In Laos lineage associations gained political power by uniting regional and national groups.

In late 1975 and 1976 the Hmong in Minnesota established a mutual assistance association — including both Hmong and Lao — known as the Lao Huam Phao, or United Lao Association. By 1977, however, some St. Paul Hmong leaders representing various lineage associations decided to form the Hmong Association in Minnesota. Of particular concern was the need to develop special educational materials for the group and to establish information networks. By 1980 Vang Pao, who had become the leader of the Hmong in the United States, was urging the formation of local associations that would include all Laotian ethnic groups. His hope was that such organizations could then be linked in a national network, providing a stronger base from which to fund service projects. In St. Paul the Hmong Association changed its name to the Lao Family Community, Incorporated, and elected a Lao to the position of vice-president.[40]

While it did not include all the lineage associations in Minnesota, the Lao Family Community became an important force in the Twin Cities Hmong settlement. Faced with the arrival of as many as 200 refugees per week in the summer of 1980, the board of directors, composed of the heads of lineage associations, appointed group leaders to recruit new members and disseminate information to refugees throughout the metropolitan area. The groups thus formed were not based on kinship, a fact which may eventually modify the association's structure. Other changes could occur if the growing Hmong community in Minneapolis should form a separate organization. Partly to offset this possibility the Lao Family Community started English classes in the Phillips neighborhood for refugees living in South Minneapolis. Similar instruction was also offered in St. Paul.[41]

Although the Hmong were generally well received in Minnesota, they have often been victims of unfair housing practices in the Twin Cities. In March, 1981, a survey of South Minneapolis' Phillips neighborhood found overcrowding of Hmong families in overpriced, poorly maintained apartments. Absentee landlords exploited the refugees because they spoke little English and were unfamiliar with accepted

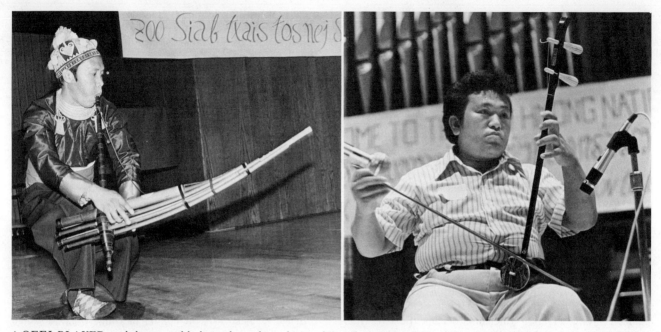

A QEEJ PLAYER and dancer added argyle socks to his traditional costume (left) and another man played the xim xos *at a national Hmong conference in St. Paul in 1981.*

housing costs. The scarcity of low-income housing also caused tensions between the Hmong and American Indians in the neighborhood who felt that the newcomers inflated rents and received unfair educational and occupational bene-fits.[42]

Although the traditional Hmong religion was animistic, a sizable number were converted to Christianity by Catholic and Protestant missionaries in Laos, and others have joined various congregations since they reached Minnesota. Members of a Hmong Christian and Missionary Alliance Church, organized in Laos in the 1950s, fled to Thailand in 1975 and later settled in St. Paul. Although many were lost along the way, new adherents gained in Minnesota have swelled the congregation to 700 or 800 persons including children. Led by four Hmong lay pastors and a missionary couple from Thailand who spoke Hmong, the alliance members met on Sunday afternoons in the denomination's Simpson Memorial Church on Charles Avenue.[43]

Two smaller congregations have also been organized in Minnesota to form the Hmong Catholic Community. One met at St. Leonard of Port Maurice Church on Clinton Avenue in Minneapolis and the other at St. Mary's Church on 8th Street in St. Paul. The former, begun in 1979 with six Hmong families, had 100 members in 1981; more recently organized St. Mary's totaled 40. In February, 1981, Father Daniel Taillez, a Hmong-speaking French priest, arrived to serve both congregations.

The political concerns of the Hmong immigrants in 1981 were focused largely on Southeast Asia and a persistent hope that some day they might return to Laos and drive the Vietnamese from their homelands. On the local scene they have made a collective effort to develop a favorable public image and to protect their rights. While struggling to retain traditional elements of their culture, the Hmong have consistently welcomed people from the larger society to their celebrations and festivals, often issuing public invitations via the press and radio. During the 1980 New Year's celebration, which was held in the St. Paul Civic Center, Mayor Latimer and General Vang Pao shared the speakers' table, and many Americans were in the audience.[44]

Certain inevitable changes were apparent in the conduct of the celebration. In Laos, for example, the New Year's festivities lasted for three days and included sports, special foods, and travel from village to village. In Minnesota the 1980 event was limited to one day, and the special foods could not be accommodated at Civic Center concession stands. Moreover, while the program featured traditional music and dancing, it concluded with several hours of enter-tainment by a Hmong rock band.[45]

The Lao and Cambodians

Small but distinctive groups of Lao and Cambodians may be found within Minnesota's larger Indochinese population. In March, 1981, the Lao numbered about 2,800 and the Cambodians about 2,000 people. The largest concentrations of Lao were located in the Twin Cities suburbs of Burnsville and Eagan, in South Minneapolis, and in St. Cloud, although others lived in small towns here and there throughout the state. A majority of the Cambodians lived in St. Paul or Minneapolis; Duluth, St. Cloud, Rochester, Faribault, and Austin had smaller numbers.[46]

The cultures of both the Lao and Cambodians combined influences from India with indigenous elements. Although their languages belonged to entirely different families (that of the Lao to Tai and that of the Cambodians to the Austroasi-

AMERICANS joined Hmong people at a table laden with traditional foods to celebrate the Hmong New Year in a St. Paul home on December 27, 1980.

atic), each was influenced by the classical Indian languages of Sanskrit and Pali. Both used alphabets of Indian origin and have borrowed Sanskrit and Pali words. Indic influences also resulted in the conversion of both peoples first to Hinduism and later to Theravada Buddhism.[47]

The Lao are the dominant group in Laos, comprising about half the population; the remainder consists of various hill tribes (such as the Hmong), who are scattered throughout the mountainous areas. Like the Hmong, the Lao may be migrants of Mongolian origin who made their way to Laos from the southern provinces of China in the late 13th century. They live in the Mekong River Valley and along its tributaries, where they cultivate rice (see Map 32.1).[48]

The area of present-day Laos was a Buddhist kingdom as early as the 14th century. Like much of Southeast Asia, it was under French authority from the late 19th century until 1953, when it achieved independence. At once the country became engaged in civil war, which essentially continued until a cease-fire was arranged in 1975.[49]

Unlike the Hmong, the Lao have no well-defined clans or lineages, and some households consist only of parents and children, while others may include a more extended family. Paternal and maternal kin are considered equally important. Respect for the elderly prevails in Laos, as it does throughout Asia, but moral obligations to parents are not as compelling as they are for the Hmong or the Vietnamese.

Religious practices include both Buddhism and cults of spirits, traditionally believed to be omnipresent. In public festivals both beliefs are blended in ceremonies such as the *baci* (calling back the soul), which is often included in New Year's celebrations in Minnesota. During this ceremony one of the wandering souls or spirits (each person is believed to have 32 souls) is called back and kept in place by tying a cotton string to the wrist.

In 1981 the group's organizations included the Lao Association for Mutual Assistance and the Lao Association in Minnesota, both formed in 1978. The former was created by immigrants from northern Laos who lived in South St. Paul, Eagan, and Burnsville, while the latter was established by those from central or southern Laos who lived in Minneapolis. Both sought to aid new arrivals by providing interpreters, transportation, and help in locating housing and employment. Both have also been active in sponsoring Lao refugees. Each held a New Year's celebration in mid-April. These events, which included religious ceremonies, traditional dances, and special foods, have occurred annually in the Twin Cities since 1976. In 1981 for the first time Lao in Minneapolis celebrated the Buddhist pre-Lenten festival on February 7. The service was conducted in a high school gymnasium by a Buddhist monk from Wisconsin. A Protestant group, known as the Lao Community Church, was

OTTO WERNER of New Ulm was among the Americans who taught English to Cambodian and other refugees in Minnesota in 1975.

organized in 1980. It grew out of the Peace Reformed Church of Eagan, which had sponsored most of the Lao congregation.[50]

Both the Lao and Cambodian immigrant communities in Minnesota in 1981 were composed of two subgroups. The 1975 arrivals were for the most part highly educated, spoke English, and were well acquainted with Western ways. Many had worked for American agencies in Vientiane and Phnom Penh, the capital cities of the two countries. Later arrivals were farmers from the countryside who did not accept the Communist system of collectivization or former soldiers of the Royal Laotian or Cambodian armies. The later immigrants, who frequently did not speak English, had more difficulty in finding employment.[51]

Like the Lao, the Cambodians (or Khmer) are the dominant group in their homeland, where they are distributed throughout the country. Their origins are obscure, but it is known that a great Cambodian civilization flourished in Southeast Asia from the 9th to the 13th centuries. In that period the Khmer Empire established its capital at Angkor and extended its rule over much of what later became South Vietnam, Laos, and Thailand. The famous temple, Angkor Wat, built during this period in the 13th century, has become a national symbol for Cambodians. By the 15th century the Khmer Empire had declined, and its power was limited to Phnom Penh. From 1863 until it achieved independence in 1953, Cambodia was ruled by France. Its ancient monarchy was overthrown in 1970, at which time the country was renamed the Khmer Republic.[52]

Organizations in Minnesota in 1981 included the Cambodian Association of Minnesota and Friends, and the Cambodian American Association in Minnesota. Leaders of the first focused a great deal of attention on the political situation in the homeland, while those of the second stressed improvement of the living conditions of Cambodian refugees in Minnesota. Organized in 1975, the first group was the larger of the two. Its members included many working-class Cambodians and a few professionals, and it carried on an active program of sponsoring additional refugees from camps in Thailand. The second group was formed in 1978 as a cultural association. Its members included younger, generally more acculturated professionals, and its program emphasized aid for new arrivals.[53]

Like the Lao, both organizations sponsored New Year's celebrations each April with traditional dances, music, and foods. In Cambodia the holiday was primarily regarded as a holy day when people attended Buddhist services and took food to the monks. In Minnesota New Year's has become a day when Cambodians relax and remember their relatives and friends.

While it is too early to attempt more than a survey of Minnesota's Indochinese peoples, a number of important developments in their history had taken place by 1981. In the Twin Cities they formed cultural, religious, and mutual assistance associations, and the first community leaders emerged. Throughout the state informal compatibility groups also appeared. Communication networks were estab-lished, and Indochinese organizations undertook the task of sponsoring new refugees from Southeast Asia.

The impact of the refugees on Minnesota was significant. Although racial tensions arose in various areas — exacerbated by economic recessions — families, congregations, and civic groups nevertheless responded to the emergency needs of the Indochinese with compassion and energy. In small towns the incorporation of the new immigrants was often an effort of the entire community, and Indochinese New Year celebrations were attended by as many Americans as refugees. In the Twin Cities metropolitan area the larger number of Indochinese organized impressive cultural events, including plays, concerts, and exhibits. New Year festivities featured special foods, demonstrations by traditional dancers and musicians, addresses by American and Indochinese leaders, and rock bands reflecting the influences of East and West. These events have introduced a distinctive new element into Minnesota's cultural life.

The 20th-century influx of Asian refugees is an unfinished story. Like earlier migrants from Europe, Africa, and the Western Hemisphere, the Asian peoples seem to be following the dual paths of acculturation and retention. Like the earlier immigrants, too, they have formed various organizations to aid their survival in a new environment — an environment that promised them both hardships and rewards.

As we have seen, the Minnesota immigrant story is an ongoing saga. In this book we have barely touched the surface of the rich material from which countless future books will doubtless be written. In the more than a century that has passed since the Indian people were pushed aside and white Europeans claimed the land we now call Minnesota, much has happened. Additional chapters featuring the immigrants who arrived only yesterday and who will arrive tomorrow will modify and reinterpret the history of the people who chose Minnesota.

Reference notes

Much of the information in this chapter is from the author's interviews of service workers and members of the various Indochinese communities in Minnesota. Those interviews that were recorded on tape are so identified; tapes are in the Audio-Visual Library, MHS. The author's notes for both the taped and untaped interviews are in the MEHP Papers, MHS.

[1] *Indochinese Refugee Reports*, February 17, 1981, p. 8; information on settlement in Minnesota from Sandra Duvander, Refugee Program Office, Minnesota Dept. of Public Welfare (DPW), March 31, 1981, and from directors of DPW's Area Co-ordinating Centers: Robert Jones, Rochester, February 17, March 17, 1981; Janice Rein, St. Cloud, Eleanor Graves, Austin, James Langworthy, Duluth, Gayle Holman, Willmar, and Sylvia Oie, Moorhead — all February 17, 1981; Ross Graves, Austin, March 12, 1981; Victor Purcell, *The Chinese in Southeast Asia*, 176 (London, Eng., 1965). The author wishes to acknowledge the helpful suggestions received from Josée Cung and Timothy Dunnigan.

"Indochinese" is a generic term referring to the peoples of Vietnam, Laos, and Cambodia, within the larger region of Southeast Asia. It was arbitrarily imposed by French colonialists in 1887 when the three countries were united to form the French Indochina Union. Because of its origin, the term was resented by nationalists in the post-World War II era when the countries became independent. Since 1975, however, it has been widely used in the U.S. by government officials, service providers, scholars, and the Indochinese settlers themselves.

A note on naming should be added. In traditional Cambodian and Vietnamese usage, the last name is given first. Lao use the same order as Americans. The family name is used infrequently in these cultures. The Hmong had no family names until their arrival in the U.S., when clan names were adopted as surnames. In Minnesota, however, many of these people have adopted American name order. This chapter reports the Americanized format except in cases of well-known artists and writers who have maintained the traditional name order for professional use.

[2] Interviews of Jane Kretzmann, state co-ordinator of refugee programs, DPW, March 11, 1980; Bich-Ngoc Nguyen, DPW, January 9; Josée Cung, January 14 (taped); Duvander, March 31 — all 1981; *Indochinese Refugee Reports,* January 15, 1980, p. 10, October 31, 1980, p. 1; DPW, "Historical Highlights of the Resettlement Program in Minnesota," mimeographed page [1980], copy in MEHP Papers; *St. Paul Dispatch,* April 6, 1979, p. 33.

[3] Interviews of Socheat Sar, January 8, February 12; Khaeng Sinakone, February 11; Josée Cung, February 13 (taped) — all 1981; Stanley Karnow, "Free No More: The Allies America Forgot," in *Geo: A New View of Our World,* 2:14 (January, 1980).

[4] Here and below, see Darell Montero and Marsha T. Weber, *Vietnamese Americans: Patterns of Resettlement and Socioeconomic Adaptation in the United States,* xiii–xiv (Boulder, Colo., 1979); Thomas C. Fox, "The War and Vietnamese Society," in John K. Whitmore, ed., *An Introduction to Indochinese History, Culture, Language and Life,* 71–76 (Ann Arbor, 1979); Committee of Concerned Asian Scholars, *The Indochina Story,* 45, 48 (New York, 1970); George C. Hildebrand and Gareth Porter, *Cambodia: Starvation and Revolution,* 19–38 (New York, 1976); Nina S. Adams and Alfred W. McCoy, eds., *Laos: War and Revolution,* xxii (New York, 1970); Cung interview, February 13, 1981.

[5] Here and below, see Arthur M. Schlesinger, Jr., *The Bitter Heritage: Vietnam and American Democracy 1941–1966,* 22–31 (Greenwich, Conn., 1967); Asian Scholars, *Indochina Story,* 22–24, 331–334; American Friends Service Committee, *Indochina 1971,* 5 (n.p., 1970); Hildebrand and Porter, *Cambodia,* 13.

[6] Hildebrand and Porter, *Cambodia,* 12; Asian Scholars, *Indochina Story,* 324; American Friends Service Committee, *Indochina 1971,* 26; Peter Thiel and Evert Fowle, comps., "Vietnam and Beyond at a Glance: A Chronology of the Events that Surrounded the Vietnam Conflict," prepared for a symposium at Macalester College, St. Paul, March 1–10, 1979, copy in MEHP Papers.

[7] Here and below, see Mary Bowen Wright, "Indochinese," in Stephan Thernstrom, ed., *Harvard Encyclopedia of American Ethnic Groups,* 509–512 (Cambridge, Mass., 1980); Robert E. Marsh, "Socioeconomic Status of Indochinese Refugees in the United States: Progress and Problems," in *Social Security Bulletin,* October, 1980, p. 12; Montero and Weber, *Vietnamese Americans,* 24, 26; *Indochinese Refugee Reports,* December 21, 1979, p. 1; Kretzmann interview, March 11, 1980. Federal assistance to Indochinese refugees followed a precedent established in the 1960s when 700,000 Cuban refugees reached the U.S.

For resettlement problems in summer, 1981, see *St. Paul Sunday Pioneer Press,* July 26, 1981, Metro/Region sec., 1, 5; *Minneapolis Tribune,* July 27, 1981, pp. 3B, 4B.

[8] *Minneapolis Tribune,* July 1, 1979, p. 1A, July 18, 1979, p. 8A, February 10, 1980, p. 13A; *Minneapolis Star,* February 17, 1979, *Saturday Magazine,* 1–15. Most of the Indochinese were admitted to the U.S. without visas under the attorney general's discretionary parole authority, which permits an unlimited number of persons to enter the country during an emergency.

[9] Kretzmann interview, March 11, 1980; DPW, "Minnesota Consortium: A Multi-Agency Effort to Provide Assistance to Indo-Chinese Refugees," 1, and "Area Coordinating Centers," undated typescripts, copies in MEHP Papers. See also Glenn Hendricks, *Indochinese Refugee Settlement Patterns in Minnesota* (Minneapolis, 1981).

[10] Interviews of Sandra Duvander, March 31, April 6, 1981.

[11] Here and two paragraphs below, see United States Asian Statistics, in MEHP Papers, compiled by Jon A. Gjerde from U.S. Dept. of Labor, Bureau of Immigration, *Annual Reports,* 1909–39, and U.S. Justice Dept., Immigration and Naturalization Service, *Annual Reports,* 1940–78; interviews of Cao Dam Nguyen and Johannes Huyen, director, St. Paul Dept. of Human Rights, both February 26, 1981; Nga Truitner interview, March 3, 1981.

[12] Interviews of Nga Truitner, January 19, 1981; Vu Khac Khoan, April 5, 1979 (taped).

[13] Here and below, see interview of Rev. Peter Thanh, September 2, 1980.

[14] Interview of Rev. John Van Tranberg, March 2, 1981.

[15] Handwritten notes, Cung Thuc Tien (VICAM member) to the author, January 16, 1981, in MEHP Papers; interview of Cung Thuc Tien, April 5, 1981. The play, with incidental music by Tien, was performed in English by the Powderhorn Players at Walker Church in Minneapolis. In 1976 another of Khan's plays, *The Last Three Days of Genghis Khan,* was produced in Minneapolis by the Theater in the Round Players. Pham Dinh Chuong (Hoai Bac) and the husband and wife duo Le Uyen and Phuong performed at the December event.

[16] Interviews of former presidents Tran Thoi, Vietnamese Alliance, March 2, 1981, and Pham Vy, Vietnamese League, March 4, 1981. Both men became members of the executive board of the Vietnamese Community in Minnesota.

[17] Interviews of Quang Vu, fellowship president, January 19, March 3, 1981.

[18] Interview of François Toan, president of Vietnamese American Friendship Assn., March 2, 1981.

[19] Interview of Thinh Tran, student association president (1979–80), February 28, 1981.

[20] Interview of Bich-Ngoc Nguyen, February 5, 1981.

[21] Jones, Rein, Langworthy, and Holman interviews — all February 17, 1981.

[22] Interviews of James Langworthy and Nguyen The Hung, both Duluth, March 11; Rev. Bruce Dissell, Holy Trinity Lutheran Church, Hibbing, and Rev. Jack Harris, United Methodist Church, Chisholm, both March 2; Langworthy and Rein, both February 17; Jones, March 17 — all 1981.

[23] Interviews of Cung Thuc Tien, February 26, March 3, 1981.

[24] Here and below, see interviews of B. Dissell, March 2, and Marilyn Dissell, April 5, 1981.

[25] *Minneapolis Star,* August 10, 1979, p. 1A.

[26] *St. Paul Dispatch,* November 15, 1979, p. 1; *Minneapolis Tribune,* November 16, 1979, p. 15C; interview of Josée Cung, March 4, 1981.

[27] Thanh interview, September 2, 1980; Truitner interview, January 19, 1981.

[28] Bich-Ngoc Nguyen interview, February 5, 1981.

[29] Taped interview of Vu Khac Khoan, June 22, 1979; *St. Paul Pioneer Press-Dispatch,* June 16, 1979, p. 1.

[30] Here and below, see *St. Paul Pioneer Press,* October 31, 1980, p. 1B; Vu Khac Khoan interview, June 22, 1979; Truitner interview, January 19, 1981.

[31] Norman G. Owen, ''The Western Impact,'' in Whitmore, ed., *Introduction to Indochinese History*, 30; W. E. Willmott, ''The Chinese in Indochina,'' in Elliot L. Tepper, ed., *Southeast Asian Exodus: From Tradition to Resettlement, Understanding Refugees from Laos, Kampuchea, and Vietnam in Canada*, 71 (Ottawa, 1980); Purcell, *Chinese in Southeast Asia*, 174; Jones interview, March 17, 1981.

[32] Here and below, see *Minneapolis Tribune*, February 27, p. 17A; June 12, p. 3A; July 18, p. 8A; August 10, p. 3A; October 21, p. 13A — all 1979; Bruce Grant, *The Boat People: An 'Age' Investigation*, 3 (Melbourne, Austral., 1979).

[33] Here and two paragraphs below, see interviews of Xi Sou, an owner of Vietnam Hong Kong International, March 5, 14, 1981; Jones, February 17, March 17, 1981. Surveys of refugees by ethnic group in nonmetropolitan Minnesota were in process in 1981.

[34] Here and below, see interview of Trieu Tran, May 15, 1979.

[35] Here and below, see taped interview of Van Tong Sam, September 9, 1980.

[36] Here and below, see interviews of Jane Kretzmann, March 11, 1980, January 15, 1981; Bich-Ngoc Nguyen, January 9; Langworthy, February 17; Duvander, April 6 — all 1981; DPW, ''Historical Highlights''; *Minnesota Daily*, February 2, 1981, p. 9.

[37] Here and below, see Dept. of the Army, *Minority Groups in Thailand*, 573, 583–586, 637–645 (*pamphlet no. 550–107* — Washington, D.C., 1970); Yang See Koumarn, ''The Hmongs of Laos: 1896–1978,'' in National Indochinese Clearinghouse, *Glimpses of Hmong History and Culture*, 3 (Indochinese Refugee Education Guides, General Information Series, no. 16 — Arlington, Va., [1978]), copy in MEHP Papers; William J. Gedney, ''Linguistic Diversity in Indochina,'' in Whitmore, ed., *Introduction to Indochinese History*, 42. Neighboring peoples have referred to the Hmong by names such as *Miao, Meo*, or *Miao-tze*. The Hmong consider these terms derogatory and prefer to be called *Hmong*, which means ''free''; see Army, *Minority Groups*, 573.

On the Hmong language and oral tradition, see interviews of Chia Vang, March 9; Timothy Dunnigan, March 16 — both 1981; Timothy Dunnigan to the author, March 27, 1981, in MEHP Papers. The Romanized Popular Alphabet was developed by Father Ives Bertrais and Dr. William A. Smalley, professor at Bethel College in Arden Hills, Minnesota. It was used extensively in Laos during the Indochina War, and in Minnesota after 1975.

[38] Here and two paragraphs below, see Koumarn, in Indochinese Clearinghouse, *Glimpses*, 4–6; John Lewallen, ''The Reluctant Counterinsurgents: International Voluntary Services in Laos,'' in Adams and McCoy, eds., *Laos*, 361; Karnow, in *Geo*, 2:23; interview of Cynthia Westbrook, March 5, 1981; Tou-Fu Vang, ''The Hmong from Laos,'' 5, typescript, [1978?], photocopy in MEHP Papers. The figure 30,000 for Hmong casualties is probably a conservative estimate.

[39] Here and below, see Tou-Fu Vang, ''The Hmong of Laos,'' 8, undated typescript prepared for the Illinois Governor's Center for Asian Assistance, copy in MEHP Papers; Timothy Dunnigan, ''Continuity and Change in the Social Organization of Hmong Refugees,'' 3–5, paper presented at American Anthropological Assn. annual meeting, Washington, D.C., December, 1980.

[40] Interviews of Ya Yang, March 15, 1981; Leng Vang, March 17, 1981; Vang, ''Hmong from Laos,'' 5; Dunnigan, ''Continuity and Change,'' 6. In 1979 Vang Pao and other Hmong leaders from all over the U.S. gathered in St. Paul for an unprecedented conference in which they undertook to make policies to direct the immigrant group's acculturation. At the urging of Vang Pao it was decided, for example, to abolish the bride price traditionally paid to a woman's family, not only because the refugees could not afford it, but also because the custom might lead to divisions among the people or encourage marriage outside the group; see interviews of Diana Rankin, January 16, 26, 1981. Vang Pao's 1980 proposal for local associations was modeled on the Lao Family Community of Santa Ana, California; see interview of Cynthia Westbrook, August 22, 1980.

[41] Rankin interview, January 26, 1981.

[42] *St. Paul Pioneer Press*, October 22, 1979, p. 17; *Minneapolis Tribune*, March 16, 1980, p. 1H, March 25, 1981, p. 1A; March 26, 1981, p. 1A; *Minnesota Daily*, February 2, 1981, p. 9.

[43] Here and below, see interviews of Rev. Marvin Martin, December 26, 1980; Phay Vang, February 2, 1981. The two Catholic churches joined in celebrating the Hmong New Year, traditionally a religious event, at the College of St. Thomas (St. Paul) on December 28, 1980. After an address by Phay Vang, lay president of the Hmong Catholic Community, the congregations shared a meal, which was followed by traditional music and dancing.

[44] Author's observations at Hmong New Year celebration, St. Paul, December 27, 1980, notes in MEHP Papers.

[45] *St. Paul Pioneer Press*, December 28, 1980, Metro/Region sec., 5.

[46] Interviews of Sar, January 8, March 16; Sinakone, February 11; Rein, February 17; Duvander, March 31 — all 1981.

[47] Gedney, in Whitmore, ed., *Introduction to Indochinese History*, 38–44.

[48] Tipawan Truong-Quang Reed and Tou-Fu Vang, ''The Hmong Highlanders and the Lao Lowlanders,'' 3–6, typescript, July, 1978, copy in MEHP Papers.

[49] Here and two paragraphs below, see Georges Condominas, ''The Lao,'' and Philippe Devillers, ''The Laotian Conflict in Perspective,'' in Adams and McCoy, eds., *Laos*, 13–15, 38–51; Vang, ''Hmong from Laos,'' 3.

[50] Interviews of Rev. Berend Vander Woude, February 26; Bounleng Daoheung, March 18; Sinakone, February 11 — all 1981. The St. Cloud area had about 250 Lao in 1981.

[51] Interviews of Koy Chhoeurn, February 7, 1981; Sinakone, February 11, 1981.

[52] Lutheran Immigration and Refugee Service, *Cambodia: The Land and Its People*, 3 (Cambodian Series, Orientation Supplement, no. 3 — New York, 1976), and Chin Sreav Nou, ''Cambodia: Some Information about its History,'' 1, undated typescript, copies of both in MEHP Papers; Hildebrand and Porter, *Cambodia*, 14.

[53] Here and below, see interviews of Soteng Chim, March 17; Jones, March 17; Chhoeurn, February 7 — all 1981.

Appendix on Statistics

Jon A. Gjerde

BASIC TO ANY EFFORT to discern trends in the movements of ethnic groups to and within Minnesota are the statistical data incorporated into the text, tables, and maps of this book. Numerous pitfalls and problems are, however, inherent both in their presentation and in their use. This appendix is intended to provide a brief explanation.

Data on migrating peoples have been collected and published in the United States and Europe for nearly two centuries. The three sources most useful to this project, despite their shortcomings, were the United States federal censuses, the Minnesota state censuses, and the reports of the United States Immigration and Naturalization Service. Using them we have pieced together from various statistical points of view the outlines of the demographic development of the state's ethnic groups, prepared a series of maps showing the dispersion of selected ethnic groups in 1880 and 1905, and constructed tables that (1) give a picture of the size and growth of the first and second generations in Minnesota counties and major urban areas; (2) show the growth of some ethnic minorities or language groups in the state; and (3) suggest in bar graphs the immigration to Minnesota and remigration back to the country of origin of selected groups between 1899 and 1932.

The federal censuses, conducted every decade since 1790, and the Minnesota state censuses, taken at 10-year intervals from 1865 to 1905, vary widely in the completeness of ethnic information recorded. Until 1960 the censuses were conducted by enumerators who went from door to door collecting information about each household on a prescribed form, which was regularly changed to suit the needs of the census bureau. The reliability of the data thus gathered depended entirely upon the accuracy with which it was given and recorded. Limited knowledge on the part of the census takers of various languages, not to mention dialects, and of world geography, including shifting national boundaries, were only a few of the factors that affected the results in regard to nationality groups. It is apparent that enumerators often misunderstood the responses they received and consequently reported them incorrectly. When birthplaces such as "Luxemburg, Germany" were repeatedly listed, for example, undercounts of Luxembourgers and inflated numbers of Germans resulted. Such errors were commonplace.

With each successive decade the manuscript census forms were expanded, and as immigration picked up in the last half of the 19th century, the information collected on ethnic groups became more extensive. The 1860 census recorded the countries of birth of Minnesota residents. Ten years later population tabulations were broken down to the city level. The following census tabulated the birthplaces of foreign born (countries of origin) by county and state and published the first tables on children of the foreign born. The 1910 census volumes for the first time gave a county-by-county breakdown of "foreign white stock" — that is, first and second generations. To the eternal frustration of immigration historians, however, the lack of consistency in the data reported from census to census makes it virtually impossible to do comparative studies or to arrive at total population figures for some ethnic groups.

Available statistics on Slavic peoples are especially confusing. Before 1918, for example, census tallies, by listing only countries of origin, counted Slovaks as Austrians and Hungarians since they — along with Magyars, Bohemians, Moravians, Albanians, Jews, Germans, Rusins, Romanians, Bulgarians, Serbs, Croats, Slovenes, Macedonians, and Italians — were part of the Austro-Hungarian Empire. After Slovakia, Bohemia, and Moravia were combined to form Czechoslovakia in 1918, their populations were lumped together in the census as Czechoslovakians.

In 1910 the census began collecting "mother tongue" information by identifying the language spoken by white people of foreign birth (and later of foreign parentage). This information should have facilitated the study of Slovaks, as it did of certain other language groups whose ethnic allegiance was not necessarily the same as their nationality or country of origin. Unfortunately, however, the enumerators' unfamiliarity with eastern European nations plus the Slovaks' lack of a well-defined self-identity led to the recording of their language variously as Slovak, Slav, Slavish, Slavic, and Slavonian — and probably as "Austrian" and "Hungarian" as well.

Other inconsistencies in mother-tongue statistics over the decades also presented problems for comparative studies. In 1910 and 1920, when queries solicited the "customary" or "ancestral" language spoken, the figures represented foreign white stock, which included both immigrants and their children. In 1930, when immigrants were asked what language they spoke before arrival in the United States, only foreign-born whites were tallied, while in 1940 not only the immigrants but also children, grandchildren, and succeeding generations were reported. The 1950 census omitted the mother-tongue category entirely. In 1960 all foreign born were questioned, and if both English and another language were reported, preference was given to the latter. The 1970 census calculated mother-tongue figures from a sample of 15% of the population — native and foreign born — that was asked to supply the language spoken as children in the home.

Using country-of-origin and mother-tongue data in counting Middle Eastern peoples offered yet another set of problems. Figures on speakers of Arabic, Armenian, and Turkish appear in this work, reflecting some of the many groups included in the Ottoman Empire before World War I. But mother-tongue distinctions were insufficient to delineate the ethnic groups of the Middle East, where religion is a vital factor in determining ethnicity. An Arabic-speaking Coptic Christian in Egypt is not an Arab, for instance, nor do many Lebanese American Christians consider themselves Arabs, although their ancestral language was Arabic. Religion was also an important factor in the ethnicity of South Slavs, for Bosnians, Hercegovinans, and Dalmatians may be either Croats, Serbs, or neither and members of quite different ethnically oriented faiths.

From 1906 to 1936 the census bureau issued 10-year special reports on religious bodies in the United States. It also published *Nativity and Parentage of the White Population* for 1940 and *Mother Tongue of Foreign Born* for 1960. These, along with such monographs as *Immigrants and Their Children* (1927 and 1956) and special reports on specific groups (Blacks, Mexicans, Indians, Asians) and other topics, are basic sources for the study of ethnic communities in the United States. Used in conjunction with census figures for country of origin, they provided statistics that gave a clearer picture of some ethnic minorities, including, for example, Lebanese Maronite Catholics in Minnesota.

Where the federal censuses lacked data, the manuscript schedules and published volumes of Minnesota censuses proved to be useful supplements. As early as 1875 the printed state census listed the country or state of birth of residents, tabulated at first by county and beginning in 1895 by county, township, and city. In 1905 the manuscript forms recorded not only Minnesotans' places of birth but also those of both parents. (The published version, however, gave only the father's birthplace.) This state census along with the 1880 federal manuscript census schedules provided data for the series of detailed Minnesota maps that appear in Chapters 3, 7, 8, 11, 12, 13, 15, and 19.

Quite apart from their statistical value, the manuscript census schedules provided other useful information. From the census takers' notations, relationships between families, individuals' social status and occupations, and even prevalent illnesses could be discovered. Habitual misspellings could be puzzled out from the census takers' usages throughout the entries.

To find usable statistics collected by the Immigration and Naturalization Service (INS), it was first necessary to trace the agency's movement through various federal departments. Established by Congress in 1891, the Bureau of Immigration assumed responsibility for duties performed earlier by state officials under the secretary of the treasury. It was transferred to the new Department of Commerce and Labor in 1903, and its name was changed to Bureau of Immigration and Naturalization in 1906. When the Department of Labor, created in 1913, assumed jurisdiction, the agency was divided into the Bureaus of Immigration and Naturalization, which functioned separately until they were consolidated into the Immigration and Naturalization Service in 1933. The latest move occurred in 1940, when the service shifted from the Labor Department to the Department of Justice.

From 1899 to 1952 the INS published information collected from immigrants at points of entry to the United States. Arrivals were queried regarding their country of origin, "race" or ethnic group, and the state to which they intended to go. In addition, from 1907 to 1952 the INS recorded by ethnic group or by race the number of aliens who remigrated. Because the INS information was supplied by the immigrants themselves, it delineated ethnic groups that earlier had been either ignored or not extensively reported by the censuses. For example, immigrants who declared themselves to be Jews or Rusins would have been counted by the census as members of various national groups in eastern Europe. Thus the INS data revealed a more accurate picture of the emigrating ethnic elements in certain European nations.

Such information, which was published in INS annual reports, improved the over-all outlines of immigration data. But like the censuses, the reports varied in quality and consistency. They were most complete during the first third of the 20th century, when direct recording of immigrants and alien emigrants by ethnic origin and intended destination suggested their movements with greater clarity than did the more static census figures. Then gaps began to appear in the information. After 1932, 23 years elapsed before immigrants were again reported by "nation of origin" and state of destination. Moreover the INS reports, at least through 1979, listed only the larger groups. More specific and more complete data were retrieved for the Minnesota Ethnic History Project from records on file in INS offices in Washington, D.C. They provided figures on immigrants headed for the state after 1970.

Certain inadequacies in the INS records should be noted. The reported number of immigrants to Minnesota reflected only those who declared their *intention* to go there at the time they entered the country. Whether they actually arrived in the state is not known, nor can it be determined how many reached it as "secondary migrants" — those who named a different state as their destination but eventually moved to Minnesota. Both situations undoubtedly existed.

For Asian immigrants, however, INS information proved to be both more detailed and more up to date than that in the federal censuses. Although Chinese were enumerated beginning in 1860, published population figures after 1880 were too low for several reasons. The Chinese are known to have avoided census takers throughout the 61 years the Exclusion Act of 1882 was in force and during the 22 years that restrictive legislation applied to them. Moreover those Chinese who responded to enumerators or filled out questionnaires were more likely to be American born, English speaking, and better educated, rather than the early or recent immigrants. Like those from other Asian nations, Chinese arrived in large numbers after 1970, so that the census data collected that year quickly became outdated.

Population statistics on Koreans were first collected by enumerators in 1910 (and intermittently thereafter), but they were not set out in published census volumes. Only national and major metropolitan area figures for 1970 appeared in a special census report on Japanese, Chinese, and Filipinos in the United States. The two national Korean population figures for 1970 — 69,510 computed from a 20% sample and 70,598 from a 15% sample — are both underestimations. Korean demographer Eui-Young Yu has suggested that 113,000 would be more accurate, but even this larger figure did not take into consideration those missed by census takers, Koreans who were not counted separately in Alaska, and miscalculations committed in the allocation procedures for race and in the editing process.

In the 1970 census, respondents were asked to classify themselves with regard to race. If, however, the race entry on the questionnaire was not filled for anyone in a specific household (*Subject Report*, p. xi), "the race of the head of the preceding household was assigned." In Minnesota, where Koreans (as well as Filipinos, Chinese, and Japanese) have not clustered within residential areas, this procedure led to distortions and undercounting.

The South Slavs epitomized most of the shortcomings of the statistical census data. Like the Slovaks, South Slavs are impossible to trace in either country-of-origin or mother-tongue listings. Until the close of World War I, they were largely invisible statistically, lumped with other groups that were part of the Austro-Hungarian or Ottoman empires. At times provinces were grouped across ethnic lines, and countries such as Montenegro and Serbia, which came into being and quickly disappeared, added further complications. Mother-tongue figures in the published censuses grouped Serbo-Croatian speakers separately from those who spoke Slovenian or Bulgarian. To add to the the problem, religion was also an important factor in the ethnicity of the South Slavs; Bosnians, Hercegovinans, and Dalmatians may be either Croats or Serbs and members of quite different ethnically oriented faiths. Nor did the INS avoid muddying the ethnic waters in its annual reports. Between 1899 and 1952, it counted Serbs, Montenegrins, and Bulgarians in a single group, Croatians and Slovenians in another, and Dalmatians, Bosnians, and Hercegovinans in a third.

Additional caveats and qualifications regarding the reliability of the statistics used are provided by the authors of the preceding chapters. Care has been taken to produce the most accurate available picture of the demographic growth of ethnic groups in Minnesota based whenever possible on several sources of information. Although we have given actual (rather than rounded) figures just as they appeared in the sources, we realize that the inherent original confusions and errors beyond our power to remedy make them less accurate than such specific numbers would imply. Because the census reported 14,812 South Slavs in Minnesota in 1910, for example, does not mean that exactly that number were present. In truth, there were probably more, since South Slavs are among the confused groups believed to have been badly underreported.

Tables and Their Sources

In preparing the tables, we attempted to utilize the strengths of the available data. Tables recording the distribution of groups by Minnesota counties list the foreign born (fb) and the native born of foreign or mixed parentage ("foreign mixed" or fm) as given in published state or federal censuses from 1890 to 1970 and in tabulations of the 1860 and 1880 manuscript census schedules. In each table, figures representing the total population of the group in a given year were computed by adding the county populations as they appeared in the source; occasionally these figures differed from the published totals, which have been printed within parentheses. The tables are particularly valuable for the larger, earlier immigrant groups in the state. They offer previously unavailable glimpses of the regional distribution of rarely reported smaller groups as well.

Nevertheless they, too, contain unavoidable variations. The figures for total foreign stock in these tables include only the first and second generations, while those counts based on "race" (Blacks, for example) include members of first, second, and succeeding generations. In addition, during the 130 years covered by the tables, new counties were formed and others changed boundaries. (The last Minnesota county to be organized, for instance, was Lake of the Woods in 1922.) The changes may be traced in Mary Ellen Lewis, "The Establishment of County Boundaries in Minnesota," a 1946 University of Minnesota master's thesis. Counties that reported no members of the ethnic group in question throughout the period covered were omitted from the tables.

Several tables summarizing the population growth of some ethnic groups in Minnesota were based on mother-tongue statistics instead of country-of-origin figures when the latter were clearly misleading or were not available. In two instances — Table 22.1 on the Hungarians and Table 23.3 on the Romanians — both mother-tongue and country-of-origin data are presented to provide concrete examples of the differences and to enable the reader to draw his or her own conclusions.

While there may be truth in the overused adage that there are "lies, damned lies, and statistics," the demographic picture of Minnesota's ethnic groups presented here is as reliable as possible. With all their faults, the statistics clearly sketch the principal trends and trace what we believe to be accurate broad outlines. At the very least the overview of the state's ethnic communities, combined with the more detailed tables, offer tools for further research.

Index

PICTURE SOURCES

We wish to thank the institutions and individuals named below for permission to publish pictures in their collections, some of which will be copied for the collections of the Minnesota Historical Society. In the following list the names of the photographers, when known, appear in parentheses.

Pages 5 (Office of Alien Property), 6 left, 7 top left and right, 365 (all U.S. Public Health Service) — National Archives, Washington, D.C.

Page 6 right (B. G. Phillips) — Museum of the City of New York.

Pages 7 bottom, 10 (Norton & Peel), 11 top, 22 left, 24 left (courtesy National Anthropological Archives, Smithsonian Institution), 26 top (Monroe Killy), 28 top (Monroe Killy), 30 left, 42 left (W. A. Riechel) and right (Ray H. Mattison), 43, 45 (Eugene D. Becker), 49, 57 (Kenneth M. Wright), 63, 64 (Clifford Renshaw), 69, 75, 79 (*St. Paul Appeal*), 81 (Joseph Zalusky), 82, 83, 96 (courtesy St. Paul Dispatch-Pioneer Press), 99 left (Cindy Karp) and right, 102 (Roy D. Young), 120, 139 (B. F. Childs), 145 (courtesy James Furlong), 147 top (Ann Regan) and bottom (Dennis Magnuson/courtesy St. Paul Dispatch-Pioneer Press), 162, 164, 166 top and bottom (courtesy Brown County Historical Society), 169 (E. D. Becker), 173 bottom left (Charles P. Gibson) and right, 176 (George Gastler), 192, 194, 196, 197, 203 (B. C. Golling/courtesy Frank Thill), 217, 230, 231, 238, 241, 252 (W. Rand), 261, 262, 263 left and right (Herman A. Larson), 269 (David Peterson), 271 (courtesy American Swedish Institute), 281 (Everett E. Edwards), 283, 284, 285 left, 292, 305 top (courtesy *Mesabi Daily News*), 307, 339, 343, 344, 345 (Ken Carley), 354, 356, 358, 366 (Great Northern Railway Papers), 371 (Tom Lutz), 385 (Deborah L. Miller), 386, 388, 394 (WPA photo by Jack Loveland), 396 (Deborah L. Miller), 397 top and bottom (Hill Studios/both courtesy Mr. and Mrs. John Kendall), 409, 418 (Deborah L. Miller), 444, 454–455, 459, 462 (Kenneth Wright Studios), 475 (Edmund A. Brush/courtesy Elsie Boosalis), 482 (courtesy *Minneapolis Tribune*), 495, 496, 497, 503 (Norton & Peel), 516 (all Deborah L. Miller), 517, 519 (Deborah L. Miller), 521 (courtesy Nakashian family), 534, 535 (C. J. Hibbard/courtesy Woo family), 536, 542 (rubbing by Virginia Hyvarinen), 548, 565 (Thatcher Studios), 582 and 588 (all Alan Ominsky), 589 bottom — Minnesota Historical Society.

Pages 11 bottom, 445 — Northeast Minnesota Historical Center, University of Minnesota-Duluth.

Page 22 right (Richard Frear) — National Park Service.

Page 24 right — Red School House, St. Paul.

Pages 26 bottom, 30 right — American Indian Center, Minneapolis.

Page 28 bottom — *Ourselves*, Minnesota Chippewa Tribe, Inc.

Page 117 — Blue Earth County Historical Society, Mankato.

Pages 124–125 — Mrs. John MacArthur, Duluth.

Page 143 — *Minneapolis Journal*, November 14, 1893.

Page 168 all (bottom right, John Decker) — Stearns County Historical Society, St. Cloud.

Page 173 top (F. W. Zertler) — Adam Simmon, comp., "Historische Ereignisse des Ordens der Hermanns-Söhne im State Minnesota" (scrapbook, 1873–98, in MHS).

Pages 201, 204 — Winona County Historical Society, Winona.

Pages 214, 218 top — Wayne C. Blesi, Minneapolis.

Page 218 bottom — Ethel Brand, Duluth.

Pages 224, 233 (A. Larson) — Norwegian-American Historical Association Archives, Northfield.

Page 285 right (Herman A. Larson) — Danish-American Fellowship, Minneapolis.

Pages 298, 311, 374 (Benedict A. Schumacher), 390, 433 — Immigration History Research Center, University of Minnesota.

Pages 302, 305 bottom (both Will S. Horton) — E. V. Smalley, "A Finnish Settlement in Minnesota," in *Northwest Illustrated Monthly Magazine*, March, 1889.

Page 309 top — Tyomies Society, Superior, Wis.

Page 309 bottom (courtesy Bob Allison) — *Aurora Diamond Jubilee Historical Souvenir Booklet, 1903–1978* (Aurora, 1978).

Page 331 — Erik Dundurs, Minneapolis.

Page 332 (Arvi T. Treude) — Mai Treude, Minneapolis.

Page 347 (Zora K. Chrislock) — Zora K. Chrislock, St. Paul.

Pages 416 (*Minneapolis Tribune*, March 26, 1948), 561 — Minneapolis Public Library.

Pages 427, 431 — International Institute of Minnesota.

Page 456 — *Duluth Illustrated, 1887* ([Duluth?], 1887).

Page 465 (Ken Moran) — Jacqueline Rocchio Moran, "The Italian-Americans of Duluth," master's thesis, University of Minnesota, 1979.

Page 476 — Frank Lagios, Duluth.

Page 477 — Margaret Apostole, Duluth.

Page 515 — Southwest Minnesota Historical Center, Southwest State University, Marshall.

Page 551 (Camera Craft Studios) — Rudolph S. Runez, White Bear Lake.

Page 552 (Rich Photo Service) — Paul C. Borge, Minneapolis.

Page 568 (Richard Young) — Normandale Community College, Bloomington.

Page 574 (Philip C. Ahn) — Philip C. Ahn, St. Paul.

Page 575 — Minneapolis Star and Tribune.

Page 584 (Wing Young Huie) — Wing Young Huie.

Page 589 top (Ly Fu Vang) — Sarah Mason, Marine on St. Croix.

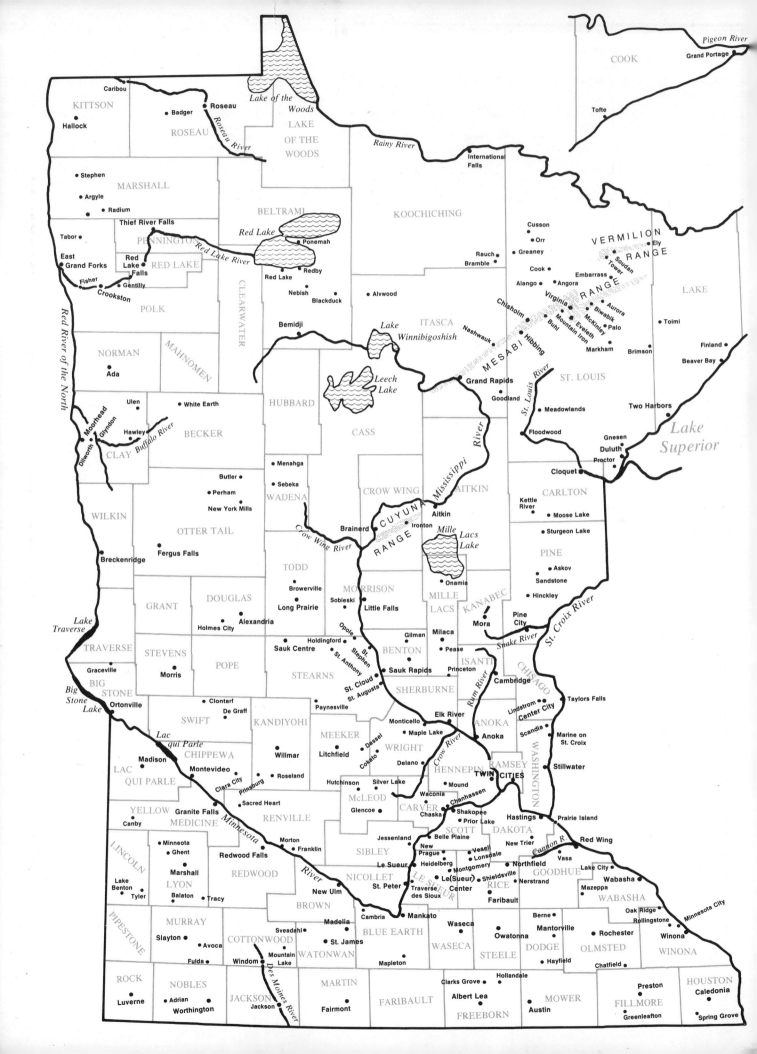